ScottForesman
LITERATURE
AND INTEGRATED STUDIES

Middle School: Grade Six

Middle School: Grade Seven

Middle School: Grade Eight

Forms of Literature

World Literature

American Literature

English Literature

The cover features a detail of Filippino Lippi's *Portrait of a Young Man,* which appears in full on this page. The son of a painter, Filippino Lippi (c. 1457–1504) began his career at the age of twelve, completing works his father left unfinished when he died. *National Gallery of Art, Washington, DC*

ScottForesman
LITERATURE
AND INTEGRATED STUDIES

Forms of Literature

Senior Consultants

Alan C. Purves
State University of New York at Albany

Carol Booth Olson
University of California, Irvine

Carlos E. Cortés
University of California, Riverside (Emeritus)

ScottForesman

Editorial Offices: Glenview, Illinois
Regional Offices: San Jose, California • Tucker, Georgia
Glenview, Illinois • Oakland, New Jersey • Dallas, Texas

ACKNOWLEDGMENTS

Texts

xxii "All the Years of Her Life" from *Morley Callaghan Stories* by Morley Callaghan. Copyright © 1959 by Morley Callaghan. Reprinted by permission of Macmillan Canada. **6** Reprinted by permission of G. P. Putnam's Sons from "Rules of the Game" from *The Joy Luck Club* by Amy Tan. Copyright © 1989 by Amy Tan. **18** "The Most Dangerous Game" by Richard Connell. Copyright 1924 by Richard Connell. Copyright renewed 1952 by Louise Fox Connell. Reprinted by permission of Brandt & Brandt Literary Agents, Inc. **47** "Checkouts" from *A Couple of Kooks and Other Stories About Love* by Cynthia Rylant. Copyright © 1990 by Cynthia Rylant. Reprinted by permission of the publisher, Orchard Books, New York. **53** Reprinted from *A Rosario Castellanos Reader* by Rosario Castellanos, edited by Maureen Ahern, translated by Maureen Ahern and others, Copyright © 1988. Originally published in Spanish in "Poesía No Eres Tú" by Rosario Castellanos, Copyright © 1972 by Fondo de Cultura Económica. By permission of the editor, the University of Texas Press and Fondo de Cultura Económica. **54** Yusef Komunyakaa, "Slam, Dunk, & Hook" from *Magic City.* Copyright © 1992 by Yusef Komunyakaa, Wesleyan University Press by permission of University Press of New England. **59** "Breaking the Ice" from *Dave Barry Is Not Making This Up* by Dave Barry. Copyright © 1991 by Dave Barry. Reprinted by permission of Crown Publishers, Inc. **64** Adapted from "Everyone's a winner when it comes to sports for the brain," by David M. Schwartz, *Smithsonian,* December 1994. Copyright © 1994 by David M. Schwartz. Reprinted by permission of the author. **66** From *Math for Smarty Pants* by Marilyn Burns. Copyright © 1992 by the Yolla Bolly Press. By permission of Little, Brown and Company. **78** "The Rule of Names" from *The Wind's Twelve Quarters* by Ursula K. Le Guin.

Copyright © 1964, 1975 by Ursula K. Le Guin. Reprinted by permission of the author and the author's agent, Virginia Kidd. **97** "The Necklace" from *The Collected Novels and Short Stories of Guy de Maupassant* by Guy de Maupassant, trans., E. Boyd. Copyright 1924 and renewed 1952 by Alfred A. Knopf Inc. Reprinted by permission of the publisher. **107** "My Delicate Heart Condition" from *Gorilla, My Love* by Toni Cade Bambara. Copyright © 1960, 1963, 1964, 1965, 1968, 1970, 1971, 1972 by Toni Cade Bambara. Reprinted by permission of Crown Publishers, Inc. **116** "Like Mexicans," from *Small Faces* by Gary Soto. Copyright © 1986 by Gary Soto. Used by permission of Bantam Doubleday Dell Books for Young Readers. **120** Abridgment of "If those cobras don't get you, the alligators will" by Richard Wolkomir. Copyright © 1992 by Richard Wolkomir. Reprinted from *Smithsonian* Magazine with the permission of the author. **134** "The Scarlet Ibis" by James Hurst. Reprinted from *The Atlantic Monthly,* July 1960. Reprinted by permission of the author. **148** "Waiting" from *The Leaving and Other Stories* by Budge Wilson. Copyright © 1990 by Budge Wilson. Reprinted by permission of Philomel Books and Stoddart Publishing Company Limited, Don Mills, Ontario, Canada. **161** "The Man to Send Rain Clouds" by Leslie Marmon Silko. Copyright © 1981 by Leslie Marmon Silko, reprinted with the permission of Wylie, Aitken & Stone, Inc. **169** "A Day's Wait" by Ernest Hemingway. Reprinted with permission of Scribner, an imprint of Simon & Schuster, Inc., from *Winner Take Nothing* by Ernest Hemingway. Copyright 1933 Charles Scribner's Sons. Copyright renewed © 1961 by Mary Hemingway.

continued on page 862

ISBN: 0-673-29447-1

http://www.sf.aw.com

3 4 5 6 7 8 9 10 DR 03 02 01 00 99 98 97

Senior Consultants

Alan C. Purves

Professor of Education and Humanities, State University of New York at Albany; Director of the Center for Writing and Literacy. Dr. Purves developed the concept and philosophy of the literature lessons for the series, consulted with editors, reviewed tables of contents and lesson manuscript, wrote the Assessment Handbooks, and oversaw the development and writing of the series testing strand.

Carol Booth Olson

Director, California Writing Project, Department of Education, University of California, Irvine. Dr. Olson conceptualized and developed the integrated writing strand of the program, consulted with editors, led a team of teachers in creating literature-based Writing Workshops, and reviewed final manuscript.

Carlos E. Cortés

Professor Emeritus, History, University of California, Riverside. Dr. Cortés designed and developed the multicultural strand embedded in each unit of the series and consulted with grade-level editors to implement the concepts.

Series Consultants

Visual and Media Literacy/Speaking and Listening/Critical Thinking

Harold M. Foster. Professor of English Education and Secondary Education, The University of Akron, Akron. Dr. Foster developed and wrote the Beyond Print features for all levels of the series.

ESL and LEP Strategies

James Cummins. Professor, Modern Language Centre and Curriculum Department, Ontario Institute for Studies in Education, Toronto.

Lily Wong Fillmore. Professor, Graduate School of Education, University of California at Berkeley.

Drs. Cummins and Fillmore advised on the needs of ESL and LEP students, helped develop the Building English Proficiency model for the program, and reviewed strategies and manuscript for this strand of the program.

Fine Arts/Humanities

Neil Anstead. Coordinator of the Humanitas Program, Cleveland Humanities Magnet School, Reseda, California. Mr. Anstead consulted on the fine art used in the program.

Reviewers and Contributors

Pupil and Teacher Edition

Jay Amberg, Glenbrook South High School, Glenview, Illinois **Edison Barber,** St. Anne Community High School, St. Anne, Illinois **Lois Barliant,** Albert G. Lane Technical High School, Chicago, Illinois **James Beasley,** Plant City Senior High School, Plant City, Florida **Linda Belpedio,** Oak Park/River Forest High School, Oak Park, Illinois **Richard Bruns,** Burges High School, El Paso, Texas **Kay Parks Bushman,** Ottawa High School, Ottawa, Kansas **Jesús Cardona,** John F. Kennedy High School, San Antonio, Texas **Marlene Carter,** Dorsey High School, Los Angeles, California **Patrick Cates,** Lubbock High School, Lubbock, Texas **Timothy Dohrer,** New Trier Township High School, Winnetka, Illinois **Margaret Doria,** Our Lady of Perpetual Help High School, Brooklyn, New York **Lucila Dypiangco,** Bell Senior High School, Bell, California **Judith Edminster,** Plant City High School, Plant City, Florida **Mary Alice Fite,** Columbus School for Girls, Columbus, Ohio **Montserrat Fontes,** Marshall High School, Los Angeles, California **Diane Fragos,** Turkey Creek Middle School, Plant City, Florida **Joan Greenwood,** Thornton Township High School, Harvey, Illinois **William Irvin,** Pittsfield Public Schools, Pittsfield, Massachusetts **Carleton Jordan,** Montclair High School, Montclair, New Jersey **Mark Kautz,** Chapel Hill High School, Chapel Hill, North Carolina **Elaine Kay,** Bartow High School, Bartow, Florida **Roslyn Kettering,** West Lafayette Junior/Senior High School, West Lafayette, Indiana **Kristina Kostopoulos,** Lincoln Park High School, Chicago, Illinois **Julia Lloyd,** Harwood Junior High School, Bedford, Texas **John Lord,** Ocean Township High School, Oakhurst, New Jersey **Dolores Mathews,** Bloomingdale High School, Valrico, Florida **Jim McCallum,** Milford High School, Milford, Massachusetts **Monette Mehalko,** Plant City Senior High School, Plant City, Florida **Lucia Podraza,** DuSable High School, Chicago, Illinois **Frank Pool,** Anderson High School, Austin, Texas **Alice Price,** Latin School, Chicago, Illinois **Anna J. Roseboro,** The Bishop's School, La Jolla, California **Peter Sebastian,** Granite Hills High School, El Cajon, California **Rob Slater,** East Forsyth High School, Winston-Salem, North Carolina **Catherine Small,** Nicolet High School, Glendale, Wisconsin **Dennis Symkowiak,** Mundelein High School, Mundelein, Illinois **Rosetta Tetteh,** Senn High School, Chicago, Illinois **Pamela Vetters,** Harlandale High School, San Antonio, Texas **Polly Walwark,** Oak Park High School, Oak Park, Illinois **Karen Wrobleski,** San Diego High School, San Diego, California **Dru Zimmerman,** Chapel Hill High School, Chapel Hill, North Carolina

CONTENTS

UNIT 1

FACING REALITY

PART ONE: THE GAMES PEOPLE PLAY

PART TWO: MISTAKEN IMPRESSIONS

PART THREE: DEALING WITH DIFFERENCES

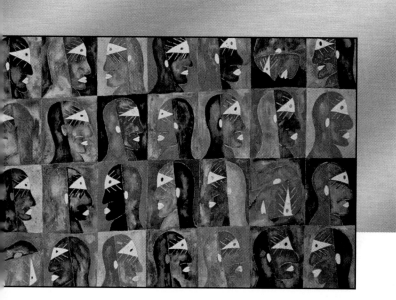

UNIT 2

GETTING THE MESSAGE

GENRE OVERVIEW:
READING A MODERN PLAY   **206**

PART ONE: DISTANT VOICES

Part Two: Reaching Out

*T*AKING A CLOSER LOOK

**GENRE OVERVIEW:
READING POETRY**   **338**

PART ONE: FAMILY MATTERS

PART TWO: SONGS OF HOPE

PART THREE: WAYS OF SEEING

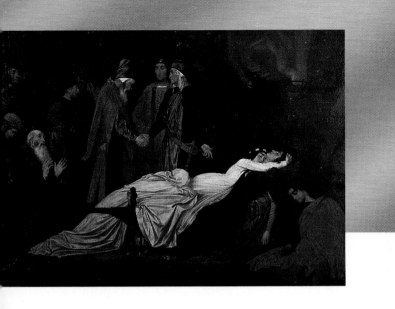

LOVE CONQUERS

GENRE OVERVIEW:
READING A SHAKESPEAREAN PLAY 476

LOVE AND SACRIFICE

MAKING A DIFFERENCE

GENRE OVERVIEW:
READING NONFICTION   **606**

PART ONE: UNEXPECTED HEROES

PART TWO: THE PRICE OF WISDOM

Literature

Exploring the Theme in Other Genres

Integrated Studies

FATEFUL JOURNEYS

**GENRE OVERVIEW:
READING A GREEK EPIC   730**

THE LONG WAY HOME

GLOSSARIES, HANDBOOKS, AND INDEXES

GENRE OVERVIEW

Short Stories

Poetry

Plays

Nonfiction

Folklore

FEATURE OVERVIEW

Genre Overviews

Interdisciplinary Studies

Reading Mini-Lessons

Writing Workshops

Beyond Print

Model for Active Reading

Good readers read actively. They jump right in by getting involved, picturing the action, and reacting to the characters or ideas. They question, evaluate, predict, and in other ways think about the story, poem, or article they are reading.

These three students agreed to let us in on their thoughts as they read "All the Years of Her Life" by Morley Callaghan. You might not have the same questions or ideas that they did about this story. However, their responses may give you ideas on how you can strengthen your skills as an active reader.

DAVID HERRMANN I'm fourteen years old. What are my hobbies? I like to play the piano, and I like volleyball. I also like to read and watch TV. I enjoy reading science fiction. I want to be a musician when I grow up.

LAUREN TEICHNER I do a lot of sports. I love to play softball. I play the piano, and I'm in the high school band. I want to be a doctor when I grow up. I'm fourteen years old. I love to read for enjoyment—I like mysteries and humorous books.

JOHN JONES   I'm fourteen. I want to be a real estate developer when I grow up. I'm on the cross-country team, and I'm interested in trying out for basketball and track. I like watching TV and relaxing with my family. I enjoy reading realistic fiction and science fiction.

Six Reading Strategies

Following are some of the techniques that good readers use often without being aware of them.

Question Ask questions that arise as you read.

Example: Why would Alfred steal things from Sam Carr's drugstore?

Predict Make reasoned guesses, based on what's happened so far, about what might happen next.

Example: I bet that Alfred will be arrested and taken to jail.

Clarify Clear up confusion and answer questions.

Example: Although Alfred doesn't go to school anymore, I think he's still pretty young.

Summarize Review some of the main ideas or events.

Example: Alfred is a troublemaker, and his behavior creates a great deal of worry and unhappiness for his mother.

Evaluate Use your common sense and evidence from the selections to form opinions and draw conclusions.

Example: I think Sam Carr is just bluffing when he says he knows Alfred has been stealing steadily. If he had known before, he would have put a stop to it.

Connect Compare the text with something in your own experience, with another text, or with ideas within the text.

Example: If I were caught stealing, I would get into a lot more trouble with my parents than Alfred did.

All the years OF HER LIFE

MORLEY CALLAGHAN

▲ Fairfield Porter, *Anne* (c. 1939). What do details in this painting reveal about the woman who is portrayed in it?

They were closing the drugstore, and Alfred Higgins, who had just taken off his white jacket, was putting on his coat and getting ready to go home. The little gray-haired man, Sam Carr, who owned the drugstore, was bending down behind the cash register, and when Alfred Higgins passed him, he looked up and said softly, "Just a moment, Alfred. One moment before you go."

The soft, confident, quiet way in which Sam Carr spoke made Alfred start to button his coat nervously. He felt sure his face was white. Sam Carr usually said, "Good night," brusquely,[1] without looking up. In the six months he had been working in the drugstore Alfred had never heard his employer speak softly like that. His heart began to beat so loud it was hard for him to get his breath. "What is it, Mr. Carr?" he asked.

"Maybe you'd be good enough to take a few things out of your pocket and leave them here before you go," Sam Carr said.

"What things? What are you talking about?"

"You've got a compact and a lipstick and at least two tubes of toothpaste in your pockets, Alfred."

"What do you mean? Do you think I'm crazy?" Alfred blustered. His face got red and he knew he looked fierce with indignation.[2] But Sam Carr, standing by the door with his blue eyes shining brightly behind his glasses and his lips moving underneath his gray moustache, only nodded his head a few times, and then Alfred grew very frightened and he didn't know what to say. Slowly he raised his hand and dipped it into his pocket, and with his eyes never meeting Sam Carr's eyes, he took out a blue compact and two tubes of toothpaste and a lipstick, and he laid them one by one on the counter.

"Petty[3] thieving, eh, Alfred?" Sam Carr said. "And maybe you'd be good enough to tell me how long this has been going on."

"This is the first time I ever took anything."

"So now you think you'll tell me a lie, eh? What kind of a sap do I look like, huh? I don't know what goes on in my own store, eh? I tell you you've been doing this pretty steady," Sam Carr said as he went over and stood behind the cash register.

Ever since Alfred had left school he had been getting into trouble wherever he worked. He lived at home with his mother and his father, who was a printer. His two older brothers were married and his sister had got married last year, and it would have been all right for his parents now if Alfred had only been able to keep a job.

While Sam Carr smiled and stroked the side of his face very delicately with the tips of his fingers, Alfred began to feel that familiar terror growing in him that had been in him every time he had got into such trouble.

"I liked you," Sam Carr was saying. "I liked you and would have trusted you, and now look what I got to do." While Alfred watched with his alert, frightened blue eyes, Sam Carr drummed with his

1. **brusquely** (brusk′lē), *adv.* abruptly; bluntly.
2. **indignation** (in′dig nā′shən), *n.* anger at something unjust, unfair, or mean.
3. **petty** (pet′ē), *adj.* having little importance or value; small.

LAUREN   I wonder what Alfred has done. Why does Mr. Carr want him to stay? (question)

JOHN   Why is Mr. Carr speaking so softly? Alfred must be guilty of something. (predict)

LAUREN   Oh, now I understand what Alfred has done—he's been stealing, and Mr. Carr has caught him. I don't think he expected to be caught. (clarify)

DAVID   I'm really surprised. I thought Sam was going to take Alfred to a movie or something. I didn't think he was going to be in trouble. (clarify)

LAUREN   Alfred is really afraid when Mr. Carr starts accusing him. I wonder what type of person Mr. Carr is. Maybe he's a really weird person. (question)

JOHN   I'm wondering about the title of this story. It doesn't make sense so far, since the two characters are males. (question)

LAUREN   I wonder what's going to happen next. I think Mr. Carr will fire Alfred, because he was stealing. (predict)

fingers on the counter. "I don't like to call a cop in point-blank,"[4] he was saying as he looked very worried. "You're a fool, and maybe I should call your father and tell him you're a fool. Maybe I should let them know I'm going to have you locked up."

"My father's not at home. He's a printer. He works nights," Alfred said.

"Who's at home?"

"My mother, I guess."

"Then we'll see what she says." Sam Carr went to the phone and dialed the number. Alfred was not so much ashamed, but there was that deep fright growing in him, and he blurted out arrogantly,[5] like a strong, full-grown man, "Just a minute. You don't need to draw anybody else in. You don't need to tell her." He wanted to sound like a swaggering,[6] big guy who could look after himself, yet the old, childish hope was in him, the longing that someone at home would come and help him. "Yeah, that's right, he's in trouble," Mr. Carr was saying. "Yeah, your boy works for me. You'd better come down in a hurry." And when he was finished Mr. Carr went over to the door and looked out at the street and watched the people passing in the late summer night. "I'll keep my eye out for a cop," was all he said.

Alfred knew how his mother would come rushing in; she would rush in with her eyes blazing, or maybe she would be crying, and she would push him away when he tried to talk to her, and make him feel her dreadful contempt;[7] yet he longed that she might come before Mr. Carr saw the cop on the beat passing the door.

While they waited—and it seemed a long time—they did not speak, and when at last they heard someone tapping on the closed door, Mr. Carr, turning the latch, said crisply, "Come in, Mrs. Higgins." He looked hard-faced and stern.

Mrs. Higgins must have been going to bed when he telephoned, for her hair was tucked in loosely under her hat, and her hand at her throat held her light coat tight across her chest so her dress would not show. She came in, large and plump, with a little smile on her friendly face. Most of the store lights had been turned out and at first she did not see Alfred, who was standing in the shadow at the end of the counter. Yet as soon as she saw him she did not look as Alfred thought she would look: she smiled, her blue eyes never wavered, and with a calmness and dignity that made them forget that her clothes seemed

---

JOHN This is strange. I thought Alfred was a grown man. But he can't be, because Mr. Carr threatens to call his father. How old do you think he is? (clarify, question)

DAVID I think he's a teenager. (evaluate)

DAVID I'm not surprised that Mr. Carr calls Alfred's mom, even though Alfred doesn't want him to draw other people in. It happens all the time when a kid gets into trouble. (connect)

LAUREN I don't know where this story is leading. As I read, I keep learning things. The story seems to be happening right "in the moment." (evaluate)

DAVID I'm scared for Alfred. I think his mom will start yelling at him. (predict)

---

4. **point-blank** (point′blangk′), *adv.* plainly and bluntly; directly.
5. **arrogantly** (ar′ə gənt lē), *adv.* proudly; haughtily.
6. **swaggering** (swag′ər ing), *adj.* with a bold, rude, or superior air.
7. **contempt** (kən tempt′), *n.* the feeling that a person, act, or thing is mean, low, or worthless; scorn.

to have been thrown on her, she put out her hand to Mr. Carr and said politely, "I'm Mrs. Higgins. I'm Alfred's mother."

Mr. Carr was a bit embarrassed by her lack of terror and her simplicity, and he hardly knew what to say to her, so she asked, "Is Alfred in trouble?"

"He is. He's been taking things from the store. I caught him red-handed. Little things like compacts and toothpaste and lipsticks. Stuff he can sell easily," the proprietor said.

As she listened Mrs. Higgins looked at Alfred sometimes and nodded her head sadly, and when Sam Carr had finished she said gravely,[8] "Is it so, Alfred?"

"Yes."

"Why have you been doing it?"

"I been spending money, I guess."

"On what?"

"Going around with the guys, I guess," Alfred said.

Mrs. Higgins put out her hand and touched Sam Carr's arm with an understanding gentleness, and speaking as though afraid of disturbing him, she said, "If you would only listen to me before doing anything." Her simple earnestness made her shy; her humility made her falter[9] and look away, but in a moment she was smiling gravely again, and she said with a kind of patient dignity, "What did you intend to do, Mr. Carr?"

"I was going to get a cop. That's what I ought to do."

"Yes, I suppose so. It's not for me to say, because he's my son. Yet I sometimes think a little good advice is the best thing for a boy when he's at a certain period in his life," she said.

Alfred couldn't understand his mother's quiet composure,[10] for if they had been at home and someone had suggested that he was going to be arrested, he knew she would be in a rage and would cry out against him. Yet now she was standing there with that gentle, pleading smile on her face, saying, "I wonder if you don't think it would be better just to let him come home with me. He looks a big fellow, doesn't he? It takes some of them a long time to get any sense," and they both stared at Alfred, who shifted away with a bit of light shining for a moment on his thin face and the tiny pimples over his cheekbone.

But even while he was turning away uneasily Alfred was realizing that Mr. Carr had become aware that his mother was really a fine woman; he knew that Sam Carr was puzzled by his mother, as if he had expected her to come in and plead with him tearfully,

---

8. **gravely** (grāv lē), *adv.* thoughtfully; seriously.
9. **falter** (fôl′tər), *v.* hesitate; draw back; waver.
10. **composure** (cəm pō′zhər), *n.* calmness; quietness; self-control.

DAVID I'm really surprised that Alfred's mom seems so calm. (clarify)

LAUREN She seems so strong on the outside. But maybe she's putting on an act. (evaluate)

JOHN I think she is putting on an act. I hope she can hold up the act the whole way through, because Mr. Carr seems to believe her. (evaluate)

LAUREN But I do think that Alfred's mom seems to like Mr. Carr. (evaluate)

DAVID I think she's trying to soothe his anger. Mr. Carr is really angry and fed up. (clarify)

JOHN I don't think Mr. Carr will call the police. The rest of the story isn't long enough to allow time for that. (predict)

and instead he was being made to feel a bit ashamed by her vast tolerance.[11] While there was only the sound of the mother's soft, assured voice in the store, Mr. Carr began to nod his head encouragingly at her. Without being alarmed, while being just large and still and simple and hopeful, she was becoming dominant there in the dimly lit store. "Of course, I don't want to be harsh," Mr. Carr was saying, "I'll tell you what I'll do. I'll just fire him and let it go at that. How's that?" and he got up and shook hands with Mrs. Higgins, bowing low to her in deep respect.

There was such warmth and gratitude in the way she said, "I'll never forget your kindness," that Mr. Carr began to feel warm and genial[12] himself.

"Sorry we had to meet this way," he said. "But I'm glad I got in touch with you. Just wanted to do the right thing, that's all," he said.

"It's better to meet like this than never, isn't it?" she said. Suddenly they clasped hands as if they liked each other, as if they had known each other a long time. "Good night, sir," she said.

"Good night, Mrs. Higgins. I'm truly sorry," he said.

The mother and son walked along the street together, and the mother was taking a long, firm stride as she looked ahead with her stern face full of worry. Alfred was afraid to speak to her, he was afraid of the silence that was between them, so he only looked ahead too, for the excitement and relief was still pretty strong in him; but in a little while, going along like that in silence made him terribly aware of the strength and the sternness in her; he began to wonder what she was thinking of as she stared ahead so grimly; she seemed to have forgotten that he walked beside her; so when they were passing under the Sixth Avenue elevated and the rumble of the train seemed to break the silence, he said in his old, blustering[13] way, "Thank God it turned out like that. I certainly won't get in a jam like that again."

"Be quiet. Don't speak to me. You've disgraced me again and again," she said bitterly.

"That's the last time. That's all I'm saying."

"Have the decency to be quiet," she snapped. They kept on their way, looking straight ahead.

When they were at home and his mother took off her coat, Alfred saw that she was really only half-dressed, and she made him feel afraid again when she said, without even looking at him, "You're a bad lot. God forgive you. It's one thing after another and always has been. Why do you stand there stupidly? Go to bed, why

---

11. **tolerance** (tol′ər əns), *n.* a willingness to let others do as they think best.
12. **genial** (jē′nyəl), *adj.* smiling and pleasant; friendly.
13. **blustering** (blus′tər ing), *adj.* in a noisy and violent way.

LAUREN   Mr. Carr is probably wondering how Alfred could have such a fine mother and yet grow up to be such a fool, which is what Mr. Carr called Alfred earlier. But after meeting Mrs. Higgins, Mr. Carr figures Alfred can't be all that bad. (evaluate)

JOHN   I wonder: If Alfred had just admitted stealing in the beginning, would Mr. Carr have let him off scot-free? (question)

LAUREN   I'm surprised that Alfred and his mom are completely silent. I was afraid that she'd start yelling at him immediately. (evaluate)

JOHN   I was hoping that Alfred wasn't going to say something stupid to his mother—but he did. (summarize)

DAVID   It's amazing how Alfred's mom stays calm all the way home. Once she gets there, she wants to be left alone. (summarize)

don't you?" When he was going, she said, "I'm going to make myself a cup of tea. Mind, now, not a word about tonight to your father."

While Alfred was undressing in his bedroom, he heard his mother moving around the kitchen. She filled the kettle and put it on the stove. She moved a chair. And as he listened there was no shame in him, just wonder and a kind of admiration of her strength and repose.[14] He could still see Sam Carr nodding his head encouragingly to her; he could hear her talking simply and earnestly, and as he sat on his bed he felt a pride in her strength. "She certainly was smooth," he thought. "Gee, I'd like to tell her she sounded swell."

And at last he got up and went along to the kitchen, and when he was at the door he saw his mother pouring herself a cup of tea. He watched and he didn't move. Her face, as she sat there, was a frightened, broken face utterly[15] unlike the face of the woman who had been so assured a little while ago in the drugstore. When she reached out and lifted the kettle to pour hot water in her cup, her hand trembled and the water splashed on the stove. Leaning back in the chair, she sighed and lifted the cup to her lips, and her lips were groping loosely as if they would never reach the cup. She swallowed the hot tea eagerly, and then she straightened up in relief, though her hand holding the cup still trembled. She looked very old.

It seemed to Alfred that this was the way it had been every time he had been in trouble before, that this trembling had really been in her as she hurried out half-dressed to the drugstore. He understood why she had sat alone in the kitchen the night his young sister had kept repeating doggedly that she was getting married. Now he felt all that his mother had been thinking of as they walked along the street together a little while ago. He watched his mother, and he never spoke, but at that moment his youth seemed to be over; he knew all the years of her life by the way her hand trembled as she raised the cup to her lips. It seemed to him that this was the first time he had ever looked upon his mother.

JOHN   I wonder what the father would do if he found out about this. (question)

LAUREN   This family seems really unstable. Maybe the father would get very upset or outraged, or he would do something to Alfred. (evaluate)

JOHN   I'm hoping that Alfred will finally see how sad he's making his mom, and that he'll learn something from this experience. (evaluate)

DAVID   It seems like the father is never around, and the mother has to deal with everything. She seems to be thinking to herself, How am I going to get through this? (evaluate)

LAUREN   It seems like the mom will have a breakdown if this ever happens again—she'll go out of her mind. (predict)

DAVID   I think Alfred has learned a lesson. I think he knows that if he gets his mom this upset again she may totally lose it. (summarize, evaluate)

---

14. **repose** (ri pōz′), *n.* quietness; ease; calmness.
15. **utterly** (ut′ər lē), *adv.* completely; totally.

Discussion After Reading

General Comments

DAVID The turning point in this story comes at the end, when Alfred sees his mother sitting alone at the kitchen table and finally understands how she feels about him and his actions. (summarize)

JOHN I think that may be one way that people grow, when they see things as they really are, like Alfred finally does. I think that Alfred grows as a person. I'm glad that he finally realizes the effect his behavior has on his mother. (connect)

DAVID Why do you think Alfred steals? I think it's just to show off to his friends. (evaluate)

LAUREN He's young and immature. I think that's why he does it. (evaluate)

DAVID If I had gotten into as much trouble as Alfred did, something worse would have happened to me. But I think Alfred has learned his lesson. (connect)

LAUREN When Alfred's mom is talking to Mr. Carr, she seems so strong and forceful. But then when she's sitting alone in the kitchen, she seems insecure and timid. That's when Alfred sees his mother as she really is, when she's by herself. I know that when I'm alone, that's the real me—it's who I really am. (connect)

JOHN What meaning did you get from the last sentence of the story? (question)

LAUREN I think it shows that Alfred finally sees the true person inside of his mother. He finally realizes that maybe he should listen to her, because she's been through a lot, and she's trying to do what's best for him. (summarize, evaluate)

Is it sometimes difficult for you to talk about literature once you've read it? Take some cues from active readers, who reflect and respond in a variety of ways. After reading "All the Years of Her Life," David, Lauren, and John discuss their personal reactions (Shaping Your Response) and literary responses (Analyzing the Story), along with the connections they have made to their own experiences (Extending the Ideas). These are the types of questions you will find after the selections in this book.

Shaping Your Response

1 Do you think Alfred will be a better son after this? Explain why or why not.

DAVID Yes, definitely. Alfred knows what he did was bad, and I think he was just waiting to be caught, like a lot of kids. He's definitely learned a lesson from this experience.

LAUREN Alfred came to the realization that he needs to stop and think before he does things, because his actions deeply affect his parents. I think he will now give his parents the respect they deserve.

JOHN At the end of the story, I think Alfred went to the kitchen, ready to pat his mom on the back and say: "Good job, you got me off that time." But when he saw his mom's face he figured it was time for him to make a change.

Analyzing the Story

2 Explain the significance of the title of the story.

LAUREN At the end of the story, it says that Alfred's mom looked really old as she sat at the kitchen table. The title lets us know that the mom has lived and knows what life is all about.

JOHN I think that when Alfred sees his mom sitting at the kitchen table, he sees all the years of her life at once. He recalls that she looks like this every time he does something bad. He realizes that if his mom has to go through this every time he messes up, maybe it's time to do things differently.

Extending the Ideas

3 Compare Alfred's new understanding of his mother with a fresh insight you've had about someone you thought you knew well.

JOHN I think when Alfred saw his mother at the kitchen table he finally understood how she felt. A similar thing happened to me with a friend I used to tease a lot. One day he was sad and down, and I asked what the problem was. He said, "Everyone's making fun of me, ganging up on me, and I can't take it anymore." He was just breaking down. I realized that some people take teasing harder than others. After that, I didn't mess with people as much.

FACING REALITY

The Games People Play

Mistaken Impressions

Dealing with Differences

Reading a

The fact that short stories so often provide enjoyable reading experiences does not happen by accident. Usually an author carefully constructs a story to keep you involved. Recognizing the elements of a short story—whether it is sad, suspenseful, or fanciful—can increase your appreciation.

...when he ventured upon insult, I vowed revenge.

—*Edgar Allan Poe, "The Cask of Amontillado"*

PLOT

Without a **plot**, you have no story. A plot is a sequence, or organized pattern, of events. The pattern of these events reveals a **conflict**—a physical or emotional struggle between two forces.

A conflict may be external, with one character pitted against another or the pressures of society. In "The Cask of Amontillado," for example, the conflict is between the narrator and his unsuspecting friend, Fortunato. Conflicts may also be internal, with a character struggling against indecision or a nagging conscience. Sometimes a story will have both external and internal conflicts.

The events in a story build to a **climax**, where the conflict is directly confronted. Then, in a story's **resolution**, the conflict is usually resolved and the action winds down.

She just stood there a long time looking at me, trying to figure me out, the way mothers are always doing....

—*Toni Cade Bambara, "My Delicate Heart Condition"*

CHARACTER

Your interest in a story stems naturally from your interest in the **characters**. The development of vivid personalities is done through various methods of characterization. Sometimes an author will directly describe a character. At other times, an author may reveal a character's personality indirectly through the character's actions, dialogue, and thoughts, as well as through the reactions of other characters. In "My Delicate Heart Condition," the narrator reveals a lot about her mother's personality and her own when she describes her mother looking at her.

Short Story

> But I guess I really loved Henrietta anyway, slowpoke though she was.
>
> —*Budge Wilson, "Waiting"*

POINT OF VIEW

When you read a story, ask yourself who is telling it. Is it a character in the story? Someone outside the story? An author's choice of narrator determines the **point of view** of a story.

If the narrator is a character, then this first-person point of view will give you a very personal and limited view of events in the story. "Waiting," for example, is told from a first person point of view. When the narrator describes her twin sister for us, we know that she may be biased or have a limited perspective.

If the story is told by a third-person narrator outside the story, the point of view may still be limited—you may learn about the actions or inner thoughts of only a few characters. But a third-person narrator may also be omniscient—knowing everything about the characters and being able to communicate their thoughts to the reader. In some stories, authors may actually switch back and forth between different points of view.

> I did not know then that pride is a wonderful, terrible thing, a seed that bears two vines, life and death.
>
> –*James Hurst, "The Scarlet Ibis"*

THEME

As you read a story, you may discover a main idea or an underlying meaning in a story—its **theme**. In "The Scarlet Ibis," for example, the idea that pride can lead to destruction is stated in different ways throughout the story.

A story may have one theme or many. An author may write a story with certain themes in mind, but as a reader, you may also discover themes in a story that connect with other literature you have read or with your own life experiences.

> Twenty feet below him the sea rumbled and hissed.
>
> —*Richard Connell, "The Most Dangerous Game"*

SETTING

The **setting** of a story is the time and the place where the events in the story occur. A setting may be described directly, or it may be suggested through action and dialogue.

The setting may be crucial to the plot of a story—characters can't be lost in a blizzard, for example, if the setting of a story is the tropics. Details about the setting may also help to establish a particular mood, or feeling. For example, Connell's description of the sea in "The Most Dangerous Game" helps establish an eerie, suspenseful mood in the story.

Part One

The Games People Play

Are you a person who thrives on competition, or do you take a different approach to life? The characters in the following selections are playing games in which the stakes are high, and sometimes even deadly.

Multicultural Connection **Communication** among people of different cultures, beliefs, and social groups can be complicated. In the following selections, what kinds of obstacles to communication exist? When is miscommunication part of a character's competitive strategy?

Before Reading

Rules of the Game

by Amy Tan

Amy Tan
born 1952

Amy Tan is the American-born daughter of Chinese immigrants. Although her novels focusing on the lives of Chinese American women have been enthusiastically received by both critics and the public, her literary career was not planned. Writing fiction was initially a form of therapy for her, something that helped relieve the pressure of her job as a technical writer. But the success of her early stories soon led to a new career as a novelist. "Rules of the Game" is from Tan's first novel, *The Joy Luck Club,* which Tan wrote to gain a better understanding of the cultural tensions between herself and her mother.

Building Background

Chinatown, San Francisco "Rules of the Game" takes place in the Chinatown community of San Francisco. This 24-square-block area is the oldest and most famous Chinese American community in the United States. Established in the mid-1800s, Chinatown's first settlers came to America to work in the mines during the California Gold Rush. Workers from this area also helped build the Transcontinental Railroad in the 1860s. Although the original Chinatown was destroyed in the 1906 California earthquake, it was rebuilt and has continued to be a dynamic, thriving community.

Literary Focus

Protagonist/Antagonist The chief character of a story, play, or novel is the **protagonist.** The rival or adversary that works against the protagonist is called an **antagonist.** An antagonist may be a character, an internal force, or an external force. As you read "Rules of the Game," determine who is the story's protagonist. Then decide what character or other force is working against him or her.

Writer's Notebook

Keeping Score People play games for many different reasons—for the thrill of victory, for fun and challenge, to pass the time, and so on. Favorite games may range from purely physical activities to sophisticated mental exercises. Before you read "Rules of the Game," write down some of your ideas about games. Choose a favorite game and consider these questions as you write: Why do you enjoy playing the game? What does it take to be good at this game—luck, skill, or both? Is winning the most important result of playing this game?

RULES OF THE GAME

Amy Tan

I was six when my mother taught me the art of invisible strength. It was a strategy for winning arguments, respect from others, and eventually, though neither of us knew it at the time, chess games.

"Bite back your tongue," scolded my mother when I cried loudly, yanking her hand toward the store that sold bags of salted plums. At home, she said, "Wise guy, he not go against wind. In Chinese we say, Come from South, blow with wind—poom!—North will follow. Strongest wind cannot be seen."

The next week I bit back my tongue as we entered the store with the forbidden candies. When my mother finished her shopping, she quietly plucked a small bag of plums from the rack and put it on the counter with the rest of the items.

My mother imparted her daily truths so she could help my older brothers and me rise above our circumstances. We lived in San Francisco's Chinatown. Like most of the other Chinese children who played in the back alleys of restaurants and curio shops, I didn't think we were poor. My bowl was always full, three five-course meals every day, beginning with a soup full of mysterious things I didn't want to know the names of.

We lived on Waverly Place, in a warm, clean, two-bedroom flat that sat above a small Chinese bakery specializing in steamed pastries and dim sum.[1] In the early morning, when the alley was still quiet, I could smell fragrant red beans as they were cooked down to a pasty sweetness. By daybreak, our flat was heavy with the odor of fried sesame balls and sweet curried chicken crescents. From my bed, I would listen as my father got ready for work, then locked the door behind him, one-two-three clicks.

At the end of our two-block alley was a small sandlot playground with swings and slides well-shined down the middle with use. The play area was bordered by wood-slat benches where old-country people sat cracking roasted watermelon seeds with their golden teeth and scattering the husks to an impatient gathering of gurgling pigeons. The best playground, however, was the dark alley itself. It was crammed with daily mysteries and adventures. My brothers and I would peer into the medicinal

---

1. **dim sum** (dim sum), *n.* crescents or buns filled with meat or seafood, and fried pastries, served on small plates. "Dim sum" means "delight your heart."

Celebration, Chinatown was painted in watercolors by Dong Kingman in the 1950s. What do you think is the significance of the American flag in this scene? ➤

herb shop, watching old Li dole out onto a stiff sheet of white paper the right amount of insect shells, saffron-colored seeds, and pungent leaves for his ailing customers. It was said that he once cured a woman dying of an ancestral curse that had eluded[2] the best of American doctors. Next to the pharmacy was a printer who specialized in gold-embossed wedding invitations and festive red banners.

Farther down the street was Ping Yuen Fish Market. The front window displayed a tank crowded with doomed fish and turtles struggling to gain footing on the slimy green-tiled sides. A hand-written sign informed tourists, "Within this store, is all for food, not for pet." Inside, the butchers with their bloodstained white smocks deftly gutted the fish while customers cried out their orders and shouted, "Give me your freshest," to which the butchers always protested, "All are freshest." On less crowded market days, we would inspect the crates of live frogs and crabs which we were warned not to poke, boxes of dried cuttlefish, and row upon row of iced prawns, squid, and slippery fish. The sanddabs made me shiver each time; their eyes lay on one flattened side and reminded me of my mother's story of a careless girl who ran into a crowded street and was crushed by a cab. "Was smash flat," reported my mother.

At the corner of the alley was Hong Sing's, a four-table café with a recessed stairwell in front that led to a door marked "Tradesmen." My brothers and I believed the bad people emerged from this door at night. Tourists never went to Hong Sing's, since the menu was printed only in Chinese. A Caucasian man with a big camera once posed me and my playmates in front of the restaurant. He had us move to the side of the picture window so the photo would capture the roasted duck with its head dangling from a juice-covered rope. After he took the picture, I told him he should go into Hong Sing's and eat dinner. When he smiled and asked me what they served, I shouted, "Guts and duck's feet and octopus gizzards!" Then I ran off with my friends, shrieking with laughter as we scampered across the alley and hid in the entryway grotto of the China Gem Company, my heart pounding with hope that he would chase us.

My mother named me after the street that we lived on: Waverly Place Jong, my official name for important American documents. But my family called me Meimei, "Little Sister." I was the youngest, the only daughter. Each morning before school, my mother would twist and yank on my thick black hair until she had formed two tightly wound pigtails. One day, as she struggled to weave a hard-toothed comb through my disobedient hair, I had a sly thought.

I asked her, "Ma, what is Chinese torture?" My mother shook her head. A bobby pin was wedged between her lips. She wetted her palm and smoothed the hair above my ear, then pushed the pin in so that it nicked sharply against my scalp.

"Who say this word?" she asked without a trace of knowing how wicked I was being. I shrugged my shoulders and said, "Some boy in my class said Chinese people do Chinese torture."

"Chinese people do many things," she said simply. "Chinese people do business, do medicine, do painting. Not lazy like American people. We do torture. Best torture."

My older brother Vincent was the one who actually got the chess set. We had gone to the annual Christmas party held at the First Chinese Baptist Church at the end of the alley. The missionary ladies had put together a Santa bag of gifts donated by members of another church. None of the gifts had names on them. There were separate sacks for boys and girls of different ages.

One of the Chinese parishioners had donned a Santa Claus costume and a stiff paper beard with cotton balls glued to it. I think the

---

2. **elude** (i lüd/), *v.* slip away from; baffle.

only children who thought he was the real thing were too young to know that Santa Claus was not Chinese. When my turn came up, the Santa man asked me how old I was. I thought it was a trick question; I was seven according to the American formula and eight by the Chinese calendar. I said I was born on March 17, 1951. That seemed to satisfy him. He then solemnly[3] asked if I had been a very, very good girl this year and did I believe in Jesus Christ and obey my parents. I knew the only answer to that. I nodded back with equal solemnity.

Having watched the other children opening their gifts, I already knew that the big gifts were not necessarily the nicest ones. One girl my age got a large coloring book of biblical characters, while a less greedy girl who selected a smaller box received a glass vial of lavender toilet water. The sound of the box was also important. A ten-year-old boy had chosen a box that jangled when he shook it. It was a tin globe of the world with a slit for inserting money. He must have thought it was full of dimes and nickels, because when he saw that it had just ten pennies, his face fell with such undisguised disappointment that his mother slapped the side of his head and led him out of the church hall, apologizing to the crowd for her son who had such bad manners he couldn't appreciate such a fine gift.

As I peered into the sack, I quickly fingered the remaining presents, testing their weight, imagining what they contained. I chose a heavy, compact one that was wrapped in shiny silver foil and a red satin ribbon. It was a twelve-pack of Life Savers and I spent the rest of the party arranging and rearranging the candy tubes in the order of my favorites. My brother Winston chose wisely as well. His present turned out to be a box of intricate plastic parts; the instructions on the box proclaimed that when they

The chessboard seemed to hold elaborate secrets....

were properly assembled he would have an authentic miniature replica[4] of a World War II submarine.

Vincent got the chess set, which would have been a very decent present to get at a church Christmas party, except it was obviously used and, as we discovered later, it was missing a black pawn and a white knight. My mother graciously thanked the unknown benefactor, saying, "Too good. Cost too much." At which point, an old lady with fine white, wispy hair nodded toward our family and said with a whistling whisper, "Merry, merry Christmas."

When we got home, my mother told Vincent to throw the chess set away. "She not want it. We not want it," she said, tossing her head stiffly to the side with a tight, proud smile. My brothers had deaf ears. They were already lining up the chess pieces and reading from the dog-eared instruction book.

I watched Vincent and Winston play during Christmas week. The chessboard seemed to hold elaborate secrets waiting to be untangled. The chessmen were more powerful than Old Li's magic herbs that cured ancestral curses. And my brothers wore such serious faces that I was sure something was at stake that was greater than avoiding the tradesmen's door to Hong Sing's.

"Let me! Let me!" I begged between games when one brother or the other would sit back with a deep sigh of relief and victory, the other annoyed, unable to let go of the outcome. Vincent at first refused to let me play, but when I offered my Life Savers as replacements for the buttons that filled in for the missing pieces, he

---

3. **solemnly** (sol′əm lē), *adv.* in a serious, grave, or earnest way.
4. **replica** (rep′lə kə), *n.* a copy or close reproduction.

relented.[5] He chose the flavors: wild cherry for the black pawn and peppermint for the white knight. Winner could eat both.

As our mother sprinkled flour and rolled out small doughy circles for the steamed dumplings that would be our dinner that night, Vincent explained the rules, pointing to each piece. "You have sixteen pieces and so do I. One king and queen, two bishops, two knights, two castles, and eight pawns. The pawns can only move forward one step, except on the first move. Then they can move two. But they can only take men by moving crossways like this, except in the beginning, when you can move ahead and take another pawn."

"Why?" I asked as I moved my pawn. "Why can't they move more steps?"

"Because they're pawns," he said.

"But why do they go crossways to take other men? Why aren't there any women and children?"

"Why is the sky blue? Why must you always ask stupid questions?" asked Vincent. "This is a game. These are the rules. I didn't make them up. See. Here. In the book." He jabbed a page with a pawn in his hand. "Pawn. P-A-W-N. Pawn. Read it yourself."

My mother patted the flour off her hands. "Let me see book," she said quietly. She scanned the pages quickly, not reading the foreign English symbols, seeming to search deliberately for nothing in particular.

"This American rules," she concluded at last. "Every time people come out from foreign country, must know rules. You not know, judge say, Too bad, go back. They not telling you why so you can use their way go forward. They say, Don't know why, you find out yourself. But they knowing all the time. Better you take it, find out why yourself." She tossed her head back with a satisfied smile.

I found out about all the whys later. I read the rules and looked up all the big words in a dictionary. I borrowed books from the Chinatown library. I studied each chess piece, trying to absorb the power each contained.

I learned about opening moves and why it's important to control the center early on; the shortest distance between two points is straight down the middle. I learned about the middle game and why tactics between two adversaries[6] are like clashing ideas; the one who plays better has the clearest plans for both attacking and getting out of traps. I learned why it is essential in the endgame[7] to have foresight, a mathematical understanding of all possible moves, and patience; all weaknesses and advantages become evident to a strong adversary and are obscured to a tiring opponent. I discovered that for the whole game one must gather invisible strengths and see the endgame before the game begins.

I also found out why I should never reveal "why" to others. A little knowledge withheld is a great advantage one should store for future use. That is the power of chess. It is a game of secrets in which one must show and never tell.

I loved the secrets I found within the sixty-four black and white squares. I carefully drew a handmade chessboard and pinned it to the wall next to my bed, where at night I would stare for hours at imaginary battles. Soon I no longer lost any games or Life Savers, but I lost my adversaries. Winston and Vincent decided they were more interested in roaming the streets after school in their Hopalong Cassidy cowboy hats.

On a cold spring afternoon, while walking home from school, I detoured through the playground at the end of our alley. I saw a group of old men, two seated across a folding table playing a game of chess, others smoking pipes, eating peanuts, and watching. I ran home and grabbed Vincent's chess set,

---

5. **relent** (ri lent′), v. become less harsh or cruel; become more tender and merciful.
6. **adversary** (ad′vər ser′ē), n. person or group on the other side in a contest; opponent.
7. **endgame** (end′gām), n. the last stage of a chess game, characterized by the presence of only a few pieces left on the board.

which was bound in a cardboard box with rubber bands. I also carefully selected two prized rolls of Life Savers. I came back to the park and approached a man who was observing the game.

"Want to play?" I asked him. His face widened with surprise and he grinned as he looked at the box under my arm.

"Little sister, been a long time since I play with dolls," he said smiling benevolently.[8] I quickly put the box down next to him on the bench and displayed my retort.[9]

Lau Po, as he allowed me to call him, turned out to be a much better player than my brothers. I lost many games and many Life Savers. But over the weeks, with each diminishing roll of candies, I added new secrets. Lau Po gave me the names. The Double Attack from the East and West Shores. Throwing Stones on the Drowning Man. The Sudden Meeting of the Clan. The Surprise from the Sleeping Guard. The Humble Servant Who Kills the King. Sand in the Eyes of Advancing Forces. A Double Killing Without Blood.

There were also the fine points of chess etiquette.[10] Keep captured men in neat rows, as well-tended prisoners. Never announce "Check" with vanity, lest someone with an unseen sword slit your throat. Never hurl pieces into the sandbox after you have lost a game, because then you must find them again, by yourself, after apologizing to all around you. By the end of the summer, Lau Po had taught me all he knew, and I had become a better chess player.

A small weekend crowd of Chinese people and tourists would gather as I played and defeated my opponents one by one. My mother would join the crowds during these outdoor exhibition games. She sat proudly on the bench, telling my admirers with proper Chinese humility,[11] "Is luck."

A man who watched me play in the park suggested that my mother allow me to play in local chess tournaments. My mother smiled graciously, an answer that meant nothing. I desperately wanted to go, but I bit back my tongue. I knew she would not let me play among strangers. So as we walked home I said in a small voice that I didn't want to play in the local tournament. They would have American rules. If I lost, I would bring shame on my family.

"Is shame you fall down nobody push you," said my mother.

During my first tournament, my mother sat with me in the front row as I waited for my turn. I frequently bounced my legs to unstick them from the cold metal seat of the folding chair. When my name was called, I leapt up. My mother unwrapped something in her lap. It was her *chang*, a small tablet of red jade which held the sun's fire. "Is luck," she whispered, and tucked it into my dress pocket. I turned to my opponent, a fifteen-year-old boy from Oakland. He looked at me, wrinkling his nose.

As I began to play, the boy disappeared, the color ran out of the room, and I saw only my white pieces and his black ones waiting on the other side. A light wind began blowing past my ears. It whispered secrets only I could hear.

"Blow from the South," it murmured. "The wind leaves no trail." I saw a clear path, the traps to avoid. The crowd rustled. "Shh! Shh!" said the corners of the room. The wind blew stronger. "Throw sand from the East to distract him." The knight came forward ready for the sacrifice. The wind hissed, louder and louder. "Blow, blow, blow. He cannot see. He is blind now. Make him lean away from the wind so he is easier to knock down."

"Check," I said, as the wind roared with laughter. The wind died down to little puffs, my own breath.

---

8. **benevolently** (bə nev′ə lənt lē), *adv.* kindly.
9. **retort** (ri tôrt′), *n.* a sharp or witty reply.
10. **etiquette** (et′ə ket), *n.* the formal rules for governing a profession, official ceremony, or a game.
11. **humility** (hyü mil′ə tē), *n.* humbleness of mind; meekness.

My mother placed my first trophy next to a new plastic chess set that the neighborhood Tao society[12] had given to me. As she wiped each piece with a soft cloth, she said, "Next time win more, lose less."

"Ma, it's not how many pieces you lose," I said. "Sometimes you need to lose pieces to get ahead."

"Better to lose less, see if you really need."

At the next tournament, I won again, but it was my mother who wore the triumphant grin.

"Lost eight piece this time. Last time was eleven. What I tell you? Better off lose less!" I was annoyed, but I couldn't say anything.

I attended more tournaments, each one farther away from home. I won all games, in all divisions. The Chinese bakery downstairs from our flat displayed my growing collection of trophies in its window, amidst the dust-covered cakes that were never picked up. The day after I won an important regional tournament, the window encased a fresh sheet cake with whipped-cream frosting and red script saying "Congratulations, Waverly Jong, Chinatown Chess Champion." Soon after that, a flower shop, headstone engraver, and funeral parlor offered to sponsor me in national tournaments. That's when my mother decided I no longer had to do the dishes. Winston and Vincent had to do my chores.

"Why does she get to play and we do all the work," complained Vincent.

"Is new American rules," said my mother. "Meimei play, squeeze all her brains out for win chess. You play, worth squeeze towel."

By my ninth birthday, I was a national chess champion. I was still some 429 points away from grand-master status, but I was touted as the Great American Hope, a child prodigy[13] and a girl to boot. They ran a photo of me in *Life* magazine next to a quote in which Bobby Fischer[14] said, "There will never be a woman grand master." "Your move, Bobby," said the caption.

The day they took the magazine picture I wore neatly plaited braids clipped with plastic barrettes trimmed with rhinestones. I was playing in a large high school auditorium that echoed with phlegmy coughs and the squeaky rubber knobs of chair legs sliding across freshly waxed wooden floors. Seated across from me was an American man, about the same age as Lau Po, maybe fifty. I remember that his sweaty brow seemed to weep at my every move. He wore a dark, malodorous suit. One of his pockets was stuffed with a great white kerchief on which he wiped his palm before sweeping his hand over the chosen chess piece with great flourish.

In my crisp pink-and-white dress with scratchy lace at the neck, one of two my mother had sewn for these special occasions, I would clasp my hands under my chin, the delicate points of my elbows poised lightly on the table in the manner my mother had shown me for posing for the press. I would swing my patent leather shoes back and forth like an impatient child riding on a school bus. Then I would pause, suck in my lips, twirl my chosen piece in midair as if undecided, and then firmly plant it in its new threatening place, with a triumphant smile thrown back at my opponent for good measure.

I no longer played in the alley of Waverly Place. I never visited the playground where the pigeons and old men gathered. I went to school, then directly home to learn new chess secrets, cleverly concealed advantages, more escape routes.

But I found it difficult to concentrate at home. My mother had a habit of standing over me while I plotted out my games. I think she thought of herself as my protective ally. Her lips would be

---

12. **Tao** (tou) **society.** Taoism, one of China's three main religions, teaches simplicity and humility as a way to peace and harmony in life.

13. prodigy (prod′ə jē), *n.* person endowed with amazing brilliance, talent, etc., especially a remarkably talented child.

14. **Bobby Fischer,** one of the most controversial chess players of all time, was the first American to become Chess Champion of the World.

This film still from the 1993 movie *The Joy Luck Club* features Tsai Chin and Vu Mai in the roles of Waverly Jong and her mother. Compare this depiction with your own mental picture about what the daughter and mother look like. ➤

sealed tight, and after each move I made, a soft "Hmmmmph" would escape from her nose.

"Ma, I can't practice when you stand there like that," I said one day. She retreated to the kitchen and made loud noises with the pots and pans. When the crashing stopped, I could see out of the corner of my eye that she was standing in the doorway. "Hmmmph!" Only this one came out of her tight throat.

My parents made many concessions to allow me to practice. One time I complained that the bedroom I shared was so noisy that I couldn't think. Thereafter, my brothers slept in a bed in the living room facing the street. I said I couldn't finish my rice; my head didn't work right when my stomach was too full. I left the table with half-finished bowls and nobody complained. But there was one duty I couldn't avoid. I had to accompany my mother on Saturday market days when I had no tournament to play. My mother would proudly walk with me, visiting many shops, buying very little. "This my daughter Wave-ly Jong," she said to whoever looked her way.

One day after we left a shop I said under my breath, "I wish you wouldn't do that, telling everybody I'm your daughter." My mother stopped walking. Crowds of people with heavy bags pushed past us on the sidewalk, bumping into first one shoulder, then another.

"Aiii-ya. So shame be with mother?" She grasped my hand even tighter as she glared at me.

I looked down. "It's not that, it's just so obvious. It's just so embarrassing."

"Embarrass you be my daughter?" Her voice was cracking with anger.

"That's not what I meant. That's not what I said."

"What you say?"

I knew it was a mistake to say anything more, but I heard my voice speaking. "Why do you have to use me to show off? If you want to show off, then why don't you learn to play chess?"

My mother's eyes turned into dangerous black slits. She had no words for me, just sharp silence.

I felt the wind rushing around my hot ears. I jerked my hand out of my mother's tight grasp and spun around, knocking into an old woman. Her bag of groceries spilled to the ground.

"Aii-ya! Stupid girl!" my mother and the

woman cried. Oranges and tin cans careened down the sidewalk. As my mother stooped to help the old woman pick up the escaping food, I took off.

I raced down the street, dashing between people, not looking back as my mother screamed shrilly, "Meimei! Meimei!" I fled down an alley, past dark, curtained shops and merchants washing the grime off their windows. I sped into the sunlight, into a large street crowded with tourists examining trinkets and souvenirs. I ducked into another dark alley, down another street, up another alley. I ran until it hurt and I realized I had nowhere to go, that I was not running from anything. The alleys contained no escape routes.

My breath came out like angry smoke. It was cold. I sat down on an upturned plastic pail next to a stack of empty boxes, cupping my chin with my hands, thinking hard. I imagined my mother, first walking briskly down one street or another looking for me, then giving up and returning home to await my arrival. After two hours, I stood up on creaking legs and slowly walked home.

The alley was quiet and I could see the yellow lights shining from our flat like two tiger's eyes in the night. I climbed the sixteen steps to the door, advancing quietly up each so as not to make any warning sounds. I turned the knob; the door was locked. I heard a chair moving, quick steps, the locks turning—click! click! click!—and then the door opened.

"About time you got home," said Vincent. "Boy, are you in trouble."

He slid back to the dinner table. On a platter were the remains of a large fish, its fleshy head still connected to bones swimming upstream in vain escape. Standing there waiting for my punishment, I heard my mother speak in a dry voice.

"We not concerning this girl. This girl not have concerning for us."

Nobody looked at me. Bone chopsticks clinked against the insides of bowls being emptied into hungry mouths.

I walked into my room, closed the door, and lay down on my bed. The room was dark, the ceiling filled with shadows from the dinnertime lights of neighboring flats.

In my head, I saw a chessboard with sixty-four black and white squares. Opposite me was my opponent, two angry black slits. She wore a triumphant smile. "Strongest wind cannot be seen," she said.

Her black men advanced across the plane, slowly marching to each successive level as a single unit. My white pieces screamed as they scurried and fell off the board one by one. As her men drew closer to my edge, I felt myself growing light. I rose up into the air and flew out the window. Higher and higher, above the alley, over the tops of tiled roofs, where I was gathered up by the wind and pushed up toward the night sky until everything below me disappeared and I was alone.

I closed my eyes and pondered my next move.

After Reading

Making Connections

Shaping Your Response

1. Who do you think is more justified in being angry at the end of the story—Meimei or her mother? Why?

2. If you were Meimei, what would your next move be?

3. On a scale of 1 to 10, with 10 being what you consider a perfect mother or daughter, rate Meimei and her mother. Be ready to explain your ratings.

Analyzing the Story

4. Amy Tan creates a vivid picture of Chinatown. Find three examples of details that help convey the **setting** of the story.

5. 🐾 How does culture influence the way Meimei and her mother **communicate** with each other?

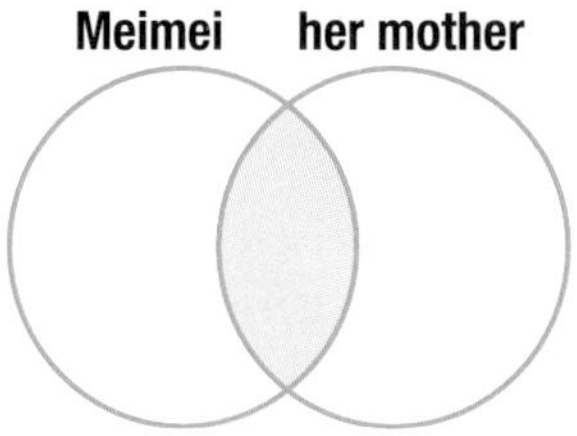

Meimei   her mother

6. In what ways are the **characters** of Meimei and her mother similar? In what ways are they different? Jot down your ideas on a Venn diagram like the one pictured here. Record the traits Meimei and her mother share in the area where the circles intersect.

7. Tan uses the image of wind several times in the story (see pages 6, 11, and 13–14). Find one example and explain what the wind **symbolizes,** or represents.

Extending the Ideas

8. Meimei talks about using "invisible strengths" to get what she wants. Describe a way you could apply this strategy to your own life.

9. The shops and services in the neighborhood reflect what is important to the culture of its residents. Do the stores and services in your neighborhood reflect the cultural heritage of your community? If so, how?

Literary Focus: Protagonist and Antagonist

A story's main character is the **protagonist,** while a rival character or force that works against the protagonist is called the **antagonist.** With these definitions in mind, answer these questions about "Rules of the Game."

- Who is the story's protagonist?

- Who is the antagonist?

- Are there any other persons or forces that work against the protagonist? What are those forces?

- How do these antagonistic forces affect the protagonist? Does change or growth occur as a result?

Vocabulary Study

adversary
benevolently
elude
etiquette
humility
prodigy
relent
replica
retort
solemnly

The first word in each word pair given below is a vocabulary word. On a separate sheet of paper, write down whether the second word is a synonym or an antonym of the vocabulary word. Then write a paragraph or two about the etiquette of playing games using as many vocabulary words as you can. Use your Glossary, if necessary, to understand the meanings of the vocabulary words.

1. solemnly—seriously
2. replica—duplicate
3. relent—restrict
4. adversary—friend
5. humility—conceit
6. prodigy—genius
7. retort—reply
8. elude—avoid
9. benevolently—harshly
10. etiquette—rules

Expressing Your Ideas

Writing Choices

Writer's Notebook Update Now that you have read the story, write a short piece that compares and contrasts yours and Meimei's ideas about games. You might also detail how your ideas about competition are similar to and different from Meimei's mother's ideas.

Dear Blabby Imagine that you are an advice columnist. Meimei has written to you, asking for some tips on how to solve her problem with her mother. What do you think Meimei's next move should be? Write a **reply letter** for your column. Be sure to give some specific ideas for Meimei to try.

Rules of Your Game At first, Meimei's family has difficulty playing chess because they don't know all the rules. Think of a game—a popular game or one that you devise—and write clear, concise **rules** for playing the game. To "test" your work, classmates can try to play the game using your rules.

Other Options

Square Off A **debate** is a formal way to argue both sides of an issue. With a partner, consider an issue that arises in "Rules of the Game" and develop an argument for each side of the issue. (Sample issues: Winning is the most satisfying result of playing a game. A prodigy upsets the balance in a family. Success makes people uncomfortable.) Present your debate to the class.

In the News You and a group of your classmates are television news anchors, reporting on events that happen in "Rules of the Game." Develop a lead story around one of the following ideas: a sportscast of one of Meimei's chess matches, an interview with a family member (or even a sports psychologist!), or any other creative ideas of your own. Present your **newscast** to the class. Videotape it so you can see yourself on the news.

The Most Dangerous Game

by Richard Connell

Richard Connell
1893–1949

Richard Connell's writing career took many interesting turns. He began writing at the age of ten as a baseball reporter for his father's newspaper. Later, Mr. Connell was secretary to his father, who was serving in Congress. Connell then finished his schooling at Harvard. After spending years on a newspaper staff in New York, he became a freelance writer, writing short stories, novels, and motion picture scripts from his home in Beverly Hills, California. "The Most Dangerous Game," by far his most famous story, has been made into many film versions.

Building Background

Living By the Sword Have you ever heard or read the quotation, "He who lives by the sword dies by the sword"? What do you think it means? Explain it in your own words. Then discuss with a partner some situations you have heard or read about that illustrate this quotation. As you read "The Most Dangerous Game," think about how the story might relate to this quotation.

Literary Focus

Plot The **plot** of a story is a series of events that presents a problem or **conflict**, builds to a **climax**, and then brings about a **resolution**. Note the usual structure of a plot provided in the diagram. As you read "The Most Dangerous Game," consider how the author develops the plot. What conflict or problem is established? What events lead to the climax? How is the conflict resolved?

Climax

Falling Action

Rising Action

Conflict

Resolution

Writer's Notebook

Friend or Foe? "The Most Dangerous Game" focuses on two men who become opponents in a conflict. Before you read "The Most Dangerous Game," write about an opponent you have faced. What kind of game were you playing? What strategies did you use against your adversary: "mind games," athletic skill, intelligence, or something else?

THE MOST DANGEROUS GAME

RICHARD CONNELL

"Off there to the right—somewhere—is a large island," said Whitney. "It's rather a mystery—"

"What island is it?" Rainsford asked.

"The old charts call it 'Ship-Trap Island,'" Whitney replied. "A suggestive name, isn't it? Sailors have a curious dread of the place. I don't know why. Some superstition—"

"Can't see it," remarked Rainsford, trying to peer through the dank tropical night that was palpable[1] as it pressed its thick warm blackness in upon the yacht.

"You've good eyes," said Whitney, with a laugh, "and I've seen you pick off a moose moving in the brown fall brush at four hundred yards, but even you can't see four miles or so through a moonless Caribbean night."

"Nor four yards," admitted Rainsford. "Ugh! It's like moist black velvet."

"It will be light enough in Rio," promised Whitney. "We should make it in a few days. I hope the jaguar guns have come from Purdey's. We should have some good hunting up the Amazon. Great sport, hunting."

"The best sport in the world," agreed Rainsford.

"For the hunter," amended Whitney. "Not for the jaguar."

"Don't talk rot, Whitney," said Rainsford. "You're a big-game hunter, not a philosopher. Who cares how a jaguar feels?"

"Perhaps the jaguar does," observed Whitney.

---

1. palpable (pal′pə bəl), *adj.* that can be touched or felt; tangible.

"Bah! They've no understanding."

"Even so, I rather think they understand one thing—fear. The fear of pain and the fear of death."

"Nonsense," laughed Rainsford. "This hot weather is making you soft, Whitney. Be a realist. The world is made up of two classes—the hunters and the huntees. Luckily, you and I are hunters. Do you think we've passed that island yet?"

Henri Rousseau, *The Hungry Lion* (1905). Though French painter Henri Rousseau never traveled, his imagination and frequent trips to the Paris zoo inspired him to paint exotic animals and lush jungle scenes. What does this painting say about life in the jungle?

"I can't tell in the dark. I hope so."

"Why?" asked Rainsford.

"The place has a reputation—a bad one."

"Cannibals?" suggested Rainsford.

"Hardly. Even cannibals wouldn't live in such a God-forsaken place. But it's gotten into sailor lore, somehow. Didn't you notice that the crew's nerves seemed a bit jumpy today?"

"They were a bit strange, now you mention it. Even Captain Nielsen—"

"Yes, even that tough-minded old Swede, who'd go up to the devil himself and ask him for a light. Those fishy blue eyes held a look I never saw there before. All I could get out of him was: 'This place has an evil name among seafaring men, sir.' Then he said to me, very gravely: 'Don't you feel anything?'—as if the air about us was actually poisonous. Now, you mustn't laugh when I tell you this—I did feel something like a sudden chill.

"There was no breeze. The sea was as flat as a plate-glass window. We were drawing near the island then. What I felt was a—a mental chill; a sort of sudden dread."

"Pure imagination," said Rainsford. "One superstitious sailor can taint[2] the whole ship's company with his fear."

"Maybe. But sometimes I think sailors have an extra sense that tells them when they are in danger. Sometimes I think evil is a tangible[3] thing—with wave lengths, just as sound and light have. An evil place can, so to speak, broadcast vibrations of evil. Anyhow, I'm glad we're getting out of this zone. Well, I think I'll turn in now, Rainsford."

"I'm not sleepy," said Rainsford. "I'm going to smoke another pipe up on the afterdeck."

"Good night, then, Rainsford. See you at breakfast."

"Right. Good night, Whitney."

There was no sound in the night as Rainsford sat there, but the muffled throb of the engine that drove the yacht swiftly through the darkness, and the swish and ripple of the wash of the propeller.

Rainsford, reclining in a steamer chair, indolently[4] puffed on his favorite brier.[5] The sensuous drowsiness of the night was on him. "It's so dark," he thought, "that I could sleep without closing my eyes; the night would be my eyelids—"

An abrupt sound startled him. Off to the right he heard it, and his ears, expert in such matters, could not be mistaken. Again he heard the sound, and again. Somewhere, off in the blackness, someone had fired a gun three times.

Rainsford sprang up and moved quickly to the rail, mystified. He strained his eyes in the direction from which the reports had come, but it was like trying to see through a blanket. He leaped upon the rail and balanced himself there, to get greater elevation; his pipe, striking a rope, was knocked from his mouth. He lunged for it; a short, hoarse cry came from his lips as he realized he had reached too far and had lost his balance. The cry was pinched off short as the blood-warm waters of the Caribbean Sea closed over his head.

He struggled up to the surface and tried to cry out, but the wash from the speeding yacht slapped him in the face and the salt water in his open mouth made him gag and strangle. Desperately he struck out with strong strokes after the receding lights of the yacht, but he stopped before he had swum fifty feet. A certain cool-headedness had come to him; it was not the first time he had been in a tight place. There was a chance that his cries could be heard by someone aboard the yacht, but that chance was slender, and grew more slender as the yacht raced on. He wrestled himself out of some of his clothes, and shouted with all his power. The lights of the yacht became faint

---

2. taint (tānt), v. spoil, corrupt, or contaminate.
3. tangible (tan′jə bəl), adj. that can be touched or felt.
4. indolently (in′dl ənt lē), adv. lazily.
5. brier (brī′ər), n. a tobacco pipe made of brier wood.

and ever-vanishing fireflies; then they were blotted out entirely by the night.

Rainsford remembered the shots. They had come from the right, and doggedly he swam in that direction, swimming with slow, deliberate strokes, conserving his strength. For a seemingly endless time he fought the sea. He began to count his strokes; he could do possibly a hundred more and then—

Rainsford heard a sound. It came out of the darkness, a high screaming sound, the sound of an animal in an extremity of anguish and terror.

He did not recognize the animal that made the sound; he did not try to; with fresh vitality he swam toward the sound. He heard it again; then it was cut short by another noise, crisp, staccato.

"Pistol shot," muttered Rainsford, swimming on.

Ten minutes of determined effort brought another sound to his ears—the most welcome he had ever heard—the muttering and growling of the sea breaking on a rocky shore. He was almost on the rocks before he saw them; on a night less calm he would have been shattered against them. With his remaining strength he dragged himself from the swirling waters. Jagged crags appeared to jut into the opaqueness; he forced himself upward, hand over hand. Gasping, his hands raw, he reached a flat place at the top. Dense jungle came down to the very edge of the cliffs. What perils that tangle of trees and underbrush might hold for him did not concern Rainsford just then. All he knew was that he was safe from his enemy, the sea, and that utter weariness was on him. He flung himself down at the jungle edge and tumbled headlong into the deepest sleep of his life.

When he opened his eyes, he knew from the position of the sun that it was late in the afternoon. Sleep had given him new vigor; a sharp hunger was picking at him. He looked about him, almost cheerfully.

"Where there are pistol shots, there are men. Where there are men, there is food," he thought. But what kind of men, he wondered, in so forbidding a place? An unbroken front of snarled and ragged jungle fringed the shore.

He saw no sign of a trail through the closely knit web of weeds and trees; it was easier to go along the shore, and Rainsford floundered along by the water. Not far from where he had landed, he stopped.

Some wounded thing, by the evidence a large animal, had thrashed about in the underbrush; the jungle weeds were crushed down and the moss was lacerated; one patch of weeds was stained crimson. A small, glittering object not far away caught Rainsford's eye and he picked it up. It was an empty cartridge.

"PISTOL SHOT," MUTTERED RAINSFORD, SWIMMING ON.

"A twenty-two," he remarked. "That's odd. It must have been a fairly large animal too. The hunter had his nerve with him to tackle it with a light gun. It's clear that the brute put up a fight. I suppose the first three shots I heard was when the hunter flushed his quarry[6] and wounded it. The last shot was when he trailed it here and finished it."

He examined the ground closely and found what he had hoped to find—the print of hunting boots. They pointed along the cliff in the direction he had been going. Eagerly he hurried along, now slipping on a rotten log or a loose stone, but making headway; night was beginning to settle down on the island.

Bleak darkness was blacking out the sea and jungle when Rainsford sighted the lights. He came upon them as he turned a crook in the coastline, and his first thought was that he had come upon a village, for there were many lights.

6. **quarry** (kwôr′ē), *n.* a pursued animal.

But as he forged along he saw to his great astonishment that all the lights were in one enormous building—a lofty structure with pointed towers plunging upward into the gloom. His eyes made out the shadowy outlines of a palatial château;[7] it was set on a high bluff, and on three sides of it cliffs dived down to where the sea licked greedy lips in the shadows.

"Mirage,"[8] thought Rainsford. But it was no mirage, he found, when he opened the tall spiked iron gate. The stone steps were real enough; the massive door with a leering gargoyle for a knocker was real enough; yet about it all hung an air of unreality.

He lifted the knocker, and it creaked up stiffly, as if it had never before been used. He let it fall, and it startled him with its booming loudness. He thought he heard steps within; the door remained closed. Again Rainsford lifted the heavy knocker, and let it fall. The door opened then, opened as suddenly as if it were on a spring, and Rainsford stood blinking in the river of glaring gold light that poured out. The first thing Rainsford's eyes discerned[9] was the largest man he had ever seen—a gigantic creature, solidly made and black-bearded to the waist. In his hand the man held a long-barreled revolver, and he was pointing it straight at Rainsford's heart.

Out of the snarl of beard two small eyes regarded Rainsford.

"Don't be alarmed," said Rainsford, with a smile which he hoped was disarming. "I'm no robber. I fell off a yacht. My name is Sanger Rainsford of New York City."

The menacing look in the eyes did not change. The revolver pointed as rigidly as if the giant were a statue. He gave no sign that he understood Rainsford's words, or that he had even heard them. He was dressed in uniform, a black uniform trimmed with gray astrakhan.[10]

"I'm Sanger Rainsford of New York," Rainsford began again. "I fell off a yacht. I am hungry."

The man's only answer was to raise with his thumb the hammer of his revolver. Then Rainsford saw the man's free hand go to his forehead in a military salute, and he saw him click his heels together and stand at attention. Another man was coming down the broad marble steps, an erect, slender man in evening clothes. He advanced to Rainsford and held out his hand.

In a cultivated voice marked by a slight accent that gave it added precision and deliberateness, he said: "It is a very great pleasure and honor to welcome Mr. Sanger Rainsford, the celebrated hunter, to my home."

Automatically Rainsford shook the man's hand.

"I've read your book about hunting snow leopards in Tibet, you see," explained the man. "I am General Zaroff."

Rainsford's first impression was that the man was singularly handsome; his second was that there was an original, almost bizarre quality about the general's face. He was a tall man past middle age, for his hair was a vivid white; but his thick eyebrows and pointed military mustache were as black as the night from which Rainsford had come. His eyes, too, were black and very bright. He had high cheekbones, a sharp-cut nose, a spare, dark face, the face of a man used to giving orders, the face of an aristocrat. Turning to the giant in uniform, the general made a sign. The giant put away his pistol, saluted, withdrew.

"Ivan is an incredibly strong fellow," remarked the general, "but he has the misfortune to be deaf and dumb. A simple fellow, but, I'm afraid, like all his race, a bit of a savage."

7. **château** (sha tō′), *n.* a large country house, usually found in France or elsewhere in Europe.
8. **mirage** (mə räzh′), *n.* an optical illusion in which a distant scene appears to be much closer than it actually is; or something that does not exist.
9. **discern** (də sėrn′), *v.* see clearly; distinguish or recognize.
10. **astrakhan** (as′trə kən), *n.* a rough woolen cloth that looks like curly furlike wool.

▲ Like General Zaroff, the man portrayed in Cuban American painter Julio Larraz's *Casanova* (1987) has a proud, aristocratic look. What clues tell you he might be a hunter? If you know that a "Casanova" is a man who pursues many women, what new insight do you have about the man in the painting?

"Is he Russian?"

"He is a Cossack,"[11] said the general, and his smile showed red lips and pointed teeth. "So am I."

"Come," he said, "we shouldn't be chatting here. We can talk later. Now you want clothes, food, rest. You shall have them. This is a most restful spot."

Ivan had reappeared, and the general spoke to him with lips that moved but gave forth no sound.

"Follow Ivan, if you please, Mr. Rainsford,"

---

11. **He is a Cossack** (kos′ak). The Cossacks, who lived in southern Russia, were noted for their love of fighting and their excellent horsemanship.

said the general. "I was about to have my dinner when you came. I'll wait for you. You'll find that my clothes will fit you, I think."

It was to a huge, beam-ceilinged bedroom with a canopied bed big enough for six men that Rainsford followed the silent giant. Ivan laid out an evening suit, and Rainsford, as he put it on, noticed that it came from a London tailor who ordinarily cut and sewed for none below the rank of duke.

The dining room to which Ivan conducted him was in many ways remarkable. There was a medieval magnificence about it; it suggested a baronial hall of feudal times with its oaken panels, its high ceiling, its vast refectory table where twoscore men[12] could sit down to eat. About the hall were the mounted heads of many animals—lions, tigers, elephants, moose, bears; larger or more perfect specimens Rainsford had never seen. At the great table the general was sitting, alone.

"You'll have a cocktail, Mr. Rainsford," he suggested. The cocktail was surpassingly good; and, Rainsford noted, the table appointments were of the finest—the linen, the crystal, the silver, the china.

They were eating *borsch*,[13] the rich, red soup with whipped cream so dear to Russian palates. Half apologetically General Zaroff said: "We do our best to preserve the amenities[14] of civilization here. Please forgive any lapses. We are well off the beaten track, you know. Do you think the champagne has suffered from its long ocean trip?"

"Not in the least,' declared Rainsford. He was finding the general a most thoughtful and affable[15] host, a true cosmopolite.[16] But there was one small trait of the general's that made Rainsford uncomfortable. Whenever he looked up from his plate he found the general studying him, appraising him narrowly.

"Perhaps," said General Zaroff, "you were surprised that I recognized your name. You see,

I read all books on hunting published in English, French, and Russian. I have but one passion in my life, Mr. Rainsford, and it is the hunt."

"You have some wonderful heads here," said Rainsford as he ate a particularly well-cooked filet mignon. "That Cape buffalo is the largest I ever saw."

"YOU HAVE SOME WONDERFUL HEADS HERE," SAID RAINSFORD.

"Oh, that fellow. Yes, he was a monster."

"Did he charge you?"

"Hurled me against a tree," said the general. "Fractured my skull. But I got the brute."

"I've always thought," said Rainsford, "that the Cape buffalo is the most dangerous of all big game."

For a moment the general did not reply; he was smiling his curious red-lipped smile. Then he said slowly: "No. You are wrong, sir. The Cape buffalo is not the most dangerous big game." He sipped his wine. "Here in my preserve on this island," he said in the same slow tone, "I hunt more dangerous game."

Rainsford expressed his surprise. "Is there big game on this island?"

The general nodded. "The biggest."

"Really?"

"Oh, it isn't here naturally, of course. I have to stock the island."

"What have you imported, general?" Rainsford asked. "Tigers?"

---

12. **twoscore men,** forty men.
13. *borsch* (bôrsh).
14. **amenities** (ə men′ə tēz), *n.* pleasant ways; polite acts.
15. affable (af′ə bəl), *adj.* courteous, pleasant, and gracious to others.
16. **cosmopolite** (koz mop′ə līt), *n.* a person who feels at home in all parts of the world.

The general smiled. "No," he said. "Hunting tigers ceased to interest me some years ago. I exhausted their possibilities, you see. No thrill left in tigers, no real danger. I live for danger, Mr. Rainsford."

The general took from his pocket a gold cigarette case and offered his guest a long black cigarette with a silver tip; it was perfumed and gave off a smell like incense.

"We will have some capital hunting, you and I," said the general. "I shall be most glad to have your society."

"But what game—" began Rainsford.

"I'll tell you," said the general. "You will be amused, I know. I think I may say, in all modesty, that I have done a rare thing. I have invented a new sensation. May I pour you another glass of port, Mr. Rainsford?"

"Thank you, general."

The general filled both glasses, and said: "God makes some men poets. Some He makes kings, some beggars. Me He made a hunter. My hand was made for the trigger, my father said. He was a very rich man with a quarter of a million acres in the Crimea,[17] and he was an ardent sportsman. When I was only five years old he gave me a little gun, specially made in Moscow for me, to shoot sparrows with. When I shot some of his prize turkeys with it, he did not punish me; he complimented me on my marksmanship. I killed my first bear in the Caucasus[18] when I was ten. My whole life has been one prolonged hunt. I went into the army—it was expected of noblemen's sons—and for a time commanded a division of Cossack cavalry, but my real interest was always the hunt. I have hunted every kind of game in every land. It would be impossible for me to tell you how many animals I have killed."

The general puffed at his cigarette.

"After the debacle in Russia[19] I left the country, for it was imprudent for an officer of the Czar to stay there. Many noble Russians lost everything. I, luckily, had invested heavily in American securities, so I shall never have to open a tea room in Monte Carlo or drive a taxi in Paris. Naturally, I continued to hunt—grizzlies in your Rockies, crocodiles in the Ganges,[20] rhinoceroses in East Africa. It was in Africa that the Cape buffalo hit me and laid me up for six months. As soon as I recovered I started for the Amazon to hunt jaguars, for I had heard they were unusually cunning. They weren't." The Cossack sighed. "They were no match at all for a hunter with his wits about him, and a high-powered rifle. I was bitterly disappointed. I was lying in my tent with a splitting headache one night when a terrible thought pushed its way into my mind. Hunting was beginning to bore me! And hunting, remember, had been my life. I have heard that in America businessmen often go to pieces when they give up the business that has been their life."

"Yes, that's so," said Rainsford.

The general smiled. "I had no wish to go to pieces," he said. "I must do something. Now, mine is an analytical mind, Mr. Rainsford. Doubtless that is why I enjoy the problems of the chase."

"No doubt, General Zaroff."

"So," continued the general, "I asked myself why the hunt no longer fascinated me. You are much younger than I am, Mr. Rainsford, and have not hunted as much, but you perhaps can guess the answer."

"What was it?"

"Simply this: hunting had ceased to be what you call 'a sporting proposition.' It had become too easy. I always got my quarry. Always. There is no greater bore than perfection."

---

17. **the Crimea** (krī mē′ə), a peninsula in southwestern Russia, jutting down into the Black Sea.
18. **the Caucasus** (kô′kə səs), mountain range extending from the Black Sea to the Caspian Sea.
19. **debacle** (di bäk′əl) **in Russia.** In the Russian Revolution of 1917, the government of the Czar was overthrown, the property of the nobles confiscated, and most of the nobility driven into exile.
20. **the Ganges** (gan′jēz′), a river in India regarded by the Hindus as being sacred.

The general lit a fresh cigarette.

"No animal had a chance with me any more. That is no boast; it is a mathematical certainty. The animal had nothing but his legs and his instinct. Instinct is no match for reason. When I thought of this it was a tragic moment for me, I can tell you."

Rainsford leaned across the table, absorbed in what his host was saying.

"It came to me as an inspiration what I must do," the general went on.

"And that was?"

The general smiled the quiet smile of one who has faced an obstacle and surmounted it with success. "I had to invent a new animal to hunt," he said.

"A new animal? You're joking."

"Not at all," said the general. "I never joke about hunting. I needed a new animal. I found one. So I bought this island, built this house, and here I do my hunting. The island is perfect for my purposes—there are jungles with a maze of trails in them, hills, swamps—"

"But the animal, General Zaroff?"

"Oh," said the general, "it supplies me with the most exciting hunting in the world. No other hunting compares with it for an instant. Every day I hunt, and I never grow bored now, for I have a quarry with which I can match my wits."

Rainsford's bewilderment showed in his face.

"I wanted the ideal animal to hunt," explained the general. "So I said: 'What are the attributes of an ideal quarry?' And the answer was, of course: 'It must have courage, cunning, and, above all, it must be able to reason.'"

"But no animal can reason," objected Rainsford.

"My dear fellow," said the general, "there is one that can."

"But you can't mean—" gasped Rainsford.

"And why not?"

"I can't believe you are serious, General Zaroff. This is a grisly joke."

"Why should I not be serious? I am speaking of hunting."

"Hunting? Good heavens, General Zaroff, what you speak of is murder."

The general laughed with entire good nature. He regarded Rainsford quizzically. "I refuse to believe that so modern and civilized a young man as you seem to be harbors romantic ideas about the value of human life. Surely your experiences in the war—"

"Did not make me condone[21] cold-blooded murder," finished Rainsford stiffly.

Laughter shook the general. "How extraordinarily droll you are!" he said. "One does not expect nowadays to find a young man of the educated class, even in America, with such a naive, and, if I may say so, mid-Victorian point of view. It's like finding a snuff-box[22] in a limousine. Ah, well, doubtless you had Puritan ancestors. I'll wager you'll forget your notions when you go hunting with me. You've a genuine new thrill in store for you, Mr. Rainsford."

"Thank you, I'm a hunter, not a murderer."

"Dear me," said the general, quite unruffled, "again that unpleasant word. But I think I can show you that your scruples[23] are quite ill-founded."

"Yes?"

"Life is for the strong, to be lived by the strong, and, if need be, taken by the strong. The weak of the world were put here to give the strong pleasure. I am strong. Why should I not use my gift? If I wish to hunt, why should I not? I hunt the scum of the earth—sailors from tramp ships—lascars,[24] blacks, Chinese, whites, mongrels—a thoroughbred horse or hound is worth more than a score of them."

---

21. condone (kən dōn′), v. forgive or overlook.
22. **snuff-box,** a small box once used for holding snuff, a form of powdered tobacco.
23. **scruple** (skrü′pəl), n. feeling of uneasiness that keeps a person from doing something.
24. **lascar** (las′kər), n. East Indian sailor.

"But they are men," said Rainsford hotly.

"Precisely," said the general. "That is why I use them. It gives me pleasure. They can reason, after a fashion. So they are dangerous."

"But where do you get them?"

The general's left eyelid fluttered down in a wink. "This island is called Ship-Trap," he answered. "Sometimes an angry god of the high seas sends them to me. Sometimes, when Providence is not so kind, I help Providence a bit. Come to the window with me."

Rainsford went to the window and looked out toward the sea.

"Watch! Out there!" exclaimed the general, pointing into the night. Rainsford's eyes saw only blackness, and then, as the general pressed a button, far out to sea Rainsford saw the flash of lights.

The general chuckled. "They indicate a channel," he said, "where there's none: giant rocks with razor edges crouch like a sea monster with wide-open jaws. They can crush a ship as easily as I crush this nut." He dropped a walnut on the hardwood floor and brought his heel grinding down on it. "Oh, yes," he said, casually, as if in answer to a question, "I have electricity. We try to be civilized here."

"Civilized? And you shoot down men?"

A trace of anger was in the general's black eyes, but it was there for but a second, and he said, in his most pleasant manner: "Dear me, what a righteous young man you are! I assure you I do not do the thing you suggest. That would be barbarous.[25] I treat these visitors with every consideration. They get plenty of good food and exercise. They get into splendid physical condition. You shall see for yourself tomorrow."

"What do you mean?"

"We'll visit my training school," smiled the general. "It's in the cellar. I have about a dozen pupils down there now. They're from the Spanish bark *San Lucar* that had the bad luck to go on the rocks out there. A very inferior lot, I regret to say. Poor specimens and more accustomed to the deck than to the jungle."

He raised his hand, and Ivan, who served as waiter, brought thick Turkish coffee. Rainsford, with an effort, held his tongue in check.

"It's a game, you see," pursued the general blandly. "I suggest to one of them that we go hunting. I give him a supply of food and an excellent hunting knife. I give him three hours' start. I am to follow, armed only with a pistol of the smallest caliber and range. If my quarry eludes me for three whole days, he wins the game. If I find him"—the general smiled—"he loses."

"Suppose he refuses to be hunted?"

"Oh," said the general, "I give him his option, of course. He need not play that game if he doesn't wish to. If he does not wish to hunt, I turn him over to Ivan. Ivan once had the honor of serving as official knouter to the Great White Czar,[26] and he has his own ideas of sport. Invariably, Mr. Rainsford, invariably they choose the hunt."

"And if they win?"

The smile on the general's face widened. "To date I have not lost," he said.

Then he added, hastily: "I don't wish you to think me a braggart, Mr. Rainsford. Many of them afford only the most elementary sort of problem. Occasionally I strike a tartar.[27] One almost did win. I eventually had to use the dogs."

---

25. barbarous (bär′bər əs), *adj.* not civilized; savage.
26. **Ivan once had the honor of serving as official knouter** (nout′ər) **to the Great White Czar** (zär). During the reign of Alexander III (1881–1894), a knouter was the official flogger of those doomed to be lashed with a knout, a terrible whip made of plaited leather thongs and wire.
27. **strike a tartar** (tär′tər). The general means that sometimes he encounters a man who isn't easily manageable.

"The dogs?"

"This way, please. I'll show you."

The general steered Rainsford to a window. The lights from the windows sent a flickering illumination that made grotesque patterns on the courtyard below, and Rainsford could see moving about there a dozen or so huge black shapes; as they turned toward him, their eyes glittered greenly.

"A rather good lot, I think," observed the general. "They are let out at seven every night. If anyone should try to get into my house—or out of it—something extremely regrettable would occur to him." He hummed a snatch of song from the Folies Bergère.[28]

"And now," said the general, "I want to show you my new collection of heads. Will you come with me to the library?"

"I hope," said Rainsford, "that you will excuse me tonight, General Zaroff. I'm really not feeling at all well."

"Ah, indeed?" the general inquired solicitously.[29] "Well, I suppose that's only natural, after your long swim. You need a good, restful night's sleep. Tomorrow you'll feel like a new man, I'll wager. Then we'll hunt, eh? I've one rather promising prospect—"

Rainsford was hurrying from the room.

"Sorry you can't go with me tonight," called the general. "I expect rather fair sport—a big, strong black. He looks resourceful—Well, good night, Mr. Rainsford; I hope you have a good night's rest."

The bed was good, and the pajamas of the softest silk, and he was tired in every fiber of his being, but nevertheless Rainsford could not quiet his brain with the opiate[30] of sleep. He lay, eyes wide open. Once he thought he heard stealthy steps in the corridor outside his room. He sought to throw open the door; it would not open. He went to the window and looked out. His room was high up in one of the towers. The lights of the château were out now, and it was dark and silent, but there was a fragment of sallow moon, and by its wan light he could see, dimly, the courtyard; there, weaving in and out in the pattern of shadow, were black, noiseless forms; the hounds heard him at the window and looked up, expectantly, with their green eyes. Rainsford went back to the bed and lay down. By many methods he tried to put himself to sleep. He had achieved a doze when, just as morning began to come, he heard, far off in the jungle, the report of a pistol.

General Zaroff did not appear until luncheon. He was dressed faultlessly in the tweeds of a country squire. He was solicitous about the state of Rainsford's health.

"As for me," sighed the general, "I do not feel so well. I am worried, Mr. Rainsford. Last night I detected traces of my old complaint."

To Rainsford's questioning glance the general said: "Ennui.[31] Boredom."

Then, taking a second helping of crêpes suzette,[32] the general explained: "The hunting was not good last night. The fellow lost his head. He made a straight trail that offered no problems at all. That's the trouble with these sailors; they have dull brains to begin with, and they do not know how to get about in the woods. They do excessively stupid and obvious things. It's most annoying. Will you have another glass of Chablis,[33] Mr. Rainsford?"

"General," said Rainsford firmly, "I wish to leave this island at once."

The general raised his thickets of eyebrows; he seemed hurt. "But, my dear fellow," he protested, "you've only just come. You've had no hunting—"

"I wish to go today," said Rainsford. He saw

---

28. **the Folies Bergère** (fô′lē ber zher′), a famous music hall in Paris.
29. solicitously (sə lis′ə təs lē), *adv.* showing concern.
30. **opiate** (o′pē it), *n.* anything that quiets or soothes.
31. **ennui** (on wē′), boredom. [French]
32. **crêpes suzette** (krāps′ sü zet′), thin dessert pancakes, usually rolled, sometimes served with a flaming brandy sauce. [French]
33. **Chablis** (shä blē′), a dry white wine.

the dead black eyes of the general on him, studying him. General Zaroff's face suddenly brightened.

He filled Rainsford's glass with venerable Chablis from a dusty bottle.

"Tonight," said the general, "we will hunt—you and I."

Rainsford shook his head. "No, general," he said. "I will not hunt."

The general shrugged his shoulders and delicately ate a hothouse grape. "As you wish, my friend," he said. "The choice rests entirely with you. But may I not venture to suggest that you will find my idea of sport more diverting than Ivan's?"

He nodded toward the corner to where the giant stood, scowling, his thick arms crossed on his hogshead of a chest.

"You don't mean—" cried Rainsford.

"My dear fellow," said the general, "have I not told you I always mean what I say about hunting? This is really an inspiration. I drink to a foeman worthy of my steel—at last."

The general raised his glass, but Rainsford sat staring at him.

"You'll find this game worth playing," the general said enthusiastically. "Your brain against mine. Your woodcraft against mine. Your strength and stamina against mine. Outdoor chess! And the stake is not without value, eh?"

"And if I win—" began Rainsford huskily.

"I'll cheerfully acknowledge myself defeated if I do not find you by midnight of the third day," said General Zaroff. "My sloop will place you on the mainland near a town."

The general read what Rainsford was thinking.

"Oh, you can trust me," said the Cossack. "I will give you my word as a gentleman and a sportsman. Of course you, in turn, must agree to say nothing of your visit here."

"I'll agree to nothing of the kind," said Rainsford.

"Oh," said the general, "in that case—But why discuss that now? Three days hence we can discuss it over a bottle of Veuve Cliquot,[34] unless—"

The general sipped his wine.

Then a businesslike air animated him. "Ivan," he said to Rainsford, "will supply you with hunting clothes, food, a knife. I suggest you wear moccasins; they leave a poorer trail. I suggest too that you avoid the big swamp in the southeast corner of the island. We call it Death Swamp. There's quicksand there. One foolish fellow tried it. The deplorable part of it was that Lazarus followed him. You can imagine my feelings, Mr. Rainsford. I loved Lazarus; he was the finest hound in my pack. Well, I must beg you to excuse me now. I always take a siesta after lunch. You'll hardly have time for a nap, I fear. You'll want to start, no doubt. I shall not follow till dusk. Hunting at night is so much more exciting than by day, don't you think? *Au revoir,*[35] Mr. Rainsford, *au revoir.*"

General Zaroff, with a deep courtly bow, strolled from the room.

From another door came Ivan. Under one arm he carried khaki hunting clothes, a haversack of food, a leather sheath containing a long-bladed hunting knife; his right hand rested on a cocked revolver thrust in the crimson sash about his waist. . . .

Rainsford had fought his way through the bush for two hours. "I must keep my nerve. I must keep my nerve," he said through tight teeth.

He had not been entirely clear-headed when the château gates snapped shut behind him. His whole idea at first was to put distance between himself and General Zaroff, and, to this end, he had plunged along, spurred on by the sharp rowels[36] of something very like panic. Now he

---

34. **Veuve Cliquot** (vœv klē′kō), a fine champagne.
35. *Au revoir* (ō rə vwär′), good-by; till I see you again. [French]
36. **rowel** (rou′əl), *n.* a small wheel with sharp points, attached to the end of a spur.

had got a grip on himself, had stopped, and was taking stock of himself and the situation.

He saw that straight flight was futile; inevitably it would bring him face to face with the sea. He was in a picture with a frame of water, and his operations, clearly, must take place within that frame.

"I'll give him a trail to follow," muttered Rainsford, and he struck off from the rude paths he had been following into the trackless wilderness. He executed a series of intricate loops; he doubled on his trail again and again, recalling all the lore of the fox hunt, and all the dodges of the fox. Night found him leg-weary, with hands and face lashed by the branches, on a thickly wooded ridge. He knew it would be insane to blunder on through the dark, even if he had the strength. His need for rest was imperative[37] and he thought: "I have played the fox, now I must play the cat of the fable." A big tree with a thick trunk and outspread branches was nearby, and, taking care to leave not the slightest mark, he climbed up into the crotch, and stretching out on one of the broad limbs, after a fashion, rested. Rest brought him new confidence and almost a feeling of security. Even so zealous a hunter as General Zaroff could not trace him there, he told himself; only the devil himself could follow that complicated trail through the jungle after dark. But, perhaps, the general was a devil—

An apprehensive night crawled slowly by like a wounded snake, and sleep did not visit Rainsford, although the silence of a dead world was on the jungle. Toward morning when a dingy gray was varnishing the sky, the cry of some startled bird focused Rainsford's attention in that direction. Something was coming through the bush, coming slowly, carefully, coming by the same winding way Rainsford had come. He flattened himself down on the limb, and through a screen of leaves almost as thick as tapestry, he watched. The thing that was approaching was a man.

It was General Zaroff. He made his way along with his eyes fixed in utmost concentration on the ground before him. He paused, almost beneath the tree, dropped to his knees and studied the ground. Rainsford's impulse was to hurl himself down like a panther, but he saw that the general's right hand held something metallic—a small automatic pistol.

The hunter shook his head several times, as if he were puzzled. Then he straightened up and took from his case one of his black cigarettes; its pungent incense-like smoke floated up to Rainsford's nostrils.

Rainsford held his breath. The general's eyes had left the ground and were traveling inch by inch up the tree. Rainsford froze there, every muscle tensed for a spring. But the sharp eyes of the hunter stopped before they reached the limb where Rainsford lay; a smile spread over his brown face. Very deliberately he blew a smoke ring into the air; then he turned his back on the tree and walked carelessly away, back along the trail he had come. The swish of the underbrush against his hunting boots grew fainter and fainter.

The pent-up air burst hotly from Rainsford's lungs. His first thought made him feel sick and numb. The general could follow a trail through the woods at night; he could follow an extremely difficult trail; he must have uncanny powers; only by the merest chance had the Cossack failed to see his quarry.

Rainsford's second thought was even more terrible. It sent a shudder of cold horror through his whole being. Why had the general smiled? Why had he turned back?

Rainsford did not want to believe what his reason told him was true, but the truth was as evident as the sun that by now had pushed through the morning mists. The general was playing with him! The general was saving him for another day's sport! The Cossack was the cat;

---

37. imperative (im per′ə tiv), *adj.* that must be done; urgent; necessary.

he was the mouse. Then it was that Rainsford knew the full meaning of terror.

"I will not lose my nerve. I will not."

He slid down from the tree, and struck off again into the woods. His face was set and he forced the machinery of his mind to function. Three hundred yards from his hiding place he stopped where a huge dead tree leaned precariously on a smaller, living one. Throwing off his sack of food, Rainsford took his knife from its sheath and began to work with all his energy.

The job was finished at last, and he threw himself down behind a fallen log a hundred feet away. He did not have to wait long. The cat was coming again to play with the mouse.

Following the trail with the sureness of a bloodhound, came General Zaroff. Nothing escaped those searching black eyes, no crushed blade of grass, no bent twig, no mark, no matter how faint, in the moss. So intent was the Cossack on his stalking that he was upon the thing Rainsford had made before he saw it. His foot touched the protruding bough that was the trigger. Even as he touched it, the general sensed his danger and leaped back with the agility of an ape. But he was not quite quick enough; the dead tree, delicately adjusted to rest on the cut living one, crashed down and struck the general a glancing blow on the shoulder as it fell; but for his alertness, he must have been smashed beneath it. He staggered, but he did not fall; nor did he drop his revolver. He stood there, rubbing his injured shoulder, and Rainsford, with fear again gripping his heart, heard the general's mocking laugh ring through the jungle.

"Rainsford," called the general, "if you are within sound of my voice, as I suppose you are, let me congratulate you. Not many men know how to make a Malay man-catcher. Luckily, for me, I too have hunted in Malacca.[38] You are proving interesting, Mr. Rainsford. I am going now to have my wound dressed; it's only a slight one. But I shall be back. I shall be back."

When the general, nursing his bruised shoulder, had gone, Rainsford took up his flight again. It was flight now, a desperate, hopeless

THEN IT WAS THAT RAINSFORD KNEW THE FULL MEANING OF TERROR.

flight, that carried him on for some hours. Dusk came, then darkness, and still he pressed on. The ground grew softer under his moccasins; the vegetation grew ranker, denser; insects bit him savagely. Then, as he stepped forward, his foot sank into the ooze. He tried to wrench it back, but the muck sucked viciously at his foot as if it were a giant leech. With a violent effort, he tore his foot loose. He knew where he was now. Death Swamp and its quicksand.

His hands were tight closed as if his nerve were something tangible that someone in the darkness was trying to tear from his grip. The softness of the earth had given him an idea. He stepped back from the quicksand a dozen feet or so and, like some huge prehistoric beaver, he began to dig.

Rainsford had dug himself in in France when a second's delay meant death. That had been a placid pastime compared to his digging now. The pit grew deeper; when it was above his shoulders, he climbed out and from some hard saplings cut stakes and sharpened them to a fine point. These stakes he planted in the bottom of the pit with the points sticking up. With flying fingers he wove a rough carpet of weeds and branches and with it he covered the mouth of the pit. Then, wet with sweat and aching with tiredness, he crouched behind the stump of a lightning-charred tree.

---

38. **Malacca** (mə lak′ə), an area in the southeastern part of the Malay Peninsula.

▲ *Green Tide* (1989) by David Hockney measures 24 in. X 72.5 in. Why might the artist choose these dimensions for a painting of the ocean?

He knew his pursuer was coming; he heard the padding sound of feet on the soft earth, and the night breeze brought him the perfume of the general's cigarette. It seemed to Rainsford that the general was coming with unusual swiftness; he was not feeling his way along, foot by foot. Rainsford, crouching there, could not see the general, nor could he see the pit. He lived a year in a minute. Then he felt an impulse to cry aloud with joy, for he heard the sharp crackle of the breaking branches as the cover of the pit gave way; he heard the sharp scream of pain as the pointed stakes found their mark. He leaped up from his place of concealment. Then he cowered back. Three feet from the pit a man was standing, with an electric torch in his hand.

"You've done well, Rainsford," the voice of the general called. "Your Burmese tiger pit[39] has claimed one of my best dogs. Again you score. I think, Mr. Rainsford, I'll see what you can do against my whole pack. I'm going home for a rest now. Thank you for a most amusing evening."

At daybreak Rainsford, lying near the swamp, was awakened by a sound that made him know that he had new things to learn about fear. It was a distant sound, faint and wavering, but he knew it. It was the baying of a pack of hounds.

Rainsford knew he could do one of two things. He could stay where he was and wait. That was suicide. He could flee. That was postponing the inevitable. For a moment he stood there, thinking. An idea that held a wild chance

---

39. **Burmese** (ber′mēz′) **tiger pit,** a deep pit covered by brush; used for trapping tigers in Burma.

came to him, and, tightening his belt, he headed away from the swamp.

The baying of the hounds drew nearer, then still nearer, nearer, ever nearer. On a ridge Rainsford climbed a tree. Down a watercourse, not a quarter of a mile away, he could see the bush moving. Straining his eyes, he saw the lean figure of General Zaroff; just ahead of him Rainsford made out another figure whose wide shoulders surged through the tall jungle weeds; it was the giant Ivan, and he seemed pulled forward by some unseen force; Rainsford knew that Ivan must be holding the pack in leash.

They would be on him any minute now. His mind worked frantically. He thought of a native trick he had learned in Uganda.[40] He slid down the tree. He caught hold of a springy young sapling and to it he fastened his hunting knife, with the blade pointing down the trail; with a bit of wild grapevine he tied back the sapling. Then he ran for his life. The hounds raised their voices as they hit the fresh scent. Rainsford knew now how an animal at bay feels.

He had to stop to get his breath. The baying of the hounds stopped abruptly; and Rainsford's heart stopped, too. They must have reached the knife.

He shinned excitedly up a tree and looked back. His pursuers had stopped. But the hope that was in Rainsford's brain when he had climbed died, for he saw in the shallow valley that General Zaroff was still on his feet. But Ivan was not. The knife, driven by the recoil of the springing tree, had not wholly failed.

---

40. **Uganda** (yŭ gan′də), formerly a British protectorate in eastern Africa, now an independent state.

Rainsford had hardly tumbled to the ground when the pack took up the cry again.

"Nerve, nerve, nerve!" he panted, as he dashed along. A blue gap showed between the trees dead ahead. Ever nearer drew the hounds. Rainsford forced himself on toward that gap. He reached it. It was the shore of the sea. Across a cove he could see the gloomy gray stone of the château. Twenty feet below him the sea rumbled and hissed. Rainsford hesitated. He heard the hounds. Then he leaped far out into the sea. . . .

When the general and his pack reached the place by the sea, the Cossack stopped. For some minutes he stood regarding the blue-green expanse of water. He shrugged his shoulders. Then he sat down, took a drink of brandy from a silver flask, lit a perfumed cigarette, and hummed a bit from *Madame Butterfly.*[41]

General Zaroff had an exceedingly good dinner in his great paneled dining hall that evening. With it he had a bottle of Pol Roger and half a bottle of Chambertin.[42] Two slight annoyances kept him from perfect enjoyment. One was the thought that it would be difficult to replace Ivan; the other was that his quarry had escaped him; of course the American hadn't played the game—so thought the general as he tasted his after-dinner liqueur. In his library he read, to soothe himself, from the works of Marcus Aurelius.[43] At ten he went up to his bedroom. He was deliciously tired, he said to himself, as he locked himself in. There was a little moonlight; so, before turning on his light, he went to the window and looked down at the courtyard. He could see the great hounds, and he called: "Better luck another time," to them. Then he switched on the light.

A man, who had been hiding in the curtains of the bed, was standing there.

"Rainsford!" screamed the general. "How did you get here?"

"Swam," said Rainsford. "I found it quicker than walking through the jungle."

The general sucked in his breath and smiled. "I congratulate you," he said. "You have won the game."

Rainsford did not smile. "I am still a beast at bay," he said in a low, hoarse voice. "Get ready, General Zaroff."

The general made one of his deepest bows. "I see," he said. "Splendid! One of us is to furnish a repast[44] for the hounds. The other will sleep in this very excellent bed. On guard, Rainsford . . ."

He had never slept in a better bed, Rainsford decided.

---

41. *Madame Butterfly,* a tragic opera by Puccini.
42. **Pol Roger** (pōl rō′zhā) **. . . and Chambertin** (shăm′ber taN), fine French wines.
43. **Marcus Aurelius** (mär′kəs ô rē′lē əs), Roman emperor (A.D. 161–180) and famous philosopher.
44. **repast** (ri past′) *n.* meal; food.

After Reading

Making Connections

Shaping Your Response

1. In your opinion, does Rainsford have the right to kill Zaroff?

2. In your notebook, write three words that describe Rainsford and three words that describe Zaroff. Share your words with a partner.

3. Do you think the ideas Rainsford expresses about hunting at the beginning of the story will change after his experiences on the island? Explain your answer.

Analyzing the Story

4. Connell uses language that creates a **mood** of dread and suspense. Find three descriptions that convey such a mood.

5. Why do you think the general is or is not a believable **character?**

6. Compare and contrast Rainsford's and Zaroff's attitudes toward hunting.

7. Define *game* in two different ways, giving two meanings to the title of the story.

8. Interpret the meaning of the last line of the story.

Extending the Ideas

9. While still on the ship, Rainsford says that "the world is made up of two classes—the hunter and the huntee." Challenge or support this view based on what you see in the world.

Literary Focus: Plot

The **plot** of a story is the series of events that begin with a problem or conflict, build to a climax, and lead to a resolution of the conflict. Make a plot structure map like this one and fill in each important event from the story at its appropriate point on the map.

Climax

Rising
Action

Falling
Action

Conflict
**Rainsford falls overboard;
fights for survival**

Resolution

Vocabulary Study

The following questions contain vocabulary words in italic type. Answer the questions, using the Glossary if necessary.

affable
barbarous
condone
discern
imperative
indolently
palpable
solicitously
taint
tangible

1. In what situations might you *discern* that tension is *palpable?*
2. Would a company want to *taint* its products? Why or why not?
3. What things might an *affable* person do?
4. Do you *condone barbarous* behavior? Why or why not?
5. What are some of the *tangible* effects of exercise?
6. Describe a time when you treated someone *solicitously.*
7. How would someone who worked *indolently* be viewed by the supervisor?
8. Is it *imperative* that you attend college? Explain.

Expressing Your Ideas

Writing Choices

Writer's Notebook Update Now that you've read the story, think about whether Rainsford's strategies were similar to strategies you use in dealing with conflict. What do you think he'll do next? In your notebook, write a continuation of "The Most Dangerous Game." Will Rainsford leave the island? What will he tell his companions about his adventures? Has his experience changed him?

Spine-Tingling Adventures When you read "The Most Dangerous Game," what kept you turning pages? Look back to see how Richard Connell "hooked" you to keep you interested in the story. Now try your own hand at an adventure story. Write an **opening scene,** being sure to leave a "hook" that would interest readers in continuing the story.

Other Options

Talk Radio Rainsford is a guest on a radio call-in show. With a small group, create the **radio broadcast,** acting as Rainsford, the host, and various callers. What topic would they discuss? (Sample ideas: "Hunting: A Cruel Sport?"; "My Vacation Was a Nightmare") Rehearse your segment and then prepare an audiotape for the class.

Help Wanted General Zaroff has mysteriously returned, and has hired your ad agency. Your first assignment: write an **advertisement** to recruit a replacement for Ivan. Be sure to include specific details about the job.

Vacation Paradise? General Zaroff has another assignment for your ad agency: develop an **advertising campaign** for the Ship-Trap Island Tourist Resort. With a small group, produce maps, brochures, magazine ads, or other materials that will entice tourists to visit the island.

Before Reading

The Cask of Amontillado

by Edgar Allan Poe

Edgar Allan Poe
1809–1849

Edgar Allan Poe lived a short, passionate, and tragic life. At the age of two, when his mother died, Poe was taken into the home of John Allan, a wealthy merchant in Richmond, Virginia. When Poe was older, his arguments with Allan and unpredictable behavior led to a break with the family.

Poe's alcoholism interfered with his work, and he was prone to rages and deep depressions. Nevertheless, he was a true innovator in the American literary scene. His reviews, poems, and short stories received favorable attention. He might have gained even more recognition before his death if his sharp criticism of other writers had not earned him so many enemies.

Building Background

Scary Tales Although Edgar Allan Poe considered himself to be primarily a poet, he enjoyed writing chilling tales of horror like the one you are about to read. Poe was a master at building spine-tingling **suspense** in his stories, and many of the techniques he invented are still used in horror stories and movies today. In fact, the Edgar Awards, given each year by the Mystery Writers of America for the best mystery books, are named for him. "The Cask of Amontillado," inspired by a true story Poe heard while serving in the Army, illustrates Poe's mastery of the horror story.

Literary Focus

Irony "The Cask of Amontillado" makes extensive use of **irony,** the contrast between what appears and what really is. With **verbal irony,** there is a contrast between what is said and what is actually meant. In a horror story, for example, the villain might say to the victim, "I'd love to have you for dinner next week." The verbal irony is that the victim thinks he will be served dinner, not that he *is* dinner, as the villain intends. **Irony of situation** occurs when things turn out contrary to what is expected or intended. For example, in movies it's often the awkward, bumbling misfit who (ironically) turns out to be the only person who can save the whole town, or the country, or the planet. As you read "The Cask of Amontillado," look for examples of how Edgar Allan Poe uses both verbal irony and irony of situation. How does the irony contribute to the total effect of the story?

Writer's Notebook

Sweet Revenge? "The Cask of Amontillado" focuses on one man's act of revenge. Describe a situation in which you or someone you know sought revenge. What led to the revenge? Did taking revenge help or hurt the situation?

The Cask of AMONTILLADO

Edgar Allan Poe

The thousand injuries of Fortunato I had borne as I best could; but when he ventured upon insult, I vowed revenge. You, who so well know the nature of my soul, will not suppose, however, that I gave utterance to a threat. *At length* I would be avenged;[1] this was a point definitively settled—but the very definitiveness with which it was resolved, precluded[2] the idea of risk. I must not only punish, but punish with impunity.[3] A wrong is unredressed when retribution overtakes its redresser.[4] It is equally unredressed when the avenger fails to make himself felt as such to him who has done the wrong.

It must be understood, that neither by word nor deed had I given Fortunato cause to doubt my goodwill. I continued, as was my wont, to smile in his face, and he did not perceive that my smile *now* was at the thought of his immolation.[5]

CLARIFY: What is the narrator's goal?

He had a weak point—this Fortunato—although in other regards he was a man to be respected and even feared. He prided himself on his connoisseurship[6] in wine. Few Italians have the true virtuoso[7] spirit. For the most part their enthusiasm is adopted to suit the time and opportunity—to practice imposture upon the British and Austrian millionaires. In painting and gemmary[8] Fortunato, like his countrymen, was a quack—but in the matter of old wines he was sincere. In this respect I did not differ from him materially: I was skillful in the Italian vintages myself, and bought largely whenever I could.

It was about dusk, one evening during the supreme madness of the carnival season,[9] that I encountered my friend. He accosted[10] me with excessive warmth, for he had been drinking

1. **avenge** (ə venj′), *v.* take revenge for or on behalf of.
2. **preclude** (pri klüd′), *v.* shut out; make impossible; prevent.
3. **impunity** (im pyü′nə tē), *n.* freedom from punishment, injury, or other bad consequences.
4. **A wrong . . . redresser.** A wrong is not righted when the person who rights the wrong is punished for doing so.
5. **immolation** (im′ə lā′shən), *n.* the act of being killed as a sacrifice.
6. **connoisseurship** (kon′ə sėr′ship), *n.* an expertise in matters of art or taste.
7. **virtuoso** (vėr′chü ō′sō), *adj.* showing the qualities of a virtuoso, a person who has a cultivated appreciation of artistic excellence.
8. **gemmary** (jem′ər ē), *n.* scientific knowledge of gems.
9. **carnival season,** a time of feasting and merrymaking celebrated just before Lent.
10. **accost** (ə kôst′), *v.* approach and speak to first.

French and Italian Jokers (1670). Like the characters in "The Cask of Amontillado," some of the actors portrayed in this painting are in carnival costumes. What kind of a mood do these costumes suggest?

much. The man wore motley.[11] He had on a tight-fitting parti-striped dress, and his head was surmounted by the conical cap and bells. I was so pleased to see him, that I thought I should never have done wringing his hand.

I said to him: "My dear Fortunato, you are luckily met. How remarkably well you are looking today! But I have received a pipe[12] of what passes for Amontillado,[13] and I have my doubts."

"How?" said he. "Amontillado? A pipe? Impossible! And in the middle of the carnival!"

"I have my doubts," I replied; "and I was silly enough to pay the full Amontillado price without consulting you in the matter. You were not

to be found, and I was fearful of losing a bargain."

"Amontillado!"

"I have my doubts."

"Amontillado!"

"And I must satisfy them."

"Amontillado!"

"As you are engaged, I am on my way to

---

11. **motley** (mot'lē), *n*. the multi-colored costume characteristic of the professional jester.
12. **pipe** (pīp), *n*. a specialized term for a large container of wine or oils.
13. **Amontillado** (ə mon'tē yä'dō), a dry, pale sherry wine.

The Cask of Amontillado   **39**

Luchesi. If anyone has a critical turn, it is he. He will tell me——"

"Luchesi cannot tell Amontillado from sherry."

"And yet some fools will have it that his taste is a match for your own."

"Come, let us go."

"Whither?"

"To your vaults."

"My friend, no; I will not impose upon your good nature. I perceive you have an engagement. Luchesi——"

"I have no engagement—come."

"My friend, no. It is not the engagement, but the severe cold with which I perceive you are afflicted. The vaults are insufferably[14] damp. They are encrusted with nitre."[15]

"Let us go, nevertheless. The cold is merely nothing. Amontillado! You have been imposed upon. And as for Luchesi, he cannot distinguish sherry from Amontillado."

Thus speaking, Fortunato possessed himself of my arm. Putting on a mask of black silk, and drawing a *roquelaure*[16] closely about my person, I suffered him to hurry me to my palazzo.[17]

There were no attendants at home; they had absconded[18] to make merry in honor of the time. I had told them that I should not return until the morning, and had given them explicit orders not to stir from the house. These orders were sufficient, I well knew, to insure their immediate disappearance, one and all, as soon as my back was turned.

I took from their sconces two flambeaux,[19] and giving one to Fortunato, bowed him through several suites of rooms to the archway that led into the vaults. I passed down a long and winding staircase, requesting him to be cautious as he followed. We came at length to the foot of the descent, and stood together on the damp ground of the catacombs[20] of the Montresors.

The gait of my friend was unsteady, and the bells upon his cap jingled as he strode.

"The pipe?" said he.

"It is farther on," said I; "but observe the white web-work which gleams from these cavern walls."

He turned toward me, and looked into my eyes with two filmy orbs that distilled the rheum of intoxication.

"Nitre?" he asked, at length.

"Nitre," I replied. "How long have you had that cough?"

"Ugh! ugh! ugh!—ugh! ugh! ugh!—ugh! ugh! ugh!—ugh! ugh! ugh!—ugh! ugh! ugh!"

My poor friend found it impossible to reply for many minutes.

"It is nothing," he said, at last.

"Come," I said, with decision, "we will go back; your health is precious. You are rich, respected, admired, beloved; you are happy, as once I was. You are a man to be missed. For me it is no matter. We will go back; you will be ill, and I cannot be responsible. Besides, there is Luchesi——"

"Enough," he said; "the cough is a mere nothing; it will not kill me. I shall not die of a cough."

SUMMARIZE: How does Montresor lure Fortunato to the vault?

"True—true," I replied; "and, indeed, I had no intention of alarming you unnecessarily; but you should use all proper caution. A draught[21] of this Medoc will defend us from the damps."

---

14. **insufferably** (in suf′ər ə blē), *adv.* intolerably or unbearably.

15. **nitre** (nī′tər), *n.* potassium nitrate. Also spelled niter.

16. **roquelaure** (rōk′e lär), *n.* a knee-length cloak buttoned in front.

17. **palazzo** (pä lät′sō), *n.* palace, mansion, or large town house in Italy.

18. **abscond** (ab skond′), *v.* go away hurriedly and secretly.

19. **I took from their sconces two flambeaux . . . .** A sconce (skons) is a candlestick projecting from a wall bracket. Flambeaux (flam bō′) are flaming torches.

20. **catacombs** (kat′ə kōmz), *n.* network of underground galleries with recesses in which to place the dead.

21. **draught** (draft), *n.* amount taken in a single drink; drink or dose; also draft.

Here I knocked off the neck of a bottle which I drew from a long row of its fellows that lay upon the mould.

"Drink," I said, presenting him the wine.

He raised it to his lips with a leer. He paused and nodded to me familiarly, while his bells jingled.

"I drink," he said, "to the buried that repose around us."

"And I to your long life."

He again took my arm, and we proceeded.

"These vaults," he said, "are extensive."

"The Montresors," I replied, "were a great and numerous family."

"I forget your arms."

"A huge human foot d'or, in a field azure; the foot crushes a serpent rampant[22] whose fangs are imbedded in the heel."

"And the motto?"

Nemo me impune lacessit.[23]

"Good!" he said.

The wine sparkled in his eyes and the bells jingled. My own fancy grew warm with the Medoc. We had passed through walls of piled bones, with casks and puncheons[24] intermingling, into the inmost recesses of the catacombs. I paused again, and this time I made bold to seize Fortunato by an arm above the elbow.

"The nitre!" I said; "see, it increases. It hangs like moss upon the vaults. We are below the river's bed. The drops of moisture trickle among the bones. Come, we will go back ere it is too late. Your cough——"

"It is nothing," he said; "let us go on. But first, another draught of the Medoc."

I broke and reached him a flagon of De Grâve. He emptied it at a breath. His eyes flashed with a fierce light. He laughed and threw the bottle upward with a gesticulation I did not understand.

I looked at him in surprise. He repeated the movement—a grotesque one.

"You do not comprehend?" he said.

"Not I," I replied.

"Then you are not of the brotherhood."

"How?"

"You are not of the masons."[25]

"Yes, yes," I said; "yes, yes."

"You? Impossible! A mason?"

"A mason," I replied.

"A sign," he said.

"It is this," I answered, producing a trowel from beneath the folds of my *roquelaure.*

"You jest," he exclaimed, recoiling[26] a few paces. "But let us proceed to the Amontillado."

"Be it so," I said, replacing the tool beneath the cloak, and again offering him my arm. He leaned upon it heavily. We continued our route in search of the Amontillado. We passed through a range of low arches, descended, passed on, and descending again, arrived at a deep crypt, in which the foulness of the air caused our flambeaux rather to glow than flame.

At the most remote end of the crypt there appeared another less spacious. Its walls had been lined with human remains, piled to the vault overhead, in the fashion of the great catacombs of Paris. Three sides of this interior crypt were still ornamented in this manner. From the fourth the bones had been thrown down, and lay promiscuously upon the earth, forming at one point a mound of some size. Within the wall thus exposed by the displacing of the bones, we perceived a still interior recess, in depth about four feet, in width three, in height six or seven. It seemed to have been constructed for no especial use within itself, but formed merely the interval between two of the colossal supports of the roof

---

22. **A huge human foot . . . rampant.** The Montresor coat-of-arms shows, on a blue background, a golden foot crushing a snake reared up to strike.

23. **Nemo me impune lacessit** (nā′mō mā im pū′nā lä kes′it). "No one can harm me unpunished." [Latin]

24. **puncheon** (pun′chən), *n.* a large cask for liquor.

25. **masons** (mā′snz). In this play on words, Fortunato refers to a member of a fraternal society. Montresor implies one who builds with stone or brick.

26. **recoil** (ri koil′), *v.* draw or shrink back.

of the catacombs, and was backed by one of their circumscribing walls of solid granite.

PREDICT: What act of revenge do you think Montresor has planned for Fortunato? Why do you think so?

It was in vain that Fortunato, uplifting his dull torch, endeavored[27] to pry into the depth of the recess. Its termination the feeble light did not enable us to see.

"Proceed," I said; "herein is the Amontillado. As for Luchesi——"

"He is an ignoramus," interrupted my friend, as he stepped unsteadily forward, while I followed immediately at his heels. In an instant he had reached the extremity of the niche, and finding his progress arrested by the rock, stood stupidly bewildered. A moment more and I had fettered[28] him to the granite. In its surface were two iron staples, distant from each other about two feet, horizontally. From one of these depended a short chain, from the other a padlock. Throwing the links about his waist, it was but the work of a few seconds to secure it. He was too much astounded to resist. Withdrawing the key I stepped back from the recess.

"Pass your hand," I said, "over the wall; you cannot help feeling the nitre. Indeed it is *very* damp. Once more let me *implore* you to return. No? Then I must positively leave you. But I must first render you all the little attentions in my power."

"The Amontillado!" ejaculated my friend, not yet recovered from his astonishment.

"True," I replied; "the Amontillado."

As I said these words I busied myself among the pile of bones of which I have before spoken. Throwing them aside, I soon uncovered a quantity of building stone and mortar. With these materials and with the aid of my trowel, I began vigorously to wall up the entrance of the niche.

I had scarcely laid the first tier[29] of the masonry when I discovered that the intoxica-

tion of Fortunato had in a great measure worn off. The earliest indication I had of this was a low moaning cry from the depth of the recess. It was *not* the cry of a drunken man. There was then a long and obstinate[30] silence. I laid the second tier, and the third, and the fourth; and then I heard the furious vibrations of the chain. The noise lasted for several minutes, during which, that I might hearken to it with the more satisfaction, I ceased my labors and sat down upon the bones. When at last the clanking subsided, I resumed the trowel, and finished without interruption the fifth, the sixth, and the seventh tier. The wall was now nearly upon a level with my breast. I again paused, and holding the flambeaux over the mason-work, threw a few feeble rays upon the figure within.

A succession of loud and shrill screams, bursting suddenly from the throat of the chained form, seemed to thrust me violently back. For a brief moment I hesitated—I trembled. Unsheathing my rapier,[31] I began to grope with it about the recess; but the thought of an instant reassured me. I placed my hand upon the solid fabric of the catacombs, and felt satisfied. I reapproached the wall. I replied to the yells of him who clamored. I re-echoed—I aided—I surpassed them in volume and in strength. I did this, and the clamorer grew still.

> A succession of loud and shrill screams... seemed to thrust me violently back.

---

27. **endeavor** (en dev′ər), *v.* make an effort; try hard.
28. **fetter** (fet′ər), *v.* chain or shackle the feet to prevent escape.
29. **tier** (tir), *n.* one of a series of rows arranged one above another.
30. **obstinate** (ob′stə nit), *adj.* not giving in; stubborn.
31. **rapier** (rā′pē ər), *n.* a long and light sword used for thrusting.

It was now midnight, and my task was drawing to a close. I had completed the eighth, the ninth, and the tenth tier. I had finished a portion of the last and the eleventh; there remained but a single stone to be fitted and plastered in. I struggled with its weight; I placed it partially in its destined position. But now there came from out the niche a low laugh that erected the hairs upon my head. It was succeeded by a sad voice, which I had difficulty in recognizing as that of the noble Fortunato. The voice said——

"Ha! ha! ha!—he! he!—a very good joke indeed—an excellent jest. We will have many a rich laugh about it at the palazzo—he! he! he!—over our wine—he! he! he!"

"The Amontillado!" I said.

"He! he! he!—he! he! he!—yes, the Amontillado. But is it not getting late? Will not they be awaiting us at the palazzo, the Lady Fortunato and the rest? Let us be gone."

"Yes," I said, "let us be gone."

"For the love of God, Montresor!"

"Yes," I said, "for the love of God!"

But to these words I hearkened in vain for a reply. I grew impatient. I called aloud:

"Fortunato!"

No answer. I called again:

"Fortunato!"

No answer still. I thrust a torch through the remaining aperture and let it fall within. There came forth in return only a jingling of the bells. My heart grew sick—on account of the dampness of the catacombs. I hastened to make an end of my labor. I forced the last stone into its position; I plastered it up. Against the new masonry I re-erected the old rampart of bones. For the half of a century no mortal has disturbed them. *In pace requiescat!*[32]

▲ Bob Baumgartner, illustration for *The Cask of Amontillado.* What clues help you identify which figure is Montresor and which is Fortunato?

32. **In pace requiescat** (in pä kā reˊkwi esˊkät). "May he rest in peace." [Latin]

After Reading

Making Connections

Shaping Your Response

1. Be Fortunato when the moment of realization hits—Montresor is leaving you in the vault. What will you say, think, and do?

2. Who will suffer more, Fortunato or Montresor? Why do you think so?

Analyzing the Story

3. Poe has the narrator state his basic plan for revenge in the first paragraph of the story, yet the story is still full of **suspense.** Identify three moments in the story that are suspenseful, and explain what makes them that way.

4. Fortunato does not suspect that Montresor is seeking revenge. Give two reasons why.

5. 👁 Is there honest **communication** between Montresor and Fortunato? Explain.

6. Why do you think Poe chooses not to reveal the evils that were committed by Fortunato?

Extending the Ideas

7. Which **character** do you think is more evil—Montresor, or General Zaroff from "The Most Dangerous Game"? Explain.

8. "The Cask of Amontillado" reveals how thoughts of revenge can change a person. Think of a modern character from a book, a movie, or real life who is driven by revenge. (Batman, for example, fights crime to avenge the murder of his parents.) Compare and contrast the modern character to Montresor.

Literary Focus: Irony

Irony is the contrast between what appears and what really is. Answer these questions about **verbal irony** and **irony of situation** in "The Cask of Amontillado."

1. What is ironic about Fortunato's name? his costume?

2. Explain how each of the following is ironic:

   • Fortunato says of his cough, "It will not kill me."

   • Montresor drinks to Fortunato's long life.

   • Both men are "masons."

3. Look back through the story and jot down other examples of both verbal irony and irony of situation.

Vocabulary Study

Rewrite each of the following quotations from the story in your own words, replacing the italicized vocabulary word with another word or phrase that has the same meaning. Your Glossary may be helpful.

accost
avenge
endeavor
impunity
insufferably
obstinate
preclude
recoil
tier
virtuoso

1. At length, I would be *avenged*. . . .
2. . . . the very definitiveness with which it was resolved, *precluded* the idea of risk.
3. I must not only punish, but punish with *impunity*.
4. Few Italians have the true *virtuoso* spirit.
5. He *accosted* me with excessive warmth, for he had been drinking much.
6. "The vaults are *insufferably* damp."
7. "You jest," he exclaimed, *recoiling* a few paces.
8. It was in vain that Fortunato . . . *endeavored* to pry into the depth of the recess.
9. I had scarcely laid the first *tier* of masonry . . .
10. There was then a long and *obstinate* silence.

Expressing Your Ideas

Writing Choices

Writer's Notebook Update What did Fortunato gain (or lose) by inflicting his revenge on Montresor? Think of another (perhaps more appropriate!) method Montresor could have used to solve his problem. Write a short synopsis of a story that shows Montresor's new way of handling his problem.

Dear Diary What did Fortunato do to earn Montresor's hatred? Poe doesn't say, so you can invent your own reasons. As Montresor, write a few **diary entries** in which you discuss the offenses Fortunato has committed and your reaction to them.

Other Options

The Musical Score Think about the feelings that "The Cask of Amontillado" evokes. What kind of music would make an appropriate background for the story? Prepare a **soundtrack** and play it as you do a dramatic reading of part of "The Cask of Amontillado."

The Jury Is Out Montresor is on trial for murdering Fortunato, and you and the members of your small group are the jury. Montresor's lawyer has argued that Montresor is innocent by reason of insanity. Discuss the case and present your **verdict** to the class.

Before Reading

Checkouts

by Cynthia Rylant

Cynthia Rylant
born 1954

Cynthia Rylant grew up in the Appalachian Mountains of West Virginia. After her parents separated, her mother left her with her grandparents in a home without electricity or indoor plumbing. Rylant was never able to reunite with her father. When she was eight, Rylant and her mother moved to the town of Beaver, West Virginia, a town that Rylant has called "a small, sparkling universe that gave me a lifetime's worth of material for my writing." Both critics and readers have acclaimed her books for children and young adults. Rylant asserts that writing "has given me a sense of self-worth that I didn't have my whole childhood."

Building Background

What problem does the girl in the cartoon have? Do you think the cartoon is realistic? Why or why not? In a small group, discuss some of the other "games" people play in their quests for romance.

Literary Focus

Characterization
When you read, it's often the **characters** in a story that draw you in and keep your interest. A skillful writer creates characters who are so vivid and realistic that you feel like you'd recognize them if they walked past you. An author may use many methods to reveal how and why characters act as they do. In "Checkouts," Cynthia Rylant introduces us to a boy and a girl who, though they remain nameless, are nevertheless memorable characters.

Writer's Notebook

Stars in Your Eyes Can you recall a time when you developed a "crush"—a sudden attraction to someone? In a paragraph or two, describe the crush. Why were you attracted to the person? Describe some of the things you did while you liked him or her. Why do you think you acted as you did? How did the other person react to your crush? As you read "Checkouts," compare your experiences to those of the characters. Do the characters' actions seem realistic?

CYNTHIA RYLANT

Her parents had moved her to Cincinnati, to a large house with beveled glass windows[1] and several porches and the *history* her mother liked to emphasize. You'll love the house, they said. You'll be lonely at first, they admitted, but you're so nice you'll make friends fast. And as an impulse tore at her to lie on the floor, to hold to their ankles and tell them she felt she was dying, to offer anything, anything at all, so they might allow her to finish growing up in the town of her childhood, they firmed their mouths and spoke from their chests and they said, It's decided.

They moved her to Cincinnati, where for a month she spent the greater part of every day in a room full of beveled glass windows, sifting through photographs of the life she'd lived and left behind. But it is difficult work, suffering, and in its own way a kind of art, and finally she didn't have the energy for it anymore, so she emerged from the beautiful house and fell in love with a bag boy at the supermarket. Of course, this didn't happen all at once, just like that, but in the sequence of things that's exactly the way it happened.

She liked to grocery shop. She loved it in the way some people love to drive long country roads, because doing it she could think and relax and wander. Her parents wrote up the list and handed it to her and off she went without complaint to perform what they regarded as a great sacrifice of her time and a sign that she was indeed a very nice girl. She had never told them how much she loved grocery shopping, only that she was "willing" to do it. She had an intuition[2] which told her that her parents were not safe for sharing such strong, important facts about herself. Let them think they knew her.

Once inside the supermarket, her hands firmly around the handle of the cart, she would lapse into a kind of reverie[3] and wheel toward the produce. Like a Tibetan monk in solitary meditation, she calmed to a point of deep, deep happiness; this feeling came to her, reliably, if strangely, only in the supermarket.

Then one day the bag boy dropped her jar of mayonnaise and that is how she fell in love.

He was nervous—first day on the job—and along had come this fascinating girl, standing in the checkout line with the unfocused stare one often sees in young children, her face turned enough away that he might take several full looks at her as he packed sturdy bags full of food and the goods of modern life. She interested him because her hair was red and thick, and in it she had placed a huge orange bow, nearly the size of a small hat. That was enough to distract him, and when finally it was her groceries he was packing, she looked at him and smiled and he could respond only by busting her jar of mayonnaise on the floor, shards[4] of glass and oozing cream decorating the area around his feet. She loved him at exactly that moment, and if he'd known this perhaps he wouldn't have fallen into the brown depression he fell into, which lasted the rest of his shift. He believed he must have looked the jackass in her

---

1. **beveled** (bevʹəld) **glass windows.** The glass in these windows has sloped edges.
2. **intuition** (inʹ tü ishʹən), *n.* immediate perception of truths, facts, etc., without reasoning.
3. **reverie** (revʹər ē), *n.* dreamy thoughts; dreamy thinking of pleasant things.
4. **shard** (shärd), *n.* broken piece; fragment.

eyes, and he envied the sureness of everyone around him: the cocky cashier at the register, the grim and harried[5] store manager, the bland butcher, and the brazen[6] bag boys who smoked in the warehouse on their breaks. He wanted a second chance. Another chance to be confident and say witty things to her as he threw tin cans into her bags, persuading her to allow him to help her to her car so he might learn just a little about her, check out the floor of the car for signs of hobbies or fetishes[7] and the bumpers for clues as to beliefs and loyalties.

But he busted her jar of mayonnaise and nothing else worked out for the rest of the day.

*S*trange, how attractive clumsiness can be. She left the supermarket with stars in her eyes, for she had loved the way his long nervous fingers moved from the conveyor belt to the bags, how deftly (until the mayonnaise) they had picked up her items and placed them into her bags. She had loved the way the hair kept falling into his eyes as he leaned over to grab a box or a tin. And the tattered brown shoes he wore with no socks. And the left side of his collar turned in rather than out.

The bag boy seemed a wonderful contrast to the perfectly beautiful house she had been forced to accept as her home, to the *history* she hated, to the loneliness she had become used to, and she couldn't wait to come back for more of his awkwardness and dishevelment.[8]

Incredibly, it was another four weeks before they saw each other again. As fate would have it, her visits to the supermarket never coincided with his schedule to bag. Each time she went to the store, her eyes scanned the checkouts at once, her heart in her mouth. And each hour he worked, the bag boy kept one eye on the door, watching for the red-haired girl with the big orange bow.

Yet in their disappointment these weeks there was a kind of ecstasy. It is reason enough to be alive, the hope you may see again some face which has meant something to you. The anticipation of meeting the bag boy eased the girl's painful transition into her new and jarring life in Cincinnati. It provided for her an anchor amid all that was impersonal and unfamiliar, and she spent less time on thoughts of what she had left behind as she concentrated on what might lie ahead. And for the boy, the long and often tedious[9] hours at the supermarket which provided no challenge other than that of showing up the following workday . . . these hours became possibilities of mystery and romance for him as he watched the electric doors for the girl in the orange bow.

And when finally they did meet up again, neither offered a clue to the other that he, or she, had been the object of obsessive thought for weeks. She spotted him as soon as she came into the store, but she kept her eyes strictly in front of her as she pulled out a cart and wheeled it toward the produce. And he, too, knew the instant she came through the door—though the orange bow was gone, replaced by a small but bright yellow flower instead—and he never once turned his head in her direction but watched her from the corner of his vision as he tried to swallow back the fear in his throat.

It is odd how we sometimes deny ourselves the very pleasure we have longed for and which is finally within our reach. For some perverse[10] reason she would not have been able to articulate,[11] the girl did not bring her cart up to the bag boy's checkout when her shopping was

---

5. **harried** (har′ēd), *adj.* worried; having lots of problems.
6. **brazen** (brā′zn), *adj.* having no shame; shameless; bold.
7. **fetish** (fet′ ish), *n.* object regarded with unreasoning reverence or blind devotion.
8. **dishevelment** (də shev′əl mənt), *n.* a state of not being neat; rumpled; disordered.
9. **tedious** (tē′dē əs), *adj.* long and tiring; boring; wearisome.
10. **perverse** (pər vėrs′), *adj.* contrary and willful.
11. **articulate** (är tik′yə lāt), *v.* express in words.

▲ Roger Mason, The Red-Haired Girl (1990). How might the girl in the painting and the girl in "Checkouts" be alike?

done. And the bag boy let her leave the store, pretending no notice of her.

This is often the way of children, when they truly want a thing, to pretend that they don't. And then they grow angry when no one tries harder to give them this thing they so casually rejected, and they soon find themselves in a rage simply because they cannot say yes when they mean yes. Humans are very complicated. (And perhaps cats, who have been known to react in the same way, though the resulting rage can only be guessed at.)

The girl hated herself for not checking out at the boy's line, and the boy hated himself for not catching her eye and saying hello, and they most sincerely hated each other without having ever exchanged even two minutes of conversation.

Eventually—in fact, within the week—a kind and intelligent boy who lived very near her beautiful house asked the girl to a movie and she gave up her fancy for the bag boy at the supermarket. And the bag boy himself grew so bored with his job that he made a desperate search for something better and ended up in a bookstore where scores of fascinating girls lingered[12] like honeybees about a hive. Some months later the bag boy and the girl with the orange bow again crossed paths, standing in line with their dates at a movie theater, and, glancing toward the other, each smiled slightly, then looked away, as strangers on public buses often do, when one is moving off the bus and the other is moving on.

---

12. **linger** (ling′gər), *v.* stay on; go slowly, as if unwilling to leave.

After Reading

Making Connections

Shaping Your Response

1. What did you expect to happen at the end of the story? How were your expectations different from what actually happens?

2. What do you think the girl and the boy like about each other?

3. In your opinion, why don't the girl and boy speak after waiting so long to see each other again?

Analyzing the Story

4. If you were the girl or boy in the story, what would you have done differently?

5. Compare Rylant's writing **style** with that of Edgar Allan Poe and Amy Tan. Which do you find the most interesting? the easiest to read? Explain why.

6. What do you think is the most important element in the development of this story—**character, setting,** or **plot?** Explain why.

Extending the Ideas

7. What kind of game do the characters in "Checkout" play? How is this game similar to and different from the games people play in "Rules of the Game" or "The Most Dangerous Game"? Compare and contrast the games in these or other selections you have read.

8. Are the experiences that the characters have in "Checkouts" typical of people their age in their situation? Explain.

Literary Focus: Characterization

Characterization is the process through which an author develops the qualities and personalities of a story's characters. An author may describe the characters directly or reveal them indirectly through their actions, speech, thoughts, or the reactions of other characters.

• What qualities of the girl and the bag boy does the author tell us about directly?

• What qualities are revealed through their actions and thoughts?

• Describe how the two main characters interact with each other. What motivates them to act as they do?

• Do these characters seem realistic? Why or why not?

Vocabulary Study

articulate
brazen
dishevelment
harried
intuition
linger
perverse
reverie
shard
tedious

Use the vocabulary words from "Checkouts" to complete the brief assignments below. Use your Glossary for words you don't know. If you cannot include all the suggested words, make up another note that uses the leftover words.

1. Use the words *reverie, harried,* and *articulate* in a yearbook description of an imaginary teacher or classmate.

2. You are an archeologist, a scientist who studies ancient ruins. Use the words *intuition, shard,* and *tedious* in a letter to your mother, explaining how you discovered a lost city.

3. Use the words *dishevelment, perverse, brazen,* and *linger* in your review of a new rock band.

Expressing Your Ideas

Writing Choices

Writer's Notebook Update Now that you have read the story, think about the crush each character had. Imagine that either the girl or boy had spoken to each other the second time they saw each other in the supermarket. Write a new ending for the story, describing what would have happened if the girl had gone to the boy's checkout line or the boy had said "hello."

Popular Opinion It's acceptable for a girl to ask a guy for a first date. It's okay to pretend to like someone to make someone else jealous. Do you agree with these statements? Why or why not? With others in a small group, write a short **opinion survey** for your classmates, using these statements along with statements of your own. For cross-generational findings, ask people of different ages to complete your survey. Tabulate the results and present them to the class. Which answers surprise you?

Other Options

Body Language Body language refers to how a person communicates through gestures, postures, eye contact or eye movements, and personal space. Do some research on body language. Then present a **demonstration** of various types of body language to your class. Ask the audience members to share their interpretations of each pose.

Vanity Plate The bag boy regretted that he wasn't able to learn more about the girl by checking out the floor and the bumper of her car. Some people express themselves through personalized license plates. Create the **license plate** for a car you might own someday that reveals something about your hobbies, beliefs, or loyalties.

Talk It Over With a partner, improvise the **dialogue** that might have occurred if the boy and girl had actually had a conversation. If you need ideas, refer back to your Writer's Notebook Update assignment.

Before Reading

Ajedrez/Chess by Rosario Castellanos
Slam, Dunk, & Hook by Yusef Komunyakaa

Rosario Castellanos
1925–1974

Mexican writer Rosario Castellanos (cäs te yä′nōs) was interested in women's issues and the plight of the poor. In addition to writing and teaching, Castellanos served as Mexico's ambassador to Israel.

Yusef Komunyakaa
born 1947

The poetry of Yusef Komunyakaa (kō mun yä′kä) tackles complex subjects such as war and racial prejudice. Komunyakaa won a Pulitzer Prize for his book *Neon Vernacular* in 1994.

Building Background

In the Roundhouse One of the poems you are about to read, "Slam, Dunk, & Hook," contains language unique to the game of basketball. With a small group, make a web of terms that pertain to the game of basketball, being sure to provide a short definition for each term. The web below should help you get started.

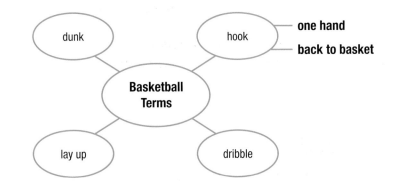

Literary Focus

Imagery A writer who uses **imagery** describes what can be seen, heard, touched, smelled, or tasted, as well as what can be felt inside (such as pain or happiness). Imagery appeals to the emotions as well as to the senses. In "Chess" and "Slam, Dunk, & Hook," the poets use imagery to appeal to your senses and your feelings.

Writer's Notebook

It's Your Move Do games and competition draw people closer together? Or do they split people apart? Choose one side of this issue and write a paragraph or two that supports your position. As you read the poems, pay attention to what the poets seem to be saying about the connection between games and relationships.

Ajedrez

Rosario Castellanos

Porque éramos amigos y, a ratos, nos amábamos;
quizá para añadir otro interés
a los muchos que ya nos obligaban
decidimos jugar juegos de inteligencia.

5 Pusimos un tablero enfrente de nosotros:
equitativo en piezas, en valores,
en posibilidad de movimientos.
Aprendimos las reglas, les juramos respeto
y empezó la partida.

10 Henos aquí hace un siglo, sentados, meditando
encarnizadamente
cómo dar el zarpazo último que aniquile
de modo inapelable y, para siempre, al otro.

Chess

Rosario Castellanos

Because we were friends and sometimes loved each other,
perhaps to add one more tie
to the many that already bound us,
we decided to play games of the mind.

5 We set up a board between us:
equally divided into pieces, values,
and possible moves.
We learned the rules, we swore to respect them,
and the match began.

10 We've been sitting here for centuries, meditating[1]
ferociously
how to deal the one last blow that will finally
annihilate[2] the other one forever.

---

1. meditate (med′ə tāt′), v. think about; consider; plan.
2. annihilate (ə nī′ə lāt), v. destroy completely; wipe out of existence.

SLAM, DUNK, & HOOK

YUSEF KOMUNYAKAA

Fast breaks. Lay ups. With Mercury's[1]
Insignia[2] on our sneakers,
We outmaneuvered the footwork
Of bad angels. Nothing but a hot
5 Swish of strings like silk
Ten feet out. In the roundhouse[3]
Labyrinth[4] our bodies
Created, we could almost
Last forever, poised in midair
10 Like storybook sea monsters.
A high note hung there
A long second. Off
The rim. We'd corkscrew
Up & dunk balls that exploded
15 The skullcap of hope & good
Intention. Bug-eyed, lanky,[5]
All hands & feet . . . sprung rhythm.
We were metaphysical[6] when girls
Cheered on the sidelines.
20 Tangled up in a falling,
Muscles were a bright motor
Double-flashing to the metal hoop
Nailed to our oak.
When Sonny Boy's mama died
25 He played nonstop all day, so hard
Our backboard splintered.
Glistening[7] with sweat, we jibed
& rolled the ball off our
Fingertips. Trouble

30 Was there slapping a blackjack[8]
Against an open palm.
Dribble, drive to the inside, feint,
& glide like a sparrowhawk.
Lay ups. Fast breaks.
35 We had moves we didn't know
We had. Our bodies spun
On swivels of bone & faith,
Through a lyric slipknot
Of joy, & we knew we were
40 Beautiful & dangerous.

▲ Red Grooms, *Fast Break* (1983-84). What details in this sculpture of painted wood and metal convey the action of a basketball game?

1. **Mercury** (mėr′kyer ē). In Roman myths, Mercury was the messenger of the gods, the god of commerce, skillful hands, quickness of wit, and speed.
2. insignia (in sig′nē ə), *n.* medal, badge, or other distinguishing mark of a position, honor, etc.
3. **roundhouse** (round′hous′), *n.* the area on the court beneath the basket.
4. **labyrinth** (lab′ə rinth′), *n.* a confusing, complicated arrangement.
5. lanky (lang′kē), *adj.* awkwardly long and thin; tall and ungraceful.
6. **metaphysical** (met′ə fiz′ə kəl), *adj.* beyond the physical or material world.
7. glisten (glis′n), *v.* shine with a twinkling light; glitter.
8. **blackjack** (blak′jak′), *n.* a small, weighted, leather-covered weapon, used for striking someone.

After Reading

Making Connections

Shaping Your
Response

1. Which of the poems do you like better? Why?

2. What **mood** does each poem bring to mind? Choose one of the poems and draw a picture that represents the feelings it conveys.

Analyzing the Poems

3. How do the structure and **rhythm** of "Slam, Dunk, & Hook" suggest an actual game of basketball?

4. What role does basketball play in the lives of the players? Cite passages from the poem that support your opinion.

5. What does Castellanos seem to imply about competition and friendship in "Chess"?

Extending the Ideas

6. "Slam, Dunk, & Hook" makes references to mythology. Find out about the god Mercury and the Labyrinth on the island of Crete. Then discuss what these mythological allusions add to the poem.

7. Both "Rules of the Game" and "Chess" highlight the game of chess and its effect on a player. Discuss what **themes,** if any, the two works have in common.

Literary Focus: Imagery

Good writing often includes **imagery,** language about sensory experiences. Imagery makes it possible for you to "participate" in a story or poem by imagining what could be seen, heard, smelled, tasted, or touched. Look for imagery in "Chess" and "Slam, Dunk, & Hook," and record your findings on a chart like the one pictured here.

Title of Poem	Image	Sense it appeals to
Ajedrez/Chess		
Slam, Dunk, & Hook		

Vocabulary Study

The questions below use the vocabulary words. Answer the questions, using your Glossary if necessary.

annihilate
glisten
insignia
lanky
meditate

1. What objects might appear to *glisten?*
2. What are some *insignia* of royalty?
3. Would you rather be called thin or *lanky?* Explain.
4. Where might you expect to find people *meditating?*
5. What occurrences could *annihilate* an entire town? Explain.

Expressing Your Ideas

Writing Choices

Writer's Notebook Update Now that you have read the poems, explain some of the ideas that both poets have about the connection between games and relationships. In each poem, does the game draw the players closer together or push them apart? Write a few sentences to answer this question.

Be a Sport Both of the poems highlight a game or sport. Think of a game or sport about which you have strong feelings. Then write your own **poem** about it. Try to show your feelings about the subject through the words and images you choose for your poem. Use vivid verbs to move the action along.

Another Option

Sports Art What feelings does this photograph convey about baseball and its fans? Make a **drawing, painting,** or **photograph** that expresses your feelings about a sport.

Scott Mlyn, *Two Fans and Wally Joyner, Memorial Stadium, Baltimore* ➤

Before Reading

Breaking the Ice

by Dave Barry

Dave Barry
born 1947

Although Dave Barry is known for his humorous observations, he first wrote "serious" news for West Chester, Pennsylvania's *Daily Local News.* He began writing humor columns for the paper while teaching "effective writing" to business executives. Barry moved to the *Miami Herald* in 1983, and his columns now appear in over 400 newspapers worldwide. Barry won the 1988 Pulitzer Prize for Distinguished Commentary, even though one of his entries made fun of the Pulitzers.

Building Background

A Date with History In "Breaking the Ice," humorist Dave Barry looks back at his early dating experiences. Barry became a teenager in 1960. To find out about dating customs at that time, interview some adults you know who had dates in the late 1950s and early 1960s. Where did teenagers go on dates? What did they wear? What rules did parents have about dating? Share your findings with the class.

Literary Focus

Satire "Breaking the Ice" is an essay that uses **satire.** Satire is the art of ridiculing an aspect of human nature or life in general. Although satire can be used to expose human weaknesses or evil institutions, satire can also be written to entertain or amuse. As you read "Breaking the Ice," consider Dave Barry's purpose for writing the satire. What topic does he satirize?

Writer's Notebook

How Do You Break the Ice? Imagine that your friend wants to ask out a girl or guy in your class, but doesn't know how to approach that person. What advice would you give? Write down some ideas that would help your friend. After you read "Breaking the Ice," you can compare your suggestions with those given by the author.

BREAKING THE ICE

Dave Barry

As a mature adult, I feel an obligation to help the younger generation, just as the mother fish guards her unhatched eggs, keeping her lonely vigil[1] day after day, never leaving her post, not even to go to the bathroom, until her tiny babies emerge and she is able, at last, to eat them. "She may be your mom, but she's still a fish" is a wisdom nugget that I would pass along to any fish eggs reading this column.

But today I want to talk about dating. This subject was raised in a letter to me from a young person named Eric Knott, who writes:

> I have got a big problem. There's this girl in my English class who is *really* good-looking. However, I don't think she knows I exist. I want to ask her out, but I'm afraid she will say no, and I will be the freak of the week. What should I do?

Eric, you have sent your question to the right mature adult, because as a young person I spent a lot of time thinking about this very problem. Starting in about eighth grade, my time was divided as follows:

Academic Pursuits: 2 percent.
Zits: 16 percent.
Trying to Figure Out How to Ask Girls Out: 82 percent.

The most sensible way to ask a girl out is to walk directly up to her on foot and say, "So, you want to go out? Or what?" I never did this. I knew, as Eric Knott knows, that there was always the possibility that the girl would say no, thereby leaving me with no viable[2] option but to leave Harold C. Crittenden Junior High School forever and go into the woods and become a bark-eating hermit whose only companions would be the gentle and understanding woodland creatures.

"Hey, ZITFACE!" the woodland creatures would shriek in cute little Chip 'n' Dale voices while raining acorns down upon my head. "You wanna DATE? HAHAHAHAHAHA."

So the first rule of dating is: Never risk direct contact with the girl in question. Your role model should be the nuclear submarine, gliding silently beneath the ocean surface, tracking an enemy target that does not even begin to suspect that the submarine would like to date it. I spent the vast majority of 1960 keeping a girl named Judy under surveillance,[3] maintaining a minimum distance of 50 lockers to avoid the danger that I might somehow get into a conversation with her, which could have led to disaster:

JUDY: Hi.

ME: Hi.

JUDY: Just in case you have ever thought about having a date with me, the answer is no.

WOODLAND CREATURES: HAHAHAHAHAHA.

The only problem with the nuclear-submarine technique is that it's difficult to get a date with a girl who has never, technically, been asked. This is why you need Phil Grant. Phil was a friend of mine who had the ability to talk to

---

1. vigil (vij′əl), *n.* a staying awake for some purpose; a watching.
2. viable (vī′ə bəl), *adj.* usable; workable.
3. surveillance (sər vā′ləns), *n.* watch kept over a person.

girls. It was a mysterious superhuman power he had, comparable to X-ray vision. So, after several thousand hours of intense discussion and planning with me, Phil approached a girl he knew named Nancy, who approached a girl named Sandy, who was a direct personal friend of Judy's and who passed the word back to Phil via Nancy that Judy would be willing to go on a date with me. This procedure protected me from direct humiliation, similar to the way President Reagan was protected from direct involvement in the Iran-Contra scandal[4] by a complex White House chain of command that at one point, investigators now believe, included his horse.

Thus it was that, finally, Judy and I went on an actual date, to see a movie in White Plains, New York. If I were to sum up the romantic ambiance[5] of this date in four words, those words would be: "My mother was driving." This made for an extremely quiet drive, because my mother, realizing that her presence was hideously embarrassing, had to pretend she wasn't there. If it had been legal, I think she would have got out and sprinted alongside the car, steering through the window. Judy and I, sitting in the backseat about 75 feet apart, were also silent, unable to communicate without the assistance of Phil, Nancy, and Sandy.

After what seemed like several years we got to the movie theater, where my mother went off to sit in the Parents and Lepers Section. The movie was called *North to Alaska,* but I can tell you nothing else about it because I spent the whole time wondering whether it would be necessary to amputate my right arm, which was not getting any blood flow as a result of being perched for two hours like a petrified snake on the back of Judy's seat exactly one molecule away from physical contact.

So it was definitely a fun first date, featuring all the relaxed spontaneity[6] of a real-estate closing, and in later years I did regain some feeling in my arm. My point, Eric Knott, is that the key to successful dating is *self-confidence.* I bet that good-looking girl in your English class would LOVE to go out with you. But YOU have to make the first move. So just do it! Pick up that phone! Call Phil Grant.

◄ These teenagers of the late 1950s or early 60s are enjoying themselves at a dance. Is this your idea of a good time?

4. **Iran-contra scandal.** In 1986, when Ronald Reagan was President, it was revealed that the U.S. government was selling weapons to Iran in exchange for the release of American hostages, and was using the money raised from the arms sales to help the Contras fight against the government in Nicaragua.
5. ambiance (am′bē əns), *n.* surroundings; atmosphere.
6. spontaneity (spon′tə nē′ə tē), *n.* condition of acting out of natural impulse or desire without being forced and without planning beforehand.

After Reading

Making Connections

Shaping Your Response

1. Do you think the "advice" offered in this essay is valuable? Why or why not?

Analyzing the Essay

2. Dave Barry uses **exaggeration;** in other words, he makes things look much better or worse than they actually are. Find two examples of exaggeration in this essay and explain their effect.

3. How does Barry use **capitalization?** What effect does this have?

Extending the Ideas

4. 🐾 In your opinion, do teenagers today experience the same **communication** problems that Barry's generation did? Explain.

Literary Focus: Satire

Satire is the art of making fun of something. Writers of satire use tools such as exaggeration, sarcasm, and humor to entertain readers while showing how ridiculous something is.

- What topic is Dave Barry satirizing in his essay? Why do you think he would write a satire about this topic?

- Explain whether or not you think "Breaking the Ice" is a successful satire.

ambience
spontaneity
surveillance
viable
vigil

Vocabulary Study

Use the vocabulary words listed here to write your own humorous account of a first date. If necessary, use your Glossary.

Expressing Your Ideas

Writing Choice

Writer's Notebook Update Now that you have read Dave Barry's advice, what do you think of it? Write a short note to Eric Knott and offer some advice of your own.

Other Options

Act It Out How can you introduce yourself to someone you think you might like? With a partner, practice techniques that you think would work and present your **role-plays** to the class.

The Dating Game Because of your great wisdom, everyone is asking you for advice on dating etiquette. Prepare an illustrated **brochure** with your "rules."

The Games People Play

Mind Games

Career Connection

Computer games, anyone? These pages offer a behind-the-scenes look at the work of computer game artist Tom Miecznikowski (myech⁄ni kuv⁄skē), who creates "invented worlds" for others to explore.

What do you do as a computer game artist?

I create the environments, images, characters, and the animations that you see in a computer game, with the help of desktop computers, sophisticated software, a tablet, and a digital pen.

Why do you like working on computer games?

As an artist and an animator, it seems to me that the most exciting work coming out now is in the new interactive media. Computer games are a kind of new frontier— there's freedom to let your imagination run wild.

What preparation did you need?

A good understanding of computers is important, but it's not the main thing. You have to be an artist first, with a strong arts education. Most importantly, you have to have

the hunger to do it. It's very competitive. You have to constantly observe the world around you so that you can give your images what the classic animators call, "the illusion of life."

Everywhere I go, I notice how things move and look and what their textures are, how the light falls on them

and into the shadows behind them, how things interact with each other. I try to be aware of the subtleties that make something seem real.

When I worked on *Panic in the Park* (Warner Brothers, 1995), I had to create a magical secret chamber in an old attic. To give the room

You may someday find yourself in the cargo bay of the spaceship that artist Tom Miecznikowski designed and animated for a computer game.

WORLDS

time, we started seeing actual images from outer space, with the pictures sent back by the astronauts. *2001* felt even more real than that. Before that, you could always tell that science fiction movies were faked. I've always liked science fiction. In fact, the image I've created here is for a proposed science fiction game.

What do you see in the future for computer games?

I think the future of computer games will be multiple-player games on networks like the World Wide Web. They'll be completely immersive. You'll design your own character and play against other people all over the world, in environments set in any place or time.

a realistic, "lived-in" look, I avoided parallel lines. In reality, nothing is truly straight, so I made sure that things were a little bit crooked here and there. A table rests at an angle, objects are in danger of falling off of tables, etc. Small details like that will make a scene seem real.

What were your early influences as an artist?

When I was ten years old, my neighbor took me to see Stanley Kubrick's *2001: A Space Odyssey*. It was a fantastic science fiction movie and it changed my view of everything. They paid so much attention to the details. Around that

Responding

1. What qualities do you think a successful computer game artist needs to have?

2. Explain whether you would rather create computer games or play them.

INTERDISCIPLINARY STUDY

Science Connection
An unusual competition called
Odyssey of the Mind inspires
students to solve problems with
creativity, teamwork, and a sense
of style.

Sports for the Brain

by David M. Schwartz

"Y ou won't have any trouble finding *our* team," Elaine Yenne told me
on the telephone a week before I caught up with her at the Odyssey
of the Mind World Finals. "Just look for six 5½-foot chickens."

The "chickens" were junior high school boys participating in
Odyssey of the Mind, an international competition that challenges students,
kindergarten through college, to find creative solutions to bizarre problems.
Yenne, a teacher at Parkhill Junior High School in Dallas, served as coach for
a team of ninth-graders working on a problem called "Mini Terrain Vehicles."
They had to design and build several small vehicles that could move in an arc,
survive sand traps and speed bumps, release a smaller car carried atop one of

the vehicles, flip onto another surface and keep going, dive off a ramp into a pool of water—and pop a balloon at the end of each 20-foot obstacle course. And it all had to be done for less than $90 in materials, without adult assistance.

But chickens? You thought designing and building trick cars would be creative enough? Obviously you've never attended the Odyssey of the Mind World Finals.

More than a million students in all 50 states and 20 other countries have participated in Odyssey of the Mind—or "OM." After choosing one of five long-term problems, students work as a team for months, seeking original solutions that will wow the judges.

For those who take first-place honors at local, state, and national competitions, the reward is a chance to compete in the World Finals, a dizzying four-day thinkathon that looks like some kind of kooky cross between science fair, masquerade party, performing arts fest and the Olympics.

Whatever it is exactly, one truth is evident from watching the 5,000 "OMers" who invaded the campus of Iowa State University in Ames in June 1994 for the World Finals: simply being creative and clever is not enough. You've got to be creative with *style*.

The ninth-graders from Parkhill Junior High School cobbled together six mini terrain vehicles from wheels, gears, axles, motors, circuit boards and other parts scavenged out of discarded cash registers, copy machines, and assorted junk they picked up at a local warehouse. The cars are about a foot long and, like the boys, are dressed as chickens. That's *style*.

"We wanted to come up with a reason to have these cars going down these different roads," explains Mark Waterston from under his feathery headpiece, "and we thought of the old joke, 'Why did the chicken cross the road?' "

And so it goes, road after road, one chicken joke after another, until the final car has completed its course. The vehicles have popped five of the eight balloons, and the flock of 5½-foot chickens takes a final jaunty strut to wildly enthusiastic cheers (and a few squawks) from the bleachers. Another eight-minute presentation at the Odyssey of the Mind World Finals is over.

By the end of the week, more than 700 such presentations will be given, each a unique solution to one of the five problems dreamed up by OM's founder and chief impresario, C. Samuel Micklus. A former professor of technology and design, Micklus believes that the future belongs to those who learn creative problem-solving skills as children. The key is what he calls "divergent" thinking. It is this ability to take mental risks and explore multiple solutions to a problem that is the essential foundation for creativity. "What problems will today's second-graders face 20 or 60 years from now?" he asks. "I don't know. No one knows because tomorrow's problems are inconceivable today. So we have to encourage creativity through divergent thinking and foster the discipline needed to pursue solutions."

Finals judge Rick Rand listens attentively as chicken-impersonating teammates Philip Wong (left) and Tad Dunn from Parkhill Junior High in Dallas, Texas, explain the design of one of their mini terrain vehicles.

Responding
Based on what you've read, do you agree that Odyssey of the Mind is a valuable learning activity? Explain.

Math Connection

Are you looking for a fun way to challenge your brain and sharpen your math skills? Try these little numbers: two games from *Math for Smarty Pants* by Marilyn Burns.

Mental Puzzles

The Thirty-one Game

This is a card game for two people. You don't need the entire deck to play. You need only 24 cards, ace through 6 of each of the four suits. If you don't have playing cards, you can make a set of 24 cards, with four of them numbered 1, four numbered 2, and so on up to four cards numbered 6. Lay out the 24 cards face up.

Decide who goes first. The first player turns any card face down and says that number out loud. The second player turns over any other card, adding that number to the first one. Continue taking turns turning a card face down and keeping a running total. Whoever reaches the sum of exactly 31 wins. If neither player hits 31, or if no one goes over 31, then no one wins that round.

There's a winning strategy to this game (you might have suspected as much). Which of you goes first is one important factor of the winning strategy, and which cards to turn over is the other.

If this game gets tiresome, change the total you're aiming for to 30, or 22, or 50. If you were to play for a total of 84, would you want to go first or second?

Looping

This is a numerical looping that also uses words. You start with any number, 39, for example. Write it as a word: thirty-nine. Then continue as shown.

Start with any number	.39
Write it as a word	.thirty-nine
Count the letters	.10
Write that as a word	.ten
Count the letters	.3
Write that as a word	.three
Count the letters	.5
Write that as a word	.five
Count the letters	.4
Write that as a word	.four
Count the letters	.4

You'll get a 4 forever and ever now. As a matter of mathematical fact, you'll get to 4, no matter what number you start with originally. Try a different number and see. Convince yourself with some examples, then see if you can figure out why you'll always get to four.

Responding

1. Can you figure out the winning strategy for the Thirty-one Game?

2. Explain why you will always end up with the number 4 when you play Looping.

Reading Mini-Lesson

Troubleshooting Strategies

When reading complex or highly technical material, there are a number of techniques you can use to aid your comprehension.

- If you become confused about what you're reading, don't panic. Read a bit further to see if your confusion clears up.

- If that doesn't work, go back and reread the confusing material. Concentrate on the parts of the text that are causing you trouble.

- Slow down. Sometimes confusion stems from the simple fact that you are reading too fast.

- Keep a dictionary close at hand and look up problem words.

- Try to visualize, or create a mental picture, of what you're reading. For example, when reading "Sports for the Brain," you might visualize each requirement that the Mini Terrain Vehicles had to fulfill.

- If the text has pictures, captions, or headings, use them to help you grasp difficult sections.

- If you come to a section you don't understand, ask yourself questions about it and read on to try to answer them. For example, in "Sports for the Brain," you read that one of the teams dressed up as chickens. Ask yourself why. Then read with the purpose of answering your own question.

Strategies like these will help you understand difficult material. Don't be afraid to come up with special techniques of your own.

Activity Options

1. Use your visualization skills to create a poster about the Mini Terrain Vehicles mentioned in "Sports for the Brain." Illustrate and caption each of the six requirements the vehicles had to fulfill.
2. Bring in a textbook from a science or social studies class. Working with a partner, assign each other a difficult passage to read. Use some of the comprehension strategies described above. Then paraphrase the passage for your partner.

Writing Workshop

Interpreting an Event

Assignment You have read about how people sometimes treat life as a game. Now write an essay that looks at a familiar part of your life, such as a date or an evening of baby-sitting, as if it were a game with rules, players, goals, and strategies. See the Writer's Blueprint for details.

WRITER'S BLUEPRINT

Product   An interpretive essay
Purpose   To interpret a familiar event as if it were a game
Audience   Your teacher, classmates, and friends
Specs   As the writer of a successful essay, you should:

❑ Begin by identifying the familiar event you have chosen and stating your purpose for writing.

❑ Go on to describe this event in detail as if it were a game, including the goals, players, rules, and special strategies for success.

❑ Conclude by sharing what you have learned about this familiar event by viewing it as a game.

❑ Write paragraphs that each keep to one main idea, not two or three.

❑ Follow the rules of grammar, usage, spelling, and mechanics. Avoid sentence fragments.

The instructions that follow are designed to lead you to a successful essay.

STEP **1**  PREWRITING

Discuss the concept of game playing in the literature. In a group, review the plots of the selections you have read. Then discuss the elements of the plots that are similar to playing games. Fill in a game-playing chart, like the partial one on the next page, for each plot. Share your charts with other groups.

Selection	Goal	Players	Rules	Strategies
"Breaking the Ice"	–to get a date	–boy & girl	–no direct contact –avoid humiliation	–surveillance –a network of friends

Choose a familiar event to write about and make a game-playing chart for it like the chart above.

Discuss your event. Tell a partner or small group what you have in mind. Go over the ideas in your chart one at a time and ask for comments.

Brainstorm a vocabulary of game words. With a partner, jot down all the game-playing words and phrases you can think of. Use a thesaurus for help. Here are some words to get you started:

Game Vocabulary

goals, players, rules, strategies, compete, time out, playing field, rally, offense, defense, scrimmage, halftime, end zone, referee, slam dunk, home run, fair play, cheating, fair, foul, spectators, scoreboard, stadium

Plan your essay. Look back at your game-playing charts, discussion notes, and game words as you make your writing plan. Use categories like these to organize your ideas.

OR . . .
You might draw a game board that shows your event as a game.

Introduction
- My event
- My purpose for writing

Body
- Goals of the event
- Players
- Rules
- Strategies

Conclusion
- Things I've learned about the event by viewing it as a game

Ask a partner to review your plan.

✔ Am I looking at a familiar event as if it were a game?

✔ Am I following the Specs in the Writer's Blueprint?

Use your partner's most helpful comments to revise your plan.

STEP 2 DRAFTING

Before you draft, review your game-playing charts, game words, writing plan, and any other notes. Then reread the Writer's Blueprint.

As you draft, don't look for mistakes in spelling and punctuation. For now just concentrate on getting the ideas from your writing plan down on paper. Here are some drafting tips.

- To capture your reader's attention, begin with something dramatic, such as a brief exchange of dialogue between people who are playing the "game," or a quotation about games from a book of quotations, or a vivid description of the "game" as seen by a radio sportscaster.
- In the body, use transition words such as *next*, *then*, and *finally* when you explain how the game is played.
- Before writing your conclusion, read over what you've written so far.

Notice how this writer began her essay with a quote she overheard. (She'll correct a spelling mistake later.)

STUDENT MODEL

The statement of "I'm going with him" is a quote that I have heard used many times for the past six years of my life. Most of the people my age say this alot with great satisfaction in their voices, as if they have found the one love of their lives. But in reality dating is just a social game I think. It's a competition in which some people follow the rules and others cheat.

3 REVISING

Ask a partner to comment on your draft before you revise it. Use this checklist as a guide.

✔ Have I followed the Specs in the Writer's Blueprint?

✔ Did I describe the event as a game with goals, rules, players, and strategies?

✔ Did I end by sharing what I learned by seeing this event as a game?

✔ Does each paragraph keep to one main idea?

Revising Strategy

Keeping to the Main Idea

A paragraph in an essay like this should be a single unit of information. It should present and elaborate on one main idea, not two or three.

Notice that in the Student Model below, the paragraph as first drafted jumps back and forth between two main ideas (social class and rules). This is confusing. Based on a partner's comment, the writer revised the paragraph so it now deals with just one main idea (rules).

STUDENT MODEL

~~I picture dating behavior between teeage boys and girls as a struggle for popularity in your "social class."~~ This typical "game of love" has many confusing but mutually understood rules of the game. For instance, you may hold hands or go to a movie together maybe once or twice. But most "couples" don't have any kind of activity together regularly like a steady couple would. The rules won't allow them to be truly together. ~~Most likely, when the girl told her friends about her "new love" they might have discouraged her that her choice was a good one because of his social class.~~

Is this about social class or rules?

Look at your work one paragraph at a time and make sure that each paragraph keeps to one main idea. When you spot sentences that stray from the main idea, rewrite them, delete them, or move them to a paragraph where they belong.

STEP 4 EDITING

Ask a partner to review your revised draft before you edit. When you edit, look for errors in grammar, usage, spelling, and mechanics. Look over each sentence to make that it's complete and not a sentence fragment.

Editing Strategy

Avoiding Sentence Fragments

A fragment may look like a complete sentence, with a capital letter at the beginning and a period or other end punctuation, but its meaning is incomplete. It cannot stand alone because it does not make sense.

| **Fragment** | Since you asked me. (*Asked me what?*) |
| **Fragment** | If you don't play by the rules. (*What will happen?*) |

Dependent, or subordinate, clauses written as complete sentences are sentence fragments, as in the examples above. They do not express a complete thought. Subordinate clauses begin with subordinate conjunctions such as *since, if, although,* and *because.* You can correct these kinds of fragments by combining them with an independent clause.

| **Fragment** | You can't break the rules. Although you might want to. |
| **Corrected** | You can't break the rules, although you might want to. |

Sometimes you can also delete the conjunction and make two complete sentences.

| **Fragment** | Life is like a game. Because you must play by the rules. |
| **Corrected** | Life is like a game. You must play by the rules. |

 PRESENTING

Consider these ideas for presenting your essay.

- Suggest to the editors of your school paper that they run a page called "The Games People Play" and include several of these essays.

- Create a cover sheet with graphics to enhance your essay. Look at game boxes and boards and see how they use graphics to reflect the topic and mood of a game.

  LOOKING BACK

Self-evaluate. What grade would *you* give your paper? Look back at the Writer's Blueprint and evaluate yourself on each point, from 6 (superior) down to 1 (inadequate).

Reflect. Think about what you've learned from writing this essay as you write answers to these questions.

- The next time you take part in the familiar event you wrote about, what will you do differently, if anything, to change the dynamics of the game?

- How did your writing plan work out? How helpful was it? If you could start over, would you use another kind of plan?

For Your Working Portfolio Add your essay and reflection responses to your working portfolio.

> **COMPUTER TIP**
> Use a different type size to make the cover page of your essay more visually striking. You might add a border or a piece of clip art for illustration.

Beyond Print

Computer Jargon

Do you need a surfboard to surf on the Net?
  When you visit a home page, should you bring flowers?
    Will hypertext make you hyper?

If you can answer these questions, you know your way around a computer. If you can't answer them, this glossary of technology terms will help you master some computer jargon—a language that changes every day as we discover more and more ways to put computers to work for us.

Application A particular computer program or piece of software.

CD-ROM Compact Disc Read Only Memory. A CD-ROM is used to store information such as text, sound, pictures, and movies. While CD-ROMs look like audio CDs, they are only readable with a computer.

CPU The Central Processing Unit of a computer. It contains the chips, wires, power, and memory needed to operate the computer.

Database An organized collection of information.

Desktop The area on a computer screen that contains icons, menus, and windows.

Download To copy a file from a server or network.

Electronic Mail Messages sent over the Internet from one user to another.

Hard Drive A storage device usually found inside your computer.

Home Page The first screen that appears when accessing a server on the World Wide Web. A home page may contain text, graphics, and sound.

Hypertext Words that can be selected and clicked on to receive further information. Hypertext is used on the World Wide Web and in multimedia presentations.

Internet A series of computer servers connected together across the country and world. A user who is connected to the Internet can access any information stored on those servers.

Log on The procedure for gaining access to a computer or network.

Menu A pull-down list of items at the top of the computer screen.

Modem A device that uses a phone line to connect your computer with a variety of online services or other computers.

Multimedia Any combination of media, including text, sound, pictures, and video.

Network Two or more computers connected together by cables, allowing them to communicate with each other.

Online Information available to a user through a network or telephone connection.

RAM Random Access Memory. A type of computer memory that allows information to be accessed in any order for a limited period of time.

Server A computer that operates a network.

Surfing the Net The act of moving from one server to another on the Internet.

Upload Copying a file onto a server or network.

User Any person who is using a computer or similar device.

World Wide Web A particular way to access the Internet by allowing users to click on words or graphics to gather information.

Activities

1. Remember the three questions at the top of page 74? Use the glossary to answer them.

2. Create a dialogue between two people in "computerspeak." How many of these terms you can use and still make sense?

3. Create a glossary of your own with other technology terms, and add new terms as you come across them.

Part Two

Mistaken Impressions

Nobody's perfect, and everyone makes mistakes. But if you don't want to repeat your mistakes, it's important to understand why you made them.

 **Multicultural Connection** **Perspective** involves seeing people and events from diverse viewpoints. One's culture can greatly influence the perspective one has. In the following selections, how do the social and cultural perspectives of the characters help create some "mistaken impressions"?

Before Reading

The Rule of Names

by Ursula Le Guin

Ursula Le Guin
born 1929

Born in Berkeley, California, Ursula Le Guin (ėr′sə lə le gwin′) has been a prolific writer of science fiction and fantasy since 1964, when she published her first book, *Rocannon's World.* Many of her books have received special awards and recognitions. Although most critics classify Le Guin's work as science fiction, Le Guin herself has commented, "I write science fiction because that is what publishers call my books. Left to myself, I should call them novels." Her novels present worlds based on many settings and characters, some realistic and some fantastical. Inhabitants of her worlds range from green, furry apes to winged creatures, wizards, and dragons.

Building Background

What's In a Name? Have you ever made up a secret language or code with a friend, so that you could communicate without other people understanding? As you read Ursula Le Guin's work, you will notice strange names for people, animals, places, and ordinary everyday items that you have never heard or read before. Le Guin herself explains, "People often ask how I think of names in fantasies, and again I have to answer that I find them, that I hear them. There are words, like rushwash tea, for which I can offer no explanation. They simply drink rushwash tea. . . ." As you read "The Rule of Names," consider how Le Guin coins new words for a new land. Do any of her words seem familiar to you?

Literary Focus

Setting The **setting** of a story is the time and place in which the story's events take place. The narrator or one of the characters may describe the setting specifically, or the setting may be suggested through dialogue and action. One critic has described the work of Ursula Le Guin as being "full of the sense of place." In "The Rule of Names," she creates a fantasy world that may seem both strange and familiar.

Writer's Notebook

That's Fantastic! Quests for treasures, gargoyles, superheroes, strange worlds, thinking animals—when you think of **fantasy,** you may think of these elements and many more. You might have seen fantasy movies or read books or comic books that deal with fantasy. Before you read "The Rule of Names," write down your impressions of what elements you would find in a fantasy story. Later you may want to compare your notions with Le Guin's depiction of a fantasy world.

The Rule of Names

Ursula Le Guin

Mr. Underhill came out from under his hill, smiling and breathing hard. Each breath shot out of his nostrils as a double puff of steam, snow-white in the morning sunshine. Mr. Underhill looked up at the bright December sky and smiled wider than ever, showing snow-white teeth. Then he went down to the village.

"Morning, Mr. Underhill," said the villagers as he passed them in the narrow street between houses with conical, overhanging roofs like the fat red caps of toadstools. "Morning, morning!" he replied to each. (It was of course bad luck to wish anyone a *good* morning; a simple statement of the time of day was quite enough, in a place so permeated[1] with Influences as Sattins Island, where a careless adjective might change the weather for a week.) All of them spoke to him, some with affection, some with affectionate disdain.[2] He was all the little island had in the way of a wizard, and so deserved respect—but how could you respect a little fat man of fifty who waddled along with his toes turned in, breathing steam and smiling? He was no great shakes as a workman either. His fireworks were fairly elaborate but his elixirs[3] were weak. Warts he charmed off frequently reappeared after three days; tomatoes he enchanted grew no

bigger than canteloupes; and those rare times when a strange ship stopped at Sattins Harbor, Mr. Underhill always stayed under his hill—for fear, he explained, of the evil eye. He was, in other words, a wizard the way walleyed[4] Gan was a carpenter: by default.[5] The villagers made do with badly-hung doors and inefficient spells, for this generation, and relieved their annoyance by treating Mr. Underhill quite familiarly, as a mere fellow-villager. They even asked him to dinner. Once he asked some of them to dinner, and served a splendid repast,[6] with silver, crystal, damask,[7] roast goose, sparkling Andrades '639, and plum pudding with hard sauce; but he was so nervous all through the

---

1. **permeate** (pėr′mē āt), *v.* spread through the whole of; pass through; pervade.
2. **disdain** (dis dān′), *n.* a feeling of scorn; a regarding with contempt.
3. **elixir** (i lik′sər), *n.* medicine made of drugs or herbs mixed with alcohol and syrup.
4. **walleyed** (wôl′īd′), *adj.* having one or both eyes turned away from the nose, so as to show much white.
5. **default** (di fôlt′), *n.* in the absence of; lacking.
6. **repast** (ri past′), *n.* meal; food.
7. **damask** (dam′əsk), *n.* a firm, shiny, reversible linen, silk, or cotton fabric with woven designs, used especially for tablecloths and napkins.

Thomas McKnight delights in creating imaginary landscapes, as his 1983 painting, *The Lighthouse,* demonstrates. Compare and contrast the mood of this painting with the mood in the opening paragraphs of "The Rule of Names."

meal that it took the joy out of it, and besides, everybody was hungry again half an hour afterward. He did not like anyone to visit his cave, not even the anteroom,[8] beyond which in fact nobody had ever got. When he saw people approaching the hill he always came trotting out to meet them. "Let's sit out here under the pine trees!" he would say, smiling and waving towards the fir grove, or if it was raining, "Let's go have a drink at the inn, eh?" though everybody knew he drank nothing stronger than well-water.

Some of the village children, teased by that locked cave, poked and pried and made raids while Mr. Underhill was away; but the small door that led into the inner chamber was spell-shut, and it seemed for once to be an effective spell. Once a couple of boys, thinking the wizard was over on the West Shore curing Mrs. Ruuna's sick donkey, brought a crowbar and a hatchet up there, but at the first whack of the hatchet on the door there came a roar of wrath from inside, and a cloud of purple steam. Mr. Underhill had got home early. The boys fled. He did not come out, and the boys came to no harm, though they said you couldn't believe what a huge hooting howling hissing horrible bellow that little fat man could make unless you'd heard it.

SUMMARIZE: How do the villagers view Mr. Underhill?

His business in town this day was three dozen fresh eggs and a pound of liver; also a stop at Seacaptain Fogeno's cottage to renew the seeing-charm on the old man's eyes (quite useless when applied to a case of detached retina,[9] but Mr. Underhill kept trying), and finally a chat with old Goody Guld, the concertina-maker's widow. Mr. Underhill's friends were mostly old people. He was timid with the strong young men of the village, and the girls were shy of him. "He makes me nervous, he smiles so much," they all said, pouting, twisting silky ringlets round a finger. "Nervous" was a new-fangled word, and their mothers all replied grimly, "Nervous my foot, silliness is the word for it. Mr. Underhill is a very respectable wizard!"

After leaving Goody Guld, Mr. Underhill passed by the school, which was being held this day out on the common. Since no one on Sattins Island was literate, there were no books to learn to read from and no desks to carve initials on and no blackboards to erase, and in fact no schoolhouse. On rainy days the children met in the loft of the Communal Barn, and got hay in their pants; on sunny days the schoolteacher, Palani, took them anywhere she felt like. Today, surrounded by thirty interested children under twelve and forty uninterested sheep under five, she was teaching an important item on the curriculum: the Rules of Names. Mr. Underhill, smiling shyly, paused to listen and watch. Palani, a plump, pretty girl of twenty, made a charming picture there in the wintry sunlight, sheep and children around her, a leafless oak above her, and behind her the dunes and sea and clear, pale sky. She spoke earnestly, her face flushed pink by wind and words. "Now you know the Rules of Names already, children. There are two, and they're the same on every island in the world. What's one of them?"

"It ain't polite to ask anybody what his name is," shouted a fat, quick boy, interrupted by a little girl shrieking, "You can't never tell your own name to nobody my ma says!"

"Yes, Suba. Yes, Popi dear, don't screech. That's right. You never ask anybody his name. You never tell your own. Now think about that a minute and then tell me why we call our wizard

---

8. **anteroom** (an′ti rüm′), *n.* a small room leading to a larger or more important one.
9. **retina** (ret′n ə), *n.* the inner membrane at the back of the eye, which is sensitive to light and receives optical images.

Mr. Underhill." She smiled across the curly heads and the woolly backs at Mr. Underhill, who beamed, and nervously clutched his sack of eggs.

"'Cause he lives under a hill!" said half the children.

"But is it his truename?"

"No!" said the fat boy, echoed by little Popi shrieking, "No!"

"How do you know it's not?"

"'Cause he came here all alone and so there wasn't anybody knew his truename so they couldn't tell us, and *he* couldn't—"

"Very good, Suba. Popi, don't shout. That's right. Even a wizard can't tell his truename. When you children are through school and go through the Passage, you'll leave your child-names behind and keep only your truenames, which you must never ask for and never give away. Why is that the rule?"

The children were silent. The sheep bleated gently. Mr. Underhill answered the question: "Because the name is the thing," he said in his shy, soft, husky voice, "and the truename is the true thing. To speak the name is to control the thing. Am I right, Schoolmistress?"

She smiled and curtseyed, evidently a little embarrassed by his participation. And he trotted off towards his hill, clutching his eggs to his bosom. Somehow the minute spent watching Palani and the children had made him very hungry. He locked his inner door behind him with a hasty <u>incantation</u>,[10] but there must have been a leak or two in the spell, for soon the bare anteroom of the cave was rich with the smell of frying eggs and sizzling liver.

The wind that day was light and fresh out of the west, and on it at noon a little boat came skimming the bright waves into Sattins Harbor. Even as it rounded the point a sharp-eyed boy spotted it, and knowing, like every child on the island, every sail and spar of the forty boats of the fishing fleet, he ran down the street calling out, "A foreign boat, a foreign boat!" Very seldom was the lonely isle visited by a boat from some equally lonely isle of the East Reach, or an adventurous trader from the Archipelago.[11] By the time the boat was at the pier half the village was there to greet it, and fishermen were following it homewards, and cowherds and clam-diggers and herb-hunters were puffing up and down all the rocky hills, heading towards the harbor.

But Mr. Underhill's door stayed shut.

There was only one man aboard the boat. Old Seacaptain Fogeno, when they told him that, drew down a bristle of white brows over his unseeing eyes. "There's only one kind of man," he said, "that sails the Outer Reach alone. A wizard, or a warlock, or a Mage . . ."

So the villagers were breathless hoping to see for once in their lives a Mage, one of the mighty White Magicians of the rich, towered, crowded inner islands of the Archipelago. They were disappointed, for the voyager was quite young, a handsome black-bearded fellow who hailed them cheerfully from his boat, and leaped ashore like any sailor glad to have made port. He introduced himself at once as a sea-peddlar. But when they told Seacaptain Fogeno that he carried an oaken walking-stick around with him, the old man nodded. "Two wizards in one town," he said. "Bad!" And his mouth snapped shut like an old carp's.

CONNECT: Why does Seacaptain Fogeno conclude that the stranger is a wizard?

As the stranger could not give them his name, they gave him one right away: Blackbeard. And they gave him plenty of attention. He had a small mixed cargo of cloth and sandals and piswi feathers for trimming cloaks

---

10. incantation (in/kan tā/shən), *n.* set of words spoken as magic charm or to cast a magic spell.
11. **Archipelago** (är/kə pel/ə gō), refers to a group of many islands.

and cheap incense and levity stones and fine herbs and great glass beads from Venway—the usual peddlar's lot. Everyone on Sattins Island came to look, to chat with the voyager, and perhaps to buy something—"Just to remember him by!" cackled Goody Guld, who like all the women and girls of the village was smitten with Blackbeard's bold good looks. All the boys hung round him too, to hear him tell of his voyages to far, strange islands of the Reach or describe the great rich islands of the Archipelago, the Inner Lanes, the roadsteads white with ships, and the golden roofs of Havnor. The men willingly listened to his tales; but some of them wondered why a trader should sail alone, and kept their eyes thoughtfully upon his oaken staff.

But all this time Mr. Underhill stayed under his hill.

"This is the first island I've ever seen that had no wizard," said Blackbeard one evening to Goody Guld, who had invited him and her nephew and Palani in for a cup of rushwash tea. "What do you do when you get a toothache, or the cow goes dry?"

"Why, we've got Mr. Underhill!" said the old woman.

"For what that's worth," muttered her nephew Birt, and then blushed purple and spilled his tea. Birt was a fisherman, a large, brave, wordless young man. He loved the schoolmistress, but the nearest he had come to telling her of his love was to give baskets of fresh mackerel to her father's cook.

"Oh, you do have a wizard?" Blackbeard asked. "Is he invisible?"

"No, he's just very shy," said Palani. "You've only been here a week, you know, and we see so few strangers here. . . ." She also blushed a little, but did not spill her tea.

Blackbeard smiled at her. "He's a good Sattinsman, then, eh?"

"No," said Goody Guld, "no more than you are. Another cup, nevvy?[12] Keep it in the cup this time. No, my dear, he came in a little bit of a boat, four years ago was it? Just a day after the

end of the shad run, I recall, for they was taking up the nets over in East Creek, and Pondi Cowherd broke his leg that very morning—five years ago it must be. No, four. No, five it is, 'twas the year the garlic didn't sprout. So he sails in on a bit of a sloop[13] loaded full up with great chests and boxes and says to Seacaptain Fogeno, who wasn't blind then, though old enough goodness knows to be blind twice over, 'I hear tell,' he says, 'you've got no wizard nor warlock at all, might you be wanting one?' 'Indeed, if the magic's white!' says the Captain, and before you could say cuttlefish Mr. Underhill had settled down in the cave under the hill and was charming the mange off Goody Beltow's cat. Though the fur grew in grey, and 'twas an orange cat. Queer-looking thing it was after that. It died last winter in the cold spell. Goody Beltow took on so at that cat's death, poor thing, worse than when her man was drowned on the Long Banks, the year of the long herring-runs, when nevvy Birt here was but a babe in petticoats." Here Birt spilled his tea again, and Blackbeard grinned, but Goody Guld proceeded undismayed, and talked on till nightfall.

Next day Blackbeard was down at the pier, seeing after the sprung board in his boat which he seemed to take a long time fixing, and as usual drawing the taciturn[14] Sattinsmen into talk. "Now which of these is your wizard's craft?" he asked. "Or has he got one of those the Mages fold up into a walnut shell when they're not using it?"

"Nay," said a stolid[15] fisherman. "She's oop in his cave, under hill."

"He carried the boat he came in up to his cave?"

---

12. **nevvy** (nev′ē), nephew.
13. **sloop** (slūp), *n.* a type of sailboat.
14. **taciturn** (tas′ə tėrn′), *adj.* speaking very little; not fond of talking.
15. **stolid** (stol′id), *adj.* not easily excited; showing no emotion; seeming dull; impassive.

"Aye. Clear oop. I helped. Heavier as lead she was. Full oop with great boxes, and they full oop with books o' spells, he says. Heavier as lead she was." And the stolid fisherman turned his back, sighing stolidly. Goody Guld's nephew, mending a net nearby, looked up from his work and asked with equal stolidity, "Would ye like to meet Mr. Underhill, maybe?"

Blackbeard returned Birt's look. Clever black eyes met candid blue ones for a long moment; then Blackbeard smiled and said, "Yes. Will you take me up to the hill, Birt?"

"Aye, when I'm done with this," said the fisherman. And when the net was mended, he and the Archipelagan set off up the village street towards the high green hill above it. But as they crossed the common Blackbeard said, "Hold on a while, friend Birt. I have a tale to tell you, before we meet your wizard."

"Tell away," says Birt, sitting down in the shade of a live-oak.

"It's a story that started a hundred years ago, and isn't finished yet—though it soon will be, very soon. . . . In the very heart of the Archipelago, where the islands crowd thick as flies on honey, there's a little isle called Pendor. The sealords of Pendor were mighty men, in the old days of war before the League. Loot and ransom and tribute came pouring into Pendor, and they gathered a great treasure there, long ago. Then from somewhere away out in the West Reach, where dragons breed on the lava isles, came one day a very mighty dragon. Not one of those overgrown lizards most of you Outer Reach folk call dragons, but a big, black, winged, wise, cunning monster, full of strength and subtlety, and like all dragons loving gold and precious stones above all things. He killed the Sealord and his soldiers, and the people of Pendor fled in their ships by night. They all fled away and left the dragon coiled up in Pendor

> **The bones of the old Sealord and his men lay about in the castle courts and on the stairs.**

Towers. And there he stayed for a hundred years, dragging his scaly belly over the emeralds and sapphires and coins of gold, coming forth only once in a year or two when he must eat. He'd raid nearby islands for his food. You know what dragons eat?"

Birt nodded and said in a whisper, "Maidens."

"Right," said Blackbeard. "Well, that couldn't be endured forever, nor the thought of him sitting on all that treasure. So after the League grew strong, and the Archipelago wasn't so busy with wars and piracy, it was decided to attack Pendor, drive out the dragon, and get the gold and jewels for the treasury of the League. They're forever wanting money, the League is. So a huge fleet gathered from fifty islands, and seven Mages stood in the prows of the seven strongest ships, and they sailed towards Pendor. . . . They got there. They landed. Nothing stirred. The houses all stood empty, the dishes on the tables full of a hundred years' dust. The bones of the old Sealord and his men lay about in the castle courts and on the stairs. And the Tower rooms reeked of dragon. But there was no dragon. And no treasure, not a diamond the size of a poppy-seed, not a single silver bead . . . Knowing that he couldn't stand up to seven Mages, the dragon had skipped out. They tracked him, and found he'd flown to a deserted island up north called Udrath; they followed his trail there, and what did they find? Bones again. His bones—the dragon's. But no treasure. A wizard, some unknown wizard from somewhere, must have met him singlehanded, and defeated him—and then made off with the treasure, right under the League's nose!"

The fisherman listened, attentive and expressionless.

"Now that must have been a powerful wizard and a clever one, first to kill a dragon, and second to get off without leaving a trace. The lords and Mages of the Archipelago couldn't track him at all, neither where he'd come from nor where he'd made off to. They were about to give up. That was last spring; I'd been off on a three-year voyage up in the North Reach, and got back about that time. And they asked me to help find the unknown wizard. That was clever of them. Because I'm not only a wizard myself, as I think some of the oafs here have guessed, but I am also a descendant of the Lords of Pendor. That treasure is mine. It's mine, and knows that it's mine. Those fools of the League couldn't find it, because it's not theirs. It belongs to the House of Pendor, and the great emerald, the star of the hoard, Inalkil the Greenstone, knows its master. Behold!" Blackbeard raised his oaken staff and cried aloud, "Inalkil!" The tip of the staff began to glow green, a fiery green radiance, a dazzling haze the color of April grass, and at the same moment the staff tipped in the wizard's hand, leaning, slanting till it pointed straight at the side of the hill above them.

"It wasn't so bright a glow, far away in Havnor," Blackbeard murmured, "but the staff pointed true. Inalkil answered when I called. The jewel knows its master. And I know the thief, and I shall conquer him. He's a mighty wizard, who could overcome a dragon. But I am mightier. Do you want to know why, oaf? Because I know his name!"

As Blackbeard's tone got more arrogant, Birt had looked duller and duller, blanker and blanker; but at this he gave a twitch, shut his mouth, and stared at the Archipelagan. "How did you . . . learn it?" he asked very slowly.

Blackbeard grinned, and did not answer.

"Black magic?"

"How else?"

Birt looked pale, and said nothing.

"I am the Sealord of Pendor, oaf, and I will have the gold my fathers won, and the jewels my mothers wore, and the Greenstone! For they are mine.—Now, you can tell your village bobbies the whole story after I have defeated this wizard

and gone. Wait here. Or you can come and watch, if you're not afraid. You'll never get the chance again to see a great wizard in all his power." Blackbeard turned, and without a backward glance strode off up the hill towards the entrance to the cave.

CLARIFY: What does Blackbeard believe about Mr. Underhill?

Very slowly, Birt followed. A good distance from the cave he stopped, sat down under a hawthorn tree, and watched. The Archipelagan had stopped; a stiff, dark figure alone on the green swell of the hill before the gaping cave-mouth, he stood perfectly still. All at once he swung his staff up over his head, and the emerald radiance shone about him as he shouted, "Thief, thief of the Hoard of Pendor, come forth!"

There was a crash, as of dropped crockery, from inside the cave, and a lot of dust came spewing out. Scared, Birt ducked. When he looked again he saw Blackbeard still standing motionless, and at the mouth of the cave, dusty and disheveled,[16] stood Mr. Underhill. He looked small and pitiful, with his toes turned in as usual, and his little bowlegs in black tights, and no staff—he never had had one, Birt suddenly thought. Mr. Underhill spoke. "Who are you?" he said in his husky little voice.

"I am the Sealord of Pendor, thief, come to claim my treasure!"

At that, Mr. Underhill slowly turned pink, as he always did when people were rude to him. But he then turned something else. He turned yellow. His hair bristled out, he gave a coughing roar—and was a yellow lion leaping down the hill at Blackbeard, white fangs gleaming.

But Blackbeard no longer stood there. A gigantic tiger, color of night and lightning, bounded to meet the lion. . . .

---

16. **disheveled** (də shev′ əld), *adj.* not neat; rumpled; mussed; disordered.

▲ This watercolor illustration for *Tanglewood Tales* (1918) by Edmund Dulac shows the Greek hero Cadmus killing a dragon. A Frenchman who moved to England, Dulac was deeply influenced by Asian and Persian art. Does his dragon seem more menacing or ornamental?

The lion was gone. Below the cave all of a sudden stood a high grove of trees, black in the winter sunshine. The tiger, checking himself in mid-leap just before he entered the shadow of the trees, caught fire in the air, became a tongue of flame lashing out at the dry black branches. . . .

But where the trees had stood a sudden cataract[17] leaped from the hillside, an arch of silvery crashing water, thundering down upon the fire. But the fire was gone. . . .

For just a moment before the fisherman's staring eyes two hills rose—the green one he knew, and a new one, a bare, brown hillock ready to drink up the rushing waterfall. That passed so quickly it made Birt blink, and after blinking he blinked again, and moaned, for what he saw now was a great deal worse. Where the cataract had been there hovered a dragon. Black wings darkened all the hill, steel claws reached groping, and from the dark, scaly, gaping lips fire and steam shot out.

Beneath the monstrous creature stood Blackbeard, laughing.

"Take any shape you please, little Mr. Underhill!" he taunted. "I can match you. But the game grows tiresome. I want to look upon my treasure, upon Inalkil. Now, big dragon, little wizard, take your true shape. I command you by the power of your truename—Yevaud!"

Birt could not move at all, not even to blink. He cowered, staring whether he would or not. He saw the black dragon hang there in the air above Blackbeard. He saw the fire lick like many tongues from the scaly mouth, the steam jet from the red nostrils. He saw Blackbeard's face grow white, white as chalk, and the beard-fringed lips trembling.

"Your name is Yevaud!"

"Yes," said a great, husky, hissing voice.

"My truename is Yevaud, and my true shape is this shape."

"But the dragon was killed—they found dragon-bones on Udrath Island—"

"That was another dragon," said the dragon, and then swooped like a hawk, talons outstretched. And Birt shut his eyes.

When he opened them the sky was clear, the hillside empty, except for a reddish-blackish trampled spot, and a few talon-marks in the grass.

Birt the fisherman got to his feet and ran. He ran across the common, scattering sheep to right and left, and straight down the village street to Palani's father's house. Palani was out in the garden weeding the nasturtiums. "Come with me!" Birt gasped. She stared. He grabbed her wrist and dragged her with him. She screeched a little, but did not resist. He ran with her straight to the pier, pushed her into his fishing-sloop the *Queenie,* untied the painter, took up the oars and set off rowing like a demon. The last that Sattins Island saw of him and Palani was the *Queenie*'s sail vanishing in the direction of the nearest island westward.

The villagers thought they would never stop talking about it, how Goody Guld's nephew Birt had lost his mind and sailed off with the schoolmistress on the very same day that the peddlar Blackbeard disappeared without a trace, leaving all his feathers and beads behind. But they did stop talking about it, three days later. They had other things to talk about, when Mr. Underhill finally came out of his cave.

Mr. Underhill had decided that since his truename was no longer a secret, he might as well drop his disguise. Walking was a lot harder than flying, and besides, it was a long, long time since he had had a real meal.

17. cataract (kat′ə rakt′), *n.* a large, steep waterfall; a violent rush or downpour of water.

After Reading

Making Connections

Shaping Your Response

1. Do you think the ending of the story is effective? Why or why not?
2. How did your impressions of Mr. Underhill change as you read?
3. What do you **predict** will happen next?

Analyzing the Story

4. What clues in the first three paragraphs of the story **foreshadow,** or hint, that Mr. Underhill may not be what he seems?
5. How does Ursula Le Guin create a **surprise ending?**
6. Why doesn't the Rule of Names help Blackbeard win the battle?

Extending the Ideas

7. ☝ Throughout the story, the characters stress the importance of names. How might our names affect how other people treat us?

Literary Focus: Setting

The time and place in which a story occurs make up the story's **setting.** How can we tell that Sattins Island is an imaginary setting? Draw a larger version of the Venn diagram shown here and fill it in by answering the first three questions below. Then use your completed diagram to answer the final question.

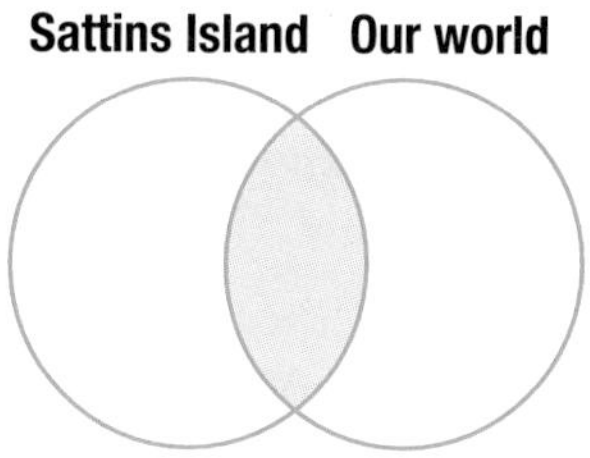

Sattins Island   Our world

- What are some activities and items on Sattins Island that do not exist in the real world? List them in the left half of the left circle.
- What are some aspects of life in the real world that are not part of life on Sattins Island? List them in the right half of the right circle.
- What aspects of life on Sattins Island also exist in the real world? List them in the area where the two circles intersect.
- What details of the setting make it clear that the story is a **fantasy,** set in an imaginary place and time?

Vocabulary Study

cataract
default
disdain
disheveled
elixir
incantation
permeate
repast
stolid
taciturn

Use the vocabulary words to complete the sentences below.

1. Mr. Underhill's appearance was always a bit____. Any ____ or ____ prepared by Mr. Underhill seemed weak and ineffective, and the villagers felt ____ for him.
2. Since there were no better wizards around, Mr. Underhill became the island's wizard by ____.
3. The ____ that Mr. Underhill served to the villagers left them feeling hungry a little while later.
4. Sattins Island may have had a ____ or other beautiful sights.

5. When Blackbeard and Mr. Underhill faced each other, magic seemed to ____ the air.

6. Normally a ____ and ____ man, Birt surprised Palani with his ravings.

Expressing Your Ideas

Writing Choices

Writer's Notebook Update Jot down details of an imaginary setting for your own fantasy story. When and where will it take place? Describe the scene, being sure to provide unusual details that define your strange new world.

The Perfect Name If you could choose your own name, what name would you choose for yourself? In a few paragraphs, write an **explanation** of your new name. First tell what name you would choose for yourself. Then give specific reasons for your choice.

Sing a Song A **ballad** is a song that tells a story. One type of ballad is the historical ballad, which relates events that are in the past. Imagine that you are a resident of Sattins Island and you want to pass down the story of Blackbeard, Mr. Underhill, and the treasure to future generations. Write a ballad, or song, that recounts the major events in the story. You might write your lyrics to go with the tune of a popular song.

Other Options

Plot It Out Sattins Island and its surroundings in the Outer Reach are imaginary places that Ursula Le Guin vividly describes. Make a detailed **map** of these places, showing where the major events of the story occur. Include a legend, or key, for your map.

Dragons Around the World Dragons hold an important place in many cultures. Do some research on how various cultures, including the Japanese and Chinese, have viewed dragons. Present an **oral report** detailing your findings.

▲ Detail of a dragon wall in China.

Before Reading

The Open Window

by Saki

Saki
1870–1916

"Saki" (sä′kē) is the pen name of H. H. (Hector Hugh) Munro, a British writer known for short stories that range from comic situations to grim supernatural events. When Munro was very young, his mother died, so his father sent him and his brother and sister to live with their grandmother and two aunts. His aunts enforced strict rules, including permanently closed windows and little time to play outside. Their strictness and tyranny are believed to have contributed to his unpredictable and rebellious story plots, in which adults are often victimized by wiser children. Munro was shot and killed while serving in the British army during World War I.

Building Background

Calling Cards The story you are about to read takes place in England in the late 1800s, a time marked by intricate rituals in the daily life of the upper classes. One such custom was paying social calls. When a person was new to town, he or she would have the footman drive them to the houses of those the new person wished to meet. Once there, the newcomer would leave a card, so that the lady of the house could decide whether to return a card or actually pay a visit. The whole process could be sidestepped by getting a letter of introduction from a friend to a prominent person. The letters were sometimes called "tickets for soup," because they required, as a minimum, that the recipient of the letter invite the bearer to dinner. As "The Open Window" begins, Framton Nuttel arrives at the home of the Sappletons with just such a letter of introduction.

Literary Focus

Tone The **tone** of a piece of writing reflects the author's attitude toward a subject or an audience. Tone can be conveyed in speech as well as in writing, as the diagram reveals. As you read "The Open Window," think about what the author's tone is and how he conveys the tone to the reader.

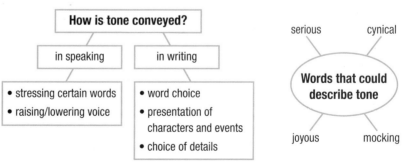

Writer's Notebook

The Joker What is a practical joke? Write a paragraph or two describing a practical joke you or someone you know played on someone else. What effect did the joke have?

The Open Window

SAKI

My aunt will be down presently, Mr. Nuttel," said a very self-possessed young lady of fifteen; "in the meantime you must try and put up with me."

Framton Nuttel endeavoured to say the correct something which should duly flatter the niece of the moment without unduly discounting the aunt that was to come. Privately he doubted more than ever whether these formal visits on a succession of total strangers would do much towards helping the nerve cure which he was supposed to be undergoing.

"I know how it will be," his sister had said when he was preparing to migrate to this rural retreat; "you will bury yourself down there and not speak to a living soul, and your nerves will be worse than ever from moping. I shall just give you letters of introduction to all the people I know there. Some of them, as far as I can remember, were quite nice."

Oscar de Mejo, *The Tiny Suitor* (1990). In this painting what do the proportions, or size relationships, imply? Decide whether or not this painting is a good illustration of the way that Mr. Nuttel and Mrs. Sappleton's niece relate to each other. ➤

Framton wondered whether Mrs. Sappleton, the lady to whom he was presenting one of the letters of introduction, came into the nice division.

"Do you know many of the people round here?" asked the niece, when she judged that they had had sufficient silent communion.

"Hardly a soul," said Framton. "My sister was staying here, at the rectory,[1] you know, some four years ago, and she gave me letters of introduction to some of the people here."

He made the last statement in a tone of distinct regret.

"Then you know practically nothing about my aunt?" pursued the self-possessed young lady.

"Only her name and address," admitted the caller. He was wondering whether Mrs. Sappleton was in the married or widowed state. An undefinable something about the room seemed to suggest masculine habitation.

HER GREAT TRAGEDY HAPPENED JUST THREE YEARS AGO. . . .

"Her great tragedy happened just three years ago," said the child; "that would be since your sister's time."

"Her tragedy?" asked Framton; somehow in this restful country spot tragedies seemed out of place.

"You may wonder why we keep that window wide open on an October afternoon," said the niece, indicating a large French window[2] that opened on to a lawn.

"It is quite warm for the time of the year," said Framton; "but has that window got anything to do with the tragedy?"

"Out through that window, three years ago to a day, her husband and her two young brothers went off for their day's shooting. They never came back. In crossing the moor[3] to their favorite snipe-shooting ground they were all three engulfed in a treacherous[4] piece of bog. It had been that dreadful wet summer, you know, and places that were safe in other years gave way suddenly without warning. Their bodies were never recovered. That was the dreadful part of it." Here the child's voice lost its self-possessed note and became falteringly human. "Poor aunt always thinks that they will come back some day, they and the little brown spaniel that was lost with them, and walk in at that window just as they used to do. That is why the window is kept open every evening till it is quite dusk. Poor dear aunt, she has often told me how they went out, her husband with his white waterproof coat over his arm, and Ronnie, her youngest brother, singing, 'Bertie, why do you bound?' as he always did to tease her, because she said it got on her nerves. Do you know, sometimes on still, quiet evenings like this, I almost get a creepy feeling that they will all walk in through that window—"

She broke off with a little shudder. It was a relief to Framton when the aunt bustled into the room with a whirl of apologies for being late in making her appearance.

"I hope Vera has been amusing you?" she said.

"She has been very interesting," said Framton.

"I hope you don't mind the open window," said Mrs. Sappleton briskly; "my husband and brothers will be home directly from shooting, and they always come in this way. They've been out for snipe in the marshes today, so they'll make a fine mess over my poor carpets. So like you menfolk, isn't it?"

---

1. **rectory** (rek′tər ē), *n*. the house of a clergyman who has charge of a parish.
2. **French window,** a pair of long windows like doors, hinged at the sides and opening in the middle.
3. moor (mûr), *n*. an expanse of open rolling infertile land, usually boggy and dominated by grasses.
4. treacherous (trech′ər əs), *adj*. not reliable; deceptive.

She rattled on cheerfully about the shooting and the scarcity of birds, and the prospects for duck in the winter. To Framton it was all purely horrible. He made a desperate but only partially successful effort to turn the talk on to a less ghastly[5] topic; he was conscious that his hostess was giving him only a fragment of her attention, and her eyes were constantly straying past him to the open window and the lawn beyond. It was certainly an unfortunate coincidence that he should have paid his visit on this tragic anniversary.

"The doctors agree in ordering me complete rest, an absence of mental excitement, and avoidance of anything in the nature of violent physical exercise," announced Framton, who labored under the tolerably widespread delusion[6] that total strangers and chance acquaintances are hungry for the least detail of one's ailments and infirmities,[7] their cause and cure. "On the matter of diet they are not so much in agreement," he continued.

"No?" said Mrs. Sappleton, in a voice which only replaced a yawn at the last moment. Then she suddenly brightened into alert attention—but not to what Framton was saying.

"Here they are at last!" she cried. "Just in time for tea, and don't they look as if they were muddy up to the eyes!"

Framton shivered slightly and turned towards the niece with a look intended to convey sympathetic comprehension. The child was staring out through the open window with dazed horror in her eyes. In a chill shock of nameless fear Framton swung round in his seat and looked in the same direction.

In the deepening twilight three figures were walking across the lawn towards the window; they all carried guns under their arms, and one of them was additionally burdened with a white coat hung over his shoulders. A tired brown spaniel kept close at their heels. Noiselessly they neared the house, and then a hoarse young voice chanted out of the dusk: "I said, Bertie, why do you bound?"

Framton grabbed wildly at his stick and hat; the hall door, the gravel drive, and the front gate were dimly noted stages in his headlong retreat. A cyclist coming along the road had to run into the hedge to avoid imminent[8] collision.

"Here we are, my dear," said the bearer of the white mackintosh, coming in through the window; "fairly muddy, but most of it's dry. Who was that who bolted out as we came up?"

"A most extraordinary man, a Mr. Nuttel," said Mrs. Sappleton; "could only talk about his illnesses, and dashed off without a word of good-bye or apology when you arrived. One would think he had seen a ghost."

"I expect it was the spaniel," said the niece calmly; "he told me he had a horror of dogs. He was once hunted into a cemetery somewhere on the banks of the Ganges by a pack of pariah[9] dogs, and had to spend the night in a newly dug grave with the creatures snarling and grinning and foaming just above him. Enough to make any one lose their nerve."

Romance at short notice was her speciality.

---

5. **ghastly** (gast′lē), *adj.* causing terror; horrible; shocking.
6. delusion (di lü′zhən), *n.* a false belief or opinion.
7. infirmity (in fèr′mə tē), *n.* sickness; illness.
8. imminent (im′ə nənt), *adj.* likely to happen soon; about to happen.
9. **pariah** (pə rī′ə), *n.* a person or animal that is generally despised; an outcast.

After Reading

Making Connections

Shaping Your Response

1. Work with partners to demonstrate the expressions you think Nuttel, Vera, and Mrs. Sappleton would have on their faces at the end of the story. Have the rest of your class decide what feelings you are trying to convey.

2. Do you think Vera's stories hurt other people, or are they just harmless practical jokes? Explain.

Analyzing the Story

3. Describe Mrs. Sappleton's reaction to Nuttel's sudden departure.

4. How would you **interpret** the meaning of the last line of the story?

5. How does Saki's **characterization** of Vera fool the reader?

Extending the Ideas

6. Imagine that Nuttel has discovered the truth about the "tragedy." What will he say or do if he sees the Sappletons again?

7. Think of another character you have read about in this book who turned out to be different than you initially expected. Compare and contrast that character to Vera.

Literary Focus: Tone

The **tone** of a story expresses the author's attitude toward a subject or an audience. Tone can be directly stated, but, more often, the author's attitude is implied. An author establishes tone through word choice, presentation of characters and events, and choice of details.

- What is Saki's attitude toward Nuttel? What words, details, and events in the story show how Saki feels about him?

- How does Saki feel about Vera? Cite specific examples from the story that reveal his attitude.

- Judging from the tone of the story, what do you think Saki's attitude was toward the custom of making social calls?

Vocabulary Study

The questions below contain vocabulary words in italic type. Answer the questions, using your Glossary if necessary to understand the italicized words.

delusion
imminent
infirmity
moor
treacherous

1. Would you rather take a walk on a *moor* or in a garden? Explain.
2. What weather conditions might make roads *treacherous*?
3. Can a *delusion* be harmful? Explain.
4. From whom would you seek help if you had an *infirmity*?
5. What signs show that rain is *imminent*?

Expressing Your Ideas

Writing Choices

Writer's Notebook Update Before reading "The Open Window," you wrote about the effects of a practical joke played by you or someone you know. What effect do you think Vera's joke will have on Nuttel? Write a short continuation of the story, being sure to detail the aftermath of Vera's joke.

A Chilling Tale Vera tells a supernatural tale about the "tragedy" that happened to her aunt. Write an **opening** for your own chilling story. Establish an appropriate tone right in the first few sentences.

Introducing . . . Nuttel's sister writes letters of introduction for her brother so that he can meet people. Imagine that you are moving to a new neighborhood. Write a modern **letter of introduction,** telling a new neighbor all about yourself. Include interesting details that will win you an invitation to dinner.

Other Options

Making Tracks Think about the feelings that "The Open Window" evokes as you read. What parts are eerie? lighthearted? Choose appropriate music and prepare a **soundtrack** for part of the story. You might play your soundtrack as you read part of the story aloud for your class.

Q and A Why do you think Vera wanted to shock Nuttel? Where did she learn to tell such scary but believable tales? With a partner, stage an **interview** with Vera to ask these questions and others. After you polish your questions and responses, do your interview "live" in front of classmates.

Drawing Rooms Do some research to find out what furnishings would be appropriate in an English country home at the turn of the century. Then create an **illustration** for a memorable scene from "The Open Window."

The Necklace

by Guy de Maupassant

Guy de Maupassant
1850–1893

Born in Normandy, France, Guy de Maupassant (gē də mō pə saⁿ´) was one of the most productive writers of all time. In ten years, he wrote nearly three hundred short stories and close to three hundred articles, as well as novels, plays, verses, and travel journals. For the most part, he chose the subjects for his stories from everyday life, the Franco-Prussian War, and the fashionable world of Paris. He is known for a writing style that is objective, realistic, and ironic. As Maupassant's literary life became more triumphant, his personal life was clouded by problems, including declining health. He died in an asylum at the age of 43.

Building Background

Touch of Class A group of persons who have about the same standing in society is called a social class. Almost all societies have some system of social ranking. Some class structures are informal and fluid, with no clearly defined characteristics for each rank. Others are rigidly formal, and individuals who are born into a certain class have little or no chance of moving into a different class. Social class might be based on factors such as wealth, power, prestige, religion, occupation, or ancestry. As you read "The Necklace," pay attention to the importance of social class.

Literary Focus

Point of View All stories must be told by someone, and an author must decide who that someone, the narrator, will be. The author's selection of a narrator determines the **point of view** from which the story will be told. A story told by a character in the story is told from the **first-person** point of view. If the narrator is outside the action, then the story is told in the **third-person** point of view. The author's decision about the point of view affects what we learn about the events and the characters.

Writer's Notebook

Words of Wisdom Shakespeare wrote, "Neither a borrower nor a lender be." Why do you think it might be a problem to be a borrower? a lender? In your log, write about a real or imaginary situation that shows the consequences of being a borrower or lender.

The Necklace

Guy de Maupassant

She was one of those pretty, charming young ladies, born, as if through an error of destiny, into a family of clerks. She had no dowry,[1] no hopes, no means of becoming known, appreciated, loved and married by a man either rich or distinguished; and she allowed herself to marry a petty clerk in the office of the Board of Education.

She was simple, not being able to adorn herself, but she was unhappy, as one out of her class; for women belong to no caste,[2] no race; their grace, their beauty, and their charm serving them in the place of birth and family. Their inborn finesse, their instinctive elegance, their suppleness of wit, are their only aristocracy,[3] making some daughters of the people the equal of great ladies.

She suffered incessantly,[4] feeling herself born for all delicacies and luxuries. She suffered from the poverty of her apartment, the shabby walls, the worn chairs and the faded stuffs.[5] All these things, which another woman of her station would not have noticed, tortured and angered her. The sight of the little Breton,[6] who made this humble home, awoke in her sad regrets and desperate dreams. She thought of quiet antechambers[7] with their oriental hangings lighted by high bronze torches and of the two great footmen in short trousers who sleep in the large armchairs, made sleepy by the heavy air from the heating apparatus. She thought of large drawing rooms hung in old silks, of graceful pieces of furniture carrying bric-a-brac of inestimable value and of the little perfumed coquettish apartments made for five o'clock chats with most intimate friends, men known and sought after, whose attention all women envied and desired.

When she seated herself for dinner before the round table, where the tablecloth had been used three days, opposite her husband who uncovered the tureen[8] with a delighted air, saying: "Oh! the good potpie! I know nothing better than that," she would think of the elegant dinners, of the shining silver, of the tapestries peopling the walls with

---

1. **dowry** (dou′rē), *n.* money or property that a woman brings to the man she marries.
2. **caste** (kast), *n.* an exclusive social group; distinct class.
3. **aristocracy** (ar′ə stok′rə sē), *n.* nobility; class of people with a high position in society.
4. **incessantly** (in ses′nt lē), *adv.* never stopping; repeating without interruption.
5. **stuffs** (stufs), *n.* in this context, any woven material, such as drapes and rugs.
6. **Breton** (bret′n), a native of Brittany, a coastal region of western France.
7. **antechamber** (an′ti chām′bər), *n.* waiting room; room leading to a larger or more important room.
8. **tureen** (tə rēn′), *n.* a deep covered dish for serving soup, etc.

ancient personages and rare birds in the midst of fairy forests; she thought of the exquisite food served on marvelous dishes, of the whispered gallantries, listened to with the smile of the Sphinx[9] while eating the rose-colored flesh of the trout or a chicken's wing.

She had neither frocks nor jewels, nothing. And she loved only those things. She felt that she was made for them. She had such a desire to please, to be sought after, to be clever and courted.

She had a rich friend, a schoolmate at the convent, whom she did not like to visit; she suffered so much when she returned. And she wept for whole days from chagrin,[10] from regret, from despair and disappointment.

One evening her husband returned, elated,[11] bearing in his hand a large envelope.

"Here," he said, "here is something for you."

She quickly tore open the wrapper and drew out a printed card on which were inscribed these words:

The Minister of Public Instruction and Madame George Ramponneau[12] ask the honor of M. and Mme. Loisel's[13] company Monday evening, January 18, at the Minister's residence.

Instead of being delighted, as her husband had hoped, she threw the invitation spitefully upon the table, murmuring:

"What do you suppose I want with that?"

"But, my dearie, I thought it would make you happy. You never go out, and this is an occasion, and a fine one! I had a great deal of trouble to get it. Everybody wishes one, and it is very select; not many are given to employees. You will see the whole official world there."

She looked at him with an irritated eye and declared impatiently:

She had neither frocks nor jewels, nothing. And she loved only those things.

"What do you suppose I have to wear to such a thing as that?"

He had not thought of that; he stammered:

"Why, the dress you wear when we go to the theater. It seems very pretty to me."

He was silent, stupefied,[14] in dismay, at the sight of his wife weeping. Two great tears fell slowly from the corners of her eyes toward the corners of her mouth; he stammered:

"What is the matter? What is the matter?"

By a violent effort she had controlled her vexation[15] and responded in a calm voice, wiping her moist cheeks:

"Nothing. Only I have no dress and consequently I cannot go to this affair. Give your card to some colleague whose wife is better fitted out than I."

He was grieved but answered:

"Let us see, Matilda. How much would a suitable costume cost, something that would serve for other occasions, something very simple?"

She reflected for some seconds, making estimates and thinking of a sum that she could ask for without bringing with it an immediate refusal and a frightened exclamation from the economical clerk.

Finally she said in a hesitating voice:

---

9. **Sphinx** (sfingks), a mythical monster with the head of a woman, man, hawk, or ram, and the body of a lion. It also refers to a puzzling or mysterious person, as it does in this context.

10. chagrin (shə grin′), *n.* a feeling of disappointment, failure, or humiliation.

11. elated (i lā′tid), *adj.* in high spirits; joyful or proud.

12. **Ramponneau** (ram′pə nō).

13. **M. and Mme. Loisel** (lwä zel′), *M.* and *Mme.* are the abbreviations for *Monsieur* (mə syœ′) and *Madame* (mä däm′), respectively.

14. stupefied (stūp′ə fīd), *adj.* overwhelmed with shock or amazement; astounded.

15. **vexation** (vek sā′shən), *n.* a being vexed (troubled or annoyed).

"I cannot tell exactly, but it seems to me that four hundred francs[16] ought to cover it."

He turned a little pale, for he had saved just this sum to buy a gun that he might be able to join some hunting parties the next summer, on the plains at Nanterre,[17] with some friends who went to shoot larks up there on Sunday. Nevertheless, he answered:

"Very well. I will give you four hundred francs. But try to have a pretty dress."

The day of the ball approached, and Mme. Loisel seemed sad, disturbed, anxious. Nevertheless, her dress was nearly ready. Her husband said to her one evening:

"What is the matter with you? You have acted strangely for two or three days."

And she responded: "I am vexed[18] not to have a jewel, not one stone, nothing to adorn myself with. I shall have such a poverty-laden look. I would prefer not to go to this party."

He replied: "You can wear some natural flowers. At this season they look very chic.[19] For ten francs you can have two or three magnificent roses."

She was not convinced. "No," she replied, "there is nothing more humiliating than to have a shabby air in the midst of rich women."

Then her husband cried out: "How stupid we are! Go and find your friend Madame Forestier[20] and ask her to lend you her jewels. You are well enough acquainted with her to do this."

She uttered a cry of joy. "It is true!" she said. "I had not thought of that."

The next day she took herself to her friend's house and related her story of distress. Mme. Forestier went to her closet with the glass doors, took out a large jewel case, brought it, opened it and said: "Choose, my dear."

She saw at first some bracelets, then a collar of pearls, then a Venetian cross of gold and jewels and of admirable workmanship. She tried the jewels before the glass, hesitated, but could neither decide to take them nor leave them. Then she asked:

"Have you nothing more?"

"Why, yes. Look for yourself. I do not know what will please you."

Suddenly she discovered in a black satin box a superb necklace of diamonds, and her heart beat fast with an immoderate[21] desire. Her hands trembled as she took them up. She placed them about her throat, against her dress, and remained in ecstasy before them. Then she asked in a hesitating voice full of anxiety:

"Could you lend me this? Only this?"

"Why, yes, certainly."

She fell upon the neck of her friend, embraced her with passion, then went away with her treasure.

The day of the ball arrived. Mme. Loisel was a great success. She was the prettiest of all, elegant, gracious, smiling and full of joy. All the men noticed her, asked her name and wanted to be presented. All the members of the Cabinet wished to waltz with her. The minister of education paid her some attention.

She danced with enthusiasm, with passion, intoxicated with pleasure, thinking of nothing, in the triumph of her beauty, in the glory of her success, in a kind of cloud of happiness that came of all this homage and all this admiration, of all these awakened desires and this victory so complete and sweet to the heart of woman.

She went home toward four o'clock in the morning. Her husband had been half asleep in one of the little salons since midnight with three other gentlemen whose wives were enjoying themselves very much.

---

16. **four hundred francs** (frangks), about $240 in U. S. currency at the time of the story. The franc itself was worth about sixty cents.
17. **Nanterre** (näN ter′).
18. vexed (vekst), *adj.* annoyed.
19. **chic** (shēk), *adj.* stylish; fashionable.
20. **Forestier** (fôr es tyā′).
21. immoderate (i mod′ər it), *adj.* not moderate; extreme or excessive.

He threw around her shoulders the wraps they had carried for the coming home, modest garments of everyday wear, whose poverty clashed with the elegance of the ball costume. She felt this and wished to hurry away in order not to be noticed by the other women who were wrapping themselves in rich furs.

Loisel detained her. "Wait," said he. "You will catch cold out there. I am going to call a cab."

But she would not listen and descended the steps rapidly. When they were in the street they found no carriage, and they began to seek for one, hailing the coachmen whom they saw at a distance.

They walked along toward the Seine,[22] hopeless and shivering. Finally they found on the dock one of those old nocturnal coupés[23] that one sees in Paris after nightfall, as if they were ashamed of their misery by day.

It took them as far as their door in Martyr Street, and they went wearily up to their apartment. It was all over for her. And on his part he remembered that he would have to be at the office by ten o'clock.

She removed the wraps from her shoulders before the glass for a final view of herself in her glory. Suddenly she uttered a cry. Her necklace was not around her neck.

Her husband, already half undressed, asked: "What is the matter?"

She turned toward him excitedly:

"I have—I have—I no longer have Madame Forestier's necklace."

He arose in dismay: "What! How is that? It is not possible."

And they looked in the folds of the dress, in the folds of the mantle, in the pockets, everywhere. They could not find it.

He asked: "You are sure you still had it when we left the house?"

"Yes, I felt it in the vestibule[24] as we came out."

"But if you had lost it in the street we should have heard it fall. It must be in the cab."

"Yes. It is probable. Did you take the number?"

"No. And you, did you notice what it was?"

"No."

They looked at each other, utterly cast down. Finally Loisel dressed himself again.

"I am going," said he, "over the track where we went on foot, to see if I can find it."

And he went. She remained in her evening gown, not having the force to go to bed, stretched upon a chair, without ambition or thoughts.

Toward seven o'clock her husband returned. He had found nothing.

He went to the police and to the cab offices and put an advertisement in the newspapers, offering a reward; he did everything that afforded them a suspicion of hope.

She waited all day in a state of bewilderment before this frightful disaster. Loisel returned at evening, with his face harrowed[25] and pale, and had discovered nothing.

"It will be necessary," said he, "to write to your friend that you have broken the clasp of the necklace and that you will have it repaired. That will give us time to turn around."

She wrote as he dictated.

At the end of a week they had lost all hope. And Loisel, older by five years, declared:

"We must take measures to replace this jewel."

The next day they took the box which had enclosed it to the jeweler whose name was on the inside. He consulted his books.

---

22. **Seine** (sān), river that flows through the center of Paris.
23. **nocturnal coupé** (nok tėr′nl küp ā′), a closed two-door carriage that could be hired during the night.
24. **vestibule** (ves′tə byül), *n.* a passage or hall between the outer door and the inside of a building.
25. **harrowed** (har′ōd), *adj.* pained or tormented; distressed.

"It is not I, madame," said he, "who sold this necklace; I only furnished the casket."[26]

Then they went from jeweler to jeweler, seeking a necklace like the other one, consulting their memories, and ill, both of them, with chagrin and anxiety.

In a shop of the Palais-Royal[27] they found a chaplet of diamonds which seemed to them exactly like the one they had lost. It was valued at forty thousand francs. They could get it for thirty-six thousand.

They begged the jeweler not to sell it for three days. And they made an arrangement by which they might return it for thirty-four thousand francs if they found the other one before the end of February.

Loisel possessed eighteen thousand francs which his father had left him. He borrowed the rest.

He borrowed it, asking for a thousand francs of one, five hundred of another, five louis[28] of this one and three louis of that one. He gave notes, made ruinous promises, took money of usurers[29] and the whole race of lenders. He compromised his whole existence, in fact, risked his signature without even knowing whether he could make it good or not, and, harassed by anxiety for the future, by the black misery which surrounded him and by the prospect of all physical privations and moral torture, he went to get the new necklace, depositing on the merchant's counter thirty-six thousand francs.

When Mme. Loisel took back the jewels to Mme. Forestier the latter said to her in a frigid tone:

"You should have returned them to me sooner, for I might have needed them."

She did open the jewel box as her friend feared she would. If she should perceive the substitution what would she think? What would she say? Would she take her for a robber?

Mme. Loisel now knew the horrible life of necessity. She did her part, however, completely, heroically. It was necessary to pay this frightful debt. She would pay it. They sent away the maid; they changed their lodgings; they rented some rooms under a mansard roof.[30]

She learned the heavy cares of a household, the odious[31] work of a kitchen. She washed the dishes, using her rosy nails upon the greasy pots and the bottoms of the stewpans. She washed the soiled linen, the chemises and dishcloths, which she hung on the line to dry; she took down the refuse to the street each morning and brought up the water, stopping at each landing to breathe. And, clothed like a woman of the people, she went to the grocer's, the butcher's and the fruiterer's with her basket on her arm, shopping, haggling[32] to the last sou[33] her miserable money.

Every month it was necessary to renew some notes, thus obtaining time, and to pay others.

The husband worked evenings, putting the books of some merchants in order, and nights he often did copying at five sous a page.

And this life lasted for ten years.

At the end of ten years they had restored all, all, with interest of the usurer, and accumulated interest, besides.

Mme. Loisel seemed old now. She had become a strong, hard woman, the crude woman of the poor household. Her hair badly

---

26. **casket** (kas′kit), *n.* in this context, a small box for jewels.
27. **Palais-Royal** (pä lā′ rwä yal′), a Parisian shopping district.
28. **louis** (lü′ē), *n.* a French gold coin equal in value to twenty francs. At the time of the story, five louis were worth about sixty dollars.
29. **usurer** (yü′zhər ər), *n.* person who lends money at an extremely high or unlawful rate of interest.
30. **mansard** (man′särd) **roof,** roof with two slopes on each side, named after François Mansard (1598-1666), French architect.
31. **odious** (ō′dē əs), *adj.* very displeasing; offensive.
32. **haggle** (hag′əl), *v.* argue or dispute, especially about a price or the terms of a bargain.
33. **sou** (sü), *n.* a former French coin that was worth one-twentieth of a franc, or about a penny.

dressed, her skirts awry,[34] her hands red, she spoke in a loud tone and washed the floors in large pails of water. But sometimes, when her husband was at the office, she would seat herself before the window and think of that evening party of former times, of that ball where she was so beautiful and so flattered.

How would it have been if she had not lost that necklace? Who knows? Who knows? How singular is life and how full of changes! How small a thing will ruin or save one!

One Sunday, as she was taking a walk in the Champs Elysées[35] to rid herself of the cares of the week, she suddenly perceived a woman walking with a child. It was Mme. Forestier, still young, still pretty, still attractive. Mme. Loisel was affected. Should she speak to her? Yes, certainly. And now that she had paid, she would tell her all. Why not?

She approached her. "Good morning, Jeanne."

Her friend did not recognize her and was astonished to be so familiarly addressed by this common personage. She stammered:

"But, madame—I do not know—You must be mistaken."

"No, I am Matilda Loisel."

Her friend uttered a cry of astonishment:

Oh! My poor Matilda! How you have changed.

"Oh! My poor Matilda! How you have changed."

"Yes, I have had some hard days since I saw you, and some miserable ones—and all because of you."

"Because of me? How is that?"

"You recall the diamond necklace that you loaned me to wear to the minister's ball?"

"Yes, very well."

"Well, I lost it."

"How is that, since you returned it to me?"

"I returned another to you exactly like it. And it has taken us ten years to pay for it. You can understand that it was not easy for us who have nothing. But it is finished, and I am decently content."

Mme. Forestier stopped short. She said:

"You say that you bought a diamond necklace to replace mine?"

"Yes. You did not perceive it then? They were just alike?"

And she smiled with a proud and simple joy. Mme. Forestier was touched and took both her hands as she replied:

"Oh, my poor Matilda! Mine were false. They were not worth over five hundred francs!"

---

34. awry (ə rī′), *adj.* wrong; out of order.
35. **Champs Elysées** (chaN zā lē zā′), a famous avenue in Paris.

After Reading

Making Connections

Shaping Your
Response

1. With a partner, pose for a snapshot of Mme. Loisel and Mme. Forestier at the end of the story. What expressions and body language does each woman display?

2. In your opinion, is the ending of the story happy or unhappy? Explain.

Analyzing the Story

3. Explain what is **ironic** in "The Necklace."

4. In your opinion, are the things that happen to Matilda the result of fate, or are they caused by her own **character?** Explain.

5. The narrator asks, "How would it have been if she had not lost the necklace? . . . How small a thing will ruin or save one!" Explain in what ways Matilda was ruined, saved, or both ruined and saved.

6. Name some clues that hint at the story's **surprise ending.**

7. ☝ A **stereotype** is a simplified, preconceived idea about a group of people, such as saying that all men like sports. Do you think this portrayal of Matilda is stereotypical of women? Explain.

Extending the Ideas

8. ☝ Fine clothing, jewelry, and fancy invitations are status symbols that Matilda feels she must have. From your **perspective,** are these things important? What are some status symbols that young people today think they must have?

Literary Focus: Point of View

Because "The Necklace" is told by a narrator outside of the story, it is told from the **third-person point of view.** There are three different types of third-person point of view. In **third-person omniscient,** the narrator is an outsider who knows everything about all the characters and knows all their thoughts. In **third-person limited,** the narrator records the thoughts and feelings of just one character. In **third-person objective,** the narrator is an outsider who merely relates facts without recording the thoughts and feelings of the characters.

- What kind of third-person point of view—omniscient, limited, or objective—does de Maupassant use in "The Necklace"?

- How does the point of view help keep the outcome secret?

- Imagine that the story were written in the first-person point of view of Mme. Forestier. How would the story be different?

Vocabulary Study

Use the listed vocabulary words to fill in the blanks in these sentences. Your Glossary may be helpful.

awry
chagrin
dowry
elated
haggle
immoderate
incessantly
odious
stupefied
vexed

1. Because of her limited ____, Matilda could only marry a clerk.
2. Matilda thought ____ about all the things she wanted but could not have.
3. Matilda's husband did not want her to spend an ____ amount on her party dress.
4. Matilda was ____ when Mme. Forestier allowed her to borrow a beautiful necklace.
5. To their ____, the Loisels could not find the lost necklace.
6. The Loisels were ____ by the replacement cost of the necklace.
7. Mme. Forestier was ____ when her necklace was returned so late.
8. Matilda found cleaning, washing, and cooking to be ____ tasks.
9. The Loisels had to ____ for their food at the market.
10. Mme. Loisel, with her features hardened by work and her skirts ____, didn't look familiar to Mme. Forestier.

Expressing Your Ideas

Writing Choices

Writer's Notebook Update Think back to the quotation "Neither a borrower nor a lender be." How does "The Necklace" illustrate this? Imagine that you are Matilda or Mme. Forestier. Write a short letter to a friend in which you agree or disagree with the quotation, explaining how you learned that it is (or is not) wise to be a borrower or a lender.

Lost and Found The Loisels tried many different things to get back the lost jewels, including advertisements. Write a lost and found **advertisement** of your own for the lost necklace. You might use classified advertisements from a newspaper as models.

Other Options

Act It Out The scene in which Mme. Loisel realizes she has lost the necklace provides some tension and frantic dialogue that could be acted out. With a partner, practice acting out the scene, deciding what facial expressions and tone of voice would work with the dialogue. Present your **dramatic scene** to others in a group.

The Honor of Your Presence Design an **invitation** for the party at the Minister's residence or for another occasion. Include all the important details. You might use calligraphy or materials such as glitter, flower petals, and so on, to enhance your invitation.

My Delicate Heart Condition

by Toni Cade Bambara

Toni Cade Bambara
1939–1995

Toni Cade Bambara (bam ber′ə) described herself as "a writer since childhood who nevertheless planned to be a doctor, lawyer, artist, musician, and everything else." Originally Toni Cade, she took the name Bambara from a signature on a sketchbook she found in her great-grand-mother's trunk. She was praised for her portrayals of characters and the affection-ate warmth and pride she showed in handling their situ-ations. Critic Laura Marcus wrote, "Bambara depicts black communities in which ties of blood and friendship are fiercely defended."

Building Background

Chills and Thrills In what situations do you think it's fun to be scared? For example, people intentionally scare themselves by riding on roller coasters or seeing suspenseful movies. Why do you think people might find it enjoyable to be frightened sometimes? Discuss these questions in a small group, trying to arrive at a theory explaining why people intentionally scare themselves.

Literary Focus

Style The way a writer expresses ideas to correspond to the audience and the purpose shapes the writer's **style.** The web below shows how the many choices an author makes determine the style of a piece of writing: which words to use and how to arrange them, whether or not to use imagery and figurative language, what point of view to use, and what tone to create. As you read "My Delicate Heart Condition," pay attention to the author's style. Why do you think the author chose to write in this particular style?

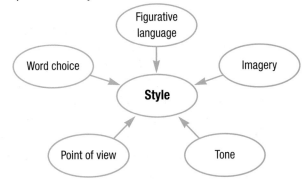

Writer's Notebook

Friendly Persuasion The narrator of "My Delicate Heart Condition" says, "For all the years my mother's known me, she still doesn't understand that my behaving has got nothing to do with who I hang out with." How do you think your friends influence your beliefs and your actions? Write a paragraph or two explaining whether or not the narrator's statement applies to you.

My Delicate Heart Condition

Toni Cade Bambara

My cousin Joanne has not been allowed to hang
out with me for some time because she went and
told Aunt Hazel that I scare her to death whenever
she sleeps over at our house or I spend the weekend at hers.
The truth is I sometimes like to tell stories about bloodthirsty
vampires or ugly monsters that lurk[1] in clothesclosets or
giant beetles that eat their way through the shower
curtain, like I used to do at camp to entertain the
kids in my bunk. But Joanne always cries and that
makes the stories even weirder, like background music
her crying. And too—I'm not going to lie about it—I get
spookier on purpose until all the little crybabies are stuffing
themselves under their pillows and throwing their sneakers
at me and making such a racket that Mary the counselor has
to come in and shine her flashlight around the bunkhouse.
I play like I'm asleep. The rest of them are too busy
blubbering[2] and finding their way out from under
blankets to tell Mary that it's me. Besides, once they
get a load of her standing against the moonlight in
that long white robe of hers looking like a ghost,
they just start up again and pretty soon the
whole camp is awake. Anyway, that's what
I do for fun. So Joanne hasn't been around. And this year I'll
have to go to the circus by myself and to camp without her.
My mother said on the phone to Aunt Hazel—"Good, keep
Jo over there and maybe Harriet'll behave herself if she's got
no one to show off to." For all the years my mother's known
me, she still doesn't understand that my behaving has got
nothing to do with who I hang out with. A private thing

---

1. lurk (lėrk), *v.* wait out of sight; be hidden.
2. **blubber** (blub′ər), *v.* cry.

between me and me or maybe between me and the Fly family since they were the ones that first got me to sit through monster movies and withstand all the terror I could take.

For four summers now, me and the Fly family have had this thing going. A battle of nerves, you might say. Each year they raise the rope closer and closer to the very top of the tent—I hear they're going to perform outdoors this year and be even higher—and they stretch the rope further across the rings where the clowns and the pony riders perform. Each year they get bolder and more daring with their rope dancing and swinging by the legs and flinging themselves into empty space making everyone throw up their hands and gasp for air until Mr. Fly at the very last possible second swings out on his bar to catch them up by the tips of their heels. Everyone just dies and clutches at their hearts. Everybody but me. I sit there calmly. I've trained myself. Joanne used to die and duck her head under the benches and stay there till it was all over.

Last summer they really got bold. On the final performance just before the fair closed, and some revival type tent show[3] comes in and all the kids go off to camp, the Fly family performed without a net. I figured they'd be up to something so I made sure my stomach was like steel. I did ten push-ups before breakfast, twenty sit-ups before lunch, skipped dinner altogether. My brother Teddy kidded me all day—"Harriet's trying out for the Olympics." I passed up the icie man[4] on the corner and the pizza and sausage stand by the schoolyard and the cotton candy and jelly apple lady and the pickle and penny candy boy; in fact I passed up all the stands that lead from the street down the little roadway to the fair grounds that used to be a swamp when we first moved from Baltimore to Jamaica, Long Island. It wasn't easy, I'm not going to lie, but I was taking no chances. Between the balloon man and the wheel of fortune was the usual clump of ladies from church who came night after night to try to win the giant punch bowl set on the top

shelf above the wheel, but had to settle night after night for a jar of gumdrops or salt and pepper shakers or some other little thing from the bottom shelf. And from the wheel of fortune to the tent was at least a million stands selling B. B. bats and jawbreakers and gingerbread and sweet potato pie and frozen custard and—like I said it wasn't easy. A million ways to tempt you, to unsettle your stomach, and make you lose the battle with the Fly family.

I sat there almost enjoying the silly clowns who came tumbling out of a steamer trunk no bigger than the one we have in the basement where my mother keeps my old report cards and photographs and letters and things. And I almost enjoyed the fire-eater and the knife thrower, but I was so close up I could see how there wasn't any real thrill. I almost enjoyed the fat-leg girls who rode the ponies two at a time and standing up, but their costumes weren't very pretty—just an ordinary polo shirt like you get if you run in the PAL meets[5] and short skirts you can wear on either side like the big girls wear at the roller rink. And I almost enjoyed the jugglers except that my Uncle Bubba can juggle the dinner plates better any day of the week so long as Aunt Hazel isn't there to stop him. I was impatient and started yawning. Finally all the clowns hitched up their baggy pants and tumbled over each other out of the ring and into the dark, the jugglers caught all the things that were up in the air and yawning just like me went off to the side. The pony girls brought their horses to a sudden stop that raised a lot of dust, then jumped down into the dirt and bowed. Then the ringmaster stepped into the circle of light and tipped his hat which was a little raggedy from where I was sitting and said—"And now, Ladieeez and Gentlemen, what you've alll been waiting forrr,

---

3. **revival type tent show.** Revivals are special services or efforts made to increase interest in religion.
4. **icie man,** ice cream man.
5. **PAL meets,** sports events organized for neighborhood children by the Police Athletic League.

▲ JoAnn Scott, *Erika*. What does the artist's choice of background colors imply about the personality of young woman she portrays?

the Main aTTRACtion, the FLY FAMILEEE." And everyone jumped up to shout like crazy as they came running out on their toes to stand in the light and then climb the ropes. I took a deep breath and folded my arms over my chest and a kid next to me went into hiding, acting like she was going to tie her shoelaces.

There used to be four of them—the father, a big guy with a bald head and bushy mustache and shoulders and arms like King Kong; a tall lanky mother whom you'd never guess could even climb into a high chair or catch anything heavier than a Ping-Pong ball to look at her; the oldest son who looked like his father except he had hair on his head but none on his face and a big face it was, so that no matter how high up he got you could always tell whether he was smiling or frowning or counting; the younger boy about thirteen, maybe, had a vacant[6] stare like he was a million miles away feeding his turtles or something, anything but walking along a tightrope or flying through the air with his family. I had always liked to watch him because he was as cool as I was. But last summer the little girl got into the act. My grandmother says she's probably a midget 'cause no self-respecting mother would allow her child to be up there acting like a bird. "Just a baby," she'd say. "Can't be more than six years old. Should be home in bed. Must be a midget." My grandfather would give me a look when she started in and we'd smile at her together.

They almost got to me that last performance, dodging around with new routines and two at a time so that you didn't know which one Mr. Fly was going to save at the last minute. But he'd fly out and catch the little boy and swing over to the opposite stand where the big boy was flying out to catch them both by the wrists and the poor woman would be left kind of dangling there, suspended, then she'd do this double flip which would kill off everyone in the tent except

me, of course, and swing out on the very bar she was on in the first place. And then they'd mess around two or three flying at once just to confuse you until the big drum roll started and out steps the little girl in a party dress and a huge blindfold wrapped around her little head and a pink umbrella like they sell down in Chinatown. And I almost—I won't lie about it—I almost let my heart thump me off the bench. I almost thought I too had to tie my shoelaces. But I sat there. Stubborn. And the kid starts bouncing up and down on the rope like she was about to take off and tear through the canvas roof. Then out swings her little brother, and before you know it, Fly Jr. like a great eagle with his arms flapping grabs up the kid, eyeband in his teeth, and swoops her off to the bar that's already got Mrs., Mr., and Big Bro on it, and surely there's no room for him. And everyone standing on their feet clutching at their faces. Everyone but me. 'Cause I know from the getgo[7] that Mr. and Mrs. are going to leave the bar to give Jr. room and fly over to the other side. Which is exactly what

 **And I almost—I won't lie about it—I almost let my heart thump me off the bench.**

they do. The lady in front of me, Mrs. Perez, who does all the sewing in our neighborhood, gets up and starts shaking her hands like ladies do to get the fingernail polish dry and she says to me with her eyes jammed shut "I must go finish the wedding gowns. Tell me later who died." And she scoots through the aisle, falling all over everybody with her eyes still shut and never looks up. And Mrs. Caine taps me on the back and leans over and says, "Some people just can't take it." And I smile at her and at her twins who're sitting there with their mouths open. I

---

6. **vacant** (vā′kənt), *adj.* empty of thought or intelligence.
7. **getgo**, slang for start; beginning.

fold my arms over my chest and just dare the Fly family to do their very worst.

The minute I got to camp, I ran up to the main house where all the counselors gather to say hello to the parents and talk with the directors. I had to tell Mary the latest doings with the Fly family. But she put a finger to her mouth like she sometimes does to shush me. "Let's not have any scary stuff this summer, Harriet," she said, looking over my shoulder at a new kid. This new kid, Willie, was from my old neighborhood in Baltimore so we got friendly right off. Then he told me that he had a romantic heart so I quite naturally took him under my wing and decided not to give him a heart attack with any ghost tales. Mary said he meant "rheumatic"[8] heart, but I don't see any difference. So I told Mary to move him out of George's tent and give him a nicer counselor who'd respect his romantic heart. George used to be my play boyfriend when I first came to camp as a little kid and didn't know any better. But he's not a nice person. He makes up funny nicknames for people which aren't funny at all. Like calling Eddie Michaels the Watermelon Kid or David Farmer Charcoal Plenty which I really do not appreciate and especially from a counselor. And once he asked Joanne, who was the table monitor, to go fetch a pail of milk from the kitchen. And the minute she got up, he started hatching a plot, trying to get the kids to hide her peanut butter sandwich and put spiders in her soup. I had to remind everyone at the table that Joanne was my first cousin by blood, and I would be forced to waste the first bum that laid a hand on her plate. And ole George says, "Oh don't be a dumbhead, Harriet. Jo's so stupid she won't even notice." And I told him right then and there that I was not his play girlfriend anymore and would rather marry the wolfman than grow up and be his wife. And just in case he didn't get the message, that night around the campfire when we were all playing Little Sally Walker sittin' in a saucer and it was my turn to shake it

to the east and to shake it to the west and to shake it to the very one that I loved the best—I shook straight for Mr. Nelson the lifeguard, who was not only the ugliest person in camp but the arch enemy of ole George.

And that very first day of camp last summer when Willie came running up to me to get in line for lunch, here comes George talking some simple stuff about "What a beautiful head you have, Willie. A long, smooth, streamlined[9] head. A sure sign of superior gifts. Definitely genius proportions." And poor Willie went for it, grinning and touching his head, which if you want to know the truth is a bullet head and that's all there is to it. And he's turning to me every which way, like he's modeling his head in a fashion show. And the minute his back is turned, ole George makes a face about Willie's head and all the kids in the line burst out laughing. So I had to beat up a few right then and there and finish off the rest later in the shower for being so stupid, laughing at a kid with a romantic heart.

One night in the last week of August when the big campfire party is held, it was very dark and the moon was all smoky, and I just couldn't help myself and started in with a story about the great caterpillar who was going to prowl through the tents and nibble off everybody's toes. And Willie started this whimpering in the back of his throat so I had to switch the story real quick to something cheerful. But before I could do that, ole George picked up my story and added a wicked witch who puts spells on city kids who come to camp, and a hunchback dwarf that chopped up tents and bunk beds, and a one-eyed phantom giant who gobbled up the hearts of underprivileged[10] kids. And every time

---

8. **rheumatic** (rü mat′ik), *adj.* painfully inflamed.
9. streamlined (strēm′līnd′), *adj.* having a shape that offers the least possible resistance to air or water.
10. underprivileged (un′dər priv′ə lijd), *adj.* having fewer advantages than others, especially because of poverty.

he got to the part where the phantom ripped out a heart, poor Willie would get louder and louder until finally he started rolling around in the grass and screaming and all the kids went crazy and scattered behind the rocks almost kicking the fire completely out as they dashed off into the darkness yelling bloody murder. And the counselors could hardly round us all up—me, too, I'm not going to lie about it. Their little circles of flashlight bobbing in and out of the bushes along the patches of pine, bumping into each other as they scrambled for us kids. And poor Willie rolling around something awful, so they took him to the infirmary.[11]

I was sneaking some gingersnaps in to him later that night when I hear Mary and another senior counselor fussing at ole George in the hallway.

"You've been picking on that kid ever since he got here, George. But tonight was the limit—"

"I wasn't picking on him, I was just trying to tell a story—"

"All that talk about hearts, gobblin' up hearts, and underpriv—"

"Yeh, you were directing it all at the little kid. You should be—"

"I wasn't talking about him. They're all underprivileged kids, after all. I mean all the kids are underprivileged."

I huddled back into the shadows and almost banged into Willie's iron bed. I was hoping he'd open his eyes and wink at me and tell me he was just fooling. That it wasn't so bad to have an underprivileged heart. But he just slept. "I'm an underprivileged kid too," I thought to myself. I knew that it was a special camp, but I'd never realized. No wonder Aunt Hazel screamed so about my scary stories and my mother flicked off the TV when the monsters came on and Mary was always shushing me. We all had bad hearts. I crawled into the supply cabinet to wait for Willie to wake up so I could ask him about it all. I ate all the gingersnaps but I didn't feel any

better. You have a romantic heart, I whispered to myself settling down among the bandages. You will have to be very careful.

It didn't make any difference to Aunt Hazel that I had changed, that I no longer told scary stories or dragged my schoolmates to the latest creature movie, or raced my friends to the edge of the roof, or held my breath, or ran under the train rail when the train was already in sight. As far as she was concerned, I was still the same ole spooky kid I'd always been. So Joanne was kept at home. My mother noticed the difference, but she said over the phone to my grandmother, "She's acting very ladylike these days, growing up." I didn't tell her about my secret, that I knew about my heart. And I was kind of glad Joanne wasn't around 'cause I would have blabbed it all to her and scared her to death. When school starts again, I decided, I'll ask my teacher how to outgrow my underprivileged heart. I'll train myself, just like I did with the Fly family.

"Well, I guess you'll want some change to go to the fair again, hunh?" my mother said coming into my room and dumping things in her pocketbook.

"No," I said. "I'm too grown up for circuses."

She put the money on the dresser anyway. I was lying, of course. I was thinking what a terrible strain it would be for Mrs. Perez and everybody else if while sitting there, with the Fly family zooming around in the open air a million miles above the ground, little Harriet Watkins should drop dead with a fatal heart attack behind them.

"I lost," I said out loud.

"Lost what?"

"The battle with the Fly family."

She just stood there a long time looking at me, trying to figure me out, the way mothers are always doing but should know better. Then she kissed me goodbye and left for work.

---

11. infirmary (in fėr′mər ē), *n.* place for the care of the sick or injured; hospital or dispensary in a school or institution.

After Reading

Making Connections

Shaping Your Response

1. Would you want Harriet Watkins to be your friend? Why or why not?

2. Do you think this story is realistic? Why or why not?

Analyzing the Story

3. Harriet faces an **internal conflict** in the story. Explain what that conflict is and what role the Fly family plays in that conflict.

4. 👁 Describe George's **perspective** on the kids at camp. How does his attitude affect the way he deals with them?

5. Explain Harriet's confusion in the story. Why does she believe that she has a heart problem?

6. How does the **point of view** in this story influence your impressions of the events?

Extending the Ideas

7. Compare Harriet's "mistaken impression" about her heart with Madame Loisel's "mistaken impression" in "The Necklace." How does each character's life change as a result of her error?

Literary Focus: Style

The choice of words in a piece of writing and the manner in which they are combined and arranged help determine the **style.** Examine Toni Cade Bambara's style in "My Delicate Heart Condition" by answering the following questions.

- Does Bambara use simple or complex words? formal or informal words?

- What impression do you have of the narrator based on the words she uses and the way she tells the story?

- Think back to either "The Rule of Names" or "The Open Window." Compare the style of that piece with the style of "My Delicate Heart Condition."

Vocabulary Study

A **word analogy** is a relationship between two words that is similar to the relationship between two other words. For example, two words that are antonyms *(hot, cold)* have the same relationship as two other words that are antonyms *(tall, short).* Such an analogy can be expressed this way: *"Hot* is to *cold* as *tall* is to *short."* Complete the following analogies using the vocabulary words. If necessary, use your Glossary to decide which word best fits each analogy.

infirmary
lurk
streamlined
underprivileged
vacant

1. stroll : walk :: hide : ____

2. spotless : filthy :: full : ____

3. school : academy :: hospital : ____

4. smooth : ____ :: rough : jagged

5. ____ : wealthy :: hungry : overfed

Expressing Your Ideas

Writing Choices

Writer's Notebook Update Do you think that Harriet is someone whose opinions or actions could easily be swayed by others? Why or why not? As Harriet, write a diary entry about how you feel when your mother and Aunt Hazel imply that you are "showing off."

I Like Your Style "My Delicate Heart Condition" is written in a style that makes you feel as if Harriet is talking directly to you. How would the style vary if a different character in the story were telling the events? Rewrite a **scene** from the story, using a style appropriate for a different narrator. You might, for example, write from the point of view of Harriet's mother, Joanne, or one of the camp counselors.

Other Options

Memories Harriet details some events from her past in a colorful way that brings them alive for readers. Choose photos or produce pictures that capture a memorable time from your past in a **photo essay.** Be sure to include captions to explain your photos. You might try to imitate Bambara's style—conversational language that draws your reader into the events.

Camping Out Part of "My Delicate Heart Condition" is set at a summer camp. Reread the story for details about the camp. Then make a **model** of Harriet's camp that shows the location of the main house, the tents, the campfire circle, and any other spots that may have been part of Harriet's camp experience.

Like Mexicans

by Gary Soto

Gary Soto
born 1952

Gary Soto's decision to become a writer was a surprise even to him. Says Soto, "I don't think I had any literary aspirations when I was a kid. In fact, we were pretty much an illiterate family. We didn't have books, and no one encouraged us to read." Soto overcame such obstacles to become a well-respected author of prose and poetry for children and adults. His work reflects his Mexican American heritage, and ranges from grim depictions of urban life to humorous anecdotes drawn from his childhood in Fresno, California. In addition to writing, Soto teaches English and Chicano studies at the University of California at Berkeley.

Building Background

Memories Are Made of This The selection you are about to read is a **memoir** by writer Gary Soto. A memoir is a narrative or series of narratives drawn from the real-life experiences of the writer. The success of a memoir depends upon the writer's ability to bring the past to life with vivid images and interesting details. In the following selection, Soto presents an amusing picture of his struggle to figure out what kind of girl he should marry.

Literary Focus

Irony In general, **irony** is a contrast between what appears to be and what really is. An ironic situation occurs when events turn out differently than expected. For example, if you stayed up all night studying for a test, only to learn it had been canceled, you would be in the ironic situation of being prepared for a test you were not going to take. As you read "Like Mexicans," note the ironic situations that Gary Soto encounters as he pursues his quest for the right girl.

Writer's Notebook

That's Ironic Think about a time when an event turned out differently than you expected. In your notebook, write about the experience. What did you expect would happen? What really did happen? How did you feel about it? After you read "Like Mexicans," you can compare your experience with Gary Soto's.

Like Mexicans

GARY SOTO

My grandmother gave me bad advice and good advice when I was in my early teens. For the bad advice, she said that I should become a barber because they made good money and listened to the radio all day. "Honey, they don't work como burros,"[1] she would say every time I visited her. She made the sound of donkeys braying. "Like that, honey!" For the good advice, she said that I should marry a Mexican girl. "No Okies, hijo"[2]—she would say—"Look my son. He marry one and they fight every day about I don't know what and I don't know what." For her, everyone who wasn't Mexican, black, or Asian were Okies. The French were Okies, the Italians in suits were Okies. When I asked about Jews, whom I had read about, she asked for a picture. I rode home on my bicycle and returned with a calendar depicting the important races of the world. "Pues sí, son Okies también!"[3] she said, nodding her head. She waved the calendar away and we went to the living room where she lectured me on the virtues of the Mexican girl: first, she could cook and, second, she acted like a woman, not a man, in her husband's home. She said she would tell me about a third when I got a little older.

I asked my mother about it—becoming a barber and marrying Mexican. She was in the kitchen. Steam curled from a pot of boiling beans, the radio was on, looking as squat as a loaf of bread. "Well, if you want to be a barber—they say they make good money." She slapped a round steak with a knife, her glasses slipping down with each strike. She stopped and looked up. "If you find a good Mexican girl, marry her of course." She returned to slapping the meat and I went to the backyard where my brother and David King were sitting on the lawn.

I ignored them and climbed the back fence to see my best friend, Scott, a second-generation Okie. I called him, and his mother pointed to the side of the house where his bedroom was a small aluminum trailer, the kind you gawk at when they're flipped over on the freeway, wheels spinning in the air. I went around to find Scott pitching horseshoes.

I picked up a set of rusty ones and joined him. While we played, we talked about school and friends and record albums. The horseshoes scuffed up dirt, sometimes ringing the iron that threw out a meager[4] shadow like a sundial. After three argued-over games, we pulled two oranges apiece from his tree and started down the alley still talking school and friends and record albums. We pulled more oranges from the alley and talked about who we would marry. "No offense, Scott," I said with an orange slice in my mouth, "but I would never marry an Okie." We walked in step, almost touching, with a sled of shadows dragging behind us. "No offense, Gary," Scott said, "but I would *never* marry a Mexican." I looked at him: a fang of orange slice showed from his munching mouth. I didn't think anything of it. He had his girl and I had mine. But our seventh-grade vision was the same: to marry, get jobs, buy cars and maybe a house if we had money left over.

We talked about our future lives until, to our surprise, we were on the downtown mall, two

1. **como burros** (kō′mō bü′rōs), like donkeys. [Spanish]
2. **No Okies, hijo** (nō ō′kēs ē′hō), Not Okies, son. "Okies" is a derogatory term for people from Oklahoma.
3. **Pues sí, son Okies también!** (pwes sē′ sōn ō′kēs täm byen′), Well, yes, they are Okies too! [Spanish]
4. **meager** (mē′gər), *adj.* thin; lean.

miles from home. We bought a bag of popcorn at Penney's and sat on a bench near the fountain watching Mexican and Okie girls pass. "That one's mine." I pointed with my chin when a girl with eyebrows arched into black rainbows ambled by. "She's cute," Scott said about a girl with yellow hair and a mouthful of gum. We dreamed aloud, our chins busy pointing out girls. We agreed that we couldn't wait to become men and lift them onto our laps.

But the woman I married was not Mexican but Japanese. It was a surprise to me. For years, I went about wide-eyed in my search for the brown girl in a white dress at a dance. I searched the playground at the baseball diamond. When the girls raced for grounders,[5] their hair bounced like something that couldn't be caught. When they sat together in the lunchroom, heads pressed together, I knew they were talking about us Mexican guys. I saw them and dreamed them. I threw my face into my pillow, making up sentences that were good as in the movies.

But when I was twenty, I fell in love with this other girl who worried my mother, who had my grandmother asking once again to see the calendar of the Important Races of the World. I told her I had thrown it away years before. I took a much-glanced-at snapshot from my wallet. We looked at it together, in silence. Then grandma reclined in her chair, lit a cigarette, and said, "Es pretty."[6] She blew and asked with all her worry pushed up to her forehead: "Chinese?"

I was in love and there was no looking back. She was the one. I told my mother who was slapping hamburger into patties. "Well, sure if you want to marry her," she said. But the more

I talked, the more concerned she became. Later I began to worry. Was it all a mistake? "Marry a Mexican girl," I heard my mother say in my mind. I heard it at breakfast. I heard it over math problems, between Western Civilization and cultural geography. But then one afternoon while I was hitchhiking home from school, it struck me like a baseball in the back: my mother wanted me to marry someone of my own social class—a poor girl. I considered my fiancée,[7] Carolyn, and she didn't look poor, though I knew she came from a family of farm workers and pull-yourself-up-by-your-bootstraps ranchers. I asked my brother, who was marrying Mexican poor that fall, if I should marry a poor girl. He screamed "Yeah" above his terrible guitar playing in his bedroom. I considered my sister who had married Mexican. Cousins were dating Mexican. Uncles were remarrying poor women. I asked Scott, who was still my best friend, and he said, "She's too good for you, so you better not."

I worried about it until Carolyn took me home to meet her parents. We drove in her Plymouth until the houses gave way to farms and ranches and finally her house fifty feet from

---

5. **grounder** (groun′dər), *n.* in baseball, a hit that makes the ball roll or bounce along the ground.
6. **Es pretty.** She is pretty.
7. **fiancée** (fē′än sā′), *n.* woman engaged to be married.

the highway. When we pulled into the drive, I panicked and begged Carolyn to make a U-turn and go back so we could talk about it over a soda. She pinched my cheek, calling me a "silly boy." I felt better, though, when I got out of the car and saw the house: the chipped paint, a cracked window, boards for a walk to the back door. There were rusting cars near the barn. A tractor with a net of spiderwebs under a mulberry. A field. A bale of barbed wire like children's scribbling leaning against an empty chicken coop. Carolyn took my hand and pulled me to my future mother-in-law who was coming out to greet us.

We had lunch: sandwiches, potato chips, and iced tea. Carolyn and her mother talked mostly about neighbors and the congregation at the Japanese Methodist Church in West Fresno. Her father, who was in khaki work clothes, excused himself with a wave that was almost a salute and went outside. I heard a truck start, a dog bark, and then the truck rattle away.

Carolyn's mother offered another sandwich, but I declined with a shake of my head and a smile. I looked around when I could, when I was not saying over and over that I was a college student, hinting that I could take care of her daughter. I shifted my chair. I saw newspapers piled in corners, dusty cereal boxes and vinegar bottles in corners. The wallpaper was bubbled from rain that had come in from a bad roof. Dust. Dust lay on lamp shades and window sills. These people are just like Mexicans, I thought. Poor people.

Carolyn's mother asked me through Carolyn if I would like a *sushi*.[8] A plate of black and white things were held in front of me. I took one, wide-eyed, and turned it over like a foreign coin. I was biting into one when I saw a kitten crawl up the window screen over the sink. I chewed and the kitten opened its mouth of terror as she crawled higher, wanting in to paw the leftovers from our plates. I looked at Carolyn, who said that the cat was just showing off. I looked up in time to see it fall. It crawled up, then fell again.

We talked for an hour and had apple pie and coffee, slowly. Finally, we got up with Carolyn taking my hand. Slightly embarrassed, I tried to pull away but her grip held me. I let her have her way as she led me down the hallway with her mother right behind me. When I opened the door, I was startled by a kitten clinging to the screen door, its mouth screaming "cat food, dog biscuits, *sushi*. . . ." I opened the door and the kitten, still holding on, whined in the language of hungry animals. When I got into Carolyn's car, I looked back: the cat was still clinging. I asked Carolyn if it was possibly hungry, but she said the cat was being silly. She started the car, waved to her mother, and bounced us over the rain-poked drive, patting my thigh for being her lover baby. Carolyn waved again. I looked back, waving, then gawking at a window screen where there were now three kittens clawing and screaming to get in. Like Mexicans, I thought. I remembered the Molinas and how the cats clung to their screens—cats they shot down with squirt guns. On the highway, I felt happy, pleased by it all. I patted Carolyn's thigh. Her people were like Mexicans, only different.

---

8. *sushi* (sū′shē), a Japanese dish of bite-sized cakes consisting of cold, boiled rice wrapped in seaweed, with slices of raw fish and vegetables inside or on top.

After Reading

Making Connections

Shaping Your Response

1. What advice would you give the narrator about the kind of person he should marry?

2. Gary Soto includes many vivid details in his memoir. Jot down five favorite **images** from the selection and share your list with others.

Analyzing the Selection

3. 👣 A **stereotype** is a fixed, narrow view of what a person or a certain group of persons is like. What are some of the stereotypes held by the narrator's grandmother?

4. How do the actions of the kitten affect Soto's impressions of his fiancée's family?

5. Why is he happy at the end of the selection?

Extending the Ideas

6. 👣 At the end, Soto says about his fiancée, "Her people were like Mexicans, only different." How has his **perspective** changed?

7. In your opinion, should a person only marry someone in the same social class? Explain.

Literary Focus: Irony

Irony occurs when there is a contrast between what is expected and what really is. In "Like Mexicans," it is ironic when Gary Soto marries a Japanese American woman because for years he has imagined marrying another Mexican American like himself.

- Explain what is ironic about Gary Soto's doubts about his fiancée.

- What other ironic situations can you identify in the selection?

Expressing Your Ideas

Writing Choice

Writer's Notebook Update Look back at the situation you wrote about before reading the selection. Write a few paragraphs to point out some of the ironies in your situation. Compare your experience with one of the ironic situations in "Like Mexicans."

Another Option

I Do, I Do Although Gary Soto's relatives gave him advice about getting married, they didn't make the decision for him. In some cultures, marriages are arranged by parents or other family members. Do some research on arranged marriages and share your findings in an **oral presentation.**

Mistaken Impressions

To Err is Human

Popular Culture Connection
Truth may be stranger than fiction, but some "true" stories are pure fiction. This article may make you a bit suspicious of the next wild story you hear.

URBAN LEGENDS

by Richard Wolkomir

A woman's at the mall here last week, in that big discount store. She's looking at these rolled-up carpets from Asia. She sticks her hand into one to feel the thickness, and something pricks her finger. Then her hand swells up. Whole arm turns black. She falls on the floor dead.

So they unroll the carpet. Inside's a cobra, and about ten baby cobras.

A friend of mine told me. His cousin knows one of the salesclerks.

Hey, it's a jungle out there.

Just ask Jan Harold Brunvand—"Mr. Urban Legend." A University of Utah folklorist, Brunvand collects modern told-as-true tall tales like the cobra-in-the-carpet story. More come in every day from his informants around the world. They are weird whoppers we tell one another, believing them to be factual. Haunted airliners. A hundred-miles-per-gallon car the oil companies keep secret. How about that guy who stole a frozen chicken at the supermarket and hid it under his hat, then fainted in the checkout line because his brain froze?

The Pied Piper is still piping. But in our fiber-optic age he pipes an MTV tune. "These stories are like traditional legends—they reflect our concerns," says Brunvand, author

New York City has its own urban legends, including rumors of huge albino alligators in city sewers.

of *The Vanishing Hitchhiker* (1981) and four other collections of urban legends. "But now we live in cities and drive cars."

Urban legends are kissing cousins of myths, fairy tales, and rumors. Legends differ from rumors because the legends are stories, with a plot. And unlike myths and fairy tales, they are supposed to be current and true, events rooted in everyday reality that at least *could* happen.

Sometimes these tall tales have hints of real roots. For instance, we've all heard about the alligators in the New York City sewers. Vacationers returning from Florida supposedly flush away their unwanted reptile pets, and the alligators feed on rats in the darkness under the streets. They grow into huge, blind albinos.

Folklorists studying the alligator legend have unearthed a February 10, 1934, *New York Times* story reporting that city workers found an eight-foot alligator in a sewer. Teddy May, who was New York sewer commissioner during the 1930s, told Robert Daley, author of the 1959 book *The World Beneath the City,* that he had found alligators in the sewers but had exterminated them by 1937. However, a sewer official told Brunvand that Teddy May was "almost as much of a legend as the alligators," a spinner of colorful yarns.

Professor Bill Ellis of Pennsylvania State University at Hazleton says the stories often are true in the sense that they express real stresses in a community. Last year he turned his attention to a legend that had upset several college campuses. Supposedly, the 16th-century seer Nostradamus had prophesied that in 1991 a massacre would occur at an unspecified university on

Halloween. At each university where the legend flared up, it contained details—such as a peculiar building—that clearly identified the doomed school as the very one.

Ellis was struck that the legend sprang up only on certain campuses. He discovered that these were schools that had previously had an episode of real violence against students, such as a mugging or rape. He theorizes that such legends serve to crystallize anxieties in the air. Before Halloween, vigilance soared on some of the affected campuses. Students telephoned campus police whenever a stray cat rustled the grass or a door slammed. But after Halloween, vigilance plummeted. Ellis says it shows how an urban legend expresses a population's anxieties, and then clears the mental air like a midsummer thunderstorm.

Warning: Stealing chickens may cause brain freeze.

Clearly, urban legends run deep. And they keep coming, crying out for analysis. "I can't stop—as long as I open my mail and answer my phone, I'm going to get more stories," says Jan Brunvand. "And when a story's hot, suddenly it's all over the country, with allusions in newspapers and on talk shows." It's fascinating to watch the stories spread, he adds: "You're seeing the living tradition as it develops and changes."

Responding

Share some urban legends you've heard with classmates and discuss what might have inspired them.

Science Connection

Have you ever pursued one goal only to achieve a completely different result? Don't worry. As these pages reveal, some well-known products have been invented that way.

Lucky

So Why Aren't They Called Potato Crumbs?

As the story goes, if it weren't for a very picky dinner guest, potato chips might never have been invented.

George Crumb was annoyed. As a chef at Moon's Lake House in Saratoga Springs, New York, in 1853, he was a busy man. When a restaurant customer kept sending back his fried potatoes, complaining that they were too thick, Crumb decided to get even. He cut the potatoes into very thin strips, fried them to a crisp, and sent them back to the customer. To his surprise, the customer loved them, and so did everyone else.

Crumb's "Saratoga Chips" were soon famous. And today the chip industry is no small potatoes. In the United States alone, 3.468 billion pounds of potatoes are used each year to make potato chips.

A Military Secret You Can Cook With

Teflon is the slipperiest substance on earth. It is also absolutely stable; nothing reacts with it. Those qualities and others make Teflon an extremely valuable chemical compound. But Teflon might never have been invented if Roy J. Plunkett hadn't goofed on a recipe.

Plunkett, a chemist at DuPont, was trying to find a nontoxic gas for use as a refrigerant. On April 6, 1938, he opened the valve on a cylinder containing a special mix of Freon gas that he had concocted. But although the cylinder weighed the same amount as before, no gas came whistling out of the valve. Puzzled, Plunkett and his assistant sawed apart the cylinder. Out came a greasy white powder—the first Teflon.

The properties of the new compound soon attracted the interest of the U.S. government. Because of its stability, Teflon was an ideal material for the gaskets on the first nuclear bomb. The existence of Teflon became a military secret, hidden from the rest of the world until the end of World War II.

Today Teflon is a material used to make everything from spaceships to non-stick cooking pans, including waterproof clothing, tents, camping gear, bridges, and even artificial body parts such as arteries and ligaments.

Mistakes

How Do You Spell Relief? A-C-E-T-Y-L-S-A-L-I-C-Y-L-I-C

Have you ever worked a math problem and gotten the right answer for the wrong reasons? If you have, you have something in common with the Reverend Edward Stone, an English minister who "rediscovered" the healing properties of willow bark.

Rev. Stone was an enthusiastic fan of the dubious scientific theory known as the Doctrine of Signatures, which held that God would always put a cure for a disease close to the place where the disease occurred. In 1763, he observed that willow trees were common in swampy areas where many people suffered from rheumatism, or stiffening of the joints. Inspired by the Doctrine of Signatures, Stone developed a medicinal preparation from willow bark. It worked! (In fact, willow bark had already been used to relieve pain for thousands of years.)

Some years later, scientists discovered that the real source of relief was actually the salicylic acid in the bark. Unfortunately, salicylic acid on its own caused severe stomach and mouth irritation. It took nearly another hundred years for chemists to develop a compound—acetylsalicylic (ə sē′tl sal′ə sil′ik) acid, or "aspirin" as it came to be known—that relieved pain and caused less stomach irritation.

A Not-So-Sticky Situation

Spencer Silver had an assignment: as a researcher at 3M Company in 1970, he was supposed to develop a super-strong adhesive. He developed a new adhesive, all right, but there was one problem: it was even weaker than the adhesives the company already had. If you glued pieces of paper together with it, they easily peeled apart. Spencer had no idea what his new glue would be good for, but he didn't throw it away.

A few years later, Arthur Fry, another 3M scientist, was frustrated because his place markers always fell out of his hymn book in church. He used some of Spencer's adhesive to coat his markers. Now he could keep his place and move his markers around as he needed to.

Fry and others soon realized the potential of this weak new adhesive. Today, offices can't survive without it—because it's the glue that keeps Post-it Notes in place.

Responding

You are trying to make shatterproof glass, but your new glass breaks up into tiny beads whenever someone whistles. What can you do with it? Brainstorm the possibilities.

Writing Workshop

False Impressions

Assignment You've read about how first impressions can change. Write a memoir in which you compare and contrast your first impressions of someone from your life with the picture you got of that person later on, after getting to know him or her better.

WRITER'S BLUEPRINT

Product   A memoir
Purpose   To compare and contrast first impressions with later ones
Audience   Yourself, family, friends
Specs   As the writer of a successful paper, you should:

❑ Write a narrative about someone from your life who made a strong first impression on you. Choose a person who surprised you when you got to know him or her better later on.

❑ Begin by introducing your subject. Go on to describe (1) the circumstances under which you first encountered this person and (2) your first impressions of this person, based on physical appearance, words and actions, and your expectations.

❑ Compare and contrast these first impressions with the impressions you later formed. Use specific details about this person to illustrate these impressions. Present your impressions in a clear comparison-contrast format.

❑ Conclude by giving your general thoughts about first impressions, based on what you learned from getting to know this person better.

❑ Follow the rules of grammar, usage, spelling, and mechanics. Pay special attention to avoiding comma splices and run-ons.

---

1 PREWRITING

Revisit the literature with a partner to find examples of first impressions and how they changed. Record your findings in a chart like the one shown.

Story	Character	First Impressions	Later Impressions
"The Rule of Names"	Mr. Underhill	People thought he was a weak, mediocre wizard.	He turned out to be a powerful dragon in disguise.

LITERARY SOURCE
" 'Yes,' said a great, husky, hissing voice. 'My truename is Yevaud, and my true shape is this shape.'
" 'But the dragon was killed—they found dragon-bones on Udrath Island—'
" 'That was another dragon,' said the dragon . . ."
from "The Rule of Names" by Ursula Le Guin

Make a chart, similar to the last one, of people from your life who made a distinct first impression on you. Consider close friends, relatives, teachers, storekeepers, etc. For your memoir, choose the person who surprised you the most.

Try a quickwrite. Write for five minutes about your first meeting with your subject. Tell why you formed your first impressions.

Plan your memoir. Look back at the information you gathered in the prewriting stage and then make a writing plan similar to this one. Jot down notes for each point.

OR . . .
In addition to the quick-write, re-create your first meeting in comic strip form. Use cartoon balloons to summarize your first impressions.

Introduction
- Setting where we first met
- Vivid details to introduce the person
- A first impression
  Specific details that illustrate this impression (See the Revising Strategy in Step 3 of this lesson.)
- Another first impression
  Specific details that illustrate this impression
  and so on . . .

Body
- A later impression
  How it differs from first impression
  Specific details that illustrate this difference
- Another later impression
  How it differs from first impression
  Specific details that illustrate this difference
  and so on . . .

Conclusion
- General thoughts about first impressions

Ask a partner to review your plan.

✔ Do I compare and contrast first impressions with later impressions?

✔ Have I followed all the Specs in the Writer's Blueprint?

Use your partner's comments to help you revise your plan.

STEP 2 DRAFTING

Before you draft, review your charts, quickwrite, and writing plan. Then reread the Writer's Blueprint.

As you draft, don't concentrate on spelling and punctuation. Focus on expanding the ideas in your writing plan. Here are a few tips for getting started:

- To capture your reader's interest, begin with a few lines of dialogue from the first meeting.

- In the body, show contrast with transitional expressions such as *although, and yet, however,* and *but.*

In the model, notice how the writer began with a line of dialogue. Spelling and punctuation errors will be corrected later.

OR . . .
Begin by summarizing your later impressions of your subject in a sentence or two. Then write the rest of your memoir as a flashback.

> "This is my brother," Joe said proudly, "but he doesn't talk. He's autistic."
>
> "Really?" I replied weakly. It was all I could think to say. I didn't know much about being autistic, but his announcement surprised me just the same. I found out later that this fact explained alot about Joseph's life.
>
> I had gone to Joseph Murphy's house to tutor him. Most people didn't like Joseph because he was different. He had alot of trouble in school, and that's where he got his nickname Slow Joe from. Joe wasn't dumb, really. he was just absent a whole lot. And when he wasn't absent, he was sleeping in class. I don't think I ever saw Joe turn in a completed homework assignment, but he looked very embarrassed about not having it done.

STUDENT MODEL

Ask a partner for comments on your draft before you revise it.

✔ Have I followed the Specs in the Writer's Blueprint?

✔ Does the body of my memoir contrast my first impressions with the impressions I formed later on?

✔ Have I included specific details to illustrate my impressions?

Revising Strategy

Using Specific Details

Specific details such as personal anecdotes help your reader understand the impression you formed and bring your subject to life. Don't just say that your subject was fun or generous. Show the reader exactly what you mean.

ORIGINAL VERSION: Aunt Hester was fun to be with. She was also a generous person. She was my mother's sister, one of three, and the oldest. I got to know her well and always liked her.

IMPROVED VERSION: Aunt Hester was fun to be with. She wouldn't just take you to a carnival, she'd ride all the rides with you. "Come on," she'd say, "let's ride the roller coaster again." She was also generous. I don't mean just with money, I mean with her time. She'd read us stories and take us for long walks in the woods.

Look back at your memoir to see if you can add specific details. Notice that the student model has been revised to include specific details to show what the writer means by "withdrawn."

STUDENT MODEL

I don't think I ever saw Joe turn in a completed homework assignment,

but he looked very embarrassed about not having it done.
He was never at games or dances. He always walked home alone.
Joseph was also very withdrawn from the people around him. The

teachers ignored him, mostly because they'd given up, and the rest of

the school seemed to follow their example.

Ask a partner to review your revised draft before you edit. As you edit, look for errors in grammar, usage, spelling, and mechanics. Look closely for comma splices and run-on sentences.

Editing Strategy

Correcting Run-on Sentences and Comma Splices

Run-on sentences are made up of two or more independent clauses without the necessary punctuation. Comma splices occur when two independent clauses are joined with a comma.

Run-on I thought the roller coaster ride would never end my Aunt Hester was laughing and not even holding on.

Comma splice I thought the roller coaster ride would never end, my Aunt Hester was laughing and not even holding on.

Here are two ways you can correct these mistakes:

Turn the clauses into two separate sentences: I thought the roller coaster ride would never end. My Aunt Hester was laughing and not even holding on.

Insert a comma and coordinating conjunction: I thought the roller coaster ride would never end, **but** my Aunt Hester was laughing and not even holding on.

Notice how the writer of the student model has corrected comma splices and run-on sentences.

FOR REFERENCE
For more information on correcting comma splices and run-on sentences, see the Language and Grammar Handbook at the back of this text.

I listened to all of Joseph's stories with great interest. as soon as I was able to, I talked to Mr. Wilson about it. "A problem indeed" was all he would say to me. ~~soon enough~~ *However, I soon* noticed changes in Joseph's attendance and work patterns. the kids stopped calling him Slow Joe. He finally managed to get the help he needed.

STUDENT MODEL

STEP  PRESENTING

Consider these ideas for presenting your memoir.

- Share your memoirs in small groups. Make some generalizations about how people form first impressions and how often those impressions prove to be correct or incorrect.

- Create an illustrated book cover for your memoir featuring pictures, drawings, or photographs of your subject.

STEP **6** LOOKING BACK

Self-Evaluate. What grade would *you* give your paper? Look back at the Writer's Blueprint and give yourself a score for each point, from 6 (superior) to 1 (inadequate).

Reflect. Think about what you've learned from writing this memoir as you write answers to these questions.

✔ After writing about how first impressions can change, do you think you will have a different attitude about meeting someone for the first time? Explain.

✔ What did you learn about writing a personal memoir? Was it easier to write about someone you know since you had familiar material to work with? Why or why not?

For Your Working Portfolio Add your memoir and your reflection responses to your working portfolio.

Beyond Print

Looking at Advertising

One of the main ways that consumers learn about products is through advertising. But don't believe everything you see (or hear). Although ads seldom lie to you, they may often mislead you. The shiny hair on a shampoo commercial may get its gleam from the special lighting in the studio, and not from the product. Or the action figures that look huge on Saturday morning TV commercials may be much smaller in real life. And so the ancient lesson, *Caveat emptor*, still holds true—let the buyer beware.

Advertisers use different types of **propaganda,** or persuasive techniques, to persuade you to believe in their products. Here are some of the propaganda techniques you can watch for:

Testimonial—uses the endorsement of famous people.

- Does the ad use celebrities? If so, who and why?

- What group of consumers will these celebrities appeal to?

Bandwagon—tells you that everyone else is already using the product.

- Does the ad use good-looking people who are having a great time while using the product?

- Does the ad try to convince you that if you buy the product, you will be just like those beautiful people?

Emotional appeal—implies that you will be happier if you use the product.

- Does the ad associate the product with something you value, like good family relationships, popularity, or financial success?

- Does the ad seem to imply that if you buy this product, these good things will happen to you?

All right. You've resisted the hype, ignored the glamour, and now you're shopping for ice cream. There's lite, low fat, sugarless, lecithin free, or "all natural ingredients" to choose from, and you haven't even looked at the flavors yet. What do all these labels really mean? Fortunately, there are legal standards for many of these terms. The chart on the next page provides some examples.

What it says	What it means
low fat	The food has 3 grams of fat or less per serving.
light, lite	The food has one-third fewer calories than a comparable product.
cholesterol free	One serving has less than 2 milligrams of cholesterol and 2 grams or less of saturated fat.
low calorie	The food has fewer than 40 calories per serving and per 100 grams.
fresh	The food is raw, not processed, frozen, or otherwise preserved.

But even with legal standards, a few loopholes still exist. For example:

- "Low fat" TV dinners may have far more than 3 grams of fat. The law only applies to individual foods, not entrees.

- Milk is exempt under the labeling law. So 2% milk can be labeled low fat even though one glass actually has 5 grams of fat.

- The ice cream you're considering may be labeled "healthy" and contain less fat and calories than other brands, but it may also have lots of sugar and artificial flavors, hardly "healthy" ingredients.

So whether you are watching ads or reading labels, take a close look at the products you're buying.

Activity Options

1. Clip a sampling of ads from magazines and newspapers. Use them to make a poster with three columns. In the first column, paste the ads or summarize them. In the second column, give examples of the persuasive techniques used in the ads. In the third column, give your opinion about whether the products will really live up to the advertisers' claims. Display your poster and lead a class discussion about the ads.

2. Choose a certain food product and carry out a comparison study of different brands. Prepare a report that compares the price, the ingredients, and the nutritional value of each brand. In your report, rate each brand and explain which one you would recommend.

3. Develop a campaign for an imaginary product. Identify the market you want to reach (athletes, computer users, children under ten, etc.) and decide which propaganda techniques you will use. Then prepare some print or broadcast ads that will reach those customers.

Part Three

Dealing with Differences

It isn't always easy to understand or accept people whose lives are very different from your own. In the following selections, the characters strive, with varying degrees of success, to bridge the personal, social, and cultural differences that threaten to divide them.

 **Multicultural Connection** **Groups** may develop common beliefs or traditions based on collective experience. An individual belongs to many groups, including one's family, peers, cultural group, and nation. In what ways do characters in these selections rely on group traditions? In what ways do conflicts arise within the groups?

The Scarlet Ibis

by James Hurst

James Hurst
born 1922

James Hurst was originally educated as an engineer. His first career was as a banker in New York City. The setting of "The Scarlet Ibis" reflects Hurst's birthplace and childhood home—a farm near the ocean in North Carolina. Because of his experiences there, Hurst has firsthand knowledge of some of the events that happen in the story: a hurricane and a rare, yet beautiful, bird that flies before it.

Building Background

A Rare Bird The title of this story might confuse you if you are not familiar with a particular species of bird. A scarlet ibis (ī′bis) is a bright red tropical bird with a long neck and beak. It generally lives far inland in the swamps of northern South America. The brilliant feathers of the scarlet ibis make it a striking sight. Ancient Egyptians worshipped the ibis because they believed it could destroy crocodiles.

Literary Focus

Symbol When you see a red rose, what do you think it means? What do you think of when you see a white dove? Both the red rose and the white dove are common **symbols.** A symbol is an object, person, or action that stands for something abstract, such as an idea or a feeling. The red rose, for example, is a concrete object that stands for an abstract idea: love. The white dove often symbolizes peace. As you read "The Scarlet Ibis," consider the author's use of symbols. What symbols do you find in the story? What abstract ideas do those symbols convey?

Writer's Notebook

All in the Family Consider the following questions about family relationships, writing your ideas in your notebook: What might cause a person to be cruel to someone he or she loves? Why are people sometimes ashamed of family members or friends? What are some tips for developing good relationships with family members?

THE SCARLET IBIS

JAMES HURST

I t was in the clove of seasons,[1] summer was dead but autumn had not yet been born, that the ibis[2] lit in the bleeding tree. The flower garden was stained with rotting brown magnolia petals and ironweeds grew rank amid the purple phlox. The five o'clocks

---

1. **clove of seasons,** the interval between two seasons.
2. **ibis** (ī′bis), *n.* any of various large, long-legged birds of warm regions having long, downward-curving bills. The ancient Egyptians regarded the ibis as sacred.

◄ Eola Willis (1856–1952), *A Carolina Vista.* Willis was influenced by Impressionist painters, whose work emphasized nature and the changing effects of light. Find some Impressionistic elements in this painting.

by the chimney still marked time, but the oriole nest in the elm was untenanted and rocked back and forth like an empty cradle. The last grave-yard flowers were blooming, and their smell drifted across the cotton field and through every room of our house, speaking softly the names of our dead.

PREDICT: What kind of events are foreshadowed by this first paragraph of the story?

It's strange that all this is still so clear to me, now that that summer has long since fled and time has had its way. A grindstone stands where the bleeding tree stood, just outside the kitchen door, and now if an oriole sings in the elm, its song seems to die up in the leaves, a silvery dust. The flower garden is prim, the house a gleaming white, and the pale fence across the yard stands straight and spruce. But sometimes (like right now), as I sit in the cool, green-draped parlor, the grindstone begins to turn, and time with all its changes is ground away—and I remember Doodle.

Doodle was just about the craziest brother a boy ever had. Of course, he wasn't a crazy crazy like old Miss Leedie, who was in love with President Wilson and wrote him a letter every day, but was a nice crazy, like someone you meet in your dreams. He was born when I was six and was, from the outset, a disappointment. He seemed all head, with a tiny body which was red and shriveled like an old man's. Everybody thought he was going to die—everybody except Aunt Nicey, who had delivered him. She said he would live because he was born in a caul[3] and cauls were made from Jesus' nightgown. Daddy had Mr. Heath, the carpenter, build a little mahogany coffin for him. But he didn't die, and when he was three months old Mama and Daddy decided they might as well name him. They named him William Armstrong, which was

like tying a big tail on a small kite. Such a name sounds good only on a tombstone.

I thought myself pretty smart at many things, like holding my breath, running, jumping, or climbing the vines in Old Woman Swamp, and I wanted more than anything else someone to race to Horsehead Landing, someone to box with, and someone to perch with in the top fork of the great pine behind the barn, where across the fields and swamps you could see the sea. I wanted a brother. But Mama, crying, told me that even if William Armstrong lived, he would never do these things with me. He might not, she sobbed, even be "all there." He might, as long as he lived, lie on the rubber sheet in the center of the bed in the front bedroom where the white marquisette curtains billowed out in the afternoon sea breeze, rustling like pal-metto fronds.[4]

It was bad enough having a invalid[5] brother, but having one who possibly was not all there was unbearable, so I began to make plans to kill him by smothering him with a pillow. However, one afternoon as I watched him, my head poked between the iron posts of the foot of the bed, he looked straight at me and grinned. I skipped through the rooms, down the echoing halls, shouting, "Mama, he smiled. He's all there! He's all there!" and he was.

When he was two, if you laid him on his stomach, he began to try to move himself, straining terribly. The doctor said that with his weak heart this strain would probably kill him, but it didn't. Trembling, he'd push himself up, turning first red, then a soft purple, and finally collapse back onto the bed like an old worn-out doll. I can still see Mama watching him, her

---

3. **caul** (kôl), *n.* a portion of the membrane enclosing a child in the womb that is sometimes found clinging to the head at birth. According to some, it is sup-posed to bring good luck and to safeguard against drowning.
4. **frond** (frond), *n.* the leaf of a fern or palm.
5. **invalid** (in′və lid), *adj.* weak because of sickness or injury; infirm or sickly.

hand pressed tight across her mouth, her eyes wide and unblinking. But he learned to crawl (it was his third winter), and we brought him out of the front bedroom, putting him on the rug before the fireplace. For the first time he became one of us.

As long as he lay all the time in bed, we called him William Armstrong, even though it was formal and sounded as if we were referring to one of our ancestors, but with his creeping around on the deerskin rug and beginning to talk, something had to be done about his name. It was I who renamed him. When he crawled, he crawled backwards, as if he were in reverse and couldn't change gears. If you called him, he'd turn around as if he were going in the other direction, then he'd back right up to you to be picked up. Crawling backward made him look like a doodlebug, so I began to call him Doodle, and in time even Mama and Daddy thought it was a better name than William Armstrong. Only Aunt Nicey disagreed. She said caul babies should be treated with special respect since they might turn out to be saints. Renaming my brother was perhaps the kindest thing I ever did for him, because nobody expects much from someone called Doodle.

Although Doodle learned to crawl, he showed no signs of walking, but he wasn't idle. He talked so much that we all quit listening to what he said. It was about this time that Daddy built him a go-cart and I had to pull him around. At first I just paraded him up and down the piazza, but then he started crying to be taken out into the yard and it ended up by my having to lug him wherever I went. If I so much as picked up my cap, he'd start crying to go with me and Mama would call from wherever she was, "Take Doodle with you."

He was a burden in many ways. The doctor had said that he mustn't get too excited, too hot, too cold, or too tired and that he must always be treated gently. A long list of don'ts went with him, all of which I ignored once we got out of the house. To discourage his coming with me, I'd run with him across the ends of the cotton rows and careen him around corners on two wheels. Sometimes I accidentally turned him over, but he never told Mama. His skin was very sensitive, and he had to wear a big straw hat whenever he went out. When the going got rough and he had to cling to the sides of the go-cart, the hat slipped all the way down over his ears. He was a sight. Finally, I could see I was licked. Doodle was my brother and he was going to cling to me forever, no matter what I did, so I dragged him across the

Doodle was my brother and he was going to cling to me forever, no matter what I did. . . .

burning cotton field to share with him the only beauty I knew, Old Woman Swamp. I pulled the go-cart through the sawtooth fern, down into the green dimness where the palmetto fronds whispered by the stream. I lifted him out and set him down in the soft rubber grass beside a tall pine. His eyes were round with wonder as he gazed about him, and his little hands began to stroke the rubber grass. Then he began to cry.

"For heaven's sake, what's the matter?" I asked, annoyed.

"It's so pretty," he said. "So pretty, pretty, pretty."

After that day Doodle and I often went down into Old Woman Swamp. I would gather wild flowers, wild violets, honeysuckle, yellow jasmine, snakeflowers, and water lilies, and with wire grass we'd weave them into necklaces and crowns. We'd bedeck ourselves with our handiwork and loll about thus beautified, beyond the touch of the everyday world. Then when the slanted rays of the sun burned orange in the tops of the pines, we'd drop our jewels into the stream and watch them float away toward the sea.

There is within me (and with sadness I have watched it in others) a knot of cruelty borne by the stream of love, much as our blood sometimes bears the seed of our destruction, and at times I was mean to Doodle. One day I took him up to the barn loft and showed him his casket, telling him how we all had believed he would die. It was covered with a film of Paris green[6] sprinkled to kill the rats, and screech owls had built a nest inside it.

Doodle studied the mahogany box for a long time, then said, "It's not mine."

"It is," I said. "And before I'll help you down from the loft, you're going to have to touch it."

"I won't touch it," he said sullenly.[7]

"Then I'll leave you here by yourself," I threatened, and made as if I were going down.

Doodle was frightened of being left. "Don't go leave me, Brother," he cried, and he leaned toward the coffin. His hand, trembling, reached out, and when he touched the casket he screamed. A screech owl flapped out of the box into our faces, scaring us and covering us with Paris green. Doodle was paralyzed, so I put him on my shoulder and carried him down the ladder, and even when we were outside in the bright sunshine, he clung to me, crying, "Don't leave me. Don't leave me."

CLARIFY: Characterize the narrator. What kind of person is he? How does he feel about his brother?

When Doodle was five years old, I was embarrassed at having a brother of that age who couldn't walk, so I set out to teach him. We were down in Old Woman Swamp and it was spring and the sick-sweet smell of bay flowers hung everywhere like a mournful[8] song. "I'm going to teach you to walk, Doodle," I said.

He was sitting comfortably on the soft grass, leaning back against the pine. "Why?" he asked.

I hadn't expected such an answer. "So I won't have to haul you around all the time."

"I can't walk, Brother," he said.

"Who says so?" I demanded.

"Mama, the doctor—everybody."

"Oh, you can walk," I said, and I took him by the arms and stood him up. He collapsed onto the grass like a half-empty flour sack. It was as if he had no bones in his little legs.

"Don't hurt me, Brother," he warned.

"Shut up. I'm not going to hurt you. I'm going to teach you to walk." I heaved him up again, and again he collapsed.

This time he did not lift his face up out of the rubber grass. "I just can't do it. Let's make honeysuckle wreaths."

"Oh yes you can, Doodle," I said. "All you got to do is try. Now come on," and I hauled him up once more.

It seemed so hopeless from the beginning that it's a miracle I didn't give up. But all of us must have something or someone to be proud of, and Doodle had become mine. I did not know then that pride is a wonderful, terrible thing, a seed that bears two vines, life and death. Every day that summer we went to the pine beside the stream of Old Woman Swamp, and I put him on his feet at least a hundred times each afternoon. Occasionally I too became discouraged because it didn't seem as if he was trying, and I would say, "Doodle, don't you *want* to learn to walk?"

He'd nod his head, and I'd say, "Well, if you don't keep trying, you'll never learn." Then I'd paint for him a picture of us as old men, white-haired, him with a long white beard and me still pulling him around in the go-cart. This never failed to make him try again.

Finally one day, after many weeks of practicing, he stood alone for a few seconds. When he fell, I grabbed him in my arms and hugged him,

---

6. **Paris green,** a poisonous emerald-green powder used to kill insects and rodents.
7. sullenly (sul′ən lē), *adv.* in a way that shows bad humor or anger.
8. mournful (môrn′fəl), *adj.* full of grief; sad; sorrowful.

our laughter pealing through the swamp like a ringing bell. Now we knew it could be done. Hope no longer hid in the dark palmetto thicket but perched like a cardinal in the lacy toothbrush tree, brilliantly visible. "Yes, yes," I cried, and he cried it too, and the grass beneath us was soft and the smell of the swamp was sweet.

With success so imminent, we decided not to tell anyone until he could actually walk. Each day, barring rain, we sneaked into Old Woman Swamp, and by cotton-picking time Doodle was ready to show what he could do. He still wasn't able to walk far, but we could wait no longer. Keeping a nice secret is very hard to do, like holding your breath. We chose to reveal all on October eighth, Doodle's sixth birthday, and for weeks ahead we mooned around the house, promising everybody a most spectacular surprise. Aunt Nicey said that, after so much talk, if we produced anything less tremendous than the Resurrection, she was going to be disappointed.

At breakfast on our chosen day, when Mama, Daddy, and Aunt Nicey were in the dining room, I brought Doodle to the door in the go-cart just as usual and had them turn their backs, making them cross their hearts and hope to die if they peeked. I helped Doodle up, and when he was standing alone I let them look. There wasn't a sound as Doodle walked slowly across the room and sat down at his place at the table. Then Mama began to cry and ran over to him, hugging him and kissing him. Daddy hugged him too, so I went to Aunt Nicey, who was thanks praying in the doorway, and began to waltz her around. We danced together quite well until she came down on my big toe with her brogans,[9] hurting me so badly I thought I was crippled for life.

Doodle told them it was I who had taught him to walk, so everyone wanted to hug me, and I began to cry.

"What are you crying for?" asked Daddy, but I couldn't answer. They did not know that I did it for myself; that pride, whose slave I was, spoke to me louder than all their voices; and that Doodle walked only because I was ashamed of having a crippled brother.

Within a few months Doodle had learned to walk well and his go-cart was put up in the barn loft (it's still there) beside his little mahogany coffin. Now, when we roamed off together, resting often, we never turned back until our destination had been reached, and to help pass the time, we took up lying. From the beginning Doodle was a terrible liar and he got me in the habit. Had anyone stopped to listen to us, we would have been sent off to Dix Hill.

My lies were scary, involved, and usually pointless; but Doodle's were twice as crazy. People in his stories all had wings and flew wherever they wanted to go. His favorite lie was about a boy named Peter who had a pet peacock with a ten-foot tail. Peter wore a golden robe that glittered so brightly that when he walked through the sunflowers they turned away from the sun to face him. When Peter was ready to go to sleep, the peacock spread his magnificent tail, enfolding the boy gently like a closing go-to-sleep flower, burying him in the gloriously iridescent,[10] rustling vortex.[11] Yes, I must admit it, Doodle could beat me lying.

CONNECT: What do the "lying" episodes reveal about the brothers?

Doodle and I spent lots of time thinking about our future. We decided that when we were grown we'd live in Old Woman Swamp and pick dog-tongue for a living. Beside the stream,

---

9. **brogan** (brō′gən), *n.* a strong work shoe made of heavy leather.
10. **iridescent** (ir′ə des′nt), *adj.* displaying changing colors.
11. **vortex** (vôr′teks), *n.* a whirling mass that sucks in everything near it.

The Scarlet Ibis   **139**

he planned, we'd build us a house of whispering leaves and the swamp birds would be our chickens. All day long (when we weren't gathering dog-tongue) we'd swing through the cypresses[12] on the rope vines, and if it rained we'd huddle beneath an umbrella tree and play stickfrog. Mama and Daddy could come and live with us if they wanted to. He even came up with the idea that he could marry Mama and I could marry Daddy. Of course, I was old enough to know this wouldn't work out, but the picture he painted was so beautiful and serene that all I could do was whisper Yes, yes.

Once I had succeeded in teaching Doodle to walk, I began to believe in my own infallibility[13] and I prepared a terrific development program for him, unknown to Mama and Daddy, of course. I would teach him to run, to swim, to climb trees, and to fight. He, too, now believed in my infallibility, so we set the deadline for these accomplishments less than a year away, when, it had been decided, Doodle could start to school.

That winter we didn't make much progress, for I was in school and Doodle suffered from one bad cold after another. But when spring came, rich and warm, we raised our sights again. Success lay at the end of summer like a pot of gold, and our campaign got off to a good start. On hot days, Doodle and I went down to Horsehead Landing and I gave him swimming lessons or showed him how to row a boat. Sometimes we descended into the cool greenness of Old Woman Swamp and climbed the rope vines or boxed scientifically beneath the pine where he had learned to walk. Promise hung about us like the leaves, and wherever we looked, ferns unfurled and birds broke into song.

That summer, the summer of 1918, was blighted.[14] In May and June there was no rain and the crops withered, curled up, then died under the thirsty sun. One morning in July a hurricane came out of the east, tipping over the oaks in the yard and splitting the limbs of the elm trees. That afternoon it roared back out of the west, blew the fallen oaks around, snapping their roots and tearing them out of the earth like a hawk at the entrails[15] of a chicken. Cotton bolls were wrenched from the stalks and lay like green walnuts in the valleys between the rows, while the cornfield leaned over uniformly so that the tassels touched the ground. Doodle and I followed Daddy out into the cotton field, where he stood, shoulders sagging, surveying the ruin. When his chin sank down onto his chest, we were frightened, and Doodle slipped his hand into mine. Suddenly Daddy straightened his shoulders, raised a giant knuckly fist, and with a voice that seemed to rumble out of the earth itself began cursing heaven, hell, the weather, and the Republican Party. Doodle and I, prodding each other and giggling, went back to the house, knowing that everything would be all right.

And during that summer, strange names were heard through the house: Château-Thierry, Amiens, Soissons, and in her blessing at the supper table, Mama once said, "And bless the Pearsons, whose boy Joe was lost at Belleau Wood."[16]

So we came to that clove of seasons. School was only a few weeks away, and Doodle was far behind schedule. He could barely clear the ground when climbing up the rope vines and his swimming was certainly not passable. We decided to double our efforts, to make that last drive and reach our pot of gold. I made him

---

12. **cypress** (sī′prəs), *n.* a kind of evergreen tree with hard wood and small, dark, scalelike leaves.
13. **infallibility** (in fal′ə bil′ə tē) *n.* freedom from error; inability to be mistaken.
14. **blighted** (blīt′əd), *adj.* suffering from decay, deterioration, destruction, or ruin.
15. **entrails** (en′trālz), *n.* the inner parts of the body of a human being or animal.
16. **Chateau-Thierry** (shä tō′ tyä rē′), **Amiens** (ä myaɴ′), **Soissons** (swä sôɴ′), **Belleau** (bel ō′) **Wood,** locations in France where certain World War I battles were fought.

Herbjörn Gausta, *Setting the Trap* (c. 1908). Gausta emigrated from Norway at the age of thirteen and lived on a farm in Minnesota. What message do you think this painting conveys about boyhood on a farm?

swim until he turned blue and row until he couldn't lift an oar. Wherever we went, I purposely walked fast, and although he kept up, his face turned red and his eyes became glazed. Once, he could go no further, so he collapsed on the ground and began to cry.

"Aw, come on, Doodle," I urged. "You can do it. Do you want to be different from everybody else when you start school?"

"Does it make any difference?"

"It certainly does," I said "Now, come on," and I helped him up.

As we slipped through dog days,[17] Doodle began to look feverish, and Mama felt his forehead, asking him if he felt ill. At night he didn't sleep well, and sometimes he had nightmares,

_____

17. **dog days,** period of very hot and uncomfortable weather during July and August, referring to the rising of Sirius, the Dog Star.

crying out until I touched him and said, "Wake up, Doodle. Wake up."

It was Saturday noon, just a few days before school was to start. I should have already admitted defeat, but my pride wouldn't let me. The excitement of our program had now been gone for weeks, but still we kept on with a tired doggedness.[18] It was too late to turn back, for we had both wandered too far into a net of expectations and had left no crumbs behind.

Daddy, Mama, Doodle, and I were seated at the dining-room table having lunch. It was a hot day, with all the windows and doors open in case a breeze should come. In the kitchen Aunt Nicey was humming softly. After a long silence, Daddy spoke. "It's so calm, I wouldn't be surprised if we had a storm this afternoon."

"I haven't heard a rain frog," said Mama, who believed in signs, as she served the bread around the table.

"I did," declared Doodle. "Down in the swamp."

"He didn't," I said contrarily.

"You did, eh?" said Daddy, ignoring my denial.

"I certainly did," Doodle reiterated,[19] scowling at me over the top of his iced-tea glass, and we were quiet again.

Suddenly, from out in the yard, came a strange croaking noise. Doodle stopped eating, with a piece of bread poised ready for his mouth, his eyes popped round like two blue buttons. "What's that?" he whispered.

I jumped up, knocking over my chair, and had reached the door when Mama called, "Pick up the chair, sit down again, and say excuse me."

By the time I had done this, Doodle had excused himself and had slipped out into the yard. He was looking up into the bleeding tree. "It's a great big red bird!" he called.

The bird croaked loudly again, and Mama and Daddy came out into the yard. We shaded our eyes with our hands against the hazy glare of the sun and peered up through the still leaves. On the topmost branch a bird the size of a chicken, with scarlet feathers and long legs, was perched precariously. Its wings hung down loosely, and as we watched, a feather dropped away and floated slowly down through the green leaves.

"It's not even frightened of us," Mama said.

"It looks tired," Daddy added. "Or maybe sick."

Doodle's hands were clasped at his throat, and I had never seen him stand still so long. "What is it?" he asked.

Daddy shook his head. "I don't know, maybe it's—"

At that moment the bird began to flutter, but the wings were uncoordinated, and amid much flapping and a spray of flying feathers, it tumbled down, bumping through the limbs of the bleeding tree and landing at our feet with a thud. Its long, graceful neck jerked twice into an S, then straightened out, and the bird was still. A white veil came over the eyes and the long white beak unhinged. Its legs were crossed and its clawlike feet were delicately curved at rest. Even death did not mar its grace, for it lay on the earth like a broken vase of red flowers, and we stood around it, awed by its exotic beauty.

"It's dead," Mama said.

"What is it?" Doodle repeated.

"Go bring me the bird book," said Daddy.

I ran into the house and brought back the bird book. As we watched, Daddy thumbed through its pages. "It's a scarlet ibis," he said, pointing to a picture. "It lives in the tropics—South America to Florida. A storm must have brought it here."

Sadly, we all looked back at the bird. A scarlet ibis! How many miles it had traveled to die like this, in *our* yard, beneath the bleeding tree.

---

18. doggedness (dô′gid nes), *n.* stubbornness.
19. reiterate (rē it′ə rāt′), *v.* say or do several times; repeat again and again.

"Let's finish lunch," Mama said, nudging us back toward the dining room.

"I'm not hungry," said Doodle, and he knelt down beside the ibis.

"We've got peach cobbler for dessert," Mama tempted from the doorway.

Doodle remained kneeling. "I'm going to bury him."

"Don't you dare touch him," Mama warned. "There's no telling what disease he might have had."

"All right," said Doodle. "I won't."

Daddy, Mama, and I went back to the dining room table, but we watched Doodle through the open door. He took out a piece of string from his pocket and, without touching the ibis, looped one end around its neck. Slowly, while singing softly "Shall We Gather at the River," he carried the bird around to the front yard and dug a hole in the flower garden, next to the petunia bed. Now we were watching him through the front window, but he didn't know it. His awkwardness at digging a hole with a shovel whose handle was twice as long as he was made us laugh, and we covered our mouths with our hands so he wouldn't hear.

When Doodle came into the dining room, he found us seriously eating our cobbler. He was pale and lingered just inside the screen door. "Did you get the scarlet ibis buried?" asked Daddy.

Doodle didn't speak but nodded his head.

"Go wash your hands, and then you can have some peach cobbler," said Mama.

"I'm not hungry," he said.

"Dead birds is bad luck," said Aunt Nicey, poking her head from the kitchen door. "Specially *red* dead birds!"

As soon as I had finished eating, Doodle and I hurried off to Horsehead Landing. Time was short, and Doodle still had a long way to go if he was going to keep up with the other boys when he started school. The sun, gilded with the yellow cast of autumn, still burned fiercely, but the dark green woods through which we passed were shady and cool. When we reached the landing, Doodle said he was too tired to swim, so we got into a skiff and floated down the creek with the tide. Far off in the marsh a rail was scolding, and over on the beach locusts were singing in the myrtle trees. Doodle did not speak and kept his head turned away, letting one hand trail limply in the water.

After we had drifted a long way, I put the oars in place and made Doodle row back against the tide. Black clouds began to gather in the southwest, and he kept watching them, trying to pull the oars a little faster. When we reached Horsehead Landing, lightning was playing across half the sky and thunder roared out, hiding even the sound of the sea. The sun disappeared and darkness descended, almost like night. Flocks of marsh crows flew by, heading inland to their roosting

Black clouds began to gather in the southwest, and he kept watching them, trying to pull the oars a little faster.

trees, and two egrets, squawking, arose from the oyster-rock shallows and careened away.

Doodle was both tired and frightened, and when he stepped from the skiff he collapsed onto the mud, sending an armada of fiddler crabs rustling off into the marsh grass. I helped him up, and as he wiped the mud off his trousers, he smiled at me ashamedly. He had failed and we both knew it, so we started back home, racing the storm. We never spoke (What are words that can solder[20] cracked pride?), but I knew he was watching me, watching for a sign of mercy. The lightning was near now, and from fear he walked so close behind me he kept

---

20. **solder** (sod′ər), *v.* unite firmly; join closely.

stepping on my heels. The faster I walked, the faster he walked, so I began to run. The rain was coming, roaring through the pines, and then like a bursting Roman candle,[21] a gum tree ahead of us was shattered by a bolt of lightning. When the deafening peal of thunder had died, and in the moment before the rain arrived, I heard Doodle, who had fallen behind, cry out, "Brother, Brother, don't leave me! Don't leave me!"

The knowledge that Doodle's and my plans had come to naught[22] was bitter, and that streak of cruelty within me awakened. I ran as fast as I could, leaving him far behind with a wall of rain dividing us. The drops stung my face like nettles, and the wind flared the wet glistening leaves of the bordering trees. Soon I could hear his voice no more.

CONNECT: If you were the narrator, what would you have done in this situation?

I hadn't run too far before I became tired, and the flood of childish spite evanesced[23] as well. I stopped and waited for Doodle. The sound of rain was everywhere, but the wind had died and it fell straight down in parallel paths like ropes hanging from the sky. As I waited, I peered through the downpour, but no one came. Finally I went back and found him hud-

dled beneath a red nightshade bush beside the road. He was sitting on the ground, his face buried in his arms, which were resting on his drawn-up knees. "Let's go, Doodle," I said.

He didn't answer, so I placed my hand on his forehead and lifted his head. Limply, he fell backwards onto the earth. He had been bleeding from the mouth, and his neck and the front of his shirt were stained a brilliant red.

"Doodle! Doodle!" I cried, shaking him; but there was no answer but the ropy rain. He lay very awkwardly, with his head thrown far back, making his vermilion[24] neck appear unusually long and slim. His little legs, bent sharply at the knees, had never before seemed so fragile, so thin.

I began to weep, and the tear-blurred vision in red before me looked very familiar. "Doodle!" I screamed above the pounding storm and threw my body to the earth above his. For a long, long time, it seemed forever, I lay there crying, sheltering my fallen scarlet ibis from the heresy of rain.

---

21. **Roman candle,** kind of firework consisting of a tube that shoots out balls of fire and sparks.
22. naught (nôt), *n.* nothing; zero (also spelled *nought*).
23. **evanesce** (ev/ə nes/), *v.* disappear gradually; fade away; vanish.
24. vermilion (vər mil/yən), *n.* a bright red.

After Reading

Making Connections

1. Do you think that the narrator should be blamed for Doodle's death? Why or why not?

2. Discuss the relationship between the brothers, focusing on what each seems to need from the other.

3. What do we learn about the **character** of Doodle from the incidents listed on the chart? Copy the chart and jot down your ideas.

What Happens	What We Learn About Doodle
Doodle visits Old Woman Swamp for the first time.	
Doodle lies about the boy and his pet peacock.	
Doodle buries the scarlet ibis.	

4. What does the narrator mean when he says that Doodle's lifeless body "looked very familiar"?

5. Explain the role that pride plays in "The Scarlet Ibis." What happens as a result of the narrator's pride—are the effects positive, negative, or both?

6. 🐾 The narrator and his brother belong to the same **group,** their family. Could other members of their family have done anything to prevent the tragedy? Explain your answer.

7. Have you ever known someone like Doodle? Describe how you think people should treat children with special needs like Doodle.

Literary Focus: Symbol

Symbols, objects that represent abstract ideas, appear regularly in literature. Writers might use symbols to make a point or create a mood, as James Hurst does in the "Scarlet Ibis."

- What qualities are represented by the scarlet ibis?
- How does the ibis represent Doodle?
- How do the events of the time—World War I, the drought, and the storm—symbolize what happens between the brothers?

Vocabulary Study

blighted
doggedness
frond
infallibility
invalid
mournful
naught
reiterate
sullenly
vermilion

Complete the following writing assignments using the vocabulary words. Use the Glossary, if necessary. If you can not use all the words suggested, use the leftover words in a note to a friend.

1. Use the words *invalid, frond, mournful,* and *vermilion* in an advertisement describing the services of a new florist shop.

2. Use the words *infallibility, doggedness,* and *naught* in a note describing your team's loss in the league championships.

3. Use the words *blighted, sullenly,* and *reiterate* in a review of a movie you don't like.

Expressing Your Ideas

Writing Choices

Writer's Notebook Update Think about why the narrator treats Doodle as he does. What are the motivations behind his actions? Now imagine that you are Doodle. Write a paragraph in which you describe your feelings toward your brother and how you feel about his rigorous "program." What do you think is motivating your brother?

What a Character! An author uses characterization to develop the qualities and personalities of people in a story. What do you learn about the characters in "The Scarlet Ibis" through their words, actions, and the reactions of other characters? Write a **character sketch**—a paragraph or two in which you tell what one of the characters in the story is like and provide some evidence to back up your opinions.

Other Options

This Is Your Life The final events in the story happen during the summer of 1918—a summer that, for the narrator's family, was marred by the fighting in Europe, a drought, and a major storm. Think of the major historical events that have happened during your lifetime. On an illustrated **time line,** show both important events in your life and significant historical events. Note whether or not there is any connection between the historical events and your personal history.

Q and A "The Scarlet Ibis" describes a close sibling relationship. In a small group, do research to learn strategies for getting along with siblings. Then, as a panel of experts, hold a **press conference** for your classmates and answer their questions about sibling relationships.

Waiting

by Budge Wilson

Budge Wilson
born 1927

Budge (Marjorie) Wilson began to write books for teenagers when she was fifty, and worked as a teacher before launching her writing career. "Waiting" is taken from *The Leaving,* a short story collection that won the Canadian Library Association's prestigious Young Adult Book Award for 1991. Another collection, *The Dandelion Garden and Other Stories,* was published in 1995. Wilson sets many of her stories in Nova Scotia, the Canadian province where she was born and where she lives and writes today. As one critic notes, "A flavor of Nova Scotia permeates the stories, although they are universal in theme."

Building Background

Sisterly Love The story you are about to read, set in Canada during World War II, concerns the relationship between twin sisters. Sibling relationships are often intense, with brothers and sisters alternately loving and hating one another, playing and fighting, or teasing and defending each other. Why do you think some siblings get along and are good friends, while other siblings fight constantly with each other? Do you think it's because of gender? age difference? birth order? other factors? In small groups, discuss the question of why siblings do and do not get along.

Literary Focus

Idioms "He was so angry, he lost his head!" Does this sentence suggest that someone's head became detached from his body? Probably not. "He lost his head" is an example of an **idiom,** an expression that does not follow normal language patterns or that has a meaning that differs from the literal meanings of the separate words. Writers may use idioms to create a certain tone in a piece of writing. The narrator in "Waiting" often uses idioms to express her thoughts. As you read the story, decide how the use of idioms affects your impressions of the narrator.

Writer's Notebook

Mom Likes You Best Do you agree or disagree with the following statement? "Favoritism always exists in families—one child is favored over the other (or others)." In your notebook, state your position on the topic. Then back up your position with some specific examples or evidence.

WAITING

BUDGE WILSON

"You must realize, of course, that Juliette is a very complex child." My mother was talking on the telephone. Shouting, to be more exact. She always spoke on the phone as though the wires had been disconnected, as though she were trying to be heard across the street through an open window. "She's so many-*sided*," she continued. "Being cute, of course, is not enough, although heaven knows she could charm the legs off a table. But you have to have something more than personality."

I was not embarrassed by any of this. Lying on the living room floor on my stomach, I was pretending to read *The Bobbsey Twins at the Seashore*. But after a while I closed the book. Letting her words drop around me, I lay there like a plant enjoying the benefit of a drenching and beneficial rain. My sister sat nearby in the huge wingback chair, legs tucked up under her, reading the funnies.

"I hope you don't regard this as *boasting*, but she really is so very, *very* talented. Bright as a button in school—three prizes, can you believe it, at the last school closing—and an outstanding athlete, even at eight years old."

Resting my head on my folded arms, I smiled quietly. I could see myself eight years from now, receiving my gold medal, while our country's flag rose in front of the Olympic flame. The applause thundered as the flag reached its peak, standing straight out from the pole, firm and strong. As the band broke into a moving rendition of "O Canada,"[1] I wept softly. I stood wet and waterlogged from my last race, my tears melding[2] with the chlorine and coursing slowly down my face. People were murmuring, "So young, so small, and so attractive."

"And such a leader!" My mother's voice hammered on. "Even at her age, she seems forever to be president of this and director of that.

I feel very blessed indeed to be the mother of such a child." My sister stirred in her chair and coughed slightly, carefully turning a page.

It was true. I was president of grade 4, and manager of the Lower Slocum Elementary School Drama Club. I had already starred in two productions, one of them a musical. In an ornate[3] crêpe paper costume composed of giant overlapping yellow petals, I had played Lead Buttercup to a full house. Even Miss Prescott's aggressive piano playing had failed to drown me out, had not prevented me from stealing the show from the Flower Queen. My mother kept the clipping from *The Shelburne Coast Guard* up on the kitchen notice board. It included a blurred newspaper picture of me with extended arms and open mouth. Below it, the caption read, "Juliette Westhaver was the surprise star of the production, with three solos and a most sprightly little dance, performed skillfully and with gusto. Broadway, look out!"

Mama was still talking. "Mm? Oh. Henrietta. Yes, well, she's fine, I guess, just fine. Such a serious, responsible little girl, and so fond of her sister." I looked up at Henrietta, who was surveying me over the top of her comics. There was no expression on her face at all.

But then Henrietta was not often given to expression of any kind. She was my twin, but apart from the accident of our birth, or the coincidence, we had almost nothing in common. It was incredible to me that we had been born to the same parents at almost the same moment, and that we had been reared in the same house.

But Henrietta was my friend and I hers. We were, in fact, best friends, as is so often the case with twins. And as with most close childhood friendships, there was one dominant member,

---

◀ Yuri Podlyaski, *Marusia* (1955). Notice the steady gaze of the young woman in this Russian Realist painting. Name some personal qualities you think she would have.

1. **"O Canada,"** the Canadian national anthem.
2. meld (meld), *v.* merge; blend.
3. ornate (ôr nāt′), *adj.* much adorned; much ornamented.

one submissive.[4] There was no doubt in this case as to who played the leading role.

Henrietta even looked submissive. She was thin and pale. She had enormous sky-blue eyes surrounded by a long fringe of totally colorless eyelashes. Her hair was a dim beige color without gradations of light or dark, and it hung straight and lifeless from two barrettes. Her fingers were long and bony, and she kept them folded in her lap, motionless, like a tired old lady. She had a straight little nose, and a mouth that seldom smiled—it was serious and still and oddly serene. She often looked as though she were waiting for something.

Untidy and flamboyant,[5] my personality and my person flamed hotly beside her cool apathy.[6] My temper flared, my joys exploded. With fiery red cheeks and a broad snub nose, I grinned and hooted my way through childhood, dragging and pushing Henrietta along as I raced from one adventure to the next. I had a mop

In the fog, it wasn't hard to believe that the Nazis were coming....

of wild black curls that no comb could tame. I was small, compact, sturdy, well-coordinated and extremely healthy. Henrietta had a lot of colds.

When I start talking about Henrietta and me, I always feel like I'm right back there, a kid again. Sometimes, you know, I got fed up with her. If you have a lot of energy, for instance, it's no fun to go skiing with someone who's got lead in her boots. And for heaven's sake, she kept falling all the time. Scared to death to try the hills, and likely as not going down them on the seat of her pants. "Fraidy-cat! Fraidy-cat!" I'd yell at her from the bottom of the hill where I had landed right side up, and she would start down the first part of the slope with straight and trembling knees, landing in a snowbank before the hill even got started. There were lots of fields

and woods around our town, and good high hills if you were looking for thrills. You could see the sea from the top of some of them, and the wild wind up there made me feel like an explorer, a brave Micmac[7] hunter, the queen of the Maritime Provinces.[8] Sometimes I would let out a yell just for the joy of it all—and there, panting and gasping and falling up the hill would be old Henrietta, complaining, forever complaining, about how tired she was, how cold.

But I guess I really loved Henrietta anyway, slowpoke though she was. I had lots and lots of other friends who were more interesting than she was. But it's a funny thing—she was nearly always my first choice for someone to play with.

There was a small woodlot to the east of the village, on land owned by my father. We called it The Grove. It had little natural paths in it, and there were open spaces under the trees like rooms or houses or castles, or whatever you wanted them to be that day. The grove of trees was on the edge of a cliff overhanging some big rocks, and at high tide the sea down there was never still, even when it was flat oil calm. So it could be a spooky kind of place to play in, too. I loved to go there when it was foggy, and play spy. It was 1940 and wartime, and by then we were ten, going on eleven. From The Grove we could sometimes see destroyers, and once even a big aircraft carrier. In the fog, it wasn't hard to believe that the Nazis were coming, and that we were going to be blown to bits any minute.

We never told Mama or Papa about going to

---

4. **submissive** (səb mis′iv), *adj.* yielding to the power, control, or authority of another; obedient; humble.
5. **flamboyant** (flam boi′ənt), *adj.* given to display; ostentatious; showy.
6. **apathy** (ap′ə thē), *n.* lack of interest in or desire for action; indifferent.
7. **Micmac,** an Algonquian Indian tribe in eastern Canada.
8. **Maritime** (mar′ə tīm) **Provinces,** provinces of Canada along the Atlantic Coast.

the cliff when the mist was thick. Henrietta hardly ever wanted to go on those foggy days. She was afraid of falling off the cliff onto the rocks, sure she would drown in the churned-up water, nervous about the ghostly shapes in the thick gray-white air. But she always went. I used to blackmail her. "If you don't go, I'll tell Mama about the time you pretended to be sick and stayed home from school because you didn't have your homework done and were scared of Miss Garrison." Or I would just plain order her around. "I'm *going*, Henrietta, so get a move on and *hurry!*" She'd come padding out of the house in her stupid yellow raincoat, so that she wouldn't get a cold in the wet wind, and off we'd go—me fast and complaining about her slowness, and her slow and complaining about my speed. But she'd be there and we'd be together and we'd have fun. I'd be the spy, and she'd be the poor agonized prisoner of war, tied up to a tree by a bunch of Nazis. Sometimes I'd leave her tethered good and long, so she'd look *really* scared instead of pretend scared, while I prowled around and killed Nazis and searched for hidden weapons. Or we'd play Ghost, and I'd be the ghost—floating along on the edge of the cliff, and shrieking in my special death shriek that I saved for ghost games. It started out low like a groan, and then rose to a wail, ending in a scream so thin and high that it almost scared *me*. Sometimes, if she was especially wet and tired, Henrietta would start to cry, and that *really* made me mad. Even now, I can't stand cry babies. But you had to have a victim, and this was something she was extra good at. No point in wasting my death shriek on a person who wasn't afraid of ghosts. No fun to have the Nazis tying up someone who was big and strong and brave, particularly when the Nazis weren't actually there and you had to think them up and pretend the whole thing.

One time when we went there with a bunch of kids instead of just us two, I forgot all about her being tied up to the tree, and got nearly home before I raced back the whole half mile to untie her. She never said a word. It was snowing, and there were big fat snowflakes on those long white lashes of hers, and her eyes looked like they were going to pop right out of her head. I said I was real sorry, and next week I even bought her a couple of comic books out of my own allowance money, when she was home sick with bronchitis.[9] Mama said she should have had the sense to wear a scarf and a warm hat, being as she was so prone to colds, and that's certainly true. She never told on me, and I don't know why. She sat up against the pillows and colored in her coloring book or read her funnies, or more often she just lay there on the bed, her hands lying limp on the quilt, with that patient, quiet, waiting look of hers.

When the spring came, a gang of us would always start going out to The Grove on weekends to start practicing for our summer play. Year after year we did this, and it had nothing to do with those school plays in which I made such a hit. We'd all talk about what stories we liked, and then we'd pick one of them and make a play out of it. I would usually select the play because I was always the one who directed it, so it was only fair that I'd get to do the choosing. If there was a king or a queen, I'd usually be the queen. If you're the director, you can't be something like a page or a minor fairy, because then you don't seem important enough to be giving out instructions and bossing people around, and the kids maybe won't pay attention to all the orders. Besides, as my mother pointed out, I was smart and could learn my lines fast, and you couldn't expect some slow dummy to memorize all that stuff.

Henrietta's voice was so soft and quiet that no one could ever hear her unless they were almost sitting on her lap; so of course it would have been stupid to give her a part. She couldn't

---

9. **bronchitis** (brong kīʹtis), *n*. inflammation of the bronchial tubes, usually accompanied by a deep cough.

even be the king's horse or the queen's milk-white mule because she was so darn scrawny. You can't have the lead animal looking as though it should be picked up by the Humane Society and put in quarantine.[10] But she was really useful to the production, and it must have been very satisfying for her. She got to find all the costume parts, and rigged up the stage in the biggest cleared space among the trees, making it look like a ballroom or a throne room or whatever else we needed. She did a truly good job, and if it weren't for the fact that I can't stand conceited people, I probably would even have told her so. I liked Henrietta the way she was. I didn't want her strutting around looking proud of herself and putting on airs. One time one of the kids said, "Hey, Henrietta, that's a really great royal bedroom you made," and right away she started standing and moving around in a way that showed she thought she was a pretty smart stage manager.

I hate that kind of thing, and I knew the others wouldn't like it either. So I said, "Oh, sure! And the king must have just lost his kingdom in

I always think that laughter is very important.

the wars. Who ever heard of a king sleeping on a pile of branches or having an old torn dishtowel at the window? Some king!" And everyone laughed. I always think that laughter is very important. It makes everyone happy right away, and is a good way to ease tensions.

We had a lot of fun practicing for those plays. No one went away for the summer. No one needed to. The sea was right there alongside the village, with a big sandy beach only a quarter mile away. Some of the fishermen let us use their smaller flats for jigging,[11] and we could always swim or dig for clams or collect mussels. Besides, the war was on; people weren't spending money on cottages or trips. Seems to me

that everyone just stuck around home and saved paper and counted their ration stamps[12] and listened to the news on the radio. There was a navy base nearby, and sometimes sailors came to dinner. They'd tell us about life on the base, and all the dangers they were expecting and hoping to experience when they started sailing to Europe. I envied them like anything, and couldn't for the life of me see why you had to be eighteen before you joined the navy, or why they wouldn't let girls run the ships or use the guns. Henrietta said she didn't want to be a sailor anyway, because she'd be too scared, which of course is only what you'd expect. Apart from that, there wasn't much excitement. So the play practices were our main entertainment during those years. In the summer, we practiced on most fine days, and in August we put on the play in front of all our mothers and fathers and uncles and aunts, and for the sisters and brothers too young to take part.

The play we put on in 1942 was about a rich nobleman called Alphonse who falls in love with an exquisitely beautiful but humble country girl called Genevieve. I played the part of Genevieve, and it was the nicest part I had ever played. In the last scene, Genevieve and the nobleman become engaged, and she gets to dress up in a very gorgeous gown for a big court ball. I had a real dress for this scene, instead of the usual pieced-together scraps of material dug out of old trunks from our attics. My mother let me use one of her long dance dresses from when she was young. It was covered with sequins

10. **quarantine** (kwôr′ən tēn′), *n.* the isolation of a person, animal, plant, ship, etc., for a time to prevent the spread of an infectious disease.
11. **jigging** (jig′ing). *n.* A jig is a fishing lure consisting of a fishhook or a set of fishhooks weighted with a spoon-shaped piece of bright metal. When you are jigging, you bob the lure up and down or pull it through the water to catch fish.
12. **ration** (rash′ən) **stamps.** During the Second World War, households were allowed a certain allotment of food, fuel, and other items that were in short supply.

and even had some sort of fluffy feather stuff around the hem; and it was pale sapphire blue and very romantic looking. I had trouble getting into it because I was almost thirteen now and sort of big through the middle. But my mother put in a new zipper instead of the buttons, and I was able to wear it after all. I had to move a little carefully and not take very deep breaths, but I was as tall as Mama now, and I felt like a real woman, a true beauty. The neck was kind of low, but I was pretty flat, so I didn't need to worry about being indecent in front of Harold Boutilier, who played the part of Alphonse. Mama put a whole lot of makeup on me, covering up the pimples I was starting to get, and I thought I looked like a movie star, a genuine leading lady. The zipper wasn't put into the dress in time for the dress rehearsal, but Harold wore a big bow at his neck and his mother's velvet shorty coat, with a galvanized chain around his waist that shone like real sil-

ver. He had on his sister's black stockings and a pair of high rubber boots, and he looked very handsome. Up until this year he had just seemed like an okay boy to me, as boys go, but this summer I'd spent a lot of time watching him and thinking about him when I went to bed at night. I guess I had a big crush on him. And I was pretty sure that when he saw me in that blue dress, he'd have a crush on me right away, too.

On the day of the play, all our families started arriving at The Grove theater a full hour before we got started. It didn't rain, and there wasn't even one of those noisy Nova Scotian winds that shake the trees and keep you from hearing the lines. My mother was hustling around backstage helping with clothes and makeup. Mostly she was fussing with my face and my first costume and telling me how pretty I looked. We had rigged up eight bedspreads, some torn and holey, some beautiful, depending on the fear or the pride of the mothers who lent them, and behind this strung-out curtain, we prepared ourselves for the two o'clock production. Henrietta was moving quietly about on the stage, straightening furniture, moving props, standing back to look at the effect. Later on, just before the curtain went up, or rather was drawn aside, she went off and sat down against a tree, where she'd have a good view of the performance, but where she'd be out of sight. If any of us needed anything, she could get it for us without the audience seeing what she was doing.

In the first part of the play, the nobleman ignores the beautiful peasant girl, who comes on dressed in rags but heavily made up and therefore beautiful. He is of course looking for a wife, but no one even thinks of her as a possible candidate. She does a lot of sighing and weeping, and Alphonse rides around on his horse (George Cruikshank) looking handsome and tragic. Harold did this very well. Still, I could hardly wait for the last scene in which I could get out of those rags and emerge as the radiant court butterfly. But I put all I had into this first scene, because when Alphonse turns down all the eligible and less beautiful women of the land and retires to a corner of the stage to brood (with George Cruikshank standing nearby, munching grass), Genevieve arrives on the scene to a roll of drums (our wooden spoon on Mrs. Eisner's pickling kettle). As Alphonse turns to look at her dazzling beauty, he recognizes her for what she is—not just a poor commoner, but a young woman of great charm and loveliness, worthy of his hand. At this point, she places her hand on her breast and does a deep and graceful curtsy. He stands up, bends to help her rise, and in a tender and significant gesture kisses her outstretched hand.

And that's exactly how we did it, right there on the foxberry patch, which looked like a rich green carpet with a red pattern, if you happened to have the kind of imagination to see it that way. I thought I would faint with the beauty of it all. Then the string of bedspreads was drawn across the scene, curtain hoops squeaking, and the applauding audience awaited the final scene.

I didn't waste any time getting into my other costume. Dressed in my blue gown, I peeked through the hole in Mrs. Powell's bedspread to assess the audience. I had not had time to look until now, but Mama had dressed me first, and she had six other girls to get ready for the ball scene. The crowd outside was large. There must have been forty-five or fifty people of various sizes and ages, sitting on the cushions placed on top of the pine needles. The little kids were crawling and squirming around like they always do, and mothers were passing out pacifiers and bags of chips and jelly beans and suckers to keep them quiet during intermission. One little boy—Janet Morash's brother—was crying his head off, and I sure as fire hoped he'd stop all that racket before the curtain went up. While I watched all this, I looked over to the left, and saw three sailors coming through the woods. I knew them. They'd been to our house for supper a couple of times, but I never dreamt we'd be lucky enough to have the navy at our play. My big scene was going to be witnessed by more than just a bunch of parents and kids. There was even a little group of grade 12 boys in the back row.

We were almost ready to begin. Backstage, most of the makeup was done, and Mrs. Elliot was standing by the tree, making up Henrietta just for the heck of it. Henrietta had set up the stage and handed out the costumes, and she was putting in time like some of the rest of us. She just had on that old blue sweatshirt of hers and her dungarees,[13] and it seemed to me that all that makeup was going to look pretty silly on

---

13. **dungarees** (dung/gə rēs/), *n.* work pants made from coarse cotton cloth.

someone who didn't have a costume on; but I didn't really care. If Henrietta wanted to make a fool of herself, it wasn't going to bother *me*.

In the last scene, all the courtiers[14] and aristocrats are milling around in the ballroom, waiting for the nobleman to arrive with his betrothed.[15] The orchestra is playing Strauss waltzes (on Mrs. Corkum's portable wind-up gramophone)[16] and you can see that everyone is itchy footed and dying to dance, but they have to wait around until Alphonse arrives with Genevieve. It is a moment full of suspense, and I had to do a lot of smart and fierce directing to get that bunch of kids to look happy and excited and impatient all at the same time. But they did a really good job that afternoon. You could see that they thought they actually *were* lords and ladies and that it was a real live ball they had come to.

Suddenly there is a sound of trumpets (little Horace Miller's Halloween horn) and Alphonse comes in, very slow and stately, with Genevieve on his arm. She is shy, and enters with downcast eyes; but he turns around, bows to her, and she raises her head with new pride and confidence, lifting her arms to join him in the dance. We did all this beautifully, if I do say so myself, and as I started to raise my arms, I though I would burst with the joy and splendor of that moment.

As it turned out, burst is just about exactly what I did. The waltz record was turned off during this intense scene, and there was total silence on the stage and in the audience. As my arms reached shoulder level, a sudden sound of ripping taffeta reached clear to the back of the audience. (Joannie Sherman was sitting in the last row, and she told me about it later.) I knew in one awful stupefying moment that my dress had ripped up the back, the full length of that long zipper. I can remember standing there on the stage with my arms half raised, unable to think or feel anything beyond a paralyzed horror. After that day, whenever I heard that someone was in a state of shock, I never had to ask the meaning of that term. I knew. Joannie told

me later that the whole stageful of people looked like they had been turned to stone, and that it really had been a scream to see.

Suddenly, as quiet and as quick as a cat, Henrietta glided onstage. She was draped in one of the classier bedspreads from the curtain, and no one would have known that she wasn't supposed to be there. I don't know how anyone as slow-moving as Henrietta could have done so much fast thinking. But she did. She was carrying the very best bedspread—a lovely blue woven one that exactly matched my dress. She stopped in front of me, and lifting the spread with what I have to admit was a lot of ceremony and grace, she placed it gravely over my shoulders. Fastening it carefully with one of the large safety pins that she always kept attached to her sweatshirt during performances, she then moved backward two paces, and bowed first to me and then to Harold, before moving slowly and with great dignity toward the exit.

Emerging from my shock with the kind of presence of mind for which I was noted, I raised my arms and prepared to start the dance with Alphonse. But Harold, eyes full of amazement, was staring at Henrietta as she floated off the stage. From the back of the audience, I could hear two long low whistles, followed by a deep male voice exclaiming, "Hubba, *hubba!*" to which I turned and bowed in graceful acknowledgement of what I felt to be a vulgar but nonetheless sincere tribute. The low voice, not familiar to me, spoke again. "Not *you*, pie-face!" he called, and then I saw three or four of the big boys from grade 12 leave the audience and run into the woods.

Somehow or other I got through that scene.

---

14. **courtier** (côr′tē ər), *n.* person who is often present at a royal court.
15. betrothed (bi trōᴛнd′), *n.* person engaged to be married.
16. **gramophone** (gram′ə fōn), *n.* trademark name for a type of phonograph, or record player.

Harold pulled his enchanted eyes back onstage, and the gramophone started the first few bars of "The Blue Danube" as we began to dance. Mercifully, the scene was short, and before long we were taking our curtain calls. "Stage manager! Stage manager!" shouted one of the sailors, and after a brief pause, old Henrietta came shyly forward, bedspread gone, dressed once more in her familiar blue sweatshirt and dungarees. The applause from the audience went on and on, and as we all bowed and curtsied, I stole a look at Henrietta. Slender, I thought, throat tight. Slender, not skinny anymore. All in an instant I saw everything, right in the midst of all that clapping and bowing. It was like one of those long complicated dreams that start and finish within the space of five minutes, just before you wake up in the morning. Henrietta was standing serenely, quietly. As the clapping continued, while the actors and actresses feverishly bobbed up and down to acknowledge the applause, she just once, ever so slightly, inclined her head, gazing at

All in an instant I saw everything, right in the midst of all that clapping and bowing.

the audience out of her astonishing eyes—enormous, arresting,[17] fringed now with long dark lashes. Mrs. Elliot's makeup job had made us all see what must have been there all the time—a strikingly beautiful face. But there was something else there now that was new. As I continued to bow and smile, the word came to me to describe that strange new thing. *Power.* Henrietta had power. And what's more, she had it without having to *do* a single thing. All she needs to do, I thought, is *be.* The terrible injustice of it all stabbed me. There I was, the lead role, the director, the brains and vigor of our twinship, and suddenly, after all my years in first place, it was she who had the power. Afterwards I looked at them—the boys, the sailors, *Harold*—

as they gazed at her. All she was doing was sauntering[18] around the stage picking up props. But they were watching, and I knew, with a stunning accuracy, that there would always be watchers now, wherever she might be, whatever she wore, regardless of what she would be doing. And I also knew in that moment, with the same sureness, that I would never have that kind of power, not ever.

The next day, Mama stationed herself at the telephone, receiving all the tributes that came pouring in. A few moments per call were given over to a brief recognition of my acting talents and to an uneasy amusement over the split dress. The rest of the time was spent in shouted discussion of Henrietta's startling and surprising beauty. I lay face downward on my bed and let the words hail down upon me. "Yes, indeed. *Yes.* I quite agree. Simply beautiful. And a real bolt from the blue. She quite astonished all of us. Although of course I recognized this quality in her all along.

I've often sat and contemplated her lovely eyes, her milky skin, her delicate hands, and thought, 'Your time will come, my dear! Your time will come!'"

"Delicate hands!" I whispered fiercely into the mattress. "Bony! Bony!"

I suppose, in a way, that nothing changed too drastically for me after that play. I continued to lead groups, direct shows, spark activities with my ideas, my zeal. In school I did well in all my subjects, and was good at sports, too. Henrietta's grades were mediocre,[19] and she never even tried out for teams or anything, while I was on the swim team, the baseball team, the basketball

---

17. **arresting** (ə rest′ing), *adj.* catching and holding attention; striking.

18. **saunter** (sôn′tər), *v.* walk along slowly and happily; stroll.

19. **mediocre** (mē′dē ō′kər), *adj.* neither good nor bad; of average or lower than average quality; ordinary.

team. She still moved slowly, languidly,[20] as though her energy was in short supply, but there was a subtle difference in her that was hard to put your finger on. It wasn't as though she went around covered with all that highly flattering greasepaint that Mrs. Elliot had supplied. In fact, she didn't really start wearing makeup until she was fifteen or sixteen. Apparently she didn't need to. That one dramatic walk-on part with the blanket and the safety pin had done it all, although I'm sure I harbored a hope that we might return to the old Henrietta as soon as she washed her face. Even the sailors started coming to the house more often. They couldn't take her out, of course, or *do* anything with her. But they seemed to enjoy just looking at her, contemplating her. They would sit there on our big brown plush chesterfield[21] under the stern picture of Great-great-grandmother Logan in the big gold frame, smoking cigarette after cigarette, and watching Henrietta as she moved about with her infuriatingly slow, lazy grace, her grave confidence. Her serenity soothed and excited them, all at the same time. Boys from grades 9 and 10 hung around our backyard, our verandah,[22] the nearest street corner. They weren't mean to me. They simply didn't know I was there, not really.

didn't spend much time with Henrietta anymore, or boss her, or make her go to The Grove in the fog or try to scare her. I just wasn't all that crazy about having her around the entire time, with those eyes looking out at me from under those long lashes, quiet, mysterious, full of power. And of course you had to trip over boys if you so much as wanted to ask her what time it was. Every once in a while I'd try to figure out what the thing was that made her so different now; and then, one day, all of a sudden, I understood. We were down at the beach, and she was just sitting on a rock or something, arms slack and resting on her knees, in a position I had often seen over the years. And in that moment I knew. Everything else was the same—the drab white skin, the bony, yes, bony hands, the limp hair. But she had lost her waiting look. Henrietta didn't look as though she were waiting for anything at all anymore.

---

20. languidly (lang′gwid lē), *adv.* in a manner that is not brisk or lively; sluggishly; dully.
21. **chesterfield** (ches′tər fēld′), *n.* a sofa (in Great Britain and Canada).
22. **verandah** (və ran′də), *n.* a large porch or gallery along one or more sides of a house.

After Reading

Making Connections

Shaping Your Response

1. With a group of classmates, form a tableau, or a posed picture, showing the reactions of Juliette and the others when Juliette's dress splits. Form another tableau depicting the instant that Juliette realizes that the applause at the end of the play is for Henrietta.

2. How does Juliette feel about the change in Henrietta? Why do you think she feels that way?

3. Whom would you rather have as a friend, Juliette or Henrietta? Explain.

Analyzing the Story

4. Describe how Juliette feels about Henrietta when the girls are young, citing specific examples.

5. Why do you think Henrietta does not tell their mother when Juliette leaves her out in the cold?

6. How does the relationship between the two girls change after the play?

Extending the Ideas

7. Compare and contrast Juliette and Henrietta with the brothers you read about in "The Scarlet Ibis."

8. 🐾 "Waiting" details a specific time in which the dynamics of a family relationship change. What event in a family **group** you know about caused a definite change? What change did the event bring about?

Literary Focus: Idioms

An **idiom** is an expression with a literal meaning that does not correspond with its figurative meaning. Many idioms would not make sense if they were interpreted literally. For example, if you said that your sister "caught a cold," you would not literally mean that she reached out with her hands to catch something. Rather, you would mean that she developed an illness.

- List three or four idioms that you found in "Waiting." One example is "lead in her feet," an idiom that Juliette uses to describe how Henrietta skis. Restate the meaning of each idiom you find in your own words. For example, when Henrietta skis with "lead in her feet," that means she skis slowly.

- Describe how the use of idioms affects the **tone** of the story.

Vocabulary Study

On a separate sheet of paper, state whether each of the following sentences is true or false. If a statement is false, rewrite it as a true statement, using the italicized vocabulary word correctly.

apathy
arresting
betrothed
flamboyant
languidly
mediocre
meld
ornate
saunter
submissive

1. A team will improve if the players *meld* into a unified group.
2. An *ornate* tapestry has intricate patterns and *arresting* designs.
3. A *submissive* person would make a good leader.
4. Someone who is *flamboyant* is shy and retiring.
5. A person who felt *apathy* would work hard to support a cause.
6. A *mediocre* student would not be the best or the worst in his class.
7. It would be a good idea to introduce your *betrothed* to your parents.
8. If a hurricane strikes, you should *saunter* to shelter.
9. A competitive runner would move *languidly* toward the finish line.

Expressing Your Ideas

Writing Choices

Writer's Notebook Update Are the ideas you wrote about favoritism shown in "Waiting"? In what ways? In your notebook, write what you would like to say to Juliette and Henrietta's mother if you met her. What do you think of the way she talks to other people about her daughters?

Seen Through Other Eyes "Waiting" is told from the point of view of Juliette. How do you think Henrietta views the events in the story? As Henrietta, write a **diary entry** describing an event from the story that reveals your inner thoughts and feelings.

Other Options

First, Last, and Only Much has been written about the characteristics of children who are the oldest, the youngest, in the middle, or the only child. Do some **research** on the topic of birth order. Present your findings in the form that makes the most sense—a chart, a graph, a report, or something else.

The Girl Most Likely to . . . Imagine that Juliette and Henrietta are seniors in high school. Project their lives into the future and write their **yearbook entries.** Draw a picture of each sister. Then write captions for the pictures that list each girl's activities and includes predictions about their future lives.

The Man to Send Rain Clouds

by Leslie Marmon Silko

Leslie Marmon Silko
born 1948

Leslie Marmon Silko was born in Albuquerque and grew up at Laguna Pueblo, about forty miles west of Albuquerque. She states that although she is descended from several American Indian peoples, she considers Laguna Pueblo the force that shaped "everything I am as a writer and human being." Now a teacher of English at the University of Arizona, Silko began writing in the fifth grade. She has written many stories and poems and is also a film producer.

Building Background

"The Man to Send Rain Clouds" takes place in New Mexico, where the main characters live in a pueblo. In past centuries the Pueblo Indians (*pueblo* is

Spanish for *village)* lived in villages of large, many-storied homes made of rocks and sun-dried clay. The homes could hold many families, and, in some cases, entire villages. Entry was usually through doors on the roofs. In pueblos today, most families live in modern houses, although the communities may still have large communal buildings where families can gather together.

Literary Focus

Setting The time and place in which the events of a story occur is called the **setting.** A narrator or one of the characters may describe the setting directly, or the setting may be suggested through dialogue and events. The story's setting provides an atmosphere in which action and conflict develop. As you read "The Man to Send Rain Clouds," consider how the setting contributes to the story. How would the story be different if it were in a different time and place?

Writer's Notebook

Getting Along Imagine that you and your family are going to live in a place among people whose beliefs are very different from yours. What would you do to better understand your new neighbors? Write a few paragraphs describing some strategies for getting along with people who may not have the same beliefs or goals as you.

The Man to Send RAIN CLOUDS

Leslie Marmon Silko

One

They found him under a big cottonwood tree. His Levi jacket and pants were faded light blue so that he had been easy to find. The big cottonwood tree stood apart from a small grove of winterbare cottonwoods which grew in the wide, sandy arroyo.[1] He had been dead for a day or more, and the sheep had wandered and scattered up and down the arroyo. Leon and his brother-in-law, Ken, gathered the sheep and left them in the pen at the sheep camp before they returned to the cottonwood tree. Leon waited under the tree while Ken drove the truck through the deep sand to the edge of the arroyo. He squinted up at the sun and unzipped his jacket—it sure was hot for this time of year. But high and northwest the blue mountains were still deep in snow. Ken came sliding down the low, crumbling bank about fifty yards down, and he was bringing the red blanket.

Before they wrapped the old man, Leon took a piece of string out of his pocket and tied a small gray feather in the old man's long white hair. Ken gave him the paint. Across the brown wrinkled forehead he drew a streak of white and along the high cheekbones he drew a strip of blue paint. He paused and watched Ken throw pinches of corn meal and pollen into the wind that fluttered the small gray feather. Then Leon painted with yellow under the old man's broad nose, and finally, when he had painted green across the chin, he smiled.

"Send us rain clouds, Grandfather." They laid the bundle in the back of the pickup and covered it with a heavy tarp[2] before they started back to the pueblo.[3]

---

1. **arroyo** (ə roi′ō), *n.* the dry bed of a stream; gully. [Spanish]
2. **tarp** (tärp), *n.* informal form of *tarpaulin,* a sheet of canvas, plastic, or other strong waterproof material, used as a protective covering.
3. **pueblo** (pweb′lō), *n.* an Indian village consisting of houses built of adobe and stone. [Spanish]

▲ Maynard Dixon, *Cloud World* (1925). Dixon wanted his art to interpret "the poetry and pathos of the life of Western people seen amid the grandeur, sternness and loneliness of their country." Comment on whether or not this painting achieves that goal.

They turned off the highway onto the sandy pueblo road. Not long after they passed the store and post office they saw Father Paul's car coming toward them. When he recognized their faces he slowed his car and waved for them to stop. The young priest rolled down the car window.

"Did you find old Teofilo?" he asked loudly.

Leon stopped the truck. "Good morning, Father. We were just out to the sheep camp. Everything is O.K. now."

"Thank God for that. Teofilo is a very old man. You really shouldn't allow him to stay at the sheep camp alone."

"No, he won't do that any more now."

"Well, I'm glad you understand. I hope I'll be seeing you at Mass this week—we missed you last Sunday. See if you can get old Teofilo to come with you." The priest smiled and waved at them as they drove away.

Two

Louise and Teresa were waiting. The table was set for lunch, and the coffee was boiling on the black iron stove. Leon looked at Louise and then at Teresa.

"We found him under a cottonwood tree in the big arroyo near sheep camp. I guess he sat down to rest in the shade and never got up again." Leon walked toward the old man's bed. The red plaid shawl had been shaken and spread carefully over the bed, and a new brown flannel shirt and pair of stiff new Levis were arranged neatly beside the pillow. Louise held the screen door open while Leon and Ken carried in the red blanket. He looked small and shriveled, and after they dressed him in the new shirt and pants he seemed more shrunken.

It was noontime now because the church bells rang the Angelus.[4] They ate the beans and

---

4. **Angelus** (an′jə ləs), prayer said by Roman Catholics in memory of Christ's assuming human form. [Latin]

The Man to Send Rain Clouds　**163**

hot bread, and nobody said anything until after Teresa poured the coffee.

Ken stood up and put on his jacket. "I'll see about the gravediggers. Only the top layer of soil is frozen. I think it can be ready before dark."

Leon nodded his head and finished his coffee. After Ken had been gone for a while, the neighbors and clanspeople came quietly to embrace Teofilo's family and to leave food on the table because the gravediggers would come to eat when they were finished.

Three

The sky in the west was full of pale-yellow light. Louise stood outside with her hands in the pockets of Leon's green army jacket that was too big for her. The funeral was over, and the old men had taken their candles and medicine bags[5] and were gone. She waited until the body was laid into the pickup before she said anything to Leon. She touched his arm, and he noticed that her hands were still dusty from the corn meal that she had sprinkled around the old man. When she spoke, Leon could not hear her.

"What did you say? I didn't hear you."

"I said that I had been thinking about something."

"About what?"

"About the priest sprinkling holy water for Grandpa. So he won't be thirsty."

Leon stared at the new moccasins that Teofilo had made for the ceremonial dances in the summer. They were nearly hidden by the red blanket. It was getting colder, and the wind pushed gray dust down the narrow pueblo road. The sun was approaching the long mesa[6] where it disappeared during the winter. Louise stood there shivering and watching his face. Then he zipped his jacket and opened the truck door. "I'll see if he's there."

Four

Ken stopped the pickup at the church, and Leon got out; and then Ken drove down the hill to the graveyard where people were waiting. Leon knocked at the old carved door with its symbols of the Lamb.[7] While he waited he looked up at the twin bells from the king of Spain with the last sunlight pouring around them in their tower.

The priest opened the door and smiled when he saw who it was. "Come in! What brings you here this evening?"

The priest walked toward the kitchen, and Leon stood with his cap in his hand, playing with the earflaps and examining the living room—the brown sofa, the green armchair, and the brass lamp that hung down from the ceiling by links of chain. The priest dragged a chair out of the kitchen and offered it to Leon.

"No thank you, Father. I only came to ask you if you would bring your holy water to the graveyard."

The priest turned away from Leon and looked out the window at the patio full of shadows and the dining-room windows of the nuns' cloister across the patio. The curtains were heavy, and the light from within faintly penetrated; it was impossible to see the nuns inside eating supper. "Why didn't you tell me he was dead? I could have brought the Last Rites[8] anyway."

Leon smiled. "It wasn't necessary, Father."

The priest stared down at his scuffed brown loafers and the worn hem of his cassock. "For a Christian burial it was necessary."

---

5. **medicine bag,** bag containing objects believed to provide power to protect or to heal.
6. **mesa** (mā′sə), *n.* a small, isolated, high plateau with a flat top and steep sides, common in dry regions of the western and southwestern United States. [Spanish]
7. **Lamb,** the Lamb of God, or Christ.
8. **Last Rites,** religious rites performed for a dying or recently dead person.

His voice was distant, and Leon thought that his blue eyes looked tired.

"It's O.K. Father, we just want him to have plenty of water."

The priest sank down into the green chair and picked up a glossy missionary magazine. He turned the colored pages full of lepers and pagans without looking at them.

"You know I can't do that, Leon. There should have been the Last Rites and a funeral Mass at the very least."

Leon put on his green cap and pulled the flaps down over his ears. "It's getting late, Father. I've got to go."

When Leon opened the door Father Paul stood up and said, "Wait." He left the room and came back wearing a long brown overcoat. He followed Leon out the door and across the dim churchyard to the adobe[9] steps in front of the church. They both stooped to fit through the low adobe entrance. And when they started down the hill to the graveyard only half of the sun was visible above the mesa.

The priest approached the grave slowly, wondering how they had managed to dig into the frozen ground; and then he remembered that this was New Mexico, and saw the pile of cold loose sand beside the hole. The people stood close to each other with little clouds of steam puffing from their faces. The priest looked at them and saw a pile of jackets, gloves, and scarves in the yellow, dry tumbleweeds that grew in the graveyard. He looked at the red blanket, not sure that Teofilo was so small, wondering if it wasn't some perverse Indian trick—something they did in March to ensure a good harvest—wondering if maybe old Teofilo was actually at sheep camp corralling[10] the sheep for the night. But there he was, facing into a cold dry wind and squinting at the last sunlight, ready to bury a red wool blanket while the faces of his parishioners were in shadow with the last warmth of the sun on their backs.

His fingers were stiff, and it took him a long time to twist the lid off the holy water. Drops of water fell on the red blanket and soaked into dark icy spots. He sprinkled the grave and the water disappeared almost before it touched the dim, cold sand; it reminded him of something—he tried to remember what it was, because he thought if he could remember he might understand this. He sprinkled more water; he shook the container until it was empty, and the water fell through the light from sundown like August rain that fell while the sun was still shining, almost evaporating before it touched the wilted squash flowers.

The wind pulled at the priest's brown Franciscan[11] robe and swirled away the corn meal and pollen that had been sprinkled on the blanket. They lowered the bundle into the ground, and they didn't bother to untie the stiff pieces of new rope that were tied around the ends of the blanket. The sun was gone, and over on the highway the eastbound lane was full of headlights. The priest walked away slowly. Leon watched him climb the hill, and when he had disappeared within the tall, thick walls, Leon turned to look up at the high blue mountains in the deep snow that reflected a faint red light from the west. He felt good because it was finished, and he was happy about the sprinkling of the holy water; now the old man could send them big thunderclouds for sure.

---

9. **adobe** (ə dō′bē), *n.* brick made of sun-dried clay. [Spanish]

10. **corral** (kə ral′), *v.* drive into or keep in a corral, a holding pen for horses, cattle, etc. [Spanish]

11. **Franciscan** (fran sis′kən), The Franciscan religious order was founded in 1209 by Saint Francis of Assisi.

After Reading

Making Connections

Shaping Your Response

1. Imagine that you are Leon or Father Paul, standing by Teofilo's grave. What are you thinking about? Speak in the first person, sharing "your" thoughts and feelings.

2. Do you think that Father Paul is successful at his job? Why or why not?

3. How does the author convey the importance of water to the community?

Analyzing the Story

4. 👁 Explain what you think the family's treatment of the old man reveals about community attitudes toward the elderly.

5. The community's attitude toward Father Paul is complex. Describe this attitude, using examples from the story to support your answer.

6. In the end, Father Paul agrees to sprinkle the holy water. What does this reveal about his **character?**

7. Father Paul's beliefs differ from those of the community. At the end of the story, do you think he has resolved those differences? Explain.

Extending the Ideas

8. 👁 Think about a story you have read or a movie you have seen that shows a "clash" between **groups** of people. How is the conflict handled? How is the treatment of that conflict similar to and different from the conflict in "The Man to Send Rain Clouds"?

Literary Focus: Setting

Authors do not always directly state the **setting** of a story. Sometimes you have to pick up details about the setting from the characters' actions and dialogue. The setting itself may influence events in the story.

• Find three examples in "The Man to Send Rain Clouds" where details of the setting are revealed by the actions or dialogue of the characters.

• Find three examples in the story where the actions of the characters are influenced by the setting.

• How is Father Paul affected by the setting of the story?

• Could this story have taken place in another setting? Explain.

Expressing Your Ideas

Writing Choices

Writer's Notebook Update Look back at the strategies for getting along with people that you wrote down before reading the story. Write a letter to Father Paul and give him some advice on how he can gain a better understanding of the people in the pueblo.

You Are There Leslie Silko uses specific details to paint a picture of the southwestern United States. Think of a place that is special to you. Write a short **description** of the place, using colorful details so that a reader could picture the place as he or she reads. Read your description to a partner. Can he or she tell what place you are describing?

View and Review Contemporary movies and television shows often feature characters who have to learn to work together despite cultural or social differences. Write a **review** of one of these films or programs. In your review, analyze whether or not the film or program presents a realistic portrayal of how people can learn to understand and overcome their differences.

Other Options

Stormy Weather The people in the village believe that sprinkling holy water on Teofilo's body will help bring rain. What atmospheric conditions are necessary for rain and other natural phenomena? After doing some research, make a **3-D model** that shows how a certain weather pattern (such as snow, rain, a tornado, and so on) forms. Use your model to present your weather information to the class.

Site Seeing You are a travel agent, and one of your clients would like to take a trip to the southwest United States. Do some research and create an **itinerary** for your client. The itinerary should include the following: maps showing the area in which your client will travel and the locations of particular attractions, the attractions you recommend that your client should visit (along with the historical significance of the sites), and photos of some of these attractions. You might use brochures from a travel agency as models for your itinerary.

Artful Response Paintings and other artwork often reflect the culture and important rituals of the artists. Paint or draw a **picture** of an important ceremony in your community. How can you convey the significance of the ritual in your artwork?

Before Reading

A Day's Wait by Ernest Hemingway
The Stolen Party by Liliana Heker

Ernest Hemingway
1899–1961

Ernest Hemingway lived an adventurous life. He drove an ambulance during World War I, began his writing career in Paris, later worked as a war correspondent, and hunted big game in Africa. He won both the Pulitzer Prize and Nobel Prize for literature. "A Day's Wait" is based on a true experience—his son's illness.

Liliana Heker
born 1943

Argentinean writer Liliana Heker published her first book as a teenager. In the 1970s, a period of military oppression in Argentina, she refused to flee her country, saying, "To be heard, we must shout from within." Heker remains politically active, and has published four collections of short stories and two novels.

Building Background

A Touch of Class One of the stories you are about to read, "The Stolen Party," may present a situation that is unfamiliar to you. In this story from Argentina, the main character is a young girl whose mother works as a maid in the home of a wealthy family. In Argentina, as in other Latin American countries, it is customary for upper- and middle-class families to hire people to work for them. These employees may live with the family or maintain their own homes. There is often a strong sense of class distinction between the household staff and their employers. Before reading "The Stolen Party," discuss whether or not you believe similar class differences exist in the United States.

Literary Focus

Theme A **theme** is a statement that expresses a main idea or an underlying meaning of a literary work. The writer may have some themes in mind when he or she creates a literary work, and the reader may discover other themes. As you read "A Day's Wait" and "The Stolen Party," consider whether or not the two stories share any common themes.

Writer's Notebook

Communication Gap Although it is often difficult to get an idea across to people your own age, it sometimes seems even more difficult for adults and younger people to communicate with each other. What do you think causes the breakdown in communication between children and adults? How do you think communication might be improved? Make a list of tips for both adults and younger people—ideas that would help them communicate more effectively.

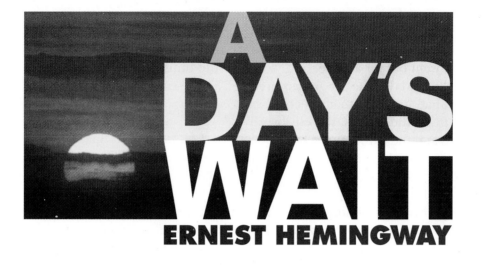

A DAY'S WAIT

ERNEST HEMINGWAY

He came into the room to shut the windows while we were still in bed and I saw he looked ill. He was shivering, his face was white, and he walked slowly as though it ached to move.

"What's the matter, Schatz?"[1]

"I've got a headache."

"You better go back to bed."

"No. I'm all right."

"You go to bed. I'll see you when I'm dressed."

But when I came downstairs he was dressed, sitting by the fire, looking a very sick and miserable boy of nine years. When I put my hand on his forehead I knew he had a fever.

"You go up to bed," I said, "you're sick."

"I'm all right," he said.

When the doctor came he took the boy's temperature.

"What is it?" I asked him.

"One hundred and two."

Downstairs, the doctor left three different medicines in different colored capsules with instructions for giving them. One was to bring down the fever, another a purgative,[2] the third to overcome an acid condition. The germs of influenza can only exist in an acid condition, he explained. He seemed to know all about influenza and said there was nothing to worry about if the fever did not go above one hundred and four degrees. This was a light epidemic of flu and there was no danger if you avoided pneumonia.

Back in the room I wrote the boy's temperature down and made a note of the time to give the various capsules.

"Do you want me to read to you?"

"All right. If you want to," said the boy. His face was very white and there were dark areas under his eyes. He lay still in the bed and seemed very detached from what was going on.

I read aloud from Howard Pyle's *Book of Pirates;* but I could see he was not following what I was reading.

"How do you feel, Schatz?" I asked him.

"Just the same, so far," he said.

I sat at the foot of the bed and read to myself while I waited for it to be time to give another capsule. It would have been natural for him to go to sleep, but when I looked up he was looking at the foot of the bed, looking very strangely.

"Why don't you try to go to sleep? I'll wake you up for the medicine."

"I'd rather stay awake."

After a while he said to me, "You don't have to stay in here with me, Papa, if it bothers you."

"It doesn't bother me."

"No, I mean you don't have to stay if it's going to bother you."

---

1. **Schatz** (shäts), German for *treasure,* a term of endearment often used for children.
2. **purgative** (pėr′gə tiv), *n.* medicine that causes emptying of the bowels.

I thought perhaps he was a little lightheaded and after giving him the prescribed capsules at eleven o'clock I went out for a while.

It was a bright, cold day, the ground covered with a sleet that had frozen so that it seemed as if all the bare trees, the bushes, the cut brush and all the grass and the bare ground had been varnished with ice. I took the young Irish setter for a little walk up the road and along a frozen creek, but it was difficult to stand or walk on the glassy surface and the red dog slipped and slithered and I fell twice, hard, once dropping my gun and having it slide away over the ice.

We flushed a covey[3] of quail under a high clay bank with overhanging brush and I killed two as they went out of sight over the top of the bank. Some of the covey lit in trees, but most of them scattered into brush piles and it was necessary to jump on the ice-coated mounds of brush several times before they would flush. Coming out while you were poised unsteadily on the icy, springy brush they made difficult shooting and I killed two, missed five, and started back pleased to have found a covey close to the house and happy there were so many left to find on another day.

At the house they said the boy had refused to let any one come into the room.

"You can't come in," he said. "You mustn't get what I have."

I went up to him and found him in exactly the position I had left him, white-faced, but with the tops of his cheeks flushed by the fever, staring still, as he had stared, at the foot of the bed.

I took his temperature.

"What is it?"

"Something like a hundred," I said. It was one hundred and two and four tenths.

"It was a hundred and two," he said.

"Who said so?"

"The doctor."

"Your temperature is all right," I said. "It's nothing to worry about."

"I don't worry," he said, "but I can't keep from thinking."

"Don't think," I said. "Just take it easy."

"I'm taking it easy," he said and looked straight ahead. He was evidently holding tight onto himself about something.

"Take this with water."

"Do you think it will do any good?"

"Of course it will."

I sat down and opened the *Pirate* book and commenced[4] to read, but I could see he was not following, so I stopped.

"About what time do you think I'm going to die?" he asked.

"What?"

"About how long will it be before I die?"

"You aren't going to die. What's the matter with you?"

"Oh, yes, I am. I heard him say a hundred and two."

"People don't die with a fever of one hundred and two. That's a silly way to talk."

"I know they do. At school in France the boys told me you can't live with forty-four degrees. I've got a hundred and two."

He had been waiting to die all day, ever since nine o'clock in the morning.

"You poor Schatz," I said. "Poor old Schatz. It's like miles and kilometers. You aren't going to die. That's a different thermometer.[5] On that thermometer thirty-seven is normal. On this kind it's ninety-eight."

"Are you sure?"

"Absolutely," I said. "It's like miles and kilometers. You know, like how many kilometers we make when we do seventy miles in the car?"

"Oh," he said.

But his gaze at the foot of the bed relaxed slowly. The hold over himself relaxed too, finally, and the next day it was very slack and he cried very easily at little things that were of no importance.

---

3. covey (kuv′ē), *n.* a brood, or family group, of partridge, quail, etc.
4. commence (kə mens′), *v.* make a start, begin.
5. **different thermometer.** The doctor took the boy's temperature with a Fahrenheit thermometer, while his French schoolmates used a Celsius thermometer.

The Stolen Party

Liliana Heker
(Translated by Alberto Manguel)

As soon as she arrived she went straight to the kitchen to see if the monkey was there. It was: what a relief! She wouldn't have liked to admit that her mother had been right. *Monkeys at a birthday?* her mother had sneered. *Get away with you, believing any nonsense you're told!* She was cross, but not because of the monkey, the girl thought; it's just because of the party.

"I don't like you going," she told her. "It's a rich people's party."

"Rich people go to Heaven too," said the girl, who studied religion at school.

"Get away with Heaven," said the mother.

The girl didn't approve of the way her mother spoke. She was barely nine, and one of the best in her class.

"I'm going because I've been invited," she said. "And I've been invited because Luciana[1] is my friend. So there."

"Ah yes, your friend," her mother grumbled. She paused. "Listen, Rosaura,"[2] she said at last. "That one's not your friend. You know what you are to them? The maid's daughter, that's what."

Rosaura blinked hard: she wasn't going to cry. Then she yelled: "Shut up! You know nothing about being friends!"

Every afternoon she used to go to Luciana's house and they would both finish their homework while Rosaura's mother did the cleaning. They had their tea in the kitchen and they told each other secrets. Rosaura loved everything in the big house, and she also loved the people who lived there.

"I'm going because it will be the most lovely party in the whole world, Luciana told me it would. There will be a magician, and he will bring a monkey and everything."

The mother swung around to take a good look at her child, and pompously[3] put her hands on her hips.

"Monkeys at a birthday?" she said. "Get away with you, believing any nonsense you're told!"

Rosaura was deeply offended. She thought it

---

1. **Luciana** (lü syä′nä).
2. **Rosaura** (rō sou′rä).
3. pompously (pom′pəs lē), *adv.* in a self-important way.

unfair of her mother to accuse other people of being liars simply because they were rich. Rosaura too wanted to be rich, of course. If one day she managed to live in a beautiful palace, would her mother stop loving her? She felt very sad. She wanted to go to that party more than anything else in the world.

"I'll die if I don't go," she whispered, almost without moving her lips.

And she wasn't sure whether she had been heard, but on the morning of the party she discovered that her mother had starched her Christmas dress. And in the afternoon, after washing her hair, her mother rinsed it in apple vinegar so that it would be all nice and shiny. Before going out, Rosaura admired herself in the mirror, with her white dress and glossy hair, and thought she looked terribly pretty.

Señora Ines[4] also seemed to notice. As soon as she saw her, she said:

"How lovely you look today, Rosaura."

Rosaura gave her starched skirt a slight toss with her hands and walked into the party with a firm step. She said hello to Luciana and asked about the monkey. Luciana put on a secretive look and whispered into Rosaura's ear: "He's in the kitchen. But don't tell anyone, because it's a surprise."

Rosaura wanted to make sure. Carefully she entered the kitchen and there she saw it: deep in thought, inside its cage. It looked so funny that the girl stood there for a while, watching it, and later, every so often, she would slip out of the party unseen and go and admire it. Rosaura was the only one allowed into the kitchen. Senora Ines had said: "You yes, but not the others, they're much too boisterous, they might break something." Rosaura had never broken anything. She even managed the jug of orange juice, carrying it from the kitchen into the dining room. She held it carefully and didn't spill a single drop. And Señora Ines had said: "Are you sure you can manage a jug as big as that?" Of course she could manage. She wasn't a but-

terfingers, like the others. Like that blonde girl with the bow in her hair. As soon as she saw Rosaura, the girl with the bow had said:

"And you? Who are you?"

"I'm a friend of Luciana," said Rosaura.

"No," said the girl with the bow, "you are not a friend of Luciana because I'm her cousin and I know all her friends. And I don't know you."

"So what," said Rosaura. "I come here every afternoon with my mother and we do our homework together."

"You and your mother do your homework together?" asked the girl, laughing.

"I and Luciana do our homework together," said Rosaura, very seriously.

The girl with the bow shrugged her shoulders.

"That's not being friends," she said. "Do you go to school together?"

"No."

"So where do you know her from?" said the girl, getting impatient.

Rosaura remembered her mother's words perfectly. She took a deep breath.

"I'm the daughter of the employee," she said.

Her mother had said very clearly: "If someone asks, you say you're the daughter of the employee; that's all." She also told her to add: "And proud of it." But Rosaura thought that never in her life would she dare say something of the sort.

"What employee?" said the girl with the bow. "Employee in a shop?"

"No," said Rosaura angrily. "My mother doesn't sell anything in any shop, so there."

"So how come she's an employee?" said the girl with the bow.

---

4. **Señora Ines** (se nyōr′ä ē nes′).

Frida Kahlo, *Niña* (1929). Compare this portrait with the description of Rosaura. To what social class does each girl seem to belong? ➤

Just then Señora Ines arrived saying *shh shh,* and asked Rosaura if she wouldn't mind helping serve out the hot dogs, as she knew the house so much better than the others.

"See?" said Rosaura to the girl with the bow, and when no one was looking she kicked her in the shin.

Apart from the girl with the bow, all the others were delightful. The one she liked best was Luciana, with her golden birthday crown; and then the boys. Rosaura won the sack race, and nobody managed to catch her when they played tag. When they split into two teams to play charades, all the boys wanted her for their side. Rosaura felt she had never been so happy in all her life.

But the best was still to come. The best came after Luciana blew out the candles. First the cake. Señora Ines had asked her to help pass the cake around, and Rosaura had enjoyed the task immensely, because everyone called out to her, shouting "Me, me!" Rosaura remembered a story in which there was a queen who had the power of life or death over her subjects. She had always loved that, having the power of life or death. To Luciana and the boys she gave the largest pieces, and to the girl with the bow she gave a slice so thin one could see through it.

"You, with the Spanish eyes," said the magician.

After the cake came the magician, tall and bony, with a fine red cape. A true magician: he could untie handkerchiefs by blowing on them and make a chain with links that had no openings. He could guess what cards were pulled out from a pack, and the monkey was his assistant. He called the monkey "partner." "Let's see here, partner," he would say, "Turn over a card." And, "Don't run away, partner: time to work now."

The final trick was wonderful. One of the children had to hold the monkey in his arms and the magician said he would make him disappear.

"What, the boy?" they all shouted.

"No, the monkey!" shouted the magician.

Rosaura thought that this was truly the most amusing party in the whole world.

The magician asked a small fat boy to come and help, but the small fat boy got frightened almost at once and dropped the monkey on the floor. The magician picked him up carefully, whispered something in his ear, and the monkey nodded almost as if he understood.

"You mustn't be so unmanly, my friend," the magician said to the fat boy.

"What's unmanly?" said the fat boy.

The magician turned around as if to look for spies.

"A sissy," said the magician. "Go sit down."

Then he stared at all the faces, one by one. Rosaura felt her heart tremble.

"You, with the Spanish eyes," said the magician. And everyone saw that he was pointing at her.

She wasn't afraid. Neither holding the monkey, nor when the magician made him vanish; not even when, at the end, the magician flung his red cape over Rosaura's head and uttered a few magic words . . . and the monkey reappeared, chattering happily, in her arms. The children clapped furiously. And before Rosaura returned to her seat, the magician said:

"Thank you very much, my little countess."

She was so pleased with the compliment that a while later, when her mother came to fetch her, that was the first thing she told her.

"I helped the magician and he said to me, 'Thank you very much, my little countess.'"

It was strange because up to then Rosaura had thought that she was angry with her mother.

All along Rosaura had imagined that she would say to her: "See that the monkey wasn't a lie?" But instead she was so thrilled that she told her mother all about the wonderful magician.

Her mother tapped her on the head and said: "So now we're a countess!"

But one could see that she was beaming.

And now they both stood in the entrance, because a moment ago Señora Ines, smiling, had said: "Please wait here a second."

Her mother suddenly seemed worried.

"What is it?" she asked Rosaura.

"What is what?" said Rosaura. "It's nothing; she just wants to get the presents for those who are leaving, see?"

She pointed at the fat boy and at a girl with pigtails who were also waiting there, next to their mothers. And she explained about the presents. She knew, because she had been watching those who left before her. When one of the girls was about to leave, Señora Ines would give her a bracelet. When a boy left, Señora Ines gave him a yo-yo. Rosaura preferred the yo-yo because it sparkled, but she didn't mention that to her mother. Her mother might have said: "So why don't you ask for one, you blockhead?" That's what her mother was like. Rosaura didn't feel like explaining that she'd be horribly ashamed to be the odd one out. Instead she said:

"I was the best-behaved at the party."

And she said no more because Señora Ines came out into the hall with two bags, one pink and one blue.

First she went up the fat boy, gave him a yo-yo out of the blue bag, and the fat boy left with his mother. Then she went up to the girl and gave her a bracelet out of the pink bag, and the girl with the pigtails left as well.

Finally she came up to Rosaura and her mother. She had a big smile on her face and Rosaura liked that. Señora Ines looked down at her, then looked up at her mother, and then said something that made Rosaura proud:

"What a marvelous daughter you have, Herminia."[5]

For an instant, Rosaura thought that she'd give her two presents: the bracelet and the yo-yo. Señora Ines bent down as if about to look for something. Rosaura also leaned forward, stretching out her arm. But she never completed the movement.

Señora Ines didn't look in the pink bag. Nor did she look in the blue bag. Instead she rummaged[6] in her purse. In her hand appeared two bills.

"You really and truly earned this," she said handing them over. "Thank you for all your help, my pet."

Rosaura felt her arms stiffen, stick close to her body, and then she noticed her mother's hand on her shoulder. Instinctively she pressed herself against her mother's body. That was all. Except her eyes. Rosaura's eyes had a cold, clear look that fixed itself on Señora Ines's face.

Señora Ines, motionless, stood there with her hand outstretched. As if she didn't dare draw it back. As if the slightest change might shatter an infinitely[7] delicate balance.

---

5. **Herminia** (er mē nyä′).
6. rummage (rum′ij), v. search thoroughly by moving things about.
7. infinitely (in′fə nit lē), adv. in a way that is without limits; endlessly.

After Reading

Making Connections

Shaping Your Response

1. In "A Day's Wait," why do you think the boy cries easily the next day?

2. At the end of "The Stolen Party," what do you think Rosaura is feeling? Explain.

Analyzing the Stories

3. What clues in "A Day's Wait" hint that the boy believes he is very ill?

4. Reread the last paragraph of "The Stolen Party." What do you think is the "infinitely delicate balance" that could be shattered?

5. Explain what you think is the significance of the **title** of each story.

6. How does the main **character** in each story "deal with differences"?

Extending the Ideas

7. Rosaura and Luciana belong to different **groups**—different social classes. How do you think this will affect their future relationship?

8. What different social classes exist in your community?

Literary Focus: Theme

A **theme** in a literary work is a statement about the underlying meaning or message of the story. Read the following theme statements. Decide whether each statement could be a theme for "A Day's Wait," "The Stolen Party," both stories, or neither story. Then write down at least one more theme for each story. Be prepared to defend your decisions in a class discussion.

1. Some people judge others by their social class.

2. Difficult experiences can be caused by misunderstandings.

3. Good friendships will last a lifetime.

4. Sometimes parents don't understand what their children are feeling.

Vocabulary Study

commence
covey
infinitely
pompously
rummage

A **word analogy** is a relationship between two words that is similar to the relationship between two other words. Analogies may reflect relationships such as antonyms (*poor : rich*); synonyms (*speak: talk*); part-to-whole (*toe : foot*); place—activity (*racetrack : run*); and thing—quality (*snow: cold*).

For each item on the next page, the first word in capital letters is a vocabulary word. Study the relationship of each pair of words in capital letters. Then choose another pair that has the same relationship. You may refer to the Glossary if necessary.

1. COMMENCE : END ::
   a. break : fix
   b. fight : struggle
   c. book : read
   d. kitchen : stove

2. RUMMAGE : SEARCH ::
   a. hide : find
   b. diamond : valuable
   c. chase : escape
   d. duplicate : copy

3. COVEY : BIRD ::
   a. teacher : student
   b. herd : sheep
   c. tiger : lion
   d. costume : actor

4. INFINITELY : ENDLESSLY ::
   a. quickly : rapidly
   b. harshly : softly
   c. truthfully : carefully
   d. forever : never

5. POMPOUSLY : HUMBLY ::
   a. stylishly : elegantly
   b. friendly : outgoing
   c. party : dance
   d. sadly : happily

Expressing Your Ideas

Writing Choices

Writer's Notebook Update Think about how each story shows the importance of communication. Write a paragraph explaining how the communication gaps in one of the stories could have been prevented.

Dear Mom Rosaura is angry with her mother at the beginning of "The Stolen Party." How do you think she feels about her mother at the end of the story? Be Rosaura and write a **letter** to your mother. Tell her how you feel after your experience at Luciana's party. Tell whether or not you still have angry feelings toward your mother, and explain why or why not.

How Hot Is It? Investigate the story behind the Fahrenheit and Celsius measurement scales. Present your findings in a **research report** that includes a graph or chart comparing the two methods.

Other Options

Different Points of View Imagine that one of these two stories is being told by a different character in the story. As this character, prepare a **monologue** that describes the events in the story from your particular point of view. Perform your monologue for your class.

Guest Speakers Luciana and her mother *think* they're appearing on a well-known talk show to tell how to plan a birthday party. Instead, they come face to face with Rosaura, who confronts them with the way she was treated at Luciana's party. What happens next? With a small group, prepare a **talk show segment** with Luciana, Señora Ines, Rosaura, and a famous talk show host. If possible, videotape your scene for presentation to the class.

Before Reading

Theme for English B by Langston Hughes
In Response to Executive Order 9066 by Dwight Okita
Fire and Ice by Robert Frost

Building Background

Executive Order 9066 One of the poems you are about to read refers to Executive Order 9066, enacted by President Franklin D. Roosevelt in 1942. After the Japanese attacked Pearl Harbor on December 7, 1941, many Americans were suspicious of immigrants from countries allied with the Axis powers, including Germany, Italy, and especially Japan. Executive Order 9066 allowed military commanders to designate areas from which "any or all persons may be excluded." The effect of this order was that 120,000 persons, most of Japanese descent and two-thirds of them American citizens, were confined in relocation camps for up to four years. Many Japanese Americans lost their homes and possessions as a result of their forced move. Years after the war, in the 1980s, the United States government admitted the injustice of these actions and paid damages to many who had been forcibly removed from their homes.

Literary Focus

Mood Do you have a favorite piece of music that makes you feel a certain way whenever you hear it? It may be the **mood** of the piece that influences your feelings. In literature as well as in music, mood is the atmosphere or general feeling of a work. The mood of a piece may be anything from giddy happiness to paralyzing fear. As you read the following selections, think about the mood of each poem and the methods the author might be using to create it.

Writer's Notebook

How to Get Along In two of the following poems, the speaker is describing himself or herself to another person. In your notebook, write a letter to someone you don't know very well but would like to know better. Describe yourself to that person.

Langston Hughes
1902–1967

Langston Hughes was a leading figure in the Harlem Renaissance, a period in the 1920s that saw the emergence of writers, musicians, and artists who portrayed the beauty and vigor of life in Harlem, an African American neighborhood in New York City. Born in Joplin, Missouri, Hughes brought a variety of experiences to his writing. By the time his first book was published, he had already worked as a truck farmer, cook, waiter, sailor, and doorman at a nightclub in Paris. Hughes's writing was highly praised for its rich and musical portrayal of everyday life in the African American community. Despite encounters with racism, Hughes never lost his conviction that *"most people are generally good, in every race and in every country where I have been."*

Dwight Okita
born 1958

A third-generation Japanese American who grew up in Chicago, Dwight Okita is a poet and playwright. He was inspired to write "In Response to Executive Order 9066" after he found out about the death of a friend three months after his funeral. He wrote a good-by letter to his friend and became intrigued by the idea of writing other letters that had not been written. Okita wrote "In Response . . ." in the voice of his mother, trying to imagine what she might have written to the government upon finding out she was to go to an internment camp.

Robert Frost
1874–1963

Born and raised in San Francisco, California, Robert Frost was ten when his family moved to New England. At the age of twenty, he published his first book, *Twilight,* consisting of six poems. Only two copies were printed—one for Frost, and one for Elinor White, his fiancée. Frost had paid for the printing himself. His writing received little attention until 1912, when Frost moved his family to England, hoping to win notice there. His gamble paid off—two of his books were published in two years, and he was a celebrated literary figure by the time he returned to the U. S. in 1915. By the end of his life, Robert Frost was one of the best-loved poets in the United States.

THEME FOR ENGLISH B

LANGSTON HUGHES

The instructor said,

> Go home and write
> a page tonight
> And let that page come out of you—
> 5 Then, it will be true.

I wonder if it's that simple?
I am twenty-two, colored, born in Winston-Salem.
I went to school there, then Durham, then here
to this college[1] on the hill above Harlem.
10 I am the only colored student in my class.
The steps from the hill lead down into Harlem,
through a park, then I cross St. Nicholas,
Eighth Avenue, Seventh, and I come to the Y,
the Harlem Branch Y, where I take the elevator
15 up to my room, sit down, and write this page.

It's not easy to know what is true for you or me
at twenty-two, my age. But I guess I'm what
I feel and see and hear, Harlem, I hear you:
hear you, hear me—we two—you, me, talk on this page.
20 (I hear New York, too.) Me—who?
Well, I like to eat, sleep, drink and be in love.
I like to work, read, learn, and understand life.
I like a pipe for a Christmas present,
or records—Bessie, bop, or Bach.[2]
25 I guess being colored doesn't make me *not* like
the same things other folks like who are other races.

---

1. **college,** Columbia University, where Hughes studied for one year.
2. **Bessie, bop, or Bach.** Bessie Smith was one of the greatest blues singers of the early twentieth century. Bop is a form of jazz. Johann Sebastian Bach (1685–1750) was an important composer of classical music.

So will my page be colored that I write?
Being me, it will not be white.
But it will be
30 a part of you, instructor.
You are white—
yet a part of me, as I am a part of you.

That's American.
Sometimes perhaps you don't want to be a part of me.
35 Nor do I often want to be a part of you.
But we are, that's true!
As I learn from you,
I guess you learn from me—
although you're older—and white—
40 and somewhat more free.

This is my page for English B.

▲ Blues singer Bessie Smith was known as the "Empress of the Blues," which is
also the title of this 1974 collage by Romare Bearden. What does the collage
express about Smith's performances?

In Response to Executive Order 9066:
All Americans of Japanese Descent Must Report to Relocation Centers

Dwight Okita

Dear Sirs:
Of course I'll come. I've packed my galoshes
and three packets of tomato seeds. Denise calls them
love apples. My father says where we're going
5 they won't grow.

I am a fourteen-year-old girl with bad spelling
and a messy room. If it helps any, I will tell you
I have always felt funny using chopsticks
and my favorite food is hot dogs.
10 My best friend is a white girl named Denise—
we look at boys together. She sat in front of me
all through grade school because of our names:
O'Connor, Ozawa. I know the back of Denise's head very well.

I tell her she's going bald. She tells me I copy on tests.
15 We're best friends.

I saw Denise today in Geography class.
She was sitting on the other side of the room.
"You're trying to start a war," she said, "giving secrets
away to the Enemy.[1] Why can't you keep your big
20 mouth shut?"

I didn't know what to say.
I gave her a packet of tomato seeds
and asked her to plant them for me, told her
when the first tomato ripened
25 she'd miss me.

▲ Tanforan Assembly Center, San Bruno, California, 1942.

---

1. **the Enemy,** the Japanese, who were at war against the United States during World War II.

Fire AND ICE

ROBERT FROST

Some say the world will end in fire,
Some say in ice.
From what I've tasted of desire
I hold with those who favor fire.
But if it had to perish twice,
5 I think I know enough of hate
To say that for destruction ice
Is also great
And would suffice.[1]

---

1. **suffice** (sə fīs′), v. be enough; be sufficient.

▲ John P. Stewart, *The Age of Ice & Fire, 1975*. Compare
the mood of this piece with the mood of the poem.

After Reading

Making Connections

Shaping Your Response

1. Which narrator do you identify with the most? Why?

2. Imagine you are Langston Hughes's instructor. Tell what grade you will give him for "Theme for English B" and explain why.

Analyzing the Poems

3. What characteristics of the speaker make the poem "In Response to Executive Order 9066" **ironic?**

4. What do fire and ice **symbolize,** or represent, in "Fire and Ice"?

Extending the Ideas

5. 👣 If you wanted to reach someone who had strong prejudices against certain **groups** of people, which of these three poems would you share with that person? Explain.

Literary Focus: Mood

Writers establish a **mood,** or atmosphere, through the images, tone, and word choice in a piece. Use a graphic organizer like this one to analyze the mood of "Theme for English B" and "Fire and Ice."

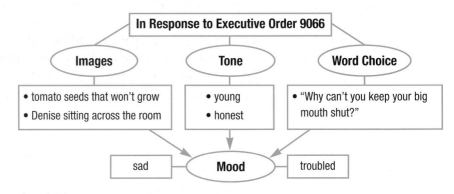

Expressing Your Ideas

Writing Choice

Writer's Notebook Update Let yourself be inspired by what the speakers in "Theme for English B" and "In Response to Executive Order 9066" revealed about themselves, and add a few more details about yourself to the letter you wrote before reading.

Another Option

Collage Effect Study "Empress of the Blues," the collage that appears on page 181, and discuss its mood, theme, and possible connection with "Theme for English B." Then make a **collage** that portrays the theme of one of the selections you have read in Unit 1.

Before Reading

I Chose to Remain by Rosa Parks, with Jim Haskins
Tolerance by E. M. Forster

Rosa Parks
born 1913

Rosa Parks, the daughter of a carpenter and a school-teacher, was active in the civil rights movement even before her historic arrest in 1955. Since then, she has received many honors for her continued dedication to civil rights.

E. M. Forster
1879–1970

Freedom was a common theme in the short stories, novels, essays, and radio broadcasts written by E. M. (Edward Morgan) Forster. His most famous novel, *A Passage to India* (1924), depicts the injustices of British rule in India.

Building Background

Overcoming Differences The two selections you are about to read present unique reflections on dealing with social and cultural differences. In the first piece, Rosa Parks recalls the historic evening in 1955 when she broke an Alabama state law by refusing to give up her bus seat to a white person. At that time in the South, "Jim Crow" laws legalized the segregation of schools, train cars, restaurants, buses, and even drinking fountains. African Americans either had limited access or were barred completely from these and other facilities. By the mid-1950s, a civil rights movement was under way to overturn these oppressive laws and work toward racial equality.

The second piece, "Tolerance," is taken from a collection of essays that E. M. Forster broadcast over the radio during World War II. World War II was a global conflict, lasting from 1939–1945. It was the most destructive war in history, with battles fought in Europe, Asia, Africa, and the islands of the Pacific. In the essay, Forster contemplates what it will take to heal from the wounds of war.

Literary Focus

Theme The main idea in a piece of writing is called its **theme.** The theme is what links a story you have read to your own experiences. Not everyone finds the same theme in a work or gives it the same label, and many stories have more than one theme. To determine the theme of a piece, ask yourself while you read, "What does this situation remind me of? What kind of message about life's experiences can I glean from this piece?"

Writer's Notebook

Paradise *Utopia* (yü tō′pē ə) means an ideal place with perfect laws. In your notebook, write a list of laws that could make up the framework of a utopian society. As you read the selections, consider what laws you think each author would recommend for an ideal society.

Rosa Parks *with* Jim Haskins
I CHOSE TO REMAIN

One evening late in 1955, Rosa Parks was riding the bus home from work in Montgomery, Alabama. When the driver asked her to give up her seat to a white person, she refused, and was arrested for violating local segregation laws. The news of her arrest triggered a massive boycott by the African American community of all city buses in Montgomery. The boycott became a turning point in the struggle for civil rights, and Rosa Parks took her case all the way to the Supreme Court. In November, 1956, the Court outlawed segregation on local bus lines. In the following excerpt from her autobiography, Rosa Parks explains why she made her historic decision that fateful evening.

When I got off from work that evening of December 1, I went to Court Square as usual to catch the Cleveland Avenue bus home. I didn't look to see who was driving when I got on, and by the time I recognized him, I had already paid my fare. It was the same driver who had put me off the bus back in 1943, twelve years earlier. He was still tall and heavy, with red, rough-looking skin. And he was still mean-looking. I didn't know if he had been on that route before—they switched the drivers around sometimes. I do know that most of the time if I saw him on a bus, I wouldn't get on it.

I saw a vacant seat in the middle section of the bus and took it. I didn't even question why there was a vacant seat even though there were quite a few people standing in the back. If I had thought about it at all, I would probably have figured maybe someone saw me get on and did not take the seat but left it vacant for me. There was a man sitting next to the window and two women across the aisle.

The next stop was the Empire Theater, and some whites got on. They filled up the white seats, and one man was left standing. The driver looked back and noticed the man standing.

◄ One year after her arrest, Rosa Parks could legally sit anywhere she wanted to on the bus. The photographer was actually the man seated behind Rosa Parks. Why do you think he composed the picture in this way?

Then he looked back at us. He said, "Let me have those front seats," because they were the front seats of the black section. Didn't anybody move. We just sat right where we were, the four of us. Then he spoke a second time: "Y'all better make it light on yourselves and let me have those seats."

The man in the window seat next to me stood up, and I moved to let him pass by me, and then I looked across the aisle and saw that the two women were also standing. I moved over to the window seat. I could not see how standing up was going to "make it light" for me. The more we gave in and complied, the worse they treated us.

I thought back to the time when I used to sit up all night and didn't sleep, and my grandfather would have his gun right by the fireplace, or if he had his one-horse wagon going anywhere, he always had his gun in the back of the wagon. People always say that I didn't give up my seat because I was tired, but that isn't true. I was not tired physically, or no more tired than I usually was at the end of a working day. I was not old, although some people have an image of me as being old then. I was forty-two. No, the only tired I was, was tired of giving in.

The driver of the bus saw me still sitting there, and he asked was I going to stand up. I said, "No." He said, "Well, I'm going to have you arrested." Then I said, "You may do that." These were the only words we said to each other. I didn't even know his name, which was James Blake, until we were in court together. He got out of the bus and stayed outside for a few minutes, waiting for the police.

As I sat there, I tried not to think about what might happen. I knew that anything was possible. I could be manhandled or beaten. I could be arrested. People have asked me if it occurred to me then that I could be the test case the NAACP had been looking for. I did not think about that at all. In fact if I had let myself think too deeply about what might happen to me, I might have gotten off the bus. But I chose to remain.

tolerance

E. M. Forster

Surely the only sound foundation for a civilization is a sound state of mind. Architects, contractors, international commissioners, marketing boards, broadcasting corporations will never, by themselves, build a new world. They must be inspired by the proper spirit, and there must be the proper spirit in the people for whom they are working.

What, though, is the proper spirit? There must be a sound state of mind before diplomacy or economics or trade conferences can function. But what state of mind is sound? Here we may differ. Most people, when asked what spiritual quality is needed to rebuild civilization, will reply, "Love." People must love one another, they say; nations must do likewise, and then the series of cataclysms[1] which is threatening to destroy us will be checked.

Respectfully but firmly, I disagree. Love is a great force in private life; it is indeed the greatest of all things. But love in public affairs does not work. It has been tried again and again: by the Christian civilizations of the Middle Ages, and also by the French Revolution,[2] a secular[3] move-

---

1. **cataclysm** (kat′ə kliz′əm), *n.* violent upheaval.
2. **French Revolution,** bloody revolution (1789–1799) that ousted the French monarchy and set up a republic.
3. **secular** (sek′yə lər), *adj.* not religious or sacred.

◄ The title of this painting by George Giusti is *"Civilization is a method of living, an attitude of equal respect for all men."–Jane Addams, 1933.* How does the painting portray the spirit of Jane Addams's remark?

ment which reasserted the Brotherhood of Man. And it has always failed. The idea that nations should love one another, or that a person in Portugal should love an unknown person in Peru—it is absurd, unreal, dangerous. It leads us into perilous and vague sentimentalism. "Love is what is needed," we chant, and then sit back and the world goes on as before. The fact is we can only love what we know personally. And we cannot know much. In public affairs, in the rebuilding of civilization, something much less dramatic and emotional is needed, namely, tolerance. Tolerance is a very dull virtue. It is boring. Unlike love, it has always had a bad press. It is negative. It merely means putting up with people, being able to stand things. No one has ever written an ode[4] to tolerance, or raised a statue to her. Yet this is the quality which will be most needed after the war. This is the state of mind which we are looking for. This is the only force which will enable different races and classes and interests to settle down together to the work of reconstruction.

The world is very full of people—appallingly[5] full; it has never been so full before, and they are all tumbling over each other. Most of these people one doesn't know and some of them one doesn't like; doesn't like the color of their skins, say, or the shapes of their noses, or the way they blow them or don't blow them, or the way they talk, or their clothes, or their fondness for jazz or their dislike of jazz, and so on. Well, what is one to do? There are two solutions. One of them is the Nazi solution. If you don't like people, kill them, banish them, segregate them, and then strut up and down proclaiming that you are the salt of the earth. The other way is much less thrilling, but it is on the whole the way of the democracies, and I prefer it. If you don't like people, put up with them as well as you can. Don't try to love them. You can't, and you'll only strain yourself. But try

to tolerate them. On the basis of that tolerance a civilized future may be built. Certainly I can see no other foundation for the postwar world.

For what it will most need is the negative virtues: not being huffy, touchy, irritable, revengeful. I have lost all faith in positive militant ideals; they can so seldom be carried out without thousands of human beings getting maimed or imprisoned. Phrases like "I will purge[6] this nation," "I will clean up this city," terrify and disgust me. They might not have mattered when the world was emptier; they are horrifying now, when one nation is mixed up with another, when one city cannot be organically separated from its neighbors.

I don't regard tolerance as a great eternally established divine principle, though I might perhaps quote "In My Father's House are many mansions"[7] in support of such a view. It's just a makeshift, suitable for an overcrowded and overheated planet. It carries on when love gives out, and love generally gives out as soon as we move away from our home and our friends, and stand among strangers in a queue[8] for potatoes. Tolerance is wanted in the queue; otherwise we think, "Why will people be so slow?" It is wanted in the tube,[9] or "Why will people be so fat?" It's wanted at the telephone, or "Why are they so deaf?" or conversely, "Why do they mumble?" It is wanted in the street, in the office, at the factory, and it is wanted above all between classes, races, religions, and nations. It's dull. And yet it entails[10] imagination. For you have all the time to be putting yourself in someone else's place. Which is a desirable spiritual exercise.

---

4. ode (ōd), *n.* a lyric poem full of noble feeling.
5. appallingly (ə pô′ling lē), *adv.* in a way that causes consternation and horror, dismay, or terror.
6. purge (pėrj), *v.* remove an undesired thing or person.
7. **In My . . . mansions,** from the Bible, John 14:2. There is room for people of all kinds in Heaven.
8. queue (kyü), *n.* British term for a line of people, automobiles, etc.
9. tube (tüb), *n.* British term for subway.
10. entail (en tāl′), *v.* impose or require.

After Reading

Making Connections

Shaping Your Response

1. If you were in Rosa Parks's situation, would you have kept your seat on the bus or given it up? Give some reasons for your answer.

2. Draw this continuum and place an X in response to this question: How tolerant do you think the world will be one hundred years from now? Compare your answer with your classmates' in a discussion.

Much less tolerant ———————————————— **Much more tolerant**

3. Which do you think will help people get along better—love or tolerance? Explain your answer.

Analyzing the Selections

4. As an African American, Rosa Parks belongs to a **group** that has experienced discrimination. How did this influence her decision to stay in her seat?

5. Describe the **tone** of "I Chose to Remain" and find three or four examples from the selection that convey it.

6. Explain the circumstances under which Forster delivered his essay. Why was it important to him to share these ideas with people?

Extending the Ideas

7. When has tolerance worked? Give some examples from history or from your own experience.

8. What are some aspects of today's world where you feel more tolerance is needed? Make a list and share it with a small group.

Literary Focus: Theme

An idea that links a literary work to real-life issues is its **theme.** A writer may directly state the theme, but the theme may also be implied. A piece of writing may have more than one theme.

- What is the topic, or subject, of Forster's essay? of Parks's memoir?

- What main idea, or **theme,** does each author express about the topic?

- Find and quote where the theme is either stated or implied in each selection.

- Do the two selections have any common themes? If so, state them.

Vocabulary Study

Write the word from the vocabulary list that best completes the meaning of each sentence.

appallingly
cataclysm
entail
ode
purge

1. A poet might write an ____ to love.

2. Building tolerance in a society can be an ____ difficult task.

3. A dictator might ____ his country of people who disagree with him.

4. Rebuilding a country after a war would probably ____ a lot of hard work.

5. An unexpected ____ may threaten the stability of a nation and its people.

Expressing Your Ideas

Writing Choices

Writer's Notebook Update Before you read the selections, you made a list in your notebook of "laws" that would make a perfect society. Based on what you learned from the selections, write down a brief list of the laws that either Rosa Parks or E. M. Forster would expect a utopia to have.

Read My Plates Using heavy paper or cardboard, design a personalized **license plates** that contains your message for peace. You can use shortened forms of words (TOLERNCE) or letters and numbers that sound like words (RU4PEACE). Remember: you are limited to a total of eight letters, numbers, and spaces. Display your license plate for the rest of the class.

Other Options

Picture This Choose pictures from magazines or newspapers that show situations that E. M. Forster would view as exemplifying love and situations that would exemplify tolerance. Use them to make two separate **collages.** Can a classmate tell which collage is which?

Nice to Meet You What might Rosa Parks and E. M. Forster have to say to each other? With a small group, stage a **talk show segment** in which Parks and Forster talk with each other and answer questions from the audience.

Dealing with Differences

Strength in Diversity

Multicultural Connection
In the United States, cultural diversity is spicing up the arts, as this article from *Time* magazine illustrates.

The Art of Diversity

by Christopher John Farley

Culture in America is likely to be spelled these days with a hyphen. Watch it on TV. There's Cuban-American singing star Gloria Estefan in a music video on MTV Latino. See it at the cinema. The film version of *The Joy Luck Club,* based on the popular novel by Chinese-American author Amy Tan, could be playing nearby. Theater? There's the modern-dance show *Griot New York,* directed by Jamaican-American choreographer Garth Fagan. Poetry? Buy a book of verse by St. Lucian-born, Nobel-prize-winning poet Derek Walcott, who teaches at Boston University. Painting? New York's Asia Society is holding a show that tours the country featuring Asian-American visual artists who emigrated from Vietnam, Thailand, and elsewhere in Asia.

And that's just the beginning. American culture used to be depicted as a Eurocentric melting pot into which other cultures were stirred and absorbed. The recent waves of new-comers have changed that. Today it seems more like a street

Choreographer Garth Fagan celebrates the immigrant experience through dance.

© Jonathan Atkin

fair, with various booths, foods, and peoples, all mixing on common sidewalks.

The new cultural carnival is most apparent in music. The New York-based, Irish-American group Black 47, which mixes rap, reggae and traditional Irish melodies, has appeared on both the *Tonight Show* and *Late Night with Conan O'Brien*. The Los Angeles rap trio Cypress Hill, which includes an Italian American, a Cuban American, and a member who is of Cuban and Mexican descent, released a hit album that started out at No. 1 on *Billboard* magazine's album chart. Latin music has become such a significant force in pop music that MTV launched MTV Latino as a separate Spanish-language edition.

Cuban-born Estefan, with her dance-floor blend of R. and B. and Cuban polyrhythms, has established herself as the queen of the new Latin sound. Arriving in Miami from Havana when she was two years old, she grew up in a household immersed in traditional Cuban ballads. By the first grade, she was also listening to British-invasion bands. "It was natural to blend both elements," says Estefan. "When immigrants come to America they bring their culture, and that culture becomes part of a new country. It makes everyone stronger."

The fashion industry has also felt the impact of newcomers. Immigrants from Asia have brought a clean, elegant new look to clothing design. Among them is Han Feng, who left Hangzhou, China, in 1985. Now head of her own design company, she sells easy-to-wear, simply shaped clothes to Bloomingdale's and Saks.

African clothing, filtered through rap culture, influences fashion as well. The L.A.-based firm Threads for Life (also known as Cross Colours) sells hip-hop fashion inspired by urban youth and African designers, such as overalls with colorful *kente*-cloth patches. "It becomes not just a pair of jeans, but something that *means* something," says firm co-owner Carl Jones.

Gloria Estefan blends Cuban rhythms with American pop music in her widely popular songs.

Other artists have turned their sights on the nature of the immigrant experience itself. Choreographer Fagan's touring show *Griot New York* features sets by noted sculptor Martin Puryear and music by trumpet virtuoso Wynton Marsalis. Employing a multiethnic troupe, *Griot* seeks to capture the drama of immigration. Says Fagan: "It's a celebration of New York City, of West Indians, Indians, and Africans, of big urban metropolises that are always being dumped on."

The celebration was a long time coming. To be an immigrant artist is to be a hyphen away from one's roots, and still a thousand miles away. But it is often that link to a foreign land—another way of seeing things—that allows such artists to contribute ideas to American culture that are fresh and new. That slim hyphen, that thin line that joins individual Americans to their past, is also what connects all America to its future.

Responding

1. What are some of the unique perspectives that immigrants can bring to the arts?

2. Who are your favorite artists? How do their cultural backgrounds influence their art?

Science Connection

The diverse forms of plant and animal life found in the world's rain forests have already changed and enriched our lives, and may be essential to our future survival.

Treasures of the Rain Forest

You won't find buried treasure or lost cities of gold in the rain forest. Nevertheless, it may be the most valuable land on earth. The greatest treasures of the rain forest are its trees and plants. Green plants take in carbon dioxide and give off oxygen—the very reverse of what human beings do. Without the oxygen produced by plants, we'd have a hard time staying alive.

Besides the very air we breathe, the rain forest also produces many of the things that we like to eat— bananas and chocolate, for example. About one fourth of all medicines come from plants found in the rain forest. And so far, only 1 percent of rain forest plants have been examined for their healing properties.

The leaves of the rosy periwinkle are used to treat certain forms of cancer. The plant once grew only in the rain forest of Madagascar. Its medicinal properties came to light when native healers told researchers about it.

Manioc is a root that provides many people in tropical rain forests with their main source of starch. You may have eaten a product of the manioc root for dessert. What is it? ➤

Care to try an iguanaburger? Dr. Dagmar Werner encourages Central American rain forest farmers to raise iguanas for meat. She hopes to encourage people to stop clearing the forest for cattle ranching. ➤

"Sustainable harvesting" means getting products from trees every year instead of cutting down the trees. One study showed that a two-and-a-half-acre plot in Peru would yield $1,000 worth of timber or $425 worth of nuts, fruit, and rubber. But the $425 could be earned every year if the trees weren't cut down. ➤

About 80 percent of what we eat first grew in the tropics. Bananas came from Southeast Asia, though they are now grown wherever the climate is suitable. Still, only a small percentage of fruits growing wild in rain forests has been grown for sale around the world. Imagine how many undiscovered taste sensations are still to be found. ▼

▲ No human-made rubber substitute resists heat as well as natural rubber, which is a necessity for airplane tires, among other products.

The copaiba tree gives off a sap that is pure diesel oil. As of 1990, twenty percent of Brazil's diesel fuel came from the copaiba. The difference between this and fossil fuels (gas, oil, coal) is that the tree will produce oil as long as it lives.

Responding

1. Name three ways that your life might be different if the rain forests disappeared.

2. Explain how a rain forest is an example of "strength in diversity."

Writing Workshop

A Plea for Tolerance

Assignment In this part of the unit, E.M. Forster writes about one strategy for dealing with differences: tolerance. Write a letter to one of the fictional characters in this part of the unit persuading him or her to adopt Forster's views on tolerance.

WRITER'S BLUEPRINT

Product	A letter of advice and encouragement
Purpose	To persuade someone to be more tolerant
Audience	A fictional character
Specs	To write an effective letter, you should:

❑ Write to the narrator in "The Scarlet Ibis" or Juliette in "Waiting" about the difficulties this character has with being tolerant. Imagine that your letter could influence the character and change the course of his or her life.

❑ Use standard friendly letter format. Begin by introducing yourself and stating your purpose for writing.

❑ Describe the character's difficulties with tolerance. Use specific details from the story, including quotations where appropriate, to illustrate each difficulty. Take care not to overgeneralize and make extreme statements that aren't really true.

❑ Give the character advice on how he or she might have handled things better. Take care not to use an accusing tone that might put your audience on the defensive. Be sympathetic and constructive.

❑ Conclude by speculating on what might have happened differently if the character had followed your advice, and give convincing reasons why. Include some words of encouragement.

❑ Follow the rules of grammar, usage, spelling, and mechanics. Take special care to use apostrophes correctly.

Review the literature and take notes on Forster's essay and on the difficulties that the narrator in "The Scarlet Ibis" and Juliette in "Waiting" have with being tolerant. In a small group, discuss the examples you found.

Chart a character's problems with tolerance. Complete the following chart with notes about the character you'll be writing to.

Character	Difficulties with Being Tolerant	How the Character Reacts	My Advice to the Character	If You Had Followed My Advice . . .
narrator in "The Scarlet Ibis"				

LITERARY SOURCE

" 'Aw, come on, Doodle,' I urged. 'You can do it. Do you want to be different from everybody else when you start school?'

" 'Does it make any difference?'

" 'It certainly does,' I said. 'Now come on,' and I helped him up."

from "The Scarlet Ibis" by James Hurst

As you make notes about your character, think carefully about the conclusions you're drawing and the opinions you're expressing. Make sure you've thought things through thoroughly. Otherwise, you might end up going to extremes and **overgeneralizing.** See the Revising Strategy in Step 3 of this lesson.

Plan your letter. First, review your notes and chart. Think about the tone you will use in addressing your audience. Then use a plan like the following to help organize your letter.

Introduction
- The character you're writing to
- A friendly way to introduce yourself
- Why you're writing

Body
- A difficulty the character had with being tolerant
  Specific detail or quotation to illustrate it
- Another difficulty the character had with being tolerant
  Specific detail or quotation to illustrate it
  and so on . . .
- Advice on how to handle these difficulties better

Conclusion
- Speculations on what might have happened if advice had been followed
- Reasons why
- Words of encouragement
- A friendly closing

OR . . .
Instead of just showing your partner your plan, talk through it together. Try to compose your letter out loud as you talk, in bits and pieces, and have your partner respond.

Ask a partner to review your plan.

✔ Have I identified my character's difficulties with being tolerant? Have I given sound advice on how to handle these difficulties better?

✔ Have I followed the Specs in the Writer's Blueprint?

Use your partner's comments to help you revise your plan.

STEP 2 DRAFTING

Before you write, review the form for a friendly letter in the Language and Grammar Handbook. Then review your prewriting notes and writing plan. Finally, look over the Writer's Blueprint one more time.

As you draft, don't spend a lot of time correcting mistakes in spelling or punctuation. Remember, this is just a first draft. For now, concentrate on getting the ideas from your writing plan down on paper. Here are some drafting tips.

OR . . .
You might want to come right out and say something like, "I don't mean to sound bossy" if you think it will help make the tone of your letter more friendly. If you do, make sure your letter lives up to this statement.

- As you introduce yourself, set a friendly tone by mentioning something you might have in common with your character.

- As you give advice, use expressions like *although, in contrast,* and *on the contrary* to contrast what the character did with what you think he or she should have done.

- To avoid sounding bossy or accusing, phrase sentences of advice as "I might . . ." rather than "You should . . . ."

STEP 3 REVISING

Ask a partner for comments on your draft before you revise it.

✔ Have I followed the Specs in the Writer's Blueprint?

✔ Have I made it clear exactly who I'm writing to and why?

✔ Have I used the standard form for a friendly letter?

✔ Have I taken care not to go to extremes and overgeneralize?

Revising Strategy

Avoiding Overgeneralizing

When you draw conclusions, take care not to go to extremes and overgeneralize—make absolute statements that aren't really true. Overgeneralizations are often introduced by absolute words such as *everyone, all, always,* and *never.*

OVERGENERALIZATION: You **always** made Henrietta cry.
CORRECTED VERSION: You **sometimes** made Henrietta cry.

The story does *not* say that Juliette made Henrietta cry *all* the time. To avoid overgeneralizing like this, make sure you can back up absolute statements with plenty of evidence. Also, reserve absolute words like *always* for statements that you are completely sure about. Notice how this writer corrected an extreme statement that a partner spotted.

> I can understand why you wouldn't want to pull around your
>
> handicapped brother everywhere you go, but you should have realized
>
> that he didn't like being handicapped any more than you liked to lug him
>
> around. I saw that you resented your brother because of his disabilities
>
> by being mean to him ~~all the time.~~ *sometimes* An example was when you showed
>
> him his coffin and made him touch it.
>
> *Are you sure he was mean all the time?*

STEP 4 EDITING

Ask a partner to review your revised draft before you edit. When you edit, look for errors in grammar, usage, spelling, and mechanics. Make sure you've used apostrophes correctly.

Editing Strategy

Using Apostrophes Correctly

Use apostrophes to make nouns possessive.

- Singular nouns are usually made possessive by adding an apostrophe and *s:* **one girl's raincoat.**

  Plural nouns that end in *s* are usually made possessive by adding an apostrophe after the *s:* **five girls' raincoats**.

  Apostrophes are also used to form contractions with pronouns and verbs and with verbs and *not:*   **he will→he'll   is not→isn't**

- Caution: Don't use apostrophes to make nouns plural.

FOR REFERENCE
Turn to the Language and Grammar Handbook at the back of this text for more information about the use of apostrophes.

COMPUTER TIP
Use the Find function to locate apostrophes in your letter so you can doublecheck whether you've used them correctly.

STEP 5 PRESENTING

- In your group, role-play a scene in wnich the character you chose reads your letter aloud and then responds to it.

- Make a poster to encourage tolerance that includes images of intolerance from the literature and images of your tolerant advice in action.

STEP 6 LOOKING BACK

Self-Evaluate. How would *you* evaluate your letter? Look back at the Writer's Blueprint and give yourself a score for each point, from 6 (superior) to 1 (inadequate).

Reflect. Think about what you learned from writing this letter as you write answers to these questions.

✔ How could you apply your advice about tolerance in your own life?

✔ What was the hardest step in writing your letter? How could you have made it easier?

For Your Working Portfolio Add your advice letter and your Reflect responses to your working portfolio.

Beyond Print

Tips for effective listening:

Pay attention. Look in the speaker's eyes. Watch the person's expressions and body language as he or she speaks.

Think as you listen. Relate what the speaker is saying to your personal experience.

Form a mental picture. Try to visualize what the speaker is telling you.

Take notes. Don't try to record the interview word for word. Just write down the highlights as you hear them.

Give the speaker feedback. Report back to the speaker what you have heard until you get it right.

Interviewing a Classmate

Good listening skills are essential in many situations. For example, members of an athletic team have to listen to the coach and to each other. Pilots have to listen to air traffic controllers. Doctors have to listen to their patients, and vice versa.

Listening to your classmates is also important. Good listening skills will help you discover the similarities you share and the differences that make your relationships with each other that much more interesting. The following activity is designed to help you learn a little more about your classmates as you develop effective listening skills.

1. Find a partner, preferably someone you don't know very well. One of you will be the listener/reporter, and the other will be the interviewee.

2. The listener/reporter should prepare about six questions for the interviewee concerning a special occasion. Consider questions like these:

   - What is your favorite special occasion? Why?

   - What do you do to celebrate it?

   - Do you prepare special foods? Describe them.

   - Are there special ceremonies? Can you describe them?

   - When does this event occur? How long does it last?

3. Conduct the interview.

4. Repeat the activity, but switch roles.

5. Present an oral report to the class that describes your partner's special occasion.

Activity Options

1. After hearing the oral reports, discuss the similarities and differences in the ways you and your classmates celebrate special occasions.

2. Learn a song, dance, or game from a classmate by following spoken instructions.

Multicultural Connections

Communication

Part One: The Games People Play In "Rules of the Game," communication between Meimei and her mother is hampered by generational and cultural differences. In "The Cask of Amontillado," Montresor deliberately blocks honest communication with Fortunato as part of his plan for revenge.

▪ Compare and contrast how Meimei, Fortunato, the boy and girl in "Checkouts," and Dave Barry deal with obstacles to communication.

Perspective

Part Two: Mistaken Impressions In "The Necklace," Mme. Loisel's bitter perspective on life is the result of her desire to be a member of the richest social class.

▪ Explain what social, cultural, or other factors influence the perspectives of three of these characters from the unit: Meimei, General Zaroff, Vera, Harriet Watkins, and Juliette.

Groups

Part Three: Dealing with Differences Each character in these selections belongs to a number of different groups, based on culture, values, age, gender, nationality, religion, and other aspects of identity.

▪ In "A Stolen Party," how do the groups that Rosaura and Luciana belong to both bring them together and pull them apart?

Activities

1. Identify a scene that shows a communication problem in one of the stories in Unit 1. With a small group, present a skit showing how the outcome of the story might have been different if real communication had taken place.

2. On a chart, show how the perspectives of three characters change in the selections, and what factors influence that change.

3. Choose a character, and make a badge for each group your character belongs to: social class, culture, nationality, and so on. Attend a class mixer wearing your badges, and find out whether you have anything in common with other characters in the unit.

Independent and Group Projects

Writing

Inspired by Life Ernest Hemingway based his short story "A Day's Wait" on an incident that occurred when his young son was ill. Try writing a short story inspired by a real-life event you have observed. Don't feel you must tell exactly what happened; instead, use the actual event as a launching pad toward an interesting, imaginative story, full of realistic details.

Role Play

Literary Luncheon As a class, plan a "literary luncheon," and come dressed as the authors and characters you met in Unit 1. Before the luncheon, plan the menu, which could include food mentioned in the selections such as rushwash tea. During the luncheon, talk with the people around you about your life, hobbies, beliefs, problems, and plans for the future. Be sure to stay in character throughout the meal.

Media

Facing Reality—on TV The characters in the selections must deal with the realities of life in many different ways. Plan a talk show segment that features a number of the characters from Unit 1. Each character should explain to the host and to the audience how he or she had to "face reality" and what was learned from the experience. If possible, videotape the show.

Drama

A Change of Setting The actions of characters are often affected by the setting of the story. But what if the same characters are placed in a very different setting? Imagine what might happen, for example, if Framton Nuttel from "The Open Window" ended up on Shiptrap Island from "The Most Dangerous Game." With a small group, prepare a skit that shows one or more characters from one story placed in the setting of another story. Present your dramatization to the class.

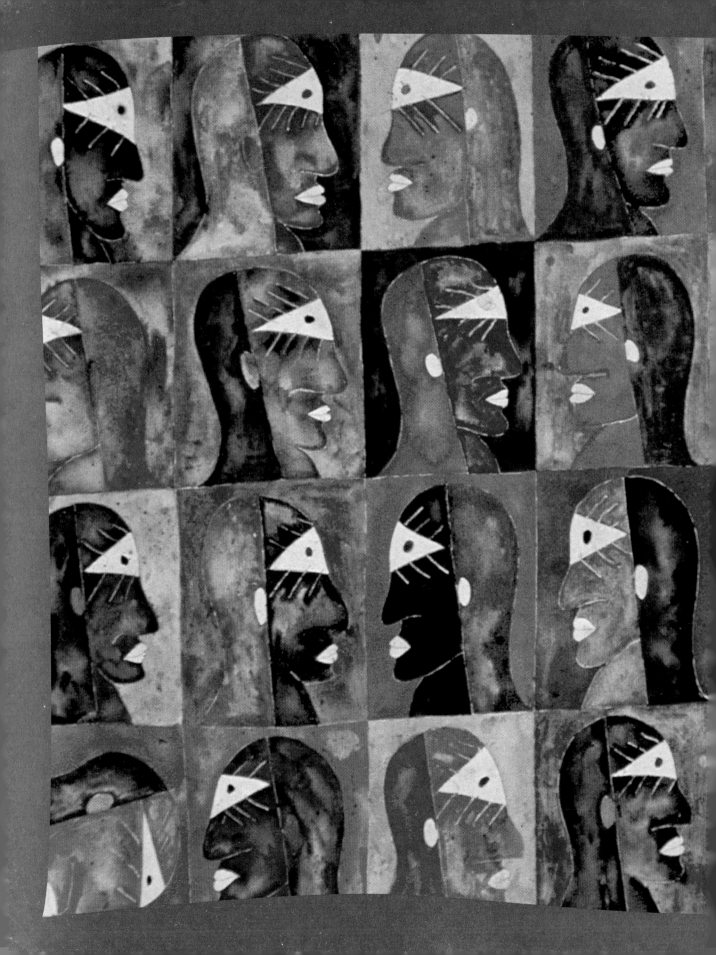

Getting the Message

Distant Voices

Reaching Out

READING A

Plays offer us a chance to experience the drama of life as actors convey it to us. For the few hours that a play or a film unfolds before us, we can lose ourselves in another world. When the lights go on again, we're back to our own reality, a bit changed, perhaps, by what we've experienced.

The first play in this unit, *Sorry, Right Number,* is actually a screenplay—a play that has been created for film or television. The second play, *The Miracle Worker,* was written for the stage. While there are some differences between a screenplay and a stage play, both have been written to be performed for an audience. Both types of drama can open the door to worlds you might otherwise never visit.

DIALOGUE AND STAGE DIRECTIONS

The written text of a play is a kind of guidebook for the director, actors, and all the technical people involved in the production. It consists mainly of **stage directions,** suggestions on how to stage a play, and **dialogue,** lines or speeches for the actors.

Stage directions have a number of functions:
- to describe the **setting**—where and when the action takes place;
- to describe the **characters;**
- to tell the actors how and when to say their lines and move around onstage;
- to give instructions for **lighting** and **sound effects;**
- in screenplays, to give instructions for **camera moves.**

In this book, stage directions are set in *italic type*. Within speeches, they are further set off by parentheses. Characters' names appear in SMALL CAPITAL LETTERS.

Since much of what happens in a play is revealed through the conversation of the characters, the dialogue in a play usually has several purposes:
- to reveal the **characters** through their words;
- to create a **mood;**
- to move the **plot** along.

MODERN PLAY

ACTS AND SCENES

Longer plays are often divided into acts and scenes. These divisions may be purely technical—to give the audience a chance to rest and the stagehands time to change the set. But in some plays, the divisions also mark stages in plot and character development. For example, in a three-act play, the first act usually provides **exposition**, or background information, and introduces one or more **conflicts**. The second act develops the conflict and ends with some sort of **climax**. The third act shows a **resolution**, or ending.

TIPS FOR READING PLAYS

Study the cast of characters. Examine the cast of characters and refer back to it when necessary. You might also keep track of characters and critical events in your notebook. For example, as you read *The Miracle Worker*, jot down a list of the key events and how Helen is affected by them.

Pay attention to stage directions. Stage directions indicate how lines are to be delivered and provide insights into setting and characters. In *Sorry, Right Number*, Dennis speaks to his younger brother Jeff "with the utter finality only a big brother can manage." What does that tell you about the brothers?

Remember that a play is written to be acted. "Stage the play" in your imagination as you read.

The brilliant costumes and make-up in the Broadway musical *Cats* (far left) have captivated audiences for years. In Alfred Hitchcock's classic suspense film, *North by Northwest* (center), camera angles and special effects heighten the drama. In the play *The Miracle Worker* (above), the stage directions help re-create a meal-time battle between Helen Keller and Annie Sullivan.

Part One

Distant Voices

Are you a good listener? Do you know what to listen for? The following selections deal with real or imaginary situations where important messages arrive from the past, the future, or somewhere outside of time.

🐾 **Multicultural Connection** **Communication** is not always easy, especially across barriers imposed by culture, language, and time. What kinds of barriers to communication exist for the characters in the following selections? What role do language, culture, and other factors play in creating and overcoming these obstacles?

Before Reading

Sorry, Right Number

by Stephen King

Stephen King
born 1947

Growing up in Portland, Maine, Stephen King had a dark sense of humor and a fascination for horror films. His first writing venture was a satiric newspaper called *The Village Vomit,* which led to his suspension from high school. After college, he worked as a high school English teacher, spending his evenings writing fiction. His first published novel was *Carrie,* which was later made into a movie. King has written many popular novels, short stories, and screenplays. Some of his best-known books include *The Shining, The Stand, It,* and *Misery.* King lives in Maine with his wife and three children.

Building Background

What Number Were You Calling? The title of the screenplay you are about to read, *Sorry, Right Number,* was inspired by a famous 1948 movie called *Sorry, Wrong Number.* In that film, a phone call made to a wrong number leads a bedridden woman to discover she is marked for murder. In the screenplay you are about to read, a phone call again leads to unexpected and frightening events. After reading *Sorry, Right Number,* you can decide whether or not the title is appropriate.

Literary Focus

Foreshadowing Writers often indicate what will happen in a story by giving clues early on. This technique is called **foreshadowing** because the author creates "shadows" that represent or hint at events before they happen. Foreshadowing is common in horror stories, since it helps create a sense of impending disaster. As you read *Sorry, Right Number,* note how Stephen King uses foreshadowing to heighten the suspense.

Writer's Notebook

Frightfully Good You've probably experienced the strange thrill of watching a horror movie. But what makes a movie frightening? Think of a scary event in your life and jot down some notes about the specific circumstances that made it scary. Based on your notes, make a list of elements you would include in a horror film.

SORRY, RIGHT NUMBER

Stephen King

Author's Note: Screenplay abbreviations are simple and exist, in this author's opinion, mostly to make those who write screenplays feel like lodge brothers.[1] In any case, you should be aware that CU *means* close-up; ECU *means* extreme close-up; INT. *means* interior; EXT. *means* exterior; B.G. *means* background; POV *means* point of view. *Probably most of you knew all that stuff to begin with, right?*

CHARACTERS

KATIE ⎫
BILL ⎪
POLLY ⎪
DENNIS ⎬ THE WEIDERMANS
CONNIE ⎪
JEFF ⎭

SOBBING VOICE ⎫
FRIEDA ⎪
KATIE'S MOTHER ⎪
OPERATOR ⎬ VOICES
MINISTER ⎪
ANNOUNCER ⎭

DAWN

GROUNDSKEEPER

HANK

GROOM AND ASSORTED WEDDING GUESTS

FADE IN ON:

KATIE WEIDERMAN'S MOUTH, ECU

She's speaking into the telephone. Pretty mouth; in a few seconds we'll see that the rest of her is just as pretty.

KATIE. Bill? Oh, he says he doesn't feel very well, but he's always like that between books . . . can't sleep, thinks every headache is the first symptom of a brain tumor . . . once he gets going on something new, he'll be fine.

SOUND, B.G: THE TELEVISION

THE CAMERA DRAWS BACK. KATIE *is sitting in the kitchen phone nook, having a good gab with her*

---

1. **lodge brothers,** members of the same club.

▲ In this illustration by John Nickle, how does the perspective, or angle of view, affect the mood?

*sister while she idles through some catalogues. We should notice one not-quite-ordinary thing about the phone she's on: it's the sort with two lines. There are lighted buttons to show which ones are engaged. Right now only one—*KATIE'*s—is. As* KATIE *continues her conversation,* THE CAMERA SWINGS AWAY FROM HER, TRACKS ACROSS THE KITCHEN, *and through the arched doorway that leads into the family room.*

KATIE *(voice, fading).* Oh, I saw Janie Charlton today . . . yes! Big as a *house!* . . .

She fades. The TV gets louder. There are three kids: JEFF, *eight,* CONNIE, *ten, and* DENNIS, *thirteen.* Wheel of Fortune *is on, but they're not watching. Instead they're engaged in that great pastime, Fighting About What Comes On Later.*

JEFF. Come *onnn!* It was his first *book!*

CONNIE. His first *gross* book.

DENNIS. We're gonna watch *Cheers* and *Wings,* just like we do every week, Jeff.

DENNIS *speaks with the utter finality only a big brother can manage. "Wanna talk about it some more and see how much pain I can inflict on your scrawny body, Jeff?" his face says.*

JEFF. Could we at least tape it?

CONNIE. We're taping CNN for Mom. She said she might be on the phone with Aunt Lois for quite awhile.

JEFF. How can you tape CNN, for God's sake? It *never stops!*

DENNIS. That's what she likes about it.

CONNIE. And don't say God's sake, Jeffie—you're not old enough to talk about God except in church.

JEFF. Then don't call me Jeffie.

CONNIE. Jeffie, Jeffie, Jeffie.

JEFF *gets up, walks to the window, and looks out into the dark. He's really upset.* DENNIS *and* CONNIE, *in the grand tradition of older brothers and sisters, are delighted to see it.*

DENNIS. Poor Jeffie.

CONNIE. I think he's gonna commit suicide.

JEFF *(turns to them).* It was his *first* book! Don't you guys even care?

CONNIE. Rent it down at the Video Stop tomorrow, if you want to see it so bad.

JEFF. They don't rent R-rated pictures to little kids and you know it!

CONNIE *(dreamily).* Shut up, it's Vanna! I *love* Vanna!

JEFF. Dennis—

DENNIS. Go ask Dad to tape it on the VCR in his office and quit being such a totally annoying little booger.

JEFF *crosses the room, poking his tongue out at Vanna White as he goes.* THE CAMERA FOLLOWS *as he goes into the kitchen.*

KATIE. . . . so when he asked me if *Polly* had tested strep positive,[2] I had to remind him she's away at prep school . . . and gosh, Lois, I miss her . . .

JEFF *is just passing through, on his way to the stairs.*

KATIE. Will you kids *please* be quiet?

JEFF *(glum).* They'll be quiet. *Now.*

He goes up the stairs, a little dejected. KATIE *looks after him for a moment, loving and worried.*

KATIE. They're squabbling again. Polly used to keep them in line, but now that she's away at school . . . I don't know . . . maybe sending her to Bolton wasn't such a hot idea. Sometimes when she calls home she sounds so *unhappy* . . .

INT. BELA LUGOSI[3] AS DRACULA, CU

Drac's standing at the door of his Transylvanian castle. Someone has pasted a comic-balloon coming out of his mouth which reads: "Listen! My children of the night! What music they make!" The poster is on a door but we only see this as JEFF *opens it and goes into his father's study.*

---

2. **tested strep positive,** found out from a medical test that she had the strep throat virus.
3. **Bela Lugosi** (bĕ′lä lü gō′zē), well-known actor who played the character of Dracula in the early film version of the book.

INT. A PHOTOGRAPH OF KATIE, CU

THE CAMERA HOLDS, THEN PANS[4] SLOWLY RIGHT. *We pass another photo, this one of* POLLY, *the daughter away at school. She's a lovely girl of sixteen or so. Past* POLLY *is* DENNIS . . . *then* CONNIE . . . *then* JEFF.

THE CAMERA CONTINUES TO PAN AND ALSO WIDENS OUT *so we can see* BILL WEIDERMAN, *a man of about forty-four. He looks tired. He's peering into the word-processor on his desk, but his mental crystal ball must be taking the night off, because the screen is blank. On the walls we see framed book-covers. All of them are spooky. One of the titles is* Ghost Kiss.

JEFF *comes up quietly behind his dad. The carpet muffles his feet.* BILL *sighs and shuts off the word-cruncher.[5] A moment later* JEFF *claps his hands on his father's shoulders.*

JEFF. BOOGA-BOOGA!

BILL. Hi, Jeffie.

He turns in his chair to look at his son, who is disappointed.

JEFF. How come you didn't get scared?

BILL. Scaring is my business. I'm case-hardened.[6] Something wrong?

JEFF. Daddy, can I watch the first hour of *Ghost Kiss* and you tape the rest? Dennis and Connie are hogging *everything*.

BILL *swivels to look at the book-jacket,* <u>*bemused.*</u>[7]

BILL. You sure you want to watch *that*, champ? It's pretty—

JEFF. *Yes!*

INT. KATIE, IN THE PHONE NOOK

In this shot, we clearly see the stairs leading to her husband's study behind her.

KATIE. I *really* think Jeff needs the orthodontic[8] work but you know Bill—

The other line rings. The other light stutters.

KATIE. That's just the other line, Bill will—

But now we see BILL *and* JEFF *coming downstairs behind her.*

BILL. Honey, where're the blank videotapes? I can't find any in the study and—

KATIE (*to* BILL). *Wait!* (*to* LOIS) Gonna put you on hold a sec, Lo.

She does. Now both lines are blinking. She pushes the top one, where the new call has just come in.

KATIE. Hello, Weiderman residence.

SOUND: DESPERATE SOBBING.

SOBBING VOICE (*filter*). Take . . . please take . . . t-t-

KATIE. Polly? Is that you? What's wrong?

SOUND: SOBBING. *It's awful, heartbreaking.*

SOBBING VOICE (*filter*). Please—quick—

SOUND: SOBBING . . . *Then,* CLICK! *A broken connection.*

KATIE. Polly, calm down! Whatever it is can't be that b—

HUM OF AN OPEN LINE.

JEFF *has wandered toward the TV room, hoping to find a blank tape.*

BILL. Who was that?

Without looking at her husband or answering him, KATIE *slams the lower button in again.*

KATIE. Lois? Listen, I'll call you back. That was Polly, and she sounded very upset. No . . . she hung up. Yes. I will. Thanks.

She hangs up.

BILL (*concerned*). It was Polly?

KATIE. Crying her head off. It sounded like she was trying to say "Please take me home" . . . I knew that damn school was bumming her out . . . Why I ever let you talk me into it . . .

She's rummaging frantically on her little phone desk. Catalogues go slithering to the floor around her stool.

---

4. **pan** (pan), *v.* move horizontally or vertically to take in a larger scene.
5. **word-cruncher** (wėrd crunch′ər), *n.* slang term for a computer.
6. **case-hardened** (kās härd′nd), *adj.* made callous or unfeeling from use or experience.
7. **bemused** (bi myüzd′), *adj.* confused; absorbed in thought.
8. **orthodontic** (ôr′thə don′tik), *adj.* of or having to do with a branch of dentistry that deals with straightening and adjusting teeth.

KATIE. *Connie did you take my address book?*

CONNIE *(voice)*. No, Mom.

BILL *pulls a battered book out of his back pocket and pages through it.*

BILL. I got it. Except—

KATIE. I know, damn dorm phone is always busy. Give it to me.

BILL. Honey, calm down.

KATIE. I'll calm down after I talk to her. She is sixteen, Bill. Sixteen-year-old girls are prone to depressive interludes.[9] Sometimes they even k . . . just give me the damn number!

BILL. 617-555-8641.

As she punches the numbers, THE CAMERA SLIDES IN TO CU.

KATIE. Come on, come on . . . don't be busy . . . just this once . . .

SOUND: CLICKS. *A pause. Then . . . the phone starts ringing.*

KATIE *(eyes closed)*. Thank You, God.

VOICE *(filter)*. Hartshorn Hall, this is Frieda. If you want Christine the Sex Queen, she's still in the shower, Arnie.

KATIE. Could you call Polly to the phone? Polly Weiderman? This is Kate Weiderman. Her mother.

VOICE *(filter)*. Oh, jeez! Sorry. I thought—hang on, please, Mrs. Weiderman.

SOUND: THE PHONE CLUNKS DOWN.

VOICE *(filter, and very faint)*. Polly? Pol? . . . Phone call! . . . It's your mother!

INT. A WIDER ANGLE ON THE PHONE NOOK, WITH BILL

BILL. Well?

KATIE. Somebody's getting her. I hope.

JEFF *comes back in with a tape.*

JEFF. I found one, Dad. Dennis hid 'em. As usual.

BILL. In a minute, Jeff. Go watch the tube.

JEFF. But—

BILL. I won't forget. Now go *on.*

JEFF *goes.*

KATIE. Come on, come on, come on . . .

BILL. Calm down, Katie.

KATIE *(snaps)*. If you'd heard her, you wouldn't tell me to calm down! She sounded—

POLLY *(filter, cheery voice)*. Hi, mom!

KATIE. Pol? Honey? Are you all right?

POLLY *(happy, bubbling voice)*. Am I *all right?* I aced my bio exam, got a B on my French Conversational Essay, and Ronnie Hansen asked me to the Harvest Ball. I'm so all right that if one more good thing happens to me today, I'll probably blow up like the *Hindenburg.*[10]

KATIE. You didn't just call me up, crying your head off?

We see by KATIE*'s face that she already knows the answer to this question.*

POLLY *(filter)*. Heck no!

KATIE. I'm glad about your test and your date, honey. I guess it was someone else. I'll call you back, okay?

POLLY *(filter)*. 'Kay. Say hi to Dad!

KATIE. I will.

INT. THE PHONE NOOK, WIDER

BILL. She okay?

KATIE. Fine. I could have *sworn* it was Polly, but . . . *she's* walking on air.

BILL. So it was a prank. Or someone who was crying so hard she dialed a wrong number . . . "through a shimmering film of tears," as we veteran[11] hacks[12] like to say.

KATIE. It was not a prank and it was not a wrong number! It was someone in *my family.*

BILL. Honey, you can't know that.

KATIE. No? If Jeffie called up, just crying, would you know it was him?

BILL *(struck by this)*. Yeah, maybe. I guess I might.

---

9. **depressive interlude,** period of depression.

10. *Hindenburg* (hin′dən bėrg′), famous inflated airship, or zeppelin, that exploded in flight in 1937.

11. veteran (vet′ər ən), *n.* person who has had much experience in some position, occupation, etc.

12. **hack** (hak), *n.* person hired to do routine work, especially literary work.

▲ David Hockney, *Unfinished Painting in Finished Photograph(s) 2nd April 1982*. From reading the title, can you figure out how the artist produced this piece?

She's not listening. She's punching numbers, fast.

BILL. Who you calling?

She doesn't answer him. SOUND: PHONE RINGS TWICE. *Then:*

OLDER FEMALE VOICE *(filter)*. Hello?

KATIE. Mom? Are you . . . *(She pauses.)* Did you call just a few seconds ago?

VOICE *(filter)*. No, dear . . . why?

KATIE. Oh . . . you know these phones. I was talking to Lois and I lost the other call.

VOICE *(filter)*. Well, it wasn't me. Kate, I saw the *prettiest* dress in La Boutique today, and—

KATIE. We'll talk about it later, Mom, okay?

VOICE *(filter)*. Kate, are you all right?

KATIE. I have . . . Mom, I think maybe I've got diarrhea. I have to go. 'Bye.

She hangs up. BILL *hangs on until she does, then he bursts into wild donkey-brays[13] of laughter.*

BILL. Oh boy . . . diarrhea . . . I gotta remember that the next time my agent calls . . . oh Katie, that was so cool—

KATIE *(almost screaming). This is not funny!*

BILL *stops laughing.*

INT. THE TV ROOM

JEFF *and* DENNIS *have been tussling.[14] They stop. All three kids look toward the kitchen.*

INT. THE PHONE NOOK, WITH BILL AND KATIE

KATIE. *I tell you it was someone in my family and she sounded*—oh, you don't understand. I *knew* that voice.

BILL. But if Polly's okay and your mom's okay . . .

KATIE *(positive).* It's Dawn.

BILL. Come on, hon, a minute ago you were sure it was Polly.

KATIE. It *had* to be Dawn. I was on the phone with Lois and Mom's okay so Dawn's the only other one it *could* have been. She's the youngest . . . I could have mistaken her for Polly . . . and she's out there in that farmhouse alone with the baby!

BILL *(startled).* What do you mean, alone?

KATIE. Jerry's in Burlington! It's Dawn! *Something's happened to Dawn!*

CONNIE *comes into the kitchen, worried.*

CONNIE. Mom? Is Aunt Dawn okay?

BILL. So far as we know, she's fine. Take it easy, doll. Bad to buy trouble before you know it's on sale.

KATIE *punches numbers and listens.* SOUND: *The* DAH-DAH-DAH *of a busy signal.* KATIE *hangs up.* BILL *looks a question at her with raised eyebrows.*

KATIE. Busy.

BILL. Katie, are you sure—

KATIE. She's the only one left—it had to be her. Bill, I'm scared. Will you drive me out there?

BILL *takes the phone from her.*

BILL. What's her number?

KATIE. 555-6169.

BILL *dials. Gets a busy. Hangs up and punches 0.*

OPERATOR *(filter).* Operator.

BILL. I'm trying to reach my sister-in-law, operator. The line is busy. I suspect there may be a problem. Can you break into the call, please?

INT. THE DOOR TO THE TV ROOM

All three kids are standing there, silent and worried.

INT. THE PHONE NOOK, WITH BILL AND KATIE

OPERATOR *(filter).* What is your name, sir?

BILL. William Weiderman. My number is—

OPERATOR *(filter).* Not the William Weiderman that wrote *Spider Doom?*

BILL. Yes, that was mine. If—

OPERATOR *(filter).* Oh my God. I just *loved* that book! I love *all* your books! I—

BILL. I'm delighted you do. But right now my wife is very worried about her sister. If it's possible for you to—

OPERATOR *(filter).* Yes, I can do that. Please give me your number, Mr. Weiderman, for the records. *(She giggles.)* I *promise* not to give it out.

BILL. It's 555-4408.

OPERATOR *(filter).* And the call number?

BILL *(looks at* KATIE*).* Uh . . .

KATIE. 555-6169.

BILL. 555-6169.

OPERATOR *(filter).* Just a moment, Mr. Weiderman . . . *Night of the Beast* was also great, by the way. Hold on.

SOUND: TELEPHONIC CLICKS AND CLACKS

KATIE. Is she—

BILL. Yes. Just . . .

There's one final CLICK.

OPERATOR *(filter).* I'm sorry, Mr. Weiderman, but that line is not busy. It's off the hook. I wonder if I sent you my copy of *Spider Doom*—

BILL *hangs up the phone.*

---

13. **bray** (brā), *n.* loud, harsh cry or noise.
14. **tussle** (tus′əl), *v.* struggle or wrestle.

KATIE. Why did you hang up?

BILL. She can't break in. Phone's not busy. It's off the hook.

They stare at each other bleakly.[15]

EXT. NIGHT. A LOW-SLUNG SPORTS CAR PASSES THE CAMERA.

INT. THE CAR, WITH KATIE AND BILL

KATIE*'s scared.* BILL, *at the wheel, doesn't look exactly calm.*

KATIE. Hey, Bill—tell me she's all right.

BILL. She's all right.

KATIE. Now tell me what you really think.

BILL. Jeff snuck up behind me tonight and put the old booga-booga on me. He was disappointed as hell when I didn't jump. I told him I was case-hardened. *(Pause)* I lied.

KATIE. Why did Jerry have to move out there when he's gone half the time? Just her and that little tiny baby? *Why?*

BILL. Shh, Kate. We're almost there.

KATIE. Go faster.

EXT. THE CAR

He does. That car is smokin.

INT. THE WEIDERMAN TV ROOM

The tube's still on and the kids are still there, but the horsing around has stopped.

CONNIE. Dennis, do you think Aunt Dawn's okay?

DENNIS *(thinks she's dead, decapitated*[16] *by a maniac).* Yeah. Sure she is.

INT. THE PHONE, POV FROM THE TV ROOM

Just sitting there on the wall in the phone nook, lights dark, looking like a snake ready to strike.

FADE OUT

---

15. bleakly (blēk′lē), *adv.* cheerlessly and depressingly.
16. **decapitated** (di kap′ə tāt əd), *adj.* with the head cut off.

After Reading

Making Connections

1. Describe how your emotions changed while you were reading the first act of the play.

2. If you were in Katie's situation, would you have reacted in the same way? Why or why not?

3. What do you **predict** will happen in the final half of the play?

4. What is Bill's first reaction when Katie tells him about the upsetting telephone call? What changes his attitude?

5. Describe four ways that King creates a **mood** of tension and disorder in the Weiderman household.

6. What do you think is the moment of greatest suspense in the play so far? Why?

7. Several of the characters in the play are having trouble **communicating.** Describe three examples of a failure to communicate in the first act and explain how the characters might have avoided these failures.

8. Writing a screenplay differs from writing a novel because the writer has to visualize how the camera will help tell the story. For example, in *Sorry, Right Number,* the camera shows framed book covers in Bill's office to indicate that he is a famous author. Make a chart like the one shown here and give at least two other examples of how King uses the camera to tell his story.

What the camera does	What this reveals
Shows framed book covers	Bill is a famous author.

9. Do the members of the Weiderman family seem like a typical family? Are there any ways in which they do *not* seem typical? If so, what are they?

10. Compare Act 1 of *Sorry, Right Number* with the opening scenes of a suspenseful movie you have seen. How does each draw you into the action? What events in each contribute to the feeling of suspense?

Vocabulary Study

bemused
bleakly
bray
tussle
veteran

Use the listed vocabulary words from Act 1 to write a short horror story in one or two paragraphs. You may change the form of the words: for example, *bleakly* can be changed to *bleak* or *bleaker* in your story. If needed, use your Glossary to understand word meanings.

Expressing Your Ideas

Writing Choices

Writer's Notebook Update Look back at your list of elements in a horror film. What do you think of your ideas now that you've read Act 1 of this screenplay? Take this opportunity to change or add to your list.

Scream Scene Use your updated list of elements of a horror story to write an **opening scene** for your own scary screenplay. Keep in mind King's use of the camera, his strategies for building suspense, and the ways he creates a mood of fear and impending doom.

Other Options

Who's the Best Boy Here? Filmmaking has a vocabulary of its own, and the people who help make a film sometimes go by rather unusual titles. Do some research to learn what the jobs such as the following involve: the focus puller, the grips and key grips, the loader, and the best boy. Find an entertaining way to share your information in an **oral presentation.**

Second-Guessing In question 3 on the opposite page, you made some predictions about what might happen in the second act of *Sorry, Right Number.* With a small group, prepare and present a brief **skit** that dramatizes your predictions.

▲ Billy Morrow Jackson, *Spring Field* (1981). Does the mood of this painting seem hopeful or ominous to you? Explain.

ACT TWO

EXT. AN ISOLATED FARMHOUSE

A long driveway leads up to it. There's one light on in the living room. Car lights sweep up the driveway. The WEIDERMAN *car pulls up close to the garage and stops.*

INT. THE CAR, WITH BILL AND KATIE

KATIE. I'm scared.

BILL *bends down, reaches under his seat, and brings out a pistol.*

BILL (*solemnly*). Booga-booga.

KATIE (*total surprise*). How long have you had that?

BILL. Since last year. I didn't want to scare you or the kids. I've got a license to carry. Come on.

EXT. BILL AND KATIE

They get out. KATIE *stands by the front of the car while* BILL *goes to the garage and peers in.*

BILL. Her car's here.

THE CAMERA TRACKS WITH THEM *to the front door. Now we can hear the* TV, PLAYING LOUD. BILL *pushes the doorbell. We hear it inside. They wait.* KATIE *pushes it. Still no answer. She pushes it again and doesn't take her finger off.* BILL *looks down at:*

EXT. THE LOCK, BILL'S POV

Big scratches on it.

EXT. BILL AND KATIE

BILL (*low*). The lock's been tampered with.

KATIE *looks, and whimpers.* BILL *tries the door. It opens. The TV is louder.*

BILL. Stay behind me. Be ready to run if something happens. God, I wish I'd left you home, Kate.

He starts in. KATIE *comes after him, terrified, near tears.*

INT. DAWN AND JERRY'S LIVING ROOM

From this angle we see only a small section of the room. The TV is much louder. BILL *enters the room, gun up. He looks to the right . . . and suddenly all the tension goes out of him. He lowers the gun.*

KATIE (*draws up beside him*). Bill . . . what . . .

He points.

INT. THE LIVING ROOM, WIDE, BILL AND KATIE'S POV

The place looks like a cyclone hit it . . . but it wasn't robbery and murder that caused this mess; only a healthy eighteen-month-old baby. After a strenuous day of trashing the living room, Baby got tired and Mommy got tired and they fell asleep on the couch together. The baby is in DAWN's *lap. There is a pair of Walkman earphones on her head. There are toys— tough plastic Sesame Street and PlaySkool stuff, for the most part—scattered hell to breakfast. The baby has also pulled most of the books out of the bookcase. Had a good munch on one of them, too, by the look.* BILL *goes over and picks it up. It is* Ghost Kiss.

BILL. I've had people say they just eat my books up, but this is ridiculous.

He's amused. KATIE *isn't. She walks over to her sister, ready to be mad . . . but she sees how really exhausted* DAWN *looks and softens.*

INT. DAWN AND THE BABY, KATIE'S POV

Fast asleep and breathing easily, like a Raphael[1] painting of Madonna and Child. THE CAMERA PANS DOWN TO: *the Walkman. We can hear the faint strains of Huey Lewis and the News.* THE CAMERA PANS A BIT FURTHER TO *a Princess telephone on the table by the chair. It's off the cradle. Not much; just enough to break the connection and scare people to death.*

INT. KATIE

She sighs, bends down, and replaces the phone. Then she pushes the STOP *button on the Walkman.*

INT. DAWN, BILL, AND KATIE

DAWN *wakes up when the music stops. Looks at* BILL *and* KATIE, *puzzled.*

DAWN (*fuzzed out*). Well . . . hi.

She realizes she's got the Walkman phones on and removes them.

BILL. Hi, Dawn.

DAWN (*still half asleep*). Shoulda called, guys. Place is a mess.

She smiles. She's radiant when she smiles.

---

1. **Raphael** (raf′ē əl), famous Italian Renaissance painter (1483–1520).

KATIE. We *tried.* The operator told Bill the phone was off the hook. I thought something was wrong. How can you sleep with that music blasting?

DAWN. It's restful. *(Sees the gnawed book* BILL's *holding.)* Oh, my God, Bill, I'm sorry! Justin's teething and—

BILL. There are critics who'd say he picked just the right thing to teethe on. I don't want to scare you, beautiful, but somebody's been at your front door lock with a screwdriver or something. Whoever it was forced it.

DAWN. Gosh, no! That was Jerry, last week. I locked us out by mistake and he didn't have his key and the spare wasn't over the door like it's supposed to be. He was mad so he took the screwdriver to it. It didn't work, either—that's one tough lock.

BILL. If it wasn't forced, how come I could just open the door and walk in?

DAWN *(guiltily).* Well . . . sometimes I forget to lock it.

KATIE. You didn't call me tonight, Dawn?

DAWN. Gee, no! I didn't call *anyone!* I was too busy chasing Justin around! He kept wanting to eat the fabric softener! Then he got sleepy and I sat down here and thought I'd listen to some tunes while I waited for your movie to come on, Bill, and I fell asleep—

At the mention of the movie BILL *starts visibly and looks at the book. Then he glances at his watch.*

BILL. I promised to tape it for Jeff. Come on, Katie, we've got time to get back.

KATIE. Just a second.

She picks up the phone and dials.

DAWN. Gee, Bill, do you think Jeffie's old enough to watch something like that?

BILL. It's network. They take out the blood-bags.[2]

DAWN *(confused but amiable).* Oh. That's good.

INT. KATIE, CU

DENNIS *(filter).* Hello?

KATIE. Just thought you'd like to know your Aunt Dawn's fine.

DENNIS *(filter).* Oh! Cool. Thanks, Mom.

INT. THE PHONE NOOK, WITH DENNIS AND THE OTHERS

He looks very relieved.

DENNIS. Aunt Dawn's okay.

INT. THE CAR, WITH BILL AND KATIE

They drive in silence for awhile.

KATIE. You think I'm a <u>hysterical</u>[3] idiot, don't you?

BILL *(genuinely surprised).* No! I was scared, too.

KATIE. You sure you're not mad?

BILL. I'm too relieved. *(Laughs.)* She's sort of a scatterbrain, old Dawn, but I love her.

KATIE *(leans over and kisses him).* I love *you.* You're a sweet man.

BILL. I'm the *boogeyman!*

KATIE. I am not fooled, sweetheart.

EXT. THE CAR PASSES THE CAMERA AND WE DISSOLVE TO:

INT. JEFF, IN BED

His room is dark. The covers are pulled up to his chin.

JEFF. You *promise* to tape the rest?

CAMERA WIDENS OUT *so we can see* BILL, *sitting on the bed.*

BILL. I promise.

JEFF. I especially liked the part where the dead guy ripped off the punk rocker's head.

BILL. Well . . . they *used* to take out all the blood-bags.

JEFF. What, Dad?

BILL. Nothing. I love you, Jeffie.

JEFF. I love you, too. So does Rambo.

JEFF *holds up a stuffed dragon of decidedly unmilitant[4] aspect.[5]* BILL *kisses the dragon, then* JEFF.

BILL. 'Night.

---

2. **blood-bags,** props that burst open to simulate bleeding, used in making movies.
3. hysterical (hi ster′ə kəl), *adj.* excited or emotional; showing an unnatural lack of self-control.
4. **unmilitant** (un mil′ə tənt), *adj.* unaggressive; not warlike.
5. **aspect** (as′pekt), *n.* appearance; facial expression.

JEFF. 'Night. *(As BILL reaches the door)* Glad Aunt Dawn was okay.

BILL. Me too.

He goes out.

INT. TV, CU

A guy who looks like he died in a car crash about two weeks prior to filming (and has since been subjected to a lot of hot weather) is staggering out of a crypt.[6] THE CAMERA WIDENS *to show* BILL, *releasing the VCR pause button.*

KATIE *(voice).* Booga-booga.

BILL *looks around companionably.[7]* THE CAMERA WIDENS OUT MORE *to show* KATIE, *wearing a nightgown.*

BILL. Same to you. I missed the first forty seconds or so after the break. I had to kiss Rambo.

KATIE. You sure you're not mad at me, Bill?

He goes to her and kisses her.

BILL. Not even a smidge.

KATIE. It's just that I could have sworn it was one of mine. You know what I mean? One of mine?

BILL. Yes.

KATIE. I can still hear those sobs. So lost . . . so heartbroken.

BILL. Kate, have you ever thought you recognized someone on the street, and called her, and when she finally turned around it was a total stranger?

KATIE. Yes, once. In Seattle. I was in a mall and I thought I saw my old roommate. I . . . oh. I see what you're saying.

BILL. Sure. There are sound-alikes as well as look-alikes.

KATIE. But . . . *you know your own.* At least I thought so until tonight.

She puts her cheek on his shoulder, looking troubled.

KATIE. I was so *positive* it was Polly . . .

BILL. Because you've been worried about her getting her feet under her at the new school . . . but judging from the stuff she told

you tonight, I'd say she's doing just fine in that department. Wouldn't you?

KATIE. Yes . . . I guess I would.

BILL. Let it go, hon.

KATIE *(looks at him closely).* I hate to see you looking so tired. Hurry up and have an idea, you.

BILL. Well, I'm trying.

KATIE. You coming to bed?

BILL. Soon as I finish taping this for Jeff.

KATIE *(amused).* Bill, that machine was made by Japanese technicians who think of damned near everything. It'll run on its own.

BILL. Yea, but it's been a long time since I've seen this one, and . . .

KATIE. Okay. Enjoy. I think I'll be awake for a little while. *(Pause)* I've got a few ideas of my own.

BILL *(smiles).* Yeah?

KATIE. Yeah.

She starts out, then turns in the doorway as something else strikes her.

KATIE. If they show that part where the punk's head gets—

BILL *(guiltily).* I'll edit it.

KATIE. 'Night. And thanks again. For everything.

She leaves. BILL *sits in his chair.*

INT. TV, CU

A couple is necking in a car. Suddenly the passenger door is ripped open by the dead guy and we DISSOLVE TO:

INT. KATIE, IN BED

It's dark. She's asleep. She wakes up . . . sort of.

KATIE *(sleepy).* Hey, big guy—

She feels for him, but his side of the bed is empty, the coverlet still pulled up. She sits up. Looks at:

INT. A CLOCK ON THE NIGHT-TABLE, KATIE'S POV

It says 2:03 A.M. Then it flashes 2:04.

---

6. crypt (kript), *n.* underground room or vault.
7. **companionably** (kəm pan′yən ə blē), *adv.* agreeably; socially.

INT. KATIE

Fully awake now. And concerned. She gets up, puts on her robe, and leaves the bedroom.

INT. THE TV SCREEN, CU

Snow.

KATIE *(voice, approaching).* Bill? Honey? You okay? Bill? Bi—

INT. KATIE, IN BILL'S STUDY

She's frozen, wide-eyed with horror.

INT. BILL, IN HIS CHAIR

He's slumped to one side, eyes closed, hand inside his shirt. DAWN *was sleeping.* BILL *is not.*

EXT. A COFFIN, BEING LOWERED INTO A GRAVE

MINISTER *(voice).* And so we commit the earthly remains of William Weiderman to the ground, confident of his spirit and soul. "Be ye not cast down, brethren . . ."

EXT. GRAVESIDE

All the WEIDERMANS *are ranged here.* KATIE *and* POLLY *wear identical black dresses and veils.* CONNIE *wears a black skirt and white blouse.* DENNIS *and* JEFF *wear black suits.* JEFF *is crying. He has Rambo the Dragon under his arm for a little extra comfort.*

CAMERA MOVES IN ON KATIE. *Tears course slowly down her cheeks. She bends and gets a handful of earth. Tosses it into the grave.*

KATIE. Love you, big guy.

EXT. JEFF

Weeping.

EXT. LOOKING DOWN INTO THE GRAVE

Scattered earth on top of the coffin.

DISSOLVE TO:

EXT. THE GRAVE

A groundskeeper pats the last sod into place.

GROUNDSKEEPER. My wife says she wishes you'd written a couple more before you had your heart attack, mister. *(Pause.)* I like Westerns, m'self.

The GROUNDSKEEPER *walks away, whistling.*

DISSOLVE TO:

EXT. DAY. A CHURCH

TITLE CARD: FIVE YEARS LATER

The Wedding March is playing. POLLY, *older and radiant with joy, emerges into a pelting[8] shower of rice. She's in a wedding gown, her new husband by her side.*

Celebrants throwing rice line either side of the path. From behind the bride and groom come others. Among them are KATIE, DENNIS, CONNIE, *and* JEFF . . . *all five years older. With* KATIE *is another man. This is* HANK. *In the interim,[9]* KATIE *has also taken a husband.*

POLLY *turns and her mother is there.*

POLLY. Thank you, Mom.

KATIE *(crying).* Oh doll, you're so welcome.

They embrace. After a moment POLLY *draws away and looks at* HANK. *There is a brief moment of tension, and then* POLLY *embraces* HANK, *too.*

POLLY. Thank you too, Hank. I'm sorry I was such a creep for so long . . .

HANK *(easily).* You were never a creep, Pol. A girl only has one father.

CONNIE. Throw it! Throw it!

After a moment, POLLY *throws her bouquet.*

EXT. THE BOUQUET, CU, SLOW MOTION

Turning and turning through the air.

DISSOLVES TO:

INT. NIGHT. THE STUDY, WITH KATIE

The word-processor has been replaced by a wide lamp looming over a stack of blueprints.[10] The book jackets have been replaced by photos of buildings. Ones that have first been built in HANK's *mind, presumably.[11]*

KATIE *is looking at the desk, thoughtful and a little sad.*

HANK *(voice).* Coming to bed, Kate?

She turns and THE CAMERA WIDENS OUT *to give us*

---

8. **pelting** (pelt ing), *adj.* hitting with objects thrown one after another.
9. interim (in′tər im), *n.* time between; the meantime.
10. **blueprints** (blū′prints), *n.* photographic prints of white lines on a blue background or blue lines on a white background, used chiefly in copying building plans, mechanical drawings, maps, etc.
11. **presumably** (pri züm′ə blē), *adv.* that is taken for granted; probably.

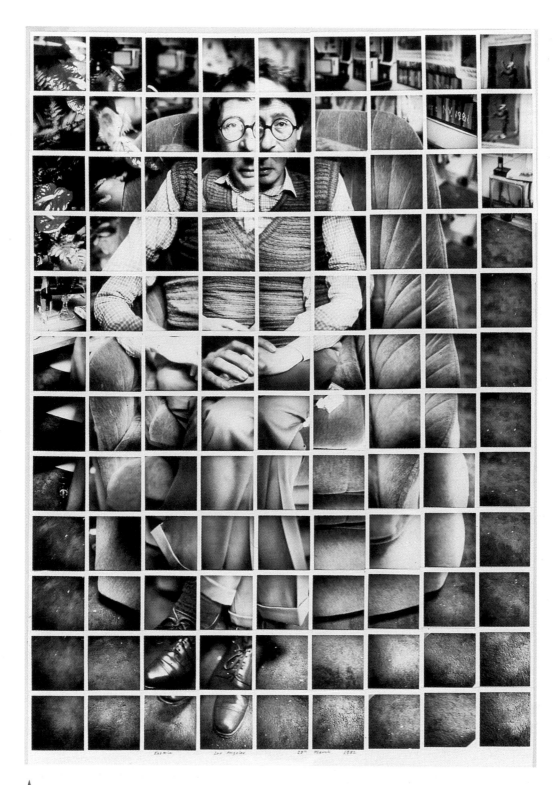

▲ David Hockney, *Kasmin Los Angeles 28th March 1982.* Hockney made more than 140 photocollages between March and May of 1982, including the one on page 215, the one pictured here, and the one on page 226. Explain why you do or don't like this approach.

▲ David Hockney, *Celia Los Angeles, April 10th 1982.* In this photocollage, what mood is conveyed by the subject's raised arms and the expression on her face?

HANK. *He's wearing a robe over pajamas. She comes to him and gives him a little hug, smiling. Maybe we notice a few streaks of gray in her hair; her pretty pony has done its fair share of running*[12] *since* BILL *died.*

KATIE. In a little while. A woman doesn't see her first one get married every day, you know.

HANK. I know.

THE CAMERA FOLLOWS *as they walk from the work area of the study to the more informal area. This is much the same as it was in the old days, with a coffee table, stereo, TV, couch, and* BILL*'s old easy-chair. She looks at this.*

HANK. You still miss him, don't you?

KATIE. Some days more than others. You didn't know, and Polly didn't remember.

HANK *(gently).* Remember what, doll?

KATIE. Polly got married on the five-year anniversary of Bill's death.

HANK *(hugs her).* Come on to bed, why don't you?

KATIE. In a little while.

HANK. Okay. Maybe I'll still be awake.

KATIE. Got a few ideas, do you?

HANK. I might.

KATIE. That's nice.

He kisses her, then leaves, closing the door behind him. KATIE *sits in* BILL*'s old chair. Close by, on the coffee table, is a remote control for the TV and an extension phone.* KATIE *looks at the blank TV, and* THE CAMERA MOVES IN *on her face. One tear rims one eye, sparkling like a sapphire.*[13]

KATIE. I *do* still miss you, big guy. Lots and lots. Every day. And you know what? It hurts.

The tear falls. She picks up the TV remote and pushes the ON *button.*

---

12. **her pretty pony . . . running,** time has passed for her.
13. **sapphire** (saf′ĭr), *n.* clear, hard, bright-blue precious stone.

INT. TV, KATIE'S POV

An ad for Ginsu Knives comes to an end and is replaced by a STAR LOGO.

ANNOUNCER *(voice).* Now back to Channel 63's Thursday night Star Time Movie . . . *Ghost Kiss.*

The logo DISSOLVES INTO *a guy who looks like he died in a car crash about two weeks ago and has since been subjected to a lot of hot weather. He comes staggering out of the same old crypt.*

INT. KATIE

Terribly startled—almost horrified. She hits the OFF *button on the remote control. The TV blinks off.*

KATIE*'s face begins to work. She struggles against the* impending[14] *emotional storm, but the coincidence of the movie is just one thing too many on what must have already been one of the most emotionally trying days of her life. The dam breaks and she begins to sob . . . terrible heartbroken sobs. She reaches out for the little table by the chair, meaning to put the remote control on it, and knocks the phone onto the floor.*

SOUND: THE HUM OF AN OPEN LINE

Her tear-stained face grows suddenly still as she looks at the telephone. Something begins to fill it . . . an idea? an intuition? Hard to tell. And maybe it doesn't matter.

INT. THE TELEPHONE, KATIE'S POV

THE CAMERA MOVES IN TO ECU . . . MOVES IN *until the dots in the off-the-hook receiver look like* chasms.[15]

SOUND OF OPEN-LINE BUZZ UP TO LOUD.

WE GO INTO THE BLACK . . . *and hear:*

BILL *(voice).* Who are you calling? Who do you *want* to call? Who *would* you call, if it wasn't too late?

INT. KATIE

There is now a strange hypnotized look on her face. She reaches down, scoops the telephone up, and punches in numbers, seemingly at random.

SOUND: RINGING PHONE

KATIE *continues to look hypnotized. The look holds until the phone is answered . . . and she hears herself on the other end of the line.*

KATIE *(voice; filter).* Hello, Weiderman residence.

KATIE*—our present-day* KATIE *with streaks of gray in her hair—goes on sobbing, yet an expression of desperate hope is trying to be born on her face. On some level she understands that the depth of her grief has allowed a kind of telephonic-time-travel. She's trying to talk, to force the words out.*

KATIE *(sobbing).* Take . . . please take . . . t-t-

INT. KATIE, IN THE PHONE NOOK, REPRISE[16]

It's five years ago. BILL *is standing beside her, looking concerned.* JEFF *is wandering off to look for a blank tape in the other room.*

KATIE. Polly? What's wrong?

INT. KATIE, IN THE STUDY

KATIE *(sobbing).* Please—quick—

SOUND: CLICK OF A BROKEN CONNECTION

KATIE *(screaming).* Take him to the hospital! If you want him to live, take him to the hospital! He's going to have a heart attack. He—

SOUND: HUM OF AN OPEN LINE

Slowly, very slowly, KATIE *hangs up the telephone. Then, after a moment, she picks it up again. She speaks aloud with no self-consciousness whatever. Probably doesn't even know she's doing it.*

KATIE. I dialed the old number. I dialed—

SLAM CUT TO:

INT. BILL, IN THE PHONE NOOK WITH KATIE BESIDE HIM

He's just taken the phone from KATIE *and is speaking to the operator.*

OPERATOR *(filter, giggles).* I *promise* not to give it out.

BILL. It's 555-

SLAM CUT TO:

INT. KATIE, IN BILL'S OLD CHAIR, CU

KATIE *(finishes).* -4408.

INT. THE PHONE, CU

KATIE*'s trembling finger carefully picks out the number, and we hear the corresponding tones: 555-4408.*

---

14. impending (im pen′ding), *adj.* threatening; about to occur.
15. chasm (kaz′əm), *n.* deep opening or crack; gap.
16. reprise (rə prēz′), *n.* repetition.

INT. KATIE, IN BILL'S OLD CHAIR, CU

She closes her eyes as the PHONE BEGINS TO RING. *Her face is filled with an agonizing mixture of hope and fear. If only she can have one more chance to pass the vital message on, it says . . . just one more chance.*

KATIE *(low).* Please . . . please . . .

RECORDED VOICE *(filter).* You have reached a non-working number. Please hang up and dial again. If you need assistance—

KATIE *hangs up again. Tears stream down her cheeks.* THE CAMERA PANS AWAY AND DOWN *to the telephone.*

INT. THE PHONE NOOK, WITH KATIE AND BILL, REPRISE

BILL. So it was a prank. Or someone who was crying so hard she dialed a wrong number . . . "through a shimmering film of tears," as we veteran hacks like to say.

KATIE. It was not a prank and it was not a wrong number! It was someone in *my family!*

INT. KATIE (PRESENT DAY) IN BILL'S STUDY

KATIE. Yes. Someone in my family. Someone who is close. *(Pause.)* Me.

She suddenly throws the phone across the room. She starts to sob again and puts her hands over her face. CAMERA HOLDS *on her for a moment, then* DOLLIES[17] ACROSS.

INT. THE PHONE

It lies on the carpet, looking both bland and somber. CAMERA MOVES IN TO ECU—*the holes in the receiver look like huge dark chasms. We* HOLD, *then*

FADE TO BLACK.

---

17. **dolly** (dol′ē), *v.* move on a platform on wheels.

Act 2

After Reading

Shaping Your Response

Making Connections

1. Did the ending of the screenplay surprise you? Why or why not?

2. After reading the entire play, what do you think is its scariest moment? Why?

3. 👁 How could better **communication** help Katie and the others in the family prevent a similar tragedy from happening again?

Analyzing the Screenplay

4. Do you think the **title** fits the screenplay? Why or why not?

5. What does the telephone **symbolize?** Tell whether you think it is an effective symbol.

6. King often makes interesting breaks between scenes, shifting abruptly from one event to another. Describe a scene break that you think is effective and explain why you think so.

7. To diagram the **plot** of *Sorry, Right Number,* which of the following shapes would you use: a linked chain, a circle, a spiral, or something else? Prepare a plot diagram that shows the major events in *Sorry, Right Number.*

Extending the Ideas

8. How would you rate this screenplay against other suspenseful stories or movies you have seen? Compare *Sorry, Right Number* to at least two other films or stories.

Literary Focus

Foreshadowing Think back to what you learned about **foreshadowing** before you read the screenplay. King uses foreshadowing in *Sorry, Right Number* to create a mood of horror. For example, in Act 1, King foreshadows Bill's death by showing him sitting in front of a blank computer screen looking tired. On a chart like the one below, list two other examples of foreshadowing in the play and briefly describe what later event is being foreshadowed.

Event that foreshadows something else	Event that is being foreshadowed
Bill looks tired.	Bill will die of a heart attack.

Vocabulary Study

Complete the following sentences using the listed vocabulary words. If necessary, use your Glossary for help with word meanings.

chasm
crypt
hysterical
impending
interim

1. You might find a dead body or two, a crazy killer, and a burial ____ in one of Bill's horror films.

2. The unknown voice on the phone is upset and ____.

3. After the phone call, Katie feels a sense of ____ doom.

4. For the Weidermans, losing Bill may feel like falling into a bottomless ____.

5. In the ____ between Bill's death and Polly's wedding, Katie marries again.

Expressing Your Ideas

Writing Choices

Writer's Notebook Update Now that you have finished reading the screenplay, take a final look at your list of elements in a horror film. Make any further revisions you think are necessary. Then write a brief response to the following statement: In a movie, camera moves and lighting are as important as the dialogue for creating suspense.

Dear Lois How do you think Katie feels at the end of *Sorry, Right Number* when she realizes she had heard her own distressed voice on the telephone? Imagine that you are Katie. Write a **letter** about the experience to your sister Lois. What will you say? What feelings will you express?

Communication Breakdown Write a brief **article** for a self-help magazine about an experience you've had where your efforts to communicate either failed or were only partially successful. Include advice for your readers on how to achieve better communication.

Other Options

Mood Music *Sorry, Right Number* ranges in mood from playful to chilling, and a **soundtrack** for this screenplay would have to reflect those different moods. Find or create appropriate music for key moments in the screenplay. Play your **soundtrack** for the class as you do a dramatic reading from those scenes.

The Art of Listening Collect some "quotable quotes" about the fine art of listening and use them in a **collage** about communication. The following quotations may help get you started.

"Bore: a person who talks when you wish him to listen."
   —Ambrose Bierce

"I listen to the wind of my soul."
   —Cat Stevens

"It is the province of knowledge to speak and it is the privilege of wisdom to listen."
   —Oliver Wendell Holmes

Before Reading

The Ghostly Rhyme

by Laurence Yep

Laurence Yep
born 1948

Growing up Chinese American in an African American neighborhood of San Francisco, Laurence Yep felt like an outsider. Even among his Chinese American friends he felt different because he didn't speak Chinese. Since he only felt at home when he was reading books, it's not surprising he became a writer. Yep believes that all writers are outsiders in some way, calling them "professional daydreamers who get paid to write down their dreams." He thinks that teenagers like his books because they often deal with "the theme of being an outsider—an alien— and many teenagers feel they're aliens."

Building Background

Chinese Religions The religions of Taoism and Buddhism have influenced Chinese thought, culture, and literature for thousands of years. Although the two religions differ, their basic philosophies are similar and continue to influence the Chinese way of life even today. One of the major beliefs held by Taoists and Buddhists alike is the importance of letting go of all striving and desire. To attain the ideal state of being, one must live simply and humbly, without attachment to material things. Pride, greed, and vanity are considered obstacles to attaining spiritual enlightenment. As you read "The Ghostly Rhyme," consider whether the main character seems to be influenced by these beliefs.

Literary Focus

Character Authors show us things about their **characters** in different ways. A writer may describe characters directly or reveal them through their actions, speech, and thoughts, as well as through the reactions of other characters. Laurence Yep uses all these methods of characterization in "The Ghostly Rhyme."

Writer's Notebook

Wising Up "The Ghostly Rhyme" is a story about a wise man. What do you think of when you imagine a wise person? In your notebook, write down your ideas about what makes someone wise. If you wish, write about someone you know who you think is wise and explain why you think so.

THE GHOSTLY RHYME

Laurence Yep

Long ago a wise man once wrote a letter to the emperor. In it, the wise man criticized an imperial[1] minister as corrupt and gave examples as proof. However, because the official was the emperor's favorite, it was the wise man and not the minister who was punished.

The wise man was sent south, where much of the land was still jungle. At first, he settled in a town that had grown up outside the walls of a Chinese fort. There he made friends with the other exiles.[2]

Eventually, though, he moved into the jungle itself, where he built a small thatched[3] hut among the cinnamon trees. Near his hut a stream ran, its water still fresh and cool from the mountains.

With a little bamboo dipper he had made himself, he would fetch the water for his tea, and then, cup in hand, he would spend all day reading.

For food, he fished in the nearby stream or picked wild fruit or gathered the vegetables he grew in a small patch outside his hut. And for wine, he had the scent of the surrounding cinnamon trees, which was so thick it would make anyone drunk. But even when he was fishing or picking fruit or gardening, he would insist that he was thinking about what he read.

Once when a friend asked him why he lived in such a lonely spot, he was surprised. "But I'm not alone," he said. "My books have told me all about these hills. I have the spirits of the woods and the dragons in the water for company." He motioned to some spotted bamboo. "And it's said these are the family of an emperor; they were transformed into these plants as they mourned him."

Meditating about what he had read, he would go for walks in the shadowy pines among the hills to where the icy rivers exploded from between the sharp, craggy mountains; and he would stand there as the spray of the waterfall fell about him like rain. And at night he would

---

1. **imperial** (im pir′ē əl), *adj.* of an empire or its ruler.
2. **exile** (eg′zīl), *n.* person who is forced to leave his or her country or home.
3. **thatched** (thacht), *adj.* covered with straw, rushes, palm leaves, etc.

stare up at the night sky and his mind would go voyaging among the stars.

When he developed a cough, his friends tried to get him to come down to the city to see a doctor, but he refused. "The smell of pine is the best medicine."

One day, he picked up a book by his favorite poet. Unfortunately, worms had gotten at the book and eaten away the outside edges of the pages. Annoyed, he opened the book to examine the damage, and his eye happened to fall upon a particular page. Most of the poems he knew by heart, but as he read the poem, he found he could not remember the last line, which was missing.

He prided himself upon his knowledge, so he sat there through the long afternoon and into the evening, trying to remember the last line. To prod[4] his memory, he kept reciting the next to the last line over and over:

"The sun on my old garden shines . . ."

He forgot to eat and even sleep. His friends, bringing some food and books up to him, found him still inside his hut, the worm-eaten book

---

4. **prod** (prod), *v.* stir up; urge on.

In this inkwash painting, *Reading in the Autumn* (c. 1470), artist Shen Chou portrays himself reading a book. In the upper left-hand corner is a poem he composed about autumn. Do you think the ink characters in the poem add to the painting or clash with it? Explain. ▼

upon his lap. He had died with a very annoyed look on his face.

Sadly, they buried him with the book; but that night as the wind shook the cinnamon and pine trees, people thought it sounded like someone sighing. And as the rain began to fall, the drops pattered down like someone impatiently tapping a finger.

His friends saw his ghost reading the poem out loud; but he stopped just before the last line. Then, with a very irritated look on his face, the ghost disappeared. At first people were frightened, but they realized that as a ghost he was just as harmless as he had been in real life.

However, when the rainy season came, his ghost would walk out of the jungle and into town to visit his friends' houses, where he would recite his one line. Eventually, though, he began to haunt the main street itself and speak the words in a loud voice. It didn't take long before the ghost started to wear on people's nerves. "If only he would recite something else—a limerick[5] or a riddle or even a jingle.[6] But it's always the same line." There were some nights when the poetical[7] ghost kept everyone up.

They pleaded with the ghost to go away; or if he wouldn't go away, at least he could quote something else. They tried bribes and threats. He ignored them, though, as obsessed in death as he had been in life.

Reluctantly, they called in a priest to exorcise[8] the ghost; but the ghost insisted on reading his ghostly rhyme over and over until it was the priest who finally banged his head against the wall in frustration and gave up.

At last, a poet heard about the literate[9] ghost. Having a taste for the strange and fantastical, the poet went up to the wise man's home.

Sitting down by the now ruined hut, he waited as the storm clouds rolled in overhead.

The wind rushed through the trees like someone sighing heavily. And the raindrops fell like someone tapping his finger impatiently. As the poet sat up, he saw the old man in his tattered robe with the worm-eaten book in his hand.

As he watched, the ghost began to read from the book. Now it happened that the poet liked the same writer. As the ghost spoke, the poet thought he had never heard the poem read better or more movingly.

When the ghost stopped just before the last line, the poet urged him, "Go on."

However, the ghost started to recite the poem over again, halting at the same place. "The sun on my old garden shines . . ."

"But I am gone," the poet finished. "No flesh confines."

The wind roared through the trees, and the rain fell in showers. Standing in the middle of the storm, the ghost smiled in relief and clapped his book shut. Tucking it under his arm, the ghost disappeared, and no one ever saw or heard him again.

> Then, with a very irritated look on his face, the ghost disappeared.

5. **limerick** (lim′ər ik), *n.* humorous nonsense verse of five lines.
6. **jingle** (jing′gəl), *n.* a song that has pleasant or catchy rhymes or repetitions.
7. **poetical** (pō et′ə kəl), *adj.* poetic; having to do with poems or poets.
8. **exorcise** (ek′sôr sīz), *v.* drive out an evil spirit by prayers, ceremonies, etc.
9. **literate** (lit′ər it), *adj.* able to read and write; educated.

After Reading

Making Connections

Shaping Your Response

1. How did you feel when the ghost finally heard the last line of the poem? Why?

2. What do you like most about this story? Least? Why?

Analyzing the Folk Tale

3. The last line of the poem is "But I am gone, no flesh confines." What is **ironic** about this line?

4. Does the wise man rely too much on books? Explain your answer.

5. Do you think the wise man is really wise? Why or why not?

Extending the Ideas

6. Does this story seem to reflect the Chinese Taoist and Buddhist teachings you learned about on page 231? Why or why not?

7. 🐾 Compare the barriers to **communication** in this story with those in *Sorry, Right Number*. How are they similar? How are they different?

Literary Focus: Characterization

Think back to what you learned earlier about **characterization.** How does Laurence Yep reveal the character of the old man in his story? Copy the chart pictured here. Show how Yep develops his character by giving one example from the story for each item on the chart.

Characterization in "The Ghostly Rhyme"	
Methods	**Example from story**
Direct description	
Through the character's speech	
Through the character's actions	
Through the reactions of others	

Expressing Your Ideas

Writing Choices

Writer's Notebook Update Look back at your notes about what it means to be wise. After reading the story, is there anything you want to change or add to your ideas? Once you've reviewed your notes, use them to write a one-page story about a foolish character who becomes wise. Consider what makes the character foolish and what changes the character. You may want to refer back to Yep's story as a model.

Last Words In most poems, the last line is very important. What happens to a poem when you take out or change its last line? Find a short poem you like and read it to a small group, but leave out the last line. Then write your own **last line** for each poem others have read. After sharing your last lines with your group, read the original last lines of the poems. Compare and contrast your new lines with the original lines. How do the new endings change the overall meaning and effect of the poems?

Other Options

Wise Guys and Know-It-Alls

Knowledge is proud that he has learned so much;
Wisdom is humble that he knows no more.
—William Cowper

What is this writer saying about the difference between wisdom and knowledge? Prepare a speech about the nature of wisdom, using the quotation as a starting point. If you wish, you may include your own personal experiences in your speech.

Scared On the Air Imagine that your group has been hired to perform a ghost story on a local radio station. Work with others in a small group to find a ghost story to perform. One group member could narrate the story while others perform creepy sound effects to accompany it. You may use recordings, musical instruments, household objects, or voices to create sound effects. Record your **radio ghost story** and play it for the class.

Elena by Pat Mora

Etymology by Amy Kashiwabara

Pat Mora
born 1942

Mexican American poet Pat Mora often explores Mexican values and customs in her writing. She says she writes "so that the stories and ideas of our people won't quietly disappear." Mora speaks English and Spanish and lives in El Paso, Texas.

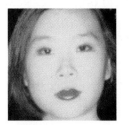

Amy Kashiwabara
born 1973

Amy Kashiwabara wrote her award-winning poem "Etymology" as a high school senior in New Jersey. She believes one of the most important things a young writer can do is to get to know other writers.

Building Background

Korea: A Divided Nation The poem "Etymology" refers to Korea, an Asian country that was divided after World War II into Soviet (Northern) and U.S. (Southern) zones of occupation. Political tensions between the communist government in North Korea and the noncommunist government in South Korea eventually led to the Korean War, which lasted from 1950 to 1953. During the war, hundreds of thousands of Korean civilians were killed, cities and villages were destroyed, and many families fled the country, seeking refuge in other nations. Since the war, North and South Korea have remained bitterly divided. Many Koreans have been forced to flee the country or have left in search of safety and economic security.

Literary Focus

Tone Imagine that a guy named Marcus says to you, "I really like your bike." Imagine Marcus saying this in a **tone** that is sarcastic, or hesitant, or hinting. Each tone, or attitude, would give a different meaning to his words. Since writers can't convey tone by speaking aloud, they rely on other techniques, such as word choice, presentation of characters and events, and choice of details. As you read the poems "Elena" and "Etymology," consider what each author's tone reveals about the characters and events in her poem.

Writer's Notebook

Tongue-tied Have you ever been in a place where people were speaking a language unfamiliar to you? Have you ever felt unable to communicate your thoughts or understand what someone else is saying to you? Try to remember how that felt and write down some words to express the feelings. List as many words as you can think of in your notebook.

▲ Carmen Lomas Garza, *Camas para Sueños (Beds for Dreams)*, 1985. Compare and contrast what the children on the roof might be thinking and feeling with what their mother may be thinking and feeling.

Elena
Pat Mora

My Spanish isn't enough.
I remember how I'd smile
listening to my little ones,
understanding every word they'd say,
5　their jokes, their songs, their plots.
Vamos a pedirle dulces a mamá. Vamos.[1]
But that was in Mexico.
Now my children go to American
　　high schools.
They speak English. At night they
　　sit around
10　the kitchen table, laugh at one another.
I stand by the stove and feel dumb, alone.
I bought a book to learn English.
My husband frowned, drank more beer.
My oldest said, "*Mamá*, he doesn't
　　want you
15　to be smarter than he is." I'm forty,
embarrassed at mispronouncing words,
embarrassed at the laughter of my
　　children,
the grocer, the mailman. Sometimes I take
my English book and lock myself in the
　　bathroom,
20　say the thick words softly,
for if I stop trying, I will be deaf
when my children need my help.

Etymology[2]
Amy Kashiwabara

What language is that?
I do not know

the language my mother whispered
when soldiers raided
5　the house looking for contraband[3]
radios and children

the language my grandmother shouted
at a careless sea who stole
my refugee[4] aunt

10　My older sister speaks it low over
　　the phone

the language they try to teach me

　　　It is Korean, and I can learn it.
　　　It is Korea, and I cannot.

1. *Vamos a pedirle dulces a mamá. Vamos.* (vä′mōs ä pe
   dēr′lā dül′säs ä mä mä′. Vä′mōs.) Let's go ask
   Mama for candy. Let's go. [Spanish]
2. **etymology** (et′ə mol′ə jē), *n.* the derivation of a
   word; explanation of the origin and history of a word.
3. **contraband** (kon′trə band), *n.* goods imported or
   exported contrary to law; smuggled goods.
4. **refugee** (ref′yə jē′), *n.* a person who flees for refuge
   or safety.

After Reading

Making Connections

Shaping Your Response

1. Do you sympathize with Elena? Why or why not?

2. Describe the emotions felt by the speaker in "Etymology."

Analyzing the Poems

3. 🖋 Compare and contrast the mother in "Elena" with the daughter in "Etymology." What obstacles to **communication** does each face?

4. The speaker in "Elena" feels "dumb" and worries that she will be "deaf." Explain what she means and how these words are related.

5. What does the speaker in "Etymology" mean when she says she can learn Korean but not Korea?

Extending the Ideas

6. How would you feel if people in your family grew up in a different country and spoke a different language than you? Why?

Literary Focus: Tone

Read the adjectives in the list below and choose two or three that best describe the speaker's **tone** in each poem. Explain why you chose the words you did and give examples from the poems to support your answers. You may add your own words to the list.

angry	confused	desperate	questioning
calm	curious	lonely	resigned
confident	defensive	loving	sad

Expressing Your Ideas

Writing Choice

Writer's Notebook Update Look back at the list of words you wrote to describe how it feels not being able to communicate with others. Trade lists with a partner and use the words from your partner's list to write a journal entry. Your entry should be from the point of view of someone in a situation where he or she doesn't speak the language being spoken by others. Share your journal entry with your partner.

Another Option

How Many Languages? Take a class poll to find out the languages spoken by all the students and their family members. Use the information you gather to create a **class mural** representing the languages and cultures of your classmates and their families. Include drawings, writings, photographs, or other items that depict the various languages and cultures.

Distant Voices

The Written Word

Social Studies Connection
How would history be different if we had never learned to write? This essay describes how written language has evolved through the ages.

SYMBOLS OF HUMANKIND

by Don Lago

Many thousands of years ago, a man quietly resting on a log reached down and picked up a stick and with it began scratching upon the sand at his feet. He moved the stick slowly back and forth and up and down, carefully guiding it through curves and straight lines. He gazed upon what he had made, and a gentle satisfaction lighted his face.

Other people noticed this man drawing on the sand. They gazed upon the figures he had made, and though they at once recognized the shapes of familiar things such as fish or birds or humans, they took a bit longer to realize what the man had meant to say by arranging these familiar shapes in this particular way. Understanding what he had done, they nodded or smiled in recognition.

This small band of humans didn't realize what they were beginning. The images these people left in the sand would soon be swept away by the wind, but their new idea would slowly grow until it had

Spanish cave paintings of hunters or warriors, 6000 B.C.

Cylinder seals from ancient Mesopotamia, used to seal letters written on clay tablets.

Hieroglyphs from the Kom Ombo Temple in Egypt.

Interdisciplinary Study   **241**

remade the human species. These people had discovered writing.

Writing, early people would learn, could contain much more information than human memory could and contain it more accurately. It could carry thoughts much farther than mere sounds could—farther in distance and in time. Profound thoughts born in a single mind could spread and endure.

The first written messages were simply pictures relating familiar objects in some meaningful way—pictographs. Yet there were no images for much that was important in human life. What, for instance, was the image for sorrow or bravery? So from pictographs humans developed ideograms to represent more abstract ideas. An eye flowing with tears could represent sorrow, and a man with the head of a lion might be bravery.

The next leap occurred when the figures became independent of things or ideas and came to stand for spoken sounds. Written figures were free to lose all resemblance to actual objects. Some societies developed syllabic systems of writing in which several hundred signs corresponded to several hundred spoken sounds. Others discovered the much simpler alphabetic system, in which a handful of signs represented the basic sounds the human voice can make.

At first, ideas flowed only slightly faster when written than they had through speech. But as technologies evolved, humans embodied their thoughts in new ways: through the printing press, in Morse code, in electromagnetic waves bouncing through the atmosphere and

PROFOUND THOUGHTS BORN IN A SINGLE MIND COULD SPREAD AND ENDURE.

Musical notation allows us to learn and perform songs by "reading" the music.

The Maya in Mexico and Central America made painted books of their history. Here, warriors cross a lake to capture an island.

People in China and elsewhere may use a personalized stamp called a "chop." The chop shown here reflects the birthdate and personality traits of the person for whom it was designed. ➤

in the binary language of computers.

Today, when the Earth is covered with a swarming interchange of ideas, we are even trying to send our thoughts beyond our planet to other minds in the Universe. Our first efforts at sending our thoughts beyond Earth have taken a very ancient form: pictographs. The first message, on plaques aboard Pioneer spacecraft launched in 1972 and 1973, featured a simple line drawing of two humans, one male and one female, the male holding up his hand in greeting. Behind them was an outline of the Pioneer spacecraft, from which the size of the humans could be judged. The plaque also included the "address" of the two human figures: a picture of the solar system, with a spacecraft emerging from the third planet. Most exobiologists believe that when other civilizations attempt to communicate with us they too will use pictures.

All the accomplishments since humans first scribbled in the sand have led us back to where we began. Written language only works when two individuals know what the symbols mean. We can only return to the simplest form of symbol available and work from there. In interstellar communication, we are at the same stage our ancestors were when they used sticks to trace a few simple images in the sand.

We still hold their sticks in our hands and draw pictures with them. But the stick is no longer made of wood; over the ages that piece of wood has been transformed into a massive radio telescope. And we no longer scratch on sand; now we write our thoughts onto the emptiness of space itself.

NOW WE WRITE OUR THOUGHTS ONTO THE EMPTINESS OF SPACE ITSELF.

ISBN 0-673-29447-1

The vertical lines and spaces in a bar code, readable by machine, contain a wealth of information about the product.

International signs use pictographic images to communicate in every language.

Before the telephone, messages in Morse Code traveled over telegraph wires in a series of dots and dashes. The word here is "communication." ➤

Responding

1. Describe what life might be like today if we had never learned to write.

2. Give your predictions about how the process of writing will change in the next hundred years.

Reading Mini-Lesson

Cause and Effect

Good readers look for organizational patterns in what they read. One common pattern that authors use is **cause and effect.** An event (the cause) leads to another event or to a whole series of events (the effect).

In "Symbols of Humankind," author Don Lago uses cause and effect to describe the history of written communication. In the first paragraph of the article, he describes how a human being draws a picture story in the sand. He then explains how this event causes other people to realize that it is possible to communicate through written pictures. That discovery then causes other events to occur. The following diagram illustrates some of the cause-effect relationships in "Symbols of Humankind."

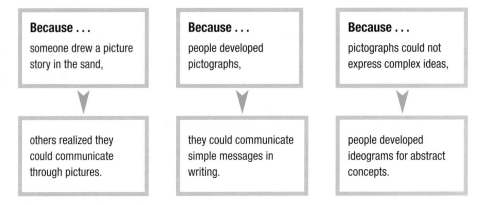

Because . . .	**Because . . .**	**Because . . .**
someone drew a picture story in the sand,	people developed pictographs,	pictographs could not express complex ideas,
↓	↓	↓
others realized they could communicate through pictures.	they could communicate simple messages in writing.	people developed ideograms for abstract concepts.

Activity Options

1. Add to the cause-effect diagram for "Symbols of Humankind." Share your findings with classmates.

2. Work with a small group of classmates to write a comic skit that uses cause-and-effect relationships. A typical skit might begin with a dog getting loose in an antique shop, a person trying to perform a simple task in the dark, or some similar event.

Writing Workshop

Lights, Camera, Action!

Assignment Write a scene for a screenplay about people struggling to communicate across barriers imposed by differences in age, culture, gender, or personal values. Use an event from a fictional or real-life source. Here are some examples:

- "Rules of the Game" by Amy Tan, pages 6–14
- a children's story such as "Goldilocks and the Three Bears" or "Cinderella"
- a short story or journal entry you have written
- a newspaper or magazine article

WRITER'S BLUEPRINT

Product	A scene for a screenplay
Purpose	To dramatize communication problems
Audience	People who see a lot of movies
Specs	To write a successful scene, you should:

❑ Write a summary of the plot and a description of the characters so your audience will know the whole story.

❑ Write your scene—a portion of the whole story. Use dialogue and screen directions that help your readers "see" and "hear" the action as vividly as possible. Use *Sorry, Right Number* as a model.

❑ Write dialogue that signals how the characters are feeling.

❑ Follow the rules of grammar, usage, spelling, and mechanics. Take care to distinguish screen directions from dialogue.

Discuss communication barriers. In a group, review the literature from this part of the unit and other stories that focus on communication problems. Discuss these problems and their causes. Use a chart like this one to keep track of your ideas.

Story	Barriers to Communication	Results
Goldilocks and the Three Bears	—Goldilocks's fear of the bears	—Goldilocks runs away without explaining herself.

OR • • •
Assign roles to different members of your group and dramatize scenes from the stories you're discussing. Then discuss why the characters have problems communicating. Make notes on the discussion.

Find your story. On your own, choose a story that you think has the best possibilities for a screenplay. You might also choose a journal entry or a news article. To help you decide, keep these questions in mind.

✔ Does this story focus on a communication problem that I could dramatize with action and dialogue?

✔ Which characters do I understand well enough to imagine their dialogue—the actual words they will speak?

Make notes on your story, using a chart like the one above.

Choose your scene. Look over your chart and decide which scene you will write as a screenplay. Look carefully at the Barriers to Communication column. Remember, you'll want to dramatize these barriers.

Visualize your scene. At the beginning of *Sorry, Right Number,* you'll find explanations of screen directions. Visualize your scene and jot down ideas about how you might use the directions. What things are important enough that they might be shown in a CU (closeup)? What INT (interior) camera shots do you want to include?—and so on. You don't have to have ideas for every category. Just make notes on what comes to mind as you visualize your scene.

Review screenplay format. Look over *Sorry, Right Number* and notice how it follows this format:

• Names of characters and technical directions, such as camera moves and sound effects, are in SMALL CAPITAL LETTERS.

- Other stage directions are in *italic type,* which you can create on a computer. If you're writing by hand, you might underline the stage directions to set them off from the dialogue. (Stage directions within dialogue should also be enclosed in parentheses.)

Make a writing plan. Use your charts as you make your writing plan. You might use a plan that looks like this one. Make notes for each item.

Introduction
- Title of story
- Plot summary of story with emphasis on barriers to communication
- Main characters, their personalities and feelings and how they relate to communication problems

Scene
- Summary of what happens in the scene
- Some key screenplay directions I'll be using
- Some key dialogue I'll be using

OR . . .
Draw a storyboard that shows the sequence of events in your scene. Make simple drawings with notes alongside that summarize the dialogue and screen directions. See pages 250–251.

STEP 2 DRAFTING

Before you draft, look over your prewriting notes and writing plan, the Writer's Blueprint, and *Sorry, Right Number* (for screenplay format).

As you draft, try these ideas.

- Try to write dialogue that reveals characters' feelings. (See the Revising Strategy in Step 3 of this lesson.)

- Take care to distinguish between dialogue and screen directions. (See the Editing Strategy in Step 4 of this lesson.)

STEP 3 REVISING

Ask a partner for comments on your draft before you revise it.

✔ Have I followed the Specs in the Writer's Blueprint?

✔ Does the summary give my audience enough background to understand the scene?

✔ Do my screen directions dramatize the communication problem?

✔ Does the dialogue reveal how each character is feeling?

Revising Strategy

Writing Dialogue That Reveals Feelings

Effective dialogue signals how the characters are feeling. Often these feelings are not directly stated, but can be inferred from the dialogue. For example, look at the first lines the children speak in *Sorry, Right Number*.

LITERARY SOURCE

JEFF. Come *onnn!* It was his first *book!*
CONNIE. His first *gross* book.

From these two short lines of dialogue we can infer that Connie and Jeff are children, that they've been having an argument, and that Connie has said things to upset Jeff. See if you can revise your dialogue so that it reveals characters' feelings without directly stating them.

STEP 4 EDITING

Ask a partner to review your revised draft before you edit. When you edit, look for errors in grammar, usage, spelling, and mechanics. Pay special attention to distinguishing between dialogue and screen directions.

Editing Strategy

Distinguishing Between Dialogue and Screen Directions

The screenplay format in *Sorry, Right Number* makes it easy to distinguish between dialogue and screen directions. When you edit your scene, be sure you've followed this format. Notice how this writer has marked changes to clear up confusion between screen directions and dialogue.

OLD WOMAN. One of my grandaughters is about your age.

You'd like her.

TEENAGER. (Looks sideways at her and half smiles.) I'm sure I would.
→ *Enclose in parentheses and change to italic type.*

5 PRESENTING

A screenplay is a visual art form. Look for ways to enhance your words with visual experiences for your audience. Here are some options.

- Videotape your scene or present the scene live for your class.

- Read your scene to the class, using different actors to read each part. Ask classmates to try to visualize the action as you read.

6 LOOKING BACK

Self-Evaluate. What grade would *you* give your paper? Look back at the Writer's Blueprint and give yourself a score on each point, from 6 (superior) to 1 (inadequate).

Reflect. Think about what you've learned from writing this scene for a screenplay as you write answers to these questions.

✔ What have you learned about communication problems from this assignment?

✔ Was writing the dialogue easier or harder than you expected? Give reasons for your answer.

For Your Working Portfolio Add your scene and your reflection responses to your working portfolio.

Beyond Print

Looking at Movies

In the screenplay *Sorry, Right Number*, Stephen King provides suggestions for props, camera moves, lighting, and other aspects important for filming each scene. While these written instructions are helpful, it's also important to have a visual guide when planning how to shoot each scene.

Film directors use **storyboards** to help plan the look and pace of a film. A storyboard is a sequence of cartoonlike panels that depict what the camera will see as each scene is filmed. These storyboards provide a step-by-step guide for the director, camera operators, and film editors.

Storyboards for the opening scene of *Sorry, Right Number* appear on the opposite page. Notice the action is plotted out panel by panel. Brief notes alongside each panel describe what is in the shot and how the camera moves.

Prepare your own set of storyboards for a scene in *Sorry, Right Number*. Label the camera moves by using the abbreviations from page 210 that Stephen King says will make you feel like a lodge brother. Remember that storyboards do not have to be artistic masterpieces. Stick figures will do, as long as you show how each camera shot will help tell the story and build the feeling of suspense. After preparing your storyboards, present them to the rest of the class.

Activity Options

1. Assemble a movie crew, including a director, actors, a camera operator, and a lighting and props person. Using the storyboards you created for *Sorry, Right Number* as a guide, videotape the scene. Then arrange a special screening for the rest of your class.

2. Movie theaters often show brief previews, called trailers, of coming attractions. Create and display storyboards for the trailer of a frightening new film.

1. **ECU.** KATIE WEIDERMAN'S MOUTH

    KATIE: "BILL? OH, HE SAYS THAT . . ."

2. **INT.** WEIDERMAN KITCHEN

    CAMERA PANS TO SHOW KATIE ON
    PHONE, THEN ZOOMS THROUGH
    DOORWAY INTO FAMILY ROOM.

    KATIE: "BIG AS A <u>HOUSE</u>!"

3. **INT.** FAMILY ROOM

    CAMERA ZOOMS IN ON THE THREE
    KIDS ARGUING IN FRONT OF THE T.V.

    JEFF: "COME <u>ON</u>! IT WAS HIS
    FIRST <u>BOOK</u>!"

4. **INT.** FAMILY ROOM

    CU OF JEFF; THEN CAMERA PANS
    TO FOLLOW JEFF TO WINDOW

    DENNIS: "POOR JEFFIE."

Part Two

Reaching Out

Have you ever had a hard time getting through to someone? Have you given up, or have you looked for a different way to reach that person? Sometimes the search for new ways to communicate can be difficult and even controversial.

 **Multicultural Connection** **Change** challenges people to reassess their behaviors, beliefs, and traditions. People may resist change, particularly when introduced by an outsider, because it threatens to upset accepted cultural patterns. In the following selections, how do the characters grapple with change and its challenge to their ways of life?

Literature

Interdisciplinary Study The Power of Language

Writing Workshop Expository Writing

Beyond Print Technology

Before Reading

The Miracle Worker

by William Gibson

William Gibson
born 1914

William Gibson brings a variety of experiences to his writing. After two years of college, he worked at various jobs, including jazz pianist at a night club and amateur actor. In 1940, he moved to Topeka, Kansas, where he wrote a verse play that was produced by a local theater. His first popular success came with his first novel *The Cobweb* (1954). In 1957, *The Miracle Worker* was presented as a play on television. It was so well received that it was rewritten for the stage (1959) and for the movies (1962). The film version won two Academy Awards.

Building Background

Reliving the Past The play you are about to read, *The Miracle Worker,* takes place in the southern United States in the 1880s, not long after the end of the Civil War in 1865. You will notice many details about everyday life that are different from the present day. Before you read, copy the chart on this page and record your predictions about daily chores, household items, and so on during the 1880s. You will fill in the last two columns of the chart after reading the play.

Life in the 1880s	What I Predict	True?	What Else I Learned
Daily chores	pumping well water		
Common household items			
Transportation			

Literary Focus

Conflict In every story there is a **conflict** of opposing forces, a struggle, a problem to be resolved. Conflicts that pit a main character against an outside factor—another character or thing, the forces of nature, the power of society, etc.—are called **external** conflicts. Conflicts that occur within the main character—struggles of emotion or conscience—are called **internal** conflicts. Like many stories and plays, *The Miracle Worker* contains several conflicts, both internal and external.

Writer's Notebook

Don't Give Up In your notebook, write about a time when you or someone you know refused to give up. Describe the situation in detail: When and where did it take place? Why was the person so determined to "hang in there"? What was the result?

The Miracle Worker

William Gibson

Act One

CHARACTERS

A DOCTOR	JAMES
KATE	ANAGNOS
ARTHUR KELLER	ANNIE SULLIVAN
HELEN	VINEY
MARTHA	BLIND GIRLS
PERCY	A SERVANT
AUNT EV	OFFSTAGE VOICES

TIME   *The 1880s*

PLACE   *In and around the Keller homestead in Tuscumbia, Alabama; also, briefly, the Perkins Institution for the Blind, in Boston.*

◄ An 1888 photograph of eight-year-old Helen Keller and Annie Sullivan.

SCENE 1

It is night over the Keller homestead. Inside, three adults in the bedroom are grouped around a crib, in lamplight. They have been through a long vigil, and it shows in their tired bearing and disarranged clothing. One is a young gentlewoman with a sweet girlish face, KATE KELLER; *the second is an elderly* DOCTOR, *stethoscope at neck, thermometer in fingers; the third is a hearty gentleman in his forties with chin whiskers,* CAPTAIN ARTHUR KELLER.

DOCTOR. She'll live.

KATE. Thank God.

(The DOCTOR *leaves them together over the crib, packs his bag.)*

DOCTOR. You're a pair of lucky parents. I can tell you now, I thought she wouldn't.

KELLER. Nonsense, the child's a Keller, she has the constitution of a goat. She'll outlive us all.

DOCTOR *(amiably).*[1] Yes, especially if some of you Kellers don't get a night's sleep. I mean you, Mrs. Keller.

KELLER. You hear, Katie?

KATE. I hear.

KELLER *(indulgent).*[2] I've brought up two of them, but this is my wife's first, she isn't battle-scarred yet.

KATE. Doctor, don't be merely considerate, will my girl be all right?

DOCTOR. Oh, by morning she'll be knocking down Captain Keller's fences again.

KATE. And isn't there anything we should do?

KELLER *(jovial).* Put up stronger fencing, ha?

---

1. amiably (ā′mē ə blē), *adv.* with a friendly attitude; peaceably.
2. indulgent (in dul′jənt), *adj.* making allowances; not critical; lenient.

DOCTOR. Just let her get well, she knows how to do it better than we do.

(*He is packed, ready to leave.*)

Main thing is the fever's gone, these things come and go in infants, never know why. Call it acute congestion of the stomach and brain.

KELLER. I'll see you to your buggy, Doctor.

DOCTOR. I've never seen a baby, more vitality, that's the truth.

(*He beams a good night at the baby and* KATE, *and* KELLER *leads him downstairs with a lamp. They go down the porch steps, and across the yard, where the* DOCTOR *goes off left;* KELLER *stands with the lamp aloft.* KATE *meanwhile is bent lovingly over the crib, which emits a bleat; her finger is playful with the baby's face.*)

KATE. Hush. Don't you cry now, you've been trouble enough. Call it acute congestion, indeed. I don't see what's so cute about a congestion, just because it's yours. We'll have your father run an editorial in his paper, the wonders of modern medicine, they don't know what they're curing even when they cure it. Men, men and their battle scars, we women will have to—

(*But she breaks off, puzzled, moves her finger before the baby's eyes.*)

Will have to—Helen?

(*Now she moves her hand, quickly.*)

Helen.

(*She snaps her fingers at the baby's eyes twice, and her hand falters; after a moment she calls out, loudly.*)

Captain. Captain, will you come—

(*But she stares at the baby, and her next call is directly at her ears.*)

Captain!

(*And now, still staring,* KATE *screams.* KELLER *in the yard hears it, and runs with the lamp back to the house.* KATE *screams again, her look intent on the baby and terrible.* KELLER *hurries in and up.*)

KELLER. Katie? What's wrong?

KATE. Look.

(*She makes a pass with her hand in the crib, at the baby's eyes.*)

KELLER. What, Katie? She's well, she needs only time to—

KATE. She can't see. Look at her eyes.

(*She takes the lamp from him, moves it before the child's face.*)

She can't *see!*

KELLER (*hoarsely*). Helen.

KATE. Or hear. When I screamed she didn't blink. Not an eyelash—

KELLER. Helen. Helen!

KATE. She can't *hear* you!

KELLER. *Helen!*

(*His face has something like fury in it, crying the child's name;* KATE *almost fainting presses her knuckles to her mouth, to stop her own cry.*

The room dims out quickly.)

SCENE 2

Time, in the form of a slow tune of distant belfry chimes which approaches in a crescendo and then fades, passes; the light comes up again on a day five years later, on three kneeling children and an old dog outside around the pump.

The dog is a setter named BELLE, *and she is sleeping. Two of the children are Negroes,* MARTHA *and* PERCY. *The third child is* HELEN, *six and a half years old, quite unkempt, in body a vivacious[3] little person with a fine head, attractive, but noticeably blind, one eye larger and protruding; her gestures are abrupt, insistent, lacking in human restraint, and her face never smiles. She is flanked by the other two, in a litter of paper-doll cutouts, and while they speak* HELEN's *hands thrust at their faces in turn, feeling baffledly at the movements of their lips.*

MARTHA (*snipping*). First I'm gonna cut off this doctor's legs, one, two, now then—

PERCY. Why you cuttin' off that doctor's legs?

MARTHA. I'm gonna give him a operation. Now

---

3. **vivacious** (vī vā′shəs), *adj.* lively; sprightly; animated.

I'm gonna cut off his arms, one, two. Now I'm gonna fix up—

(She pushes HELEN's *hand away from her mouth.)*

You stop that.

PERCY. Cut off his stomach, that's a good operation.

MARTHA. No, I'm gonna cut off his head first, he got a bad cold.

PERCY. Ain't gonna be much of that doctor left to fix up, time you finish all them opera—

(But HELEN *is poking her fingers inside his mouth, to feel his tongue; he bites at them, annoyed, and she jerks them away.* HELEN *now fingers her own lips, moving them in imitation, but soundlessly.)*

MARTHA. What you do, bite her hand?

PERCY. That's how I do, she keep pokin' her fingers in my mouth, I just bite 'em off.

MARTHA. What she tryin' do now?

PERCY. She tryin' *talk.* She gonna get mad. Looka her tryin' talk.

*(*HELEN *is scowling, the lips under her fingertips moving in ghostly silence, growing more and more frantic, until in a bizarre rage she bites at her own fingers. This sends* PERCY *off into laughter, but alarms* MARTHA.)*

MARTHA. Hey, you stop now.

(She pulls HELEN's *hand down.)*

You just sit quiet and—

(But at once HELEN *topples* MARTHA *on her back, knees pinning her shoulders down, and grabs the scissors.* MARTHA *screams.* PERCY *darts to the bell string on the porch, yanks it, and the bell rings.*

Inside, the lights have been gradually coming up on the main room, where we see the family informally gathered, talking, but in pantomine: KATE *sits darning socks near a cradle, occasionally rocking it;* CAPTAIN KELLER *in spectacles is working over newspaper pages at a table; a benign visitor in a hat,* AUNT EV, *is sharing the sewing basket, putting the finishing touches on a big shapeless doll made out of towels; an indolent young man,* JAMES KELLER, *is at the window watching the children.*

With the ring of the bell, KATE *is instantly on her feet and out the door onto the porch, to take in the scene;*

now we see what these five years have done to her, the girlish playfulness is gone, she is a woman steeled in grief.)

KATE *(for the thousandth time).* Helen.

(She is down the steps at once to them, seizing HELEN's *wrists and lifting her off* MARTHA; MARTHA *runs off in tears and screams for Momma, with* PERCY *after her.)*

Let me have those scissors.

(Meanwhile the family inside is alerted, AUNT EV *joining* JAMES *at the window;* CAPTAIN KELLER *resumes work.)*

JAMES *(blandly).* She only dug Martha's eyes out. Almost dug. It's always almost, no point worrying till it happens, is there?

(They gaze out, while KATE *reaches for the scissors in* HELEN's *hand. But* HELEN *pulls the scissors back, they struggle for them a moment, then* KATE *gives up, lets* HELEN *keep them. She tries to draw* HELEN *into the house.* HELEN *jerks away.* KATE *next goes down on her knees, takes* HELEN's *hands gently, and using the scissors like a doll, makes* HELEN *caress and cradle them; she points* HELEN's *finger housewards.* HELEN's *whole body now becomes eager; she surrenders the scissors,* KATE *turns her toward the door and gives her a little push.* HELEN *scrambles up and toward the house, and* KATE *rising follows her.)*

AUNT EV. How does she stand it? Why haven't you seen this Baltimore man? It's not a thing you can let go on and on, like the weather.

JAMES. The weather here doesn't ask permission of me, Aunt Ev. Speak to my father.

AUNT EV. Arthur. Something ought to be done for that child.

KELLER. A refreshing suggestion. What?

*(*KATE *entering turns* HELEN *to* AUNT EV, *who gives her the towel doll.)*

AUNT EV. Why, this very famous oculist[4] in Baltimore I wrote you about, what was his name?

---

4. **oculist** (ok′yə list), *n.* doctor who examines and treats defects and diseases of the eye; ophthalmologist.

KATE. Dr. Chisholm.[5]

AUNT EV. Yes, I heard lots of cases of blindness people thought couldn't be cured he's cured, he just does wonders. Why don't you write to him?

KELLER. I've stopped believing in wonders.

KATE *(rocks the cradle).* I think the Captain will write to him soon. Won't you Captain?

KELLER. No.

JAMES *(lightly).* Good money after bad, or bad after good. Or bad after bad—

AUNT EV. Well, if it's just a question of money, Arthur, now you're marshal you have this Yankee money.[6] Might as well—

KELLER. Not money. The child's been to specialists all over Alabama and Tennessee, if I thought it would do good I'd have her to every fool doctor in the country.

KATE. I think the Captain will write to him soon.

KELLER. Katie. How many times can you let them break your heart?

KATE. Any number of times.

(HELEN meanwhile sits on the floor to explore the doll with her fingers, and hand pauses over the face: this is no face, a blank area of towel, and it troubles her. Her hand searches for features, and taps questioningly for eyes, but no one notices. She then yanks at her AUNT*'s dress, and taps again vigorously for eyes.)*

AUNT EV. What, child?

(Obviously not hearing, HELEN *commences to go around, from person to person, tapping for eyes, but no one attends or understands.)*

KATE *(no break).* As long as there's the least chance. For her to see. Or hear, or—

KELLER. There isn't. Now I must finish here.

KATE. I think, with your permission, Captain, I'd like to write.

◄ Production still from the 1962 film *The Miracle Worker,* starring Anne Bancroft as Annie Sullivan and Patty Duke as Helen Keller. Helen asks for eyes for her doll as her mother and Aunt Ev look on uncomprehendingly.

KELLER. I said no, Katie.

AUNT EV. Why, writing does no harm, Arthur, only a little bitty letter. To see if he can help her.

KELLER. He can't.

KATE. We won't know that to be a fact, Captain, until after you write.

KELLER *(rising, emphatic[7]).* Katie, he can't. *(He collects his papers.)*

JAMES *(facetiously).* Father stands up, that makes it a fact.

KELLER. You be quiet! I'm badgered enough here by females without your impudence.

*(*JAMES *shuts up, makes himself scarce.* HELEN *now is groping among things on* KELLER*'s desk, and paws his papers to the floor.* KELLER *is exasperated.)*

Katie.

*(*KATE *quickly turns* HELEN *away, and retrieves the papers.)*

I might as well try to work in a henyard as in this house—

JAMES *(placating[8]).* You really ought to put her away, Father.

KATE *(staring up).* What?

JAMES. Some asylum. It's the kindest thing.

AUNT EV. Why, she's your sister, James, not a nobody—

JAMES. Half sister, and half—mentally defective, she can't even keep herself clean. It's not pleasant to see her about all the time.

KATE. Do you dare? Complain of what you *can* see?

KELLER *(very annoyed).* This discussion is at an end! I'll thank you not to broach it again, Ev.

(Silence descends at once. HELEN *gropes her way with the doll, and* KELLER *turns back for a final word, explosive.)*

---

5. **Chisholm** (chiz′əm).
6. **now you're marshal you have this Yankee money.** Though Keller owned property, he lacked cash until he was appointed federal marshal.
7. **emphatic** (em fat′ik), *adj.* said or done with force or stress; strongly expressed.
8. placating (plā′kāt′ing), *adj.* soothing or satisfying the anger of; appeasing.

I've done as much as I can bear, I can't give my whole life to it! The house is at sixes and sevens[9] from morning till night over the child, it's time some attention was paid to Mildred here instead!

KATE (*gently dry*). You'll wake her up, Captain.

KELLER. I want some peace in the house, I don't care how, but one way we won't have it is by rushing up and down the country every time someone hears of a new quack. I'm as sensible to this affliction as anyone else, it hurts me to look at the girl.

KATE. It was not our affliction I meant you to write about, Captain.

(HELEN *is back at* AUNT EV, *fingering her dress, and yanks two buttons from it.*)

AUNT EV. Helen! My buttons.

(HELEN *pushes the buttons into the doll's face.* KATE *now sees, comes swiftly to kneel, lifts* HELEN*'s hand to her own eyes in question.*)

KATE. Eyes?

(HELEN *nods energetically.*)

She wants the doll to have eyes.

(*Another kind of silence now, while* KATE *takes pins and buttons from the sewing basket and attaches them to the doll as eyes.* KELLER *stands, caught, and watches morosely.* AUNT EV *blinks, and conceals her emotion by inspecting her dress.*)

AUNT EV. My goodness me, I'm not decent.

KATE. She doesn't know better, Aunt Ev. I'll sew them on again.

JAMES. Never learn with everyone letting her do anything she takes it into her mind to—

KELLER. You be quiet!

JAMES. What did I say now?

KELLER. You talk too much.

JAMES. I was agreeing with you!

KELLER. Whatever it was. Deprived child, the least she can have are the little things she wants.

(JAMES, *very wounded, stalks out of the room onto the porch; he remains there, sulking.*)

AUNT EV (*indulgently*). It's worth a couple of buttons, Kate, look.

(HELEN *now has the doll with eyes, and cannot contain herself for joy; she rocks the doll, pats it vigorously, kisses it.*)

This child has more sense than all these men Kellers, if there's ever any way to reach that mind of hers.

(*But* HELEN *suddenly has come upon the cradle, and unhesitatingly overturns it; the swaddled baby tumbles out, and* CAPTAIN KELLER *barely manages to dive and catch it in time.*)

KELLER. *Helen!*

(*All are in commotion, the baby screams, but* HELEN *unperturbed is laying her doll in its place.* KATE *on her knees pulls her hands off the cradle, wringing them;* HELEN *is bewildered.*)

KATE. Helen, Helen, you're not to do such things, how can I make you understand—

KELLER (*hoarsely*). Katie.

KATE. How can I get it into your head, my darling, my poor—

KELLER. Katie, some way of teaching her an iota[10] of discipline has to be—

KATE (*flaring*). How can you discipline an afflicted child? Is it her fault?

(HELEN*'s fingers have fluttered to her mother's lips, vainly trying to comprehend their movements.*)

KELLER. I didn't say it was her fault.

KATE. Then whose? I don't know what to do! How can I teach her, beat her—until she's black and blue?

KELLER. It's not safe to let her run around loose. Now there must be a way of confining her, somehow, so she can't—

KATE. Where, in a cage? She's a growing child, she has to use her limbs!

KELLER. Answer me one thing, is it fair to Mildred here?

---

9. **at sixes and sevens,** chaotic or full of confusion.
10. **iota** (ī ō′tə), *n.* a very small part or quantity; bit.

KATE (*inexorably*). Are you willing to put her away?

(*Now* HELEN's *face darkens in the same rage as at herself earlier, and her hand strikes at* KATE's *lips.* KATE *catches her hand again, and* HELEN *begins to kick, struggle, twist.*)

KELLER. Now what?

KATE. She wants to talk, like—*be* like you and me. (*She holds* HELEN *struggling until we hear from the child her first sound so far, an inarticulate weird noise in her throat such as an animal in a trap might make; and* KATE *releases her. The second she is free* HELEN *blunders away, collides violently with a chair, falls, and sits weeping.* KATE *comes to her, embraces, caresses, soothes her, and buries her own face in her hair, until she can control her voice.*)

Every day she slips further away. And I don't know how to call her back.

AUNT EV. Oh, I've a mind to take her up to Baltimore myself. If that doctor can't help her, maybe he'll know who can.

KELLER (*presently, heavily*). I'll write the man, Katie.

(*He stands with the baby in his clasp, staring at* HELEN's *head, hanging down on* KATE's *arm.*

The lights dim out, except the one on KATE *and* HELEN. *In the twilight,* JAMES, AUNT EV, *and* KELLER *move off slowly, formally, in separate directions;* KATE *with* HELEN *in her arms remains motionless in an image which overlaps into the next scene and fades only when it is well under way.*)

SCENE 3

Without pause, from the dark down left we hear a man's voice with a Greek accent speaking:

ANAGNOS. —who could do nothing for the girl, of course. It was Dr. Bell who thought she might somehow be taught.[11] I have written the family only that a suitable governess, Miss Annie Sullivan, has been found here in Boston—

(*The lights begin to come up, down left, on a long table and chair. The table contains equipment for*

teaching the blind by touch—a small replica of the human skeleton, stuffed animals, models of flowers and plants, piles of books. The chair contains a girl of twenty, ANNIE SULLIVAN, *with a face which in repose is grave and rather obstinate, and when active is impudent,[12] combative, twinkling with all the life that is lacking in* HELEN's, *and handsome; there is a crude vitality to her. Her suitcase is at her knee.* ANAGNOS, *a stocky bearded man, comes into the light only toward the end of his speech.*)

ANAGNOS. —and will come. It will no doubt be difficult for you there, Annie. But it has been difficult for you at our school too, hm? Gratifying, yes, when you came to us and could not spell your name, to accomplish so much here in a few years, but always an Irish battle.[13] For independence.

(*He studies* ANNIE, *humorously; she does not open her eyes.*)

This is my last time to counsel you, Annie, and you do lack some—by some I mean *all*—what, tact or talent to bend. To others. And what has saved you on more than one occasion here at Perkins is that there was nowhere to expel you to. Your eyes hurt?

ANNIE. My ears, Mr. Anagnos.

(*And now she has opened her eyes; they are inflamed, vague, slightly crossed, clouded by the granular growth of trachoma,[14] and she often keeps them closed to shut out the pain of light.*)

---

11. **It was Dr. Bell who thought she might somehow be taught.** Dr. Chisholm, the oculist in Baltimore, urged Captain Keller to contact Alexander Graham Bell, the inventor of the telephone. Bell, whose lifelong interest was the teaching of deaf people, advised Keller to write to Michael Anagnos, the director of the Perkins Institute for the Blind in Boston.

12. **impudent** (im′pyə dənt), *adj.* shamelessly bold; very rude and insolent.

13. **Irish battle,** Ireland had been striving for independence from English rule as early as the 1500s. In 1886, Home Rule, allowing the Irish to govern themselves, was defeated by England. The metaphor suggests that Annie is fiercely independent.

14. **trachoma** (trə kō′mə), *n.* a contagious inflammation of the eyeball and eyelids.

ANAGNOS *(severely)*. Nowhere but back to Tewksbury,[15] where children learn to be saucy. Annie, I know how dreadful it was there, but that battle is dead and done with, why not let it stay buried?

ANNIE *(cheerily)*. I think God must owe me a resurrection.

ANAGNOS *(a bit shocked)*. What?

ANNIE *(taps her brow)*. Well, He keeps digging up that battle!

ANAGNOS. That is not a proper thing to say, Annie. It is what I mean.

ANNIE *(meekly)*. Yes. But I know what I'm like, what's this child like?

ANAGNOS. Like?

ANNIE. Well—Bright or dull, to start off.

ANAGNOS. No one knows. And if she is dull, you have no patience with this?

ANNIE. Oh, in grown-ups you have to, Mr. Anagnos. I mean in children it just seems a little—precocious,[16] can I use that word?

ANAGNOS. Only if you can spell it.

ANNIE. Premature. So I hope at least she's a bright one.

ANAGNOS. Deaf, blind, mute—who knows? She is like a little safe, locked, that no one can open. Perhaps there is a treasure inside.

ANNIE. Maybe it's empty, too?

ANAGNOS. Possible. I should warn you, she is much given to tantrums.

ANNIE. Means something is inside. Well, so am I, if I believe all I hear. Maybe you should warn *them*.

ANAGNOS *(frowns)*. Annie. I wrote them no word of your history. You will find yourself among strangers now, who know nothing of it.

ANNIE. Well, we'll keep them in a state of blessed ignorance.

ANAGNOS. Perhaps *you* should tell it?

ANNIE *(bristling)*. Why? I have enough trouble with people who *don't* know.

ANAGNOS. So they will understand. When you have trouble.

ANNIE. The only time I have trouble is when I'm right.

(But she is amused at herself, as is ANAGNOS.*)*

Is it my fault it's so often? I won't give them trouble, Mr. Anagnos, I'll be so ladylike they won't notice I've come.

ANAGNOS. Annie, be—humble. It is not as if you have so many offers to pick and choose. You will need their affection, working with this child.

ANNIE *(humorously)*. I hope I won't need their pity.

ANAGNOS. Oh, we can all use some pity.

(Crisply.)

So. You are no longer our pupil, we throw you into the world, a teacher. *If* the child can be taught. No one expects you to work miracles, even for twenty-five dollars a month. Now, in this envelope a loan, for the railroad, which you will repay me when you have a bank account. But in this box, a gift. With our love.

*(*ANNIE *opens the small box he extends, and sees a garnet ring. She looks up, blinking, and down.)*

I think other friends are ready to say good-bye.

(He moves as though to open doors.)

ANNIE. Mr. Anagnos.

(Her voice is trembling.)

Dear Mr. Anagnos, I—

(But she swallows over getting the ring on her finger, and cannot continue until she finds a woebegone[17] joke.)

Well, what should I say, I'm an ignorant

---

15. **Tewksbury,** a poorhouse maintained by the state of Massachusetts.
16. **precocious** (pri kō′shəs), *adj.* developed too early; occurring before the natural time.
17. **woebegone** (wō′bi gôn′), *adj.* looking sad, sorrowful, or wretched.

opinionated girl, and everything I am I owe to you?

ANAGNOS *(smiles).* That is only half true, Annie.

ANNIE. Which half? I crawled in here like a drowned rat, I thought I died when Jimmie died, that I'd never again— come alive. Well, you say with love so easy, and I haven't *loved* a soul since and I never will, I suppose, but this place gave me more than my eyes back. Or taught me how to spell, which I'll never learn anyway, but with all the fights and the trouble I've been here it taught me what help is, and how to live again, and I don't want to say goodbye. Don't open the door, I'm crying.

ANAGNOS *(gently).* They will not see.

(He moves again as though opening doors, and in comes a group of girls, eight-year-olds to seventeen-year-olds; as they walk we see they are blind. ANAGNOS *shepherds them in with a hand.)*

A CHILD. Annie?

ANNIE *(her voice cheerful).* Here, Beatrice.

(As soon as they locate her voice they throng joyfully to her, speaking all at once; ANNIE *is down on her knees to the smallest, and the following are the more intelligible fragments in the general hubbub.)*

CHILDREN. There's a present. We brought you a going-away present. Annie!

ANNIE. Oh, now you shouldn't have—

CHILDREN. We did, we did, where's the present?

SMALLEST CHILD *(mournfully).* Don't go, Annie, away.

CHILDREN. Alice has it. Alice! Where's Alice? Here I am! Where? Here!

(An arm is aloft out of the group, waving a present; ANNIE *reaches for it.)*

ANNIE. I have it. I have it, everybody, should I open it?

In this photograph of the real Annie Sullivan, what does the expression on her face reveal about her character? ▼

CHILDREN. Open it! Everyone be quiet! Do, Annie! She's opening it. Ssh!

(A settling of silence while ANNIE *unwraps it. The present is a pair of smoked glasses, and she stands still.)*

Is it open, Annie?

ANNIE. It's open.

CHILDREN. It's for your eyes, Annie. Put them on, Annie! 'Cause Mrs. Hopkins said your eyes hurt since the operation. And she said you're going where the sun is *fierce.*

ANNIE. I'm putting them on now.

SMALLEST CHILD (*mournfully*). Don't go, Annie, where the sun is fierce.

CHILDREN. Do they fit all right?

ANNIE. Oh, they fit just fine.

CHILDREN. Did you put them on? Are they pretty, Annie?

ANNIE. Oh, my eyes feel hundreds of per cent better already, and pretty, why, do you know how I look in them? Splendiloquent.[18] Like a race horse!

CHILDREN (*delighted*). There's another present! Beatrice! We have a present for Helen, too! Give it to her, Beatrice. Here, Annie!

(*This present is an elegant doll, with movable eyelids and a momma sound.*)

It's for Helen. And we took up a collection to buy it. And Laura dressed it.

ANNIE. It's beautiful!

CHILDREN. So don't forget, you be sure to give it to Helen from us, Annie!

ANNIE. I promise it will be the first thing I give her. If I don't keep it for myself, that is, you know I can't be trusted with dolls!

SMALLEST CHILD (*mournfully*). Don't go, Annie, to her.

ANNIE (*her arm around her*). Sarah, dear. I don't *want* to go.

SMALLEST CHILD. Then why are you going?

ANNIE (*gently*). Because I'm a big girl now, and big girls have to earn a living. It's the only way I can. But if you don't smile for me first, what I'll just have to do is—

(*She pauses, inviting it.*)

SMALLEST CHILD. What?

ANNIE. Put *you* in my suitcase, instead of this doll. And take *you* to Helen in Alabama!

(*This strikes the children as very funny, and they begin to laugh and tease the smallest child, who after a moment does smile for* ANNIE.)

ANAGNOS (*then*). Come, children. We must get the trunk into the carriage and Annie into her train, or no one will go to Alabama. Come, come.

(*He shepherds them out and* ANNIE *is left alone on her knees with the doll in her lap. She reaches for her suitcase, and by a subtle change in the color of the light, we go with her thoughts into another time. We hear a boy's voice whispering; perhaps we see shadowy intimations of these speakers in the background.*)

BOY'S VOICE. Where we goin', Annie?

ANNIE (*in dread*). Jimmie.

BOY'S VOICE. Where we goin'?

ANNIE. I said—I'm takin' care of you—

BOY'S VOICE. Forever and ever?

MAN'S VOICE (*impersonal*). Annie Sullivan, aged nine, virtually blind. James Sullivan, aged seven—What's the matter with your leg, Sonny?

ANNIE. Forever and ever.

MAN'S VOICE. Can't he walk without that crutch?

(ANNIE *shakes her head, and does not stop shaking it.*)

Girl goes to the women's ward. Boy to the men's.

BOY'S VOICE (*in terror*). Annie! Annie, don't let them take me—Annie!

ANAGNOS (*offstage*). Annie! Annie?

(*But this voice is real, in the present, and* ANNIE *comes up out of her horror, clearing her head with a final shake; the lights begin to pick out* KATE *in the* KELLER *house, as* ANNIE *in a bright tone calls back.*)

ANNIE. Coming!

(*This word catches* KATE, *who stands half turned and attentive to it, almost as though hearing it. Meanwhile* ANNIE *turns and hurries out, lugging the suitcase.*)

SCENE 4

The room dims out; the sound of railroad wheels begins from off left, and maintains itself in a constant rhythm underneath the following scene; the remaining

---

18. **Splendiloquent** (splend′el′ə kwənt). Annie has invented a word for the occasion by combining *splendid* and *eloquent.*

lights have come up on the KELLER *homestead.* JAMES *is lounging on the porch, waiting. In the upper bedroom which is to be* ANNIE's, HELEN *is alone, puzzledly exploring, fingering, and smelling things, the curtains, empty drawers in the bureau, water in the pitcher by the washbasin, fresh towels on the bedstead. Downstairs in the family room* KATE *turning to a mirror hastily adjusts her bonnet, watched by a Negro servant in an apron,* VINEY.

VINEY. Let Mr. Jimmie go by hisself, you been pokin' that garden all day, you ought to rest your feet.

KATE. I can't wait to see her, Viney.

VINEY. Maybe she ain't gone be on this train neither.

KATE. Maybe she is.

VINEY. And maybe she ain't.

KATE. And maybe she is. Where's Helen?

VINEY. She upstairs, smellin' around. She know somethin' funny's goin' on.

KATE. Let her have her supper as soon as Mildred's in bed, and tell Captain Keller when he comes that we'll be delayed tonight.

VINEY. Again.

KATE. I don't think we need say *again.* Simply delayed will do.

(She runs upstairs to ANNIE's *room,* VINEY *speaking after her.)*

VINEY. I mean that's what he gone say. "What, again?"

*(*VINEY *works at setting the table. Upstairs* KATE *stands in the doorway, watching* HELEN's *groping explorations.)*

KATE. Yes, we're expecting someone. Someone for my Helen.

*(*HELEN *happens upon her skirt, clutches her leg;* KATE *in a tired dismay kneels to tidy her hair and soiled pinafore.)*

Oh dear, this was clean not an hour ago.

*(*HELEN *feels her bonnet, shakes her head darkly, and tugs to get it off.* KATE *retains it with one hand, diverts* HELEN *by opening her other hand under her nose.)*

Here. For while I'm gone.

*(*HELEN *sniffs, reaches, and pops something into her mouth, while* KATE *speaks a bit guiltily.)*

I don't think one peppermint drop will spoil your supper.

(She gives HELEN *a quick kiss, evades[19] her hands, and hurries downstairs again. Meanwhile* CAPTAIN KELLER *has entered the yard from around the rear of the house, newspaper under arm, cleaning off and munching on some radishes; he sees* JAMES *lounging at the porch post.)*

KELLER. Jimmie?

JAMES *(unmoving).* Sir?

KELLER *(eyes him).* You don't look dressed for anything useful, boy.

JAMES. I'm not. It's for Miss Sullivan.

KELLER. Needn't keep holding up that porch, we have wooden posts for that. I asked you to see that those strawberry plants were moved this evening.

JAMES. I'm moving your—Mrs. Keller, instead. To the station.

KELLER *(heavily).* Mrs. Keller. Must you always speak of her as though you haven't met the lady?

*(*KATE *comes out on the porch, and* JAMES *inclines his head.)*

JAMES *(ironic).* Mother.

(He starts off the porch, but sidesteps KELLER's *glare like a blow.)*

I said Mother!

KATE. Captain.

KELLER. Evening, my dear.

KATE. We're off to meet the train, Captain. Supper will be a trifle delayed tonight.

KELLER. What, again?

KATE *(backing out).* With your permission, Captain?

(And they are gone. KELLER *watches them offstage, morosely. Upstairs* HELEN *meanwhile has groped for*

---

19. **evade** (i vād'), *v.* get away from; avoid by cleverness.

her mother, touched her cheek in a meaningful gesture, waited, touched her cheek, waited, then found the open door, and made her way down. Now she comes into the family room, touches her cheek again; VINEY *regards her.*)

VINEY. What you want, honey, your momma?

(HELEN *touches her cheek again.* VINEY *goes to the sideboard, gets a tea-cake, gives it into* HELEN's *hand;* HELEN *pops it into her mouth.*)

Guess one little tea-cake ain't gone ruin your appetite.

(*She turns* HELEN *toward the door.* HELEN *wanders out onto the porch, as* KELLER *comes up the steps. Her hands encounter him, and she touches her cheek again, waits.*)

KELLER. She's gone.

(*He is awkward with her; when he puts his hand on her head, she pulls away.* KELLER *stands regarding her, heavily.*)

She's gone, my son and I don't get along, you don't know I'm your father, no one likes me, and supper's delayed.

(HELEN *touches her cheek, waits.* KELLER *fishes in his pocket.*)

Here. I brought you some stick candy, one nibble of sweets can't do any harm.

(*He gives her a large stick candy;* HELEN *falls to it.* VINEY *peers out the window.*)

VINEY (*reproachfully*). Cap'n Keller, now how'm I gone get her to eat her supper you fill her up with that trash?

KELLER (*roars*). Tend to your work!

(VINEY *beats a rapid retreat.* KELLER *thinks better of it, and tries to get the candy away from* HELEN, *but* HELEN *hangs on to it; and when* KELLER *pulls, she gives his leg a kick.* KELLER *hops about,* HELEN *takes refuge with the candy down behind the pump, and* KELLER *then irately flings his newspaper on the porch floor, stamps into the house past* VINEY *and disappears.*)

SCENE 5

The lights half dim on the homestead, where VINEY *and* HELEN *going about their business soon find their*

way off. Meanwhile, the railroad sounds off left have mounted in a crescendo to a climax typical of a depot at arrival time, the lights come up on stage left, and we see a suggestion of a station. Here ANNIE *in her smoked glasses and disarrayed by travel is waiting with her suitcase, while* JAMES *walks to meet her; she has a battered paper-bound book, which is a Perkins report,[20] under her arm.*

JAMES (*coolly*). Miss Sullivan?

ANNIE (*cheerily*). Here! At last, I've been on trains so many days I thought they must be backing up every time I dozed off—

JAMES. I'm James Keller.

ANNIE. James?

(*The name stops her.*)

I had a brother Jimmie. Are you Helen's?

JAMES. I'm only half a brother. You're to be her governess?

ANNIE (*lightly*). Well. Try!

JAMES (*eyeing her*). You look like half a governess.

(KATE *enters.* ANNIE *stands moveless, while* JAMES *takes her suitcase.* KATE's *gaze on her is doubtful, troubled.*)

Mrs. Keller, Miss Sullivan.

(KATE *takes her hand.*)

KATE (*simply*). We've met every train for two days.

(ANNIE *looks at* KATE's *face, and her good humor comes back.*)

ANNIE. I changed trains every time they stopped, the man who sold me that ticket ought to be tied to the tracks—

JAMES. You have a trunk, Miss Sullivan?

ANNIE. Yes.

(*She passes* JAMES *a claim check, and he bears the suitcase out behind them.* ANNIE *holds the battered book.* KATE *is studying her face, and* ANNIE *returns the gaze;*

---

20. **Perkins report,** report written by Dr. Samuel G. Howe, the founder of the Perkins Institute. During the 1830s Dr. Howe had taught Laura Bridgman, a young woman who was both blind and deaf, to communicate. He described his teaching methods and his progress in his annual reports to the directors of the Perkins Institute.

this is a mutual appraisal, Southern gentlewoman and working-class Irish girl, and ANNIE *is not quite comfortable under it.*)

You didn't bring Helen, I was hoping you would.

KATE. No, she's home.

(*A pause.* ANNIE *tries to make ladylike small talk, though her energy now and then erupts; she catches herself up whenever she hears it.*)

ANNIE. You—live far from town, Mrs. Keller?

KATE. Only a mile.

ANNIE. Well. I suppose I can wait one more mile. But don't be surprised if I get out to push the horse!

KATE. Helen's waiting for you, too. There's been such a bustle in the house, she expects something, heaven knows what.

(*Now she voices part of her doubt, not as such, but* ANNIE *understands it.*)

I expected—a desiccated[21] spinster. You're very young.

ANNIE (*resolutely[22]*). Oh, you should have seen me when I left Boston. I got much older on this trip.

KATE. I mean, to teach anyone as difficult as Helen.

ANNIE. *I* mean to try. They can't put you in jail for trying!

KATE. Is it possible, even? To teach a deaf-blind child *half* of what an ordinary child learns—has that ever been done?

ANNIE. Half?

KATE. A tenth.

ANNIE (*reluctantly*). No.

(KATE*'s face loses its remaining hope, still appraising her youth.*)

Dr. Howe did wonders, but—an ordinary child? No, never. But then I thought when I was going over his reports—

(*She indicates the one in her hand.*)

—he never treated them like ordinary chil-

dren. More like—eggs everyone was afraid would break.

KATE (*a pause*). May I ask how old you are?

ANNIE. Well, I'm not in my teens, you know! I'm twenty.

KATE. All of twenty.

(ANNIE *takes the bull by the horns, valiantly.*)

ANNIE. Mrs. Keller, don't lose heart just because I'm not on my last legs. I have three big advantages over Dr. Howe that money couldn't buy for you. One is his work behind me, I've read every word he wrote about it and he wasn't exactly what you'd call a man of few words. Another is to *be* young, why, I've got energy to do anything. The third is, I've been blind.

(*But it costs her something to say this.*)

KATE (*quietly*). Advantages.

ANNIE (*wry*). Well, some have the luck of the Irish, some do not.

(KATE *smiles; she likes her.*)

KATE. What will you try to teach her first?

ANNIE. First, last, and—in between, language.

KATE. Language.

ANNIE. Language is to the mind more than light is to the eye. Dr. Howe said that.

KATE. Language.

(*She shakes her head.*)

We can't get through to teach her to sit still. You *are* young, despite your years, to have such—confidence. Do you, inside?

(ANNIE *studies her face; she likes her, too.*)

ANNIE. No, to tell you the truth I'm as shaky inside as a baby's rattle!

(*They smile at each other, and* KATE *pats her hand.*)

KATE. Don't be.

(JAMES *returns to usher them off.*)

We'll do all we can to help, and to make you

---

21. **desiccated** (des′ə kāt′əd), *adj.* dried up.
22. **resolutely** (rez′ə lüt lē), *adv.* determinedly; firmly.

feel at home. Don't think of us as strangers, Miss Annie.

ANNIE *(cheerily).* Oh, strangers aren't so strange to me. I've know them all my life!

(KATE smiles again, ANNIE smiles back, and they precede JAMES offstage.)

SCENE 6

The lights dim on them, having simultaneously risen full on the house; VINEY has already entered the family room, taken a water pitcher, and come out and down to the pump. She pumps real water. As she looks offstage, we hear the clop of hoofs, a carriage stopping, and voices.

VINEY. Cap'n Keller! Cap'n Keller, they comin'!

(She goes back into the house, as KELLER comes out on the porch to gaze.)

She sure 'nuff came, Cap'n.

(KELLER descends, and crosses toward the carriage; this conversation begins offstage and moves on.)

KELLER *(very courtly).* Welcome to Ivy Green, Miss Sullivan. I take it you are Miss Sullivan—

KATE. My husband, Miss Annie, Captain Keller.

ANNIE *(her best behavior).* Captain, how do you do.

KELLER. A pleasure to see you, at last. I trust you had an agreeable journey?

ANNIE. Oh, I had several! When did this country get so big?

JAMES. Where would you like the trunk, Father?

KELLER. Where Miss Sullivan can get at it, I imagine.

ANNIE. Yes, please. Where's Helen?

KELLER. In the hall, Jimmie—

KATE. We've put you in the upstairs corner room, Miss Annie, if there's any breeze at all this summer, you'll feel it—

(In the house the setter BELLE flees into the family room, pursued by HELEN with groping hands; the dog doubles back out the same door, and HELEN still groping for her makes her way out to the porch; she is messy, her hair tumbled, her pinafore now ripped, her shoelaces untied. KELLER acquires the suitcase,

and ANNIE gets her hands on it too, though still endeavoring to live up to the general air of propertied manners.[23])

KELLER. *And* the suitcase—

ANNIE *(pleasantly).* I'll take the suitcase, thanks.

KELLER. Not at all, I have it, Miss Sullivan.

ANNIE. I'd like it.

KELLER *(gallantly).* I couldn't think of it, Miss Sullivan. You'll find in the South we—

ANNIE. Let me.

KELLER. —view women as the flowers of civiliza—

ANNIE *(impatiently).* I've got something in it for Helen!

(She tugs it free; KELLER stares.)

Thank you. When do I see her?

KATE. There. There is Helen.

(ANNIE turns, and sees HELEN on the porch. A moment of silence. Then Annie begins across the yard to her, lugging her suitcase.)

KELLER *(sotto voce[24]).* Katie—

(KATE silences him with a hand on his arm. When ANNIE finally reaches the porch steps she stops, contemplating HELEN for a last moment before entering her world. Then she drops the suitcase on the porch with intentional heaviness, HELEN starts with the jar, and comes to grope over it. ANNIE puts forth her hand, and touches HELEN's. HELEN at once grasps it, and commences to explore it, like reading a face. She moves her hand on to ANNIE's forearm, and dress; and ANNIE brings her face within reach of HELEN's fingers, which travel over it, quite without timidity, until they encounter and push aside the smoked glasses. ANNIE's gaze is grave, unpitying, very attentive. She puts her hands on HELEN's arms, but HELEN at once pulls away, and they confront each other with a distance between. Then HELEN returns to the suitcase, tries to open it, cannot. ANNIE points HELEN's hand overhead. HELEN pulls away, tries to

---

23. **general air of propertied manners,** atmosphere of wealth and distinction.
24. *sotto voce* (sot′ō vō′chē), in a low tone. [Latin]

open the suitcase again; ANNIE *points her hand over-head again.* HELEN *points overhead, a question, and* ANNIE, *drawing* HELEN*'s hand to her own face, nods.* HELEN *now begins tugging the suitcase toward the door; when* ANNIE *tries to take it from her, she fights her off and backs through the doorway with it.* ANNIE *stands a moment, then follows her in, and together they get the suitcase up the steps into* ANNIE*'s room.)*

KATE. Well?

KELLER. She's very rough, Katie.

KATE. I like her, Captain.

KELLER. Certainly rear a peculiar kind of young woman in the North. How old is she?

KATE *(vaguely).* Ohh—Well, she's not in her teens, you know.

KELLER. She's only a child. What's her family like, shipping her off alone this far?

KATE. I couldn't learn. She's very closemouthed about some things.

KELLER. Why does she wear those glasses? I like to see a person's eyes when I talk to—

KATE. For the sun. She was blind.

KELLER. Blind.

KATE. She's had nine operations on her eyes. One just before she left.

KELLER. Blind, good heavens, do they expect one blind child to teach another? Has she experience at least, how long did she teach there?

KATE. She was a pupil.

KELLER *(heavily).* Katie, Katie. This is her first position?

KATE *(bright voice).* She was valedictorian[25]—

KELLER. Here's a houseful of grownups can't cope with the child, how can an inexperienced half-blind Yankee schoolgirl manage her?

*(*JAMES *moves in with the trunk on his shoulder.)*

JAMES *(easily).* Great improvement. Now we have two of them to look after.

KELLER. You look after those strawberry plants!

*(*JAMES *stops with the trunk.* KELLER *turns from him without another word, and marches off.)*

JAMES. Nothing I say is right.

KATE. Why say anything?

(She calls.)

Don't be long, Captain, we'll have supper right away—

(She goes into the house, and through the rear door of the family room. JAMES *trudges in with the trunk, takes it up the steps to* ANNIE*'s room, and sets it down outside the door. The lights elsewhere dim somewhat.)*

SCENE 7

Meanwhile, inside, ANNIE *has given* HELEN *a key; while* ANNIE *removes her bonnet,* HELEN *unlocks and opens the suitcase. The first thing she pulls out is a voluminous shawl. She fingers it until she perceives what it is; then she wraps it around her, and acquiring* ANNIE*'s bonnet and smoked glasses as well, dons the lot: the shawl swamps her, and the bonnet settles down upon the glasses, but she stands before a mirror cocking her head to one side, then to the other, in a mockery of adult action.* ANNIE *is amused, and talks to her as one might to a kitten, with no trace of company manners.*

ANNIE. All the trouble I went to and that's how I look?

*(*HELEN *then comes back to the suitcase, gropes for more, lifts out a pair of female drawers.)*

Oh, no. Not the drawers!

(But HELEN *discarding them comes to the elegant doll. Her fingers explore its features, and when she raises it and finds its eyes open and close, she is at first startled, then delighted. She picks it up, taps its head vigorously, taps her own chest, and nods questioningly.* ANNIE *takes her finger, points it to the doll, points it to* HELEN, *and touching it to her own face, also nods.* HELEN *sits back on her heels, clasps the doll to herself, and rocks it.* ANNIE *studies her, still in bonnet and smoked glasses like a caricature of herself, and addresses her humorously.)*

---

25. **valedictorian** (val′ə dik tôr′ē ən), *n.* student who gives the farewell address at the graduating exercises, often the highest ranking student in the class.

All right, Miss O'Sullivan. Let's begin with doll.

(*She takes* HELEN*'s hand; in her palm* ANNIE*'s forefinger points, thumb holding her other fingers clenched.*)

D.

(*Her thumb next holds all her fingers clenched, touching* HELEN*'s palm.*)

O.

(*Her thumb and forefinger extend.*)

L.

(*Same contact repeated.*)

L.

(*She puts* HELEN*'s hand to the doll.*)

Doll.

JAMES. You spell pretty well.

(ANNIE *in one hurried move gets the drawers swiftly back into the suitcase, the lid banged shut, and her head turned, to see* JAMES *leaning in the doorway.*)

Finding out if she's ticklish? She is.

(ANNIE *regards him stonily, but* HELEN *after a scowling moment tugs at her hand again,* imperious.[26] ANNIE *repeats the letters, and* HELEN *interrupts her fingers in the middle, feeling each of them, puzzled.* ANNIE *touches* HELEN*'s hand to the doll, and begins spelling into it again.*)

JAMES. What is it, a game?

ANNIE (*curtly*). An alphabet.

JAMES. Alphabet?

ANNIE. For the deaf.

(HELEN *now repeats the finger movements in air, exactly, her head cocked to her own hand, and* ANNIE*'s eyes suddenly gleam.*)

Ho. How *bright* she is!

JAMES. You think she knows what she's doing?

(*He takes* HELEN*'s hand, to throw a meaningless gesture into it; she repeats this one too.*)

She imitates everything, she's a monkey.

◄ Production still from the 1962 film *The Miracle Worker*. Annie gives Helen a doll and tries to teach her the word for it.

ANNIE (*very pleased*). Yes, she's a bright little monkey, all right.

(*She takes the doll from* HELEN, *and reaches for her hand;* HELEN, *instantly grabs the doll back.* ANNIE *takes it again, and* HELEN*'s hand next, but* HELEN *is incensed*[27] *now; when* ANNIE *draws her hand to her face to shake her head no, then tries to spell to her,* HELEN *slaps at* ANNIE*'s face.* ANNIE *grasps* HELEN *by both arms, and swings her into a chair, holding her pinned there, kicking, while glasses, doll, bonnet fly in various directions.* JAMES *laughs.*)

JAMES. She wants her doll back.

ANNIE. When she spells it.

JAMES. Spell, she doesn't know the thing has a name, even.

ANNIE. Of course not, who expects her to, now? All I want is her fingers to learn the letters.

JAMES. Won't mean anything to her.

(ANNIE *gives him a look. She then tries to form* HELEN*'s fingers into the letters, but* HELEN *swings a haymaker*[28] *instead, which* ANNIE *barely ducks, at once pinning her down again.*)

Doesn't like that alphabet, Miss Sullivan. You invent it yourself?

(HELEN *is now in a rage, fighting tooth and nail to get out of the chair, and* ANNIE *answers while struggling and dodging her kicks.*)

ANNIE. Spanish monks under a—vow of silence. Which I wish *you'd* take!

(*And suddenly releasing* HELEN*'s hands, she comes and shuts the door in* JAMES*'s face.* HELEN *drops to the floor, groping around for the doll.* ANNIE *looks around desperately, sees her purse on the bed, rummages in it, and comes up with a battered piece of cake wrapped in newspaper; with her foot she moves the doll deftly out of the way of* HELEN*'s groping, and going on her knee she lets* HELEN *smell the cake. When* HELEN *grabs for*

---

26. **imperious** (im pir′ē əs), *adj.* haughty or arrogant; overbearing.
27. **incensed** (in senst′), *adj.* very angry; filled with rage.
28. **haymaker** (hā′mā′kər), *n.* (slang) a hard, swinging, upward blow with the fist.

it, ANNIE *removes the cake and spells quickly into the reaching hand.*)

Cake. From Washington up north, it's the best I can do.

(HELEN*'s hand waits, baffled.* ANNIE *repeats it.*)

C,a,k,e. Do what my fingers do, never mind what it means.

(*She touches the cake briefly to* HELEN*'s nose, pats her hand, presents her own hands.* HELEN *spells the letters rapidly back.* ANNIE *pats her hand enthusiastically, and gives her the cake;* HELEN *crams it into her mouth with both hands.* ANNIE *watches her, with humor.*)

Get it down fast, maybe I'll steal that back too. Now.

(*She takes the doll, touches it to* HELEN*'s nose, and spells again into her hand.*)

D, o, l, l. Think it over.

(HELEN *thinks it over, while* ANNIE *presents her own hand. Then* HELEN *spells three letters.* ANNIE *waits a second, then completes the word for* HELEN *in her palm.*)

L.

(*She hands over the doll, and* HELEN *gets a good grip on its leg.*)

Imitate now, understand later. End of the first les—

(*She never finishes, because* HELEN *swings the doll with a furious energy, it hits* ANNIE *squarely in the face, and she falls back with a cry of pain, her knuckles up to her mouth.* HELEN *waits, tensed for further combat. When* ANNIE *lowers her knuckles she looks at blood on them; she works her lips, gets to her feet, finds the mirror, and bares her teeth at herself. Now she is furious herself.*)

You little wretch, no one's taught you *any* manners? I'll—

(*But rounding from the mirror she sees the door slam.* HELEN *and the doll are on the outside, and* HELEN *is turning the key in the lock.* ANNIE *darts over, to pull the knob; the door is locked fast. She yanks it again.*)

Helen! Helen, let me out of—

(*She bats her brow at the folly of speaking, but* JAMES, *now downstairs, hears her and turns to see* HELEN *with the key and doll groping her way down the steps;* JAMES *takes in the whole situation, makes a move to intercept* HELEN, *but then changes his mind, lets her pass, and amusedly follows her out onto the porch. Upstairs* ANNIE *meanwhile rattles the knob, kneels, peers through the keyhole, gets up. She goes to the window, looks down, frowns.* JAMES *from the yard sings gaily up to her:*)

JAMES. Buffalo girl, are you coming out tonight, Coming out tonight, Coming out—

(*He drifts back into the house.* ANNIE *takes a handkerchief, nurses her mouth, stands in the middle of the room, staring at door and window in turn, and so catches sight of herself in the mirror, her cheek scratched, her hair disheveled, her handkerchief bloody, her face disgusted with herself. She addresses the mirror, with some irony.*)

ANNIE. Don't worry. They'll find you, you're not lost. Only out of place.

(*But she coughs, spits something into her palm, and stares at it, outraged.*)

And toothless.

(*She winces.*)

Oo! It hurts.

(*She pours some water into the basin, dips the handkerchief, and presses it to her mouth. Standing there, bent over the basin in pain—with the rest of the set dim and unreal, and the lights upon her taking on the subtle color of the past—she hears again, as do we, the faraway voices, and slowly she lifts her head to them; the boy's voice is the same, the others are cracked old crones in a nightmare, and perhaps we see their shadows.*)

BOY'S VOICE. It hurts. Annie, it hurts.

FIRST CRONE'S VOICE. Keep that brat shut up, can't you, girlie, how's a body to get any sleep in this damn ward?

BOY'S VOICE. It hurts. It hurts.

SECOND CRONE'S VOICE. Shut up, you!

BOY'S VOICE. Annie, when are we goin' home? You promised!

ANNIE. Jimmie—

BOY'S VOICE. Forever and ever, you said forever—

(ANNIE *drops the handkerchief, averts to the window, and is arrested there by the next cry.*)

Annie? Annie, you there? Annie! It *hurts!*

THIRD CRONE'S VOICE. Grab him, he's fallin'!

BOY'S VOICE. *Annie!*

DOCTOR'S VOICE (*a pause, slowly*). Little girl. Little girl, I must tell you your brother will be going on a—

(But ANNIE *claps her hands to her ears, to shut this out; there is instant silence. As the lights bring the other areas in again,* JAMES *goes to the steps to listen for any sound from upstairs.* KELLER *reentering from left crosses toward the house; he passes* HELEN *en route to her retreat under the pump.* KATE *reenters the rear door of the family room, with flowers for the table.*)

KATE. Supper is ready, Jimmie, will you call your father?

JAMES. Certainly.

(*But he calls up the stairs, for* ANNIE'*s benefit:*)

Father! Supper!

KELLER (*at the door*). No need to shout, I've been cooling my heels for an hour. Sit down.

JAMES. Certainly.

KELLER. Viney!

(VINEY *backs in with a roast, while they get settled around the table.*)

VINEY. Yes, Cap'n, right here.

KATE. Mildred went directly to sleep, Viney?

VINEY. Oh yes, that babe's a angel.

KATE. And Helen had a good supper?

VINEY (*vaguely*). I dunno, Miss Kate, somehow she didn't have much of a appetite tonight—

KATE (*a bit guilty*). Oh. Dear.

KELLER (*hastily*). Well, now. Couldn't say the same for my part, I'm famished.[29] Katie, your plate.

KATE (*looking*). But where is Miss Annie?

(*A silence.*)

JAMES (*pleasantly*). In her room.

KELLER. In her room? Doesn't she know hot food must be eaten hot? Go bring her down at once, Jimmie.

JAMES (*rising*). Certainly, I'll get a ladder.

KELLER (*stares*). What?

JAMES. I'll need a ladder. Shouldn't take me long.

KATE (*stares*). What shouldn't take you—

KELLER. Jimmie, do as I say! Go upstairs at once and tell Miss Sullivan supper is getting cold—

JAMES. She's locked in her room.

KELLER. Locked in her—

KATE. What on earth are you—

JAMES. Helen locked her in and made off with the key.

KATE (*rising*). And you sit here and say nothing?

JAMES. Well, everyone's been telling me not to say anything.

(*He goes serenely out and across the yard, whistling.* KELLER *thrusting up from his chair makes for the stairs.*)

KATE. Viney, look out in back for Helen. See if she has that key.

VINEY. Yes, Miss Kate.

(VINEY *goes out the rear door.*)

KELLER (*calling down*). She's out by the pump!

(KATE *goes out on the porch after* HELEN, *while* KELLER *knocks on* ANNIE'*s door, then rattles the knob, imperiously.*)

Miss Sullivan! Are you in there?

ANNIE. Oh, I'm in here, all right.

KELLER. Is there no key on your side?

ANNIE (*with some asperity*). Well, if there was a key in here, *I* wouldn't be in here. Helen took it, the only thing on my side is me.

KELLER. Miss Sullivan. I—

(*He tries, but cannot hold it back.*)

---

29. **famished** (fam′isht), *adj.* very hungry; starving.

Not in the house ten minutes, I don't see *how* you managed it!

(*He stomps downstairs again, while* ANNIE *mutters to herself.*)

ANNIE. And even I'm not on my side.

KELLER (*roaring*). Viney!

VINEY (*reappearing*). Yes Cap'n?

KELLER. Put that meat back in the oven!

(VINEY *bears the roast off again, while* KELLER *strides out onto the porch.* KATE *is with* HELEN *at the pump, opening her hands.*)

KATE. She has no key.

KELLER. Nonsense, she must have the key. Have you searched in her pockets?

KATE. Yes. She doesn't have it.

KELLER. Katie, she must have the key.

KATE. Would you prefer to search her yourself, Captain?

KELLER. No, I would not prefer to search her! She almost took my kneecap off this evening, when I tried merely to—

(JAMES *reappears carrying a long ladder, with* PERCY *running after him to be in on things.*)

Take the ladder back!

JAMES. Certainly.

(*He turns around with it.* MARTHA *comes skipping around the upstage corner of the house to be in on things, accompanied by the setter* BELLE.)

KATE. She could have hidden the key.

KELLER. Where?

KATE. Anywhere. Under a stone. In the flower beds. In the grass—

KELLER. Well, I can't plow up the entire grounds to find a missing key! Jimmie!

JAMES. Sir?

KELLER. Bring me a ladder!

JAMES. Certainly.

(VINEY *comes around the downstage side of the house to be in on things; she has* MILDRED *over her shoulder, bleating.* KELLER *places the ladder against* ANNIE'*s window and mounts.* ANNIE *meanwhile is running*

about making herself presentable, washing the blood off her mouth, straightening her clothes, tidying her hair. Another Negro servant enters to gaze in wonder, increasing the gathering ring of spectators.)

KATE (*sharply*). What is Mildred doing up?

VINEY. Cap'n woke her, ma'am, all that hollerin'.

KELLER. Miss Sullivan!

(ANNIE *comes to the window, with as much air of gracious normality as she can manage;* KELLER *is at the window.*)

ANNIE (*brightly*). Yes, Captain Keller?

KELLER. Come out!

ANNIE. I don't see how I can. There isn't room.

KELLER. I intend to carry you. Climb onto my shoulder and hold tight.

ANNIE. Oh, no. It's—very chivalrous of you, but I'd really prefer to—

KELLER. Miss Sullivan, follow instructions! I will not have you also tumbling out of our windows.

(ANNIE *obeys, with some misgivings.*)

I hope this is not a sample of what we may expect from you. In the way of simplifying the work of looking after Helen.

ANNIE. Captain Keller. I'm perfectly able to go down a ladder under my own—

KELLER. I doubt it, Miss Sullivan. Simply hold onto my neck.

(*He begins down with her, while the spectators stand in a wide and somewhat awe-stricken circle, watching.* KELLER *half-misses a rung, and* ANNIE *grabs at his whiskers.*)

My *neck*, Miss Sullivan!

ANNIE. I'm sorry to inconvenience you this way—

KELLER. No inconvenience, other than having that door taken down and the lock replaced, if we fail to find that key.

ANNIE. Oh, I'll look everywhere for it.

KELLER. Thank you. Do not look in any rooms that can be locked. There.

(*He stands her on the ground.* JAMES *applauds.*)

ANNIE. Thank you very much.

(She smoothes her skirt, looking as composed and lady-like as possible. KELLER *stares around at the spectators.)*

KELLER. Go, go, back to your work. What are you looking at here? There's nothing here to look at.

(They break up, move off.)

Now would it be possible for us to have supper, like other people?

(He marches into the house.)

KATE. Viney, serve supper. I'll put Mildred to sleep.

(They all go in. JAMES *is the last to leave, murmuring to* ANNIE *with a gesture.)*

JAMES. Might as well leave the l, a, d, d, e, r, hm?

*(*ANNIE *ignores him, looking at* HELEN; JAMES *goes in too. Imperceptibly the lights commence to narrow down.* ANNIE *and* HELEN *are now alone in the yard,* HELEN *seated at the pump, where she has been oblivious to it all, a battered little savage, playing with the doll in a picture of innocent contentment.* ANNIE *comes near, leans against the house, and taking off her smoked glasses, studies her, not without awe. Presently* HELEN *rises, gropes around to see if anyone is present;* ANNIE *evades her hand, and when* HELEN *is satisfied she is alone, the key suddenly protrudes out of her mouth. She takes it in her fingers, stands thinking, gropes to the pump, lifts a loose board, drops the key into the well, and hugs herself gleefully.* ANNIE *stares. But after a moment she shakes her head to herself, she cannot keep the smile from her lips.)*

ANNIE. You *devil.*

(Her tone is one of great respect, humor, and acceptance of challenge.)

You think I'm so easily gotten rid of? You have a thing or two to learn, first. I have nothing else to do.

(She goes up the steps to the porch, but turns for a final word, almost of warning.)

And nowhere to go.

(And presently she moves into the house to the others, as the lights dim down and out, except for the small circle upon HELEN *solitary at the pump, which ends the act.)*

After Reading

Making Connections

Annie   Helen

1. Make a Venn diagram for Annie and Helen, showing their differences and the traits they have in common.

2. If you were Annie, what would you do next? Why?

3. What signs of intelligence does Helen show?

4. How does Annie Sullivan hope to educate Helen? Explain.

5. Describe Kate's first impression of Annie, and how it changes.

6. If Helen were a child today, how would her circumstances be different? What aspects of her situation would remain the same?

Vocabulary Study

Match each vocabulary word on the left with its synonym on the right. Use your Glossary if necessary.

1. amiably   a. avoid
2. evade   b. soothing
3. famished   c. lenient
4. imperious   d. angry
5. impudent   e. hungry
6. incensed   f. nicely
7. indulgent   g. firmly
8. placating   h. lively
9. resolutely   i. overbearing
10. vivacious   j. rude

Expressing Your Ideas

Writing Choice

Dear Diary As Annie, write a **diary entry** that tells about your first day on the job. Describe your first impressions and concerns.

Another Option

Dramatic Action With others in a small group, act out a scene or part of a scene in Act 1. Be sure to study both the dialogue and stage directions to prepare for a **performance** in front of your class.

Photograph of Helen Keller as a child, at about the time the events in *The Miracle Worker* took place. Contrast how Helen appears in this photo with the way she is portrayed at this point in the play. ➤

Act Two

SCENE 1

It is evening. The only room visible in the Keller house is ANNIE*'s, where by lamplight* ANNIE *in a shawl is at a desk writing a letter; at her bureau* HELEN *in her customary unkempt state is tucking her doll in the bottom drawer as a cradle, the contents of which she has dumped out, creating as usual a fine disorder.* ANNIE *mutters each word as she writes her letter, slowly, her eyes close to and almost touching the page, to follow with difficulty her penwork.*

ANNIE. ". . . and, nobody, here, has, attempted, to, control, her. The, greatest, problem, I, have, is, how, to, discipline, her, without, breaking, her, spirit."

(Resolute voice.)

"But, I, shall insist, on, reasonable, obedience, from, the, start—"

(At which point HELEN*, groping about on the desk, knocks over the inkwell.* ANNIE *jumps up, rescues her letter, rights the inkwell, grabs a towel to stem the spillage, and then wipes at* HELEN*'s hands;* HELEN *as always pulls free, but not until* ANNIE *first gets three letters into her palm.)*

Ink.

*(*HELEN *is enough interested in and puzzled by this spelling that she proffers her hand again; so* ANNIE *spells and impassively dunks it back in the spillage.)*

The Miracle Worker—Act Two, Scene 1   277

Ink. It has a name.

(*She wipes the hand clean, and leads* HELEN *to her bureau, where she looks for something to engage her. She finds a sewing card, with needle and thread, and going to her knees, shows* HELEN*'s hand how to connect one row of holes.*)

Down. Under. Up. And be careful of the needle—

(HELEN *gets it and* ANNIE *rises.*)

Fine. You keep out of the ink and perhaps I can keep out of—the soup.[1]

(*She returns to the desk, tidies it, and resumes writing her letter, bent close to the page.*)

"These, blots, are, her, handiwork. I—"

(*She is interrupted by a gasp.* HELEN *has stuck her finger, and sits sucking at it, darkly. Then with vengeful resolve she seizes her doll, and is about to dash its brains out on the floor when* ANNIE *diving catches it in one hand, which she at once shakes with hopping pain but otherwise ignores, patiently.*)

All right, let's try temperance.[2]

(*Taking the doll, she kneels, goes through the motion of knocking its head on the floor, spells into* HELEN*'s hand.*)

Bad, girl.

(*She lets* HELEN *feel the grieved expression on her face.* HELEN *imitates it. Next she makes* HELEN *caress the doll and kiss the hurt spot and hold it gently in her arms, then spells into her hand.*)

Good, girl.

(*She lets* HELEN *feel the smile on her face.* HELEN *sits with a scowl, which suddenly clears; she pats the doll, kisses it, wreathes her face in a large artificial smile, and bears the doll to the washstand, where she carefully sits it.* ANNIE *watches, pleased.*)

Very good girl—

(*Whereupon* HELEN *elevates the pitcher and dashes it on the floor instead.* ANNIE *leaps to her feet, and stands inarticulate;* HELEN *calmly gropes back to sit to the sewing card and needle.*)

ANNIE *manages to achieve self-control. She picks up a fragment or two of the pitcher, sees* HELEN *is puzzling over the card, and resolutely kneels to demonstrate it again. She spells in* HELEN*'s hand.*

KATE *meanwhile coming around the corner with folded sheets on her arm, halts at the doorway and watches them for a moment in silence; she is moved, but level.*)

KATE (*presently*). What are you saying to her?

(ANNIE *glancing up is a bit embarrassed, and rises from the spelling, to find her company manners.*)

ANNIE. Oh, I was just making conversation. Saying it was a sewing card.

KATE. But does that—

(*She imitates with her fingers.*)

—mean that to her?

ANNIE. No. No, she won't know what spelling is till she knows what a word is.

KATE. Yet you keep spelling to her. Why?

ANNIE (*cheerily*). I like to hear myself talk!

KATE. The Captain says it's like spelling to the fence post.

ANNIE. (*a pause*). Does he, now.

KATE. Is it?

ANNIE. No, it's how I watch you talk to Mildred.

KATE. Mildred.

ANNIE. Any baby. Gibberish, grown-up gibberish, baby-talk gibberish, do they understand one word of it to start? Somehow they begin to. If they hear it. I'm letting Helen hear it.

KATE. Other children are not—impaired.

ANNIE. Ho, there's nothing impaired in that head, it works like a mousetrap!

KATE. (*smiles*). But after a child hears how many words, Miss Annie, a million?

ANNIE. I guess no mother's ever minded enough to count.

(*She drops her eyes to spell into* HELEN*'s hand, again

---

1. **keep out of—the soup,** stay out of trouble.
2. temperance (tem′pər əns), *n.* a being moderate in action, speech, habits, etc.; self-control.

indicating the card; HELEN *spells back, and* ANNIE *is amused.)*

KATE *(too quickly).* What did she spell?

ANNIE. I spelt card. She spelt cake!

(She takes in KATE*'s quickness, and shakes her head, gently.)*

No, it's only a finger-game to her, Mrs. Keller. What she has to learn first is that things have names.

KATE. And when will she learn?

ANNIE. Maybe after a million and one words.

(They hold each other's gaze; KATE *then speaks quietly.)*

KATE. I should like to learn those letters, Miss Annie.

ANNIE *(pleased).* I'll teach you tomorrow morning. That makes only half a million each!

KATE *(then).* It's her bedtime.

*(*ANNIE *reaches for the sewing card,* HELEN *objects,* ANNIE *insists, and* HELEN *gets rid of* ANNIE*'s hand by jabbing it with the needle.* ANNIE *gasps, and moves to grip* HELEN*'s wrist; but* KATE *intervenes with a proffered sweet, and* HELEN *drops the card, crams the sweet into her mouth, and scrambles up to search her mother's hands for more.* ANNIE *nurses her wound staring after the sweet.)*

I'm sorry, Miss Annie.

ANNIE *(indignantly).* Why does she get a reward? For stabbing me?

KATE. Well—

(Then, tiredly.)

We catch our flies with honey, I'm afraid. We haven't the heart for much else, and so many times she simply cannot be compelled.

ANNIE *(ominous[3]).* Yes. I'm the same way myself.

*(*KATE *smiles, and leads* HELEN *off around the corner.* ANNIE *alone in her room picks up things and in the act of removing* HELEN*'s doll gives way to unmannerly temptation; she throttles it. She drops it on her bed, and stands pondering. Then she turns back, sits decisively, and writes again, as the light dim on her.)*

(Grimly.)

"The, more, I, think, the, more, certain, I,

am, that, obedience, is, the, gateway, through, which, knowledge, enters, the, mind, of, the, child—"

SCENE 2

On the word "obedience" a shaft of sunlight hits the water pump outside, while ANNIE*'s voice ends in the dark, followed by a distant cockcrow; daylight comes up over another corner of the sky, with* VINEY*'s voice heard at once.*

VINEY. Breakfast ready!

*(*VINEY *comes down into the sunlight beam, and pumps a pitcherful of water. While the pitcher is brimming we hear conversation from the dark; the light grows to the family room of the house where all are either entering or already seated at breakfast, with* KELLER *and* JAMES *arguing the war.[4]* HELEN *is wandering around the table to explore the contents of the other plates. When* ANNIE *is in her chair, she watches* HELEN. VINEY *re-enters, sets the pitcher on the table;* KATE *lifts the almost empty biscuit plate with an inquiring look,* VINEY *nods and bears it off back, neither of them interrupting the men.* ANNIE *meanwhile sits with fork quiet, watching* HELEN, *who at her mother's plate pokes her hand among some scrambled eggs.* KATE *catches* ANNIE*'s eyes on her, smiles with a wry gesture.* HELEN *moves on to* JAMES*'s plate, the male talk continuing,* JAMES *deferential and* KELLER *overriding.)*

JAMES. —no, but shouldn't we give the devil his due, Father? The fact is we lost the South two years earlier when he outthought us behind Vicksburg.

KELLER. Outthought is a peculiar word for a butcher.

JAMES. Harness maker, wasn't he?

KELLER. I said butcher, his only virtue as a soldier was numbers and he led them to slaughter with no more regard than for so many sheep.

JAMES. But even if in that sense he was a butcher, the fact is he—

---

3. **ominous** (om′ə nəs), *adj.* unfavorable; threatening.
4. **the war,** the Civil War.

KELLER. And a drunken one, half the war.

JAMES. Agreed, Father. If his own people said he was I can't argue he—

KELLER. Well, what is it you find to admire in such a man, Jimmie, the butchery or the drunkenness?

JAMES. Neither, Father, only the fact that he beat us.

KELLER. He didn't.

JAMES. Is it your contention we won the war, sir?

KELLER. He didn't beat us at Vicksburg. We lost Vicksburg because Pemberton gave Bragg five thousand of his cavalry and Loring, whom I knew personally for a nincompoop before you were born, marched away from Champion's Hill with enough men to have held them, we lost Vicksburg by stupidity verging on treason.

JAMES. I would have said we lost Vicksburg because Grant was one thing no Yankee general was before him—

KELLER. Drunk? I doubt it.

JAMES. Obstinate.

KELLER. Obstinate. Could any of them compare even in that with old Stonewall?[5] If he'd been there we would still have Vicksburg.

JAMES. Well, the butcher simply wouldn't give up, he tried four ways of getting around Vicksburg and on the fifth try he got around. Anyone else would have pulled north and—

KELLER. He wouldn't have got around if we'd had a Southerner in command, instead of a half-breed Yankee traitor like Pemberton—

(While this background talk is in progress, HELEN *is working around the table, ultimately toward* ANNIE'*s plate. She messes with her hands in* JAMES'*s plate, then in* KELLER'*s, both men taking it so for granted they hardly notice. Then* HELEN *comes groping with soiled hands past her own plate, to* ANNIE'*s; her hand goes to it, and* ANNIE, *who has been waiting, deliberately lifts and removes her hand.* HELEN *gropes again,*

ANNIE *firmly pins her by the wrist, and removes her hand from the table.* HELEN *thrusts her hands again,* ANNIE *catches them, and* HELEN *begins to flail[6] and makes noises; the interruption brings* KELLER'*s gaze upon them.)*

What's the matter there?

KATE. Miss Annie. You see, she's accustomed to helping herself from our plates to anything she—

ANNIE *(evenly).* Yes, but *I'm* not accustomed to it.

KELLER. No, of course not. Viney!

KATE. Give her something, Jimmie, to quiet her.

JAMES *(blandly).* But her table manners are the best she has. Well.

(He pokes across with a chunk of bacon at HELEN'*s hand, which* ANNIE *releases; but* HELEN *knocks the bacon away and stubbornly thrusts at* ANNIE'*s plate,* ANNIE *grips her wrists again, the struggle mounts.)*

KELLER. Let her this time, Miss Sullivan, it's the only way we get any adult conversation. If my son's half merits that description.

(He rises.)

I'll get you another plate.

ANNIE *(gripping* HELEN*).* I have a plate, thank you.

KATE *(calling).* Viney! I'm afraid what Captain Keller says is only too true, she'll persist in this until she get her own way.

KELLER *(at the door).* Viney, bring Miss Sullivan another plate—

ANNIE *(stonily).* I have a plate, nothing's wrong with the *plate,* I intend to keep it.

(Silence for a moment, except for HELEN'*s noises as she struggles to get loose; the* KELLERS *are a bit nonplussed,[7] and* ANNIE *is too darkly intent on* HELEN'*s manners to have any thoughts now of her own.)*

JAMES. Ha. You see why they took Vicksburg?

---

5. **Stonewall,** Thomas J. "Stonewall" Jackson (1824-1863), a general in the Confederate Army.

6. flail (flāl), *v.* beat; thrash.

7. nonplussed (non plust′), *adj.* puzzled completely; made unable to say or do anything; perplexed.

▲ Production still from the 1962 film *The Miracle Worker*. Annie struggles with Helen at breakfast as the horrified family looks on. What is each character looking at, and what does this reveal about the scene?

The Miracle Worker—Act Two, Scene 2   **281**

KELLER (*uncertainly*). Miss Sullivan. One plate or another is hardly a matter to struggle with a deprived child about.

ANNIE. Oh, I'd sooner have a more—

(HELEN *begins to kick,* ANNIE *moves her ankles to the opposite side of the chair.*)

—heroic issue myself, I—

KELLER. No, I really must insist you—

(HELEN *bangs her toe on the chair and sinks to the floor, crying with rage and feigned injury;* ANNIE *keeps hold of her wrists, gazing down, while* KATE *rises.*)

Now she's hurt herself.

ANNIE (*grimly*). No, she hasn't.

KELLER. Will you please let her hands go?

KATE. Miss Annie, you don't know the child well enough yet, she'll keep—

ANNIE. I know an ordinary tantrum well enough, when I see one, and a badly spoiled child—

JAMES. Hear, hear.

KELLER (*very annoyed*). Miss Sullivan! You would have more understanding of your pupil if you had some pity in you. Now kindly do as I—

ANNIE. Pity?

(*She releases* HELEN *to turn equally annoyed on* KELLER *across the table; instantly* HELEN *scrambles up and dives at* ANNIE*'s plate. This time* ANNIE *intercepts her by pouncing on her wrists like a hawk, and her temper boils.*)

For this *tyrant?* The whole house turns on her whims, is there anything she wants she doesn't get? I'll tell you what I pity, that the sun won't rise and set for her all her life, and every day you're telling her it will, what good will your pity do her when you're under the strawberries, Captain Keller?

KELLER (*outraged*). Kate, for the love of heaven will you—

KATE. Miss Annie, please. I don't think it serves to lose our—

ANNIE. It does you good, that's all. It's less trouble to feel sorry for her than to teach her anything better, isn't it?

KELLER. I fail to see where you have taught her anything yet, Miss Sullivan!

ANNIE. I'll begin this minute, if you'll leave the room, Captain Keller!

KELLER (*astonished*). Leave the—

ANNIE. Everyone, please.

(*She struggles with* HELEN, *while* KELLER *endeavors to control his voice.*)

KELLER. Miss Sullivan, you are here only as a paid teacher. Nothing more, and not to lecture—

ANNIE. I can't *unteach* her six years of pity if you can't stand up to one tantrum! Old Stonewall, indeed. Mrs. Keller, you promised to help.

KATE. Indeed I did, we truly want to—

ANNIE. Then leave me alone with her. Now!

KELLER (*in a wrath*). Katie, will you come outside with me? At once, please.

(*He marches to the front door.* KATE *and* JAMES *follow him. Simultaneously* ANNIE *releases* HELEN*'s wrists, and the child again sinks to the floor, kicking and crying her weird noises;* ANNIE *steps over her to meet* VINEY *coming in the rear doorway with biscuits and a clean plate, surprised at the general commotion.*)

VINEY. Heaven sakes—

ANNIE. Out, please.

(*She backs* VINEY *out with one hand, closes the door on her astonished mouth, locks it, and removes the key.* KELLER *meanwhile snatches his hat from a rack, and* KATE *follows him down the porch steps.* JAMES *lingers in the doorway to address* ANNIE *across the room with a bow.*)

JAMES. If it takes all summer, General.[8]

(ANNIE *comes over to his door in turn, removing her glasses grimly; as* KELLER *outside begins speaking,* ANNIE *closes the door on* JAMES, *locks it, removes the key, and turns with her back against the door to stare ominously at* HELEN, *kicking on the floor.*

---

8. **If it takes all summer,** a quote from General Grant, who, after a series of terrible battles during the Civil War, said, "I propose to fight it out on this line if it takes all summer."

JAMES *takes his hat from the rack, and going down the porch steps joins* KATE *and* KELLER *talking in the yard,* KELLER *in a sputter of ire.*[9])

KELLER. This girl, this—cub of a girl—*presumes!* I tell you, I'm of half a mind to ship her back to Boston before the week is out. You can inform her so from me!

KATE (*eyebrows up*). I, Captain?

KELLER. She's a *hireling!* Now I want it clear, unless there's an apology and complete change of manner she goes back on the next train! Will you make that quite clear?

KATE. Where will you be, Captain, while I am making it quite—

KELLER. At the office!

(*He begins off left, finds his napkin still in his irate hand, is uncertain with it, dabs his lips with dignity, gets rid of it in a toss to* JAMES, *and marches off.* JAMES *turns to eye* KATE.)

JAMES. Will you?

(KATE*'s mouth is set, and* JAMES *studies it lightly.*)

I thought what she said was exceptionally intelligent. I've been saying it for years.

KATE (*not without scorn*). To his face?

(*She comes to relieve him of the white napkin, but reverts again with it.*)

Or will you take it, Jimmie? As a flag?

SCENE 3

JAMES *stalks out, much offended, and* KATE *turning stares across the yard at the house; the lights narrowing down to the following pantomime in the family room leaves her motionless in the dark.*

ANNIE *meanwhile has begun by slapping both keys down on a shelf out of* HELEN*'s reach; she returns to the table, upstage.* HELEN*'s kicking has subsided, and when from the floor her hand finds* ANNIE*'s chair empty she pauses.* ANNIE *clears the table of* KATE*'s,* JAMES*'s, and* KELLER*'s plates; she gets back to her own across the table just in time to slide it deftly away from* HELEN*'s pouncing hand. She lifts the hand and moves it to* HELEN*'s plate, and after an instant's exploration,* HELEN *sits again on the floor and drums her heels.*

ANNIE *comes around the table and resumes her chair. When* HELEN *feels her skirt again, she ceases kicking, waits for whatever is to come, renews some kicking, waits again.* ANNIE *retrieving her plate takes up a forkful of food, stops it halfway to her mouth, gazes at it devoid of appetite, and half-lowers it; but after a look at* HELEN *she sighs, dips the forkful toward* HELEN *in a for-your-sake toast, and puts it in her own mouth to chew, not without an effort.*

HELEN *now gets hold of the chair leg, and half-succeeds in pulling the chair out from under her.* ANNIE *bangs it down with her rear, heavily, and sits with all her weight.* HELEN*'s next attempt to topple it is unavailing, so her fingers dive in a pinch at* ANNIE*'s flank.* ANNIE *in the middle of her mouthful almost loses it with startle, and she slaps down her fork to round on* HELEN. *The child comes up with curiosity to feel what* ANNIE *is doing, so* ANNIE *resumes eating, letting* HELEN*'s hand follow the movement of her fork to her mouth; whereupon* HELEN *at once reaches into* ANNIE*'s plate.* ANNIE *firmly removes her hand to her own plate.* HELEN *in reply pinches* ANNIE*'s thigh, a good mean pinchful that makes* ANNIE *jump.* ANNIE *sets the fork down, and sits with her mouth tight.* HELEN *digs another pinch into her thigh, and this time* ANNIE *slaps her hand smartly away;* HELEN *retaliates with a roundhouse fist that catches* ANNIE *on the ear, and* ANNIE*'s hand leaps at once in a forceful slap across* HELEN*'s cheek;* HELEN *is the startled one now.* ANNIE*'s hand in compunction*[10] *falters to her own face, but when* HELEN *hits at her again,* ANNIE *deliberately slaps her again.* HELEN *lifts her fist irresolute for another roundhouse,* ANNIE *lifts her hand resolute for another slap, and they freeze in this posture, while* HELEN *mulls it over. She thinks better of it, drops her fist, and giving* ANNIE *a wide berth, gropes around to her mother's chair, to find it empty; she blunders her way along the table upstage, and encountering the empty chairs and missing plates, she looks bewildered; she gropes back to her mother's chair, again touches her cheek and indicates the chair, and waits for the world to answer.*

---

9. **ire** (īr), *n.* anger; wrath.
10. **compunction** (kəm pungk′shən), *n.* uneasiness of the mind because of wrongdoing; remorse.

ANNIE *now reaches over to spell into her hand, but* HELEN *yanks it away; she gropes to the front door, tries the knob, and finds the door locked, with no key. She gropes to the rear door, and finds it locked, with no key. She commences to bang on it.* ANNIE *rises, crosses, takes her wrists, draws her resisting back to the table, seats her, and releases her hands upon her plate; as* ANNIE *herself begins to sit,* HELEN *writhes out of her chair, runs to the front door, and tugs and kicks at it.* ANNIE *rises again, crosses, draws her by one wrist back to the table, seats her, and sits;* HELEN *escapes back to the door, knocking over her mother's chair en route.* ANNIE *rises again in pursuit, and this time lifts* HELEN *bodily from behind and bears her kicking to her chair. She deposits her, and once more turns to sit.* HELEN *scrambles out, but as she passes* ANNIE *catches her up again from behind and deposits her in the chair;* HELEN *scrambles out on the other side, for the rear door, but* ANNIE *at her heels catches her up and deposits her again in the chair. She stands behind it.* HELEN *scrambles out to her right, and the instant her feet hit the floor* ANNIE *lifts and deposits her back; she scrambles out to her left, and is at once lifted and deposited back. She tries right again and is deposited back, and tries left again and is deposited back, and now feints* ANNIE *to the right but is off to her left, and is promptly deposited back. She sits a moment, and then starts straight over the tabletop, dishware notwithstanding;* ANNIE *hauls her in and deposits her back, with her plate spilling in her lap, and she melts to the floor and crawls under the table, laborious among its legs and chairs; but* ANNIE *is swift around the table and waiting on the other side when she surfaces, immediately bearing her aloft;* HELEN *clutches at* JAMES*'s chair for anchorage but it comes with her, and halfway back she abandons it to the floor.* ANNIE *deposits her in her chair, and waits.* HELEN *sits tensed motionless. Then she tentatively puts out her left foot and hand,* ANNIE *interposes her own hand, and at the contact* HELEN *jerks hers in. She tries her right foot,* ANNIE *blocks it with her own, and* HELEN *jerks hers in. Finally, leaning back she slumps down in her chair, in a sullen biding.*

ANNIE *backs off a step, and watches;* HELEN *offers no move.* ANNIE *takes a deep breath. Both of them and the*

room *are in considerable disorder, two chairs down and the table a mess, but* ANNIE *makes no effort to tidy it; she only sits on her own chair, and lets her energy refill. Then she takes up knife and fork, and resolutely addresses her food.* HELEN*'s hand comes out to explore, and seeing it* ANNIE *sits without moving; the child's hand goes over her hand and fork, passes—*ANNIE *still does not move—and withdraws. Presently it moves for her own plate, slaps about for it, and stops, thwarted.[11] At this,* ANNIE *again rises, recovers* HELEN*'s plate from the floor and a handful of scattered food from the deranged tablecloth, drops it on the plate, and pushes the plate into contact with* HELEN*'s fist. Neither of them now moves for a pregnant moment—until* HELEN *suddenly takes a grab of food and wolfs it down.* ANNIE *permits herself the humor of a minor bow and warming of her hands together; she wanders off a step or two, watching.* HELEN *cleans up the plate.*

After a glower of indecision, she holds the empty plate out for more. ANNIE *accepts it, and crossing to the removed plates, spoons food from them onto it; she stands debating the spoon, tapping it a few times on* HELEN*'s plate; and when she returns with the plate she brings the spoon, too. She puts the spoon first into* HELEN*'s hand, then sets the plate down.* HELEN *discarding the spoon reaches with her hand, and* ANNIE *stops it by the wrist; she replaces the spoon in it.* HELEN *impatiently discards it again, and again* ANNIE *stops her hand, to replace the spoon in it. This time* HELEN *throws the spoon on the floor.* ANNIE *after considering it lifts* HELEN *bodily out of the chair, and in a wrestling match on the floor closes her fingers upon the spoon, and returns her with it to the chair.* HELEN *again throws the spoon on the floor.* ANNIE *lifts her out of the chair again; but in the struggle over the spoon* HELEN *with* ANNIE *on her back sends her sliding over her head;* HELEN *flees back to her chair and scrambles into it. When* ANNIE *comes after her she clutches it for dear life;* ANNIE *pries one hand loose, then the other, then the first again, then the other again, and then lifts* HELEN *by the waist, chair and all, and shakes the*

---

11. **thwarted** (thwôrt′əd), *adj.* prevented from doing something; opposed and defeated.

▲ Production still from the 1962 film *The Miracle Worker.* Alone together, Annie and Helen continue their breakfast battle. At this point, do you think Annie is going too far?

chair loose. HELEN *wrestles to get free, but* ANNIE *pins her to the floor, closes her fingers upon the spoon, and lifts her kicking under one arm; with her other hand she gets the chair in place again, and plunks* HELEN *back on it. When she releases her hand,* HELEN *throws the spoon at her.*

ANNIE *now removes the plate of food.* HELEN *grabbing finds it missing, and commences to bang with her fists on the table.* ANNIE *collects a fistful of spoons and descends with them and the plate on* HELEN; *she lets her smell the plate, at which* HELEN *ceases banging, and* ANNIE *puts the plate down and a spoon in* HELEN*'s hand.* HELEN *throws it on the floor.* ANNIE *puts another spoon in her hand.* HELEN *throws it on the floor. When* ANNIE *comes to her last spoon she sits next to* HELEN, *and gripping the spoon in* HELEN*'s hand compels her to take food in it up to her mouth.* HELEN *sits with lips shut.* ANNIE *waits a stolid moment, then lowers* HELEN*'s hand. She tries again; this time* HELEN *suddenly opens her mouth and accepts the food.* ANNIE *lowers the spoon with a sigh of relief, and* HELEN *spews the mouthful out at her face.* ANNIE *sits a moment with eyes closed, then takes the pitcher and dashes its water into* HELEN*'s face, who gasps astonished.* ANNIE *with* HELEN*'s hand takes up another spoonful, and shoves it into her open mouth.* HELEN *swallows involuntarily, and while she is catching her breath* ANNIE *forces her palm open, throws four swift letters into it, then another four, and bows toward her with devastating pleasantness.*

ANNIE. Good girl.

(ANNIE *lifts* HELEN*'s hand to feel her face nodding;* HELEN *grabs a fistful of her hair, and yanks. The pain brings* ANNIE *to her knees, and* HELEN *pummels her; they roll under the table, and the lights commence to dim out on them.*)

SCENE 4

Simultaneously the light at left has been rising slowly, so slowly that it seems at first we only imagine what is intimated in the yard: a few ghostlike figures, in silence, motionless, waiting. Now the distant belfry chimes commence to toll the hour, also very slowly, almost—it is twelve—interminably; the sense is that of a long time passing. We can identify the figures before the twelfth stroke, all facing the house in a kind of watch. KATE *is standing exactly as before, but now with the baby* MILDRED *sleeping in her arms, and placed here and there, unmoving, are* AUNT EV *in her hat with a hanky to her nose, and the two Negro children,* PERCY *and* MARTHA *with necks outstretched eagerly, and* VINEY *with a knotted kerchief on her head and a feather duster in her hand.*

The chimes cease, and there is silence. For a long moment none of the group moves.

VINEY *(presently).* What am I gone do, Miss Kate? It's noontime, dinner's comin', I didn't get them breakfast dishes out of there yet.

(KATE *says nothing, stares at the house.* MARTHA *shifts* HELEN*'s doll in her clutch, and it plaintively says* momma.)

KATE *(presently).* You run along, Martha.

(AUNT EV *blows her nose.*)

AUNT EV *(wretchedly).* I can't wait out here a minute longer, Kate, why, this could go on all afternoon, too.

KATE. I'll tell the Captain you called.

VINEY *(to the children).* You hear what Miss Kate say? Never you mind what's going on here.

(*Still no one moves.*)

You run along tend your own bizness.

(*Finally* VINEY *turns on the children with the feather duster.*)

Shoo!

(*The two children divide before her. She chases them off.* AUNT EV *comes to* KATE, *on her dignity.*)

AUNT EV. Say what you like, Kate, but that child is a *Keller.*

(*She opens her parasol, preparatory to leaving.*)

I needn't remind you that all the Kellers are cousins to General Robert E. Lee. I don't know *who* that girl is.

(*She waits; but* KATE *staring at the house is without response.*)

The only Sullivan I've heard of—from Boston too, and I'd think twice before locking her up with that kind—is that man John L.[12]

(*And* AUNT EV *departs, with head high. Presently* VINEY *comes to* KATE, *her arms out for the baby.*)

VINEY. You give me her, Miss Kate, I'll sneak her in back, to her crib.

(*But* KATE *is moveless, until* VINEY *starts to take the baby;* KATE *looks down at her before relinquishing her.*)

KATE (*slowly*). This child never gives me a minute's worry.

VINEY. Oh yes, this one's the angel of the family, no question bout *that*.

(*She begins off rear with the baby, heading around the house; and* KATE *now turns her back on it, her hand to her eyes. At this moment there is the slamming of a door, and when* KATE *wheels* HELEN *is blundering down the porch steps into the light, like a ruined bat out of hell.* VINEY *halts, and* KATE *runs in;* HELEN *collides with her mother's knees, and reels off and back to clutch them as her savior.* ANNIE *with smoked glasses in hand stands on the porch, also much undone, looking as though she had indeed just taken Vicksburg.* KATE *taking in* HELEN*'s ravaged state becomes steely in her gaze up at* ANNIE.)

KATE. What happened?

(ANNIE *meets* KATE*'s gaze, and gives a factual report, too exhausted for anything but a flat voice.*)

ANNIE. She ate from her own plate.

(*She thinks a moment.*)

She ate with a spoon. Herself.

(KATE *frowns, uncertain with thought, and glances down at* HELEN.)

And she folded her napkin.

(KATE*'s gaze now wavers from* HELEN *to* ANNIE, *and back.*)

KATE (*softly*). Folded—her napkin?

ANNIE. The room's a wreck, but her napkin is folded.

(*She pauses, then:*)

I'll be in my room, Mrs. Keller.

(*She moves to reenter the house; but she stops at* VINEY*'s voice.*)

VINEY (*cheery*). Don't be long, Miss Annie. Dinner be ready right away!

(VINEY *carries* MILDRED *around the back of the house.* ANNIE *stands unmoving, takes a deep breath, stares over her shoulder at* KATE *and* HELEN, *then inclines her head graciously, and goes with a slight stagger into the house. The lights in her room above steal up in readiness for her.* KATE *remains alone with* HELEN *in the yard, standing protectively over her, in a kind of wonder.*)

KATE (*slowly*). Folded her napkin.

(*She contemplates the wild head in her thighs, and moves her fingertips over it, with such a tenderness, and something like a fear of its strangeness, that her own eyes close; she whispers, bending to it.*)

My Helen—folded her napkin—

(*And still erect, with only her head in surrender,* KATE *for the first time that we see loses her protracted war with grief; but she will not let a sound escape her, only the grimace of tears comes, and sobs that shake her in a grip of silence. But* HELEN *feels them, and her head comes up in its own wondering, to interrogate her mother's face, until* KATE *buries her lips in the child's palm.*)

SCENE 5

Upstairs, ANNIE *enters her room, closes the door, and stands back against it; the lights, growing on her with their special color, commence to fade on* KATE *and* HELEN. *Then* ANNIE *goes wearily to her suitcase, and lifts it to take it toward the bed. But it knocks an object to the floor, and she turns back to regard it. A new voice comes in a cultured murmur, hesitant as with the effort of remembering a text.*

MAN'S VOICE. This—soul—

(ANNIE *puts the suitcase down, and kneels to the object: it is the battered Perkins report, and she stands with it in her hand, letting memory try to speak.*)

This—blind, deaf, mute—woman—

---

12. **John L.,** John L. Sullivan (1858–1918), the world heavyweight boxing champion from 1882–1892.

(ANNIE *sits on her bed, opens the book, and finding the passage, brings it up an inch from her eyes to read, her face and lips following the overheard words, the voice quite factual now.*)

Can nothing be done to disinter this human soul? The whole neighborhood would rush to save this woman if she were buried alive by the caving in of a pit, and labor with zeal until she were dug out. Now if there were one who had as much patience as zeal, he might awaken her to a consciousness of her immortal—

(*When the boy's voice comes,* ANNIE *closes her eyes, in pain.*)

BOY'S VOICE. Annie? Annie, you there?

ANNIE. Hush.

BOY'S VOICE. Annie, what's that noise?

(ANNIE *tries not to answer; her own voice is drawn out of her, unwilling.*)

ANNIE. Just a cot, Jimmie.

BOY'S VOICE. Where they pushin' it?

ANNIE. To the deadhouse.

BOY'S VOICE. Annie. Does it hurt, to be dead?

(ANNIE *escapes by opening her eyes, her hand works restlessly over her cheek; she retreats into the book again, but the cracked old crones interrupt, whispering.* ANNIE *slowly lowers the book.*)

FIRST CRONE'S VOICE. There is schools.

SECOND CRONE'S VOICE. There is schools outside—

THIRD CRONE'S VOICE. —schools where they teach blind ones, worse'n you—

FIRST CRONE'S VOICE. To read—

SECOND CRONE'S VOICE. To read and write—

THIRD CRONE'S VOICE. There is schools outside where they—

FIRST CRONE'S VOICE. There is schools—

(*Silence.* ANNIE *sits with her eyes shining, her hand almost in a caress over the book. Then:*)

BOY'S VOICE. You ain't goin' to school, are you, Annie?

ANNIE (*whispering*). When I grow up.

BOY'S VOICE. You ain't either, Annie. You're goin' to stay here take care of me.

ANNIE. I'm goin' to school when I grow up.

BOY'S VOICE. You said we'll be together, forever and ever and ever—

ANNIE (*fierce*). I'm goin' to school when I grow up!

DOCTOR'S VOICE (*slowly*). Little girl. Little girl, I must tell you. Your brother will be going on a journey, soon.

(ANNIE *sits rigid, in silence. Then the boy's voice pierces it, a shriek of terror.*)

BOY'S VOICE. Annie!

(*It goes into* ANNIE *like a sword, she doubles onto it; the book falls to the floor. It takes her a racked moment to find herself and what she was engaged in here; when she sees the suitcase she remembers, and lifts it once again toward the bed. But the voices are with her, as she halts with suitcase in hand.*)

FIRST CRONE'S VOICE. Goodbye, Annie.

DOCTOR'S VOICE. Write me when you learn how.

SECOND CRONE'S VOICE. Don't tell anyone you came from here. Don't tell anyone—

THIRD CRONE'S VOICE. Yeah, don't tell anyone you come from—

FIRST CRONE'S VOICE. Yeah, don't tell anyone—

SECOND CRONE'S VOICE. Don't tell any—

(*The echoing voices fade. After a moment* ANNIE *lays the suitcase on the bed; and the last voice comes faintly, from far away.*)

BOY'S VOICE. Annie. It hurts, to be dead. Forever.

(ANNIE *falls to her knees by the bed, stifling her mouth in it. When at last she rolls blindly away from it, her palm comes down on the open report; she opens her eyes, regards it dully, and then, still on her knees, takes in the print.*)

MAN'S VOICE (*factual*). —might awaken her to a consciousness of her immortal nature. The chance is small indeed; but with a smaller chance they would have dug desperately for her in the pit; and is the life of the soul of less import than that of the body?

(ANNIE *gets to her feet. She drops the book on the bed,*

and pauses over her suitcase; after a moment she unclasps and opens it. Standing before it, she comes to her decision; she at once turns to the bureau, and taking her things out of its drawers, commences to throw them into the open suitcase.)

SCENE 6

In the darkness down left a hand strikes a match, and lights a hanging oil lamp. It is KELLER*'s hand, and his voice accompanies it, very angry; the lights rising here before they fade on* ANNIE *show* KELLER *and* KATE *inside a suggestion of a garden house, with a bay-window seat toward center and a door at back.*

KELLER. Katie, I will not *have* it! Now you did not see when that girl after supper tonight went to look for Helen in her room—

KATE. No.

KELLER. The child practically climbed out of her window to escape from her! What kind of teacher *is* she? I thought I had seen her at her worst this morning, shouting at me, but I come home to find the entire house disorganized by her—Helen won't stay one second in the same room, won't come to the table with her, won't let herself be bathed or undressed or put to bed by her, or even by Viney now, and the end result is that *you* have to do more for the child than before we hired this girl's services! From the moment she stepped off the train she's been nothing but a burden, incompetent, impertinent,[13] ineffectual, immodest—

KATE. She folded her napkin, Captain.

KELLER. What?

KATE. Not ineffectual. Helen did fold her napkin.

KELLER. What in heaven's name is so extraordinary about folding a napkin?

KATE *(with some humor).* Well. It's more than you did, Captain.

KELLER. Katie. I did not bring you all the way out here to the garden house to be frivolous. Now, how does Miss Sullivan propose to teach a deaf-blind pupil who won't let her even touch her?

KATE *(a pause).* I don't know.

KELLER. The fact is, today she scuttled any chance she ever had of getting along with the child. If you can see any point or purpose to her staying on here longer, it's more than—

KATE. What do you wish me to do?

KELLER. I want you to give her notice.

KATE. I can't.

KELLER. Then if you won't, I must. I simply will not—

(He is interrupted by a knock at the back door. KELLER *after a glance at* KATE *moves to open the door;* ANNIE *in her smoked glasses is standing outside.* KELLER *contemplates her, heavily.)*

Miss Sullivan.

ANNIE. Captain Keller.

(She is nervous, keyed up to seizing the bull by the horns again, and she assumes a cheeriness which is not unshaky.)

Viney said I'd find you both over here in the garden house. I thought we should—have a talk?

KELLER *(reluctantly).* Yes I—Well, come in.

*(*ANNIE *enters, and is interested in this room; she rounds on her heel, anxiously, studying it.* KELLER *turns the matter over to* KATE, *sotto voce.)*

Katie.

KATE *(turning it back, courteously).* Captain.

*(*KELLER *clears his throat, makes ready.)*

KELLER. I, ah—wanted first to make my position clear to Mrs. Keller, in private. I have decided I—am not satisfied—in fact, am deeply dissatisfied—with the manner in which—

ANNIE *(intent).* Excuse me, is this little house ever in use?

---

13. **impertinent** (im pėrt'n ənt), *adj.* rudely bold; impudent; insolent.

KELLER (*with patience*). In the hunting season. If you will give me your attention, Miss Sullivan.

(ANNIE *turns her smoked glasses upon him; they hold his unwilling stare.*)

I have tried to make allowances for you because you come from a part of the country where people are—women, I should say—come from who—well, for whom—

(*It begins to elude him.*)

—allowances must—be made. I have decided, nevertheless, to—that is, decided I—

(*Vexedly.*)

Miss Sullivan, I find it difficult to talk through those glasses.

ANNIE (*eagerly, removing them*). Oh, of course.

KELLER (*dourly*). Why do you wear them, the sun has been down for an hour.

ANNIE (*pleasantly, at the lamp*). Any kind of light hurts my eyes.

(*A silence;* KELLER *ponders her, heavily.*)

KELLER. Put them on. Miss Sullivan, I have decided to—give you another chance.

ANNIE (*cheerfully*). To do what?

KELLER. To—remain in our employ.

(ANNIE*'s eyes widen.*)

But on two conditions. I am not accustomed to rudeness in servants or women, and that is the first. If you are to stay, there must be a radical change of manner.

ANNIE (*a pause*). Whose?

KELLER (*exploding*). Yours, young lady, isn't it obvious? And the second is that you persuade me there's the slightest hope of your teaching a child who flies from you now like the plague, to anyone else she can find in this house.

ANNIE (*a pause*). There isn't.

(KATE *stops sewing, and fixes her eyes upon* ANNIE.)

KATE. What, Miss Annie?

ANNIE. It's hopeless here. I can't teach a child who runs away.

KELLER (*nonplussed*). Then—do I understand you—propose—

ANNIE. Well, if we all agree it's hopeless, the next question is what—

KATE. Miss Annie.

(*She is leaning toward* ANNIE, *in deadly earnest; it commands both* ANNIE *and* KELLER.)

I am not agreed. I think perhaps you—underestimate Helen.

ANNIE. I think everybody here does.

KATE. She did fold her napkin. She learns, she learns, do you know she began talking when she was six months old? She could say "water." Not really—"wahwah." "Wahwah," but she meant water, she knew what it meant, and only six months old, I never saw a child so—bright, or outgoing—

(*Her voice is unsteady, but she gets it level.*)

It's still in her, somewhere, isn't it? You should have seen her before her illness, such a good-tempered child—

ANNIE (*agreeably*). She's changed.

(*A pause,* KATE *not letting her eyes go; her appeal at last is unconditional, and very quiet.*)

KATE. Miss Annie, put up with it. And with us.

KELLER. Us!

KATE. Please? Like the lost lamb in the parable, I love her all the more.

ANNIE. Mrs. Keller, I don't think Helen's worst handicap is deafness or blindness. I think it's your love. And pity.

KELLER. Now what does that mean?

ANNIE. All of you here are so sorry for her you've kept her—like a pet, why, even a dog you housebreak. No wonder she won't let me come near her. It's useless for me to try to teach her language or anything else here. I might as well—

KATE (*cuts in*). Miss Annie, before you came we spoke of putting her in an asylum.

(ANNIE *turns back to regard her. A pause.*)

ANNIE. What kind of asylum?

KELLER. For mental defectives.

KATE. I visited there. I can't tell you what I saw, people like—animals, with—*rats*, in the halls, and—

(She shakes her head on her vision.)

What else are we to do, if you give up?

ANNIE. Give up?

KATE. You said it was hopeless.

ANNIE. Here. Give up, why, I only today saw what has to be done, to begin!

(She glances from KATE *to* KELLER, *who stare, waiting; and she makes it as plain and simple as her nervousness permits.)*

I—want complete charge of her.

KELLER. You already have that. It has resulted in—

ANNIE. No, I mean day and night. She has to be dependent on me.

KATE. For what?

ANNIE. Everything. The food she eats, the clothes she wears, fresh—

(She is amused at herself, though very serious.)

—air, yes, the air she breathes, whatever her body needs is a—primer, to teach her out of. It's the only way, the one who lets her have it should be her teacher.

(She considers them in turn; they digest it, KELLER *frowning,* KATE *perplexed.)*

Not anyone who *loves* her, you have so many feelings they fall over each other like feet, you won't use your chances and you won't let me.

KATE. But if she runs from you—*to us*—

ANNIE. Yes, that's the point. I'll have to live with her somewhere else.

KELLER. What!

ANNIE. Till she learns to depend on and listen to me.

KATE *(not without alarm).* For how long?

ANNIE. As long as it takes.

(A pause. She takes a breath.)

I packed half my things already.

KELLER. Miss—Sullivan!

(But when ANNIE *attends upon him he is speechless, and she is merely earnest.)*

ANNIE. Captain Keller, it meets both your conditions. It's the one way I can get back in touch with Helen, and I don't see how I can be rude to you again if you're not around to interfere with me.

KELLER *(red-faced).* And what is your intention if I say no? Pack the other half, for home, and abandon your charge to—to—

ANNIE. The asylum?

(She waits, appraises KELLER'*s glare and* KATE'*s uncertainty, and decides to use her weapons.)*

I grew up in such an asylum. The state almshouse.

*(*KATE'*s head comes up on this, and* KELLER *stares hard;* ANNIE'*s tone is cheerful enough, albeit*[14] *level as gunfire.)*

Rats—why, my brother Jimmie and I used to play with the rats because we didn't have toys. Maybe you'd like to know what Helen will find there, not on visiting days? One ward was full of the—old women, crippled, blind, most of them dying, but even if what they had was catching there was nowhere else to move them, and that's where they put us. There were younger ones across the hall, prostitutes mostly, with T.B.,[15] and epileptic fits, and a couple of the kind who—keep after other girls, especially young ones, and some insane. Some just had the D.T.'s.[16] The youngest were in another ward to have babies they didn't want, they started at thirteen, fourteen. They'd leave afterwards, but the babies stayed and we played with them, too, though a lot of them had—sores all over from diseases you're not supposed to talk about, but not many of

---

14. **albeit** (ôl bē′it), *conj.* although.
15. **T. B.,** tuberculosis, an infectious disease, usually affecting the lungs.
16. **D.T.'s,** delirium tremens; tremblings and hallucinations, caused by excessive use of drugs or alcohol.

▼ Photograph of the Keller garden house.

them lived. The first year we had eighty, seventy died. The room Jimmie and I played in was the deadhouse, where they kept the bodies till they could dig—

KATE *(closes her eyes).* Oh, my dear—

ANNIE. —the graves.

(She is immune to KATE*'s compassion.)*

No, it made me strong. But I don't think you need send Helen there. She's strong enough.

(She waits again; but when neither offers her a word, she simply concludes.)

No, I have no conditions, Captain Keller.

KATE *(not looking up).* Miss Annie.

ANNIE. Yes.

KATE *(a pause).* Where would you—take Helen?

ANNIE. Ohh—

(Brightly.)

Italy?

KELLER *(wheeling).* What?

ANNIE. Can't have everything, how would this garden house do? Furnish it, bring Helen here after a long ride so she won't recognize it, and you can see her every day. If she doesn't know. Well?

KATE *(a sigh of relief).* Is that all?

ANNIE. That's all.

KATE. Captain.

*(*KELLER *turns his head; and* KATE*'s request is quiet but firm.)*

With your permission?

KELLER *(teeth in cigar).* Why must she depend on you for the food she eats?

ANNIE *(a pause).* I want control of it.

KELLER. Why?

ANNIE. It's a way to reach her.

KELLER *(stares).* You intend to *starve* her into letting you touch her?

ANNIE. She won't starve, she'll learn. All's fair in love and war, Captain Keller, you never cut supplies?

KELLER. This is hardly a war!

ANNIE. Well, it's not love. A siege[17] is a siege.

KELLER *(heavily).* Miss Sullivan. Do you *like* the child?

ANNIE *(straight in his eyes).* Do you?

(A long pause.)

KATE. You could have a servant here—

ANNIE *(amused).* I'll have enough work without looking after a servant! But that boy Percy could sleep here, run errands—

KATE *(also amused).* We can let Percy sleep here, I think, Captain?

ANNIE *(eagerly).* And some old furniture, all our own—

KATE *(also eager).* Captain? Do you think that walnut bedstead in the barn would be too—

KELLER. I have not yet consented to Percy! Or to the house, or to the proposal! Or to Miss Sullivan's—staying on when I—

(But he erupts in an irate surrender.)

---

17. **siege** (sēj), *n.* long or persistent effort to overcome resistance; a long-continued attack.

Very well, I consent to everything!

(*He shakes the cigar at* ANNIE.)

For two weeks. I'll give you two weeks in this place, and it will be a miracle if you get the child to tolerate you.

KATE. Two weeks? Miss Annie, can you accomplish anything in two weeks?

KELLER. Anything or not, two weeks, then the child comes back to us. Make up your mind, Miss Sullivan, yes or no?

ANNIE. Two weeks. For only one miracle?

(*She nods at him, nervously.*)

I'll get her to tolerate me.

(KELLER *marches out, and slams the door.* KATE *on her feet regards* ANNIE, *who is facing the door.*)

KATE (*then*). You can't think as little of love as you said.

(ANNIE *glances, questioning.*)

Or you wouldn't stay.

ANNIE (*a pause*). I didn't come here for love. I came for money!

(KATE *shakes her head to this, with a smile; after a moment she extends her open hand.* ANNIE *looks at it, but when she puts hers out it is not to shake hands, it is to set her fist in* KATE'*s palm.*)

KATE (*puzzled*). Hm?

ANNIE. A. It's the first of many. Twenty-six!

(KATE *squeezes her fist, squeezes it hard, and hastens out after* KELLER. ANNIE *stands as the door closes behind her, her manner so apprehensive that finally she slaps her brow, holds it, sighs, and, with her eyes closed, crosses herself for luck.*)

SCENE 7

The lights dim into a cool silhouette scene around her, the lamp paling out, and now, in formal entrances, persons appear around ANNIE *with furniture for the room.* PERCY *crosses the stage with a rocking chair and waits;* MARTHA *from another direction bears in a stool,* VINEY *bears in a small table, and the other Negro servant rolls in a bed partway from left; and* ANNIE, *opening her eyes to put her glasses back on, sees them. She turns around in the room once, and goes into*

action, pointing out locations for each article; the servants place them and leave, and ANNIE *then darts around, interchanging them. In the midst of this—while* PERCY *and* MARTHA *reappear with a tray of food and a chair, respectively—*JAMES *comes down from the house with* ANNIE'*s suitcase, and stands viewing the room and her quizzically;* ANNIE *halts abruptly under his eyes, embarrassed, then seizes the suitcase from his hand, explaining herself brightly.*)

ANNIE. I always wanted to live in a doll's house!

(*She sets the suitcase out of the way, and continues;* VINEY *at left appears to position a rod with drapes for a doorway, and the other servant at center pushes in a wheelbarrow loaded with a couple of boxes of* HELEN'*s toys and clothes.* ANNIE *helps lift them into the room, and the servant pushes the wheelbarrow off. In none of this is any heed taken of the imaginary walls of the garden house, the furniture is moved in from every side and itself defines the walls.* ANNIE *now drags the box of toys into center, props up the doll conspicuously on top; with the people melted away, except for* JAMES, *all is again still. The lights turn again without pause, rising warmer.*)

JAMES. You don't let go of things easily, do you? How will you—win her hand now, in this place?

ANNIE (*curtly*). Do I know? I lost my temper, and here we are!

JAMES (*lightly*). No touching, no teaching. Of course you *are* bigger—

ANNIE. I'm not counting on force, I'm counting on her. That little imp is dying to know.

JAMES. Know what?

ANNIE. Anything. Any and every crumb in God's creation. I'll have to use that appetite too.

(*She gives the room a final survey, straightens the bed, arranges the curtains.*)

JAMES (*a pause*). Maybe she'll teach you.

ANNIE. Of course.

JAMES. That she isn't. That there's such a thing as—dullness of heart. Acceptance. And letting go. Sooner or later we all give up, don't we?

ANNIE. Maybe you all do. It's my idea of the original sin.

JAMES. What is?

ANNIE (*witheringly*). Giving up.

JAMES (*nettled*). You won't open her. Why can't you let her be? Have some—pity on her, for being what she is—

ANNIE. If I'd ever once thought like that, I'd be dead!

JAMES (*pleasantly*). You will be. Why trouble?

(ANNIE *turns to glare at him; he is mocking.*)

Or will you teach me?

(*And with a bow, he drifts off. Now in the distance there comes the clopping of hoofs, drawing near, and nearer, up to the door; and they halt.* ANNIE *wheels to face the door. When it opens this time, the* KELLERS— KATE *in traveling bonnet,* KELLER *also hatted—are standing there with* HELEN *between them; she is in a cloak.* KATE *gently cues her into the room.* HELEN *comes in groping, baffled, but interested in the new surroundings;* ANNIE *evades her exploring hand, her gaze not leaving the child.*)

ANNIE. Does she know where she is?

KATE (*shakes her head*). We rode her out in the country for two hours.

KELLER. For all she knows, she could be in another town—

(HELEN *stumbles over the box on the floor and in it discovers her doll and other battered toys, is pleased, sits to them, then becomes puzzled and suddenly very wary. She scrambles up and back to her mother's thighs, but* ANNIE *steps in, and it is hers that* HELEN *embraces.* HELEN *recoils, gropes, and touches her cheek instantly.*)

KATE. That's her sign for me.

ANNIE. I know.

(HELEN *waits, then recommences her groping, more urgently.* KATE *stands indecisive, and takes an abrupt step toward her, but* ANNIE*'s hand is a barrier.*)

In two weeks.

KATE. Miss Annie, I—Please be good to her. These two weeks, try to be very good to her—

ANNIE. I will.

(KATE, *turning then, hurries out. The* KELLERS *cross back of the main house.*

ANNIE *closes the door.* HELEN *starts at the door jar, and rushes it.* ANNIE *holds her off.* HELEN *kicks her, breaks free, and careens around the room like an imprisoned bird, colliding with furniture, groping wildly, repeatedly touching her cheek in a growing panic. When she has covered the room, she commences her weird screaming.* ANNIE *moves to comfort her, but her touch sends* HELEN *into a paroxysm of rage; she tears away, falls over her box of toys, flings its contents in handfuls in* ANNIE*'s direction, flings the box too, reels to her feet, rips curtains from the window, bangs and kicks at the door, sweeps objects off the mantelpiece and shelf, a little tornado incarnate, all destruction, until she comes upon her doll and, in the act of hurling it, freezes. Then she clutches it to herself, and in exhaustion sinks sobbing to the floor.* ANNIE *stands contemplating her, in some awe.*)

Two weeks.

(*She shakes her head, not without a touch of disgusted bewilderment.*)

What did I get into now?

(*The lights have been dimming throughout, and the garden house is lit only by the moonlight now, with* ANNIE *lost in the patches of dark.*)

SCENE 8

KATE, *now hatless and coatless, enters the family room by the rear door, carrying a lamp.* KELLER, *also hatless, wanders simultaneously around the back of the main house to where* JAMES *has been waiting, in the rising moonlight, on the porch.*

KELLER. I can't understand it. I had every intention of dismissing that girl, not setting her up like an empress.

JAMES. Yes, what's her secret, sir?

KELLER. Secret?

JAMES (*pleasantly*). That enables her to get anything she wants out of you? When I can't.

(JAMES *turns to go into the house, but* KELLER *grasps*

his wrist, twisting him half to his knees. KATE comes from the porch.)

KELLER (angrily). She does *not* get anything she—

JAMES (in pain). Don't—don't—

KATE. Captain.

KELLER. He's afraid.

(He throws JAMES away from him, with contempt.)

What *does* he want out of me?

JAMES (an outcry). My God, don't you know?

(He gazes from KELLER to KATE.)

Everything you forgot, when you forgot my mother.

KELLER. What!

(JAMES wheels into the house. KELLER takes a stride to the porch, to roar after him.)

One thing that girl's secret is not, she doesn't fire one shot and disappear!

(KATE stands rigid, and KELLER comes back to her.)

Katie. Don't mind what he—

KATE. Captain, *I* am proud of you.

KELLER. For what?

KATE. For letting this girl have what she needs.

KELLER. Why can't my son be? He can't bear me, you'd think I treat him as hard as this girl does Helen—

(He breaks off, as it dawns in him.)

KATE (gently). Perhaps you do.

KELLER. But he has to learn some respect!

KATE (a pause, wryly). Do you like the child?

(She turns again to the porch, but pauses, reluctant.)

How empty the house is, tonight.

(After a moment she continues on in. KELLER stands moveless, as the moonlight dies on him.)

SCENE 9

The distant belfry chimes toll, two o'clock, and with them, a moment later, comes the boy's voice on the wind, in a whisper.

BOY'S VOICE. Annie. Annie.

(In her patch of dark ANNIE, now in her nightgown, hurls a cup into a corner as though it were her grief, getting rid of its taste through her teeth.)

ANNIE. No! No pity, I won't have it.

(She comes to HELEN, prone on the floor.)

On either of us.

(She goes to her knees, but when she touches HELEN's hand the child starts up awake, recoils, and scrambles away from her under the bed. ANNIE stares after her. She strikes her palm on the floor, with passion.)

I *will* touch you!

(She gets to her feet, and paces in a kind of anger around the bed, her hand in her hair, and confronting HELEN at each turn.)

How, how? How do I—

(ANNIE stops. Then she calls out urgently, loudly.)

Percy! Percy!

(She moves swiftly to the drapes, at left.)

Percy, wake up!

(PERCY's voice comes in a thick sleepy mumble, unintelligible.)

Get out of bed and come in here. I need you.

(ANNIE darts away, finds and strikes a match, and touches it to the hanging lamp; the lights come up dimly in the room, and PERCY stands bare to the waist in torn overalls between the drapes, with eyes closed, swaying. ANNIE goes to him, pats his cheeks vigorously.)

Percy. You awake?

PERCY. No'm.

ANNIE. How would you like to play a nice game?

PERCY. Whah?

ANNIE. With Helen. She's under the bed. Touch her hand.

(She kneels PERCY down at the bed, thrusting his hand under it to contact HELEN's; HELEN emits an animal sound and crawls to the opposite side, but commences sniffing. ANNIE rounds the bed with PERCY and thrusts his hand again at HELEN; this time HELEN clutches it, sniffs in recognition, and comes scrambling out after PERCY, to hug him with delight. PERCY alarmed struggles, and HELEN's fingers go to his mouth.)

Production still from the 1962 film *The Miracle Worker.* In the garden house, Annie tries again to communicate with Helen. Does the relationship between Annie and Helen appear to have changed in any way? Explain.

PERCY. Lemme go. Lemme go—

(HELEN *fingers her own lips, as before, moving them in dumb imitation.*)

She tryin' talk. She gonna hit me—

ANNIE (*grimly*). She *can* talk. If she only knew, I'll show you how. She makes letters.

(*She opens* PERCY'*s other hand, and spells into it.*)

This one is C. C.

(*She hits his palm with it a couple of times, her eyes upon* HELEN *across him;* HELEN *gropes to feel what* PERCY'*s hand is doing, and when she encounters* ANNIE'*s she falls back from them.*)

She's mad at me now, though, she won't play. But she knows lots of letters. Here's another, A. C, a. C, a.

(*But she is watching* HELEN, *who comes groping, consumed with curiosity;* ANNIE *makes the letters in* PERCY'*s hand, and* HELEN *pokes to question what they are up to. Then* HELEN *snatches* PERCY'*s other hand, and quickly spells four letters into it.* ANNIE *follows them aloud.*)

C, a, k, e! She spells cake, she gets cake.

(*She is swiftly over to the tray of food, to fetch cake and a jug of milk.*)

She doesn't know yet it means this. Isn't it funny she knows how to spell it and doesn't *know* she knows?

(*She breaks the cake in two pieces, and extends one to each;* HELEN *rolls away from her offer.*)

Well, if she won't play it with me, I'll play it

with you. Would you like to learn one she doesn't know?

PERCY. No'm.

(*But* ANNIE *seizes his wrist, and spells to him.*)

ANNIE. M, i, l, k. M is this. I, that's an easy one, just the little finger. L is this—

(*And* HELEN *comes back with her hand, to feel the new word.* ANNIE *brushes her away and continues spelling aloud to* PERCY. HELEN*'s hand comes back again, and tries to get in;* ANNIE *brushes it away again.* HELEN*'s hand insists, and* ANNIE *puts it away rudely.*)

No, why should I talk to you? I'm teaching Percy a new word. L. K is this—

(HELEN *now yanks their hands apart; she butts* PERCY *away, and thrusts her palm out insistently.* ANNIE*'s eyes are bright, with glee.*)

Ho, you're *jealous*, are you!

(HELEN*'s hand waits, intractably[18] waits.*)

All *right*.

(ANNIE *spells into it, milk; and* HELEN *after a moment spells it back to* ANNIE. ANNIE *takes her hand, with her whole face shining. She gives a great sigh.*)

Good! So I'm finally back to where I can touch you, hm? Touch and go! No love lost, but here we go.

(*She puts the jug of milk into* HELEN*'s hand and squeezes* PERCY*'s shoulder.*)

You can go to bed now, you've earned your sleep. Thank you.

(PERCY *stumbling up weaves his way out through the drapes.* HELEN *finishes drinking, and holds the jug out, for* ANNIE; *when* ANNIE *takes it,* HELEN *crawls onto the bed, and makes for sleep.* ANNIE *stands, looks down at her.*)

Now all I have to teach you is—one word. Everything.

(*She sets the jug down. On the floor now* ANNIE *spies the doll, stoops to pick it up, and with it dangling in her hand, turns off the lamp. A shaft of moonlight is left on* HELEN *in the bed, and a second shaft on the rocking chair; and* ANNIE, *after putting off her smoked glasses, sits in the rocker with the doll. She is rather happy, and dangles the doll on her knee, and it makes its momma sound.* ANNIE *whispers to it in mock solicitude.*)

Hush, little baby. Don't—say a word—

(*She lays it against her shoulder, and begins rocking with it, patting its diminutive behind; she talks the lullaby to it, humorously at first.*)

Momma's gonna buy you—a mockingbird.
If that—mockingbird don't sing—

(*The rhythm of the rocking takes her into the tune, softly, and more tenderly.*)

Momma's gonna buy you a diamond ring.
If that diamond ring turns to brass—

(*A third shaft of moonlight outside now rises to pick out* JAMES *at the main house, with one foot on the porch step; he turns his body, as if hearing the song.*)

Momma's gonna buy you a looking glass.
If that looking glass gets broke—

(*In the family room a fourth shaft picks out* KELLER *seated at the table, in thought; and he, too, lifts his head, as if hearing.*)

Momma's gonna buy you a billy goat.
If that billy goat won't pull—

(*The fifth shaft is upstairs in* ANNIE'S *room, and picks out* KATE, *pacing there; and she halts, turning her head, too, as if hearing.*)

Momma's gonna buy you a cart and bull.
If that cart and bull turns over,
Momma's gonna buy you a dog named Rover.
If that dog named Rover won't bark—

(*With the shafts of moonlight on* HELEN, *and* JAMES, *and* KELLER, *and* KATE, *all moveless, and* ANNIE *rocking the doll, the curtain ends the act.*)

---

18. **intractably** (in trak′tə blē), *adv.* in a hard-to-manage way; stubbornly.

After Reading

Making Connections

1. Explain whether or not Annie has been an effective teacher so far.

2. Are blindness and deafness Helen's worst handicaps? Explain.

3. What does the battle between Annie and Helen in Scene 3 reveal about these **characters?**

4. Annie's experiences in a state asylum are revealed in a **flashback** in Scene 5 and in her **dialogue** in Scene 6. How have these experiences affected Annie?

5. Think about a time when you had to work closely with someone with whom you did not get along. Compare your relationship with the relationship between Helen and Annie.

6. Based on what you know about the characters, what do you **predict** will happen in Act 3?

Vocabulary Study

compunction
flail
impertinent
intractably
ire
nonplussed
ominous
siege
temperance
thwarted

Decide if the following pairs of words are synonyms or antonyms. Use your Glossary, if necessary, to understand the meanings of the italicized vocabulary words.

1. *compunction*—regret
2. *flail*—thrash
3. *impertinent*—respectful
4. *intractably*—stubbornly
5. *ire*—anger

6. *nonplussed*—certain
7. *ominous*—threatening
8. *siege*—surrender
9. *temperance*—indulgence
10. *thwarted*—assisted

Expressing Your Ideas

Writing Choice

Silent Words Imagine that you are Helen. Record your inner feelings about what has happened since the stranger has come to your house.

Another Option

Be an Expert You and a group of classmates are teachers, and Helen is your new student. How will you help her? Hold a parent-teacher conference, with group members acting as Helen's parents and teachers. Come up with an **action plan** to help Helen succeed.

Act Three

SCENE 1

The stage is totally dark, until we see ANNIE *and* HELEN *silhouetted on the bed in the garden house.* ANNIE *'s voice is audible, very patient, and worn; it has been saying this for a long time.*

ANNIE. Water, Helen. This is water. W, a, t, e, r.

It has a *name*.

(A silence. Then:)

Egg, e, g, g. It has a *name*, the name stands for the thing. Oh, it's so simple, simple as birth, to explain.

(The lights have commenced to rise, not on the garden house but on the homestead. Then:)

Helen, Helen, the chick *has* to come out of its shell, sometime. You come out, too.

(In the bedroom, upstairs, we see VINEY *unhurriedly washing the window, dusting, turning the mattress, readying the room for use again; then in the family room a diminished group at one end of the table—* KATE, KELLER, JAMES—*finishing up a quiet breakfast; then outside, down right, the other Negro servant on his knees, assisted by* MARTHA, *working with a trowel around a new trellis and wheelbarrow. The scene is one of everyday calm, and all are oblivious to* ANNIE *'s voice.)*

There's only one way out, for you, and it's language. To learn that your fingers can talk. And say anything, anything you can name. This is a mug. Mug, m, u, g. Helen, it has a *name*. It—has—a—name—

(KATE rises from the table.)

KELLER *(gently).* You haven't eaten, Katie.

KATE *(smiles, shakes her head).* I haven't the appetite. I'm too—restless, I can't sit to it.

KELLER. You should eat, my dear. It will be a long day, waiting.

JAMES *(lightly).* But it's been a short two weeks. I never thought life could be so—noiseless, went much too quickly for me.

(KATE and KELLER gaze at him, in silence. JAMES becomes uncomfortable.)

ANNIE. C, a, r, d. Card. C, a—

JAMES. Well, the house has been practically normal, hasn't it?

KELLER *(harshly).* Jimmie.

JAMES. Is it wrong to enjoy a quiet breakfast, after five years? And you two even seem to enjoy each other—

KELLER. It could be even more noiseless, Jimmie, without your tongue running every minute. Haven't you enough feeling to imagine what Katie has been undergoing, ever since—

(KATE stops him, with her hand on his arm.)

KATE. Captain.

(To JAMES.)

It's true. The two weeks have been normal,

quiet, all you say. But not short. Interminable.[1]

(She rises, and wanders out; she pauses on the porch steps, gazing toward the garden house.)

ANNIE *(fading).* W, a, t, e, r. But it means *this.* W, a, t, e, r. *This.* W, a, t—

JAMES. I only meant that Miss Sullivan is a boon.[2] Of contention,[3] though, it seems.

KELLER *(heavily).* If and when you're a parent, Jimmie, you will understand what separation means. A mother loses a—protector.

JAMES *(baffled).* Hm?

KELLER. You'll learn, we don't just keep our children safe. They keep us safe.

(He rises, with his empty coffee cup and saucer.)

There are of course all kinds of separation, Katie has lived with one kind for five years. And another is disappointment. In a child.

(He goes with the cup out the rear door. JAMES *sits for a long moment of stillness. In the garden house the lights commence to come up;* ANNIE, *haggard[4] at the table, is writing a letter, her face again almost in contact with the stationery;* HELEN, *apart on the stool, and for the first time as clean and neat as a button, is quietly crocheting an endless chain of wool, which snakes all around the room.)*

ANNIE. "I, feel, every, day, more, and, more, in—"

(She pauses, and turns the pages of a dictionary open before her; her finger descends the words to a full stop. She elevates her eyebrows, then copies the word.)

"—adequate."

(In the main house JAMES *pushes up, and goes to the front doorway, after* KATE.*)*

JAMES. Kate?

(KATE turns her glance, JAMES *is rather weary.)*

I'm sorry. Open my mouth, like that fairy tale, frogs jump out.

KATE. No. It has been better. For everyone.

(She starts away, up center.)

ANNIE *(writing).* "If, only, there, were, someone, to, help, me, I, need, a, teacher, as, much, as, Helen—"

JAMES. Kate.

(KATE halts, waits.)

What does he want from me?

KATE. That's not the question. Stand up to the world, Jimmie, that comes first.

JAMES *(a pause, wryly).* But the world is him.

KATE. Yes. And no one can do it for you.

JAMES. Kate.

(His voice is humble.)

At least we—Could you—be my friend?

KATE. I am.

(KATE turns to wander, up back of the garden house. ANNIE*'s murmur comes at once; the lights begin to die on the main house.)*

ANNIE. "—my, mind, is, undisciplined, full, of, skips, and, jumps, and—"

(She halts, rereads, frowns.)

Hm.

(ANNIE puts her nose again in the dictionary, flips back to an earlier page, and fingers down the words; KATE *presently comes down toward the bay window with a trayful of food.)*

Disinter—disinterested—disjoin—dis—

(She backtracks, indignant.)

Disinterested, disjoin—Where's disipline?

(She goes a page or two back, searching with her finger, muttering.)

What a dictionary, have to know how to spell it before you can look up how to spell it, disciple, *discipline!* Diskipline.

(She corrects the word in her letter.)

Undisciplined.

(But her eyes are bothering her, she closes them in exhaustion and gently fingers the eyelids. KATE *watches her through the window.)*

---

1. interminable (in′tėr′mə nə bəl), *adj.* endless.
2. **boon** (bün), *n.* a great benefit; blessing.
3. contention (kən ten′shən), *n.* an arguing; disputing; quarreling. James makes a play on the phrase "bone of contention" when he says "boon of contention."
4. haggard (hag′ərd), *adj.* looking worn from pain, fatigue, worry, and so on.

KATE. What are you doing to your eyes?

(ANNIE *glances around; she puts her smoked glasses on, and gets up to come over, assuming a cheerful energy.*)

ANNIE. It's worse on my vanity! I'm learning to spell. It's like a surprise party, the most unexpected characters turn up.

KATE. You're not to overwork your eyes, Miss Annie.

ANNIE. Well.

(*She takes the tray, sets it on her chair, and carries chair and tray to* HELEN.)

Whatever I spell to Helen I'd better spell right.

KATE (*almost wistful*). How—serene she is.

ANNIE. She learned this stitch yesterday. Now I can't get her to stop!

(*She disentangles one foot from the wool chain, and sets the chair before* HELEN. HELEN *at its contact with her knee feels the plate, promptly sets her crocheting down, and tucks the napkin in at her neck, but* ANNIE *withholds the spoon; when* HELEN *finds it missing, she folds her hands in her lap, and quietly waits.* ANNIE *twinkles at* KATE *with mock devoutness.*)

Such a little lady, she'd sooner starve than eat with her fingers.

(*She gives* HELEN *the spoon, and* HELEN *begins to eat, neatly.*)

KATE. You've taught her so much, these two weeks. I would never have—

ANNIE. Not enough.

(*She is suddenly gloomy, shakes her head.*)

Obedience isn't enough. Well, she learned two nouns this morning, key and water, brings her up to eighteen nouns and three verbs.

KATE (*hesitant*). But—not—

ANNIE. No. Not that they mean things. It's still a finger-game, no meaning.

(*She turns to* KATE, *abruptly.*)

Mrs. Keller—

(*But she defers it; she comes back, to sit in the bay and lift her hand.*)

Shall we play our finger-game?

KATE. How will she learn it?

ANNIE. It will come.

(*She spells a word;* KATE *does not respond.*)

KATE. How?

ANNIE (*a pause*). How does a bird learn to fly?

(*She spells again.*)

We're born to use words, like wings, it has to come.

KATE. How?

ANNIE (*another pause, wearily*). All right. I don't know how.

(*She pushes up her glasses, to rub her eyes.*)

I've done everything I could think of. Whatever she's learned here—keeping herself clean, knitting, stringing beads, meals, setting-up exercises each morning, we climb trees, hunt eggs, yesterday a chick was born in her hands—all of it I spell, everything we do, we never stop spelling. I go to bed with—writer's cramp from talking so much!

KATE. I worry about you, Miss Annie. You must rest.

ANNIE. Now? She spells back in her *sleep,* her fingers make letters when she doesn't know! In her bones those five fingers know, that hand aches to—speak out, and something in her mind is asleep, how do I—nudge that awake? That's the one question.

KATE. With no answer.

ANNIE (*long pause*). Except keep at it. Like this.

(*She again begins spelling—"I, need"—and* KATE*'s brows gather, following the words.*)

KATE. More—time?

(*She glances at* ANNIE, *who looks her in the eyes, silent.*)

Here?

ANNIE. Spell it.

(KATE *spells a word—no—shaking her head;* ANNIE *spells two words—why, not—back, with an impatient question in her eyes; and* KATE *moves her head in pain to answer it.*)

KATE. Because I can't—

ANNIE. Spell it! If she ever learns, you'll have a lot to tell each other, start now.

(KATE *painstakingly spells in air. In the midst of this the rear door opens, and* KELLER *enters with the setter* BELLE *in tow.*)

KELLER. Miss Sullivan? On my way to the office, I brought Helen a playmate—

ANNIE. Outside please, Captain Keller.

KELLER. My dear child, the two weeks are up today, surely you don't object to—

ANNIE *(rising).* They're not up till six o'clock.

KELLER *(indulgent).* Oh, now. What difference can a fraction of one day—

ANNIE. An agreement is an agreement. Now you've been very good, I'm sure you can keep it up for a few more hours.

(*She escorts* KELLER *by the arm over the threshold; he obeys, leaving* BELLE.)

KELLER. Miss Sullivan, you are a tyrant.

ANNIE. Likewise, I'm sure. You can stand there, and close the door if she comes.

KATE. I don't think you know how eager we are to have her back in our arms—

ANNIE. I do know, it's my main worry.

KELLER. It's like expecting a new child in the house. Well, she *is* so—composed, so—

(*Gently.*)

Attractive. You've done wonders for her, Miss Sullivan.

ANNIE *(not a question).* Have I.

KELLER. If there's anything you want from us in repayment tell us, it will be a privilege to—

ANNIE. I just told Mrs. Keller. I want more time.

KATE. Miss Annie—

ANNIE. Another week.

(HELEN *lifts her head, and begins to sniff.*)

KELLER. We miss the child. *I* miss her, I'm glad to say, that's a different debt I owe you—

ANNIE. Pay it to Helen. Give *her* another week.

KATE *(gently).* Doesn't she miss us?

KELLER. Of course she does. What a wrench this unexplainable—exile must be to her, can you say it's not?

ANNIE. No. But I—

(HELEN *is off the stool, to grope about the room; when she encounters* BELLE, *she throws her arms around the dog's neck in delight.*)

KATE. Doesn't she need affection too, Miss Annie?

ANNIE *(wavering).* She—never shows me she needs it, she won't have any—caressing or—

KATE. But you're not her mother.

KELLER. And what would another week accomplish? We are more than satisfied, you've done more than we ever thought possible, taught her constructive—

ANNIE. I can't promise anything. All I can—

KELLER *(no break).* —things to do, to behave like—even look like—a human child, so manageable, contented, cleaner, more—

ANNIE *(withering).* Cleaner.

KELLER. Well. We say cleanliness is next to godliness, Miss—

ANNIE. Cleanliness is next to nothing, she has to learn that everything has its name! That words can be her *eyes*, to everything in the world outside her, and inside too, what is she without words? With them she can think, have ideas, be reached, there's not a thought or fact in the world that can't be hers. You publish a newspaper, Captain Keller, do I have to tell you what words are? And she has them already—

KELLER. Miss Sullivan—

ANNIE. —eighteen nouns and three verbs, they're in her fingers now, I need only time to push *one* of them into her mind! One, and everything under the sun will follow. Don't you see what she's learned here is only clearing the way for that? I can't risk her unlearning it, give me more time alone with her, another week to—

KELLER. Look.

(He points, and ANNIE *turns.* HELEN *is playing with* BELLE*'s claws; she makes letters with her fingers, shows them to* BELLE*, waits with her palm, then manipulates the dog's claws.)*

What is she spelling?

(A silence.)

KATE. Water?

*(*ANNIE *nods.)*

KELLER. Teaching a dog to spell.

(A pause.)

The dog doesn't know what she means, any more than she knows what you mean, Miss Sullivan. I think you ask too much, of her and yourself. God may not have meant Helen to have the—eyes you speak of.

ANNIE *(toneless).* I mean her to.

KELLER *(curiously).* What is it to you?

*(*ANNIE*'s head comes slowly up.)*

You make us see how we indulge her for our sake. Is the opposite true, for you?

ANNIE *(then).* Half a week?

KELLER. An agreement *is* an agreement.

ANNIE. Mrs. Keller?

KATE *(simply).* I want her back.

(A wait; ANNIE *then lets her hands drop in surrender, and nods.)*

KELLER. I'll send Viney over to help you pack.

ANNIE. Not until six o'clock. I have her till six o'clock.

KELLER *(consenting).* Six o'clock. Come, Katie.

*(*KATE *leaving the window joins him around back, while* KELLER *closes the door; they are shut out. Only the garden house is daylit now, and the light on it is narrowing down.* ANNIE *stands watching* HELEN *work* BELLE*'s claws. Then she settles beside them on her knees, and stops* HELEN*'s hand.)*

ANNIE *(gently).* No.

(She shakes her head, with HELEN*'s hand to her face, then spells.)*

Dog. D, o, g. Dog.

(She touches HELEN*'s hand to* BELLE. HELEN *dutifully pats the dog's head, and resumes spelling to its paw.)*

Not water.

*(*ANNIE *rolls to her feet, brings a tumbler of water back from the tray, and kneels with it, to seize* HELEN*'s hand and spell.)*

Here. Water. *Water.*

(She thrusts HELEN*'s hand into the tumbler.* HELEN *lifts her hand out dripping, wipes it daintily on* BELLE*'s hide, and taking the tumbler from* ANNIE*, endeavors to thrust* BELLE*'s paw into it.* ANNIE *sits watching, wearily.)*

I don't know how to tell you. Not a soul in the world knows how to tell you. Helen, Helen.

(She bends in compassion to touch her lips to HELEN*'s temple, and instantly* HELEN *pauses, her hands off the dog, her head slightly averted. The lights are still narrowing, and* BELLE *slinks off. After a moment* ANNIE *sits back.)*

Yes, what's it to me? They're satisfied. Give them back their child and dog, both house-broken, everyone's satisfied. But me, and you.

*(*HELEN*'s hand comes out into the light, groping.)*

Reach. *Reach!*

*(*ANNIE *extending her own hand grips* HELEN*'s; the two hands are clasped, tense in the light, the rest of the room changing in shadows.)*

I wanted to teach you—oh, everything that earth is full of, Helen, everything on it that's ours for a wink and it's gone, and what we are on it, the—light we bring to it and leave behind in—words, why, you can see five thousand years back in a light of words, everything we feel, think, know—and share, in words, so not a soul is in darkness, or done with, even in the grave. And I know, I *know,* one word and I can put the world in your hand—and whatever it is to me, I won't take less! How, how, how do I tell you that *this—*

(She spells.)

—means a *word,* and the word means this *thing,* wool?

(She thrusts the wool at HELEN*'s hand;* HELEN *sits, puzzled.* ANNIE *puts the crocheting aside.)*

Or this—s, t, o, o, l—means this *thing,* stool?

(She claps HELEN*'s palm to the stool.* HELEN *waits, uncomprehending.* ANNIE *snatches up her napkin, spells.)*

Napkin!

(She forces it on HELEN*'s hand, waits, discards it, lifts a fold of the child's dress, spells.)*

Dress!

(She lets it drop, spells.)

F, a, c, e, face!

(She draws HELEN*'s hand to her cheek, and pressing it there, staring into the child's responseless eyes, hears the distant belfry begin to toll, slowly. one, two, three, four, five, six.)*

SCENE 2

On the third stroke the lights stealing in around the garden house show us figures waiting. VINEY, *the other servant,* MARTHA, PERCY *at the drapes, and* JAMES *on the dim porch.* ANNIE *and* HELEN *remain, frozen. The chimes die away. Silently* PERCY *moves the drape-rod back out of sight;* VINEY *steps into the room—not using the door—and unmakes the bed; the other servant brings the wheelbarrow over, leaves it handy, rolls the bed off;* VINEY *puts the bed linens on top of a waiting boxful of* HELEN*'s toys, and loads the box on the wheelbarrow;* MARTHA *and* PERCY *take out the chairs, with the trayful, then the table; and* JAMES, *coming down and into the room, lifts* ANNIE*'s suitcase from its corner.* VINEY *and the other servant load the remaining odds and ends on the wheelbarrow, and the servant wheels it off.* VINEY *and the children departing leave only* JAMES *in the room with* ANNIE *and* HELEN. JAMES *studies the two of them, without mockery, and then, quietly going to the door and opening it, bears the suitcase out, and housewards. He leaves the door open.*

KATE *steps into the doorway, and stands.* ANNIE *lifting her gaze from* HELEN *sees her; she takes* HELEN*'s hand from her cheek, and returns it to the child's own, stroking it there twice, in her mother-sign, before spelling slowly into it.*

M, o, t, h, e, r. Mother.

*(*HELEN *with her hand free strokes her cheek, suddenly forlorn.* ANNIE *takes her hand again.)*

M, o, t, h—

(But KATE *is trembling with such impatience that her voice breaks from her, harsh.)*

KATE. Let her *come!*

*(*ANNIE *lifts* HELEN *to her feet, with a turn, and gives her a little push. Now* HELEN *begins groping, sensing something, trembling herself; and* KATE *falling one step in onto her knees clasps her, kissing her.* HELEN *clutches her, tight as she can.* KATE *is inarticulate, choked, repeating* HELEN*'s name again and again. She wheels with her in her arms to stumble away out the doorway;* ANNIE *stands unmoving, while* KATE *in a blind walk carries* HELEN *like a baby behind the main house, out of view.*

ANNIE *is now alone on the stage. She turns, gazing around at the stripped room, bidding it silently farewell, impassively, like a defeated general on the deserted battlefield. All that remains is a stand with a basin of water; and here* ANNIE *takes up an eyecup, bathes each of her eyes, empties the eyecup, drops it in her purse, and tiredly locates her smoked glasses on the floor. The lights alter subtly; in the act of putting on her glasses* ANNIE *hears something that stops her, with head lifted. We hear it too, the voices out of the past, including her own, now, in a whisper.)*

BOY'S VOICE. You said we'd be together, forever—You promised, forever and—*Annie!*

ANAGNOS'S VOICE. But that battle is dead and done with, why not let it stay buried?

ANNIE'S VOICE *(whispering).* I think God must owe me a resurrection.

ANAGNOS'S VOICE. What?

(A pause, and ANNIE *answers it herself, heavily.)*

ANNIE. And I owe God one.

BOY'S VOICE. Forever and ever—

*(*ANNIE *shakes her head.)*

—forever, and ever, and—

*(*ANNIE *covers her ears.)*

—forever, and ever, and ever—

(It pursues ANNIE; *she flees to snatch up her purse, wheels to the doorway, and* KELLER *is standing in it. The lights have lost their special color.)*

KELLER. Miss—Annie.

(He has an envelope in his fingers.)

I've been waiting to give you this.

ANNIE *(after a breath)*. What?

KELLER. Your first month's salary.

(He puts it in her hand.)

With many more to come, I trust. It doesn't express what we feel, it doesn't pay our debt. For what you've done.

ANNIE. What have I done?

KELLER. Taken a wild thing, and given us back a child.

ANNIE *(presently)*. I taught her one thing, "no." Don't do this, don't do that—

KELLER. It's more than all of us could, in all the years we—

ANNIE. I wanted to teach her what language is. I wanted to teach her "yes."

KELLER. You will have time.

ANNIE. I don't know how. I know without it to do nothing but obey is—no gift, obedience without understanding is a—blindness, too. Is that all I've wished on her?

KELLER *(gently)*. No, no—

ANNIE. Maybe. I don't know what else to do. Simply go on, keep doing what I've done, and have—faith that inside she's—That inside it's waiting. Like water, underground. All you can do is keep on.

KELLER. It's enough. For us.

ANNIE. You can help, Captain Keller.

KELLER. How?

ANNIE. Even learning "no" has been at a cost. Of much trouble and pain. Don't undo it.

KELLER. Why should we wish to—

ANNIE *(abruptly)*. The world isn't an easy place for anyone, I don't want her just to obey but to let her have her way in everything is a lie, to *her,* I can't—

(Her eyes fill, it takes her by surprise, and she laughs through it.)

And I don't even love her, she's not my child! Well. You've got to stand between that lie and her.

KELLER. We'll try.

ANNIE. Because *I* will. As long as you let me stay, that's one promise I'll keep.

KELLER. Agreed. We've learned something too, I hope.

(A pause.)

Won't you come now, to supper?

ANNIE. Yes.

(She wags the envelope, ruefully.)

Why doesn't God pay His debts each month?

KELLER. I beg your pardon?

ANNIE. Nothing. I used to wonder how I could—

(The lights are fading on them, simultaneously rising on the family room of the main house, where VINEY *is polishing glassware at the table set for dinner.)*

—earn a living.

KELLER. Oh, you do.

ANNIE. I really do. Now the question is, can I survive it!

*(*KELLER *smiles, offers his arm.)*

KELLER. May I?

*(*ANNIE *takes it, and the lights lose them as he escorts her out.)*

SCENE 3

Now in the family room the rear door opens, and HELEN *steps in. She stands a moment, then sniffs in one deep grateful breath, and her hands go out vigorously to familiar things, over the door panels, and to the chairs around the table, and over the silverware on the table, until she meets* VINEY; *she pats her flank approvingly.*

VINEY. Oh, we glad to have you back too, prob'ly.

*(*HELEN *hurries groping to the front door, opens and closes it, removes its key, opens and closes it again to be sure it is unlocked, gropes back to the rear door and repeats the procedure, removing its key and hugging herself gleefully.)*

AUNT EV *is next in by the rear door, with a relish tray; she bends to kiss* HELEN's *cheek.* HELEN *finds* KATE *behind her, and thrusts the keys at her.)*

KATE. What? Oh.

(To EV.*)*

Keys.

(She pockets them, lets HELEN *feel them.)*

Yes, I'll keep the keys. I think we've had enough of locked doors, too.

*(*JAMES, *having earlier put* ANNIE's *suitcase inside her door upstairs and taken himself out of view around the corner, now reappears and comes down the stairs as* ANNIE *and* KELLER *mount the porch steps. Following them into the family room, he pats* ANNIE's *hair in passing, rather to her surprise.)*

JAMES. Evening, General.

(He takes his own chair opposite. VINEY *bears the empty water pitcher out to the porch. The remaining suggestion of garden house is gone now, and the water pump is unobstructed;* VINEY *pumps water into the pitcher.* KATE *surveying the table breaks the silence.)*

KATE. Will you say grace, Jimmie?

(They bow their heads, except for HELEN, *who palms her empty plate and then reaches to be sure her mother is there.* JAMES *considers a moment, glances across at* ANNIE, *lowers his head again, and obliges.)*

JAMES *(lightly).* And Jacob was left alone, and wrestled with an angel until the breaking of the day; and the hollow of Jacob's thigh was out of joint, as he wrestled with him; and the angel said, Let me go, for the day breaketh. And Jacob said, I will not let thee go, except thou bless me. Amen.

*(*ANNIE *has lifted her eyes suspiciously at* JAMES, *who winks expressionlessly and inclines his head to* HELEN.*)*

Oh, you angel.

(The others lift their faces; VINEY *returns with the pitcher, setting it down near* KATE, *then goes out the rear door; and* ANNIE *puts a napkin around* HELEN.*)*

AUNT EV. That's a very strange grace, James.

KELLER. Will you start the muffins, Ev?

JAMES. It's from the Good Book, isn't it?

AUNT EV *(passing a plate).* Well, of course it is. Didn't you know?

JAMES. Yes, I knew.

KELLER *(serving).* Ham, Miss Annie?

ANNIE. Please.

AUNT EV. Then why ask?

JAMES. I meant it *is* from the Good Book, and therefore a fitting grace.

AUNT EV. Well, I don't know about *that.*

KATE *(with the pitcher).* Miss Annie?

ANNIE. Thank you.

AUNT EV. There's an awful *lot* of things in the Good Book that I wouldn't care to hear just before eating.

(When ANNIE *reaches for the pitcher,* HELEN *removes her napkin and drops it to the floor.* ANNIE *is filling* HELEN's *glass when she notices it; she considers* HELEN's *bland expression a moment, then bends, retrieves it, and tucks it around* HELEN's *neck again.)*

JAMES. Well, fitting in the sense that Jacob's thigh was out of joint, and so is this piggie's.

AUNT EV. I declare, James—

KATE. Pickles, Aunt Ev?

AUNT EV. Oh, I should say so, you know my opinion of your pickles—

KATE. This is the end of them, I'm afraid. I didn't put up nearly enough last summer, this year I intend to—

(She interrupts herself, seeing HELEN *deliberately lift off her napkin and drop it again to the floor. She bends to retrieve it, but* ANNIE *stops her arm.)*

KELLER *(not noticing).* Reverend looked in at the office today to complain his hens have stopped laying. Poor fellow, *he* was out of joint, all he could—

(He stops too, to frown down the table at KATE, HELEN, *and* ANNIE *in turn, all suspended in midmotion.)*

JAMES *(not noticing).* I've always suspected those hens.

AUNT EV. Of what?

JAMES. I think they're Papist.[5] Has he tried—

(*He stops, too, following* KELLER's *eyes.* ANNIE *now stops to pick the napkin up.*)

AUNT EV. James, now you're pulling my—lower extremity, the first thing you know we'll be—

(*She stops, too, hearing herself in the silence.* ANNIE, *with everyone now watching, for the third time puts the napkin on* HELEN. HELEN *yanks it off, and throws it down.* ANNIE *rises, lifts* HELEN's *plate, and bears it away.* HELEN, *feeling it gone, slides down and commences to kick up under the table; the dishes jump.* ANNIE *contemplates this for a moment, then coming back takes* HELEN's *wrists firmly and swings her off the chair.* HELEN *struggling gets one hand free, and catches at her mother's skirt; when* KATE *takes her by the shoulders,* HELEN *hangs quiet.*)

KATE. Miss Annie.

ANNIE. No.

KATE (*a pause*). It's a very special day.

ANNIE (*grimly*). It will be, when I give in to that.

(*She tries to disengage* HELEN's *hand;* KATE *lays hers on* ANNIE's.)

KATE. Please. I've hardly had a chance to welcome her home—

ANNIE. Captain Keller.

KELLER (*embarrassed*). Oh, Katie, we—had a little talk, Miss Annie feels that if we indulge Helen in these—

AUNT EV. But what's the child done?

ANNIE. She's learned not to throw things on the floor and kick. It took us the best part of two weeks and—

AUNT EV. But only a napkin, it's not as if it were breakable!

ANNIE. And everything she's learned *is?* Mrs. Keller, I don't think we should—play tug-of-war for her, either give her to me or you keep her from kicking.

KATE. What do you wish to do?

ANNIE. Let me take her from the table.

AUNT EV. Oh, let her stay, my goodness, she's only a child, she doesn't have to wear a napkin if she doesn't want to her first evening—

ANNIE (*level*). And ask outsiders not to interfere.

AUNT EV (*astonished*). Out—outsi—I'm the child's *aunt!*

KATE (*distressed*). Will once hurt so much, Miss Annie? I've—made all Helen's favorite foods, tonight.

(*A pause.*)

KELLER (*gently*). It's a homecoming party, Miss Annie.

(ANNIE *after a moment releases* HELEN. *But she cannot accept it, at her own chair she shakes her head and turns back, intent on* KATE.)

ANNIE. She's testing you. You realize?

JAMES (*to* ANNIE). She's testing you.

KELLER. Jimmie, be quiet.

(JAMES *sits, tense.*)

Now she's home, naturally she—

ANNIE. And wants to see what will happen. At your hands. I said it was my main worry, is this what you promised me not half an hour ago?

KELLER (*reasonably*). But she's *not* kicking, now—

ANNIE. And not learning not to. Mrs. Keller, teaching her is bound to be painful, to everyone. I know it hurts to watch, but she'll live up to just what you demand of her, and no more.

JAMES (*palely*). She's testing *you.*

KELLER (*testily*). Jimmie.

JAMES. I have an opinion. I think I should—

KELLER. No one's interested in hearing your opinion.

ANNIE. *I'm* interested, of course she's testing me. Let me keep her to what she's learned and she'll go on learning from me. Take her out of my hands and it all comes apart.

(KATE *closes her eyes, digesting it;* ANNIE *sits again, with a brief comment for her.*)

---

5. **Papist** (pā′pist), derogatory term for a Roman Catholic.

Production still from the 1962 film *The Miracle Worker.* Annie and Helen at the pump.

Be bountiful, it's at her expense.

(She turns to JAMES, *flatly.)*

Please pass me more of—her favorite foods.

(Then KATE *lifts* HELEN*'s hands, and turning her toward* ANNIE, *surrenders her;* HELEN *makes for her own chair.)*

KATE *(low).* Take her, Miss Annie.

ANNIE *(then).* Thank you.

(But the moment ANNIE *rising reaches for her hand,* HELEN *begins to fight and kick, clutching to the tablecloth, and uttering laments.* ANNIE *again tries to loosen her hand, and* KELLER *rises.)*

KELLER *(tolerant).* I'm afraid you're the difficulty, Miss Annie. Now I'll keep her to what she's learned, you're quite right there—

(He takes HELEN*'s hands from* ANNIE, *pats them;* HELEN *quiets down.*

—but I don't see that we need send her from the table, after all, she's the guest of honor. Bring her plate back.

ANNIE. If she was a seeing child, none of you would tolerate one—

KELLER. Well, she's not, I think some compromise is called for. Bring her plate, please.

*(*ANNIE*'s jaw sets, but she restores the plate, while* KELLER *fastens the napkin around* HELEN*'s neck; she permits it.)*

There. It's not unnatural, most of us take some aversion⁶ to our teachers, and occasionally another hand can smooth things out.

(He puts a fork in HELEN*'s hand;* HELEN *takes it. Genially.⁷)*

Now. Shall we start all over?

---

6. **aversion** (ə vėr′zhən), *n.* a strong or fixed dislike; antipathy.
7. **genially** (jē′nyəl ē), *adv.* in a way that is smiling and pleasant; cheerful and friendly; kindly.

(He goes back around the table, and sits. ANNIE *stands watching.* HELEN *is motionless, thinking things through, until with a wicked glee she deliberately flings the fork on the floor. After another moment she plunges her hand into her food, and crams a fistful into her mouth.)*

JAMES *(wearily).* I think we've started all over—

*(*KELLER *shoots a glare at him, as* HELEN *plunges her other hand into* ANNIE*'s plate.* ANNIE *at once moves in, to grasp her wrist, and* HELEN *flinging out a hand encounters the pitcher; she swings with it at* ANNIE; ANNIE *falling back, blocks it with an elbow, but the water flies over her dress.* ANNIE *gets her breath, then snatches the pitcher away in one hand, hoists* HELEN *up bodily under the other arm, and starts to carry her out, kicking.* KELLER *stands.)*

ANNIE *(savagely polite).* Don't get up!

KELLER. Where are you going?

ANNIE. Don't smooth anything else out for me, don't interfere in any way! I treat her like a seeing child because I *ask* her to see, I *expect* her to see, don't undo what I do!

KELLER. Where are you taking her?

ANNIE. To make her fill this pitcher again!

(She thrusts out with HELEN *under her arm, but* HELEN *escapes up the stairs and* ANNIE *runs after her.* KELLER *stands rigid.* AUNT EV *is astounded.)*

AUNT EV. You let her speak to you like that, Arthur? A creature who *works* for you?

KELLER *(angrily).* No. I don't.

(He is starting after ANNIE *when* JAMES, *on his feet with shaky resolve,* interposes[8] *his chair between them in* KELLER*'s path.)*

JAMES. Let her go.

KELLER. What!

JAMES *(a swallow).* I said—let her go. She's right.

*(*KELLER *glares at the chair and him.* JAMES *takes a deep breath, then headlong.)*

She's right, Kate's right, I'm right, and you're wrong. If you drive her away from here it will be over my dead—chair, has it

never occurred to you that on one occasion you might be consummately wrong?

*(*KELLER*'s stare is unbelieving, even a little fascinated.* KATE *rises in* trepidation,[9] *to mediate.)*

KATE. Captain.

*(*KELLER *stops her with his raised hand; his eyes stay on* JAMES*'s pale face, for a long hold. When he finally finds voice, it is gruff.)*

KELLER. Sit down, everyone.

(He sits. KATE *sits.* JAMES *holds onto his chair.* KELLER *speaks mildly.)*

Please sit down, Jimmie.

(JAMES *sits, and a moveless silence prevails;* KELLER*'s eyes do not leave him.* ANNIE *has pulled* HELEN *downstairs again by one hand, the pitcher in her other hand, down the porch steps, and across the yard to the pump. She puts* HELEN*'s hand on the pump handle, grimly.)*

ANNIE. All right. Pump.

*(*HELEN *touches her cheek, waits uncertainly.)*

No, she's not here. Pump!

(She forces HELEN*'s hand to work the handle, then lets go. And* HELEN *obeys. She pumps till the water comes, then* ANNIE *puts the pitcher in her other hand and guides it under the spout, and the water tumbling half into and half around the pitcher douses* HELEN*'s hand.* ANNIE *takes over the handle to keep water coming, and does automatically what she has done many times before, spells into* HELEN*'s free palm.)*

Water. W, a, t, e, r. *Water.* It has a—*name*—

And now the miracle happens. HELEN *drops the pitcher on the slab under the spout, it shatters. She stands transfixed.* ANNIE *freezes on the pump handle; there is a change in the sundown light, and with it a change in* HELEN*'s face, some light coming into it we have never seen there, some struggle in the depths behind it; and her lips tremble, trying to remember something the muscles around them once knew, till at last it finds its way out, painfully, a baby sound buried under the debris of years of dumbness.)*

---

8. **interpose** (in′tər pōz′), *v.* come between other things.
9. **trepidation** (trep′ə dā′shən), *n.* nervous dread; fear; fright.

HELEN. Wah. Wah.

(And again, with great effort.)

Wah. Wah.

(HELEN plunges her hand into the dwindling water, spells into her own palm. Then she gropes frantically, ANNIE reaches for her hand, and HELEN spells into ANNIE's hand.)

ANNIE *(whispering).* Yes.

(HELEN spells it out again.)

Yes!

(HELEN grabs at the handle, pumps for more water, plunges her hand into its spurt and grabs ANNIE's to spell it again.)

Yes! Oh, my dear—

(She falls to her knees to clasp HELEN's hand, but HELEN pulls it free, stands almost bewildered, then drops to the ground, pats it swiftly, holds up her palm, imperious. ANNIE spells into it.)

Ground.

(HELEN spells it back.)

Yes!

(HELEN whirls to the pump, pats it, holds up her palm, and ANNIE spells into it.)

Pump.

(HELEN spells it back.)

Yes! Yes!

(Now HELEN is in such an excitement she is possessed, wild, trembling, cannot be still, turns, runs, falls on the porch step, claps it, reaches out her palm, and ANNIE is at it instantly to spell.)

Step.

(HELEN has no time to spell back now, she whirls groping, to touch anything, encounters the trellis, shakes it, thrusts out her palm, and ANNIE while spelling to her cries wildly at the house.)

Trellis. Mrs. Keller! *Mrs. Keller.*

(Inside KATE starts to her feet. HELEN scrambles back on to the porch, groping, and finds the bell string, tugs it; the bell rings, the distant chimes begin tolling the hour, all the bells in town seem to break into speech while HELEN reaches out and ANNIE spells feverishly into her hand. KATE hurries out, with KELLER after her; AUNT EV

is on her feet, to peer out the window; only JAMES remains at the table, and with a napkin wipes his damp brow. From up right and left the servants—VINEY, the two Negro children, the other servant—run in, and stand watching from a distance as HELEN, ringing the bell, with her other hand encounters her mother's skirt; when she throws a hand out, ANNIE spells into it.)

Mother.

(KELLER now seizes HELEN's hand, she touches him, gestures a hand, and ANNIE again spells.)

Papa—she *knows!*

(KATE and KELLER go to their knees, stammering, clutching HELEN to them, and ANNIE steps unsteadily back to watch the threesome, HELEN spelling wildly into KATE's hand, then into KELLER's, KATE spelling back into HELEN's; they cannot keep their hands off her, and rock her in their clasp.

Then HELEN gropes, feels nothing, turns all around, pulls free, and comes with both hands groping, to find ANNIE. She encounters ANNIE's thighs, ANNIE kneels to her, HELEN's hand pats ANNIE's cheek impatiently, points a finger, and waits; and ANNIE spells into it.)*

Teacher.

(HELEN spells it back, slowly; ANNIE nods.)

Teacher.

(She holds HELEN's hand to her cheek. Presently HELEN withdraws it, not jerkily, only with reserve, and retreats a step. She stands thinking it over, then turns again and stumbles back to her parents. They try to embrace her, but she has something else in mind, it is to get the keys, and she hits KATE's pocket until KATE digs them out for her.

ANNIE *with her own load of emotion has retreated, her back turned, toward the pump, to sit;* KATE *moves to* HELEN, *touches her hand questioningly, and* HELEN *spells a word to her.* KATE *comprehends it, their first act of verbal communication, and she can hardly utter the word aloud, in wonder, gratitude, and* deprivation;[10] *it is a moment in which she* simultaneously[11] *finds and loses a child.)*

---

10. **deprivation** (dep′rə vā′shən), *n.* a loss.
11. **simultaneously** (sī′məl tā′nē əs lē), *adv.* at the same time.

Production still from the 1962 film *The Miracle Worker.* Helen asks Annie for more words as her amazed family looks on. Compare and contrast this scene with the family scene in Act 2, Scene 2.

KATE. Teacher?

(ANNIE *turns; and* KATE, *facing* HELEN *in her direction by the shoulders, holds her back, holds her back, and then relinquishes[12] her.* HELEN *feels her way across the yard, rather shyly, and when her moving hands touch* ANNIE*'s skirt she stops. Then she holds out the keys and places them in* ANNIE*'s hand. For a moment neither of them moves. Then* HELEN *slides into* ANNIE*'s arms, and lifting away her smoked glasses, kisses her on the cheek.* ANNIE *gathers her in.*

KATE *torn both ways turns from this, gestures the servants off, and makes her way into the house, on* KELLER*'s arm. The servants go, in separate directions. The lights are half down now, except over the pump.* ANNIE *and* HELEN *are here, alone in the yard.* ANNIE *has found* HELEN*'s hand, almost without knowing it, and she spells slowly into it, her voice unsteady, whispering.*)

ANNIE. I, love, Helen.

(*She clutches the child to her, tight this time, not spelling, whispering into her hair.*)

Forever, and—

(*She stops. The lights over the pump are taking on the color of the past, and it brings* ANNIE*'s head up, her eyes opening, in fear; and as slowly as though drawn she rises, to listen, with her hand on* HELEN*'s shoulders. She waits, waits, listening with ears and eyes both, slowly here, slowly there: and hears only silence. There are no voices. The color passes on, and when her eyes come back to* HELEN *she can breathe the end of her phrase without fear.*)

—ever.

---

12. **relinquish** (ri ling′kwish), *v.* give up; let go; release.

After Reading

Making Connections

Shaping Your
Response

1. For which of the **characters** do you feel the most sympathy? Explain.

2. What progress do you **predict** Helen can make after these events?

Analyzing the Play

3. On page 305, what does Annie mean when she tells Captain Keller, ". . . obedience without understanding is a—blindness too"?

4. Explain the meaning of this statement in the **stage directions** on page 310: ". . . it is a moment in which she [Kate] simultaneously finds and loses a child."

5. 👆 Compare how Helen and the other members of the Keller family each react to the **changes** that Annie Sullivan brings into their lives.

Extending the Ideas

6. Part 2 of Unit 2, which includes this play, is called "Reaching Out." What does this play show about reaching out?

7. Go back to the chart about life in the 1880s that you started before reading *The Miracle Worker.* Fill in the rest of the chart using the information you learned from reading the play.

Life in the 1880s	What I Predict	True?	What Else I Learned
Daily chores	pumping well water	yes	pitcher and basin for water in bedrooms
Common household items	no electricity	yes	lamps and lanterns used
Transportation			

Literary Focus: Conflict

The **conflict** in a story or play may be physical, such as two people fighting or a person fighting against nature. A conflict may also be emotional or a struggle of conscience. Seldom is the conflict in a story exclusively external or internal. Answer these questions about the conflicts in *The Miracle Worker.*

• What do you think is the major conflict in the play?

• Describe the conflict between Captain Keller and his son James.

• What different conflicts does Annie Sullivan face? How do these conflicts change throughout the play?

• Which conflicts in the play are resolved by the end, and how?

Vocabulary Study

Complete each of the following sentences with one of the vocabulary words listed here. Use your Glossary, if necessary.

**aversion
contention
deprivation
genially
haggard
interminable
interpose
relinquish
simultaneously
trepidation**

1. The long train ride to Alabama seems ____ to Annie.
2. When she arrives, Annie hopes to be greeted ____ by Helen.
3. Annie has a strong ____ to bright light.
4. Poverty led Annie to experience a great deal of ____ as a child.
5. The Kellers do not want to ____ control over their daughter.
6. Battles with Helen leave Annie looking worn and ____.
7. The Kellers feel much ____ about Annie's plans for Helen.
8. When Annie spells words to Percy, Helen wants to ____ herself between them.
9. Ideas about discipline are a main ____ between Annie and Kate.
10. At the end of the play, Kate is ____ happy and sad.

Expressing Your Ideas

Writing Choices

Writer's Notebook Update
Compare the situation you wrote about before reading with Annie's desire to succeed with Helen.

Ask the Expert In the photo, actress Patty Duke is meeting the real Helen Keller. Imagine that you have won the part of one of the main characters in *The Miracle Worker*. Write down the **questions** you would like to ask Helen Keller to prepare yourself for the role.

Another Option

Set Design Build a model stage set for *The Miracle Worker*. Show how the different settings in the play can be depicted in a limited space.

Before Reading

W-a-t-e-r by Helen Keller

Hearing the Sweetest Songs by Nicolette Toussaint

Helen Keller
1880–1968

The dramatic story told in *The Miracle Worker* was only the beginning of the real Helen Keller's remarkable journey. Keller, who later learned to speak and lip-read, traveled all over the world as a noted author, lecturer, and fund-raiser. Her teacher, Annie Sullivan, remained with her until Sullivan's death in 1936.

Nicolette Toussaint

Nicolette Toussaint is founder of Public Relations for Social Change, a consulting group. She lectures frequently on widely varying topics.

Building Background

Sounds of Silence Nicolette Toussaint, the author of "Hearing the Sweetest Sounds," uses a hearing aid. Her account of life with a hearing aid may differ from your ideas of what it would be like to use one. A hearing aid is a small electronic amplifier, so it amplifies—makes louder—*everything* it picks up, including unwanted background noises. If a radio was on while someone was talking to you, for example, a hearing aid would not distinguish between the noise of the radio and the voice of the person you want to hear. A hearing aid cannot make sounds sharper or clearer, only louder.

Literary Focus

Connotation/Denotation What comes to your mind when you hear the word *tree?* The **denotation** of a word is the meaning you would find in a dictionary: "a woody plant with a single stem or trunk." The emotional response to a word and the associations a word carries make up a word's **connotation**. Connotations of the word *tree* include shade, coolness, shelter, and so on. Some words carry definite connotations, while other words trigger different associations in different people. For example, would you rather be called "thin" or "scrawny"? What connotations does each word have?

Writer's Notebook

Sense Deprivation What do you think your life would be like if you lost one of your senses? In your notebook, describe how a typical day in your life would be different if you were unable to see, to hear, to taste, to feel, or to smell. As you read, think about how each author observes the world around her.

W·A·T·E·R

HELEN KELLER

The most important day I remember in all my life is the one on which my teacher, Anne Mansfield Sullivan, came to me. I am filled with wonder when I consider the immeasurable contrast between the two lives which it connects. It was the third of March, 1887, three months before I was seven years old.

On the afternoon of that eventful day, I stood on the porch, dumb, expectant. I guessed vaguely from my mother's signs and from the hurrying to and fro in the house that something unusual was about to happen, so I went to the door and waited on the steps. The afternoon sun penetrated the mass of honeysuckle that covered the porch, and fell on my upturned face. My fingers lingered almost unconsciously on the familiar leaves and blossoms which had just come forth to greet the sweet southern spring. I did not know what the future held of marvel or surprise for me. Anger and bitterness had underlined(underline)preyed[1] upon me continually for weeks and a deep languor[2] had succeeded this passionate struggle.

Have you ever been at sea in a dense fog, when it seemed as if a tangible white darkness shut you in, and the great ship, tense and anxious,

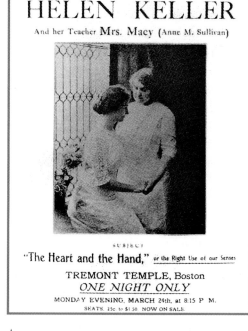

The First Appearance on the Lecture Platform of

HELEN KELLER

And her Teacher **Mrs. Macy** (Anne M. Sullivan)

SUBJECT

"The Heart and the Hand," or the Right Use of our Senses

TREMONT TEMPLE, Boston

ONE NIGHT ONLY

MONDAY EVENING, MARCH 24th, at 8:15 P. M.

SEATS, 25c to $1.50 NOW ON SALE

▲ This poster advertises Helen Keller's first speaking tour. Throughout her adult life, Keller gave lectures all over the world. Why do you think the public was so interested in her?

groped her way toward the shore with plummet and sounding-line,[3] and you waited with beating heart for something to happen? I was like that ship before my education began, only I was without compass or sounding-line, and had no way of knowing how near the harbor was. "Light! give me light!" was the wordless cry of my soul, and the light of love shone on me in that very hour.

I felt approaching footsteps. I stretched out my hand as I supposed to my mother. Someone took it, and I was caught up and held close in the arms of her who had come to reveal all things to me, and, more than all things else, to love me.

The morning after my teacher came she led me into her room and gave me a doll. The little blind children at the Perkins Institution had sent it and Laura Bridgman had dressed it; but

---

1. **prey** (prā), *v.* be a strain upon; injure; irritate.
2. **languor** (lāng′gər), *n.* lack of energy; weakness; weariness.
3. **plummet** (plum′it) **and sounding-line.** Ships once used these instruments to navigate in waters of unknown depth. A plummet was a weight fastened to a sounding-line, which was marked in fathoms and used to measure the depth of water.

I did not know this until afterward. When I had played with it a little while, Miss Sullivan slowly spelled into my hand the word "d-o-l-l." I was at once interested in the finger play and tried to imitate it. When I finally succeeded in making the letters correctly I was flushed with childish pleasure and pride. Running downstairs to my mother I held up my hand and made the letters for doll. I did not know that I was spelling a word or even that words existed; I was simply making my fingers go in monkey-like imitation. In the days that followed I learned to spell in this uncomprehending way a great many words, among them *pin, hat, cup,* and a few verbs like *sit, stand* and *walk.* But my teacher had been with me several weeks before I understood that everything has a name.

One day, while I was playing with my new doll, Miss Sullivan put my big rag doll into my lap also, spelled "d-o-l-l" and tried to make me understand that "d-o-l-l" applied to both. Earlier in the day we had had a tussle over the words "m-u-g" and "w-a-t-e-r." Miss Sullivan had tried to impress it upon me that "m-u-g" is *mug* and that "w-a-t-e-r" is *water,* but I persisted in confounding[4] the two. In despair she had dropped the subject for the time, only to renew it at the first opportunity. I became impatient at her repeated attempts and seizing the new doll, I dashed it upon the floor. I was keenly delighted when I felt the fragments of the broken doll at my feet. Neither sorrow nor regret followed my passionate outburst. I had not loved the doll. In the still, dark world in which I lived there was no strong sentiment or tenderness. I felt my teacher sweep the fragments to one side of the hearth, and I had a sense of satisfaction that the cause of my discomfort was removed. She brought me my hat, and I knew I was going out into the warm sunshine. This thought, if a wordless sensation may be called a thought, made me hop and skip with pleasure.

We walked down the path to the well-house, attracted by the fragrance of the honeysuckle with which it was covered. Someone was drawing water and my teacher placed my hand under the spout. As the cool stream gushed over one hand she spelled into the other the word *water,* first slowly then rapidly. I stood still, my whole attention fixed upon the motions of her fingers. Suddenly I felt a misty consciousness as of something forgotten—a thrill of returning thought; and somehow the mystery of language was revealed to me. I knew then that "w-a-t-e-r" meant the wonderful cool something that was flowing over my hand. That living word awakened my soul, gave it light, hope, joy, set it free! There were barriers still, it is true, but barriers that could in time be swept away.

I left the well-house eager to learn. Everything had a name, and each name gave birth to a new thought. As we returned to the house every object which I touched seemed to quiver with life. That was because I saw everything with the strange, new sight that had come to me. On entering the door I remembered the doll I had broken. I felt my way to the hearth and picked up the pieces. I tried vainly to put them together. Then my eyes filled with tears; for I realized what I had done, and for the first time I felt repentance and sorrow.

I learned a great many new words that day. I do not remember what they all were; but I do know that *mother, father, sister, teacher* were among them—words that were to make the world blossom for me, "like Aaron's rod, with flowers."[5] It would have been difficult to find a happier child than I was as I lay in my crib at the close of that eventful day and lived over the joys it had brought me, and for the first time longed for a new day to come.

> I did not know what the future held of marvel or surprise for me.

---

4. confound (kon found′), *v.* confuse; mix up.
5. **like Aaron's rod, with flowers.** A biblical allusion to Numbers 17:23, in which Aaron's branch sprouts with buds as a sign that God has chosen him to be a leader.

Hearing the Sweetest Songs

Nicolette Toussaint

Every year when I was a child, a man brought a big, black, squeaking machine to school. When he discovered I couldn't hear all his peeps and squeaks, he would get very excited. The nurse would draw a chart with a deep canyon in it. Then I would listen to the squeaks two or three times, while the adults—who were all acting very, very nice—would watch me raise my hand. Sometimes I couldn't tell whether I heard the squeaks or just imagined them, but I liked being the center of attention.

My parents said I lost my hearing to pneumonia[1] as a baby, but I knew I hadn't *lost* anything. None of my parts had dropped off. Nothing had changed: if I wanted to listen to Beethoven, I could put my head between the speakers and turn the dial up to 7. I could hear jets at the airport a block away. I could hear my mom when she was in the same room—if I wanted to. I could even hear my cat purr if I put my good ear right on top of him.

I wasn't aware of *not* hearing until I began to wear a hearing aid at the age of 30. It shattered my peace: shoes creaking, papers crackling, pencils tapping, phones ringing, refrigerators humming, people cracking knuckles, clearing throats and blowing noses! Cars, bikes, dogs, cats, kids all seemed to appear from nowhere and fly right at me.

> . . . I knew I hadn't lost anything.
>
> None of my parts had dropped off.

I was constantly startled, unnerved,[2] agitated[3]—exhausted. I felt as though inquisitorial[4] Nazis in an old World War II film were burning the side of my head with a merciless white spotlight. Under that onslaught, I had to break down and confess: I couldn't hear. Suddenly, I began to discover many things I couldn't do.

I couldn't identify sounds. One afternoon, while lying on my side watching a football game on TV, I kept hearing a noise that sounded like my cat playing with a flexible-spring doorstop. I checked, but the cat was asleep. Finally, I happened to lift my head as the noise occurred. Heard through my good ear, the metallic buzz turned out to be the referee's whistle.

---

1. **pneumonia** (nü mō′nyə), *n.* a bacterial or viral disease in which the lung becomes inflamed, often accompanied by chills, a pain in the chest, a hard, dry cough, and a high fever.
2. unnerved (un nėrvd′), *adj.* deprived of nerve, firmness, or self-control.
3. agitated (aj′ə tāt əd), *adj.* disturbed or upset very much.
4. **inquisitorial** (in kwiz′ə tôr′ē əl), *adj.* unduly curious; prying.

I couldn't tell where sounds came from. I couldn't find my phone under the blizzard of papers on my desk. The more it rang, the deeper I dug. I shoveled mounds of paper onto the floor and finally had to track it down by following the cord from the wall.

When I lived alone, I felt helpless because I couldn't hear alarm clocks, vulnerable because I couldn't hear the front door open and frightened because I wouldn't hear a burglar until it was too late.

Then one day I missed a job interview because of the phone. I had gotten off the subway twenty minutes early, eager and dressed to the nines. But the address I had written down didn't exist! I must have misheard it. I searched the street, becoming overheated, late and frantic, knowing that if I confessed that I couldn't hear on the phone, I would make my odds of getting hired even worse.

For the first time, I felt unequal, disadvantaged and disabled. Now that I had something to compare, I knew that I *had* lost something; not just my hearing, but my independence and

In *Night Flowers* (1918), German artist Paul Klee expresses his vision of a garden at night. Do you believe that artists have unique ways of seeing and hearing reality? Explain.

my sense of wholeness. I had always hated to be seen as inferior, so I never mentioned my lack of hearing. Unlike a wheelchair or a white cane, my disability doesn't announce itself. For most of my life, I chose to pass as abled, and I thought I did it quite well.

But after I got the hearing aid, a business friend said, "You know, Nicolette, you think you get away with not hearing, but you don't. Sometimes in meetings you answer the wrong question. People don't know you can't hear, so they think you're daydreaming, eccentric,[5] stupid—or just plain rude. It would be better to just tell them."

I wondered about that then, and I still do. If I tell, I risk being seen as *un*able rather than *dis*abled. Sometimes, when I say I can't hear, the waiter will turn to my companion and say, "What does she want?" as though I have lost my power of speech.

If I tell, people may see *only* my disability. Once someone is labeled "deaf," "crippled," "mute" or "aged," that's too often all they are. I'm a writer, a painter, a slapdash housekeeper, a gardener who grows wondrous roses; my hearing is just part of the whole. It's a tender part, and you should handle it with care. But like most people with a disability, I don't mind if you ask about it.

> **Songs imagined are as sweet as songs heard, and songs shared are sweeter still.**

In fact, you should ask, because it's an important part of me, something my friends see as part of my character. My friend Anne always rests a hand on my elbow in parking lots, since several times, drivers who assume that I hear them have nearly run me over. When I hold my head at a certain angle, my husband, Mason, will say, "It's a plane" or "It's a siren." And my mother loves to laugh about the things I *thought* I heard: last week I was told that "the Minotaurs[6] in the garden are getting out of hand." I imagined capering bullmen and I was disappointed to learn that all we had in the garden were overgrown "baby tears."

Not hearing can be funny, or frustrating. And once in a while, it can be the cause of something truly transcendent.[7] One morning at the shore I was listening to the ocean when Mason said, "Hear the bird?" What bird? I listened hard until I heard a faint, unbirdlike, croaking sound. If he hadn't mentioned it, I would never have noticed it. As I listened, slowly I began to hear—or perhaps imagine—a distant song. Did I *really* hear it? Or just hear in my heart what he shared with me? I don't care. Songs imagined are as sweet as songs heard, and songs shared are sweeter still.

That sharing is what I want for all of us. We're all just temporarily abled, and every one of us, if we live long enough, will become disabled in some way. Those of us who have gotten there first can tell you how to cope with phones and alarm clocks. About ways of holding a book, opening a door and leaning on a crutch all at the same time. And what it's like to give up in despair on Thursday, then begin all over again on Friday, because there's no other choice—and because the roses are beginning to bud in the garden.

These are conversations we all should have, and it's not that hard to begin. Just let me see your lips when you speak. Stay in the same room. Don't shout. And ask what you want to know.

---

5. eccentric (ek sen′trik), *adj.* out of the ordinary; not usual; odd; peculiar.
6. **Minotaur** (min′ə tôr), in Greek legends, a monster with a bull's head and a man's body.
7. **transcendent** (tran sen′ dənt), *adj.* surpassing ordinary limits; superior; extraordinary.

After Reading

Making Connections

Shaping Your
Response

1. Jot down anything that surprises you about the **tone** and **style** of Helen Keller's writing.

2. Nicolette Toussaint wonders whether she should tell other people about her disability. Would you tell? Why or why not?

Analyzing the
Selections

3. Why didn't Helen Keller feel any "strong sentiment or tenderness" before the arrival of Annie Sullivan?

4. Toussaint writes, "We're all just temporarily abled. . . ." What does she mean? Do you agree with her? Explain why or why not.

5. Do these two selections share any common **themes?** Explain.

Extending the Ideas

6. Compare Helen Keller's account of her language breakthrough with the one given in *The Miracle Worker*.

7. 🐾 What kind of **change** is Toussaint asking for in the way people with disabilities are treated by society?

Literary Focus: Connotation and Denotation

A **denotation** is the literal or dictionary meaning of a word. A **connotation** is an association made with a word. A cake, for example, has the denotation of being a baked mixture of flour, sugar, eggs, and butter. A cake may suggest connotations of a celebration, a special dessert, or a high-calorie temptation.

• What connotations does the word *water* have for Helen Keller?

• Toussaint makes a distinction between the terms *unable* and *disabled*. What are the denotations of the two words? What connotations of these words does Toussaint object to?

Vocabulary Study

Choose the vocabulary word from the list that best completes each sentence. Use your Glossary, if necessary.

agitated
confound
eccentric
prey
unnerved

1. The despair that would _____ upon Helen Keller disappeared when she learned to communicate.

2. At first, Helen would _____ the words for different objects.

3. The jumble of sounds that Nicolette Toussaint could hear with her hearing aid left her feeling _____ and _____.

4. People who didn't know that Toussaint could not hear assumed from her actions that she was an _____ person.

Expressing Your Ideas

Writing Choices

Writer's Notebook Update In your notebook, write a few paragraphs comparing your daily perceptions of the world with those that Helen Keller and Nicolette Toussaint might have.

Claims to Fame Find out about a famous deaf or hearing-impaired person and write a **profile** of him or her. Your profile might include a chronology of the person's life as well as his or her major accomplishments. Some good subjects for your profile might include: composer Ludwig von Beethoven, actress Marlee Matlin, artist Francisco Goya, or inventor Thomas Edison.

Other Options

Loud, Louder, Loudest A decibel is a unit of measurement that describes the intensity of sounds. A sound that is barely perceptible would measure zero decibels, while a sound that is painfully loud would measure around 130 decibels. Use reference materials to find the decibel ranges for some common sounds. Record your findings on a **chart.**

Another Language Helen Keller learned to communicate through fingerspelling, in which each letter of the alphabet has one distinct sign. Learn the **fingerspelling** for yours and your classmates' names, and practice spelling and reading each other's names.

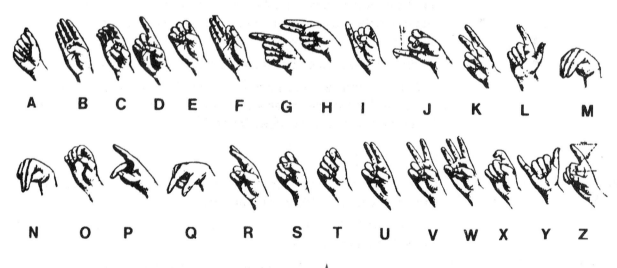

A B C D E F G H I J K L M

N O P Q R S T U V W X Y Z

▲ The Manual Alphabet

Humanities Connection

You might think that any language is built from spoken sounds. But as this article about American Sign Language explains, languages can also be formed from movement.

It's Brain Stuff

American Sign Language

by Richard Wolkomir

When Bill Stokoe started teaching English at Gallaudet University in Washington, D.C., the world's only liberal arts university for deaf people, the school enrolled him in a course in signing. But Stokoe noticed something odd: among themselves, students signed differently from his classroom teacher.

Stokoe had been taught a sort of gestural code, each movement of the hands representing a word in English. At the time, American Sign Language (ASL) was thought to be no more than a form of pidgin English. But Stokoe believed the "hand talk"

Diodes on her arm and fingertip enable Salk researcher Kathy Say to trace the graceful pattern of ASL words.

his students used looked richer. He wondered: Might deaf people actually have a genuine language? And could that language be unlike any other on Earth? It was 1955, when even deaf people dismissed their signing as "slang." Stokoe's idea was academic heresy.

It is 37 years later. Stokoe is having lunch at a café near the Gallaudet campus and explaining how he started a revolution. For decades educators fought his idea that signed languages are natural languages like English, French, and Japanese. They assumed language must be based on speech. But sign language is based on the movement of hands. "What I said," Stokoe explains, "is that language is not mouth stuff—it's brain stuff."

When Stokoe analyzed his students' signing, he found it was like spoken language, which combines bits of sound—each meaningless by itself—into meaningful words. Signers, following similar rules, combine individually meaningless hand and body movements into words. They choose from a palette of hand shapes, such as a fist or a pointing index finger. They also choose where to make a sign: for example, on the face or on the chest. They choose how to orient the hand and arm. And each sign has a movement—it might begin at the cheek and finish at the chin. A shaped hand executing a particular motion creates a word.

At the Salk Institute in San Diego, California, Dr. Ursula Bellugi and her associates found that ASL has a key language ingredient: a grammar to regulate its flow. For example, in a conversation a signer might make the sign for "Joe" at an arbitrary spot in space. Now that spot stands for "Joe." By pointing to it, the signer creates the pronoun "he" or "him," meaning "Joe." A sign moving toward the spot means something done *to* "him." A sign moving away from the spot means an action *by* Joe, something "he" did.

By the 1980s, most linguists had accepted sign languages as natural languages on an equal footing with English, Italian, Hindi and

In a huddle at Gallaudet: the huddle originated here in the 1890s so players could hide signs from other teams.

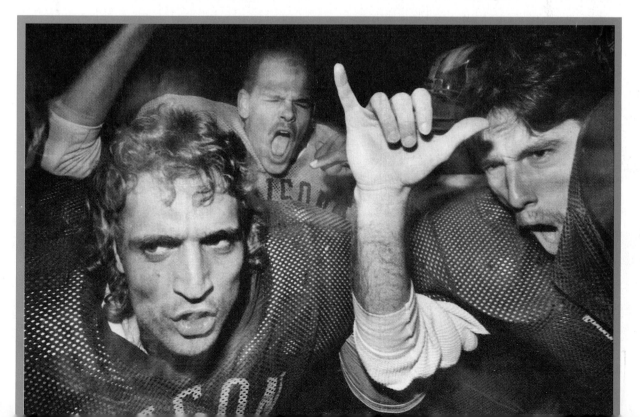

Ruth Benedict and her daughter Rachel play out a story using sign. The entire family is deaf and fluent in ASL. Rachel started to sign words when she was 11 months old.

others of the world. Signed languages like ASL were as powerful, subtle, and intricately structured as spoken ones.

Just as no one can pinpoint the origins of spoken language in prehistory, the roots of sign language remain hidden from view. What linguists do know is that sign languages have sprung up independently in many different places. Signing probably began with simple gestures, but then evolved into a true language with structured grammar. "In every place we've ever found deaf people, there's sign," says anthropological linguist Bob Johnson. But it's not the same language. "I went to a Mayan village where, out of 400 people, 13 were deaf, and they had their own Mayan Sign—I'd guess it's been maintained for thousands of years." Today at least 50 native sign languages are "spoken" worldwide, all mutually incomprehensible, from ASL and Israeli Sign to Chinese Sign.

Freda Norman, formerly an actress with the National Theater of the Deaf and now a Salk research associate, puts it like this: "I love to read books, but ASL is my first language." She adds, smiling: "Sometimes I forget that the hearing are different."

Responding

1. What clues have shown researchers that American Sign Language is a "real" language like English or Chinese?

2. As a project, learn some words or phrases in ASL and practice them with others.

3. What might poetry in sign language be like?

Social Studies Connection

Because the Navajo language is a complex, difficult language spoken only by Navajos and a few outsiders, it became a powerful secret weapon during World War II.

Navajo Code Talkers

by Harry Gardiner

Code talkers like these two young Marines helped the United States defeat Japan in World War II.

W hen Japanese planes attacked Pearl Harbor on the morning of December 7, 1941, most members of the United States' largest Indian tribe were isolated from the problems of the day. When they heard the news, though, they picked up their guns and headed for the nearest recruiting station. In New Mexico, one group of fighting men cleaned and oiled their rifles, packed their saddlebags, and rode off to Gallup, ready to do battle with the enemy.

More than three thousand Navajo would eventually serve their country throughout the world. They would be found in the Aleutian Islands, in North Africa, on the Normandy beaches, in Italy and Sicily, and, most of all, in the Central and South Pacific. They were better prepared to deal with conditions on the Pacific islands than most U.S. soldiers. For example, they could crawl through the jungle without making noise, hiding behind bushes their Anglo comrades had not even noticed. Because they were used to desert darkness instead of lighted streets, they were able to move around in the dark with great accuracy in almost any kind of terrain. They often amazed their white companions with their ability to spot a snake by smell or sound.

One man, Philip Johnston, a civil engineer from Los Angeles, changed the lives of many young Navajo men in a unique way. The son of a missionary father, Johnston had spent a large part of his early life living among the Navajo and spoke their language fluently. This was not easy to do, since the language is extremely complex, very difficult to learn, and nearly impossible to imitate. Johnston proposed that the Marine Corps use a code based on the Navajo language to prevent Japanese and German cryptographers from decoding U.S. messages. His plan was approved, and during the next five years, he helped turn more than four hundred Navajo into Marine "code talkers" and the Navajo language into one of the United States' more successful secret weapons.

The Navajo were chosen for several reasons. First, Johnston had an intimate knowledge of their language and culture.

Interdisciplinary Study **325**

Second, the tribe was big enough to provide a large number of speakers. Third, only twenty-eight non-Navajo, mainly missionaries and anthropologists, could speak the language—and none of these was Japanese or German.

The Navajo language developed over the many centuries, making it very complex. For example, the same word spoken with four different alterations in pitch or tone of voice has four different meanings. Depending on how you pronounce the Navajo word written *ni'á*, it can have meanings as different as "A set of round objects extends off in a horizontal line" and "I bought it." This complexity, combined with fluent speakers who could transmit the code more quickly than an artificial code, made it difficult to decode.

Because it might fall into enemy hands, this new code was to be spoken only over the radio or telephone and never to be put into writing. Since the plan was to develop a code of Indian words, not merely to use translations of Indian words, there had to be complete agreement on the meanings of all words used. Any variation in interpretation could spell disaster.

The code talkers had to memorize the entire vocabulary of 411 terms. In competitions with Anglo Marines, the Navajo code talkers always won in both speed and accuracy. Even the most complicated reports and instructions were transmitted without a single error—an achievement that regular communications men speaking code were unable to duplicate. The code was so successful that the Japanese and Germans failed to decipher a single syllable of the thousands of messages sent with it.

In the September 18, 1945, issue of the *San Diego Union*, it was stated, "For three years, wherever the Marines landed, the Japanese got an earful of strange gurgling noises interspersed with other sounds resembling the call of a Tibetan monk and the sound of a hot water bottle being emptied."

The importance of the role played by the Navajo code talkers was noted by Major Howard Conner when he said, "Were it not for the Navajos, the Marines would never have taken Iwo Jima!" The capture of this island was crucial to U.S. forces in the last stages of the war because Japanese planes had continually attacked U.S. bombers from there. The entire military operation was directed by Navajo code talkers. During the first forty-eight hours, they sent and received more than eight hundred messages without error. When the famous flag raising took place on Mount Suribachi, the news came in the Navajo code, with the name of Suribachi pronounced as Sheep-uncle-ram-ice-bear-ant-cat-horse-itch.

Navajo code remained a secret until 1965. In March 1989, the surviving code talkers were reunited in Phoenix, Arizona, and honored by the commandant of the Marine Corps.

Military Term	Navajo Word	Navajo Meaning
Corps	Din-neh-ih	Clan
Dive Bomber	Gini	Chicken hawk
Battleship	Lo-tso	Whale
Submarine	Besh-lo	Iron fish
Mine Sweeper	Cha	Beaver
Bombs	A-ye-shi	Eggs
Grenades	Ni-ma-si	Potatoes

Responding

1. What were some of the factors that made it impossible to decode the Navajo code talkers' secret messages?

2. With a team, invent a secret code. Exchange messages with another team and see if you can break each other's code.

Writing Workshop

Evaluating Annie Sullivan

Assignment What do you think of the way Annie Sullivan dealt with Helen Keller in *The Miracle Worker?* Evaluate her methods in an essay.

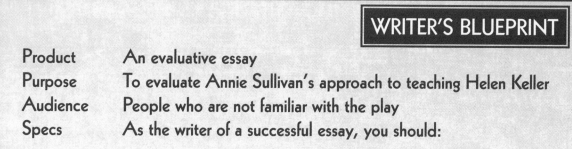

WRITER'S BLUEPRINT

Product   An evaluative essay
Purpose   To evaluate Annie Sullivan's approach to teaching Helen Keller
Audience   People who are not familiar with the play
Specs   As the writer of a successful essay, you should:

- ❑ Begin by giving your audience the background they'll need to follow your train of thought. Do this by describing the situation in the Keller household as it existed before Annie Sullivan arrived.

- ❑ Go on to describe the methods Annie Sullivan used to deal with Helen.

- ❑ Evaluate these methods. Do you approve or disapprove? Were they effective? Were they humane? Should Annie Sullivan have used other methods? Why or why not? Support your conclusions with specific examples from the play, including quotations where appropriate.

- ❑ Conclude by summarizing Annie Sullivan's overall approach and giving your evaluation of it.

- ❑ Be sure to make solid connections between one idea and another.

- ❑ Follow the rules of grammar, usage, spelling, and mechanics. Take special care to avoid improper shifts in verb tense.

STEP **1** PREWRITING

Review the play. In a small group, discuss the situation in the Keller household prior to the arrival of Annie Sullivan. Focus on answering questions like the ones on the next page.

- Was Helen born deaf and blind? If not, what happened to her?

- What was Helen's family doing for her? Had she been taken to doctors?

- How did the various members of the family react to Helen? (See the Literary Source.)

LITERARY SOURCE
"**KELLER:** I've done as much as I can bear, I can't give my whole life to it! The house is at sixes and sevens from morning to night over the child. . . ."
from *The Miracle Worker* by William Gibson

Try a quickwrite. After your discussion, write for five minutes to briefly describe the Keller household before Annie Sullivan arrived. Use the questions above to help you get going.

Chart Annie Sullivan's teaching methods. Create a chart, like the one shown, that gives examples of the methods Annie used in working with Helen. In the first column, identify the method. In the second column, briefly describe a scene in which the method is used. In the third column, describe Helen's reaction to the method.

Method	Scene	Helen's Reaction
being firm	Annie grabs Helen's hands when Helen tries to eat from Annie's plate. (Act 2, Scene 2)	She cries with rage.

COMPUTER TIP
Use the "table" function of your word processor to create charts like these if you need a neat way to organize information for your essay.

Evaluate the methods in the first column of your chart by adding a fourth column, headed Pro/Con. Write *pro* for methods you approve of and *con* for methods you disagree with, and explain why.

Plan your essay. Look back at your prewriting activities as you develop your writing plan. Organize your notes into an informal outline like the one shown here.

Introduction
- Background information about the Kellers' situation

Body
- First method
  - Example of how it was used
  - Your evaluation
  - Supporting quote or example from the play
- Second method
and so on . . .

OR . . .
For planning the body, draw four scenes from *The Miracle Worker* showing different methods Annie used and Helen's reaction to them. Include lines of dialogue. Label each picture to describe the scene.

Conclusion
- Summary of Annie Sullivan's approach
- Your overall evaluation of her approach

Ask a partner to review your plan.

✔ Have I planned to describe the situation in the Keller household as it was before Annie Sullivan's arrival?

✔ Have I presented and evaluated methods Annie used in dealing with Helen?

✔ Have I included examples and quotations from the play?

Use any helpful comments from your partner to revise your plan.

STEP 2 DRAFTING

Before you draft, review your prewriting notes and writing plan. Be sure to reread the Writer's Blueprint.

As you draft, consider these tips.

- Begin in a dramatic manner by describing a scene from the play that vividly illustrates conditions at the Keller household when Annie arrived.

- Concentrate on making solid connections between different ideas. (See the Revising Strategy in Step 3 of this lesson.)

STEP 3 REVISING

Ask a partner to comment on your draft before you revise it. Use this checklist as a guide.

✔ Did I begin by describing the Kellers' situation?

✔ Did I go on to describe the methods Annie Sullivan used with Helen?

✔ Did I clearly state my evaluation of her approach and support it with examples and quotations?

✔ Have I made solid connections between ideas?

Revising Strategy

Connecting Ideas

Essays are full of ideas. When you make connections between ideas, you leave your readers feeling secure. They know where you're taking them. When you leave your ideas unconnected, you leave your readers feeling lost and confused. For example:

> Right from the start, Annie Sullivan felt sympathy for Helen. Annie couldn't stand bright light and had to wear sunglasses. Annie believed in herself. Helen couldn't eat with a knife and fork. She didn't know what words were. She couldn't see or hear. Annie was determined to get her there.

The writer gives us disconnected facts and leaves us wondering how they fit together. See what happens when the writer adds connections.

> Right from the start, Annie Sullivan felt sympathy for Helen. *Annie too had vision problems*—she couldn't stand bright light and had to wear sunglasses. Annie believed in herself, *but she was also a realist. She knew that* Helen couldn't eat with a knife and fork, that Helen didn't know what words were, that she couldn't see or hear. *Helen had a long way to go, but* Annie was determined to get her there.

Notice how the addition of a short, simple phrase helps correct ideas in the student model below.

STUDENT MODEL

Annie Sullivan's approach worked because she believed that

"obedience is the gateway through which knowledge enters the mind of a

In keeping with this philosophy,

child."ᴧ She knew that she had to address Helen's behavior problems

before she could teach her anything. Even though trying to make Helen

behave was difficult, Annie approached it as a job and was able to do it.

As you revise, pay special attention to spots where you switch from one idea to another, and add connections if you need to.

Ask a partner to review your revised draft before you edit. When you edit, look for errors in grammar, usage, spelling, and mechanics. Look over each sentence to make sure you have used consistent verb tense.

Editing Strategy

Keeping Consistent Verb Tense

The tense of a verb tells when the action takes place—in the present, in the past, or in the future. Be consistent by using the same verb tense within a sentence.

Mixed tenses	Helen points and ran toward the house.
Edited	Helen points and runs toward the house.
Mixed tenses	James often criticizes Helen but never corrected her.
Edited	James often criticizes Helen but never corrects her.

FOR REFERENCE
See the Language and Grammar Handbook for more information on consistent verb tense.

Notice how mixed verb tenses have been corrected in the model that follows.

Annie Sullivan took a much different approach, and her arrival sent

the household into more of an uproar than it already ~~is,~~ *was in* if that was possible.

Annie's goal was to teach Helen to finger spell so she could begin to

communicate and learn about the world around her. Annie began on the

very first afternoon by trying to finger spell d-o-l-l onto Helen's palm. Helen

was confused and angry and ~~ends~~ *ended* the lesson by cracking the doll across

Annie's face. Annie soon realized that before she could teach Helen anything

she would first have to teach her how to behave properly. This ~~will~~ *would* not be

easy because Helen was used to getting her way most of the time.

STUDENT MODEL

STEP **5** PRESENTING

Consider these ideas for presenting your essay.

- Create a cover sheet with sketches of the characters, symbols from the sign alphabet, or other appropriate illustrations.

- Choose a few papers to be reviewed by a special education teacher. Ask him/her to respond and talk about current methods of teaching people like Helen.

STEP **6** LOOKING BACK

Self-evaluate. What grade would *you* give your paper? Look back at the Writer's Blueprint and give yourself a score for each point, from 6 (superior) to 1 (inadequate).

Reflect. Think about what you've learned from writing this essay as you write answers to these questions.

✔ How do you think the teaching methods you evaluated compare to modern methods for educating people with disabilities?

✔ Look back at your writing plan. Did you follow it closely, or did you go off in other directions? How useful do you think writing plans are in general? Why?

For Your Working Portfolio Add your essay and reflection responses to your working portfolio.

Beyond Print

Basic Word Processing

When Ernest Hemingway was a young writer struggling to make a living in Paris, a suitcase full of his manuscripts was lost on a train. Since Hemingway had no other copies, he lost several years' worth of work. Today, thanks to word-processing programs, writers can easily save their work. A loss like Hemingway's would be an inconvenience, not a tragedy.

Word processors not only allow writers to preserve their work, but also help simplify the tasks of revising, editing, and proofreading. Consider these word-processing tips.

- When you're working on a rough draft, don't worry about mistakes. You can correct, move, and edit text later with a few keystrokes.

- Use the spell checker on your word processor, but proofread your work as well. Why? Be cause they spill checker wood knot find any miss steaks in this sentience, that's way. Are you convinced?

- Save your documents frequently as you work, since power outages and system errors can wipe out unsaved work.

- When revising a document, you may want to save it under a new name. Then make all your corrections on the new version. If you change your mind about something you've cut, you can copy it from the original file and paste it back into the new document.

- Limit your use of fonts. You might choose one font for the body text and another for headings. More than that may be confusing to read.

- Learn how to use word-processing tools such as automatic page numbers, footnotes, centered headings, and even charts and graphs.

Activity Options

1. Try to compose a writing assignment entirely on the computer.

2. Create a new document called Brilliant Ideas. Whenever you have an inspiration for a story, poem, or writing topic, briefly record your idea on that document. Later, when you want to expand on the idea, copy it from your Brilliant Ideas document and paste it into a new document that will become your rough draft.

Multicultural Connections

Communication

Part One: Distant Voices The characters in these selections face a number of obstacles that prevent open communication. In *Sorry, Right Number,* for example, Katie is unable to interpret the mysterious message she receives in an upsetting phone call.

■ In the poems "Elena" and "Etymology," what barriers to communication exist for the speakers?

Change

Part Two: Reaching Out People may resist change when it threatens their behaviors, beliefs, and traditions. In *The Miracle Worker,* the Keller family must deal with the changes that are introduced by an outsider, Annie Sullivan.

■ Which character seems best able to accept the changes brought in by Annie Sullivan? Why is he or she able to handle them?

Activities

1. In a small group, describe a communication problem you or someone you know has faced. Explain what factors led to the problem, what you did to try to improve communication, and what the results were.

2. Write the letters that spell *communication* down the length of a poster. Then, next to each letter, write a word beginning with that letter that refers to something that will help communication. For example, "C is for caring, O is for openness," etc. Decorate your poster and present it to the class.

3. Think about the selections you have read so far this year. Identify three characters who face changes. Make a chart like the following to record their response to those changes.

Character	Type of change	Character's response to change	Why the character responded that way

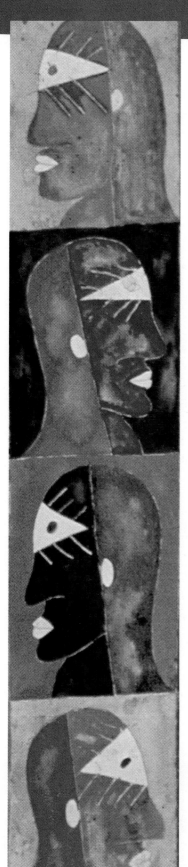

Independent and Group Projects

Drama

Reader's Theater In a small group, choose an act from *Sorry, Right Number* or *The Miracle Worker* and stage a dramatic reading. After deciding who will read each role, practice reading your lines smoothly and with appropriate expression. Invite the other members of your class or another class to attend your final presentation.

Writing

In Review Find an opportunity to view a film at a movie theater or watch a "made for TV" movie. Write a critical review of the play or film, paying special attention to the quality of the dialogue, the development of the plot, and the use of the camera to tell the story.

Art

Ready to Wear Choose one of the plays you read in this unit or another play you know and design costumes for one or more of the main characters. Include accessories such as shoes and jewelry, and make sure the details are historically accurate. Show your designs in a series of sketches.

Research

Getting the Word Out You have explored many different forms of communication in Unit 2. Choose a form of communication from any time in history that you would like to research further—perhaps the Pony Express, Esperanto, or current satellite technology. After researching your topic, prepare a oral report for your classmates that summarizes what you learned. Include graphic aids such as charts or photographs that will help illustrate the information you present.

Taking a Closer Look

Poetry looks <u>into</u> things, not just <u>at</u> them.

—Naomi Shihab Nye

Imagery

Poets create vivid images to reach all your senses. In "I Am Singing Now," Luci Tapahonso describes how her daughters are "breathing clouds of white in the dark" as they sleep in the back of a pickup truck, dreaming of "the scent of fire/the smell of mutton." When the reader can see, hear, taste, touch, and smell the images, the poem becomes much more than mere words on a page.

Reading

It's found in the quietest classrooms and the loudest streetcorners. It is as old as the human voice, and as new as the words scribbled on today's lunch napkin. What are we talking about? Poetry. In a few words, a poem might bring to life a single moment, or a season, or an entire life. Poets rely on a number of tools to accomplish this task. Four of the main ones are described here: imagery, sound, form, and figurative language.

Learn to ride your memories as a bird rides the sky...

Poetry is the search for syllables to shoot at the barriers of the unknown and the unknowable.

—Carl Sandburg

Figurative Language

Simile, metaphor, and **personification** are three kinds of **figurative language**. A **simile** is a direct comparison between two things using *like* or *as;* for example, Edna St. Vincent Millay speaks of "courage like a rock." A **metaphor** is an indirect or implied comparison between two things. In "The Runaway," Robert Frost uses a metaphor when he describes a snowfall as "a curtain of falling flakes." When an object in a poem is **personified**, it is given human qualities. In "Postage Stamp Connections," two stamps are personified.

Chicago poet Cin Salach performs one of her poems.

Form

A poet deals with form when considering the look of a poem on the page. Lines may be long, short, or of varying lengths. The poem may be divided into stanzas, or groups of lines. The number of lines in each stanza may or may not follow a set formula. Form also includes capitalization and punctuation. Some poets follow traditional rules, while others, like E. E. Cummings, break the rules on purpose.

If it's real, it's simple usually, and if it's simple, it's true.

—John Lennon

Tips for Reading Poetry

- **Read the poem straight through to get a sense of where it goes.**
- **Consider the title. Does it hold a clue to the meaning of the poem?**
- **Read the poem aloud, and notice how the author uses the sound of the words to enhance the poem.**
- **Go back to the images in the poem that confuse you or fascinate you. Reread them carefully and try to visualize them.**
- **Try restating each line in your own words.**
- **If you've tried all these techniques and still can't "get" a certain poem, don't despair. Even Carl Sandburg admitted, "I've written some poetry I don't understand myself."**

Our problems are all about communication, and that's what rap is.

—Queen Latifah

Sound

Poets use sound to create a kind of word music. **Rhyme** and **rhythm** will set up a beat within a poem, as in "My Papa's Waltz" by Theodore Roethke. **Alliteration**, when a series of words begin with the same letter, and **onomatopoeia**, when the sound of a word imitates the sound of an object, create other sound effects. These and other **sound devices** enrich a poem.

339

Part One

Family Matters

The following selections highlight rich moments in family histories, and point out how members of the same family may have different ways of recalling the past.

Multicultural Connection **Individuality** involves the development of one's personal identity within different cultural settings. In these selections, how is individuality influenced by cultural and family experiences?

Before Reading

Making a Fist by Naomi Shihab Nye

Knoxville, Tennessee by Nikki Giovanni

Fifth Grade Autobiography by Rita Dove

Mnemonic by Li-Young Lee

Building Background

Memories The four poems that follow are about childhood memories, a popular subject for poetry. Some poets write about childhood to understand the past, others to share or celebrate a meaningful experience. Think of a childhood experience that was significant for you, and not too personal to share. Find or create a visual image that reminds you of the experience. You might bring in a family photograph, copy a photograph or illustration from a book or magazine, or draw a picture or cartoon. Share your piece with the class and describe the experience it represents.

Literary Focus

Imagery One of the basic rules of good writing is "Show, don't tell." So instead of simply *telling* your audience that, for example, the kitchen is dirty, use **imagery** that involves all the senses. *Show* your readers through your words that a week's worth of grimy dishes is piled up in the sink, a rusty faucet drips steadily, layers of grime coat the countertops, and an ancient meatball is slowly decaying in a dusty corner. Not only will your readers know that the kitchen is dirty, they'll feel like they're standing right there in the room. Powerful imagery brings a scene to life by appealing directly to the reader's senses and emotions.

Writer's Notebook

Writing About Childhood Think of experiences from your childhood that you'd like to write about and list them in your notebook. As you read the following poems, compare them with your own experiences. Do they resemble any that you recorded in your notebook?

Naomi Shihab Nye
born 1952

Naomi Shihab Nye's poetry reflects her heritage as the daughter of a Palestinian father and an American mother. Nye grew up in St. Louis, Jerusalem, and Texas, where she lives today with her husband and son. She thinks of poets as explorers and pilgrims, traveling into new territory. She has published several books of poetry and was featured on "The Language of Life," a popular PBS television series about poetry.

Nikki Giovanni
born 1943

Nikki Giovanni was born in Tennessee and grew up in an African American community in Lincoln Heights, Ohio. Her poetry is conversational in tone and reflects rhythm and blues influences. Giovanni frequently writes about childhood: "I hope my poetry reaches both the heart and the mind of a child who is a child and the adult who still nurtures the child within." She has published numerous books of poetry.

Rita Dove
born 1952

Reading is an important part of writer Rita Dove's life. "First and foremost, now, then, and always, I have been passionate about books," she says. In 1986, she won the Pulitzer Prize for *Thomas and Beulah,* a book of poems loosely based on the lives of her grandparents. In 1993, she was named Poet Laureate of the United States, the youngest person ever awarded that honor.

Li-Young Lee
born 1957

Li-Young Lee was born in Jakarta, Indonesia, the son of Chinese parents and the grandson of the first president of the Republic of China. When Lee was a baby, his father was imprisoned in Indonesia for political reasons. The family later fled the country and eventually settled in the United States. Lee, who currently lives in Chicago, has received numerous honors for his writing, including the Lamont Poetry Prize in 1990. His recent memoir, *Winged Seed,* like much of his poetry, explores his relationship with his father.

Making a Fist

Naomi

Shihab

Nye

For the first time, on the road north of Tampico,[1]
I felt the life sliding out of me,
a drum in the desert, harder and harder to hear.
I was seven, I lay in the car
5 watching palm trees swirl a sickening pattern past the glass.
My stomach was a melon split wide inside my skin.

"How do you know if you are going to die?"
I begged my mother.
We had been traveling for days.
10 With strange confidence she answered,
"When you can no longer make a fist."

Years later I smile to think of that journey,
the borders we must cross separately,
stamped with our unanswerable woes.
15 I who did not die, who am still living,
still lying in the backseat behind all my questions,
clenching and opening one small hand.

---

1. **Tampico** (tăm pē′kō), seaport on the eastern coast of Mexico.

Knoxville, Tennessee

Nikki Giovanni

I always like summer
best
you can eat fresh corn
from daddy's garden
5 and okra[1]
and greens
and cabbage
and lots of
barbecue
10 and buttermilk
and homemade ice-cream
at the church picnic
and listen to
gospel music
15 outside
at the church
homecoming
and go to the mountains with
your grandmother
20 and go barefooted
and be warm
all the time
not only when you go to bed
and sleep

---

1. **okra** (ō′krə), *n.* a tall plant cultivated for its sticky pods,
which are used in soups and as a vegetable.

Fifth Grade Autobiography

Rita Dove

I was four in this photograph fishing
with my grandparents at a lake in Michigan.
My brother squats in poison ivy.
His Davy Crockett cap
5 sits squared on his head so the raccoon tail
flounces down the back of his sailor suit.

My grandfather sits to the far right
in a folding chair,
and I know his left hand is on
10 the tobacco in his pants pocket
because I used to wrap it for him
every Christmas. Grandmother's hips
bulge from the brush, she's leaning
into the ice chest, sun through the trees
15 printing her dress with soft
luminous[1] paws.

I am staring jealously at my brother;
the day before he rode his first horse, alone.
I was strapped in a basket
20 behind my grandfather.
He smelled of lemons. He's died—

but I remember his hands.

---

1. luminous (lü′mə nəs), *adj.* bathed in or exposed to light; emitting or reflecting light.

(above left and below) Anna Belle Lee Washington, *Games We Played.* The artist chose to depict these scenes on attached panels instead of eight separate paintings. What effect did she create in this way?

Mnemonic[1] Li-Young Lee

I was tired. So I lay down.
My lids grew heavy. So I slept.
Slender memory, stay with me.

I was cold once. So my father took off his blue sweater.
5 He wrapped me in it, and I never gave it back.
It is the sweater he wore to America,
this one, which I've grown into, whose sleeves are too long,
whose elbows have thinned, who outlives its rightful owner.
Flamboyant[2] blue in daylight, poor blue by daylight,
10 it is black in the folds.

A serious man who devised[3] complex systems of numbers and rhymes
to aid him in remembering, a man who forgot nothing, my father
would be ashamed of me.
Not because I'm forgetful,
15 but because there is no order
to my memory, a heap
of details, uncatalogued, illogical.
For instance:
God was lonely. So he made me.
20 My father loved me. So he spanked me.
It hurt him to do so. He did it daily.

The earth is flat. Those who fall off don't return.
The earth is round. All things reveal themselves to men only gradually.

I won't last. Memory is sweet.
25 Even when it's painful, memory is sweet.

Once, I was cold. So my father took off his blue sweater.

---

1. mnemonic (ni mon′ik), *n.* device or strategy for aiding the memory.
2. flamboyant (flam boi′ənt), *adj.* gorgeously brilliant; striking.
3. devise (di vīz′), *v.* think out; plan.

After Reading

Making Connections

Shaping Your Response

1. Do you think "Making a Fist" ends on an optimistic or pessimistic note? Explain.

2. Write three words that you think describe the **tone** of the speaker in "Knoxville, Tennessee."

3. How do you think the speaker in "Mnemonic" feels about his father? What makes you think so?

Analyzing the Poems

4. Why do you think the speaker in "Making a Fist" smiles when she remembers the journey from her childhood?

5. How old do you think the speaker in "Knoxville, Tennessee" is meant to be? How do the **tone** and **word choice** lead you to that conclusion?

6. Describe how the **mood** changes in "Fifth Grade Autobiography."

7. What does the speaker in "Mnemonic" mean when he says, "Even when it's painful, memory is sweet"? Explain.

Extending the Ideas

8. Describe an experience or feeling of yours that resembles that of the speaker in one of the four poems. Explain why you think the experiences or feelings are similar.

Literary Focus: Imagery

Think back to what you learned about **imagery** before reading the selections. Each poet uses images to involve the reader's emotions and senses. For example, in "Making a Fist" the speaker describes "watching palm trees whirl a sickening pattern past the glass." On the chart below, list an example of effective imagery in each poem and explain what senses and emotions it reaches.

Poem	Image	Senses and feelings
Making a Fist	palm trees in a sickening, swirling pattern	sense of sight; feelings of dizziness or nausea
Knoxville, Tennessee		
Fifth Grade Autobiography		
Mnemonic		

Vocabulary Study

Complete each of the following sentences with the correct vocabulary word. If necessary, use your Glossary for help with word meanings.

devise
flamboyant
luminous
mnemonic
okra

1. A family picnic wouldn't be complete without lots of vegetables like corn on the cob, potatoes, and ____.

2. The lemonade pitcher was ____ in the afternoon sunlight.

3. Aunt Rachel, who was always dressed in polka dots, was one of the more ____ members of the family.

4. Greg made up a ____ to remember the names of all his cousins.

5. The family wished they could ____ a way to get together more often.

Expressing Your Ideas

Writing Choices

Writer's Notebook Update Review the childhood experiences you recorded in your notebook. Choose one and create a list of images that you associate with the experience, as Giovanni does in "Knoxville, Tennessee."

I Remember . . . Use your list of images of a childhood experience to write a **poem.** You can write from your own viewpoint as a child or a teenager remembering, or from someone else's viewpoint. To get started, you may want to look again at the approaches used in the poems you have just read. When you've finished writing, trade poems with a partner and respond to each other's piece. Does your partner's response to your poem surprise you? Are you achieving what you want to say? Revise your poem based on your conversation with your partner.

Other Options

Food for Thought Many of the pleasant childhood memories in Nikki Giovanni's "Knoxville, Tennessee" have to do with food. What kind of food brings back pleasant memories for you? Hold a class **food festival,** with each person bringing a special dish that triggers good memories. Take turns explaining why the food you brought is significant to you.

Childhood Documentaries Ask a young child you know to describe an important experience that they want to share in a **documentary** you will prepare. You may tape the interview on a video or audio recorder, take photographs, draw, or write notes. Use your materials to create a documentary presentation of the child's story. If possible, invite the child to see the presentation.

Kids in the News Work with your group to collect newspaper or magazine articles that involve stories about children. Present an **oral report** to the class about the types of stories you found and what they indicate about the lives and experience of children living today. Discuss whether these stories relate to the poems about childhood that you read.

Before Reading

My Papa's Waltz by Theodore Roethke

The Courage That My Mother Had by Edna St. Vincent Millay

The Funeral by Gordon Parks

Like Bookends by Eve Merriam

Building Background

Parents and Children Each of the following poems describes a parent or parents. For most people, the relationship they have with their parents is one of life's most important and influential bonds. Before you read the poems, take a few minutes to think about the kind of parent you might want to be someday. In a small group, share your list of the top five qualities you would hope to have as a parent.

Literary Focus

Hyperbole and Rhyme Exaggerating to emphasize a point or to create a comic effect is called **hyperbole,** and it is common in speech and writing. In fact, hyperbole is so common often people don't even notice it. For example, when you say "I'm starving!" to express hunger, you are using hyperbole. Look for examples of hyperbole in the following poems.

A major part of the music of poetry is **rhyme,** or the repetition of certain sounds. Poets rhyme to create a sense of order, for emphasis, to slow down or speed up, or to lull or even jolt the reader. As you read the following poems, notice whether or not the writers use rhyme, and what the effect of its presence or absence is.

Writer's Notebook

Let's Talk The following poems deal with parent-child relationships in different ways. In your notebook, record a meaningful dialogue between a parent and a child. The child (and the parent) can be of any age.

Theodore Roethke
1908–1963

As a child, Theodore Roethke (ret′kə) was frail and prone to illness, often staying indoors by himself. While Roethke was in high school, his father died of cancer. Although Roethke attempted to shake the pain and shyness of his youth, he remained an introspective adult who struggled for years with alcoholism and manic depression. He taught literature at colleges and universities for many years and was known as an excellent teacher. Roethke's numerous books of poetry earned him many awards and prizes.

Edna St. Vincent Millay
1892–1950

Edna St. Vincent Millay began writing poetry as a young child and published poems regularly as she was growing up. Her first book of poetry was published in 1917, on the day she graduated from Vassar College. Millay was one of the first serious American poets to win a wide national readership. She enjoyed her greatest popularity during the 1920s, receiving the Pulitzer Prize in 1923. Her poetry is still read widely today.

Gordon Parks
born 1912

Gordon Parks, originally named Alexander Buchanan, grew up the youngest of fifteen children in a poor family in Kansas. Parks has worked as a photographer, writer, film director, songwriter, and composer. In 1968, his autobiographical novel *The Learning Tree* was made into a motion picture. Parks adapted and directed the film himself, becoming the first African American director for a major Hollywood studio.

Eve Merriam
1916–1992

Growing up in Philadelphia, Eve Merriam loved poetry and soon began writing her own. Although she published poems in her high school magazine, it didn't occur to her until college that she would be a writer. After college, Merriam worked as an advertising copywriter and later as a magazine editor. In addition to writing poetry for adults, she wrote numerous books for children. Her writing often explored social issues such as feminism, racial equality, and environmentalism.

MY PAPA'S WALTZ

Theodore Roethke

The whiskey on your breath
Could make a small boy dizzy;
But I hung on like death:
Such waltzing was not easy.

5 We romped until the pans
Slid from the kitchen shelf;
My mother's countenance[1]
Could not unfrown itself.

The hand that held my wrist
10 Was battered on one knuckle;
At every step you missed
My right ear scraped a buckle.

You beat time on my head
With a palm caked hard by dirt,
15 Then waltzed me off to bed
Still clinging to your shirt.

---

1. **countenance** (koun′tə nəns), *n.*
expression of the face; features.

Carroll Cloar, *My Father Was Big as a Tree*
(1955). How do you think the son feels
toward his father? Explain. ➤

Frank W. Benson, *My Daughter Elisabeth* (1915). What aspects of his daughter's character does the artist express in this painting? Compare this depiction with Millay's portrayal of her mother in her poem.

The Courage That My Mother Had

Edna St. Vincent Millay

The courage that my mother had
Went with her, and is with her still:
Rock from New England quarried;[1]
Now granite[2] in a granite hill.

5 The golden brooch[3] my mother wore
She left behind for me to wear;
I have no thing I treasure more:
Yet, it is something I could spare.

Oh, if instead she'd left to me
10 The thing she took into the grave!—
That courage like a rock, which she
Has no more need of, and I have.

THE Funeral

Gordon Parks

After many snows I was home again.
Time had whittled[4] down to mere hills
The great mountains of my childhood.
Raging rivers I once swam trickled now
5   like gentle streams.
And the wide road curving on to China or
          Kansas City or perhaps Calcutta,[5]
Had withered to a crooked path of dust
Ending abruptly at the county burying ground.
10 Only the giant who was my father
                    remained the same.
A hundred strong men strained beneath his coffin
When they bore him to his grave.

▲ Hubert Shuptrine, *Alf* (1975). How do the angle and the intensity of the light affect your impression of the man portrayed here?

1. **quarried** (kwôr′ēd), *adj.* dug out from a quarry, a place where stone is dug out or blasted out for use in building.
2. **granite** (gran′it), *n.* very hard igneous rock formation, often used for tombstones.
3. **brooch** (brōch), *n.* an ornamental pin that can be fastened to a garment.
4. **whittle** (hwit′l), *v.* cut down little by little.
5. **Calcutta,** a seaport on the eastern coast of India, near the Bay of Bengal.

LIKE BOOKENDS

Eve Merriam

Like bookends
my father at one side
my mother at the other

propping me up
5 but unable to read
what I feel.

Were they born with clothes on?
Born with rules on?

When we sit at the dinner table
10 we smooth our napkins into polite folds.
How was your day dear
     Fine
And how was yours dear
     Fine
15 And how was school
     The same

Only once in a while
when we're not trying so hard
when we're not trying at all
20 our napkins suddenly whirl away
and we float up to the ceiling
where we sing and dance until it hurts from laughing

and then we float down
with our napkin parachutes
25 and once again spoon our soup
and pass the bread please.

After Reading

Making Connections

Shaping Your Response

1. On a scale of 1 to 10 (10 being best), rate how much you like each poem. Explain your ratings.

2. Go back to your "top five" list of qualities you would like to have as a parent (page 349). Explain whether or not the parents in these poems have any of those qualities.

Analyzing the Poems

3. What emotions do you think the boy is feeling in "My Papa's Waltz"? What words and **images** does Roethke use to convey these feelings?

4. Why is *granite* an appropriate **word choice** in "The Courage That My Mother Had"?

5. In "The Funeral," how long has it been since the speaker has visited his home? Support your answer with evidence from the text.

6. Compare and contrast the **character** of the father in "My Papa's Waltz" and "The Funeral."

7. In "Like Bookends," do you think bookends are an appropriate **symbol** for the speaker's parents? Explain.

Extending the Ideas

8. In "The Courage That My Mother Had," the speaker wishes she had inherited her mother's courage. Do you think it's possible to "inherit" courage from another person? Why or why not?

9. In your opinion, how would the **individuality** of each speaker be influenced by the parent or parents mentioned in the poem?

Literary Focus: Hyperbole and Rhyme

You've learned that **hyperbole** is a figure of speech that uses exaggeration to emphasize a point or create comic or satiric effect. Gordon Parks uses hyperbole in "The Funeral" when he says a hundred men strained to carry his father's coffin. Find another example of hyperbole from one of the poems you have just read.

Rhyme is the repetition of the sounds at the end of words. Which of the four poems use rhyme? How does the rhyme or lack of rhyme affect the tone of each poem?

Expressing Your Ideas

Writing Choices

Writer's Notebook Update Look back at the dialogue you wrote between a parent and a child. Choose some elements from that dialogue and use them as inspiration for writing a poem about a parent/child relationship.

Unforgettable Moments Some of the poems you have just read describe a memorable moment for the speaker and a parent (or parents). For example, in "My Papa's Waltz" the speaker describes an experience he had as a young boy dancing wildly with his father. Think of someone you know well, and write a short **essay** about an interesting or unforgettable moment you shared with that person.

Penny for Your Thoughts This untitled painting by French painter Suzanne Valadon (1867–1938) portrays a family. Study the faces of the persons in the painting. Then write a **dialogue** that records the thoughts of each family member as he or she is posing for the painting.

Other Options

Fitting Image Find visual **images** from a magazine or book to represent one or more of the parents in the four poems. Share your images with the class and explain why you think each is a good representation of the character or characters you chose.

Symbolic Art Choose a character from a story you have read. Think of a symbol that could represent that character, in the way that New England rock represents the mother in "The Courage That My Mother Had." Make a piece of **art** that relates the story character to the symbol you have chosen. Share your artwork with the class.

Before Reading

The Last Word by Judith Ortiz Cofer

Alligator by Bailey White

Judith Ortiz Cofer
born 1952

Judith Ortiz Cofer was born in Puerto Rico and moved to New Jersey with her family when she was four. Cofer, who has published several books, often explores the differences between Puerto Rican village life and American urban life.

Bailey White
born 1950

Bailey White, a first-grade teacher, often reads her stories and essays on National Public Radio. Her reflections on southern life are characterized by tenderness and humor. She lives in Georgia with her mother.

Building Background

Re-imagining Memoir In "Alligator," Bailey White describes the somewhat unusual behavior of an aunt of hers. Families often enjoy telling stories about the idiosyncracies, or unusual habits, of other relatives. Before reading the following selections, think of a story you've heard about someone with some unique habits or qualities and share it with a partner.

Literary Focus

Mood The atmosphere or general feeling of a piece of writing is known as its **mood.** Possibilities for mood are as broad as the range of human emotion. For example, a story's mood might be gloomy, excited, lonely, furious, sarcastic, or playful. Writers create mood through choice of setting, details, images, and words. As you read the following selections, think about the mood of each piece and how the author creates it.

Writer's Notebook

Memory Games What does it mean to remember something? How do you know whether a memory is actually yours, or something someone else has told you about the past? In your notebook, write about a "memory" you have of the past that might be based mostly on what other people have told you about the event.

> "I did that," says my memory.
>
> "I did not," says my pride; and memory yields.
>
> — Nietzche, *Beyond Good and Evil*

THE LAST WORD

Judith Ortiz Cofer

My mother opens the photo album to a picture of my father as a very young man in an army uniform. She says to me, "You had not met your father yet when this photograph was taken. He left for Panama when I was a couple of months pregnant with you, and didn't get back until you were two years old."

I have my own "memories" about this time in my life, but I decide to ask her a few questions, anyway. It is always fascinating to me to hear her version of the past we shared, to see what shades of pastel she will choose to paint my childhood's "summer afternoon."

"How did I react to his homecoming?" I ask my mother whose eyes are already glazing over with grief and affection for her husband, my father, dead in a car wreck now for over a decade. There are few pictures of him in middle age in her album. She prefers to remember him as the golden boy she married, forever a young man in military uniform coming home laden with gifts from exotic places for us.

"You were the happiest little girl on the island, I believe," she says smiling down at his picture. "After a few days of getting acquainted, you two were inseparable. He took you everywhere with him."

"Mother . . ." In spite of my resolve, I am jarred by the disparity[1] of our recollections[2] of this event. "Was there a party for him when he returned? Did you roast a pig out in the backyard? I remember a fire . . . and an accident . . . involving me."

She lifts her eyes to meet mine. She looks mildly surprised.

"You were only a baby . . . what is it that you think happened on that day?"

"I remember that I was put in a crib and left alone. I remember many people talking, music, laughter." I want her to finish the story. I want my mother to tell me that

---

1. **disparity** (dis par′ə tē), *n.* difference; being unalike; inequality.
2. **recollection** (rek′ə lek′shən), *n.* memory.

Julio Rosado del Valle, *Saro and Aita* (1949). How do the lines and shapes in this painting show a connection between the mother and daughter? ▼

what I remember is true. But she is stubborn too. Her memories are precious to her and although she accepts my explanations that what I write in my poems and stories is mainly the product of my imagination, she wants certain things she believes are true to remain sacred, untouched by my fictions.

"And what is this accident you remember? What do you think happened at your father's homecoming party?" Her voice has taken on the deadly serious tone that has always made me swallow hard. I am about to be set straight. I decide to forge ahead. *This is just an experiment,* I tell myself. I am comparing notes on the past with my mother. This can be managed without resentment. After all, we are both intelligent adults.

"I climbed out of the crib, and walked outside. I think . . . I fell into the fire."

My mother shakes her head. She is now angry, and worse, disappointed in me. She turns the pages of the book until she finds my birthday picture. A short while after his return from Panama, my father is supposed to have spent a small fortune giving me the fanciest birthday party ever seen in our pueblo.[3] He wanted to make up for all the good times together we had missed. My mother has told me the story dozens of times. There are many photographs documenting the event. Every time I visit a relative someone brings out an album and shows me a face I've memorized: that of a very solemn two-year-old dressed in a fancy dress sent by an aunt from New York just for the occasion, surrounded by toys and decorations, a huge, ornate cake in front of me. I am not smiling in any of these pictures.

My mother turns the album toward me. "Where were you burned?" she asks, letting a little irony sharpen the hurt in her voice. "Does that look like a child who was neglected for one moment?"

"So what really happened on that day, Mami?"[4] I look at the two-year-old's face again. There is a celebration going on around her, but her eyes—and my memory—tell me that she is not a part of it.

"There was a little accident involving the fire that day, Hija,"[5] my mother says in a gentler voice. She is the Keeper of the Past. As the main witness of my childhood, she has the power to refute my claims.

"This is what happened. You were fascinated by a large book your father brought home from his travels. I believe it was a foreign language dictionary. We couldn't pry it away from you, though it was almost as big as you. I took my eyes off you for one moment, *un momentito, nada más, Hija,*[6] and you somehow dragged that book to the pit where we were roasting a pig, and you threw it in."

"Do you know why I did that, Mother?" I am curious to hear her explanation. I dimly recall early mentions of a valuable book I supposedly did away with in the distant past.

"Why do children do anything they do? The fire attracted you. Maybe you wanted attention. I don't know. But," she shakes her finger at me in mock accusation, "if you remember a burning feeling, the location of this fire was your little behind after I gave you some *pan-pan*[7] to make sure you didn't try anything like that ever again."

We both laugh at her use of the baby word for a spanking that I had not heard her say in three decades.

"That is what really happened?"

"Es la pura verdad,"[8] she says. "Nothing but the truth."

But that is not how *I* remember it.

---

3. **pueblo** (pweb′lō), small town or village. [Spanish]
4. **Mami** (mä′mē), Mom, Mother. [Spanish]
5. **Hija** (ē′hä), daughter. [Spanish]
6. *un momentito, nada más, Hija* (un mō men tē′tō nä′dä mäs, ē′ha), no more than a moment, Daughter. [Spanish]
7. *pan-pan* (pän′pän′), a spanking. [Spanish]
8. *Es la pura verdad* (es lä pü′rä ver däd′). It is the pure truth. [Spanish]

Alligator

Bailey White

I remember as a little child watching my Aunt Belle's wide rump disappear into the cattails and marsh grass at the edge of a pond as she crawled on her hands and knees to meet a giant alligator face to face. She was taming him, she said. We children would wait high up on the bank with our eyes and mouths wide open, hoping that the alligator wouldn't eat her up, but not wanting to miss it if he did.

Finally, Aunt Belle would get as close to him as she wanted, and they would stare at each other for some minutes. Then my aunt would jump up, wave her arms in the air, and shout, "Whoo!" With a tremendous leap and flop the alligator would throw himself into the water. The little drops from that splash would reach all the way to where we were standing, and my aunt would come up the bank drenched and exul-tant. "I have to show him who's boss," she would tell us.

Later, Aunt Belle taught that alligator to bel-low on command. She would drive the truck down to the edge of the pond and gun the engine. We would sit in the back, craning our necks to see him coming. He would come fast across the pond, raising two diagonal waves

Later, Aunt Belle taught that alligator to bellow on command.

behind him as he came. He would haul himself into the shallow water and get situated just right. His back was broad and black. His head was as wide as a single bed. His tail would

This Burmese wood and ivory carving of a crocodile is actually a zither, a stringed musical instrument. Do this crocodile and the alligator in "Alligator" seem frightening? Why or why not? ▼

But sometimes, on the nights of the full moon in springtime, I can hear an alligator bellow.

disappear into the dark pond water. He was the biggest alligator anyone had ever seen.

Then my aunt would turn off the engine. We would all stop breathing. The alligator would swell up. He would lift his head, arch his tail, and bellow. The sound would come from deep inside. It was not loud, but it had a carrying quality. It was like a roar, but with more authority than a lion's roar. It was a sound you hear in your bones. If we were lucky, he would bellow ten times. Then Aunt Belle would throw him a dead chicken.

The day came when she could just walk down to the pond and look out across the water. The alligator would come surging up to the bank, crawl out, and bellow.

By this time he was very old. My aunt got old, too. Her children had all grown up. She got to where she was spending a lot of time down at the pond. She'd go down there and just sit on the bank. When the alligator saw her, he'd swim over and climb out. He never bellowed anymore. They would just sit and look at each other. After a while my aunt would walk back to the house. The alligator would swim out to where the water was deep and black, and float for a minute; then he'd just disappear, without even a ripple. That's how he did.

But one day he didn't come when Aunt Belle went to the pond. He didn't come the next day, or the day after. All that summer, Aunt Belle walked around and around the pond looking, listening, and sniffing. "Something as big as that, you'd know if he was dead, this hot weather," she'd say. Finally, she stopped going down to the pond.

But sometimes, on the nights of the full moon in springtime, I can hear an alligator bellow. It comes rolling up through the night. It's not loud, but it makes me sit up in bed and hold my breath. Sometimes I hear it ten times. It's a peaceful sound.

After Reading

Making Connections

Shaping Your Response

1. After reading "The Last Word," do you believe the daughter or the mother? Explain.

2. In "Alligator," how do you think the narrator feels about the alligator? Cite evidence from the story.

Analyzing the Memoirs

3. Use a Venn diagram like the one pictured here to represent the similarities and differences of the mother's and daughter's memories of the accident in "The Last Word."

Mother's memories   Daughter's memories

4. Who do you think gets the last word in "The Last Word"? Explain.

5. How does the relationship between the alligator and Aunt Belle change over the years? Explain.

Extending the Ideas

6. In Part 1 of Unit 3, you have met a number of memorable and sometimes unusual family members. If you were stranded on a desert island, which of these people would you want to share the island with? Give reasons for your choices.

Literary Focus: Mood

You've learned that **mood** is the atmosphere or general feeling of a piece of writing. For example, the mood of "The Last Word" is troubled and somewhat mysterious. Describe the mood of "Alligator" and give specific examples of how Bailey White creates it.

Expressing Your Ideas

Writing Choice

Writer's Notebook Update Ask someone you've known for a long time to tell you their version of something you remember from childhood. In your notebook, write down both versions of the event and, if the two versions differ, explain why you would have different memories of the same event.

Another Option

On the Air Bailey White often reads her stories on National Public Radio. Practicing with a partner, prepare to do a **radio broadcast** of "Alligator" or one of the poems you've read in this unit. Tape your piece and play it for the class.

Before Reading

A Christmas Memory

by Truman Capote

Truman Capote
1924–1984

Truman Capote (kä pō′tē) was born in New Orleans, Louisiana, but grew up in a small Alabama town. He hated school, especially the military schools he was forced to attend. From childhood, Capote loved to write. At seventeen, he published his first story in a major magazine. Three years later, he won the prestigious O. Henry Award. Much of Capote's writing was autobiographical, often about his experiences living in the South. He was a versatile writer, whose work ranged from light comedy to nightmarish tragedy.

Building Background

The Best of Friends "A Christmas Memory" is a story about a memorable friendship. Think about someone in your life whom you consider a close friend. How did you become friends? What is he or she like? What kinds of things do you do together? What makes this friendship different from others? As a class, generate a list of qualities necessary for a good friendship.

Literary Focus

Simile A **simile** is a figure of speech, usually using the words *like* or *as,* that directly compares two unlike things. By appealing to the imagination and senses, an effective simile makes readers look at something in a fresh way. Here is an example of a simile: *Christmas shoppers filled the mall like bees in a hive.* Sometimes a sentence contains *like* or *as,* but does not have a simile, as in this example: *The mall looked like it was crowded.* In that sentence, the mall is not being compared to anything else.

Writer's Notebook

Old Friends Think of a friendship you have now, or have had in the past, with a person significantly older than you, such as a relative, teacher, or neighbor. Write a brief description of the friendship in your notebook. How does it differ from your friendships with people your own age? As you read "A Christmas Memory," think about how the ages of the two characters shape their friendship.

A very young Truman Capote poses for a photograph with his beloved cousin and friend. ➤

A Christmas Memory

TRUMAN CAPOTE

Imagine a morning in late November.

A coming of winter morning more than

twenty years ago. Consider the kitchen of a

spreading old house in a country town.

A great black stove is its main feature;

but there is also a big round table and a

fireplace with two rocking chairs placed in

front of it. Just today the fireplace commenced its seasonal roar.

A woman with shorn white hair is standing at the kitchen window. She is wearing tennis shoes and a shapeless gray sweater over a summery calico dress. She is small and sprightly, like a bantam hen; but, due to a long youthful illness, her shoulders are pitifully hunched. Her face is remarkable—not unlike Lincoln's, craggy like that, and tinted by sun and wind; but it is delicate too, finely boned, and her eyes are sherry-colored and timid. "Oh my," she exclaims, her breath smoking the windowpane, "it's fruitcake weather!"

The person to whom she is speaking is myself. I am seven; she is sixty-something. We are cousins, very distant ones, and we have lived together—well, as long as I can remember. Other people inhabit the house, relatives; and though they have power over us, and frequently make us cry, we are not, on the whole, too much aware of them. We are each other's best friend. She calls me Buddy, in memory of a boy who was formerly her best friend. The other Buddy died in the 1880s, when she was still a child. She is still a child.

"I knew it before I got out of bed," she says, turning away from the window with a purposeful excitement in her eyes. "The courthouse bell sounded so cold and clear. And there were no birds singing; they've gone to warmer country, yes indeed. Oh, Buddy, stop stuffing biscuit and fetch our buggy. Help me find my hat. We've thirty cakes to bake."

*I*t's always the same: a morning arrives in November, and my friend, as though officially inaugurating[1] the Christmas time of year that exhilarates her imagination and fuels the blaze of her heart, announces: "It's fruitcake weather! Fetch our buggy. Help me find my hat."

The hat is found, a straw cartwheel corsaged[2] with velvet roses out-of-doors has faded: it once belonged to a more fashionable relative. Together, we guide our buggy, a dilapidated[3] baby carriage, out to the garden and into a

"It's fruitcake weather!"

grove of pecan trees. The buggy is mine; that is, it was bought for me when I was born. It is made of wicker, rather unraveled, and the wheels wobble like a drunkard's legs. But it is a faithful object; springtimes, we take it to the woods and fill it with flowers, herbs, wild fern for our porch pots; in the summer, we pile it with picnic paraphernalia[4] and sugar-cane fishing poles and roll it down to the edge of a creek; it has its winter uses, too: as a truck for hauling firewood from the yard to the kitchen, as a warm bed for Queenie, our tough little orange and white rat terrier who has survived distemper[5] and two rattlesnake bites. Queenie is trotting beside it now.

Three hours later we are back in the kitchen hulling a heaping buggyload of windfall pecans. Our backs hurt from gathering them: how hard they were to find (the main crop having been shaken off the trees and sold by the orchard's owners, who are not us) among the concealing leaves, the frosted, deceiving grass. Caarackle! A cheery crunch, scraps of miniature thunder sound as the shells collapse and the golden

---

1. inaugurate (in ô′gyə rāt′), *v.* make a formal beginning of.
2. **corsaged** (kôr säzhd′), *adj.* decorated with flowers.
3. dilapidated (də lap′ə dā′tid), *adj.* fallen into ruin; decayed through neglect.
4. **paraphernalia** (par′ə fər nā′lyə), *n.* equipment.
5. **distemper** (dis tem′pər), *n.* an infectious viral disease of dogs and other animals, accompanied by fever, coughing, and loss of strength.

mound of sweet oily ivory meat mounts in the milk-glass bowl. Queenie begs to taste, and now and again my friend sneaks her a mite, though insisting we deprive ourselves. "We mustn't, Buddy. If we start, we won't stop. And there's scarcely enough as there is. For thirty cakes." The kitchen is growing dark. Dusk turns the window into a mirror: our reflections mingle with the rising moon as we work by the fireside in the firelight. At last, when the moon is quite high, we toss the final hull into the fire and, with joined sighs, watch it catch flame. The buggy is empty, the bowl is brimful.

We eat our supper (cold biscuits, bacon, blackberry jam) and discuss tomorrow. Tomorrow the kind of work I like best begins: buying. Cherries and citron,[6] ginger and vanilla and canned Hawaiian pineapple, rinds and raisins

thought it perhaps sacrilegious,[8] the slogan "A.M.! Amen!" To tell the truth, our only *really* profitable enterprise was the Fun and Freak Museum we conducted in a backyard woodshed two summers ago. The Fun was a stereopticon[9] with slide views of Washington and New York lent us by a relative who had been to those places (she was furious when she discovered why we'd borrowed it); the Freak was a three-legged biddy chicken hatched by one of our own hens. Everybody hereabouts wanted to see that biddy: we charged grownups a nickel, kids two cents. And took in a good twenty dollars before the museum shut down due to the decease[10] of the main attraction.

But one way and another we do each year accumulate Christmas savings, a Fruitcake Fund. These moneys we keep hidden in an ancient bead purse under a loose board under the floor under a chamber pot under my friend's bed. The purse is seldom removed from this

At last, when the moon is quite high, we toss the final hull into the fire. . . .

and walnuts and whiskey and oh, so much flour, butter, so many eggs, spices, flavorings: why, we'll need a pony to pull the buggy home.

But before these purchases can be made, there is the question of money. Neither of us has any. Except for skinflint[7] sums persons in the house occasionally provide (a dime is considered very big money); or what we earn ourselves from various activities: holding rummage sales, selling buckets of hand-picked blackberries, jars of homemade jam and apple jelly and peach preserves, rounding up flowers for funerals and weddings. Once we won seventy-ninth prize, five dollars, in a national football contest. Not that we know a fool thing about football. It's just that we enter any contest we hear about: at the moment our hopes are centered on the fifty-thousand-dollar Grand Prize being offered to name a new brand of coffee (we suggested "A.M."; and after some hesitation, for my friend

safe location except to make a deposit, or, as happens every Saturday, a withdrawal; for on Saturdays I am allowed ten cents to go to the picture show. My friend has never been to a picture show, nor does she intend to: "I'd rather hear you tell the story, Buddy. That way I can imagine it more. Besides, a person my age shouldn't squander[11] their eyes. When the Lord comes, let me see him clear." In addition to

---

6. **citron** (sit′rən), *n.* a pale-yellow citrus fruit somewhat like a lemon but larger, with less acid and a thicker rind.
7. **skinflint** (skin′flint′), *adj.* mean and stingy.
8. **sacrilegious** (sak′rə lij′əs), *adj.* injurious or insulting to sacred persons or things.
9. **stereopticon** (ster′ē op′tə kən), *n.* hand-held viewer that combines two images to create a three-dimensional effect.
10. decease (di sēs′), *n.* death.
11. squander (skwon′dər), *v.* waste; spend foolishly.

never having seen a movie, she has never: eaten in a restaurant, traveled more than five miles from home, received or sent a telegram, read anything except funny papers and the Bible, worn cosmetics, cursed, wished someone harm, told a lie on purpose, let a hungry dog go hungry. Here are a few things she has done, does do: killed with a hoe the biggest rattlesnake ever seen in this county (sixteen rattles), dip snuff[12] (secretly), tame hummingbirds (just try it) till they balance on her finger, tell ghost stories (we both believe in ghosts) so tingling they chill you in July, talk to herself, take walks in the rain, grow the prettiest japonicas[13] in town, know the recipe for every sort of old-time Indian cure, including a magical wart-remover.

Now, with supper finished, we retire to the room in a faraway part of the house where my friend sleeps in a scrap-quilt-covered iron bed painted rose pink, her favorite color. Silently, wallowing in the pleasures of conspiracy, we take the bead purse from its secret place and spill its contents on the scrap quilt. Dollar bills, tightly rolled and green as May buds. Somber fifty-cent pieces, heavy enough to weight a dead man's eyes. Lovely dimes, the liveliest coin, the one that really jingles. Nickels and quarters, worn smooth as creek pebbles. But mostly a hateful heap of bitter-odored pennies. Last summer others in the house contracted to pay us a penny for every twenty-five flies we killed. Oh, the carnage[14] of August: the flies that flew to heaven! Yet it was not work in which we took pride. And, as we sit counting pennies, it is as though we were back tabulating dead flies. Neither of us has a head for figures; we count slowly, lose track, start again. According to her

Silently, wallowing in the pleasures of conspiracy, we take the bead purse from its secret place. . . .

calculations, we have $12.73. According to mine, exactly $13. "I do hope you're wrong, Buddy. We can't mess around with thirteen. The cakes will fall. Or put somebody in the cemetery. Why, I wouldn't dream of getting out of bed on the thirteenth." This is true: she always spends thirteenths in bed. So, to be on the safe side, we subtract a penny and toss it out the window.

Of the ingredients that go into our fruitcakes, whiskey is the most expensive, as well as the hardest to obtain: state laws forbid its sale. But everybody knows you can buy a bottle from Mr. Haha Jones. And the next day, having completed our more prosaic[15] shopping, we set out for Mr. Haha's business address, a "sinful" (to quote public opinion) fish-fry and dancing café down by the river. We've been there before, and on the same errand; but in previous years our dealings have been with Haha's wife, an iodine-dark Indian woman with brassy peroxided hair and a dead-tired disposition. Actually, we've never laid eyes on her husband, though we've heard that he's an Indian too. A giant with razor scars across his cheeks. They call him Haha because he's so gloomy, a man who never laughs. As we approach his café (a large log cabin festooned[16] inside and out with chains of garish-gay naked lightbulbs and standing by the

---

12. **snuff** (snuf), *n.* powdered tobacco, often scented, taken into the nose.
13. **japonica** (jə pon′ə kə), *n.* camellia; Asiatic shrub of the rose family, with showy red, pink, or white flowers.
14. **carnage** (kär′nij), *n.* slaughter of a great number.
15. **prosaic** (prō zā′ik), *adj.* ordinary, not exciting.
16. **festooned** (fe stünd′), *adj.* decorated with strings or chains of flowers, leaves, ribbons, etc.

river's muddy edge under the shade of river trees where moss drifts through the branches like gray mist) our steps slow down. Even Queenie stops prancing and sticks close by. People have been murdered in Haha's café. Cut to pieces. Hit on the head. There's a case coming up in court next month. Naturally these goings-on happen at night when the colored lights cast crazy patterns and the Victrola wails. In the daytime Haha's is shabby and deserted. I knock at the door, Queenie barks, my friend calls: "Mrs. Haha, ma'am? Anyone to home?"

Footsteps. The door opens. Our hearts overturn. It's Mr. Haha Jones himself! And he *is* a giant; he *does* have scars; he *doesn't* smile. No, he glowers[17] at us through Satan-tilted eyes and demands to know: "What you want with Haha?"

For a moment we are too paralyzed to tell. Presently my friend half-finds her voice, a whispery voice at best: "If you please, Mr. Haha, we'd like a quart of your finest whiskey."

His eyes tilt more. Would you believe it? Haha is smiling! Laughing, too. "Which one of you is a drinkin' man?"

"It's for making fruitcakes, Mr. Haha. Cooking."

This sobers him. He frowns. "That's no way to waste good whiskey." Nevertheless, he retreats into the shadowed café and seconds later appears carrying a bottle of daisy yellow unlabeled liquor. He demonstrates its sparkle in the sunlight and says: "Two dollars."

We pay him with nickels and dimes and pennies. Suddenly, jangling the coins in his hand like a fistful of dice, his face softens. "Tell you what," he proposes, pouring the money back into our bead purse, "just send me one of them fruitcakes instead."

"Well," my friend remarks on our way home, "there's a lovely man. We'll put an extra cup of raisins in *his* cake."

The black stove, stoked with coal and firewood, glows like a lighted pumpkin. Eggbeaters whirl, spoons spin round in bowls of butter and sugar, vanilla sweetens the air, ginger spices it; melting, nose-tingling odors saturate the kitchen, suffuse[18] the house, drift out to the world on puffs of chimney smoke. In four days our work is done. Thirty-one cakes, dampened with whiskey, bask on window sills and shelves.

Who are they for?

Friends. Not necessarily neighbor friends: indeed, the larger share are intended for persons we've met maybe once, perhaps not at all. People who've struck our fancy. Like President Roosevelt. Like the Reverend and Mrs. J. C. Lucey, Baptist missionaries to Borneo[19] who lectured here last winter. Or the little knife grinder who comes through town twice a year. Or Abner Packer, the driver of the six o'clock bus from Mobile, who exchanges waves with us every day as he passes in a dust-cloud whoosh. Or the young Wistons, a California couple whose car one afternoon broke down outside the house and who spent a pleasant hour chatting with us on the porch (young Mr. Wiston snapped our picture, the only one we've ever had taken). Is it because my friend is shy with everyone *except* strangers that these strangers, and merest acquaintances, seem to us our truest friends? I think yes. Also, the scrapbooks we keep of thank-you's on White House stationery, time-to-time communications from California and Borneo, the knife grinder's

> The black stove, stoked with coal and firewood, glows like a lighted pumpkin.

---

17. **glower** (glou′ər), *v.* stare angrily; scowl fiercely.
18. **suffuse** (sə fyūz′), *v.* cover or spread through.
19. **Borneo** (bôr′nē ō), a large island in the East Indies, between Java and the Philippines.

penny post cards, make us feel connected to eventful worlds beyond the kitchen with its view of a sky that stops.

*N*ow a nude December fig branch grates against the window. The kitchen is empty, the cakes are gone; yesterday we carted the last of them to the post office, where the cost of stamps turned our purse inside out. We're broke. That rather depresses me, but my friend insists on celebrating—with two inches of whiskey left in Haha's bottle. Queenie has a spoonful in a bowl of coffee (she likes her coffee chicory-flavored and strong). The rest we divide between a pair of jelly glasses. We're both quite awed at the prospect of drinking straight whiskey; the taste of it brings screwed-up expressions and sour shudders. But by and by we begin to sing, the two of us singing different songs simultaneously. I don't know the words to mine, just: *Come on along, come on along, to the dark-town strutters' ball.* But I can dance: that's what I mean to be, a tap dancer in the movies. My dancing shadow rollicks[20] on the walls; our voices rock the chinaware; we giggle: as if unseen hands were tickling us. Queenie rolls on her back, her paws plow the air, something like a grin stretches her black lips. Inside myself, I feel warm and sparky as those crumbling logs, carefree as the wind in the chimney. My friend waltzes round the stove, the hem of her poor calico skirt pinched between her fingers as though it were a party dress: *Show me the way to go home,* she sings, her tennis shoes squeaking on the floor. *Show me the way to go home.*

Enter: two relatives. Very angry. Potent[21] with eyes that scold, tongues that scald.[22] Listen to what they have to say, the words tumbling together into a wrathful tune: "A child of seven! whiskey on his breath! are you out of your mind? feeding a child of seven! must be loony! road to ruination![23] remember Cousin Kate? Uncle Charlie? Uncle Charlie's brother-in-law? shame! scandal! humiliation! kneel, pray, beg the Lord!"

Queenie sneaks under the stove. My friend gazes at her shoes, her chin quivers, she lifts her skirt and blows her nose and runs to her room. Long after the town has gone to sleep and the house is silent except for the chimings of clocks and the sputter of fading fires, she is weeping into a pillow already as wet as a widow's handkerchief.

"Don't cry," I say, sitting at the bottom of her bed and shivering despite my flannel nightgown that smells of last winter's cough syrup, "don't cry," I beg, teasing her toes, tickling her feet, "you're too old for that."

"It's because," she hiccups, "I *am* too old. Old and funny."

"Not funny. Fun. More fun than anybody. Listen. If you don't stop crying you'll be so tired tomorrow we can't go cut a tree."

She straightens up. Queenie jumps on the bed (where Queenie is not allowed) to lick her cheeks. "I know where we'll find pretty trees, Buddy. And holly, too. With berries big as your eyes. It's way off in the woods. Farther than we've ever been. Papa used to bring us Christmas trees from there: carry them on his shoulder. That's fifty years ago. Well, now: I can't wait for morning."

---

20. **rollick** (rol′ik), *v.* enjoy oneself in a free, hearty way; frolic.
21. potent (pōt′nt), *adj.* powerful; strong.
22. scald (skôld), *v.* burn as if with boiling water.
23. **ruination** (rü′ə nā′shən), *n.* ruin; destruction; downfall.

orning. Frozen rime[24] lusters the grass; the sun, round as an orange and orange as hot-weather moons, balances on the horizon, burnishes[25] the silvered winter woods. A wild turkey calls. A renegade[26] hog grunts in the undergrowth. Soon, by the edge of knee-deep, rapid-running water, we have to abandon the buggy. Queenie wades the stream first, paddles across barking complaints at the swiftness of the current, the pneumonia-making coldness of it. We follow, holding our shoes and equipment (a hatchet, a burlap sack) above our heads. A mile more: of chastising[27] thorns, burs and briers that catch at our clothes; of rusty pine needles brilliant with gaudy fungus and molted feathers. Here, there, a flash, a flutter, an ecstasy of shrillings reminds us that not all the birds have flown south. Always, the path unwinds through lemony sun pools and pitch vine tunnels. Another creek to cross: a disturbed armada[28] of speckled trout froths the water round us, and frogs the size of plates practice belly flops; beaver workmen are building a dam. On the farther shore, Queenie shakes herself and trembles. My friend shivers, too: not with cold but enthusiasm. One of her hat's ragged roses sheds a petal as she lifts her head and inhales the pine-heavy air. "We're almost there; can you smell it, Buddy?" she says, as though we were approaching an ocean.

And, indeed, it is a kind of ocean. Scented acres of holiday trees, prickly-leafed holly. Red berries shiny as Chinese bells: black crows swoop upon them screaming. Having stuffed our burlap sacks with enough greenery and crimson to garland a dozen windows, we set about choosing a tree. "It should be," muses my friend, "twice as tall as a boy. So a boy can't steal the star." The one we pick is twice as tall as me. A brave handsome brute that survives thirty hatchet strokes before it keels with a creaking rending cry. Lugging it like a kill, we commence the long trek out. Every few yards we abandon the struggle, sit down and pant. But we have the strength of triumphant huntsmen; that and the tree's virile, icy perfume revive us, goad[29] us on. Many compliments accompany our sunset return along the red clay road to town; but my friend is sly and noncommittal[30] when passers-by praise the treasure perched on our buggy: what a fine tree and where did it come from? "Yonderways," she murmurs vaguely. Once a car stops and the rich mill owner's lazy wife leans out and whines: "Give ya two-bits cash for that ol' tree." Ordinarily my friend is afraid of saying no; but on this occasion she promptly shakes her head: "We wouldn't take a dollar." The mill owner's wife persists. "A dollar, my foot! Fifty cents. That's my last offer. Goodness, woman, you can get another one." In answer, my friend gently reflects: "I doubt it. There's never two of anything."

Home: Queenie slumps by the fire and sleeps till tomorrow, snoring loud as a human.

A trunk in the attic contains: a shoebox of ermine tails (off the opera cape of a curious lady who once rented a room in the house), coils of frazzled tinsel gone gold with age, one silver star, a brief rope of dilapidated, undoubtedly dangerous candylike light bulbs. Excellent decorations, as far as they go, which isn't far enough: my friend wants our tree to blaze "like a Baptist window," droop with weighty snows of ornament. But we can't afford the made-in-Japan splendors at the five-and-dime.[31] So we do what we've always done: sit for days at the kitchen table with scissors and crayons and stacks of colored paper. I make sketches and my friend cuts them out: lots of cats, fish too

---

24. **rime** (rīm), *n.* white frost.
25. **burnish** (ber′nish), *v.* make bright and glossy; polish.
26. **renegade** (ren′ə gād), *adj.* in this context, refers to a domestic animal living in the wild.
27. **chastising** (cha stīz′ing), *adj.* punishing.
28. **armada** (är mä′də), *n.* large fleet of warships.
29. **goad** (gōd), *v.* drive or urge on.
30. **noncommittal** (non′kə mit′l), *adj.* not committing oneself; not saying yes or no.
31. **five-and-dime,** a store that sells small, cheaply priced goods.

▲ Jean-Baptiste Simeon Chardin, *Utensiles de Cuisine (Kitchen Utensils)*. Unlike most artists of his day, Chardin (1699–1779) believed that even simple objects were worth painting. Explain whether or not the objects shown here would be "simple" to paint.

(because they're easy to draw), some apples, some watermelons, a few winged angels devised from saved-up sheets of Hershey-bar tin foil. We use safety pins to attach these creations to the tree; as a final touch, we sprinkle the branches with shredded cotton (picked in August for this purpose). My friend, surveying the effect, clasps her hands together. "Now honest, Buddy. Doesn't it look good enough to eat?" Queenie tries to eat an angel.

After weaving and ribboning holly wreaths for all the front windows, our next project is the fashioning of family gifts. Tie-dye scarves for the ladies, for the men a home-brewed lemon and licorice and aspirin syrup to be taken "at the first Symptoms of a Cold and after Hunting." But when it comes time for making each other's gifts, my friend and I separate to work secretly. I would like to buy her a pearl-handled knife, a radio, a whole pound of chocolate-covered cherries (we tasted some once, and she always swears: "I could live on them, Buddy, Lord yes I could—and that's not taking His name in vain"). Instead, I am building her a kite. She would like to give me a bicycle (she's said so on several million occasions: "If only I could, Buddy. It's bad enough in life to do without something *you* want: but confound it, what gets my goat is not being able to give somebody something you want *them* to have. Only one of these days I will, Buddy. Locate you a bike. Don't ask how. Steal it, maybe"). Instead, I'm fairly certain that she is building me a kite—the same as last year, and the year before: the year before that we exchanged slingshots. All of which is fine by me. For we are champion kite-fliers who study the wind like sailors; my friend, more accomplished than I, can get a kite aloft when there isn't enough breeze to carry clouds.

Christmas Eve afternoon we scrape together a nickel and go to the butcher's to buy Queenie's traditional gift, a good gnawable beef bone. The bone, wrapped in funny paper, is placed high in the tree near the silver star. Queenie knows it's there. She squats at the foot of the tree staring up in a trance of greed: when bedtime arrives she refuses to budge. Her excitement is equaled by my own. I kick the covers and turn my pillow as though it were a scorching summer's night. Somewhere a rooster crows: falsely, for the sun is still on the other side of the world.

"Buddy, are you awake?" It is my friend, calling from her room, which is next to mine; and an instant later she is sitting on my bed holding a candle. "Well, I can't sleep a hoot," she declares. "My mind's jumping like a jack rabbit. Buddy, do you think Mrs. Roosevelt will serve our cake at dinner?" We huddle in the bed, and she squeezes my hand I-love-you. "Seems like your hand used to be so much smaller. I guess I hate to see you grow up. When you're grown up, will we still be friends?" I say always. "But I feel so bad, Buddy.

"Well, I can't sleep a hoot," she declares. "My mind's jumping like a jack rabbit. . . ."

I wanted so bad to give you a bike. I tried to sell my cameo[32] Papa gave me. Buddy"—she hesitates, as though embarrassed—"I made you another kite." Then I confess that I made her one, too; and we laugh. The candle burns too short to hold. Out it goes, exposing the starlight, the stars spinning at the window like a visible caroling that slowly, slowly daybreak silences. Possibly we doze; but the beginnings of dawn splash us like cold water: we're up, wide-eyed and wandering while we wait for others to waken. Quite deliberately my friend drops a kettle on the kitchen floor. I tap-dance in front of closed doors. One by one the household emerges, looking as though they'd like to kill us both; but it's Christmas, so they can't. First, a gorgeous breakfast: just everything you can imagine—from flapjacks and fried squirrel to hominy grits and honey-in-the-comb. Which puts everyone in a good humor except my friend and I. Frankly, we're so impatient to get at the presents we can't eat a mouthful.

Well, I'm disappointed. Who wouldn't be? With socks, a Sunday school shirt, some handkerchiefs, a hand-me-down sweater and a year's subscription to a religious magazine for children. *The Little Shepherd*. It makes me boil. It really does.

---

32. **cameo** (kam′ē ō), *n.* semi-precious stone carved so that there is a raised design on a background usually of a different color.

My friend has a better haul. A sack of Satsumas,[33] that's her best present. She is proudest, however, of a white wool shawl knitted by her married sister. But she *says* her favorite gift is the kite I built her. And it *is* very beautiful; though not as beautiful as the one she made me, which is blue and scattered with gold and green Good Conduct stars; moreover, my name is painted on it, "Buddy."

"Buddy, the wind is blowing."

The wind is blowing, and nothing will do till we've run to a pasture below the house where Queenie has scooted to bury her bone (and where, a winter hence, Queenie will be buried, too). There, plunging through the healthy waist-high grass, we unreel our kites, feel them twitching at the string like sky fish as they swim into the wind. Satisfied, sun-warmed, we sprawl in the grass and peel Satsumas and watch our kites cavort.[34] Soon I forget the socks and hand-me-down sweater. I'm as happy as if we'd already won the fifty-thousand-dollar Grand Prize in that coffee-naming contest.

"My, how foolish I am!" my friend cries, suddenly alert, like a woman remembering too late she has biscuits in the oven. "You know what I've always thought?" she asks in a tone of discovery, and not smiling at me but a point beyond. "I've always thought a body would have to be sick and dying before they saw the Lord. And I imagined that when He came it would be like looking at the Baptist window: pretty as colored glass with the sun pouring through, such a shine you don't know it's getting dark. And it's been a comfort: to think of that shine taking away all the spooky feeling. But I'll wager[35] it never happens. I'll wager at the very end a body realizes the Lord has already shown Himself. That things as they are"—her hand circles in a gesture that gathers

"As for me, I could leave the world with today in my eyes."

clouds and kites and grass and Queenie pawing earth over her bone—"just what they've always seen, was seeing Him. As for me, I could leave the world with today in my eyes."

This is our last Christmas together.

Life separates us. Those who Know Best decide that I belong in a military school. And so follows a miserable succession of bugle-blowing prisons, grim reveille-ridden[36] summer camps. I have a new home too. But it doesn't count. Home is where my friend is, and there I never go.

And there she remains, puttering around the kitchen. Alone with Queenie. Then alone. ("Buddy dear," she writes in her wild hard-to-read script, "yesterday Jim Macy's horse kicked Queenie bad. Be thankful she didn't feel much. I wrapped her in a Fine Linen sheet and rode her in the buggy down to Simpson's pasture where she can be with all her Bones. . . .") For a few Novembers she continues to bake her fruitcakes single-handed; not as many, but some: and, of course, she always sends me "the best of the batch." Also, in every letter she encloses a dime wadded in toilet paper: "See a picture show and write me the story." But gradually in her letters she tends to confuse me with her other friend, the Buddy who died in the 1880s; more and more thirteenths are not the only days she stays in bed: a morning arrives in November, a leafless birdless coming

---

33. **Satsuma** (sat süm′ä), *n.* a type of tangerine.
34. **cavort** (kə vôrt′), *v.* prance about; jump around.
35. **wager** (wā′jər), *v.* make a bet; gamble.
36. **reveille-ridden.** Reveille (rev′ə lē) is the bugle or drum signal used to wake up soldiers; to be reveille-ridden is a way of saying the camp has too many disciplinary routines such as the daily reveille.

▲ GG Kopilak, *The Way It Is.* What do you think the title of this painting could mean?

of winter morning, when she cannot rouse herself to exclaim: "Oh my, it's fruitcake weather!"

And when that happens, I know it. A message saying so merely confirms a piece of news some secret vein had already received, severing[37] from me an irreplaceable part of myself, letting it loose like a kite on a broken string. That is why, walking across a school campus on this particular December morning, I keep searching the sky. As if I expected to see, rather like hearts, a lost pair of kites hurrying toward heaven.

37. **sever** (sev′ər), *v.* cut off.

After Reading

Making Connections

Shaping Your Response

1. What are the most memorable parts of the story for you? Why?

2. Do you think it was right for Buddy and his friend to be separated? Why or why not?

3. This story deals with a series of rather ordinary events. Why do you think they made such a lasting impression on Buddy?

Analyzing the Story

4. Why do you think Buddy's friend is shy with everyone but strangers?

5. The list of things Buddy's friend *never* does tells as much about her as the list of things she "has done, does do." What do the lists on page 369 reveal about her **character?**

6. The others in the house pay Buddy and his friend to swat flies. What does this reveal about how they view Buddy's friend?

7. 👁 What are some ways that Buddy and his friend express their **individuality?**

8. At the end of the story, Buddy expects to see "a lost pair of kites hurrying toward heaven." What do you think he means?

9. Capote uses vivid **imagery** to describe different scenes in the story. Find five examples of imagery in "A Christmas Memory." Explain which senses they appeal to and what feelings they evoke.

Extending the Ideas

10. Go back to the list of qualities for a good friendship that you developed before reading the story. Decide whether the friendship between Buddy and his cousin has any of those qualities.

Literary Focus: Simile

A **simile** is a figure of speech, usually using *like* or *as,* that compares unlike things and reveals similarities between them. Truman Capote uses similes in "A Christmas Memory" to help create a vivid portrait of Buddy's wonderful and unlikely friendship. For example, after his friend dies, Buddy compares his feelings of loss and loneliness to being "loose like a kite on a broken string." Find two other similes that you think contribute to the vividness of the story and explain what they reveal.

Vocabulary Study

decease
dilapidated
festooned
inaugurate
noncommittal
potent
prosaic
scald
sever
squander

Use each of the listed vocabulary words in brief pieces written for your local newspaper. You can use the suggestions given below or make up your own articles. If necessary, use your Glossary for help with word meanings.

1. Use the words *festooned, noncommittal,* and *inaugurate* in a feature story describing the opening of a new shopping mall.

2. Use the words *decease, sever, dilapidated,* and *squander* in an editorial about an abandoned house in your neighborhood.

3. Use the words *prosaic, potent,* and *scald* to describe a new first-aid technique in the "Better Health" column.

Expressing Your Ideas

Writing Choices

Writer's Notebook Update One of the things that makes "A Christmas Memory" a great story is the unforgettable character of Buddy's friend. Look at what you wrote in your notebook about your older friend. Make a list of things that person has never done and another list of things that person has done or does do, like the lists Buddy creates about his friend.

Opposites Attract Sometimes people who seem to be very different can become good friends. Choose two characters or speakers from this unit who don't seem very much alike on the surface. Write the **valentines** they send to one another, revealing what each character values in the other.

Thanks, Buddy Buddy and his friend receive thank-you letters from all over the world for the fruitcakes they send to their special friends. With a partner, put together an **album** of the letters they receive over the years.

Other Options

Scene Soundtrack Capote uses rich sensory images to describe the places and events in "A Christmas Memory." Choose a favorite scene and reread it carefully, noting all the details Capote provides. Then create an **illustration** of the scene.

The Other Side of the Story Buddy says that the "others" in his family decide to send him away to military school. Who are these "others"? Why do they make such a decision? In a small group, improvise the conversation Buddy's relatives have when they decide to send him away to school. Present your **improvisation** to the class.

Family Matters

All in the Family

Social Studies Connection
As this article explains, learning about your ancestors can help make history come alive and enrich your sense of identity.

IN THE SHADE OF A *Family Tree*

Pleasures of Genealogy

by Robert D. San Souci

People have long been interested in where they came from—who their ancestors were, where these people lived, how and why they traveled often great distances. Recording one's family history is an ancient tradition. The biblical book Genesis lists the genealogy (a record of family descent from an ancestor or ancestors) of the great patriarchs (male heads of families), while the Gospel of St. Matthew lists the ancestors of Jesus. The *Anglo-Saxon Chronicle* recounts the descendants of the Saxon chieftains.

In traditional Chinese and Japanese ancestor worship, wooden tablets inscribed with the names and birth and death dates of the deceased are kept in the ancestral hall of a clan or in a household shrine. Many peoples without written records recall their ancestry through spoken recitations, such as those of African *griots* (grē′ōz), or elders. It is said that when a griot dies, it is as if a library has been burned to the ground.

Throughout history, keeping accurate accounts of royal family trees has been a vital means of establishing a person's right to rule.

From the pharaohs of Egypt to the British monarchs, certain families have steered the course of empires, and the fate of nations has been directly linked to the rulers' bloodlines. Today a person's ancestors may determine his or her place in society.

In Colonial America, settlers from Europe tended to stay in the same place. Children often raised their families near their parents' and grandparents' home. It was easy to keep tabs on where a person came from because there were always relatives and friends to remember.

But as frontiers expanded, new territories opened, and transportation became cheaper and less hazardous, people began to move greater distances in greater numbers. Sometimes they moved to better themselves, seeking land, gold, or new business opportunities. Sometimes they were forced to migrate because of war, famine, or social and political unrest. New immigrants arrived from Europe and scattered all across the country. Former slaves from the southern states moved in great numbers after the Civil War.

Today moving is a part of life for many

Several generations of the Solomon family gathered for this photograph taken at a family reunion. Have you seen similar photos of your own extended family?

families. It is not unusual for an American family to move every few years. In the process, many people lose a sense of their extended family because they lose touch with their ancestors and know little about how their family came to be where it is now.

Yet the desire to know remains a widespread human urge. There is great interest in uncovering one's family tree. Perhaps the most dramatic recent example was Alex Haley's *Roots,* in which he told how, as a boy in Tennessee, he would listen to his grandmother tell him stories that traced his family back for generations to a man she called "the African."

After ten years of research, Haley discovered that the name of "the African" was Kunta

Kinte; that he had been kidnapped from the village of Juffure in Gambia, West Africa, in 1767; and that he had been carried to Maryland and sold to a Virginia planter. Tracing the family history from his great-great-great-great-great-grandfather to himself, Haley uncovered generations of slaves, freedmen, farmers, blacksmiths, lumber mill workers, Pullman porters, lawyers, architects, and, finally, a writer—himself. Along the way, he discovered numerous relatives, living and dead, eventually even meeting his own African sixth cousins.

For some of us, tracing our family history back to our own roots may uncover a similar thicket of ancestral branches. For others, limited access to relatives or documents may produce a trail that peters out after a generation or two. However far back we can go, the rewards of finding out about our past make the effort worthwhile.

Several of my friends have traced their family histories, with some dramatic results. One discovered that his family name, Whitmore, came from the old English White Mere, meaning "white lake" or "white pond," and connected him with an old British family. Another friend cherishes the fact that he can trace his family name back to one of the families that arrived on the *Fortune,* the second ship to reach Plymouth colony in 1621.

A third friend followed his family back beyond the "melting pot" of Ellis Island (for years, the first stop for immigrants from Europe to America) to a small Russian village. His people had come to America to escape anti-Jewish pogroms (persecutions). Three years ago, he and his family returned to Russia for a visit. Though no family members remained in the region, he said that walking where his relatives once walked, breathing the air they breathed, and touching the stonework of buildings that were standing when they lived there was a moving and unforgettable experience.

When I was a child, I learned of a great castle named Sans Souci (the name, in French, means "without care" or "carefree"), built by King Frederick II of Prussia. I taped a photograph of that fairy-tale castle to my wall. I felt sure that, when I was old enough, I would trace my bloodline back to Frederick. Then I would lay claim to at least one wing of the castle.

In later years, I began checking my family tree. My mother's side of the family led me back to the south coast of Ireland and the small fishing village of Skibbereen, from which my maternal grandfather sailed to San Fran-

cisco in the early part of this century. There I felt a part of my past come alive.

Pursuing my "castle in Germany" dream through my father's family (in New England), I found that, to the best of an elder female relative's recollection, the family name, San Souci (no one can account for the missing "s" on "San") went back only to my great-great-great-grandfather and his brother (my

. . . I FELT A PART OF MY PAST COME ALIVE.

great-great-great-granduncle). They had emigrated from England and settled in Quebec (French-speaking Canada). There they learned French and made a good living as barbers. They also were great jesters and became know as *les frères sans souci* (the carefree brothers). Before they changed the name to San Souci, the family name was Fraham.

At first I was disappointed to find my German castle replaced by a barbershop. But the story is such a delightful one that, in a way, I feel richer for knowing it.

Responding

1. According to the author, why are people so interested in their family trees?

2. Do some research on a grandparent, great-grandparent, or someone even further back in your family's history. Interview relatives to learn more about the person, and present what you learn in an interesting narrative.

INTERDISCIPLINARY STUDY

Fine Art Connection
Artists around the world have
explored the concept of family in
their work, as the images on these
pages demonstrate.

THE *Family* IN Art

▲ *Different Generations,* a 1992 painting by Chickasaw
painter Mike Larsen, uses strong color and sweeping
images to depict several generations in a family.

In *Midnight Mother and Sleepy Child,* a wood-
block print, Japanese artist Kitagawa Utamaro
(1753–1806) captures a tender moment between
mother and child. ➤

Family members of different generations are also portrayed in *The Banjo Lesson* (1893) by Henry O. Tanner. Notice the artist's use of light.

The relaxed pose of the children in *Two Children at the Seashore* (1884) was characteristic of the work of American Impressionist painter Mary Cassatt. What elements hint that the two children are sisters?

Henry Moore's bronze sculpture, *Family Group* (1948–1949), stands nearly five feet tall. What does the "body language" of the three figures reveal about them?

Responding

1. Describe the mood of each of these works of art.

2. What different aspects of family relationships are revealed in these images?

Writing Workshop

Moments in Time

Assignment In a saturation recall paper, the writer recreates an event from memory so vividly that the reader comes away with a *you are there* feeling. Now that you've read about other writers' memories, write a saturation recall paper about a memory of your own.

WRITER'S BLUEPRINT

Product	A saturation recall paper
Purpose	To describe a childhood memory in vivid detail
Audience	Family members and friends
Specs	As the writer of a successful paper, you should:

❏ Choose a memorable event from your childhood, such as a picnic, a reunion, or a vacation. Saturate yourself in the event—recall every detail you can about the experience.

❏ Tell what happened in time order, from start to finish, using first-person ("I") point of view.

❏ Use vivid sensory details to tell the reader how things sounded, felt, and smelled, as well as how they looked.

❏ Show, rather than tell, how you were feeling as the event took place.

❏ End by explaining why this memory has special significance for you.

❏ Follow the rules of grammar, usage, spelling, and mechanics. Use adjectives and adverbs correctly.

STEP **1** PREWRITING

Revisit the literature and react to it. Reread some of the selections and make a list of key sensory details that each author uses to bring memories to life. Then imagine yourself at the scene and write how you, as a child, might have reacted to these details. For example, here are details and reactions you might have noted from the Literary Source:

- crunch of pecans—excited at the sound

- sweet oily ivory meat—full of hungry anticipation

Brainstorm childhood memories with friends and family members. You might look through old photo albums, letters, and other memorabilia for ideas. Make a list. Rate each memory in terms of how well you remember it, from 10 (in great detail) down to 1 (in little detail). Then choose the one you'll write about.

Plan your writing. Create a moment-by-moment outline of your memory from start to finish. Make a chart as shown, using the number of boxes appropriate for your event. Fill in each box with pencil so you can change it. To complete the chart, explain why the event is special to you.

What happened first	Details
What happened next *and so on . . .*	Details
Why this event is special	

LITERARY SOURCE
"Caarackle! A cheery crunch, scraps of miniature thunder sound as the shells collapse and the golden mound of sweet oily ivory meat mounts in the milk-glass bowl."
    from "A Christmas Memory" by Truman Capote

OR . . .
Describe the event, using a tape recorder, as if you were telling a friend about it. Then listen to the tape and create a chart like the one here, or make an index card for each happening.

STEP 2 DRAFTING

As you draft, keep these drafting tips in mind:

- Write in present tense, as if the event were happening now, or in past tense, looking back on it as a memory.

- Keep family photos or artifacts that relate to the event in front of you. They should help jog your memory.

STEP 3 REVISING

Ask a partner for comments on your draft before you revise it.

✔ Have I told about the event in time order, from start to finish?

✔ Does my writing show rather than tell?

Revising Strategy

Showing, Not Telling

To give your readers a *you are there* feeling, don't just tell them what happened. Use descriptive words and phrases to *show* them what happened.

Telling   Christmas morning was always exciting for us kids. The Christmas tree was beautiful and loaded with presents.

Showing   At last, Christmas morning. We waited—whispering, giggling, and shaking with the cold and excitement. We crept downstairs, holding hands, afraid to breathe. Suddenly, we could see it! The Christmas tree—glowing and twinkling, and holding all the visions that had danced inside our heads for weeks.

Notice how the student model was revised to *show* the event in greater detail.

STUDENT MODEL

Finally it was time to leave. We ~~loaded up our luggage and got into~~ *squeezed ourselves and about a ton of luggage into* the car. ~~We had a lot of stuff and it was pretty crowded. It made riding in~~ *We were packed in like sardines. My brother and I jammed the* ~~the car uncomfortable for my brother and me and we fought a lot.~~ *cooler Mom had packed between us and argued bitterly about who had more room.* My dad

was never one to make a lot of stops so we knew we had a long ride ahead

of us. Space was at a premium. Finally, we each settled into our respective

corners and braced ourselves for another family vacation.

STEP 4 EDITING

Ask a partner to review your revised draft before you edit. When you edit, look for errors in grammar, usage, spelling, and mechanics. Be sure to use adjectives and adverbs correctly.

Editing Strategy

Using Adjectives and Adverbs Correctly

Use adjectives and adverbs correctly when you write. Remember that the adjectives *good* and *bad* modify nouns and that the adverbs *well* and *badly* modify verbs. Don't confuse them.

Don't write: This car runs bad.
Write: This car runs badly.

Don't write: This car runs good.
Write: This car runs well.

> **FOR REFERENCE**
> See the Language and Grammar Handbook at the back of this book for more information on the correct use of adjectives and adverbs.

STEP 5 PRESENTING

- Collect the essays of classmates who grew up in several different cultures. Create displays and present essays to show the similarities and differences between life in these various cultures.

- Re-create the special event you wrote about by turning your paper into a script. Have classmates help you act out the scene.

STEP 6 LOOKING BACK

Self-evaluate. What grade would *you* give your paper? Look back at the Writer's Blueprint and give your paper a score for each point, from 6 (superior) to 1 (inadequate).

Reflect. What have you learned from writing this paper? Write your responses to these questions.

 Did writing this paper change the way you remember the event? Explain.

✔ Put your paper away for a few days and then take it out and read it again. How does it look to you now? What do you see about it now that you didn't see a few days ago?

For Your Working Portfolio Add your paper and your reflection responses to your working portfolio.

Beyond Print

Looking at Television Families

Generations of television viewers have grown up watching situation comedies about families. Early family sitcoms such as *I Love Lucy* provided an amusing escape from reality by presenting silly characters in unrealistic situations that came to a happy conclusion in thirty minutes. While many sitcoms still follow that formula, others tackle issues in a more realistic way, or even exaggerate the *worst* aspects of family life. Can you name shows that fit into each of those categories?

Imagine that you have been asked to create a new family sitcom for a ten- to fifteen-year-old TV audience. Prepare a report that describes your new show by listing "ingredients" such as these:

The Jetson family enjoyed all the comforts of space-age living in *The Jetsons*, a popular show in the 1960s. ▼

The Characters. Describe the characters in your show, including family members, neighbors, friends, and other recurring characters.

The Costumes. Make sketches or clip images from magazines that show what your characters will wear.

The Set. Make a diagram or write a description of the interior and exterior appearance of your television family's home. Include details about furniture, decorations, and even color schemes.

The Problems. Briefly describe some of the main conflicts and issues among the characters. Describe the tone of your show—are you aiming for silly escapism, realistic humor, or dark comedy?

Activity Options

1. Write a script and videotape the opening episode of your new sitcom.

2. Choose a classic family sitcom and list its "ingredients." Compare that list with the list you created for your own sitcom.

Part Two

Songs of Hope

Do you see a glass of water as being half full, or half empty? The following selections will introduce you to people who refuse to give up on life, and who choose instead to work toward a future full of hope.

Multicultural Connection **Choice** may be influenced by cultural situations and settings. In the following selections, what are the cultural and social situations that the speakers find themselves in? What choices do the speakers make to affirm hopeful possibilities in life?

Literature

Interdisciplinary Study Seeds of Change

Writing Workshop Persuasive Writing

Beyond Print Effective Speaking

Before Reading

The Exhibit by Lisel Mueller

Lucinda Matlock by Edgar Lee Masters

Oye Mundo/ Sometimes by Jesús Papoleto Meléndez

Saturday Afternoon, When Chores Are Done by Harryette Mullen

Building Background

Daring to Believe The following poems speak of hope in the face of grief or adversity. Lisel Mueller's poem "The Exhibit" is about a man who was a prisoner of war during World War II. Prisoners of war often lived in filthy conditions with little food or water for months or years at a time. Hope for freedom and peace was all that kept them alive. In Edgar Lee Masters's poem "Lucinda Matlock," a woman speaks of life from her grave. The poem is from *Spoon River Anthology,* Masters's most famous book, in which the poems are narrated by the deceased residents of the imaginary town of Spoon River.

Literary Focus

Rhythm Like music, spoken and written language have **rhythm.** You use rhythm all the time in conversation to express ideas or convey emotion. Poets achieve rhythm in the way they arrange stressed and unstressed sounds. The rhythm in a poem may have a regular, predictable beat; it may be varied to emphasize different moods or situations; or it may be irregular to resemble natural speech or conversation. Pay attention to the use of rhythm in the following poems. What effects does each author achieve through rhythm?

Writer's Notebook

Hope Is Where You Find It The speakers in the following poems find hope in different ways. Before you begin reading, consider what makes you feel hopeful, even in the most difficult circumstances. Jot down some sources of hope in your life.

Lisel Mueller
born 1924

Lisel Mueller has published five books of poetry and has translated several works from German into English. Her awards for poetry include the American Book Award, the Lamont Poetry Prize, and the Theodore Roethke Prize. Born in Germany, Mueller is now a U.S. citizen, and has taught in a number of universities as a visiting writer.

Edgar Lee Masters
1868–1950

Though Edgar Lee Masters loved writing, his father urged him to become a lawyer. Masters worked for eight years in partnership with the renowned liberal lawyer Clarence Darrow. He never abandoned his writing, however, and published his poems and stories in magazines for many years while practicing law. *Spoon River Anthology,* a collection of Masters's poems and short stories about small town life in Illinois, was published in 1915 and became immediately popular.

Jesús Papoleto Meléndez
born 1950

Originally a high school dropout, Puerto Rican writer Jesús Papoleto Meléndez eventually went back to school and continued his studies at City College of New York and Hunter College. He grew interested in writing while participating in the Fieldston School Upward Bound Program and Teachers & Writers Collaborative. In addition to publishing several volumes of poetry, Meléndez writes plays. He currently lives in New York City.

Harryette Mullen
born 1953

Born in Florence, Alabama, Harryette Mullen has lived over the years in Texas, California, and New York. While living in Austin, Texas, she taught creative writing classes in local schools through a poets-in-the-schools program. She has written many articles on African American literature, and her poems and prose have been widely published in magazines, journals, and anthologies. Mullen earned a Ph.D. in literature in 1990, and she currently teaches at the University of Southern California in Los Angeles.

The last of a series of late medieval tapestries depicting a hunt for a unicorn, this shows the magical beast in captivity. One writer described this unicorn as being "in captivity, yet free." What do you think she meant?

The Exhibit

L I S E L   M U E L L E R

My uncle in East Germany
points to the unicorn in the painting
and explains it is now extinct.
We correct him, say such a creature
5 never existed. He does not argue,
but we know he does not believe us.
He is certain power and gentleness
must have gone hand in hand
once. A prisoner of war
10 even after the war was over,
my uncle needs to believe in something
that could not be captured except by love,
whose single luminous horn
redeemed¹ the murderous forest
15 and, dipped into foul water,
would turn it pure. This world,
this terrible world we live in,
is not the only possible one,
his eighty-year-old eyes insist,
20 dry wells that fill so easily now.

---

1. **redeem** (ri dēm′), *v.* make up for; set free, save, or rescue.

Lucinda Matlock

EDGAR LEE MASTERS

I went to dances at Chandlerville,
And played snap-out at Winchester.
One time we changed partners,
Driving home in the moonlight of middle June,
5 And then I found Davis.
We were married and lived together for seventy years,
Enjoying, working, raising the twelve children,
Eight of whom we lost
Ere[1] I had reached the age of sixty.
10 I spun, I wove, I kept the house, I nursed the sick,
I made the garden, and for holiday

Rambled over the fields where sang the larks,
And by Spoon River[2] gathering many a shell,
And many a flower and medicinal[3] weed——
15 Shouting to the wooded hills, singing to the green valleys.
At ninety-six I had lived enough, that is all,
And passed to a sweet repose.[4]
What is this I hear of sorrow and weariness,
Anger, discontent, and drooping hopes?
20 Degenerate[5] sons and daughters,
Life is too strong for you——
It takes life to love Life.

---

1. **ere** (er), old English for *before.*
2. **Spoon River,** small stream near the town where Edgar Lee Masters grew up and where his grandmother, Lucinda Matlock, lived.
3. **medicinal** (mə dis′n əl), *adj.* having value as medicine; healing; helping; relieving.
4. **repose** (ri pōz′), *n.* rest or sleep; peace, calmness.
5. **degenerate** (di jen′ər it′), *adj.* showing a decline in physical, mental, or moral strength.

OYE MUNDO/ SOMETIMES

JESÚS
PAPOLETO
MELÉNDEZ

sometimes (
      when the night air feels *chévere*[1]
) when i can hear the real sound
of *el barrio*[2]
5 on *la conga   y timbales*[3]
coke bottles
& garbage can tops

      when i can feel
      & reallyreally touch
10   *la música latina/   africana*[4]

& the fingerpoppin soul
emergin from tears/   sweet tears of laughter

      & i can feel
      a conglomeration[5] of vibrations/
15   heat waves
      body waves
      people waves
      of real *gente*[6]
      /& i feel goooooooood

20 when i can taste the rare culture
of *cuchifritos   y lechón*[7]
chitterlins[8]   & black-eyed peas
& corn bread

      & *la pompa*[9] is open
25   & cooooooools the hot tar
      of summer heated streets
      where children play
      kick-the-can (
& sirens
30 cannot be heard)

      /sometimes

sometimes
when the last of the ghetto[10] poets
writes of flowers
35 growin in gutters   /& i know it's real

      /sometimes

A Romare Bearden, detail from *The Block* (1971). This collage depicts the busy life of a big-city neighborhood. Is the attitude toward urban life reflected in this image positive or negative? Explain.

sometimes/ sometimes
when i can almost hear /being echoed back
an answer
40 to my ghetto cry

sometimes/ sometimes
i run up the fire escape/ not to escape
& climb on the roof
& stand on the ledge
45 & look down
& yell out
to the midnight world
below
above
50 around
within:

OYE MUNDO TU ERES BONITO!!![11]

& i forget about the junkies
on the stoop.

1. *chévere* (che′ve rā), good, happy. [Spanish]
2. *el barrio* (el bä′rē ō), the neighborhood. [Spanish]
3. *la conga y timbales* (lä kōn′gä ē tēm bä′läs), conga music and kettledrums. [Spanish]
4. *la música latina/ africana* (la mŭ′sē kä lä tē′nä ä frē kä′nä), Latin/African music. [Spanish]
5. conglomeration (kən glom′ə rā′shən), *n.* a mixed-up mass of various things or persons; mixture.
6. *gente* (hen′tā), people. [Spanish]
7. *cuchifritos y lechón. Cuchifritos* (cŭ′chē frē′tōs) refers to fried food sold on the street. *Lechón* (le chōn′) is pork. [Spanish]
8. chitterlins (chit′ėr lins), *n.* slang for *chitterlings,* intestines of animals cooked as food.
9. *la pompa* (lä pōm′pä), slang for fire hydrant (from *pump).* [Spanish]
10. ghetto (get′ō), *n.* part of a city where a particular racial group or nationality lives.
11. *Oye mundo tú eres bonito* (ō′yā mün′dō tü e′res bō nē′tō), Listen world you are beautiful. [Spanish]

▲ *Braids* (1995) by American painter Arnold Rice shows a quiet domestic scene of a mother braiding her daughter's hair. How do the shapes of the chair and the mother's arms contribute to the mood of this painting?

Saturday Afternoon, When Chores Are Done

HARRYETTE MULLEN

I've cleaned house
and the kitchen smells like pine.
I can hear the kids yelling
through the back screen door.
5   While they play tug-of-war
with an old jumprope
and while these blackeyed peas
boil on the stove,
I'm gonna sit here at the table
10 and plait[1] my hair.

I oil my hair and brush it soft.
Then, with the brush in my lap,
I gather the hair in my hands,
pull the strands smooth and tight,
15 and weave three sections into a fat
   shiny braid
that hangs straight down my back.

I remember mama teaching me to plait
   my hair
one Saturday afternoon when chores
   were done.
My fingers were stubby and short.
20 I could barely hold three strands at once,
and my braids would fray apart
no sooner than I'd finished them.
Mama said, "Just takes practice, is all."
Now my hands work swiftly, doing easy
25 what was once so hard to do.

Between time on the job,
keeping house, and raising two girls
   by myself,
there's never much time like this,
for thinking and being alone.
30 Time to gather life together
before it unravels like an old jumprope
and comes apart at the ends.

Suddenly I notice the silence.
The noisy tug-of-war has stopped.
35 I get up to check out back,
see what my girls are up to now.
I look out over the kitchen sink,
where the sweet potato plant
spreads green in the window.
40 They sit quietly on the back porch steps,
Melinda plaiting Carla's hair
into a crooked braid.

Older daughter,
you are learning what I am learning:
45 to gather the strands together
with strong fingers,
to keep what we do
from coming apart at the ends.

---

1. **plait** (plāt), *v.* braid.

After Reading

Making Connections

Shaping Your Response

1. What music would you choose to represent the **tone** of "The Exhibit"? Why?

2. Write three words to describe the **character** Lucinda Matlock.

3. Do you think "Oye Mundo/ Sometimes" ends on an optimistic or pessimistic note? Explain.

4. Describe the **mood** of "Saturday Afternoon, When Chores Are Done."

Analyzing the Poems

5. Why does the uncle in "The Exhibit" need to believe in the unicorn?

6. What do you think the speaker in "Lucinda Matlock" means when she says, "It takes life to love Life"?

7. What **images** does the speaker of "Oye Mundo/ Sometimes" use to convey joy and sadness? Give examples.

8. In your own words, state a **theme** that you find in "Saturday Afternoon, When Chores Are Done."

Extending the Ideas

9. Draw a larger version of the web shown here. Then fill in the circles to show the sources of hope in each poem.

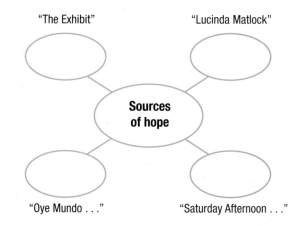

"The Exhibit"   "Lucinda Matlock"

Sources of hope

"Oye Mundo . . ."   "Saturday Afternoon . . ."

Literary Focus: Understanding Rhythm

Think back to what you learned about **rhythm** before reading the poems. Each poet uses rhythm to emphasize ideas or create a particular mood. For example, Edgar Lee Masters uses an irregular rhythm to resemble ordinary conversational speech—the way you would expect Lucinda Matlock to speak. Choose one of the poems and describe its rhythm and the effect its rhythm creates. Support your answer with specific examples.

Vocabulary Study

Write the letter of the word that is most nearly the opposite in meaning to the italicized vocabulary word. If necessary, use your Glossary for help with word meanings.

conglomeration
degenerate
medicinal
redeem
repose

1. *conglomeration:* (A) separation (B) gathering (C) clarity (D) mixture
2. *degenerate:* (A) obedient (B) decayed (C) careless (D) vigorous
3. *medicinal:* (A) poisonous (B) healthy (C) natural (D) dry
4. *redeem:* (A) retrieve (B) destroy (C) betray (D) save
5. *repose:* (A) sleep (B) agitation (C) anticipation (D) patience

Expressing Your Ideas

Writing Choices

Writer's Notebook Update Review the sources of hope you wrote about in your notebook. Then come up with a symbol to represent the source of hope you wrote about. For example, in "The Exhibit," the unicorn is a symbol of purity and gentleness. In your notebook, explain why your symbol represents hope to you.

To Whom It May Concern Choose one of the poems and write a **letter** to the speaker or one of the characters. You may write whatever you like, as long as it relates to the poem. For example, you may argue with the speaker, express sympathy, ask questions, or share a related experience of your own.

Points of View Edgar Lee Masters based his poem "Lucinda Matlock" on his real-life grandmother. "The Exhibit" gives the point of view of the speaker's elderly uncle. Think of an older person you know and write a **poem** from his or her point of view. You may write about the past, the state of the world today, or both.

Other Options

This Must Be the Place Many people carry an image in their mind of a place they find beautiful, peaceful, or inspiring, like the Spoon River in "Lucinda Matlock" or the rooftop in "Oye Mundo/ Sometimes." Find or make a **visual image,** such as a drawing, photograph, sculpture, etc., of a place that is inspiring or meaningful to you. On a separate notecard, provide a brief explanation of where the place is (even if it is in your imagination) and why it is important to you. You might create an exhibit of the images with your classmates.

On the Issues With a small group, plan a **panel discussion** with characters from the four poems appearing as speakers. Determine what character each of you will play and what issues you will discuss in the panel. Some possible speakers for the panels are the uncle in "The Exhibit" and the speaker in "Saturday Afternoon, When Chores Are Done."

Before Reading

Jazz Fantasia by Carl Sandburg
Nothing but Drums by Oscar Hijuelos
I Am Singing Now by Luci Tapahonso

Building Background

Music Dreams The following poems are about music, and the language used in them has strong musical qualities. Language and music have a lot in common. Both have rhythm, tone, and mood, which help convey meaning and affect our emotions. Although music generally has a more regular rhythm than language, some types of language, such as poetry, are more rhythmic than others. Some song lyrics, even without musical accompaniment, still have a strong musical rhythm. Bring in some examples of rhythmic lyrics to share with the class.

Literary Focus

Onomatopoeia and Rhythm Bike spokes hum, bears galumph, raindrops plip, and sand shishes: These are examples of **onomatopoeia,** words whose sound resembles or imitates their meaning. A poem's **rhythm** can also imitate its meaning, or subject. Alexander Pope illustrates this idea in his *Essay on Criticism:*

> When Ajax strives, some rock's vast weight to throw,
> The line too labors, and the words move slow;
> Not so, when swift Camilla scours the plain,
> Flies o'er th' unbending corn, and skims along the main.

In this example, the sound and rhythm of the lines reinforce their meaning: The first two lines move slowly (like throwing a huge rock), while the third and fourth lines move quickly (like running). Listen for onomatopoeia and rhythm as you read the poems in this section.

Writer's Notebook

Word Inventions When onomatopoetic words or phrases are overused, they become clichéd and uninteresting and lose their effectiveness. For example, how many times have you heard these expressions: buzzing bees, chirping birds, or roaring lions? Being as creative and original as possible, make a list of onomatopoetic words. You may use words you know or make up your own.

Carl Sandburg
1878–1967

Carl Sandburg was born in Galesburg, Illinois, the son of Swedish parents. He didn't distinguish himself in school, but received recognition for his writing ability at an early age. As a young man, he traveled widely, fought in the Spanish-American War, and worked as an organizer for the Social Democratic Party. When his first book of poetry was published in 1916, he quickly became a popular national figure, particularly in Chicago, the setting for many of the poems. In addition to poetry, Sandburg wrote articles, children's books, biographies, and an autobiography.

Oscar Hijuelos
born 1951

As a young boy, Oscar Hijuelos (ē hwe′lōs) became severely ill and spent two years in a hospital for terminally ill children. Although he recovered and returned home, he often missed school and spent much of his childhood inside drawing and reading comic books. Today, he says he still views life as a solitary experience. In 1990, his best-selling book *The Mambo Kings Play Songs of Love* won the Pulitzer Prize, making Hijuelos the first Latino to win the prestigious award. The son of Cuban immigrants, Hijuelos still lives in the New York City neighborhood where he grew up.

Luci Tapahonso
born 1953

Luci Tapahonso, a Navajo Indian, believes that for people like herself who live apart from their homelands, "writing is a means for . . . restoring our spirits to the state of *hozho,* or beauty, which is the basis of Navajo philosophy." Tapahonso has written several books of poetry. Born in Shiprock, New Mexico, Tapahonso currently teaches English at the University of New Mexico in Albuquerque. Her writing often combines poetry, songs, prayers, and stories about Navajo life.

▲ American artist Gil Mayers gave no title to this painting of musicians and instruments. What title would you give to it?

JAZZ FANTASIA

CARL SANDBURG

Drum on your drums, batter on your banjoes,
sob on the long cool winding saxophones.
Go to it, O jazzmen.

Sling your knuckles on the bottoms of the happy
5   tin pans, let your trombones ooze, and go husha-
husha-hush with the slippery sand-paper.

Moan like an autumn wind high in the lonesome treetops, moan soft like
you wanted somebody terrible, cry like a racing car slipping away from a
motorcycle cop, bang-bang! you jazzmen, bang altogether drums, traps,
10 banjoes, horns, tin cans—make two people fight on the top of a stairway
and scratch each other's eyes in a clinch tumbling down the stairs.

Can the rough stuff . . . now a Mississippi steamboat pushes up the night
river with a hoo-hoo-hoo-oo . . . and the green lanterns calling to the high
soft stars . . . a red moon rides on the humps of the low river hills . . .
15 go to it, O jazzmen.

Nothing but Drums

OSCAR HIJUELOS

And now nothing but drums,
a battery of drums, the conga drums jamming out,
in a *descarga*,[1]
and the drummers lifting their heads and
5   shaking under some kind of spell.
There's rain drums, like pitter-patter pitter-patter
but a hundred times faster, and then
slamming-the-door-drums
and dropping-the-bucket-drums, kicking-the-car-fender
10 drums. Then circus drums,
then coconuts-falling-out-of-the-trees-and
thumping-against-the-ground-drums, then lion-skin drums,
then the-whacking-of-a-hand-against-a-wall drums,
the beating-of-a-pillow drums, heavy-stones-against-a-wall drums,
15 then the-mountain-rumble drums, then the-little-birds-learning
to-fly drums and the big-birds-alighting-on-a-rooftop
and fanning-their-immense-wings drums, then a-boat
down-the-river-with
its-oars-dropping-heavily
20 into-the-water
drums.

---

1. *descarga* (des cär′gä), release or discharge. [Spanish]

▲ Sherri Silverman, *Crescent Moon over the Southwest.* What elements in the painting draw the viewer into the desert landscape?

I Am Singing Now

LUCI TAPAHONSO

the moon is a white sliver
balancing the last of its contents
in the final curve of the month
my daughters sleep
5 in the back of the pickup
breathing small clouds of white in the dark
they lie warm and soft
under layers of clothes and blankets
how they dream, precious ones, of grandma
10   and the scent of fire
the smell of mutton[1]
they are already home

i watch the miles dissolve behind us
in the hazy glow of taillights and
15 the distinct shape of hills and mesas[2] loom above
          then recede slowly in the clear winter night.

i sing to myself and
think of my father
          teaching me, leaning towards me
20   listening as i learned.
          "just like this," he would say
and he would sing those old songs

          into the fiber of my hair,
          into the pores of my skin,
25   into the dreams of my children
and i am singing now
for the night
          the almost empty moon
and the land swimming beneath cold bright stars.

---

1. **mutton** (mut′n), *n.* the meat of a mature sheep.
2. **mesa** (mā′sə), *n.* flat-topped natural elevation.

After Reading

Making Connections

Shaping Your Response

1. Choose the most memorable **image** from one of these poems and read it aloud to a partner. Explain why it is memorable for you.

2. What is your favorite drumming sound in "Nothing but Drums"? Why?

3. Write two questions for the speaker in "I Am Singing Now."

Analyzing the Poems

4. Describe the different moods of jazz represented in the third and fourth stanzas of "Jazz Fantasia."

5. How does "Nothing but Drums" convey the **rhythm** of everyday life? Give examples.

6. Describe the **mood** of each of these three poems.

Extending the Ideas

7. Explain what you think music **symbolizes** in each of these poems.

Literary Focus: Onomatopoeia and Rhythm

You have learned that **onomatopoeia** is the use of words whose sound suggests their meaning or imitates associated sounds. Writers use onomatopoeia to create precise, vivid images or dramatic effects. For example, in "Jazz Fantasia," Carl Sandburg uses the words "drum," "batter," and "sob" to imitate jazz sounds. He also imitates different moods of jazz music by changing the poem's **rhythm** from fast and jumpy to slow and romantic. Find other examples of onomatopoeia and rhythm in one of the poems and explain their effect.

Expressing Your Ideas

Writing Choices

Writer's Notebook Update You've learned a lot about **onomatopoeia** from reading the poems in this section. Use your list of onomatopoetic words to write a few lines of descriptive poetry. Share your piece with the class.

Another Option

Beat of Life Work with students in your group to think of other kinds of drumming from everyday life that could be added to "Nothing but Drums." Combine your ideas in a **performance piece,** with each member of the group reciting a line of poetry and then playing a corresponding drum sound. Perform your piece for the class.

I Have a Dream

by Martin Luther King, Jr.

Martin Luther King, Jr.
1929–1968

In 1964, the Nobel Peace Prize was awarded to American Baptist minister Martin Luther King, Jr., for his accomplishments as a civil rights leader. Born in Atlanta, Georgia, King attended Morehouse College, Crozer Theological Seminary, and Boston University. He first achieved national prominence in 1955 when he led a nonviolent boycott of a bus line in Montgomery, Alabama, protesting the policy of segregating black and white passengers. The protest helped bring about the U.S. Supreme Court ruling that segregation on public transit facilities was unconstitutional. Although King was assassinated in 1968, his teachings continue to inspire people throughout the world.

Building Background

King's Dream As a graduate student at Boston University, Martin Luther King, Jr., was deeply influenced by two well-known advocates of civil disobedience and passive resistance—American writer Henry David Thoreau and Indian leader Mohandas Gandhi. After King's successful leadership of the Montgomery bus boycott of 1955, he founded the Southern Christian Leadership Conference (SCLC), a civil rights organization committed to nonviolent protest and action. With the SCLC as a base, King built a powerful nonviolent civil rights movement in the United States. One of the high points of the civil rights struggle was the March on Washington on August 28, 1963. Nearly a quarter of a million blacks and whites gathered at the Lincoln Memorial to show solidarity and pressure Congress to pass a strong civil rights bill. The massive crowd listened in hushed awe as King delivered his now famous "I Have a Dream" speech.

Literary Focus

Metaphor A **metaphor** is an implied comparison between two essentially unlike things. Metaphors are like similes except they do not use the words *like* or *as.* Writers use metaphor to highlight certain aspects of the subject they are writing about. If you talk about a "valley of despair" or an "oasis of freedom," as King does in his speech, you are using metaphors to describe aspects of despair and freedom. As you read, look for other metaphors in King's speech.

Writer's Notebook

What's Your Impression? You've probably heard of Martin Luther King, Jr.'s "I Have a Dream" speech. Perhaps you have read or heard parts of it before. Write down what you think the speech is about based on what you've heard or remember. You might also jot down any questions you have about the speech.

I Have a Dream . . .

MARTIN LUTHER KING, JR.

I am happy to join with you today in what will go down in history as the greatest demonstration for freedom in the history of our nation.

Fivescore[1] years ago, a great American, in whose symbolic shadow we stand, signed the Emancipation Proclamation.[2] This momentous decree came as a great beacon light of hope to millions of Negro slaves who had been seared[3] in the flames of withering injustice. It came as a joyous daybreak to end the long night of their captivity.

But one hundred years later, the Negro is still not free; one hundred years later, the life of the Negro is still sadly crippled by the manacles[4] of segregation and the chains of discrimination; one hundred years later, the Negro lives on a lonely island of poverty in the midst of a vast ocean of material prosperity; one hundred years later, the Negro is still languished[5] in the corners of American society and finds himself an exile in his own land.

So we've come here today to dramatize a shameful condition. In a sense we've come to our

---

1. **fivescore** (fīv′ skôr), *adj.* one hundred.
2. **Emancipation Proclamation,** an executive order issued by Abraham Lincoln on January 1, 1863, that outlawed slavery in many parts of the U.S.
3. **seared** (sird), *adj.* burned or charred.
4. **manacle** (man′ə kəl), *n.* restraint or cuff for the hands.
5. **languished** (lang′gwisht), *adj.* neglected; diminished; dispirited.

At the climax of the 1963 civil rights March on Washington, more than 250,000 people listened to Martin Luther King, Jr., deliver his celebrated "I Have a Dream" speech. In his speech Dr. King uses a roll call of American landscapes to help express his message of freedom. Do you think the setting of his speech reinforced that message?

nation's capital to cash a check. When the architects of our republic wrote the magnificent words of the Constitution and the Declaration of Independence, they were signing a promissory note[6] to which every American was to fall heir. This note was the promise that all men, yes, black men as well as white men, would be

Now is the time to make real the promises of democracy. . . .

guaranteed the unalienable[7] rights of life, liberty, and the pursuit of happiness.

It is obvious today that America has defaulted[8] on this promissory note insofar as her citizens of color are concerned. Instead of honoring this sacred obligation, America has given the Negro people a bad check; a check which has come back marked "insufficient funds." We refuse to believe that there are insufficient funds in the great vaults of opportunity of this nation. And so we've come to cash this check, a check that will give us upon demand the riches of freedom and the security of justice.

We have also come to this hallowed spot to remind America of the fierce urgency of now. This is no time to engage in the luxury of cooling off or to take the tranquilizing[9] drug of gradualism.[10] Now is the time to make real the promises of democracy; now is the time to rise from the dark and desolate[11] valley of segregation to the sunlit path of racial justice; now is the time to lift our nation from the quicksands of racial injustice to the solid rock of brotherhood; now is the time to make justice a reality for all of God's children. It would be fatal for the nation to overlook the urgency of the moment. This sweltering[12] summer of the Negro's legitimate[13] discontent will not pass until there is an invigorating[14] autumn of freedom and equality.

Nineteen sixty-three is not an end, but a beginning. And those who hope that the Negro needed to blow off steam and will now be content, will have a rude awakening if the nation returns to business as usual.

There will be neither rest nor tranquility in America until the Negro is granted his citizenship rights. The whirlwinds of revolt will continue to shake the foundations of our nation until the bright day of justice emerges.

But there is something that I must say to my people who stand on the warm threshold which leads into the palace of justice. In the process of gaining our rightful place we must not be guilty of wrongful deeds.

Let us not seek to satisfy our thirst for freedom by drinking from the cup of bitterness and hatred. We must forever conduct our struggle on the high plane of dignity and discipline. We must not allow our creative protest to degenerate[15] into physical violence. Again and again we must rise to the majestic heights of meeting physical force with soul force.

The marvelous new militancy[16] which has engulfed the Negro community must not lead

---

6. **promissory note** (prom′ə sôr′ē nōt′), written promise to pay a stated sum of money to a certain person or persons at a certain time.
7. **unalienable** (un ā′lyə nə bəl), *adj.* that cannot be given or taken away. Also, **inalienable**.
8. default (di fôlt′), *v.* fail to do something or to appear somewhere when due; neglect.
9. **tranquilizing** (trang′kwə līz ing), *adj.* calming, quieting.
10. **gradualism** (graj′ü ə liz′əm), *n.* principle or method of gradual, as opposed to immediate, change.
11. desolate (des′ə lit), *adj.* joyless; barren, lifeless; without warmth, comfort, or hope.
12. sweltering (swel′tər ing), *adj.* extremely and unpleasantly hot.
13. legitimate (lə jit′ə mit), *adj.* rightful; valid; logical.
14. invigorating (in vig′ə rā′ting), *adj.* energizing.
15. **degenerate** (di jen′ə rāt′), *v.* grow worse.
16. **militancy** (mil′ə tən sē), *n.* warlike behavior or tendency; militant spirit.

us to a distrust of all white people, for many of our white brothers, as evidenced by their presence here today, have come to realize that their destiny is tied up with our destiny and they have come to realize that their freedom is inextricably[17] bound to our freedom. This offense we share mounted to storm the battlements of injustice must be carried forth by a biracial army. We cannot walk alone.

And as we walk, we must make the pledge that we shall always march ahead. We cannot turn back. There are those who are asking the devotees[18] of civil rights, "When will you be satisfied?" We can never be satisfied as long as the Negro is the victim of the unspeakable horrors of police brutality.

We can never be satisfied as long as our bodies, heavy with the fatigue of travel, cannot gain lodging in the motels of the highways and the hotels of the cities. We cannot be satisfied as long as the Negro's basic mobility[19] is from a smaller ghetto to a larger one.

Let us not seek to satisfy our thirst for freedom by drinking from the cup of bitterness and hatred.

We can never be satisfied as long as our children are stripped of their selfhood and robbed of their dignity by signs stating "for whites only." We cannot be satisfied as long as a Negro in Mississippi cannot vote and a Negro in New York believes he has nothing for which to vote. No, we are not satisfied, and we will not be satisfied until justice rolls down like waters and righteousness like a mighty stream.

I am not unmindful that some of you have come here out of excessive trials and tribulation.[20] Some of you have come fresh from narrow jail cells. Some of you have come from areas where your quest for freedom left you battered by the storms of persecution and staggered by the winds of police brutality. You have been the veterans of creative suffering. Continue to work with the faith that unearned suffering is redemptive.[21]

Go back to Mississippi; go back to Alabama; go back to South Carolina; go back to Georgia; go back to Louisiana; go back to the slums and ghettos of our northern cities, knowing that somehow this situation can, and will be changed. Let us not wallow[22] in the valley of despair.

So I say to you today, my friends, that even though we must face the difficulties of today and tomorrow, I still have a dream. It is a dream deeply rooted in the American dream that one day this nation will rise up and live out the true meaning of its creed—we hold these truths to be self-evident; that all men are created equal.

I have a dream that one day on the red hills of Georgia the sons of former slaves and the sons of former slaveowners will be able to sit down together at the table of brotherhood.

I have a dream that one day, even the state of Mississippi, a state sweltering with the heat of injustice, sweltering with the heat of oppression, will be transformed into an oasis of freedom and justice.

17. inextricably (in ek′strə kə blē), *adv.* incapable of being disentangled.
18. **devotee** (dev′ə tē′), *n.* person who is strongly devoted to something; enthusiast.
19. **mobility** (mō bil′ə tē), *n.* ability or readiness to move or be moved.
20. **tribulation** (trib′yə lā′shən), *n.* great trouble; severe trial; affliction.
21. redemptive (ri demp′tiv), *adj.* bringing about reform, freedom, or compensation; restorative.
22. wallow (wol′ō), *v.* flounder; become or remain helpless; indulge oneself excessively.

I have a dream that my four little children will one day live in a nation where they will not be judged by the color of their skin but by the content of their character. I have a dream today!

I have a dream that one day, down in Alabama, with its vicious racists, with its governor having his lips dripping with the words of

This is our hope. This is the faith that I go back to the South with.

interposition and nullification,[23] that one day, right there in Alabama, little black boys and black girls will be able to join hands with little white boys and white girls as sisters and brothers. I have a dream today!

I have a dream that one day every valley shall be exalted,[24] every hill and mountain shall be made low, the rough places shall be made plain, and the crooked places shall be made straight and the glory of the Lord will be revealed and all flesh shall see it together.

This is our hope. This is the faith that I go back to the South with.

With this faith we will be able to hew out of the mountain of despair a stone of hope. With this faith we will be able to transform the jangling discords[25] of our nation into a beautiful symphony of brotherhood.

With this faith we will be able to work together, to pray together, to struggle together, to go to jail together, to stand up for freedom together, knowing that we will be free one day. This will be the day when all of God's children will be able to sing with new meaning—"my country, 'tis of thee; sweet land of liberty; of thee I sing; land where my fathers died; land of the

pilgrim's pride; from every mountainside; let freedom ring"—and if America is to be a great nation, this must become true.

So let freedom ring from the prodigious[26] hilltops of New Hampshire.

Let freedom ring from the mighty mountains of New York.

Let freedom ring from the heightening Alleghenies of Pennsylvania.

Let freedom ring from the snow-capped Rockies of Colorado.

Let freedom ring from the curvacious[27] peaks of California.

But not only that.

Let freedom ring from Stone Mountain of Georgia.

Let freedom ring from Lookout Mountain of Tennessee.

Let freedom ring from every hill and molehill of Mississippi, from every mountainside, let freedom ring.

When we let freedom ring, when we let it ring from every village and hamlet,[28] from every state and city, we will be able to speed up that day when all of God's children—black men and white men, Jews and Gentiles, Catholics and Protestants—will be able to join hands and to sing in the words of the old Negro spiritual, "Free at last, free at last; thank God Almighty, we are free at last."

---

23. **interposition** (in′tər pə zish′ən) **and nullification** (nul′ə fə kā′shən), the threat to resist federal desegregation laws by declaring them unconstitutional.
24. exalted (eg zôlt′ əd), *adj.* elevated; praised; glorified.
25. **discord** (dis′kôrd), *n.* disagreement; dissension.
26. prodigious (prə dij′əs), *adj.* enormous; causing amazement or wonder.
27. **curvacious** (kėr′vā′shəs), *adj.* having curves suggestive of a full-figured woman.
28. **hamlet** (ham′lit), *n.* a small country village.

After Reading

Making Connections

Shaping Your Response

1. Write three or four words that describe your response to "I Have a Dream."

2. Identify the most memorable image, in your opinion, from the speech. Explain why it is memorable for you.

Analyzing the Speech

3. Do you agree with King that people should be judged by "the content of their character"? Explain.

4. If African Americans were legally emancipated one hundred years before King spoke, why does he call for action in his speech?

5. What reasoning does King use to defend nonviolent protest?

6. What does King mean when he says that the freedom of whites is "inextricably bound" to the freedom of blacks?

7. Find three moments in the speech when King uses **repetition** to make a point. What effect does the repetition have?

Extending the Ideas

8. 🐾 What kind of **choice** does King urge his audience to make? How is that choice related to events in U.S. history?

Literary Focus: Metaphor

You have learned that a **metaphor** is a comparison of unlike things. Writers use metaphor to reveal certain qualities of the subject they are writing about. Martin Luther King, Jr., was a master of metaphor. Complete the following chart about the use of metaphor in "I Have a Dream," and add at least three examples of your own.

Metaphor	What two things are being compared?	What is revealed by the comparison?
(p. 408) "flames of withering injustice"	fire and injustice	People can be hurt by injustice just as they can be hurt by the flames of a fire.
(p. 408) "a lonely island of poverty"	an island and poverty	

Vocabulary Study

default
desolate
exalted
inextricably
invigorating
legitimate
prodigious
redemptive
sweltering
wallow

Imagine you are a speechwriter working for a politician. For each event described below, write the opening sentences of a speech your boss will give. Use each of the ten listed vocabulary words at least once in your speeches.

1. A press conference about the failure of a local bank, which has caused the loss of millions of dollars.

2. The opening of a new school for artistically gifted students.

3. A benefit dinner for a local civil rights group.

4. The ground-breaking ceremony for a new community swimming pool.

Expressing Your Ideas

Writing Choices

Writer's Notebook Update Now that you've read King's speech, look back at your notes about it. Were your expectations accurate? Work with a partner to briefly outline the major points of the speech.

A Simple Message Imagine that you have an eight-year-old sister. She asks you to tell her what the "I Have a Dream" speech is all about. Summarize the speech in simple language so that she can understand its major ideas. Describe the occasion in which King delivered the speech and what his purpose was. If you have younger sisters or brothers, share your **summary** to see how they respond.

Other Options

How Civil Are We? Hold a **panel discussion** about the present situation of civil rights in the United States. Consider the status of such groups as cultural minorities, women, senior citizens, and children. Before you begin, determine with your classmates what point of view each of you will represent on the panel. Make sure to examine the current economic, political, and social status of the groups you discuss.

Fighters for Change There have been many Americans like Martin Luther King, Jr., who dedicated their lives to working for social justice. Do some research on an American you'd like to learn more about and prepare an **oral report** that explains how he or she contributed (or contributes) to social justice.

Free Spirit Create a piece of art that you think captures the spirit of freedom. Bring in your piece or a copy of it to share with the class. Work with your classmates to create an **art exhibit** on the spirit of freedom.

Songs of Hope

Seeds of Change

Social Studies Connection

Not long ago, the South Bronx in New York City was a place of hopelessness and fear. But life there is changing for the better, thanks to the efforts of some hard-working people.

Charlotte Street in 1981. Abandoned buildings and trash-filled vacant lots like these were a typical sight all over the South Bronx.

HOPE RETURNS to the SOUTH BRONX

by Patrick Breslin

B urned out buildings. Acres of trash. Gunfire in the streets. A war zone? No, the South Bronx, in New York City. Or at least, that *was* the South Bronx. For a while.

In the 1800s, the Bronx, one of New York City's five boroughs, or districts, was a rural retreat for wealthy New York families. By the 1950s, the Bronx was a gritty, bustling, hopeful place, home to thousands of immigrant families. Every day, workers jammed the elevated trains that linked the Bronx to jobs in Manhattan. People felt safe and neighborhoods were stable.

But by the late 1960s, the situation had changed. Jobs were lost to cheaper labor in the southern United States. Crime increased. Drug dealers invaded the neighborhoods. The Bronx, which had been a place of hope for generations of immigrants and their families, became a disaster zone. In the South Bronx especially, the combined problems of unemployment, crime, and illegal drugs threatened to completely destroy the community.

Interdisciplinary Study **415**

Those who could, fled. Some landlords torched their buildings for the insurance money before they left, adding to the devastation. The situation grew even worse. Alexandra Immanuel came to the South Bronx from the island of St. Lucia in 1971, when she was fourteen. Now she recalls, "We couldn't go out. There was a feeling of despair. I felt like a prisoner in my own house."

But not everyone gave up. In the 1960s, Father Louis Gigante, a Catholic priest at St. Athanasius Parish in the South Bronx, brought busloads of protesters to the Manhattan offices of city officials, and eventually founded the Southeast Bronx Community Organization (SEBCO). With funds from private foundations and government agencies, SEBCO rebuilt and restored much of the housing in the neighborhood around St. Athanasius. SEBCO's success inspired community organizations in other parts of the Bronx, including groups

(far left) Charlotte Street in 1984. Community organizations were working tirelessly to renovate old buildings and to construct new housing for Bronx residents. The beginnings of change were noticeable on Charlotte Street.

(left) Charlotte Street in 1994. It's hard to believe that these tree-lined streets with well-kept homes were a dangerous wasteland only a few years before.

with colorful names like Banana Kelly, so-called because Kelly Street in the Bronx curves like a banana, and the Mid-Bronx Desperadoes, who chose their name after realizing they were "desperate" about neighborhood problems.

For more than two decades, groups like these have worked hard to clean up vacant lots, renovate housing, and improve community services, while keeping the neighborhood affordable for its original residents. For Alexandra Immanuel, the changes are obvious, and exciting. In 1991, she and her husband purchased a new town house that had been built by a local community organization in the South Bronx. "The kids love it," she says. "They can play in the yard, and I don't have to worry. The neighbors are good. Everybody looks out for each other."

Individuals, churches, and community organizations have fought for years to make the South Bronx a good place to live again.

As the pictures on these pages show, their struggle has not been in vain. Not all of the problems have been solved—issues such as jobs, education, and medical care must still be tackled. But where despair and fear once ruled, hope and determination have come to live.

Responding

1. Imagine that you have lived near Charlotte Street for twenty years. Write a newspaper editorial that expresses how you feel about the changes on the street.

2. Based on this article, what would you say are some necessary ingredients for bringing about positive change in a community?

Making a
Difference

Interview with Martha Jiménez

As a civil rights lawyer for the Mexican American Legal Defense and Education Fund (MALDEF) in San Francisco, Martha Jiménez knows she's using every ounce of her talents to help others. "I use my Spanish and English skills, write persuasively, do educational outreach, and work with Latino businesses and the larger community," she says. "I'm really challenged to use my abilities!"

Born in 1961 in San Antonio, Texas, Jiménez grew up on the predominantly Mexican American west side of San Antonio. Even as a child, Jiménez realized that although Mexican Americans were a majority of the local population, they had little representation in positions of power. "I remember my parents saying, 'We pay taxes. We live here. But we don't get the same services.'" Jiménez knew that she wanted to make a difference.

"I wanted to use whatever talents I had to serve the community," Jiménez recalls. "I thought about medicine, but I realized that my strengths lay in persuasiveness and talking to people and writing. So I decided to study law."

Now, as a civil rights lawyer, Jiménez deals with controversial issues such as immigration policy, equal access to education, and racism. "I'm always on TV talking about cases in our community," she says. She has a lot of respect for her clients. "I learn so much about dignity and strength from them, and I'm always humbled by people who are willing to face retaliation and harassment after lawsuits. We go through all these years of law school, but I don't know how many of us lawyers would be willing to face the same amount of harassment. I feel very lucky to know these people."

When Jiménez visits schools, she offers a challenging message: "Indifference really kills. You must care passionately about life, whatever you do. Whether you become a factory worker or a university president, keep working for change. One person really can make a difference."

Martha Jiménez (right) engages in a courtroom discussion with two other civil rights lawyers.

Responding

1. How did Jiménez's background influence her decision to become a civil rights lawyer?

2. Jiménez says, "Keep working for change." What kind of social change would you like to work toward?

Writing Workshop

My Dream of a Perfect World

Assignment Use Dr. Martin Luther King, Jr.'s speech, "I Have a Dream," as a model to create a persuasive essay and speech of your own.

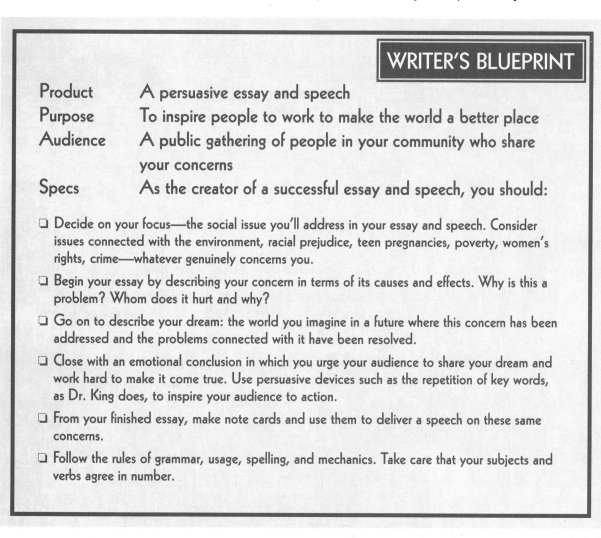

WRITER'S BLUEPRINT

Product   A persuasive essay and speech

Purpose   To inspire people to work to make the world a better place

Audience   A public gathering of people in your community who share your concerns

Specs   As the creator of a successful essay and speech, you should:

❑ Decide on your focus—the social issue you'll address in your essay and speech. Consider issues connected with the environment, racial prejudice, teen pregnancies, poverty, women's rights, crime—whatever genuinely concerns you.

❑ Begin your essay by describing your concern in terms of its causes and effects. Why is this a problem? Whom does it hurt and why?

❑ Go on to describe your dream: the world you imagine in a future where this concern has been addressed and the problems connected with it have been resolved.

❑ Close with an emotional conclusion in which you urge your audience to share your dream and work hard to make it come true. Use persuasive devices such as the repetition of key words, as Dr. King does, to inspire your audience to action.

❑ From your finished essay, make note cards and use them to deliver a speech on these same concerns.

❑ Follow the rules of grammar, usage, spelling, and mechanics. Take care that your subjects and verbs agree in number.

Chart Dr. King's concerns. With a small group, reread the "I Have a Dream" speech and make a chart like the one that follows.

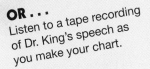

OR . . .
Listen to a tape recording of Dr. King's speech as you make your chart.

Concerns	Causes	Effects
discrimination against blacks	history of slavery and prejudice	unequal opportunities

Create a personal concerns chart. Make it similar to the one you made from Dr. King's speech, but this time note your own concerns and their causes and effects. When your chart is complete, select the concern that you feel most strongly about.

Collect information on your concern. Watch for newspaper, magazine, and television reports. Take notes on causes and effects.

Formulate a vision. Imagine what the world would be like if the concern you selected was no longer a problem. Visualize this better world and make notes on what you see.

Analyze Dr. King's speech for the use of repetition as a persuasive device. Notice the examples in the Literary Source here and in Step 3 of this lesson. Look for other examples in the speech and jot them down.

LITERARY SOURCE
"Go back to Mississippi; go back to Alabama; . . . go back to the slums and ghettos of the northern cities, knowing that somehow this situation can, and will be changed."
from "I Have a Dream" by Dr. Martin Luther King, Jr.

Plan your essay. Reread the Writer's Blueprint. Then organize your notes into a writing plan like the one that follows, which addresses each point in the blueprint.

Introduction
Your concern
    Its causes
    Its effects

Body
What the world would look like if the problem were solved
    First difference
    Second difference
    and so on

Conclusion
Urge audience to share your vision and work toward it.

DRAFTING

Start Writing. Here are some drafting tips.

- After writing the introduction, take a few minutes to revise it before going on to the body, or write the body first and the introduction later.

- Use repetition of key words and phrases to help persuade and inspire.

Ask a partner for comments on your draft before you revise it. See the Revising Strategy below.

Revising Strategy

LITERARY SOURCE

"... for many of our white brothers, as evidenced by their presence here today, have come to realize that their *destiny* is tied up with our *destiny* and they have come to realize that their *freedom* is inextricably bound to our *freedom.*"

from "I Have a Dream" by Dr. Martin Luther King, Jr.

Repetition as a Persuasive Device

See if you can use repetition to emphasize important ideas when you revise. Notice how repetition was used in the Literary Sources and in the student model below.

Parents must influence their children positively.

Parents
~~They~~ must show their children what is right and wrong and

teach them what will happen if they make the wrong choices.
Parents must teach their children
~~Children must be taught~~ about values—their priorities and

STUDENT MODEL

what should be important to them.

Ask a partner to review your revised draft before you edit. Look carefully for errors in subject-verb agreement.

Editing Strategy

FOR REFERENCE
For more information on subject-verb agreement, see the Language and Grammar Handbook in the back of this text.

Subject-Verb Agreement

When you edit, make sure that you follow these rules:

- A singular subject takes a singular verb.
  (*Crime* in big cities *is* a problem.)

- A plural subject takes a plural verb.
  (The *crimes* of theft and vandalism *are* increasing.)

STEP 5 PRESENTING

Prepare a speech based on your essay. Read your essay paragraph by paragraph and make note cards for your speech. Include the important points. Highlight significant words and items you want to emphasize. Arrange and number your note cards in the order you will use them. See the Beyond Print article on the next page for more information on preparing note cards.

Give your speech. See the Beyond Print article on the next page for pointers on delivering an effective speech.

COMPUTER TIP
Make sure your note cards are easy to read. Use a word processor to print them with bold, clear type, using a font size of 14 points or more.

STEP 6 LOOKING BACK

Self-evaluate. Look back at the Writer's Blueprint and give your paper a score for each point, from 6 (superior) to 1 (inadequate).

Reflect. Write your responses to these questions.

✔ Think about what life would be like if we lived in a perfect world. Can you think of any disadvantages? Anything you'd miss?

✔ How did the content of your essay differ from that of your speech?

For Your Working Portfolio Add your persuasive essay, your note cards, your reflection responses, and perhaps a tape or video recording of your speech to your working portfolio.

Beyond Print

Tips for Making a Speech

When Martin Luther King, Jr., delivered his "I Have a Dream" speech in 1963, his words had a tremendous impact on American society. Part of the reason why his message was so effective was that Reverend King knew how to deliver a speech in a way that made his words even more powerful and memorable. The following tips will help you deliver a speech in a way that will have a positive impact on your audience.

Prepare note cards. Outline your speech on a series of note cards. Don't write out what you will say word for word; instead, summarize each point on a separate card. Number your cards in the correct order. Notice how one student has summarized a point about parental responsibilities on the sample note card shown here.

(#4)

Parents must:

- *have positive influence*
- *teach right and wrong*
- *teach values and priorities*
- *serve as guides*

Rehearse. You may feel silly giving your speech in front of a mirror or your cat, but it's a great idea. Rehearsing will help you deliver your speech smoothly, without depending too much on your note cards.

Maintain eye contact. When you deliver your speech, you'll be much more convincing if you look directly at your audience.

Speak clearly. Don't mumble. You don't have to shout, but try to project your voice to the back of the room. Say your words clearly and with expression, and avoid filling in the gaps with "ums" and "uhs."

Ask for feedback. After giving your speech, ask the audience for feedback. If possible, videotape your speech so that you can observe yourself. Make a list of points to keep in mind your next speech.

Activity Options

1. Practice your speech in front of a partner. Give each other feedback on both the content and the delivery of your speeches.

2. Find a famous speech and prepare to deliver it to your class.

Part Three

Ways of Seeing

Painters and poets, engineers and scientists, thinkers and dreamers: all have unique ways of perceiving reality.

🐾 Multicultural Connection **Perspective** involves seeing and interpreting a situation from different viewpoints. In the selections, notice the factors that help shape the perspectives of the speakers.

Literature

Interdisciplinary Study Through Different Eyes

Reading Mini-Lesson

Writing Workshop Narrative Writing

Beyond Print Technology

Before Reading

My Grandfather Was a Quantum Physicist by Duane BigEagle

The Bean Eaters by Gwendolyn Brooks

Miss Rosie by Lucille Clifton

maggie and milly and molly and may by E. E. Cummings

Building Background

Portraits When creating a portrait, a painter works with color and line to reveal inner qualities of the person being painted. Though writers use different kinds of tools, such as imagery and figurative language, they also can create portraits that go beyond the outward appearance of a person. The four poems that follow are character portraits. As you read them, consider how the poets create their characters. Do the characters seem real to you? Why or why not?

Literary Focus

Alliteration and Rhyme Alliteration is the repetition of sounds at the beginnings of words or in accented syllables: *Lila likes to alliterate with the lovely letter l*. Like alliteration, **rhyme** involves the repetition of sounds—specifically, the sounds at the end of words: *It's time to rhyme or pay a dime.* Alliteration and rhyme work well together to create melody, establish a mood and tone, and to emphasize certain words or ideas.

Writer's Notebook

Tongue Teasers Alliteration and **rhyme** are good ways to create emphasis or echo meaning in spoken or written language. Aside from their usefulness, however, alliteration and rhyme can be just plain fun. Such wordplay is common in everyday speech because it is pleasing to say and listen to. Record in your notebook some lists of pleasing tongue-teasing words that alliterate or rhyme.

Duane BigEagle
born 1946

Native American writer Duane BigEagle says that his Osage heritage taught him "an awareness of the natural world and the spiritual world that today we ignore most of the time." He won a scholarship to study physics at the University of California at Berkeley, but became interested in poetry and changed his major to English. Today, BigEagle writes poetry and fiction and works as a teacher, lecturer, magazine editor, and community arts organizer in California.

Gwendolyn Brooks
born 1917

Gwendolyn Brooks was born in Topeka, Kansas, but grew up on the South Side of Chicago, where she still lives today. She began to write poetry at the age of seven. Today, as one of America's most distinguished poets, Brooks has written many books of poetry and was the first African American to win the Pulitzer Prize. As Poet Laureate of Illinois, Brooks has helped young writers by sponsoring the Illinois Poet Laureate Awards and awards for student writers.

Lucille Clifton
born 1936

In simple, powerful language, Lucille Clifton's poems trace black experience in America from before the 1960s. Because she often writes in the richly varied voices of different characters, her poems are particularly effective when read aloud. Clifton has read her work in colleges and universities throughout the country. In addition to poetry, she has written family memoirs and many children's books. Clifton has six children and lives in California.

E. E. Cummings
1894–1962

Throughout his impressive career as a poet, E. E. (Edward Estlin) Cummings criticized and satirized what he saw as artificial or pretentious in the world. A true nonconformist, Cummings celebrated the spontaneous in his poetry by making up words and experimenting with word order, line lengths, and punctuation. His collection *Poems: 1923–1954* received the National Book Award in 1955.

My Grandfather Was a Quantum Physicist[1]

Duane BigEagle

I can see him now
smiling
in full dance regalia,[2]
an eagle feather fan in his hand.
5 He's standing with the other men
on the grassy field
in front of the round house
on a sunny afternoon.

Scientists have finally discovered
10 that the intimate details
of our lives
are influenced by things
behind the physical world,
beyond the stars
15 and beyond time.

My grandfather knew this.

---

1. **quantum physicist** (kwon′təm fiz′ə sist),
   specialist in the area of physics dealing
   with energy and its transference and
   transformation.
2. **regalia** (ri gā′lē ə), *n.* special dress.

The ***Bean*** Eaters

Gwendolyn Brooks

They eat beans mostly, this old yellow pair.
Dinner is a casual affair.
Plain chipware on a plain and creaking wood,
Tin flatware.

5 Two who are Mostly Good.
Two who have lived their day,
But keep on putting on their clothes
And putting things away.

And remembering . . .
10 Remembering, with twinklings and twinges,
As they lean over the beans in their rented back room that
     is full of beads and receipts and dolls and cloths,
     tobacco crumbs, vases and fringes.

Tom Heflin, *After All These Years.* The artist uses light and shadow to blur and fade several sections of the painting. What does the sense of fading and blurring tell you about the two people depicted here?

Miss Rosie

Lucille Clifton

When I watch you
wrapped up like garbage
sitting, surrounded by the smell
of too old potato peels
5 or
when I watch you
in your old man's shoes
with the little toe cut out
sitting, waiting for your mind
10 like next week's grocery
I say
when I watch you
you wet brown bag of a woman
who used to be the best looking gal
     in Georgia
15 used to be called the Georgia Rose
I stand up
through your destruction
I stand up

△ In *Best Friends*, artist Diane Leonard uses a beach setting and intense color to evoke a moment of friendship. Come up with several words that describe both a beach and a friendship.

m a g g i e
and milly
and molly
and may

E. E. Cummings

maggie and milly and molly and may
went down to the beach(to play one day)

and maggie discovered a shell that sang
so sweetly she couldn't remember her troubles,and

5 milly befriended a stranded star
whose rays five languid[1] fingers were;

and molly was chased by a horrible thing
which raced sideways while blowing bubbles:and

may came home with a smooth round stone
10 as small as a world and as large as alone.

For whatever we lose(like a you or a me)
it's always ourselves we find in the sea

---

1. **languid** (lang′gwid), *adj.* without energy; weak; sluggish.

After Reading

Making Connections

Shaping Your Response

1. Do you think the couple in "The Bean Eaters" is happy? Explain.

2. What do you think the speaker in "Miss Rosie" means when she says, "I stand up"?

3. What do you know about each of the four girls in "maggie and milly and molly and may"?

Analyzing the Poems

4. The grandfather in "My Grandfather Was a Quantum Physicist" probably never studied physics. Why would the speaker call him a quantum physicist?

5. **Characterize** the bean eaters, citing evidence from the poem.

6. The speaker in "Miss Rosie" calls Miss Rosie a "wet brown bag of a woman" and says she used to be called "the Georgia Rose." What do these **metaphors** tell you about Miss Rosie's past and present life?

7. Describe the **mood** of "maggie and milly and molly and may."

Extending the Ideas

8. ☝ Choose two of the poems and tell how the speaker's **perspective** might be influenced by social or cultural factors.

Literary Focus: Alliteration and Rhyme

You have learned that **alliteration** and **rhyme** both involve the repetition of sounds. Most of the poems in this section make use of alliteration, rhyme, or both. For example, in the first stanza of "The Bean Eaters," *pair, affair, chipware,* and *flatware* all rhyme. Identify four examples of alliteration or rhyme that you particularly like in these poems.

Expressing Your Ideas

Writing Choices

Writer's Notebook Update Using your lists of alliterative and rhyming words, write some lines of alliteration, rhyme, or both. Share your favorite lines with the class.

Picture This You've read four portrait poems. Now write a **portrait poem** yourself, and use the tools of figurative language and imagery to create a picture in words.

Another Option

At the Beach Create a **visual** or **audio image** that expresses your feelings about a day at the beach.

Before Reading

To Look at Any Thing by John Moffitt
Tiburón by Martín Espada
The Runaway by Robert Frost

Building Background

Observations Good writers observe their environments and think about how to communicate their observations effectively in words. The following poems include vivid, specific details that allow the reader to "see" what the writer has observed. For example, in "The Runaway," Robert Frost uses powerful language and strong images to describe a frightened young horse. What qualities do you think make someone a good observer? Share your thoughts with the class.

Literary Focus

Simile A **simile** is a figure of speech in which two unlike things are directly compared with the words *like* or *as*. When a simile is effective, it reveals something new about the things it compares. Similes are common in speech and writing, as in phrases such as *cry like a baby*, *smooth as silk*, and *quiet as a mouse*. Make a list of other similes that have become common in everyday language. Then look for similes as you read the poems on the following pages.

Writer's Notebook

What Do You See? Work with a partner to find a classroom object to observe and write about. Each of you should study the object carefully and think about how to describe it in words as creatively as possible. For example, you might imagine what the object looks like in different kinds of light or what it might say if it could speak. Remember that the kind of "seeing" a writer does involves looking beyond the surface of things.

John Moffitt
1908–1987

John Moffitt, who was born in Harrisburg, Pennsylvania, lived as a Hindu monk for nearly thirty years before converting to Christianity in 1963. Throughout his life, Moffitt wrote extensively about religion in essays, poems, journals, travelogues, and letters to other writers. Moffitt viewed life and writing as a journey. His poems reflect his capacity for careful observation and his search for inner peace.

Martín Espada
born 1957

Martín Espada was born in Brooklyn, New York. At thirteen, he moved with his family to a suburb on Long Island, where he was frequently harassed for being Puerto Rican. Espada began writing poetry to cope with being treated like an outsider in school. In college, however, he quit writing after finding he couldn't relate to the writers he was studying in his English classes. He began writing again when a friend showed him an inspirational book of Latin American poetry. Espada has written four books and currently teaches creative writing at the University of Massachusetts in Amherst.

Robert Frost
1874–1963

One of the most honored American poets, Robert Frost received four Pulitzer Prizes and was asked by John F. Kennedy to read at the 1961 presidential inauguration ceremony. Frost wrote most of his poems about life in rural New England, imitating the ordinary speech of the people who lived there. While living briefly in England, he became acquainted with some of the leading poets of his time, including Ezra Pound, William Butler Yeats, and Amy Lowell. For more information about Frost, see page 179.

TO LOOK AT ANY THING

John Moffitt

To look at any thing,
If you would know that thing,
You must look at it long:
To look at this green and say
5 'I have seen spring in these
Woods,' will not do—you must
Be the thing you see:
You must be the dark snakes of
Stems and ferny plumes of leaves,
10 You must enter in
To the small silences between
The leaves,
You must take your time
And touch the very peace
15 They issue from.

TIBURÓN[1]   Martín Espada

East 116th
and a long red car
stalled with the hood up
roaring salsa[2]
5 like a prize shark
mouth yanked open
and down in the stomach
the radio
of the last fisherman
10 still tuned
to his lucky station

---

1. **tiburón** (tē bü rōn′), shark. [Spanish]
2. **salsa** (säl′sä), form of Latin American music
   with characteristics of rhythm and blues, jazz,
   and rock.

The angle of this photograph makes the car seem powerful and even a bit
dangerous. How does this relate to the description of the car in "Tiburón"?

THE
Runaway

Robert Frost

In his painting *Horses,* Ceylonese artist Senaka Senanayake depicts horses in various active poses and surrounds them with vibrant swirls of color. What do these things tell you about the artist's feelings about horses?

Once when the snow of the year was beginning to fall,
We stopped by a mountain pasture to say, 'Whose colt?'
A little Morgan[1] had one forefoot on the wall,
The other curled at his breast. He dipped his head
5 And snorted at us. And then he had to bolt.
We heard the miniature thunder where he fled,
And we saw him, or thought we saw him, dim and gray,
Like a shadow against the curtain of falling flakes.
'I think the little fellow's afraid of the snow.
10 He isn't winter-broken. It isn't play
With the little fellow at all. He's running away.
I doubt if even his mother could tell him, "Sakes,
It's only weather." He'd think she didn't know!
Where is his mother? He can't be out alone.'
15 And now he comes again with clatter of stone,
And mounts the wall again with whited eyes
And all his tail that isn't hair up straight.
He shudders his coat as if to throw off flies.
'Whoever it is that leaves him out so late,
20 When other creatures have gone to stall and bin,
Ought to be told to come and take him in.'

---

1. **Morgan** (môr′gən), sturdy, strong horse kept for work on farms, of a breed originating in Vermont.

After Reading

Making Connections

Shaping Your Response

1. Write two or three words to describe the **mood** of "To Look at Any Thing."

2. To which senses do the **images** in "Tiburón" appeal? Give examples.

3. What are your feelings toward the colt in "The Runaway"?

Analyzing the Poems

4. Write a sentence or two that expresses the **theme** of "To Look at Any Thing."

5. Describe the attitude of the observers in "The Runaway."

Extending the Ideas

6. "To Look at Any Thing" offers advice on how to observe life. Name a few other selections in this book in which it seems as though the author took Moffitt's advice.

Literary Focus: Simile

You know that a **simile** is a comparison of unlike things using *like* or *as*. Frost uses a simile when he compares the colt to a shadow. Identify the major simile in "Tiburón" and explain why you think it is or is not effective.

Expressing Your Ideas

Writing Choices

Writer's Notebook Update Look back at the observations you wrote before reading, and discuss them with your partner. What do you like about each other's piece? What have you learned from the poems that could improve your observation skills? Then write a second draft to polish your observations.

The Poem and I Everyone's experience of poetry is different. Write an **essay** about what poetry is like for you. Is it, for example, a puzzle, a tightrope walk, or a journey?

Another Option

Ways of Seeing Like writers, artists use their powers of observation. Choose an object, a person, or a landscape to observe closely. After doing some preliminary sketches, make a **drawing, painting,** or **sculpture** that incorporates your observations.

Before Reading

Postage Stamp Connections by Nancy Lee Pulley
Write About a Radish by Karla Kuskin
Keeping Things Whole by Mark Strand
There is no Frigate like a Book by Emily Dickinson

Building Background

Fresh Perspectives The poems on the next pages look at familiar or ordinary things with fresh perspectives. Karla Kuskin wrote "Write About a Radish" because she wanted to write about something no one else had ever written a poem about. Although she chose something rather ordinary—a radish—her poem is interesting because she writes about the radish in a surprising way. Good writers write about familiar themes with originality by developing their own unique voice, which is shaped by their particular way of seeing the world.

Literary Focus

Personification is a figure of speech that assigns human characteristics to nonhuman things, or life to inanimate objects. We assign human characteristics to nonhuman things when we refer to the *hands* of a clock or an *angry* sky. Personification allows the writer to present abstract qualities, emotions, events, or objects in familiar and understandable terms. As you read the following poems, look for instances of personification.

Writer's Notebook

From the Usual to the Strange Choose an ordinary object, such as a chair, a potato, or an ice cube. In your mind, put this object in an unusual situation: the potato, for example, has been stuffed into the mouth of a very small volcano. Try freewriting—writing every idea that comes into your head without stopping to change or fix anything—for five minutes about this strange situation involving an everyday item.

Nancy Lee Pulley
born 1948

Nancy Lee Pulley first published "Postage Stamp Connections" under her pen name, Lee Douglass. She began sending out poems as Lee Douglass to see whether using a man's name would improve her chances of being published. Some editors who had rejected her poems in the past did indeed accept poems by Lee Douglass! For Pulley, who lives in Indiana, writing poetry involves speaking from the deepest part of the self.

Karla Kuskin
born 1932

Award-winning author and illustrator Karla Kuskin began writing poetry as a young girl, receiving encouragement from her parents and teachers. While studying at Yale University, Kuskin wrote and illustrated a children's book, which was later published. Since then, she has published children's books, essays, book reviews, and screenplays. Kuskin remembers ideas by writing them down on whatever paper is handy, including grocery lists and newspapers.

Mark Strand
born 1934

Mark Strand's poems have a clear yet dreamlike quality, and often include unusual events that seem oddly unsurprising. Strand, who has published nine books of poetry, has won numerous awards, including a MacArthur Foundation Fellowship. From 1990 to 1991, Strand served as Poet Laureate of the United States. He currently teaches writing at the University of Utah.

Emily Dickinson
1830–1886

Emily Dickinson lived her entire life in her family's home in Amherst, Massachusetts. Although she traveled very little, she had many close friends and wrote nearly ten thousand letters. Of her nearly two thousand poems, Dickinson published only a few during her lifetime. After her death, when her family published a small volume of her poems, her work began to reach a wider audience. Today, Dickinson is one of the most respected and influential American poets. Her poetry is characterized by its precise language and utterly original voice.

POSTAGE STAMP
Connections

Nancy Lee Pulley

Elvis curls his lip at Mary Cassatt[1]
but she is unmoved,
regal[2] in a feathered hat. They
have flown all night together
5 from Vermont that way, him singing
into his microphone,
her face a little severe, perhaps
seeing ahead to the next painting.
Elvis just mumbles in her left ear.
10 They have come to the same place
in space and time, for better
or worse, and she is making
the best of it, eyes looking far beyond
the square given her, a woman
15 with a vision, while the king croons[3]
wrapped in white sequins, soft
and a little undeserving of this honor.

1. **Mary Cassatt** (kə sat′), American figure painter and
   etcher (1844–1926). She lived mostly in France and
   was influenced by the French Impressionists. You can
   find an example of her work on page 383.
2. **regal** (rē′gəl), *adj.* belonging to or fit for a king or
   queen; royal; stately; splendid; magnificent.
3. **croon** (krün), *v.* hum, sing, or murmur in a low
   tone; sing in a low, sentimental voice.

▲ Christian Pierre, *Global Seat* (1992). How does the familiar image of a simple, straight-backed chair help make an observation about the world?

Write About a Radish   **Karla Kuskin**

Write about a radish
Too many people write about the moon.

The night is black
The stars are small and high
5 The clock unwinds its ever-ticking tune
Hills gleam dimly
Distant nighthawks cry.
A radish rises in the waiting sky.

Keeping Things Whole   **Mark Strand**

In a field
I am the absence
of field.
This is
5 always the case.
Wherever I am
I am what is missing.

When I walk
I part the air
10 and always
the air moves in
to fill the spaces
where my body's been.

We all have reasons
15 for moving.
I move
to keep things whole.

There is no *Frigate* like a *Book*

Emily Dickinson

There is no Frigate[1] like a Book
To take us Lands away
Nor any Coursers[2] like a Page
Of prancing Poetry.—

10 This Traverse[3] may the poorest take
Without oppress of Toll—
How frugal[4] is the Chariot
That bears the Human soul.

1. frigate (frig′it), *n.* light boat propelled by sails.
2. **courser** (kôr′sər), *n.* swift, spirited horse.
3. traverse (trav′ərs), *n.* the act of passing across, over, or through.
4. frugal (frü′gəl), *adj.* requiring or costing little; avoiding waste or unnecessary spending.

After Reading

Making Connections

Shaping Your Response

1. Rate how well you liked the four poems on a scale of 1–10, 10 being best. Why did you choose the ratings you did?

2. What do you think the speaker means in the last line of "Postage Stamp Connections"?

Analyzing the Poems

3. In each of these poems, the poet takes a familiar object and looks at it in a new way. Describe the fresh perspective of each poem in a chart like the one shown.

Familiar object	What the poet imagines
radish	A radish rises in the sky like the moon.

4. A **cliché** is a phrase or expression with overused language or images, such as *I was scared to death*. How does Kuskin avoid clichés in "Write About a Radish"?

5. What do you think the speaker in "Keeping Things Whole" means when he says he moves to keep things whole?

6. Give your own interpretation of the meaning of the last two lines of Dickinson's poem.

Extending the Ideas

7. 🐾 Choose one of the poems. Tell how the writer's fresh **perspective** has affected the way *you* view some aspect of life.

Literary Focus: Personification

Personification is a figure of speech that attributes human characteristics to nonhuman things, or living characteristics to non-living things. Emily Dickinson personifies poetry when she describes it as "prancing." Find another example of personification that you like from one of the poems and explain what is being personified.

Vocabulary Study

The poems you have read depict some odd situations. Explain what is unusual about each of the following scenes. For help with the italicized vocabulary words, consult the Glossary.

croon
frigate
frugal
regal
traverse

1. Elephants at the zoo *croon* popular songs for peanuts.

2. A *frigate* is pulled over for speeding on the highway.

3. A *frugal* mother buys a limousine for each of her children.

4. A *regal* dinner guest eats peas with her fingers.

5. An actor looks younger and younger with the *traverse* of time.

Expressing Your Ideas

Writing Choices

Writer's Notebook Update Look back at the freewriting you did before reading the poems. Highlight the "golden lines" in your writing—lines that you like a lot for their imagery and power. Use those golden lines as the starting point for a poem about an ordinary object in an extraordinary situation.

Close Encounters In "Postage Stamp Connections," Nancy Lee Pulley imagines an encounter between postage stamps of rock star Elvis Presley and painter Mary Cassatt. Write your own **dialogue** about a conversation between two other famous people on postage stamps.

Other Options

Music, Anyone? Work with a partner to find or create a piece of music that you think complements or dramatizes one of the poems you have just read. Work together to prepare a **performance** of the poem along with the musical accompaniment you have selected. Perform your piece for the class.

Transported by Language In her poem, Emily Dickinson compares a book to a frigate that takes the reader to other lands. What kind of image most resembles your own experience of reading? Create a two- or three-dimensional **model** that symbolizes your feelings about reading. Display your model in a class exhibit.

Before Reading

Nameless, Tennessee

by William Least Heat Moon

**William Least Heat Moon
(William Trogdon)**
born 1939

William Trogdon, the son of an Osage Indian father and an Anglo-Irish mother, grew up in two spiritual worlds. For a pen name, he took the name *William* to represent his Anglo-Irish side and *Least Heat Moon* from his father, Heat Moon, to represent his Osage Indian side. During the travels that inspired his best-selling book *Blue Highways*, Least Heat Moon says he discovered the importance of letting go of egoism and embracing new experiences. His second book, *PrairyErth*, was published in 1991. Formerly a literature professor, Least Heat Moon now spends his time traveling and writing.

Building Background

Seeing America In March of 1978, at the age of thirty-eight, William Least Heat Moon left his home in Columbia, Missouri, and set off on a remarkable journey around the United States. Driving a 1975 Econoline Ford van, he traveled America's "blue highways," the back roads marked in blue on old highway maps. He named his van Ghost Dancing after ceremonies of Plains Indians in the 1890s, who danced for the return of the old Indian way of life. Least Heat Moon's book *Blue Highways* is a record of his journey through what remains of small-town America. The map shows his circular route, which started and ended in Columbia, Missouri.

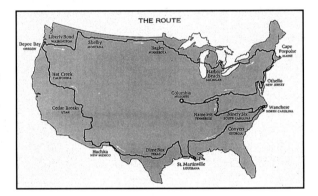

Literary Focus

Dialect is the form of speech characteristic of people in a particular class, racial group, or geographic region. In the United States, many dialects of English exist across the country. A writer can make the setting seem more realistic by having characters speak in the dialect of the region where the action takes place. As you read the selection, notice how Least Heat Moon brings to life the unusual setting of Nameless, Tennessee, and the dialect of the people who live there.

Writer's Notebook

Travel Log Think of a memorable journey you've taken, perhaps to another country or state or simply to a building, park, or neighborhood you'd never seen before. Consider what made the trip memorable for you. What new things did you see? What were the people, trees, or animals like? Write some notes about the major details of your trip and why it was significant in your life.

Marilyn, Thurmond, Virginia, and Hilda Watts in Nameless, Tennessee, in a photograph taken by William Least Heat Moon.

"Nameless, Tennessee"

William Least Heat Moon

Nameless, Tennessee, was a town of maybe ninety people if you pushed it, a dozen houses along the road, a couple of barns, same number of churches, a general merchandise store selling Fire Chief gasoline, and a community center with a lighted volleyball court. Behind the center was an open-roof, rusting metal privy[1] with PAINT ME on the door; in the hollow of a nearby oak lay a full pint of Jack Daniel's Black Label. From the houses, the odor of coal smoke.

Next to a red tobacco barn stood the general merchandise with a poster of Senator Albert Gore, Jr., smiling from the window. I knocked. The door opened partway. A tall, thin man said, "Closed up. For good," and started to shut the door.

"Don't want to buy anything. Just a question for Mr. Thurmond Watts."

The man peered through the slight opening. He looked me over. "What question would that be?"

"If this is Nameless, Tennessee, could he tell me how it got that name?"

The man turned back into the store and called out, "Miss Ginny! Somebody here wants to know how Nameless come to be Nameless."

Miss Ginny edged to the door and looked me and my truck over. Clearly, she didn't approve. She said, "You know as well as I do, Thurmond. Don't keep him on the stoop in the damp to tell him." Miss Ginny, I found out, was Mrs. Virginia Watts, Thurmond's wife.

I stepped in and they both began telling the story, adding a detail here, the other correcting a fact there, both smiling at the foolishness of it all. It seems the hilltop settlement went for years without a name. Then one day the Post Office Department told the people if they wanted mail up on the mountain they would have to give the place a name you could properly address a letter to. The community met; there were only a handful, but they commenced debating. Some wanted patriotic names, some names from nature, one man recommended in all serious-ness his own name. They couldn't agree, and they ran out of names to argue about. Finally, a fellow tired of the talk; he didn't like the mail he

"This here's a nameless place if I ever seen one...."

received anyway. "Forget the durn Post Office," he said. "This here's a nameless place if I ever seen one, so leave it be." And that's just what they did.

Watts pointed out the window. "We used to have signs on the road, but the Halloween boys kept tearin' them down."

"You think Nameless is a funny name," Miss Ginny said. "I see it plain in your eyes. Well, you take yourself up north a piece to Difficult or Defeated or Shake Rag. Now them are silly names."

The old store, lighted only by three fifty-watt bulbs, smelled of coal oil and baking bread. In the middle of the rectangular room, where the oak floor sagged a little, stood an iron stove. To the right was a wooden table with an unfinished game of checkers and a stool made from an apple-tree stump. On shelves around the walls sat earthen[2] jugs with corncob stoppers, a few canned goods, and some of the two thousand old clocks and clockworks Thurmond Watts owned. Only one was ticking; the others he just looked at. I asked how long he'd been in the store.

"Thirty-five years, but we closed the first day of the year. We're hopin' to sell it to a churchly couple. Upright people. No athians.[3]"

"Did you build this store?"

"I built this one, but it's the third general store on the ground. I fear it'll be the last. I take no pleasure in that. Once you could come in here for a gallon of paint, a pickle, a pair of shoes, and a can of corn."

"Or horehound candy," Miss Ginny said. "Or corsets and salves. We had cough syrups and all that for the body. In season, we'd buy and sell blackberries and walnuts and chestnuts, before

---

1. **privy** (priv′ē), *n.* outhouse, outdoor toilet.
2. **earthen** (ėr′thən), *adj.* made of packed clay.
3. **athians** (ā′thē ənz), atheists, people who do not believe in God.

the blight[4] got them. And outside, Thurmond milled corn and sharpened plows. Even shoed a horse sometimes."

"We could fix up a horse or a man or a baby," Watts said.

"Thurmond, tell him we had a doctor on the ridge in them days."

"We had a doctor on the ridge in them days. As good as any doctor alivin'. He'd cut a crooked toenail or deliver a woman. Dead these last years."

"I got some bad ham meat one day," Miss Ginny said, "and took to vomitin'. All day, all night. Hangin' on the drop edge of yonder. I said to Thurmond, 'Thurmond, unless you want shut of me, call the doctor.'"

"I studied on it," Watts said.

"You never did. You got him right now. He come over and put three drops of iodeen[5] in half a glass of well water. I drank it down and the vomitin' stopped with the last swallow. Would you think iodeen could do that?"

"He put Miss Ginny on one teaspoon of spirits of ammonia in well water for her nerves. Ain't nothin' works better for her to this day."

"Calms me like the hand of the Lord."

Hilda, the Wattses' daughter, came out of the backroom. "I remember him," she said. "I was just a baby. Y'all were talkin' to him, and he lifted me up on the counter and gave me a stick of Juicy Fruit and a piece of cheese."

"Knew the old medicines," Watts said. "Only drugstore he needed was a good kitchen cabinet. None of them antee-beeotics[6] that hit you worsen your ailment. Forgotten lore now, the old medicines, because they ain't profit in iodeen."

Miss Ginny started back to the side room where she and her sister Marilyn were taking apart a duck-down mattress to make bolsters.[7] She stopped at the window for another look at Ghost Dancing.[8] "How do you sleep in that thing? Ain't you all cramped and cold?"

"How does the clam sleep in his shell?" Watts said in my defense.

"Thurmond, get the boy a piece of buttermilk pie afore he goes on."

"Hilda, get him some buttermilk pie." He looked at me. "You like good music?" I said I did. He cranked up an old Edison phonograph, the kind with the big morning-glory blossom for a speaker, and put on a wax cylinder. "This will be 'My Mother's Prayer,'" he said.

While I ate buttermilk pie, Watts served as disc jockey of Nameless, Tennessee. "Here's 'Mountain Rose.'" It was one of those moments that you know at the time will stay with you to the grave: the sweet pie, the gaunt man playing the old music, the coals in the stove glowing orange, the scent of kerosene and hot bread. "Here's 'Evening Rhapsody.'" The music was so heavily romantic we both laughed. I thought: It is for this I have come.

Feathered over and giggling, Miss Ginny stepped from the side room. She knew she was a sight. "Thurmond, give him some lunch. Still looks hungry."

Hilda pulled food off the woodstove in the backroom: home-butchered and canned whole-hog sausage, home-canned June apples, turnip greens, cole slaw, potatoes, stuffing, hot cornbread. All delicious.

Watts and Hilda sat and talked while I ate. "Wish you would join me."

"We've ate," Watts said. "Cain't beat a woodstove for flavorful cookin'."

He told me he was raised in a one-hundred-fifty-year-old cabin still standing in one of the hollows. "How many's left," he said, "that grew up in a log cabin? I ain't the last surely, but I must be climbin' on the list."

---

4. **blight** (blīt), *n.* disease or insect that causes plants to wither or die.
5. **iodeen,** iodine, medicine used to prevent infection.
6. **antee-beeotics,** antibiotics, medicines for fighting infection.
7. **bolster** (bōl′stər), *n.* pillow, cushion, or pad.
8. **Ghost Dancing,** the name of the author's van.

Hilda cleared the table. "You Watts ladies know how to cook."

"She's in nursin' school at Tennessee Tech. I went over for one of them football games last year there at Coevul." To say *Cookeville,* you let the word collapse in upon itself so that it comes out "Coevul."

"Do you like football?" I asked.

"Don't know. I was so high up in that stadium, I never opened my eyes."

Watts went to the back and returned with a fat spiral notebook that he set on the table. His expression had changed. "Miss Ginny's *Deathbook.*"

The thing startled me. Was it something I was supposed to sign? He opened it but said nothing. There were scads of names written in a tidy hand over pages incised[9] to crinkliness by a ballpoint. Chronologically,[10] the names had piled up: wives, grandparents, a stillborn infant, relatives, friends close and distant. Names, names. After each, the date of *the* unknown finally known and transcribed.[11] The last entry bore yesterday's date.

"She's wrote out twenty years' worth. Ever day she listens to the hospital report on the radio and puts the names in. Folks come by to check a date. Or they just turn through the books. Read them like a scrapbook."

Hilda said, "Like Saint Peter at the gates inscribin'[12] the names."

Watts took my arm. "Come along." He led me to the fruit cellar under the store. As we went down, he said, "Always take a newborn baby upstairs afore you take him downstairs, otherwise you'll incline him downwards."

The cellar was dry and full of cobwebs and jar after jar of home-canned food, the bottles organized as a shopkeeper would: sausage, pumpkin, sweet pickles, tomatoes, corn, relish, blackberries, peppers, squash, jellies. He held a hand out toward the dusty bottles. "Our tomorrows."

I thought: It is for this I have come.

Upstairs again, he said, "Hope to sell the store to the right folk. I see now, though, it'll be somebody offen the ridge. I've studied on it, and maybe it's the end of our place." He stirred the coals. "This store could give a comfortable livin', but not likely get you rich. But just gettin' by is dice rollin' to people nowadays. I never did see my day guaranteed."

When it was time to go, Watts said, "If you find anyone along your way wants a good store—on the road to Cordell Hull Lake—tell them about us."

I said I would. Miss Ginny and Hilda and Marilyn came out to say goodbye. It was cold and drizzling again. "Weather to give a man the weary dismals," Watts grumbled. "Where you headed from here?"

"I don't know."

"Cain't get lost then."

Miss Ginny looked again at my rig. It had worried her from the first as it had my mother. "I hope you don't get yourself kilt in that durn thing gallivantin' around the country."

"Come back when the hills dry off," Watts said. "We'll go lookin' for some of them round rocks all sparkly inside."

I thought a moment. "Geodes?"[14]

"Them's the ones. The county's properly full of them."

---

9. **incise** (in sīz′), *v.* cut into, engrave.
10. **chronologically** (kron′ə loj′ə kə lē), *adv.* being arranged according to the order of time.
11. **transcribed** (tran skrībd′), *adj.* copied; set down in writing or print.
12. **inscribin'**, inscribing, writing or engraving on paper, stone, metal, etc.
13. **gallivantin'**, gallivanting, traveling or roaming about for pleasure.
14. **geode** (jē′ōd), *n.* rock that usually has a cavity lined with crystals or other mineral matter.

After Reading

Making Connections

Shaping Your
Response

1. Do you think Nameless is a fitting name for the town? Why or why not?

2. Why do you think Thurmond Watts cares about who will buy his store?

Analyzing the
Selection

3. **Characterize** Least Heat Moon and the Watts family.

4. Mr. Watts tells the author that he never saw his day "guaranteed." What does this reveal about his attitude toward life?

5. List at least five **images** from the selection that help bring the **setting** to life. Tell which of the five senses each image appeals to.

Extending the Ideas

6. Compare Nameless to the community where you live. Are there any similarities? What are some of the differences?

7. 🐾 As an outsider, how might Least Heat Moon's **perspective** on Nameless differ from that of local residents?

Literary Focus: Dialect

You have learned **dialect** is the characteristic speech of a particular group of people. List some examples of dialect that you found in the selection. How do these details about dialect enrich your understanding of the setting?

Expressing Your Ideas

Writing Choice

Writer's Notebook Update Use your notes about your memorable journey to write an essay about the experience. Model your piece after "Nameless, Tennessee." Include a map to show where you went and the route you took.

Another Option

Useless Bay, Washington The name of a town may or may not reveal a lot about its spirit. Look at a map of the United States or a state map and make a list of towns with unusual names. Choose one whose name you find especially intriguing and create a **poster** of images to show how you envision the town.

The Rocket

by Ray Bradbury

Ray Bradbury
born 1920

From the time Ray Bradbury was a boy growing up in Waukegan, Illinois, he knew he wanted to be a writer. After high school, he was so determined to get published that he wrote a story every week, a pattern that continued for many years. At twenty, he sold his first story, and at twenty-four he was earning enough money from writing to quit his part-time job selling newspapers. Bradbury has written novels, short stories, plays, screenplays, and poetry. He is perhaps best known for his highly popular science-fiction novel *The Martian Chronicles.*

Building Background

Flights of the Imagination Long before the technology for space flight was developed, generations of writers published stories about rockets and space travel. The lack of technical information did not hinder their storytelling abilities. Jules Verne and H. G. Wells, writing in the late 1800s and early 1900s, depended more on imagination than on science to fuel their fictional spacecraft. By 1950, when "The Rocket" was written, Ray Bradbury and other science-fiction writers could envision a world where a flight to the moon would become nearly as commonplace as a bus ride across town. Of course, it was still more than a decade before the first manned space flight took place.

Literary Focus

Dialogue Conversation among characters is called **dialogue.** When writing dialogue, authors must consider the background and personality of the characters, as well as the particular situation in the narrative. Good dialogue moves the story along and reveals information about the characters. As you read the selection, notice how Bradbury uses dialogue to shape the characters and advance the plot.

Writer's Notebook

Science Fiction or Fiction? What do you think of when you encounter the term *science fiction?* What's the difference between science fiction and just plain fiction? Make some notes about what you think science fiction is and how it differs from other forms of writing.

THE ROCKET

Ray Bradbury

Many nights Fiorello Bodoni[1] would awaken to hear the rockets sighing in the dark sky. He would tiptoe from bed, certain that his kind wife was dreaming, to let himself out into the night air. For a few moments he would be free of the smells of old food in the small house by the river. For a silent moment he would let his heart soar alone into space, following the rockets.

Now, this very night, he stood half naked in the darkness, watching the fire fountains murmuring in the air. The rockets on their long wild way to Mars and Saturn and Venus!

"Well, well, Bodoni."

Bodoni started.

On a milk crate, by the silent river, sat an old man who also watched the rockets through the midnight hush.

---

1. **Fiorello Bodoni** (fē ə rel′ō bō dō′nē).

"Oh, it's you, Bramante!"[2]

"Do you come out every night, Bodoni?"

"Only for the air."

"So? I prefer the rockets myself," said old Bramante. "I was a boy when they started. Eighty years ago, and I've never been on one yet."

"I will ride up in one someday," said Bodoni.

"Fool!" cried Bramante. "You'll never go. This is a rich man's world." He shook his gray head, remembering. "When I was young they wrote it in fiery letters: THE WORLD OF THE FUTURE! Science, Comfort, and New Things for All! Ha! Eighty years. The Future becomes Now! Do *we* fly rockets? No! We live in shacks like our ancestors before us."

"Perhaps my *sons*—" said Bodoni.

"No, nor *their* sons!" the old man shouted. "It's the rich who have dreams and rockets!"

Bodoni hesitated. "Old man, I've saved three thousand dollars. It took me six years to save it. For my business, to invest in machinery. But every night for a month now I've been awake. I hear the rockets. I think. And tonight I've made up my mind. One of us will fly to Mars!" His eyes were shining and dark.

"Idiot," snapped Bramante. "How will you choose? Who will go? If you go, your wife will hate you, for you will be just a bit nearer God, in space. When you tell your amazing trip to her, over the years, won't bitterness gnaw at her?"

"No, no!"

"Yes! And your children? Will their lives be filled with the memory of Papa, who flew to Mars while they stayed here? What a senseless task you will set your boys. They will think of the rocket all their lives. They will lie awake. They will be sick with wanting it. Just as you are sick now. They will want to die if they cannot go. Don't set that goal, I warn you. Let them be content with being poor. Turn their eyes down to their hands and to your junkyard, not up to the stars."

"But—"

"Suppose your wife went? How would you feel, knowing she had *seen* and you had not? She would become holy. You would think of throwing her in the river. No, Bodoni, buy a new wrecking machine, which you need, and pull your dreams apart with it, and smash them to pieces."

The old man subsided,[3] gazing at the river in which, drowned, images of rockets burned down the sky.

"Good night," said Bodoni.

"Sleep well," said the other.

When the toast jumped from its silver box, Bodoni almost screamed. The night had been sleepless. Among his nervous children, beside his mountainous wife, Bodoni had twisted and stared at nothing. Bramante was right. Better to invest the money. Why save it when only one of the family could ride the rocket, while the others remained to melt in frustration?

"Fiorello, eat your toast," said his wife, Maria.

"My throat is shriveled," said Bodoni.

The children rushed in, the three boys fighting over a toy rocket, the two girls carrying dolls which duplicated the inhabitants of Mars, Venus, and Neptune, green mannequins with three yellow eyes and twelve fingers.

"I saw the Venus rocket!" cried Paolo.

"It took off, *whoosh!*" hissed Antonello.

"Children!" shouted Bodoni, hands to his ears.

They stared at him. He seldom shouted.

Bodoni arose. "Listen, all of you," he said. "I have enough money to take one of us on the Mars rocket."

Everyone yelled.

"You understand?" he asked. "Only *one* of us. Who?"

"Me, me, me!" cried the children.

"You," said Maria.

"You," said Bodoni to her.

They all fell silent.

---

2. **Bramante** (brä mänʹtā).

3. subside (səb sīdʹ), *v.* settle down, become quiet.

The children reconsidered. "Let Lorenzo go—he's oldest."

"Let Miriamne[4] go—she's a girl!"

"Think what you would see," said Bodoni's wife to him. But her eyes were strange. Her voice shook. "The meteors, like fish. The universe. The Moon. Someone should go who could tell it well on returning. You have a way with words."

"Nonsense. So have you," he objected.

Everyone trembled.

"Here," said Bodoni unhappily. From a broom he broke straws of various lengths. "The short straw wins." He held out his tight fist. "Choose."

Solemnly each took his turn.

"Long straw."

"Long straw."

Another.

"Long straw."

The children finished. The room was quiet.

Two straws remained. Bodoni felt his heart ache in him.

"Now," he whispered. "Maria."

She drew.

"The short straw," she said.

"Ah," sighed Lorenzo, half happy, half sad. "Mama goes to Mars."

Bodoni tried to smile. "Congratulations. I will buy your ticket today."

"Wait, Fiorello—"

"You can leave next week," he murmured.

She saw the sad eyes of her children upon her, with the smiles beneath their straight, large noses. She returned the straw slowly to her husband. "I cannot go to Mars."

"But why not?"

"I will be busy with another child."

"What!"

She would not look at him. "It wouldn't do for me to travel in my condition."

He took her elbow. "Is this the truth?"

"Draw again. Start over."

"Why didn't you tell me before?" he said <u>incredulously</u>.[5]

▲ Phil Huling, *The Pull of Gravity*, 1995. What do you think the title of this painting could mean?

"I didn't remember."

"Maria, Maria," he whispered, patting her face. He turned to the children. "Draw again."

Paolo immediately drew the short straw.

"I go to Mars!" He danced wildly. "Thank you, Father!"

The other children edged away. "That's swell, Paolo."

---

4. **Miriamne** (mir´ē äm´ne).
5. incredulously (in krej´ə ləs lē), *adv.* disbelievingly; skeptically.

Paolo stopped smiling to examine his parents and his brothers and sisters. "I *can* go, can't I?" he asked uncertainly.

"Yes."

"And you'll *like* me when I come back?"

"Of course."

Paolo studied the precious broomstraw on his trembling hand and shook his head. He threw it away. "I forgot. School starts. I can't go. Draw again."

But no one would draw. A full sadness lay on them.

"None of us will go," said Lorenzo.

"That's best," said Maria.

"Bramante was right," said Bodoni.

With his breakfast curdled[6] within him, Fiorello Bodoni worked in his junkyard, ripping metal, melting it, pouring out usable ingots.[7] His equipment flaked apart; competition had kept him on the insane edge of poverty for twenty years.

It was a very bad morning.

In the afternoon a man entered the junkyard and called up to Bodoni on his wrecking machine. "Hey, Bodoni, I got some metal for you!"

"What is it, Mr. Mathews?" asked Bodoni, listlessly.[8]

"A rocket ship. What's wrong? Don't you want it?"

"Yes, yes!" He seized the man's arm, and stopped, bewildered.

"Of course," said Mathews, "it's only a mockup. *You* know. When they plan a rocket they build a full-scale model first, of aluminum. You might make a small profit boiling her down. Let you have her for two thousand—"

Bondoni dropped his hand. "I haven't the money."

"Sorry. Thought I'd help you. Last time we talked you said how everyone outbid you on junk. Thought I'd slip this to you on the q.t.[9] Well—"

"I need new equipment. I saved money for that."

"I understand."

"If I bought your rocket, I wouldn't even be able to melt it down. My aluminum furnace broke down last week—"

"Sure."

"I couldn't possibly use the rocket if I bought it from you."

"I know."

Bodoni blinked and shut his eyes. He opened them and looked at Mr. Mathews. "But I am a great fool. I will take my money from the bank and give it to you."

The rocket was white and big in the junkyard.

"But if you can't melt the rocket down—"

"Deliver it," said Bodoni.

"All right, if you say so. Tonight?"

"Tonight," said Bodoni, "would be fine. Yes, I would like to have a rocket ship tonight."

There was a moon. The rocket was white and big in the junkyard. It held the whiteness of the moon and the blueness of the stars. Bodoni looked at it and loved all of it. He wanted to pet it and lie against it, pressing it with his cheek, telling it all the secret wants of his heart.

He stared up at it. "You are all mine," he said. "Even if you never move or spit fire, and just sit there and rust for fifty years, you are mine."

The rocket smelled of time and distance. It

---

6. **curdled** (kẻr′dld), *adj.* thickened; formed into curds.
7. **ingot** (ing′gət), *n.* mass of metal cast into a block or bar to be recast, rolled, or forged at a later time.
8. listlessly (list′lis lē), *adv.* inactively, carelessly; languidly.
9. **on the q.t.** quietly; in confidence, in secret.

was like walking into a clock. It was finished with Swiss delicacy. One might wear it on one's watch fob. "I might even sleep here tonight," Bodoni whispered excitedly.

He sat in the pilot's seat.

He touched a lever.

He hummed in his shut mouth, his eyes closed.

The humming grew louder, louder, higher, higher, wilder, stranger, more exhilarating, trembling in him and leaning him forward and pulling him and the ship in a roaring silence and in a kind of metal screaming, while his fists flew over the controls, and his shut eyes quivered,[10] and the sound grew and grew until it was a fire, a strength, a lifting and a pushing of power that threatened to tear him in half. He gasped. He hummed again and again, and did not stop, for it could not be stopped, it could only go on, his eyes tighter, his heart furious. "Taking off!" he screamed. *The jolting concussion![11] The thunder!* "The Moon!" he cried, eyes blind, tight. "The meteors!" *The silent rush in volcanic light.* "Mars. Oh, yes! Mars! Mars!"

He fell back, exhausted and panting. His shaking hands came loose of the controls and his head tilted wildly. He sat for a long time, breathing out and in, his heart slowing.

Slowly, slowly, he opened his eyes.

The junkyard was still there.

He sat motionless. He looked at the heaped piles of metal for a minute, his eyes never leaving them. Then, leaping up, he kicked the levers. "Take off, blast you!"

The ship was silent.

"I'll show you!" he cried.

Out in the night air, stumbling, he started the fierce motor of his terrible wrecking machine and advanced upon the rocket. He maneuvered[12] the massive weights into the moonlit sky. He readied his trembling hands to plunge the weights, to smash, to rip apart this insolently[13] false dream, this silly thing for which he had paid his money, which would not move, which would not do his bidding. "I'll teach you!" he shouted.

But his hand stayed.

The silver rocket lay in the light of the moon. And beyond the rocket stood the yellow lights of his home, a block away, burning warmly. He heard the family radio playing some distant music. He sat for half an hour considering the rocket and the house lights, and his eyes narrowed and grew wide. He stepped down

"It will fly," he said, looking at it.

from the wrecking machine and began to walk, and as he walked he began to laugh, and when he reached the back door of his house he took a deep breath and called, "Maria, Maria, start packing. We're going to Mars!"

"Oh!"

"Ah!"

"I can't *believe* it!"

"You will, you will."

The children balanced in the windy yard, under the glowing rocket, not touching it yet. They started to cry.

Maria looked at her husband. "What have you done?" she said. "Taken our money for this? It will never fly."

"It will fly," he said, looking at it.

"Rocket ships cost millions. Have you millions?"

"It will fly," he repeated steadily. "Now, go to the house, all of you. I have phone calls to make,

---

10. **quiver** (kwiv′ər), *v.* shake with a light but rapid motion; shiver; tremble.

11. **concussion** (kən kush′ən), *n.* sudden, violent shaking; shock.

12. **maneuver** (mə nü′vər), *v.* make a series of changes in position or direction for a specific purpose; manipulate; manage skillfully.

13. **insolently** (in′sə lənt lē), *adv.* contemptuously; impudently; overbearingly.

work to do. Tomorrow we leave! Tell no one, understand? It is a secret."

The children edged off from the rocket, stumbling. He saw their small, feverish faces in the house windows, far away.

Maria had not moved. "You have ruined us," she said.

"Our money used for this—this thing. When it should have been spent on equipment."

"You will see," he said.

Without a word she turned away.

"God help me," he whispered, and started to work.

Through the midnight hours trucks arrived, packages were delivered, and Bodoni, smiling, exhausted his bank account. With blowtorch and metal stripping he assaulted the rocket, added, took away, worked fiery magics

"This will be the one trip of your life. Keep your eyes wide."

and secret insults upon it. He bolted nine ancient automobile motors into the rocket's empty engine room. Then he welded the engine room shut, so none could see his hidden labor.

At dawn he entered the kitchen. "Maria," he said, "I'm ready for breakfast."

She would not speak to him.

At sunset he called to the children. "We're ready! Come on!" The house was silent.

"I've locked them in the closet," said Maria.

"What do you mean?" he demanded.

"You'll be killed in that rocket," she said. "What kind of rocket can you buy for two thousand dollars? A bad one!"

"Listen to me, Maria."

"It will blow up. Anyway, you are no pilot."

"Nevertheless, I can fly *this* ship. I have fixed it."

"You have gone mad," she said.

"Where is the key to the closet?"

"I have it here."

He put out his hand. "Give it to me."

She handed it to him. "You will kill them."

"No, no."

"Yes, you will. I *feel* it."

He stood before her. "You won't come along?"

"I'll stay here," she said.

"You will understand; you will see then," he said, and smiled. He unlocked the closet. "Come, children. Follow your father."

"Good-bye, good-bye, Mama!"

She stayed in the kitchen window, looking out at them, very straight and silent.

At the door of the rocket the father said, "Children, this is a swift rocket. We will be gone only a short while. You must come back to school, and I to my business." He took each of their hands in turn. "Listen. This rocket is very old and will fly only *one* more journey. It will not fly again. This will be the one trip of your life. Keep your eyes wide."

"Yes, Papa."

"Listen, keep your ears clean. Smell the smells of a rocket. *Feel. Remember.* So when you return you will talk of it all the rest of your lives."

"Yes, Papa."

The ship was quiet as a stopped clock. The airlock hissed shut behind them. He strapped them all, like tiny mummies, into rubber hammocks. "Ready?" he called.

"Ready!" all replied.

"Blast-off!" He jerked ten switches. The rocket thundered and leaped. The children danced in their hammocks, screaming. "We're moving! We're off! Look!"

"Here comes the Moon!"

The moon dreamed by. Meteors broke into fireworks. Time flowed away in a serpentine[14] of gas. The children shouted. Released from their hammocks, hours later, they peered from the ports. "There's Earth!" "There's Mars!"

---

14. **serpentine** (sėr′pən tēn′), *n.* something that winds, turns, or twists like a snake.

The rocket dropped pink petals of fire while the hour dials spun; the child eyes dropped shut. At last they hung like drunken moths in their cocoon hammocks.

"Good," whispered Bodoni, alone.

He tiptoed from the control room to stand for a long moment, fearful, at the airlock door.

He pressed a button. The airlock door swung wide. He stepped out. Into space? Into inky tides of meteor and gaseous torch? Into swift mileages and infinite dimensions?

No. Bodoni smiled.

All about the quivering rocket lay the junkyard.

Rusting, unchanged, there stood the padlocked junkyard gate, the little silent house by the river, the kitchen window lighted, and the river going down to the same sea. And in the center of the junkyard, manufacturing a magic dream, lay the quivering, purring rocket. Shaking and roaring, bouncing the netted children like flies in a web.

Maria stood in the kitchen window.

He waved to her and smiled.

He could not see if she waved or not. A small wave, perhaps. A small smile.

The sun was rising.

Bodoni withdrew hastily into the rocket. Silence. All still slept. He breathed easily. Tying himself into a hammock, he closed his eyes. To himself he prayed, Oh, let nothing happen to the illusion in the next six days. Let all of space come and go, and red Mars come up under our ship, and the moons of Mars, and let there be no flaws in the color film. Let there be three dimensions; let nothing go wrong with the hidden mirrors and screens that mold the fine illusion. Let time pass without crisis.

He awoke.

Red Mars floated near the rocket.

"Papa!" The children thrashed to be free.

Bodoni looked and saw red Mars and it was good and there was no flaw in it and he was very happy.

At sunset on the seventh day the rocket stopped shuddering.

"We are home," said Bodoni.

They walked across the junkyard from the open door of the rocket, their blood singing, their faces glowing. Perhaps they knew what he had done. Perhaps they guessed his wonderful magic trick. But if they knew, if they guessed, they never said. Now they only laughed and ran.

"I have ham and eggs for all of you," said Maria, at the kitchen door.

"Mama, Mama, you should have come, to see it, to see Mars, Mama, and meteors, and everything!"

"Yes," she said.

At bedtime the children gathered before Bodoni. "We want to thank you, Papa."

"It was nothing."

"We will remember it for always, Papa. We will never forget."

Very late in the night Bodoni opened his eyes. He sensed that his wife was lying beside him, watching him. She did not move for a very long time, and then suddenly she kissed his cheeks and his forehead. "What's this?" he cried.

"You're the best father in the world," she whispered.

"Why?"

"Now I see," she said. "I understand."

She lay back and closed her eyes, holding his hand. "Is it a very lovely journey?" she asked.

"Yes," he said.

"Perhaps," she said, "perhaps, some night, you might take me on just a little trip, do you think?"

"Just a little one, perhaps," he said.

"Thank you," she said. "Good night."

"Good night," said Fiorello Bodoni.

After Reading

Making Connections

Shaping Your Response

1. Do you think the Bodoni children realize their trip in space was an illusion? Why or why not?

2. Bodoni spends his savings on the rocket instead of investing it in new equipment. Do you agree with his decision? Why or why not?

Analyzing the Story

3. Why do Maria and Paolo turn down the chance to go on the Mars rocket?

4. 👣 What factors—social, economic, and cultural—affect Fiorello Bodoni's **perspective** on space travel?

Extending the Ideas

5. "The Rocket" takes place eighty years after space travel begins, which in actual history would be around the year 2040. Compare your vision of what life on Earth will be like then with Bradbury's.

6. Most of the selections you have read in Unit 3 have been poems. Does "The Rocket" have any poetic qualities? Explain.

Literary Focus: Dialogue

You have learned that **dialogue** helps develop characters and move the plot along. List qualities of Bodoni and his family that are revealed through dialogue. Then find one example where the dialogue helps develop the plot.

Vocabulary Study

incredulously
listlessly
maneuver
quiver
subside

Use the listed vocabulary words to write an opening scene for a science-fiction story of your own. If necessary, use your Glossary for help with word meanings.

Expressing Your Ideas

Writing Choices

Writer's Notebook Update In your notebook, explain whether or not "The Rocket" meets your expectations about science fiction.

Another Option

Fly Me to the Moon Investigate current techniques for creating special effects in movies, video games, or flight simulators, and present your findings in a **multimedia presentation.**

Ways of Seeing

Through Different Eyes

Career Connection
An architect must "see" a building long before it is ever constructed. In this article, architect Maura Donnelly explains how she has turned an early love for drawing houses into an ever-expanding career.

Architecture as Sculpture
by Maura Donnelly

Architecture is related to sculpture, but in sculpture, you create by reducing something. You start with a piece of marble or wood and carve it or chisel it *down* to the form you want. With architecture, you build *up* with bricks and mortar.

As a kid, I was always drawing houses. I remember that when I was nine, my parents decided to build a house. I worked for weeks and presented them with a design, but they said my ideas were too expensive!

In high school, I signed up for drafting class. At the time—this was in the 1970s—my high school did not encourage girls to become architects or engineers. In fact, my drafting teacher said that women didn't belong in architecture. When I mentioned his remark to my eighty-seven-year-old grandmother, she said, "Women certainly do belong in architecture, because women clean houses. If a woman built a house, she wouldn't put the laundry in the basement!"

When I went to college, I found a school that specialized in environmental design—Parsons School of Design in New York City. After graduation, I moved to Chicago and worked for a well-known architect, Harry Weese, who designed the Metro system in Washington, D.C. I worked mostly on individual rooms in large buildings, such as hotels and courthouses. Like many recent architecture graduates, I dealt with details such as where sprinkler heads would fit, or what type of wood trim would go on a judge's bench.

After a few years of on-the-job experience, I was eligible to take the professional licensing exam for architects. It's a very difficult exam —only 10 percent of the people who take it pass the entire exam the first time. I had to take some parts over, and I was relieved once I made it through!

Since then, I've worked as a construction project administrator. I hire the architect, supervise the design, hire contractors, and supervise the construction. I've worked on mental health institutions, colleges, prisons, and now, at my current job, on schools.

I'm also studying for a master's degree in urban planning. I guess my interests keep expanding. As an architect, I've designed rooms; as a construction administrator, I've overseen the building of those rooms from beginning to end; and now, with urban planning, I consider how entire buildings will fit into an urban landscape.

Architect Maura Donnelly

Responding
Take a look at floor plans in some architectural magazines, and try designing a room, a home, or a building of your dreams.

Fine Art Connection

Many people think of art as something that will fit on a wall, a shelf, or a tabletop. The art on these two pages reflects the vision of some creative people with big ideas about art. Very big ideas.

BIG ART

460

(opposite page) Sculptor Claes Oldenburg and Coosje Van Bruggen created *Spoonbridge and Cherry* (1985–1988), which spans a reflecting pool in Minneapolis.

(left) To create *Sunflower Still Life* (1986), artist Stan Herd planted and later harvested sunflowers, soybeans, and alfalfa on land borrowed from a Kansas farmer.

(lower left) Designed by sculptor Gutzon Borglum, Mount Rushmore in South Dakota is a massive memorial to four U.S. presidents.

(below) For his 1981 project *Surrounded Islands,* the artist Christo wrapped islands in Biscayne Bay, Florida, in miles of bright pink fabric.

Responding

1. How does size affect the impact of these works of art?

2. Make a sketch or mock-up of your own giant-size work of art. Give a sense of scale by showing buildings or people in the background.

Social Studies Connection

Across generations and cultures, the way we see the world has influenced the way we make our maps. And our maps have influenced the way we see the world! The maps on these pages not only depict certain places, but also reflect the world-views and values of the cultures that produced them.

MAPPING OUR WORLDS

The images on this page look at first like abstract art, but they are actually maps. The one above was produced by an Australian Aborigine and represents the lakes and other landmarks of the mapmaker's tribal homeland.

The ones below, carved from driftwood by the Inuit people of the Arctic region, provide highly accurate models of the coastline, necessary to a culture dependent on fishing.

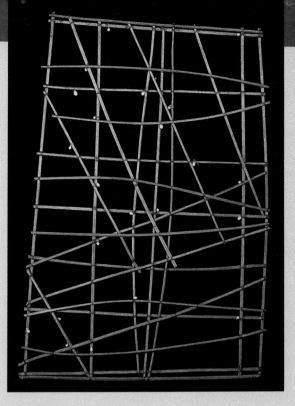

◄ Like the Inuit, the island peoples of the Pacific have needed maps for sea travel. These peoples have navigated immense distances over the open ocean using maps made of palmsticks and shells like the one shown here. The shells represent islands, and the sticks mark the prevailing movements of the ocean waves. Threads tied around the sticks indicate at what point an island would come into view on the horizon.

Maps such as this one guided European explorers to the New World. This one is French and is oriented to emphasize the part of North America that would become New France. Turn the map upside-down and it reveals a more familiar view of the Atlantic coastline. ▼

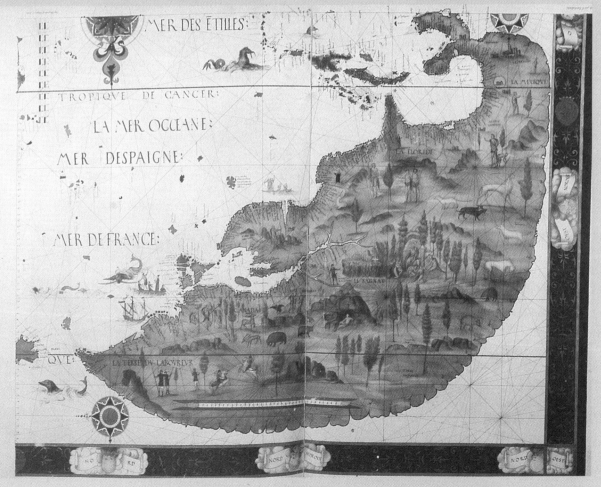

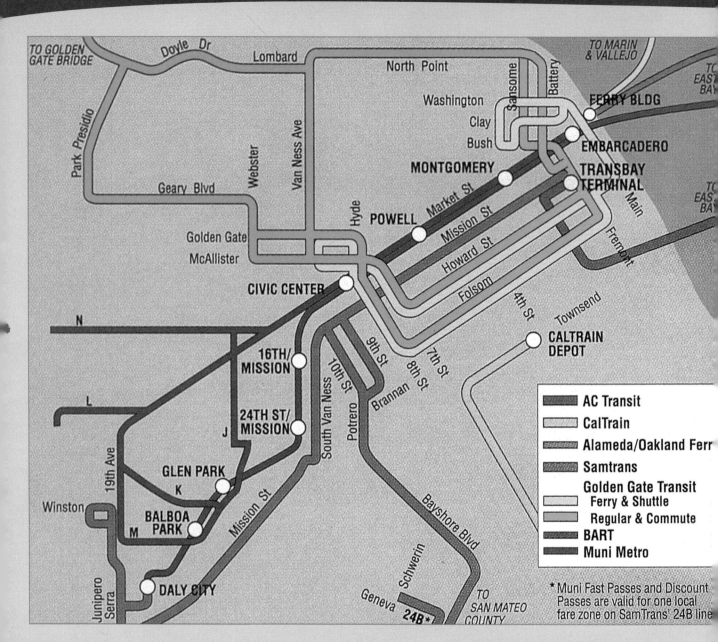

Public transit maps serve the same function as the other maps you have seen—guiding people from one place to another. This map contains useful information about public transportation in and around San Francisco, California.

Responding

1. Which of these maps do you find the most appealing as art? Explain.

2. Look at a map of a familiar area from an unusual perspective. (Try turning it upside-down, for example.) How does this change your sense of the relationships between places?

3. Create a stick-and-shell style map of your neighborhood.

Reading Mini-Lesson

Graphic Aids

Writers often use **graphic aids** to show readers a visual image of what they are trying to explain in words. There are many types of graphic aids, including illustrations, diagrams, charts, and graphs. Maps such as the ones shown on pages 462–464 are another commonly used graphic aid.

Modern maps usually have a feature known as a **key.** The key may use symbols, color codes, compass points, and mileage scales to help the viewer better understand the more intricate details of the map. For example, the key to a map of the United States will show symbols for important places such as capital cities and state parks. The key will probably show different colors for various highway and superhighway routes. Always look closely at a map key. You may find details that you didn't notice upon first glance.

Take a look at the map on the opposite page. It shows eight public transit routes within the San Francisco Bay Area. Each route is represented by a different color, as illustrated in the key at the bottom-right-hand corner of the map. Notice that this map does not provide information about distances. Can you think of any reasons for that?

Activity Options

1. Choose two spots on the map on page 464. Write out directions on how to get from one place to the other. Be sure to mention important landmarks and cross streets along the way. Give your written directions to a partner and see if he or she can trace the route you are recommending on the map.

2. Work with a partner to create a map of your school for new students. Show important locations such as the school's entrances, classrooms, the gymnasium, and the principal's office. Decide on symbols to represent water fountains, bathrooms, and other features, and include these symbols in your map key. To test your map, make a copy of it and mark a route for someone else to follow.

Writing Workshop

Reflections in a Poet's Eye

Assignment Use the medium of poetry to reflect on someone or something that is close and important to you.

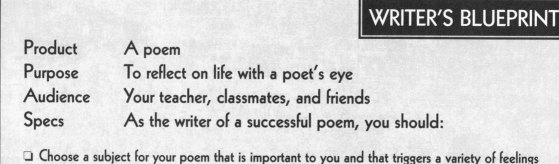

WRITER'S BLUEPRINT

Product   A poem

Purpose   To reflect on life with a poet's eye

Audience   Your teacher, classmates, and friends

Specs   As the writer of a successful poem, you should:

❏ Choose a subject for your poem that is important to you and that triggers a variety of feelings and thoughts. Your subject could be something specific and concrete, such as a seashell, a friend, or a place in nature. Or it might be an abstract idea or a concern, such as friendship or prejudice.

❏ Use poetic devices, such as imagery and figures of speech, to help bring your subject to life.

❏ Be sure to show the reader how and why your subject is important to you.

❏ Use punctuation suitable for the kind of poem you're writing. Make sure everything is spelled correctly.

STEP 1 PREWRITING

Brainstorm subjects for your poem. First, look back at the literature and list the subjects the poets deal with. Then list things that are important to you. A journal or diary would be a good source to look into. Consider people, places, things, activities, special moments in time, and things you've seen, done, and dreamed. Choose your subject from this list.

Draw your subject. If your subject is concrete, draw it from different angles. If it's abstract, draw images that it brings to mind.

Search out figures of speech in the poems in this unit. Here are some examples from one of the prose selections, "The Rocket."

Figures of Speech	Purpose	Example
imagery	to paint pictures in the reader's mind by appealing to the senses	"green mannequins with three yellow eyes and twelve fingers"
simile	to state a likeness between two things that are very different from each other (uses *like* or *as*)	"The rocket smelled of time and distance. It was like walking into a clock."
metaphor	like a simile, but does not use *like* or *as*	"The sound grew and grew until it was a fire. . . ."
personification	give an object lifelike qualities	"the rockets sighing in the dark sky"

Return to your drawings and brainstorm figures of speech about them. List images that appeal to the senses and comparisons that help bring your subject to life.

Quickwrite about your subject for five minutes or so in prose. Don't try to write a poem yet. Work on simply getting your ideas down for right now. Be sure you deal with why your subject is important to you.

Find the golden lines. Look back at your quickwrite and highlight your favorite lines. Look especially for lively figures of speech.

Make a writing plan. Assemble your golden lines in the order you'll want to present them. Then make notes on other ideas you'll want to deal with.

STEP 2 DRAFTING

Before you draft, look back at the poems in this unit one more time and notice the form of each poem. Get an idea of the many possibilities for the form your poem might take. Also, review the Writer's Blueprint and your prewriting materials.

As you draft, remember that writing poetry takes time. Be prepared to make changes in your draft. Here are some drafting tips.

- Prop your drawings up in front of you so you can look at them as you draft.

- Keep in mind that one of your prime objectives is to show the reader why your subject is important to you. See the Revising Strategy in Step 3 of this lesson.

3 REVISING

Ask a partner for comments on your draft before you revise it.

✔ Have I used figures of speech effectively?

✔ Have I shown the reader how and why my subject is important to me?

Revising Strategy

Getting Your Message Across

Poetry is personal. Poets want readers to see and hear and feel what they, personally, see, hear, and feel. They also want readers to understand why something is important to them. Have you done this in your poem? With a partner, follow these three steps to test how well you've gotten your message across.

1. Read your draft again and, on a separate piece of paper, complete this sentence:

   This subject is important to me because _____.

2. Fold this paper over and keep it with you. Then have your partner read your draft and respond to it by completing this sentence:

   This subject is important to you because _____.

3. Compare your response and your partner's to see how well you've gotten your message across. See if you can use your partner's response when you revise. Notice how one writer used a partner's response to improve a poem in the student model that follows.

To listen is our job

If you cannot hear its fierce roar   *I'm not sure what kind of battle you mean.*

Then you are not at peace

But a victim of war.   *The battles are as wicked as a demon's face*
                          It is a battle of color and race

If you are a part of this battle of fate

You must save yourself before it's too late

STUDENT MODEL

4 EDITING

Ask a partner to review your revised draft before you edit. Look especially for spelling errors that occur because letters are not in the right order.

Editing Strategy

Spelling: Getting Letters in the Right Order

We misspell some words because they have combinations of letters that are easy to write in the wrong order. When you edit your poem, pay attention to words like these:

believe	neutral	their	weird
through	glimpse	like	because
doesn't	tremendous	fail	real

STEP 5 PRESENTING

- Find music that supports the imagery in your poem and use it as background music as you read to the class.

- Decorate your poem. Draw your own illustration or photocopy a picture of a famous painting and put it on the page with your poem. Copy the two items together.

STEP 6 LOOKING BACK

Self-evaluate. Look back at the Writer's Blueprint and give yourself a score for each item, from 6 (superior) to 1 (inadequate).

Reflect. Write your responses to these questions.

✔ What did writing a poem about your particular subject reveal to you about that subject that you hadn't realized before? Explain.

✔ Wait a few days and read your poem again. Explain how your view of your poem changed over this brief span of time.

For Your Working Portfolio Add your poem and your reflection responses to your working portfolio.

Beyond Print

Multimedia Presentations

Modern technology makes it possible to add some zip to your classroom presentations. Using multimedia tools such as slides, audiotapes, videos, overhead projectors, computers, and CD-ROMs, you can transform a routine report into an exciting media event.

A computer is an especially powerful tool for producing a multimedia presentation. Linking the computer with a projection unit allows you to add animation, special effects, sound, and video to an oral report. Through some software and CD-ROM products, you can even create an interactive program that viewers can explore at their own pace and in the order they determine.

Whether or not you have access to a computer, organization is the key to an effective multimedia presentation. Here are some tips for success:

- Begin planning by developing an outline and a clear thesis. Try to create a strong beginning, middle, and end that will make your point clear to the audience, just as you would in a written essay.

- Remember that good writing skills are important. Text should be concise and clear, especially since viewers may have only a few seconds to read. Headings should be spelled correctly.

- Use pictures and music to enrich the information, not to distract from it. Don't overload on "busy" images or sounds. Use colors that will stand out across the room.

- Use the media to create clear transitions from one section to another. For example, as you are finishing the current section, you could fade in some music that relates to the next section.

- Use large text in projections so everyone will be able to read it. Don't try to put all your information on the screen; instead, summarize your major points in a series of headings and present the details orally.

CD-ROM products such as **AuthorWorks**, shown here, may contain a multimedia tool that allows you to design your own interactive presentations.

- Project your voice clearly so everyone will hear and understand you.

- Before beginning a presentation, double-check all your equipment. Is everything plugged in and turned on? Are slides, tapes, discs, or files loaded and ready to go?

- Each piece of media you add will make your presentation more complicated, so practice is essential. Be sure to carry out several "dress rehearsals" of your presentation. In the case of multimedia, practice really does make for perfection.

Activity Options

1. Prepare a multimedia presentation based on a selection, an author, or a theme found in Unit 3. Start by preparing an outline that lists the information you will provide and the different media you will use to provide it.

2. Using a multimedia program such as **AuthorWorks** or HyperCard, create an interactive presentation that viewers can navigate on their own. Your presentation should include images, text, and clear instructions on how to move from section to section.

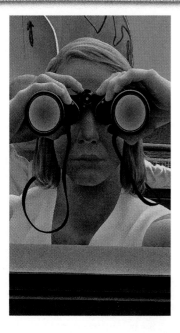

Multicultural Connections

Individuality

Part One: Family Matters These selections describe how a person's individuality can be influenced by family relationships.

■ Compare and contrast the lessons learned from family members in "Making a Fist," "The Courage That My Mother Had," and "Alligator."

Choice

Part Two: Songs of Hope In "The Exhibit," the speaker's elderly uncle chooses to believe that a better world is possible.

■ In "Oye Mundo/ Sometimes" and "Saturday Afternoon, When Chores Are Done," what choices do the speakers make to affirm hopeful possibilities in life?

Perspective

Part Three: Ways of Seeing "Nameless, Tennessee" hints at the factors that influence the perspectives of author William Least Heat Moon and of the Watts family. What are some of those factors?

■ The poems by Duane BigEagle, John Moffitt, and Emily Dickinson each reveal a certain attitude toward life. Reread the biographical information and explain what cultural, spiritual, or social factors might affect these authors' perspectives.

Activities

1. Consider this statement: Expressions of individuality should not be allowed to conflict with cultural or family traditions. With a small group, stage a debate that examines both sides of this question.

2. Making a choice about who to be or what to believe in is a theme that appears throughout this unit. For at least three of the selections, identify what kind of a choice is made and what cultural values, if any, influence that choice. Present your findings on a chart.

3. With a partner, choose three artists whose artwork appears in this book. Do some research to answer these questions about each artist: What is his or her perspective on art? How has that perspective been influenced by the artist's cultural heritage?

Independent and Group Projects

Writing

Poetic Thoughts The poetry in this unit represents a wide range of styles and approaches. Some poems rhyme, others do not. Some are written in stanzas of a certain length, while others have no set form. Uses of punctuation and capitalization vary. Some of the poems can be understood right away, while others require a few readings. In a brief paper, explain which of the styles of poetry found in this unit appeal to you most, and why. Be sure to use specific examples from the poems.

Dance

A Moving Message A dance expresses feelings about a subject through the movements of the dancers. Alone or with others, choreograph and present a dance that expresses your feelings about one aspect of life. Possible subjects include sports, the environment, life in your community, dreams for the future, and so on.

Art

Artistic Visions The art that appears in this unit presents some unique visions of reality. Create a piece of art, whether a painting, sculpture, weaving, diorama, or another form, that reflects your own unique perspective on the world.

Discussion

Taking Another Look The selections you have read in Unit 3 represent only a tiny sampling from the works of these authors. With a small group, choose three authors from this unit and read at least one other poem, story, or memoir by each author. Then hold a discussion to compare the new selections with the ones you have already read.

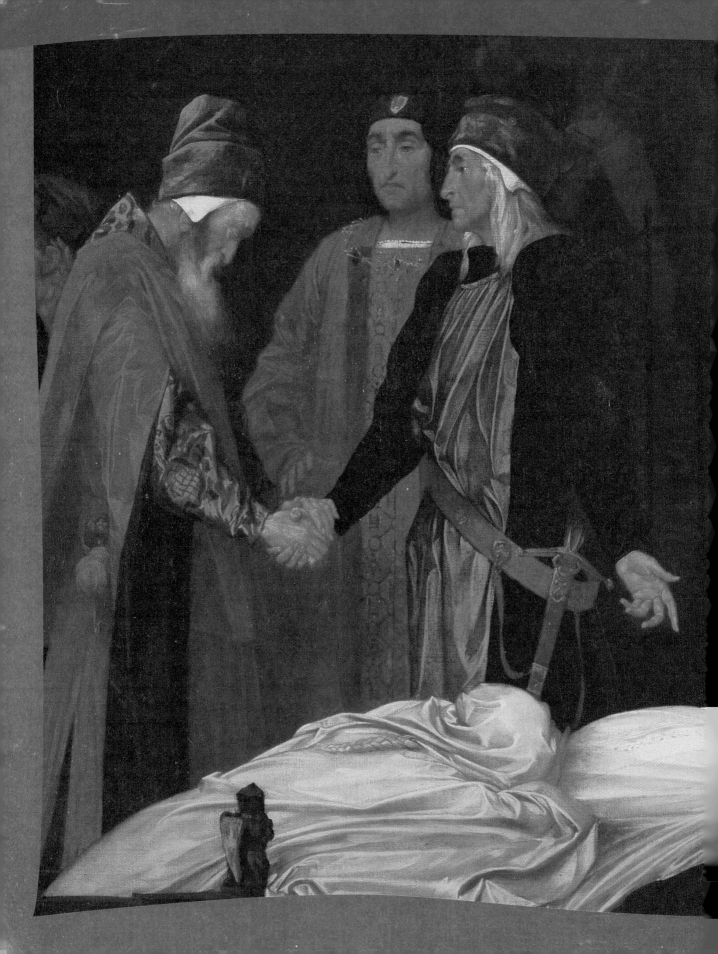

LOVE
CONQUERS

Love and Sacrifice
Pages 478–603

Reading

Love, hatred, death, destiny—the themes of William Shakespeare's tragic play *Romeo and Juliet* are as timely today as they were four hundred years ago. But many people are intimidated by Shakespeare's plays. "The words are too big!" "Everyone talks funny!" "I don't get it!" The tips you'll find on these pages may help you set aside your fears, so that you can experience the drama, beauty, and excitement of a Shakespearean play.

Read the scene summary.

At the beginning of each scene, a brief summary gives you the highlights. Read the summaries to know what to expect as you read the play.

Use the notes.

In the margins, you will find definitions and pronunciations of unfamiliar words and phrases, as well as questions to help your understanding.

Keep reading.

Shakespeare's audience could hear the words and see the accompanying action. They probably didn't "get" every word, but could follow the general flow of events. When you read, go through several speeches or a whole page before going back to reread. Pay attention to the **stage directions** in order to visualize the action.

a *Shakespearean Play*

Learn Shakespeare's vocabulary.
Some pronouns and verbs have changed in form or in meaning over the centuries. For example, Shakespeare's characters sometimes use other pronouns for *you: thou* or *thee* for the subject and object in a sentence; *thy* or *thine* for *your* and *yours.* Verbs may appear in unfamiliar forms, often ending in *t, st,* or *th.* Thus, *has = hast* or *hath; can = canst; are = art; will = wilt; do* or *does = dost; were = wert.*

Rearrange sentences.
The order of words and phrases is sometimes unusual. The verb may come before the subject. Phrases may be separated from the subject or verb they modify. Consider this example:

> "At this same ancient feast of Capulet's
> Sups the fair Rosaline whom thou so loves,
> With all the admirèd beauties of Verona."

The verb, *sups,* comes before the subject, *Rosaline.* The clause that follows, "whom thou so lovest," describes Rosaline. But the last phrase, "With all the admirèd beauties of Verona," refers back to the verb *sups* again. When you come across a confusing passage, try rearranging the phrases in an order that makes more sense to you.

Note the rhythm of the lines.
Most of *Romeo and Juliet* is written in **blank verse** (also called **iambic pentameter**), a form of poetry in which unrhymed lines have ten syllables. Stressed syllables usually alternate with unstressed syllables, as in this line: "O, she doth teach the torches to burn bright!"

In the line, "That I must love a loathèd enemy," the accent mark indicates that *loathed* should have two syllables—loath-ed—to give the line ten syllables. Elsewhere, Shakespeare contracts words to make them fit the rhythm: *o'er* for *over; is't* for *is it.*

Think about the characters.
As you read the play, form a picture in your mind of each major character. What does the dialogue reveal? What are the character's strengths and weaknesses? How does the character change in the course of the play? Seeing the characters as if they were real people will help you enter into the play.

Interpret figurative language.
Shakespeare often uses figurative language to convey important ideas. Ask yourself what the comparison is and what it suggests. For example, Romeo says "Love is a smoke made with the fume of sighs." What is he saying about love?

Read passages aloud.
Shakespeare wrote *Romeo and Juliet* for the stage, not the page. As you read the play, read passages aloud to better appreciate the wordplay, rhythm, and meaning. If possible, see a production of the play or rent it on video—the 1968 film directed by Franco Zeffirelli, from which the photographs in this book are taken, is a well-known version.

Love and Sacrifice

Love weaves joy and sorrow into our lives, bringing tears as well as laughter. The characters in the following selections believe in the transformative power of love despite the hardships they encounter.

🐾 Multicultural Connection **Interactions** between groups of people may involve either cooperation or conflict, depending on how the groups resolve their differences. Sometimes a group demands that, as a sign of loyalty, its members reject the members of another group. What group pressures do Romeo and Juliet face? How do those pressures affect their lives?

Before Reading

Romeo and Juliet

by William Shakespeare

William Shakespeare
1564–1616

Nearly four hundred years after his death, William Shakespeare remains the best-known author in English literature. Born in Stratford, England, Shakespeare married Anne Hathaway at eighteen and had three children. Several years later, he moved to London, where he became a successful man of the theater: actor, playwright, producer, and theater owner. He retired at forty-six and died of unknown causes at fifty-two.

Although many details about Shakespeare's life are unknown, records show that he was generous, easygoing, and well-liked. In addition to writing poetry, Shakespeare wrote and produced thirty-eight plays, averaging two each year. The play you are about to read, *Romeo and Juliet,* was probably written between 1594 and 1596.

Building Background

The Globe Theater

Many of William Shakespeare's plays were first performed at the Globe Theater in London, pictured in the illustration. The main acting area, called the platform, or cockpit, jutted out over the brick-paved courtyard about 5½ feet above the ground. At either side were large permanent doors that served as the main stage entrances. A number of trap doors in the floor of the platform led to the area below stage known as Hell. From these trap doors arose apparitions, smoke, and fog, and through them actors descended when the action required them to go underground. The rooms on the top two floors could be curtained or not, depending on the requirements of a particular play. The middle room of the top floor was used as a musicians' gallery or as an acting area.

Sound effects such as thunder or battle "alarums" were produced in the three rooms above the top floor, called the huts. The huts also housed a pulley system used to suspend items in midair when

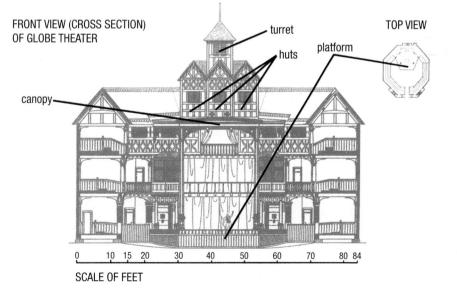

FRONT VIEW (CROSS SECTION) OF GLOBE THEATER

TOP VIEW

turret

huts

platform

canopy

SCALE OF FEET
0 10 15 20 30 40 50 60 70 80 84

necessary. Above them was the turret, from which the flag was flown to indicate that a performance was to be given.

Surrounding the entire stage was a hollow eight-sided structure three stories high. (See the "top view.") This building formed a circle—a "wooden O," as Shakespeare called it. While the structure itself had a roof, the area it enclosed did not. People who bought the cheapest tickets—known as groundlings—stood in the exposed yard to watch the play. Those who could afford higher admission fees sat within the structure, on benches placed on each of the three floors. The theater could accommodate about 2000 spectators.

The first Globe Theater, completed around 1599, burned down in 1613. A new Globe, promptly built on the same spot, stood until 1644, when it was torn down, and houses were erected on its site. Today a new Globe, a replica of the earlier theaters, is being built near its original site south of the Thames River.

Literary Focus

Theme The **theme** of a literary work, or its underlying meaning, often helps us make a connection between the literature and our own lives. Because every reader's personality and experiences are unique, certain themes in a story may be more meaningful for one person than for others. Some of the best stories can be understood in different ways, depending on the individual perspective of the reader. As you begin reading *Romeo and Juliet*, consider what theme or themes in the play are most meaningful to you.

Writer's Notebook

Ties That Bind Have you ever heard the expression, "Children pay for the sins of their parents"? Briefly explain in your notebook what you think this statement means. Then explain why you agree or disagree with it. If possible, use examples to support your opinion.

This photograph and the others that appear throughout the play are film stills from Franco Zeffirelli's 1968 film *Romeo and Juliet,* starring Leonard Whiting and Olivia Hussey in the title roles. What is your first impression of this young couple? ➤

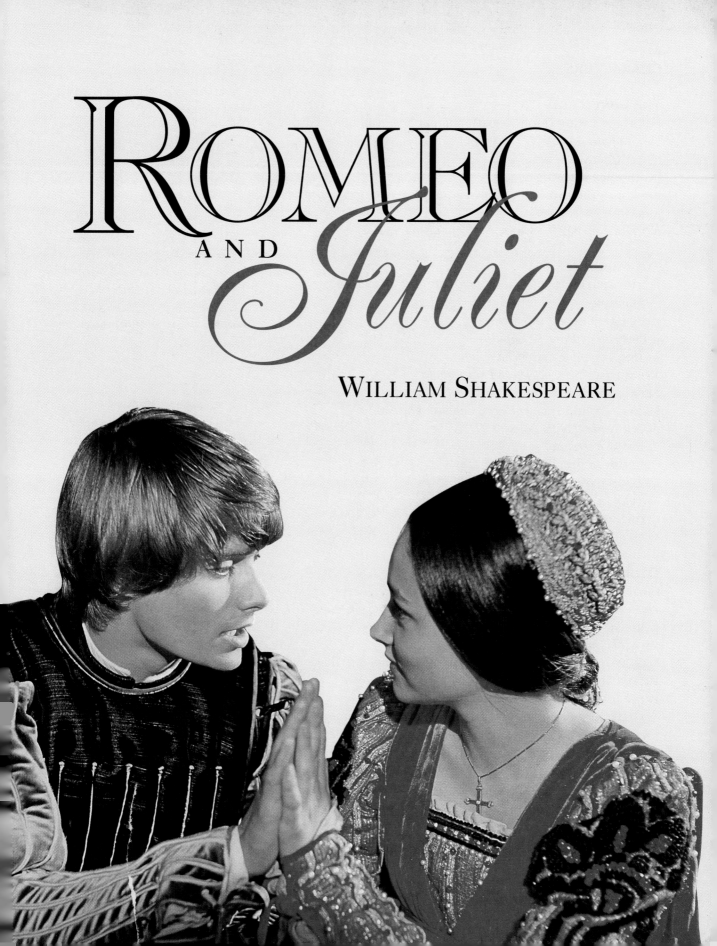

ROMEO
AND *Juliet*

WILLIAM SHAKESPEARE

CHARACTERS

THE MONTAGUES

LORD MONTAGUE (mon′tə gyü), *father of Romeo and sworn enemy of the house of Capulet*

LADY MONTAGUE, *his wife*

ROMEO, *son of the Montagues*

BENVOLIO (ben vōl′ē ō), *Montague's nephew and Romeo's friend*

ABRAHAM, *a servant*

BALTHASAR (bäl′thə zär′), *a servant attending Romeo*

THE CAPULETS

LORD CAPULET (kap′yü let), *father of Juliet and sworn enemy of the house of Montague*

LADY CAPULET, *his wife*

JULIET, *daughter of the Capulets*

NURSE, *servant to and friend of Juliet*

TYBALT (tib′əlt), *nephew of Lady Capulet*

PETRUCHIO (pə trüch′ē ō), *Capulet's kinsman*

SECOND CAPULET, *an old man, Capulet's kinsman*

PETER, *servant of the Nurse*

SAMSON, *a servant*

GREGORY, *a servant*

ANTHONY, *a servant*

POTPAN, *a servant*

CLOWN *or* SERVANT

Other SERVANTS

OTHERS

CHORUS, *actor who introduces Acts 1 and 2*

PRINCE, *Prince Escalus* (es′kə ləs), *ruler of Verona*

PARIS, *a young count (or county) and kinsman of the Prince*

PAGE *to Count Paris*

MERCUTIO (mėr kyü′shē ō), *the Prince's kinsman and Romeo's friend*

FRIAR LAURENCE, *Franciscan priest and friend to Romeo*

FRIAR JOHN, *trusted messenger of Friar Laurence*

APOTHECARY (ə poth′ə ker′ē), *a pharmacist in Mantua*

Three MUSICIANS *(Simon Catling, Hugh Rebeck, and James Soundpost)*

Three WATCHMEN

CITIZENS, MASKERS, TORCHBEARERS, GUARDS, SERVANTS, *and* ATTENDANTS

ACT ONE

PROLOGUE

Summary *The Chorus, a single actor, summarizes the plot of the play, and suggests its themes.*

Enter CHORUS.

CHORUS. Two households, both alike in dignity,
    In fair Verona, where we lay our scene,
    From ancient grudge break to new mutiny,
        Where civil blood makes civil hands unclean.
5   From forth the fatal loins of these two foes
        A pair of star-crossed lovers take their life;
    Whose misadventured piteous overthrows
        Doth with their death bury their parents' strife.
    The fearful passage of their death-marked love,
10   And the continuance of their parents' rage,
    Which, but their children's end, naught could remove,
        Is now the two hours' traffic of our stage;
    The which if you with patient ears attend,
    What here shall miss, our toil shall strive to mend.   *(Exit.)*

3 mutiny (myūt′n ē), *n.* rioting.

6 star-crossed, ill-fated. In Shakespeare's day, it was commonly believed that the stars controlled people's lives.

11 but, except for.
11 naught (nôt), *n.* nothing; zero. Also, **nought.**

■ What does the Prologue **foreshadow** about the end of the play?

SCENE 1

Summary *When a sword fight breaks out between the servants of two feuding houses, Prince Escalus of Verona threatens both Capulet and Montague with death should such a disturbance occur again. Lord and Lady Montague ask Benvolio if he knows the cause of Romeo's depression. When Benvolio asks Romeo, he is told that the woman Romeo loves has refused him.*

A public square in Verona. Enter SAMSON *and* GREGORY, *servants of the house of Capulet, armed with swords and small shields.*

SAMSON. Gregory, on my word, we'll not carry coals.

GREGORY. No, for then we should be colliers.

SAMSON. I mean, an we be in choler, we'll draw.

GREGORY. Ay, while you live, draw your neck out of collar.

5 **SAMSON** *(with mock belligerence).* I strike quickly, being moved.

GREGORY. But thou art not quickly moved to strike.

SAMSON. A dog of the house of Montague moves me.

GREGORY. To move is to stir, and to be valiant is to stand. Therefore, if thou art moved, thou runn'st away.

10 **SAMSON.** A dog of that house shall move me to stand. I will take the wall of any man or maid of Montague's.

GREGORY. That shows thee a weak slave, for the weakest goes to the wall.

1 carry coals, endure insults.
2 collier (kol′yər), *n.* coal or charcoal dealer; person looked down upon.
3 an we . . . draw, if we are angry, we'll draw (our swords).
4 collar, a halter used by the hangman.
5 belligerence (bə lij′ər - əns), *n.* fighting attitude.

10 take the wall of, get the better of.
12 weakest . . . wall. The weakest are always forced to give way.

SAMSON. 'Tis true, and therefore women, being the weaker vessels, are
15   ever thrust to the wall. Therefore I will push Montague's men from
the wall and thrust his maids to the wall.

GREGORY. The quarrel is between our masters and us their men.

SAMSON. 'Tis all one. I will show myself a tyrant: when I have fought with
the men, I will be civil with the maids—I will cut off their heads.

20 **GREGORY.** The heads of the maids?

SAMSON. Ay, the heads of the maids, or their maidenheads. Take it in
what sense thou wilt.

GREGORY. They must take it in sense that feel it.

SAMSON. Me they shall feel while I am able to stand, and 'tis known I
25   am a pretty piece of flesh.

GREGORY. 'Tis well thou art not fish; if thou hadst, thou hadst been
Poor John. Draw thy tool. Here comes of the house of Montagues.

(Enter ABRAHAM *and* BALTHASAR, *servants of the Montagues.)*

SAMSON. My naked weapon is out. Quarrel, I will back thee.

GREGORY. How, turn thy back and run?

30 **SAMSON.** Fear me not.

GREGORY. No, marry. I fear thee!

SAMSON. Let us take the law of our side. Let them begin.

GREGORY. I will frown as I pass by, and let them take it as they list.

SAMSON. Nay, as they dare. I will bite my thumb at them, which is
35   disgrace to them if they bear it.

*(*SAMSON *makes taunting gestures.)*

ABRAHAM. Do you bite your thumb at us, sir?

SAMSON. I do bite my thumb, sir.

ABRAHAM. Do you bite your thumb at us, sir?

SAMSON *(aside to* GREGORY*)*. Is the law of our side if I say ay?

40 **GREGORY.** No.

SAMSON *(to* ABRAHAM*)*. No, sir, I do not bite my thumb at you, sir, but
I bite my thumb, sir.

GREGORY *(to* ABRAHAM*)*. Do you quarrel, sir?

ABRAHAM. Quarrel, sir? No, sir.

45 **SAMSON.** But if you do, sir, I am for you. I serve as good a man as you.

ABRAHAM. No better.

SAMSON. Well, sir.

GREGORY *(aside to* SAMSON*)*. Say "better." Here comes one of my master's kinsmen.

50 **SAMSON** *(to* ABRAHAM*)*. Yes, better, sir.

ABRAHAM. You lie.

(Enter BENVOLIO, *a nephew of* MONTAGUE *and hence a first cousin of*
ROMEO.*)*

SAMSON. Draw, if you be men. Gregory, remember thy washing blow.

(The four SERVANTS *fight.)*

BENVOLIO. Part, fools!

---

17 masters . . . men, only between the men of the household, not the women.

27 Poor John, dried and salted hake, a poor kind of fish.

30 Fear me not. Don't mistrust me.
31 marry, by the Virgin Mary; a mild oath.
32 take the law of, have the law on.
33 list, wish.
34 bite my thumb, an insulting gesture.

■ How do Samson and Gregory taunt Abraham into starting a fight?

■ Both Samson and Gregory are cowards at heart. What suddenly gives them the courage to draw their swords?

52 washing, crushing.

Put up your swords. You know not what you do.
(He beats down their swords.)
(Enter TYBALT, *a hot-headed youth, nephew of* LADY CAPULET *and first cousin of* JULIET.*)*

TYBALT *(contemptuously).* What, art thou drawn among these heartless
55   hinds?
Turn thee, Benvolio. Look upon thy death.
BENVOLIO *(quietly).* I do but keep the peace. Put up thy sword,
Or manage it to part these men with me.
TYBALT *(scornfully).* What, drawn and talk of peace? I hate the word
60   As I hate hell, all Montagues, and thee.
(They fight.)
Have at thee, coward!
(Enter several of both houses, who join the fray; then enter an OFFICER *and* CITIZENS *with clubs or other weapons.)*
CITIZENS. Clubs, bills, and partisans! Strike! Beat them down!
Down with the Capulets! Down with the Montagues!
(Enter old CAPULET *in his dressing gown, and* LADY CAPULET.*)*
CAPULET *(who cannot resist joining in the quarrel).* What noise is this?
Give me my long sword, ho!
LADY CAPULET *(scornfully).* A crutch, a crutch! Why call you for
65   a sword?
CAPULET. My sword, I say! Old Montague is come
And flourishes his blade in spite of me.
(Enter old MONTAGUE *and* LADY MONTAGUE.*)*
MONTAGUE. Thou villain Capulet! *(To his wife.)* Hold me not, let me go.
LADY MONTAGUE. Thou shalt not stir one foot to seek a foe.
(Enter PRINCE ESCALUS, *head of Verona's government, with* ATTENDANTS.*)*
70   PRINCE *(sternly).* Rebellious subjects, enemies to peace,
Profaners of this neighbor-stainèd steel—
Will they not hear? What, ho! You men, you beasts,
That quench the fire of your <u>pernicious</u> rage
With purple fountains issuing from your veins,
75   On pain of torture, from those bloody hands
Throw your mistempered weapons to the ground
And hear the sentence of your movèd prince.
Three civil brawls, bred of an airy word,
By thee, old Capulet, and Montague,
80   Have thrice disturbed the quiet of our streets
And made Verona's ancient citizens
Cast by their grave-beseeming ornaments
To wield old partisans in hands as old,
Cankered with peace, to part your cankered hate.
85   If ever you disturb our streets again
Your lives shall pay the forfeit of the peace.

55 heartless hinds (hīnds), cowardly servants.

61 Have at thee. I shall attack you; be on your guard.

62 bills . . . partisans (pär′tə-zəns), long-handled spears with sharp cutting blades.

65 crutch. Lady Capulet implies that a crutch is better suited to her aged husband than is a sword.
67 flourish (flėr′ish), *v.* make a showy display.

■ Escalus breaks off his speech in line 72 to ask a question. Why do you think he does this?

73 pernicious (pər nish′əs), *adj.* destructive; fatal, deadly.

78 airy, merely a breath, trivial.
82–83 Cast . . . partisans, give up the staffs old men carry and take up spears.
84 Cankered (kang′kərd), *adj.* corroded.
84 cankered, malignant.
86 forfeit (fôr′fit) **of the peace,** penalty for disturbing the peace.

For this time all the rest depart away.
You, Capulet, shall go along with me,
And Montague, come you this afternoon,
90   To know our farther pleasure in this case,
To old Freetown, our common judgment-place.
Once more, on pain of death, all men depart.
(*Exit all but* MONTAGUE, LADY MONTAGUE, *and* BENVOLIO.)

MONTAGUE. Who set this ancient quarrel new abroach?
(*To* BENVOLIO.) Speak, nephew, were you by when it began?

95 **BENVOLIO.** Here were the servants of your adversary,
And yours, close fighting ere I did approach.
I drew to part them. In the instant came
The fiery Tybalt with his sword prepared,
Which, as he breathed defiance to my ears,
100   He swung about his head and cut the winds
Who, nothing hurt withal, hissed him in scorn.
While we were interchanging thrusts and blows,
Came more and more, and fought on part and part
Till the Prince came, who parted either part.

105 **LADY MONTAGUE.** O, where is Romeo? Saw you him today?
Right glad I am he was not at this fray.

BENVOLIO. Madam, an hour before the worshiped sun
Peered forth the golden window of the east,
A troubled mind drave me to walk abroad,
110   Where, underneath the grove of sycamore
That westward rooteth from this city's side,
So early walking did I see your son.
Towards him I made, but he was ware of me
And stole into the covert of the wood.
115   I, measuring his affections by my own,
Which then most sought where most might not be found,
Being one too many by my weary self,
Pursued my humor, not pursuing his,
And gladly shunned who gladly fled from me.

120 **MONTAGUE.** Many a morning hath he there been seen,
With tears augmenting the fresh morning's dew,
Adding to clouds more clouds with his deep sighs;
But all so soon as the all-cheering sun
Should in the farthest east begin to draw
125   The shady curtains from Aurora's bed,
Away from light steals home my heavy son
And private in his chamber pens himself,
Shuts up his windows, locks fair daylight out,
And makes himself an artificial night.

---

93 set . . . abroach, reopened this old quarrel.

95 adversary (ad′vər ser′ē), *n.* enemy, foe.

101 Who . . . withal (wi ᴛʜôl′), the winds, hurt not at all by Tybalt's swinging of his sword.
103 on . . . part, on one side and then the other.
106 fray, noisy quarrel.

109 drave, drove.
110 sycamore, a tree symbolic of unhappy lovers.

113 ware, wary.

115 affections, wishes, feelings.
116 most . . . found, chiefly yearned for a place where others would not be found.
118 humor, mood, whim.

121 augment (ôg ment′), *v.* increase; add to.

125 Aurora (ô rôr′ə), goddess of the dawn.
126 heavy, sad.

130   Black and <u>portentous</u> must this humor prove
       Unless good counsel may the cause remove.
    BENVOLIO. My noble uncle, do you know the cause?
    MONTAGUE. I neither know it nor can learn of him.
    BENVOLIO. Have you importuned him by any means?
135 **MONTAGUE.** Both by myself and many other friends.
       But he, his own affections' counselor,
       Is to himself—I will not say how true,
       But to himself so secret and so close,
       So far from sounding and discovery,
140   As is the bud bit with an envious worm
       Ere he can spread his sweet leaves to the air
       Or dedicate his beauty to the sun.
       Could we but learn from whence his sorrows grow,
       We would as willingly give cure as know.
    (Enter ROMEO *absorbed in thought.)*
145 **BENVOLIO.** See where he comes. So please you, step aside.
       I'll know his grievance or be much denied.
    MONTAGUE. I would thou wert so happy by thy stay
       To hear true shrift. Come, madam, let's away.
    (Exit MONTAGUE *and* LADY MONTAGUE.*)*
    BENVOLIO. Good morrow, cousin.
    ROMEO.   Is the day so young?
    BENVOLIO. But new struck nine.
150 **ROMEO.**   Ay me! Sad hours seem long.
       Was that my father that went hence so fast?
    BENVOLIO. It was. What sadness lengthens Romeo's hours?
    ROMEO. Not having that which, having, makes them short.
    BENVOLIO. In love?
155 **ROMEO.** Out—
    BENVOLIO. Of love?
    ROMEO. Out of her favor where I am in love.
    BENVOLIO. Alas, that Love, so gentle in his view,
       Should be so tyrannous and rough in proof!
160 **ROMEO.** Alas, that Love, whose view is muffled still,
       Should without eyes see pathways to his will!
       Where shall we dine?—O me! What fray was here?
       Yet tell me not, for I have heard it all.
       Here's much to do with hate, but more with love.
165   Why, then, O brawling love, O loving hate,
       O anything of nothing first create,
       O heavy lightness, serious vanity,
       Misshapen <u>chaos</u> of well-seeming forms,
       Feather of <u>lead</u>, bright smoke, cold fire, sick health,

130 portentous (pôr-ten′təs), *adj.* indicating upcoming evil; threatening; ominous.

134 importune (im-pôr′chən), *v.* ask urgently.

139 sounding and discovery, responding to efforts to understand his views.
141 Ere . . . leaves, before the bud can open its sweet leaves.

146 be much denied. He will find it difficult to refuse me an answer.
147 happy by thy stay, fortunate in your waiting.
148 To hear true shrift, to hear true confession.
149 Good morrow, cousin. Good morning, cousin (any relative).

■ How does Shakespeare's **characterization** of the Montagues show them to be concerned parents?

159 proof, experience.
160 Love . . . still, Love, who is always blindfolded.

166 create, created.

168 chaos (kā′os), *n.* complete disorder; great confusion.

170 Still-waking sleep, that is not what it is!
This love feel I, that feel no love in this.
Dost thou not laugh?

BENVOLIO.   No, coz, I rather weep.

ROMEO. Good heart, at what?

BENVOLIO.   At thy good heart's oppression.

ROMEO. Why, such is love's transgression.

175 Griefs of mine own lie heavy in my breast,
Which thou wilt propagate, to have it pressed
With more of thine. This love that thou hast shown
Doth add more grief to too much of mine own.
Love is a smoke made with the fume of sighs;

180 Being purged, a fire sparkling in lovers' eyes;
Being vexed, a sea nourished with lovers' tears.
What is it else? A madness most discreet,
A choking gall, and a preserving sweet.
Farewell, my coz.

BENVOLIO.   Soft! I will go along.

185 And if you leave me so, you do me wrong.

ROMEO. Tut, I have lost myself. I am not here.
This is not Romeo; he's some other where.

BENVOLIO. Tell me in sadness, who is that you love?

ROMEO. What, shall I groan and tell thee?

190 **BENVOLIO.** Groan? Why, no, but sadly tell me who.

ROMEO. Bid a sick man in sadness make his will—
A word ill urged to one that is so ill!
In sadness, cousin, I do love a woman.

BENVOLIO (smiling). I aimed so near when I supposed you loved.

195 **ROMEO.** A right good markman! And she's fair I love.

BENVOLIO. A right fair mark, fair coz, is soonest hit.

ROMEO. Well, in that hit you miss. She'll not be hit
With Cupid's arrow. She hath Dian's wit,
And, in strong proof of chastity well armed,

200 From love's weak childish bow she lives unharmed.
She will not stay the siege of loving terms,
Nor bid th' encounter of assailing eyes,
Nor ope her lap to saint-seducing gold.
O, she is rich in beauty, only poor

205 That when she dies, with beauty dies her store.

BENVOLIO. Then she hath sworn that she will still live chaste?

ROMEO. She hath, and in that sparing makes huge waste,
For beauty starved with her severity
Cuts beauty off from all posterity.

210 She is too fair, too wise, wisely too fair,
To merit bliss by making me despair.

170 still-waking, always awake.
171 that feel . . . this, that cannot take any pleasure in this love.
172 coz, a short form of *cousin.*
174 transgression (trans-gresh′ən), *n.* the act of breaking a law, command, commitment, etc.
176 propagate (prop′ə gāt), *v.* increase in number or intensity; multiply.

■ Note the many metaphors in this speech. Is Shakespeare making fun of Romeo's infatuation?

184 soft, wait.

188 sadness, seriousness.

195 fair, beautiful.
196 fair, clear, distinct. A play on words.
198 Dian's wit, the wisdom of Diana, goddess of chastity and the moon.
201 She . . . terms. She will not listen to avowals of love.
202 assailing (ə sāl′ing), *adj.* attacking; overpowering.
205 with beauty . . . store. She will die without children, and therefore her beauty will die with her.
206 chaste (chāst), *adj.* pure; virtuous.
209 posterity (po ster′ə tē), *n.* generations of the future.

She hath forsworn to love, and in that vow
Do I live dead, that live to tell it now.
BENVOLIO. Be ruled by me. Forget to think of her.
215 **ROMEO.** O, teach me how I should forget to think!
BENVOLIO. By giving liberty unto thine eyes:
Examine other beauties.
ROMEO. 'Tis the way
To call hers, exquisite, in question more.
These happy masks that kiss fair ladies' brows,
220 Being black, puts us in mind they hide the fair.
He that is strucken blind cannot forget
The precious treasure of his eyesight lost.
Show me a mistress that is passing fair:
What doth her beauty serve but as a note
225 Where I may read who passed that passing fair?
Farewell. Thou canst not teach me to forget.
BENVOLIO. I'll pay that doctrine, or else die in debt.   *(Exit.)*

217–218 **'Tis the way . . . more.** To look at others only makes me more aware of how exquisite her beauty is.
219–220 **These happy masks . . . fair.** The black masks that women sometimes wear in public (a common practice in Shakespeare's time) remind us of the beauty they hide.
223 **passing,** exceedingly.
225 **who . . . fair,** who surpassed that beauty.
227 **pay that doctrine,** teach Romeo to forget.

SCENE 2

Summary *Lord Capulet and Count Paris discuss a possible marriage between Paris and Juliet, Capulet's daughter. Capulet sends a servant to invite various people to a party at his house. The servant meets Romeo and Benvolio in the street and, not recognizing them as Montagues, invites them.*

A street in Verona. Enter CAPULET, PARIS, *and* SERVANT.
CAPULET (*addressing* PARIS). But Montague is bound as well as I,
In penalty alike, and 'tis not hard, I think,
For men so old as we to keep the peace.
PARIS. Of honorable reckoning are you both,
5 And pity 'tis you lived at odds so long.
But now, my lord, what say you to my suit?
CAPULET. But saying o'er what I have said before:
My child is yet a stranger in the world;
She hath not seen the change of fourteen years.
10 Let two more summers wither in their pride
Ere we may think her ripe to be a bride.
PARIS. Younger than she are happy mothers made.
CAPULET. And too soon marred are those so early made.
The earth hath swallowed all my hopes but she;
15 She is the hopeful lady of my earth.
But woo her, gentle Paris, get her heart;
My will to her consent is but a part;
And, she agreed, within her scope of choice
Lies my consent and fair-according voice.
20 This night I hold an old accustomed feast,

1 **bound,** obliged to keep the peace.

4 **reckoning,** reputation.

■ Is Capulet eager to renew the feud with Montague? Explain.

15 **hopeful lady of my earth,** center of my existence.
17 **My will . . . part.** My wishes are of secondary importance to her consent.
19 **fair-according,** agreeing.

Paris and Lord Capulet talk over Paris's offer of marriage to Juliet. While Shakespeare stages their discussion on a street, Zeffirelli brings the scene inside for the film version. What effect might the change in **setting** have on the scene?

Whereto I have invited many a guest
Such as I love; and you among the store,
One more, most welcome, makes my number more.
At my poor house look to behold this night
25   Earth-treading stars that make dark heaven light.
Such comfort as do lusty young men feel
When well-appareled April on the heel
Of limping winter treads, even such delight
Among fresh fennel buds shall you this night
30   Inherit at my house. Hear all, all see,
And like her most whose merit most shall be;
Which on more view of many, mine, being one,
May stand in number, though in reckoning none.
Come, go with me. (*To* SERVANT, *giving him a paper.*) Go sirrah,
     trudge about
35   Through fair Verona; find those persons out
Whose names are written there, and to them say,
My house and welcome on their pleasure stay.
(*Exit* CAPULET *and* PARIS.)
SERVANT (*peering at the paper*). Find them out whose names are written
     here! It is written that the shoemaker should meddle with his yard
40   and the tailor with his last, the fisher with his pencil, and the
     painter with his nets; but I am sent to find those persons whose
     names are here writ, and can never find what names the writing
     person hath here writ. I must to the learned.—In good time!
(*Enter* BENVOLIO *and* ROMEO.)
BENVOLIO. Tut, man, one fire burns out another's burning,
45   One pain is lessened by another's anguish;
     Turn giddy, and be holp by backward turning;
          One desperate grief cures with another's languish.
     Take thou some new infection to thy eye,
     And the rank poison of the old will die.
50 ROMEO. Your plaintain leaf is excellent for that.
BENVOLIO. For what, I pray thee?
ROMEO.   For your broken shin.
BENVOLIO. Why, Romeo, art thou mad?
ROMEO. Not mad, but bound more than a madman is;
     Shut up in prison, kept without my food,
55   Whipped and tormented and—Good e'en, good fellow.
SERVANT. God gi' good e'en. I pray, sir, can you read?
ROMEO. Ay, mine own fortune in my misery.
SERVANT. Perhaps you have learned it without book. But, I pray, can
     you read anything you see?
60 ROMEO. Ay, if I know the letters and the language.

30 inherit, enjoy.
32–33 Which . . . none, my daughter will be one among the company but may not be the one you will prefer.
34 sirrah (sir′ə), customary form of address to servants.

■ In some editions of the play, this servant is called Clown. His confusion of the terms of various professions is another example of word play. Try to match the proper term with its profession.

46 holp, helped.

50 plantain (plan′tən) **leaf,** used as a salve for bruises.

56 God gi' good e'en, God give you a good evening.

SERVANT. Ye say honestly. Rest you merry!

(He thinks ROMEO *is not taking him seriously, and starts to leave.)*

ROMEO. Stay, fellow, I can read. *(He reads the paper.)*

 "Signor Martino and his wife and daughters,

 County Anselme and his beauteous sisters,

65 The lady widow of Vitruvio,

 Signor Placentio and his lovely nieces,

 Mercutio and his brother Valentine,

 Mine uncle Capulet, his wife, and daughters,

 My fair niece Rosaline, and Livia,

70 Signor Valentio and his cousin Tybalt,

 Lucio and the lively Helena."

(He returns the paper to the servant.)

 A fair assembly. Whither should they come?

SERVANT. Up.

ROMEO. Whither?

75 **SERVANT.** To supper; to our house.

ROMEO. Whose house?

SERVANT. My master's.

ROMEO. Indeed, I should have asked thee that before.

SERVANT. Now I'll tell you without asking. My master is the great rich

80 Capulet; and if you be not of the house of Montagues, I pray, come

 and crush a cup of wine. Rest you merry! *(Exit.)*

BENVOLIO. At this same ancient feast of Capulet's

 Sups the fair Rosaline whom thou so loves,

 With all the admirèd beauties of Verona.

85 Go thither, and with unattainted eye

 Compare her face with some that I shall show,

 And I will make thee think thy swan a crow.

ROMEO. When the devout religion of mine eye

  Maintains such falsehood, then turn tears to fires;

90 And these who, often drowned, could never die,

  Transparent heretics, be burnt for liars!

 One fairer than my love? The all-seeing sun

 Ne'er saw her match since first the world begun.

BENVOLIO. Tut, you saw her fair, none else being by,

95 Herself poised with herself in either eye;

 But in that crystal scales let there be weighed

 Your lady's love against some other maid

 That I will show you shining at this feast,

 And she shall scant show well that now seems best.

100 **ROMEO.** I'll go along, no such sight to be shown,

 But to rejoice in splendor of mine own. *(Exit.)*

61 **Rest you merry!** May you continue happy.

81 **crush a cup,** have a drink.

82 **ancient,** customary.

85 **unattainted,** unprejudiced, impartial.

90 **these . . . drowned,** these eyes, that have often drowned in tears.

91 **heretic** (her′ə tik), *n.* person who maintains opinions contrary to generally accepted beliefs.

96 **crystal scales,** Romeo's eyes, in which ladies are balanced and compared.

101 **splendor of mine own,** the beauty of the lady I love.

SCENE 3

Summary *Lady Capulet tries to talk to her daughter about Count Paris, but the talkative Nurse interrupts with lengthy anecdotes of Juliet as a child. Lady Capulet asks Juliet if she favors the Count as a possible husband.*

A room in Capulet's house. Enter LADY CAPULET *and* NURSE.

LADY CAPULET. Nurse, where's my daughter? Call her forth to me.

NURSE. Now, by my maidenhead at twelve year old,
    I bade her come. What, lamb! What, ladybird!
    God forbid. Where's this girl? What, Juliet!

(*Enter* JULIET.)

5 **JULIET.** How now? Who calls?

NURSE. Your mother.

JULIET. Madam, I am here. What is your will?

LADY CAPULET. This is the matter.—Nurse, give leave awhile,
    We must talk in secret.—Nurse, come back again;

10   I have remembered me, thou's hear our counsel.
    Thou knowest my daughter's of a pretty age.

NURSE. Faith, I can tell her age unto an hour.

LADY CAPULET. She's not fourteen.

NURSE.   I'll lay fourteen of my teeth—
    And yet, to my teen be it spoken, I have but four—

15   She's not fourteen. How long is it now
    To Lammastide?

LADY CAPULET.   A fortnight and odd days.

NURSE. Even or odd, of all days in the year,
    Come Lammas Eve at night shall she be fourteen.
    Susan and she—God rest all Christian souls!—

20   Were of an age. Well, Susan is with God;
    She was too good for me. But, as I said,
    On Lammas Eve at night shall she be fourteen,
    That shall she, marry, I remember it well.
    'Tis since the earthquake now eleven years,

25   And she was weaned—I never shall forget it—
    Of all the days of the year, upon that day;
    For I had then laid wormwood to my dug,
    Sitting in the sun under the dovehouse wall.
    My lord and you were then at Mantua—

30   Nay, I do bear a brain! But, as I said,
    When it did taste the wormwood on the nipple
    Of my dug and felt it bitter, pretty fool,
    To see it tetchy and fall out wi' th' dug!
    "Shake" quoth the dovehouse. 'Twas no need, I trow,

35   To bid me trudge!
    And since that time it is eleven years,

---

3 What, an exclamation meaning "Oh."

8 give leave, leave us alone.

10 thou's, thou shalt.

14 teen, sorrow, grief.

16 Lammastide (lam′əs tīd), August 1.
16 fortnight, fourteen days.

■ Who was Susan? What probably happened to her?

30 bear a brain, have a good brain or memory.

33 tetchy, fretful.
34 trow, believe, assure you.
35 trudge, be off quickly.

For then she could stand high-lone; nay, by the rood,
She could have run and waddled all about.
For even the day before, she broke her brow,
40 And then my husband—God be with his soul!
'A was a merry man—took up the child.
"Yea," quoth he, "dost thou fall upon thy face?
Thou wilt fall backward when thou hast more wit,
Wilt thou not, Jule?" and, by my halidom,
45 The pretty wretch left crying and said "Ay."
To see now how a jest shall come about!
I warrant, an I should live a thousand years,
I never should forget it. "Wilt thou not, Jule?" quoth he,
And, pretty fool, it stinted and said "Ay."
50 **LADY CAPULET.** Enough of this. I pray thee, hold thy peace.
NURSE. Yes, madam. Yet I cannot choose but laugh
To think it should leave crying and say "Ay."
And yet, I warrant, it had upon its brow
A bump as big as a young cockerel's stone—
55 A perilous knock—and it cried bitterly.
"Yea," quoth my husband, "fall'st upon thy face?
Thou wilt fall backward when thou comest to age,
Wilt thou not, Jule?" It stinted and said "Ay."
JULIET. And stint thou too, I pray thee, Nurse, say I.
60 **NURSE.** Peace, I have done. God mark thee to his grace!
Thou was the prettiest babe that e'er I nursed.
An I might live to see thee married once,
I have my wish.
LADY CAPULET. Marry, that "marry" is the very theme
65 I came to talk of. Tell me, daughter Juliet,
How stands your disposition to be married?
JULIET. It is an honor that I dream not of.
NURSE. An honor? Were not I thine only nurse,
I would say thou hadst sucked wisdom from thy teat.
70 **LADY CAPULET.** Well, think of marriage now. Younger than you
Here in Verona, ladies of esteem,
Are made already mothers. By my count
I was your mother much upon these years
That you are now a maid. Thus then in brief:
75 The valiant Paris seeks you for his love.
NURSE. A man, young lady! Lady, such a man
As all the world—why, he's a man of wax.
LADY CAPULET. Verona's summer hath not such a flower.
NURSE. Nay, he's a flower, in faith, a very flower.
80 **LADY CAPULET** (*to* JULIET). What say you? Can you love the gentleman?
This night you shall behold him at our feast.

---

37 high-lone, without help.
37 rood (rōod), the Holy Cross.
39 even . . . brow, just the day before, she cut her forehead.
41 'A, He.
42 quoth (kwōth), said.

44 by my halidom, a mild oath.
45 wretch, unfortunate or unhappy person.

49 stinted, stopped crying.

64 Marry, indeed.

73 much upon these years, almost at the same age. Note that Lady Capulet is only about twenty-eight years old, much younger than Lord Capulet.
77 a man of wax, as handsome as if modeled in wax.

Juliet, Lady Capulet, and the Nurse discuss the possibility of Juliet's marriage to Paris. What do the expressions on the faces of the women reveal about their **characters?**

Read o'er the volume of young Paris' face,
And find delight writ there with beauty's pen;
Examine every married lineament,
85 And see how one another lends content;
And what obscured in this fair volume lies
Find written in the margent of his eyes.
This precious book of love, this unbound lover,
To beautify him, only lacks a cover.
90 The fish lives in the sea, and 'tis much pride
For fair without the fair within to hide.
That book in many's eyes doth share the glory,
That in gold clasps locks in the golden story;
So shall you share all that he doth possess

84 lineament (lin′ē ə mənt), *n.* part or feature.

87 margent (mär′jənt), *n.* margin.

95   By having him, making yourself no less.

NURSE. No less? Nay, bigger. Women grow by men.

LADY CAPULET. Speak briefly, can you like of Paris' love?

JULIET. I'll look to like, if looking liking move;
        But no more deep will I endart mine eye
100   Than your consent gives strength to make it fly.
        (*Enter a* SERVANT.)

SERVANT. Madam, the guests are come, supper served up, you called,
        my young lady asked for, the Nurse cursed in the pantry, and every-
        thing in extremity. I must hence to wait. I beseech you, follow
        straight.

LADY CAPULET. We follow thee. (*Exit* SERVANT.) Juliet, the County
105   stays.

NURSE. Go, girl, seek happy nights to happy days.   (*Exit.*)

SCENE 4

> **Summary** *Outside the Capulet house, Romeo is in no mood to go to the
> Capulet party. The others argue with him; Mercutio tells of a fanciful dream
> he has had about Queen Mab; and Romeo agrees to accompany them.*

A street in Verona that same evening. Enter ROMEO, MERCUTIO, BENVOLIO,
TORCHBEARERS, *and five or six friends; all but* MERCUTIO *are in masks.*

ROMEO. What, shall this speech be spoke for our excuse?
        Or shall we on without apology?

BENVOLIO. The date is out of such prolixity.
        We'll have no Cupid hoodwinked with a scarf,
5   Bearing a Tartar's painted bow of lath,
        Scaring the ladies like a crowkeeper,
        Nor no without-book prologue, faintly spoke
        After the prompter, for our entrance;
        But let them measure us by what they will,
10   We'll measure them a measure, and be gone.

ROMEO. Give me a torch. I am not for this ambling.
        Being but heavy, I will bear the light.

MERCUTIO. Nay, gentle Romeo, we must have you dance.

ROMEO. Not I, believe me. You have dancing shoes
15   With nimble soles; I have a soul of lead
        So stakes me to the ground I cannot move.

MERCUTIO. You are a lover; borrow Cupid's wings,
        And soar with them above a common bound.

ROMEO. I am too sore enpiercèd with his shaft
20   To soar with his light feathers, and so bound
        I cannot bound a pitch above dull woe.
        Under love's heavy burden do I sink.

MERCUTIO. And, to sink in it, should you burden love—

---

98 I'll look . . . move. I am ready to look on him favorably—if just looking at him can inspire liking.

99 endart, look as if penetrating with darts.

■ How does Juliet respond to her mother's suggestion?

103 beseech, beg; implore.
104 straight, immediately.
105 the County stays. Count Paris awaits you. (Count Paris is commonly referred to as "County.")

1–3 speech . . . prolixity (prō lik′sə tē). It was once customary for maskers to be preceded by a messenger who made an elaborate excuse for their appearance at the party. Benvolio says this is old-fashioned.
4 hoodwinked, blindfolded.
6 crowkeeper, scarecrow.
7 without-book, memorized.
10 measure . . . measure, dance for them.
11 ambling, dancing in an affected manner.

18 bound, leap; also limit, or boundary.

Too great oppression for a tender thing.

25 **ROMEO** (*sighing*). Is love a tender thing? It is too rough,
Too rude, too boisterous, and it pricks like thorn.

MERCUTIO. If love be rough with you, be rough with love;
Prick love for pricking, and you beat love down.
Give me a case to put my visage in.   (*He puts on a mask.*)

30 A visor for a visor! What care I
What curious eye doth quote deformities?
Here are the beetle brows shall blush for me.

BENVOLIO. Come, knock and enter, and no sooner in
But every man betake him to his legs.

35 **ROMEO.** A torch for me. Let wantons light of heart
Tickle the senseless rushes with their heels,
For I am proverbed with a grandsire phrase:
I'll be a candle holder and look on.
The game was ne'er so fair, and I am done.

40 **MERCUTIO.** Tut, dun's the mouse, the constable's own word.
If thou art dun, we'll draw thee from the mire
Of—save your reverence—love, wherein thou stickest
Up to the ears. Come, we burn daylight, ho!

ROMEO. Nay, that's not so.

MERCUTIO.   I mean, sir, in delay

45 We waste our lights in vain, like lamps by day.
Take our good meaning, for our judgment sits
Five times in that ere once in our five wits.

ROMEO. And we mean well in going to this masque,
But 'tis no wit to go.

MERCUTIO.   Why, may one ask?

ROMEO. I dreamt a dream tonight.

50 **MERCUTIO.**   And so did I.

ROMEO. Well, what was yours?

MERCUTIO.   That dreamers often lie.

ROMEO. In bed asleep, while they do dream things true.

MERCUTIO. O, then, I see Queen Mab hath been with you.
She is the fairies' midwife, and she comes

55 In shape no bigger than an agate stone
On the forefinger of an alderman,
Drawn with a team of little atomi
Over men's noses as they lie asleep.
Her chariot is an empty hazelnut,

60 Made by the joiner squirrel or old grub,
Time out o' mind the fairies' coachmakers.
Her wagon spokes made of long spinners' legs,
The cover of the wings of grasshoppers,
Her traces of the smallest spider web,

29 case, mask.
29 visage (viz′ij), *n.* face; appearance or aspect.
30 A visor (vi′zər) **. . . visor,** a mask for an ugly, masklike face.
31 quote, take notice of.

36 senseless rushes, unfeeling fibers used as floor coverings.
37 proverbed . . . phrase, taught by an old saying.
38 candle holder, spectator.
40 dun . . . mouse, keep still; also a pun in that "Dun is in the mire" alludes to a Christmas game in which Dun, a horse, was represented by a heavy log pulled by actors in a play.

46–47 Take . . . wits. Try to understand what I intend to say, relying on common sense instead of the five senses.

50 tonight, last night.

53 Queen Mab, the fairy queen.

57 atomi (a′təm ē), *n.* tiny creatures.

62 spinners', spiders'.

65   Her collars of the moonshine's watery beams,
      Her whip of cricket's bone, the lash of film,
      Her wagoner a small gray-coated gnat,
      Not half so big as a round little worm
      Pricked from the lazy finger of a maid.
70   And in this state she gallops night by night
      Through lovers' brains, and then they dream of love;
      O'er courtiers' knees, that dream on curtsies straight;
      O'er lawyers' fingers, who straight dream on fees;
      O'er ladies' lips, who straight on kisses dream,
75   Which oft the angry Mab with blisters plagues
      Because their breaths with sweetmeats tainted are.
      Sometimes she gallops o'er a courtier's nose,
      And then dreams he of smelling out a suit.
      And sometimes comes she with a tithe-pig's tail
80   Tickling a parson's nose as 'a lies asleep;
      Then dreams he of another benefice.
      Sometimes she driveth o'er a soldier's neck,
      And then dreams he of cutting foreign throats,
      Of breaches, ambuscadoes, Spanish blades,
85   Of healths five fathom deep, and then anon
      Drums in his ear, at which he starts and wakes,
      And being thus frighted swears a prayer or two
      And sleeps again. This is that very Mab
      That plats the manes of horses in the night,
90   And bakes the elflocks in foul sluttish hairs,
      Which once untangled much misfortune bodes.
      This is the hag, when maids lie on their backs,
      That presses them and learns them first to bear,
      Making them women of good carriage.
      This is she—
95   **ROMEO.**   Peace, peace, Mercutio, peace!
      Thou talk'st of nothing.

      MERCUTIO.   True, I talk of dreams,
      Which are the children of an idle brain,
      Begot of nothing but vain fantasy,
      Which is as thin of substance as the air,
100   And more inconstant than the wind, who woos
      Even now the frozen bosom of the north,
      And being angered, puffs away from thence,
      Turning his side to the dew-dropping south.

      BENVOLIO. This wind you talk of blows us from ourselves.
105   Supper is done, and we shall come too late.

      ROMEO. I fear, too early; for my mind misgives
      Some consequence yet hanging in the stars

---

66 film, delicate thread.
67 wagoner (wag′ə nər), *n.* coachman.
68–69 worm . . . maid. It was popularly believed that worms would breed in the fingers of the idle.
70 state, pomp, dignity.

75 plague (plāg), *v.* vex; annoy; bother.

78 smelling out a suit, seeing an opportunity to gain royal favor.
79 tithe-pig (tīтн′pig), pig given to a parson instead of tax money.
80 'a, he.
81 benefice (ben′ə fis), *n.* permanent position in a church.
84 ambuscadoes (am′bəs-cä′dōz), surprise attacks.
84 Spanish blades, fine swords made in Toledo, Spain.
90 bakes . . . hairs, mats together and tangles the hair.

106 misgives . . . stars, dreads some future misfortune not yet determined.

Shall bitterly begin his fearful date
With this night's revels, and expire the term
110 Of a despisèd life closed in my breast
By some vile forfeit of untimely death.
But He that hath the steerage of my course
Direct my suit! On, lusty gentlemen.
BENVOLIO. Strike, drum.   *(Exit.)*

108 **his fearful date,** its dreaded time.
109 **revel** (rev′əl), *n.* merry-making.
109–111 **expire . . . death,** bring my unhappy life to an untimely end.

SCENE 5

Summary *The servants clear the tables; Lord Capulet welcomes an old relative; and Romeo enters, sees Juliet, and instantly falls in love. Tybalt, recognizing Romeo's voice, is outraged and calls for his sword. His uncle, Lord Capulet, prevents the fight. Romeo makes his way to Juliet, and they exchange teasing words and kisses. Before he leaves, Romeo discovers that Juliet is a Capulet. The Nurse tells Juliet that Romeo is a Montague.*

A spacious room in Capulet's house. SERVANTS *enter with napkins.*

FIRST SERVANT. Where's Potpan, that he helps not to take away? He shift a trencher? He scrape a trencher?

SECOND SERVANT. When good manners shall lie all in one or two men's hands, and they unwashed too, 'tis a foul thing.

5 **FIRST SERVANT.** Away with the joint stools, remove the court cupboard, look to the plate. *(To another servant.)* Good thou, save me a piece of marchpane, and as thou loves me, let the porter let in Susan Grindstone and Nell. *(To the other servants.)* Anthony and Potpan!

10 **SECOND SERVANT.** Ay, boy, ready.

FIRST SERVANT. You are looked for and called for, asked for and sought for, in the great chamber.

THIRD SERVANT. We cannot be here and there too. Cheerly, boys! Be brisk awhile, and the longest liver take all.   *(Exit.)*

(Enter CAPULET, LADY CAPULET, *with* JULIET, *the* NURSE, TYBALT, *and others of the* CAPULET *clan, mingling with, and talking to, the* GUESTS. *In the background,* MUSICIANS.*)*

15 **CAPULET.** Welcome, gentlemen! Ladies that have their toes
Unplagued with corns will walk a bout with you.
Ah, my mistresses, which of you all
Will now deny to dance? She that makes dainty,
She, I'll swear, hath corns. Am I come near ye now?

*(*ROMEO, BENVOLIO, *and* MERCUTIO *enter the room.)*

20 Welcome, gentlemen! I have seen the day
That I have worn a visor and could tell
A whispering tale in a fair lady's ear
Such as would please. 'Tis gone, 'tis gone, 'tis gone.

2 **trencher,** a wooden dish or plate.

5 **joint stools,** stools on which the dinner guests were seated.
6 **plate,** silverplate.
7 **marchpane,** a cake made from sugar and almonds; i.e., marzipan.

14 **liver,** survivor.

16 **walk a bout,** dance a turn.

18 **makes dainty,** affectedly hesitates to dance.
19 **Am . . . now?** Have I hit home to the truth?

■ How does Capulet urge his female guests to dance?

You are welcome, gentlemen! Come, musicians, play.
25 A hall, a hall! Give room! And foot it, girls.
(Music plays, the guests dance, and CAPULET *walks around the room.)*
(*To* SERVANTS.) More light, you knaves, and turn the tables up,
And quench the fire; the room is grown too hot.
Ah, sirrah, this unlooked-for sport comes well.
(*To an elderly kinsman.*) Nay, sit, nay, sit, good cousin Capulet,
30 For you and I are past our dancing days.
How long is 't now since last yourself and I
Were in a mask?
SECOND CAPULET. By 'r Lady, thirty years.
CAPULET. What, man? 'Tis not so much, 'tis not so much;
'Tis since the nuptial of Lucentio,
35 Come Pentecost as quickly as it will,
Some five-and-twenty years, and then we masked.
SECOND CAPULET. 'Tis more, 'tis more. His son is elder, sir;
His son is thirty.
CAPULET. Will you tell me that?
His son was but a ward two years ago.
(ROMEO, *who has been trying to locate* ROSALINE, *catches a fleeting glimpse of* JULIET, *whose beauty dazzles him. He halts a passing* SERVANT.)
40 **ROMEO.** What lady's that which doth enrich the hand
Of yonder knight?
SERVANT. I know not, sir.
ROMEO. O, she doth teach the torches to burn bright!
It seems she hangs upon the cheek of night
45 As a rich jewel in an Ethiop's ear—
Beauty too rich for use, for earth too dear!
So shows a snowy dove trooping with crows
As yonder lady o'er her fellows shows.
The measure done, I'll watch her place of stand,
50 And, touching hers, make blessèd my rude hand.
Did my heart love till now? Forswear it, sight!
For I ne'er saw true beauty till this night.
TYBALT. This, by his voice, should be a Montague.
(*To a* SERVANT.) Fetch me my rapier, boy. What dares the slave
55 Come hither, covered with an antic face,
To fleer and scorn at our solemnity?
Now, by the stock and honor of my kin,
To strike him dead I hold it not a sin.
CAPULET (*overhearing* TYBALT). Why, how now, kinsman? Wherefore
storm you so?
60 **TYBALT.** Uncle, this is a Montague, our foe,
A villain that is hither come in spite
To scorn at our solemnity this night.

25 A hall, a hall! Make room!
26 turn the tables up. The tables were flat leaves hinged together and place on trestles. When they were folded they took little space.

32 By'r Lady, by the Virgin Mary; a mild oath.

34 nuptial (nup′shəl), *n.* marriage.

42 I know not, sir. The servant has been hired for the party and does not know Juliet.

54 rapier (rā′pē ər), *n.* sword.
56 fleer, sneer.
56 solemnity (sə lem′nə tē), *n.* celebration.

CAPULET. Young Romeo is it?

TYBALT.   'Tis he, that villain Romeo.

CAPULET. Content thee, gentle coz, let him alone.

65   'A bears him like a portly gentleman,
      And, to say truth, Verona brags of him
      To be a virtuous and well governed youth.
      I would not for the wealth of all this town
      Here in my house do him <u>disparagement</u>.
70   Therefore be patient; take no note of him.
      It is my will, the which if thou respect,
      Show a fair presence and put off these frowns,
      An ill-beseeming <u>semblance</u> for a feast.

TYBALT. It fits when such a villain is a guest.
      I'll not endure him.

65 portly, dignified.

69 disparagement (dis par′ij-mənt), *n.* injurious speech; belittlement.
73 semblance (sem′bləns), *n.* outward appearance.
74 It fits, a frown is fitting.

◄ Romeo removes his mask at the Capulets' ball. How might the custom of wearing masks at a party affect the **mood** of the guests?

CAPULET (*sternly, while restraining* TYBALT).

75 He shall be endured.
What, goodman boy? I say he shall. Go to!
Am I the master here, or you? Go to.
You'll not endure him! God shall mend my soul,
You'll make a mutiny among my guests!
80 You will set cock-a-hoop! You'll be the man!
TYBALT (*grumbling*). Why, uncle, 'tis a shame.
CAPULET. Go to, go to,
You are a saucy boy. Is 't so, indeed?
This trick may chance to scathe you. I know what,
You must contrary me. Marry, 'tis time. (*To* GUESTS.)
85 Well said, my hearts! (*To* TYBALT.) You are a princox; go.
Be quiet, or—(*To* SERVANTS.) More light, more light! (*To* TYBALT.)
For shame!
I'll make you quiet. (*To* GUESTS.) What, cheerly, my hearts!
TYBALT. Patience perforce with willful choler meeting
Makes my flesh tremble in their different greeting.
90 I will withdraw. But this intrusion shall,
Now seeming sweet, convert to bitterest gall. (*Exit.*)
ROMEO (*finally reaching* JULIET *and placing his palm against hers as if to
dance. Instead, however, he ignores the music and simply speaks.*).
If I profane with my unworthiest hand
This holy shrine, the gentle fine is this:
My lips, two blushing pilgrims, ready stand
95 To smooth that rough touch with a tender kiss.
JULIET. Good pilgrim, you do wrong your hand too much,
Which mannerly devotion shows in this;
For saints have hands that pilgrims' hands do touch,
And palm to palm is holy palmers' kiss.
100 **ROMEO.** Have not saints lips, and holy palmers too?
JULIET. Ay, pilgrim, lips that they must use in prayer.
ROMEO. O, then, dear saint, let lips do what hands do.
They pray; grant thou, lest faith turn to despair.
JULIET. Saints do not move, though grant for prayers' sake.
105 **ROMEO.** Then move not, while my prayer's effect I take.
Thus from my lips, by thine, my sin is purged.
(*His lips touch hers briefly.*)
JULIET. Then have my lips the sin that they have took.
ROMEO. Sin from my lips? O trespass sweetly urged!
Give me my sin again.
(*They kiss again until* JULIET *breaks the spell by teasing* ROMEO.)
JULIET. You kiss by th' book.
110 **NURSE** (*who has made her way through the crowds to find* JULIET). Madam,
your mother craves a word with you.

76 goodman boy, a scornful term.
76 Go to, come now (a reproof).

80 You . . . cock-a-hoop, you want to be cock of the walk.

82 saucy, impudent; rude.
83 scathe (skāᴛʜ), *v.* injure.
84 You must contrary me. You insist on opposing me.
85 Well said, you have danced well.
85 princox (prin′koks), *n.* a saucy youngster.
88–89 Patience . . . greeting. The tension between forced patience and deep anger makes me tremble.
90 intrusion (in trü′zhən), *n.* act of intruding, or coming unasked or unwanted.

93 gentle fine, mild penance.

99 palmers, pilgrims who brought palm leaves back from the Holy Land. Note the wordplay around *palms* of the hand, *palmers,* and *pilgrims* in lines 94–101.

109 by th' book, according to rule.

110 crave, greatly desire.

(JULIET *reluctantly leaves* ROMEO.)

ROMEO (*to the* NURSE). What is her mother?

NURSE (*to* ROMEO).   Marry, bachelor,
    Her mother is the lady of the house,
    And a good lady, and a wise and virtuous.
    I nursed her daughter that you talked withal.

115   I tell you, he that can lay hold of her
    Shall have the chinks.

(NURSE *moves away from* ROMEO *and into the crowd.*)

ROMEO (*stricken*).   Is she a Capulet?
    O dear account! My life is my foe's debt.

BENVOLIO (*coming forward*). Away, begone! The sport is at the best.

ROMEO. Ay, so I fear; the more is my unrest.

CAPULET (*addressing the guests who are about to take their leave*).

120   Nay, gentlemen, prepare not to be gone.
    We have a trifling foolish banquet towards.

(MERCUTIO *whispers something to* CAPULET, *who laughs.*)

    Is it e'en so? Why, then, I thank you all.
    I thank you, honest gentlemen. Good night.

(BENVOLIO *and* ROMEO *join the departing guests.*)

    (*To a* SERVANT.) More torches here! Come on, then, let's to bed.

125   Ah, sirrah, by my fay, it waxes late.
    I'll to my rest.

JULIET. Come hither, Nurse. What is yond gentleman?

NURSE. The son and heir of old Tiberio.

JULIET. What's he that now is going out of door?

130 **NURSE.** Marry, that, I think, be young Petruchio.

JULIET. What's he that follows here, that would not dance?

NURSE. I know not. (*The* NURSE *does know but tries to keep* JULIET *from learning that the man is* ROMEO — *and a Montague.*)

JULIET. Go ask his name. If he be marrièd,
    My grave is like to be my wedding bed.

NURSE (*seeing that it is useless to hide* ROMEO's *identity*).

135   His name is Romeo, and a Montague,
    The only son of your great enemy.

JULIET. My only love sprung from my only hate!
    Too early seen unknown, and known too late!
    Prodigious birth of love it is to me

140   That I must love a loathèd enemy.

NURSE. What's this? What's this?

JULIET.   A rhyme I learned even now
    Of one I danced withal.

(*A call off-stage: "Juliet."*)

NURSE.   Anon, anon!
    Come, let's away. The strangers all are gone.   (*Exit.*)

---

116 chinks, money (inherited by Juliet from her father).

117 dear, costly.

117 My . . . debt. My life is at the mercy of my foe.

121 foolish banquet towards, a simple dessert about to be served.

125 fay, faith.

■ Why do you think Juliet asks the Nurse to identify two other young men at the party before asking Romeo's identity?

142 anon (ə non′), at once. Shakespeare occasionally uses *anon* in the sense of "in a minute."

After Reading

Making Connections

Shaping Your Response

1. Do you think the fight in Scene 1 will be the last instance of feuding between the Capulets and Montagues? Explain.

2. Do you think Juliet is old enough to be married? Why or why not?

3. What advice would you give Romeo and Juliet at the end of Act 1?

Analyzing the Play

4. In the Prologue, Shakespeare describes Juliet and Romeo as "star-crossed lovers." Explain what you think he means by this.

5. Identify and describe the **characters** Tybalt and Benvolio.

6. Does Capulet seem sincere in his concern for his daughter's happiness in marriage? Cite lines from the play to support your answer.

7. How does the Nurse feel about Juliet and the Capulet family? Support your answer with examples.

8. Describe the general **mood** as Scene 5 opens and then explain how it is changed by Tybalt's behavior.

9. Compare Romeo's reaction to discovering Juliet's identity to her reaction upon discovering his identity.

Extending the Ideas

10. You have known the fate of Romeo and Juliet since line 8 of the Prologue. Does knowing the outcome deepen or lessen your interest in the story? Why?

11. **Predict** the role of each of the following characters in the play based on their personalities and the events of Act 1: Tybalt, Mercutio, Paris, and Benvolio.

12. 👆 How do you think the **interactions** of the Capulets and Montagues will affect Romeo and Juliet?

Vocabulary Study

augment
belligerence
chaos
disparagement
intrusion
pernicious
portentous
semblance
transgression
visage

Choose the vocabulary word from the list that best completes each of the following sentences. Use the Glossary if you need help with word meanings.

1. The servants of the Montagues do not like to hear any _____ of their masters.

2. The quarrel among the servants of the two households causes _____ in the streets of Verona.

3. Tybalt's habit of getting into fights is a result of his general _____.

4. The Prince calls for an end to the _____ feud between the two families.

5. Any further ____ of the law by either family will be punished.

6. Before the party, Romeo believes that Rosaline's ____ is the fairest in the world.

7. Romeo doubts he will ever have even the ____ of love for anyone else.

8. Tybalt does not like Romeo's ____ at the party.

9. His anger may be ____ of tragic events to come.

10. Juliet's clever words serve to ____ her beauty.

Expressing Your Ideas

Writing Choices

Comic Effect The Nurse is one of Shakespeare's great comic characters. Review the two scenes she appears in and make a list of her qualities. Then use your list to write a **character study** in which you describe the Nurse's major traits and what makes her comic.

Chain of Events Draw a **chain diagram** like the one shown, but larger. Work with a partner to fill in the major events that occur in the play during Act 1. Save your diagram to expand on later.

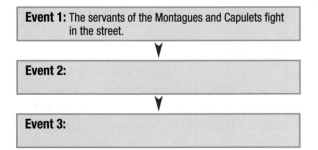

Event 1: The servants of the Montagues and Capulets fight in the street.

Event 2:

Event 3:

A Day to Remember Imagine yourself as Juliet and write a **journal entry** after the party. Be sure to record your impressions about Romeo and your feelings.

Other Options

Verona ActionNews Imagine that you are a television reporter at the party at the Capulets. Broadcast your **live report** from the scene, providing juicy details about who's there and what's happening. If possible, videotape your report.

Party Time What would the party at the Capulet's be like if it were held in this day and age? With your classmates, put on a **skit** that re-creates Scene 5 in a modern setting. Include all the major events, but update the dialogue, the costumes, the music, and the actions of the characters.

ACT TWO

PROLOGUE

Summary *The Chorus notes that Romeo's love for Rosaline has been replaced by his affection for Juliet. The Chorus suggests that even though the two families are still at odds, the young lovers will find a way to meet.*

Enter CHORUS.

CHORUS. Now old desire doth in his deathbed lie,
    And young affection gapes to be his heir;
That fair for which love groaned for and would die,
    With tender Juliet matched, is now not fair.
5 Now Romeo is beloved and loves again,
    Alike bewitchèd by the charm of looks;
But to his foe supposed he must complain,
    And she steal love's sweet bait from fearful hooks.
Being held a foe, he may not have access
10   To breathe such vows as lovers use to swear;
And she as much in love, her means much less
    To meet her new-belovèd anywhere.
But passion lends them power, time means, to meet,
Temp'ring extremities with extreme sweet. *(Exit.)*

2 **gapes,** yearns, clamors.
3 **fair,** beauty, i.e., Rosaline.

6 **alike,** equally with Juliet.
7 **complain,** declare his love.

10 **use to,** are accustomed to.

14 **temp'ring,** moderating; softening.

SCENE 1

Summary *Romeo hides from Mercutio and Benvolio. Mercutio tries to "conjure" him into appearing, but Benvolio concludes that he simply wants to be alone.*

A lane outside the wall of Capulet's orchard; after the party. Enter ROMEO.

ROMEO. Can I go forward when my heart is here?
    Turn back, dull earth, and find thy center out.
(He climbs the wall and leaps into the orchard. Enter BENVOLIO *and* MERCUTIO.)
BENVOLIO *(calling to the hidden* ROMEO*)*. Romeo! My cousin Romeo!
MERCUTIO. He is wise
5   And, on my life, hath stolen him home to bed.
BENVOLIO. He ran this way and leapt this orchard wall.
    Call, good Mercutio.
MERCUTIO *(jestingly)*.   Nay, I'll conjure too.
    Romeo! Humors! Madman! Passion! Lover!
    Appear thou in the likeness of a sigh.
10 Speak but one rhyme, and I am satisfied;
    Cry but "Ay me!" Pronounce but "love" and "dove."
    Speak to my gossip Venus one fair word,

2 **dull earth,** Romeo himself.
2 **thy center,** Juliet.

7 **conjure** (kon′jər), *v.* call up a spirit by magic.
8 **Humors,** romantic whims.

12 **gossip,** intimate friend.

One nickname for her purblind son and heir,
Young Abraham Cupid, he that shot so trim
15 When King Cophetua loved the beggar maid.—
(*To* BENVOLIO.) He heareth not, he stirreth not, he moveth not;
The ape is dead, and I must conjure him.—
(*Calls to* ROMEO.) I conjure thee by Rosaline's bright eyes,
By her high forehead and her scarlet lip,
20 By her fine foot, straight leg, and quivering thigh,
And the demesnes that there adjacent lie,
That in thy likeness thou appear to us.
BENVOLIO. An if he hear thee, thou wilt anger him.
MERCUTIO. This cannot anger him. 'Twould anger him
25 To raise a spirit in his mistress' circle
Of some strange nature, letting it there stand
Till she had laid it and conjured it down;
That were some spite. My invocation
Is fair and honest; in his mistress' name
30 I conjure only but to raise up him.
BENVOLIO. Come, he hath hid himself among these trees
To be consorted with the humorous night.
Blind is his love, and best befits the dark.
MERCUTIO. If love be blind, love cannot hit the mark.
35 Now will he sit under a medlar tree
And wish his mistress were that kind of fruit
As maids call medlars when they laugh alone.
O, Romeo, that she were, O, that she were
An open-arse, and thou a poppering pear!
40 Romeo, good night. I'll to my truckle bed;
This field bed is too cold for me to sleep.
Come, shall we go?
BENVOLIO.   Go, then, for 'tis in vain
To seek him here that means not to be found.   (*Exit.*)

SCENE 2

Summary *Wandering in the Capulet orchard, Romeo sees Juliet, who has stepped onto the balcony. He then hears her lamenting that Romeo is a Montague. When Romeo speaks to her, Juliet is simultaneously pleased by his presence but frightened for his safety. As the two pledge their love, the Nurse calls Juliet into the house. Juliet withdraws but reappears twice: once to ascertain that Romeo is serious about marrying her, and a second time just to be with him for a little longer.*

A beautiful orchard on the Capulets' grounds, with a balcony of the house prominently placed outside Juliet's bedroom. Enter ROMEO.
ROMEO. He jests at scars that never felt a wound.

---

13 purblind (pėr′blīnd′), *adj.* completely blind.
15 King Cophetua (kō fet′tü ä). In an old ballad, he fell in love with a beggar maid and made her his queen.
17 ape, Romeo is compared to a trained monkey who can "play dead."
21 demesnes (di māns′), *n.* regions.

25 circle, conjuring circle.
26 strange, belonging to another person.

28 spite, injury.

32 consorted . . . night, associated with the damp night.
33 befit, be suitable or proper for.
35 medlar (med′lər) **tree,** a fruit tree found in Asia and southern Europe.

40 truckle bed, today called a trundle bed, a small bed that fits beneath a larger one.
41 field bed, the ground.

■ Compare and contrast Benvolio's and Mercutio's attitudes toward Romeo's wish to be alone.

1 He jests . . . wound. Romeo has overheard the jests made by Mercutio, who, Romeo says, has never known the pangs of love.

(Catching sight of JULIET *at her dimly lighted window.)*

But soft, what light through yonder window breaks?
It is the east, and Juliet is the sun.
Arise, fair sun, and kill the envious moon,
5 Who is already sick and pale with grief
That thou her maid art far more fair than she.
Be not her maid, since she is envious;
Her vestal livery is but sick and green
And none but fools do wear it. Cast it off.

*(*JULIET *steps out onto the balcony.)*

10 It is my lady, O, it is my love.
O, that she knew she were!
She speaks, yet she says nothing. What of that?
Her eye discourses. I will answer it.
I am too bold. 'Tis not to me she speaks.
15 Two of the fairest stars in all the heaven,
Having some business, do entreat her eyes
To twinkle in their spheres till they return.
What if her eyes were there, they in her head?
The brightness of her cheek would shame those stars
20 As daylight doth a lamp; her eyes in heaven
Would through the airy region stream so bright
That birds would sing and think it were not night.
See how she leans her cheek upon her hand!
O, that I were a glove upon that hand,
That I might touch that cheek!

JULIET.   Ay me!
25 **ROMEO.**   She speaks.

O, speak again, bright angel, for thou art
As glorious to this night, being o'er my head,
As is a wingèd messenger of heaven
Unto the white-upturnèd wondering eyes
30 Of mortals that fall back to gaze on him
When he bestrides the lazy puffing clouds
And sails upon the bosom of the air.

JULIET *(unaware that she is being overheard).* O Romeo, Romeo,
     wherefore art thou Romeo?
Deny thy father and refuse thy name!
35 Or, if thou wilt not, be but sworn my love,
And I'll no longer be a Capulet.

ROMEO *(aside).* Shall I hear more, or shall I speak at this?

JULIET. 'Tis but thy name that is my enemy;
Thou art thyself, though not a Montague.
40 What's Montague? It is nor hand, nor foot,
Nor arm, nor face, nor any other part

■ When Romeo speaks of
and to Juliet, he uses many
images of light. Why do you
think Shakespeare chooses
this kind of **imagery?**

13 discourse (dis kôrs′), *v.*
talk; converse.

16 entreat (en trēt′), *v.* ask
earnestly.
17 spheres, the hollow,
transparent globes in which,
it was believed, the stars and
other planets were set.

39 though . . . Montague,
even if you were not a
Montague.

▲ From her balcony, Juliet looks down upon Romeo. How does
the **lighting** increase the drama in this scene?

Romeo and Juliet—Act Two, Scene 2   **509**

Belonging to a man. O, be some other name!
What's in a name? That which we call a rose
By any other word would smell as sweet;
45   So Romeo would, were he not Romeo called,
Retain that dear perfection which he owes
Without that title. Romeo, doff thy name,
And for thy name, which is no part of thee,
Take all myself.

ROMEO (*speaking loudly enough to be heard by* JULIET).
                    I take thee at thy word!
50   Call me but love, and I'll be new baptized;
Henceforth I never will be Romeo.

JULIET. What man art thou that, thus bescreened in night,
So stumblest on my counsel?

ROMEO.   By a name
I know not how to tell thee who I am.
55   My name, dear saint, is hateful to myself,
Because it is an enemy to thee;
Had I it written, I would tear the word.

JULIET. My ears have not yet drunk a hundred words
Of thy tongue's uttering, yet I know the sound:
60   Art thou not Romeo and a Montague?

ROMEO. Neither, fair maid, if either thee dislike.

JULIET. How camest thou hither, tell me, and wherefore?
The orchard walls are high and hard to climb,
And the place death, considering who thou art,
65   If any of my kinsmen find thee here.

ROMEO. With love's light wings did I o'erperch these walls,
For stony limits cannot hold love out,
And what love can do, that dares love attempt;
Therefore thy kinsmen are no stop to me.

70 **JULIET.** If they do see thee, they will murder thee.

ROMEO. Alack, there lies more peril in thine eye
Than twenty of their swords. Look thou but sweet,
And I am proof against their enmity.

JULIET. I would not for the world they saw thee here.

75 **ROMEO.** I have night's cloak to hide me from their eyes;
And but thou love me, let them find me here.
My life were better ended by their hate
Than death proroguèd, wanting of thy love.

JULIET. By whose direction found'st thou out this place?

80 **ROMEO.** By love, that first did prompt me to inquire.
He lent me counsel, and I lent him eyes.
I am no pilot; yet, wert thou as far
As that vast shore washed with the farthest sea,

46 **owes,** owns.
47 **doff,** discard.

53 **counsel,** secret thoughts.

66 **o'erperch,** fly over and
perch beyond.

73 **proof . . . enmity,**
safeguarded by armor from
their hatred.

76 **And but,** if only.

78 **proroguèd** (prō rōg′əd),
adj. postponed.
78 **wanting of,** lacking.

I should adventure for such merchandise.

85 **JULIET.** Thou knowest the mask of night is on my face,
Else would a maiden blush bepaint my cheek
For that which thou hast heard me speak tonight.
Fain would I dwell on form—fain, fain deny
What I have spoke; but farewell compliment!

90 Dost thou love me? I know thou wilt say "Ay,"
And I will take thy word. Yet if thou swear'st
Thou mayst prove false. At lovers' perjuries,
They say, Jove laughs. O gentle Romeo,
If thou dost love, pronounce it faithfully.

95 Or if thou thinkest I am too quickly won,
I'll frown and be perverse and say thee nay,
So thou wilt woo, but else not for the world.
In truth, fair Montague, I am too fond,
And therefore thou mayst think my havior light.

100 But trust me, gentleman, I'll prove more true
Than those that have more cunning to be strange.
I should have been more strange, I must confess,
But that thou overheard'st, ere I was ware,
My true-love passion. Therefore pardon me,

105 And not impute this yielding to light love,
Which the dark night hath so discoverèd.

ROMEO. Lady, by yonder blessèd moon I vow,
That tips with silver all these fruit-tree tops—

JULIET. O, swear not by the moon, th' inconstant moon,

110 That monthly changes in her circled orb,
Lest that thy love prove likewise variable.

ROMEO. What shall I swear by?

JULIET.   Do not swear at all;
Or, if thou wilt, swear by thy gracious self,
Which is the god of my idolatry,
And I'll believe thee.

115 **ROMEO.**   If my heart's dear love—

JULIET. Well, do not swear. Although I joy in thee,
I have no joy of this contract tonight.
It is too rash, too unadvised, too sudden,
Too like the lightning, which doth cease to be

120 Ere one can say it lightens. Sweet, good night!
This bud of love, by summer's ripening breath,
May prove a beauteous flower when next we meet.
Good night, good night! As sweet repose and rest
Come to thy heart as that within my breast!

125 **ROMEO.** O, wilt thou leave me so unsatisfied?

JULIET. What satisfaction canst thou have tonight?

88 **fain,** gladly.
88 **dwell on form,** follow convention.
89 **compliment,** etiquette, convention.

92 **perjury** (pėr′jər ē), *n.* act of lying under oath.
93 **Jove,** ruler of the gods.

99 **my havior light,** my behavior is unmaidenly.
101 **cunning** (kun′ing), *n.* skill; cleverness.
101 **strange,** reserved, distant.

105 **impute** (im pūt′), *v.* attribute; consider as belonging to.

117 **contract,** betrothal, engagement.

■ Why is Juliet afraid of love that is "too rash"?

ROMEO. Th' exchange of thy love's faithful vow for mine.

JULIET. I gave thee mine before thou didst request it;
    And yet I would it were to give again.

130 **ROMEO.** Wouldst thou withdraw it? For what purpose, love?

JULIET. But to be frank and give it thee again.
    And yet I wish but for the thing I have.
    My bounty is as boundless as the sea,
    My love as deep; the more I give to thee,
135   The more I have, for both are infinite.
    (NURSE *calls "Juliet" from inside the bedroom.*)
    I hear some noise within. Dear love, adieu!—
    Anon, good Nurse!—Sweet Montague, be true.
    Stay but a little; I will come again.
    (JULIET *goes into her bedroom.*)

ROMEO. O blessèd, blessèd night! I am afeard,
140   Being in night, all this is but a dream,
    Too flattering-sweet to be substantial.
    (JULIET *returns to the balcony.*)

JULIET. Three words, dear Romeo, and good night indeed.
    If that thy bent of love be honorable,
    Thy purpose marriage, send me word tomorrow,
145   By one that I'll procure to come to thee,
    Where and what time thou wilt perform the rite,
    And all my fortunes at thy foot I'll lay
    And follow thee my lord throughout the world.

NURSE *(within the bedroom).* Madam!

150 **JULIET.** I come, anon.—But if thou meanest not well,
    I do beseech thee—

NURSE *(within and more persistently).* Madam!

JULIET.   By and by, I come——
    To cease thy strife and leave me to my grief.
    Tomorrow will I send.

ROMEO. So thrive my soul——

155 **JULIET.** A thousand times good night!
    (JULIET *goes inside for a few moments.*)

ROMEO. A thousand times the worse, to want thy light.
    Love goes toward love as schoolboys from their books,
    But love from love, toward school with heavy looks.
    (ROMEO *reluctantly begins to back away when* JULIET *reappears.*)

JULIET. Hist! Romeo, hist! *(To herself.)* O, for a falconer's voice,
160   To lure this tassel-gentle back again!
    Bondage is hoarse and may not speak aloud,
    Else would I tear the cave where Echo lies
    And make her airy tongue more hoarse than mine
    With repetition of "My Romeo!"

---

129 would, wish.

131 frank, generous.

136 adieu (ə dyū′), good-by. [French]

143 thy bent of love, the intentions of your love.
145 procure (prə kyùr′), *v.* cause.

■ Briefly explain what Juliet asks Romeo to do in lines 142–148.

151 By and by, at once.

160 tassel-gentle, a male hawk.
161 Bondage . . . aloud. I must not be overheard.
162 Echo (ek′ō), a nymph who pined away for a handsome youth until only her voice was left.

---

165 **ROMEO.** It is my soul that calls upon my name.
How silver-sweet sound lovers' tongues by night,
Like softest music to attending ears!

JULIET. Romeo!

ROMEO.   My nyas?

168 **nyas** (nī as′), *v.* fledgling.

JULIET.   At what o'clock tomorrow
Shall I send to thee?

ROMEO.   At the hour of nine.

170 **JULIET.** I will not fail; 'tis twenty years till then.—
I have forgot why I did call thee back.

ROMEO. Let me stand here till thou remember it.

JULIET. I shall forget, to have thee still stand there,
Remembering how I love thy company.

175 **ROMEO.** And I'll still stay, to have thee still forget,
Forgetting any other home but this.

JULIET. 'Tis almost morning. I would have thee gone—
And yet no farther than a wanton's bird,
That lets it hop a little from his hand,

178 **wanton's,** spoiled child's.
180 **gyve** (jīv), shackle; metal band for holding a prisoner by wrists or ankles.

180 Like a poor prisoner in his twisted gyves,
And with a silken thread plucks it back again,
So loving-jealous of his liberty.

ROMEO. I would I were thy bird.

JULIET.   Sweet, so would I.
Yet I should kill thee with much cherishing.

185 Good night, good night! Parting is such sweet sorrow
That I shall say good night till it be morrow.

(She goes into her room.)

ROMEO. Sleep dwell upon thine eyes, peace in thy breast!
Would I were sleep and peace, so sweet to rest!
Hence will I to my ghostly friar's close cell,

189 **ghostly,** spiritual.
190 **dear hap,** good fortune.

190 His help to crave, and my dear hap to tell.   *(Exit.)*

SCENE 3

Summary *It is dawn and Friar Laurence, confessor to both Romeo and Juliet, is gathering herbs and meditating on good and evil. Romeo enters and bewilders the Friar with his riddling talk. Romeo confesses he is in love with Juliet and wishes to marry her. Though the Friar is surprised that Romeo has so suddenly forsaken Rosaline, he agrees to marry Romeo and Juliet in hopes that the marriage will end the feud between their families.*

Friar Laurence's cell. Enter FRIAR LAURENCE *with a basket of healing herbs.*

FRIAR LAURENCE. The gray-eyed morn smiles on the frowning night,
Check'ring the eastern clouds with streaks of light,
And fleckled darkness like a drunkard reels
From forth day's path and Titan's fiery wheels.

3 **fleckled,** dappled.
4 **Titan's.** Helios, the sun god, was one of a race of giants called Titans.

Romeo tells Friar Laurence of his new love for Juliet. Judging by the scene, do you think Romeo likes and trusts Friar Laurence? Explain.

5   Now, ere the sun advance his burning eye,
The day to cheer and night's dank dew to dry,
I must up-fill this osier cage of ours
With baleful weeds and precious-juicèd flowers.
The earth that's nature's mother is her tomb;
10   What is her burying grave, that is her womb;
And from her womb children of divers kind
We sucking on her natural bosom find,
Many for many virtues excellent,
None but for some, and yet all different.
15   O, mickle is the powerful grace that lies
In plants, herbs, stones, and their true qualities.
For naught so vile that on the earth doth live
But to the earth some special good doth give;
Nor aught so good but, strained from that fair use,
20   Revolts from true birth, stumbling on abuse.
Virtue itself turns vice, being misapplied,
And vice sometime's by action dignified.
(ROMEO *enters and stands by the door unseen.*)
Within the infant rind of this weak flower
Poison hath residence and medicine power:

7 osier (ō′zhər) **cage,** willow basket.
8 baleful (bāl′fəl), *adj.* full of hurtful or deadly influence.

11 divers (dī′vərz), *adj.* various.

14 None but for some. No plant entirely lacks value.
15 mickle, much.

17 vile (vīl), *adj.* foul; disgusting; poor.

19 strained, pulled away from.
20 Revolts . . . birth, betrays its own special purpose.

25 For this, being smelt, with that part cheers each part;
Being tasted, stays all senses with the heart.
Two such opposèd kings encamp them still
In man as well as herbs—grace and rude will;
And where the worser is <u>predominant</u>,
30 Full soon the canker death eats up that plant.
(ROMEO *advances and speaks.*)
ROMEO. Good morrow, Father.
FRIAR LAURENCE.   Benedicite!
What early tongue so sweet saluteth me?
Young son, it argues a distempered head
So soon to bid good morrow to thy bed.
35 Care keeps his watch in every old man's eye,
And where care lodges sleep will never lie;
But where unbruisèd youth with unstuffed brain
Doth couch his limbs, there golden sleep doth reign.
Therefore thy earliness doth me assure
40 Thou art uproused with some distemp'rature;
Or if not so, then here I hit it right:
Our Romeo hath not been in bed tonight.
ROMEO. That last is true. The sweeter rest was mine.
FRIAR LAURENCE. God pardon sin! Wast thou with Rosaline?
45 **ROMEO.** With Rosaline, my ghostly father? No.
I have forgot that name, and that name's woe.
FRIAR LAURENCE. That's my good son. But where hast thou been, then?
ROMEO. I'll tell thee ere thou ask it me again.
I have been feasting with mine enemy,
50 Where on a sudden one hath wounded me
That's by me wounded. Both our remedies
Within thy help and holy <u>physic</u> lies.
I bear no hatred, blessèd man, for, lo,
My <u>intercession</u> likewise steads my foe.
55 **FRIAR LAURENCE.** Be plain, good son, and homely in thy drift.
Riddling confession finds but riddling shrift.
ROMEO. Then plainly know my heart's dear love is set
On the fair daughter of rich Capulet.
As mine on hers, so hers is set on mine,
60 And all combined, save what thou must combine
By holy marriage. When and where and how
We met, we wooed, and made exchange of vow
I'll tell thee as we pass; but this I pray,
That thou consent to marry us today.
65 **FRIAR LAURENCE.** Holy Saint Francis, what a change is here!
Is Rosaline, that thou didst love so dear,
So soon forsaken? Young men's love then lies

25 that part . . . part. Its odor refreshes all parts of the body.
26 with the heart, by stopping the heart.
29 predominant (pri dom′ə-nənt), *adj.* having more power; most noticeable.
30 canker, cankerworm, which destroys plants.
31 Benedicite (ben′ə dis′ə-tā), God bless us. [Latin]
33 distempered, disturbed.

37 unstuffed brain, mind unoccupied with worries.
38 couch, rest.

■ Why does Friar Laurence assume Romeo is upset?

■ In lines 50–51, what does Romeo mean by the riddle, "one hath wounded me/ That's by me wounded"?

52 physic (fiz′ik), *n.* medicine.
54 intercession (in′tər-sesh′ən), *n.* act of pleading for another person.
54 steads (steds), helps.
55 homely . . . drift, simple and direct.
56 shrift, absolution.

60 all combined, the arrangement is complete.

Not truly in their hearts, but in their eyes.
Jesu Maria, what a deal of brine
70 Hath washed thy sallow cheeks for Rosaline!
How much salt water thrown away in waste
To season love, that of it doth not taste!
The sun not yet thy sighs from heaven clears,
Thy old groans yet ringing in mine ancient ears.
75 Lo, here upon thy cheek the stain doth sit
Of an old tear that is not washed off yet.
If e'er thou wast thyself and these woes thine,
Thou and these woes were all for Rosaline.
And art thou changed? Pronounce this sentence then:
80 Women may fall, when there's no strength in men.
ROMEO. Thou chid'st me oft for loving Rosaline.
FRIAR LAURENCE. For doting, not for loving, pupil mine.
ROMEO. And bad'st me bury love.
FRIAR LAURENCE.   Not in a grave
To lay one in, another out to have.
85 **ROMEO.** I pray thee, chide not. She whom I love now
Doth grace for grace and love for love allow.
The other did not so.
FRIAR LAURENCE.   O, she knew well
Thy love did read by rote, that could not spell.
But come, young waverer, come, go with me,
90 In one respect I'll thy assistant be;
For this alliance may so happy prove
To turn your households' rancor to pure love.
ROMEO. O, let us hence! I stand on sudden haste.
FRIAR LAURENCE. Wisely and slow. They stumble that run fast.
(ROMEO *and the* FRIAR *go out.*)

SCENE 4

Summary *Benvolio and Mercutio wonder where Romeo went after the ball. Benvolio mentions a letter Tybalt sent to Romeo; Mercutio makes fun of Tybalt's style of swordsmanship. Romeo enters but does not reveal where, or with whom, he has been. The Nurse enters, Benvolio and Mercutio exit, and once Romeo stops the Nurse from talking, he gives her a message for Juliet: Juliet is to come to Friar Laurence's cell that afternoon to be married.*

A street in Verona on the morning after the ball. Enter MERCUTIO *and* BENVOLIO.

MERCUTIO. Where the devil should this Romeo be?
Came he not home tonight?
BENVOLIO. Not to his father's. I spoke with his man.
MERCUTIO. Why, that same pale hardhearted wench, that Rosaline,

---

69 **brine,** salty tears.
70 **sallow** (sal′ō), *adj.* sickly, yellowish or brownish-yellow color.

81 **chid'st,** chided, scolded.
82 **doting,** being foolishly fond of.
83 **bad'st,** bade, ordered.

88 **did read by rote,** merely repeated conventional expressions of love.

92 **rancor** (rang′kər), *n.* bitter resentment; hatred.
93 **I stand on,** I demand.

2 **tonight,** last night.

---

5   Torments him so that he will sure run mad.

BENVOLIO. Tybalt, the kinsman to old Capulet,
     Hath sent a letter to his father's house.

MERCUTIO. A challenge, on my life.

BENVOLIO. Romeo will answer it.

10 **MERCUTIO.** Any man that can write may answer a letter.

BENVOLIO. Nay, he will answer the letter's master, how he dares, being
     dared.

MERCUTIO. Alas poor Romeo! He is already dead, stabbed with a white
     wench's black eye, run through the ear with a love song, the very

15   pin of his heart cleft with the blind bow-boy's butt shaft. And he is
     a man to encounter Tybalt?

BENVOLIO. Why, what is Tybalt?

MERCUTIO. More than prince of cats. O, he's the courageous captain
     of compliments. He fights as you sing prick song, keeps time,

20   distance, and proportion; he rests his minim rests, one, two, and
     the third in your bosom. The very butcher of a silk button, a duel-
     list, a duellist, a gentleman of the very first house, of the first and
     second cause. Ah, the immortal *passado! The punto reverso! The hay!*

BENVOLIO. The what?

25 **MERCUTIO.** The pox of such antic, lisping, affecting fantasticoes; these
     new tuners of accent! "By Jesu, a very good blade! A very tall man!
     A very good whore!" Why, is not this a lamentable thing, grandsire,
     that we should be thus afflicted with these strange flies, these fash-
     ionmongers, these pardon-me's, who stand so much on the new

30   form that they cannot sit at ease on the old bench? O, their bones,
     their bones!

(Enter ROMEO, who shows no sign of his former moodiness.)

BENVOLIO. Here comes Romeo, here comes Romeo.

MERCUTIO. Without his roe, like a dried herring. O flesh, flesh, how art
     thou fishified! Now is he for the numbers that Petrarch flowed in.

35   Laura to his lady was but a kitchen wench—marry, she had a better
     love to berhyme her—Dido a dowdy, Cleopatra a gypsy, Helen and
     Hero hildings and harlots, Thisbe a gray eye or so, but not to the
     purpose. Signor Romeo, *bonjour!* There's a French salutation to
     your French slop. You gave us the counterfeit fairly last night.

40 **ROMEO.** Good morrow to you both. What counterfeit did I give you?

MERCUTIO. The slip, sir, the slip. Can you not conceive?

ROMEO. Pardon, good Mercutio. My business was great, and in such a
     case as mine a man may strain courtesy.

(He laughs and claps MERCUTIO on the shoulder.)

MERCUTIO. That's as much as to say, such a case as yours constrains a

45   man to bow in the hams.

ROMEO. Meaning, to curtsy.

MERCUTIO. Thou hast most kindly hit it.

18 prince of cats. In a collection of fables, the name of the Prince of Cats was Tybert or Tybalt.
18–19 captain of compliments, master of rules of ceremony in duelling.
19 prick song, music written out.
19–20 time, distance, and proportion, fencing terms.
20 minim rest, a half rest in music.
21 butcher . . . button, one who can cut off any button of his adversary.
22–23 of the first . . . cause, ready to quarrel over anything—or nothing.
23 *passado* (pə sä′dō), *punto reverso* (pun′tō ri vėr′sō), *hay* (hā), fencing moves.
26 new tuners of accent, those who use new slang and foreign words.

33 roe, fish eggs, but here a possible pun on RO-meo.
34 numbers, verses.
34–38 Petrarch (pē′trärk) **. . . purpose.** Petrarch, an Italian Renaissance poet, wrote poems to Laura. Other romantic heroines are also mentioned here.
37 hildings, good-for-nothings.
38 Signor (sē′nyôr) **. . .** *bonjour* (bôN zhür′). Sir Romeo, good day.
39 slop, large breeches (a French style).
39 gave . . . counterfeit, played us a trick.
41 slip, getaway; but also, a counterfeit coin.

ROMEO. A most courteous exposition.

MERCUTIO. Nay, I am the very pink of courtesy.

50 **ROMEO.** Pink for flower.

MERCUTIO. Right.

ROMEO. Why then *(kicking him lightly)* is my pump well flowered.

MERCUTIO. Sure wit, follow me this jest now till thou hast worn out thy pump, that when the single sole of it is worn, the jest may remain,

55 after the wearing, solely singular.

ROMEO. O single-soled jest, solely singular for the singleness!

MERCUTIO. Come between us, good Benvolio. My wits faints.

ROMEO. Switch and spurs, switch and spurs! Or I'll cry a match.

MERCUTIO. Nay, if our wits run the wild-goose chase, I am done, for

60 thou hast more of the wild goose in one of thy wits than, I am sure, I have in my whole five. Was I with you there for the goose?

ROMEO. Thou wast never with me for anything when thou wast not there for the goose.

MERCUTIO. I will bite thee by the ear for that jest.

65 **ROMEO.** Nay, good goose, bite not.

MERCUTIO. Thy wit is a very bitter sweeting; it is a most sharp sauce.

ROMEO. And is it not, then, well served in to a sweet goose?

MERCUTIO. O, here's a wit of cheveril, that stretches from an inch narrow to an ell broad!

70 **ROMEO.** I stretch it out for that word "broad," which, added to the goose, proves thee far and wide a broad goose.

MERCUTIO. Why, is not this better now than groaning for love? Now art thou sociable, now art thou Romeo; now art thou what thou art, by art as well as by nature. For this driveling love is like a great natural

75 that runs lolling up and down to hide his bauble in a hole.

BENVOLIO. Stop there, stop there.

MERCUTIO. Thou desirest me to stop in my tale against the hair.

BENVOLIO. Thou wouldst else have made thy tale large.

MERCUTIO. O, thou art deceived; I would have made it short, for I was

80 come to the whole depth of my tale and meant indeed to occupy the argument no longer.

ROMEO *(seeing the* NURSE *and* PETER*).* Here's goodly gear!

(Enter NURSE *and* PETER, *her servant. He is carrying a large fan.)*

A sail, a sail!

MERCUTIO. Two, two: a shirt and a smock.

85 **NURSE.** Peter!

PETER. Anon!

NURSE. My fan, Peter.

MERCUTIO. Good Peter, to hide her face, for her fan's the fairer face.

NURSE. God gi' good morrow, gentlemen.

90 **MERCUTIO.** God gi' good e'en, fair gentlewoman.

NURSE. Is it good e'en?

---

49 pink of courtesy, perfection of manners. A pink is also a flower, and pinking is a kind of decoration used on shoes (e.g., pumps).

58 switch and spurs, keep up the pace.

59 wild-goose chase, a horse race in which the leading rider dares competitors to follow wherever he or she goes.

61 Was . . . goose? Did I score a point in calling you a goose?

66 sweeting, a tart apple.

68 cheveril (chev′ər əl), *n.* kid leather, easily stretched.

69 ell, forty-five inches.

71 broad, large, complete.

74 natural, idiot.

■ What does Mercutio mean when he says in line 72, "better now than groaning for love"?

77 against the hair, against the grain; against my wish.

84 shirt . . . smock, indicating a man and woman.

89 God . . . morrow. God give you a good morning.

MERCUTIO. 'Tis no less, I tell ye, for the bawdy hand of the dial is now upon the prick of noon.

NURSE. Out upon you! What a man are you?

95 **ROMEO.** One, gentlewoman, that God hath made for himself to mar.

NURSE. By my troth, it is well said. "For himself to mar," quoth 'a? Gentlemen, can any of you tell me where I may find the young Romeo?

ROMEO. I can tell you; but young Romeo will be older when you have 100 found him than he was when you sought him. I am the youngest of that name, for fault of a worse.

NURSE. You say well.

MERCUTIO. Yea, is the worst well? Very well took, i' faith, wisely, wisely.

NURSE. If you be he, sir, I desire some confidence with you.

105 **BENVOLIO.** She will indite him to some supper.

MERCUTIO. A bawd, a bawd, a bawd! So ho!

ROMEO. What hast thou found?

MERCUTIO. No hare, sir, unless a hare, sir, in a lenten pie, that is something stale and hoar ere it be spent.   *(He sings.)*

110   An old hare hoar,
      And an old hare hoar,
    Is very good meat in Lent.
      But a hare that is hoar
      Is too much for a score,
115   When it hoars ere it be spent.

92 bawdy (bô′dē), *adj.* indecent; lewd; obscene.
94 Out upon you, an expression of indignation.
95 mar, disfigure morally.
96 By my troth, in truth.

101 fault, lack.

103 took, understood.
104 confidence, the nurse's blunder for *conference*.
105 indite. Imitating the nurse, Benvolio jokingly misuses *indite* for *invite*.
106 So ho, cry of a hunter sighting game.
108 lenten pie, a pie that should contain no meat.
109 hoar (hôr), *adj.* moldy; also, *v.* turn moldy.
109 spent, consumed.

114 for a score, to pay good money for.

◀ In the film version, the Nurse expresses her irritation in a more physical way than Shakespeare calls for. What does this add to your understanding of her **character**?

Romeo, will you come to your father's? We'll to dinner thither.

ROMEO. I will follow you.

MERCUTIO. Farewell, ancient lady. Farewell, (*singing*) "Lady, lady, lady."
(*Exit* MERCUTIO *and* BENVOLIO.)

NURSE. I pray you, sir, what saucy merchant was this that was so full of
120   his ropery?

ROMEO. A gentleman, Nurse, that loves to hear himself talk, and will
speak more in a minute than he will stand to in a month.

NURSE. An 'a speak anything against me, I'll take him down, an 'a were
lustier than he is, and twenty such Jacks; and if I cannot, I'll find
125   those that shall. Scurvy knave! I am none of his flirt-gills. I am none
of his skains-mates. (*To* PETER.) And thou must stand by, too, and
suffer every knave to use me at his pleasure!

PETER. I saw no man use you at his pleasure. If I had, my weapon
should quickly have been out; I warrant you, I dare draw as soon
130   as another man, if I see occasion in a good quarrel, and the law on
my side.

NURSE. Now, afore God, I am so vexed that every part about me quivers. (*Muttering to herself.*) Scurvy knave! (*To* ROMEO, *after regaining her
composure.*) Pray you, sir, a word; and as I told you, my young lady bid
135   me inquire you out. What she bid me say, I will keep to myself. But
first let me tell ye, if ye should lead her in a fool's paradise, as they
say, it were a very gross kind of behavior, as they say. For the gentlewoman is young; and therefore if you should deal double with
her, truly it were an ill thing to be offered to any gentlewoman,
140   and very weak dealing.

ROMEO. Nurse, commend me to thy lady and mistress. I protest unto
thee—

NURSE. Good heart, and i' faith I will tell her as much. Lord, Lord, she
will be a joyful woman.

145 **ROMEO.** What wilt thou tell her, Nurse? Thou dost not mark me.

NURSE. I will tell her, sir, that you do protest, which, as I take it, is a
gentlemanlike offer.

ROMEO. Bid her devise
Some means to come to shrift this afternoon,
150   And there she shall at Friar Laurence' cell
Be shrived and married. Here is for thy pains. (*Offers money.*)

NURSE. No, truly, sir, not a penny.

ROMEO. Go to, I say you shall.

NURSE (*pocketing the money*). This afternoon, sir? Well, she shall be
there.

155 **ROMEO.** And stay, good Nurse, behind the abbey wall.
Within this hour my man shall be with thee
And bring thee cords made like a tackled stair,
Which to the high topgallant of my joy

---

119 saucy merchant, rude fellow.
120 ropery (rō′pər ē), *n.* vulgar humor.
122 stand to, stand to listen to.
124 Jacks, rascals.
125 scurvy knave, disease-ridden rascal.
125 flirt-gills, flirtatious women.
126 skains-mates, perhaps outlaws, dagger-mates, or gangster molls.

■ What does the Nurse mean when she warns Romeo not to "deal double" with Juliet?

140 weak, shifty and contemptible.
141 protest, vow.

145 mark me, pay attention to what I say.

151 shrived, absolved.

153 Go to, say nothing more.

157 tackled stair, rope ladder.
158 topgallant, highest mast and sail of a ship.

Must be my convoy in the secret night.

160 Farewell. Be trusty, and I'll quit thy pains.

   Farewell. Commend me to thy mistress.

NURSE. Now God in heaven bless thee! (*She turns to go but stops and calls to* ROMEO.) Hark you, sir.

ROMEO. What sayst thou my dear Nurse?

165 **NURSE.** Is your man secret? Did you ne'er hear say,

   "Two may keep counsel, putting one away"?

ROMEO. 'Warrant thee, my man's as true as steel.

NURSE. Well, sir, my mistress is the sweetest lady—Lord, Lord! When 'twas a little prating thing—O, there is a nobleman in town, one

170 Paris, that would fain lay knife aboard; but she, good soul, had as lief see a toad, a very toad, as see him. I anger her sometimes and tell her that Paris is the properer man, but I'll warrant you, when I say so, she looks as pale as any clout in the versal world. Doth not rosemary and Romeo begin both with a letter?

175 **ROMEO** (*breaking out in loud laughter*). Ay, Nurse, what of that? Both with an R.

NURSE. Ah, mocker! That's the dog's name; R is for the—No; I know it begins with some other letter; and she hath the prettiest sententious of it, of you and rosemary, that it would do you good to hear it.

180 **ROMEO.** Commend me to thy lady.

NURSE. Ay, a thousand times. (*Exit* ROMEO.) Peter!

PETER. Anon!

NURSE. Peter, take my fan, and go before, and apace. (*Exit.*)

SCENE 5

> **Summary** *After being gone three hours, the Nurse enters complaining of exhaustion and breathlessness. Eventually, she tells Juliet to meet Romeo at Friar Laurence's that afternoon since Friar Laurence has agreed to marry the young lovers.*

Capulet's orchard. Enter JULIET.

JULIET (*with rising anxiety*). The clock struck nine when I did send the nurse;

   In half an hour she promised to return.

   Perchance she cannot meet him. That's not so.

   O, she is lame! Love's heralds should be thoughts,

5   Which ten times faster glide than the sun's beams

   Driving back shadows over louring hills.

   Therefore do nimble-pinioned doves draw Love,

   And therefore hath the wind-swift Cupid wings.

   Now is the sun upon the highmost hill

10 Of this day's journey, and from nine till twelve

   Is three long hours, yet she is not come.

159 convoy, means of travel.
160 quit, reward.
161 commend, speak well of; praise.

165 secret, trustworthy.
166 Two . . . away, two may keep a secret if only one of them knows it.

169 prating (prāt′ing), *adj.* chattering.
170 fain . . . aboard, gladly seize, in the manner of a pirate, what he desires.
171 lief (lēf), willingly.
173 clout, rag.
173 versal, universal.
177 the dog's name. The sound of the letter R was thought to resemble a dog's snarl.
178 sententious (sen-ten′shəs), *adj.* full of meaning; the nurse's error for *sentences* (clever sayings).

183 apace, quickly.

■ Juliet's opening speech is a **soliloquy,** a speech representing a character's thoughts. What is Juliet's state of mind?

3 perchance, perhaps.
4 herald (her′əld), *n.* messenger.
6 louring, sullen, gloomy.
7 nimble-pinioned . . . Love. Swift-winged doves drew the chariot of Venus, goddess of love.

Had she affections and warm youthful blood,
She would be as swift in motion as a ball;
My words would bandy her to my sweet love,
15   And his to me.
But old folks, many feign as they were dead—
Unwieldy, slow, heavy, and pale as lead.
(*Enter* NURSE *and* PETER.)
       O God, she comes!—O honey Nurse, what news?
       Hast thou met with him? Send thy man away.
20 **NURSE.** Peter, stay at the gate. (*Exit* PETER.)
   JULIET. Now, good sweet Nurse—O Lord, why lookest thou sad?
       Though news be sad, yet tell them merrily;
       If good, thou shamest the music of sweet news
       By playing it to me with so sour a face.
25 **NURSE.** I am aweary. Give me leave awhile.
       Fie, how my bones ache! What a jaunce have I had!
   JULIET. I would thou hadst my bones and I thy news.
       Nay, come, I pray thee, speak. Good, good Nurse, speak.
   NURSE. Jesu, what haste! Can you not stay awhile?
30   Do you not see that I am out of breath?
   JULIET (*with exasperation*). How art thou out of breath, when thou hast
           breath
       To say to me that thou art out of breath?
       The excuse that thou dost make in this delay
       Is longer than the tale thou dost excuse.
35   Is thy news good or bad? Answer to that;
       Say either, and I'll stay the circumstance.
       Let me be satisfied: is 't good or bad?
   NURSE. Well, you have made a simple choice. You know not how to
       choose a man. Romeo? No, not he. Though his face be better than
40   any man's, yet his leg excels all men's; and for a hand, and a foot,
       and a body, though they be not talked on, yet they are past
       compare. He is not the flower of courtesy, but, I'll warrant him, as
       gentle as a lamb. Go thy ways, wench. Serve God. What, have you
       dined at home?
45 **JULIET.** No, no; but all this did I know before.
       What says he of our marriage? What of that?
   NURSE. Lord, how my head aches! What a head have I!
       It beats as it would fall in twenty pieces.
       My back o' t'other side—ah, my back, my back!
50   Beshrew your heart for sending me about
       To catch my death with jauncing up and down!
   JULIET. I' faith, I am sorry that thou art not well.
       (*Beseechingly.*) Sweet, sweet, sweet Nurse, tell me, what says my love?
   NURSE. Your love says, like an honest gentleman,

14 bandy, toss to and fro, as in tennis.

16 feign (fān), *v.* pretend; disguise.
17 unwieldy (un wēl′dē), *adj.* heavy and awkward; bulky.

22 news . . . them. News was often used in the plural.

25 give me leave, let me alone.
26 jaunce, rough jolting, hard trip.

29 stay, wait.

36 stay the circumstance, await details.
38 simple, foolish.

50 beshrew (bi shrü′), *v.* curse.

55 And a courteous, and a kind, and a handsome,
And, I warrant, a virtuous—Where is your mother?
JULIET (*bewildered*). Where is my mother? Why, she is within,
Where should she be? (*Angrily.*) How oddly thou repliest!
"Your love says, like an honest gentleman,
'Where is your mother?'"
60 **NURSE.**   O God's Lady dear!
Are you so hot? Marry, come up, I trow.
Is this the poultice for my aching bones?
Henceforward do your messages yourself.
JULIET. Here's such a coil! Come, what says Romeo?
65 **NURSE.** Have you got leave to go to shrift today?
JULIET. I have.
NURSE. Then hie you hence to Friar Laurence' cell;
There stays a husband to make you a wife.
Now comes the wanton blood up in your cheeks;
70 They'll be in scarlet straight at any news.
Hie you to church. I must another way,
To fetch a ladder, by the which your love
Must climb a bird's nest soon when it is dark.
I am the drudge, and toil in your delight,
75 But you shall bear the burden soon at night.
Go. I'll to dinner. Hie you to the cell.
JULIET. Hie to high fortune! Honest Nurse, farewell.
(*They go out in opposite directions.*)

SCENE 6

Summary *In this brief scene, Friar Laurence and Romeo await Juliet's arrival. Romeo burns with love while Friar Laurence warns him to love moderately. After Juliet arrives, she and Romeo speak of their love and then leave with the Friar to exchange marriage vows.*

Friar Laurence's cell. Enter FRIAR LAURENCE *and* ROMEO.
FRIAR LAURENCE. So smile the heavens upon this holy act
That after-hours with sorrow chide us not!
ROMEO. Amen, amen! But come what sorrow can,
It cannot countervail the exchange of joy
5 That one short minute gives me in her sight.
Do thou but close our hands with holy words,
Then love-devouring death do what he dare;
It is enough I may but call her mine.
FRIAR LAURENCE. These violent delights have violent ends
10 And in their triumph die, like fire and powder,
Which as they kiss consume. The sweetest honey
Is loathsome in his own deliciousness,

■ Although the Nurse seems to be teasing Juliet when she asks where Lady Capulet is, what serious reason might she have for asking this?

61 Are . . . trow. Are you so impatient? Indeed, come off it, I declare.
62 poultice (pōl′tis), *n.* soft, moist covering of herbs applied as medicine.
64 coil, commotion.
65 shrift, confession.

67 hie (hī), *v.* hasten.

70 in scarlet, blushing.

4 countervail (koun′tər-vāl′), *v.* balance, equal.

12 loathsome (lōŦH′səm), *adj.* hateful; sickening.

◀ Friar Laurence prepares to marry Romeo and Juliet. Why is Juliet dressed as simply as she is?

And in the taste confounds the appetite.
Therefore love moderately. Long love doth so;
15   Too swift arrives as tardy as too slow.
        (*Enter* JULIET.)
            Here comes the lady. O, so light a foot
            Will ne'er wear out the everlasting flint.
            A lover may bestride the gossamers
            That idles in the wanton summer air,
20   And yet not fall, so light is vanity.
    JULIET. Good even to my ghostly confessor.
    FRIAR LAURENCE. Romeo shall thank thee, daughter, for us both.
    JULIET. As much to him, else is his thanks too much.
    ROMEO. Ah, Juliet, if the measure of thy joy
25   Be heaped like mine, and that thy skill be more
            To blazon it, then sweeten with thy breath
            This neighbor air, and let rich music's tongue
            Unfold the imagined happiness that both
            Receive in either by this dear encounter.
30 **JULIET.** Conceit, more rich in matter than in words,
            Brags of his substance, not of ornament.
            They are but beggars that can count their worth.
            But my true love is grown to such excess
            I cannot sum up sum of half my wealth.
35 **FRIAR LAURENCE.** Come, come with me, and we will make short work;
            For, by your leaves, you shall not stay alone
            Till Holy Church incorporate two in one.   (*Exit.*)

13 **confounds,** destroys.

■ What might Friar Laurence's speech in lines 9–15 **foreshadow** about events to come?

18 **gossamer** (gos′ə mər), *n.* cobweb.
20 **so light is vanity,** so unsubstantial are the illusions of love.
21 **even,** evening.
23 **As much to him,** the same greeting to him.

25 **that,** if.
26 **blazon** (blā′zn), *v.* proclaim.

30–31 **Conceit . . . ornament.** True understanding, more enriched by the reality (of love) than by mere words, finds more worth in the reality than in outward show.

After Reading

Making Connections

1. Choose your favorite lines from Act 2 and read them to a partner, explaining why you like them.

2. Do you think Friar Laurence uses good judgment in agreeing to marry Juliet and Romeo? Explain.

3. Do you agree with the friar's advice to Romeo to "love moderately"? Why or why not?

4. Think of three adjectives to describe the **character** of Friar Laurence. Cite specific lines to support your choices.

5. Is Romeo's approach to love the same as or different from Juliet's? Explain.

6. In Scene 2, lines 109–111, why does Juliet object to Romeo's vow "by the moon"?

7. In Scene 3, line 81, Romeo tells the friar, "Thou chid'st me oft for loving Rosaline." Friar Laurence replies, "For doting, not for loving, pupil mine." What do you think the friar means?

8. Why do you think Shakespeare chose to make Scene 4 humorous? Consider the **tone** of the scenes that come before and after it.

9. Do you think the action has, in general, moved quickly or slowly in Act 2? Explain.

10. Think of a recent movie or book about young people in love. How is the contemporary version of young love similar to and different from Shakespeare's version?

11. If Romeo and Juliet lived now, do you think they would marry so quickly? Why or why not?

Vocabulary Study

baleful
cunning
entreat
feign
intercession
loathsome
predominant
sallow
unwieldy
vile

Here are some scenes that you *won't* find in *Romeo and Juliet*. Write some lines of dialogue for one or more of these scenes, or for a scene you invent. Use all of the listed vocabulary words at least once in the dialogue you write. You can either imitate Shakespeare's style or create your own.

1. Romeo runs into Rosaline after the party at the Capulets.

2. Lady Capulet overhears the balcony scene and has a talk with Juliet.

3. Tybalt finds out that Romeo and Juliet are going to marry and tells Lord Capulet.

4. Juliet tells Romeo she doesn't want to marry him so soon after they've met.

Expressing Your Ideas

Writing Choices

Love at First Sight Write the **love poem** that Romeo might write to Juliet the day after meeting her. Remember that, as Romeo, this is perhaps the most exciting event of your life.

Adding Links Expand the **chain diagram** you started previously to include the major events of Act 2. Work with the same partner and save the diagram for later.

Thoughts into Words The Nurse and Friar Laurence assist Romeo and Juliet in carrying out their plan to marry. Write a **diary entry** for either the Nurse or Friar Laurence and record your hopes and fears for the newly married couple.

Other Options

Line, Please Actors know that one of the best ways to get "inside a character" is to memorize that character's lines. Choose a speech of at least fifteen uninterrupted lines from the first two acts. Memorize the speech and add any gestures or movements you think enhance it. Perform your **speech** for the class and tell what you learned about the character from the exercise.

Little Thing Called Love In a small group, discuss the feelings Romeo and Juliet have for each other. Do you think they truly love each other? What is love and how is it different from infatuation or a "crush"? Work with your group to answer these questions and come up with a **definition of love** to share with the class.

ACT THREE

SCENE 1

Summary *Benvolio, Mercutio, and others walk in the town square. Fearing trouble, Benvolio urges that they go home. Tybalt enters and, seeing Romeo, turns to challenge him. When Romeo avoids the fight, his seeming cowardice infuriates Mercutio, who draws on Tybalt. Romeo tries to stop the fight, but Tybalt stabs Mercutio and flees. Mercutio exits, supported by Benvolio, who soon returns with word of Mercutio's death. Tybalt returns; Romeo kills him and then flees. The Prince, the Montagues, and the Capulets enter. Benvolio reveals what has happened. Prince Escalus announces that Romeo shall be exiled from Verona.*

A public place in Verona, immediately following the marriage of Romeo and Juliet. Enter MERCUTIO, BENVOLIO, PAGE, *and* SERVANTS.

BENVOLIO. I pray thee, good Mercutio, let's retire.
    The day is hot, the Capels are abroad,
    And if we meet we shall not scape a brawl,
    For now, these hot days, is the mad blood stirring.

5 **MERCUTIO.** Thou art like one of these fellows that when he enters the confines of a tavern, claps me his sword upon the table and says, "God send me no need of thee!" and by the operation of the second cup draws him on the drawer, when indeed there is no need.

BENVOLIO. Am I like such a fellow?

10 **MERCUTIO.** Come, come, thou art as hot a Jack in thy mood as any in Italy, and as soon moved to be moody, and as soon moody to be moved.

BENVOLIO. And what to?

MERCUTIO. Nay, an there were two such, we should have none shortly,
15 for one would kill the other. Thou! Why, thou wilt quarrel with a man that hath a hair more or a hair less in his beard than thou hast. Thou wilt quarrel with a man for cracking nuts, having no other reason but because thou hast hazel eyes. What eye but such an eye would spy out such a quarrel? Thy head is as full of quarrels as an
20 egg is full of meat, and yet thy head hath been beaten as addle as an egg for quarreling. Thou hast quarreled with a man for coughing in the street, because he hath wakened thy dog that hath lain asleep in the sun. Didst thou not fall out with a tailor for wearing his new doublet before Easter? With another, for tying his new shoes with
25 old ribbon? And yet thou wilt tutor me from quarreling!

BENVOLIO. An I were so apt to quarrel as thou art, any man should buy the fee simple of my life for an hour and a quarter.

MERCUTIO. The fee simple! O simple!

(*Enter* TYBALT, *and other* CAPULETS.)

---

2 Capels, Capulets.

7 by . . . the second cup, by the time the second cup of wine begins to affect him.
8 drawer, one who draws wine from its container.
10 Jack, fellow.
11–12 moved . . . moved, as inclined to get angry as to be angry when crossed.

■ Based on what you know about Benvolio, do you think Mercutio's comments about his character are accurate?

19 spy out, see the occasion for.
20 addle, confused.

24 doublet (dub′lit), *n.* jacket.
25 tutor . . . quarreling, teach me how not to quarrel.
27 fee simple, absolute ownership.
28 simple, stupid.

BENVOLIO. By my head, here comes the Capulets.

30 **MERCUTIO.** By my heel, I care not.

TYBALT *(to his kinsmen).* Follow me close, for I will speak to them.—
    Gentlemen, good e'en. A word with one of you.

MERCUTIO. And but one word with one of us? Couple it with some-
    thing: make it a word and a blow.

35 **TYBALT.** You shall find me apt enough to that, sir, an you will give me
    occasion.

MERCUTIO. Could you not take some occasion without giving?

TYBALT. Mercutio, thou consortest with Romeo.

MERCUTIO. "Consort"? What, dost thou make us minstrels? An thou
40   make minstrels of us, look to hear nothing but discords. Here's my
    fiddlestick; here's that shall make you dance. Zounds, "consort"!

BENVOLIO. We talk here in the public haunt of men.
    Either withdraw unto some private place,
    Or reason coldly of your grievances,
45   Or else depart; here all eyes gaze on us.

MERCUTIO. Men's eyes were made to look, and let them gaze.
    I will not budge for no man's pleasure, I.

(Enter ROMEO.*)*

TYBALT *(to* BENVOLIO*).* Well, peace be with you, sir. Here comes my man.

MERCUTIO. But I'll be hanged, sir, if he wear your livery.
50   Marry, go before to field, he'll be your follower;
    Your worship in that sense may call him "man."

TYBALT *(confronting* ROMEO*).* Romeo, the love I bear thee can afford
    No better term than this: thou art a villain.

ROMEO. Tybalt, the reason that I have to love thee
55   Doth much excuse the appertaining rage
    To such a greeting. Villain am I none.
    Therefore, farewell. I see thou knowest me not.

TYBALT *(contemptuously).* Boy, this shall not excuse the injuries
    That thou hast done me. Therefore turn and draw.

60 **ROMEO.** I do protest I never injured thee,
    But love thee better than thou canst devise
    Till thou shalt know the reason of my love.
    And so, good Capulet—which name I tender
    As dearly as mine own—be satisfied.

65 **MERCUTIO.** O calm, dishonorable, vile submission!
    Alla stoccado carries it away.   *(He draws his sword.)*
    Tybalt, you ratcatcher, will you walk?

TYBALT. What wouldst thou have with me?

MERCUTIO. Good king of cats, nothing but one of your nine lives, that
70   I mean to make bold withal, and, as you shall use me hereafter,
    dry-beat the rest of the eight. Will you pluck your sword out of

38 consortest with, accompany or wait upon.
39 Consort. *Consort* also means "to combine to make music."
40 discord (dis′kôrd), *n.* disagreement; clashing of sounds.
41 Zounds, a form of the oath, "By God's wounds."
45 depart, separate.

48 my man. Tybalt speaks insultingly as though Romeo were his servant.
49 if . . . livery (liv′ər ē), if Romeo wears the uniform of Tybalt's servants.
50 go . . . follower. If you went to the field of encounter, Romeo would follow you quickly enough.
55–56 appertaining . . . greeting, rage suitable to such a greeting.
57 I . . . not. Romeo realizes that Tybalt doesn't know that Romeo is now his kinsman.

63 tender, cherish.
66 *Alla stoccado* (ä′lä stō-kä′dō), Italian for "With the thrust"; Tybalt, with his bold insults, wins the day.
67 ratcatcher, an allusion to Tybalt as Prince of Cats.
67 walk, step aside with me.
69–70 that . . . withal. That I intend to take at once.
71 dry-beat . . . eight, soundly beat your other eight lives.

his pilcher by the ears? Make haste, lest mine be about your ears
ere it be out.

TYBALT (*drawing*). I am for you.

75 **ROMEO.** Gentle Mercutio, put thy rapier up.

MERCUTIO. Come, sir, your *passado*.

(TYBALT *and* MERCUTIO *fight*.)

ROMEO. Draw, Benvolio, beat down their weapons.
Gentlemen, for shame, forbear this outrage!
Tybalt, Mercutio, the Prince expressly hath
80 Forbid this bandying in Verona streets.
Hold, Tybalt! Good Mercutio!

(TYBALT, *reaching under* ROMEO'*s arm, stabs* MERCUTIO *and flees*.)

MERCUTIO. I am hurt.
A plague o' both your houses! I am sped.
Is he gone, and hath nothing?

BENVOLIO. What, art thou hurt?

MERCUTIO. Ay, ay, a scratch, a scratch; marry, 'tis enough.
85 Where is my page? Go, villain, fetch a surgeon. (*Exit* PAGE.)

ROMEO. Courage, man, the hurt cannot be much.

MERCUTIO. No, 'tis not so deep as a well, nor so wide as a church door,
but 'tis enough, 'twill serve. Ask for me tomorrow, and you shall
find me a grave man. I am peppered, I warrant, for this world. A
90 plague o' both your houses! Zounds, a dog, a rat, a mouse, a cat,
to scratch a man to death! A braggart, a rogue, a villain, that fights
by the book of arithmetic! Why the devil came you between us? I
was hurt under your arm.

ROMEO. I thought all for the best.

95 **MERCUTIO.** Help me into some house, Benvolio,
Or I shall faint. A plague o' both your houses!
They have made worm's meat of me. I have it,
And soundly too. Your houses!

(MERCUTIO *is helped off by* BENVOLIO *and some* SERVANTS.)

ROMEO. This gentleman, the Prince's near ally,
100 My very friend, hath got this mortal hurt
In my behalf; my reputation stained
With Tybalt's slander—Tybalt, that an hour
Hath been my cousin! O sweet Juliet,
Thy beauty hath made me effeminate,
105 And in my temper softened valor's steel.

(*Reenter* BENVOLIO.)

BENVOLIO. O Romeo, Romeo, brave Mercutio is dead!
That gallant spirit hath aspired the clouds,
Which too untimely here did scorn the earth.

ROMEO. This day's black fate on more days doth depend;

---

72 **his pilcher,** its scabbard.

78 **forbear,** stop.

80 **bandying,** fighting.

82 **sped,** done for.

■ What irritates Mercutio
about being wounded by
Tybalt?

84 **enough,** enough to kill
him.
85 **villain,** a form of address
to a servant.
89 **a grave man.** Mercutio
puns with his last breath.
89 **peppered,** finished.

92 **book of arithmetic,** a
textbook on fencing.

97 **I have it,** I am wounded;
similar to today's "I've had it."

99 **ally,** kinsman.
100 **very,** true.

105 valor (val′ər), *n.* bravery;
courage.

107 **aspired,** soared to.

109 **depend,** hang over
threateningly.

▲ Romeo and Tybalt face each other in a fight to the death. The young men of Verona seem to carry swords whenever they are in public. How does this affect events in the play?

110   This but begins the woe others must end.
       (*Reenter* TYBALT.)
     BENVOLIO. Here comes the furious Tybalt back again.
     ROMEO. Alive in triumph, and Mercutio slain!
       Away to heaven, respective lenity,
       And fire-eyed fury be my conduct now!
115   Now, Tybalt, take the "villain" back again
       That late thou gavest me, for Mercutio's soul
       Is but a little way above our heads,
       Staying for thine to keep him company.
       Either thou or I, or both, must go with him.
120 **TYBALT.** Thou, wretched boy, that didst consort him here,
       Shalt with him hence.
     ROMEO (*drawing his sword*). This shall determine that.
      (*They fight.* TYBALT *falls dead.*)

113 respective lenity (len′ə-tē), considerate mildness.
114 conduct, guide.

BENVOLIO. Romeo, away, begone!

    The citizens are up, and Tybalt slain.

    Stand not amazed. The Prince will doom thee death

125   If thou art taken. Hence, begone, away!

ROMEO. O, I am fortune's fool!

BENVOLIO.   Why dost thou stay? (*Exit* ROMEO.)

(*Enter several* CITIZENS.)

FIRST CITIZEN. Which way ran he that killed Mercutio?

    Tybalt, that murderer, which way ran he?

BENVOLIO. There lies that Tybalt.

FIRST CITIZEN (*to* BENVOLIO).   Up, sir, go with me.

130   I charge thee in the Prince's name, obey.

(*Enter* PRINCE ESCALUS, *attended;* MONTAGUE, CAPULET, *their* WIVES, *and* OTHERS.)

PRINCE. Where are the vile beginners of this fray?

BENVOLIO. O noble Prince, I can discover all

    The unlucky manage of this fatal brawl.

    There lies the man, slain by young Romeo,

135   That slew thy kinsman, brave Mercutio.

LADY CAPULET. Tybalt, my cousin! O my brother's child!

    O Prince! O cousin! Husband! O, the blood is spilled

    Of my dear kinsman! Prince, as thou art true,

    For blood of ours shed blood of Montague.

140   O cousin, cousin!

PRINCE. Benvolio, who began this bloody fray?

BENVOLIO. Tybalt, here slain, whom Romeo's hand did slay.

    Romeo, that spoke him fair, bid him bethink

    How nice the quarrel was, and urged withal

145   Your high displeasure. All this—utterèd

    With gentle breath, calm look, knees humbly bowed—

    Could not take truce with the unruly spleen

    Of Tybalt deaf to peace, but that he tilts

    With piercing steel at bold Mercutio's breast,

150   Who, all as hot, turns deadly point to point,

    And, with a martial scorn, with one hand beats

    Cold death aside and with the other sends

    It back to Tybalt, whose dexterity

    Retorts it. Romeo he cries aloud,

155   "Hold, friends! Friends, part!" and swifter than his tongue

    His agile arm beats down their fatal points,

    And twixt them rushes; underneath whose arm

    An envious thrust from Tybalt hit the life

    Of stout Mercutio, and then Tybalt fled;

160   But by and by comes back to Romeo,

    Who had but newly entertained revenge,

124 amazed, stupefied.

126 fortune's fool, the plaything or pawn of fate.

■ By bringing the citizens on stage, what does Shakespeare suggest about the street brawl and its effect on the lives of Verona's citizens?

132 discover, reveal.
133 manage, course.

143 fair, civilly.
144 nice, trivial.

147 take truce, make peace.
147 unruly spleen, ungovernable rage.
148 tilts, strikes.

151 martial (mär′shəl), *adj.* warlike.

153 dexterity (dek ster′-ə tē), *n.* skill in using the hands or body.
154 retort (ri tôrt′), *v.* return.

159 stout, stout-hearted; brave.

And to 't they go like lightning, for, ere I
Could draw to part them was stout Tybalt slain,
And, as he fell, did Romeo turn and fly.
165 This is the truth, or let Benvolio die.
LADY CAPULET. He is a kinsman to the Montague.
Affection makes him false; he speaks not true.
Some twenty of them fought in this black strife,
And all those twenty could but kill one life.
170 I beg for justice, which thou, Prince, must give.
Romeo slew Tybalt; Romeo must not live.
PRINCE. Romeo slew him, he slew Mercutio.
Who now the price of his dear blood doth owe?
MONTAGUE. Not Romeo, Prince, he was Mercutio's friend;
175 His fault concludes but what the law should end,
The life of Tybalt.
PRINCE.   And for that offense
Immediately we do exile him hence.
I have an interest in your hate's proceeding;
My blood for your rude brawls doth lie a-bleeding;
180 But I'll amerce you with so strong a fine
That you shall all repent the loss of mine.
(*Shouting above loud outcries from* MONTAGUES *and* CAPULETS.)
I will be deaf to pleading and excuses;
Nor tears nor prayers shall purchase out abuses.
Therefore use none. Let Romeo hence in haste,
185 Else, when he is found, that hour is his last.
Bear hence this body and attend our will.
Mercy but murders, pardoning those that kill.   (*Exit.*)

SCENE 2

Summary *Juliet awaits eagerly the coming of night and the arrival of Romeo. The nurse enters, shocked at the news of Tybalt's death. Finally she reveals that Romeo has killed Tybalt and is banished. The nurse promises that she will bring Romeo to Juliet that night. Juliet sends her forth to Romeo with a ring as token of her love.*

Capulet's orchard. Enter JULIET.
JULIET. Gallop apace, you fiery-footed steeds,
Towards Phoebus' lodging! Such a wagoner
As Phaëthon would whip you to the west
And bring in cloudy night immediately.
5 Spread thy close curtain, love-performing night,
That runaways' eyes may wink, and Romeo
Leap to these arms, untalked of and unseen.
Lovers can see to do their amorous rites

168 strife, fighting; quarreling.

■ Why do you think Lady Capulet says, "Some twenty" men fought Tybalt?

179 My blood, the blood of my kin.
180 amerce (ə mėrs′), *v.* punish by fine.
181 mine, my blood.

183 purchase out, make up for.

186 attend our will, wait for our further judgments.

1 steed, horse.
2 Phoebus (fē′bəs), the sun god.
3 Phaëthon (fā′ə thon). He was allowed to drive the chariot of the sun for a day. Too weak to control the horses, he nearly destroyed the world.

By their own beauties; or, if love be blind,

10 It best agrees with night. Come, civil night,
Thou sober-suited matron all in black,
And learn me how to lose a winning match
Played for a pair of stainless maidenhoods.
Hood my unmanned blood, bating in my cheeks,

15 With thy black mantle till strange love grown bold
Think true love acted simple modesty.
Come, night. Come, Romeo. Come, thou day in night;
For thou wilt lie upon the wings of night
Whiter than new snow upon a raven's back.

20 Come, gentle night, come, loving, black-browed night,
Give me my Romeo, and when I shall die
Take him and cut him out in little stars,
And he will make the face of heaven so fine
That all the world will be in love with night

25 And pay no worship to the garish sun.
O, I have bought the mansion of a love
But not possessed it, and though I am sold,
Not yet enjoyed. *(She looks around eagerly.)* So tedious is this day
As is the night before some festival

30 To an impatient child that hath new robes
And may not wear them. O, here comes my nurse,
And she brings news, and every tongue that speaks
But Romeo's name speaks heavenly <u>eloquence</u>.
(Enter NURSE *with the rope-ladder.)*
Now, Nurse, what news? What hast thou there the cords
That Romeo bid thee fetch?

35 **NURSE.**   Ay, ay, the cords.
(She throws down the ladder abruptly.)
JULIET. Ay me, what news? Why dost thou wring thy hands?
NURSE. Ah, weraday! He's dead, he's dead, he's dead!
We are undone, lady, we are undone!
Alack the day, he's gone, he's killed, he's dead!
JULIET. Can heaven be so envious?

40 **NURSE.**   Romeo can,
Though heaven cannot. O Romeo, Romeo!
Who ever would have thought it? Romeo!
JULIET. What devil art thou that dost torment me thus?
This torture should be roared in dismal hell.

45 Hath Romeo slain himself? Say thou but "Ay,"
And that bare vowel "I" shall poison more
Than the death-darting eye of cockatrice.
I am not I, if there be such an "Ay."
Or those eyes shut, that makes thee answer "Ay."

---

10 civil night, circumspect; well-ordered.

12 learn, teach.

14 hood, cover.
14 unmanned, untamed.
15 strange, diffident, shy.

25 garish (ger'ish), *adj.* glaring.

33 eloquence (el'ə kwəns), *n.* flow of speech that has grace and force.

37 weraday, alas.

47 cockatrice (kok'ə tris), *n.* a fabled serpent that could kill with its glance.
45–49 Say . . . "Ay." Note Juliet's wordplay in this speech: *Ay, I,* and *eye.*

50 If he be slain, say "Ay," or if not, "No."
    Brief sounds determine of my weal or woe.
    NURSE. I saw the wound. I saw it with mine eyes—
    God save the mark!—here on his manly breast.
    A piteous corpse, a bloody piteous corpse;
55 Pale, pale as ashes, all bedaubed in blood,
    All in gore-blood. I swoonèd at the sight.
    JULIET. O, break, my heart! Poor bankrupt, break at once!
    To prison, eyes; ne'er look on liberty!
    Vile earth, to earth resign; end motion here,
60 And thou and Romeo press one heavy bier!
    NURSE. O Tybalt, Tybalt, the best friend I had!
    O courteous Tybalt! Honest gentleman!
    That ever I should live to see thee dead!
    JULIET. What storm is this that blows so contrary?
65 Is Romeo slaughtered, and is Tybalt dead?
    My dearest cousin, and my dearer lord?
    Then, dreadful trumpet, sound the general doom!
    For who is living, if those two are gone?
    NURSE. Tybalt is gone, and Romeo banishèd;
70 Romeo that killed him, he is banishèd.
    JULIET. O God! Did Romeo's hand shed Tybalt's blood?
    NURSE. It did, it did. Alas the day it did!
    JULIET. O serpent heart, hid with a flowering face!
    Did ever dragon keep so fair a cave?
75 Beautiful tyrant! Fiend angelical!
    Dove-feathered raven! Wolvish-ravening lamb!
    Despisèd substance of divinest show!
    Just opposite to what thou justly seem'st,
    A damnèd saint, an honorable villain!
80 O nature, what hadst thou to do in hell
    When thou didst bower the spirit of a fiend
    In mortal paradise of such sweet flesh?
    Was ever book containing such vile matter
    So fairly bound? O, that deceit should dwell
    In such a gorgeous palace!
85 **NURSE.**   There's no trust,
    No faith, no honesty in men; all perjured,
    All forsworn, all naught, all dissemblers.
    Ah, where's my man? Give me some aqua vitae.
    These griefs, these woes, these sorrows make me old.
    Shame come to Romeo!
90 **JULIET.**   Blistered be thy tongue
    For such a wish! He was not born to shame.
    Upon his brow shame is ashamed to sit,

51 determine . . . woe, decide my well-being or my sorrow.

53 God . . . mark. God have mercy on us.

56 gore-blood, clotted blood.
59 Vile earth . . . resign. Miserable body, resign yourself to death.
59 motion, human activity.

67 trumpet . . . doom. Juliet calls for the trumpet to proclaim doomsday, or the end of the world.

■ Juliet's speech about Romeo is full of **paradoxes,** contradictory words or phrases such as "beautiful tyrant." What does this reveal about her feelings towards Romeo after learning of Tybalt's murder?

81 bower (bou′ər), *v.* give lodging to.

87 forsworn (fôr swôrn′), *adj.* untrue to one's sworn oath.
87 naught, worthless, evil.
87 dissembler (di sem′blər), *n.* one who hides or pretends.
88 aqua vitae (ä′kwä vē′tā), spirits to restore calmness. [Latin]

For 'tis a throne where honor may be crowned
Sole monarch of the universal earth.

95 O, what a beast was I to chide at him!

NURSE. Will you speak well of him that killed your cousin?

JULIET. Shall I speak ill of him that is my husband?
Ah, poor my lord, what tongue shall smooth thy name
When I, thy three-hours wife, have mangled it?
100 But wherefore, villain, didst thou kill my cousin?
That villain cousin would have killed my husband.
Back, foolish tears, back to your native spring!
Your tributary drops belong to woe,
Which you, mistaking, offer up to joy.
105 My husband lives, that Tybalt would have slain,
And Tybalt's dead, that would have slain my husband.
All this is comfort. Wherefore weep I then?
Some word there was, worser than Tybalt's death,
That murdered me. I would forget it fain,
110 But O, it presses to my memory
Like damnèd guilty deeds to sinners' minds:
"Tybalt is dead, and Romeo—banishèd."
That "banishèd," that one word "banishèd,"
Hath slain ten thousand Tybalts. Tybalt's death
115 Was woe enough if it had ended there;
Or, if sour woe delights in fellowship
And needly will be ranked with other griefs,
Why followed not, when she said "Tybalt's dead,"
"Thy father," or "thy mother," nay, or both,
120 Which modern lamentation might have moved?
But with a rearward following Tybalt's death,
"Romeo is banishèd"—to speak that word
Is father, mother, Tybalt, Romeo, Juliet,
All slain, all dead. "Romeo is banishèd!"
125 There is no end, no limit, measure, bound,
In that word's death; no words can that woe sound.
Where is my father and my mother, Nurse?

NURSE. Weeping and wailing over Tybalt's corpse.
Will you go to them? I will bring you thither.

130 **JULIET.** Wash they his wounds with tears? Mine shall be spent,
When theirs are dry, for Romeo's banishment.
Take up those cords. Poor ropes, you are beguiled,
Both you and I, for Romeo is exiled.
He made you for a highway to my bed,
135 But I, a maid, die maiden-widowèd.
Come, cords, come, Nurse. I'll to my wedding bed,
And death, not Romeo, take my maidenhead!

■ What prompts Juliet to defend Romeo? Is this sudden change of attitude believable?

103 tributary (trib′yə ter′ē), *adj.* flowing into a larger stream or body of water; paying tribute.

109 fain, gladly.

117 needly, of necessity.

120 modern lamentation, ordinary grief.
121 rearward, a guard following at the rear of a group.

126 sound, understand; express.

132 beguiled (bi gīld′), *adj.* tricked; deceived.

NURSE. Hie to your chamber. I'll find Romeo
To comfort you. I wot well where he is.
140   Hark ye, your Romeo will be here at night.
I'll to him. He is hid at Laurence' cell.
JULIET. O, find him! Give this ring to my true knight *(giving a ring)*,
And bid him come to take his last farewell.   *(Exit.)*

SCENE 3

Summary *Friar Laurence tells Romeo he has been banished from Verona;
then the nurse tells Romeo what Juliet's state of mind is. Romeo becomes so
distraught he threatens suicide. The friar restrains him and urges him to go
to Juliet but to leave by daybreak.*

Friar Laurence's cell. Enter FRIAR LAURENCE.
FRIAR LAURENCE *(calling softly)*. Romeo, come forth; come forth,
thou fearful man.
Affliction is enamored of thy parts,
And thou art wedded to calamity.
(Enter ROMEO, *coming from his hiding place.)*
ROMEO. Father, what news? What is the Prince's doom?
5   What sorrow craves acquaintance at my hand
That I yet know not?
FRIAR LAURENCE.   Too familiar
Is my dear son with such sour company.
I bring thee tidings of the Prince's doom.
ROMEO. What less than doomsday is the Prince's doom?
10 **FRIAR LAURENCE.** A gentler judgment vanished from his lips:
Not body's death, but body's banishment.
ROMEO. Ha, banishment? Be merciful, say "death";
For exile hath more terror in his look,
Much more than death. Do not say "banishment."
15 **FRIAR LAURENCE.** Here from Verona art thou banishèd.
Be patient, for the world is broad and wide.
ROMEO. There is no world without Verona walls
But purgatory, torture, hell itself.
Hence "banishèd" is banished from the world,
20   And world's exile is death. Then "banishèd"
Is death mistermed. Calling death "banishèd,"
Thou cutt'st my head off with a golden ax
And smilest upon the stroke that murders me.
FRIAR LAURENCE. O deadly sin! O rude unthankfulness!
25   Thy fault our law calls death, but the kind Prince,
Taking thy part, hath rushed aside the law
And turned that black word "death" to "banishment."
This is dear mercy, and thou seest it not.

---

139 wot, know.

2 Affliction . . . parts.
Misfortune thrives on the
qualities (parts) you are
showing—self-pity and
despair.
3 calamity (kə lam′ə tē), *n.*
great misfortune; disaster.
4 doom, punishment.

■ Why does Romeo have to
ask Friar Laurence for news
of the Prince's sentence?

9 doomsday, the end of the
world.
10 vanished, issued.

17 without, outside of.

20 world's exile, exile from
the world that is everything
to me—the world where
Juliet dwells.

26 rushed aside, thrust aside.

Friar Laurence tells Romeo he has been banished. What do Romeo's appearance and body language reveal about his state of mind?

ROMEO. 'Tis torture, and not mercy. Heaven is here
30   Where Juliet lives, and every cat and dog
   And little mouse, every unworthy thing,
   Live here in heaven and may look on her,
   But Romeo may not. More validity,
   More honorable state, more courtship lives
35   In carrion flies than Romeo. They may seize
   On the white wonder of dear Juliet's hand
   And steal immortal blessing from her lips,
   Who even in pure and vestal modesty

34 courtship, courtliness; occasion for wooing.

Romeo and Juliet—Act Three, Scene 3   **537**

Still blush, as thinking their own kisses sin;
40 But Romeo may not, he is banishèd.
Flies may do this, but I from this must fly.
They are free men, but I am banishèd.
And sayest thou yet that exile is not death?
Hadst thou no poison mixed, no sharp-ground knife,
45 No sudden mean of death, though ne'er so mean,
But "banishèd" to kill me? "Banishèd"?
O Friar, the damnèd use that word in hell;
Howling attends it. How hast thou the heart,
Being a divine, a ghostly confessor,
50 A sin absolver, and my friend professed,
To mangle me with that word "banishèd"?

FRIAR LAURENCE. Thou fond mad man, hear me a little speak.

ROMEO. O, thou wilt speak again of banishment.

FRIAR LAURENCE. I'll give thee armor to keep off that word,
55 Adversity's sweet milk, philosophy,
To comfort thee, though thou art banishèd.

ROMEO. Yet "banishèd"? Hang up philosophy!
Unless philosophy can make a Juliet,
Displant a town, reverse a prince's doom,
60 It helps not, it prevails not. Talk no more.

FRIAR LAURENCE. O, then I see that madmen have no ears.

ROMEO. How should they, when that wise men have no eyes?

FRIAR LAURENCE. Let me dispute with thee of thy estate.

ROMEO. Thou canst not speak of that thou dost not feel.
65 Wert thou as young as I, Juliet thy love,
An hour but married, Tybalt murderèd,
Doting like me, and like me banishèd,
Then mightst thou speak, then mightst thou tear thy hair,
And fall upon the ground, as I do now (*flinging himself full length
upon the floor and sobbing*),
70 Taking the measure of an unmade grave.

(*The* NURSE *knocks on the door.*)

FRIAR LAURENCE. Arise. One knocks. Good Romeo, hide thyself.

ROMEO. Not I, unless the breath of heartsick groans,
Mistlike, infold me from the search of eyes. (*The* NURSE *knocks again.*)

FRIAR LAURENCE. Hark, how they knock! Who's there? Romeo, arise.
75 Thou wilt be taken.—Stay awhile! Stand up.

(*Louder knocking.*)

Run to my study. (*Loudly.*) By and by! God's will,
What simpleness is this? I come, I come!

(*Knocking continues.*)

Who knocks so hard? Whence come you? What's your will?

(*Going to the door.*)

39 **their own kisses,** when Juliet's lips touch (kiss), it seems to them a sin.

45 **mean,** means.
45 **mean,** base, vile.

50 **absolver** (ab solv′ər), *n.* one who frees others from sin, guilt, or punishment.
52 **fond,** foolish.

■ Why does Romeo reject the friar's suggestion that he look for solace in philosophy?

63 **dispute,** reason, discuss.
63 **estate,** situation, condition.

NURSE (*speaking offstage*). Let me come in, and you shall know my
    errand.
80   I come from Lady Juliet.
FRIAR LAURENCE (*unlocking the door*). Welcome, then.
(*Enter* NURSE, *talking as she comes into the cell.*)
NURSE. O holy Friar, O, tell me, holy Friar,
    Where's my lady's lord, where's Romeo?
FRIAR LAURENCE. There on the ground, with his own tears made
    drunk.
85 **NURSE.** O, he is even in my mistress' case,
    Just in her case! O woeful sympathy!
    Piteous predicament! Even so lies she,
    Blubbering and weeping, weeping and blubbering.—
    Stand up, stand up! Stand, an you be a man.
90   For Juliet's sake, for her sake, rise and stand!
    Why should you fall into so deep an O?
(ROMEO *rises.*)
ROMEO. Nurse!
NURSE. Ah sir, ah sir! Death's the end of all.
ROMEO. Spakest thou of Juliet? How is it with her?
95   Doth not she think me an old murderer,
    Now I have stained the childhood of our joy
    With blood removed but little from her own?
    Where is she? And how doth she? And what says
    My concealed lady to our canceled love?
100 **NURSE.** O, she says nothing, sir, but weeps and weeps,
    And now falls on her bed, and then starts up,
    And "Tybalt" calls, and then on Romeo cries,
    And then down falls again.
ROMEO.   As if that name,
    Shot from the deadly level of a gun,
105   Did murder her, as that name's cursèd hand
    Murdered her kinsman. O, tell me, Friar, tell me,
    In what vile part of this anatomy
    Doth my name lodge? Tell me, that I may sack
    The hateful mansion.
(ROMEO *draws his sword.*)
FRIAR LAURENCE.   Hold thy desperate hand!
110   Art thou a man? Thy form cries out thou art;
    Thy tears are womanish, thy wild acts denote
    The unreasonable fury of a beast.
    Unseemly woman in a seeming man,
    And ill-beseeming beast in seeming both!
115   Thou hast amazed me. By my holy order,
    I thought thy disposition better tempered.

85 he is . . . case. Romeo is in the same state as Juliet.
86 woeful sympathy, sad agreement.

91 an O, a fit of groaning.

■ How does the Nurse challenge Romeo to pull himself together?

95 an old, a hardened.

99 concealed lady, secretly married wife.

104 level, aim.

107 anatomy (ə nat′ə mē), *n.* body.

111 denote (di nōt′), *v.* indicate; mean.

114 ill-beseeming, unsuitable, inappropriate.
116 tempered, blended, mixed.

Hast thou slain Tybalt? Wilt thou slay thyself,
And slay thy lady, that in thy life lives,
By doing damnèd hate upon thyself?

120 Why railest thou on thy birth, the heaven, and earth,
Since birth, and heaven, and earth, all three do meet
In thee at once, which thou at once wouldst lose?
Fie, fie, thou shamest thy shape, thy love, thy wit,
Which, like a usurer, abound'st in all,

125 And usest none in that true use indeed
Which should bedeck thy shape, thy love, thy wit.
Thy noble shape is but a form of wax,
Digressing from the valor of a man;
Thy dear love sworn but hollow perjury,

130 Killing that love which thou hast vowed to cherish;
Thy wit, that ornament to shape and love,
Misshapen in the conduct of them both,
Like powder in a skilless soldier's flask
Is set afire by thine own ignorance,

135 And thou dismembered with thine own defense.
What, rouse thee, man! Thy Juliet is alive,
For whose dear sake thou wast but lately dead;
There art thou happy. Tybalt would kill thee,
But thou slewest Tybalt; there art thou happy.

140 The law that threatened death becomes thy friend
And turns it to exile; there art thou happy.
A pack of blessings light upon thy back,
Happiness courts thee in her best array,
But, like a misbehavèd and sullen wench

145 Thou pout'st upon thy fortune and thy love.
Take heed, take heed, for such die miserable.
Go, get thee to thy love, as was decreed.
Ascend her chamber; hence and comfort her.
But look thou stay not till the watch be set,

150 For then thou canst not pass to Mantua,
Where thou shalt live till we can find a time
To blaze your marriage, reconcile your friends,
Beg pardon of the Prince, and call thee back
With twenty hundred thousand times more joy

155 Than thou went'st forth in lamentation.
Go before, Nurse. Commend me to thy lady,
And bid her hasten all the house to bed,
Which heavy sorrow makes them apt unto.
Romeo is coming.

160 **NURSE.** O Lord, I could have stayed here all the night
To hear good counsel. O, what learning is!—

120 Why railest thou on, why do you complain about.
121 heaven, and earth, soul and body.
123 wit, intellect.
124 Which, (you) who.
124 usurer (yü′zhər ər), *n.* moneylender.
127 form of wax, waxwork, mere outer form.
128 digress (dī gres′), *v.* turn away from; swerve; diverge.

132 conduct, guidance.
133 flask, powderhorn.

135 dismembered . . . defense, blown up with your own gunpowder.

138 There, in this respect.

149 watch be set, watchmen have taken their stand at the gates of Verona.
150 Mantua, a town in northern Italy about thirty miles from Verona.
152 blaze, announce.
152 reconcile (rek′ən sīl), *v.* settle a disagreement or difference; make peace.
155 lamentation (lam′ən-tā′shən), *n.* loud grief.

158 apt unto, inclined to.

■ How does the friar finally get through to Romeo?

My lord, I'll tell my lady you will come.

ROMEO. Do so, and bid my sweet prepare to chide.

NURSE. Here, sir, a ring she bid me give you, sir.
165   Hie you, make haste, for it grows very late.   *(Exit* NURSE.*)*

ROMEO *(regarding the ring tenderly).* How well my comfort is revived
    by this!

FRIAR LAURENCE *(ushering* ROMEO *to the door).* Go hence. Good night.
    And here stands all your state:
    Either be gone before the watch be set,
170   Or by the break of day disguised from hence.
    Sojourn in Mantua. I'll find out your man,
    And he shall signify from time to time
    Every good hap to you that chances here.
    Give me thy hand. 'Tis late. Farewell, good night.
175 **ROMEO.** But that a joy past joy calls out on me,
    It were a grief so brief to part with thee.
    Farewell.   *(Exit.)*

S C E N E   4

Summary *Lord Capulet speaks with the Count Paris, explaining that Juliet has been greatly affected by the death of Tybalt. Then he promises Paris that the young couple will be married on Thursday, three days hence.*

A room in Capulet's house. Enter LORD *and* LADY CAPULET *and* PARIS.

CAPULET *(to* PARIS*).* Things have fall'n out, sir, so unluckily,
    That we have had no time to move our daughter.
    Look you, she loved her kinsman Tybalt dearly,
    And so did I. Well, we were born to die.
5   'Tis very late. She'll not come down tonight.
    I promise you, but for your company
    I would have been abed an hour ago.

PARIS. These times of woe afford no times to woo.
    Madam, good night. Commend me to your daughter.

10 **LADY CAPULET.** I will, and know her mind early tomorrow.
    Tonight she's mewed up to her heaviness.

CAPULET *(suddenly).* Sir Paris, I will make a desperate tender
    Of my child's love. I think she will be ruled
    In all respects by me; nay, more, I doubt it not.
15   Wife, go you to her ere you go to bed.
    Acquaint her here of my son Paris' love,
    And bid her, mark you me, on Wednesday next—
    But soft, what day is this?

PARIS.   Monday, my lord.

CAPULET. Monday! Ha, ha! Well, Wednesday is too soon;
20   O' Thursday let it be. O' Thursday, tell her,

---

168 here stands . . . state. Your fortune depends on acting exactly as follows.
171 sojourn (sō′jėrn′), *v.* stay briefly.
171 your man, Romeo's servant, Balthasar.
173 hap, occurrence.

176 brief, quickly.

2 move our daughter, talk to Juliet about marrying you.

11 mewed . . . heaviness, confined in her room with her grief.
12 desperate tender, rash offer.

She shall be married to this noble earl.
Will you be ready? Do you like this haste?
We'll keep no great ado—a friend or two;
For hark you, Tybalt being slain so late,
25 It may be thought we held him carelessly,
Being our kinsman, if we revel much.
Therefore we'll have some half a dozen friends,
And there an end. But what say you to Thursday?
PARIS. My lord, I would that Thursday were tomorrow.
30 **CAPULET.** Well, get you gone. O' Thursday be it, then.
(*To* LADY CAPULET.) Go you to Juliet ere you go to bed;
Prepare her, wife, against this wedding day.—
Farewell, my lord.—Light to my chamber, ho!—
Afore me, it is so very late
35 That we may call it early by and by.
Good night. (*Exit.*)

23 ado (ə dū), *n.* noisy activity; bustle.
24 late, recently.
25 held him carelessly, didn't care enough for him.

■ In Act 1, Capulet says he will allow Juliet to decide who she marries. Now he promises her to Paris. Why do you think he changes his mind?

32 against, for.
34 Afore me, exclamation like "by my life," or perhaps a direction to a servant to precede him with a candle or lantern.

SCENE 5

Summary *At dawn, Romeo and Juliet reluctantly bid each other farewell before Lady Capulet enters and informs her daughter that she will be married in two days. Juliet refuses and thus angers both her parents. When Juliet turns to the nurse for comfort, the nurse counsels her to forget Romeo and to marry the Count. Juliet decides to ask Friar Laurence what to do.*

Capulet's orchard. Enter ROMEO *and* JULIET, *at the window of her bedroom.*
JULIET. Wilt thou be gone? It is not yet near day.
It was the nightingale, and not the lark,
That pierced the fearful hollow of thine ear;
Nightly she sings on yond pomegranate tree.
5 Believe me, love, it was the nightingale.
ROMEO. It was the lark, the herald of the morn,
No nightingale. Look, love, what envious streaks
Do lace the severing clouds in yonder east.
Night's candles are burnt out, and jocund day
10 Stands tiptoe on the misty mountain tops.
I must be gone and live, or stay and die.
JULIET. Yond light is not daylight, I know it, I.
It is some meteor that the sun exhaled
To be to thee this night a torchbearer
15 And light thee on thy way to Mantua.
Therefore stay yet. Thou need'st not to be gone.
ROMEO. Let me be ta'en; let me be put to death.
I am content, so thou wilt have it so.
I'll say yon gray is not the morning's eye;
20 'Tis but the pale reflex of Cynthia's brow.

2 nightingale . . . lark. The nightingale's song is associated with the night, the lark's song with dawn.

8 lace, stripe, streak.
8 severing (sev′ər ing), *adj.* scattering.
9 Night's candles, the stars.
9 jocund (jok′ənd), cheerful; merry.

13 meteor . . . exhaled. Meteors were thought to be vapors of luminous gas drawn up from the earth by the sun.

20 reflex . . . brow, reflection of the moon (Cynthia).

▲ At sunrise, Romeo and Juliet bid farewell to each other. In what way has the daytime now become their enemy?

Nor that is not the lark whose notes do beat
The vaulty heaven so high above our heads.
I have more care to stay than will to go.
Come, death, and welcome! Juliet wills it so.

25 How is 't, my soul? Let's talk. It is not day.

JULIET. It is, it is. Hie hence, begone, away!
It is the lark that sings so out of tune,
Straining harsh discords and unpleasing sharps.
Some say the lark makes sweet division;

30 This doth not so, for she divideth us.
Some say the lark and loathèd toad changed eyes;
O, now I would they had changed voices too,
Since arm from arm that voice doth us affray,
Hunting thee hence with hunt's-up to the day.

35 O, now begone! More light and light it grows.

ROMEO. More light and light, more dark and dark our woes!
(Enter the NURSE *to the bedchamber.)*

NURSE *(urgently).* Madam!

JULIET. Nurse?

NURSE. Your lady mother is coming to your chamber.

40 The day is broke; be wary, look about.   *(Exit.)*

JULIET. Then window, let day in, and let life out.

ROMEO. Farewell, farewell! One kiss, and I'll descend.
(He starts down the ladder.)

JULIET. Art thou gone so? Love, lord, ay, husband, friend!
I must hear from thee every day in the hour,

45 For in a minute there are many days.
O, by this count I shall be much in years
Ere I again behold my Romeo!

ROMEO. Farewell! *(Embracing her once again.)*
I will omit no opportunity

50 That may convey my greetings, love, to thee.

JULIET. O, think'st thou we shall ever meet again?

ROMEO. I doubt it not, and all these woes shall serve
For sweet discourses in our times to come.

JULIET. O God, I have an ill-divining soul!

55 Methinks I see thee, now thou art so low,
As one dead in the bottom of a tomb.
Either my eyesight fails or thou lookest pale.

ROMEO. And trust me, love, in my eye so do you.
Dry sorrow drinks our blood. Adieu, adieu!   *(Exit.)*

60 **JULIET.** O Fortune, Fortune! All men call thee fickle.
If thou art fickle, what dost thou with him
That is renowned for faith? Be fickle, Fortune.
For then, I hope, thou wilt not keep him long,

23 care, concern, desire.

28 sharps, high notes.
29 division, musical variety.
31 changed eyes, an allusion to an old saying that the toad and the lark had exchanged eyes, since the lark's eyes were considered ugly and the toad's beautiful.
33 affray, frighten.
34 hunt's-up, a wake-up song for hunters.

■ Compare and contrast what light **symbolizes** in the balcony scene (Act 2, Scene 2) and in this scene.

54 ill-divining, anticipating evil.

59 Dry sorrow . . . blood. It was believed that sorrow dried up the blood.
61 fickle, likely to change or give up loyalty, attachment, etc.; inconstant; uncertain.

But send him back.

LADY CAPULET. Ho, daughter, are you up?

65 **JULIET.** Who is 't that calls? It is my lady mother.
(To herself.) Is she not down so late, or up so early?
What unaccustomed cause procures her hither?
(Enter LADY CAPULET.*)*

LADY CAPULET. Why, how now, Juliet?

JULIET.   Madam, I am not well.

LADY CAPULET. Evermore weeping for your cousin's death?
70 What, wilt thou wash him from his grave with tears?
An if thou couldst, thou couldst not make him live;
Therefore, have done. Some grief shows much of love,
But much of grief shows still some want of wit.

JULIET. Yet let me weep for such a feeling loss.

75 **LADY CAPULET.** So shall you feel the loss, but not the friend
Which you weep for.

JULIET.   Feeling so the loss,
I cannot choose but ever weep the friend.

LADY CAPULET. Well, girl, thou weep'st not so much for his death
As that the villain lives which slaughtered him.

JULIET. What villain, madam?

80 **LADY CAPULET.**   That same villain, Romeo.

JULIET *(aside).* Villain and he be many miles asunder.—
(Aloud.) God pardon him! I do, with all my heart;
And yet no man like he doth grieve my heart.

LADY CAPULET. That is because the traitor murderer lives.

85 **JULIET.** Ay, madam, from the reach of these my hands.
Would none but I might venge my cousin's death!

LADY CAPULET. We will have vengeance for it, fear thou not.
Then weep no more. I'll send to one in Mantua,
Where that same banished runagate doth live,
90 Shall give him such an unaccustomed dram
That he shall soon keep Tybalt company.
And then, I hope, thou wilt be satisfied.

JULIET. Indeed, I never shall be satisfied
With Romeo till I behold him—dead—
95 Is my poor heart so for a kinsman vexed.
Madam, if you find out but a man
To bear a poison, I would temper it,
That Romeo should, upon receipt thereof,
Soon sleep in quiet. O, how my heart abhors
100 To hear him named, and cannot come to him
To wreak the love I bore my cousin
Upon his body that hath slaughtered him!

LADY CAPULET. Find thou the means, and I'll find such a man.

66 down, in bed.
67 procures her hither, leads her to come this way.

■ What is **ironic** about Lady Capulet's opinion of Juliet's behavior?

83 like, so much as.

86 venge, avenge.

89 runagate (run′ə gāt), *n.* renegade.

94 dead. Juliet arranges her words in such a way that Lady Capulet will mistakenly think that she wishes to see Romeo dead.
97 temper, mix. Juliet continues to mislead her mother, since *temper* can also mean moderate.
99 abhor (ab hôr′), *v.* regard with horror or disgust; hate; detest.
101 wreak (rēk), *v.* express; inflict.

But now I'll tell thee joyful tidings, girl.

105 **JULIET.** And joy comes well in such a needy time.

What are they, beseech your ladyship?

LADY CAPULET. Well, well, thou hast a careful father, child,

One who, to put thee from thy heaviness,

Hath sorted out a sudden day of joy

110 That thou expects not, nor I looked not for.

JULIET. Madam, in happy time, what day is that?

LADY CAPULET. Marry, my child, early next Thursday morn,

The gallant, young, and noble gentleman,

The County Paris, at Saint Peter's Church

115 Shall happily make thee there a joyful bride.

JULIET (*with vigorous spirit*). Now, by Saint Peter's Church, and Peter too,

He shall not make me there a joyful bride!

I wonder at this haste, that I must wed

Ere he that should be husband comes to woo.

120 I pray you, tell my lord and father, madam,

I will not marry yet, and when I do I swear

It shall be Romeo, whom you know I hate,

Rather than Paris. These are news indeed!

LADY CAPULET (*angrily*). Here comes your father. Tell him so yourself,

125 And see how he will take it at your hands.

(*Enter* CAPULET *and the* NURSE.)

CAPULET. When the sun sets, the earth doth drizzle dew,

But for the sunset of my brother's son

It rains downright.

How now, a conduit, girl? What, still in tears?

130 Evermore showering? In one little body

Thou counterfeits a bark, a sea, a wind;

For still thy eyes, which I may call the sea,

Do ebb and flow with tears; the bark thy body is,

Sailing in this salt flood; the winds, thy sighs,

135 Who, raging with thy tears, and they with them,

Without a sudden calm, will overset

Thy <u>tempest</u>-tossèd body.—How now, wife?

Have you delivered to her our decree?

LADY CAPULET. Ay, sir, but she will none, she gives you thanks.

140 I would the fool were married to her grave!

CAPULET. Soft, take me with you, take me with you, wife.

How? Will she none? Doth she not give us thanks?

Is she not proud? Doth she not count her blest,

Unworthy as she is, that we have wrought

145 So worthy a gentleman to be her bride?

JULIET. Not proud you have, but thankful that you have.

106 they, the "joyful tidings," in line 104.
107 careful, taking care to ensure your well-being.
109 sorted out, chosen.

129 conduit (kon′dü it), *n.* fountain.

133 bark (also barque), a boat.

136 overset, capsize.
137 tempest (tem′pist), *n.* violent storm or disturbance.
139 will none, refuses "our decree," in line 138.

141 take me with you, let me understand you.

144 wrought (rôt), *v.* arranged for.
145 bride, bridegroom.

Proud can I never be of what I hate,
But thankful even for hate that is meant love.

CAPULET. How, how, how, how, chopped logic? What is this?
150 "Proud," and "I thank you," and "I thank you not,"
And yet "not proud"? Mistress minion, you,
Thank me no thankings, nor proud me no prouds,
But fettle your fine joints 'gainst Thursday next
To go with Paris to Saint Peter's Church,
155 Or I will drag thee on a hurdle thither.
Out, you greensickness carrion! Out, you baggage!
You tallow-face! *(He raises his hand to strike her.)*

LADY CAPULET (*to* CAPULET). Fie, fie! What, are you mad?

JULIET (*kneeling*). Good father, I beseech you on my knees,
Hear me with patience but to speak a word.

160 **CAPULET.** Hang thee, young baggage, disobedient wretch!
I tell thee what: get thee to church o' Thursday
Or never after look me in the face.

(JULIET *starts to answer.*)
Speak not, reply not, do not answer me!
My fingers itch. Wife, we scarce thought us blest
165 That God had lent us but this only child;
But now I see this one is one too much,
And that we have a curse in having her.
Out on her, hilding!

NURSE.   God in heaven bless her!
You are to blame, my lord, to rate her so.

170 **CAPULET.** And why, my Lady Wisdom? Hold your tongue,
Good Prudence. Smatter with your gossips, go.

NURSE. I speak no treason.

CAPULET (*wrathfully*).   O, God-i'-good-e'en!

NURSE. May not one speak?

CAPULET.   Peace, you mumbling fool!
Utter your gravity o'er a gossip's bowl,
175 For here we need it not.

LADY CAPULET. You are too hot.

CAPULET. God's bread, it makes me mad!
Day, night, hour, tide, time, work, play,
Alone, in company, still my care hath been
180 To have her matched. And having now provided
A gentleman of noble parentage,
Of fair demesnes, youthful, and nobly liened,
Stuffed, as they say, with honorable parts,
Proportioned as one's thought would wish a man—
185 And then to have a wretched puling fool,
A whining mammet, in her fortune's tender,

---

148 thankful . . . love.
Thankful for something hateful that was done lovingly.

149 chopped logic, one who argues unfairly.

151 minion (min′yən), *n.* spoiled darling.

153 fettle, make ready.

153 'gainst, in preparation for.

155 hurdle, a conveyance for transporting criminals.

156 greensickness, an anemic ailment of young women.

156 carrion (kar′ē ən), *n.* dead and decaying flesh; rottenness; filth.

164 My fingers itch, that is, to choke or strike you.

168 hilding, good-for-nothing.

169 rate, berate, scold.

171 Good Prudence, my wise one. Capulet is speaking ironically.

171 Smatter . . . gossips, chatter with your cronies.

174 gravity, wisdom.

177 God's bread, by the sacrament; a mild oath.

182 demesnes (di māns′), *n.* estates, property.

182 liened (lēnd), *adj.* descended.

183 parts, qualities, abilities.

185 puling (pyŭl ing), *adj.* whining.

186 mammet, doll.

186 fortune's tender, offer of good fortune.

To answer, "I'll not wed, I cannot love,
I am too young; I pray you, pardon me."
But, an you will not wed, *(bitterly ironic)* I'll pardon you.
190 Graze where you will, you shall not house with me.
Look to 't, think on 't. I do not use to jest.
Thursday is near. Lay hand on heart; advise.
An you be mine, I'll give you to my friend;
An you be not, hang, beg, starve, die in the streets,
195 For, by my soul, I'll ne'er acknowledge thee,
Nor what is mine shall never do thee good.
Trust to 't, bethink you. I'll not be forsworn.
(*Exit* CAPULET.)

JULIET. Is there no pity sitting in the clouds
That sees into the bottom of my grief?
200 O sweet my Mother, cast me not away!
Delay this marriage for a month, a week;
Or if you do not, make the bridal bed
In that dim monument where Tybalt lies.

LADY CAPULET. Talk not to me, for I'll not speak a word.
205 Do as thou wilt, for I have done with thee.
(*Exit, leaving* JULIET *and the* NURSE *alone.*)

JULIET *(rising).* O God!—O Nurse, how shall this be prevented?
My husband is on earth, my faith in heaven.
How shall that faith return again to earth,
Unless that husband send it me from heaven
210 By leaving earth? Comfort me, counsel me.
Alack, alack, that heaven should practice stratagems
Upon so soft a subject as myself! (*To the* NURSE.)
What sayst thou? Hast thou not a word of joy?
Some comfort, Nurse.

NURSE.   Faith, here it is.
215 Romeo is banished, and all the world to nothing
That he dares ne'er come back to challenge you,
Or if he do, it needs must be by stealth.
Then, since the case so stands as now it doth,
I think it best you married with the County.
220 O, he's a lovely gentleman!
Romeo's a dishclout to him. An eagle, madam,
Hath not so green, so quick, so fair an eye
As Paris hath. Beshrew my very heart,
I think you are happy in this second match,
225 For it excels your first; or if it did not,
Your first is dead—or 'twere as good he were,
As living here and you no use of him.

JULIET. Speak'st thou from thy heart?

191 **I do not . . . jest.** I am unaccustomed to jesting.
192 **advise,** consider carefully.

■ How does Capulet threaten Juliet?

207 **faith in heaven.** Juliet refers to her marriage vows.

211 **practice strategems** (strat′ə jəms), contrive dreadful deeds.

215 **all . . . nothing,** the odds are.
216 **challenge,** lay claim to.
217 stealth (stelth), *n.* secret or sly action.

221 **to him,** compared to him.
222 **green.** Green eyes were admired in Shakespeare's day.
223 **beshrew,** curse.

227 **here,** on earth.

NURSE. And from my soul too. Else beshrew them both.

230 **JULIET.** Amen!

NURSE. What?

JULIET. Well, thou has comforted me marvelous much.
Go in, and tell my lady I am gone,
Having displeased my father, to Laurence' cell
235 To make confession and to be absolved.

NURSE. Marry, I will; and this is wisely done.   *(Exit.)*

JULIET. Ancient damnation! O most wicked fiend!
Is it more sin to wish me thus forsworn,
Or to dispraise my lord with that same tongue
240 Which she hath praised him with above compare
So many thousand times? Go, counselor,
Thou and my bosom henceforth shall be twain.
I'll to the Friar to know his remedy.
If all else fail, myself have power to die.   *(Exit.)*

■ Do you think the Nurse is a realist or an idealist? Why?

237 Ancient damnation, damnable old woman.
237 fiend (fēnd), *n.* a very wicked or cruel person; demon.

242 bosom . . . twain, secret thoughts shall be separated in the future; i.e., Juliet will confide in the nurse no more.

After Reading

Making Connections

1. Do you think Romeo was right to avenge Mercutio's murder by killing Tybalt? Explain.

2. On a scale of 1 (least mature) to 10 (most mature), rate how mature Romeo is and how mature Juliet is. Explain your ratings.

3. Do you think Juliet's contradictory reaction to learning about Romeo's murder of Tybalt is understandable? Why or why not?

4. In their encounter with Tybalt, do Benvolio and Mercutio react in character—that is, does each behave as you would expect? Explain.

5. How does Romeo's secret lead to disaster in Scene 1?

6. Scene 1 is commonly considered the **turning point** of the play. In your opinion, is there any way Romeo might have prevented the tragic events? Explain.

7. Compare and contrast Juliet's and Romeo's reaction to the same tragic news in Scenes 2 and 3.

8. **Dramatic irony** occurs when the audience knows something that some of the characters don't. What examples of dramatic irony can you find in Scenes 4 and 5?

9. What **character traits** does Juliet reveal in her conversations with her mother and father in Scene 5?

10. The role of a daughter in the 1300s differs greatly from the role of daughters today. List these differences and decide what advantages and disadvantages Juliet has over young women today.

Vocabulary Study

abhor
calamity
dexterity
discord
eloquence
martial
reconcile
stealth
tempest
valor

A synonym word web for the vocabulary word *abhor* is shown here. Make synonym word webs for each of the remaining vocabulary words. If necessary, use the Glossary for help with word meanings.

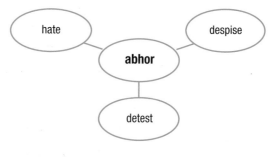

Expressing Your Ideas

Writing Choices

Dear Daughter From Act 1 to Act 3, Lord Capulet changes his attitude about Juliet and marriage. Imagine that you are Lady Capulet and Juliet has asked you to explain her father's change of heart. Write a **letter** to Juliet in which you suggest reasons why Capulet has changed his attitude about her marriage to Paris.

Reasonable Doubt? Before killing Tybalt, Romeo says, "O sweet Juliet,/Thy beauty hath made me effeminate/And in my temper softened valor's steel!" Write a short **essay** in which you respond to this statement. Do you agree or disagree with Romeo's assessment of the situation? Does love make you weak? Is fighting a show of strength? Support your argument with specific reasons.

Domino Effect Refer to the **chain diagram** of the significant events that occur during Acts 1 and 2. Expand the diagram to include the major events in Act 3. Could the characters have avoided the tragic circumstances that are beginning to unfold? If so, how?

Other Options

Fatal Flaw . . . Hold a **class debate** about what factor is most responsible for the problems that entangle Romeo, Juliet, and their families by the end of Act 3. In small groups, choose from among these or other possibilities: pride, impatience, secrecy, temper, disobedience, chance. Work with your group to prepare your arguments in advance. Use as many specific examples from the play as possible.

Gender Roles In Shakespeare's day, acting onstage was not considered proper behavior for women. Male actors—usually boys or young men—played all the female roles. Re-create this gender-bending effect by acting out a scene from the play with boys taking female roles and girls taking male roles. After your **performance,** discuss what it was like to play characters of the opposite sex. Did you learn anything from the experience?

ACT FOUR

SCENE 1

Summary *Count Paris explains to Friar Laurence that Lord Capulet desires a hasty marriage because Juliet's sorrow for Tybalt may endanger her health. Juliet enters and responds coolly to Paris's courteous statements of affection. Once Paris leaves, Juliet turns to Friar Laurence, vowing to commit suicide rather than marry Paris. Friar Laurence offers her a potion that will make her appear dead for "two and forty hours." During that time, he will send to Mantua for Romeo and when she awakens in the family tomb, he and Romeo will be there.*

Friar Laurence's cell. Enter FRIAR LAURENCE *and* PARIS.

FRIAR LAURENCE. On Thursday, sir? The time is very short.

PARIS. My father Capulet will have it so,
    And I am nothing slow to slack his haste.

FRIAR LAURENCE. You say you do not know the lady's mind?

5   Uneven is the course. I like it not.

PARIS. Immoderately she weeps for Tybalt's death,
    And therefore have I little talked of love,
    For Venus smiles not in a house of tears.
    Now, sir, her father counts it dangerous

10   That she do give her sorrow so much sway,
    And in his wisdom hastes our marriage
    To stop the inundation of her tears,
    Which, too much minded by herself alone,
    May be put from her by society.

15   Now do you know the reason of this haste.

FRIAR LAURENCE *(aside)*. I would I knew not why it should be
        slowed.—
    (*To* PARIS.) Look, sir, here comes the lady toward my cell.
    (*Enter* JULIET.)

PARIS. Happily met, my lady and my wife!

JULIET. That may be, sir, when I may be a wife.

20 **PARIS.** That "may be" must be, love, on Thursday next.

JULIET. What must be shall be.

FRIAR LAURENCE.   That's a certain text.

PARIS. Come you to make confession to this father?

JULIET. To answer that, I should confess to you.

PARIS. Do not deny to him that you love me.

25 **JULIET.** I will confess to you that I love him.

PARIS. So will ye, I am sure, that you love me.

JULIET. If I do so, it will be of more price,
    Being spoke behind your back, than to your face.

---

2 My father, my prospective father-in-law.
3 nothing slow . . . haste, anxious to do nothing that might slow down his plans to hasten the marriage.
5 Uneven . . . course, the race course is not even; i.e., not smooth sailing.
8 Venus, goddess of love.
10 do give . . . sway, allows her sorrow (over Tybalt's death) to control her feelings.
12 inundation (in′un-dā′shən), *n.* flood.
13 minded . . . alone, dwelt on by her in privacy.
14 May be . . . society, may be remedied if she mingles with others.

■ What **theme** of the play is echoed in Juliet's line, "What must be shall be"?

PARIS. Poor soul, thy face is much abused with tears.

30 **JULIET.** The tears have got small victory by that,
  For it was bad enough before their spite.

PARIS. Thou wrong'st it more than tears with that report.

JULIET. That is no slander, sir, which is a truth;
  And what I spake, I spake it to my face.

35 **PARIS.** Thy face is mine, and thou hast slandered it.

JULIET. It may be so, for it is not mine own.—
  Are you at leisure, holy Father, now,
  Or shall I come to you at evening Mass?

FRIAR LAURENCE. My leisure serves me, pensive daughter, now.

40   My lord, we must entreat the time alone.

PARIS. God shield I should disturb devotion!
  Juliet, on Thursday early will I rouse ye.
  Till then, adieu, and keep this holy kiss.   *(Exit.)*

JULIET. O, shut the door! And when thou hast done so,

45   Come weep with me—past hope, past cure, past help!

FRIAR LAURENCE. Ah, Juliet, I already know thy grief;
  It strains me past the compass of my wits.
  I hear thou must, and nothing may prorogue it,
  On Thursday next be married to this county.

50 **JULIET.** Tell me not, Friar, that thou hearest of this,
  Unless thou tell me how I may prevent it.
  If in thy wisdom thou canst give no help,
  Do thou but call my resolution wise
  And with this knife I'll help it presently.

55   God joined my heart and Romeo's, thou our hands;
  And ere this hand, by thee to Romeo sealed,
  Shall be the label to another deed,
  Or my true heart with treacherous revolt
  Turn to another, this shall slay them both.

60   Therefore, out of thy long-experienced time,
  Give me some present counsel, or, behold,
  Twixt my extremes and me this bloody knife
  Shall play the umpire, arbitrating that
  Which the commission of thy years and art

65   Could to no issue of true honor bring.
  Be not so long to speak; I long to die
  If what thou speak'st speak not of remedy.

FRIAR LAURENCE. Hold, daughter. I do spy a kind of hope,
  Which craves as desperate an execution

70   As that is desperate which we would prevent.
  If, rather than to marry County Paris,
  Thou hast the strength of will to slay thyself,
  Then is it likely thou wilt undertake

33 slander (slan′dər), *n.* a false statement spoken with intent to harm the reputation of another.

40 entreat . . . alone, request that you leave us alone.
41 shield, forbid, prevent.

47 It strains . . . wits. It exceeds the limits of my wisdom; i.e., I'm at my wit's end.

53 resolution (rez′ə-lü′shən), *n.* decision; determination.
54 presently, at once.

57 label, the seal attached to a deed; i.e., confirmation.

60 time, age.
61 present, instant.
62 extremes, extreme difficulties.
63 arbitrate (är′bə trāt), *v.* give a decision in a dispute.
64 commission, authority.
64 art, skill.

■ How is Juliet's suicide threat in this scene different from Romeo's in Act 3, Scene 3?

◄ Juliet accepts the potion from Friar Laurence. How does the position of their hands intensify the drama of the action?

A thing like death to chide away this shame,
75   That cop'st with Death himself to scape from it;
And if thou darest, I'll give thee remedy.
  JULIET. O, bid me leap, rather than marry Paris,
From off the battlements of any tower,
Or walk in thievish ways, or bid me lurk
80   Where serpents are; chain me with roaring bears,
Or hide me nightly in a charnel house,
O'ercovered quite with dead men's rattling bones,
With reeky shanks and yellow chopless skulls;
Or bid me go into a new-made grave
85   And hide me with a dead man in his tomb—
Things that, to hear them told, have made me tremble—
And I will do it without fear or doubt,
To live an unstained wife to my sweet love.
  FRIAR LAURENCE. Hold, then. Go home, be merry, give consent
90   To marry Paris. Wednesday is tomorrow.
Tomorrow night look that thou lie alone;
Let not the Nurse lie with thee in thy chamber.
Take thou this vial, being then in bed,
And this distilling liquor drink thou off,
95   When presently through all thy veins shall run
A cold and drowsy humor; for no pulse

75 cop'st with, bargains with.

79 in thievish ways, along highways where thieves hide out.
81 charnel (chär′nl) **house,** a vault where the bones of the dead were placed.
83 reeky, foul-smelling.
83 chopless, with the lower jaw missing.

96 humor, liquid.

Shall keep his native progress, but surcease;
No warmth, no breath shall testify thou livest;
The roses in thy lips and cheeks shall fade
100   To wanny ashes, thy eyes' windows fall
Like death when he shuts up the day of life;
Each part, deprived of supple government,
Shall, stiff and stark and cold, appear like death
And in this borrowed likeness of shrunk death
105   Thou shalt continue two-and-forty hours,
And then awake as from a pleasant sleep.
Now, when the bridegroom in the morning comes
To rouse thee from thy bed, there art thou dead.
Then, as the manner of our country is,
110   In thy best robes uncovered on the bier
Thou shalt be borne to that same ancient vault
Where all the <u>kindred</u> of the Capulets lie.
In the meantime, against thou shalt awake,
Shall Romeo by my letters know our drift,
115   And hither shall he come; and he and I
Will watch thy waking, and that very night
Shall Romeo bear thee hence to Mantua.
And this shall free thee from this present shame,
If no inconstant toy nor womanish fear
120   <u>Abate</u> thy valor in the acting it.

JULIET. Give me, give me! O, tell not me of fear!

FRIAR LAURENCE. Hold, get you gone. Be strong and prosperous
    In this resolve. I'll send a friar with speed
    To Mantua, with my letters to thy lord.

125 **JULIET.** Love give me strength, and strength shall help afford.
    Farewell, dear Father! *(Exit.)*

SCENE 2

Summary *As Lord Capulet organizes the wedding, Juliet enters and asks her father to pardon her previous behavior. A delighted Capulet moves the wedding from Thursday to Wednesday and Lady Capulet protests at the sudden change of plan. Lord Capulet dismisses her fears.*

A hall in Capulet's house. Enter CAPULET, LADY CAPULET, *the* NURSE, *and* SERVANTS.

CAPULET *(handing* FIRST SERVANT *a list).* So many guests invite as here
    are writ.

(Exit FIRST SERVANT.*)*
    Sirrah, go hire me twenty cunning cooks.

SECOND SERVANT. You shall have none ill, sir, for I'll try if they can lick
5   their fingers.

---

97 native, natural.
97 surcease (sər sēs′), *v.* cease.

100 wanny, wan, pale.

102 supple government, control over the flexibility of the body.

110 uncovered, with your face uncovered.
110 bier (bir), *n.* platform on which a dead body is placed before burial.
112 kindred (kin′drid), *n.* relatives.
113 against . . . awake, in preparation for your awakening.
114 drift, intentions.

119 inconstant toy, fickle, trifling fancy.
120 abate (ə bāt′), *v.* diminish.

■ Explain the friar's plan for Juliet.

4 try, test.

CAPULET. How canst thou try them so?

SECOND SERVANT. Marry, sir, 'tis an ill cook that cannot lick his own fingers; therefore he that cannot lick his fingers goes not with me.

CAPULET. Go, begone.

(*Exit* SECOND SERVANT.)

10　We shall be much unfurnished for this time.

What, is my daughter gone to Friar Laurence?

NURSE. Ay, forsooth.

CAPULET. Well, he may chance to do some good on her.

A peevish self-willed harlotry it is.

15　**NURSE.** See where she comes from shrift with merry look.

(*Enter* JULIET. *She is apparently in good spirits.*)

CAPULET. How now, my headstrong, where have you been gadding?

JULIET. Where I have learned me to repent the sin

Of disobedient opposition

To you and your behests, and am enjoined

20　By holy Laurence to fall prostrate here

And beg your pardon. (*She kneels.*) Pardon, I beseech you!

Henceforward I am ever ruled by you.

CAPULET. Send for the County! Go tell him of this.

I'll have this knot knit up tomorrow morning.

25　**JULIET.** I met the youthful lord at Laurence' cell

And gave him what becomèd love I might,

Not stepping o'er the bounds of modesty.

CAPULET. Why, I am glad on 't. This is well. Stand up.

This is as 't should be. Let me see the County;

30　Ay, marry, go, I say, and fetch him hither.

Now, afore God, this reverend holy friar,

All our whole city is much bound to him.

JULIET. Nurse, will you go with me into my closet

To help me sort such needful ornaments

35　As you think fit to furnish me tomorrow?

LADY CAPULET. No, not till Thursday. There is time enough.

CAPULET. Go, Nurse, go with her. We'll to church tomorrow.

(*Exit* JULIET *and* NURSE.)

LADY CAPULET. We shall be short in our provision.

'Tis now near night.

CAPULET.　　　　　　　Tush, I will stir about,

40　And all things shall be well, I warrant thee, wife.

Go thou to Juliet, help to deck up her.

I'll not to bed tonight. Let me alone.

I'll play the huswife for this once.—What, ho!—

(*To himself.*) They are all forth. Well, I will walk myself

45　To County Paris, to prepare up him

7–8 'tis . . . fingers. It's a poor cook who won't eat his own cooking.

14 A peevish. . . is. She (Juliet) is a selfish good-for-nothing.

16 gadding, moving about restlessly; looking for pleasure or excitement.

19 behest (bi hest′), *n.* command, order.

26 becomèd (bi kum′əd), *adj.* suitable.

32 bound, indebted.

33 closet, private room.

35 furnish me, fit me out with.

38 provision, supplies; i.e., the food and drink for the wedding guests.

■ Why do you think Capulet unexpectedly moves forward the day of Juliet's marriage to Paris?

45–46 prepare . . . tomorrow, prepare him for tomorrow.

Against tomorrow. My heart is wondrous light,
Since this same wayward girl is so reclaimed.   *(Exit.)*

Summary *Juliet dismisses her nurse. In a long soliloquy she reveals both her fears and her determination. At last she drinks the potion and slips into unconsciousness.*

Juliet's bedchamber. Enter JULIET *and the* NURSE.
JULIET. Ay, those attires are best. But, gentle Nurse,
    I pray thee, leave me to myself tonight;
    For I have need of many orisons
    To move the heavens to smile upon my state,
5   Which, well thou knowest, is cross and full of sin.
    (Enter LADY CAPULET.*)*
LADY CAPULET. What, are you busy, ho? Need you my help?
JULIET. No, madam, we have culled such necessaries
    As are behooveful for our state tomorrow.
    So please you, let me now be left alone,
10   And let the Nurse this night sit up with you,
    For I am sure you have your hands full all
    In this so sudden business.
LADY CAPULET.   Good night.
    Get thee to bed and rest, for thou hast need.
    (Exit LADY CAPULET *and the* NURSE.*)*
JULIET. Farewell! God knows when we shall meet again.
15   I have a faint cold fear thrills through my veins
    That almost freezes up the heat of life.
    I'll call them back again to comfort me.
    Nurse!—What should she do here?
    My dismal scene I needs must act alone.
20   Come, vial.
    What if this mixture do not work at all?
    Shall I be married then tomorrow morning?
    No, no, this shall forbid it. Lie thou there.
    (She lays down her dagger.)
    What if it be a poison, which the Friar
25   Subtly hath ministered to have me dead,
    Lest in this marriage he should be dishonored
    Because he married me before to Romeo?
    I fear it is; and yet methinks it should not,
    For he hath still been tried a holy man.
30   How if, when I am laid into the tomb,
    I wake before the time that Romeo

---

47 wayward (wāʹwərd), *adj.* disobedient; willful.
47 reclaimed (ri klāmdʹ), *adj.* brought back to useful, good, or fitting condition.

1 attire (ə tīrʹ), *n.* clothing.
3 orison (ôrʹə sən), *n.* prayer.
5 cross, contrary.

■ What **irony** do you see in Juliet's statement to the Nurse that she needs privacy to pray?

7 culled, picked out.
8 behooveful (bi hüvʹfəl), *adj.* needed.
8 state, ceremony.

25 ministered, applied or administered (something).

29 still been tried, always been proved to be.

Come to redeem me? There's a fearful point!
Shall I not then be stifled in the vault,
To whose foul mouth no healthsome air breathes in,
35   And there die strangled ere my Romeo comes?
Or, if I live, is it not very like
The horrible conceit of death and night,
Together with the terror of the place—
As in a vault, an ancient receptacle,
40   Where for this many hundred years the bones
Of all my buried ancestors are packed;
Where bloody Tybalt, yet but green in earth,
Lies festering in his shroud; where, as they say,
At some hours in the night spirits resort;—
45   Alack, alack, is it not like that I,
So early waking, what with loathsome smells,
And shrieks like mandrakes torn out of the earth,
That living mortals, hearing them, run mad—
O, if I wake, shall I not be distraught,
50   Environèd with all these hideous fears,
And madly play with my forefathers' joints,
And pluck the mangled Tybalt from his shroud,
And in this rage, with some great kinsman's bone
As with a club dash out my desperate brains?
55   O, look! Methinks I see my cousin's ghost
Seeking out Romeo, that did spit his body
Upon a rapier's point.—Stay, Tybalt, stay! *(Clutching the vial.)*
Romeo, Romeo, Romeo! Here's drink—I drink to thee.
(She drinks and falls upon her curtained bed.)

36 like, likely.
37 conceit, idea.

39 As, namely.

47 mandrakes, plants that resemble the human form. The mandrake was fabled to shriek when torn from the ground and to cause madness.
49 distraught (dis trôt′), *adj.* in a state of mental conflict or confusion.
50 fears, objects of fear.
52 mangled (mang′gəld), *adj.* badly cut or torn; spoiled, ruined.
53 rage, madness.

■ Summarize what Juliet fears could happen to her.

S C E N E 4

Summary *While Juliet lies still and quiet upstairs, downstairs is in a frenzy of wedding preparations. When the Count and his musicians arrive, Capulet sends the nurse to awaken Juliet.*

A hall in Capulet's house. Enter LADY CAPULET *and the* NURSE.
LADY CAPULET. Hold, take these keys, and fetch more spices, Nurse.
NURSE. They call for dates and quinces in the pastry.
(Enter CAPULET.*)*
CAPULET. Come, stir, stir, stir! The second cock hath crowed.
The curfew bell hath rung; 'tis three o'clock.
5   Look to the baked meats, good Angelica
Spare not for cost.
NURSE.   Go, you cotquean, go,
Get you to bed. Faith, you'll be sick tomorrow
For this night's watching.

2 quince (kwins), *n.* hard, yellowish, pear-shaped fruit, used for preserves and jelly.
2 pastry, room in which pastry was made.
5 baked meats, pies, pastries.
6 cotquean (kot′kwēn), a man who acts the housewife.
8 For . . . watching, because of staying up all night.

Juliet takes the potion that will make her appear to be dead. How does film director Zeffirelli establish a **mood** in this scene?

CAPULET. No, not a whit. What, I have watched ere now
10   All night for lesser cause, and ne'er been sick.
    LADY CAPULET. Ay, you have been a mouse-hunt in your time;
      But I will watch you from such watching now.
    (*Exit* LADY CAPULET *and* NURSE.)
    CAPULET. A jealous hood, a jealous hood!
    (*Enter* SERVANTS *carrying baskets of food.*)
      Now, fellow, what is there?
15 **FIRST SERVANT.** Things for the cook, sir, but I know not what.

9 whit, a very small bit.

11 mouse-hunt, hunter of women.

13 jealous hood, one who wears the hat of jealousy.

CAPULET. Make haste, make haste.

(*Exit* FIRST SERVANT.)

(*To* SECOND SERVANT.) Sirrah, fetch drier logs.
Call Peter. He will show thee where they are.

SECOND SERVANT. I have a head, sir, that will find out logs
20   And never trouble Peter for the matter. (*Exit.*)

CAPULET (*laughing*). Mass, and well said. A merry whoreson, ha!
Thou shalt be loggerhead. Good faith, 'tis day.
The County will be here with music straight,
For so he said he would. I hear him near.

(*Music sounds offstage.*)

25   Nurse! Wife! What, ho! What, Nurse, I say!

(*Enter* NURSE.)

Go waken Juliet, go and trim her up.
I'll go and chat with Paris. Hie, make haste,
Make haste. The bridegroom he is come already.
Make haste, I say.   (*Exit.*)

19 I . . . logs. My head is wooden and thus recognizes other wooden things.
21 Mass, by the Mass, a mild oath.
22 loggerhead, blockhead, a head made of logs.

S C E N E   5

Summary   *The nurse comes to awaken Juliet and is horrified to discover her apparently dead. As Juliet's parents lament their daughter's death, Friar Laurence and Count Paris enter. Friar Laurence calms and comforts the mourners with the consolations of religion. After the family leaves to make funeral arrangements, the musicians that have accompanied Paris exchange comic insults with Peter.*

Juliet's bedchamber. The curtains are drawn around Juliet's bed. Enter the NURSE.

NURSE (*urgently*). Mistress! What, mistress! Juliet! Fast, I warrant her.
Why, lamb; why, lady! Fie, you slugabed!
Why, love, I say! (*Louder.*) Madam! Sweetheart! Why, bride!
What, not a word? (*Teasingly.*) You take your pennyworths now.
5   Sleep for a week; for the next night, I warrant,
The County Paris hath set up his rest
That you shall rest but little. (*Pauses.*) God forgive me,
Marry, and amen! How sound is she asleep!
I needs must wake her. (*She opens the curtains which hang around the sides of the bed.*) Madam, madam, madam!
10   Ay, let the County take you in your bed;
He'll fright you up, i' faith. Will it not be?   (*She leans over the bed.*)
What, dressed, and in your clothes, and down again?
I must needs wake you. (*Shaking her.*) Lady, lady, lady!
Alas, alas! (*Running to the door.*) Help, help! My lady's dead!
15   O, weraday, that ever I was born!
Some aqua vitae, ho! My lord! My lady!

■ Compare the **mood** of Scene 4 with that of the previous scene.

1 fast, fast asleep.

4 pennyworths, small portions.
6 set . . . rest, firmly resolved.

12 down, back to bed.

(*Enter* LADY CAPULET.)

LADY CAPULET. What noise is here?

NURSE (*going to* LADY CAPULET). O lamentable day!

LADY CAPULET. What is the matter?

NURSE (*pointing to the bed*). Look, look! O heavy day!

LADY CAPULET. O me. O me! My child, my only life,

20 Revive, look up, or I will die with thee!

Help, help! Call help.

(*Enter* CAPULET, *still in high spirits.*)

CAPULET. For shame, bring Juliet forth. Her lord is come.

NURSE. She's dead, deceased. She's dead, alack the day!

LADY CAPULET. Alack the day, she's dead, she's dead, she's dead!

25 **CAPULET.** Ha! Let me see her. Out, alas! She's cold.

Her blood is settled, and her joints are stiff;

Life and these lips have long been separated.

Death lies on her like an untimely frost

Upon the sweetest flower of all the field.

NURSE. O lamentable day!

30 **LADY CAPULET.**   O woeful time!

CAPULET. Death, that hath ta'en her hence to make me wail,

Ties up my tongue and will not let me speak.

(*Enter* FRIAR LAURENCE *and* PARIS.)

FRIAR LAURENCE. Come, is the bride ready to go to church?

CAPULET (*bitterly*). Ready to go, but never to return.

35 O son, the night before thy wedding day

Hath Death lain with thy wife. There she lies,

Flower as she was, deflowered by him.

Death is my son-in-law, Death is my heir;

My daughter he hath wedded. I will die,

40 And leave him all; life, living, all is Death's.

PARIS. Have I thought long to see this morning's face,

And doth it give me such a sight as this?

LADY CAPULET. Accurst, unhappy, wretched, hateful day!

Most miserable hour that e'er time saw

45 In lasting labor of his pilgrimage!

But one, poor one, one poor and loving child,

But one thing to rejoice and solace in,

And cruel Death hath catched it from my sight!

NURSE. O woe! O woeful, woeful, woeful day!

50 Most lamentable day, most woeful day

That ever, ever I did yet behold!

O day, O day, O day! O hateful day!

Never was seen so black a day as this.

O woeful day, O woeful day!

55 **PARIS.** Beguiled, divorcèd, wrongèd, spited, slain!

25 Out, alas, an exclamation of grief.
26 settled, thickened.

■ Explain how the friar's words may be deliberately **ironic.**

40 living, property.
41 thought long . . . face, long looked forward to the dawn on this, my wedding day.
43 unhappy, fatal.

46 but, only.
47 solace (sol′is), *v.* find comfort.

Most detestable Death, by thee beguiled,
By cruel, cruel thee quite overthrown!
O love! O life! Not life, but love in death!
CAPULET. Despised, distressèd, hated, martyred, killed!
60 Uncomfortable time, why cam'st thou now
To murder, murder our solemnity?
O child! O child! My soul, and not my child!
Dead art thou! Alack, my child is dead,
And with my child my joys are burièd.
65 **FRIAR LAURENCE.** Peace, ho, for shame! Confusion's cure lives not
In these confusions. Heaven and yourself
Had part in this fair maid; now heaven hath all,
And all the better is it for the maid.
Your part in her you could not keep from death,
70 But heaven keeps his part in eternal life.
The most you sought was her promotion,
For 'twas your heaven she should be advanced;
And weep ye now, seeing she is advanced
Above the clouds, as high as heaven itself?
75 O, in this love, you love your child so ill
That you run mad, seeing that she is well.
She's not well married that lives married long,
But she's best married that dies married young.
Dry up your tears, and stick your rosemary
80 On this fair corpse, and, as the custom is,
And in her best array, bear her to church;
For though fond nature bids us all lament,
Yet nature's tears are reason's merriment.
CAPULET. All things that we ordainèd festival
85 Turn from their office to black funeral:
Our instruments to melancholy bells,
Our wedding cheer to a sad burial feast,
Our solemn hymns to sullen dirges change,
Our bridal flowers serve for a buried corpse,
90 And all things change them to the contrary.
FRIAR LAURENCE. Sir, go you in, and, madam, go with him,
And go, Sir Paris. Everyone prepare
To follow this fair corpse unto her grave.
The heavens do lour upon you for some ill;
95 Move them no more by crossing their high will.
(*Exit* CAPULET, LADY CAPULET, PARIS, *and* FRIAR. *The* NURSE *and the*
Count's MUSICIANS *remain.*)
FIRST MUSICIAN. Faith, we may put up our pipes and be gone.
NURSE. Honest good fellows, ah, put up, put up!

60 uncomfortable, joyless.
61 solemnity (sə lem′nə tē),
n. festive celebration.

65 Confusion's,
destruction's.

70 his part, Juliet's immortal
soul.

72 advanced, lifted up, promoted.

■ What consolation does
the friar offer the Capulets?

79 rosemary, symbol of
immortality and enduring
love.
82 fond nature, foolish
human nature.
83 nature's . . . merriment,
that which causes human
nature to weep is an
occasion of joy for reason.
84 ordainèd festival,
intended to be gay and
festive.
88 dirge, a funeral song.

94 lour . . . ill, threaten you
because of some sin committed by you.

For well you know this is a pitiful case. *(The* NURSE *exits, shaking her head sorrowfully.)*

FIRST MUSICIAN. Ay, by my troth, the case may be amended.

(Enter PETER, *the* NURSE'S *servant.)*

100 **PETER.** Musicians, O, musicians, "Heart's ease," "Heart's ease." O, an you will have me live, play "Heart's ease."

FIRST MUSICIAN. Why "Heart's ease"?

PETER. O, musicians, because my heart itself plays "My heart is full." O, play me some merry dump to comfort me.

105 **FIRST MUSICIAN.** Not a dump we! 'Tis no time to play now.

PETER. You will not, then?

FIRST MUSICIAN. No.

PETER. I will then give it you soundly.

FIRST MUSICIAN. What will you give us?

110 **PETER.** No money, on my faith, but the gleek; I will give you the minstrel.

FIRST MUSICIAN. Then will I give you the serving-creature.

PETER. Then will I lay the serving-creature's dagger on your pate. I will carry no crotchets. I'll re you, I'll fa you. Do you note me?

115 **FIRST MUSICIAN.** An you re us and fa us, you note us.

SECOND MUSICIAN. Pray you, put up your dagger and put out your wit.

PETER. Then have at you with my wit! I will dry-beat you with an iron wit, and put up my iron dagger. Answer me like men. *(He sings.)*

"When griping griefs the heart doth wound,
120   And doleful dumps the mind oppress,
Then music with her silver sound—"

Why "silver sound"? Why "music with her silver sound"? What say you, Simon Catling?

FIRST MUSICIAN. Marry, sir, because silver hath a sweet sound.

125 **PETER.** Pretty! What say you, Hugh Rebeck?

SECOND MUSICIAN. I say "silver sound" because musicians sound for silver.

PETER. Pretty too! What say you, James Soundpost?

THIRD MUSICIAN. Faith, I know not what to say.

130 **PETER.** O, I cry you mercy, you are the singer. I will say for you. It is "music with her silver sound" because musicians have no gold for sounding: *(He sings.)*

"Then music with her silver sound
    With speedy help doth lend redress."

135 **FIRST MUSICIAN.** What a pestilent knave is this same!

SECOND MUSICIAN. Hang him, Jack! Come, we'll in here, tarry for the mourners, and stay dinner. *(Exit.)*

---

99 case, with a pun on instrument case.
99 amended, repaired.
100 "Heart's ease," an old ballad.

103 "My . . . full," another old ballad.
104 dump, slow dance melody.
108 give it you, give it to you; e.g., thrash you.
110 gleek, mocking jest.
110 give . . . minstrel, call you a minstrel, or vagabond.
111 serving-creature. Peter *is* a servant.
113 pate, top of the head.
114 carry no crotchets. Endure no whims, or quarternotes.
114 re, fa, musical notes.
114 note, understand; set to music.
116 put out, display.
117 dry-beat, thrash without drawing blood.

123–128 Catling . . . Soundpost. The musicians have musical names. A catling is a small lute string made of catgut. A rebeck is a three-stringed fiddle. A soundpost is a wooden peg in a violin that supports the bridge.
130 cry you mercy, beg your pardon.
131 have . . . sounding, are paid only silver for playing.

135 pestilent (pes'tl ənt), *adj.* pesty; bothersome.
136 tarry (tar'ē), *v.* delay leaving; remain.
137 stay, await.

Romeo and Juliet—Act Four, Scene 5   **563**

After Reading

Shaping Your Response

Making Connections

1. What do you think could go wrong with the friar's plan?

2. Do you feel sympathy for Paris? Why or why not?

Analyzing the Play

3. In Scene 1, Paris speaks to Juliet affectionately. Describe Juliet's response.

4. How does Paris interpret Juliet's responses?

5. Capulet moves the wedding from Thursday to Wednesday. What effect might his change of plan have on the friar's arrangements?

6. Describe Juliet's major emotions in Scene 3.

7. Compare the reactions of Lord Capulet, Lady Capulet, and Paris to Juliet's death.

8. How does Shakespeare create a sense of haste and urgency in Act 4?

9. At the end of Act 4, are events moving according to the friar's plan? Explain.

Extending the Ideas

10. If you were directing this play, how would you instruct your actors to reinforce the sense of urgency in Act 4?

11. In Shakespeare's day, it was possible to plan a wedding on short notice. Why is that unusual today?

Vocabulary Study

The listed vocabulary words are antonyms for the underlined words in the sentences. Based on context, choose the word from the list that best completes each sentence. The Glossary may be helpful.

abate
distraught
inundation
kindred
mangled
reclaimed
resolution
slander
solace
wayward

1. Rosaline's lack of response to Romeo is like a <u>drought</u>, but Juliet's love for him is an ____.

2. Juliet does not want her words to ____ Romeo because in her heart she <u>praises</u> him.

3. The Nurse's advice about marrying Paris does not ____ Juliet but instead <u>distresses</u> her.

4. Mercutio and Paris are more than <u>acquaintances</u> of the Prince; they are his ____.

5. Juliet's optimism begins to ____ as her problems <u>increase</u>.

6. After experiencing feelings of <u>indecision</u>, Juliet forms a ____ about what to do.

7. Because Juliet agrees to marry Paris, she is not <u>abandoned</u> by her father, but is instead ____ as a daughter.

8. Lord Capulet is happy when his ____ daughter seems <u>obedient</u> again.

9. Juliet pretends to be <u>calm</u> when she goes to bed, but she is actually quite ____.

10. Juliet fears that her mind will not be <u>unharmed</u> by the shock of waking up in the tomb next to Tybalt's ____ body.

Expressing Your Ideas

Writing Choices

Dear Romeo In Scene 1, Friar Laurence tells Juliet that he will write to Romeo in Mantua. Write the friar's **letter** and include all the essential information that Romeo needs to know. Choose an appropriate tone for your letter.

The Plot Thickens Update your **chain diagram** to include the significant events that occur during Act 4, and jot down predictions about what lies ahead in Act 5. After reading Act 5, you can complete the diagram.

Other Options

What's Up, Juliet? With a small group, choose a scene or part of a scene from Act 4 to reenact in a present-day setting. Practice your **scene** with the other members of your group and then perform it for the class.

Costume Design Imagine that you are the costumer for a new production of *Romeo and Juliet*. Do some research on fourteenth-century fashions in Italy and prepare a series of **sketches** of the costumes needed for either Romeo or Juliet. Include details such as hats, hairstyles, shoes, coats, and accessories such as swords, jewelry, and purses.

ACT FIVE

SCENE 1

Summary *In Mantua, Romeo muses on his odd dream wherein he was dead but Juliet revived him with a kiss. The servant Balthasar enters with the report of Juliet's death. Romeo determines to return to Verona and join Juliet in death. To that end, he enters an apothecary's, or pharmacist's, shop and buys a vial of strong poison.*

A street in Mantua. ROMEO *enters.*

ROMEO. If I may trust the flattering truth of sleep,
My dreams presage some joyful news at hand.
My bosom's lord sits lightly in his throne,
And all this day an unaccustomed spirit
5 Lifts me above the ground with cheerful thoughts.
I dreamt my lady came and found me dead—
Strange dream, that gives a dead man leave to think!—
And breathed such life with kisses in my lips
That I revived and was an emperor.
10 Ah me, how sweet is love itself possessed
When but love's shadows are so rich in joy!
(*Enter* BALTHASAR.)
News from Verona! How now, Balthasar,
Dost thou not bring me letters from the Friar?
How doth my lady? Is my father well?
15 How fares my Juliet? That I ask again,
For nothing can be ill if she be well.
BALTHASAR. Then she is well, and nothing can be ill.
Her body sleeps in Capels' monument,
And her immortal part with angels lives.
20 I saw her laid low in her kindred's vault,
And presently took post to tell it you.
O, pardon me for bringing these ill news,
Since you did leave it for my office, sir.
ROMEO. Is it e'en so? Then I defy you, stars!
25 Thou knowest my lodging. Get me ink and paper,
And hire post-horses. I will hence tonight.
BALTHASAR. I do beseech you, sir, have patience.
Your looks are pale and wild, and do import
Some misadventure.
ROMEO.　　　　　　　Tush, thou art deceived.
30 Leave me, and do the thing I bid thee do.
Hast thou no letters to me from the Friar?

---

1 **flattering,** favorable.
2 **presage** (pri sāj′), *v.* predict.
3 **bosom's lord,** heart.

7 **leave,** permission.

10 **itself possessed,** actually enjoyed.
11 **shadows,** dreams.

■ What makes the exiled Romeo feel cheerful in the opening of this scene?

18 **Capels',** Capulets'.

21 **presently took post,** soon set out with post horses.
23 **office,** duty.

24 **Then . . . stars.** Romeo defies the destiny that has fated him to live without Juliet.

28 **import,** suggest.

BALTHASAR. No, my good lord.

ROMEO.   No matter. Get thee gone,
    And hire those horses. I'll be with thee straight.
(*Exit* BALTHASAR.)
    Well, Juliet, I will lie with thee tonight.
35 Let's see for means. O mischief, thou art swift
    To enter in the thoughts of desperate men!
    I do remember an apothecary—
    And hereabouts 'a dwells—which late I noted
    In tattered weeds, with overwhelming brows,
40 Culling of simples. Meager were his looks;
    Sharp misery had worn him to the bones;
    And in his needy shop a tortoise hung,
    An alligator stuffed, and other skins
    Of ill-shaped fishes; and about his shelves
45 A beggarly account of empty boxes,
    Green earthen pots, bladders, and musty seeds,
    Remnants of packthread, and old cakes of roses
    Were thinly scattered to make up a show.
    Noting this penury, to myself I said,
50 "An if a man did need a poison now,
    Whose sale is present death in Mantua,
    Here lives a caitiff wretch would sell it him."
    O, this same thought did but forerun my need,
    And this same needy man must sell it me.
55 As I remember, this should be the house.
    Being holiday, the beggar's shop is shut.
    What, ho! Apothecary!
(*Enter* APOTHECARY.)
APOTHECARY.   Who calls so loud?
ROMEO. Come hither, man. I see that thou art poor.
    Hold, there is forty ducats, let me have
60 A dram of poison, such soon-speeding gear
    As will disperse itself through all the veins
    That the life-weary taker may fall dead,
    And that the trunk may be discharged of breath
    As violently as hasty powder fired
65 Doth hurry from the fatal cannon's womb.
APOTHECARY. Such mortal drugs I have, but Mantua's law
    Is death to any he that utters them.
ROMEO. Art thou so bare and full of wretchedness,
    And fearest to die? Famine is in thy cheeks,
70 Need and oppression starveth in thy eyes,
    Contempt and beggary hangs upon thy back.
    The world is not thy friend, nor the world's law;

---

33 straight, immediately.

35 for means, by what means; i.e., Romeo looks for a means by which he may join Juliet in death.
37 apothecary (ə poth′ə-ker′ē), *n.* pharmacist.
39 weeds, clothes.
39 overwhelming, overhanging.
40 culling of simples, selecting medicinal herbs.
40 meager (mē′gər), *adj.* impoverished, poor.
45 beggarly account, poor or meager number.
47 cakes of roses, rose petals caked together for use as a perfume.
49 penury (pen′yər ē), *n.* great poverty; extreme want.
51 Whose . . . death, the sale of which is punished by immediate death.
52 caitiff (kā′tif), *adj.* miserable.

59 ducat (duk′ət), *n.* gold coin.
60 soon-speeding gear, quick-acting substance.
61 disperse (dis pėrs′), *v.* move in different directions; scatter.
63 trunk, body.

66 mortal, deadly.
67 any . . . utters them, anyone who distributes them.

70 starveth, show hunger.

The world affords no law to make thee rich.
Then be not poor, but break it, and take this.
75 **APOTHECARY.** My poverty but not my will consents.
ROMEO. I pay thy poverty and not thy will.
APOTHECARY. Put this in any liquid thing you will
And drink it off, and if you had the strength
Of twenty men it would dispatch you straight.
80 **ROMEO.** There is thy gold—worse poison to men's souls,
Doing more murder in this loathsome world
Than these poor compounds that thou mayst not sell.
I sell thee poison; thou hast sold me none.
Farewell. Buy food, and get thyself in flesh.   (*Exit* APOTHECARY.)
85 Come, cordial and not poison, go with me
To Juliet's grave, for there must I use thee.   (*Exit.*)

85 **cordial** (kôr′jəl), *n.* a heart stimulant; thus a restorative.

S C E N E 2

Summary *Friar Laurence had given Friar John a letter to deliver to Romeo in Mantua. Before he could go to Mantua, however, Friar John had been locked in a house that the authorities believed to contain a plague victim. Hearing this, Friar Laurence asks for a crowbar and sets off to be with Juliet in the tomb when she awakens from her sleep.*

Friar Laurence's cell. Enter FRIAR JOHN.
FRIAR JOHN. Holy Franciscan friar! Brother, ho!
(*Enter* FRIAR LAURENCE.)
FRIAR LAURENCE. This same should be the voice of Friar John.
Welcome from Mantua! What says Romeo?
Or if his mind be writ, give me his letter.
5 **FRIAR JOHN.** Going to find a barefoot brother out—
One of our order—to associate me
Here in this city visiting the sick,
And finding him, the searchers of the town,
Suspecting that we both were in a house
10 Where the infectious pestilence did reign,
Sealed up the doors and would not let us forth,
So that my speed to Mantua there was stayed.
FRIAR LAURENCE. Who bare my letter, then, to Romeo?
FRIAR JOHN. I could not send it—here it is again—
15 Nor get a messenger to bring it thee,
So fearful were they of infection.
FRIAR LAURENCE. Unhappy fortune! By my brotherhood,
The letter was not nice but full of charge,
Of dear import, and the neglecting it
20 May do much danger. Friar John, go hence.

4 **if . . . writ,** if he has sent a written message.
6 **associate,** accompany.

8 **searchers,** officials who sought out those suspected of having a highly contagious disease (the "infectious pestilence" in line 10).

■ How has fate interfered with the friar's plans?

18 **nice,** trivial.
19 **Of dear import,** having dreadful significance.

Get me an iron crow and bring it straight
Unto my cell.

FRIAR JOHN. Brother, I'll go and bring it thee.   *(Exit.)*

FRIAR LAURENCE. Now must I to the monument alone.

25 Within this three hours will fair Juliet wake.
She will beshrew me much that Romeo
Hath had no notice of these accidents;
But I will write again to Mantua,
And keep her at my cell till Romeo come—

30 Poor living corpse, closed in a dead man's tomb!   *(Exit.)*

SCENE 3

Summary *Paris and his page enter the churchyard. Paris strews flowers near the tomb but hides when his page alerts him that someone is coming. Romeo and Balthasar enter. Romeo gives Balthasar a letter to be delivered to Lord Montague after sunrise. Romeo forces open the doors of the tomb, and Paris comes forward thinking that Romeo will defile the bodies of Tybalt and Juliet. Romeo refuses to leave, Paris draws his sword, the page runs for help, and Romeo stabs Paris. Romeo carries Paris into the tomb, speaks his final loving words to Juliet, and swallows the poison he has brought with him. Friar Laurence appears and discovers the bodies of the two young men. Juliet stirs, learns that Romeo and Paris are dead, and stabs herself. The Prince, Lord Montague, Lord Capulet, and Lady Capulet arrive. The friar explains what has happened. Prince Escalus shames both Capulet and Montague, and the two men end their feud.*

The churchyard in Verona where the Capulets' tomb is located. It is nighttime. Enter PARIS *and his* PAGE *bearing flowers and a torch.*

PARIS. Give me thy torch, boy. Hence, and stand aloof.
Yet put it out, for I would not be seen.

(The PAGE *extinguishes the torch.)*

Under yond yew trees lay thee all along,
Holding thy ear close to the hollow ground.

5 So shall no foot upon the churchyard tread,
Being loose, unfirm, with digging up of graves,
But thou shalt hear it. Whistle then to me
As signal that thou hearest something approach.
Give me those flowers. Do as I bid thee. Go.

10 **PAGE** *(speaking aside).* I am almost afraid to stand alone
Here in the churchyard, yet I will adventure.   *(He retires.)*

PARIS. Sweet flower, with flowers thy bridal bed I strew—
O woe! Thy canopy is dust and stones—
Which with sweet water nightly I will dew,

15 Or, wanting that, with tears distilled by moans.

---

21 iron crow, crowbar.

27 accidents, happenings.

1 aloof (ə lüf′), *adv.* away at a distance but within view.

3 all along, at full length.

■ How has Paris been affected by Juliet's death?

12 strew, scatter or sprinkle.

14 sweet, perfumed.
14 dew, moisten.
15 wanting, lacking.

▲ Romeo enters the tomb of the Capulets. What are his thoughts at this moment?

The obsequies that I for thee will keep
Nightly shall be to strew thy grave and weep.
(The PAGE *whistles offstage.)*
　　The boy gives warning something doth approach.
　　What cursèd foot wanders this way tonight
20　To cross my obsequies and true love's rite?
　　What, with a torch? Muffle me, night, awhile.
(He withdraws to the shadowed side of the tomb, where he cannot be seen. Enter
ROMEO *and* BALTHASAR *carrying tools to open the tomb.)*

16 obsequies (ob′sə kwēz),
n. ceremonies in honor of
the dead.

20 cross, interfere with.
21 muffle, hide.

ROMEO. Give me that mattock and the wrenching iron.
Hold, take this letter. Early in the morning
See thou deliver it to my lord and father
25   Give me the light. Upon thy life I charge thee,
Whate'er thou hearest or seest, stand all aloof
And do not interrupt me in my course.
Why I descend into this bed of death
Is partly to behold my lady's face,
30   But chiefly to take thence from her dead finger
A precious ring—a ring that I must use
In dear employment. Therefore hence, begone.
But if thou, jealous, dost return to pry
In what I farther shall intend to do,
35   By heaven, I will tear thee joint by joint
And strew this hungry churchyard with thy limbs.
The time and my intents are savage-wild,
More fierce and more inexorable far
Than empty tigers or the roaring sea.
40 **BALTHASAR.** I will be gone, sir, and not trouble ye.
  ROMEO. So shalt thou show me friendship. *(Offering money.)* Take
    thou that.
Live, and be prosperous; and farewell, good fellow.
  BALTHASAR *(aside).* For all this same, I'll hide me hereabout.
His looks I fear, and his intents I doubt. *(He pretends to leave but
hides nearby.)*
45 **ROMEO.** Thou detestable maw, thou womb of death,
Gorged with the dearest morsel of the earth,
Thus I enforce thy rotten jaws to open,
And in despite I'll cram thee with more food. *(He succeeds in
prying open the doors of the tomb.)*
  PARIS. That is that banished haughty Montague
50   That murdered my love's cousin, with which grief
It is supposèd the fair creature died,
And here is come to do some villainous shame
To the dead bodies. I will apprehend him. *(He comes forward.)*
Stop thy unhallowed toil, vile Montague!
55   Can vengeance be pursued further than death?
Condemnèd villain, I do apprehend thee.
Obey and go with me, for thou must die.
  ROMEO. I must indeed, and therefore came I hither.
Good gentle youth, tempt not a desperate man.
60   Fly hence and leave me. Think upon these gone;
Let them affright thee. I beseech thee, youth,
Put not another sin upon my head
By urging me to fury. O, begone!

22 **mattock,** pickax.

■ Why do you think Romeo gives Balthasar a letter?

33 **jealous,** suspicious.

38 **inexorable** (in ek′sər ə-bəl), *adj.* relentless; unyielding.

45 **maw,** stomach.
45 **womb of death,** belly of death. (Romeo addresses the tomb.)
46 **dearest . . . earth,** i.e., Juliet.
48 **in despite,** in defiance.

53 **apprehend** (ap′ri-hend′), *v.* seize; arrest.
54 **unhallowed,** wicked; sinful; evil.

By heaven, I love thee better than myself,
65   For I come hither armed against myself.
Stay not, begone. Live, and hereafter say
A madman's mercy bid thee run away.

PARIS. I do defy thy conjuration *(drawing his sword)*,
And apprehend thee for a felon here.

70   **ROMEO.** Wilt thou provoke me? *(Drawing his own sword.)* Then have at
thee, boy!

PAGE. O Lord, they fight! I will go call the watch. *(Exit.)*

PARIS. O, I am slain! *(He falls.)* If thou be merciful,
Open the tomb, lay me with Juliet. *(He dies.)*

ROMEO. In faith, I will. Let me peruse this face.
75   Mercutio's kinsman, noble County Paris!
What said my man when my betossèd soul
Did not attend him as we rode? I think
He told me Paris should have married Juliet.
Said he not so? Or did I dream it so?
80   Or am I mad, hearing him talk of Juliet,
To think it was so? O, give me thy hand,
One writ with me in sour misfortune's book.
I'll bury thee in a triumphant grave.
A grave? O, no! A lantern, slaughtered youth,
85   For here lies Juliet, and her beauty makes
This vault a feasting presence full of light.
Death, lie thou there, by a dead man interred.

(He lays PARIS *in the tomb, not far from* JULIET.*)*
How oft when men are at the point of death
Have they been merry, which their keepers call
90   A lightening before death! O, how may I
Call this a lightening? O my love, my wife!
Death, that hath sucked the honey of thy breath,
Hath had no power yet upon thy beauty.
Thou art not conquered; beauty's ensign yet
95   Is crimson in thy lips and in thy cheeks,
And death's pale flag is not advancèd there.
Tybalt, liest thou there in thy bloody sheet?
O, what more favor can I do to thee
Than with that hand that cut thy youth in twain
100 To sunder his that was thine enemy?
Forgive me, cousin! *(Turning again to* JULIET.*)* Ah, dear Juliet,
Why art thou yet so fair? Shall I believe
That unsubstantial Death is amorous,
And that the lean abhorrèd monster keeps
105 Thee here in dark to be his paramour?
For fear of that I still will stay with thee

68 conjuration (kon′jə-rā′shən), *n.* solemn appeal.
69 felon (fel′ən), *n.* criminal.

74 peruse (pə rüz′), *v.* examine in detail.

77 attend, pay attention to.

83 triumphant, glorious, honorable.
84 lantern, a tower room with many windows.
86 feasting presence, a splendid reception room.
87 Death, the corpse of Paris.
87 interred (in tèrd′), *adj.* put into a grave or tomb; buried.
89 keepers, jailers.
90 lightening, a revival of spirit.

94 ensign (en′sīn), *n.* banner.
96 advancèd, raised.

■ What is **ironic** about Romeo's description of Juliet?

97 sheet, shroud.
100 sunder, split apart; sever.
100 his, Romeo's youth.

104 abhorrèd, hated.
105 paramour (par′ə mür), *n.* lover.
106 still, always.

And never from this palace of dim night
Depart again. Here, here will I remain
With worms that are thy chambermaids. O, here
110 Will I set up my everlasting rest
And shake the yoke of inauspicious stars
From this world-wearied flesh. Eyes, look your last!
Arms, take your last embrace! And, lips, O you
The doors of breath, seal with a righteous kiss
115 A dateless bargain to engrossing death!
Come, bitter conduct, come, <u>unsavory</u> guide,
Thou desperate pilot, now at once run on
The dashing rocks thy seasick weary bark!
Here's to my love. *(He drinks the poison.)* O true apothecary!
120 Thy drugs are quick. Thus with a kiss I die. *(Falls.)*
(Enter, at the other end of the churchyard, FRIAR LAURENCE, *with a lantern, crowbar, mattock, and spade.)*

FRIAR LAURENCE. Saint Francis be my speed! How oft tonight
Have my old feet stumbled at graves! Who's there?

BALTHASAR. Here's one, a friend, and one that knows you well.

FRIAR LAURENCE. Bliss be upon you. Tell me, good my friend,
125 What torch is yond that vainly lends his light
To grubs and eyeless skulls? As I discern,
It burneth in the Capels' monument.

BALTHASAR. It doth so, holy sir, and there's my master,
One that you love.

FRIAR LAURENCE.   Who is it?

BALTHASAR.   Romeo.

FRIAR LAURENCE. How long hath he been there?

130 BALTHASAR.   Full half hour.

FRIAR LAURENCE. Go with me to the vault.

BALTHASAR.   I dare not, sir.
My master knows not but I am gone hence,
And fearfully did menace me with death
If I did stay to look on his intents.

135 FRIAR LAURENCE. Stay, then, I'll go alone. Fear comes upon me.
O, much I fear some ill unthrifty thing.

BALTHASAR. As I did sleep under this yew tree here
I dreamt my master and another fought,
And that my master slew him.

FRIAR LAURENCE   Romeo!   *(He goes forward.)*
140 Alack, alack, what blood is this which stains
The stony entrance of this sepulcher?   *(He sees the swords.)*
What mean these masterless and gory swords
To lie discolored by this place of peace?   *(He enters the tomb.)*
Romeo! O, pale! Who else? What, Paris too?

111 **inauspicious** (in′ô-spish′əs), *adj.* unfavorable; unlucky.

115 **dateless bargain,** everlasting contract.
116 **conduct,** guide; i.e., poison.
116 unsavory (un sā′vər ē), *adj.* distasteful; morally offensive.
117 **pilot,** perhaps Romeo's soul.
118 **bark,** Romeo's body.

121 **speed,** protector.
122 **stumbled at graves.** This was an unlucky omen.

136 **unthrifty,** unfortunate.

141 **sepulcher** (sep′əl kər), *n.* burial place; tomb.

Romeo and Juliet—Act Five, Scene 3   **573**

145 And steeped in blood? Ah, what an unkind hour
Is guilty of this lamentable chance!
The lady stirs.   (*Slowly* JULIET *comes out of her trance.*)
JULIET. O comfortable Friar, where is my lord?
I do remember well where I should be,
150 And there I am. Where is my Romeo?
(*Offstage noise of the* WATCHMEN *approaching.*)
FRIAR LAURENCE. I hear some noise. Lady, come from that nest
Of death, contagion, and unnatural sleep.
A greater power than we can contradict
Hath thwarted our intents. Come, come away.
155 Thy husband in thy bosom there lies dead,
And Paris, too. Come, I'll dispose of thee
Among a sisterhood of holy nuns.   (*Voices are heard.*)
Stay not to question, for the watch is coming.
Come, go, good Juliet. I dare no longer stay.
(*He leaves* JULIET *in the tomb.*)
160 **JULIET.** Go, get thee hence, for I will not away.   (*Exit* FRIAR LAURENCE.)
What's here? A cup, closed in my true love's hand?
Poison, I see, hath been his timeless end.
O churl, drunk all, and left no friendly drop
To help me after? I will kiss thy lips;
165 Haply some poison yet doth hang on them,
To make me die with a restorative. (*Kisses him.*)
Thy lips are warm.
FIRST WATCHMAN. (*offstage*). Lead, boy. Which way?
JULIET. Yea, noise? Then I'll be brief. O happy dagger!
(*She snatches* ROMEO's *dagger.*)
170 This is thy sheath. (*Stabs herself.*) There rust, and let me die.
(*She falls on* ROMEO's *body and dies.*)
(*Enter the* PAGE *of* PARIS, *followed by the* FIRST WATCHMAN.)
PAGE. This is the place, there where the torch doth burn.
FIRST WATCHMAN. The ground is bloody. Search about the churchyard.
Go, some of you, whoe'er you find attach. (*He enters the tomb.*)
Pitiful sight! Here lies the County slain,
175 And Juliet bleeding, warm, and newly dead,
Who here hath lain these two days burièd.   (*To the* PAGE.)
Go tell the Prince. Run to the Capulets.
Raise up the Montagues. Some others search.
We see the ground whereon these woes do lie,
180 But the true ground of all these piteous woes
We cannot without circumstance descry.
(*Enter other members of the* WATCH, *with* BALTHASAR.)
SECOND WATCHMAN. Here's Romeo's man. We found him in the
churchyard.

148 comfortable, comforting.

162 timeless, untimely; also, everlasting.
163 churl, miser.

165 haply, perhaps.
166 To make . . . restorative. The very thing (a kiss) that had once restored Juliet's good cheer may now bring about her death.
169 happy, timely.

173 whoe'er . . . attach. Arrest anyone you find.

179 woes, the bodies of Romeo and Juliet.
180 ground, cause.
181 without . . . descry (di skrī′), understand without the details.

▲ Juliet prepares to join Romeo in death. Compare and contrast this image with the image of Romeo and Juliet on page 481.

FIRST WATCHMAN. Hold him in safety till the Prince come hither.

(*Enter* FRIAR LAURENCE *and another* WATCHMAN.)

THIRD WATCHMAN. Here is a friar, that trembles, sighs, and weeps.

185   We took this mattock and this spade from him
      As he was coming from this churchyard's side.

FIRST WATCHMAN. A great suspicion. Stay the Friar, too.

(*Enter* PRINCE ESCALUS *and* ATTENDANTS.)

PRINCE. What misadventure is so early up
      That calls our person from our morning rest?

(*Enter* LORD *and* LADY CAPULET.)

190 **CAPULET.** What should it be that is so shrieked abroad?

LADY CAPULET. O, the people in the street cry "Romeo,"
      Some "Juliet," and some "Paris," and all run
      With open outcry toward our monument.

PRINCE. What fear is this which startles in our ears?

195 **FIRST WATCHMAN.** Sovereign, here lies the County Paris slain,
      And Romeo dead, and Juliet, dead before,
      Warm and new killed.

PRINCE. Search, seek, and know how this foul murder comes.

FIRST WATCHMAN. Here is a friar, and slaughtered Romeo's man,

200   With instruments upon them fit to open
      These dead men's tombs.

CAPULET. O heavens! O wife, look how our daughter bleeds!
      This dagger hath mista'en, for lo, his house
      Is empty on the back of Montague,

205   And it mis-sheathèd in my daughter's bosom!

LADY CAPULET. O me! This sight of death is as a bell
      That warns my old age to a sepulcher.

(*Enter* MONTAGUE *and* OTHERS.)

PRINCE. Come, Montague, for thou art early up
      To see thy son and heir more early down.

210 **MONTAGUE.** Alas, my liege, my wife is dead tonight;
      Grief of my son's exile hath stopped her breath.
      What further woe conspires against mine age?

PRINCE. Look, and thou shalt see.

MONTAGUE. O thou untaught! What manners is in this,

215   To press before thy father to a grave?

PRINCE. Seal up the mouth of outrage for a while,
      Till we can clear these ambiguities
      And know their spring, their head, their true descent;
      And then will I be general of your woes

220   And lead you even to death. Meantime, forbear,
      And let mischance be slave to patience.
      Bring forth the parties of suspicion.

FRIAR LAURENCE. I am the greatest, able to do least,

187 A great suspicion, a most suspicious thing.

■ Why do the watchmen believe the friar might be guilty of a crime?

203 mista'en, mistaken its right target.
203 his house, its scabbard.

207 warns, orders.

210 liege (lēj), *n.* lord.

214 untaught, ill-mannered youth.

216 mouth of outrage, outcry.

218 spring, source.

221 let mischance . . . patience. Let patience control your hasty reaction to these mishaps.

Yet most suspected, as the time and place

225 Doth make against me, of this direful murder;
And here I stand, both to impeach and purge
Myself condemnèd and myself excused.

PRINCE. Then say at once what thou dost know in this.

FRIAR LAURENCE. I will be brief, for my short date of breath

230 Is not so long as is a tedious tale.
Romeo, there dead, was husband to that Juliet,
And she, there dead, that Romeo's faithful wife.
I married them, and their stol'n marriage day
Was Tybalt's doomsday, whose untimely death

235 Banished the new-made bridegroom from this city,
For whom, and not for Tybalt, Juliet pined.
You, to remove that siege of grief from her,
Betrothed and would have married her perforce
To County Paris. Then comes she to me,

240 And with wild looks bid me devise some means
To rid her from this second marriage,
Or in my cell there would she kill herself.
Then gave I her—so tutored by my art—
A sleeping potion, which so took effect

245 As I intended, for it wrought on her
The form of death. Meantime I writ to Romeo
That he should hither come as this dire night
To help to take her from her borrowed grave,
Being the time the potion's force should cease.

250 But he which bore my letter, Friar John,
Was stayed by accident, and yesternight
Returned my letter back. Then all alone
At the prefixèd hour of her waking
Came I to take her from her kindred's vault,

255 Meaning to keep her closely at my cell
Till I conveniently could send to Romeo.
But when I came, some minute ere the time
Of her awakening, here untimely lay
The noble Paris and true Romeo dead.

260 She wakes, and I entreated her come forth
And bear this work of heaven with patience.
But then a noise did scare me from the tomb,
And she, too desperate, would not go with me,
But, as it seems, did violence on herself.

265 All this I know, and to the marriage
Her nurse is privy; and if aught in this
Miscarried by my fault, let my old life

225 make, tell.
226 impeach and purge, accuse and free from blame.

238 perforce (pər fôrs′), *adv.* by force.

247 as this, on the very.
248 borrowed, used temporarily.

255 closely, secretly.

■ In summarizing the tragic events, does the friar try to protect himself?

266 privy (priv′ē), *adj.* sharing secret knowledge of something.
266 aught (ôt), *pron.* anything.

Be sacrificed some hour before his time
Unto the rigor of severest law.

270 **PRINCE.** We still have known thee for a holy man.
Where's Romeo's man? What can he say to this?

BALTHASAR. I brought my master news of Juliet's death,
And then in post he came from Mantua
To this same place, to this same monument.

275 This letter he early bid me give his father,
And threatened me with death, going in the vault,
If I departed not and left him there.

PRINCE. Give me the letter. I will look on it.
Where is the County's page, that raised the watch?

280 Sirrah, what made your master in this place?

PAGE. He came with flowers to strew his lady's grave,
And bid me stand aloof, and so I did.
Anon comes one with light to ope the tomb,
And by and by my master drew on him,

285 And then I ran away to call the watch.

PRINCE. This letter doth make good the Friar's words,
Their course of love, the tidings of her death;
And here he writes that he did buy a poison
Of a poor 'pothecary, and therewithal

290 Came to this vault to die, and lie with Juliet.
Where be these enemies? Capulet, Montague,
See what a scourge is laid upon your hate,
That heaven finds means to kill your joys with love.
And I, for winking at your discords, too

295 Have lost a brace of kinsmen. All are punished.

CAPULET. O brother Montague, give me thy hand.
This is my daughter's jointure, for no more
Can I demand.

MONTAGUE.   But I can give thee more,
For I will raise her statue in pure gold,

300 That whiles Verona by that name is known
There shall no figure at such rate be set
As that of true and faithful Juliet.

CAPULET. As rich shall Romeo's by his lady's lie;
Poor sacrifices of our enmity!

305 **PRINCE.** A glooming peace this morning with it brings;
The sun, for sorrow, will not show his head.
Go hence to have more talk of these sad things.
Some shall be pardoned, and some punishèd;
For never was a story of more woe,

310 Than this of Juliet and her Romeo.   *(Exit.)*

---

269 rigor (rig′ər), *n.* strictness; harshness.

273 in post, with the greatest possible speed.

280 made, did.

283 anon, soon.
283 ope, open.
284 by and by, almost at once.

■ What or whom does Prince Escalus blame for the deaths of Romeo and Juliet?

293 your joys, your children.
294 winking at, shutting my eyes to.
295 brace, pair.

297 jointure (join′chər), *n.* dowry.

301 at such . . . set, be valued so greatly.

Making Connections

1. If you could prevent Juliet from killing herself after finding Romeo dead, would you? Why or why not?

2. On a scale of 1 (cowardly) to 10 (brave), rate Friar Laurence. Explain your ratings.

3. What does Romeo mean when he calls the poison a "cordial," or heart stimulant, in Scene 1, line 85?

4. In Scene 2, why is Friar Laurence worried?

5. Create a chart like the one shown here to compare the opening of Act 3, Scene 2 with the opening of Act 5, Scene 1. What similarities and differences do you find?

Act 3, Scene 2	Act 5, Scene 1
Juliet awaits news of Romeo.	Romeo awaits news of Juliet.

6. Reread Romeo's description of the tomb. What examples of **personification** do you find?

7. What **irony** do you see in the duel between Paris and Romeo?

8. Why do you think Friar Laurence runs from the tomb after Juliet awakens?

9. What effect do you think the tragic events of the play will have on future **interactions** between the families?

10. Although *Romeo and Juliet* is usually categorized as a tragedy, some people think that the play's lighter tone and its celebration of young love make it more like Shakespeare's romantic comedies. Do you think *Romeo and Juliet* is more tragic or romantic?

Literary Focus: Theme

Shakespeare's plays contain many **themes,** or layers of meaning. Like all his plays, *Romeo and Juliet* can be understood in different ways. For example, some may see the story as a celebration of young love; others may interpret it as a statement about the responsibility of adults toward young people; and still others may focus on the idea of fate versus free will. Now that you've read the play, explain what themes in the play are most significant to you, and why.

Vocabulary Study

Words that people use in everyday conversation are often too casual for use in formal writing. In the following sentences, replace the underlined word or phrase with a more formal word from the list. If necessary, use the Glossary for help with word meanings.

aloof
disperse
interred
peruse
unsavory

1. Graveyards have a reputation for being <u>icky</u> places to be.
2. Balthasar stands <u>off a ways</u> while Romeo enters the tomb.
3. Romeo has to <u>check out</u> Paris's face to see if he knows him.
4. Juliet's body is <u>stashed</u> in the family tomb.
5. Romeo hopes the poison will <u>get going</u> rapidly throughout his body.

Expressing Your Ideas

Writing Choices

Writer's Notebook Update Review your notes about the expression "Children pay for the sins of their parents" (from page 480). Now write a response to this statement as Romeo or Juliet would see it.

To Tell or Not to Tell In the last scene of the play, the secret of Romeo's marriage to Juliet is finally revealed—too late to prevent the tragedy. Should the couple have revealed their marriage earlier in the play? Or would the revelation have caused an equally disastrous outcome? Address these questions in a **persuasive essay,** giving at least three reasons for your opinion. Arrange your reasons so that you focus on the strongest one last.

Letter to Young Lovers Imagine that Friar Laurence is approached by another young couple whose parents oppose their marriage. Write the friar's **letter of advice** to them. Based on his experiences with Romeo and Juliet, what would he tell another couple to do?

Other Options

Surviving the Tragedy Work with your classmates to enact a **counseling session** in which the surviving characters work through their feelings about the tragedy. One or two students should play counselors who mediate the discussion and the others should play characters in the play.

What Might Have Been Imagine that the friar's plan had worked and Romeo and Juliet ended up alive and together. Work with your classmates to create a **skit** showing the couple fifteen years later. What is their life like?

Set Design Imagine that you work as a set designer. You have been hired to design a **stage set** for a production of Shakespeare's *Romeo and Juliet*. Work with a partner to sketch or describe the set for two scenes from the play. Specify what the set would look like and what materials would be needed. Share your designs with the class.

Before Reading

Annabel Lee by Edgar Allan Poe
The Gift of the Magi by O. Henry

Edgar Allan Poe
1809–1849

Writer Edgar Allan Poe was known for his stinging criticism, but at home he lavished loving attention on his young wife. In 1836, Poe married his frail thirteen-year-old cousin, Virginia Clemm. Poe was heartbroken when she died at age 24 of tuberculosis, and he died two years later at the age of 40. For more information about Poe, see page 37.

O. Henry
1862–1910

While serving a prison term for embezzlement, William Sydney Porter began writing stories under the pseudonym O. Henry. After his release, he eventually settled in New York and wrote many stories about the people there.

Building Background

For Your Information Edgar Allan Poe wrote his poem "Annabel Lee" about his young wife Virginia Clemm, who died of tuberculosis. Poe never acknowledged the real cause of her death, merely saying that she had broken a blood vessel in a "singing accident."

The Magi (mā′jī) referred to in "The Gift of the Magi" were priests from ancient Persia. According to Matthew in the New Testament of the Bible, three Magi—or "Wise Men"—visited the infant Jesus in the stable where he was born, bearing gifts of gold, frankincense, and myrrh.

Literary Focus

Plot consists of the related events that occur in a story. A story with a conventional plot follows this pattern: a conflict or problem is established; complications arise from the conflict; a main character takes action or the situation itself brings about a climax; the conflict is resolved. Every author approaches plot in his or her own unique way. Some create loosely connected plots with little or no final resolution. Others write tightly woven plots with a clear conflict and resolution. What kind of plots do you prefer? Why? As you read "The Gift of the Magi," consider how O. Henry handles plot.

Writer's Notebook

Trials of Love The story and poem that follow are each about the obstacles faced by a young couple deeply in love. What do you think are some of the greatest obstacles a relationship can face? Record your ideas in your notebook.

Annabel Lee

Edgar

Allan

Poe

It was many and many a year ago,
    In a kingdom by the sea,
That a maiden there lived whom you may know
    By the name of Annabel Lee;—
5 And this maiden she lived with no other thought
    Than to love and be loved by me.

I was a child and *she* was a child,
    In this kingdom by the sea;
But we loved with a love that was more than love—
10   I and my Annabel Lee—
With a love that the winged seraphs[1] of Heaven
    Coveted[2] her and me.

And this was the reason that, long ago,
    In this kingdom by the sea,
15 A wind blew out of a cloud, chilling
    My beautiful Annabel Lee;
So that her high-born kinsmen came
    And bore her away from me,
To shut her up in a sepulcher,[3]
20   In this kingdom by the sea.

The angels, not half so happy in Heaven,
    Went envying her and me—
Yes!—that was the reason (as all men know,
    In this kingdom by the sea)
25 That the wind came out of the cloud by night,
    Chilling and killing my Annabel Lee.

But our love it was stronger by far than the love
    Of those who were older than we—
    Of many far wiser than we—
30 And neither the angels in Heaven above,
    Nor the demons down under the sea,
Can ever dissever[4] my soul from the soul
    Of the beautiful Annabel Lee:—

For the moon never beams, without bringing me dreams
35   Of the beautiful Annabel Lee;
And the stars never rise, but I feel the bright eyes
    Of the beautiful Annabel Lee;
And so, all the night-tide, I lie down by the side
Of my darling—my darling—my life and my bride,
40   In her sepulchre there by the sea—
    In her tomb by the sounding sea.

1. **seraph** (ser′əf), *n.* one of the highest order of angels.
2. **covet** (kuv′ət), *v.* desire something that belongs to others.
3. sepulcher (sep′əl kər), *n.* place of burial; tomb; grave.
4. **dissever** (di sev′ər), *v.* cut into parts; sever; separate.

▲ Eastman Johnson, *The Girl I Left Behind Me* (ca. 1870–1875). The title of the painting refers to an old Irish song that became a popular Civil War ballad. Do any elements in the painting hint that the young subject may have been left behind by a soldier gone off to war?

The Gift of the Magi

O. HENRY

◄ Gustave Courbet, *Portrait of Jo* (1866). What might the young woman in this painting be thinking as she gazes into the mirror?

One dollar and eighty-seven cents. That was all. And sixty cents of it was in pennies. Pennies saved one and two at a time by bulldozing the grocer and the vegetable man and the butcher until one's cheeks burned with the silent imputation of parsimony[1] that such close dealing implied. Three times Della counted it. One dollar and eighty-seven cents. And the next day would be Christmas.

There was clearly nothing to do but flop down on the shabby little couch and howl. So Della did it. Which instigates[2] the moral reflection that life is made up of sobs, sniffles, and smiles, with sniffles predominating.

While the mistress of the home is gradually subsiding from the first stage to the second, take a look at the home. A furnished flat at eight dollars per week. It did not exactly

---

1. **imputation** (im′pyŭ tā′shən) **of parsimony** (pär′sə-mō′nē), an accusation of stinginess.
2. instigate (in′stə gāt), v. urge on; stir up.

beggar description,[3] but it certainly had that word on the lookout for the mendicancy squad.[4]

In the vestibule below was a letter-box into which no letter would go, and an electric button from which no mortal finger could coax a ring. Also appertaining[5] thereunto was a card bearing the name "Mr. James Dillingham Young."

The "Dillingham" had been flung to the breeze during a former period of prosperity when its possessor was being paid thirty dollars per week. Now, when the income was shrunk to twenty dollars, the letters of "Dillingham" looked blurred, as though they were thinking seriously of contracting to a modest and unassuming D. But whenever Mr. James Dillingham Young came home and reached his flat above he was called "Jim" and greatly hugged by Mrs. James Dillingham Young, already introduced to you as Della. Which is all very good.

Della finished her cry and attended to her cheeks with the powder rag. She stood by the window and looked out dully at a gray cat walking a gray fence in a gray backyard. Tomorrow would be Christmas Day, and she had only one dollar and eighty-seven cents with which to buy Jim a present. She had been saving every penny she could for months, with this result. Twenty dollars a week doesn't go far. Expenses had been greater than she had calculated. They always are. Only one dollar and eighty-seven cents to buy a present for Jim. Her Jim. Many a happy hour she had spent planning for something nice for him. Something fine and rare and sterling—something just a little bit near to being worthy of the honor of being owned by Jim.

There was a pier-glass[6] between the windows of the room. Perhaps you have seen a pier-glass in an eight-dollar flat. A very thin and very agile person may, by observing his reflection in a rapid sequence of longitudinal[7] strips, obtain a fairly accurate conception of his looks. Della, being slender, had mastered the art.

Suddenly she whirled from the window and stood before the glass. Her eyes were shining

brilliantly, but her face had lost its color within twenty seconds. Rapidly she pulled down her hair and let it fall to its full length.

Now, there were two possessions of the James Dillingham Youngs in which they both took a mighty pride. One was Jim's gold watch that had been his father's and his grandfather's. The other was Della's hair. Had the Queen of Sheba[8] lived in the flat across the airshaft,[9] Della would have let her hair hang out the window someday to dry just to depreciate[10] Her Majesty's jewels and gifts. Had King Solomon[11] been the janitor, with all his treasures piled up in the basement, Jim would have pulled out his watch every time he passed, just to see him pluck at his beard from envy.

So now Della's beautiful hair fell about her rippling and shining like a cascade of brown waters. It reached below her knee and made itself almost a garment for her. And then she did it up again nervously and quickly. Once she faltered for a minute and stood still while a tear or two splashed on the worn red carpet.

On went her old brown jacket; on went her old brown hat. With a whirl of skirts and with the brilliant sparkle still in her eyes, she fluttered out the door and down the stairs to the street.

Where she stopped the sign read: "Mme. Sofronie. Hair Goods of All Kinds." One flight up Della ran, and collected herself, panting. Madame, large, too white, chilly, hardly looked the "Sofronie."

---

3. **beggar description,** exhaust the power to describe.
4. **mendicancy** (men′də kən sē) **squad,** a police squad that picked up illegal beggars.
5. **appertain** (ap′ər tān′), v. belong as a part.
6. **pier-glass** (pir′glas′), n. a long mirror designed for the narrow portion of wall between two windows.
7. **longitudinal** (lon′jə tüd′n əl), adj. running lengthwise.
8. **Queen of Sheba,** a wealthy, beautiful queen from northern Africa who visited King Solomon.
9. **airshaft** (er′shaft), n. an interior passageway for air.
10. depreciate (di prē′shē āt), v. lessen the value of.
11. **King Solomon,** a biblical king of Israel known for his wealth and wisdom.

"Will you buy my hair?" asked Della.

"I buy hair," said Madame. "Take yer hat off and let's have a sight at the looks of it."

Down rippled the brown cascade.

"Twenty dollars," said Madame, lifting the mass with a practiced hand.

"Give it to me quick," said Della.

Oh, and the next two hours tripped by on rosy wings. Forget the hashed metaphor. She was ransacking the stores for Jim's present.

She found it at last. It surely had been made for Jim and no one else. There was no other like it in any of the stores, and she had turned all of them inside out. It was a platinum fob chain[12] simple and chaste[13] in design, properly proclaiming its value by substance alone and not by meretricious[14] ornamentation—as all good things should do. It was even worthy of The Watch. As soon as she saw it she knew that it must be Jim's. It was like him. Quietness and value—the description applied to both. Twenty-one dollars they took from her for it, and she hurried home with the eighty-seven cents. With that chain on his watch Jim might be properly anxious about the time in any company. Grand as the watch was, he sometimes looked at it on the sly on account of the old leather strap that he used in place of a chain.

When Della reached home her intoxication gave way a little to prudence and reason. She got out her curling irons and lighted the gas and went to work repairing the ravages made by generosity added to love. Which is always a tremendous task, dear friends—a mammoth task.

Within forty minutes her head was covered with tiny, close-lying curls that made her look wonderfully like a truant schoolboy. She looked at her reflection in the mirror long, carefully, and critically.

"If Jim doesn't kill me," she said to herself, "before he takes a second look at me, he'll say I look like a Coney Island[15] chorus girl. But what could I do—oh! what could I do with a dollar and eighty-seven cents?"

At seven o'clock the coffee was made and the frying pan was on the back of the stove hot and ready to cook the chops.

Jim was never late. Della doubled the fob chain in her hand and sat on the corner of the table near the door that he always entered. Then she heard his step on the stair away down on the first flight, and she turned white for just a moment. She had a habit of saying little silent prayers about the simplest everyday things, and now she whispered "Please God, make him think I am still pretty."

The door opened and Jim stepped in and closed it. He looked thin and very serious. Poor fellow, he was only twenty-two—and to be burdened with a family! He needed a new overcoat and he was without gloves.

Jim stopped inside the door, as immovable as a setter at the scent of quail. His eyes were fixed upon Della, and there was an expression in them that she could not read, and it terrified her. It was not anger, nor surprise, nor disapproval, nor horror, nor any of the sentiments that she had been prepared for. He simply stared at her fixedly with that peculiar expression on his face.

Della wriggled off the table and went to him.

"Jim, darling," she cried, "don't look at me that way. I had my hair cut off and sold it because I couldn't have lived through Christmas without giving you a present. It'll grow out again—you won't mind, will you? I just had to do it. My hair grows awfully fast. Merry Christmas! Jim, and let's be happy. You don't know what a nice—what a beautiful, nice gift I've got for you."

"You've cut off your hair?" asked Jim, laboriously, as if he had not arrived at that patent[16] fact yet even after the hardest mental labor.

---

12. **fob chain**, a chain used to connect a pocket watch to a pocket.
13. **chaste** (chāst), *adj.* simple in style or taste.
14. **meretricious** (mer/ə trish/əs), *adj.* attractive in a showy way; alluring by false charms.
15. **Coney Island**, a beach and amusement park in Brooklyn, New York.
16. **patent** (pāt/nt), *adj.* evident; plain.

"Cut it off and sold it," said Della. "Don't you like me just as well, anyhow? I'm me without my hair, ain't I?"

Jim looked about the room curiously.

"You say your hair is gone?" he said, with an air almost of idiocy.

"You needn't look for it," said Della. "It's sold, I tell you—sold and gone, too. It's Christmas Eve, boy. Be good to me, for it went for you. Maybe the hairs of my head were numbered," she went on with a sudden serious sweetness, "but nobody could ever count my love for you. Shall I put the chops on, Jim?"

Out of his trance Jim seemed quickly to wake. He enfolded his Della. For ten seconds let us regard with discreet[17] scrutiny[18] some inconsequential object in the other direction. Eight dollars a week or a million a year—what is the difference? A mathematician or a wit would give you the wrong answer. The Magi brought valuable gifts, but that was not among them. This dark assertion will be illuminated later on.

Jim drew a package from his overcoat pocket and threw it upon the table.

"Don't make any mistake, Dell," he said, "about me. I don't think there's anything in the way of a haircut or a shave or a shampoo that could make me like my girl any less. But if you'll unwrap that package you may see why you had me going a while at first."

White fingers and nimble tore at the string and paper. And then an ecstatic scream of joy; and then, alas! a quick feminine change to hysterical tears and wails, necessitating the immediate employment of all the comforting powers of the lord of the flat.

For there lay The Combs—the set of combs, side and back, that Della had worshipped for long in a Broadway window. Beautiful combs, pure tortoise shell, with jeweled rims—just the shade to wear in the beautiful vanished hair. They were expensive combs, she knew, and her heart had simply craved and yearned over them

without the least hope of possession. And now, they were hers, but the tresses that should have adorned the coveted adornments were gone.

But she hugged them to her bosom, and at length she was able to look up with dim eyes and a smile and say: "My hair grows so fast, Jim!"

And then Della leaped up like a little singed cat and cried, "Oh, oh!"

Jim had not yet seen his beautiful present. She held it out to him eagerly upon her open palm. The dull precious metal seemed to flash with a reflection of her bright and ardent spirit.

"Isn't it a dandy, Jim? I hunted all over town to find it. You'll have to look at the time a hundred times a day now. Give me your watch. I want to see how it looks on it."

Instead of obeying, Jim tumbled down on the couch and put his hands under the back of his head and smiled.

"Della," said he, "let's put our Christmas presents away and keep 'em a while. They're too nice to use just at present. I sold the watch to get the money to buy your combs. And now suppose you put the chops on."

The Magi,[19] as you know, were wise men—wonderfully wise men—who brought gifts to the Babe in the manger. They invented the art of giving Christmas presents. Being wise, their gifts were no doubt wise ones, possibly bearing the privilege of exchange in case of duplication. And here I have lamely related to you the uneventful chronicle[20] of two foolish children in a flat who most unwisely sacrificed for each other the greatest treasures of their house. But in a last word to the wise of these days let it be said that of all who give gifts these two were the wisest. Of all who give and receive gifts, such as they are wisest. Everywhere they are wisest. They are the Magi.

---

17. **discreet** (dis krēt′), *adj.* very careful and sensible in speech and action; wisely cautious.
18. **scrutiny** (skrüt′n ē), *n.* close examination.
19. **Magi** (mā′jī, ma′jī), *n.* (in the Bible) the three wise men who brought gifts to the infant Jesus.
20. **chronicle** (kron′ə kəl), *n.* record of events in the order in which they took place; history; story.

The Gift of the Magi   **587**

After Reading

Making Connections

Shaping Your Response

1. How do the **rhythm** and **rhyme** of "Annabel Lee" affect your reaction to the poem?

2. Do you think Jim and Della are foolish to sacrifice their most prized possessions? Give reasons for your answer.

3. Point out the words and phrases that give "Annabel Lee" the qualities of a **fantasy.**

Analyzing the Selections

4. Why do you think Poe titled his poem "Annabel Lee" instead of "Virginia Clemm"?

5. Why do you think Jim has "an air almost of idiocy" when he first sees Della's short hair?

6. Even though Jim and Della are poor and have little money to buy each other Christmas presents, how does O. Henry create a humorous, optimistic **tone** in this story?

Extending the Ideas

7. Compare and contrast the endings of these love stories with the ending of *Romeo and Juliet*.

8. Do you think O. Henry would agree with the old saying "the best things in life are free"? Explain your answer.

Literary Focus: Plot

O. Henry's **plots** are known for their compactness, humorous situations, and surprise endings. Give examples of how Henry prepares readers for the surprise ending in "The Gift of the Magi." Then copy and complete the plot structure diagram for the story.

Climax

Falling
Action

Rising
Action

Conflict

Resolution

Della needs money
for Jim's present.

Vocabulary Study

Match each vocabulary word on the left with its synonym on the right. Use the Glossary if you need help with word meanings.

depreciate
discreet
instigate
scrutiny
sepulcher

1. instigate
2. depreciate
3. discreet
4. scrutiny
5. sepulcher

a. decry
b. examination
c. provoke
d. tomb
e. prudent

Expressing Your Ideas

Writing Choices

Writer's Notebook Update Look over your notes about the trials of love. Compare the issues you wrote about with the main obstacles faced by the two couples you've just read about.

Love in Verse "Annabel Lee" is a poem that tells a sad love story. Write your own **poem** about two people in love. Try to create and sustain a particular mood, whether joyful, sad, silly, or bittersweet, through your choice of words and the rhythm of the lines.

Same Time Next Year Using O. Henry's style, write a **sequel** to "The Gift of the Magi." What happens in the lives of Della and Jim next Christmas? Share your story with the class.

Other Options

Turn-of-the-Century Fashion Do some **research** to find out the fashion prevalent in New York at the time of the story's setting (1905). How did people of Jim and Della's social class dress and wear their hair? Why were a watch, a watch chain, long hair, and hair combs so significant to them? Present the results of your research to the class.

Stage Fright Edgar Allan Poe wrote many poems and short stories. His writing is famous for its mystery and terror. Memorize one of Poe's pieces and give a **performance** of it in class. Depending on the piece you choose, you may need to work with a partner.

Oh, Henry O. Henry was known for his plot twists and surprise endings. With a partner, read a few more stories by O. Henry. Then review the stories in a **class presentation,** giving a "thumbs up" or "thumbs down" rating for each story in terms of plot, characterization, and the story's general appeal.

Love and Sacrifice

The Art of Love

Popular Culture Connection

Throughout the ages, writers have been inspired by the tale of *Romeo and Juliet*. Humorist Merrill Markoe presents a very modern interpretation of that timeless tragedy.

This year, in honor of Valentine's Day, I decided to reread a true classic—*Romeo and Juliet*.

If you have not had the occasion to do so lately, please allow me to reacquaint you with the details of this timeless model of romantic love.

When we first meet the teenage Romeo, it is a Sunday night and he has decided to crash a ball just to catch a glimpse of Rosaline, a girl with whom he is desperately in love. Instead, he meets the thirteen-year-old Juliet. And even though only seconds before he was deeply in love with Rosaline, now he knows instantly that this thirteen-year-old girl is the greatest love of his life. Really. She is. He's not kidding this time.

DERANGED LOVE MUTANTS:

THE STORY OF ROMEO AND JULIET!

by MERRILL MARKOE

OH, ROMEO!
≶SIGH≶

Juliet has never been in love before. And yes, their two families hate each other. But so what? My parents never liked anyone I went out with either. The important thing is that by Monday afternoon, so beautiful is their love, they go ahead and get married.

Just one day later.

In lieu of a honeymoon, Romeo kills Juliet's cousin and Juliet goes back home to spend the night at her parents' house. Of course her parents do not know about the marriage yet, but they are so beside themselves with grief about the murdered cousin that Juliet's father decides there is no time like the present to arrange for Juliet to marry an older man.

Well, she is thirteen and not getting any younger. Soon, she'll be thirteen and a half. However, because he's an adult and not a hot-headed teenager, he really doesn't want to rush things. So he sets the wedding date for Thursday.

Naturally, the already-married Juliet realizes she must defy her father's wishes. She is no longer a co-dependent. She has boundaries and as a fully individualized adult, she must stand up to him and tell him her intentions. She takes the most sensible course of action under the circumstances. She pretends to be dead.

This also bodes very well for the future of her marriage to Romeo since we now know that the core of any "love-at-first-sight" attraction is usually "repetition compulsion"—wherein a person reenacts the identical behavior and problems first seen in the parent-child relationship.

Thank God both Romeo and Juliet killed themselves before we were able to chart their marriage any farther into the future when it most certainly would have descended into scenarios like this:

(Romeo enters parlor)

"Juliet! Juliet! My Light! I'm home! Juliet? Juliet? Juliet? Oh no. Honey. Not dead again. Don't tell me you're dead again. Please don't be playing dead again. You were just dead on Monday. I can't call 911 twice in one week. It's too embarrassing. Juliet? Juliet?"

Well, there you have this year's Valentine's Day poster couple. A thirteen-year-old girl who likes to pretend to be dead married to a teenage murderer who has no trouble falling in love with two different girls on the same Sunday night.

Which leaves us with this slightly comforting fact:

There is no reason to lament today's lack of viable romantic models. Things are no worse now than they ever were. The only difference is that back then no one watched Oprah or read psychology books. So they didn't mind calling deranged neurotic behavior "the greatest love story ever told."

Happy Valentine's Day.

Responding

1. Explain whether you agree or disagree with Markoe's analysis of Romeo and Juliet's relationship.

2. Markoe says of modern romance, "Things are no worse now than they ever were." What do you think?

2. Markoe's essay is a **satire** that pokes fun at a classic work of literature. Think of another classic you have heard or read and write a brief piece that satirizes it.

Humanities Connection

Romance during the Middle Ages centered on the ideals of courtly love, in which a knight or nobleman expressed his love for a noblewoman through great deeds, romantic songs, honorable conduct, and vows of eternal devotion. This love was usually unfulfilled, especially since the lady in question might already be married. In the 1100s, Andreas Capellanus, a court chaplain, composed a set of rules for courtly love, some of which appear here.

The Rules of Love

by Andreas Capellanus

Portrait of a Man and Woman at a Casement by Florentine painter **Fra Filippo Lippi (c.1406–1469).**

❖ Marriage is no real excuse for not loving.
❖ He who is not jealous cannot love.
❖ No one can be bound by a double love.
❖ It is well known that love is always increasing or decreasing.
❖ That which a lover takes against the will of his beloved has no relish.
❖ No one should be deprived of love without the very best of reasons.
❖ It is not proper to love any woman whom one would be ashamed to seek to marry.
❖ When made public love rarely endures.
❖ The easy attainment of love makes it of little value; difficulty of attainment makes it prized.
❖ A new love puts to flight an old one.
❖ Good character alone makes any man worthy of love.
❖ If love diminishes, it quickly fails and rarely revives.
❖ Jealousy, and therefore love, are increased when one suspects his beloved.
❖ Every act of a lover ends in the thought of his beloved.
❖ Love can deny nothing to love.
❖ A man who is vexed by too much passion usually does not love.
❖ A true lover is constantly and without intermission possessed by the thought of his beloved.
❖ Nothing forbids one woman being loved by two men or one man by two women.

Responding

1. Which of these "rules" surprise you? Explain why.

2. Would Romeo and Juliet agree with these rules? Give evidence for your answer.

Reading Mini-Lesson

Comparison and Contrast

Skilled readers often use comparison and contrast to gain a deeper understanding of what they read. In the article "Deranged Love Mutants: The Story of Romeo and Juliet," writer Merrill Markoe invites readers to compare and contrast Shakespeare's famous tragedy with her modern reinterpretation of it. By comparing and contrasting Markoe's article with Shakespeare's play, readers come away with two very different ways of looking at a classic story.

Markoe uses modern pop psychology terms to poke fun at "the greatest love story ever told." For example, she puts a modern spin on the feud between the Montagues and the Capulets: "And yes, their two families hate each other. But so what? My parents never liked anyone I went out with either." By telling the love story without much detail and without Shakespeare's poetic use of language, Markoe makes the tragedy seem ridiculous and funny. All this leads to her point—that this great love story may not be as romantic as we thought.

Now compare and contrast "The Rules of Love" on page 592 with "Deranged Love Mutants" and *Romeo and Juliet*. Do the three selections have anything in common? In what ways do they differ? Is "The Rules of Love" more similar in tone and theme to "Deranged Love Mutants" or to *Romeo and Juliet?*

Many authors use comparison and contrast to illustrate their points. Similarly, you may gain more from your reading when you find ways to compare and contrast the materials you read.

Activity Options

1. With a group of classmates, improvise a scene from *Romeo and Juliet* as Merrill Markoe might describe it. For example, in the improvisation, Romeo and Juliet should be played as typical teenagers in a modern world complete with telephones, dating, and high school.

2. With a partner, find at least two articles on the same subject in different magazines or newspapers. Compare and contrast the articles by preparing a chart that shows how they are similar and how they are different. Present your chart to the class and discuss your findings.

Writing Workshop

Examining a Tragedy

Assignment Several factors contributed to the tragic outcome of *Romeo and Juliet*. Write an essay in which you explain who or what you feel was the single most important cause of the young couple's tragic death.

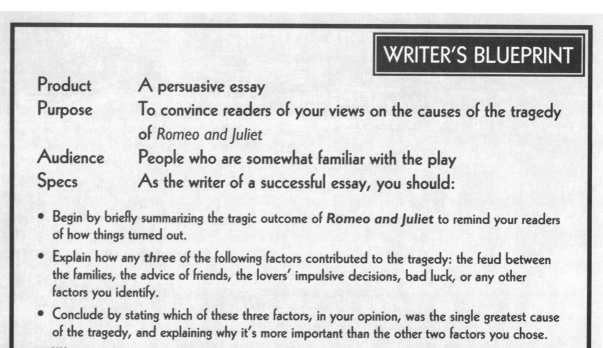

WRITER'S BLUEPRINT

Product	A persuasive essay
Purpose	To convince readers of your views on the causes of the tragedy of *Romeo and Juliet*
Audience	People who are somewhat familiar with the play
Specs	As the writer of a successful essay, you should:

- Begin by briefly summarizing the tragic outcome of **Romeo and Juliet** to remind your readers of how things turned out.

- Explain how any *three* of the following factors contributed to the tragedy: the feud between the families, the advice of friends, the lovers' impulsive decisions, bad luck, or any other factors you identify.

- Conclude by stating which of these three factors, in your opinion, was the single greatest cause of the tragedy, and explaining why it's more important than the other two factors you chose.

- Write paragraphs that each develop a general statement with specific examples.

- Follow the rules of grammar, usage, spelling, and mechanics. Pay special attention to using pronouns correctly.

Become the characters. Imagine that Romeo and Juliet came back to life and lived to adulthood. With a partner, act out a discussion between the lovers about the causes of their tragedy. Be sure to talk about each of the factors listed in the Specs of the Writer's Blueprint, as well as any new factors that might come out of your discussion. Take notes.

Examine the play. Now, working alone, examine the play and take more notes on the same factors you discussed in the first activity.

Rate each factor on a scale from 10 (a very important cause) to 1 (of little importance). Jot down reasons for your ratings. Based on these ratings, choose the three factors that you feel are the most important causes of the couple's tragic fate.

Examine the three factors closely. Jot down events and quotations from the play to support each factor you chose. Be sure to note the act and scene where your information came from. You might use a chart like this one.

Factor/Cause: Advice from friends	
Event #1	**Quote**
Friar Laurence advises Juliet to drink a potion (Act 4, Scene 1)	"Take thou this vial, being then in bed," (line 93)
Event #2	

Plan the essay. Use the information from your notes and chart to plan your essay. You might use the three-part plan that follows as a guide.

Introduction
- Key phrases that describe the tragic outcome of *Romeo and Juliet*

Body
- First factor that contributed to the outcome
- Specific events that involve this factor
- Quotes from the play for support

(Repeat for factors 2 and 3)

Conclusion
- Your choice for the greatest cause of the tragedy
- Reasons why it's more important than the other two factors

OR . . .
Write each factor on an index card and assign it a number from 1 to 3. On other cards with that same number, write the events and quotes that support that factor. Arrange the cards in order.

Ask a partner for comments on your plan before you begin drafting.

✔ Have I made it clear what three factors I chose?

✔ Have I made it clear which factor is most important?

✔ Have I cited specific examples to develop my ideas?

Use your partner's comments to revise your plan. If you need to make changes, use your chart of factors/causes for reference.

STEP 2 DRAFTING

Before you write, check your revised writing plan against the Writer's Blueprint one more time. Here are some ideas to help you as you draft.

• You may want to begin your essay with a few lines from the play. Choose lines that reflect the play's tragic outcome.

• When you draft the body, use transition words, such as *in addition, furthermore, again, also, likewise, similarly, then,* and *but,* to help you move from the discussion of one factor to the next.

Here is part of one student's draft. Notice how this writer uses transitions to connect ideas. The draft hasn't yet been proofread for spelling or punctuation; the writer will do that later.

STUDENT MODEL

Key impulsive decisions also factored into the outcome. It all starts with Romeo. He is the one who killed Tybalt in a fit of rage. Then, at the tomb, he is the one who poisoned himself. But it wasn't just Romeo's decisions that were bad. Juliet also agreed to secretly marry Romeo. This created a commitment that neither side had the power to follow through on. Furthermore, Capulet complicates the situation by offering Juliets hand in marriage to Paris.

Ask a partner for comments on your draft before you revise it.

✔ Which paragraphs could be improved by adding examples?

✔ Which paragraphs could be improved by removing examples?

✔ Are the general statements supported by specific examples?

Revising Strategy

Supporting General Statements

Readers need to see specific examples, such as facts and quotations from the play, to support your general statements. Without strong support, readers will be left wondering whether you really know what you're trying to say. Using specific examples inspires trust.

No Support   The family feud causes trouble and tragedy for everybody in the play. *(What trouble? What tragedy?)*

Support   The family feud causes much of the tragedy. It leads directly to Mercutio's death and indirectly to the death of the lovers.

Notice how the writer of this sample supports general statements with specific examples from the play.

> Many factors came together to cause the tragic deaths of Romeo
>
> and Juliet. Bad luck, impulsive decisions, and the feud between the two
>
> families all contributed to their fate. However, I think that the feud was
>
> *If the Montagues and Capulets had not feuded,*
> the most important factor. ~~It's too bad that Romeo and Juliet had to die,~~
> *then Romeo and Juliet would not have had to keep their love secret.*
> ~~but the way things were going it had to happen. And that's what~~
> *The secrets created communication problems that snowballed with*
> ~~happened in Romeo and Juliet.~~
> *each deception. If the feud had not existed, then many lives,*
>
> *including Romeo's and Juliet's, would have been spared.*

STUDENT MODEL

Ask a partner to review your revised draft before you edit. When you edit, look for errors in grammar, usage, spelling, and mechanics. Look especially for unclear pronoun references.

Editing Strategy

Using Clear Pronoun References

Sometimes readers can't tell to whom or to what a pronoun refers. As you proofread your essay, make sure that each pronoun clearly refers to a specific person, place, or thing.

Unclear   Romeo and Benvolio, Mercutio's friends, watch Tybalt flee. **He** realizes that **he** has killed **him.** *(Who realizes who has killed whom?)*

Clear   Romeo and Benvolio, Mercutio's friends, watch Tybalt flee. **Tybalt** realizes that he has killed **Mercutio.**

Notice how the writer of the draft below cleared up problems with pronoun reference.

> Bad luck also contributed to their tragic fate. Friar Laurence's plan
>
> to reunite Romeo and Juliet seemed foolproof until bad luck stepped in.
>
> First, Romeo never received his message explaining Juliet's "death."
> *Friar Laurence*
> When ~~he~~ finally heard of the mistake he sent another message but it was
> *Romeo*
> too late. ~~He~~ had already left.

STUDENT MODEL

FOR REFERENCE
See the Language and Grammar Handbook in the back of this book for more information on pronoun reference.

STEP  PRESENTING

Here are two ideas for presenting your essay.

- Write a tabloid headline to go over your essay and then post the essay on the bulletin board under its headline. One example might be "Family Feud Causes Fated Death!"

- Find a partner who chose a different factor from yours. Read your papers aloud to the class. Afterwards, the two of you can lead the class in a discussion of the differences in your views.

STEP LOOKING BACK

Self-evaluate. What grade would *you* give your essay? Look back at the Writer's Blueprint and give yourself a score for each point, from 6 (superior) to 1 (inadequate).

Reflect. Think about what you've learned from this essay and write your response to these reflections.

- Write your reactions to this statement based on what you learned about tragedy from writing your essay: "The world is a comedy to those who think, a tragedy to those who feel." (Horace Walpole).

- Which part of this paper was the easiest for you and which did you find most difficult? Explain why. What can you learn from your responses that will help you on your next writing assignment?

For Your Working Portfolio Add your persuasive essay and your reflection responses to your working portfolio.

Beyond Print

Performing Shakespeare

Of all the forms of art, drama is one that demands a high level of team-work and cooperation. To put on a play, the director, actors, musicians, designers, and members of the stage crew and technical crew must work out complex problems together. You can develop your collaborative skills by working with your classmates to present several scenes from *Romeo and Juliet* in a classroom production. Here are some tips for doing so.

Review the play. Go over the play again so that you know the story line very well. You might want to write an outline of the play on the board. Since you won't be performing the entire play, it's important to know what comes before and after the scenes you select.

Select the scenes and the actors. As a class, choose the scenes you want to perform. Reread and discuss those scenes. Assign the roles for each scene. If you have several different Romeos and Juliets, each actor can bring something different to the role. You might ask for your teacher's help in casting and in making final scene selections.

Rehearse. You will need to plan a number of rehearsals leading up to the actual performance. Your rehearsal schedule might look like this:

1. Read through the scenes and learn the language. If some of the speeches are hard to follow, ask your teacher's permission to cut some of the lines. (Shakespeare's plays are often pruned for performance.)

2. Read through the scenes again with all the language changes. Try to take on the personality and voice of the character you are playing.

3. Read through the scenes and block them, which means moving around and deciding who is standing where. Plan your entrances and exits, and decide what actions you'll carry out in each scene.

4. Memorize the lines or learn them so well that you need only glance down occasionally at a script or cards with your lines on them. Keep the dialogue moving; try not to have long pauses where everyone is lost.

5. Have a dress rehearsal—at least one run-through with no stops.

Prepare costumes and sets. Use your imagination for costumes and sets, and remember that even simple props can be quite effective. If you think it will help your audience, wear tags with your characters' names.

Perform the scenes. Perform the various scenes in the order they appear in the play. You might have a narrator introduce each scene with a brief summary of what has already taken place. When you're not on stage, become a thoughtful viewer. Observe your classmates closely and take notes for later discussion.

Activity Options

1. Discuss your performance with your classmates. What did you learn by performing *Romeo and Juliet?* What did you learn about your character? about other characters? about the themes?

2. Discuss the experience of working together on a class production of the play. What surprised you about the experience? What was easier than you expected? What was harder than you expected?

3. Put together a class album that describes, with words and pictures, the process of planning and presenting your production of scenes from *Romeo and Juliet*.

Multicultural Connections

Interactions

Love and Sacrifice If not resolved, the tensions that arise out of the interactions of different groups can sometimes lead to tragedy. In *Romeo and Juliet*, the conflict between the Montagues and the Capulets leads to the tragic death of the two young lovers.

■ Re-examine the play. What reasons might the Montagues and Capulets have had for not getting along in the first place?

■ What kinds of intergroup tensions are hinted at in "Annabel Lee"?

Activities

1. The characters in *Romeo and Juliet* have different attitudes toward the feud between the Montagues and the Capulets. On a chart like the one shown here, list each major character in the play, state his or her attitude toward the feud, and describe the probable motivation behind that attitude.

Character	Attitude toward feud	Motivation
Romeo	He wants to end it.	He is in love with Juliet.
Juliet		
Tybalt		

2. In a small group, do some research on mediation, or conflict resolution. What are some common techniques that are used to settle differences among individuals or groups? Then imagine that your group has been asked to mediate the feud between the Montagues and the Capulets. Develop a plan for helping the two families resolve their differences.

3. Romeo and Juliet, Annabel Lee and her lover, and Jim and Della are appearing on a daytime talk show to discuss the conflicts they must face in their relationships. With a small group, brainstorm what each couple would probably have to say about this topic and present a skit of the talk show segment.

Independent and Group Projects

Art

Designed by You Many famous designers have created their own unique interpretations of the costumes and set design for theater productions of *Romeo and Juliet*. Choose a memorable scene from the play. Create a series of sketches for either the costumes or the stage set that would be used in that particular scene.

Oral Presentation

Strong Words The selections in Unit 4 are full of vivid images and rhythmic language. Memorize a passage from one of the selections in Unit 4 and present it to the class. Be sure to put appropriate expression in your voice and use meaningful gestures.

Drama

Modern Interpretation Choose a scene from *Romeo and Juliet* or one of the other selections in Unit 4 and prepare a skit that presents a modern-day version of the scene. Think about how to update the language, references, and setting of the scene you choose.

Research

Wedding Bells Around the world, people have very different customs regarding courtship and marriage. Choose a culture from another part of the world and investigate courtship and marriage customs there. Consider questions like the following: At what age do the people usually marry? Who chooses a marriage partner? If a dowry is involved, what is it and who gets it? How is the marriage ceremony conducted? After the marriage, how do the bride and groom relate to the families on both sides?

Making a Difference

Unexpected Heroes

The Price of Wisdom

Reading

Nonfiction is literature about real people and events. While fiction may carry you into imaginary worlds, nonfiction offers the pleasure of exploring some aspect of the real world.

Consider, for example, Maya Angelou. This well-known writer and actress has written, in addition to poetry, screenplays, and children's stories, many nonfiction books, essays, and articles. She has told the story of her life in a series of autobiographies, beginning with *I Know Why the Caged Bird Sings*. Other people have written about Angelou in books and articles about her life, reviews of her work, interviews, biographical entries in reference books, and even articles in supermarket tabloids. All these are forms of nonfiction (though the tabloids certainly stretch the definition). If you want to learn more about Maya Angelou, you have a wealth of nonfiction sources to choose from.

The types of nonfiction you will encounter in Unit Five include autobiographies, biographies, and essays, including an excerpt from *I Know Why the Caged Bird Sings* (page 610). Other forms of nonfiction include letters, speeches, reviews, and diaries.

AUTOBIOGRAPHIES AND BIOGRAPHIES

In an **autobiography,** the writer describes significant events in his or her own life. By its nature, an autobiography is not an objective, impartial work. Instead, it offers a unique and deeply personal insight into the mind and heart of the writer.

In a **biography,** the writer describes events in another person's life from a third-person point of view. To prepare for writing, a biographer may examine thousands of documents, visit the place where the subject lived, interview the subject if possible, and talk with the person's relatives, friends, or associates. Compiling this information may take years.

While many biographers strive for an impartial view of the subject, some present biased or sensational conclusions. In reading a biography, it is important to consider what is factual information and what is the opinion of the biographer.

N o n f i c t i o n

Tips for Reading Autobiographies and Biographies

- *Keep in mind what you already know, if anything, about the person you are reading about.*
- *Look for the same elements you find in fiction—**characterization, theme, plot,** and **setting.***
- *Ask yourself why the author has chosen to describe particular incidents. What do these incidents reveal?*
- *When reading an autobiography, consider how the writer's personal feelings may affect his or her interpretation of certain events.*
- *When reading a biography, notice how the biographer weaves together factual information and opinions about the subject. Do you agree with those opinions?*

ESSAYS

In an **essay,** a writer explores a particular topic and expresses an opinion or comes to a conclusion. An essay is usually brief, reflecting the author's attitudes and knowledge at a given moment. Potential topics for an essay are virtually unlimited.

Depending on the subject, the author of an essay may choose a **formal** or an **informal** style. The formal essay is usually marked by its serious purpose, dignified tone, and logical organization. The informal essay is characterized by its rambling structure, unconventional theme, casual tone, and the author's personal involvement.

Tips for Reading Essays

- *Identify the **main idea** or **theme.** It may be stated directly, often near the beginning or the end of the essay, or merely be implied.*
- *Find the **supporting details**—facts, arguments, and examples—that the author uses to illustrate or defend the main idea.*
- *Decide which statements in the piece are **facts** and which are **opinions.***
- *Use your own knowledge and experience to decide whether or not you agree with the author's **conclusion.***

MULTICULTURAL VOICES

FOREWORD BY RITA DOVE

Angelou
WOULDN'T TAKE NOTHING FOR MY JOURNEY NOW

MAYA ANGELOU
I Know Why the Caged Bird Sings

Part One

Unexpected Heroes

Who is a hero? Someone who leaps tall buildings in a single bound, and saves a city from certain doom? Can a hero be someone who, without any super powers, works hard to make life better? The selections you are about to read may give you a new perspective on heroism.

🐾 Multicultural Focus **Individuality** may represent either a challenge or an affirmation of cultural traditions and group identity. In the following selections, does the expression of individuality threaten or strengthen the larger community?

Graduation

by Maya Angelou

Maya Angelou
born 1928

Born in St. Louis, Maya Angelou (an′jə lō) went to live with her grandmother in Stamps, Arkansas, after her parents' marriage broke up. She began a theatrical career in 1954, touring in *Porgy and Bess* and in off-Broadway shows. She has written short plays, television documentaries, and films, and has worked as a newspaper editor in Egypt, an administrator at the University of Ghana, and lecturer at various American universities. Her autobiography *I Know Why the Caged Bird Sings,* from which "Graduation" is taken, is perhaps her best-known work. Angelou was chosen by President Clinton to write a special poem for his inauguration in 1992.

Building Background

Separate But Equal? Although slavery was abolished in the U.S. after the Civil War, prejudice against African Americans still existed, especially in the South. In 1896, the U.S. Supreme Court established the principle of "separate but equal," legitimizing "Jim Crow" laws throughout the southern states. Named after a character in a minstrel show, Jim Crow laws by 1914 essentially created two societies—one black, one white. Separate facilities were established for blacks and whites, including schools, restaurants, streetcars, hospitals, and even cemeteries. In 1954, the Supreme Court decided that segregation in public schools was unconstitutional, and the Jim Crow laws eventually crumbled. The autobiography you are about to read refers to this kind of segregation, in that the county has two separate schools—one for black students and one for white students. As you read, consider whether these schools are truly "separate but equal." What kinds of opportunities exist for students at each school?

Literary Focus

Symbol A **symbol** is something concrete—a person, place, event, or object—that suggests something more abstract, such as an idea, a feeling, or an emotion. A heart, for example, is an organ in the body, but it also stands for love. Authors often use symbols to enrich their stories, poems, or dramas.

Writer's Notebook

Surprise! Describe in your log a time when something turned out differently than you expected. What was the event or circumstance? What did you expect to happen, and what happened instead? Did you learn anything from this situation?

Graduation

Maya Angelou

The children in Stamps[1] trembled visibly with anticipation. Some adults were excited too, but to be certain the whole young population had come down with graduation epidemic. Large classes were graduating from both the grammar school and the high school. Even those who were years removed from their own day of glorious release were anxious to help with preparations as a kind of dry run.[2] The junior students who were moving into the vacating classes' chairs were tradition-bound to show their talents for leadership and management. They strutted through the school and around the campus exerting pressure on the lower grades. Their authority was so new that occasionally if they pressed a little too hard it had to be overlooked. After all, next term was coming, and it never hurt a sixth grader to have a play sister in the eighth grade, or a tenth-year student to be able to call a twelfth grader Bubba. So all was endured in a spirit of shared understanding. But the graduating classes themselves were the nobility. Like travelers with exotic destinations on their minds, the graduates were remarkably forgetful. They came to school without their books, or tablets or even pencils. Volunteers fell over themselves to secure replacements for the missing equipment. When accepted, the willing workers might or might not be thanked, and it was of no importance to the pregraduation rites. Even teachers were respectful of the now quiet and aging seniors, and tended to speak to them, if not as equals, as beings only slightly lower than themselves. After tests were returned and grades given, the student body, which acted like an extended family, knew who did well, who excelled, and what piteous ones had failed.

Unlike the white high school, Lafayette County Training School distinguished itself by having neither lawn, nor hedges, nor tennis court, nor climbing ivy. Its two buildings (main classrooms, the grade school and home economics) were set on a dirt hill with no fence to limit either its boundaries or those of bordering farms. There was a large expanse to the left of the school which was used alternately as a baseball diamond or a basketball court. Rusty hoops on the swaying poles represented the permanent recreational equipment, although bats and balls could be borrowed from the P.E. teacher if the borrower was qualified and if the diamond wasn't occupied.

Over this rocky area relieved by a few shady tall persimmon trees the graduating class walked. The girls often held hands and no longer bothered to speak to the lower students.

---

1. **Stamps,** Stamps, Arkansas, where Maya Angelou lived with her grandmother.
2. **dry run,** a practice.

Stephen Scott Young, *Westwind* (1993). What personality traits would you associate with the young girl portrayed in this watercolor?

There was a sadness about them, as if this old world was not their home and they were bound for higher ground. The boys, on the other hand, had become more friendly, more outgoing. A decided change from the closed attitude they projected while studying for finals. Now they seemed not ready to give up the old school, the familiar paths and classrooms. Only a small percentage would be continuing on to college—one of the South's A & M (agricultural and mechanical) schools, which trained Negro youths to be carpenters, farmers, handymen, masons, maids, cooks and baby nurses. Their future rode heavily on their shoulders, and blinded them to the collective joy that had pervaded[3] the lives of the boys and girls in the grammar school graduating class.

Parents who could afford it had ordered new shoes and ready-made clothes for themselves from Sears and Roebuck or Montgomery Ward. They also engaged the best seamstresses to make the floating graduating dresses and to cut down secondhand pants which would be pressed to a military slickness for the important event.

Oh, it was important, all right. Whitefolks would attend the ceremony, and two or three would speak of God and home, and the Southern way of life, and Mrs. Parsons, the principal's wife, would play the graduation march while the lower-grade graduates paraded down the aisles and took their seats below the platform. The high school seniors would wait in empty classrooms to make their dramatic entrance.

In the Store I was the person of the moment. The birthday girl. The center. Bailey had graduated the year before, although to do so he had had to forfeit[4] all pleasures to make up for his time lost in Baton Rouge.[5]

My class was wearing butter-yellow piqué[6] dresses, and Momma launched out on mine. She smocked the yoke into tiny crisscrossing puckers, then shirred the rest of the bodice.

Her dark fingers ducked in and out of the lemony cloth as she embroidered raised daisies around the hem. Before she considered herself finished she had added a crocheted cuff on the puff sleeves, and a pointy crocheted collar.

It was going to be lovely. A walking model of all the various styles of fine hand sewing and it didn't worry me that I was only twelve years old and merely graduating from the eighth grade. Besides, many teachers in Arkansas Negro schools had only that diploma and were licensed to impart[7] wisdom.

The days had become longer and more noticeable. The faded beige of former times had been replaced with strong and sure colors. I began to see my classmates' clothes, their skin tones, and the dust that waved off pussy willows. Clouds that lazed across the sky were objects of great concern to me. Their shiftier shapes might have held a message that in my new happiness and with a little bit of time I'd soon decipher.[8] During that period I looked at the arch of heaven so religiously my neck kept a steady ache. I had taken to smiling more often, and my jaws hurt from the unaccustomed activity. Between the two physical sore spots, I suppose I could have been uncomfortable, but that was not the case. As a member of the winning team (the graduating class of 1940) I had outdistanced unpleasant sensations by miles. I was headed for the freedom of open fields.

---

3. **pervade** (pər vād′), v. spread throughout.
4. **forfeit** (fôr′fit), v. lose or have to give up by one's own act, neglect, or fault.
5. **Baton Rouge** (bat′n rüzh′), capital of Louisiana. The previous year, Angelou's brother Bailey had hopped a freight train hoping to get to California. Instead he was stranded for two weeks in Baton Rouge before returning home to Stamps.
6. **piqué** (pi kā′), v. fabric of cotton, rayon, or silk, with narrow ribs or raised stripes.
7. **impart** (im pärt′), v. communicate; tell.
8. **decipher** (di sī′fər), v. make out the meaning of something that is not clear.

Youth and social approval allied themselves with me and we trammeled[9] memories of slights and insults. The wind of our swift passage remodeled my features. Lost tears were pounded to mud and then to dust. Years of withdrawal were brushed aside and left behind, as hanging ropes of parasitic[10] moss.

My work alone had awarded me a top place and I was going to be one of the first called in the graduation ceremonies. On the classroom blackboard, as well as on the bulletin board in the auditorium, there were blue stars and white stars and red stars. No absences, no tardinesses, and my academic work was among the best of the year. I could say the preamble to the Constitution even faster than Bailey. We timed ourselves often: "WethepeopleoftheUnitedStatesinordertoforma moreperfectunion . . ." I had memorized the Presidents of the United States from Washington to Roosevelt in chronological as well as alphabetical order.

My hair pleased me too. Gradually the black mass had lengthened and thickened, so that it kept at last to its braided pattern, and I didn't have to yank my scalp off when I tried to comb it.

Louise and I had rehearsed the exercises until we tired out ourselves. Henry Reed was class valedictorian. He was a small, very black boy with hooded eyes, a long, broad nose and an oddly shaped head. I had admired him for years because each term he and I vied[11] for the best grades in our class. Most often he bested me, but instead of being disappointed I was pleased that we shared top places between us. Like many Southern Black children, he lived with his grandmother, who was as strict as Momma and as kind as she knew how to be. He was courteous, respectful and soft-spoken to elders, but on the playground he chose to play the roughest games. I admired him. Anyone, I reckoned, sufficiently afraid or sufficiently dull could be polite. But to be able to operate at a top level with both adults and children was admirable.

His valedictory speech was entitled "To Be or Not to Be." The rigid tenth-grade teacher had helped him write it. He'd been working on the dramatic stresses for months.

The weeks until graduation were filled with heady activities. A group of small children were to be presented in a play about buttercups and daisies and bunny rabbits. They could be heard throughout the building practicing their hops and their little songs that sounded like silver bells. The older girls (non-graduates, of course) were assigned the task of making refreshments for the night's festivities. A tangy scent of ginger, cinnamon, nutmeg and chocolate wafted around the home economics building as the budding cooks made samples for themselves and their teachers.

In every corner of the workshop, axes and saws split fresh timber as the woodshop boys made sets and stage scenery. Only the graduates were left out of the general bustle. We were free to sit in the library at the back of the building or look in quite detachedly, naturally, on the measures being taken for our event.

Even the minister preached on graduation the Sunday before. His subject was, "Let your light so shine that men will see your good works and praise your Father, Who is in Heaven." Although the sermon was purported to be addressed to us, he used the occasion to speak to backsliders,[12] gamblers and general ne'er-do-wells.[13] But since he had called our names at the beginning of the service we were mollified.[14]

Among Negroes the tradition was to give presents to children going only from one grade

---

9. **trammel** (tram′əl), *v.* restrain; hold back.
10. **parasitic** (par′ə sit′ik), *adj.* of or like a parasite; living on others.
11. **vie** (vī), *v.* strive for superiority; compete.
12. **backslider** (bak′slīd′ər), *n.* person who slides back into wrongdoing, especially to practices forbidden by the church.
13. **ne'er-do-well** (ner′dü wel′), *n.* irresponsible or good-for-nothing person.
14. **mollified** (mol′ə fīd), *adj.* softened in temper; calmed, pacified, or appeased; mitigated.

to another. How much more important this was when the person was graduating at the top of the class. Uncle Willie and Momma had sent away for a Mickey Mouse watch like Bailey's. Louise gave me four embroidered handkerchiefs. (I gave her three crocheted doilies.) Mrs. Sneed, the minister's wife, made me an underskirt to wear for graduation, and nearly every customer gave me a nickel or maybe even a dime with the instruction "Keep on moving to higher ground," or some such encouragement.

Amazingly the great day finally dawned and I was out of bed before I knew it. I threw open the back door to see it more clearly, but Momma said, "Sister, come away from that door and put your robe on."

I hoped the memory of that morning would never leave me. Sunlight was itself still young, and the day had none of the insistence maturity would bring it in a few hours. In my robe and barefoot in the backyard, under cover of going to see about my new beans, I gave myself up to the gentle warmth and thanked God that no matter what evil I had done in my life He had allowed me to live to see this day. Somewhere in my fatalism I had expected to die, accidentally, and never have the chance to walk up the stairs in the auditorium and gracefully receive my hard-earned diploma. Out of God's merciful bosom I had won reprieve.[15]

Bailey came out in his robe and gave me a box wrapped in Christmas paper. He said he had saved his money for months to pay for it. It felt like a box of chocolates, but I knew Bailey wouldn't save money to buy candy when we had all we could want under our noses.

He was as proud of the gift as I. It was a soft-leather-bound copy of a collection of poems by Edgar Allan Poe, or, as Bailey and I called him,

I hoped the memory of that morning would never leave me.

"Eap." I turned to "Annabel Lee" and we walked up and down the garden rows, the cool dirt between our toes, reciting the beautifully sad lines.

Momma made a Sunday breakfast although it was only Friday. After we finished the blessing, I opened my eyes to find the watch on my plate. It was a dream of a day. Everything went smoothly and to my credit. I didn't have to be reminded or scolded for anything. Near evening I was too jittery to attend to chores, so Bailey volunteered to do all before his bath.

Days before, we had made a sign for the Store, and as we turned out the lights Momma hung the cardboard over the doorknob. It read clearly: CLOSED. GRADUATION.

My dress fitted perfectly and everyone said that I looked like a sunbeam in it. On the hill, going toward the school, Bailey walked behind with Uncle Willie, who muttered, "Go on, Ju." He wanted him to walk ahead with us because it embarrassed him to have to walk so slowly. Bailey said he'd let the ladies walk together, and the men would bring up the rear. We all laughed, nicely.

Little children dashed by out of the dark like fireflies. Their crepe-paper dresses and butterfly wings were not made for running and we heard more than one rip, dryly, and the regretful "uh uh" that followed.

The school blazed without gaiety. The windows seemed cold and unfriendly from the lower hill. A sense of ill-fated timing crept over

---

15. **reprieve** (ri prēv′), *n.* temporary relief from any evil or trouble.

Anna Belle Lee Washington, *Sunday*. What details in this painting reveal that a special occasion is taking place?

me, and if Momma hadn't reached for my hand I would have drifted back to Bailey and Uncle Willie, and possibly beyond. She made a few slow jokes about my feet getting cold, and tugged me along to the now-strange building.

Around the front steps, assurance came back. There were my fellow "greats," the graduating class. Hair brushed back, legs oiled, new dresses and pressed pleats, fresh pocket handkerchiefs and little handbags, all homesewn. Oh, we were up to snuff,[16] all right. I joined my comrades and didn't even see my family go in to find seats in the crowded auditorium.

The school band struck up a march and all classes filed in as had been rehearsed. We stood in front of our seats, as assigned, and on a signal from the choir director, we sat. No sooner had this been accomplished than the band started to play the national anthem. We rose again and sang the song, after which we recited the pledge of allegiance. We remained standing for a brief minute before the choir director and the principal signaled to us, rather desperately I thought, to take our seats. The command was so unusual that our carefully rehearsed and smooth-running machine was thrown off. For a full minute we fumbled for our chairs and bumped into each other awkwardly. Habits change or solidify under pressure, so in our state of nervous tension we had been ready to follow our usual assembly pattern: the American national anthem, then the pledge of allegiance, then the song every Black person I knew called the Negro National Anthem.[17] All done in the same key, with the same passion and most often standing on the same foot.

16. **up to snuff,** meeting expectations or standards.
17. **Negro National Anthem,** "Lift Ev'ry Voice and Sing," by James Weldon Johnson and J. Rosamond Johnson.

F inding my seat at last, I was overcome with a presentiment[18] of worse things to come. Something unrehearsed, unplanned, was going to happen, and we were going to be made to look bad. I distinctly remember being explicit in the choice of pronoun. It was "we," the graduating class, the unit, that concerned me then.

The principal welcomed "parents and friends" and asked the Baptist minister to lead us in prayer. His invocation was brief and punchy, and for a second I thought we were getting back on the high road to right action. When the principal came back to the dais,[19] however, his voice had changed. Sounds always affected me profoundly and the principal's voice was one of my favorites. During assembly it melted and lowed weakly into the audience. It had not been in my plan to listen to him, but my curiosity was piqued[20] and I straightened up to give him my attention.

He was talking about Booker T. Washington,[21] our "late great leader," who said we can be as close as the fingers on the hand, etc. . . . Then he said a few vague things about friendship and the friendship of kindly people to those less fortunate than themselves. With that his voice nearly faded, thin, away. Like a river diminishing to a stream and then to a trickle. But he cleared his throat and said, "Our speaker tonight, who is also our friend, came from Texarkana[22] to deliver the commencement address, but due to the irregularity of the train schedule, he's going to, as they say, 'speak and run.'" He said that we understood and wanted the man to know that we were most grateful for the time he was able to give us and then something about how we were willing always to adjust to another's program, and without more ado—"I give you Mr. Edward Donleavy."

Not one but two white men came through the door offstage. The shorter one walked to the speaker's platform, and the tall one moved over to the center seat and sat down. But that was our principal's seat, and already occupied. The dislodged gentleman bounced around for a long breath or two before the Baptist minister gave him his chair, then with more dignity than the situation deserved, the minister walked off the stage.

Donleavy looked at the audience once (on reflection, I'm sure that he wanted only to reassure himself that we were really there), adjusted his glasses and began to read from a sheaf of papers.

He was glad "to be here and to see the work going on just as it was in the other schools."

At the first "Amen" from the audience I willed the offender to immediate death by choking on the word. But Amens and Yes, sir's began to fall around the room like rain through a ragged umbrella.

He told us of the wonderful changes we children in Stamps had in store. The Central School (naturally, the white school was Central) had already been granted improvements that would be in use in the fall. A well-known artist was coming from Little Rock to teach art to them. They were going to have the newest microscopes and chemistry equipment for their laboratory. Mr. Donleavy didn't leave us long in the dark over who made these improvements available to Central High. Nor were we to be ignored in the general betterment scheme he had in mind.

He said that he had pointed out to people at a very high level that one of the first-line football tacklers at Arkansas Agricultural and Mechanical College had graduated from good old Lafayette County Training School. Here fewer Amen's were heard. Those few that did break through lay dully in the air with the heaviness of habit.

He went on to praise us. He went on to say how he had bragged that "one of the best

---

18. **presentiment** (pri zen′tə mənt), *n.* a feeling that something, especially something evil, is about to happen.
19. **dais** (dā′is), *n.* a raised platform.
20. **piqued** (pēkd), *adj.* aroused, stirred up.
21. **Booker T. Washington,** 1856–1915, African American writer and educator who worked for civil rights.
22. **Texarkana,** a city in southwest Arkansas.

basketball players at Fisk sank his first ball right here at Lafayette County Training School."

The white kids were going to have a chance to become Galileos and Madame Curies and Edisons and Gauguins, and our boys (the girls weren't even in on it) would try to be Jesse Owenses and Joe Louises.[23]

Owens and the Brown Bomber were great heroes in our world, but what school official in the white-goddom of Little Rock had the right to decide that those two men must be our only heroes? Who decided that for Henry Reed to become a scientist he had to work like George Washington Carver,[24] as a bootblack,[25] to buy a lousy microscope? Bailey was obviously always going to be too small to be an athlete, so which concrete angel glued to what country seat had decided that if my brother wanted to become a lawyer he had to first pay penance for his skin by picking cotton and hoeing corn and studying correspondence books at night for twenty years?

The man's dead words fell like bricks around the auditorium and too many settled in my belly. Constrained[26] by hard-learned manners I couldn't look behind me, but to my left and right the proud graduating class of 1940 had dropped their heads. Every girl in my row had found something new to do with her handkerchief. Some folded the tiny squares into love knots, some into triangles, but most were wadding them, then pressing them flat on their yellow laps.

On the dais, the ancient tragedy was being replayed. Professor Parsons sat, a sculptor's reject, rigid. His large, heavy body seemed devoid[27] of will or willingness, and his eyes said he was no longer with us. The other teachers examined the flag (which was draped stage right) or their notes, or the windows which opened on our now-famous playing diamond.

Graduation, the hush-hush magic time of frills and gifts and congratulations and diplomas, was finished for me before my name was called. The accomplishment was nothing. The

meticulous[28] maps, drawn in three colors of ink, learning and spelling decasyllabic[29] words, memorizing the whole of *The Rape of Lucrece*[30]— it was for nothing. Donleavy had exposed us.

We were maids and farmers, handymen and washerwomen, and anything higher that we aspired to was farcical[31] and presumptuous.[32]

Then I wished that Gabriel Prosser and Nat Turner[33] had killed all whitefolks in their beds and that Abraham Lincoln had been assassinated before the signing of the Emancipation Proclamation, and that Harriet Tubman[34] had been killed by that blow on her head and Christopher Columbus had drowned in the *Santa María*.

It was awful to be Negro and have no control over my life. It was brutal to be young and already trained to sit quietly and listen to charges brought against my color with no chance of defense. We

23. **Galileos . . . Joe Louises.** Galileo (gal′ə lā′ō), 1564-1642, was an Italian astronomer, physicist, mathematician, and inventor. Polish-born Marie Curie, 1867–1934, was a physicist and chemist. Thomas Alva Edison, 1847–1931, was an American inventor. Paul Gauguin (gō gan′), 1848–1903, was a French painter. Jesse Owens, 1913–1980, an African American athlete, was the star of the 1936 Olympic games. Joe Louis (1914–1981), nicknamed "The Brown Bomber," was the first African American heavyweight boxing champion of the world.
24. **George Washington Carver,** 1864?–1943, African American botanist and chemist.
25. **bootblack** (bŭt′blak′), *n.* person whose work is shining shoes and boots.
26. constrained (kən strānd′), *adj.* restrained; forced.
27. **devoid** (di void′), *adj.* entirely without; empty.
28. meticulous (mə tik′yə ləs), *adj.* extremely careful about details.
29. **decasyllabic** (dek′ə sə lab′ik), *adj.* having ten syllables.
30. *The Rape of Lucrece*, a long poem by Shakespeare.
31. **farcical** (fär′sə kəl), *adj.* of or like a farce; ridiculous.
32. presumptuous (pri zump′chü əs), *adj.* acting without permission or right; too bold; forward.
33. **Gabriel Prosser and Nat Turner,** African Americans who led rebellions against slavery.
34. **Harriet Tubman,** an African American abolitionist who escaped from slavery and led many other people to freedom on the Underground Railroad.

should all be dead. I thought I should like to see us all dead, one on top of the other. A pyramid of flesh with the whitefolks on the bottom, as the broad base, then the Indians with their silly tomahawks and teepees and wigwams and treaties, the Negroes with their mops and recipes and cotton sacks and spirituals sticking out of their mouths. The Dutch children should all stumble in their wooden shoes and break their necks. The French should choke to death on the Louisiana Purchase (1803) while silkworms ate all the Chinese with their stupid pigtails. As a species, we were an abomination.[35] All of us.

Donleavy was running for election, and assured our parents that if he won we could count on having the only colored paved playing field in that part of Arkansas. Also—he never looked up to acknowledge the grunts of acceptance—also, we were bound to get some new equipment for the home economics building and the workshop.

He finished, and since there was no need to give any more than the most perfunctory[36] thank-you's, he nodded to the men on the stage, and the tall white man who was never introduced joined him at the door. They left with the attitude that now they were off to something really important. (The graduation ceremonies at Lafayette County Training School had been a mere preliminary.)

The ugliness they left was palpable. An uninvited guest who wouldn't leave. The choir was summoned and sang a modern arrangement of "Onward, Christian Soldiers," with new words pertaining to graduates seeking their place in the world. But it didn't work. Elouise, the daughter of the Baptist minister, recited "Invictus," and I could have cried at the impertinence[37] of "I am the master of my fate, I am the captain of my soul."

My name had lost its ring of familiarity and I had to be nudged to go and receive my diploma. All my preparations had fled. I neither marched up to the stage like a conquering Amazon,[38] nor did I look in the audience for Bailey's nod of approval. Marguerite Johnson, I heard the name again, my honors were read, there were noises in the audience of appreciation, and I took my place on the stage as rehearsed.

I thought about colors I hated: ecru, puce, lavender, beige and black.

There was shuffling and rustling around me, then Henry Reed was giving his valedictory address, "To Be or Not to Be."[39] Hadn't he heard the whitefolks? We couldn't *be*, so the question was a waste of time. Henry's voice came out clear and strong. I feared to look at him. Hadn't he got the message? There was no "nobler in the mind" for Negroes because the world didn't think we had minds, and they let us know it. "Outrageous fortune"? Now, that was a joke. When the ceremony was over I had to tell Henry Reed some things. That is, if I still cared. Not "rub," Henry, "erase." "Ah, there's the erase." Us.

Henry had been a good student in elocution.[40] His voice rose on tides of promise and fell on waves of warnings. The English teacher had helped him to create a sermon winging through Hamlet's soliloquy. To be a man, a doer, a builder, a leader, or to be a tool, an unfunny joke, a crusher of funky toadstools. I marveled that Henry could go through with the speech as if we had a choice.

---

35. **abomination** (ə bom′ə nā′shən), *n.* something that arouses strong disgust.
36. perfunctory (pər fungk′tər ē), *adj.* done for the sake of performing the duty; mechanical; indifferent.
37. **impertinence** (im pėrt′n əns), *n.* rude boldness.
38. **Amazon** (am′ə zon), in Greek legends, one of a race of women warriors.
39. **"To Be or Not to Be."** Henry's speech takes its name from the famous soliloquy in Shakespeare's play *Hamlet, Prince of Denmark,* which begins,

    "To be, or not to be: that is the question:
    Whether 'tis nobler in the mind to suffer
    The slings and arrows of outrageous fortune
    Or to take arms against a sea of troubles,
    And by opposing end them?"

40. **elocution** (el′ə kyü′shən), *n.* art of speaking or reading well in public.

had been listening and silently rebutting[41] each sentence with my eyes closed; then there was a hush, which in an audience warns that something unplanned is happening. I looked up and saw Henry Reed, the conservative, the proper, the A student, turn his back to the audience and turn to us (the proud graduating class of 1940) and sing, nearly speaking,

"Lift ev'ry voice and sing
Till earth and heaven ring
Ring with the harmonies of Liberty . . ."

It was the poem written by James Weldon Johnson. It was the music composed by J. Rosamond Johnson. It was the Negro national anthem. Out of habit we were singing it.

Our mothers and fathers stood in the dark hall and joined the hymn of encouragement. A kindergarten teacher led the small children onto the stage and the buttercups and daisies and bunny rabbits marked time and tried to follow:

"Stony the road we trod
Bitter the chastening[42] rod
Felt in the days when hope, unborn,
     had died.
Yet with a steady beat
Have not our weary feet
Come to the place for which our fathers
     sighed?"

Every child I knew had learned that song with his ABC's and along with "Jesus Loves Me This I Know." But I personally had never heard it before. Never heard the words, despite the thousands of times I had sung them. Never thought they had anything to do with me.

On the other hand, the words of Patrick Henry[43] had made such an impression on me that I had been able to stretch myself tall and trembling and say, "I know not what course others may take, but as for me, give me liberty or give me death."

And now I heard, really for the first time:

"We have come over a way that with tears
has been watered,
We have come, treading our path through
the blood of the slaughtered."

While echoes of the song shivered in the air, Henry Reed bowed his head, said "Thank you," and returned to his place in the line. The tears that slipped down many faces were not wiped away in shame.

We were on top again. As always, again. We survived. The depths had been icy and dark, but now a bright sun spoke to our souls. I was no longer simply a member of the proud graduating class of 1940; I was a proud member of the wonderful, beautiful Negro race.

Oh, Black known and unknown poets, how often have your auctioned pains sustained us? Who will compute the lonely nights made less lonely by your songs, or by the empty pots made less tragic by your tales?

If we were a people much given to revealing secrets, we might raise monuments and sacrifice to the memories of our poets, but slavery cured us of that weakness. It may be enough, however, to have it said that we survive in exact relationship to the dedication of our poets (include preachers, musicians and blues singers).

---

41. **rebut** (ri but′), *v.* try to disprove.
42. **chastening** (chā′sn ing), *adj.* punishing.
43. **Patrick Henry,** 1736–1799, American Revolutionary patriot, orator, and statesman.

After Reading

Making Connections

Shaping Your
Response

1. What image from this selection stands out most in your mind?

2. How do Maya Angelou and her family feel about her graduation from eighth grade? What specific details in the selection reveal their feelings?

Analyzing the
Autobiography

3. What hints on pages 614–615 **foreshadow** that graduation may not be what the author expects?

4. How does Donleavy's speech **stereotype** the students of the graduating class?

5. How does Donleavy's speech affect the narrator's self-image?

6. ☙ Despite the general mood of despair, Henry Reed goes through with his inspirational speech. How does this expression of his **individuality** strengthen the community?

Extending the Ideas

7. At the end of the selection, Angelou says that poets sustain and nourish the African American community. Compare her ideas with your own beliefs about the role of poets in a society.

8. Graduation was an important rite, or ceremony, in Maya Angelou's community. What ceremonies are vital in your community? Why do you think they are so important?

Literary Focus: Symbol

Symbols, objects that represent abstract ideas, appear regularly in literature. For example, Angelou describes the Negro National Anthem as a symbol of the strength that exists in her community. Sometimes, the meaning of a symbol changes within a literary work. With these ideas in mind, copy and complete the chart shown here.

Symbol	What it means:		
	before Donleavy's speech	after Donleavy's speech	after Henry Reed's speech
the school			
graduation			

Vocabulary Study

Decide if the word pairs below are synonyms or antonyms. Use your Glossary, if necessary, to understand the italicized vocabulary words.

1. *constrained*—restricted
2. *decipher*—decode
3. *forfeit*—keep
4. *meticulous*—sloppy
5. *mollified*—angry

6. *perfunctory*—indifferent
7. *pervade*—spread
8. *presentiment*—intuition
9. *presumptuous*—humble
10. *reprieve*—relief

Expressing Your Ideas

Writing Choices

Writer's Notebook Update Now that you have read the autobiography, think of how the author's expectations about her graduation did not match the outcome. In your notebook, compare and contrast your experience of having things turn out differently than expected with Angelou's experience.

Do-It-Yourself Education In "Graduation," Angelou details some of her school assignments. What subjects and topics do you think are important for students your age to learn? Write a brief **proposal** for a curriculum that describes the subjects and ideas that should be covered, along with reasons for your choices. Present your curriculum to a "school board" made up of your classmates, and be prepared to defend your proposal.

Speak to Me Think ahead to the graduation ceremonies for your class. Who do you think would be a good speaker for your ceremony? Write a **letter** inviting this person to speak to your graduating class. Be sure to include why you are choosing this person and a brief description of what you hope this person will address in his or her speech.

Other Options

Role Models In "Graduation," Angelou mentions many people who have been role models. Who do you think is a worthwhile role model for your generation? Make a **museum display** about this person. You might include a picture or drawing of the person, a biographical profile, and "artifacts" that illustrate important things he or she did.

School Funds In her autobiography, Angelou describes the spending discrepancies among schools in her county. Do some research to find out how schools in your state are funded. Find out how much money per student is allocated to several different schools in your state and area. Record your findings on **charts** and **graphs.** Are there gaps in spending among different schools? What do you think accounts for those discrepancies?

Civil Rights Do some research on U.S. civil rights legislation during the 1950s and 1960s. Then interview someone who lived through the '50s and '60s about their perceptions of the changes these laws brought to American society. (For tips on conducting interviews, see page 657.) Present your findings in an **oral report** to the class.

The Village Watchman

by Terry Tempest Williams

Terry Tempest Williams
born 1955

A fifth-generation Mormon, Terry Tempest Williams has lived in Utah all her life and is currently Naturalist-in-Residence at the Utah Museum of Natural History. She is the author of several environmental books for both adults and children. Williams says that when she first became interested in writing, she doubted her own abilities, asking, "What do I have to write about?" By keeping a journal, she realized her experiences were good materials for her writing. Williams explains, "Experience is all we have. That's what literature is built on, personal experience and perceptions."

Building Background

Family Ties A writer for *Time* magazine once wrote, "Some people are your relatives but others are your ancestors, and you choose the ones you want to have as ancestors. You create yourself out of those values." What do you think is the difference between a "relative" and an "ancestor"? Who would you choose to have as an ancestor?

Literary Focus

Flashback Sometimes a writer interrupts a scene taking place in the present to show something that took place at an earlier time. This interruption is called a **flashback.** By showing events that happen in the past, a writer can help readers better understand the characters and the present action in a story. Flashbacks may also add to the dramatic intensity of a story.

Writer's Notebook

Relatively Speaking In your notebook, write about a family member, not necessarily in your immediate family, who means a lot to you. You might use some of these questions to guide you as you write: What about this person will you always remember? What activities do you (or did you) enjoy doing with him or her? What has this family member helped you learn about yourself or about life? As you read "The Village Watchman," consider how the author might answer these questions about an important relative in her life.

THE VILLAGE WATCHMAN

Terry Tempest Williams

Stories carved in cedar rise from the deep woods of Sitka.[1] These totem poles are foreign to me, this vertical lineage[2] of clans: Eagle, Raven, Wolf, and Salmon. The Tlingit[3] craftsmen create a genealogy[4] of the Earth, a reminder from mentors[5] that we come into this world as innocents in need of proper instruction. I sit on the soft floor of this Alaskan forest and feel the presence of Other.

The totem before me is called Wolf Pole by locals. The Village Watchman sits on top of Wolf's head with his knees drawn to his chest, his hands holding them tight against his body. He wears a red-and-black-striped hat. His eyes are direct, deep-set, painted blue. The expression on his face reminds me of a man I loved, a man who was born into this world feet first.

"Breech," my mother told me of her brother's birth. "Alan was born feet first. As a result, his brain was denied oxygen. He is special."

This information impressed me as a child. I remember thinking fish live underwater; maybe Alan had gills, maybe he didn't need a face-first gulp of air like the rest of us. His sweet breath of initiation

---

1. **Sitka,** a small city in Alaska.
2. lineage (lin′ē ij), *n.* descent in a direct line from a common ancestor.
3. **Tlingit** (tling′git), a group of Indian peoples of the islands and coast of southern Alaska.
4. **genealogy** (jē′nē al′ə jē), *n.* descent of a person or family from an ancestor; pedigree; lineage.
5. mentor (men′tər), *n.* wise and trusted advisor.

came in time, slowly moving up through the soles of his tiny webbed feet. The amniotic[6] sea he had floated in for nine months delivered him with a fluid memory. He knew something. Other.

Wolf who resides in the center of this totem holds the tail of Salmon with his feet. The tongue of Wolf hangs down, blood-red, as do his front paws, black. Salmon, a sockeye, is poised downriver—a swish of a tail and he could be gone, but the clasp of Wolf is strong.

There is a story of a boy who was kidnapped from his village by the Salmon People. He was taken from his family to learn the ways of water. When he returned many years later to his home, he was recognized by his own as a holy man privy[7] to the mysteries of the unseen world. Twenty years after my uncle's death, I wonder if Alan could have been that boy.

But our culture tells a different story, more alien than those of Tlingit or Haida.[8] My culture calls people of sole-births retarded, handicapped, mentally disabled or challenged. We see them for who they are not, rather than who they are.

My grandmother, Lettie Romney Dixon, wrote in her journal,

> It wasn't until Alan was sixteen months old that a busy doctor cruelly broke the news to us. Others may have suspected our son's limitations but to those of us who loved him so unquestionably, lightning struck without warning. I hugged my sorrow to myself. I felt abandoned and lost. I wouldn't accept the verdict. Then we started the trips to a multitude of doctors. Most of them were kind and explained that our child was like a car without brakes, like an electric wire without insulation. They gave us no hope for a normal life.

Normal. Latin, *normalis; norma*, a rule; conforming with or constituting an accepted standard, model, or pattern, especially corresponding to the median or average of a large group in type, appearance, achievement, function, or development.

Alan was not normal. He was unique; one and only; single; sole; unusual; extraordinary; rare. His emotions were not measured, his curiosity was not bridled.[9] In a sense, he was wild like a mustang in the desert; and like most wild horses, he was eventually rounded up.

He was unpredictable. He created his own rules and they changed from moment to moment. Alan was twelve years old, hyperactive, mischievous, easily frustrated, and unable to learn in traditional ways. The situation was intensified by his seizures. Suddenly, without warning, he would stiffen like a rake, fall forward, and crash to the ground hitting his head. My grandparents could not keep him home any longer. They needed professional guidance and help. In 1957, they reluctantly placed their youngest child in an institution for handicapped children called the American Fork Training School. My grandmother's heart broke for the second time.

Once again, from her journal,

> Many a night my pillow is wet from tears of sorrow and senseless dreamings of "if things had only been different," or wondering if he is tucked in snug and warm, if he is well and happy, if the wind still bothers him.

The wind may have continued to bother Alan, certainly the conditions he was living under were less than ideal, but as a family there was much about his private life we never knew.

---

6. **amniotic** (am′nē ot′ik), *adj.* of or inside the fluid-filled inner sac that encloses the embryos of reptiles, birds, and mammals.
7. **privy** (priv′ē), *adj.* having secret or private knowledge of.
8. **Haida** (hī′dä), a group of Indian peoples in southern Alaska.
9. **bridled** (brī′dld), *adj.* held back; controlled.

What we did know was that Alan had an enormous capacity for adaptation.[10] We had no choice but to follow him.

I followed him for years.

Alan was ten years my senior. In my mind, growing up, he was mythic. Everything I was taught not to do, Alan did. We were taught to be polite, not to express displeasure or anger in public. Alan was sheer physical expression. Whatever was on his mind was vocalized and usually punctuated with colorful speech. We would go bowling as a family on Sundays. Each of us would take our turn, hold the black ball up, take a few steps, swing an arm back, forward, glide, and release—the ball would roll down the alley, hit a few pins, we would wait for it to return, and then take our second turn. Little emotion was shown. When it was Alan's turn, it was an event. Nothing subtle. His style was Herculean.[11] Big man. Big roll. Big bang. Whether it was a strike or a gutter, he clapped his hands, spun around on the floor, slapped his thighs and cried, "Did you see that one? Send me another ball, sweet Jesus!" And the ball was always returned.

I could always count on my uncle for a straight answer. He was my mentor in understanding that one of the remarkable aspects of being human was to hold opposing views in our minds at once.

"How are you doing?" I would ask.

"Ask me how I am feeling," he answered.

"Okay, how are you feeling?"

"Today? Right now?"

"Yes."

"I am very happy and very sad."

"How can you be happy and sad at the same time?" I asked in all seriousness, a girl of nine or ten.

"Because both require each other's company. They live in the same house. Didn't you know?"

We would laugh and then go on to another topic. Talking to my uncle was always like entering a maze of riddles. Ask a question. Answer with a question and see where it leads you.

These family photographs show Alan Romney Dixon as a boy (above) and with his brother Don (top photo).

10. **adaptation** (ad′ap tā′shən), *n.* adjustment to different circumstances or conditions.
11. **Herculean** (hėr′kyū′lē ən), *adj.* having great strength, courage, or size; very powerful. Refers to Hercules, the son of Zeus, a hero who possessed great strength and courage.

This family photograph shows Alan with some of his nieces and nephews. The girl on the left is author Terry Tempest Williams as a child. ▼

My younger brother Steve and I spent a lot of time with Alan. He offered us shelter from the conventionality[12] of a Mormon[13] family. At home during Christmas he would direct us in his own nativity plays. "More—" he would say to us, making wide gestures with his hands. "Give me more of yourself." He was not like anyone we knew. In a culture where we were taught socially to be seen and not heard, Alan was our mirror. We could be different, too. His unquestioning belief in us as children, as human beings, was in startling contrast to the way we watched the public react to him. It hurt us. What we could never tell was if it hurt him.

Each week, Steve and I would accompany our grandparents south to visit Alan. It was an hour drive to the training school from Salt Lake City, mostly through farmlands. We would enter the grounds, pull into the parking lot to a playground filled with huge papier-mâché storybook figures (a twenty-foot pied piper; a pumpkin carriage with Cinderella inside, the old woman who lived in a shoe), and nine out of ten times, Alan was standing outside his dormitory waiting for us. We would get out of the car and he would run toward us, throwing his powerful arms around us. His hugs cracked my back and at times I had to fight for my breath. My grandfather would calm him down by simply saying, "We're here, son. You can relax now."

Alan was a formidable[14] man, now in his early twenties, stocky and strong. His head was large with a protruding[15] forehead that bore many scars, a line-by-line history of seizures. He always had on someone else's clothes—a tweed jacket too small, brown pants too big, a striped golf shirt that didn't match. He showed us appearances didn't matter, personality did. If you didn't know him, he could look frightening. It was an unspoken rule in our family that the character of others was gauged in how they treated Alan. The only consistent item in his attire was a silver football helmet from Olympus High School where my grandfather was the coach. It was a loving, practical solution to protect Alan when he fell. The helmet cradled his head and absorbed the shock of the seizures.

"Part of the team," my grandfather Sanky would say as he slapped him affectionately on the back. "You're a Titan, son, and I love you—"

The windows to the dormitory were dark,

12. **conventionality** (kən ven′shən al′ə tē), *n.* behavior that conforms to commonly accepted and approved ways.
13. **Mormon** (môr′mən), refers to the Church of Jesus Christ of Latter-day Saints, founded in 1830 by Joseph Smith. The church emphasizes family unity and missionary work.
14. **formidable** (fôr′mə də bəl), *adj.* hard to overcome; hard to deal with; to be dreaded.
15. **protruding** (prō trüd′ing), *adj.* thrusting forth; projecting; sticking out.

reflecting Mount Timpanogos to the east. It was hard to see inside but I knew what the interior held. It looked like an abandoned gymnasium without bleachers, filled with hospital beds. The stained white walls and yellow-waxed floors offered no warmth to its residents. The stench was nauseating, sweat and urine trapped in the oppression of stale air. I recall the dirty sheets, the lack of privacy, and the almond-eyed children who never rose from their beds. And then I would turn around and face Alan's cheerfulness, the open and loving manner in which he would introduce me to his friends, the pride he exhibited as he showed me around his home. He demanded no judgment. I kept thinking "Doesn't he see how bad this is, how poorly they are being treated?" His words would return to me, "I am very happy and I am very sad."

For my brother and me, Alan was our guide, our elder. He was fearless. But neither one of us will ever be able to escape the image of Alan kissing his parents goodbye after an afternoon visit and slowly walking back to his dormitory. Before we drove away, he would turn toward us, take off his silver helmet, and wave. The look on his face haunts me still. Alan walked point[16] for all of us.

Alan liked to talk about God. Perhaps it was in these private conversations that our real friendship was forged.

"I know Him," he would say when all the adults were gone.

"You do?" I asked.

"I talk to Him every day."

"How so?"

"I talk to Him in my prayers. I listen and then I hear His voice."

"What does He tell you?"

"He tells me to be patient. He tells me to be kind. He tells me that he loves me."

In Mormon culture, children are baptized as members of the Church of Jesus Christ of Latter-day Saints when they turn eight years old. Alan had never been baptized because my grandparents believed it should be his choice, not something simply taken for granted. When he turned twenty-two, he expressed a sincere desire to join the Church. A date was set immediately.

The entire Dixon clan convened[17] in the Lehi chapel, a few miles north of the group home where Alan was then living. We were there to support and witness his conversion. As we walked toward the meeting house where this sacred rite was to be performed, Alan had a violent seizure. My grandfather and uncle Don, Alan's elder brother, dropped down with him, holding his head and body as every muscle thrashed on the pavement like a school of netted fish brought on deck. I didn't want to look but to walk away would have been worse. We stayed with him, all of us.

"Talk to God—" I heard myself saying under my breath. "I love you, Alan."

"Can you hear me, darling?" It was my grandmother's voice, her hand holding her son's hand.

By now many of us were gathered on our knees around him, our trembling hands on his rigid body.

And we, who have always thought
of happiness as rising, would feel
the emotion that almost overwhelms us
whenever a happy thing falls.

—Rainer Maria Rilke[18]

Alan opened his eyes. "I want to be baptized," he said. The men helped him to his feet. The gash on his left temple was deep. Blood dripped down the side of his face. He would forgo[19] stitches once again. My mother had her arm around my grandmother's waist. Shaken,

---

16. **walked point.** In war, the soldier who leads a patrol walks point.
17. convene (kən vēn′), v. meet for some purpose; gather together; assemble.
18. **Rainer Maria Rilke** (rān′ər mä rē′ə ril′ke), German poet (1875–1926).
19. **forgo** (fôr gō′), v. do without.

we all followed him inside. Alan's father and brother ministered to him, stopped the bleeding and bandaged the wound, then helped him change into the designated white garments for baptism. He entered the room with great dignity and sat in the front pew with a dozen or more eight-year-old children seated on either side. Row after row of family sat behind him.

"Alan Romney Dixon." His name was called by the presiding bishop. Alan rose from the pew and met his brother Don, also dressed in white, who took his hand and led him down the blue-tiled stairs into the baptismal font filled with water. They faced the congregation. Don raised his right arm to the square in the gesture of a holy oath as Alan placed his hands on his brother's left forearm. The sacred prayer was offered in the name of the Father, the Son, and the Holy Ghost, after which my uncle put his right hand behind Alan's head and gently lowered him into the water for baptism by immersion.[20]

Alan emerged from the holy water like an angel.

> The breaking away of childhood
> left you intact.[21] In a moment,
> you stood there, as if completed
> in a miracle, all at once.
>
> —Rainer Maria Rilke

Six years later I found myself sitting across from my uncle at the University Hospital where he was being treated for a severe ear infection. I was eighteen. He was twenty-eight.

"Alan," I asked. "What is it really like to be inside your body?"

He crossed his legs and placed both hands on the arms of the chair. His brown eyes were piercing.

"I can't tell what it's like except to say I feel pain for not being seen as the person I am."

A few days later, Alan died alone; unique; one and only; single; in American Fork, Utah.

The Village Watchman sits on top of his totem with Wolf and Salmon—it is beginning to rain in the forest. I find it curious that this spot in southeast Alaska has brought me back into relation with my uncle, this man of sole-birth, this man who came into the world feet first. He reminds me of what it means to live and love with a broken heart: how nothing is sacred, how everything is sacred. He was a weathervane, a storm and a clearing at once.

Shortly after his death, Alan appeared to me in a dream. We were standing in my grandmother's kitchen. He was leaning against the white stove with his arms folded.

"Look at me now, Terry," he said smiling. "I'm normal—perfectly normal." And then he laughed. We both laughed.

He handed me his silver football helmet that was resting on the counter, kissed me and opened the back door.

"Do you recognize who I am?"

On this day in Sitka, I remember.

---

20. **immersion** (i mėr′zhən), *n.* the act of being dipped or lowered into a liquid until covered by it. Immersion also refers to a baptism done by dipping a person completely under water.
21. intact (in takt′), *adj.* with no part missing, as if untouched; whole; uninjured.

After Reading

Making Connections

Shaping Your
Response

1. Would you want to have someone like Alan in your family? Why or why not?

2. How are Alan and the Village Watchman alike?

Analyzing the
Selection

3. Describe the author's relationship with her uncle. What was she able to receive from Alan that she could not receive from other family members?

4. Compare and contrast the views of Alan held by the family and people outside the family.

5. 👁 How did Alan's **individuality** affect the people around him?

6. Discuss the **quotations** that Williams inserts into her piece. How do they help the author make her point?

Extending the Ideas

7. Williams writes about people like Alan, "We see them for who they are not, rather than who they are." Explain this statement, and tell whether or not you agree with the author.

8. Williams describes how she was told to be quiet and polite as a child. Why do you think that, in many cultures, children are taught to be "seen but not heard"?

Literary Focus: Flashback

A **flashback** is an interruption in the action of a story or play to show a scene or event that happened at an earlier time. "The Village Watchman" is an extended flashback, a piece of writing that is almost entirely a flashback triggered by an event in the present. With these ideas in mind, answer these questions about "The Village Watchman."

- How does the totem pole trigger the author's memories of her uncle?

- How does the fact that this selection is an extended flashback affect the tone of the piece?

Vocabulary Study

Choose the vocabulary word from the list that most closely describes each idea. Use your Glossary, if necessary.

convene
conventionality
intact
lineage
mentor

1. The ____ of the clan in Alaska was shown on the totem pole.

2. Alan taught the author much about life, and she saw him as a ____.

3. Alan freely expressed himself. He did not believe in ____.

4. Though Alan's body was scarred from many falls, his generous spirit remained ____.

5. The family would often ____ at the institution where Alan lived.

Expressing Your Ideas _____

Writing Choices

Writer's Notebook Update Before you read the story, you wrote about your relationship with a relative who is special to you. In your notebook, compare and contrast that relationship with the one between Terry Tempest Williams and her uncle Alan.

Poetic Person Williams uses a simile to describe Alan, writing that he was "wild like a mustang in the desert." Use similes to describe a person you admire. Write a short **poem,** with a simile in each line that helps describe the person.

Flash of the Past Think of a song, object, event, or place that triggers a pleasant memory for you. Write a brief **memoir** that begins with the "trigger" item and then, in a flashback, describes the memory that has been recalled.

Other Options

Photo Opportunity "The Village Watchman" includes photographs that show the author's family. Draw pictures or use photographs to create a **pictorial essay** about important people or events in your life. Write captions that identify who is in the pictures, what is happening, and why the pictures show something important about your life.

Web-ster Williams uses different words and phrases to describe her uncle Alan. Choose a person that you admire and brainstorm some words that describe that person. Using the example here as a model, create a **word web** that places the person you admire at the center and gives the other words you associate with that person.

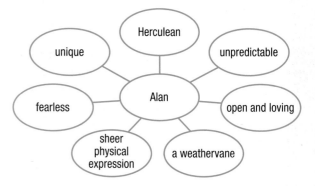

Before Reading

from When Heaven and Earth Changed Places

by Le Ly Hayslip

Le Ly Hayslip
born 1949

Le Ly (lā′lē) Hayslip was born into a close-knit Buddhist family and grew up in Central Vietnam during the long war between North and South Vietnam. The war arrived in her village when she was twelve years old. Members of her family were killed; she suffered hunger, imprisonment, torture, and rape. She escaped her war-ravaged country by marrying an American soldier and immigrating to the United States in 1970.

Hayslip's autobiography, *When Heaven and Earth Changed Places,* published in 1989, was later made into a movie by Oliver Stone. Hayslip is also the founder of East Meets West, an organization that has established a relief program near Hayslip's original home in Vietnam.

Building Background

A Troubled History After many centuries of Chinese rule, Vietnam recovered its independence in the 900s. In the late 1800s, the country was seized by the French. In the Indochina War (1946–1954), Ho Chi Minh, a Vietnamese communist, defeated the French, and the country was divided into communist North Vietnam and noncommunist South Vietnam. In the late 1950s, communist rebels known as the Viet Cong revolted against the South Vietnamese government. By 1965, the U.S. was sending combat troops to Vietnam to fight against the Viet Cong and their North Vietnamese allies. The war officially ended in 1973, but fighting continued until North Vietnamese forces defeated the South Vietnamese in 1975. In the following excerpt from her autobiography, Le Ly Hayslip describes her childhood in Vietnam during the late 1950s and early 1960s.

Literary Focus

Proverbs Have you ever heard statements like these?

> Haste makes waste.

> A stitch in time saves nine.

> Fool me once, shame on you. Fool me twice, shame on me.

These sayings are called **proverbs.** A proverb is a brief saying that expresses a general truth or practical observation about life or human behavior. All around the world, proverbs are passed down from one generation to another. Think of some examples of proverbs. What lessons can you learn from them?

Writer's Notebook

Worth Fighting For What things in life are so important that you would go to great lengths to save them? In your notebook, describe something, whether a possession or something intangible, that you feel is important enough to struggle to keep. How far would you go to protect it?

from When Heaven and

After my brother Bon went North, I began to pay more attention to my father.

He was built solidly—big-boned—for a Vietnamese man, which meant he probably had well-fed, noble ancestors. People said he had the body of a natural-born warrior. He was a year younger and an inch shorter than my mother, but just as good-looking. His face was round, like Khmer[1] or Thai,[2] and his complexion was brown as soy from working all his life in the sun. He was very easygoing about everything and seldom in a hurry. Seldom, too, did he say no to a request—from his children or his neighbors. Although he took everything in stride, he was a hard and diligent[3] worker. Even on holidays, he was always mending things or tending to our house and animals. He would not wait to be asked for help if he saw someone in trouble. Similarly, he always said what he thought, although he knew, like most honest men, when to keep silent. Because of his honesty, his empathy,[4] and his openness to people, he

Earth Changed Places

Le Ly Hayslip

understood life deeply. Perhaps that is why he was so easygoing. Only a half-trained mechanic thinks everything needs fixing.

He loved to smoke cigars and grew a little tobacco in our yard. My mother always wanted him to sell it, but there was hardly ever enough to take to market. I think for her it was the principle of the thing: smoking cigars was like burning money. Naturally, she had a song

---

1. **Khmer** (kmer), one of the native peoples of Cambodia.
2. **Thai** (tī), natives of Thailand.
3. diligent (dil′ə jənt), *adj.* hard-working; industrious.
4. empathy (em′pə thē), *n.* the quality or process of entering fully into another's feelings or motives, into the meaning of a work of art, etc.

for such gentle vices[5]—her own habit of chewing betel nuts[6] included:

> Get rid of your tobacco,
> And you will get a water buffalo.
> Give away your betel,
> And you will get more paddy land.[7]

Despite her own good advice, she never abstained[8] from chewing betel, nor my father from smoking cigars. They were rare luxuries that life and the war allowed them.

My father also liked rice wine, which we made; and enjoyed an occasional beer, which he purchased when there was nothing else we needed. After he'd had a few sips, he would tell jokes and happy stories and the village kids would flock around. Because I was his youngest daughter, I was entitled to listen from his knee—the place of honor. Sometimes he would sing funny songs about whoever threatened the village and we would feel better. For example, when the French or Moroccan soldiers[9] were near, he would sing:

> There are many kinds of vegetables,
> Why do you like spinach?
> There are many kinds of wealth,
> Why do you use Minh money?
> There are many kinds of people,
> Why do you love terrorists?

We laughed because these were all the things the French told us about the Viet Minh[10] fighters whom we favored in the war. Years later, when the Viet Cong were near, he would sing:

> There are many kinds of vegetables,
> Why do you like spinach?
> There are many kinds of money,
> Why do you use Yankee dollars?
> There are many kinds of people,
> Why do you disobey your ancestors?

This was funny because the words were taken from the speeches the North Vietnamese cadres[11] delivered to shame us for helping the Republic.[12] He used to have a song for when the Viet Minh were near too, which asked in the same way, "Why

do you use francs?" and "Why do you love French traitors?" Because he sang these songs with a comical voice, my mother never appreciated them. She couldn't see the absurdity of our situation as clearly as we children. To her, war and real life were different. To us, they were all the same.

Even as a parent, my father was more lenient[13] than our mother, and we sometimes ran to him for help when she was angry. Most of the time, it didn't work and he would lovingly rub our heads as we were dragged off to be spanked. The village saying went: "A naughty child learns more from a whipping stick than a sweet stick." We children were never quite sure about that, but agreed the whipping stick was an eloquent teacher. When he absolutely had to punish us himself, he didn't waste time. Wordlessly, he would find a long, supple bamboo stick and let us have it behind our thighs. It stung, but he could have whipped us harder. I think seeing the pain in his face hurt more than receiving his halfhearted blows. Because of that, we seldom did anything to merit a father's spanking—the highest penalty in our family. Violence in any form offended him. For this reason, I think, he grew old before his time.

One of the few times my father ever touched my mother in a way not consistent with love was during one of the yearly floods, when people came to our village for safety from the lower

---

5. **vice** (vīs), *n.* evil, immoral, or wicked habit or tendency.
6. **betel** (bē′tl) **nut,** the orange-colored nut of a tropical Asiatic palm tree.
7. **paddy land,** flooded areas with raised banks around the sides for growing rice.
8. **abstain** (ab stān′), *v.* hold oneself back voluntarily; refrain.
9. **French or Moroccan soldiers.** France occupied Vietnam in the early 1950s. The Moroccan soldiers were in Vietnam because France also controlled Morocco at that time.
10. **Viet Minh** (vē et′min′), fighters against the French.
11. **North Vietnamese cadres** (kā′drāz), representatives of communist North Vietnam.
12. **the Republic,** South Vietnam.
13. **lenient** (lē′nyənt), *adj.* mild or gentle; not harsh or stern; merciful.

ground. We sheltered many in our house, which was nothing more than a two-room hut with woven mats for a floor. I came home one day in winter rain to see refugees and Republican soldiers milling around outside. They did not know I lived there so I had to elbow my way inside. It was nearly supper time and I knew my mother would be fixing as much food as we could spare.

In the part of the house we used as our kitchen, I discovered my mother crying. She and my father had gotten into an argument outside a few minutes before. He had assured the refugees he would find something to eat for everyone and she insisted there would not be enough for her children if everyone was fed. He repeated his order to her, this time loud enough for all to hear. Naturally, he thought this would end the argument. She persisted in contradicting him, so he had slapped her.

This show of male power—we called it *do danh vo*[14]—was usual behavior for Vietnamese husbands but unusual for my father. My mother could be as strict as she wished with his children and he would seldom interfere. Now, I discovered there were limits even to his great patience. I saw the glowing red mark on her cheek and asked if she was crying because it hurt. She said no. She said she was crying because her action had caused my father to lose face in front of strangers. She promised that if I ever did what she had done to a husband, I would have both cheeks glowing: one from his blow and one from hers.

Once, when I was the only child at home, my mother went to Danang[15] to visit Uncle Nhu,[16] and my father had to take care of me. I woke up from my nap in the empty house and cried for my mother. My father came in from the yard and reassured me, but I was still cranky and continued crying. Finally, he gave me a rice cookie to shut me up. Needless to say, this was a tactic my mother never used.

The next afternoon I woke up and although I was not feeling cranky, I though a rice cookie might be nice. I cried a fake cry and my father came running in.

"What's this?" he asked, making a worried face. "Little Bay Ly[17] doesn't want a cookie?"

I was confused again.

"Look under your pillow," he said with a smile.

I twisted around and saw that, while I was sleeping, he had placed a rice cookie under my pillow. We both laughed and he picked me up like a sack of rice and carried me outside while I gobbled the cookie.

In the yard, he plunked me down under a tree and told me some stories. After that, he got some scraps of wood and showed me how to make things: a doorstop for my mother and a toy duck for me. This was unheard of—a father doing these things with a child that was not a son! Where my mother would instruct me on cooking and cleaning and tell stories about brides, my father showed me the mystery of hammers and explained the customs of our people.

is knowledge of the Vietnamese went back to the Chinese Wars in ancient times. I learned how one of my distant ancestors, a woman named Phung Thi Chinh,[18] led Vietnamese fighters against the Han. In one battle, even though she was pregnant and surrounded by Chinese, she delivered the baby, tied it to her back, and cut her way to safety wielding a sword in each hand. I was amazed at this warrior's bravery and impressed that I was her descendant. Even more, I was amazed and impressed by my father's pride in her accomplishments (she was, after all, a humble female), and his belief that I was worthy of

14. *do danh vo* (dô dän′və). Note: The pronunciations of Vietnamese words in this selection are approximations.

15. **Danang** (dä näng′), seaport in central Vietnam, on the South China Sea.

16. **Nhu** (nŭ).

17. **Bay Ly** (bī lē′). The family's name for Le Ly. In accordance with Vietnamese customs, it refers to her position as the sixth child in the family.

18. **Phung Thi Chinh** (fung tē tchin′).

her example. *"Con phai theo got chan co ta"*[19] (Follow in her footsteps), he said. Only later would I learn what he truly meant.

Never again did I cry after my nap. Phung Thi women were too strong for that. Besides, I was my father's daughter and we had many things to do together.

On the eve of my mother's return, my father cooked a feast of roast duck. When we sat down to eat it, I felt guilty and my feelings showed on my face. He asked why I acted so sad.

"You've killed one of mother's ducks," I said. "One of the fat kind she sells at the market. She says the money buys gold which she saves for her daughters' weddings. Without gold for a dowry—*con o gia*[20]—I will be an old maid!"

My father looked suitably concerned, then brightened and said, "Well, Bay Ly, if you can't get married, you will just have to live at home forever with me!"

I clapped my hands at the happy prospect.

My father cut into the rich, juicy bird and said, "Even so, we won't tell your mother about the duck, okay?"

I giggled and swore myself to secrecy.

The next day, I took some water out to him in the fields. My mother was due home any time and I used every opportunity to step outside and watch for her. My father stopped working, drank gratefully, then took my hand and led me to the top of a nearby hill. It had a good view of the village and the land beyond it, almost to the ocean. I thought he was going to show me my mother coming back, but he had something else in mind.

He said, "Bay Ly, you see all this here? This is the Vietnam we have been talking about. You understand that a country is more than a lot of dirt, rivers, and forests, don't you?"

I said, "Yes, I understand." After all, we had learned in school that one's country is as sacred as a father's grave.

"Good. You know, some of these lands are battlefields where your brothers and cousins are fighting. They may never come back. Even your sisters have all left home in search of a better life. You are the only one left in my house. If the enemy comes back, you must be both a daughter and a son. I told you how the Chinese used to rule our land. People in this village had to risk their lives diving in the ocean just to find pearls for the Chinese emperor's gown. They had to risk tigers and snakes in the jungle just to find herbs for his table. Their payment for this hardship was a bowl of rice and another day of life. That is why Le Loi, Gia Long,[21] the Trung Sisters, and Phung Thi Chinh fought so hard to expel the Chinese. When the French came, it was the same old story. Your mother and I were taken to Danang to build a runway for their airplanes. We labored from sunup to sundown and well after dark. If we stopped to rest or have a smoke, a Moroccan would come up and whip our behinds. Our reward was a bowl of rice and another day of life. Freedom is never a gift, Bay Ly. It must be won and won again. Do you understand?"

I said that I did.

"Good." He moved his finger from the patchwork of brown dikes, silver water, and rippling stalks to our house at the edge of the village. "This land here belongs to me. Do you know how I got it?"

I thought a moment, trying to remember my mother's stories, then said honestly, "I can't remember."

He squeezed me lovingly. "I got it from your mother."

"What? That can't be true!" I said. Everyone in the family knew my mother was poor and my father's family was wealthy. Her parents were dead and she had to work like a slave for her mother-in-law to prove herself worthy. Such women don't have land to give away!

---

19. *Con phai theo got chan co ta* (kôn fī tāô gôʹtchun cô tä).
20. *Con o gia* (kôn u yä).
21. **Le Loi** (lā loi), **Gia Long** (yä long).

"It's true." My father's smile widened. "When I was a young man, my parents needed someone to look after their lands. They had to be very careful about who they chose as wives for their three sons. In the village, your mother had a reputation as the hardest worker of all. She raised herself and her brothers without parents. At the same time, I noticed a beautiful woman working in the fields. When my mother said she was going to talk to the matchmaker about this hardworking village girl she'd heard about, my heart sank. I was too attracted to this mysterious tall woman I had seen in the rice paddies. You can imagine my surprise when I found out the girl my mother heard about and the woman I admired were the same.

"Well, we were married and my mother tested your mother severely. She not only had to cook and clean and know everything about children, but she had to be able to manage several farms and know when and how to take the extra produce to the market. Of course, she was testing her other daughters-in-law as well. When my parents died, they divided their several farms among their sons, but you know what? They gave your mother and me the biggest share because they knew we would take care of it best. That's why I say the land came from her, because it did."

I suddenly missed my mother very much and looked down the road to the south, hoping to see her. My father noticed my sad expression.

"Hey." He poked me in the ribs. "Are you getting hungry for lunch?"

"No. I want to learn how to take care of the farm. What happens if the soldiers come back? What did you and Mother do when the soldiers came?"

A 1960 photograph of Le Ly Hayslip's father.

My father squatted on the dusty hilltop and wiped the sweat from his forehead. "The first thing I did was to tell myself that it was my duty to survive—to take care of my family and my farm. That is a tricky job in wartime. It's as hard as being a soldier. The Moroccans were very savage. One day the rumor passed that they were coming to destroy the village. You may remember the night I sent you and your brothers and sisters away with your mother to Danang."

"You didn't go with us!" My voice still held the horror of the night I thought I had lost my father.

"Right! I stayed near the village—right on this hill—to keep an eye on the enemy and on our house. If they really wanted to destroy the village, I would save some of our things so that we could start over. Sure enough, that was their plan.

"The real problem was to keep things safe and avoid being captured. Their patrols were everywhere. Sometimes I went so deep in the forest that I worried about getting lost, but all I had to do was follow the smoke from the burning huts and I could find my way back.

"Once, I was trapped between two patrols that had camped on both sides of a river. I had to wait in the water for two days before one of them moved on. When I got out, my skin was shriveled like an old melon. I was so cold I could hardly move. From the waist down, my body was black with leeches.[22] But it was worth all the pain. When your mother came back, we still had some furniture and tools to cultivate the earth. Many people lost everything. Yes, we were very lucky."

My father put his arms around me. "My brother Huong[23]—your uncle Huong—had three sons and four daughters. Of his four daughters, only one is still alive. Of his three sons, two went north to Hanoi[24] and one went south to Saigon.[25] Huong's house is very empty. My other brother, your uncle Luc,[26] had only two sons. One went north to Hanoi, the other was killed in the fields. His daughter is deaf and dumb. No wonder he has taken to drink, eh? Who does he have to sing in his house and tend his shrine[27] when he is gone? My sister Lien[28] had three daughters and four sons. Three of the four sons went to Hanoi and the fourth went to Saigon to find his fortune. The girls all tend their in-laws and mourn slain husbands. Who will care for Lien when she is too feeble to care for herself? Finally, my baby sister Nhien[29] lost her husband

to French bombers. Of her two sons, one went to Hanoi and the other joined the Republic, then defected,[30] then was murdered in his house. Nobody knows which side killed him. It doesn't really matter."

My father drew me out to arm's length and looked me squarely in the eye. "Now, Bay Ly, do you understand what your job is?"

I squared my shoulders and put on a soldier's face. "My job is to avenge my family. To protect my farm by killing the enemy. I must become a woman warrior like Phung Thi Chinh!"

My father laughed and pulled me close. "No, little peach blossom. Your job is to stay alive—to keep an eye on things and keep the village safe. To find a husband and have babies and tell the story of what you've seen to your children and anyone else who'll listen. Most of all, it is to live in peace and tend the shrine of our ancestors. Do these things well, Bay Ly, and you will be worth more than any soldier who ever took up a sword."

---

22. **leech** (lēch), *n.* any of a class of bloodsucking or carnivorous annelid worms living chiefly in freshwater ponds and streams.
23. **Huong** (hŭ′ung).
24. **Hanoi** (hä noi′), capital of North Vietnam, now capital of Vietnam.
25. **Saigon** (sī gon′), capital of South Vietnam, now Ho Chi Minh City.
26. **Luc** (lŭk).
27. **tend his shrine.** A shrine is a place or object considered sacred because of its history, memories, etc. In some cultures, after someone dies, his or her children look after that person's or family's shrine.
28. **Lien** (lē′ung).
29. **Nhien** (nē′ung).
30. **defect** (dē′fekt), *v.* forsake one's own country, group, etc., for another, especially another that is opposed to it in political or social doctrine.

After Reading

Making Connections

Shaping Your Response

1. If you were in Bay Ly's family, would you want to stay in the village or leave? Explain.

2. How would you **characterize** Bay Ly's father and mother? Give examples from the text to support your answer.

Analyzing the Autobiography

3. Bay Ly's father describes the Vietnamese countryside to his daughter. What does the land represent to him?

4. Explain two "lessons" that Bay Ly learns from her father.

5. Jot down a list of at least five things you learned about Vietnam from this selection. What questions do you still have?

Extending the Ideas

6. Bay Ly's father wants her to find a husband, have babies, tell the stories of what she has seen, and tend the shrine of their ancestors. Compare and contrast those goals with the goals parents have for children in your community.

7. The life of Bay Ly and her family took place amidst the backdrop of the Vietnam War. How might your life and your goals be affected if you grew up in a war-torn country?

Literary Focus: Proverbs

A **proverb** is a short, wise saying used for a long time by many people. Proverbs often make observations on character or conduct and express popular wisdom. For example, when Bay Ly says "Only a half-trained mechanic thinks everything needs fixing" (page 633), she means that a truly wise person realizes that some things are fine the way they are. Find and record three other proverbs from the selection. Then restate them in your own words.

Vocabulary Study

abstain
diligent
empathy
lenient
vice

For each item below, the first word in capital letters is a vocabulary word. Study the relationship of the first word pair. Then complete the analogy by choosing another word pair that has the same relationship.

1. DILIGENT : HARD-WORKING ::
   a. peaceful : violent
   b. honest : truthful
   c. wise : proverb
   d. strength : weakness

2. EMPATHY : UNDERSTANDING ::
   a. anger : boredom
   b. forgive : forget
   c. love : caring
   d. lying : stealing

3. LENIENT : TOUGH ::
   a. friendly : mean
   b. finger : hand
   c. vice : weakness
   d. difficult : hard

4. VICE : DISHONESTY ::
   a. feeling : thinking
   b. sorrow : joy
   c. virtue : diligence
   d. tough : lenient

5. ABSTAIN : VICE ::
   a. avoid : responsibility
   b. virtue : temptation
   c. plans : ruin
   d. overcome : fear

Expressing Your Ideas

Writing Choices

Writer's Notebook Update Now that you have read the selection, think about what means the most to Bay Ly's family. Imagine that you are one of Bay Ly's parents, defending your decision to stay in the village when others had left. Write a short persuasive speech that would inspire other families to follow your example.

Fabled Lessons Choose a proverb that you think makes an important point about life. Write a **fable** that illustrates the lesson of the proverb. Remember that two common elements of fables are that they often feature animals with human characteristics and have events happen in threes. State your proverb at the end as the moral of the fable.

Other Options

Time in a Bottle Bay Ly's father asks her to tell what she has seen to her children. Make a **time capsule** for your grandchildren or great-grandchildren to find. You might include a letter that tells about important events in your family and in the world, newspaper or magazine headlines, and other artifacts that might help someone learn what the world was like in your lifetime.

This Is My Country Bay Ly learns from her father what their country means to him. What does your country mean to you? Find or draw images to make a **collage** that expresses your feelings towards your country.

Countries at War After reading the selection, you may have further questions about Vietnam or the Vietnam War. Write down a few of the questions you have, and do some **research** to answer them. Possible topics to consider include: the involvement of various countries in the Vietnam War, the adjustment of Vietnam War veterans upon their return home, the goals that were or were not accomplished by the war, the Vietnam Veterans Memorial, and so on.

Before Reading

A Lincoln Preface

by Carl Sandburg

Carl Sandburg
1878–1967

Poet Carl Sandburg's love for Abraham Lincoln led him to write a total of six volumes of Lincoln's biography, which were a culmination of thirty years of collecting information, pondering, and writing. Upon completing the first two volumes, *Abraham Lincoln: The Prairie Years,* Sandburg wrote a preface that "would begin at the death of Lincoln and work back to the day he left Illinois." But when Sandburg decided to write an additional four volumes called *Abraham Lincoln: The War Years,* which was published in 1939, he abandoned the early preface, which is reprinted here. For additional information on Sandburg, see his biography on page 401.

Building Background

A Country Divided The biography you are about to read takes place against the backdrop of the Civil War. By the time that Abraham Lincoln became President on March 4, 1861, seven Southern states had already seceded from the Union. The major causes of the war were disagreements over the power of the federal government to control the states, the separate economies of the industrial North and the agricultural South, and, of course, the continuation of slavery and its expansion into the newly formed territories of the United States.

The war lasted four years and was marked by some of the fiercest military campaigns in modern history. As you read the biography, imagine what it would be like to be the President of a country splitting in two. Do you agree with the way in which Abraham Lincoln handled the country's problems? Do you think he had the right qualities for the job?

Literary Focus

Style When a writer expresses ideas, he or she uses a particular **style** that corresponds with the purpose and intended audience for the piece. The style is determined by many choices an author makes: which words to use and how to arrange them, whether or not to use imagery and figurative language, what point of view to use, and what tone to create. You'll find that Carl Sandburg uses a somewhat unusual style in "A Lincoln Preface."

Writer's Notebook

Fourscore and Seven Years Ago Abraham Lincoln delivered "The Gettysburg Address," one of the world's most famous speeches. What else do you know about him? In your notebook, record some facts that you already know about Abraham Lincoln. Then write questions that you still may have about him or the time period during which he was President (1861–1865).

A LINCOLN PREFACE

Carl Sandburg

In the time of the April lilacs in the year 1865, a man in the City of Washington, D.C., trusted a guard to watch at a door, and the guard was careless, left the door, and the man was shot, lingered a night, passed away, was laid in a box, and carried north and west a thousand miles; bells sobbed; cities wore crepe;[1] people stood with hats off as the railroad burial car came past at midnight, dawn, or noon.

During the four years of time before he gave up the ghost,[2] this man was clothed with despotic[3] power, commanding the most powerful armies till then assembled in modern warfare, enforcing drafts of soldiers, abolishing the right of habeas corpus,[4] directing politically and spiritually the wild, massive forces loosed in civil war.

Four billion dollars' worth of property was taken from those who had been legal owners of it, confiscated,[5] wiped out as by fire, at his instigation[6] and executive direction; a class of chattel property[7] recognized as lawful for two hundred years went to the scrap pile.

When the woman who wrote *Uncle Tom's Cabin*[8] came to see him in the White House, he greeted her, "So you're the little woman who wrote the book that made this great war," and as they seated themselves at a fireplace, "I do love an open fire; I always had one to home." As they were finishing their talk of the days of blood, he said, "I shan't last long after it's over."

An Illinois Congressman looked in on him as he had his face lathered for a shave in the White House, and remarked, "If anybody had told me that in a great crisis like this the people were going out to a little one-horse town[9] and

---

1. **crepe** (krāp), *n.* a thin cloth with a finely crinkled surface. Black crepe is a sign of mourning.
2. **gave up the ghost,** died.
3. **despotic** (des pot′ik), *adj.* having unlimited power; tyrannical.
4. **habeas corpus** (hā′bē əs kôr′pəs), order requiring that a prisoner be brought into court to decide whether he or she is being held lawfully.
5. **confiscated** (kon′fə skāt′əd), *adj.* seized by authority; taken and kept.
6. **instigation** (in′stə gā′shən), *n.* an urging on.
7. **chattel** (chat′l) **property,** property that is not real estate; i. e., slaves.
8. *Uncle Tom's Cabin.* An anti-slavery novel written in 1852 by Harriet Beecher Stowe.
9. **one-horse town,** an undeveloped town with few businesses and services.

◄ At far left, a photograph of Abraham Lincoln taken on June 3, 1860. At left, a photograph taken on April 10, 1865. What does the contrast in Lincoln's physical appearance reveal about his experiences during the five years between the photographs?

who bitterly fought him politically, and accused him of blunders or crimes, were Franklin Pierce, a former President of the United States; Horatio Seymour, the governor of New York; Samuel F. B. Morse, inventor of the telegraph; Cyrus H. McCormick, inventor of the farm reaper; General George B. McClellan, a Democrat who had commanded the Army of the Potomac; and the *Chicago Times,* a daily newspaper. In all its essential propositions the Southern Confederacy had the moral support of powerful, respectable elements throughout the North, probably more than a million voters believing in the justice of the cause of the South as compared with the North.

SUMMARIZE: What controversial methods did Lincoln use to obtain his goals?

While propagandas raged, and the war winds howled, he sat in the White House, the Stubborn Man of History, writing that the Mississippi was one river and could not belong to two countries, that the plans for railroad connection from coast to coast must be pushed through and the Union Pacific realized.

His life, mind, and heart ran on contrasts. When his white kid gloves broke into tatters while shaking hands at a White House reception, he remarked, "This looks like a general bustification."[10] When he talked with an Ohio friend one day during the 1864 campaign, he mentioned one public man, and murmured, "He's a thistle! I don't see why God lets him

pick out a one-horse lawyer for President, I wouldn't have believed it." The answer was, "Neither would I. But it was a time when a man with a policy would have been fatal to the country. I never had a policy. I have simply tried to do what seemed best each day, as each day came."

"I don't intend precisely to throw the Constitution overboard, but I will stick it in a hole if I can," he told a Cabinet officer. The enemy was violating the Constitution to destroy the Union, he argued, and therefore, "I will violate the Constitution, if necessary, to save the Union." He instructed a messenger to the Secretary of the Treasury, "Tell him not to bother himself about the Constitution. Say that I have that sacred instrument here at the White House, and I am guarding it with great care."

When he was renominated, it was by the device of seating delegates from Tennessee, which gave enough added votes to seat favorable delegates from Kentucky, Missouri, Louisiana, Arkansas, and from one county in Florida. Until late in that campaign of 1864, he expected to lose the November election; military victories brought the tide his way; the vote was 2,200,000 for him and 1,800,000 against him. Among those

---

10. **bustification,** an example of regional English. This word, used in the Arkansas-Missouri area in the 1800s, was used facetiously to mean a disaster, a quarrel, or an explosion.

live." Of a devious senator, he said, "He's too crooked to lie still!" And of a New York editor, "In early life in the West, we used to make our shoes last a great while with much mending, and sometimes, when far gone, we found the leather so rotten the stitches would not hold. Greeley is so rotten that nothing can be done with him. He is not truthful; the stitches all tear out." As he sat in the telegraph office of the War Department, reading cipher dispatches,[11] and came to the words, Hosanna and Husband, he would chuckle, "Jeffy D.," and at the words, Hunter and Happy, "Bobby Lee."[12]

While the luck of war wavered[13] and broke and came again, as generals failed and campaigns were lost, he held enough forces of the Union together to raise new armies and supply them, until generals were found who made war as victorious war has always been made, with terror, frightfulness, destruction, and valor and sacrifice past words of man to tell.

A slouching, gray-headed poet, haunting the hospitals at Washington, characterized him as "the grandest figure on the crowded canvas of the drama of the nineteenth century—a Hoosier Michelangelo."[14]

His own speeches, letters, telegrams, and official messages during that war form the most significant and enduring document from any one man on why the war began, why it went on, and the dangers beyond its end. He mentioned "the politicians," over and again "the politicians," with scorn and blame. As the platoons filed before him at a review of an army corps, he asked, "What is to become of these boys when the war is over?"

He was chosen spokesman; yet there were times he was silent; nothing but silence could at those times have fitted a chosen spokesman; in the mixed shame and blame of the immense wrongs of two crashing civilizations, with nothing to say, he said nothing, slept not at all, and wept at those times in a way that made weeping appropriate, decent, majestic.

His hat was shot off as he rode alone one night in Washington; a son he loved died as he watched at the bed; his wife was accused of betraying information to the enemy, until denials from him were necessary; his best companion was a fine-hearted and brilliant son with a deformed palate[15] and an impediment[16] of speech; when a Pennsylvania congressman told him the enemy had declared they would break into the city and hang him to a lamp post, he said he had considered "the violent preliminaries" to such a scene; on his left thumb was scar where an ax had nearly chopped the thumb off when he was a boy; over one eye was a scar where he had been hit with a club in the hands of a Negro trying to steal the cargo off a Mississippi River flatboat; he threw a cashiered[17] officer out of his room in the White House, crying, "I can bear censure,[18] but not insult. I never wish to see your face again."

As he shook hands with the correspondent of the London *Times,* he drawled, "Well, I guess the London *Times* is about the greatest power on earth—unless perhaps it is the Mississippi River." He rebuked[19] with anger a woman who got on her knees to thank him for a pardon that saved her son from being shot at sunrise; and when an Iowa woman said she had journeyed out of her way to Washington just for a look at him, he grinned, "Well, in the matter of looking at one another, I have altogether the advantage."

---

11. **cipher dispatches,** messages written in a secret code.
12. **"Jeffy . . . Lee."** Refers to Jefferson Davis, president of the Confederacy, and Robert E. Lee, Confederate general.
13. **waver** (wā′vər), *v.* become unsteady; hesitate.
14. **Hoosier Michelangelo.** Hoosier (hü′zhər) is a nickname for a native or inhabitant of Indiana. Michelangelo (mī′kə lan′jə lō), 1475–1564, was a great Italian sculptor, painter, architect, and poet.
15. **palate** (pal′ət), *n.* roof of the mouth.
16. **impediment** (im ped′ə mənt), *n.* a physical defect, especially a defect in speech.
17. **cashiered** (ka shird′), *adj.* dismissed from service for some dishonorable act.
18. **censure** (sen′shər), *n.* expression of disapproval.
19. **rebuke** (ri byük), *v.* express disapproval of; reprove.

He asked his Cabinet to vote on the high military command, and after the vote, told them the appointment had already been made; one Cabinet officer, who had been governor of Ohio, came away personally baffled and frustrated from an interview, to exclaim, to a private secretary, "That man is the most cunning person I ever saw in my life"; an Illinois lawyer who had been sent on errands carrying his political secrets, said, "He is a trimmer[20] and such a trimmer as the world has never seen."

He manipulated the admission of Nevada as a state in the Union, when her votes were needed for the Emancipation Proclamation,[21] saying, "It is easier to admit Nevada than to raise another million of soldiers." At the same time he went to the office of a former New York editor, who had become Assistant Secretary of War, and said the votes of three congressmen were wanted for the required three-quarters of votes in the House of Representatives, advising, "There are three that you can deal with better than anybody else. . . . Whatever promise you make to those men, I will perform it." And in the same week, he said to a Massachusetts politician that two votes were lacking, and, "Those two votes must be procured.[22] I leave it to you to determine how it shall be done; but remember that I am President of the United States and clothed with immense power, and I expect you to procure those votes." And while he was thus employing every last resource and device of practical politics to constitutionally abolish slavery, the abolitionist[23] Henry Ward Beecher attacked him with javelins of scorn and detestation in a series of editorials that brought from him the single comment, "Is thy servant a dog?"

When the King of Siam[24] sent him a costly sword of exquisite embellishment, and two elephant tusks, along with letters and a photograph of the King, he acknowledged the gifts in a manner as lavish as the Orientals. Addressing the King of Siam as "Great and Good Friend," he wrote thanks for each of the gifts, including "also two elephants' tusks of length and magnitude such as indicate they could have belonged only to an animal which was a native of Siam." After further thanks for the tokens received, he closed the letter to the King of Siam with strange grace and humor, saying, "I appreciate most highly your Majesty's tender of good offices in forwarding to this Government a stock from which a supply of elephants might be raised on our soil. . . . Our political jurisdiction,[25] however, does not reach a latitude so low as to favor the multiplication of the elephant, and steam on land as well as water has been our best agent of transportation. . . . Meantime, wishing for your Majesty a long and happy life, and, for the generous and emulous[26] people of Siam, the highest possible prosperity, I commend both to the blessing of Almighty God."

CLARIFY: Restate the closing of Lincoln's letter in your own words.

He sent hundreds of telegrams, "Suspend death sentence," or "Suspend execution" of So-and-So, who was to be shot at sunrise. The telegrams varied oddly at times, as in one, "If Thomas Samplogh, of the First Delaware Regiment, has been sentenced to death, and is not yet executed, suspend and report the case

---

20. **trimmer,** person whose opinions, actions, etc., change to suit the circumstances.
21. **Emancipation Proclamation,** a declaration made by Abraham Lincoln on January 1, 1863, which freed all slaves residing in territory in rebellion against the federal government.
22. procure (prə kyür′), v. obtain by care or effort.
23. **abolitionist** (ab′ə lish′ə nist), n. person in the 1830s to 1860s who favored the abolition, or ending, of slavery in the United States.
24. **Siam** (sī am′), former name of Thailand.
25. **jurisdiction** (jur′is dik′shən), n. extent of authority.
26. **emulous** (em′yə ləs), adj. wishing to equal or excel.

to me." And another, "Is it Lieut. Samuel B. Davis whose death sentence is commuted?[27] If not done, let it be done."

While the war drums beat, he liked best of all the stories told of him, one of two Quakeresses[28] heard talking in a railway car. "I think that Jefferson will succeed." "Why does thee think so?" "Because Jefferson is a praying man." "And so is Abraham a praying man." "Yes, but the Lord will think Abraham is joking."

An Indiana man at the White House heard him say, "Voorhees, don't it seem strange to you that I, who could never so much as cut off the head of a chicken, should be elected, or selected, into the midst of all this blood?"

A party of American citizens, standing in the ruins of the Forum in Rome, Italy, heard there the news of the first assassination of the first American dictator, and took it as a sign of the growing up and the aging of the civilization on the North American continent. Far out in Coles County, Illinois, a beautiful, gaunt old woman in a log cabin said "I knowed he'd never come back."

Of men taking too fat profits out of the war, he said, "Where the carcass is, there will the eagles be gathered together."

An enemy general, Longstreet, after the war, declared him to have been "the one matchless man in forty millions of people," while one of his private secretaries, Hay, declared his life to have been the most perfect in its relationships and adjustments since that of Christ.

Between the days in which he crawled as a baby on the dirt floor of a Kentucky cabin, and the time when he gave his final breath in Washington, he packed a rich life with work, thought, laughter, tears, hate, love.

With vast reservoirs of the comic and the droll, and notwithstanding a mastery of mirth[29] and nonsense, he delivered a volume of addresses and letters of terrible and serious appeal, with import beyond his own day, shot through here and there with far, thin ironies, with paragraphs having raillery[30] of the quality of the Book of Job, and echoes as subtle as the whispers of wind in prairie grass.

Perhaps no human clay-pot has held more laughter and tears.

The facts and myths of his life are to be an American possession, shared widely over the world, for thousands of years, as the tradition of Knute or Alfred, Lao-tse or Diogenes, Pericles or Caesar,[31] are kept. This because he was not only a genius in the science of neighborly human relationships and an artist in the personal handling of life from day to day, but a strange friend and a friendly stranger to all forms of life that he met.

He lived fifty-six years of which fifty-two were lived in the West—the prairie years.

---

27. **commute** (kə myütʹ), v. change an obligation, penalty, etc., to a less severe one.
28. **Quakeresses** (kwāʹkər əsʹəs), female Quakers. Quakers are members of a Christian group called the Society of Friends, whose beliefs include the observance of simplicity in worship, manners, etc., and opposition to war and to the taking of oaths.
29. mirth (mėrth), n. merry fun; being joyous; merriment.
30. **raillery** (rālʹər ē), n. good-humored ridicule; joking; teasing.
31. **Knute . . . Caesar,** great statesmen and philosophers of ancient times.

After Reading

Making Connections

Shaping Your Response

1. Did this piece make your opinion of Abraham Lincoln more favorable, less favorable, or about the same? Be ready to explain your position.

2. On page 643, Sandburg calls Lincoln "the Stubborn Man of History." On page 646, he calls him "the first American dictator." What do these phrases reveal about Sandburg's attitude toward Lincoln?

Analyzing the Biography

3. Sandburg writes that Lincoln's "life, mind, and heart ran on contrasts." Use evidence from the biography to support or refute this claim.

4. Unlike many biographies, this selection does not discuss events chronologically, or in the order in which they occurred. What effect does this create?

Extending the Ideas

5. Do you think Lincoln's actions, such as manipulating Nevada's admission to the United States, were justified? Why or why not?

6. What lessons do you think today's leaders could learn from the example of Abraham Lincoln?

Literary Focus: Style

A major aspect of an author's **style** is the choice and arrangement of language and incidents to shape readers' attitudes toward a subject. With that in mind, answer these questions about "A Lincoln Preface."

1. With each of the following quotations, what attitudes or feelings toward Lincoln do you think Sandburg hoped to arouse?

— ". . . this man was clothed with despotic power . . ." (p. 642)

— ". . . [he] wept at those times in a way that made weeping appropriate, decent, majestic." (p. 644)

— "He asked his Cabinet to vote . . . and after the vote, told them the appointment had already been made. . . ." (p. 645)

— ". . . he packed a rich life with work, thought, laughter, tears, hate, love." (p. 646)

2. Count the number of single-sentence paragraphs in "A Lincoln Preface." What is their effect on the **rhythm** of the selection?

3. Explain whether you think any aspects of Sandburg's style were influenced by the fact that he was a poet.

Vocabulary Study

Choose the word that is a synonym, or most nearly the same in meaning, as the italicized vocabulary word. Use your Glossary, if necessary, to check the meanings of the vocabulary words.

confiscated
despotic
mirth
procure
waver

1. *confiscated* (a) paid (b) seized (c) given (d) assisted
2. *despotic* (a) unhappy (b) unreasonable (c) despairing (d) tyrannical
3. *mirth* (a) maliciousness (b) sadness (c) simplicity (d) merriment
4. *procure* (a) fight (b) request (c) obtain (d) deny
5. *waver* (a) vary (b) salute (c) abandon (d) dismiss

Expressing Your Ideas

Writing Choices

Writer's Notebook Update Before you read "A Lincoln Preface," you wrote some facts that you already knew about Abraham Lincoln and some questions you had about him. In your notebook, write the answers to the questions you wrote and other interesting information you learned from the biography.

Secret Admirer In only a few pages, Carl Sandburg captures the personality of Abraham Lincoln. Think about someone you admire: a relative, a friend, or someone you have read or heard about. Write a **character sketch** of that person. Be sure to describe the person and highlight the person's personality traits that you most admire. You might imitate some elements of Sandburg's style.

Words to the Wise If Abraham Lincoln were alive today, what situations in the world do you think would benefit from his knowledge and understanding? Write a **letter** to Lincoln, in which you detail a problem with which Lincoln could help. Then trade letters with a partner. As Lincoln, answer your partner's letter. What advice do you think Lincoln would give to solve the problem?

Other Options

Reformers "A Lincoln Preface" mentions Harriet Beecher Stowe's book *Uncle Tom's Cabin*. This book was Stowe's contribution to the abolitionist movement. Abolitionists were reformers who sought to end the institution of slavery. Find out more about the anti-slavery movement or one of the abolitionists. Use the information you find to write a short **chapter** for a class book on the abolitionist movement. Some famous abolitionists include William Lloyd Garrison, Frederick Douglass, Angelina Grimke, Wendell Phillips, and John Brown.

Well Said Sandburg mentions that Lincoln's speeches during the war form a clear picture of why the war began and endured and "the dangers beyond its end." Find one of Lincoln's famous speeches, such as the "Gettysburg Address." Practice reading aloud all or part of the speech, considering what words to emphasize, the tone to use when delivering the speech, and so on. Deliver your **speech** to the class.

Before Reading

The Secret Life of Walter Mitty

by James Thurber

James Thurber
1894–1961

James Thurber grew up in Columbus, Ohio, and became one of the foremost American humorists of his time. After serving in the U.S. Embassy in France during World War I, he worked as a journalist in Paris and in New York. He became associated with *The New Yorker* magazine shortly after it was founded and contributed stories and cartoons to it. For inspiration, Thurber frequently drew upon memories of his childhood in Ohio and the slightly wacky members of his family who, according to Thurber, were addicted to absurdity. "The Secret Life of Walter Mitty" served as the basis for a 1947 movie starring comic actor Danny Kaye.

Building Background

Thurber's World Many anecdotes about Thurber have been recorded, all showing his absurd sense of humor. For example, when he overdrew his bank account, he admitted that he did not keep track of the checks he wrote. When the bank manager asked him how he knew how much money he had in his account, Thurber replied, "I thought that was *your* business." Commenting on Thurber's humor, poet T. S. Eliot described Thurber's work as "a form of humor which is also a way of saying something serious." For "The Secret Life of Walter Mitty," Thurber drew inspiration from the stereotyped adventure hero of the 1920s and 1930s, who dashed from one exciting scene to the next with a cynical gleam in his eye and a careless smile on his lips.

Literary Focus

Dialogue The conversation between two or more people in a literary work is called **dialogue.** Dialogue can help develop a character in two ways: through the words that character says, and through the things that other characters say about the character. Dialogue can also serve to create mood, advance the plot, or develop the theme of a story.

Writer's Notebook

Perchance to Dream *You're on stage before one hundred thousand screaming fans. You look over toward the skyboxes, and you see every famous person from Hollywood has come to your concert. When you sing your first note, the entire stadium falls silent, and then erupts with cheers and applause at the end of every song.*

Have you ever had daydreams like that one? In your notebook, jot down some of your favorite daydreams. As you read the story, think about what roles daydreams play in the life of the main character.

THE SECRET LIFE OF Walter Mitty

JAMES THURBER

"We're going through!" The Commander's voice was like thin ice breaking. He wore his full-dress uniform, with the heavily braided white cap pulled down rakishly[1] over one cold gray eye. "We can't make it, sir. It's spoiling for a hurricane, if you ask me." "I'm not asking you, Lieutenant Berg," said the Commander. "Throw on the power light! Rev her up to 8500! We're going through!" The pounding of the cylinders increased: ta-pocketa-pocketa-pocketa-*pocketa-pocketa*. The Commander stared at the ice forming on the pilot window. He walked over and twisted a row of complicated dials. "Switch on No. 8 auxiliary!" he shouted. "Switch on No. 8 auxiliary!" repeated Lieutenant Berg. "Full strength in No. 3 turret!" shouted the Commander. "Full strength in No. 3 turret!" The crew, bending to their various tasks in the huge, hurtling eight-engined Navy hydroplane,[2] looked at each other and grinned. "The Old Man'll get us through," they said to one another. "The Old Man ain't afraid of Hell!" . . .

"Not so fast! You're driving too fast!" said Mrs. Mitty. "What are you driving so fast for?"

"Hmm?" said Walter Mitty. He looked at his wife, in the seat beside him, with shocked astonishment. She seemed grossly unfamiliar, like a strange woman who had yelled at him in a crowd. "You were up to fifty-five," she said. "You know I don't like to go more than forty. You were up to fifty-five." Walter Mitty drove on toward Waterbury in silence, the roaring of the SN202 through the worst storm in twenty years of Navy flying fading in the remote, intimate airways of his mind. "You're tensed up again," said Mrs. Mitty. "It's one of your days. I wish you'd let Dr. Renshaw look you over."

*W*alter Mitty stopped the car in front of the building where his wife went to have her hair done. "Remember to get those overshoes while I'm having my hair done," she said. "I don't need overshoes," said Mitty. She put her mirror back into her bag. "We've been all through that," she said, getting out of the car. "You're not a young man any longer." He raced the engine a little. "Why don't you wear your gloves? Have you lost your gloves?" Walter Mitty reached in a pocket and brought out the gloves. He put them on, but after she had turned and

---

1. **rakishly** (rā′kish lē), *adv.* in a dashing way; smartly; jauntily.
2. **hydroplane** (hī′drə plān), *n.* a fast motorboat that glides on the surface of the water.

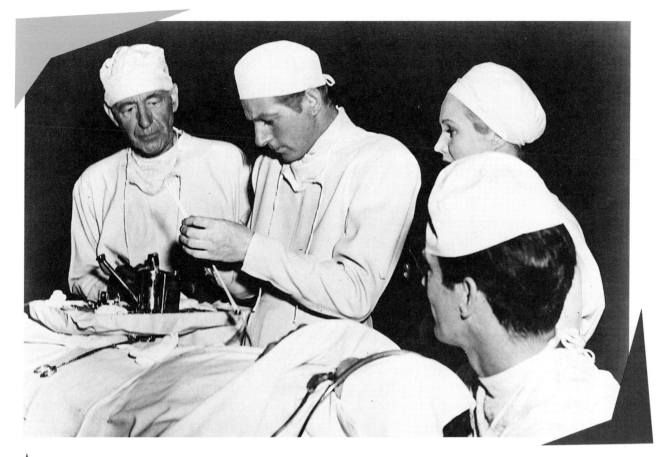

Actor Danny Kaye (center) appeared in the 1947 film adaptation of "The Secret Life of Walter Mitty." If a new film version were done today, what actor would you cast in the role of Walter Mitty?

gone into the building and he had driven on to a red light, he took them off again. "Pick it up, brother!" snapped a cop as the light changed, and Mitty hastily pulled on his gloves and lurched ahead. He drove around the streets aimlessly[3] for a time, and then he drove past the hospital on his way to the parking lot.

. . . "It's the millionaire banker, Wellington McMillan," said the pretty nurse. "Yes?" said Walter Mitty, removing his gloves slowly. "Who has the case?" "Dr. Renshaw and Dr. Benbow, but there are two specialists here, Dr. Remington from New York and Mr. Pritchard-Mitford from London. He flew over." A door opened down a long, cool corridor and Dr. Renshaw came out. He looked distraught and haggard. "Hello, Mitty," he said, "We're having the devil's own time with McMillan, the millionaire banker and close personal friend of Roosevelt.[4] Obstreosis of the ductal tract. Tertiary.[5] Wish you'd take a look at him." "Glad to," said Mitty.

In the operating room there were whispered introductions: "Dr. Remington, Dr. Mitty. Mr. Pritchard-Mitford, Dr. Mitty." "I've read your

3. **aimlessly** (ām′lis lē), *adv.* in a way that is without purpose; pointlessly.
4. **Roosevelt,** Franklin Delano, 1882–1945, 32nd President of the United States.
5. **Obstreosis** (ob′strē ō′sis) **of the ductal** (duk′təl) **tract. Tertiary** (tėr′shē er′ē). This medical diagnosis is complete nonsense.

book on streptothricosis,"[6] said Pritchard-Mitford, shaking hands. "A brilliant performance, sir." "Thank you," said Walter Mitty. "Didn't know you were in the States, Mitty," grumbled Remington. "Coals to Newcastle,[7] bringing Mitford and me up here for a tertiary." "You are very kind," said Mitty. A huge, complicated machine, connected to the operating table, with many tubes and wires, began at this moment to go pocketa-pocketa-pocketa. "The new anesthetizer is giving way!" shouted an intern. "There is no one in the East who knows how to fix it!" "Quiet, man!" said Mitty, in a low, cool voice. He sprang to the machine, which was now going pocketa-pocketa-queep-pocketa-queep. He began fingering delicately a row of glistening dials. "Give me a fountain pen!" he snapped. Someone handed him a fountain pen. He pulled a faulty piston out of the machine and inserted the pen in its place. "That will hold for ten minutes," he said. "Get on with the operation." A nurse hurried over and whispered to Renshaw, and Mitty saw the man turn pale. "Coreopsis[8] has set in," said Renshaw nervously. "If you would take over, Mitty?" Mitty looked at him and at the craven[9] figure of Benbow, who drank, and at the grave, uncertain faces of the two great specialists. "If you wish," he said. They slipped a white gown on him; he adjusted a mask and drew on thin gloves; nurses handed him shining . . .

"Back it up, Mac! Look out for that Buick!" Walter Mitty jammed on the brakes. "Wrong lane, Mac," said the parking-lot attendant, looking at Mitty closely. "Gee. Yeh," muttered Mitty. He began cautiously to back out of the lane marked "Exit Only." "Leave her sit there," said the attendant. "I'll put her away." Mitty got out of the car. "Hey, better leave the key." "Oh," said Mitty, handing the man the ignition key. The attendant vaulted into the car, backed it up with insolent skill, and put it where it belonged.

They're so damn cocky, thought Walter Mitty, walking along Main Street; they think they know everything. Once he had tried to take his chains off,[10] outside New Milford, and he had got them wound around the axles. A man had had to come out in a wrecking car and unwind them, a young, grinning garageman. Since then Mrs. Mitty always made him drive to a garage to have the chains taken off. The next time, he thought, I'll wear my right arm in a sling; they won't grin at me then. I'll have my right arm in a sling and they'll see I couldn't possibly take the chains off myself. He kicked at the slush on the sidewalk. "Overshoes," he said to himself, and he began looking for a shoe store.

When he came out into the street again, with the overshoes in a box under his arm, Walter Mitty began to wonder what the other thing was his wife had told him to get. She had told him twice, before they set out from their house for Waterbury. In a way he hated these weekly trips to town—he was always getting something wrong. Kleenex, he thought, Squibb's, razor blades? No. Toothpaste, toothbrush, bicarbonate, carborundum, initiative and referendum? He gave it up. But she would remember it. "Where's the what's-its-name?" she would ask. "Don't tell me you forgot the what's-its-name." A newsboy went by shouting something about the Waterbury trial.

. . . "Perhaps this will refresh your memory." The District Attorney suddenly thrust a heavy automatic[11] at the quiet figure on the witness stand. "Have you ever seen this before?" Walter

---

6. **streptothricosis** (strep′tō thri kō′sis). Close to *strep-tothrichosis,* once the name of a disease caused by a group of bacteria.
7. **Coals to Newcastle.** Newcastle, England, was a coal-producing area. The expression "carrying coals to Newcastle" means to do something totally unnecessary.
8. **Coreopsis** (kor′ē op′sis), a genus of herb. Its use is nonsense, but imaginative nonsense, on Mitty's part.
9. **craven** (crā′vən), *adv.* cowardly.
10. **take his chains off.** At the time of the story, it was a common practice to put chains on the tires of cars during the winter months to add traction for driving on slippery ice and snow.
11. **automatic** (ô′tə mat′ik), *n.* another name for a pistol.

Mitty took the gun and examined it expertly. "This is my Webley-Vickers 50.80," he said calmly. An excited buzz ran around the courtroom. The judge rapped for order. "You are a crack shot with any sort of firearms, I believe?" said the District Attorney, insinuatingly.[12] "Objection!" shouted Mitty's attorney. "We have shown that the defendant could not have fired the shot. We have shown that he wore his right arm in a sling on the night of the fourteenth of July." Walter Mitty raised his hand briefly and the bickering attorneys were stilled. "With any known make of gun," he said evenly, "I could have killed Gregory Fitzhurst at three hundred feet *with my left hand*." Pandemonium[13] broke loose in the courtroom. A woman's scream rose above the bedlam[14] and suddenly a lovely, dark-haired girl was in Walter Mitty's arms. The District Attorney struck at her savagely. Without rising from his chair, Mitty let the man have it on the point of the chin. "You miserable cur!"[15] . . .

"Puppy biscuit," said Walter Mitty. He stopped walking and the buildings of Waterbury rose up out of the misty courtroom and surrounded him again. A woman who was passing laughed. "He said 'Puppy biscuit,'" she said to her companion. "That man said 'Puppy biscuit' to himself." Walter Mitty hurried on. He went into an A. & P.,[16] not the first one he came to but a smaller one farther up the street. "I want some biscuit for small, young dogs," he said to the clerk. "Any special brand, sir?" The greatest pistol shot in the world thought a moment. "It says 'Puppies Bark for It' on the box," said Walter Mitty.

*H*is wife would be through at the hairdresser's in fifteen minutes, Mitty saw in looking at his watch, unless they had trouble drying it; sometimes they had trouble drying it. She didn't like to get to the hotel first; she would want him to be there waiting for her as usual. He found a big leather chair in the lobby, facing a window, and he put the overshoes and the puppy biscuit on the floor beside it. He picked up an old copy of *Liberty*[17] and sank down into the chair. "Can Germany Conquer the World Through the Air?" Walter Mitty looked at the pictures of bombing planes and of ruined streets.

. . . "The cannonading[18] has got the wind up in young Raleigh, sir," said the sergeant. Captain Mitty looked up at him through tousled hair. "Get him to bed," he said wearily. "With the others. I'll fly alone." "But you can't, sir," said the sergeant anxiously. "It takes two men to handle that bomber and the Archies are pounding hell out of the air. Von Richtman's circus is between here and Saulier."[19] "Somebody's got to get that ammunition dump," said Mitty. "I'm going over. Spot of brandy?" He poured a drink for the sergeant and one for himself. War thundered and whined around the dugout and battered at the door. There was a rending[20] of wood and splinters flew through the room. "A bit of a near thing," said Captain Mitty carelessly. "The box barrage[21] is closing in," said the sergeant. "We only live once, Sergeant," said Mitty, with his

12. **insinuatingly** (in sin′yŭ āt′ing lē), *adv.* in an indirect or hinting manner.
13. pandemonium (pan′də mō′nē əm), *n.* wild uproar.
14. **bedlam** (bed′ləm), *n.* a noisy confusion; uproar.
15. **cur** (kėr), *n.* a dog of mixed breed; also, a surly, contemptible person.
16. **A. & P.,** a regional grocery store.
17. *Liberty,* a popular magazine of the '30s and '40s.
18. **cannonading** (kan′ə nād′ing), *n.* a continued firing of cannons.
19. **Archies . . . Saulier.** Here as elsewhere, Mitty's daydream blends reality and fantasy. In World War I, *Archies* was the British nickname for anti-aircraft guns and the shells they fired. *Von Richtman* is reminiscent of Baron von Richtoven, a World War I German flying ace. *Saulier* (sô lē ā′) appears to be a fictional town in France.
20. **rending** (rend′ing), *n.* splitting.
21. barrage (bə räzh′), *n.* barrier of artillery fire used to hold back the enemy or to protect one's own soldiers when advancing or retreating.

The Secret Life of Walter Mitty **653**

faint fleeting smile. "Or do we?" He poured another brandy and tossed it off. "I never see a man could hold his brandy like you, sir," said the sergeant. "Begging your pardon, sir." Captain Mitty stood up and strapped on his huge Webley-Vickers automatic. "It's forty kilometers through hell, sir," said the sergeant. Mitty finished one last brandy. "After all," he said softly, "what isn't?" The pounding of the cannon increased; there was the rat-tat-tatting of machine guns, and from somewhere came the menacing pocketa-pocketa-pocketa of the new flame throwers. Walter Mitty walked to the door of the dugout humming "Auprès de Ma Blonde."[22] He turned and waved to the sergeant. "Cheerio!" he said. . . .

Something struck his shoulder. "I've been looking all over this hotel for you," said Mrs. Mitty. "Why do you have to hide in this old chair? How did you expect me to find you?" "Things close in," said Walter Mitty vaguely. "What?" Mrs. Mitty said. "Did you get the what's-its-name? The puppy biscuit? What's in that box?" "Overshoes," said Mitty. "Couldn't you have put them on in the store?" "I was thinking," said Walter Mitty. "Does it ever occur to you that I am sometimes thinking?" She looked at him.

"I'm going to take your temperature when I get you home," she said.

They went out through the revolving doors that made a faintly derisive[23] whistling sound when you pushed them. It was two blocks to the parking lot. At the drugstore on the corner she said, "Wait here for me. I forgot something. I won't be a minute." She was more than a minute. Walter Mitty lighted a cigarette. It began to rain, rain with sleet in it. He stood up against the wall of the drugstore, smoking. . . . He put his shoulders back and his heels together. "To hell with the handkerchief," said Walter Mitty scornfully. He took one last drag on his cigarette and snapped it away. Then, with that faint, fleeting smile playing about his lips, he faced the firing squad; erect and motionless, proud and disdainful,[24] Walter Mitty the Undefeated, inscrutable[25] to the last.

---

22. **"Auprès de Ma Blonde"** (ō prä′ də mä blôn′də), the title of a French song, "Near My Blonde."
23. derisive (di rī′siv), *adj.* that makes fun of; mocking; scornful.
24. **disdainful** (dis dān′fəl), *adj.* scornful.
25. inscrutable (in skrü′tə bəl), *adj.* incomprehensible; so mysterious or obscure that one cannot make out its meaning.

◄ Walter Mitty (played by Danny Kaye) in a moment of glory. What details in this scene make it clear that Mitty is a hero?

After Reading

Making Connections

Shaping Your Response

1. The title of Part 1 in Unit 5 is "Unexpected Heroes." Is Walter Mitty a hero? Explain.

2. Why do you think Walter Mitty daydreams?

Analyzing the Story

3. Contrast the real Walter Mitty with his imaginary self.

4. How does the author connect incidents in reality to Mitty's imaginary adventures?

5. How does the author **characterize** Mrs. Mitty?

6. What details in both Mitty's fantasies and his real life heighten the comical aspect of his character?

Extending the Ideas

7. What is your favorite daydream? Compare your daydream with Walter Mitty's.

8. If Walter Mitty were placed in a situation calling for a real hero, could he live up to the challenge? Give evidence from the story to support your answer.

Literary Focus: Dialogue

Dialogue consists of the spoken words between characters in a story or play. Dialogue serves many purposes: it can establish setting, set the tone, further the action, or reveal character traits.

- What does the dialogue in the fantasy segments show about Walter Mitty?

- How do the comments of Mrs. Mitty, the parking lot attendant, and a woman on the street help to reveal Mitty's character?

Vocabulary Study

aimlessly
barrage
derisive
inscrutable
pandemonium

Complete the following writing assignments using the listed vocabulary words. Use the Glossary, if necessary, to understand the meanings of the vocabulary words. If you are unable to use all the words, use the leftover words in a note to a friend.

1. Use the words *aimlessly* and *inscrutable* in the opening for a chilling story.

2. Use the words *pandemonium, derisive,* and *barrage* in an article describing the scene at a sold-out concert.

Expressing Your Ideas

Writing Choices

Writer's Notebook Update Now that you have read the story, think about the roles that Mitty plays in his daydreams. Why do these roles appeal to him? Imagine that you are Walter Mitty, writing in your "dream journal." Add another adventure or two.

Extra! Extra! The "adventures" of Walter Mitty would make great newspaper stories. For each daydream described in the story, write a concise, attention-grabbing **headline.** Then write additional headlines for other imaginary adventures Mitty could have.

Dream On The story focuses on the daydreams of Walter Mitty. How would this story be different if Mrs. Mitty were the daydreamer? Imagine what Mrs. Mitty might daydream about. Then write an **episode** detailing one of Mrs. Mitty's daydreams.

Other Options

The Gift of Gab Imagine that Mr. and Mrs. Mitty are guests on a television show. In a small group, create a **television segment,** acting as the Mittys, the host, and other appropriate guests. Perhaps you'll have the Mittys as a team on a game show or as the guests on a talk show about husband/wife communication. Rehearse your segment, being sure to keep "in character." Present your show to the class.

Action! "The Secret Life of Walter Mitty" was made into a successful movie. Imagine that you were staging the story as a play. How would you signal the progression from fantasy to reality? You might, for example, use lighting effects or music. Write stage directions needed for turning one section of the story into a **skit.** Use your stage directions to rehearse your skit with a small group. After rehearsing, perform your skit for the class.

Unexpected Heroes

Untold Stories

Journalism Connection

Reporters are constantly on the lookout for new stories. But in order to get those stories, they must perfect their interviewing skills. The following interview tips were written for school newspaper reporters.

Tips

for Great Interviews

by Vivian Dubrovin

1. Arrange a time and place for the interview.

2. Tell the person what the interview will be about so that he or she can prepare for it in advance.

3. Study your background material and plan your questions.

4. Be on time and be polite.

5. Let the person talk about other things if he or she wants to tell you something that relates to the subject.

6. Forget some of your questions if they don't seem appropriate after you have talked for a while. You don't have to ask everything if you think you have all the information you need.

7. Take a note pad with you and several pencils. Write down facts, numbers, dates, and names of persons and places. Take the time to be sure the spelling is correct.

8. At the end of the interview, go over your notes with the person. Be sure you have understood correctly what he or she said.

9. Write all the information down as soon as you can. You can organize it and write your story later, but get your information out of your head and onto paper as soon as possible.

Responding

1. Which of these tips do you think are the most important? Explain.

2. With a partner, role-play a celebrity interview. One of you can be the celebrity, and the other can be a magazine reporter. Try to follow the process described above.

Interdisciplinary Study   **657**

Social Studies Connection

In some professions, generations of women have struggled to be accepted on an equal footing with men. Since 1929, a group known as the 99s has welcomed women who fly in the face of convention.

In the Air with the

by David Roberts

Late in 1929, a group of pilots gathered in a hangar at a Long Island airport. Though a number of them enjoyed international fame for their record-breaking flights, all had stories to share about the discrimination they faced. Many had been told they shouldn't be piloting planes at all, for one reason: they were women.

Over the noise of airplane engines, the women fliers discussed plans to form their own organization. Amelia Earhart suggested that the group take its name from the number of pilots who joined. At the time, 126 women were licensed pilots in the United States, and all were invited to become charter members for a fee of one dollar. Of the 126, 99 signed up, and the 99s were ready for takeoff.

Those first members included some remarkable and even controversial women. Twenty-three-year-old Louise Thaden had recently won the first coast-to-coast Women's Air Derby (dubbed the "Powder Puff Derby" by humorist Will Rogers). Amelia Earhart, the 99s' first president, was already the first woman to have crossed the Atlantic in an airplane; a few years later, in 1932, she became the first female pilot to fly solo across the Atlantic. Elinor Smith had been grounded from flying for ten days by the mayor of New York City, after she flew *under* the four bridges crossing the East River. And Florence (Pancho) Barnes, disguised as a male sailor on a banana boat, had run guns for Mexican revolutionaries.

Like the male pilots in the early days of aviation, women fliers were known for their persistence and daring. During her 1931 attempt to fly solo across the Atlantic Ocean, Ruth Nichols crashed in Newfoundland, breaking several vertebrae. But three months later she broke the women's world record for distance on a nonstop flight—wearing a steel corset from her hips to her armpits. Louise Thaden amazed the nation in 1936 when she raced from New York to Los Angeles against top male pilots—and took first place, winning the coveted Bendix Trophy.

Though the public loved them, the 99s were often viewed as novelties, even freaks. Despite their achievements, women fliers had to put up with patronizing nicknames like the

Amelia Earhart mysteriously disappeared over the Pacific Ocean in 1937. She was flying the final leg of what would have been the first circumnavigation of the globe near the Equator by any flier.

In 1935, the 99s gathered to celebrate Amelia Earhart's successful solo flight across the Pacific Ocean.

Despite their achievements,
women fliers had to put up with
patronizing nicknames like the Flying
Flappers and the Petticoat Pilots.

Flying Flappers and the Petticoat Pilots. Whenever a female pilot died in a crash, newspaper headlines would announce that women were incapable of flying planes, but wouldn't mention that male pilots suffered fatal crashes in equal numbers. Flying hero Charles Lindbergh argued vehemently against allowing women to join the Air Force— even though his own wife, Anne Morrow Lindbergh, was a distinguished pilot.

Over the years, women pilots won some

battles and lost others. American women were allowed to fly military planes during World War II, though not in combat. In 1959, 25 women were allowed to undergo testing as candidates for NASA's first astronaut training program. Thirteen women passed the rigorous tests, but were then shut out of the program. It wasn't until 1983 that pilot Sally Ride became the first American woman in space. Women were first hired as commercial pilots on major airlines in 1973, but are still a small minority.

Today the basic mission of the 99s remains unchanged: to combat prejudicial attitudes toward women pilots. With 6,400 members around the world, the 99s hold races and get-togethers, perform public service, and provide scholarships for promising young female pilots. The group's headquarters in Oklahoma City also serves as a museum honoring women fliers. There the spirit and humor of the 99s is reflected even on the restroom signs: "Pilots" on the women's door, "Co-Pilots" on the men's.

◄ Elinor Smith was only seventeen when she flew under four Manhattan bridges.

Responding
1. What qualities did the early 99s have to exhibit?

2. Imagine that you are boarding a jetliner and you see that the pilot is a woman. Describe your reaction.

Reading Mini-Lesson

Main Idea and Supporting Details

The ability to find the **main idea** as you read is a useful skill, especially when reading a nonfiction article for information. The main idea gives the most important point of the article and can usually be summed up in one sentence. The **details** that a writer includes may support the main idea, clarify it, or simply add interesting information.

One strategy for identifying the main idea of an article is to look for the **topic sentence** of each paragraph within the article. A topic sentence gives the main idea of a single paragraph, and is supported by details within the paragraph. Examining the topic sentences can help you build a picture of the main idea. A topic sentence may not always be directly stated in a paragraph. When it is, however, it is often the first or last sentence.

Create a larger version of the diagram shown here for "In the Air with the 99s." Following the example that is given, identify the topic sentence of each paragraph and summarize it in a few words on the diagram. List one or two details in the paragraph that support the topic sentence. After summarizing all the topic sentences, use them to help you write a new sentence that states the main idea of the entire article.

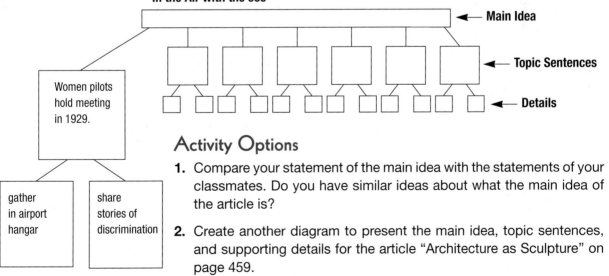

"In the Air with the 99s"

← Main Idea

← Topic Sentences

← Details

Women pilots hold meeting in 1929.

gather in airport hangar

share stories of discrimination

Activity Options

1. Compare your statement of the main idea with the statements of your classmates. Do you have similar ideas about what the main idea of the article is?

2. Create another diagram to present the main idea, topic sentences, and supporting details for the article "Architecture as Sculpture" on page 459.

Reading Mini-Lesson   **661**

Writing Workshop

Local Heroes

Assignment You have read about individuals who make a difference in the lives of the people around them. Work with a partner to write a feature article for your school newspaper about such a person from your community.

WRITER'S BLUEPRINT

Product   A feature article
Purpose   To recognize personal achievements
Audience   Members of your school and community
Specs   To write a successful article, you should:

❑ Choose a person who has made a difference in your life or in the life of your community. It might be someone like a firefighter who saves a life, or someone whose daily devotion to family or community life is extraordinary.

❑ Begin your article by briefly telling what makes this person special. Start with a lead sentence that grabs your reader's attention.

❑ Go on to give important information about this person, including personal background, character traits, heroic deeds or actions, and thoughts on the future. Include quotes from an interview with your subject. If possible, include photographs as part of the article.

❑ Close by telling what you think this person should receive as a reward for his or her achievements.

❑ Follow the rules of grammar, usage, spelling, and mechanics. Be sure to use commas correctly.

PREWRITING

Revisit the literature. Work with a partner to review the literature in this part and list the traits of characters who make a difference in the lives of others. Record traits in a chart like the one shown.

Character	Traits	Examples
Henry Reed	courteous, respectful, soft-spoken, competitive, very smart	graduation speech heartens graduates and tells them they deserve to be successful

LITERARY SOURCE
"While echoes of the song shivered in the air, Henry Reed bowed his head, said 'Thank you,' and returned to his place in the line. The tears that slipped down many faces were not wiped away in shame."

from "Graduation" by Maya Angelou

Make a similar chart for people you know. Then, with your partner, choose your subject. Contact this person right away to be sure she or he is willing to cooperate.

Research your subject by gathering information from a variety of sources, such as interviews with people who know your subject and newspaper articles about her or him. Keep notes to use when you begin drafting.

OR . . .
Make a time line listing important events in your subject's life and organize your information around these events.

Plan an interview with your subject. Make a list of the questions you plan to ask. Include a variety of topics, such as the subject's background, reminiscences and feelings about special deeds, and thoughts about the future.

Conduct your interview. See page 657 for tips on interviewing.

Plan your article by creating an outline like the one shown. Get in at least one quotation from your subject in each of the three parts.

- **Introduction**
  A lead sentence to hook the reader (See the Revising Strategy in Step 3 of this lesson.)
  What makes subject special

- **Body**
  Background information
  Exceptional deeds and traits
  Thoughts on the future

- **Conclusion**
  What this person should receive as a reward

Start writing. Here are some drafting tips.

- Begin with a lead sentence that amazes, intrigues, or amuses the reader. (See the Revising Strategy in Step 3 of this lesson.)

- Use the lead-sentence techniques shown in Step 3 in other parts of your article.

> **COMPUTER TIP**
> Some word-processing programs have a **Drag and Drop** feature that allows you to move copy around without having to cut and paste or retype it. Check to see if your program has this feature, and learn how to use it.

Ask another pair of classmates for comments on your draft before you revise it. Pay special attention to the lead sentence.

Revising Strategy

Writing a Lead Sentence

The lead sentence, the first sentence in an article, must hook the reader in some way. Three ways are shown below. (Emma Lindenmeier has been tending to sick and wounded animals for over fifty years.)

1. **Amaze the reader:** Emma Lindenmeier has saved more lives than a whole hospital full of doctors.
2. **Intrigue the reader:** One morning in May, Emma Lindenmeier woke up to find a bobcat staring back at her from across the bedroom.
3. **Amuse the reader:** In Emma Lindenmeier's medicine cabinet, where you'd expect to find cough medicine and aspirin, you find worm pills and vitamin biscuits in the shape of mail carriers.

Look over your lead sentence to be sure that it hooks the reader in some way. Notice how the writer of the student model revised the lead sentence to intrigue the reader.

You may not know Mr. Thomas MacDonald but you've probably
˄Mr. Thomas MacDonald ~~works~~ as the head greens keeper at a
seen his work. He
Park District golf course. He is not the village president, manager,

fire-fighter, or police chief, but he's no less important to his village.

STUDENT MODEL

Ask another pair of classmates to review your revised draft before you edit. When you edit, look for errors in grammar, usage, spelling, and mechanics. Look closely for errors involving misuse of commas.

Editing Strategy

Using Commas Correctly

Including unnecessary commas can make sentences choppy or confusing. Notice how misuse of commas interrupts the flow of the following sentences.

FOR REFERENCE
More information on the use of commas can be found in the Language and Grammar Handbook at the back of the book.

FAULTY   Mary and John, were surprised by all the community support. (*improper separation of subject and verb*)

REVISED   Mary and John were surprised by all the community support.

FAULTY   The survival of eagles, and other endangered species is an important consideration of the charity Brian founded. (*improper separation of words joined by a coordinating conjunction*)

REVISED   The survival of eagles and other endangered species is an important consideration of the charity Brian founded.

FAULTY   Mrs. Maxwell said, that she'd been thinking about working with young people for a number of years. (*inserted after* said *as if this were a direct, instead of an indirect, quotation*)

REVISED   Mrs. Maxwell said that she'd been thinking about working with young people for a number of years.

FAULTY   The Jensens have worked in the church's soup kitchen, since it opened. (*improper separation of a dependent clause from the rest of the sentence*)

REVISED   The Jensens have worked in the church's soup kitchen since it opened.

When you edit, check to see that when you've used a comma, you've used it for a good reason.

STEP 5 PRESENTING

Consider these ideas for presenting your feature article:

- Read your article to the class with the subject present in the classroom as an honored guest.

- Work with your teacher to make a display of your articles as part of a Local Hero Recognition Week.

- Give an illustrated copy of the article to your subject.

- Submit your article to a local newspaper or magazine for publication.

STEP 6 LOOKING BACK

Self-evaluate. What grade would *you* give your paper? Look back at the Writer's Blueprint and give yourself a score for each item, from 6 (superior) to 1 (inadequate).

Reflect. Think about what you learned from writing your article as you write answers to these questions.

✔ How can you use the subject of your article as a role model in your own life?

✔ What did you learn about the interview process? What would you do differently the next time you conduct an interview?

For Your Working Portfolio Add your feature article and your reflection responses to your working portfolio.

Beyond Print

Evaluating Sources

In Unit 5, you have read about a number of people who have tried to "make a difference." President Abraham Lincoln was one of these individuals. Through his actions and in particular through his words, he changed this country forever. The most famous of Lincoln's words are those of the Gettysburg Address, a brief speech he gave in late November 1863, at the dedication of a cemetery for the thousands of soldiers killed at the climactic Battle of Gettysburg. Today the Gettysburg Address is regarded as a masterpiece of eloquence and one of the primary expressions of American democratic ideals. But an examination of historical sources reveals that in Lincoln's time, reactions to his famous speech were quite mixed.

What are sources? Sources are the materials used in doing research. They can be historical documents, literary works, fine art, or items reflecting popular culture. The sources for the reactions to Lincoln's Gettysburg Address include such things as newspaper stories, letters, and diaries. When sources contradict each other, the following strategies will help you evaluate the information they present:

Determine whether the information is relevant. For example, if an account of the Gettysburg Address was largely devoted to describing what the President wore, its value in judging the quality of the speech would be diminished.

Look for underlying assumptions. Many times the unstated beliefs of a writer are reflected in a source. For example, the *Springfield Republican* had once made the assumption that Lincoln was "a simple Susan," not very clever or articulate. After the Gettysburg Address, the newspaper admitted: "We had grown so accustomed to homely and imperfect phrase in his [speeches] . . . but this shows he can talk handsomely as well as act sensibly."

Recognize bias. Lincoln aroused strong feelings in the people around him and these feelings are reflected in the sources dealing with the Gettysburg Address. The *Chicago Times,* a newspaper that was violently opposed to Lincoln's policies, was among those who dismissed the speech, describing it as "an offensive exhibition of boorishness and vulgarity." The newspaper's bias against Lincoln must be considered in weighing its estimate of his speech.

Consider expertise. Sources that reflect an individual's expertise may have more value. For example, Edward Everett, the famous orator who preceded Lincoln at Gettysburg, delivered a very lengthy (and much admired) speech; Lincoln's address was very brief. Everett wrote to Lincoln afterwards, "I wish I could flatter myself that I came as near to the central idea of the occasion in two hours as you did in two minutes." Everett's experience as a speaker gives weight to his high opinion of the Gettysburg Address.

Check consistency. Does the source contain obvious contradictions? For example, if an account of Lincoln at Gettysburg first said the President angered the audience and then said his speech was met with thunderous applause, its value as a source would be questionable.

Activity Options

1. With a small group, choose a book, movie, or song to review. Write your reviews individually, and then read each other's reviews. In a discussion, compare the opinions expressed in your reviews. Discuss what factors may have influenced you to have different reactions to the book, movie, or song.

2. Choose a current political figure on the local or national level. Find two pieces of writing—articles, letters to the editor, editorials, etc.— that present widely different opinions about the politician. Write an analysis of these writings that compares the attitudes of both writers and speculates on reasons for their different viewpoints. If information is available, you might look into factors such as the writers' respective backgrounds, areas of expertise, and bias.

Part Two

The Price of Wisdom

Have you heard the expression, "Ignorance is bliss"? While the authors of the following selections may not agree with that statement, they do offer reflections on the idea that the gift of knowledge sometimes means the loss of something else.

Multicultural Connection **Change** may occur when people are led to re-examine their beliefs, behavior, or traditions. What changes in attitude take place in the following selections, and what factors influence those changes?

Before Reading

What True Education Should Do by Sydney J. Harris
The Struggle to Be an All-American Girl by Elizabeth Wong

Sydney J. Harris
1917–1986

Beginning in 1944, Sydney J. Harris wrote his widely syndicated column, "Strictly Personal," for the *Chicago Daily News* and later for the Chicago *Sun-Times.* Writing on subjects ranging from war and peace to marriage and parenthood, Harris was described by *Time* magazine as "the most-quoted newsman in Chicago."

Elizabeth Wong
Playwright Elizabeth Wong based her first play, *Letters to a Student Revolutionary,* on her correspondence with a Chinese student involved in the 1989 demonstrations at Tiananmen Square. Wong also moonlights as a columnist for the *Los Angeles Times.*

Building Background

An Ancient Teacher In his essay "What True Education Should Do," Sydney Harris mentions a method of teaching that may not be familiar to you—the **Socratic** (sō krat′ik) **method.** Named after Socrates (sok′rə tēs), a Greek philosopher and teacher who lived from about 469–399 B.C., the Socratic method involves extensive questioning. Rather than giving students information, Socrates believed it was important for students to discover what they already knew. Socrates would ask questions of his students, claiming that he did not know the answers. As his pupils attempted to answer the series of questions, they would be able to examine their own knowledge and beliefs.

Literary Focus

Irony In general, **irony** describes a contrast between what appears to be and what really is. In **verbal irony,** it is plain that the speaker means the opposite of what he or she says. In **situational irony,** there is a discrepancy between what might be expected to happen and what actually happens. A writer may use irony to intensify the meaning he or she intends for the piece. As you read "The Struggle to Be an All-American Girl," consider the author's use of irony and its effect.

Writer's Notebook

Unique Lessons The following selections both deal with the learning process. In your notebook, write about something you learned in a unique way. Perhaps someone you have known has had a great effect on you, or some experience you have had caused you to learn a lesson. What did you learn? Was it a new fact or subject, a lesson about life, something about yourself, or something else? How did you learn it?

Before Reading

Two Views of the Mississippi

by Mark Twain

Mark Twain
1835–1910

A humorist, newspaperman, lecturer, and writer, Samuel Langhorne Clemens, better known as Mark Twain, grew up in the river town of Hannibal, Missouri. His boyhood along the Mississippi River inspired many of the scenes, characters, and incidents in his works. After ending his formal schooling at a young age, Twain learned the printing trade, wrote for newspapers, and became a steamboat pilot. (His pen name was river slang for "two fathoms deep"; that is, safe water.) When the Civil War ended river traffic, Twain turned to writing and lecturing. Highly regarded for his keen and humorous observations about life and people, Twain is probably best known for his novels *The Adventures of Tom Sawyer* and *The Adventures of Huckleberry Finn*.

Building Background

Reading the River In the essay you are about to read, Mark Twain describes the fascinating complexity of the Mississippi River. In Twain's day, navigating a boat on the Mississippi was much different than the modern process, which relies on sonar and other sophisticated techniques. Before 1830, steamboats were operated only during daylight, because all navigation had to be done by observation. Even later in the nineteenth century, steamboat pilots had to memorize and account for such factors as water depth, current speed, configuration of riverbeds, and locations of snags and other obstacles. As a pilot, Twain had to familiarize himself with all the landmarks along the riverbanks and needed to interpret all the wind conditions that would affect progress of boats. "Reading" the river incorrectly could cause a ship to sink or run aground.

Literary Focus

Metaphor A **metaphor** is an implied comparison between things that are essentially unalike. An **extended metaphor** is a metaphor that is developed and expanded in a literary work. In "Two Views of the Mississippi," Twain repeatedly compares the Mississippi River to a book. As you read the selection, consider how this extended metaphor helps you visualize and understand the ideas Twain presents.

Writer's Notebook

Best-Kept Secrets At first the river was a mystery to young Samuel Clemens; later, navigation became second nature to him. In your notebook, write about something that was very interesting or mysterious to you—until you really understood it. For example, as a young child, you may have been captivated by a certain magic trick. If so, you could describe how you felt when you learned how the trick worked.

Two Views of the Mississippi

Mark Twain

▲ *Champions of the Mississippi* (1866). This Currier & Ives engraving depicts steamboats on the Mississippi River. What message does this image convey about steamboats?

The face of the water, in time, became a wonderful book—a book that was a dead language to the uneducated passenger, but which told its mind to me without reserve, delivering its most cherished secrets as clearly as if it uttered them with a voice. And it was not a book to be read once and thrown aside, for it had a new story to tell every day. Throughout the long twelve hundred miles there was

It is the faintest and simplest expression the water ever makes, and the most hideous to a pilot's eye.

never a page that was void of[1] interest, never one that you could leave unread without loss, never one that you would want to skip, thinking you could find higher enjoyment in some other thing. There never was so wonderful a book written by man; never one whose interest was so absorbing, so unflagging,[2] so sparklingly renewed with every reperusal.[3] The passenger who could not read it was charmed with a peculiar sort of faint dimple on its surface (on the rare occasions when he did not overlook it altogether); but to the pilot that was an *italicized* passage; indeed, it was more than that, it was a legend of the largest capitals, with a string of shouting exclamation points at the end of it; for it meant that a wreck or a rock was buried there that could tear the life out of the strongest vessel[4] that ever floated. It is the faintest and simplest expression the water ever makes, and the most hideous to a pilot's eye. In truth, the passenger who could not read this book saw nothing but all manner of pretty pictures in it, painted by the sun and shaded by the clouds, whereas to the trained eye these were not pictures at all, but the grimmest and most dead-earnest of reading matter.

Now when I had mastered the language of this water and had come to know every trifling[5] feature that bordered the great river as familiarly as I knew the letters of the alphabet, I had made a valuable acquisition.[6]

But I had lost something, too. I had lost something which could never be restored to me while I lived. All the grace, the beauty, the poetry had gone out of the majestic river! I still keep in mind a certain wonderful sunset which I witnessed when steamboating was new to me. A broad expanse of the river was turned to blood; in the middle distance the red hue brightened into gold, through which a solitary log came floating, black and conspicuous;[7] in one place a long, slanting mark lay sparkling upon the water; in another the surface was broken by boiling, tumbling rings, that were as many-tinted as an opal; where the ruddy[8] flush was faintest, was a smooth spot that was covered with graceful circles and radiating lines, ever so delicately traced; the shore on our left was densely wooded, and the somber shadow that fell from this forest was broken in one place by a long, ruffled trail that shone like silver; and

---

1. **void of,** without; lacking.
2. **unflagging** (un flag′ing), *adj.* not weakening or failing.
3. **reperusal** (rē′pə rü′səl), *n.* a careful rereading or detailed re-examination.
4. **vessel** (ves′əl), *n.* a large boat; ship.
5. **trifling** (trī′fling), *adj.* having little value or importance.
6. **acquisition** (ak′wə zish′ən), *n.* something acquired or gained; addition to an existing group.
7. **conspicuous** (kən spik′yü əs), *adj.* easily seen; clearly visible.
8. **ruddy** (rud′ē), *adj.* red or reddish.

I stood like one bewitched. I drank it in, in a speechless rapture.

high above the forest wall a clean-stemmed dead tree waved a single leafy bough that glowed like a flame in the unobstructed splendor that was flowing from the sun. There were graceful curves, reflected images, woody heights, soft distances; and over the whole scene, far and near, the dissolving lights drifted steadily, enriching it, every passing moment, with new marvels of coloring.

I stood like one bewitched. I drank it in, in a speechless rapture. The world was new to me, and I had never seen anything like this at home. But as I have said, a day came when I began to cease from noting the glories and the charms which the moon and the sun and the twilight wrought[9] upon the river's face; another day came when I ceased altogether to note them. Then, if that sunset scene had been repeated, I should have looked upon it without rapture, and should have commented upon it, inwardly, after this fashion: This sun means that we are going to have wind tomorrow; that floating log means that the river is rising, small thanks to it; that slanting mark on the water refers to a bluff reef[10] which is going to kill somebody's steamboat one of these nights, if it keeps on stretching out like that; those tumbling "boils" show a dissolving bar[11] and a changing channel there; the lines and circles in the slick water over yonder are a warning that the troublesome place is shoaling[12] up dangerously; that silver streak in the shadow of the forest is the "break" from a new snag,[13] and he has located himself in the very best place he could

have found to fish for steamboats; that tall dead tree, with a single living branch, is not going to last long, and then how is a body ever going to get through this blind place at night without the friendly old landmark?

No, the romance and the beauty were all gone from the river. All the value any feature of it had for me now was the amount of usefulness it could furnish toward compassing[14] the safe piloting of a steamboat. Since those days, I have pitied doctors from my heart. What does the lovely flush in a beauty's cheek mean to a doctor but a "break" that ripples above some deadly disease? Are not all her visible charms sown thick with what are to him the signs and symbols of hidden decay? Does he ever see her beauty at all, or doesn't he simply view her professionally, and comment upon her unwholesome[15] condition all to himself? And doesn't he sometimes wonder whether he has gained most or lost most by learning his trade?

---

9. **wrought** (rôt), *v.* formed; a past tense form of *work*.
10. **bluff reef** (bluf rēf), *n.* a high, steep bar, which rises abruptly on one side.
11. **bar** (bär), *n.* a riverbed elevation of sand, gravel, or rock that is an obstacle to navigation.
12. **shoal** (shōl), *v.* become shallow.
13. **snag** (snag), *n.* a tree or branch embedded in the river bottom and not visible on the surface, forming a hazard to navigation.
14. **compass** (kum′pəs), *v.* accomplish; obtain.
15. **unwholesome** (un hōl′səm), *adj.* unhealthy.

After Reading

Making Connections

Shaping Your Response

1. Complete the sentence "A river is ___," both from your point of view and the point of view of Mark Twain.

2. Do you think that Mark Twain would have encouraged others to become riverboat pilots? Explain.

Analyzing the Essay

3. Explain the meaning of the **title,** "Two Views of the Mississippi."

4. 👆 What aspects of his job as a steamboat pilot **change** Twain's feelings about the river?

5. How does Twain feel that he and a doctor are alike?

Extending the Ideas

6. The **theme** for this part of Unit 5 is "The Price of Wisdom." Explain whether or not you feel this essay fits that theme.

7. What modern professions might lead to the same kind of disappointment that Twain describes in his essay? Give several examples.

Literary Focus: Metaphor

A **metaphor** highlights particular aspects of a thing or a person by making comparisons between the subject and something unlike it. Occasionally, an entire piece or part of a piece may rely on a single, prolonged comparison, called an **extended metaphor.** In his essay, Twain uses an extended metaphor that compares the Mississippi River to a book. On the chart below, list the qualities or features of a book that Twain mentions in order to describe the qualities or features of the river.

Extended metaphor: "The face of the water, in time, became a wonderful book. . . ."	
Book quality or feature mentioned by Twain	**River quality or feature he is describing**
• Offers a new story to tell every day.	• Offers something new to see every day.
• Has pretty pictures for those who can't read.	• Looks beautiful to those who can't see the danger signs.

Vocabulary Study

A synonym is a word having a meaning that is the same or nearly the same as that of another word. Choose the word that is most nearly the same in meaning as the vocabulary word.

acquisition
conspicuous
ruddy
unflagging
vessel

1. acquisition: (a) gain; (b) deposit; (c) requirement; (d) purpose
2. conspicuous: (a) suspicious; (b) noticeable; (c) unclear; (d) seaworthy
3. ruddy: (a) ready; (b) dark; (c) equipped; (d) reddish
4. unflagging: (a) waving; (b) unfurled; (c) tireless; (d) still
5. vessel: (a) boat; (b) visible; (c) blood; (d) map

Expressing Your Ideas

Writing Choices

Writer's Notebook Update Now that you have read the essay, think about how Twain's attitude toward the river changed. In your notebook, write a letter from Twain to his boss, in which Twain evaluates his own abilities as a steamboat pilot. Be sure to mention his "river-reading" skills.

Words of the Trade In the essay, Twain uses several terms particular to boating, such as *reef, bar, shoaling,* and *snag.* Think of a profession in which you are interested or a subject about which you know a great deal. What special terms are used within that profession or subject? Make a **glossary** of those terms. Be sure to provide pronunciations and, when practical, illustrations of your words.

Natural Description Mark Twain offers a vivid description of the beauty of the sunset on the river. What do you find beautiful in nature? Write a **description** of this object or place, being sure to use colorful language and vivid imagery to bring your subject to life.

Other Options

Well-Read Mark Twain was a prolific writer with many books to his credit, ranging from adventure to satire to autobiography. Read another of Twain's works (or a portion of it). Give a unique **report** on the book. For example, you could act as a salesman giving a "pitch" for the book or make a map or display that relates to the book. How is the work you chose similar to and different from "Two Views of the Mississippi"?

Old Man River Imagine that your class is contributing to a museum about steamboat travel. Do some research to make a **display** on some aspect of the subject. Topics for your display might include: the design and operation of steam engines; legendary pilots; maps of major rivers and ports that were used extensively for trade; navigational tools and techniques; social life on the steamboats; famous steamboat accidents; artwork depicting steamboat life; and so on.

Before Reading

from Woodsong

by Gary Paulsen

Gary Paulsen
born 1939

Gary Paulsen has held many jobs, including teacher, soldier, actor, director, farmer, rancher, truck driver, professional archer, migrant farm worker, singer, and sailor. Elements of nearly all of them have appeared in some form or another in his writing. Paulsen's love of the outdoors and deep respect for nature have also been reflected in many of his books.

Paulsen is a prolific writer, with nonfiction, plays, and novels for both adults and young people to his credit. Paulsen explains, "I write because it's all I can do. Every time I've tried to do something else I cannot, and have to come back to writing, though often I hate it—hate it and love it. . . . I write because it's all there is." Paulsen and his wife have homes in Wyoming, New Mexico, and Minnesota.

Building Background

When Indian people talk of animal people, we talk of our brothers and sisters. We see the same light of day. We breathe the same air and drink the same water.

　　—Allen Pinkham, Nez Percé elder.

What do you think of the quotation? Make a Venn diagram like the one shown here to illustrate similarities and differences between animals and people. After you read the excerpt from *Woodsong,* you may have more to add to your diagram.

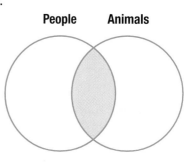

Literary Focus

Style When a writer expresses ideas, he or she uses a particular **style** to correspond with the purpose and intended audience for the piece. Many choices an author makes help determine the style: which words to use and how to arrange them, whether or not to use imagery and figurative language, what point of view to use, and what tone to create. Author Gary Paulsen's style has been described as "spare and disciplined." As you read the selection, decide whether or not you agree.

Writer's Notebook

Real-life Adventures You are about to read Gary Paulsen's account of some unusual and meaningful adventures. What has been your greatest adventure? Describe it in your notebook, being sure to recount when and where it happened and who was with you. Was the adventure planned, or was it something spontaneous (or maybe even an emergency)? What knowledge, either about the world or about yourself, did you gain from the experience?

WOODSONG

GARY PAULSEN

The adventure really begins in differences—the great differences between people and animals, between the way we live now and the way we once lived, between the Mall and the Woods.

Primarily the difference between people and animals is that people use fire. People create fire, and animals don't. Oh, there are minor things—like cars and planes and all the other inventions we seem to have come up with. But in a wild state, the real difference is that we use controlled fire.

And it was in the business of fire that I came to the first of many amazements inside the woods.

It started with a campfire.

I was on a hundred-mile run in deep winter with new dogs—pups, really, just over a year old. I had gone beyond the trapping stage and was training new dogs for a possible attempt on the Iditarod.[1] The pups had lived in kennels, mostly. They had only been on short training runs so that almost everything they saw on this run was new to them. They had to learn to understand as they ran.

A cow in a field was a marvel and had to be investigated; it took me half an hour to get untangled from the fence. A ruffled grouse that flew down the trail ahead of us had to be chased. A red squirrel took the whole team off the trail into the woods, piling into deep drifts and leaving us all upside down and packed with snow.

---

1. **Iditarod** (ī dit′ə rod), a 1,049-mile race from Anchorage to Nome, Alaska. The competitors are teams of sled-dogs and their "mushers," or drivers. Gary Paulsen and his dogs later competed in this race.

It was, in short, a day full of wonders for them and when night came and it was time to stop—you can really only do about twenty miles a day with young dogs—we found a soft little clearing in the spruce trees. I made beds for them and when they were fed and settled, or as settled as young dogs can get, I made a fire hole in the snow in the center of the clearing, next to the sled, and started a small fire with some dead popple.[2] It was not a cold night so the fire was very small, just enough to melt some snow and make tea. The flames didn't get over a foot high—but the effect was immediate and dramatic.

The dogs went crazy with fear. They lunged against their chains, slamming and screaming. I went to them and petted them and soothed them and at length they accepted the fire. I put their frozen blocks of meat around the edges of the flames to soften, and fed them warm meat. Then they sat and stared at the flames, the whole ring of them.

Of course they had never seen fire, or flame, in the kennel—it was all completely new to them. But the mystery was why they would automatically fear it. They had seen many new things that day, and they didn't fear anything but the fire.

And when they were over the fear of it, they were fascinated with it. I stretched my foam pad and sleeping bag out in the sled to settle in for the night. This is a complicated process. The felt liners for my shoepacs had to be taken off and put down inside the bag so my body heat could dry them for the next day. My parka had

_____

2. **popple** (pop′əl), *n.* a slender quick-growing tree of the willow family; also called *poplar.*

Judy Larson, *The Family Tree.* What elements in this painting make it seem more like a photograph?

to be turned inside out so all the sweat from the day could freeze and be scraped off in the morning. Any wet clothing had to be flattened and worked down into the bag to dry as well. While I was doing all this in the light from my head lamp, I let the fire die down.

Just as I started to slide into the bag one of the dogs started to sing. It was the sad song.

They have many songs and I don't know them all. There is a happy song they sing when the moon is full on the snow and they are fed and there is a rain song, which is melancholy[3]— they don't like rain very much—and there is a song they sing when you have been with them in the kennel and start to walk away, a come-back-and-don't-go-away sad song.

That was the song one dog had started to sing. When I turned to look at him he was staring where the fire had died down into a cup in the snow, and in a moment the rest of them had picked up the song and were wailing and moaning for the lost fire, all staring where the flames had been.

In an hour they had gone from some coded, genetic fear of fire, to understanding fire, to missing it when it went away.

Cave people must have gone through this same process. I wondered how long it had taken us to understand and know fire. The pups had done it in an hour and I thought as I pulled the mummy bag up over my head and went to sleep how smart they were or perhaps how smart we weren't and thought we were.

Sometimes when they run it is not believable. And even when the run is done and obviously happened it is still not believable.

On a run once when it was the perfect temperature for running, twenty below—cold enough for the dogs to run cool, but not so bitterly cold as to freeze anything exposed—I thought I would just let them go and see what they wanted to do. I wouldn't say a word, wouldn't do anything but stand on the back of

the sled—unless a bootie or a quick snack was needed. I'd let them run at an easy lope. I thought I would let them go until they wanted to stop and then only run that way from then on, and they ran to some primitive instinct, coursed[4] and ran for seventeen hours without letup.

One hundred and seventy-five miles.

And they didn't pant, weren't tired, could have done it again. I nearly froze—just a piece of meat on the back of the sled—but they ran and ran in a kind of glory and even now I can't quite believe it.

The second incident with fire was much the same—something from another world, another time. It happened, but it is not quite believable.

We had run long in a day—a hundred and fifty miles—with an adult team in good shape. The terrain[5] had been rough, with many moguls (mounds of snow) that made the sled bounce in the trail. I had taken a beating all day and I was whipped. I made beds and fed the dogs and built up a large fire. It had been a classic run but I was ready for sleep. It was nearly thirty below when I crawled into the sleeping bag.

I was just going to sleep, with my eyes heavy and the warmth from the fire in my face, when the dogs started an incredible uproar.

I opened my eyes and there was a deer standing right across the fire from me.

A doe. Fairly large—more than a year old—standing rigid, staring at me straight on in the face across the fire. She was absolutely petrified with terror.

At first I thought she had somehow stupidly blundered into the camp and run past the dogs to the fire.

But she hung there, staring at me, her ears rotating with the noise of the dogs around her. She did not run and still did not run and

---

3. **melancholy** (mel′ən kol′ē), *adj.* depressed in spirits; sad; gloomy.
4. **course** (kôrs), *v.* race; run.
5. **terrain** (te rān′), *n.* the physical features of a piece of land.

I thought she must be a medicine doe sent to me; a spirit doe come in a dream to tell me something.

Then I saw the others.

Out, perhaps thirty yards or more beyond the camp area, but close enough for the fire to shine in their eyes—the others. The wolves. There was a pack of brush wolves and they had been chasing her. I couldn't tell the number, maybe five or six; they kept moving in agitation and it was hard to pin them down, but they were clearly reluctant to let her go, although they were also clearly afraid of me and being close to me. Unlike timber wolves, brush wolves are not endangered, not protected, and are trapped heavily. We are most definitely the enemy, and they worried at seeing me.

And when I saw them I looked back at the doe and could see that she was blown. Her mouth hung open and spit smeared down both sides with some blood in it. They must have been close to getting her when she ran to the camp.

And the fire.

She must have smelled her death to make the decision she made. To run through the circle of dogs, toward the fire and the man was a mad gamble—a gamble that I wasn't a deer hunter, that the dogs weren't loose or they would have been on her like the wolves, that somehow it would be better here.

All those choices to make at a dead, frantic run with wolves pulling at her.

This time it had worked.

I sat up, half raised, afraid to move fast lest she panic and run back into the wolves. I had more wood next to the sled and I slowly put a couple of pieces on the fire and leaned back again. The wolves were very nervous now and

She must have smelled her death to make the decision she made.

they moved away when I put the wood on the fire, but the doe stayed nearby for a long time, so long that some of the dogs actually went back to lying down and sleeping.

She didn't relax. Her body was locked in fear and ready to fly at the slightest wrong move, but she stayed and watched me, watched the fire until the wolves were well gone and her sides were no longer heaving with hard breathing. She kept her eye on me, her ears on the dogs. Her nostrils flared as she smelled me and the fire and when she was ready—perhaps in half an hour but it seemed like much more—she wheeled, flashed her white tail at me, and disappeared.

The dogs exploded into noise again when she ran away, then we settled back to watching the fire until sleep took us. I would have thought it all a dream except that her tracks and the tracks of the wolves were there in the morning.

Fear comes in many forms but perhaps the worst scare is the one that isn't anticipated; the one that isn't really known about until it's there. A sudden fear. The unexpected.

And again, fire played a role in it.

We have bear trouble. Because we feed processed meat to the dogs there is always the smell of meat over the kennel. In the summer it can be a bit high because the dogs like to "save" their food sometimes for a day or two or four—burying it to dig up later. We live on the edge of wilderness and consequently the meat smell brings any number of visitors from the woods.

Skunks abound, and foxes and coyotes and wolves and weasels—all predators.[6] We once had an eagle live over the kennel for more than a week, scavenging[7] from the dogs, and a crazy group of ravens has pretty much taken over the

---

6. **predator** (pred′ə tər), *n.* animal that lives by preying on other animals.
7. **scavenge** (skav′ənj), *v.* pick over discarded objects for things to use.

puppy pen. Ravens are protected by the state and they seem to know it. When I walk toward the puppy pen with the buckets of meat it's a toss-up to see who gets it—the pups or the birds. They have actually pecked the puppies away from the food pans until they have gone through and taken what they want.

Spring, when the bears come, is the worst. They have been in hibernation through the winter, and they are hungry beyond caution. The meat smell draws them like flies, and we frequently have two or three around the kennel at the same time. Typically they do not bother us much—although my wife had a bear chase her from the garden to the house one morning—but they do bother the dogs.

They are so big and strong that the dogs fear them, and the bears trade on this fear to get their food. It's common to see them scare a dog into his house and take his food. Twice we have had dogs killed by rough bear swats that broke their necks—and the bears took their food.

We have evolved an uneasy peace with them but there is the problem of familiarity. The first time you see a bear in the kennel it is a novelty, but when the same ones are there day after day, you wind up naming some of them (old Notch-Ear, Billy-Jo, etc.). There gets to be a too relaxed attitude. We started to treat them like pets.

A major mistake.

There was a large male around the kennel for a week or so. He had a white streak across his head which I guessed was a wound scar from some hunter—bear hunting is allowed here. He wasn't all that bad so we didn't mind him. He would frighten the dogs and take their hidden stashes now and then, but he didn't harm them and we became accustomed to him hanging around. We called him Scarhead and now and again we would joke about him as if he were one of the yard animals.

At this time we had three cats, forty-two dogs, fifteen or twenty chickens, eight ducks, nineteen large white geese, a few banty hens, ten fryers which we'd raised from chicks and couldn't (as my wife put it) "snuff and eat," and six woods-wise goats.

The bears, strangely, didn't bother any of the yard animals. There must have been a rule, or some order to the way they lived because they would hit the kennel and steal from the dogs but leave the chickens and goats and other yard stock completely alone—although you would have had a hard time convincing the goats of this fact. The goats spent a great deal of time with their back hair up, whuffing and blowing snot at the bears—and at the dogs who would *gladly* have eaten them. The goats never really believed in the truce.

There is not a dump or landfill to take our trash to and so we separate it—organic, inorganic—and deal with it ourselves. We burn the paper in a screened enclosure and it is fairly efficient, but it's impossible to get all the food particles off wrapping paper, so when it's burned the food particles burn with it.

And give off a burnt food smell.

And nothing draws bears like burning food. It must be that they have learned to understand human dumps—where they spend a great deal of time foraging.[8] And they learn amazingly fast. In Alaska, for instance, the bears already know that the sound of a moose hunter's gun means there will be a fresh gut pile when the hunter cleans the moose. They come at a run when they hear the shot. It's often a close race to see if the hunter will get to the moose before the bears take it away. . . .

Because we're on the south edge of the wilderness area we try to wait until there is a northerly breeze before we burn so the food smell will carry south, but it doesn't always help. Sometimes bears, wolves, and other predators are already south, working the sheep farms down where it is more settled—they take a terrible toll of sheep—and we catch them on the way back through.

That's what happened one July morning.

---

8. **forage** (fôr′ij), *v.* hunt or search for food.

Scarhead had been gone for two or three days and the breeze was right, so I went to burn the trash. I fired it off and went back into the house for a moment—not more than two minutes. When I came back out Scarhead was in the burn area. His tracks (directly through the tomatoes in the garden) showed he'd come from the south.

He was having a grand time. The fire didn't bother him. He was trying to reach a paw in around the edges of flame to get at whatever smelled so good. He had torn things apart quite a bit—ripped one side off the burn enclosure—and I was having a bad day and it made me mad.

I was standing across the burning fire from him and without thinking—because I was so used to him—I picked up a stick, threw it at him, and yelled, "Get out of here."

I have made many mistakes in my life, and will probably make many more, but I hope never to throw a stick at a bear again.

In one rolling motion—the muscles seemed to move within the skin so fast that I couldn't take half a breath—he turned and came for me. Close. I could smell his breath and see the red around the sides of his eyes. Close on me he stopped and raised on his back legs and hung over me, his forelegs and paws hanging down, weaving back and forth gently as he took his time and decided whether or not to tear my head off.

I could not move, would not have time to react. I knew I had nothing to say about it. One blow would break my neck. Whether I lived or died depended on him, on his thinking, on his ideas about me—whether I was worth the bother or not.

I did not think then.

Looking back on it I don't remember having one coherent[9] thought when it was happening. All I knew was terrible menace. His eyes looked very small as he studied me. He looked down on me for what seemed hours. I did not move, did not breathe, did not think or do anything.

And he lowered.

Perhaps I was not worth the trouble. He lowered slowly and turned back to the trash and I walked backward halfway to the house and then ran—anger growing now—and took the rifle from the gun rack by the door and came back out.

He was still there, rummaging through the trash. I worked the bolt and fed a cartridge in and aimed at the place where you kill bears and began to squeeze. In raw anger, I began to take up the four pounds of pull necessary to send death into him.

And stopped.

Kill him for what?

That thought crept in.

Kill him for what?

For not killing me? For letting me know it is wrong to throw sticks at four-hundred-pound bears? For not hurting me, for not killing me, I should kill him? I lowered the rifle and ejected the shell and put the gun away. I hope Scarhead is still alive. For what he taught me, I hope he lives long and is very happy because I learned then—looking up at him while he made up his mind whether or not to end me—that when it is all boiled down I am nothing more and nothing less than any other animal in the woods.

---

9. **coherent** (kō hir′ənt), *adj.* logically connected; consistent.

I could smell his breath and see the red around the sides of his eyes.

After Reading

Making Connections

Shaping Your Response

1. At the beginning of the essay, Paulsen talks about the difference between the Mall and the Woods. Explain what you think he means and explain which place you prefer.

2. If you were Paulsen, would you have shot the bear? Why or why not?

Analyzing the Essay

3. What does Paulsen's attitude toward animals seem to be? Cite some examples from the text to back up your answer.

4. What common **themes** run throughout this essay?

Extending the Ideas

5. Paulsen says at the end of his essay, ". . . when it is all boiled down I am nothing more and nothing less than any other animal in the woods." Do you agree or disagree? Explain.

Literary Focus: Style

Many choices an author makes help determine the **style** of a piece of writing.

- Does Paulsen use simple or complex words? formal or informal words? Why do you think he uses those types of words?

- Comment on Paulsen's use of short sentences. Where does he use them? What effect do they have?

- Write a brief description of Paulsen's style, citing examples from the text.

Vocabulary Study

forage
melancholy
predator
scavenge
terrain

Use the listed vocabulary words to write a brief fictional account of an adventure that occurs while camping, on safari, or on a trip to the zoo. Use the Glossary, if necessary, to understand the meanings of the vocabulary words.

Expressing Your Ideas

Writing Choice

Writer's Notebook Update Think about Paulsen's adventures and what he learned from them. In your notebook, jot down newspaper headlines that would capture the flavor of Paulsen's adventures.

Another Option

A Race Like No Other Do some research and prepare a travel plan for someone who wants to watch the Iditarod race in Alaska.

Before Reading

The Inspector-General

by Anton Chekhov

Anton Chekhov
1860–1904

Anton Chekhov was a Russian playwright and short-story writer. When he needed to pay his bills for medical school, he turned to writing, selling his stories, short sketches, and jokes to journals and papers. While studying medicine, he contracted tuberculosis and spent most of his life battling the steady advance of this disease. Although Chekhov wrote some comic and satirical stories, much of his work dealt with the despair caused by his characters' inability to effectively respond to or communicate with each other.

Building Background

Setting the Scene The play you are about to read takes place in Russia in the 1800s, a time when many changes were occurring. Alexander II, who became czar—or emperor—in 1855, promoted many reforms. He freed the serfs, developed railroads, organized a banking system, and introduced a jury system and freedom of the press. When Alexander II's reforms did not go far enough for some revolutionaries, he was the target of criticism and was killed by a terrorist's bomb in 1881. The new czar, Alexander III, was a harsh leader, limiting freedom of the press, reducing the powers of self-government, and helping the rich become richer. Discontented Russians began forming political organizations with widely different ideas of how the government should be run. It is against this backdrop of political strife and harsh rule that "The Inspector-General" takes place.

Literary Focus

Satire The art of ridiculing an aspect of human nature or life in general is called **satire**. Satire may be gentle and humorous, or it may be fierce and scornful. Although primarily designed to expose and thereby correct human weaknesses and institutional evils, satire can also serve to entertain and amuse. As you read "The Inspector-General," consider what Chekhov chooses as the subject of his satire. Keep in mind what was happening in Russia during Chekhov's lifetime.

Writer's Notebook

Poking Fun Many comedy shows, movies, and comic strips use satire as a source of humor. For example, the *Naked Gun* movies have satirized police dramas, and comic strips such as *Doonesbury* have used the government and popular culture as subjects of satire. In your notebook, comment on an aspect of today's society that is worthy of satire.

This 1978 oil painting by Russian artist Ilya Glazunov is titled *The Procession.* Look for clues in the painting to figure out what kind of a procession is taking place. Then explain how Glazunov's use of color affects the mood of the piece. ➤

The Inspector-General

The curtain goes up to reveal falling snow and a cart facing away from us. Enter the STORYTELLER, *who begins to read the story. Meanwhile, the* TRAVELER *enters. He is a middle-aged man of urban appearance, wearing dark glasses and a long overcoat with its collar turned up. He is carrying a small traveling bag. He climbs into the cart and sits facing us.*

STORYTELLER. *The Inspector-General.* In deepest incognito,[1] first by express train, then along back roads, Pyotr Pavlovich Posudin[2] was hastening toward the little town of N__, to which he had been summoned by an anonymous letter. "I'll take them by surprise," he thought to himself. "I'll come down on them like a thunderbolt out of the blue. I can just imagine their faces when they hear who I am." *(Enter the* DRIVER, *a peasant, who climbs onto the cart, so that he is sitting with his back to us, and the cart begins to trundle[3] slowly away from us.)* And when he thought to himself for long enough, he fell into conversation with the driver of the cart.

What did he talk about? About himself, of course. *(Exit the* STORYTELLER.)

TRAVELER. I gather you've got a new inspector-general in these parts.

DRIVER. True enough.

TRAVELER. Know anything about him? *(The* DRIVER *turns and looks at the* TRAVELER, *who turns his coat collar up a little higher.)*

DRIVER. Know anything about him? Of course we do! We know everything about all of them up there! Every last little clerk—we know the color of his hair and the size of his boots! *(He turns back to the front, and the* TRAVELER *permits himself a slight smile.)*

TRAVELER. So, what do you reckon? Any good, is he? *(The* DRIVER *turns around.)*

---

1. **incognito** (in′kog nē′tō), *n.* a disguised condition.
2. **Pyotr Pavlovich Posudin** (pyō′tr päv lō′vich pō-sü′dən).
3. **trundle** (trun′dl), *v.* roll along; push along.

Anton Chekhov

DRIVER. Oh, yes, he's a good one, this one.

TRAVELER. Really?

DRIVER. Did one good thing straight off.

TRAVELER. What was that?

DRIVER. He got rid of the last one. Holy terror he was! Hear him coming five miles off! Let's say he's going to this little town. Somewhere like we're going, say. He'd let all the world know about it a month before. So now he's on his way, say, and it's like thunder and lightning coming down the road. And when he gets where he's going, he has a good sleep. He has a good eat and drink, and then he starts. Stamps his feet, shouts his head off. Then he has another good sleep, and off he goes.

TRAVELER. But the new one's not like that?

DRIVER. Oh, no. The new one goes everywhere on the quiet. Creeps around like a cat. Don't want no one to see him, don't want no one to know who he is. Say he's going into this town down the road here. Someone there sent him a letter on the sly, let's say. "Things going on here you should know about." Something of that kind. Well, now, he creeps out of his office, so none of them up there see him go. He hops on a train just like anyone else, just like you or me. When he gets off, he don't go jumping into a cab or nothing fancy. Oh, no. He wraps himself up from head to toe so you can't see his face, and he wheezes away like an old dog so no one can recognize his voice.

TRAVELER. Wheezes? That's not wheezing! That's the way he talks! So I gather.

DRIVER. Oh, is it? But the tales they tell about him. You'd laugh till you burst your tripes![4]

TRAVELER (*sourly*). I'm sure I would.

DRIVER. He drinks, mind!

---

4. **tripes** (trīps), *n.* the walls of the stomach. The word usually refers to the stomach of a cow or sheep.

TRAVELER (*startled*). Drinks?

DRIVER. Oh, like a hole in the ground. Famous for it.

TRAVELER. He's never touched a drop! I mean, from what I've heard.

DRIVER. Oh, not in public, no. Goes to some great ball—"No thank you, not for me." Oh, no, he puts it away at home! Wakes up in the morning, rubs his eyes, and the first thing he does, he shouts, "Vodka!" So in runs his valet[5] with a glass. Fixed himself up a tube behind his desk, he has. Leans down, takes a pull on it, no one the wiser.

TRAVELER (*offended*). How do you know all this, may I ask?

DRIVER. Can't hide it from the servants, can you? The valet and the coachman have got tongues in their heads. Then again, he's on the road, say, going about his business, and he keeps the bottle in his little bag. (*The* TRAVELER *discreetly pushes the traveling bag out of the* DRIVER'S *sight.*) And his housekeeper . . .

TRAVELER. What about her?

DRIVER. Runs circles around him, she does, like a fox round his tail. She's the one who wears the trousers.[6] The people aren't half so frightened of him as they are of her.

TRAVELER. But at least he's good at his job, you say?

DRIVER. Oh, he's a blessing from heaven, I'll grant him that.

TRAVELER. Very cunning, you were saying.

DRIVER. Oh, he creeps around, all right.

TRAVELER. And then he pounces, yes? I should think some people must get the surprise of their life, mustn't they?

DRIVER. No, no. Let's be fair, now. Give him his due. He don't make no trouble.

TRAVELER. No. I mean, if no one knows he's coming . . .

DRIVER. Oh, that's what *he* thinks, but *we* all know.

TRAVELER. You know?

DRIVER. Oh, some gentleman gets off the train at the station back there with his greatcoat up to his eyebrows and says, "No, I don't want a cab, thank you. Just an ordinary horse and cart for me." Well, we'd put two and two together, wouldn't we? Say it was you, now, creeping along down the road here. The lads would be down there in a cab by now! By the time you got there, the whole town would be as regular as clockwork! And you'd think to yourself, "Oh, look at that! As clean as a whistle! And they didn't know I was coming!" No, that's why he's such a blessing after the other one. This one believes it.

TRAVELER. Oh, I see.

DRIVER. What, you thought we didn't know him? Why, we've got the electric telegraph these days! Take today, now. I'm going past the station back there this morning, and the fellow who runs the buffet comes out like a bolt of lightning. Arms full of baskets and bottles. "Where are you off to?" I say. "Doing drinks and refreshments for the inspector-general!" he says, and he jumps into a carriage and goes flying down the road here. So there's the inspector-general, all muffled up like a roll of carpet, going secretly along in a cart somewhere, and when he gets there, nothing to be seen but vodka and cold salmon!

TRAVELER (*shouts*). Turn around!

DRIVER (*to the horse*). Whoa, boy! Whoa! (*To the* TRAVELER.) Oh, so what's this, then? Don't want to go running into the inspector-general, is that it? (*The* TRAVELER *gestures impatiently for the* DRIVER *to turn the cart around.* DRIVER *to the horse.*) Back we go, then, boy. Home we go. (*He turns the cart around and the* TRAVELER *takes a swig from his traveling bag.*) Though if I know the old devil, he's like as not turned around and gone home again himself. (*Blackout.*)

---

5. **valet** (val′ā), *n*. servant who takes care of a man's clothes and gives him personal service.

6. **wears the trousers,** who is really in charge.

After Reading

Making Connections

Shaping Your Response

1. Do you think the driver knows the traveler is the inspector-general? Why or why not?

2. If you could meet the inspector-general, what advice would you give him on how to do his job better?

Analyzing the Play

3. Compare and contrast the inspector-general with the man who held the job before him. Why isn't either one effective in the position?

4. Comment on the last line of the play. How is it **ironic?**

5. What function does the driver have in the play? What kind of **character** is he?

Extending the Ideas

6. Do you think the inspector-general has gained any wisdom from this trip? Why or why not?

7. Imagine you have been asked to re-create this play in a contemporary American setting. Instead of a driver and an inspector-general heading toward a town in a horse-drawn cart, what might the situation be?

Literary Focus: Satire

Satire is the art of criticizing a subject by ridiculing it and evoking an attitude of amusement, contempt, or scorn. Much satire has as its central purpose the reform of persons and institutions. Satirists may use such techniques as sarcasm, exaggeration, humor, and absurdity to make their points. With these ideas in mind, answer the following questions about the play.

- What subject is Chekhov satirizing in "The Inspector-General"?

- What methods does Chekhov use to satirize his subject?

- What does the satire reveal about the time period and place in which Chekhov lived?

Expressing Your Ideas

Writing Choices

Writer's Notebook Update Before you read the play, you wrote about a subject that is worthy of satire. Now that you have read the play, look back at what you wrote and make a list of additional topics that are deserving of satire.

That's Classified In your opinion, what qualities does an inspector-general need for his position? Imagine that you are the inspector-general's boss, and you are looking for a replacement. Write a **classified advertisement** that describes the qualities that a successful candidate for the position of inspector-general will have.

Playful Satire Now that you have read a satire about a subject from the past, try your hand at writing a scene from a play or story that satirizes a current situation. You might consider the list in your notebook for ideas for your writing.

Other Options

Playing Along "The Inspector-General" relies mostly on dialogue for its effect. With two partners, practice reading the play, deciding how best to read the lines. What tone of voice would be appropriate for the driver? the traveler? How would their tones change as the play progresses? After considering these questions and practicing, perform the **play** in front of your class.

Subtle Persuasion Imagine that the inspector-general decides to go to the town and do the inspection anyway. You are a resident of the town, and you and your neighbors must decide how to trick the inspector-general into believing that everything in town is fine, and that no one is doing anything to criticize or harm the government. Hold a **"town meeting"** to come up with a plan for fooling him. Then write up an outline of your plan in a top-secret memo to everyone in town.

Before Reading

The Adventure of the Speckled Band

by Sir Arthur Conan Doyle

Sir Arthur Conan Doyle
1859–1930

Born in Edinburgh, Scotland, Sir Arthur Conan Doyle worked for a time as a ship's doctor and attempted to establish a private medical practice. During this period, he also began writing, combining his interests in detection and science to create the character of detective Sherlock Holmes. Although Conan Doyle wished to be remembered principally for his political works and his carefully researched historical novels, Sherlock Holmes stories continue to overshadow all his other writings.

Building Background

The Incomparable Sherlock Holmes Sir Arthur Conan Doyle wrote sixty stories featuring Sherlock Holmes, the famous detective. Holmes—brilliant, eccentric, observant, and logical—became the model for the literary detective, and has been portrayed by more actors than any other figure from literature. In the U.S., more than one hundred Sherlock Holmes societies keep alive the memory of the master English sleuth. One "fan club," the Baker Street Irregulars, hosts an annual dinner and awards members who have shown serious interest in the many cases of their hero. Sherlock Holmes is based on Dr. Joseph Bell, one of Conan Doyle's medical school instructors. A surgeon, Bell was noted for his ability to diagnose a patient's character as well as his or her disease.

▲ Dr. Joseph Bell, the inspiration for Sherlock Holmes

Literary Focus

Point of View The author's choice of a narrator determines a story's **point of view,** and affects how much information readers will be given. If the narrator is a character in the story, for example, the reader will only know that character's thoughts. As you read "The Adventure of the Speckled Band," determine from whose point of view the story is told. How does this choice of narrator dictate how much you know about the events and the characters' thoughts?

Writer's Notebook

Elementary, Dear Watson The Case of the Missing Socks! The Mystery of the Long-lost Homework! Have you ever had to solve a mystery like one of these? In your log, write about a time you put your detective skills to work. What was the mystery? How did you solve it?

The Adventure of the Speckled Band

Sir Arthur Conan Doyle

On glancing over my notes of the seventy-odd cases in which I have during the last eight years studied the methods of my friend Sherlock Holmes, I find many tragic, some comic, a large number merely strange, but none commonplace; for, working as he did rather for the love of his art than for the acquirement of wealth, he refused to associate himself with any investigation which did not tend towards the unusual, and even the fantastic. Of all these varied cases, however, I cannot recall any which presented more singular[1] features than that which was associated with the well-known Surrey family of the Roylotts of Stoke Moran. The events in question occurred in the early days of my association with Holmes, when we were sharing rooms as bachelors in Baker Street. It is possible that I might have placed them upon record before, but a promise of secrecy was made at the time, from which I have only been freed during the last month by the untimely death of the lady to whom the pledge was given. It is perhaps as well that the facts should now come to light, for I have reasons to know that there are widespread rumors as to the death of Dr. Grimesby Roylott which tend to make the matter even more terrible than the truth.

It was early in April in the year '83 that I woke one morning to find Sherlock Holmes standing, fully dressed, by the side of my bed. He was a late riser, as a rule, and as the clock on the mantelpiece showed me that it was only a quarter past seven, I blinked up at him in some surprise, and perhaps just a little resentment, for I was myself regular in my habits.

"Very sorry to knock you up, Watson,"[2] said he, "but it's the common lot this morning. Mrs. Hudson has been knocked up, she retorted[3] upon me, and I on you."

"What is it, then—a fire?"

"No; a client. It seems that a young lady has arrived in a considerable state of excitement, who insists upon seeing me. She is waiting now in the sitting room. Now, when young ladies wander about the metropolis[4] at this hour of the morning, and knock sleepy people up out of their beds, I presume that it is something very pressing which they have to communicate. Should it prove to be an interesting case, you would, I am sure, wish to follow it from the

---

1. **singular** (sing′gyə lər), *adj.* strange; odd; peculiar.
2. **"Very sorry . . . Watson,"** Sherlock Holmes is apologizing to Watson for waking him up with his visit.
3. **retort** (ri tôrt′), *v.* reply quickly or sharply.
4. **metropolis** (mə trop′ə lis), *n.* a large city; important center, especially the center of some activity.

This illustration, which depicts actor William Gillette in the role of Sherlock, Holmes, appeared in a 1907 issue of *Vanity Fair.* Compare this image with other portrayals of Sherlock Holmes that you have seen.

outset. I thought, at any rate, that I should call you and give you the chance."

"My dear fellow, I would not miss it for anything."

I had no keener pleasure than in following Holmes in his professional investigations, and in admiring the rapid deductions, as swift as intuitions, and yet always founded on a logical basis, with which he unraveled the problems which were submitted to him. I rapidly threw on my clothes and was ready in a few minutes to accompany my friend down to the sitting room. A lady dressed in black and heavily veiled, who had been sitting in the window, rose as we entered.

"Good morning, madam," said Holmes cheerily. "My name is Sherlock Holmes. This is my intimate friend and associate, Dr. Watson, before whom you can speak as freely as before myself. Ha! I am glad to see that Mrs. Hudson has had the good sense to light the fire. Pray draw up to it, and I shall order you a cup of hot coffee, for I observe that you are shivering."

"It is not cold which makes me shiver," said the woman in a low voice, changing her seat as requested.

"What, then?"

"It is fear, Mr. Holmes. It is terror." She raised her veil as she spoke, and we could see that she was indeed in a pitiable state of agitation, her face all drawn and gray, with restless, frightened eyes, like those of some hunted animal. Her features and figure were those of a woman of thirty, but her hair was shot with premature gray, and her expression was weary and haggard. Sherlock Holmes ran her over with one of his quick, all-comprehensive glances.

"You must not fear," said he soothingly,

"It is not cold which makes me shiver," said the woman in a low voice. . . .

bending forward and patting her forearm. "We shall soon set matters right, I have no doubt. You have come in by train this morning, I see."

"You know me, then?"

"No, but I observe the second half of a return ticket in the palm of your left glove. You must have started early, and yet you had a good drive in a dogcart,[5] along heavy roads, before you reached the station."

The lady gave a violent start and stared in bewilderment at my companion.

"There is no mystery, my dear madam," said he, smiling. "The left arm of your jacket is spattered with mud in no less than seven places. The marks are perfectly fresh. There is no vehicle save a dogcart which throws up mud in that way, and then only when you sit on the left-hand side of the driver."

"Whatever your reasons may be, you are perfectly correct," said she. "I started from home before six, reached Leatherhead at twenty past, and came in by the first train to Waterloo. Sir, I can stand this strain no longer; I shall go mad if it continues. I have no one to turn to—none, save only one, who cares for me, and he, poor fellow, can be of little aid. I have heard of you, Mr. Holmes; I have heard of you from Mrs. Farintosh, whom you helped in the hour of her sore need. It was from her that I had your address. Oh, sir, do you not think that you could help me, too, and at least throw a little light through the dense darkness which surrounds me? At present it is out of my power to reward you for your services, but in a month or six weeks I shall be married, with the control of my own income, and then at least you shall not find me ungrateful."

---

5. **dogcart** (dôg kärt), *n.* a small, open, horse-drawn carriage with two seats placed back to back.

Holmes turned to his desk and, unlocking it, drew out a small casebook, which he consulted.

"Farintosh," said he. "Ah yes, I recall the case; it was concerned with an opal tiara. I think it was before your time, Watson. I can only say, madam, that I shall be happy to devote the same care to your case as I did to that of your friend. As to reward, my profession is its own reward; but you are at liberty to defray whatever expenses I may be put to, at the time which suits you best. And now I beg that you will lay before us everything that may help us in forming an opinion upon the matter."

"Alas!" replied our visitor, "the very horror of my situation lies in the fact that my fears are so vague, and my suspicions depend so entirely upon small points, which might seem trivial to another, that even he to whom of all others I have a right to look for help and advice looks upon all that I tell him about it as the fancies of a nervous woman. He does not say so, but I can read it from his soothing answers and averted[6] eyes. But I have heard, Mr. Holmes, that you can see deeply into the manifold wickedness of the human heart. You may advise me how to walk amid the dangers which encompass me."

"I am all attention, madam."

"My name is Helen Stoner, and I am living with my stepfather, who is the last survivor of one of the oldest Saxon families in England, the Roylotts of Stoke Moran, on the western border of Surrey."

Holmes nodded his head. "The name is familiar to me," said he.

"The family was at one time among the richest in England, and the estates extended over the borders into Berkshire in the north, and Hampshire in the west. In the last century, however, four successive heirs were of a dissolute[7] and wasteful disposition, and the family ruin was eventually completed by a gambler in the days of the Regency. Nothing was left save a few acres of ground, and the two-hundred-year-old house, which is itself crushed under a heavy mortgage. The last squire dragged out his exis-

tence there, living the horrible life of an aristocratic pauper;[8] but his only son, my stepfather, seeing that he must adapt himself to the new conditions, obtained an advance from a relative, which enabled him to take a medical degree and went out to Calcutta,[9] where, by his professional skill and his force of character, he established a large practice. In a fit of anger, however, caused by some robberies which had been perpetrated[10] in the house, he beat his native butler to death and narrowly escaped a capital sentence. As it was, he suffered a long term of imprisonment and afterwards returned to England a morose[11] and disappointed man.

"When Dr. Roylott was in India he married my mother, Mrs. Stoner, the young widow of Major General Stoner, of the Bengal Artillery. My sister Julia and I were twins, and we were only two years old at the time of my mother's remarriage. She had a considerable sum of money—not less than £1000 a year—and this she bequeathed[12] to Dr. Roylott entirely while we resided with him, with a provision that a certain annual sum should be allowed to each of us in the event of our marriage. Shortly after our return to England my mother died—she was killed eight years ago in a railway accident near Crewe. Dr. Roylott then abandoned his attempts to establish himself in practice in London and took us to live with him in the old ancestral house at Stoke Moran. The money which my mother had left was enough for all our wants, and there seemed to be no obstacle to our happiness.

---

6. **averted** (ə vėrt′əd), *adj.* turned away or turned aside.
7. **dissolute** (dis′ə lüt), *adj.* living an immoral life; loose in morals; licentious; dissipated.
8. **pauper** (pô′pər), *n.* a very poor person.
9. **Calcutta** (kal kut′ə), seaport in Eastern India, near the Bay of Bengal.
10. **perpetrate** (pėr′pə trāt), *v.* do or commit a crime, fraud, trick, or anything bad or foolish.
11. **morose** (mə rōs′), *adj.* gloomy; sullen; ill-humored.
12. **bequeath** (bi kwēꞭ′), *v.* give or leave (especially money or property) by a will.

"But a terrible change came over our step-father about this time. Instead of making friends and exchanging visits with our neighbors, who had at first been overjoyed to see a Roylott of Stoke Moran back in the old family seat, he shut himself up in his house and seldom came out save to indulge in ferocious quarrels with whoever might cross his path. Violence of temper approaching to mania has been hereditary in the men of the family, and in my stepfather's case it had, I believe, been intensified by his long residence in the tropics. A series of disgraceful brawls took place, two of which ended in the police court, until at last he became the terror of the village, and the folks would fly at his approach, for he is a man of immense strength, and absolutely uncontrollable in his anger.

"Last week he hurled the local blacksmith over a parapet[13] into a stream, and it was only by paying over all the money which I could gather together that I was able to avert another public exposure. He had no friends at all save the wandering gypsies, and he would give these vagabonds leave to encamp upon the few acres of bramble-covered land which represent the family estate, and would accept in return the hospitality of their tents, wandering away with them sometimes for weeks on end. He has a passion also for Indian animals, which are sent over to him by a correspondent, and he has at this moment a cheetah and a baboon, which wander freely over his grounds and are feared by the villagers almost as much as their master.

"You can imagine from what I say that my poor sister Julia and I had no great pleasure in our lives. No servant would stay with us, and for a long time we did all the work of the house. She was but thirty at the time of her death, and yet her hair had already begun to whiten, even as mine has."

"Your sister is dead, then?"

"She died just two years ago, and it is of her death that I wish to speak to you. You can understand that, living the life which I have described, we were little likely to see anyone of our own age and position. We had, however, an aunt, my mother's maiden sister, Miss Honoria Westphail, who lives near Harrow, and we were occasionally allowed to pay short visits at this lady's house. Julia went there at Christmas two years ago, and met there a half-pay major of marines, to whom she became engaged. My stepfather learned of the engagement when my sister returned and offered no objection to the marriage; but within a fortnight[14] of the day which had been fixed for the wedding, the terrible event occurred which has deprived me of my only companion."

Sherlock Holmes had been leaning back in his chair with his eyes closed and his head sunk in a cushion, but he half opened his lids now and glanced across at his visitor.

"Pray be precise as to details," said he.

"It is easy for me to be so, for every event of that dreadful time is seared into my memory. The manor house is, as I have already said, very old, and only one wing is now inhabited. The bedrooms in this wing are on the ground floor, the sitting rooms being in the central block of the buildings. Of these bedrooms the first is Dr. Roylott's, the second my sister's, and the third my own. There is no communication between them, but they all open out into the same corridor. Do I make myself plain?"

"Perfectly so."

"The windows of the three rooms open out upon the lawn. That fatal night Dr. Roylott had gone to his room early, though we knew that he had not retired to rest, for my sister was troubled by the smell of the strong Indian cigars which it was his custom to smoke. She left her room, therefore, and came into mine, where she sat for some time, chatting about her approaching wedding. At eleven o'clock she rose to leave me, but she paused at the door and looked back.

"'Tell me, Helen,' said she, 'have you ever heard anyone whistle in the dead of the night?'

---

13. **parapet** (par′ə pet), *n.* a low wall or barrier at the edge of a balcony, roof, bridge, etc.
14. **fortnight** (fôrt′nīt), *n.* two weeks.

"'Never,' said I.

"'I suppose that you could not possibly whistle, yourself, in your sleep?'

"'Certainly not. But why?'

"'Because during the last few nights I have always, about three in the morning, heard a low, clear whistle. I am a light sleeper, and it has awakened me. I cannot tell where it came from—perhaps from the next room, perhaps from the lawn. I thought that I would just ask you whether you had heard it.'

"'No, I have not. It must be those wretched gypsies in the plantation.'

"'Very likely. And yet if it were on the lawn, I wonder that you did not hear it also.'

"'Ah, but I sleep more heavily than you.'

"'Well, it is of no great consequence, at any rate.' She smiled back at me, closed my door, and a few moments later I heard her key turn in the lock."

"Indeed," said Holmes. "Was it your custom always to lock yourselves in at night?"

"Always."

"And why?"

"I think that I mentioned to you that the doctor kept a cheetah and a baboon. We had no feeling of security unless our doors were locked."

"Quite so. Pray proceed with your statement."

"I could not sleep that night. A vague feeling of impending[15] misfortune impressed me. My sister and I, you will recollect, were twins, and you know how subtle are the links which bind two souls which are so closely allied. It was a wild night. The wind was howling outside, and the rain was beating and splashing against the windows. Suddenly, amid all the hubbub of the gale, there burst forth the wild scream of a terrified woman. I knew that it was my sister's voice. I sprang from my bed, wrapped a shawl round

"Tell me, Helen," said she, "have you ever heard anyone whistle in the dead of the night?"

me, and rushed into the corridor. As I opened my door I seemed to hear a low whistle, such as my sister described, and a few moments later a clanging sound, as if a mass of metal had fallen. As I ran down the passage, my sister's door was unlocked, and revolved slowly upon its hinges. I stared at it horror-stricken, not knowing what was about to issue from it. By the light of the corridor lamp I saw my sister appear at the opening, her face blanched with terror, her hands groping for help, her whole figure swaying to and fro like that of a drunkard. I ran to her and threw my arms round her, but at that moment her knees seemed to give way and she fell to the ground. She writhed[16] as one who is in terrible pain, and her limbs were dreadfully convulsed. At first I thought that she had not recognized me, but as I bent over her she suddenly shrieked out in a voice which I shall never forget, 'Oh, my God! Helen! It was the band! The speckled band!' There was something else which she would fain[17] have said, and she stabbed with her finger into the air in the direction of the doctor's room, but a fresh convulsion seized her and choked her words. I rushed out, calling loudly for my stepfather, and I met him hastening from his room in his dressing gown. When he reached my sister's side she was unconscious, and though he poured brandy down her throat and sent for medical aid from the village, all efforts were in vain, for she slowly sank and died without having recovered her consciousness. Such was the dreadful end of my beloved sister."

"One moment," said Holmes; "are you sure

15. **impending** (im pen′ding), *adj.* likely to happen soon; threatening; about to occur.
16. writhe (rīᴛʜ), *v.* twist and turn; twist about.
17. **fain** (fān), *adv.* willingly.

about this whistle and metallic sound? Could you swear to it?"

"That was what the county coroner[18] asked me at the inquiry. It is my strong impression that I heard it, and yet, among the crash of the gale and the creaking of an old house, I may possibly have been deceived."

"Was your sister dressed?"

"No, she was in her nightdress. In her right hand was found the charred stump of a match, and her left a matchbox."

"Showing that she had struck a light and looked about her when the alarm took place. That is important. And what conclusions did the coroner come to?"

"He investigated the case with great care, for Dr. Roylott's conduct had long been notorious in the county, but he was unable to find any satisfactory cause of death. My evidence showed that the door had been fastened upon the inner side, and the windows were blocked by old-fashioned shutters with broad iron bars, which were secured every night. The walls were carefully sounded, and were shown to be quite solid all round, and the flooring was also thoroughly examined, with the same result. The chimney is wide, but is barred up by four large staples. It is certain, therefore, that my sister was quite alone when she met her end. Besides, there were no marks of any violence upon her."

"How about poison?"

"The doctors examined her for it, but without success."

"What do you think that this unfortunate lady died of, then?"

"It is my belief that she died of pure fear and nervous shock, though what it was that frightened her I cannot imagine."

"Were there gypsies in the plantation at the time?"

"Yes, there are nearly always some there."

"Ah, and what did you gather from this allusion to a band—a speckled band?"

"Sometimes I have thought that it was merely the wild talk of delirium, sometimes that it may have referred to some band of people, perhaps to those very gypsies in the plantation. I do not know whether the spotted handkerchiefs which so many of them wear over their heads might have suggested the strange adjective which she used."

EVALUATE: At this point in the story, what do you think happened to Julia?

Holmes shook his head like a man who is far from being satisfied.

"These are very deep waters," said he; "pray go on with your narrative."

"Two years have passed since then, and my life has been until lately lonelier than ever. A month ago, however, a dear friend, whom I have known for many years, has done me the honor to ask my hand in marriage. His name is Armitage—Percy Armitage—the second son of Mr. Armitage, of Crane Water, near Reading. My stepfather has offered no opposition to the match, and we are to be married in the course of the spring. Two days ago some repairs were started in the west wing of the building, and my bedroom wall has been pierced, so that I have had to move into the chamber in which my sister died, and to sleep in the very bed in which she slept. Imagine, then, my thrill of terror when last night, as I lay awake, thinking over her terrible fate, I suddenly heard in the silence of the night the low whistle which had been the herald[19] of her own death. I sprang up and lit the lamp, but nothing was to be seen in the room. I was too shaken to go to bed again, however, so I dressed, and as soon as it was daylight I slipped down, got a dogcart at the Crown Inn, which is opposite, and drove to Leatherhead, from whence I have come on this morning

---

18. **coroner** (kôr′ə nər), *n.* official of a local government whose principal function is to investigate the cause of any death not clearly due to natural causes.
19. **herald** (her′əld), *n.* something that announces or hints at what will happen.

with the one object of seeing you and asking your advice."

"You have done wisely," said my friend. "But have you told me all?"

"Yes, all."

"Miss Roylott, you have not. You are screening your stepfather."

"Why, what do you mean?"

For answer Holmes pushed back the frill of black lace which fringed the hand that lay upon our visitor's knee. Five little livid spots, the marks of four fingers and a thumb, were printed upon the white wrist.

"You have been cruelly used," said Holmes.

The lady colored deeply and covered over her injured wrist. "He is a hard man," she said, "and perhaps he hardly knows his own strength."

There was a long silence, during which Holmes leaned his chin upon his hands and stared into the crackling fire.

"This is a very deep business," he said at last. "There are a thousand details which I should desire to know before I decide upon our course of action. Yet we have not a moment to lose. If we were to come to Stoke Moran today, would it be possible for us to see over these rooms without the knowledge of your stepfather?"

"As it happens, he spoke of coming into town today upon some most important business. It is probable that he will be away all day, and that there would be nothing to disturb you. We have a housekeeper now, but she is old and foolish, and I could easily get her out of the way."

"Excellent. You are not averse[20] to this trip, Watson?"

"By no means."

"Then we shall both come. What are you going to do yourself?"

Elie Delaunay (1826–1891), *Madame Georges Bizet*. What do you think the expression on Madame Bizet's face reveals about her personality?

"I have one or two things which I would wish to do now that I am in town. But I shall return by the twelve o'clock train, so as to be there in time for your coming."

"And you may expect us early in the afternoon. I have myself some small business matters to attend to. Will you not wait and breakfast?"

"No, I must go. My heart is lightened already

---

20. **averse** (ə vėrs′), *adj.* having a strong or fixed dislike; opposed or unwilling.

since I have confided my trouble to you. I shall look forward to seeing you again this afternoon." She dropped her thick black veil over her face and glided from the room.

"And what do you think of it all, Watson?" asked Sherlock Holmes, leaning back in his chair.

"It seems to me to be a most dark and sinister business."

"Dark enough and sinister enough."

"Yet if the lady is correct in saying that the flooring and walls are sound, and that the door, window, and chimney are impassable, then her sister must have been undoubtedly alone when she met her mysterious end."

"What becomes, then, of these nocturnal whistles, and what of the very peculiar words of the dying woman?"

"I cannot think."

"When you combine the ideas of whistles at night, the presence of a band of gypsies who are on intimate terms with this old doctor, the fact that we have every reason to believe that the doctor has an interest in preventing his stepdaughter's marriage, the dying allusion to a band, and, finally, the fact that Miss Helen Stoner heard a metallic clang, which might have been caused by one of those metal bars that secured the shutters falling back into its place, I think that there is good ground to think that the mystery may be cleared along those lines."

"But what, then, did the gypsies do?"

"I cannot imagine."

"I see many objections to any such theory."

"And so do I. It is precisely for that reason that we are going to Stoke Moran this day. I want to see whether the objections are fatal, or if they may be explained away. But what in the name of the devil!"

The ejaculation had been drawn from my companion by the fact that our door had been suddenly dashed open, and that a huge man had framed himself in the aperture. His costume was a peculiar mixture of the professional and of the agricultural, having a black top hat, a long frock coat, and a pair of high gaiters,[21] with a hunting crop swinging in his hand. So tall was he that his hat actually brushed the cross bar of the doorway, and his breadth seemed to span it across from side to side. A large face, seared with a thousand wrinkles, burned yellow with the sun, and marked with every evil passion, was turned from one to the other of us, while his deep-set, bile-shot eyes, and his high, thin, fleshless nose, gave him somewhat the resemblance to a fierce old bird of prey.

"Which of you is Holmes?" asked this apparition.

"My name, sir; but you have the advantage of me," said my companion quietly.

"I am Dr. Grimesby Roylott, of Stoke Moran."

"Indeed, Doctor," said Holmes blandly. "Pray take a seat."

"I will do nothing of the kind. My stepdaughter has been here. I have traced her. What has she been saying to you?"

"It is a little cold for the time of the year," said Holmes.

"What has she been saying to you?" screamed the old man furiously.

"But I have heard that the crocuses promise well," continued my companion imperturbably.[22]

"Ha! You put me off, do you?" said our new visitor, taking a step forward and shaking his hunting crop. "I know you, you scoundrel! I

> *It seems to me to be a most dark and sinister business.*

---

21. **gaiter** (gā′tər), *n.* an outer covering for the lower leg or ankle, made of cloth, leather, etc., for outdoor wear.
22. **imperturbably** (im′pər tėr′bə blē), *adv.* not being easily excited or disturbed; calmly.

have heard of you before. You are Holmes, the meddler."

My friend smiled.

"Holmes the busybody!"

His smile broadened.

"Holmes, the Scotland Yard Jack-in-office!"

Holmes chuckled heartily. "Your conversation is most entertaining," said he. "When you go out close the door, for there is a decided draught."

"I will go when I have said my say. Don't you dare to meddle with my affairs. I know that Miss Stoner has been here. I traced her! I am a dangerous man to fall foul of! See here." He stepped swiftly forward, seized the poker, and bent it into a curve with his huge brown hands.

"See that you keep yourself out of my grip," he snarled, and hurling the twisted poker into the fireplace he strode out of the room.

"He seems a very amiable person," said Holmes, laughing. "I am not quite so bulky, but if he had remained I might have shown him that my grip was not much more feeble than his own." As he spoke he picked up the steel poker and, with a sudden effort, straightened it out again.

"Fancy his having the insolence to confound me with[23] the official detective force! This incident gives zest to our investigation, however, and I only trust that our little friend will not suffer from her imprudence[24] in allowing this brute to trace her. And now, Watson, we shall order breakfast, and afterwards I shall walk down to Doctors' Commons, where I hope to get some data which may help us in this matter."

CONNECT: What have you learned about Roylott from his visit to Holmes?

It was nearly one o'clock when Sherlock Holmes returned from his excursion. He held in his hand a sheet of blue paper, scrawled over with notes and figures.

"I have seen the will of the deceased wife," said he. "To determine its exact meaning I have been obliged to work out the present prices of the investments with which it is concerned. The total income, which at the time of the wife's death was little short of £1100, is now, through the fall in agricultural prices, not more than £750. Each daughter can claim an income of £250, in case of marriage. It is evident, therefore, that if both girls had married, this beauty would have had a mere pittance,[25] while even one of them would cripple him to a very serious extent. My morning's work has not been wasted, since it has proved that he has the very strongest motives for standing in the way of anything of the sort. And now, Watson, this is too serious for dawdling, especially as the old man is aware that we are interesting ourselves in his affairs; so if you are ready, we shall call a cab and drive to Waterloo. I should be very much obliged if you would slip your revolver into your pocket. An Eley's No. 2 is an excellent argument with gentlemen who can twist steel pokers into knots. That and a toothbrush are, I think, all that we need."

At Waterloo we were fortunate in catching a train for Leatherhead, where we hired a trap at the station inn and drove for four or five miles through the lovely Surrey lanes. It was a perfect day, with a bright sun and a few fleecy clouds in the heavens. The trees and wayside hedges were just throwing out their first green shoots, and the air was full of the pleasant smell of the moist earth. To me at least there was a strange contrast between the sweet promise of the spring and this sinister quest upon which we were engaged. My companion sat in the front of the trap, his arms folded, his hat pulled down over his eyes, and his chin sunk upon his breast, buried in the deepest thought. Suddenly, however, he started, tapped me on the shoulder, and pointed over the meadows.

"Look there!" said he.

A heavily timbered park stretched up in a

---

23. **confound me with,** get me confused with.
24. imprudence (im prüd′ns), *n.* lack of good judgment.
25. pittance (pit′ns), *n.* a small amount of money.

gentle slope, thickening into a grove at the highest point. From amid the branches there jutted out the gray gables and high rooftree of a very old mansion.

"Stoke Moran?" said he.

"Yes, sir, that be the house of Dr. Grimesby Roylott," remarked the driver.

"There is some building going on there," said Holmes; "that is where we are going."

"There's the village," said the driver, pointing to a cluster of roofs some distance to the left; "but if you want to get to the house, you'll find it shorter to get over this stile,[26] and so by the footpath over the fields. There it is, where the lady is walking."

"And the lady, I fancy, is Miss Stoner," observed Holmes, shading his eyes. "Yes, I think we had better do as you suggest."

We got off, paid our fare, and the trap rattled back on its way to Leatherhead.

"*Good heavens!*" she cried, "he has followed me, then."

"I thought it as well," said Holmes as we climbed the stile, "that this fellow should think we had come here as architects, or on some definite business. It may stop his gossip. Good afternoon, Miss Stoner. You see that we have been as good as our word."

Our client of the morning had hurried forward to meet us with a face which spoke her joy. "I have been waiting so eagerly for you," she cried, shaking hands with us warmly. "All has turned out splendidly. Dr. Roylott has gone to town, and it is unlikely that he will be back before evening."

"We have had the pleasure of making the doctor's acquaintance," said Holmes, and in a few words he sketched out what had occurred. Miss Stoner turned white to the lips as she listened.

"Good heavens!" she cried, "he has followed me, then."

"So it appears."

"He is so cunning that I never know when I am safe from him. What will he say when he returns?"

"He must guard himself, for he may find that there is someone more cunning than himself upon his track. You must lock yourself up from him tonight. If he is violent, we shall take you away to your aunt's at Harrow. Now, we must make the best use of our time, so kindly take us at once to the rooms which we are to examine."

The building was of gray, lichen[27]-blotched stone, with a high central portion and two curving wings, like the claws of a crab, thrown out on each side. In one of these wings the windows were broken and blocked with wooden boards, while the roof was partly caved in, a picture of ruin. The central portion was in little better repair, but the right-hand block was comparatively modern, and the blinds in the windows, with the blue smoke curling up from the chimneys, showed that this was where the family resided. Some scaffolding had been erected against the end wall, and the stonework had been broken into, but there were no signs of any workmen at the moment of our visit. Holmes walked slowly up and down the ill-trimmed lawn and examined with deep attention the outsides of the windows.

"This, I take it, belongs to the room in which you used to sleep, the center one to your sister's, and the one next to the main building to Dr. Roylott's chamber?"

"Exactly so. But I am now sleeping in the middle one."

"Pending the alterations, as I understand. By

---

26. **stile** (stīl), *n.* step or steps for getting over a fence or wall.

27. **lichen** (lī′kən), *n.* any of a large group of flowerless organisms that look somewhat like moss and grow in patches on trees, rocks, etc.

the way, there does not seem to be any very pressing need for repairs at that end wall."

"There were none. I believe that it was an excuse to move me from my room."

"Ah! that is suggestive. Now, on the other side of this narrow wing runs the corridor from which these three rooms open. There are windows in it, of course?"

"Yes, but very small ones. Too narrow for anyone to pass through."

"As you both locked your doors at night, your rooms were unapproachable from that side. Now, would you have the kindness to go into your room and bar your shutters?"

Miss Stoner did so, and Holmes, after a careful examination through the open window, endeavored[28] in every way to force the shutter open, but without success. There was no slit through which a knife could be passed to raise the bar. Then with his lens he tested the hinges, but they were of solid iron, built firmly into the massive masonry. "Hum!" said he, scratching his chin in some perplexity, "my theory certainly presents some difficulties. No one could pass these shutters if they were bolted. Well, we shall see if the inside throws any light upon the matter."

A small side door led into the whitewashed corridor from which the three bedrooms opened. Holmes refused to examine the third chamber, so we passed at once to the second, that in which Miss Stoner was now sleeping, and in which her sister had met with her fate. It was a homely little room, with a low ceiling and a gaping fireplace, after the fashion of old country houses. A brown chest of drawers stood in one corner, a narrow white-counterpaned bed in another, and a dressing table on the left-hand side of the window. These articles, with two small wickerwork chairs, made up all the furniture to the room save for a square of Wilton carpet in the center. The boards round and the paneling of the walls were of brown, worm-eaten oak, so old and discolored that it may have dated from the original building of the house. Holmes drew one of the chairs into

a corner and sat silent, while his eyes traveled round and round and up and down, taking in every detail of the apartment.

"Where does that bell communicate with?" he asked at last, pointing to a thick bell rope[29] which hung down beside the bed, the tassel actually lying upon the pillow.

"It goes to the housekeeper's room."

"It looks newer than the other things."

"Yes, it was only put there a couple of years ago."

"Your sister asked for it, I suppose?"

"No, I never heard of her using it. We used always to get what we wanted for ourselves."

"Indeed, it seemed unnecessary to put so nice a bellpull there. You will excuse me for a few minutes while I satisfy myself as to this floor." He threw himself down upon his face with his lens in his hand and crawled swiftly backward and forward, examining minutely the cracks between the boards. Then he did the same with the woodwork with which the chamber was paneled. Finally he walked over to the bed and spent some time in staring at it and in running his eye up and down the wall. Finally he took the bell rope in his hand and gave it a brisk tug.

"Why, it's a dummy," said he.

"Won't it ring?"

"No, it is not even attached to a wire. This is very interesting. You can see now that it is fastened to a hook just above where the little opening for the ventilator is."

"How very absurd! I never noticed that before."

"Very strange!" muttered Holmes, pulling at the rope. "There are one or two very singular points about this room. For example, what a fool a builder must be to open a ventilator into another room, when, with the same trouble, he might have communicated with the outside air!"

---

28. **endeavor** (en devʹər), *v.* make an effort; try hard.
29. **bell rope,** a cord that, when pulled, rings a bell to call for a servant.

"That is also quite modern," said the lady.

"Done about the same time as the bell rope?" remarked Holmes.

"Yes, there were several little changes carried out about that time."

"They seem to have been of a most interesting character—dummy bell ropes, and ventilators which do not ventilate. With your permission, Miss Stoner, we shall now carry our researches into the inner apartment."

Dr. Grimesby Roylott's chamber was larger than that of his stepdaughter, but was as plainly furnished. A camp bed, a small wooden shelf full of books, mostly of a technical character, an armchair beside the bed, a plain wooden chair against the wall, a round table, and a large iron safe were the principal things which met the eye. Holmes walked slowly round and examined each and all of them with the keenest interest.

"What's in here?" he asked, tapping the safe.

"My stepfather's business papers."

"Oh! you have seen inside, then?"

"Only once, some years ago. I remember that it was full of papers."

"There isn't a cat in it, for example?"

"No. What a strange idea!"

"Well, look at this!" He took up a small saucer of milk which stood on the top of it.

"No; we don't keep a cat. But there is a cheetah and a baboon."

"Ah, yes, of course! Well, a cheetah is just a big cat, and yet a saucer of milk does not go very far in satisfying its wants, I daresay. There is one point which I should wish to determine." He squatted down in front of the wooden chair and examined the seat of it with the greatest attention.

"Thank you. That is quite settled," said he, rising and putting his lens in his pocket. "Hello! Here is something interesting!"

The object which had caught his eye was a small dog lash hung on one corner of the bed. The lash, however, was curled upon itself and tied so as to make a loop of whipcord.

"What do you make of that, Watson?"

"It's a common enough lash. But I don't know why it should be tied."

"That is not quite so common, is it? Ah, me! it's a wicked world, and when a clever man turns his brains to crime it is the worst of all. I think that I have seen enough now, Miss Stoner, and with your permission we shall walk out upon the lawn."

I had never seen my friend's face so grim or his brow so dark as it was when we turned from the scene of this investigation. We had walked several times up and down the lawn, neither Miss Stoner nor myself liking to break in upon his thoughts before he roused himself from his reverie.

SUMMARIZE: What clues have Holmes and Watson gathered so far?

"It is very essential, Miss Stoner," said he, "that you should absolutely follow my advice in every respect."

"I shall most certainly do so."

"The matter is too serious for any hesitation. Your life may depend upon your compliance."[30]

"I assure you that I am in your hands."

"In the first place, both my friend and I must spend the night in your room."

Both Miss Stoner and I gazed at him in astonishment.

"Yes, it must be so. Let me explain. I believe that that is the village inn over there?"

"Yes, that is the Crown."

"Very good. Your windows would be visible from there?"

"Certainly."

"You must confine yourself to your room, on pretense of a headache, when your stepfather comes back. Then when you hear him retire for the night, you must open the shutters of your

---

30. **compliance** (kəm plī′əns), *n.* a complying or doing as another wishes; yielding to a request or command.

window, undo the hasp,[31] put your lamp there as a signal to us, and then withdraw quietly with everything which you are likely to want into the room which you used to occupy. I have no doubt that, in spite of the repairs, you could manage there for one night."

"Oh, yes, easily."

"The rest you will leave in our hands."

"But what will you do?"

"We shall spend the night in your room, and we shall investigate the cause of this noise which has disturbed you."

"I believe, Mr. Holmes, that you have already made up your mind," said Miss Stoner, laying her hand upon my companion's sleeve.

"Perhaps I have."

"Then, for pity's sake, tell me what was the cause of my sister's death."

"I should prefer to have clearer proofs before I speak."

"You can at least tell me whether my own thought is correct, and if she died from some sudden fright."

"No, I do not think so. I think that there was probably some more tangible[32] cause. And now, Miss Stoner, we must leave you, for if Dr. Roylott returned and saw us our journey would be in vain. Good-bye, and be brave, for if you will do what I have told you you may rest assured that we shall soon drive away the dangers that threaten you."

Sherlock Holmes and I had no difficulty in engaging a bedroom and sitting room at the Crown Inn. They were on the upper floor, and from our window we could command a view of the avenue gate, and of the inhabited wing of Stoke Moran Manor House. At dusk we saw Dr. Grimesby Roylott drive past, his huge form looming up beside the little figure of the lad who drove him. The boy had some slight difficulty in undoing the heavy iron gates, and we heard the hoarse roar of the doctor's voice and saw the fury with which he shook his clinched fists at him. The trap drove on, and a few min-

utes later we saw a sudden light spring up among the trees as the lamp was lit in one of the sitting rooms.

"Do you know, Watson," said Holmes as we sat together in the gathering darkness, "I have really some scruples[33] as to taking you tonight. There is a distinct element of danger."

"Can I be of assistance?"

"Your presence might be invaluable."

"Then I shall certainly come."

"It is very kind of you."

"You speak of danger. You have evidently seen more in these rooms than was visible to me."

"No, but I fancy that I may have deduced[34] a little more. I imagine that you saw all that I did."

"I saw nothing remarkable save the bell rope, and what purpose that could answer I confess is more than I can imagine."

"You saw the ventilator, too?"

"Yes, but I do not think that it is such a very unusual thing to have a small opening between two rooms. It was so small that a rat could hardly pass through."

"I knew that we should find a ventilator before ever we came to Stoke Moran."

"My dear Holmes!"

"Oh, yes, I did. You remember in her statement she said that her sister could smell Dr. Roylott's cigar. Now, of course that suggested at once that there must be a communication between the two rooms. It could only be a small one, or it would have been remarked upon at the coroner's inquiry. I deduced a ventilator."

"But what harm can there be in that?"

"Well, there is at least a curious coincidence of dates. A ventilator is made, a cord is hung, and a lady who sleeps in the bed dies. Does not that strike you?"

---

31. **hasp** (hasp), *n.* clasp or fastening for a door, window, trunk, etc.
32. **tangible** (tan′jə bəl), *adj.* that can be touched or felt by touch; real; actual; definite.
33. **scruple** (skrü′pəl), *n.* feeling of doubt about what one ought to do; a feeling of uneasiness.
34. **deduce** (di düs′), *v.* reach a conclusion by reasoning.

"I cannot as yet see any connection."

"Did you observe anything very peculiar about that bed?"

"No."

"It was clamped to the floor. Did you ever see a bed fastened like that before?"

"I cannot say that I have."

"The lady could not move her bed. It must always be in the same relative position to the ventilator and to the rope—or so we may call it, since it was clearly never meant for a bellpull."

"Holmes," I cried, "I seem to see dimly what you are hinting at. We are only just in time to prevent some subtle and horrible crime."

"Subtle enough and horrible enough. When a doctor does go wrong he is the first of criminals. He has nerve and he has knowledge. Palmer and Pritchard were among the heads of their profession. This man strikes even deeper, but I think, Watson, that we shall be able to strike deeper still. But we shall have horrors enough before the night is over; for goodness' sake let us have a quiet pipe and turn our minds for a few hours to something more cheerful."

About nine o'clock the light among the trees was extinguished, and all was dark in the direction of the Manor House. Two hours passed slowly away, and then, suddenly, just at the stroke of eleven, a single bright light shone out right in front of us.

"That is our signal," said Holmes, springing to his feet; "it comes from the middle window."

As we passed out he exchanged a few words with the landlord, explaining that we were going on a late visit to an acquaintance, and that it was possible that we might spend the night there. A moment later we were out on the dark road, a chill wind blowing in our faces, and one yellow light twinkling in front of us through the gloom to guide us on our somber errand.

There was little difficulty in entering the grounds, for unrepaired breaches gaped in the old park wall. Making our way among the trees, we reached the lawn, crossed it, and were about to enter through the window when out from a clump of laurel bushes there darted what seemed to be a hideous and distorted child, who threw itself upon the grass with writhing limbs and then ran swiftly across the lawn into the darkness.

"My God!" I whispered; "did you see it?"

Holmes was for the moment as startled as I. His hand closed like a vise upon my wrist in his agitation. Then he broke into a low laugh and put his lips to my ear.

"It is a nice household," he murmured. "That is the baboon."

I had forgotten the strange pets which the doctor affected. There was a cheetah, too; perhaps we might find it upon our shoulders at any moment. I confess that I felt easier in my mind when, after following Holmes's example and slipping off my shoes, I found myself inside the bedroom. My companion noiselessly closed the shutters, moved the lamp onto the table, and cast his eyes round the room. All was as we had seen it in the daytime. Then creeping up to me and making a trumpet of his hand, he whispered into my ear again so gently that it was all that I could do to distinguish the words:

"The least sound would be fatal to our plans."

I nodded to show that I had heard.

"We must sit without light. He would see it through the ventilator."

I nodded again.

"Do not go asleep; your very life may depend upon it. Have your pistol ready in case we should need it. I will sit on the side of the bed, and you in that chair."

I took out my revolver and laid it on the corner of the table.

Holmes had brought up a long thin cane, and this he placed upon the bed beside him. By it he laid the box of matches and the stump of a candle. Then he turned down the lamp, and we were left in darkness.

How shall I ever forget that dreadful vigil? I could not hear a sound, not even the drawing of

▲ Caspar David Friedrich, *Remembrance of Johann Bremer* (c. 1817). Compare and contrast the setting of this oil painting with the description of Stoke Moran.

a breath, and yet I knew that my companion sat open-eyed, within a few feet of me, in the same state of nervous tension in which I was myself. The shutters cut off the least ray of light, and we waited in absolute darkness. From outside came the occasional cry of a night bird, and once at our very window a long drawn catlike whine, which told us that the cheetah was indeed at liberty. Far away we could hear the deep tones of the parish clock, which boomed out every quarter of an hour. How long they seemed, those quarters! Twelve struck, and one and two and three, and still we sat waiting silently for whatever might befall.

Suddenly there was the momentary gleam of a light up in the direction of the ventilator, which vanished immediately, but was succeeded by a strong smell of burning oil and heated metal. Someone in the next room had lit a dark lantern. I heard a gentle sound of movement, and then all was silent once more, though the smell grew stronger. For half an hour I sat with straining ears. Then suddenly another sound became audible—a very gentle, soothing sound, like that of a small jet of steam escaping continually from a kettle. The instant that we heard it, Holmes sprang from the bed, struck a match, and lashed furiously with his cane at the bellpull.

"You see it, Watson?" he yelled. "You see it?"

But I saw nothing. At the moment when Holmes struck the light I heard a low, clear whistle, but the sudden glare flashing into my weary eyes made it impossible for me to tell what it was at which my friend lashed so savagely. I could, however, see that his face was deadly pale and filled with horror and loathing.

He had ceased to strike and was gazing up at the ventilator when suddenly there broke from the silence of the night the most horrible cry to which I have ever listened. It swelled up louder and louder, a hoarse yell of pain and fear and anger all mingled in the one dreadful shriek. They say that away down in the village, and even in the distant parsonage, that cry raised the sleepers from their beds. It struck cold to our hearts, and I stood gazing at Holmes, and he at me, until the last echoes of it had died away into the silence from which it rose.

"What can it mean?" I gasped.

"It means that it is all over," Holmes answered. "And perhaps, after all, it is for the best. Take your pistol, and we will enter Dr. Roylott's room."

With a grave face he lit the lamp and led the way down the corridor. Twice he struck at the chamber door without any reply from within. Then he turned the handle and entered, I at his heels, with the cocked pistol in my hand.

It was a singular sight which met our eyes. On the table stood a dark lantern with the shutter half open, throwing a brilliant beam of light upon the iron safe, the door of which was ajar. Beside this table, on the wooden chair, sat Dr. Grimesby Roylott, clad in a long gray dressing gown, his bare ankles protruding beneath, and his feet thrust into red heelless Turkish slippers. Across his lap lay the short stock with the long lash which we had noticed during the day. His chin was cocked upward and his eyes were fixed in a dreadful, rigid stare at the corner of the ceiling. Round his brow he had a peculiar yellow band, with brownish speckles, which seemed to be bound tightly round his head. As we entered he made neither sound nor motion.

"The band! the speckled band!" whispered Holmes.

I took a step forward. In an instant his strange headgear began to move, and there reared itself from among his hair the squat diamond-shaped head and puffed neck of a loathsome serpent.

"It is a swamp adder!" cried Holmes; "the deadliest snake in India. He has died within ten seconds of being bitten. Violence does, in truth, recoil upon the violent, and the schemer falls into the pit which he digs for another. Let us thrust this creature back into its den, and we can then remove Miss Stoner to some place of shelter and let the county police know what has happened."

As he spoke he drew the dog whip swiftly from the dead man's lap, and throwing the noose round the reptile's neck he drew it from its horrid perch and, carrying it at arm's length, threw it into the iron safe, which he closed upon it.

Such are the true facts of the death of Dr. Grimesby Roylott, of Stoke Moran. It is not necessary that I should prolong a narrative which has already run to too great a length by telling how we broke the sad news to the terrified girl, how we conveyed her by the morning train to the care of her good aunt at Harrow, of how the slow process of official inquiry came to the conclusion that the doctor met his fate while indiscreetly playing with a dangerous pet. The little which I had yet to learn of the case was told by Sherlock Holmes as we traveled back next day.

"I had," said he, "come to an entirely erroneous[35] conclusion which shows, my dear Watson, how dangerous it always is to reason from insufficient data. The presence of the gypsies, and the use of the word 'band,' which was used by the poor girl, no doubt to explain the appearance which she had caught a hurried

---

35. **erroneous** (ə rō′nē əs), *adj.* containing error; wrong; mistaken; incorrect.

glimpse of by the light of her match, were sufficient to put me upon an entirely wrong scent. I can only claim the merit that I instantly reconsidered my position when, however, it became clear to me that whatever danger threatened an occupant of the room could not come either from the window or the door. My attention was speedily drawn, as I have already remarked to you, to this ventilator, and to the bell rope which hung down to the bed. The discovery that this was a dummy, and that the bed was clamped to the floor, instantly gave rise to the suspicion that the rope was there as a bridge for something passing through the hold and coming to the bed. The idea of a snake instantly occurred to me, and when I coupled it with my knowledge that the doctor was furnished with a supply of creatures from India, I felt that I was probably on the right track. The idea of using a form of poison which could not possibly be discovered by any chemical test was just such a one as would occur to a clever and ruthless man who had had an Eastern training. The rapidity with which such a poison would take effect would also, from his point of view, be an advantage. It would be a sharp-eyed coroner, indeed, who could distinguish the two little dark punctures which would show where the poison fangs had done their work. Then I thought of the whistle. Of course he must recall the snake before the morning light revealed it to the victim. He had trained it, probably by the use of the milk which we saw, to return to him when summoned. He would put it through this ventilator at the hour that he thought best, with the certainty that it would crawl down the rope and land on the

"Violence does, in truth, recoil upon the violent, and the schemer falls into the pit which he digs for another."

bed. It might or might not bite the occupant, perhaps she might escape every night for a week, but sooner or later she must fall a victim.

"I had come to these conclusions before ever I had entered his room. An inspection of his chair showed me that he had been in the habit of standing on it, which of course would be necessary in order that he should reach the ventilator. The sight of the safe, the saucer of milk, and the loop of whipcord were enough to finally dispel[36] any doubts which may have remained. The metallic clang heard by Miss Stoner was obviously caused by her stepfather hastily closing the door of his safe upon its terrible occupant. Having once made up my mind, you know the steps which I took in order to put the matter to the proof. I heard the creature hiss as I have no doubt that you did also, and I instantly lit the light and attacked it."

"With the result of driving it through the ventilator."

"And also with the result of causing it to turn upon its master at the other side. Some of the blows of my cane came home and roused its snakish temper, so that it flew upon the first person it saw. In this way I am no doubt indirectly responsible for Dr. Grimesby Roylott's death, and I cannot say that it is likely to weigh very heavily upon my conscience."

---

36. **dispel** (dis pel′), *v.* drive away and scatter.

After Reading

Making Connections

Shaping Your Response

1. Do you think someone as brilliant as Holmes needs a "sidekick" like Watson? Why or why not?

2. Do you think that Holmes would be an effective member of a modern police force? Why or why not?

Analyzing the Story

3. What kind of person is Watson? How does he feel about working with Holmes?

4. Helen Stoner does not tell Holmes how she traveled to his house. Describe the **inferences,** or deductions, that Holmes makes to determine her method of travel.

5. What do you learn about Holmes's **character** from Roylott's visit?

6. What **motivation** did Roylott have for his crimes?

7. On a chart like the one begun below, show what clues certain items provided to help Holmes solve the mystery.

Item	Clue it provides
fake bell rope	used as a bridge for something
whistle	
ventilator	

Extending the Ideas

8. Compare and contrast this story with another detective story you have read or a mystery movie or television show you have seen.

9. The **theme** of this part of Unit 5 is "The Price of Wisdom." Compare and contrast Holmes's wisdom with Roylott's wisdom. Did either character pay a price for his wisdom? Explain.

Literary Focus: Point of View

Point of view, the author's choice of narrator for a story, determines the amount of information a reader will be given, as well as the angle from which this information will be presented. Watson serves as the first-person narrator of "The Adventure of the Speckled Band."

- What effect does the author's choice of narrator have on our understanding of the mystery?

- How would the story be different if Holmes told the story? if Helen told the story?

Vocabulary Study

averted
compliance
deduce
dissolute
erroneous
imperturbably
imprudence
morose
pittance
writhe

You are a world-famous author of thrilling mystery stories. Use the listed vocabulary words in brief scenes such as the ones suggested below. The Glossary will help you understand how to use these words correctly.

1. A detective and client discuss the mysterious disappearance of the client's grandmother.

2. A cab driver describes overhearing two passengers plan a murder.

3. An elegant (but guilty) model denies any knowledge of a recent jewelry theft.

4. The young heir to a fortune finds a snake in a coat pocket.

Expressing Your Ideas

Writing Choices

Writer's Notebook Update Before you read the story, you wrote about a mystery or problem you solved using reasoning. In your notebook, compare and contrast your method (and the outcome) with that of Holmes.

It Was a Dark and Stormy Night This story reflects the Gothic style popular during the 1700s and 1800s, in which settings were often mysterious, desolate, or even grotesque. Write a **description** of your own Gothic setting—perhaps a gloomy castle or a deserted old mansion. Be sure to include details that appeal to all the senses. What would you hear, see, feel, and even smell in such a place?

Mystery! Research a famous unsolved mystery, such as the disappearance of ships in the Bermuda Triangle, sightings of unidentified flying objects, or the Loch Ness monster. Write a **newspaper article** on one of these mysteries, focusing on what exactly the mystery is and what efforts have been made to solve it.

Other Options

Mapping It Out To understand how Holmes solves the mystery, it is essential to understand the layout of the Roylott mansion and its rooms and ventilation system. Make a **map** to accompany the story, showing the grounds of the estate and the floorplan of the mansion. Be sure to show on your map Roylott's room, the room in which the murder occurred, and the path taken by the snake.

Dramatic Tension The growing tension in the story would make it an interesting one to present as a **radio play.** Choose a portion of the story, and, in a small group, practice reading aloud the dialogue in character. Be sure to consider what tone of voice would be appropriate for each part. Also consider the sound effects you will add, such as the whistling and clanging, as well as music to heighten the tension. After practicing, present your radio play to the class.

The Price of Wisdom

Paths of Wisdom

Psychology Connection
Recent studies in psychology suggest that there's more to intelligence than an IQ test can accurately measure. In fact, one psychologist argues convincingly that there are actually seven different kinds of intelligence.

BODILY-KINESTHETIC

INTERPERSONAL

INTRAPERSONAL

MANY WAYS of KNOWING

Have you ever composed an original melody, caught a ball while running, or traced an imaginary route in your mind? You may not see these accomplishments as signs of intelligence, but according to Harvard psychologist Howard Gardner, they are. Gardner's 1983 book *Frames of Mind* shows how great scientists, mathematicians, artists, and politicians rely on much more than factual knowledge to accomplish their work. Successful people may have highly developed abilities in any of the seven areas of intelligence shown on the pie chart on these pages. Therefore, argues Gardner, modern education should help students develop all these areas of intelligence.

Musical
- able to appreciate and work with melody, rhythm, and tone in music
  - example: pianist Arthur Rubenstein

Spatial
- able to visualize an object and manipulate it in one's imagination; able to produce a likeness of an object
  - example: artist Georgia O'Keeffe

Linguistic
- able to understand and manipulate words and language
  - example: poet Emily Dickinson

Logical-mathematical
- able to see patterns in things; able to use logic and reasoning to solve problems
  - example: scientist Albert Einstein

Intrapersonal
- able to understand and analyze one's own thoughts and emotions
  - example: psychologist Sigmund Freud

Interpersonal
- able to understand, work with, and influence others
  - example: political leader Mahatma Gandhi

Bodily-kinesthetic
- able to use one's body in skilled ways and handle objects skillfully
  - example: choreographer Martha Graham

MUSICAL

SPATIAL

LINGUISTIC

LOGICAL-MATHEMATICAL

7

Responding
1. Which of these seven types of intelligence do you feel are your own strongest areas of ability?

2. Think of some "geniuses" you have known or read about. Discuss which areas of intelligence their work involves.

Career Connection

As a counselor, Darryl Tonemah (tō′ne mä) draws upon his cultural traditions and his music to help people learn to live healthier lives.

THE CIRCLE IN TIME

Interview with Darryl Tonemah

Tell a little bit about your background.

I'm a full-blood Native American, and a member of the Kiowa tribe. I'm Kiowa and Comanche on my dad's side, and Tuscarora on my mom's. I was born on the Tuscarora reservation in New York, but we moved around after my dad started working for the Indian Health Service. I went to high school and college in South Dakota.

After college, I worked as a drug and alcohol counselor in Oklahoma. A lot of the clients talked about difficult childhoods and not knowing what "healthy" behavior was. I thought I could give something back to my culture by working directly with young people and families. So when I went to the University of Oklahoma for graduate school, I joined a campus organization that led workshops for different Indian tribes on topics like healthy relationships, communication, and leadership training.

What approach do you use in your workshops?

I base my workshops on the medicine wheel, which is something that Native Americans of all tribes can relate to, although they have slightly different views of it. The wheel has a center and four directions, and all the elements relate to each other.

THE CIRCLE IN TIME
CONNECTS YOUR LIFE AND MINE.
I BELIEVE, I BELIEVE.

—from "Believe" by Darryl Tonemah, © 1995.

In the center of the wheel is the person's sexuality, and how the person sees his or her role in the world. The North is the home of the mind. I discuss education and learning from the elders. To the East is spirituality, which can grow through things like talking to the elders, or holding a child, or learning from those around you. In the South are the emotions, which involve a person's ability to give and receive love, to share a connection with others. The West is the physical body, your connection to the Earth. I talk about healthy eating habits, exercise, and so on.

You're also a musician. How does music fit into what you do?

About four years ago I was talking with elders and they said that traditionally, educators in a tribe would use any means possible—singing, dance, storytelling, puppets—to help young people understand their message. And I thought, "Well, I play a little guitar." I began using music at the beginning of a workshop to get people's attention, to hook them in. I like to use humor—as a culture, Indian people like to tease each other. So some of my songs are about the ways different tribes tease each other about what kinds of cars we drive, or what we eat. Now, as well as doing workshops, I'm often invited to give concerts. I really enjoy that. I couldn't pick between the two, because if the music grows I can reach a lot of people that way, too.

Responding

1. How do you think the song lyrics relate to the medicine wheel that Tonemah describes?

2. The medicine wheel is a symbol of balance and health. Create and illustrate your own symbol for a healthy lifestyle.

Writing Workshop

What I'd Like to Know Is. . . .

Assignment Write an I-Search paper, in which you research a topic of interest to you personally and report on what you learned and how you learned it.

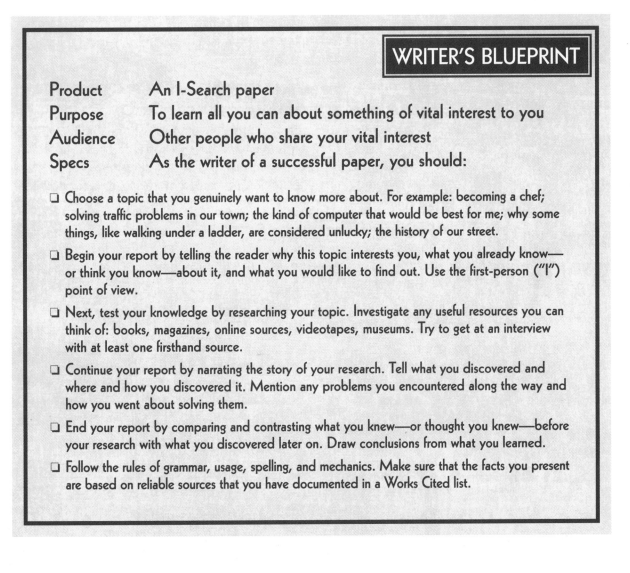

WRITER'S BLUEPRINT

Product   An I-Search paper

Purpose   To learn all you can about something of vital interest to you

Audience   Other people who share your vital interest

Specs   As the writer of a successful paper, you should:

❏ Choose a topic that you genuinely want to know more about. For example: becoming a chef; solving traffic problems in our town; the kind of computer that would be best for me; why some things, like walking under a ladder, are considered unlucky; the history of our street.

❏ Begin your report by telling the reader why this topic interests you, what you already know— or think you know—about it, and what you would like to find out. Use the first-person ("I") point of view.

❏ Next, test your knowledge by researching your topic. Investigate any useful resources you can think of: books, magazines, online sources, videotapes, museums. Try to get at an interview with at least one firsthand source.

❏ Continue your report by narrating the story of your research. Tell what you discovered and where and how you discovered it. Mention any problems you encountered along the way and how you went about solving them.

❏ End your report by comparing and contrasting what you knew—or thought you knew—before your research with what you discovered later on. Draw conclusions from what you learned.

❏ Follow the rules of grammar, usage, spelling, and mechanics. Make sure that the facts you present are based on reliable sources that you have documented in a Works Cited list.

Review the literature. Working in a small group, review the literary selections in this part and make a list of the topics these authors felt strongly about, such as what education really is (see the Literary Source). Then brainstorm ideas for your own research topic. Some of these questions may suggest more topic ideas:

- Is there something you'd like to do in your free time but don't know much about? (Examples: skydiving, gourmet cooking, surfing, volunteer work, photography, computers, sewing)

- Are you saving money to buy anything? Do you need to learn how to operate it? How could you find the best buy? (Examples: electric guitar, camera, computer)

- What controversial issues interest you? (Examples: welfare, violence in the media, healthful foods versus junk foods)

Try a quickwrite after you choose your topic. Write for five minutes. Explain what you want to know about your topic and how you plan to gather information. Share your quickwrite with your group. Perhaps they can help you refine your topic or give you more ideas about gathering information.

Create a knowledge chart. Write down what you already know, what you assume, and what you imagine about the topic, using a chart like the one shown. Also, note what you would like to find out. Remember to use the first-person ("I") point of view.

> **LITERARY SOURCE**
> "When most people think of the word 'education,' they think of a pupil as a sort of animate sausage casing. Into this empty casing, the teachers are supposed to stuff 'education.'"
> from "What True Education Should Do" by Sidney J. Harris

> **OR . . .**
> Before doing a quickwrite, do some preliminary research. Look through a library card catalogue, for instance. If you can't find much information, you may need to choose another topic.

What I Know	What I Assume	What I Imagine	What I Would Like to Find Out
I read about a study showing that kids who watch a lot of TV become more aggressive or more tolerant of aggression.	These kids must watch shows that contain violent scenes or that give a message that violence is all right.	I imagine that adults are getting more and more concerned about this issue.	What are people proposing as possible solutions to this problem?

Write the first part of your paper, in which you deal with the information you've listed in your knowledge chart. See the second point in the Blueprint. You will write the rest of your paper after testing your knowledge by researching your topic.

Research your topic. Visit libraries, museums, and other community institutions to find sources of useful information. Try to get an interview with at least one firsthand source, an expert who knows something about your topic.

For each source, make a **source card** that lists the information you'll need for your Works Cited list. Give each source card a separate number. Record relevant information on **note cards**. Include the source name and number and the appropriate page numbers. See the examples that follow.

Source Card

> 1
>
> Getchell, Leroy H., Grover D. Pippin, and Jill
> W. Varnes. *Perspectives on Health.*
> Lexington, MA: D. C. Heath and
> Company, 1994.

Note Card

> *Perspectives on Health* 1
>
> violence learned from watching
> others; tend not to learn to use
> emotions positively if movies,
> media deal with emotions in
> harmful ways   p. 97

Plan the rest of your report. Organize the information from your notes into a writing plan like this one. (Remember, you've already written the first part.)

- **Your research experience**
  The steps you took
  Problems and how you handled them
  What you discovered

- **What you already knew compared/contrasted with what you discovered**
  Similarities
  Differences
  Conclusions

OR . . .
Create a time line to show your research steps. The time line should chronicle your research and include notes about what you discovered on your journey.

STEP **2** DRAFTING

Start writing. Here are some drafting tips.

- You might want to narrate the story of your research as if it were a journey. Use words like *trip, stops, destination, arrive,* and *leave.*

- Don't just list facts. Draw conclusions from them. See the Revising Strategy in Step 3 of this lesson.

> **COMPUTER TIP**
> Your word-processing program may have an outline option. Use this feature to view the main ideas and details of your paragraphs in outline form.

STEP **3** REVISING

Ask a partner for comments on your draft before you revise it.

✔ Have I described my research experience in narrative form?

✔ Have I drawn conclusions from what I've learned in my research?

Revising Strategy

Drawing Conclusions

When you draw conclusions about your research at the end of your report, be sure you've looked carefully at the facts and dealt with the questions they raise and the thoughts they suggest. Notice how the writer of the student model revised to include conclusions based on research.

STUDENT MODEL:

In conclusion, you shouldn't worry about getting AIDS if you do not practice high-risk behavior.
AIDS is neither airborne nor highly contagious. For example, the CDC reports that you cannot contract AIDS from a mosquito bite.

It cannot be contracted through casual contact, such as kissing or

holding hands. Many people who have AIDS feel like lepers because

no one wants to be near them or touch them. However, the facts

prove that this type of contact would not put someone at risk. *So, if you know people who are HIV positive or have AIDS, don't treat them like outsiders. Just because they're losing T cells doesn't mean that they're losing their feelings.*

Ask a partner to review your revised draft before you edit. When you edit, watch for errors in grammar, usage, spelling, and mechanics. Look carefully for errors in the form of your Works Cited list.

Editing Strategy

Works Cited List

The Works Cited list is the final page of your report. All the sources you cited in your report are listed on this page. Use your source cards when you write this page. Here are examples of how to cite four different kinds of sources:

For a reference book:
Barrera, Neal S. "Television." *World Book Encyclopedia,* 1995 ed.

For a book:
Chisholm, Penelope. *Children and Violence: You Can Help.* New York: Alfred A. Knopf, 1991.

For a magazine article:
Harrison, Marci. "Please Turn Off the Television," *Time,* 24 Sept. 1993, pp. 23–4.

For a firsthand interview:
Zavaleta, Milos. Telephone interview. 28 Nov. 1995.

> **COMPUTER TIP**
> Use the computer to italicize the titles of books, magazines, and references sources instead of underlining them.

Your teacher might ask you to use **footnotes** to acknowledge sources of information within the text of your report. Find out which style of footnotes your teacher prefers. Then, be consistent. Number the footnotes consecutively with raised numerals within the text. Then place your numbered citations at the bottom of the text pages where they are cited, or at the end of your paper.

STEP 5 PRESENTING

Form a group with students who chose a similar topic and use one of the following ideas to present your paper.

- Create a true-false test based on the new information you learned about your topic. Administer the test to your classmates. Then present your essay and let them discover how many misconceptions they had. Conclude your presentation by discussing their answers.

- Compile a research handbook based on the research experiences of the class. Include tips on what worked and what didn't along with anecdotes to illustrate various points. This handbook could be published on the computer and used by classes that follow yours.

STEP 6 LOOKING BACK

Self-evaluate. What grade would *you* give your paper? Look back at the Writer's Blueprint and evaluate your paper on each point, from 6 (superior) to 1 (inadequate).

Reflect. Write your answers to these questions.

✔ As you researched your topic, what piece of information did you find to be the most surprising? How did you convey this element of surprise in your writing?

✔ What did you learn about doing research from writing this paper?

For Your Working Portfolio Add your I-Search paper and your reflection responses to your working portfolio.

Beyond Print

Electronic Research

Today a wide variety of electronic research tools such as those described here may be available at your school, library, or home. The next time you have a research project, consider using the following:

- A **magazine or newspaper index** stored on a CD-ROM. Many of these contain summaries or the full text of material in periodicals.

- **Reference materials** such as dictionaries and encyclopedias on CD-ROM. Two examples include the **AuthorWorks** CD-ROM, which offers information, photos, and video about influential authors, and the **Custom Literature Database** CD-ROM, which provides the text of many literary works.

- **Online services** that connect you with other computers, giving you access to encyclopedias, magazines, reviews, interviews, and subject-specific databases. Using online services, librarians can search other libraries for books, articles, or other research materials.

Here are some tips for successful electronic research:

- **Enter information accurately.** The computer can't read your mind, so be sure to spell names and keywords correctly.

- **If you are searching by subject, try several different keywords.** Before beginning a subject search, brainstorm a list of possible keywords. If you are looking for more information on planets, look under *planets, astronomy, exobiology*, or any number of other keywords.

- **Know how to download information.** There are several ways to move the information off the screen and into your hands. The easiest way is to print out the information. Data can also be downloaded onto a computer hard drive or disk. Finally, you may be able to request printed information that will be sent to you directly.

Activity

Prepare a brochure that describes the electronic research resources available at your school or library.

Multicultural Connections

Individuality

Part One: Unexpected Heroes In "Graduation," Henry Reed's expression of his individuality strengthens the community when he leads the graduation audience in an unplanned but uplifting rendition of "Lift Ev'ry Voice and Sing."

■ Explain how the individuality of Alan Romney Dixon, Le Ly Hayslip's father, and Abraham Lincoln both challenged and strengthened the people around them.

Change

Part Two: The Price of Wisdom Our interactions with the world around us may change our beliefs and values. In "The Struggle to Be an All-American Girl," Elizabeth Wong reveals a change in her once-critical attitude toward her Chinese heritage.

■ Explain how encounters with nature led writers Mark Twain and Gary Paulsen to experience a change in attitude.

Activities

Work in small groups on the following activities.

1. Choose three people described in the selections in this unit. How did they maintain their individuality despite pressure from others?
2. Consider some of the authors of these selections. Describe how events in their lives influenced a change in their attitudes.

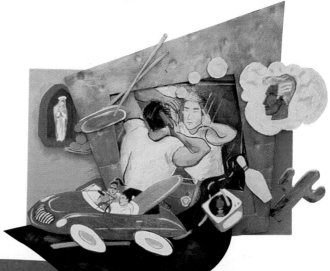

Independent and Group Projects

Writing

Changing Times Many of the authors in this unit describe places, people, or events that have influenced their lives. Think about a place, person, or event that has in some way changed the way you see yourself or the world around you. Write a brief memoir that explains how you have changed and describes the experience that brought about the change.

Media

On Camera With two or three of your classmates, become a roving band of reporters. Take a video camera into the cafeteria and the hallways of your school to interview students on the spot. (Be sure to get permission from the administration first.) Ask students a question like this one: "What person from our generation is making the greatest contribution to society today?" Show highlights of your interviews to the rest of your class. If you have access to editing equipment, edit your video footage down to a ten- or fifteen-minute program.

Research

More About the Author Choose one of the authors from this unit and do further research about that person. Prepare a chart or poster that lists details about the author's life and his or her interests, qualities of the author's writing style, and the titles of the author's best-known works. If possible, include quotes about the author's work from book reviews. For tips on how to conduct your research, read the Beyond Print articles on pages 667–668 and page 725.

Oral Presentation

Real-World Reading In Unit 5, you have read autobiographies, memoirs, biographies, and essays. Read at least one example of another form of nonfiction: a film or music review, a collection of letters, a published diary, a travel or history book, etc. Prepare an oral report that summarizes what you learned from your reading. As part of your report, describe what special kinds of information this particular form of nonfiction has to offer.

UNIT **6**

Fateful
Journeys

The Long Way Home
Pages 732–813

IN THE EPIC POEM the *Odyssey*, the Greek poet Homer spins an exciting tale about the wanderings of the hero Odysseus. Some aspects of Homer's story, such as the fights and monsters and homesickness, are found in many tales of adventure, ancient and modern. But some other characteristics of the *Odyssey* are less familiar and you may enjoy reading the poem more if you know what to expect.

HEAR MY SONG

Epic poems such as the *Odyssey* were part of an oral literature. People generally did not sit alone and read them, but instead, as the illustration portrays, gathered in groups to listen to these poems being chanted or sung. Oral poets such as Homer and those who came before him preserved the heroic traditions of the Greek people, including the tales of the heroes of the Trojan War, through the centuries before their language came to be written down.

A TALE RETOLD

The people shown in the illustration have not come to be surprised by a new story, but to hear a familiar tale retold in a way that would move them again. Since Homer's story is well known to his audience, the poem does not conceal the final outcome. There are many hints of what lies ahead.

HOMER'S WAY WITH WORDS

As a narrator, Homer rarely employs lengthy descriptions of people or places. Instead, he will focus on one or two specific details, and you must use your imagination to fill out a picture. Many of these simple descriptions, phrases such as "pale-gold Aphrodite," and "winedark sea" are used again and again. Homer also does not spend much time on characterization, again confining himself to simple formulas, such as "Penelope the Wise." What interests Homer is not appearances or personalities but action.

THE CODE OF THE WARRIOR

Homer's epic depicts a world of warrior aristocrats. Bravery in battle, a high sense of personal honor, and loyalty to one's word and one's friends, are what matter to his heroes. But while Homer celebrates these aristocratic values, he also finds virtues in ordinary people that are absent in others far wealthier and more powerful.

THE HAND OF THE GODS

One aspect of Homer's world that surprises modern readers is the frequent interference of the gods. Homer assumes the gods take sides in human affairs. The sea-god Poseidon is the bitter enemy of Odysseus, and tries to keep him from reaching home. Athena, the goddess of wisdom, loves the hero for his craftiness and aids him all she can. The gods frequently disguise themselves as human beings in the story, trying to help their friends or destroy their enemies. But when the gods become involved in human affairs, their actions are governed more by their emotions than by morality.

READING A GREEK EPIC

READING FROM HOMER BY SIR LAWRENCE ALMA-TADEMA (1885). MANY OF ALMA-TADEMA'S PAINTINGS PORTRAYED LIFE IN ANCIENT GREECE AND ROME. WHAT DOES THIS PAINTING CONVEY ABOUT THE EXPERIENCE OF "READING FROM HOMER"? EXPLAIN.

The Long Way Home

The war is over. The hero leaves for home. The theme of the returning hero has been the subject of countless stories, songs, and plays around the world and across generations. The *Odyssey* by Homer is an ancient example of this popular theme.

Multicultural Connection **Choice** is often influenced by the cultural values of the society in which we live. Our heroes are often those people who choose to demonstrate bravery, loyalty, or other virtues valued by our culture. In the *Odyssey,* how do cultural values influence the choices made by the different characters?

Before Reading

The Voyage

from the **Odyssey** by Homer

Homer
C. 725 B.C.

Homer, considered the author of the Greek epics the *Iliad* and the *Odyssey,* most likely did not write at all. As an oral poet, Homer memorized accounts of historical events and combined popular Greek expressions with his own style to create entertaining stories. Homer's epic poems were probably first written down around 725 B.C.

Robert Fitzgerald
1910–1985

Robert Fitzgerald's English version of the *Odyssey* has been immensely popular since it first appeared in 1961. Fitzgerald translated many other classical works and also published four volumes of his own poetry.

Building Background

Setting the Scene To understand the following selections from the *Odyssey*, it is important to know what has happened so far. The Achaeans (Homer's name for Greeks) have fought and won a ten-year war against Troy. On the voyage home to Ithaca, the Greek hero Odysseus and his men anger Poseidon, god of the sea, when they blind Polyphemus, the giant Cyclops who is Poseidon's son.

When the *Odyssey* begins, Odysseus has been detained for many years on the island of the nymph Calypso. Back home in Ithaca, young men have moved into Odysseus's palace, hoping to marry his wife Penelope. Penelope says she will choose a husband after weaving a funeral shroud for her father-in-law, Laertes. But each night she unravels her weaving, thereby prolonging her task.

At the urging of Athena, goddess of wisdom, the gods finally agree to help Odysseus return home. Athena sends Odysseus's son Telemachus on a journey to find out if his father is alive. While Telemachus is gone, Penelope's suitors plot to kill him.

Meanwhile, the god Hermes orders Calypso to release Odysseus. Odysseus sets sail, but is shipwrecked by Poseidon. He washes up on an island, where he is aided by the friendly Phaeacians. At a Phaeacian banquet, Odysseus tells of his adventures during the ten years since the fall of Troy. He begins by describing his encounters with the Cicones, the Lotus Eaters, and the Cyclops.

Literary Focus

Epic Hero The **epic hero** is the central character of an epic, someone whose words and actions have great significance. The character of Odysseus, one of the most famous epic heroes, was probably based on real-life Greeks who displayed courage, persistence, strength, and wisdom.

Writer's Notebook

Heroic Qualities What qualities do you think make someone heroic? Record your thoughts in your notebook. As you read the *Odyssey,* compare your ideas about heroes with the character of Odysseus.

PRINCIPAL CHARACTERS

THE ODYSSEY

MORTALS

Achaeans (ə kē′ənz), Homer's name for the Greeks.

Alcinous (al sin′ō əs), the generous, good-natured king of the Phaeacians, to whom Odysseus tells his story.

Antinous (an tin′ō əs), the most aggressive and cruel of Penelope's suitors.

Eumaeus (yü mē′əs), Odysseus's faithful swineherd.

Eurycleia (yü′rə klē′ə), Odysseus's faithful old nurse, who recognizes him in his beggar disguise.

Eurylochus (yü ri′lə kəs), one of Odysseus's crewmen.

Eurymachus (yü ri′mə kəs), a treacherous suitor.

Laertes (lā er′tēz), Odysseus's elderly father. He lives alone on a small farm outside of town.

Melanthius (mə lan′thē əs), Odysseus's chief goatherd. While Odysseus is gone, he ignores his duties and befriends the suitors.

Mentor (men′tôr), a faithful friend of Odysseus who served as Telemachus's tutor. Athena sometimes disguises herself as Mentor.

Odysseus (ō dis′ē əs), king of Ithaca and hero of the ten-year Trojan War. He is forced by the angry gods to wander for ten more years before returning home. In Latin, known as Ulysses.

Penelope (pə nel′ə pē), Odysseus's faithful wife.

Philoetius (fi lē′shəs), Odysseus's chief cowherd. He helps Odysseus fight the suitors.

Telemachus (tə lem′ə kəs), Odysseus's brave and loyal son, who fights with Odysseus against the suitors.

GODS AND SUPERNATURAL BEINGS

Athena (a thē′nə), daughter of Zeus and goddess of wisdom. She assists Odysseus during his journey and helps him defeat the suitors. See page 801.

Calypso (kə lip′sō), a sea nymph who keeps Odysseus captive for many years.

Charybdis (kə rib′dis), a huge, dangerous whirlpool.

Circe (sėr′sē), an enchantress who temporarily turns Odysseus's crew into swine. Odysseus stays with her for a year, and she helps him on his voyage home.

Cyclopes (sī klō′pēz), a race of one-eyed giants.

Helios (hē′lē os), god of the sun.

Hermes (hėr′mēz), son of Zeus and messenger of the gods. Hermes helps Odysseus resist Circe's spell. See page 802.

Polyphemus (pol′ə fē′məs), a Cyclops (sī′klops) and a son of Poseidon. Odysseus blinds Polyphemus, angering Poseidon.

Poseidon (pə sīd′n), god of the sea and earthquakes, and younger brother of Zeus. See page 801.

Scylla (sil′ə), a sea monster with six heads who eats some of Odysseus's crew.

Sirens (sī′rənz), beautiful but deadly maidens who tempt passing sailors with tantalizing singing.

Zeus (züs), the supreme god and king of Olympus. See page 801.

The Voyage

FROM THE

ODYSSEY

HOMER

Le Nef de Telemachus
(French, "The Ship of
Telemachus") shows
Odysseus's son in search
of his father. What mood
does this image convey?
lighthearted adventure?
heroic determination?

SAILING FROM TROY

"I am Laertes' son, Odysseus.

Men hold me
formidable for guile in peace and war:
this fame has gone abroad to the sky's rim.
My home is on the peaked sea-mark of Ithaca
5 under Mount Neion's wind-blown robe of leaves,
in sight of other islands—Dulichium,
Same, wooded Zacynthus—Ithaca
being most lofty in that coastal sea,
and northwest, while the rest lie east and south.

2 formidable (fôr′mə də-
bəl), *adj.* causing fear or
dread; inspiring awe or
wonder.
2 guile (gīl), *n.* crafty deceit;
sly tricks; cunning.

10　A rocky isle, but good for a boy's training;
　　I shall not see on earth a place more dear,
　　though I have been detained long by Calypso,
　　loveliest among goddesses, who held me
　　in her smooth caves, to be her heart's delight,
15　as Circe of Aeaea, the enchantress,
　　desired me, and detained me in her hall.
　　But in my heart I never gave consent.
　　Where shall a man find sweetness to surpass
　　his own home and his parents? In far lands
20　he shall not, though he find a house of gold.

　　What of my sailing, then, from Troy?
　　　　　　　　　　　　　　　　What of those years
　　of rough adventure, weathered under Zeus?
　　The wind that carried west from Ilium
　　brought me to Ismarus, on the far shore,
25　a strongpoint on the coast of the Cicones.
　　I stormed that place and killed the men who fought.
　　Plunder we took, and we enslaved the women,
　　to make division, equal shares to all—
　　but on the spot I told them: 'Back, and quickly!
30　Out to sea again!' My men were mutinous,
　　fools, on stores of wine. Sheep after sheep
　　they butchered by the surf, and shambling cattle,
　　feasting,—while fugitives went inland, running
　　to call to arms the main force of Cicones.
35　This was an army, trained to fight on horseback
　　or, where the ground required, on foot. They came
　　with dawn over that terrain like the leaves
　　and blades of spring. So doom appeared to us,
　　dark word of Zeus for us, our evil days.
40　My men stood up and made a fight of it—
　　backed on the ships, with lances kept in play,
　　from bright morning through the blaze of noon
　　holding our beach, although so far outnumbered;
　　but when the sun passed toward unyoking time,
45　then the Achaeans, one by one, gave way.
　　Six benches were left empty in every ship
　　that evening when we pulled away from death.
　　And this new grief we bore with us to sea:
　　our precious lives we had, but not our friends.
50　No ship made sail next day until some shipmate
　　had raised a cry, three times, for each poor ghost
　　unfleshed by the Cicones on that field.

■ How does Odysseus justify his years with Calypso and Circe?

23 Ilium (il′ē əm), Troy.

25 Cicones (si kō′nēz), a tribe allied with the Trojans and raided by Odysseus and his men after they leave Troy.
27 plunder (plun′dər), *n.* things taken by force or robbery.
30 mutinous (myüt′n əs), *adj.* openly rebellious against lawful authority, especially by sailors or soldiers against their officers.

37 terrain (te rān′), *n.* land; ground; territory.

44 when the sun . . . time, when the sun went down.
46 Six benches . . . empty, as many men who filled six rowing benches on each ship were killed in battle.

■ Why are so many of Odysseus's men killed in battle against the Cicones?

Now Zeus the lord of cloud roused in the north
a storm against the ships, and driving veils
55 of squall moved down like night on land and sea.
The bows went plunging at the gust; sails
cracked and lashed out strips in the big wind.
We saw death in that fury, dropped the yards,
unshipped the oars, and pulled for the nearest lee:
60 then two long days and nights we lay offshore
worn out and sick at heart, tasting our grief,
until a third Dawn came with ringlets shining.
Then we put up our masts, hauled sail, and rested,
letting the steersmen and the breeze take over.

65 I might have made it safely home, that time,
but as I came round Malea the current
took me out to sea, and from the north
a fresh gale drove me on, past Cythera.
Nine days I drifted on the teeming sea
70 before dangerous high winds. Upon the tenth
we came to the coastline of the Lotus Eaters,
who live upon that flower. We landed there
to take on water. All ships' companies
mustered alongside for the mid-day meal.
75 Then I sent out two picked men and a runner
to learn what race of men that land sustained.
They fell in, soon enough, with Lotus Eaters,
who showed no will to do us harm, only
offering the sweet Lotus to our friends—
80 but those who ate this honeyed plant, the Lotus,
never cared to report, nor to return:
they longed to stay forever, browsing on
that native bloom, forgetful of their homeland.
I drove them, all three wailing, to the ships,
85 tied them down under their rowing benches,
and called the rest: 'All hands aboard;
come, clear the beach and no one taste
the Lotus, or you lose your hope of home.'
Filing in to their places by the rowlocks
90 my oarsmen dipped their long oars in the surf,
and we moved out again on our sea faring."

55 squall (skwôl), *n.* a
sudden, violent gust of wind
often accompanied by rain,
snow, or sleet.

**58–59 dropped the yards . . .
lee,** dropped the sails, took
out the oars, and began rowing toward the nearest shelter
from the wind.

■ Do you think Odysseus's
men who ate the Lotus will
be glad he forced them to
leave?
89 rowlock (rō′lok′), *n.* slot
where oars are held in place
on a ship or boat.

After Reading

Making Connections

Shaping Your Response

1. Describe your impression of Odysseus so far.

2. Do you think Odysseus is right to force his men to leave the land of the Lotus Eaters? Why or why not?

Analyzing the Selection

3. **Characterize** Odysseus's men based on their behavior on the coast of the Cicones and in the land of the Lotus Eaters.

4. How does Odysseus seem different from his men?

Extending the Ideas

5. Do you agree with Odysseus that no place surpasses the "sweetness" of home? Why or why not?

Vocabulary Study

Write the letter of the word pair that best matches the relationship between the capitalized words. If necessary, use the Glossary for help with word meanings.

formidable
guile
mutinous
plunder
squall

1. FORMIDABLE : INTIMIDATING :: (A) greedy : starving (B) threatening : reassuring (C) deceptive : deceitful (D) angry : forgiving

2. GUILE : INNOCENCE :: (A) threat : reassurance (B) curiosity : interest (C) cunning : deception (D) trust : promise

3. MUTINOUS : OBEDIENT :: (A) willing : cooperative (B) rebellious : belligerent (C) hesitant : uncertain (D) loud : quiet

4. PLUNDER : ROB :: (A) groceries : buy (B) flowers : weeds (C) books : pages (D) flippers : dive

5. SQUALL : GUST :: (A) tree : forest (B) brook : stream (C) water : ice (D) air : land

Expressing Your Ideas

Writing Choice

That's a Different Story Choose the battle with the Cicones or the visit to the Lotus Eaters and write about what happened from the point of view of one of Odysseus's men. If you wish, read your **retelling** to the class.

Another Option

Land of the Lotus When Odysseus and his crew land on the coastline of the Lotus Eaters, some of his men fall under the spell of the intoxicating lotus flower. Create a **visual representation,** such as a drawing, painting, or cartoon, of these events.

② THE CYCLOPS

"In the next land we found were Cyclopes,
giants, louts, without a law to bless them.
In ignorance leaving the fruitage of the earth in mystery
to the immortal gods, they neither plow
5   nor sow by hand, nor till the ground, though grain—
wild wheat and barley—grows untended, and
wine-grapes, in clusters, ripen in heaven's rain.
Cyclopes have no muster and no meeting,
no consultation or old tribal ways,
10 but each one dwells in his own mountain cave
dealing out rough justice to wife and child,
indifferent to what others do. . . .

As we rowed on, and nearer to the mainland,
at one end of the bay, we saw a cavern
15 yawning above the water, screened with laurel,
and many rams and goats about the place
inside a sheepfold—made from slabs of stone
earthfast between tall trunks of pine and rugged
towering oak trees.

                              A prodigious man
20 slept in this cave alone, and took his flocks
to graze afield—remote from all companions,
knowing none but savage ways, a brute
so huge, he seemed no man at all of those
who eat good wheaten bread; but he seemed rather
25 a shaggy mountain reared in solitude.
We beached there, and I told the crew
to stand by and keep watch over the ship;
as for myself I took my twelve best fighters
and went ahead. I had a goatskin full
30 of that sweet liquor that Euanthes' son,
Maron, had given me. He kept Apollo's
holy grove at Ismarus; for kindness
we showed him there, and showed his wife and child,
he gave me seven shining golden talents
35 perfectly formed, a solid silver winebowl,
and then this liquor—twelve two-handled jars
of brandy, pure and fiery. Not a slave
in Maron's household knew this drink; only
he, his wife and the storeroom mistress knew;

3 fruitage (frü′tij), *n.* fruit.

8–9 no muster . . . ways, no political assembly or social traditions.

■ How does Odysseus **characterize** the Cyclopes?

17 sheepfold (shēp′fōld′), *n.* pen or shelter for sheep.
18 earthfast (ėrth′fast′), *adj.* held firmly in the ground.
19 prodigious (prə dij′əs), *adj.* very great; huge; vast.

34 talent (tal′ənt), *n.* an ancient unit of weight or money.

40 and they would put one cupful—ruby-colored,
   honey-smooth—in twenty more of water,
   but still the sweet scent hovered like a fume
   over the winebowl. No man turned away
   when cups of this came round.

                              A wineskin full
45 I brought along, and victuals in a bag,
   for in my bones I knew some towering brute
   would be upon us soon—all outward power,
   a wild man, ignorant of civility.

   We climbed, then, briskly to the cave. But Cyclops
50 had gone afield, to pasture his fat sheep,
   so we looked round at everything inside:
   a drying rack that sagged with cheeses, pens
   crowded with lambs and kids, each in its class:
   firstlings apart from middlings, and the 'dewdrops,'
55 or newborn lambkins, penned apart from both.
   And vessels full of whey were brimming there—
   bowls of earthenware and pails for milking.
   My men came pressing round me, pleading:

                                         'Why not
   take these cheeses, get them stowed, come back,
60 throw open all the pens, and make a run for it?
   We'll drive the kids and lambs aboard. We say
   put out again on good salt water!'

                                      Ah,
   how sound that was! Yet I refused. I wished
   to see the caveman, what he had to offer—
65 no pretty sight, it turned out, for my friends.
   We lit a fire, burnt an offering,
   and took some cheese to eat; then sat in silence
   around the embers, waiting. When he came
   he had a load of dry boughs on his shoulder
70 to stoke his fire at suppertime. He dumped it
   with a great crash into that hollow cave,
   and we all scattered fast to the far wall.
   Then over the broad cavern floor he ushered
   the ewes he meant to milk. He left his rams
75 and he-goats in the yard outside, and swung
   high overhead a slab of solid rock
   to close the cave. Two dozen four-wheeled wagons,
   with heaving wagon teams, could not have stirred

45 victuals (vit′ls), *n.*
supplies of food.

■ What might be **foreshadowed** in lines 62–65?

the tonnage of that rock from where he wedged it
80 over the doorsill. Next he took his seat
and milked his bleating ewes. A practiced job
he made of it, giving each ewe her suckling;
thickened his milk, then, into curds and whey,
sieved out the curds to drip in withy baskets,
85 and poured the whey to stand in bowls
cooling until he drank it for his supper.
When all these chores were done, he poked the fire,
heaping on brushwood. In the glare he saw us.

'Strangers,' he said, 'who are you? And where from?
90 What brings you here by sea ways—a fair traffic?
Or are you wandering rogues, who cast your lives
like dice, and ravage other folk by sea?'

We felt a pressure on our hearts, in dread
of that deep rumble and that mighty man.
95 But all the same I spoke up in reply:

'We are from Troy, Achaeans, blown off course
by shifting gales on the Great South Sea;
homeward bound, but taking routes and ways
uncommon; so the will of Zeus would have it.
100 We served under Agamemnon, son of Atreus—
the whole world knows what city
he laid waste, what armies he destroyed.
It was our luck to come here; here we stand,
beholden for your help, or any gifts
105 you give—as custom is to honor strangers.
We would entreat you, great Sir, have a care
for the gods' courtesy; Zeus will avenge
the unoffending guest.'

He answered this
from his brute chest, unmoved:

'You are a ninny,
110 or else you come from the other end of nowhere,
telling me, mind the gods! We Cyclopes
care not a whistle for your thundering Zeus
or all the gods in bliss; we have more force by far.
I would not let you go for fear of Zeus—
115 you or your friends—unless I had a whim to.
Tell me, where was it, now, you left your ship—

84 **withy baskets,** baskets made of twigs.

91 rogue (rōg), *n.* dishonest or unprincipled person; scoundrel; rascal.

100 **Agamemnon** (ag′ə-mem′non), king of Argos in southern Greece, who led the Achaeans to war against Troy.

around the point, or down the shore, I wonder?'

He thought he'd find out, but I saw through this,
and answered with a ready lie:

'My ship?

120 Poseidon Lord, who sets the earth a-tremble,
broke it up on the rocks at your land's end.
A wind from seaward served him, drove us there.
We are survivors, these good men and I.'

Neither reply nor pity came from him,
125 but in one stride he clutched at my companions
and caught two in his hands like squirming puppies
to beat their brains out, spattering the floor.
Then he dismembered them and made his meal,
gaping and crunching like a mountain lion—
130 everything: innards, flesh, and marrow bones.
We cried aloud, lifting our hands to Zeus,
powerless, looking on at this, appalled;
but Cyclops went on filling up his belly
with manflesh and great gulps of whey,
135 then lay down like a mast among his sheep.
My heart beat high now at the chance of action,
and drawing the sharp sword from my hip I went
along his flank to stab him where the midriff
holds the liver. I had touched the spot
140 when sudden fear stayed me: if I killed him
we perished there as well, for we could never
move his ponderous doorway slab aside.
So we were left to groan and wait for morning.

When the young Dawn with finger tips of rose
145 lit up the world, the Cyclops built a fire
and milked his handsome ewes, all in due order,
putting the sucklings to the mothers. Then,
his chores being all dispatched, he caught
another brace of men to make his breakfast,
150 and whisked away his great door slab
to let his sheep go through—but he behind,
reset the stone as one would cap a quiver.
There was a din of whistling as the Cyclops
rounded his flock to higher ground, then stillness.
155 And now I pondered how to hurt him worst,
if but Athena granted what I prayed for.

■ Why does Odysseus tell
the Cyclops that he and his
men are the only survivors of
a shipwreck?

142 ponderous (pon′dər əs),
adj. very heavy.

■ Why doesn't Odysseus kill
the Cyclops in his sleep?

149 brace (brās), *n.* a pair;
couple.
152 cap a quiver (kwiv′ər),
put a cap on the point of an
arrow or on the case that
holds arrows.
153 din (din), *n.* a continuing loud, confused noise.

Here are the means I thought would serve my turn:

a club, or staff, lay there along the fold—
an olive tree, felled green and left to season
160 for Cyclops' hand. And it was like a mast
a lugger of twenty oars, broad in the beam—
a deep-sea-going craft—might carry:
so long, so big around, it seemed. Now I
chopped out a six foot section of this pole
165 and set it down before my men, who scraped it;
and when they had it smooth, I hewed again
to make a stake with pointed end. I held this
in the fire's heart and turned it, toughening it,
then hid it, well back in the cavern, under
170 one of the dung piles in profusion there.
Now came the time to toss for it: who ventured
along with me? whose hand could bear to thrust
and grind that spike in Cyclops' eye, when mild
sleep had mastered him? As luck would have it,
175 the men I would have chosen won the toss—
four strong men, and I made five as captain.

At evening came the shepherd with his flock,
his woolly flock. The rams as well, this time,
entered the cave: by some sheep-herding whim—
180 or a god's bidding—none were left outside.
He hefted his great boulder into place
and sat him down to milk the bleating ewes
in proper order, put the lambs to suck,
and swiftly ran through all his evening chores.
185 Then he caught two more men and feasted on them.
My moment was at hand, and I went forward
holding an ivy bowl of my dark drink,
looking up, saying:

                              'Cyclops, try some wine.
Here's liquor to wash down your scraps of men.
190 Taste it, and see the kind of drink we carried
under our planks. I meant it for an offering
if you would help us home. But you are mad,
unbearable, a bloody monster! After this,
will any other traveller come to see you?'

195 He seized and drained the bowl, and it went down
so fiery and smooth he called for more:

161 lugger (lug′ər), large sea-going boat with a four-sided sail.

166 hew (hyü), *v.* cut with an ax, sword, etc.; chop.

'Give me another, thank you kindly. Tell me,
how are you called? I'll make a gift will please you.
Even Cyclopes know the wine-grapes grow
200 out of grassland and loam in heaven's rain,
but here's a bit of nectar and ambrosia!'

Three bowls I brought him, and he poured them down.
I saw the fuddle and flush come over him,
then I sang out in cordial tones:

                                              'Cyclops,
205 you ask my honorable name? Remember
the gift you promised me, and I shall tell you.
My name is Nohbdy: mother, father, and friends,
everyone calls me Nohbdy.'

                                    And he said:
'Nohbdy's my meat, then, after I eat his friends.
210 Others come first. There's a noble gift, now.'

Even as he spoke, he reeled and tumbled backward,
his great head lolling to one side; and sleep
took him like any creature. Drunk, hiccuping,
he dribbled streams of liquor and bits of men.

215 Now, by the gods, I drove my big hand spike
deep in the embers, charring it again,
and cheered my men along with battle talk
to keep their courage up: no quitting now.
The pike of olive, green though it had been,
220 reddened and glowed as if about to catch.
I drew it from the coals and my four fellows
gave me a hand, lugging it near the Cyclops
as more than natural force nerved them; straight
forward they sprinted, lifted it, and rammed it
225 deep in his crater eye, and I leaned on it
turning it as a shipwright turns a drill
in planking, having men below to swing
the two-handled strap that spins it in the groove.
So with our brand we bored that great eye socket
230 while blood ran out around the red hot bar.
Eyelid and lash were seared; the pierced ball
hissed broiling, and the roots popped.

200 loam (lōm), *n.* rich, fertile earth.
201 nectar (nek′tər) **and ambrosia** (am brō′zhə), *n.* the drink and food of the gods.
203 fuddle and flush, confusion and flushed complexion caused by drunkenness.

■ **Predict** why Odysseus tells the Cyclops his name is Nohbdy.

226 shipwright (ship′rīt′), *n.* carpenter skilled in ship repair and construction.

▲ *The Blinding of Polyphemus* was painted by the Italian artist Pellegrino Tibaldi (1527–1596). Do you think his version of this scene emphasizes the monstrousness of the Cyclops? Why or why not?

                                                   In a smithy
one sees a white-hot axehead or an adze
plunged and wrung in a cold tub, screeching steam—
235 the way they make soft iron hale and hard—:
just so that eyeball hissed around the spike.
The Cyclops bellowed and the rock roared round him,
and we fell back in fear. Clawing his face
he tugged the bloody spike out of his eye,
240 threw it away, and his wild hands went groping;
then he set up a howl for Cyclopes
who lived in caves on windy peaks nearby.
Some heard him; and they came by divers ways
to clump around outside and call:

                                         'What ails you,
245 Polyphemus? Why do you cry so sore

232 smithy (smith′ē), *n.* the workshop of a smith.
233 adze (adz), *n.* axelike cutting tool used chiefly for shaping wood.
235 hale (hāl), *adj.* free from defect.

243 divers (dī′vərz), *adj.* several different.

The Odyssey—The Cyclops   **745**

in the starry night? You will not let us sleep.
Sure no man's driving off your flock? No man
has tricked you, ruined you?'

                                        Out of the cave
the mammoth Polyphemus roared in answer:

250 'Nohbdy, Nohbdy's tricked me, Nohbdy's ruined me!'

To this rough shout they made a <u>sage</u> reply:

'Ah well, if nobody has played you foul
there in your lonely bed, we are no use in pain
given by great Zeus. Let it be your father,
Poseidon Lord, to whom you pray.'

255   So saying
they trailed away. And I was filled with laughter
to see how like a charm the name deceived them.
Now Cyclops, wheezing as the pain came on him,
fumbled to wrench away the great doorstone
260 and squatted in the breach with arms thrown wide
for any silly beast or man who bolted—
hoping somehow I might be such a fool.
But I kept thinking how to win the game:
death sat there huge; how could we slip away?
265 I drew on all my wits; and ran through tactics,
reasoning as a man will for dear life,
until a trick came—and it pleased me well.
The Cyclops' rams were handsome, fat, with heavy
fleeces, a dark violet.

                                        Three abreast
270 I tied them silently together, twining
cords of willow from the ogre's bed;
then slung a man under each middle one
to ride there safely, shielded left and right
So three sheep could convey each man. I took
275 the woolliest ram, the choicest of the flock,
and hung myself under his kinky belly,
pulled up tight, with fingers twisted deep
in sheepskin ringlets for an iron grip.
So, breathing hard, we waited until morning.

251 sage (sāj), *adj.* wise.

260 breach (brēch), *n.* a gap in a wall.

Greek pottery was frequently decorated with pictures of gods and heroes, like this image of Odysseus escaping from the cave of the Cyclops. Compare this with the different ways—such as movie posters or trading cards—in which heroes are depicted in American popular culture today. ➤

280　When Dawn spread out her finger tips of rose
　　　the rams began to stir, moving for pasture,
　　　and peals of bleating echoed round the pens
　　　where dams with udders full called for a milking.
　　　Blinded, and sick with pain from his head wound,
285　the master stroked each ram, then let it pass,
　　　but my men riding on the pectoral fleece
　　　the giant's blind hands blundering never found.
　　　Last of them all my ram, the leader, came,
　　　weighted by wool and me with my meditations.
290　The Cyclops patted him, and then he said:

　　　'Sweet cousin ram, why lag behind the rest
　　　in the night cave? You never linger so,
　　　but graze before them all, and go afar
　　　to crop sweet grass, and take your stately way
295　leading along the streams, until at evening
　　　you run to be the first one in the fold.
　　　Why, now, so far behind? Can you be grieving
　　　over your Master's eye? That carrion rogue
　　　and his accurst companions burnt it out
300　when he had conquered all my wits with wine.
　　　Nohbdy will not get out alive, I swear.
　　　Oh, had you brain and voice to tell
　　　where he may be now, dodging all my fury!
　　　Bashed by this hand and bashed on this rock wall

286 pectoral (pek′tər əl), *adj.* of, in, or on the breast or chest.

298 carrion (kar′e ən), *adj.* rotten; filthy.

305 his brains would strew the floor, and I should have
rest from the outrage Nohbdy worked upon me.'

He sent us into the open, then. Close by,
I dropped and rolled clear of the ram's belly,
going this way and that to untie the men.
310 With many glances back, we rounded up
his fat, stiff-legged sheep to take aboard,
and drove them down to where the good ship lay.
We saw, as we came near, our fellows' faces
shining; then we saw them turn to grief
315 tallying those who had not fled from death.
I hushed them, jerking head and eyebrows up,
and in a low voice told them: 'Load this herd;
move fast, and put the ship's head toward the breakers.'
They all pitched in at loading, then embarked
320 and struck their oars into the sea. Far out,
as far off shore as shouted words would carry,
I sent a few back to the adversary:

'O Cyclops! Would you feast on my companions?
Puny, am I, in a Caveman's hands?
325 How do you like the beating that we gave you,
you damned cannibal? Eater of guests
under your roof! Zeus and the gods have paid you!'

The blind thing in his doubled fury broke
a hilltop in his hands and heaved it after us.
330 Ahead of our black prow it struck and sank
whelmed in a spuming geyser, a giant wave
that washed the ship stern foremost back to shore.
I got the longest boathook out and stood
fending us off, with furious nods to all
335 to put their backs into a racing stroke—
row, row, or perish. So the long oars bent
kicking the foam sternward, making head
until we drew away, and twice as far.
Now when I cupped my hands I heard the crew
in low voices protesting:

340   'Godsake, Captain!
Why bait the beast again? Let him alone!'

'That tidal wave he made on the first throw
all but beached us.'

■ How does Odysseus get
himself and his men safely
out of the cave?

330 **prow** (prou), *n.* the front
of a ship or boat.
331 **whelm** (hwelm), *v.* turn
over; become submerged.
332 **stern** (stern), *n.* the back
of a ship or boat.
333 **boathook** (bōt hu̇k), *n.* a
pole with a hook used to pull
or push a boat into place.

'All but stove us in!'

'Give him our bearing with your trumpeting,
he'll get the range and lob a boulder.'

'Aye

345 He'll smash our timbers and our heads together!'

I would not heed them in my glorying spirit,
but let my anger flare and yelled:

'Cyclops,

if ever mortal man inquire
350 how you were put to shame and blinded, tell him
Odysseus, raider of cities, took your eye:
Laertes' son, whose home's on Ithaca!'

At this he gave a mighty sob and rumbled:

'Now comes the weird upon me, spoken of old,
355 A wizard, grand and wondrous, lived here—Telemus,
a son of Eurymus; great length of days
he had in wizardry among the Cyclopes,
and these things he foretold for time to come:
my great eye lost, and at Odysseus' hands.
360 Always I had in mind some giant, armed
in giant force, would come against me here.
But this, but you—small, pitiful and twiggy—
you put me down with wine, you blinded me.
Come back, Odysseus, and I'll treat you well,
365 praying the god of earthquake to befriend you—
his son I am, for he by his avowal
fathered me, and, if he will, he may
heal me of this black wound—he and no other
of all the happy gods or mortal men.'

370 Few words I shouted in reply to him:
'If I could take your life I would and take
your time away, and hurl you down to hell!
The god of earthquake could not heal you there!'

At this he stretched his hands out in his darkness
375 toward the sky of stars, and prayed Poseidon:

'O hear me, lord, blue girdler of the islands,

344 Give him our bearing, reveal our location.

354 the weird, the strange fate.

365 god of earthquake, Poseidon.
366 avowal (ə vou′əl), *n.* an open declaration or acknowledgment.

The Odyssey—The Cyclops   **749**

if I am thine indeed, and thou art father:
grant that Odysseus, raider of cities, never
see his home: Laertes' son, I mean,
380 who kept his hall on Ithaca. Should destiny
intend that he shall see his roof again
among his family in his father land,
far be that day, and dark the years between.
Let him lose all companions, and return
385 under strange sail to bitter days at home.'

In these words he prayed, and the god heard him.
Now he laid hands upon a bigger stone
and wheeled around, titanic for the cast,
to let it fly in the black-prowed vessel's track.
390 But it fell short, just aft the steering oar,
and whelming seas rose giant above the stone
to bear us onward toward the island.

                                           There

as we ran in we saw the squadron waiting,
the trim ships drawn up side by side, and all
395 our troubled friends who waited, looking seaward.
We beached her, grinding keel in the soft sand,
and waded in, ourselves, on the sandy beach.
Then we unloaded all the Cyclops' flock
to make division, share and share alike,
400 only my fighters voted that my ram,
the prize of all, should go to me. I slew him
by the sea side and burnt his long thighbones
to Zeus beyond the stormcloud, Cronus' son,
who rules the world. But Zeus disdained my offering;
405 destruction for my ships he had in store
and death for those who sailed them, my companions.
Now all day long until the sun went down
we made our feast on mutton and sweet wine,
till after sunset in the gathering dark
410 we went to sleep above the wash of ripples.

When the young Dawn with finger tips of rose
touched the world, I roused the men, gave orders
to man the ships, cast off the mooring lines;
and filing in to sit beside the rowlocks
415 oarsmen in line dipped oars in the grey sea.
So we moved out, sad in the vast offing,
having our precious lives, but not our friends."

■ Why does Polyphemus
pray to Poseidon?

388 titanic (tī tan′ik), *adj.*
having great size, strength, or
power; gigantic. The Titans
were giants who ruled the
world before being over-
thrown by Zeus, Poseidon,
and Hades.
390 aft (aft), *adj.* behind.

396 keel (kēl), *n.* a long timber or plate extending
lengthways along the center
of the bottom of a ship.

402–403 burnt . . . to Zeus. It
was customary in ancient
Greece to roast choice cuts of
meat and offer them to the
gods as a symbolic display of
respect.

413 mooring (mur′ing)
lines, ropes used to hold
boats and ships to shore.
416 offing (ô′fing), *n.* the
part of the deep sea seen
from the shore; the near or
foreseeable future.

After Reading

Making Connections

1. If you were in Odysseus's situation, would you do what he does in the land of the Cyclopes? Explain.

2. Odysseus uses detailed, vivid language to describe the actions of the Cyclops. Choose your favorite descriptive passage and read it to a partner, explaining why you like it.

3. Has your impression of Odysseus's **character** changed? Explain.

4. Identify three examples of Odysseus's cleverness and three examples of his foolhardy pride in his encounter with the Cyclops.

5. How might Odysseus's encounter with the Cyclops shape his future?

6. 🐾 How do Odysseus's cultural values affect the **choices** he makes?

Vocabulary Study

Write the letter of the word whose meaning has the least in common with the other words in the set. If necessary, refer to the Glossary for help with word meanings.

din
ponderous
rogue
sage
titanic

1. (A) din (B) serenity (C) silence (D) peace
2. (A) weighty (B) light (C) heavy (D) ponderous
3. (A) rogue (B) scoundrel (C) gentleman (D) rascal
4. (A) foolish (B) unthinking (C) sage (D) careless
5. (A) petite (B) gigantic (C) colossal (D) titanic

Expressing Your Ideas

Writing Choice

Point/Counterpoint Odysseus criticizes the Cyclopes for having no laws or society, and he describes Polyphemus as a heartless savage. Yet Odysseus himself in many ways lives the life of an outlaw. Is Odysseus more civilized than Polyphemus? Write an editorial to the *Greek Gazette* in which you address that question. Support your opinion with at least three examples from the story.

Another Option

Foolish Pride? Using Odysseus as an example, hold a **class debate** about the dangers and virtues of pride.

THE GODDESS CIRCE

After escaping the Cyclops, Odysseus and his fleet reach the island of the wind king Aeolus (ē′ə ləs), where they receive shelter and provisions to continue their journey home. As a gift to ensure good sailing, Aeolus gives Odysseus a bull-hide sack holding all the contrary winds. Within sight of Ithaca, Odysseus's men jealously open the sack, believing it will contain gold and silver. The winds blow them all the way back to Aeolus's island. Odysseus again asks Aeolus for help, but the king denies him, saying Odysseus must be cursed by the gods. When Odysseus's fleet reaches land again, they are ambushed by Laestrygonians (les′trə gōn′ē ənz), a race of man-eating giants. All the ships but Odysseus's are destroyed.

Grieving for their comrades, Odysseus and his shipmates sail on to an unfamiliar island, where they spot smoke rising from the forest. Odysseus's shipmate Eurylochus goes with half of the crew to investigate, leaving Odysseus and the others with the ship. They discover the goddess Circe's stone house, where tamed wolves and mountain lions lie at the door. Fearing foul play, Eurylochus hides nearby. He watches helplessly as Circe turns his unsuspecting shipmates into swine by giving them wine mixed with a magic potion.

When Eurylochus returns to the ship and tells what has happened, Odysseus sets out alone to rescue his men. On his way, the messenger god Hermes appears and gives him a magic herb that will counteract Circe's bewitching potion.

> ". . . Then toward Olympus through the island trees
> Hermes departed, and I sought out Circe,
> my heart high with excitement, beating hard.
> Before her mansion in the porch I stood
> 5 to call her, all being still. Quick as a cat
> she opened her bright doors and sighed a welcome;
> then I strode after her with heavy heart
> down the long hall, and took the chair she gave me,
> silver-studded, intricately carved,
> 10 made with a low footrest. The lady Circe
> mixed me a golden cup of honeyed wine,
> adding in mischief her unholy drug.
> I drank, and the drink failed. But she came forward
> aiming a stroke with her long stick, and whispered:
>
> 15 'Down in the sty and snore among the rest!'

◄ *Circe Invidiosa* (Latin, "Envious Circe"), painted by British artist J. W. Waterhouse (1849–1917), shows the sorceress poisoning the sea in order to transform Scylla, her rival for the love of a merman, into a hideous monster. How has the artist used light and color to suggest the power and menace of Circe's magical potion?

Without a word, I drew my sharpened sword
and in one bound held it against her throat.
She cried out, then slid under to take my knees,
catching her breath to say, in her distress:

20 'What champion, of what country, can you be?
Where are your kinsmen and your city?
Are you not sluggish with my wine? Ah, wonder!
Never a mortal man that drank this cup
but when it passed his lips he had succumbed.
25 Hale must your heart be and your tempered will.
Odysseus then you are, O great contender,
of whom the glittering god with golden wand
spoke to me ever, and foretold
the black swift ship would carry you from Troy.
30 Put up your weapon in the sheath. We two
shall mingle and make love upon our bed.
So mutual trust may come of play and love.'

To this I said:

                                    'Circe, am I a boy,
that you should make me soft and doting now?
35 Here in this house you turned my men to swine;
now it is I myself you hold, enticing
into your chamber, to your dangerous bed,
to take my manhood when you have me stripped.
I mount no bed of love with you upon it.
40 Or swear me first a great oath, if I do,
you'll work no more enchantment to my harm.'
She swore at once, outright, as I demanded,
and after she had sworn, and bound herself,
I entered Circe's flawless bed of love.

45 Presently in the hall her maids were busy,
the nymphs who waited upon Circe: four,
whose cradles were in fountains, under boughs,
or in the glassy seaward-gliding streams.
One came with richly colored rugs to throw
50 on seat and chairback, over linen covers;
a second pulled the tables out, all silver,
and loaded them with baskets all of gold;
a third mixed wine as tawny-mild as honey
in a bright bowl, and set out golden cups.
55 The fourth came bearing water, and lit a blaze

24 succumb (sə kum′), *v.*
give way; yield.

■ How does Circe discover
Odysseus's identity?

36 entice (en tīs′), *v.* attract
artfully; tempt; lure.

46 nymph (nimf), *n.* divine
maiden.

53 tawny (tô′nē), *adj.*
brownish-yellow.

under a cauldron. By and by it bubbled,
and when the dazzling brazen vessel seethed
she filled a bathtub to my waist, and bathed me,
pouring a soothing blend on head and shoulders,
60 warming the soreness of my joints away.
When she had done, and smoothed me with sweet oil,
she put a tunic and a cloak around me
and took me to a silver-studded chair
with footrest, all elaborately carven.
65 Now came a maid to tip a golden jug
of water into a silver finger bowl,
and draw a polished table to my side.
The larder mistress brought her tray of loaves
with many savory slices, and she gave
70 the best, to tempt me. But no pleasure came;
I huddled with my mind elsewhere, oppressed.

Circe regarded me, as there I sat
disconsolate and never touched a crust.
Then she stood over me and chided me:

75 'Why sit at table mute, Odysseus?
Are you mistrustful of my bread and drink?
Can it be treachery that you fear again,
after the gods' great oath I swore for you?'
I turned to her at once, and said:

                            'Circe,
80 where is the captain who could bear to touch
this banquet, in my place? A decent man
would see his company before him first.
Put heart in me to eat and drink—you may,
by freeing my companions. I must see them.'

85 But Circe had already turned away.
Her long staff in her hand, she left the hall
and opened up the sty. I saw her enter,
driving those men turned swine to stand before me.
She stroked them, each in turn, with some new chrism;
90 and then, behold! their bristles fell away,
the coarse pelt grown upon them by her drug
melted away, and they were men again,
younger, more handsome, taller than before.
Their eyes upon me, each one took my hands,
95 and wild regret and longing pierced them through,

---

68 larder mistress, servant in charge of the larder, or pantry, where meats and other foods are kept.
69 savory (sā′vər ē), *adj.* pleasing in taste or smell; appetizing.
73 disconsolate (dis kon′sə-lit), *adj.* without hope; forlorn; unhappy.
74 chide (chīd), *v.* find fault with; scold.

77 treachery (trech′ər ē), *n.* deceitfulness; betrayal.

■ How does clever Odysseus get Circe to free his men?

89 chrism (kriz′əm), *n.* oil.

91 pelt (pelt), *n.* animal skin.

so the room rang with sobs, and even Circe
pitied that transformation. Exquisite
the goddess looked as she stood near me, saying:

'Son of Laertes and the gods of old,
100 Odysseus, master mariner and soldier,
go to the sea beach and sea-breasting ship;
drag it ashore, full length upon the land;
stow gear and stores in rock-holes under cover;
return; be quick; bring all your dear companions.'

105 Now, being a man, I could not help consenting.
So I went down to the sea beach and the ship,
where I found all my other men on board,
weeping, in despair along the benches.
Sometimes in farmyards when the cows return
110 well fed from pasture to the barn, one sees
the pens give way before the calves in tumult,
breaking through to cluster about their mothers,
bumping together, bawling. Just that way
my crew poured round me when they saw me come—
115 their faces wet with tears as if they saw
their homeland, and the crags of Ithaca,
even the very town where they were born.
And weeping still they all cried out in greeting:

'Prince, what joy this is, your safe return!
120 Now Ithaca seems here, and we in Ithaca!
But tell us now, what death befell our friends?'

And, speaking gently, I replied:

'First we must get the ship high on the shingle,
and stow our gear and stores in clefts of rock
125 for cover. Then come follow me, to see
your shipmates in the magic house of Circe
eating and drinking, endlessly regaled.'

They turned back, as commanded, to this work;
only one lagged, and tried to hold the others:
130 Eurylochus it was, who blurted out:

'Where now, poor remnants? Is it devil's work
you long for? Will you go to Circe's hall?
Swine, wolves, and lions she will make us all,

111 tumult (tū′mult), *n.*
disorderly agitation;
commotion.

123 shingle (shing′gəl), *n.*
gravel or rocky material often
found on the seashore.

127 regaled (ri gāld′), *adj.*
agreeably entertained, especially with feasting.

beasts of her courtyard, bound by her enchantment.
135 Remember those the Cyclops held, remember
shipmates who made that visit with Odysseus!
The daring man! They died for his foolishness!'

When I heard this I had a mind to draw
the blade that swung against my side and chop him,
140 bowling his head upon the ground—kinsman
or no kinsman, close to me though he was.
But others came between, saying, to stop me,

'Prince, we can leave him, if you say the word;
let him stay here on guard. As for ourselves,
145 show us the way to Circe's magic hall.'

So all turned inland, leaving shore and ship,
and Eurylochus—he, too, came on behind,
fearing the rough edge of my tongue. Meanwhile
at Circe's hands the rest were gently bathed,
150 anointed with sweet oil, and dressed afresh
in tunics and new cloaks with fleecy linings.
We found them all at supper when we came.
But greeting their old friends once more, the crew
could not hold back their tears; and now again
155 the rooms rang with sobs. Then Circe, loveliest
of all immortals, came to counsel me:

'Son of Laertes and the gods of old,
Odysseus, master mariner and soldier,
enough of weeping fits. I know—I, too—
160 what you endured upon the inhuman sea,
what odds you met on land from hostile men.
Remain with me, and share my meat and wine;
restore behind your ribs those gallant hearts
that served you in the old days, when you sailed
165 from stony Ithaca. Now parched and spent,
your cruel wandering is all you think of,
never of joy, after so many blows.'

As we were men we could not help consenting.
So day by day we lingered, feasting long
170 on roasts and wine, until a year grew fat.
But when the passing months and wheeling seasons
brought the long summery days, the pause of summer,
my shipmates one day summoned me and said:

■ Why doesn't Eurylochus
want to enter Circe's hall?

165 parched (pärchd), *adj.*
hot, dry, or thirsty.

■ Why does Odysseus decide
to stay with Circe?

'Captain shake off this trance, and think of home—
if home indeed awaits us,

175   if we shall ever see
your own well-timbered hall on Ithaca.'

They made me feel a pang, and I agreed.
That day, and all day long, from dawn to sundown,
we feasted on roast meat and ruddy wine,
180   and after sunset when the dusk came on
my men slept in the shadowy hall, but I
went through the dark to Circe's flawless bed
and took the goddess' knees in supplication,
urging, as she bent to hear:

                                               'O Circe,

185   now you must keep your promise; it is time.
Help me make sail for home. Day after day
my longing quickens, and my company
give me no peace, but wear my heart away
pleading when you are not at hand to hear.'

190   The loveliest of goddesses replied:

'Son of Laertes and the gods of old,
Odysseus, master mariner and soldier,
you shall not stay here longer against your will;
but home you may not go
195   unless you take a strange way round and come
to the cold homes of Death and pale Persephone.
You shall hear prophecy from the rapt shade
of blind Tiresias of Thebes, forever
charged with reason even among the dead;
200   to him alone, of all the flitting ghosts,
Persephone has given a mind undarkened.'

At this I felt a weight like stone within me,
and, moaning, pressed my length against the bed,
with no desire to see the daylight more.
205   But when I had wept and tossed and had my fill
of this despair, at last I answered her:

'Circe, who pilots me upon this journey?
No man has ever sailed to the land of Death.' "

*Circe gives Odysseus instructions on how to reach the land of the dead
and what to do once he arrives there. The next morning, Odysseus and his
crew depart.*

183 supplication (sup′lə-kā′shən), *n.* a humble prayer addressed to a god.

196 Persephone (pər sef′ə-nē), the wife of Hades, god of the underworld. See the information on Demeter, her mother, on page 803.
197 shade (shād), *n.* a ghost.
198 Tiresias (tī rē′sē əs), a blind prophet whose ghost resided in the underworld.

After Reading

Making Connections

1. Is Circe a manipulative witch, a kind friend, or something else? Explain.

2. Do you find it out of character for Odysseus to cry when he hears he must visit the land of the dead? Why or why not?

3. Is the role of the god Hermes in this passage different from or similar to the role of the gods in previous passages? Explain.

4. Why do you think Circe changes her attitude toward Odysseus when he resists the spell of her potion?

5. Why do you think Odysseus wants to kill Eurylochus when Eurylochus reminds the others of Odysseus's actions in the land of the Cyclops?

6. 👣 Odysseus explains his decision to remain with Circe by saying, "Being a man, I could not help consenting." What is he saying about the **choice** he has made?

Vocabulary Study

chide
disconsolate
parched
savory
succumb

Make a **crossword puzzle** using the listed vocabulary words. Use a newspaper crossword puzzle as a model if you aren't sure how to make one. Have a friend or family member work on the puzzle. Check their answers when they are finished. For help in writing clues, refer to the Glossary.

Expressing Your Ideas

Writing Choice

Free Will or Fate? Which of the following statements do you think accurately describes Odysseus's journey up to this point? (A) Odysseus is master of his own destiny. (B) Odysseus's journey home is affected by uncontrollable forces. Write a brief **essay** to support your opinion, using examples from the *Odyssey*.

Another Option

In Her Own Words Write a **monologue,** or long speech, from Circe's point of view, telling about her encounter with Odysseus and his men. If you wish, share your piece with the class.

2 THE SIRENS

Following Circe's advice, Odysseus and his men sail to the land of the dead at the edge of the world. When Odysseus offers sacrificial blood, the blind prophet Tiresias arrives, drinks some of the blood, and tells Odysseus about his future.

Tiresias warns Odysseus that only discipline and denial will protect him from Poseidon's revenge for the blinding of his son, Polyphemus. When Odysseus and his crew reach the land of Helios, the sun god, they must not raid his cattle. If they do, many more years will pass before Odysseus, alone and unknown, reaches Ithaca. There he will face many difficulties before re-establishing himself as master of his palace. Once Odysseus has done this, Tiresias continues, he must offer a sacrifice to Poseidon, thus regaining the god's favor. Then Odysseus will enjoy a long and peaceful life.

After Tiresias departs, Odysseus remains to speak with the ghost of his mother, friends, and famous people from the past. Unable to bear the company of the dead any longer, Odysseus flees to his ship and sails with his crew back to Circe's home.

"Soon, then,
knowing us back from the Dark Land, Circe came
freshly adorned for us, with handmaids bearing
loaves, roast meats, and ruby-colored wine.
5 She stood among us in immortal beauty
jesting:

     'Hearts of oak, did you go down
alive into the homes of Death? One visit
finishes all men but yourselves, twice mortal!
Come, here is meat and wine, enjoy your feasting
10 for one whole day; and in the dawn tomorrow
you shall put out to sea. Sailing directions,
landmarks, perils, I shall sketch for you, to keep you
from being caught by land or water
in some black sack of trouble.'

     In high humor
15 and ready for carousal, we agreed;
so all that day until the sun went down
we feasted on roast meat and good red wine,
till after sunset, at the fall of night,
the men dropped off to sleep by the stern hawsers.

15 **carousal** (kə rou′zəl), *n.* a noisy revel or drinking party.

19 **hawser** (hô′zər), *n.* large stout rope, used for mooring or towing ships.

20 She took my hand then, silent in that hush,
drew me apart, made me sit down, and lay
beside me, softly questioning, as I told
all I had seen, from first to last.

                      Then said the Lady Circe:
'So: all those trials are over.

                            Listen with care

25 to this, now, and a god will arm your mind.
Square in your ship's path are Sirens, crying
beauty to bewitch men coasting by;
woe to the innocent who hears that sound!
He will not see his lady nor his children

30 in joy, crowding about him, home from sea;
the Sirens will sing his mind away
on their sweet meadow lolling. There are bones
of dead men rotting in a pile beside them
and flayed skins shrivel around the spot.

                            Steer wide;

35 keep well to seaward; plug your oarsmen's ears
with beeswax kneaded soft; none of the rest
should hear that song.

                    But if you wish to listen,
let the men tie you in the lugger, hand
and foot, back to the mast, lashed to the mast,

40 so you may hear those harpies' thrilling voices;
shout as you will, begging to be untied,
your crew must only twist more line around you
and keep their stroke up, till the singers fade.
What then? One of two courses you may take,

45 and you yourself must weigh them. I shall not
plan the whole action for you now, but only
tell you of both.

                Ahead are beetling rocks
and dark blue glancing Amphitrite, surging,
roars around them. Prowling Rocks, or Drifters,

50 the gods in bliss have named them—named them well.
Not even birds can pass them by, not even
the timorous doves that bear ambrosia
to Father Zeus; caught by downdrafts, they die
on rockwall smooth as ice.

                    Each time, the Father

55 wafts a new courier to make up his crew.

Still less can ships get searoom of these Drifters,
whose boiling surf, under high fiery winds,

34 flayed (flād), *adj.* having the skin or outer covering stripped off; skinned.

■ What happens to men who listen to the singing of the Sirens?

40 harpy (här′pē), *n.* a mythical creature that is part woman and part bird; a cruel, greedy person.

47 beetling (bē′tl ing), *adj.* projecting; jutting.
48 Amphitrite (am′fə trī′tē), goddess of the sea, wife of Poseidon.

52 timorous (tim′ər əs), *adj.* easily frightened; timid.

55 waft (waft), *v.* cause to move lightly by the impulse of wind or waves.
55 courier (kėr′ē ər), *n.* messenger.

carries tossing wreckage of ships and men.
Only one ocean-going craft, the far-famed
60 Argo, made it, sailing from Aieta;
but she, too, would have crashed on the big rocks
if Hera had not pulled her through, for love
of Jason, her captain.

                                    A second course

lies between headlands. One is a sharp mountain
65 piercing the sky, with stormcloud round the peak
dissolving never, not in the brightest summer,
to show heaven's azure there, nor in the fall.
No mortal man could scale it, nor so much
as land there, not with twenty hands and feet,
70 so sheer the cliffs are—as of polished stone.
Midway that height, a cavern full of mist
opens toward Erebus and evening. Skirting
this in the lugger, great Odysseus,
your master bowman, shooting from the deck,
75 would come short of the cavemouth with his shaft;
but that is the den of Scylla, where she yaps
abominably, a newborn whelp's cry,
though she is huge and monstrous. God or man,
no one could look on her in joy. Her legs—
80 and there are twelve—are like great tentacles,
unjointed, and upon her serpent necks
are borne six heads like nightmares of ferocity,
with triple serried rows of fangs and deep
gullets of black death. Half her length, she sways
85 her heads in air, outside her horrid cleft,
hunting the sea around that promontory
for dolphins, dogfish, or what bigger game
thundering Amphitrite feeds in thousands.
And no ship's company can claim
90 to have passed her without loss and grief; she takes,
from every ship, one man for every gullet.

The opposite point seems more a tongue of land
you'd touch with a good bowshot, at the narrows.
A great wild fig, a shaggy mass of leaves,
95 grows on it, and Charybdis lurks below
to swallow down the dark sea tide. Three times
from dawn to dusk she spews it up
and sucks it down again three times, a whirling
maelstrom; if you come upon her then
100 the god who makes earth tremble could not save you.

60–63 Argo . . . captain. The Greek hero Jason sailed on the Argo in search of the Golden Fleece. With the goddess Hera's help, the ship passed safely through the treacherous rocky place called the Drifters.

67 azure (azh′ər), *adj.* sky blue.

72 Erebus (er′ə bəs), a place of darkness in the underworld on the way to Hades.

77 abominably (ə bom′ə nə-blē), *adv.* in a way that arouses disgust and hatred; detestably; horribly.
77 whelp (hwelp), *n.* young dog, wolf, bear, lion, tiger, etc.

83 serried (ser′ēd), *adj.* crowded closely together.
84 gullet (gul′it), *n.* throat.
85 cleft (kleft), *n.* space or opening made by splitting; crack; fissure.
86 promontory (prom′ən-tôr′ē), *n.* a high point of land extending from the coast into the water; cape; headland.

99 maelstrom (māl′strəm), *n.* a great or turbulent whirlpool.

No, hug the cliff of Scylla, take your ship
through on a racing stroke. Better to mourn
six men than lose them all, and the ship, too.'

So her advice ran; but I faced her, saying:

105 'Only instruct me, goddess, if you will,
how, if possible, can I pass Charybdis,
or fight off Scylla when she raids my crew?'

Swiftly that loveliest goddess answered me:

'Must you have battle in your heart forever?
110 The bloody toil of combat? Old contender,
will you not yield to the immortal gods?
That nightmare cannot die, being eternal
evil itself—horror, and pain, and chaos;
there is no fighting her, no power can fight her,
all that <u>avails</u> is flight.

115   Lose headway there
along that rockface while you break out arms,
and she'll swoop over you, I fear, once more,
taking one man again for every gullet.
No, no, put all your backs into it, row on;
120 invoke Blind Force, that bore this <u>scourge</u> of men,
to keep her from a second strike against you.

Then you will coast Thrinacia, the island
where Helios' cattle graze, fine herds, and flocks
of goodly sheep. The herds and flocks are seven,
with fifty beasts in each.

125   No lambs are dropped,
or calves, and these fat cattle never die.
Immortal, too, their cowherds are—their shepherds—
Phaethousa and Lampetia, sweetly braided
nymphs that divine Neaira bore
130 to the overlord of high noon, Helios.
These nymphs their gentle mother bred and placed
upon Thrinacia, the distant land,
in care of flocks and cattle for their father.

Now give those kine a wide berth, keep your thoughts
135 intent upon your course for home,
and hard seafaring brings you all to Ithaca.

How has the artist conveyed the heroism of Odysseus in this
engraving of his ship passing between Scylla and Charybdis?

115 avail (ə vāl′), *v.* help;
benefit.

■ Why does Circe tell
Odysseus to steer toward
Scylla instead of Charybdis?

120 scourge (skėrj), *n.* some
thing or person that causes
great trouble or misfortune;
affliction.

128 Phaethousa (fā′ə thŭz′ə)
and Lampetia (lam pē′shə).
129 Neaira (nē ī′rə).

134 kine (kīn), *n.* cows or
cattle.
134 give . . . a wide berth,
keep well away from.

But if you raid the beeves, I see destruction
for ship and crew.
                              Rough years then lie between
you and your homecoming, alone and old,
140 the one survivor, all companions lost.'

As Circe spoke, Dawn mounted her golden throne,
and on the first rays Circe left me, taking
her way like a great goddess up the island.
I made straight for the ship, roused up the men
145 to get aboard and cast off at the stern.
They scrambled to their places by the rowlocks
and all in line dipped oars in the grey sea.
But soon an off-shore breeze blew to our liking—
a canvas-bellying breeze, a lusty shipmate
150 sent by the singing nymph with sunbright hair.
So we made fast the braces, and we rested,
letting the wind and steersman work the ship.
The crew being now silent before me, I
addressed them, sore at heart:
                                        'Dear friends,
155 more than one man, or two, should know those things
Circe foresaw for us and shared with me,
so let me tell her forecast: then we die
with our eyes open, if we are going to die,
or know what death we baffle if we can. Sirens
160 weaving a haunting song over the sea
we are to shun, she said, and their green shore
all sweet with clover; yet she urged that I
alone should listen to their song. Therefore
you are to tie me up, tight as a splint,
165 erect along the mast, lashed to the mast,
and if I shout and beg to be untied,
take more turns of the rope to muffle me.'

I rather dwelt on this part of the forecast,
while our good ship made time, bound outward down
170 the wind for the strange island of Sirens.
Then all at once the wind fell, and a calm
came over all the sea, as though some power
lulled the swell.
                        The crew were on their feet
briskly, to furl the sail, and stow it; then,
175 each in place, they poised the smooth oar blades
and sent the white foam scudding by. I carved
a massive cake of beeswax into bits

137 beeves (bēvz), *n.* plural of *beef;* i.e., the cattle.

149 canvas-bellying breeze, a breeze that fills a ship's sails.

173 the swell, the waves.

174 furl (fėrl), *v.* roll up; fold up.

▲ Compare and contrast this painting of Odysseus and the Sirens, by Edmund Dulac
(1882–1953), with the painting by J. W. Waterhouse on pages 728–729.

and rolled them in my hands until they softened—
no long task, for a burning heat came down
180 from Helios, lord of high noon. Going forward
I carried wax along the line, and laid it
thick on their ears. They tied me up, then, plumb
amidships, back to the mast, lashed to the mast,
and took themselves again to rowing. Soon,
185 as we came smartly within hailing distance,
the two Sirens, noting our fast ship
off their point, made ready, and they sang:

182–183 plumb amidships,
upright in the middle of
the ship.

The Odyssey—The Sirens | **765**

This way, oh turn your bows,
        Achaea's glory,
190 *As all the world allows—*
        Moor and be merry.

Sweet coupled airs we sing.
        No lonely seafarer
Holds clear of entering
195   *Our green mirror.*

Pleased by each purling note
        Like honey twining
From her throat and my throat,
        Who lies a-pining?

200 *Sea rovers here take joy*
        Voyaging onward,
As from our song of Troy
Greybeard and rower-boy
        Goeth more learnèd.

205 *All feats on that great field*
        In the long warfare,
Dark days the bright gods willed,
        Wounds you bore there,

Argos' old soldiery
210   *On Troy beach teeming,*
Charmed out of time we see.
No life on earth can be
        Hid from our dreaming.

The lovely voices in <u>ardor</u> appealing over the water
215 made me crave to listen, and I tried to say
'Untie me!' to the crew, jerking my brows;
but they bent steady to the oars. Then Perimedes
got to his feet, he and Eurylochus,
and passed more line about, to hold me still.
220 So all rowed on, until the Sirens
dropped under the sea rim, and their singing
dwindled away.
                    My faithful company
rested on their oars now, peeling off
the wax that I had laid thick on their ears;
225 then set me free."

196 purling (pèrl ing) *adj.*
rippling.

209 Argos, city in southern
Greece.

214 ardor (är′ dər), *n.*
passion; great enthusiasm;
eagerness.

217 Perimedes (per′ə mē′-
dēz).

★ How do the Sirens attempt
to lure Odysseus's ship to
their shore?

⊡ SCYLLA AND CHARYBDIS

"But scarcely had that island
faded in blue air than I saw smoke
and white water, with sound of waves in tumult—
a sound the men heard, and it terrified them.
5 Oars flew from their hands; the blades went knocking
wild alongside till the ship lost way,
with no oarblades to drive her through the water.

Well, I walked up and down from bow to stern
trying to put heart into them, standing over
every oarsman, saying gently,

10   'Friends,
have we never been in danger before this?
More fearsome, is it now, than when the Cyclops
penned us in his cave? What power he had!
Did I not keep my nerve, and use my wits
to find a way out for us?

15   Now I say
by hook or crook this peril too shall be
something that we remember.

                              Heads up, lads!
We must obey the orders as I give them.
Get the oarshafts in your hands, and lay back
20 hard on your benches; hit these breaking seas.
Zeus help us pull away before we founder.
You at the tiller, listen, and take in
all that I say—the rudders are your duty;
keep her out of the combers and the smoke;
25 steer for that headland; watch the drift, or we
fetch up in the smother, and you drown us.'

That was all, and it brought them round to action.
But as I sent them on toward Scylla, I
told them nothing, as they could do nothing.
30 They would have dropped their oars again, in panic,
to roll for cover under the decking. Circe's
bidding against arms had slipped my mind,
so I tied on my cuirass and took up
two heavy spears, then made my way along
35 to the foredeck—thinking to see her first from there,

---

22 tiller (til′ər), *n.* a lever used to control the rudder of a boat.
23 rudder (rud′ər), *n.* a flat piece of wood attached by a hinge to a ship's stern, used to steer.
24 comber (kō′mər), *n.* long, curling ocean wave.
26 fetch up, end up.
26 smother (smuth′ər), *n.* thick stifling smoke; a dense cloud of fog, foam, spray, snow, or dust.

33 cuirass (kwi ras′), *n.* a piece of armor covering the body from neck to waist.

the monster of the grey rock, harboring
torment for my friends. I strained my eyes
upon that cliffside veiled in cloud, but nowhere
could I catch sight of her.

                                    And all this time,
40 in travail, sobbing, gaining on the current,
we rowed into the strait—Scylla to port
and on our starboard beam Charybdis, dire
gorge of the salt sea tide. By heaven! when she
vomited, all the sea was like a cauldron
45 seething over intense fire, when the mixture
suddenly heaves and rises.

                                    The shot spume
soared to the landside heights, and fell like rain.

But when she swallowed the sea water down
we saw the funnel of the maelstrom, heard
50 the rock bellowing all around, and dark
sand raged on the bottom far below.
My men all blanched against the gloom, our eyes
were fixed upon that yawning mouth in fear
of being devoured.

                                    Then Scylla made her strike,
55 whisking six of my best men from the ship.
I happened to glance aft at ship and oarsmen
and caught sight of their arms and legs, dangling
high overhead. Voices came down to me
in anguish, calling my name for the last time.

60 A man surfcasting on a point of rock
for bass or mackerel, whipping his long rod
to drop the sinker and the bait far out,
will hook a fish and rip it from the surface
to dangle wriggling through the air:

                                    so these
65 were borne aloft in spasms toward the cliff.

She ate them as they shrieked there, in her den,
in the dire grapple, reaching still for me—
and deathly pity ran me through
at that sight—far the worst I ever suffered,
questing the passes of the strange sea.
70   We rowed on.
The Rocks were now behind; Charybdis, too,
and Scylla dropped astern. . . ."

36 harbor (här′bər), *v.* hold a thought, feeling, or intention; contain.

40 travail (trə vāl′), *n.* a physical, mental, or emotional exertion; great effort; toil.
42 dire (dīr), *adj.* inspiring horror; dismal, oppressive.
49 funnel (fun′l), *n.* a cone-like opening.
52 blanch (blanch), *v.* become pale with fear.

▲ This vase decorated with the half-woman, half-snake Scylla was done in the third century B.C. How does this image of Scylla contrast with that in the engraving on page 763?

67 grapple (grap′əl), *n.* an instrument with iron claws used to fasten onto an enemy ship; a struggle.

■ What do you think the men would have done if Odysseus had told them about Scylla?

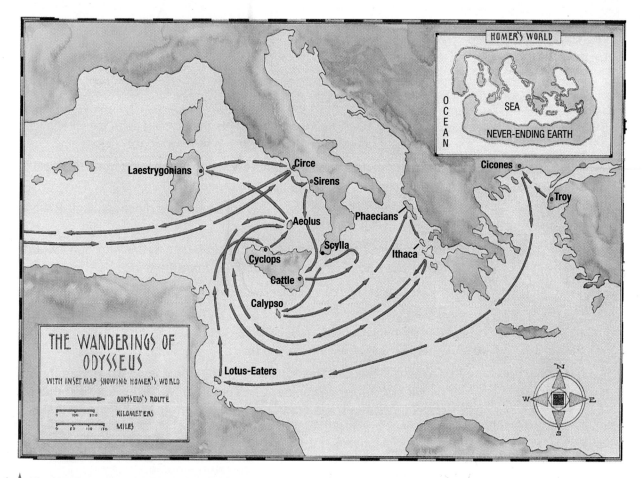

The map shows one accepted version of the route Odysseus followed on his voyage home to Ithaca. Compare the geography shown here to that of a modern map of the region.

Odysseus's ship approaches the land of the sun god's prized cattle. Odysseus agrees to go ashore, but makes his crew promise not to touch the sacred cattle. Onshore winds prevent the crew from sailing for a month, and they are forced to eat all their food supplies. One day while Odysseus is sleeping, Eurylochus persuades the hungry men to slaughter the cattle, saying it is better to risk angering the gods than to starve to death. When Helios, the sun god, learns of the crime, he demands that Zeus punish Odysseus and his men.

A few days later, the weather improves and Odysseus and his crew set out to sea. Zeus sends a deadly storm that destroys the ship and kills all the men except Odysseus. Fighting the storm, Odysseus lashes together a raft from the wreckage of his ship. He floats back toward Charybdis, where he is tossed by a wave into an overhanging fig tree. He waits for hours in the tree until his raft is spit back up again by Charybdis. With help from the gods, he then floats unnoticed past dangerous Scylla and drifts to the island of the nymph Calypso.

With this, Odysseus concludes the long story of his adventures that he has been relating to his hosts, the Phaeacians, at their banquet.

After Reading

Making Connections

1. Did you expect that Odysseus and his men would pass the Sirens without succumbing to their power? Why or why not?

2. Do you think Odysseus was right not to warn his men about Scylla? Why or why not?

3. In which adventure do you think Odysseus acts most heroically? Why do you think so?

4. **Characterize** Circe's attitude at the beginning of this passage toward Odysseus and his men. Cite examples from the text.

5. When Odysseus asks Circe how he could fight off Scylla, what is the point of her reply (lines 105–121)?

6. Do you think the crew's decision to eat the sacred cattle is consistent with their previous actions? Explain.

7. Typically in ancient Greek stories, the outcome is revealed from the beginning. Audiences enjoyed finding out *how* heroes survived their adventures. Would you prefer not knowing from the beginning that Odysseus survives? Explain.

8. Based on what you know about Odysseus so far, make a **prediction** about what might happen when he returns home.

Literary Focus: Epic Hero

An **epic hero,** the central character of an epic, has abilities that exceed those of ordinary people while still being fundamentally human. What qualities make Odysseus an epic hero? What qualities, including his weaknesses, reveal how human he is? Create a chart like the one shown here that lists Odysseus's qualities and states whether these qualities seem heroic or typically human.

Odysseus's qualities	Heroic or human?
Courage	Heroic

Vocabulary Study

Match each vocabulary word on the left with its **synonym** on the right. If necessary, use the Glossary for help with word meanings.

abominably
ardor
avail
dire
harbor
promontory
scourge
timorous
travail
waft

1. harbor
2. timorous
3. waft
4. abominably
5. promontory
6. avail
7. scourge
8. travail
9. dire
10. ardor

a. fearful
b. toil
c. passion
d. hold
e. affliction
f. cape
g. disgustingly
h. horrifying
i. float
j. help

Expressing Your Ideas

Writing Choices

Writer's Notebook Update Review the notes you wrote about what makes someone a hero. Now that you've read parts of the *Odyssey*, compare your contemporary perspective of the hero to Homer's depiction of Odysseus. How are your notions of the hero like Homer's? How are they different? Record your thoughts in your notebook.

The Forgotten Chapter Imagine that scholars discover a lost passage from Homer's *Odyssey* that describes another adventure at sea. Write the forgotten passage from Odysseus's point of view, using the chapters you have read so far as your model. Indicate where in the story your forgotten **chapter** should go.

Here Lies Odysseus . . . Now that you've done some thinking about Odysseus, write an **epitaph** for his gravestone that summarizes or briefly describes his life and character. Share your piece with the class.

Other Options

Hero or Scoundrel? What do you think of Odysseus? Is he a hero to be admired, or a lying, no-good scoundrel? Do you like him? Would you want to be like him? Hold a **class debate** about Odysseus, using these questions as a starting point.

Monster Mobile Make a hanging **mobile** of the monsters from the *Odyssey*. You may use any materials you wish. Possibilities are two-dimensional matted or papier-maché drawings, or three-dimensional figures made of clay, wood, cloth, or soap. Exhibit your mobile in a class display.

Adventure Flip Book Briefly outline the major events of Odysseus's voyage so far. Make simple drawings of the events and staple the pages together to make a **flip book.** Title your book and share it with the class.

Before Reading

The Homecoming

from the **Odyssey** by Homer

Building Background

The Hero's Return After Odysseus finishes the long tale of his years of wandering, his generous Phaeacian hosts give him many gifts and send him home to Ithaca on one of their magic ships.

On the beach in Ithaca, the goddess Athena warns Odysseus about the suitors. Athena explains that Penelope has waited faithfully for Odysseus, and that his son Telemachus is abroad seeking news of his whereabouts. She disguises Odysseus as an old beggar so that he can assess the situation at home. Odysseus visits his loyal servant, Eumaeus the swineherd, who treats him kindly despite his rough appearance. Unaware that his visitor is Odysseus, Eumaeus speaks highly of his long-absent master.

Meanwhile, Telemachus returns to Ithaca, avoiding a trap the suitors have set for him. Telemachus's travels have taught him much about the world, and he returns with a new sense of confidence and self-respect. He goes directly to Eumaeus, who greets him warmly. After sharing a meal with Eumaeus and the disguised Odysseus, Telemachus explains his predicament with the suitors. Telemachus then sends Eumaeus to tell Penelope that he has returned safely from his travels. Telemachus and Odysseus are thus alone when the goddess Athena arrives.

Literary Focus

Plot The plot of a story is the series of related events that present and eventually resolve a problem or conflict. As you read the following selections about Odysseus's homecoming, pay attention to how Homer builds suspense and resolves conflict in the plot of the *Odyssey*.

Writer's Notebook

Journey's End Odysseus's wanderings at sea have finally ended, and he must re-establish himself as king. Up to this point, you have been given many hints about the outcome of the story. Jot down what you remember hearing so far about Odysseus's homecoming. How do you think the plot will be resolved?

The Homecoming

FROM THE
ODYSSEY
HOMER

② FATHER AND SON

. . . From the air
she walked, taking the form of a tall woman,
handsome and clever at her craft, and stood
beyond the gate in plain sight of Odysseus,
5 unseen, though, by Telemachus, unguessed,
for not to everyone will gods appear.
Odysseus noticed her; so did the dogs,
who cowered whimpering away from her. She only
nodded, signing to him with her brows,
10 a sign he recognized. Crossing the yard,
he passed out through the gate in the stockade
to face the goddess. Then she said to him:

"Son of Laertes and gods of old,
Odysseus, master of land ways and sea ways,
15 dissemble to your son no longer now.
The time has come: tell him how you together
will bring doom on the suitors in the town.
I shall not be far distant then, for I
myself desire battle."

This statue of Athena *Promachos* ("Defender"), shows the goddess holding the *aegis*, the "snake-fringed shield" with which she terrifies the suitors. How does this image convey Athena's dual character as a goddess of wisdom and warfare?

11 stockade (sto kād′), *n.* a line of posts set firmly to form a defense; an enclosure or pen.

■ Why do you think Athena desires battle?

Saying no more,

20 she tipped her golden wand upon the man,
making his cloak pure white, and the knit tunic
fresh around him. Lithe and young she made him,
ruddy with sun, his jawline clean, the beard
no longer grey upon his chin. And she
withdrew when she had done.

25 Then Lord Odysseus
reappeared—and his son was thunderstruck.
Fear in his eyes, he looked down and away
as though it were a god, and whispered:

"Stranger,
you are no longer what you were just now!
30 Your cloak is new; even your skin! You are
one of the gods who rule the sweep of heaven!
Be kind to us, we'll make you fair oblation
and gifts of hammered gold. Have mercy on us!"

The noble and enduring man replied:

35 "No god. Why take me for a god? No, no.
I am that father whom your boyhood lacked
and suffered pain for lack of. I am he."

Held back too long, the tears ran down his cheeks
as he embraced his son.
Only Telemachus,
40 uncomprehending, wild
with incredulity, cried out:

"You cannot
be my father Odysseus! Meddling spirits
conceived this trick to twist the knife in me!
No man of woman born could work these wonders
45 by his own craft, unless a god came into it
with ease to turn him young or old at will.
I swear you were in rags and old,
and here you stand like one of the immortals!"

Odysseus brought his ranging mind to bear
and said:

50 "This is not princely, to be swept
away by wonder at your father's presence.
No other Odysseus will ever come,
for he and I are one, the same; his bitter

---

22 lithe (līᴛʜ), *adj.* characterized by flexibility and grace.

32 oblation (o blā′shən), *n.* something offered in worship or devotion.

41 incredulity (in′krə dü′lə- tē), *n.* disbelief; skepticism.

---

fortune and his wanderings are mine.
55 Twenty years gone, and I am back again
on my own island.

As for my change of skin,
that is a charm Athena, Hope of Soldiers,
uses as she will; she has the knack
to make me seem a beggar man sometimes
60 and sometimes young, with finer clothes about me.
It is no hard thing for the gods of heaven
to glorify a man or bring him low."

When he had spoken, down he sat.

Then, throwing
his arms around this marvel of a father
65 Telemachus began to weep. Salt tears
rose from the wells of longing in both men,
and cries burst from both as keen and fluttering
as those of the great taloned hawk,
whose nestlings farmers take before they fly.
70 So helplessly they cried, pouring out tears,
and might have gone on weeping so till sundown,
had not Telemachus said:

"Dear father! Tell me
what kind of vessel put you here ashore
on Ithaca? Your sailors, who were they?
75 I doubt you made it, walking on the sea!"

Then said Odysseus, who had borne the barren sea:

"Only plain truth shall I tell you, child.
Great seafarers, the Phaeacians, gave me passage
as they give other wanderers. By night
80 over the open ocean, while I slept,
they brought me in their cutter, set me down
on Ithaca, with gifts of bronze and gold
and stores of woven things. By the gods' will
these lie all hidden in a cave. I came
85 to this wild place, directed by Athena,
so that we might lay plans to kill our enemies.
Count up the suitors for me, let me know
what men at arms are there, how many men.
I must put all my mind to it, to see
90 if we two by ourselves can take them on
or if we should look round for help."

■ Why is Telemachus disbe-lieving at first that Odysseus has returned?

81 cutter (kut′ər), *n.* a small ship.

🔁 THE BEGGAR AT THE MANOR

Unafraid to learn that the suitors number over a hundred, Odysseus tells Telemachus of his plan for revenge with the help of Athena and Zeus. Telemachus visits Penelope and tells her he has heard Odysseus is alive but stranded on Calypso's island. Meanwhile, the suitors are angered to discover that Telemachus has outwitted their plot to ambush him, and they determine to kill him if it is the will of the gods.

The swineherd Eumaeus and the disguised Odysseus are ridiculed by Odysseus's goatherd Melanthius on their way to Odysseus's palace. Odysseus is enraged but restrains himself. As they approach the palace, Odysseus is overjoyed to see his home again but is brought to tears seeing Argus, a dog he trained as a puppy, lying neglected and ill at the front gate. Argus recognizes Odysseus, wags his tail, and dies.

Odysseus and the swineherd enter Odysseus's hall, where the suitors are feasting. Odysseus goes to each suitor and begs for food. When he reaches Antinous, the arrogant young man insults him before the entire assembly.

But here Antinous broke in, shouting:

"God!

What evil wind blew in this pest?

Get over,

stand in the passage! Nudge my table, will you?
Egyptian whips are sweet
5 to what you'll come to here, you nosing rat,
making your pitch to everyone!
These men have bread to throw away on you
because it is not theirs. Who cares? Who spares
another's food, when he has more than plenty?"

10 With guile Odysseus drew away, then said:

"A pity that you have more looks than heart.
You'd grudge a pinch of salt from your own larder
to your own handy man. You sit here, fat
on others' meat, and cannot bring yourself
15 to rummage out a crust of bread for me!"

Then anger made Antinous' heart beat hard,
and, glowering under his brows, he answered:

"Now!

You think you'll shuffle off and get away
after that impudence? Oh, no you don't!"

20 The stool he let fly hit the man's right shoulder
on the packed muscle under the shoulder blade—
like solid rock, for all the effect one saw.
Odysseus only shook his head, containing
thoughts of bloody work, as he walked on,
25 then sat, and dropped his loaded bag again
upon the door sill. Facing the whole crowd
he said, and eyed them all:

"One word only,

my lords, and suitors of the famous queen.
One thing I have to say.
30 There is no pain, no burden for the heart
when blows come to a man, and he defending
his own cattle—his own cows and lambs.
Here it was otherwise. Antinous
hit me for being driven on by hunger—
35 how many bitter seas men cross for hunger!
If beggars interest the gods, if there are Furies
pent in the dark to avenge a poor man's wrong, then may
Antinous meet his death before his wedding day!"

Then said Eupeithes' son, Antinous:

"Enough.

40 Eat and be quiet where you are, or shamble elsewhere,
unless you want these lads to stop your mouth
pulling you by the heels, or hands and feet,
over the whole floor, till your back is peeled!"

But now the rest were mortified, and someone
45 spoke from the crowd of young bucks to rebuke him:

"A poor show, that—hitting this famished tramp—
bad business, if he happened to be a god.
You know they go in foreign guise, the gods do,
looking like strangers, turning up
50 in towns and settlements to keep an eye
on manners, good or bad."

---

19 impudence (im′pyə-dəns), *n.* contemptuous or cocky disregard; insolence.

■ Why do you think Homer mentions that Odysseus doesn't even lose his stride when he is hit with the footstool?

36 Furies (fyùr′ēz), goddesses of vengeance.

44 mortified (môr′tə fīd), *adj.* severely embarrassed; shamed.
45 rebuke (ri byük′), *v.* criticize sharply; reprimand.
46 famished (fam′isht), *adj.* suffering from severe hunger; starving.
48 guise (gīz), *n.* external appearance; costume.

But at this notion
Antinous only shrugged.
                                    Telemachus,
after the blow his father bore, sat still
without a tear, though his heart felt the blow.
55 Slowly he shook his head from side to side,
containing murderous thoughts.

                                    Penelope
on the higher level of her room had heard
the blow, and knew who gave it. Now she murmured:

"Would god you could be hit yourself, Antinous—
hit by Apollo's bowshot!"

60   And Eurynome
her housekeeper, put in:
                                    "He and no other?
If all we pray for came to pass, not one
would live till dawn!"

                                    Her gentle mistress said:

"Oh, Nan, they are a bad lot; they intend
65 ruin for all of us, but Antinous
appears a blacker-hearted hound than any.
Here is a poor man come, a wanderer,
driven by want to beg his bread, and everyone
in hall gave bits, to cram his bag—only
70 Antinous threw a stool, and banged his shoulder!"

So she described it, sitting in her chamber
among her maids—while her true lord was eating.
Then she called in the forester and said:

"Go to that man on my behalf, Eumaeus,
75 and send him here, so I can greet and question him.
Abroad in the great world, he may have heard
rumors about Odysseus—may have known him!"

60 Apollo (ə pol′ō), the god Apollo was a skilled bowman whose arrows were said to cause sudden death. See page 803.

After Reading

Making Connections

1. Write two or three words to describe each of these **characters:** Athena, Telemachus, Antinous.

2. Odysseus tells Telemachus he is not being "princely" when Telemachus doubts that he is his father. Do you agree? Why or why not?

3. Were you surprised by the emotional reunion between Telemachus and Odysseus? Why or why not?

4. In the *Odyssey,* how are people's true natures revealed in the way they treat strangers? Give examples.

5. Why does the disguised Odysseus antagonize Antinous in conversation?

6. Odysseus expects heroic loyalty from his servants and family, particularly his wife Penelope, who remains alone for twenty years while he is away. Do you think such loyalty should be expected today? Explain.

Vocabulary Study

**guise
incredulity
lithe
mortified
rebuke**

The first word in each of the following pairs is a vocabulary word. First, indicate whether the words in each pair are synonyms or antonyms. Then write a sentence using each of the vocabulary words.

1. guise : costume

2. incredulity : acceptance

3. lithe : flexible

4. mortified : shamed

5. rebuke : praise

Expressing Your Ideas

Writing Choice

I Met My Father Today . . . Imagine that you are Telemachus writing a **letter** to a close friend about finally being reunited with your father after so many years. How do you feel? What do you think of Odysseus? What are your hopes and fears? Read your letter to a partner.

Another Option

Live from the Hall A television reporter visits Odysseus's banquet hall to report on events there and interview suitors and servants. With a small group, present a live **newscast** that gives the latest news from the palace.

THE TEST OF THE BOW

That afternoon, while the suitors are exercising in the courtyard, a large, ill-mannered beggar named Irus threatens Odysseus, saying there is room for only one beggar in Ithaca. For their own amusement, the suitors arrange a boxing match between Irus and Odysseus. They are amazed by Odysseus's muscular body and praise him for defeating Irus.

At dinner, Penelope, made even more beautiful by Athena, chides the suitors for continuing to exhaust the resources of her husband's estate. With growing argument and unrest among them, the men agree to go home for the night as Telemachus suggests.

That night, Odysseus and Telemachus remove all the weapons from the hall and hide them. The disguised Odysseus tells Penelope that he believes her husband is alive and on his way home. Penelope explains that for the safety of her household she must finally agree to marry one of the suitors. She decides she will select the man who can string her husband's bow and shoot an arrow through a straight row of twelve axes.

Later, Penelope prays to Artemis (är′tə mis), goddess of chastity and hunting, saying she would rather die than marry another man. Elsewhere in the palace, Eurycleia, Odysseus's aged nurse, recognizes him by a scar on his foot. He makes her swear to keep his identity secret. Athena appears to reassure the fretful Odysseus that he will be victorious.

The next day, Odysseus appeals to Zeus for a sign of his favor, and Zeus answers with a rumbling of thunder. During lunch, one of the suitors insults Odysseus and throws a bone at him. Outraged, Telemachus delivers an angry speech at the group, telling them he knows of their plot to kill him. The men are too stunned and drowsy with overeating to respond, and they fall into a fit of uncontrollable laughter. Later, during the contest of the bow, none of the suitors is strong enough to string it. Odysseus requests a try and, though the suitors deny him, Penelope assents. As Odysseus confidently takes up his old bow, his faithful servants Eumaeus and Philoetius lock the palace gates and doors.

> And Odysseus took his time,
> turning the bow, tapping it, every inch,
> for borings that termites might have made
> while the master of the weapon was abroad.
> 5 The suitors were now watching him, and some
> jested among themselves:
>
> "A bow lover!"
>
> "Dealer in old bows!"

3 **boring** (bôr ing), *n.* a hole.

"Maybe he has one like it
at home!"

"Or has an itch to make one for himself."

"See how he handles it, the sly old buzzard!"

10 And one disdainful suitor added this:

"May his fortune grow an inch for every inch he bends it!"

10 **disdainful** (dis dān′fəl),
adj. full of contempt; scornful.

◄ N. C. Wyeth, *The Trial
of the Bow.* Why do you
think the artist posed
the onlookers in the
way he did?

But the man skilled in all ways of contending,
satisfied by the great bow's look and heft,
like a musician, like a harper, when
15 with quiet hand upon his instrument
he draws between his thumb and forefinger
a sweet new string upon a peg: so effortlessly
Odysseus in one motion strung the bow.
Then slid his right hand down the cord and plucked it,
20 so the taut gut vibrating hummed and sang
a swallow's note.
            In the hushed hall it smote the suitors
and all their faces changed. Then Zeus thundered
overhead, one loud crack for a sign.
And Odysseus laughed within him that the son
25 of crooked-minded Cronus had flung that omen down.
He picked one ready arrow from his table
where it lay bare: the rest were waiting still
in the quiver for the young men's turn to come.
He nocked it, let it rest across the handgrip,
30 and drew the string and grooved butt of the arrow,
aiming from where he sat upon the stool.
                  Now flashed
arrow from twanging bow clean as a whistle
through every socket ring, and grazed not one,
to thud with heavy brazen head beyond.
             Then quietly
Odysseus said:

35   "Telemachus, the stranger
you welcomed in your hall has not disgraced you.
I did not miss, neither did I take all day
stringing the bow. My hand and eye are sound,
not so contemptible as the young men say.
40 The hour has come to cook their lordships' mutton—
supper by daylight. Other amusements later,
with song and harping that adorn a feast."

He dropped his eyes and nodded, and the prince
Telemachus, true son of King Odysseus,
45 belted his sword on, clapped hand to his spear,
and with a clink and glitter of keen bronze
stood by his chair, in the forefront near his father.

---

13 heft (heft), *n.* weight, heaviness.

■ Do you think Homer's comparison of Odysseus to a musician is an effective **simile** here? Why or why not?

21 smote (smōt), *v.* struck sharply; delivered a blow (past tense of *smite*).

25 omen (ō′mən), *n.* a sign of what is to happen.

29 nock (nok), *v.* fit against a bowstring.

39 contemptible (kən-temp′tə bəl), *adj.* deserving scorn; mean; low; worthless.

DEATH IN THE GREAT HALL

Now shrugging off his rags the wiliest fighter of the islands
leapt and stood on the broad door sill, his own bow in his hand.
He poured out at his feet a rain of arrows from the quiver
and spoke to the crowd:

> "So much for that. Your clean-cut game is over.
> 5 Now watch me hit a target that no man has hit before,
> if I can make this shot. Help me, Apollo."

He drew to his fist the cruel head of an arrow for Antinous
just as the young man leaned to lift his beautiful drinking cup,
embossed, two-handled, golden: the cup was in his fingers:
10 the wine was even at his lips: and did he dream of death?
How could he? In that revelry amid his throng of friends
who would imagine a single foe—though a strong foe indeed—
could dare to bring death's pain on him and darkness on his eyes?
Odysseus' arrow hit him under the chin
15 and punched up to the feathers through his throat.

Backward and down he went, letting the winecup fall
from his shocked hand. Like pipes his nostrils jetted
crimson runnels, a river of mortal red,
and one last kick upset his table
20 knocking the bread and meat to soak in dusty blood.
Now as they craned to see their champion where he lay
the suitors jostled in uproar down the hall,
everyone on his feet. Wildly they turned and scanned
the walls in the long room for arms; but not a shield,
25 not a good ashen spear was there for a man to take and throw.
All they could do was yell in outrage at Odysseus:

"Foul! to shoot at a man! That was your last shot!"

"Your own throat will be slit for this!"

> "Our finest lad is down!
You killed the best on Ithaca."

> "Buzzards will tear your eyes out!"

1 wily (wī′lē), *adj.* crafty;
cunning; tricky.

9 embossed (em bossd′),
adj. decorated with a design,
pattern, etc., that stands out
from the surface.
11 revelry (rev′əl rē), *n.* boisterous reveling or festivity.
11 throng (thrông), *n.*
crowd; multitude.

■ Why do you think Homer
includes details about the
cup Antinous drinks from?

18 runnel (run′əl), *n.* small
stream or brook; rivulet;
runlet.

30　For they imagined as they wished—that it was a wild shot,
　　an unintended killing—fools, not to comprehend
　　they were already in the grip of death.
　　But glaring under his brows Odysseus answered:

　　"You yellow dogs, you thought I'd never make it
35　home from the land of Troy. You took my house to plunder,
　　twisted my maids to serve your beds. You dared
　　bid for my wife while I was still alive.
　　Contempt was all you had for the gods who rule wide heaven,
　　contempt for what men say of you hereafter.
40　Your last hour has come. You die in blood."

　　As they all took this in, sickly green fear
　　pulled at their entrails, and their eyes flickered
　　looking for some hatch or hideaway from death.
　　Eurymachus alone could speak. He said:

45　"If you are Odysseus of Ithaca come back,
　　all that you say these men have done is true.
　　Rash actions, many here, more in the countryside.
　　But here he lies, the man who caused them all.
　　Antinous was the ringleader, he whipped us on
50　to do these things. He cared less for a marriage
　　than for the power Cronion has denied him
　　as king of Ithaca. For that
　　he tried to trap your son and would have killed him.
　　He is dead now and has his portion. Spare
55　your own people. As for ourselves, we'll make
　　restitution of wine and meat consumed,
　　and add, each one, a tithe of twenty oxen
　　with gifts of bronze and gold to warm your heart.
　　Meanwhile we cannot blame you for your anger."

60　Odysseus glowered under his black brows
　　and said:

　　　　　　　　　　"Not for the whole treasure of your fathers,
　　all you enjoy, lands, flocks, or any gold
　　put up by others, would I hold my hand.
　　There will be killing till the score is paid.
65　You forced yourselves upon this house. Fight your way out,
　　or run for it, if you think you'll escape death.
　　I doubt one man of you skins by."

　　They felt their knees fail, and their hearts—but heard
　　Eurymachus for the last time rallying them.

51 Cronion (krō′nē ən),
another name for Zeus, the
supreme god and son of
Cronus.

57 tithe (tīтн), *n.* a portion,
often one-tenth, of yearly
income paid as a tax or
donation.

70　"Friends," he said, "the man is <u>implacable</u>.
　　Now that he's got his hands on bow and quiver
　　he'll shoot from the big door stone there
　　until he kills us to the last man.

　　　　　　　　　　　　　　　　　　　　　Fight, I say,
　　let's remember the joy of it. Swords out!
75　Hold up your tables to <u>deflect</u> his arrows.
　　After me, everyone: rush him where he stands.
　　If we can budge him from the door, if we can pass
　　into the town, we'll call out men to chase him.
　　This fellow with his bow will shoot no more."

　　He drew his own sword as he spoke, a broadsword of fine bronze,
80　honed like a razor on either edge. Then crying hoarse and loud
　　he hurled himself at Odysseus. But the kingly man let fly
　　an arrow at that instant, and the quivering feathered butt
　　sprang to the nipple of his breast as the barb stuck in his liver.
　　The bright broadsword clanged down. He lurched and fell aside,
85　pitching across his table. His cup, his bread and meat,

70 implacable (im plā′kə-
bəl), *adj.* unable to be
appeased; refusing to be
reconciled; unyielding.

■ What makes Eurymachus
decide to fight?

75 deflect (di flekt′), *v.* turn
aside.

◄ N. C. Wyeth, *The
Slaughter of the Suitors.*
The artist has positioned
two hands—one has
just flung a spear and
the other reaches up for
mercy—at the center
of his illustration of the
combat in the great
hall. What does this
focus add to the mood
of his painting?

were spilt and scattered far and wide, and his head slammed on
    the ground.
Revulsion, anguish in his heart, with both feet kicking out,
he downed his chair, while the shrouding wave of mist closed on
    his eyes. . . .

*Odysseus fells many more men with arrows, while Telemachus fetches
shields and spears for himself, his father, Eumaeus, and the cowherd.
Meanwhile, the treacherous goatherd Melanthius escapes to the storage room
and brings arms for twelve of the suitors. Eumaeus and the cowherd discover
Melanthius returning for more arms and string him up to the ceiling. Aided
by Athena, the four men defeat the suitors. The few survivors beg for mercy.*

     One more who had avoided furious death
90 was the son of Terpis, Phemius, the minstrel,
  singer by compulsion to the suitors.
  He stood now with his harp, holy and clear,
  in the wall's recess, under the window, wondering
  if he should flee that way to the courtyard altar,
95 sanctuary of Zeus, the Enclosure God.
  Thighbones in hundreds had been offered there
  by Laertes and Odysseus. No, he thought;
  the more direct way would be best—to go
  humbly to his lord. But first to save
100 his murmuring instrument he laid it down
  carefully between the winebowl and a chair,
  then he betook himself to Lord Odysseus,
  clung hard to his knees, and said:

                               "Mercy,
  mercy on a suppliant, Odysseus!
105 My gift is song for men and for the gods undying.
  My death will be remorse for you hereafter.
  No one taught me: deep in my mind a god
  shaped all the various ways of life in song.
  And I am fit to make verse in your company
110 as in the god's. Put aside lust for blood.
  Your own dear son Telemachus can tell you,
  never by my own will or for love
  did I feast here or sing amid the suitors.
  They were too strong, too many; they compelled me."

115 Telemachus in the elation of battle
  heard him. He at once called to his father:

87 revulsion (ri vul′shən), *n.* a sudden, violent change or reaction, especially of disgust; repugnance.

91 compulsion (kəm-pul′shən), *n.* a being compelled; use of force.

95 the Enclosure God, or god of the courtyard. It was thought that a statue of Zeus in a courtyard would protect the home.

104 suppliant (sup′lē ənt), *n.* one who makes humble entreaty or begs.
106 remorse (ri môrs′), *n.* sorrowful regret.

115 elation (i lā′shən), *n.* high spirits; joy or pride.

"Wait: that one is innocent: don't hurt him.
And we should let our herald live—Medon;
he cared for me from boyhood. Where is *he?*
120 Has he been killed already by Philoetius
or by the swineherd? Else he got an arrow
in that first gale of bowshots down the room."

Now this came to the ears of prudent Medon
under the chair where he had gone to earth,
125 pulling a new-flayed bull's hide over him.
Quiet he lay while blinding death passed by.
Now heaving out from under
he scrambled for Telemachus' knees and said:

"Here I am, dear prince; but rest your spear!
130 Tell your great father not to see in me
a suitor for the sword's edge—one of those
who laughed at you and ruined his property!"

The lord of all the tricks of war surveyed
this fugitive and smiled. He said:

135 "Courage: my son has dug you out and saved you.
Take it to heart, and pass the word along:
fair dealing brings more profit in the end.
Now leave this room. Go and sit down outdoors
where there's no carnage, in the court,
140 you and the poet with his many voices,
while I attend to certain chores inside."

At this the two men stirred and picked their way
to the door and out, and sat down at the altar,
looking around with wincing eyes
145 as though the sword's edge hovered still.
And Odysseus looked around him, narrow-eyed,
for any others who had lain hidden
while death's black fury passed.
                              In blood and dust
he saw that crowd all fallen, many and many slain.

150 Think of a catch that fishermen haul in to a halfmoon bay
in a fine-meshed net from the white-caps of the sea:
how all are poured out on the sand, in throes for the salt sea,
twitching their cold lives away in Helios' fiery air:
so lay the suitors heaped on one another.

133 survey (sər vā′), *v.* look over; view; examine.

139 carnage (kär′nij), *n.* slaughter of a great number of people.

152 throes (thrōz), *n.* a desperate struggle.

■ What **simile** does Homer use to describe the fallen suitors?

After Reading

Making Connections

1. What do you think Odysseus is thinking and feeling when he first handles his bow?

2. Do you think Odysseus's actions are justified? Explain.

3. After Odysseus completes the test of the bow, he says there will be "other amusements later." What is **ironic** about this statement?

4. What does Eurymachus's speech to Odysseus (lines 45–59) reveal about his **character?** Explain.

5. Describe the changes in attitude that the suitors experience.

6. Why do you think Homer included the passage in which Telemachus and Odysseus spare the lives of Phemius and Medon?

7. Describe how the **plot** moves toward a climax and resolution.

Vocabulary Study

**contemptible
deflect
implacable
remorse
wily**

Complete the synonym word web for the word *wily.* Then make synonym word webs for each of the remaining words in the vocabulary list. If necessary, refer to a thesaurus for help with synonyms.

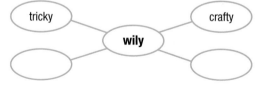

Expressing Your Ideas

Writing Choice

An Eye for an Eye Do you think Odysseus is justified in killing the suitors, or is his revenge too brutal? Write a **letter** to the *Ithaca Times* criticizing or defending Odysseus's actions. Consider issues such as the possibility that the suitors would have killed Odysseus.

Other Options

Bow Master Create a **visual representation** of the climactic moment when Odysseus strings his bow.

Summit on Violence Hold a **summit meeting** on violence. What is the effect of violence in the media? Is the *Odyssey*'s violence different from that in society today? If so, how?

THE TRUNK OF THE OLIVE TREE

After the fighting ends, Odysseus's old servant Eurycleia comes out and begins to rejoice, but Odysseus stops her, saying such a massacre is no reason for rejoicing. Odysseus then orders the woman servants who consorted with suitors to remove the dead bodies and clean up the bloody hall. Afterward, Telemachus hangs the women outside. Odysseus orders Eurycleia to burn fire and brimstone to cleanse the palace. He then sends for Penelope, who has been sleeping under Athena's spell. Penelope greets Odysseus, who is still blood-stained from the fight, but she is not sure he really is her husband.

Greathearted Odysseus, home at last,
was being bathed now by Eurynome
and rubbed with golden oil, and clothed again
in a fresh tunic and a cloak. Athena
5 lent him beauty, head to foot. She made him
taller, and massive, too, with crisping hair
in curls like petals of wild hyacinth
but all red-golden. Think of gold infused
on silver by a craftsman, whose fine art
10 Hephaestus taught him, or Athena: one
whose work moves to delight: just so she lavished
beauty over Odysseus' head and shoulders.
He sat then in the same chair by the pillar,
facing his silent wife, and said:

                            "Strange woman,
15 the immortals of Olympus made you hard,
harder than any. Who else in the world
would keep aloof as you do from her husband
if he returned to her from years of trouble,
cast on his own land in the twentieth year?

20 Nurse, make up a bed for me to sleep on.
Her heart is iron in her breast."

8 infused (in fyüzd′), *adj.* poured into; instilled.
10 Hephaestus (hi fes′təs), god of fire and metalworking. See page 803.
11 lavish (lav′ish), *v.* give or spend very freely or generously.
17 aloof (ə lüf′), *adj.* unsympathetic; not interested; reserved.

This statue of Penelope, a Roman copy of a Greek original, was done in the first century A.D. What is the chief emotion conveyed by this image? ➤

Penelope
spoke to Odysseus now. She said:

"Strange man,
if man you are . . . This is no pride on my part
nor scorn for you—not even wonder, merely.
25 I know so well how you—how he—appeared
boarding the ship for Troy. But all the same . . .

Make up his bed for him, Eurycleia.
Place it outside the bedchamber my lord
built with his own hands. Pile the big bed
30 with fleeces, rugs, and sheets of purest linen."

With this she tried him to the breaking point,
and he turned on her in a flash raging:

"Woman, by heaven you've stung me now!
Who dared to move my bed?
35 No builder had the skill for that—unless
a god came down to turn the trick. No mortal
in his best days could budge it with a crowbar.
There is our pact and pledge, our secret sign,
built into that bed—my handiwork
and no one else's!
40   An old trunk of olive
grew like a pillar on the building plot,
and I laid out our bedroom round that tree,
lined up the stone walls, built the walls and roof,
gave it a doorway and smooth-fitting doors.
45 Then I lopped off the silvery leaves and branches,
hewed and shaped that stump from the roots up
into a bedpost, drilled it, let it serve
 as model for the rest. I planed them all,
inlaid them all with silver, gold and ivory,
50 and stretched a bed between—a <u>pliant</u> web
of oxhide thongs dyed crimson.
                                              There's our sign!
I know no more. Could someone else's hand
have sawn that trunk and dragged the frame away?"

Their secret! as she heard it told, her knees
55 grew <u>tremulous</u> and weak, her heart failed her.
With eyes brimming tears she ran to him,
throwing her arms around his neck, and kissed him,
murmuring:

■ Why does Penelope question that Odysseus is a man?

49 inlay (in′lā), *v.* decorate with a design or material set in the surface.
50 pliant (plī′ənt), *adj.* bending easily; flexible; supple.
51 crimson (krim′zən), *n.* deep red.

55 tremulous (trem′yə ləs), *adj.* trembling; quivering.

"Do not rage at me, Odysseus!
No one ever matched your caution! Think
60 what difficulty the gods gave: they denied us
life together in our prime and flowering years,
kept us from crossing into age together.
Forgive me, don't be angry. I could not
welcome you with love on sight! I armed myself
65 long ago against the frauds of men,
impostors who might come—and all those many
whose underhanded ways bring evil on!
Helen of Argos, daughter of Zeus and Leda,
would she have joined the stranger, lain with him,
70 if she had known her destiny? known the Achaeans
in arms would bring her back to her own country?
Surely a goddess moved her to adultery,
her blood unchilled by war and evil coming,
the years, the desolation; ours, too.
75 But here and now, what sign could be so clear
as this of our own bed?
No other man has ever laid eyes on it—
only my own slave, Actoris, that my father
sent with me as a gift—she kept our door.
80 You make my stiff heart know that I am yours."

Now from his breast into his eyes the ache
of longing mounted, and he wept at last,
his dear wife, clear and faithful, in his arms,
longed for
85   as the sunwarmed earth is longed for by a swimmer
spent in rough water where his ship went down
under Poseidon's blows, gale winds and tons of sea.
Few men can keep alive through a big surf
to crawl, clotted with brine, on kindly beaches
90 in joy, in joy, knowing the abyss behind:
and so she too rejoiced, her gaze upon her husband,
her white arms round him pressed as though forever.

65 fraud (frôd), *n.* dishonest
dealing; trickery; cheating.

68 Helen of Argos . . . Leda
(lē′də). Helen is the wife of
Achaean king Menelaus; her
abduction by Paris and adultery with him led to the
Trojan War. Leda became
pregnant with Helen after
Zeus appeared to her as a
swan and seduced her.
74 desolation (des′ə-
lā′shən), *n.* grief, sadness;
loneliness; barrenness.

89 clotted (klot′əd), *adj.*
covered with thick clumps or
masses.
89 brine (brīn), *n.* very salty
water.
90 abyss (ə bis′), *n.* a
bottomless or very great
depth; chasm.

After Reading

Making Connections

1. What do you learn about Penelope in this scene?

2. **Characterize** Odysseus's behavior toward Penelope in this scene. Do you think he is fair to her?

3. Why is it **ironic** that Odysseus is frustrated by Penelope's shrewd caution?

4. Do you think the marriage between Odysseus and Penelope is a fair arrangement? Why or why not?

5. Work with a partner to list Odysseus's greatest triumphs and major mistakes; then use the examples to write a **definition** of an epic hero.

6. Throughout the *Odyssey*, Homer uses **epithets,** or repeated words or phrases, such as "grey-eyed Athena," to describe characters. Work with a partner to identify common epithets used for Odysseus throughout the *Odyssey.* Then tell how they reinforce your understanding of his character.

7. Throughout the *Odyssey,* do you think the gods are just in their dealings with mortals? Support your answer with examples.

8. ☝ What cultural values and ideals are reflected in the conclusion of the *Odyssey?*

9. Compare and contrast Odysseus to some popular present-day action heroes.

Literary Focus

Plot The elements of a plot in a story include a conflict or conflicts, a climax, and a resolution. On a chart like the one shown here, compare the plot elements in the first part of the *Odyssey* with the plot elements in this part of the epic. Then explain which plot appeals to you more, and why.

Plot element	"The Voyage"	"The Homecoming"
conflict(s)	Odysseus angers Poseidon.	
climax		
resolution		

Vocabulary Study

Write the letter of the phrase that best demonstrates the meaning of the vocabulary word. Use the Glossary for help with word meanings.

abyss
desolation
lavish
pliant
tremulous

1. ABYSS: (A) a mountain peak; (B) a pact between brothers; (C) a chasm between glaciers

2. DESOLATION: (A) a woman greeting a friend; (B) a child abandoned by its parents; (C) a girl writing a poem

3. LAVISH: (A) a child receiving many birthday presents; (B) a coach scolding a player; (C) a person fainting from hunger

4. PLIANT: (A) a stiff metal bar; (B) a rainbow; (C) an old leather belt

5. TREMULOUS: (A) a boy seeing his father after many years; (B) a girl watching a dull movie; (C) a child nodding off to sleep

Expressing Your Ideas

Writing Choices

Writer's Notebook Update Now that you know how the conflict of the *Odyssey* is resolved, how close were your predictions about what would happen? Do you find the resolution satisfying? Why or why not? Record your thoughts in your notebook.

Will Odysseus Stay Home? Many writers, including Dante, Alfred Lord Tennyson, and Nikos Kazantzakis, have written sequels to the *Odyssey*. Try your hand at writing an **outline** for *Odyssey 2: The Adventure Continues*.

The Women of the *Odyssey* Some of the most complex and interesting characters in the *Odyssey* are women. Write a **character study** in which you compare and contrast two of the story's major female characters.

Other Options

I Remember When . . . After living to a ripe old age, Odysseus has finally died. Everyone who has known him is gathering to pay their respects and say a few words about the famous hero. Choose a character from the *Odyssey* you wish to play and work with your classmates to enact Odysseus's funeral. Take some time to prepare your **speech** in advance.

Odyssey: The Game Would the *Odyssey* make a good computer game? Pick a key scene from the epic and create **storyboards** to show how you would turn that scene into a computer game.

Before Reading

Siren Song by Margaret Atwood

An Ancient Gesture by Edna St. Vincent Millay

Sea Canes by Derek Walcott

The Tide Rises, the Tide Falls by Henry Wadsworth Longfellow

Building Background

Timeless Themes The poems on the following pages relate to the *Odyssey* or themes in the *Odyssey*, offering new perspectives on Homer's epic story. In "Siren Song," Margaret Atwood writes from the point of view of one of the Sirens. In "An Ancient Gesture," Edna St. Vincent Millay writes about how Penelope might have felt during Odysseus's twenty-year absence. In Derek Walcott's poem "Sea Canes," the speaker walks by the sea, lamenting the loss of friends who have died. And in Henry Wadsworth Longfellow's poem "The Tide Rises, the Tide Falls," a traveler returns home. As you read these poems, compare them to the *Odyssey*. What new perspectives on Homer's famous story do they offer?

Literary Focus

Mood The **mood** of a piece of writing is the atmosphere of feeling that it creates. Moods of poems can range from joyous to desperate to darkly comic. Authors create particular moods through their choice of setting, details, images, and words. For example, a poem set on a roller coaster is likely to have a mood of excitement or fear, whereas a poem full of details about standing in line at the post office might have a mood of bored frustration. Pay attention to how the authors of the following poems create mood.

Writer's Notebook

At the Sea Three of the poems you are about to read take place by the sea. What do the sea and shore represent to you? What thoughts and feelings do you associate with them? Record your ideas in your notebook.

Margaret Atwood
born 1939

Canadian writer Margaret Atwood began her writing career as a poet, publishing her first book in 1961. Since then, she has published numerous poetry collections, novels, essays, and short stories. Her popular novel *The Handmaid's Tale* was made into a major motion picture in 1990. Atwood, who has taught writing in Canada, the United States, and Australia, has won numerous literary awards and honorary degrees. She lives in Toronto with her husband and daughter.

Edna St. Vincent Millay
1892–1950

Edna St. Vincent Millay planned to become a concert pianist, but started writing after her piano teacher said her hands were too small. After graduating from college and publishing her first book, Millay moved to Greenwich Village in New York City. Her artistic talent and unconventional lifestyle made her a key figure in the Village, which was home to many artists and writers. For more information about Millay, see page 350.

Derek Walcott
born 1930

Derek Walcott's father died shortly after he and his twin brother were born on the Caribbean island of St. Lucia. Walcott's mother, believing in her son's talent, scraped together money for him to publish a booklet of his poems when he was nineteen. Now considered one of the finest living poets, Walcott was honored in 1992 with the Nobel Prize for literature. Much of his poetry explores life for people of the Caribbean.

Henry Wadsworth Longfellow
1807–1882

Henry Wadsworth Longfellow was born in Portland, Maine, and educated at Bowdoin College, where he was in class with young Nathaniel Hawthorne. His life was marred by tragedy: his first wife died shortly after they were married, and his second wife was tragically killed in a fire. He taught modern languages and literature at Harvard for eighteen years. His most popular book, *Hiawatha,* was published in 1855. Longfellow was an extremely popular poet in his lifetime, and his poetry is still appreciated for its simple, romantic storytelling.

Woman in a Greek Chair (Penelope) was painted in 1984 by David Ligare. How does the mood of this modern painting differ from the classical statue of Penelope on page 789? ➤

Siren Song

Margaret Atwood

This is the one song everyone
would like to learn: the song
that is irresistible:

the song that forces men
5 to leap overboard in squadrons[1]
even though they see the beached skulls

the song nobody knows
because anyone who has heard it
is dead, and the others can't remember.

An Ancient Gesture

Edna St. Vincent Millay

I thought, as I wiped my eyes on the
    corner of my apron:
Penelope did this too.
And more than once: you can't keep
    weaving all day
And undoing it all through the night;
5 Your arms get tired, and the back of your
    neck gets tight;

And along towards morning, when you
    think it will never be light,
And your husband has been gone, and you
    don't know where, for years,
Suddenly you burst into tears;
There is simply nothing else to do.

10 And I thought, as I wiped my eyes on the
    corner of my apron:
This is an ancient gesture, authentic,
    antique,
In the very best tradition, classic, Greek;
Ulysses did this too.
But only as a gesture,—a gesture which
    implied
15 To the assembled throng that he was
    much too moved to speak.
He learned it from Penelope . . .
Penelope, who really cried.

10 Shall I tell you the secret
and if I do, will you get me
out of this bird suit?

I don't enjoy it here
squatting on this island
15 looking picturesque[2] and mythical

with these two feathery maniacs,
I don't enjoy singing
this trio, fatal and valuable.

I will tell the secret to you,
20 to you, only to you.
Come closer. This song

is a cry for help: Help me!
Only you, only you can,
you are unique

25 at last. Alas
it is a boring song
but it works every time.

---

1. **squadron** (skwod′rən), *n.* unit of military organization.
2. **picturesque** (pik′chə resk′), *adj.* resembling a picture or painted scene; charming or quaint in appearance.

Sea Canes

Derek Walcott

Half my friends are dead.
I will make you new ones, said earth.
No, give me them back, as they were, instead,
with faults and all, I cried.

5 Tonight I can snatch their talk
from the faint surf's drone[1]
through the canes, but I cannot walk

on the moonlit leaves of ocean
down that white road alone,
10 or float with the dreaming motion

of owls leaving earth's load.
O earth, the number of friends you keep
exceeds those left to be loved.

The sea canes by the cliff flash green and silver;
15 they were the seraph[2] lances of my faith,
but out of what is lost grows something stronger

that has the rational[3] radiance of stone,
enduring moonlight, further than despair,
strong as the wind, that through dividing canes

20 brings those we love before us, as they were,
with faults and all, not nobler, just there.

---

1. **drone** (drōn), *n.* a deep sustained or monotonous sound; hum.
2. **seraph** (ser′əf), *n.* one of the highest order of angels.
3. **rational** (rash′ə nəl), *adj.* having reason or understanding; reasonable.

▲ What feelings about the sea are conveyed in *Storm on the Reef*, by the modern American painter John David Hawver?

The Tide Rises, the Tide Falls

Henry Wadsworth Longfellow

The tide rises, the tide falls,
The twilight darkens, the curlew[1] calls;
Along the sea-sands damp and brown
The traveller hastens toward the town,
5   And the tide rises, the tide falls.

Darkness settles on roofs and walls,
But the sea, the sea in the darkness calls;
The little waves, with their soft, white hands,
Efface[2] the footprints in the sands,
10   And the tide rises, the tide falls.

The morning breaks; the steeds in their stalls
Stamp and neigh, as the hostler[3] calls;
The day returns, but nevermore
Returns the traveller to the shore,
15   And the tide rises, the tide falls.

---

1. **curlew** (ker′lŭ), *n.* a migratory, brown, long-legged bird related to the woodcock.
2. **efface** (ə fās′), *v.* erase or make indistinct by wearing away a surface.
3. **hostler** (os′lər), *n.* one who takes care of horses or mules.

After Reading

Making Connections

Shaping Your
Response

1. Were you surprised by what the speaker says in "Siren Song"? Explain.

2. Do you agree with the **characterization** of Penelope and Odysseus in "An Ancient Gesture"?

3. Write two or three words to describe the **tone** of "Sea Canes."

4. Explain how the **rhythm** affects the **mood** in "The Tide Rises, the Tide Falls."

Analyzing the Poems

5. Explain the meaning of the last two lines of "Siren Song."

6. What is the gesture in "An Ancient Gesture," and how does Odysseus's gesture differ from Penelope's?

7. What is lost and what is gained in "Sea Canes"?

8. Why do you think the traveler in the last poem never returns to the shore?

Extending the Ideas

9. What new perspective of the *Odyssey* does each poem offer?

Literary Focus

Mood You have learned that the mood of a piece of writing is the atmosphere of feeling it creates. Briefly describe the mood of each of the poems you have just read.

Expressing Your Ideas

Writing Choice

Writer's Notebook Update Three of these poems are set by the sea. Write your own **poem** about the sea and share it with a classmate.

Another Option

Visual Illustration All the poems in this section create striking images. Choose your favorite image from one of the poems and create a **visual representation** of it. Your piece could be a drawing, photograph, mural, collage, cartoon, mobile, or sculpture.

The Long Way Home

The World of Homer

Humanities Connection

The creativity of the ancient Greeks ranged from the poetic to the practical. The following pages deal with two aspects of their inventiveness: first, how the ancient Greeks viewed their gods; second, how the ships of Odysseus might have looked.

THE ANCIENT GREEKS BELIEVED THAT THEIR PRINCIPAL GODS LIVED IN BEAUTIFUL PALACES ON OLYMPUS, A HIGH MOUNTAIN IN THE NORTH. THESE GODS, KNOWN AS THE OLYMPIANS, WERE EACH ASSOCIATED WITH PARTICULAR DOMAINS, SYMBOLS, AND POWERS.

THE 12 OLYMPIANS

POSEIDON
(pə sīd′n)

Family Ties: son of Cronus; brother of Zeus
Domain: god of the sea
Nickname: Earthshaker
Weapons: storm, earthquake
Symbols: trident, horse, dolphin
Profile: Poseidon drew lots with his brothers Zeus and Hades for domains of power: Zeus got heaven and earth; Poseidon got the sea; Hades got the Underworld.
Odyssey link: Poseidon hated Odysseus because the hero had blinded his son, the Cyclops Polyphemus. He did everything he could to keep Odysseus from reaching home.
Roman name: Neptune (nep′tün)

ZEUS (züs)

Family Ties: son of Cronus and Rhea
Domain: god of heaven and earth; king of the gods
Nickname: Lord of Lightning
Weapon: thunderbolt
Symbols: eagle, oak
Profile: As they were born, Cronus devoured each of his children. Zeus's mother Rhea hid him until he was old enough to overcome Cronus and force him to disgorge Zeus's brothers and sisters.
Odyssey link: At the opening of the poem, Athena gets her father Zeus's permission to aid Odysseus. Later, Zeus sends omens in the form of flights of eagles and peals of thunder.
Roman names: Jupiter (jüp′ə ter), Jove (jōv)

ATHENA
(ə thē′nə)

Family Ties: daughter of Zeus
Domain: goddess of wisdom and war
Nicknames: Pallas (from the name of a giant she had killed), Grey-eyed
Weapon: the aegis (ē′jəs), a snake-fringed shield that drives people mad with terror
Symbols: owl, olive tree
Profile: At her birth, Athena sprang fully armed from the head of her father Zeus; she was the patron of Athens.
Odyssey link: Athena loved Odysseus because of his cunning and aided him and his family whenever possible. In Odysseus's battle with the suitors, she terrifies them with the aegis.
Roman name: Minerva (mə nėr′və)

HERMES
(hèr′mēz)

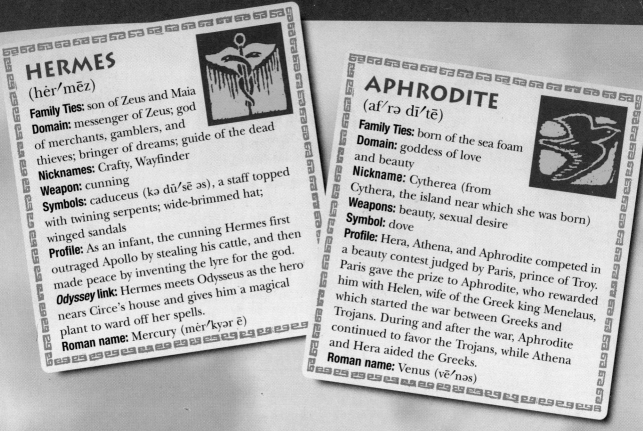

Family Ties: son of Zeus and Maia
Domain: messenger of Zeus; god of merchants, gamblers, and thieves; bringer of dreams; guide of the dead
Nicknames: Crafty, Wayfinder
Weapon: cunning
Symbols: caduceus (kə dü′sē əs), a staff topped with twining serpents; wide-brimmed hat; winged sandals
Profile: As an infant, the cunning Hermes first outraged Apollo by stealing his cattle, and then made peace by inventing the lyre for the god.
Odyssey link: Hermes meets Odysseus as the hero nears Circe's house and gives him a magical plant to ward off her spells.
Roman name: Mercury (mèr′kyər ē)

APHRODITE
(af′rə dī′tē)

Family Ties: born of the sea foam
Domain: goddess of love and beauty
Nickname: Cytherea (from Cythera, the island near which she was born)
Weapons: beauty, sexual desire
Symbol: dove
Profile: Hera, Athena, and Aphrodite competed in a beauty contest judged by Paris, prince of Troy. Paris gave the prize to Aphrodite, who rewarded him with Helen, wife of the Greek king Menelaus, which started the war between Greeks and Trojans. During and after the war, Aphrodite continued to favor the Trojans, while Athena and Hera aided the Greeks.
Roman name: Venus (vē′nəs)

HERA (hir′ə)

Family Ties: daughter of Cronus; sister and wife of Zeus
Domain: queen of the gods
Nicknames: Ox-eyed, White-armed
Weapon: transformation
Symbol: peacock
Profile: Hera was very jealous of Zeus, who was frequently unfaithful to her. She turned Io, one of the women he loved, into a bull, and then tormented her in the form of a gadfly. She transformed another, Callisto, into a bear. She tormented Heracles, Zeus's son by Alcmene, throughout his life, first sending serpents to strangle him in his cradle and then forcing him to perform his 12 Labors.
Roman name: Juno (jü′nō)

ARTEMIS
(är′tə məs)

Family Ties: daughter of Zeus and Leto; sister of Apollo
Domain: goddess of the hunt, the forests, wild animals, the moon, virginity, and childbirth
Nicknames: Huntress, the Pure
Weapon: death-dealing arrows
Symbols: bow and quiver of arrows, crescent moon
Profile: Niobe boasted of her six children, pointing out that Leto had only two. In revenge, Artemis killed Niobe's three daughters and Apollo her three sons.
Roman name: Diana (dī ä′nə)

ARES (er′ēz)

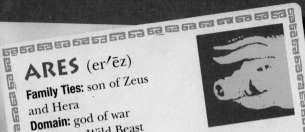

Family Ties: son of Zeus and Hera

Domain: god of war

Nickname: Wild Beast

Weapon: rage

Symbols: spear, blazing torch, vulture, dog, boar

Profile: The brutal Ares was disliked by his parents and the other Olympians. Among the gods, he was valued only by Hades, ruler of the dead, since Ares's activities as promoter of war provided him with many subjects. Although fierce, Ares was basically a bully, and was outmatched by the disciplined bravery of Athena. Among the Greeks, Ares was most venerated by the warlike Spartans.

Roman name: Mars (märz)

DIONYSUS (dī′ō nī′səs)

Family Ties: son of Zeus and Semele, the youngest of the Olympians and the only one to have a mortal parent

Domain: god of wine

Nickname: Loosener (from the relaxing effects of wine)

Weapon: madness

Symbols: clusters of grapes, ivy, roses, tiger, panther

Profile: Dionysus traveled through the world, spreading his cult of wine-induced ecstasy. When King Pentheus rejected his cult, the god's female followers in their madness mistook the king for a wild beast and tore him to pieces.

Roman name: Bacchus (bäk′əs)

HEPHAESTUS (hə fes′təs)

Family Ties: son of Zeus and Hera; husband of Aphrodite

Domain: god of fire and metalworking

Nicknames: Melter, Gamelegs (from his lameness)

Weapon: inventiveness

Symbols: smith's hammer and tongs

Profile: Outraged by his ugliness, Zeus threw the infant Hephaestus from Olympus and his fall to earth crippled him. Among the beautiful things Hephaestus crafted was the armor of the Greek hero Achilles.

Roman name: Vulcan (vul′kən)

APOLLO (ə pol′ō)

Family Ties: son of Zeus; brother of Artemis

Domain: god of the sun, music, poetry, prophecy, and healing

Nicknames: Bright, Far-striker

Weapon: death-dealing arrows

Symbols: lyre, bow, laurel wreath

Profile: Apollo tried to win the love of Cassandra, daughter of Priam, king of Troy, by giving her the power to see the future. When she refused his love, he turned the gift into a curse by fating that her prophecies would never be believed. Apollo's best-known link with prophecy was his shrine at Delphi, the most sacred site in the Greek world, where his priestess delivered mysterious oracles.

Roman name: Apollo (ə pol′ō)

DEMETER (di mē′tər)

Family Ties: daughter of Cronus; mother of Persephone

Domain: goddess of agriculture

Nicknames: Mother Earth, Great Goddess

Weapon: famine

Symbols: stalks of wheat, poppy

Profile: When her child Persephone was carried off to the underworld by Hades to be his wife, the grieving Demeter caused crops to wither, threatening humanity with starvation. The Olympians negotiated an agreement whereby Persephone spent half of each year (summer) with Demeter and the other half (winter) in the underworld with Hades.

Roman name: Ceres (sir′ēz)

HOMERIC SHIPS

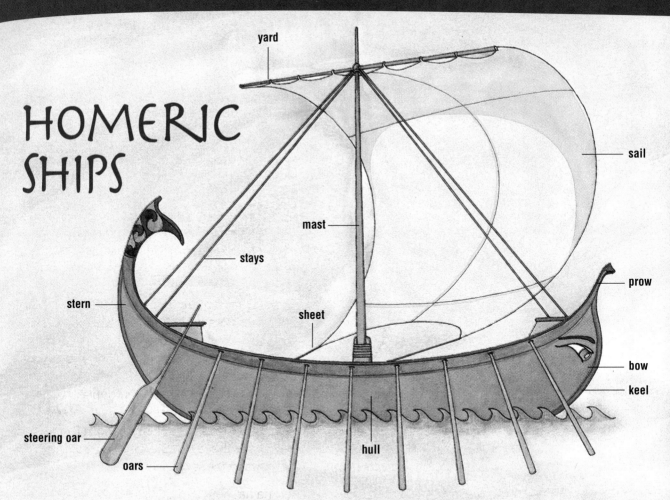

yard

sail

mast

stays

stern

sheet

prow

bow

keel

steering oar

oars

hull

What did Odysseus's ships look like? The evidence from the *Odyssey* and a few surviving vase paintings shows that they were light, open boats, certainly built for speed. Their **hulls** had a narrow flat bottom—which made it easy to pull them up on a beach at night or in bad weather—and were usually black, either painted or smeared with pitch. The ribs forming the hull were attached to the **keel,** a strong timber running the length of the ship. The ships were curved at the **prow** and **stern**—Homer compares them to the horns of cattle. The front or **bow** of the ship might have an eye painted on it, to "guide" the ship.

These ships were propelled by both sails and oars, often used together. A single **mast** was set in a box **amidships** (the center of the ship) and secured with ropes called **stays.** To the mast was attached the **yard,** a pole which held the large square white sail. The sail was held in place by ropes called **sheets.** The rowers sat on narrow planks, or **benches,** and pulled at the oars. Small boats might have ten oarsmen on a side; larger ships as many as 25. Large ships might be 100 feet in length and 10 to 12 feet across at their widest point. A steersman standing **aft,** or toward the stern, guided the ship using a **steering oar** or **tiller.**

Responding

1. Look up the meanings of the following words, which are formed from the names of the Greek and Roman gods: *mercurial, jovial, saturnine, martial, Junoesque.*

2. Use the information on Homeric ships to create an illustration for the scene in which Odysseus flees the island of the Cyclops.

Reading Mini-Lesson

Classifying

Have you ever organized your CD collection, stored documents in folders on a computer, or sorted your laundry before washing it? To do any of these tasks, you are using classification skills. Classification also makes it possible to find books at the library, cereal at the supermarket, and phone numbers in the telephone book.

When you classify, you arrange information in categories or break large categories into smaller ones. Classifying is a basic thinking skill that good readers use to understand the information they read. Classification is also a tool for mentally storing knowledge, such as details about each of the Greek gods.

The "cards" displayed on pages 801–803 present information about the twelve Olympians that has already been classified into categories such as family ties, symbols, and weapons. This classification allows you to quickly locate information about these gods. For example, quickly scan the cards to find the answers to these questions:

- What nicknames does Athena have?

- What symbol is associated with Aphrodite?

- Which god has the Roman name of Vulcan?

Activity Options

1. Play a game that will test how quickly you can locate information that is classified. Choose one person to be the moderator, and divide the rest of the class into teams of four or five students. Each team should prepare ten questions about the Olympians that can be answered by studying pages 801–803. (You can use the questions provided above as models.) When one team reads a question aloud, the first opposing team that answers correctly wins a point. After all the questions have been answered, the team with the most points wins.

2. In a small group, choose ten characters from this book and classify information about them on cards similar to the ones used to describe the twelve Olympians. Use your cards as a basis for a group discussion that compares and contrasts these characters.

Writing Workshop

Grecian Getaway

Assignment Imagine that you have been given the job of persuading travelers to take a vacation trip that visits places mentioned in the *Odyssey*.

WRITER'S BLUEPRINT

Product   A travel brochure

Purpose   To sell a prepackaged tour

Audience   People who like to travel

Specs   As the creator of a successful brochure, you should:

❑ Give a description of the stops on the tour, which will visit places mentioned in the **Odyssey**.

❑ Include a map showing the various stops along the way and a day-by-day schedule, list of activities, transportation, lodging and eating arrangements, and advice on what to pack.

❑ Make your brochure as persuasive as you can. You might include quotes from the text and make up testimonials from Odysseus, Circe, and other characters telling how exciting and enriching this tour will be.

❑ Combine eye-catching illustrations with the writing to create an enticing design.

❑ Use a persuasive, enthusiastic tone throughout.

❑ Follow the rules of grammar, usage, spelling, and mechanics. Be sure to capitalize proper nouns and proper adjectives correctly.

STEP 1 PREWRITING

Create an itinerary. Review the literature and the map on page 769 with a partner and choose places along Odysseus's route for a vacation tour. Create a rough sketch of a map showing the various stops. Use your map to make an itinerary, like the one shown.

Tour Itinerary

Where	Day 1: Ithaca	Day 2:
Description from text	"A rocky isle, but good for a boy's training." page 736, line 10	
Ideas for tourist activity	Survival course; cross-country hike	
Persuasive slogan, testimonial, or quote	Visit the place Odysseus himself called "more dear."	

Visit a travel agency and pick up travel brochures. (While you're at it, see if you can get a travel agent to come and talk to your class.) Maybe you can even find a description of a tour to Greece.

Make a rough model of your brochure. Here is one way to do this. Fold a piece of notebook paper in thirds to create a brochure with six panels (three panels on the front, three on the back). This will serve as a model where you can make notes and rough sketches.

Use the front panel as an enticing cover. Use the inside panels to describe the itinerary, including travel times, transportation, food, and lodging. Use the back panel to show the company logo and address.

STEP 2 DRAFTING

Before you draft, review the Writer's Blueprint and your prewriting materials. Here are some ideas to help you as you begin writing.

- Write with precise, descriptive words so that each panel conveys as much information as possible in a limited space. Consult the brochures you obtained from the travel agency.

- Visualize each stop on the tour as you write about what your readers will find appealing about that location.

- Write with an enthusiastic tone that will help persuade travelers to take your tour. See the Revising Strategy in Step 3 of this lesson.

As you draft, keep your illustrations in mind. Remember, your writing and visuals will have to work together. Keep the travel brochures open in front of you for inspiration.

As you draw your final illustrations, be sure to leave enough space to accommodate the writing.

COMPUTER TIP
Use clip art or a drawing program to help illustrate your brochure.

Ask a partner for comments on your draft before you revise it.

✔ Would this brochure persuade readers to visit places mentioned in the *Odyssey*? How could I make it more persuasive?

✔ Did I include a map and a list of activities?

✔ Have I used a persuasive, enthusiastic tone throughout?

Revising Strategy

Using an Enthusiastic Tone

Tone reflects a writer's attitude toward the subject or audience. A travel brochure should show the writer's enthusiasm for the subject (the destination) and the audience (the traveler). A neutral tone isn't fitting for something like a travel brochure. How has the writer's choice of words made the tone in the revised version more enthusiastic and engaging?

NEUTRAL While in Ithaca, you can walk along the rocky coastline and observe the historic sights along the way.

REVISED Picture yourself in historic Ithaca, enjoying an invigorating hike along the rugged, scenic coastline.

When you revise, make sure you use a tone that reflects enthusiasm. Notice how the writer of the student model revised with this idea in mind.

Next we come to Olympus, ~~a mountain of trees.~~ *an inviting mountain of majestic trees* In the center is a ^*magnificent* mansion where we can stay for the evening. While at Olympus we will visit Persephone. There we will ~~have~~ *enjoy a feast of* milk, honey sweet wine, water, and white barley.

STUDENT MODEL

STEP **4** EDITING

Ask a partner to review your revised draft before you edit. Be sure to capitalize proper nouns and proper adjectives correctly.

Editing Strategy

Proper Nouns and Proper Adjectives

When you edit your brochure, make sure you've capitalized proper nouns and proper adjectives.

FOR REFERENCE
For more tips on capitalizing proper nouns and adjectives, see the Language and Grammar Handbook.

- Capitalize words that name a particular person, place, or thing. Capitalize only the important words in a two-or-more-word noun:

  Circe   **Aegean Sea**   **Fun and Sun Cruises**

- Capitalize proper adjectives—but not the nouns they modify.

  the Greek isles   **Athenian culture**   **Greek architecture**

STEP **5** PRESENTING

- Present the highlights of your brochure to the class as if you were a travel agent addressing a group of potential customers.

- Send your brochure to a local travel agency and ask for comments.

STEP **6** LOOKING BACK

Self-evaluate. Look back at the Writer's Blueprint and give your paper a score for each item, from 6 (superior) to 1 (inadequate).

Reflect. Write your responses to these questions.

✔ Which do you think was the more persuasive advertising tool in your brochure, your words or your illustrations? Why?

✔ Now that you've created your brochure, where would you like to spend your next vacation and what would you like to do there?

For Your Working Portfolio Add your brochure and your reflection responses to your working portfolio.

Beyond Print

Looking at Paintings

Artists are often inspired by the work of other artists. Sometimes an artist re-creates and reinterprets an existing piece of art as a way to both pay tribute to the earlier work, and to explore new dimensions of the original idea or form. As you can see here, the two paintings on these pages depict the same scene from the *Odyssey:* Odysseus (or Ulysses) returning home to Penelope. The Romare Bearden piece on the right is clearly modeled after the Bernardino Pintoricchio piece below. By comparing the two paintings, you can reach a deeper understanding of each individual work. Some of the elements to consider in your comparison are the following: the subject matter, the media or materials used to make the painting, and the composition.

Subject Matter Both of these works tell a story. Do they tell the same story? Do they tell it in the same way? Notice that the same number of people appear in both paintings. What is similar and different about the way they are portrayed?

Choice of Media Pintoricchio's painting is a fresco, a watercolor painting done on fresh plaster. Bearden's painting is a serigraph (ser′ə graf), a handmade print produced by pressing different colors of oil paint through a series of silk screens. How do these different choices of media affect the level of detail in each painting?

Composition Study the colors, shapes, and objects in each painting. In some ways, the two works are quite similar. For instance, in both pictures the loom separates Penelope from

Bernardino Pintoricchio, scene from the *Odyssey* (1509). Fresco, 125.5 cm. x 150 cm. ▼

Romare Bearden, *The Return of Ulysses* (1976). Serigraph on paper, 18.5 in. x 22.5 in. ➤

Odysseus and the other men in the painting. How does this separation fit the story of the *Odyssey?* Also, in both works the ship centers the picture and leads your eyes up and out, while the cat at the bottom balances the ship at the top. There are also significant differences, however, in the composition of each painting. Notice how the use of color is quite different. How do the colors affect the mood of each painting? You might also compare the sizes of the paintings. (You will have to know how to convert inches and centimeters to do this!) How do you think the size of each painting would affect your overall impression of each work?

Activity Options

1. Imagine you must choose one of these paintings to illustrate a new edition of the *Odyssey.* Explain which work appeals to you more, referring to the elements described above to defend your choice.

2. Choose a work of art that interests you, perhaps one of the illustrations in this book. Let that work inspire the creation of your own piece of art, whether a drawing, painting, sculpture, or something else. Be prepared to discuss how elements in your piece were influenced by the work that inspired you.

Multicultural Connections

Choice

The Long Way Home Cultural values may affect the choices we make in life. In the *Odyssey*, cultural values about honor, heroism, and loyalty influence some of the choices Odysseus makes as he struggles to return home.

■ What cultural values may have prompted Odysseus's decision to seek out and confront the Cyclops?

■ How do you think Odysseus's decision to slaughter the suitors might have reflected the cultural values of the ancient Greeks?

Activities

Work in small groups on the following activities.

1. Choose at least three authors or characters you have encountered in this book who were faced with some kind of choice. On a chart like the following, list who the character was, what the choice was, and what values or beliefs influenced the character's decision.

Name of author or character	Choice that was made	Values/beliefs that influenced the decision
Gary Paulsen *(Woodsong)*	He decided not to shoot the bear in his yard.	Respect for nature; sense of fairness

2. Find several news stories about ordinary people who have performed acts of heroism: saving someone from a fire, speaking out against racism or hate crimes, providing medical help on a battlefield, etc. After reading interviews and articles about these people, discuss what kinds of values influenced their decisions to act in a heroic way.

Independent and Group Projects

Writing

Epic Attempts Now that you have read portions of the *Odyssey*, an epic poem, try writing an epic poem yourself. Choose an exciting event, real or imaginary, that you will tell about in a long narrative poem. For an extra challenge, mimic the form used by Robert Fitzgerald in his translation of the *Odyssey* and write in blank verse—unrhymed lines of iambic pentameter.

Art

Comic Adventures Draw a series of cartoon panels depicting one of the episodes from the *Odyssey*. Study some comic books for ideas on how to convey a sense of adventure and high-speed action in your drawings. Display your work on a poster or in booklet form.

Research

Boat Business Even before Homer's day, sea voyages had an important economic role in coastal communities. Do some research about the shipping industry today. What kinds of goods are transported by boat? What costs are involved in building and operating a shipping fleet? What are the risks? Are there still pirates on the high seas? Present the results of your research in an oral report.

Drama

Drama at Sea With a small group, present a Reader's Theater version of one of the episodes from the *Odyssey*. After selecting an episode, assign each speaking part to a different member of your group and choose a narrator. While no memoriza___ ___ necessary, each person should practice reading his or her p_____ ___and with appropriate expression. To present the epi___ facing your audience and read the episode al___ end, with each person reading his or her cha___

Glossaries, Handbooks, and Indexes

Glossary of Literary Terms

Words within entries in SMALL CAPITAL LETTERS refer to other entries in the Glossary of Literary Terms.

A

alliteration (ə lit′ə rā′shən), the repetition of consonant sounds at the beginnings of words or within words, particularly in accented syllables. It can be used to reinforce meaning, unify thought, or create a musical effect. "The sand slid silently into the sea" is an example of alliteration.

   See also SOUND DEVICES.

allusion (ə lü′zhən), a brief reference to a person, event, or place, real or fictitious, or to a work of art. "Theme for English B" (page 180) contains an allusion to blues singer Bessie Smith.

analogy (ə nal′ə jē), a comparison made between two objects, situations, or ideas that are somewhat alike but unlike in most respects. Frequently an unfamiliar or complex object or idea will be explained through comparison to a familiar or simpler one. In "Architecture as Sculpture" (page 459), Maura Donnelly draws an analogy between architecture and sculpture.

antagonist (an tag′ə nist), a character in a story or play who opposes the chief character or PROTAGONIST. In "The Most Dangerous Game" (page 18), General Zaroff is the antagonist.

assonance (as′n əns), the repetition of similar vowel sounds followed by different consonant sounds. It is often used instead of RHYME. *Fade* and *stayed* are examples of rhyme; *fade* and *pale,* examples of assonance.

   See also SOUND DEVICES.

autobiography *See* BIOGRAPHY.

B

ballad, a NARRATIVE song or poem passed on in the oral tradition. It often makes use of REPETITION and DIALOGUE. If the author of a ballad is unknown, it is called a *folk ballad;* if the author is known, it is called a *literary ballad.*

biography, an account of a person's life. "A Lincoln Preface" (page 642) is an example of biography. Autobiography is the story of all or part of a person's life written by the person who lived it. Maya Angelou's "Graduation" (page 610) is an example of autobiography. MEMOIR is a form of autobiography.

blank verse, unrhymed IAMBIC PENTAMETER, a line of five feet, or ten syllables. Much of *Romeo and Juliet* (page 481) is written in blank verse.

C

characterization (kar′ik tər ə zā′shən), the methods an author uses to develop characters. An author may directly describe characters' personality or physical appearance, as in "The Scarlet Ibis" (page 134). An author may reveal characters through their actions and speech, as in "My Delicate Heart Condition" (page 107), or through their thoughts, as in "The Secret Life of Walter Mitty" (page 650). Or an author may reveal characters through the reactions of others, as in "The Man to Send Rain Clouds" (page 161).

climax, the turning point in a story or play when the central problem or CONFLICT in the PLOT is most intense or exciting. In "Checkouts" (page 47), the problem to be solved is whether the girl and the bag boy will meet again. The climax occurs when they see each other a second time but do not speak. Not every story or play has a dramatic climax. Sometimes a character may simply resolve a problem in his or her mind. At times there is no RESOLUTION of the PLOT; the climax may come when a character realizes that a resolution is impossible.

comedy, a play written primarily to amuse the audience. In addition to arousing laughter, comic writing often appeals to the intellect. "The Inspector-General" (page 690) is a comedy.

comic relief, an amusing episode in a serious or tragic literary work, especially a DRAMA, that is introduced to relieve tension. In *Romeo and Juliet* the Nurse provides comic relief in Act 2, Scene 5.

conflict, the struggle between two opposing forces. The four basic kinds of conflict are these: 1. a person against another person or ANTAGONIST, as in "Rules of the Game" (page 6); 2. a person against nature, as in the excerpt from *Woodsong* (page 682); 3. a person against society, as in "I Chose to Remain" (page 186); and 4. two elements within a person struggling for mastery, as in "The Struggle to Be an All-American Girl" (page 672).

connotation (kon′ə tā′shən), the emotional associations surrounding a word, as opposed to the word's literal meaning or DENOTATION. Some connotations are fairly universal, others quite personal. In Nikki Giovanni's poem "Knoxville, Tennessee" (page 344), the connotations of the words that help to describe summer are quite personal.

consonance (kon′sə nəns), the repetition of consonant sounds that are preceded by different vowel sounds. Consonance may occur within a line as well as at the end of lines.

> Within our be*d*s awhile we hear*d*
> The win*d* that roun*d* the gables roare*d*,
> With now and then a ru*d*er shock,
> Which ma*d*e our very be*d*stea*d*s rock.
> Whittier, from "Snowbound"

Consonance is an effective device for linking sound, MOOD, and meaning.
See also SOUND DEVICES.

D

denotation (dē′nō tā′shən), the strict, literal meaning of a word.
See also CONNOTATION.

dialect, a form of speech characteristic of a particular region or class, differing from the standard language in pronunciation, vocabulary, and grammatical form. "Nameless, Tennessee" (page 445) contains several examples of dialect.

dialogue, conversation between two or more people in a literary work. Dialogue can develop CHARACTERIZATION, as in "The Open Window" (page 90); create MOOD, as in "The Cask of Amontillado" (page 38); advance PLOT, as in "The Adventure of the Speckled Band" (page 696); and develop

THEME, as in the excerpt from *When Heaven and Earth Changed Places* (page 632).

diary, a record of daily happenings and inner thoughts that is written by a person for his or her own use.

diction, an author's choice of words and phrases in a literary work. Diction may be casual or formal, simple or complex, old-fashioned or modern.

drama, a literary work, written to be acted, that tells a story through the speech and actions of the characters. A drama may be a TRAGEDY, such as *Romeo and Juliet* (page 481), or a COMEDY, such as "The Inspector-General" (page 690).

E

end rhyme, the rhyming of words at the ends of lines of poetry, as in "Fire and Ice" (page 183).
See also RHYME *and* INTERNAL RHYME.

epic, a long NARRATIVE poem (originally handed down in oral tradition—later a literary form) dealing with great heroes and adventures; having a national, world-wide, or cosmic setting; involving supernatural forces; and written in a deliberately ceremonial STYLE. The *Odyssey* by Homer (page 734) is an epic.

epic hero, the main character in an EPIC, who is a courageous force for good, is frequently on a quest, and must overcome great odds. An epic hero often has a series of adventures while traveling. In the *Odyssey,* Odysseus is an epic hero.
See also HERO.

epitaph (ep′ə taf), a short statement written in memory of a dead person, often inscribed on a tombstone.

epithet (ep′ə thet), a descriptive expression, usually mentioning a quality or attribute of the person or thing being described. In the *Odyssey,* Homer describes Odysseus through epithets such as "the man skilled in all ways of contending" (page 782) and "the wiliest fighter of the islands" (page 783).

essay, a prose composition that presents a personal viewpoint. An essay may present a viewpoint through formal analysis and argument, as in "What True Education Should Do" (page 671), or it may be more informal in style, as in "Breaking the Ice" (page 59).

extended metaphor, a comparison that is developed at great length, often through a whole work or a great part of it. It is common in POETRY but is used in PROSE as well. "Two Views of the Mississippi" (page 676) is an example of extended metaphor.
See also METAPHOR.

F

fable, a brief TALE in which the characters are often animals, told to point out a moral truth.

falling action, the events leading toward the resolution of a PLOT, which take place after the CLIMAX.

fantasy, a work that takes place in an unreal world, concerns incredible characters, or employs fictional scientific principles. "The Rule of Names" (page 78) is fantasy.
See also SCIENCE FICTION.

fiction, a type of literature drawn from the imagination of the author that tells about imaginary people and happenings. NOVELS and SHORT STORIES are forms of fiction.

figurative language, language used in a nonliteral way to express a suitable relationship between essentially unlike things, in order to furnish new effects or fresh insights. The more common figures of speech are SIMILE, METAPHOR, PERSONIFICATION, and HYPERBOLE.

flashback, interruption of the NARRATIVE to show an episode that happened before that particular point in the story. In *The Miracle Worker* (page 254), the author makes use of flashbacks to reveal Annie Sullivan's past.

folk literature, a type of early literature that has been passed orally from generation to generation and written down some centuries later. The authorship of folk literature, which includes MYTHS, FABLES, fairy tales, EPICS, and LEGENDS, is unknown.

foot, a group of syllables in VERSE usually consisting of one accented syllable and one or more unaccented syllables. A foot may occasionally have two accented syllables or two unaccented syllables. In the following lines the feet are separated by slanted lines:

> At mid-/night, in/the month/of June,/
> I stand/beneath/the mys-/tic moon.
> > Poe, from "The Sleeper"

The most common line lengths are five feet (pentameter), four feet (tetrameter), and three feet (trimeter). The lines quoted above are iambic tetrameter.
See also RHYTHM *and* IAMBIC PENTAMETER.

foreshadowing, a hint or clue given to the reader of what is to come. In "The Adventure of the Speckled Band" (page 696), the reader begins to suspect as early as paragraph 9 that some sinister events are about to take place.

free verse, a type of poetry written with RHYTHM and other poetic devices but without a fixed pattern of METER and RHYME. "Slam, Dunk, & Hook" (page 54) is free verse.

G

genre (zhän′rə), a form or type of literary work. For example, the SHORT STORY and POETRY are two literary genres.

H

hero, the central character in a NOVEL, SHORT STORY, DRAMA, or other work of fiction. When the central character is a woman, she is sometimes called a *heroine.*
See also EPIC HERO.

humor, in literature, writing whose purpose is to amuse or to evoke laughter. Humorous writing can be sympathetic to human nature or satirical. "Breaking the Ice" (page 59) is a humorous ESSAY.

hyperbole (hī pėr′bə lē), a figure of speech involving great exaggeration. The effect may be serious or comic. For example, in "My Delicate Heart Condition," the main character, on her way to a circus tent, says there were "at least a million stands selling . . . jawbreakers and gingerbread and sweet potato pie. . . ."

See also FIGURATIVE LANGUAGE.

I

iambic pentameter (ı am′bik pen tam′ə tər), a verse line of five metrical feet. Each FOOT has an unaccented syllable followed by an accented syllable. The following lines, which portray the tired journey home of cattle and plowman after a long day, are in iambic pentameter:

The low-/ing herd/wind slow-/ly o'er/the lea.
The plow-/man home-/ward plods/his wear-/y
way. . . .

Gray, from "Elegy Written in a
Country Churchyard"

Much of *Romeo and Juliet* (page 481) and the Fitzgerald translation of the *Odyssey* (page 734) is written in iambic pentameter.

idiom (id′ē əm), an expression whose meaning cannot be understood from the ordinary meaning of the words in it. For example, "to rub elbows" means to mingle with other people.

imagery (im′ij rē), concrete words or details that provide vividness in a literary work. Imagery tends to arouse emotions or feelings in a reader that abstract language does not. The poem "I Am Singing Now" (page 405) contains vivid imagery that describes a ride home through the desert on a moonlit night.

inference (in′fər əns), reasonable conclusion about the behavior of a character or the meaning of an event, drawn from the limited information presented by the author.

internal rhyme, the rhyming of words or accented syllables within a line that may or may not have a RHYME at the end as well: "We three shall flee across the sea to Italy."

irony (ī′rə nē), the term used to describe a contrast between what appears to be and what really is. In *verbal irony,* the intended meaning of a statement or work is different from (often the opposite of) what the statement or work literally says. *Irony of situation* refers to an occurrence that is contrary to what is expected or intended. *Dramatic irony* refers to a situation in which events or facts not known to a character are known to the audience or reader. For example, in *Romeo and Juliet*, the audience knows Romeo has killed Tybalt before Juliet knows it.

J

journal, a formal record of a person's daily experiences. It is less intimate or personal than a DIARY and more chronological than an AUTOBIOGRAPHY.

L

legend, a story handed down from the past, often associated with some period in the history of a people. A legend differs from a MYTH in that it may contain some historical truth and refer less to supernatural events.

M

memoir (mem′wär), a form of AUTOBIOGRAPHY, a record of one's own experiences. A memoir may not have the chronological structure of many autobiographies. Sometimes a memoir is more concerned with personalities, events, and actions of public importance than with the private life of the writer. "Alligator" (page 361) is an example of memoir.

metaphor, a figure of speech involving an implied comparison between two unlike things. This comparison may be stated (She was a stone) or implied (Her stony silence filled the room).

See also SIMILE and FIGURATIVE LANGUAGE.

meter, the pattern of stressed and unstressed syllables in POETRY.

See also RHYTHM, FOOT, and IAMBIC PENTAMETER.

mood, the overall atmosphere or emotional aura of a work. Words such as *gloomy, calm, sad*, and *joyful* can be used to describe mood.

moral, the lesson or inner meaning to be learned from a FABLE, TALE, or other story.

motivation, the portrayal of circumstances and aspects of personality that makes a character's actions and reactions believable. In "The Gift of the Magi" (page 584), the characters are motivated by love and concern for each other.

mystery, a work of FICTION that contains a puzzling problem or an event not explained until the end, so as to keep the reader in SUSPENSE. "The Adventure of the Speckled Band" (page 696) is a mystery.

myth, a traditional story connected with the religion of a people, usually attempting to account for something in nature. A myth has less historical background than a LEGEND.

N

narrative, a story or account of an event or a series of events. It may be told either in POETRY or in PROSE, and it may be either fictional or true. "The Most Dangerous Game" (page 18) is a narrative, as is the *Odyssey* (page 734).

narrator, the teller of a story. The teller may be a character in the story, as "My Delicate Heart Condition" (page 107); an anonymous voice outside the story, as in "The Open Window" (page 90); or the author, as in "The Last Word" (page 358).
See also POINT OF VIEW.

nonfiction, any type of writing that deals with real people and happenings. BIOGRAPHY, ESSAY, and history are types of nonfiction.

novel, a long work of NARRATIVE fiction dealing with characters, situations, and SETTINGS that imitate those of real life. Among the authors in this text who have written novels are Stephen King, Ursula Le Guin, Ernest Hemingway, and Amy Tan.

O

onomatopoeia (on′ə mat′ə pē′ə), a word or words used in such a way that the sound imitates the sound of the thing spoken of. Some single words in which sound suggests meaning are *hiss, smack, buzz, murmur,* and *hum.* The italicized words in the following lines all imitate the sounds

associated with them.

> *Bang-whang-whang* goes the drum,
>   *tootle-te-tootle* the fife,
> Oh, a day in the city square, there is no
>   such pleasure in life!
>   Browning, from "Up at a Villa—Down
>   in the City"

See also SOUND DEVICES.

P

personification (pər son′ə fə kā′shən), the representation of abstractions, ideas, animals, or inanimate objects as if alive, as in the poem "Tiburón" (page 434), in which a car is made to seem alive.
See also FIGURATIVE LANGUAGE.

play *See* DRAMA.

plot, in the simplest sense, a series of happenings in a literary work. The term is also used to refer to the action as it is organized around a CONFLICT and builds to a CLIMAX followed by a RESOLUTION.

poetry, a type of literature that creates an emotional response. The response is achieved by the imaginative use of words patterned to produce a desired effect through RHYTHM, sound, and meaning. Poetry may be rhymed or unrhymed.

point of view, the author's choice of a narrator for a story. The story may be related by a character (the *first-person* point of view), as in "The Scarlet Ibis" (page 134); or the story may be told by a NARRATOR who does not participate in the action (the *third-person* point of view), as in "The Necklace" (page 97). A third-person narrator may be *omniscient* (om nish′ənt)—able to see into the minds of all characters. Or the third-person narrator may be *limited*—confined to a single character's perceptions, as in "The Stolen Party" (page 171). An author who describes only what can be seen, like a newspaper reporter, is said to use an *objective* point of view.

prose, the ordinary form of spoken or written language. Almost any literature that is not POETRY is prose.

protagonist (prō tag′ə nist), the leading character in a literary work. Rainsford is the protagonist of "The Most Dangerous Game" (page 18).

See also ANTAGONIST.

pun, a play on words; a humorous use of a word that has different meanings *(bear/bear),* or of two or more words with the same or nearly the same sound but different meanings *(right/write).* In the opening scene of *Romeo and Juliet,* Capulet's servants pun on words such as *choler* and *collar.*

R

repetition, a poetic device in which a sound, word, or phrase is repeated for style and emphasis, as in "The Tide Rises, the Tide Falls" (page 799), where the repeated lines imitate the motion of the tides.

See also SOUND DEVICES.

resolution (rez′ə lü′shən), the part of a PLOT following the CLIMAX in which the complications are resolved or settled. In "The Necklace" (page 97), the resolution occurs when Mme. Loisel meets her old friend, Mme. Forestier, and learns the truth about the necklace.

rhyme, the exact repetition of sounds in at least the final accented syllables of two or more words.

See also END RHYME, INTERNAL RHYME, *and* SOUND DEVICES.

rhyme scheme, any pattern of rhyme in a poem. The rhyme scheme of a poem can be shown by using a different letter of the alphabet for each END RHYME. For example, the rhyme scheme of "The Courage That My Mother Had" (page 353) is *abab cdcd efef.*

rhythm, the arrangement of stressed and unstressed sounds into patterns in speech or writing. Rhythm, or METER, may be regular, as in "My Papa's Waltz" (page 351), or it may vary within a line or work, as in "Jazz Fantasia" (page 403).

See also SOUND DEVICES.

rising action, the part of a PLOT that leads up to the CLIMAX. In rising action, the complication caused by the CONFLICT of opposing forces is developed.

S

satire (sat′īr), the technique that employs wit to ridicule a subject, usually some social institution or human foible, often with the intention of inspiring reform. "The Inspector-General" (page 690) is an example of a satire.

science fiction, a fictional literary work that uses scientific and technological facts and theories as a basis for stories about such subjects as extraterrestrial beings, adventures in the future or on other planets, and travel through space and time. "The Rocket" (page 451) is an example of science fiction.

See also FANTASY.

setting, the time (both time of day or season and period in history) and place in which the action of a NARRATIVE occurs. The setting may be suggested through DIALOGUE and action, or it may be described by the NARRATOR or one of the characters. Setting contributes strongly to the MOOD, atmosphere, and plausibility of a work.

short story, a short prose NARRATIVE that is carefully crafted and usually tightly constructed.

simile (sim′ə lē), a figure of speech involving a direct comparison, using *like* or *as,* between two basically unlike things that have something in common, as in "The Runaway" (page 435), in which a colt is compared to a shadow.

See also FIGURATIVE LANGUAGE.

soliloquy (sə lil′ə kwē), a speech made by an actor when alone on the stage. It reveals the actor's thoughts and feelings to the audience but not to the other characters in the play. Juliet has a soliloquy at the beginning of Act 3, Scene 2 of *Romeo and Juliet.*

sound devices, the techniques an author uses to enhance the sound of a work when it is read aloud. Sound devices include ALLITERATION, ASSONANCE, CONSONANCE, ONOMATOPOEIA, REPETITION, RHYME, and RHYTHM.

speaker, the person who is speaking in a poem. In "Like Bookends" (page 354), the speaker is probably a teenage son or daughter.

stage directions, directions given by the author of a PLAY to indicate the action, costumes, SETTING, arrangement of the stage, and so on. For examples of stage directions, see *The Miracle Worker* (page 254), where they are printed in italic type.

stanza, a group of lines that are set off and form a division in a poem.

stereotype (ster′ē ə tīp′), a conventional character, PLOT, or SETTING that possesses little or no individuality. "The Secret Life of Walter Mitty" (page 650) pokes fun at the stereotype of a dashing hero.

style, the distinctive handling of language by an author. It involves the specific choices made with regard to words and phrases, sentence structure, FIGURATIVE LANGUAGE, and so on. For a comparison of two different styles, see "Rules of the Game" (page 6) and "The Open Window" (page 90).

suspense, any device used by an author to maintain a reader's interest or heighten anxiety. The reader of "The Adventure of the Speckled Band" (page 696) is kept in suspense by not learning what the speckled band is until the end of the story.

symbol, a person, place, event, or object that has a meaning in itself but suggests other meanings as well. Many symbols, such as a national flag, have a common meaning. Writers use symbols that are more personal to help them express a memory, a THEME, or a feeling. For example, in "A Christmas Memory" (page 365), a "lost pair of kites" becomes a symbol for the narrator and his elderly friend.

T

tale, a spoken or written NARRATIVE, usually less complicated than a SHORT STORY. "The Ghostly Rhyme" (page 232) is a tale.

theme, the underlying meaning of a literary work. A theme may be directly stated but more often is implied. A work may have a number of themes, and the interpretation of these themes is often influenced by a reader's personal experience. In "The Scarlet Ibis" (page 134), an important theme is the danger of selfish pride.

tone, the author's attitude, either stated or implied, toward his or her subject matter and toward the audience. Words to describe tone include these: *serious, bitter, cynical, humorous,* and *ironic.* For example, the tone of "The Courage That My Mother Had" (page 353) might be described as regretful.

tragedy, dramatic or NARRATIVE writing in which the main character suffers disaster after a serious and significant struggle, but faces his or her downfall in such a way as to attain heroic stature. *Romeo and Juliet* (page 481) is considered a tragedy because of the fate of the lovers.

V

verse, a synonym for POETRY.

Glossary of Vocabulary Words

a hat	o hot		
ā age	ō open	ch child	
ä far	ô order, all	ng long	
e let	oi oil	sh she	
ē equal	ou out	th thin	
ė term	u cup	ŦH then	
i it	ů put	zh measure	
ī ice	ü rule		

ə { a in about / e in taken / i in pencil / o in lemon / u in circus }

A

abate (ə bāt′), *v.* diminish.

abhor (ab hôr′), *v.* regard with horror or disgust; hate; detest.

abominably (ə bom′ə nə blē), *adv.* in a way that arouses disgust and hatred; detestably; horribly.

abstain (ab stān′), *v.* hold oneself back voluntarily; refrain.

abyss (ə bis′), *n.* a bottomless or very great depth; chasm.

accost (ə kôst′), *v.* approach and speak to first.

acquisition (ak′wə zish′ən), *n.* something acquired or gained; addition to an existing group.

adversary (ad′vər ser′ē), *n.* person or group on the other side in a contest; opponent.

affable (af′ə bəl), *adj.* courteous, pleasant, and gracious to others.

agitated (aj′ə tāt əd), *adj.* disturbed or upset very much.

aimlessly (ām′lis lē), *adv.* in a way that is without purpose; pointlessly.

aloof (ə lüf′), *adv.* away at a distance but within view.

ambiance (am′bē əns), *n.* surroundings; atmosphere.

amiably (ā′mē ə blē), *adv.* with a friendly attitude; peaceably.

annihilate (ə nī′ə lāt), *v.* destroy completely; wipe out of existence.

apathy (ap′ə thē), *n.* lack of interest in or desire for action; indifferent.

appallingly (ə pô′ling lē), *adv.* in a way that causes consternation and horror, dismay, or terror.

ardor (är′dər), *n.* passion; great enthusiasm; eagerness.

arresting (ə rest′ing), *adj.* catching and holding attention; striking.

articulate (är tik′yə lāt), *v.* express in words.

augment (ôg ment′), *v.* increase; add to.

avail (ə vāl′), *v.* help; benefit.

avenge (ə venj′), *v.* take revenge for or on behalf of.

aversion (ə vėr′zhən), *n.* a strong or fixed dislike; antipathy.

averted (ə vėrt′əd), *adj.* turned away or turned aside.

awry (ə rī′), *adj.* wrong; out of order.

B

baleful (bāl′fəl), *adj.* full of hurtful or deadly influence.

barbarous (bär′bər əs), *adj.* not civilized; savage.

barrage (bə räzh′), *n.* barrier of artillery fire used to hold back the enemy or to protect one's own soldiers when advancing or retreating.

belligerence (bə lij′ər əns), *n.* fighting attitude.

bemused (bi myüzd′), *adj.* confused; absorbed in thought.

benevolently (bə nev′ə lənt lē), *adv.* kindly.

betrothed (bi trōŦHd′), *n.* person engaged to be married.

bleakly (blēk′lē), *adv.* cheerlessly and depressingly.

blighted (blīt′əd), *adj.* suffering from decay, deterioration, destruction, or ruin.

bray (brā), *n.* loud, harsh cry or noise.

brazen (brā′zn), *adj.* having no shame; shameless; bold.

C

calamity (kə lam′ə tē), *n.* great misfortune; disaster.

cataclysm (kat′ə kliz′əm), *n.* violent upheaval.

cataract (kat′ə rakt′), *n.* a large, steep waterfall; a violent rush or downpour of water.

chagrin (shə grin′), *n.* a feeling of disappointment, failure, or humiliation.

chaos (kā′os), *n.* complete disorder; great confusion.

chasm (kaz′əm), *n.* deep opening or crack; gap.

chide (chīd), *v.* find fault with; scold.

commence (kə mens′), *v.* make a start, begin.

compliance (kəm plī′əns), *n.* a complying or doing as another wishes; yielding to a request or command.

compunction (kəm pungk′shən), *n.* uneasiness of mind because of wrongdoing; remorse.

condone (kən dōn′), *v.* forgive or overlook.

confiscated (kon′fə skāt′əd), *adj.* seized by authority; taken and kept.

confound (kon found′), *v.* confuse; mix up.

conglomeration (kən glom′ə rā′shən), *n.* a mixed-up mass of various things or persons; mixture.

conspicuous (kən spik′yü əs), *adj.* easily seen; clearly visible.

constrained (kən strānd′), *adj.* restrained; forced.

contemptible (kən temp′tə bəl), *adj.* deserving scorn; mean; low; worthless.

contention (kən ten′shən), *n.* an arguing; disputing; quarreling.

convene (kən vēn′), *v.* meet for some purpose; gather together; assemble.

conventionality (kən ven′shən al′ə tē), *n.* behavior that conforms to commonly accepted and approved ways.

covey (kuv′ē), *n.* a brood, or family group, of partridge, quail, etc.

croon (krün), *v.* hum, sing, or murmur in a low tone; sing in a low, sentimental voice.

crypt (kript), *n.* underground room or vault.

cunning (kun′ing), *n.* skill; cleverness.

D

decease (di sēs′), *n.* death.

decipher (di sī′fər), *v.* make out the meaning of something that is not clear.

deduce (di düs′), *v.* reach a conclusion by reasoning.

default (di fôlt′), *n.* in the absence of; lacking.

default (di fôlt′), *v.* fail to do something or to appear somewhere when due; neglect.

deflect (di flekt′), *v.* turn aside.

degenerate (di jen′ər it′), *adj.* showing a decline in physical, mental, or moral strength.

delusion (di lü′zhən), *n.* a false belief or opinion.

depreciate (di prē′shē āt), *v.* lessen the value of.

deprivation (dep′rə vā′shən), *n.* a loss.

derisive (di rī′siv), *adj.* that makes fun of; mocking; scornful.

desolate (des′ə lit), *adj.* joyless; barren, lifeless; without warmth, comfort, or hope.

desolation (des′ə lā′shən), *n.* grief, sadness; loneliness; barrenness.

despotic (des pot′ik), *adj.* having unlimited power; tyrannical.

devise (di vīz′), *v.* think out; plan.

dexterity (dek ster′ə tē), *n.* skill in using the hands or body.

dilapidated (də lap′ə dā′tid), *adj.* fallen into ruin; decayed through neglect.

diligent (dil′ə jənt), *adj.* hard-working; industrious.

din (din), *n.* a continuing loud, confused noise.

dire (dīr), *adj.* inspiring horror; dismal, oppressive.

discern (də sėrn′), *v.* see clearly; distinguish or recognize.

disconsolate (dis kon′sə lit), *adj.* without hope; forlorn; unhappy.

discord (dis′kôrd), *n.* disagreement; clashing of sounds.

discreet (dis krēt′), *adj.* very careful and sensible in speech and action; wisely cautious.

disdain (dis dān′), *n.* a feeling of scorn; a regarding with contempt.

disheveled (də shev′ əld), *adj.* not neat; rumpled; mussed; disordered.

dishevelment (də shev′əl mənt), *n.* a state of not being neat; rumpled; disordered.

disparagement (dis par′ij mənt), *n.* injurious speech; belittlement.

disperse (dis pėrs′), *v.* move in different directions; scatter.

dissolute (dis′ə lüt), *adj.* living an immoral life; loose in morals; licentious; dissipated.

dissuade (di swād′), *v.* persuade not to do something.

distraught (dis trôt′), *adj.* in a state of mental conflict or confusion.

doggedness (dô′gid nes), *n.* stubbornness.

dowry (dou′rē), *n.* money or property that a woman brings to the man she marries.

E

eccentric (ek sen′trik), *adj.* out of the ordinary; not usual; odd; peculiar.

elated (i lā′tid), *adj.* in high spirits; joyful or proud.

elicit (i lis′it), *v.* draw forth; bring out.

elixir (i lik′sər), *n.* medicine made of drugs or herbs mixed with alcohol and syrup.

eloquence (el′ə kwəns), *n.* flow of speech that has grace and force.

elude (i lüd′), *v.* slip away from; baffle.

empathy (em′pə thē), *n.* the quality or process of entering fully into another's feelings or motives, into the meaning of a work of art, etc.

endeavor (en dev′ər), *v.* make an effort; try hard.

entail (en tāl′), *v.* impose or require.

entreat (en trēt′), *v.* ask earnestly.

erroneous (ə rō′nē əs), *adj.* containing error; wrong; mistaken; incorrect.

etiquette (et′ə ket), *n.* the formal rules for governing a profession, official ceremony, or a game.

evade (i vād′), *v.* get away from; avoid by cleverness.

exalted (eg zôlt′əd), *adj.* elevated; praised; glorified.

F

famished (fam′isht), *adj.* very hungry; starving.

fanatical (fə nat′ə kəl), *adj.* unreasonably enthusiastic or zealous.

feign (fān), *v.* pretend; disguise.

festooned (fe stünd′), *adj.* decorated with strings or chains of flowers, leaves, ribbons, etc.

flail (flāl), *v.* beat; thrash.

flamboyant (flam boi′ənt), *adj.* given to display; ostentatious; showy; also, gorgeously brilliant; striking.

forage (fôr′ij), *v.* hunt or search for food.

forfeit (fôr′fit), *v.* lose or have to give up by one's own act, neglect, or fault.

formidable (fôr′mə də bəl), *adj.* causing fear or dread; inspiring awe or wonder.

frigate (frig′it), *n.* light boat propelled by sails.

frond (frond), *n.* the leaf of a fern or palm.

frugal (frü′gəl), *adj.* requiring or costing little; avoiding waste or unnecessary spending.

G

genially (jē′nyəl ē), *adv.* in a way that is smiling and pleasant; cheerful and friendly; kindly.

glisten (glis′n), *v.* shine with a twinkling light; glitter.

guile (gīl), *n.* crafty deceit; sly tricks; cunning.

guise (gīz), *n.* external appearance; costume.

H

haggard (hag′ərd), *adj.* looking worn from pain, fatigue, worry, and so on.

haggle (hag′əl), *v.* argue or dispute, especially about a price or the terms of a bargain.

harbor (här′bər), *v.* hold a thought, feeling, or intention; contain.

harried (har′ēd), *adj.* worried; having lots of problems.

humility (hyü mil′ə tē), *n.* humbleness of mind; meekness.

hysterical (hi ster′ə kəl), *adj.* excited or emotional; showing an unnatural lack of self-control.

I

imminent (im′ə nənt), *adj.* likely to happen soon; about to happen.

immoderate (i mod′ər it), *adj.* not moderate; extreme or excessive.

impending (im pen′ding), *adj.* threatening; about to occur.

imperative (im per′ə tiv), *adj.* that must be done; urgent; necessary.

imperious (im pir′ē əs), *adj.* haughty or arrogant; overbearing.

impertinent (im pėrt′n ənt), *adj.* rudely bold; impudent; insolent.

imperturbably (im′pər tėr′bə blē), *adv.* not being easily excited or disturbed; calmly.

implacable (im plā′kə bəl), *adj.* unable to be appeased; refusing to be reconciled; unyielding.

imprudence (im prüd′ns), *n.* lack of good judgment.

impudent (im′pyə dənt), *adj.* shamelessly bold; very rude and insolent.

impunity (im pyü′nə tē), *n.* freedom from punishment, injury, or other bad consequences.

inaugurate (in ô′gyə rāt′), *v.* make a formal beginning of.

incantation (in′kan tā′shən), *n.* set of words spoken as a magic charm or to cast a magic spell.

incensed (in senst′), *adj.* very angry; filled with rage.

incessantly (in ses′nt lē), *adv.* never stopping; repeating without interruption.

incredulity (in′krə dü′lə tē), *n.* disbelief; skepticism.

incredulously (in krej′ə ləs lē), *adv.* disbelievingly; skeptically.

indolently (in′dl ənt lē), *adv.* lazily.

indulgent (in dul′jənt), *adj.* making allowances; not critical; lenient.

inextricably (in ek′strə kə blē), *adv.* incapable of being disentangled.

infallibility (in fal′ə bil′ə tē), *n.* freedom from error; inability to be mistaken.

infinitely (in′fə nit lē), *adv.* in a way that is without limits; endlessly.

infirmary (in fėr′mər ē), *n.* place for the care of the sick or injured; hospital or dispensary in a school or institution.

infirmity (in fėr′mə tē), *n.* sickness; illness.

inscrutable (in skrü′tə bəl), *adj.* incomprehensible; so mysterious or obscure that one cannot make out its meaning.

insignia (in sig′nē ə), *n.* medal, badge, or other distinguishing mark of a position, honor, etc.

instigate (in′stə gāt), *v.* urge on; stir up.

insufferably (in suf′ər ə blē), *adv.* intolerably or unbearably.

intact (in takt′), *adj.* with no part missing, as if untouched; whole; uninjured.

intercession (in′tər sesh′ən), *n.* act of pleading for another person.

interim (in′tər im), *n.* time between; the meantime.

interminable (in′tėr′mə nə bəl), *adj.* endless.

interpose (in′tər pōz′), *v.* come between other things.

interred (in tėrd′), *adj.* put into a grave or tomb; buried.

intractably (in trak′tə blē), *adv.* in a hard-to-manage way; stubbornly.

intrusion (in trü′zhən), *n.* act of intruding, or coming unasked or unwanted.

intuition (in′ tü ish′ən), *n.* immediate perception of truths, facts, etc., without reasoning.

inundation (in′un dā′shən), *n.* flood.

invalid (in′və lid), *adj.* weak because of sickness or injury; infirm or sickly.

invigorating (in vig′ə rā′ting), *adj.* energizing.

ire (īr), *n.* anger; wrath.

K

kindred (kin′drid), *n.* relatives.

L

languidly (lang′gwid lē), *adv.* in a manner that is not brisk or lively; sluggishly; dully.

lanky (lang′kē), *adj.* awkwardly long and thin; tall and ungraceful.

latent (lāt′nt), *adj.* present but not active; hidden; concealed.

lavish (lav′ish), *v.* give or spend very freely or generously.

legitimate (lə jit′ə mit), *adj.* rightful; valid; logical.

lenient (lē′nyənt), *adj.* mild or gentle; not harsh or stern; merciful.

lineage (lin′ē ij), *n.* descent in a direct line from a common ancestor.

linger (ling′gər), *v.* stay on; go slowly, as if unwilling to leave.

listlessly (list′lis lē), *adv.* inactively, carelessly; languidly.

lithe (līтн), *adj.* characterized by flexibility and grace.

loathsome (lōтн′səm), *adj.* hateful; sickening.

luminous (lü′mə nəs), *adj.* bathed in or exposed to light; emitting or reflecting light.

lurk (lėrk), *v.* wait out of sight; be hidden.

M

maneuver (mə nü′vər), *v.* make a series of changes in position or direction for a specific purpose; manipulate; manage skillfully.

mangled (mang′gəld), *adj.* badly cut or torn; spoiled, ruined.

martial (mär′shəl), *adj.* warlike.

medicinal (mə dis′n əl), *adj.* having value as medicine; healing; helping; relieving.

mediocre (mē′dē ō′kər), *adj.* neither good nor bad; of average or lower than average quality; ordinary.

meditate (med′ə tāt′), *v.* think about; consider; plan.

melancholy (mel′ən kol′ē), *adj.* depressed in spirits; sad; gloomy.

meld (meld), *v.* merge; blend.

mentor (men′tər), *n.* wise and trusted advisor.

meticulous (mə tik′yə ləs), *adj.* extremely careful about details.

mirth (mėrth), *n.* merry fun; being joyous; merriment.

mnemonic (ni mon′ik), *n.* device or strategy for aiding the memory.

mollified (mol′ə fīd), *adj.* softened in temper; calmed, pacified, or appeased; mitigated.

moor (mùr), *n.* an expanse of open rolling infertile land, usually boggy and dominated by grasses.

morose (mə rōs′), *adj.* gloomy; sullen; ill-humored.

mortified (môr′tə fīd), *adj.* severely embarrassed; shamed.

mournful (môrn′fəl), *adj.* full of grief; sad; sorrowful.

mutinous (myüt′n əs), *adj.* openly rebellious against lawful authority, especially by sailors or soldiers against their officers.

N

naught (nôt), *n.* nothing; zero (also spelled *nought).*

noncommittal (non′kə mit′l), *adj.* not committing oneself; not saying yes or no.

nonplussed (non plust′), *adj.* puzzled completely; made unable to say or do anything; perplexed.

O

obstinate (ob′stə nit), *adj.* not giving in; stubborn.

ode (ōd), *n.* a lyric poem full of noble feeling.

odious (ō′dē əs), *adj.* very displeasing; offensive.

okra (ō′krə), *n.* a tall plant cultivated for its sticky pods, which are used in soups and as a vegetable.

ominous (om′ə nəs), *adj.* unfavorable; threatening.

ornate (ôr nāt′), *adj.* much adorned; much orna-mented.

P

palpable (pal′pə bəl), *adj.* that can be touched or felt; tangible.

pandemonium (pan′də mō′nē əm), *n.* wild uproar.

parched (pärchd), *adj.* hot, dry, or thirsty.

perfunctory (pər fungk′tər ē), *adj.* done for the sake of performing the duty; mechanical; indifferent.

permeate (pėr′mē āt), *v.* spread through the whole of; pass through; pervade.

pernicious (pər nish′əs), *adj.* destructive; fatal, deadly.

peruse (pə rüz′), *v.* examine in detail.

pervade (pər vād′), *v.* spread throughout.

perverse (pər vėrs′), *adj.* contrary and willful.

pittance (pit′ns), *n.* a small amount of money.

placating (plā′kāt′ing), *adj.* soothing or satisfying the anger of; appeasing.

pliant (plī′ənt), *adj.* bending easily; flexible; supple.

plunder (plun′dər), *n.* things taken by force or robbery.

pompously (pom′pəs lē), *adv.* in a self-important way.

ponderous (pon′dər əs), *adj.* very heavy.

portentous (pôr ten′təs), *adj.* indicating upcoming evil; threatening; ominous.

potent (pōt′nt), *adj.* powerful; strong.

preclude (pri klüd′), *v.* shut out; make impossible; prevent.

predator (pred′ə tər), *n.* animal that lives by preying on other animals.

predominant (pri dom′ə nənt), *adj.* having more power; most noticeable.

presentiment (pri zen′tə mənt), *n.* a feeling that something, especially something evil, is about to happen.

presumptuous (pri zump′chü əs), *adj.* acting without permission or right; too bold; forward.

prey (prā), *v.* be a strain upon; injure; irritate.

procure (prə kyür′), *v.* obtain by care or effort.

prodigious (prə dij′əs), *adj.* enormous; causing amazement or wonder.

prodigy (prod′ə jē), *n.* person endowed with amazing brilliance, talent, etc., especially a remarkably talented child.

promontory (prom′ən tôr′ē), *n.* a high point of land extending from the coast into the water; cape; headland.

prosaic (prō zā′ik), *adj.* ordinary, not exciting.

purge (pėrj), *v.* remove an undesired thing or person.

Q

quiver (kwiv′ər), *v.* shake with a light but rapid motion; shiver; tremble.

R

rebuke (ri byük′), *v.* criticize sharply; reprimand.

reclaimed (ri klāmd′), *adj.* brought back to useful, good, or fitting condition.

recoil (ri koil′), *v.* draw or shrink back.

reconcile (rek′ən sīl), *v.* settle a disagreement or difference; make peace.

redeem (ri dēm′), *v.* make up for; set free, save, or rescue.

redemptive (ri demp′tiv), *adj.* bringing about reform, freedom, or compensation; restorative.

regal (rē′gəl), *adj.* belonging to or fit for a king or queen; royal; stately; splendid; magnificent.

reiterate (rē it′ə rāt′), *v.* say or do several times; repeat again and again.

relent (ri lent′), *v.* become less harsh or cruel; become more tender and merciful.

relinquish (ri ling′kwish), *v.* give up; let go; release.

remorse (ri môrs′), *n.* sorrowful regret.

repast (ri past′), *n.* meal; food.

replica (rep′lə kə), *n.* a copy or close reproduction.

repose (ri pōz′), *n.* rest or sleep; peace, calmness.

reprieve (ri prēv′), *n.* temporary relief from any evil or trouble.

resolutely (rez′ə lüt′lē), *adv.* determinedly; firmly.

resolution (rez′ə lü′shən), *n.* decision; determination.

retort (ri tôrt′), *n.* a sharp or witty reply.

reverie (rev′ər ē), *n.* dreamy thoughts; dreamy thinking of pleasant things.

rogue (rōg), *n.* dishonest or unprincipled person; scoundrel; rascal.

ruddy (rud′ē), *adj.* red or reddish.

rummage (rum′ij), *v.* search thoroughly by moving things about.

S

sage (sāj), *adj.* wise.

sallow (sal′ō), *adj.* sickly, yellowish or brownish-yellow color.

saunter (sôn′tər), *v.* walk along slowly and happily; stroll.

savory (sā′vər ē), *adj.* pleasing in taste or smell; appetizing.

scald (skôld), *v.* burn as if with boiling water.

scavenge (skav′ənj), *v.* pick over discarded objects for things to use.

scourge (skėrj), *n.* some thing or person that causes great trouble or misfortune; affliction.

scrutiny (skrüt′n ē), *n.* close examination.

semblance (sem′bləns), *n.* outward appearance.

sepulcher (sep′əl kər), *n.* place of burial; tomb; grave.

sever (sev′ər), *v.* cut off.

shard (shärd), *n.* broken piece; fragment.

siege (sēj), *n.* long or persistent effort to overcome resistance; a long-continued attack.

simultaneously (sī′məl tā′nē əs lē), *adv.* at the same time.

slander (slan′dər), *n.* a false statement spoken with intent to harm the reputation of another.

solace (sol′is), *v.* find comfort.

solemnly (sol′əm lē), *adv.* in a serious, grave, or earnest way.

solicitously (sə lis′ə təs lē), *adv.* showing care or concern.

spontaneity (spon′tə nē′ə tē), *n.* condition of acting out of natural impulse or desire without being forced and without planning beforehand.

squall (skwôl), *n.* a sudden, violent gust of wind often accompanied by rain, snow, or sleet.

squander (skwon′dər), *v.* waste; spend foolishly.

stealth (stelth), *n.* secret or sly action.

stolid (stol′id), *adj.* not easily excited; showing no emotion; seeming dull; impassive.

streamlined (strēm′līnd′), *adj.* having a shape that offers the least resistance to air or water.

stupefied (stūp′ə fīd), *adj.* overwhelmed with shock or amazement; astounded.

submissive (səb mis′iv), *adj.* yielding to the power, control, or authority of another; obedient; humble.

subside (səb sīd′), *v.* settle down, become quiet.

succinctly (sək singkt′ lē), *adv.* expressed in a brief and clear manner; concisely.

succumb (sə kum′), *v.* give way; yield.

sullenly (sul′ən lē), *adv.* in a way that shows bad humor or anger.

surveillance (sər vā′ləns), *n.* watch kept over a person.

sweltering (swel′tər ing), *adj.* extremely and unpleasantly hot.

T

taciturn (tas′ə tėrn′), *adj.* speaking very little; not fond of talking.

taint (tānt), *v.* spoil, corrupt, or contaminate.

tangible (tan′jə bəl), *adj.* that can be touched or felt.

tedious (tē′dē əs), *adj.* long and tiring; boring; wearisome.

temperance (tem′pər əns), *n.* a being moderate in action, speech, habits, etc.; self-control.

tempest (tem′pist), *n.* violent storm or disturbance.

terrain (te rān′), *n.* the physical features of a piece of land.

thwarted (thwôrt′əd), *adj.* prevented from doing something; opposed and defeated.

tier (tir), *n.* one of a series of rows arranged one above another.

timorous (tim′ər əs), *adj.* easily frightened; timid.

titanic (tī tan′ik), *adj.* having great size, strength, or power; gigantic. The Titans were giants who ruled the world before being overthrown by Zeus and his brothers Poseidon and Hades.

transgression (trans gresh′ən), *n.* the act of breaking a law, command, commitment, etc.

travail (trə vāl′), *n.* a physical, mental, or emotional exertion; great effort; toil.

traverse (trav′ərs), *n.* the act of passing across, over, or through.

treacherous (trech′ər əs), *adj.* not reliable; deceptive.

tremulous (trem′yə ləs), *adj.* trembling; quivering.

trepidation (trep′ə dā′shən), *n.* nervous dread; fear; fright.

tussle (tus′əl), *v.* struggle or wrestle.

U

underprivileged (un′dər priv′ə lijd), *adj.* having fewer advantages than others, especially because of poverty.

unflagging (un flag′ing), *adj.* not weakening or failing.

unnerved (un nėrvd′), *adj.* deprived of nerve, firmness, or self-control.

unsavory (un sā′vər ē), *adj.* distasteful; morally offensive.

unwieldy (un wēl′dē), *adj.* heavy and awkward; bulky.

V

vacant (vā′kənt), *adj.* empty of thought or intelligence.

valor (val′ər), *n.* bravery; courage.

vermilion (vər mil′yən), *n.* a bright red.

vessel (ves′əl), *n.* a large boat; ship.

veteran (vet′ər ən), *n.* person who has had much experience in some position, occupation, etc.

vexed (vekst), *adj.* annoyed.

viable (vī′ə bəl), *adj.* usable; workable.

vice (vīs), *n.* evil, immoral, or wicked habit or tendency.

vigil (vij′əl), *n.* a staying awake for some purpose; a watching.

vile (vīl), *adj.* foul; disgusting; poor.

virtuoso (vėr′chü ō′sō), *adj.* showing the qualities of a virtuoso, a person who has a cultivated appreciation of artistic excellence.

visage (viz′ij), *n.* face; appearance or aspect.

vivacious (vī vā′shəs), *adj.* lively; sprightly; animated.

W

waft (waft), *v.* cause to move lightly by or as if by the impulse of wind or waves.

wallow (wol′ō), *v.* flounder; become or remain helpless; indulge oneself excessively.

waver (wā′vər), *v.* become unsteady; hesitate.

wayward (wā′wərd), *adj.* disobedient; willful.

wily (wī′lē), *adj.* crafty; cunning; tricky.

writhe (rīᴛʜ), *v.* twist and turn; twist about.

Language and Grammar Handbook

This Handbook will help you as you edit your writing. It is alphabetically arranged with each entry explaining a term or concept. For example, if you can't remember when to use *accept* and *except,* look up the entry **accept, except.** You'll find an explanation and an example (often from the selections in this book) of the meaning of each word.

A

accept, except The similarity in sound causes these words to be confused. *Accept* means "to take or receive; consent to receive; say yes to." It is always a verb. *Except* is most commonly used as a preposition meaning "but."

◆ The dogs went crazy with fear. . . . I went to them and petted them and soothed them and at length they accepted the fire.
from *Woodsong* by Gary Paulsen

◆ The pawns can only move forward one step, except on the first move.
from "Rules of the Game" by Amy Tan

active and passive voice A verb is said to be in the active voice when its subject is the doer of the action, and in the passive voice when its subject is the receiver of the action. A passive verb is a form of the verb *be* plus the past participle of the verb: *is* told, *had been* told, *will be* told, and so on.

ACTIVE: The drum major led the band.
PASSIVE: The band was led by the drum major.

Active verbs are more direct and forceful than passive verbs. Passive verbs are effective, however, when the doer of the action is unknown, unimportant, or obvious, or when the receiver of the action should be emphasized:

◆ At the end of our two-block alley was a small sandlot playground. . . .
from "Rules of the Game" by Amy Tan

◆ The hat is found, a straw cartwheel corsaged with velvet roses. . . .
from "A Christmas Memory" by Truman Capote

adjective Adjectives are modifiers that describe nouns and pronouns and make their meaning more exact. Adjectives tell *what kind, which one,* or *how many.*

What kind:	grey clouds	blowing snow	strong winds
Which one:	this locker	that uniform	those players
How many:	two minutes	several years	many crowds

See also **comparative forms of adjectives and adverbs.**

adverb Adverbs modify verbs, adjectives, or other adverbs. They tell *how, when,* or *where* about verbs.

How:	carefully	wisely	quickly
When:	tomorrow	now	soon
Where:	here	there	beside

See also **comparative forms of adjectives and adverbs.**

affect, effect *Affect* is a verb. It is most frequently used to mean "to influence." *Effect* is mainly used as a noun meaning "result" or "consequence."

◆ The weather is certain to affect attendance.
◆ The flames didn't get over a foot high—but the effect was immediate and dramatic.
　　　from *Woodsong* by Gary Paulsen

agreement

1. subject-verb agreement When the subject and verb of a sentence are both singular or both plural, they agree in number. This is called subject-verb agreement. Usually, singular verbs in the present tense end in *s.* Plural verbs do not have the *s* ending.

Darnell drives. (singular subject; singular verb)
Darnell and his brother drive. (plural subject; plural verb)

Pronouns generally follow the same rule. However, *I* and *you* always take plural verbs.

	Singular	Plural
1st person	I drive	we drive
2nd person	you drive	you drive
3rd person	he/she/it drives	they drive

Changes also occur with the verb *to be* in both the present and past tense.

Present Tense		Past Tense	
I am	we are	I was	we were
you are	you are	you were	you were
he/she/it is	they are	he/she/it was	they were

a. Most compound subjects joined by *and* or *both . . . and* are plural and are followed by plural verbs.

◆ A book and a candle were on the table.

b. A compound subject joined by *or, either . . . or,* or *neither . . . nor* is followed by a verb that agrees in number with the closer subject.

　　　　　　　　　S　　　　　　S　　V
◆ Neither Mark nor his cousins work there.

　　　　　　　　　　S　　　　S　　V
◆ Neither his cousins nor Mark works there.

Problems arise when it isn't obvious what the subject is. The following rules should help you with some of the most troublesome situations.

c. Phrases or clauses coming between the subject and the verb do not affect the subject-verb agreement.

　　　　　　S　　　　　　　　　　V
◆ The weeks until graduation were filled with heady activities.
　　from "Graduation" by Maya Angelou

d. Singular verbs are used with singular indefinite pronouns—*each, every, either, neither, anyone, anybody, one, everyone, everybody, someone, somebody, nobody, no one.*

　　　　　　S　　　V
◆ Neither of us has any money.

e. Plural indefinite pronouns take plural verbs. They are *both, few, many,* and *several.*

　　　　　S　　　　　　　　　　V
◆ Several of the band members are late.

f. The indefinite pronouns *all, any, most, none,* and *some* can be either singular or plural depending on their meaning in a sentence.

Singular	Plural
Some of the food *was* left.	*Some* of the guests *were* lost.
All of the wood *was* rotten.	*All* of the logs *were* burned.
None of the snow *was* removed.	*None* of the streets *were* plowed.

g. The verb agrees with the subject regardless of the number of the predicate complement (after a form of a linking verb).

　　　　　　　　　S　　　V
◆ The biggest attraction was the bears.

　　S　　　V
◆ Bears were the biggest attraction.

h. Unusual word order does not affect agreement; the verb generally agrees with the subject, whether the subject follows or precedes it.

　　　　V　　　　S
◆ Now came a maid to tip a golden jug of water into a silver finger bowl. . . .
　　from the *Odyssey* by Homer

In informal English, you may often hear sentences like "There's a book and some paper for you on my desk." *There's* is a contraction for "There is." Technically, since the subject is *a book and some paper,* the verb should be plural and the sentence should begin, "There are. . . ." Since this may sound strange, you may want to revise the sentence to something like "A book and some paper are on my desk." Be especially careful of sentences beginning with *There;* be sure the verb agrees with the subject.

◆ There ^v was a ^s chance that his cries could be heard. . . .
  from "The Most Dangerous Game" by Richard Connell

◆ There ^v are few ^s pictures of him in middle age in her album.
  from "The Last Word" by Judith Ortiz Cofer

2. Pronoun-antecedent agreement An *antecedent* is a word, clause, or phrase to which a pronoun refers. The pronoun agrees with its antecedent in person, number, and gender.

◆ My ^a mother patted the flour off her ^p hands.
  from "Rules of the Game" by Amy Tan

a. Singular pronouns are generally used to refer to the indefinite pronouns *one, anyone, each, either, neither, everybody, everyone, somebody, someone, nobody,* and *no one.*

◆ Neither ^a of the men could eat his ^p dinner.

◆ Everybody ^a brought his ^p lunch that day.

The second sentence poses problems. It is clearly plural in meaning, and *everybody* may not refer to men only. To avoid the latter problem, you could write "Everybody brought his or her ticket to the gate." This solution is clumsy and wordy, though. Sometimes it is best to revise:

◆ All students brought their lunches that day.

This sentence is now clear and nonsexist.

all right *All right* is generally used as an adjective and should always be spelled as two words.

◆ Max said that he was feeling all right.

ambiguity An ambiguous sentence is one that has two or more possible meanings. One of the most common causes of ambiguity is unclear pronoun reference.

Ambiguous: She told her sister that she would be late.

Since it is not clear who will be late, the sentence should be revised.

Clear: "I will be late," she told her sister.
Clear: "You will be late," she told her sister.

among, between *Among* implies more than two persons, places, or things. *Between* usually refers to two, followed either by a plural or by two expressions joined by *and*—not by *or.*

- Jenny was among the ten students who visited the White House.
- Shafts of sunlight slanted down between the two buildings.

See also **between you and me.**

apostrophe (') An apostrophe is used in possessive words, both singular and plural, and in contractions. It is also used to form the plurals of letters and numbers.

Paul's chess set   A's and B's   weren't

It may be used to indicate places in words in which certain letters are omitted.

- This store could give a comfortable livin', but not likely get you rich.
  from "Nameless, Tennessee" by William Least Heat Moon

appositive An *appositive* is a word or phrase that follows another word or phrase and explains it more fully. It is usually set off by commas or dashes.

- He was built solidly—big-boned—for a Vietnamese man, which meant he probably had well-fed, noble ancestors.
  from *When Heaven and Earth Changed Places* by Le Ly Hayslip

- Two assistants, Rachel and Ben, work with the librarian.

If, however, the appositive is used to specify a particular person or thing, it is not set off.

- Dad is reading a biography of Peter the Great.

as, like *See* **like, as.**

awkward writing A general term (abbreviated *awk*) sometimes used to indicate such faults as inappropriate word choice, unnecessary repetition, clumsy phrasing, confusing word order, or any other weakness or expression that makes reading difficult and obscures meaning. Many writers have found that reading their first drafts aloud helps them detect clumsy or unclear phrasing in their work. Once identified, awkward construction can almost always be improved by rethinking and rewording.

bad, badly In formal English and in writing, *bad* (the adjective) is used to modify a noun or pronoun and is used after a linking verb. *Badly* (the adverb) modifies a verb.

- She felt bad about missing the meeting. (Adjective used with linking verb *felt*)
- The play was badly performed. (Adverb modifying a verb)

HINT: To check yourself, realize that you would never say "between we." You would say "between us," *us* being the objective form of the pronoun *we*.

between you and me   After prepositions such as *between,* use the objective form of the personal pronouns: *between you and* **me,** *between you and* **her,** *between you and* **us,** *between you and* **them.**

- ◆ The decision is between you and him.
- ◆ Was the understanding between you and them?

borrow, lend   To *borrow* means to "get something from someone else with the understanding that it will be returned." To *lend* means to "let another have or use something temporarily."

- ◆ Yusef said I could borrow his stopwatch.
- ◆ "Go and find your friend Madame Forestier and ask her to lend you her jewels."
  from "The Necklace" by Guy de Maupassant

Borrow is often followed by *from*—never by *off* or *off of.*

bring, take   To *bring* means to "carry something toward." To *take* means to "carry something away."

- ◆ Ken came sliding down the low, crumbling bank about fifty yards down, and he was bringing the red blanket.
  from "The Man to Send Rain Clouds" by Leslie Marmon Silko

- ◆ She tried the jewels before the glass, hesitated, but could neither decide to take them nor leave them.
  from "The Necklace" by Guy de Maupassant

C capitalization

1. Capitalize all proper nouns and adjectives.

Proper Nouns	Proper Adjectives
Mexico	Mexican
Hawaii	Hawaiian
Japan	Japanese

2. Capitalize people's names and titles.

Dr. Jiménez	Governor Walsh
Justice Black	Aunt Rose
Rabbi Epstein	Grandpa

3. Capitalize the names of ethnic groups, languages, religions, revered persons, deities, religious bodies, buildings, and writings. Also capitalize any adjectives made from these names.

Portuguese	Jewish traditions
Asian American	Baptist
St. Mark's Church	the Koran

Language and Grammar Handbook   **837**

4. Capitalize geographical names (except for articles and prepositions) and any adjectives made from these names.

Cambodia	French doors
Mississippi River	Italian language
Padre Island	the Alamo
the Czech Republic	Canadian waters

5. Capitalize the names of structures, organizations, and bodies in the universe.

New York Public Library	Big Dipper
Golden Gate Bridge	Lincoln Memorial
the Senate	Venus
the United Nations	the Milky Way

6. Capitalize the names of historical events, times, and documents.

the Depression	Vietnam War
Gettysburg Address	Russian Revolution
the Monroe Doctrine	the Harlem Renaissance

7. Capitalize the names of months, days, holidays, and time abbreviations.

July	Friday
Memorial Day	A.M. P.M.

8. Capitalize the first letters in sentences, lines of poetry, and direct quotations.

◆ The tide rises, the tide falls,
  The twilight darkens, the curlew calls;
    from "The Tide Rises, the Tide Falls" by Henry Wadsworth Longfellow

◆ The coach said, "Practice will begin at 7 a.m."

9. Capitalize certain parts of letters and outlines.

Dear Mr. Henley,   Yours truly,

I. North American Trees
  A. Coniferous
    1. Pine
    2. Spruce
    3. Balsam
  B. Deciduous

10. Capitalize the first, last, and all other important words in titles.
See also **italics.**

book	Dickens's *David Copperfield*
newspaper	story in the *Mesa Tribune*
play and movie	starred in *Citizen Kane*
television series	liked *Friends*
short story	read "The Necklace"
music (long)	saw *Cats*
music (short)	sang "Shenandoah"
work of art	Wyeth's *From Mt. Kearsarge*
magazine	*People* magazine

clause A clause is a group of words that has a subject and a verb. A clause is independent when it can stand alone and make sense. A dependent clause has a subject and a verb, but when it stands alone it is incomplete, and the reader is left wondering about the meaning.

<u>Independent Clause</u>   <u>Dependent Clause</u>

$\overset{s}{}\quad\overset{v}{}$ $\overset{s}{}\quad\overset{v}{}$

Homer wrote the *Odyssey.*   Although Homer wrote the *Odyssey.*

colon (:) A colon is often used to explain or clarify what has preceded it.

◆ My friend shivers, too: not with cold but enthusiasm.
    from "A Christmas Memory" by Truman Capote

A colon is also used after phrases that introduce a list or quotation.

◆ I wasn't aware of not hearing until I began to wear a hearing aid at the age of thirty. It shattered my peace: shoes creaking, papers crackling, pencils tapping, phones ringing, refrigerators humming, people cracking knuckles, clearing throats, and blowing noses!
    from "Hearing the Sweetest Songs" by Nicolette Toussaint

comma (,) Commas are used to show a pause or separation between words and word groups in sentences, to avoid confusion in sentences, to separate items in addresses, in dialogue, and in figures.

NOTE: If the items in a series are all separated by *and* or *or,* no comma is necessary: Rain and wind and sleet all hampered the rescue.

1. Use commas between items in a series. Words, phrases, and clauses in a series are separated by commas.

◆ I would gather wild flowers, wild violets, honeysuckle, yellow jasmine, snakeflowers, and water lilies, and with wire grass we'd weave them into necklaces and crowns.
    from "The Scarlet Ibis" by James Hurst

2. Use a comma after certain introductory words and groups of words such as clauses and prepositional phrases of five words or more.

♦ When he opened his eyes, he knew from the position of the sun that it was late in the afternoon.
   from "The Most Dangerous Game" by Richard Connell

3. Use a comma to set off nouns of direct address. The name or title by which persons (or animals) are addressed is called a noun of direct address.

♦ After a while he said to me, "You don't have to stay in here with me, Papa, if it bothers you."
   from "A Day's Wait" by Ernest Hemingway

4. Use commas to set off interrupting elements and appositives. Any phrase or clause that interrupts the flow of a sentence is often set off by commas. Parenthetical expressions like *of course, after all, to be sure, on the other hand, I suppose,* and *as you know;* and words like *yes, no, oh,* and *well* are all set off by commas.

♦ A lady dressed in black and heavily veiled, who had been sitting in the window, rose as we entered.
   from "The Adventure of the Speckled Band" by Arthur Conan Doyle

5. Use a comma before a coordinating conjunction *(and, but, for, or, nor, yet, so)* **in a compound sentence.**

♦ Some of the fishermen let us use their smaller flats for jigging, and we could always swim or dig for clams or collect mussels.
   from "Waiting" by Budge Wilson

6. Use a comma after a dependent clause that begins a sentence. Do not use a comma before a dependent clause that follows the independent clause.

♦ If I were to sum up the romantic ambience of this date in four words, those words would be: "My mother was driving."
   from "Breaking the Ice" by Dave Barry

♦ We had to stop skating because it was getting dark.

7. Use a comma to separate items in an address. The number and street are considered one item. The state and zip code are also considered one item. Use a comma after the zip code if it is within a sentence.

Hector Cruz, 4723 Elmwood Pl., Evanston, IL 60202

Anna's address is 1332 Oak St, Columbus, OH 73215, but I don't have her phone number.

8. Use a comma to separate numerals greater than three digits.

79,000   3,500

9. Use commas in punctuating dialogue. *See* **dialogue.**

comma splice *See* **run-on sentence.**

comparative forms of adjectives and adverbs To show a greater degree of the quality or characteristic named by an adjective or adverb, *-er* or *-est* is added to the word, or *more* or *most* is put before it.

> Positive: Amy is tall.
> Comparative: Amy is taller than her sister.
> Superlative: Amy is the tallest child in the family.

More and *most* are generally used with longer adjectives and adverbs, and with all adverbs ending in *-ly.*

> Positive: The race was exciting.
> Comparative: The second race was more exciting than the first.
> Superlative: The third race was the most exciting one I have ever seen.

> ◆ Jan is more likely than Pat to enter the marathon.

The *comparative* forms are usually used in comparing two things or people, and the *superlative* in comparing more than two.

> ◆ Of the two drawings, Rachel's was the better one.
> ◆ Mrs. Forestieri is the best cook in the neighborhood.

Writers sometimes have trouble phrasing comparisons so that a reader can see immediately what things are being compared.

> Faulty: The trails in the state park are longer than Pine Woods.
> (Trails are being compared to a woods.)

> Corrected: The trails in the state park are longer than those in Pine Woods.

conjunction A conjunction is a word that links one part of a sentence to another. It can join words, phrases, or entire sentences.

D

dash (—) A dash is used to indicate a sudden break or change of thought.

> ◆ In one rolling motion—the muscles seemed to move within the skin so fast that I couldn't take half a breath—he turned and came for me.
> from *Woodsong* by Gary Paulsen

dialogue Dialogue is often used to enliven many types of writing. Notice the paragraphing and punctuation of the following passage.

> ◆ . . . at this he gave a twitch, shut his mouth, and stared at the Archipelagan. "How did you . . . learn it?" he asked very slowly.
>   Blackbeard grinned, and did not answer.
>   "Black magic?"
>   "How else?"
>   from "The Rule of Names" by Ursula Le Guin

See also **quotation marks.**

direct address *See* **comma 3.**

ellipsis (. . .) An ellipsis is used to indicate that words (or sentences or paragraphs) have been omitted. An ellipsis consists of three dots, but if the omitted portion would have completed the sentence, a fourth dot is added for the period.

> ◆ . . . From the air
>   she walked, taking the form of a tall woman. . . .
>   from the *Odyssey* by Homer

exclamation point (!) An exclamation mark is used at the end of an exclamatory sentence—one that shows excitement or strong emotion. Exclamation points can also be used with strong interjections.

F

fragment *See* **sentence fragment.**

friendly letter form A typical form for a friendly letter contains five parts: the heading, which provides the writer's address and the date, the greeting, the body of the letter, the closing, and the signature. Note the sample below.

heading ——————

> 134 River Dr.
> Cairo, IL 62914
> September 10, 1997

greeting ——————

> Dear Diana,

body ——————

> I have already started school. Have you? This year I'm taking algebra, botany, history, and English. Plus, I'm going to try out for the school orchestra. Hope I make it! I'd also like to take swimming lessons, but Mom thinks I'll be too busy to do that.
>
> Please write and let me know how school is going. We'll probably see you at Thanksgiving.

closing ——————

> Love,

signature ——————

> Lynne

G

gerund A verb form usually ending in *-ing* that is used as a noun. In the following sentence, *grieving* is the object of the preposition *with.*

> ◆ Her nights and days are wearied out with grieving.
>   from the *Odyssey* by Homer

A gerund used as the object of a preposition should be related to the subject. Otherwise the phrase will dangle.

> Dangling: After hearing the warning, the window was shut.
> Corrected: After hearing the warning, we shut the window.

good, well *Good* is used as an adjective to modify a noun or pronoun. Do not use it to modify a verb. *Well* is usually used as an adverb to modify a verb.

◆ My grandmother gave me bad advice and good advice. . . .
from "Like Mexicans" by Gary Soto

◆ My aunt asked whether I was doing well in school.

When you are referring to health, use *well* if the meaning is "not ill." If the meaning is "pleasant" or "in good spirits," use *good:*

◆ I feel really good today!

H

hopefully This is often used to mean "it is hoped," or "I hope," as in the sentence, "Hopefully she will be able to console herself." However, in formal writing, avoid this usage and follow this example:

◆ I hope that the storm will end tomorrow.

however Words like *however, moreover, nevertheless,* and *consequently,* (known as conjunctive adverbs) require special punctuation. If the word comes within a clause, it is generally set off by commas.

◆ In the last century, however, four successive heirs were of a dissolute and wasteful disposition. . . .
from "The Adventure of the Speckled Band" by Sir Arthur Conan Doyle

If the conjunctive adverb separates two independent clauses, a semicolon is used preceding the word.

◆ He can speak French; however, he rarely has the opportunity to do so.

interjection An interjection is a word or phrase used to express strong emotion. It is followed by an exclamation point.

Look out!   Oh, no! Rain!

NOTE: In handwritten or non-computer writing, use underlining to indicate italics.

italics *Italic type* is used to indicate titles of whole works such as books, magazines, newspapers, plays, films, and so on. It is also used to indicate foreign words and phrases.

◆ Just a moment, Mr. Weiderman . . . *Night of the Beast* was also great, by the way.
from *Sorry, Right Number* by Stephen King

NOTE: The correct way to respond to a question such as, "Who's there?" is "It is I." This sounds too formal in some situations, however. "It's me" is generally accepted as standard usage, although it is not correct to say, "It's them," "It's him," "It's us," or "It's her."

its, it's *Its* is the possessive form of the personal pronoun *it; it's* is the contraction meaning "it is."

◆ He pulled a faulty piston out of the machine and inserted the pen in its place.
from "The Secret Life of Walter Mitty" by James Thurber

◆ It's common to see them scare a dog into his house and take his food.
from *Woodsong* by Gary Paulsen

L

lay, lie This verb pair presents problems because, in addition to the similarity between the words, the past tense of *lie* is *lay*.

The verb *to lay* means "to put or place something somewhere."

Present	Past	Past Participle
lay	laid	(has) laid

NOTE: *Lied* refers only to not telling the truth: Many people thought he *lied* on the witness stand.

The principal parts of the verb *to lie,* which means "to rest," "to be at rest," or "to be in a reclining position," are the following:

Present	Past	Past Participle
lie	lay	(has) lain

Notice how the verbs are used in the following sentences.

◆ He lay still in the bed and seemed very detached from what was going on. (He was in a reclining position.)
   from "A Day's Wait" by Ernest Hemingway

◆ "I believe, Mr. Holmes, that you have already made up your mind," said Miss Stoner, laying her hand upon my companion's sleeve. (placing her hand on his sleeve)
   from "The Adventure of the Speckled Band" by Sir Arthur Conan Doyle

◆ Ivan laid out an evening suit. . . . (He put out an evening suit.)
   from "The Most Dangerous Game" by Richard Connell

like, as *Like* is used as a preposition in phrases of comparison. *As, as if,* and *as though* are used as conjunctions—to introduce clauses.

◆ I figured they'd be up to something so I made sure my stomach was like steel.
   from "My Delicate Heart Condition" by Toni Cade Bambara

◆ I marveled that Henry could go through with the speech as if we had a choice.
   from "Graduation" by Maya Angelou

Hint: Remember that *lose* often means the opposite of *gain.* Each word has just four letters.

lose, loose *Lose* (to lose one's way, to lose a watch) is a verb; *loose* (to come loose, loose-fitting) is an adjective.

◆ To run through the circle of dogs, toward the fire and the man was a mad gamble—a gamble that I wasn't a deer hunter, that the dogs weren't loose. . . .
   from *Woodsong* by Gary Paulsen

◆ Until late in that campaign of 1864, he expected to lose the November election. . . .
   from "A Lincoln Preface" by Carl Sandburg

M **modifier** A modifier is a word or group of words that restrict, limit, or make more exact the meaning of other words. The modifiers of nouns and pronouns are usually adjectives, participles, adjective phrases, and adjective clauses. The modifiers of verbs, adjectives, and adverbs are adverbs, adverb phrases, and adverb clauses. In the following examples, the italicized words modify the words that directly follow them in boldface type.

◆ *Nine* **days** I drifted on the *teeming* **sea** before *dangerous high* **winds.**
from the *Odyssey* by Homer

myself (and himself, herself, and so on) Be careful not to use *myself* and the other reflexive and intensive pronouns when you simply need to use the personal pronoun *I* or its objective form *me.*

Incorrect: Michael and myself are leaving tomorrow.
Correct: Michael and I are leaving tomorrow.

Incorrect: Luis walked to school with Marta and myself.
Correct: Luis walked to school with Marta and me.

HINT: When trying to decide which pronoun to use, remember that you would not say "Myself am going to the game." You would say *I.*

N **none, no one** When *none* tells how many, a plural verb is generally used.

◆ Well, now, he creeps out of his office, so none of them up there see him go.
from "The Inspector-General" by Anton Chekhov

No one is singular and is often used for emphasis.

◆ No one, absolutely no one, believes the Rangers will win tonight.

See also **agreement 1f.**

noun A noun is a word that names a person, place, thing, or idea. Most nouns are made plural by adding *-s* or *-es* to the singular. When you are unsure about a plural form, check a dictionary.

P **parallel construction** Items in a sentence that are of equal importance should be expressed in parallel (or similar) forms. These can take the form of noun phrases, verb phrases, infinitive phrases, and prepositional phrases.

◆ I have a dream that one day every valley shall be exalted, every hill and mountain shall be made low, the rough places shall be made plain, and the crooked places shall be made straight. . . .
from "I Have a Dream" by Martin Luther King, Jr.

parentheses ( ) Parentheses are used to enclose words that interrupt or add explanation to a sentence. They are also used to enclose references to page numbers, chapters, or dates. Punctuation marks that belong to the sentence come after the parentheses, not before.

Language and Grammar Handbook **845**

◆ Its two buildings (main classrooms, the grade school and home economics) were set on a dirt hill with no fence. . . .
from "Graduation" by Maya Angelou

◆ Arthur Conan Doyle (1859–1930) wrote sixty stories featuring Sherlock Holmes.

participle A participle is a verb form used in forming various tenses of verbs. The present participle ends in *-ing: growing.* The past participle usually ends in *-ed, -t, -d, -en,* or *-n: scared, kept, said, risen, blown.*

I am thinking.   We were running.   Leaves have blown away.

Participles are also used as adjectives, modifying nouns and pronouns.

◆ . . . in my bones I knew some towering brute would be upon us soon. . . .
from the *Odyssey* by Homer

NOTE: Apostrophes are not used with personal pronouns to show possession: The jewelry box is yours, but its contents are mine.

possessive case The possessive case is formed in various ways. For singular nouns and indefinite pronouns, add an apostrophe and *s.*

my sister's car   someone's shoe   everybody's grade

For plural nouns ending in an *s,* add only an apostrophe.

the doctors' offices   the babies' pool   the churches' members

However, if the plural does not end in *s,* add an apostrophe and an *s.*

◆ The children's shouts rang out in the clear, cold air.

preposition Prepositions are words such as *about, between, during, from, in, of, over, through, until,* and *with* that show the relationship between a noun or pronoun and some other word in a sentence.

prepositional phrase Prepositional phrases are groups of words that begin with a preposition and end with a noun or pronoun. These phrases act as modifiers and create vivid pictures for the reader. Notice the three prepositional phrases in the following sentence.

◆ The child was staring out through the open window with dazed horror in her eyes.
from "The Open Window" by Saki

HINT: When you are uncertain about whether to use a subject pronoun or an object pronoun in a sentence, take out the first pronoun to test the sentence. (You wouldn't say "The coach asked *he* to arrive early.")

pronoun Subject pronouns are used as subjects of sentences. Object pronouns can be used as direct objects, indirect objects, or objects of prepositions.

When a pronoun is used as the subject of a sentence, the pronoun is in the nominative case and is called a subject pronoun: *He* and *I* met at the movies.

Subject Pronouns

Singular	I	you	he, she, it
Plural	we	you	they

When a pronoun is used as an object, the pronoun is in the objective case and is called an object pronoun: The coach asked *him* and *me* to arrive early.

Object Pronouns

Singular	me	you	him, her, it
Plural	us	you	them

See also **agreement 2** *for pronoun-antecedent agreement.*

Q **quotation marks (" ")** Quotation marks enclose a speaker's exact words. They are also used to enclose some titles. When you use someone's exact words in your writing, use the following rules:

1. Enclose all quoted words within quotation marks.

◆ Gary Soto wrote, "I was in love and there was no looking back."

2. The first word of a direct quotation begins with a capital letter.
When a quotation is broken into two parts, use two sets of quotation marks. Use one capital letter if the quote is one sentence. Use two capital letters if it is two sentences.

◆ "What's this?" he asked, making a worried face. "Little Bay Ly doesn't want a cookie?"

from *When Heaven and Earth Changed Places* by Le Ly Hayslip

3. Use a comma between the words that introduce the speaker and the words that are quoted. Place the end punctuation or the comma that ends the quotation inside the quotation marks. Put question marks and exclamation points inside the quotation marks only if they are a part of the quotation. Begin a new paragraph each time the speaker changes.

◆ "Why?" I asked as I moved my pawn. "Why can't they move more steps?"
"Because they're pawns," he said.
from "Rules of the Game" by Amy Tan

When a quoted passage is made up of more than one paragraph, opening quotation marks are put at the beginning of each paragraph, but closing marks are put only at the end of the last paragraph. *See also* **dialogue.**

R **reflexive pronouns** Reflexive pronouns reflect the action of the verb back to the subject. An intensive pronoun adds emphasis to the noun or pronoun just named.

◆ If Henrietta wanted to make a fool of herself, it wasn't going to bother *me.* (reflexive)
from "Waiting" by Budge Wilson

◆ Only you yourself know your real feelings. (intensive)

run-on sentence A run-on sentence occurs when there is only a comma or no punctuation between two independent clauses. Separate the clauses into two complete sentences, join them with a semicolon, or join them with a comma and a coordinating conjunction.

Run-on: Jason picked up his lunch then he headed for school.
Run-on: Jason picked up his lunch, then he headed for school.

Correct: Jason picked up his lunch. Then he headed for school.
Correct: Jason picked up his lunch; then he headed for school.
Correct: Jason picked up his lunch, and then he headed for school.

Sometimes, in narrative writing, authors choose to use run-ons for effect, as in the following passage.

◆ Here's a houseful of grownups can't cope with the child, how can an inexperienced half-blind Yankee schoolgirl manage her?
from *The Miracle Worker* by William Gibson

See also **stringy sentences.**

semicolon (;) Use this punctuation mark to separate the two parts of a compound sentence when they are not joined by a comma and a conjunction.

◆ He was chosen spokesman; yet there were times he was silent. . . .
from "A Lincoln Preface" by Carl Sandburg

sentence fragment A fragment often occurs when one sentence is finished, but another thought occurs to the writer. That thought is written and punctuated as a complete sentence, even though it may be missing a subject, verb, or both.

Fragment: He spent a lot of time talking on the telephone. Especially during the evening.

Correct: He spent a lot of time talking on the telephone, especially during the evening.

As with run-ons, fragments are sometimes used by writers for effect.

◆ We were on top again. As always, again.
from "Graduation" by Maya Angelou

sit, set Use *sit* to mean "to sit down"; use *set* to mean "to put something somewhere."

Present	Past	Past Participle	Present Participle
sit	sat	had sat	is sitting
set	set	had set	is setting

◆ We had to sit at the back of the theater.
◆ Amy set her popcorn on the floor and knocked it over.

stringy sentences A stringy sentence is one in which several independent clauses are strung together with *and.* Since all the ideas seem to be treated equally, a reader may have difficulty seeing how they are related. Correct a stringy sentence by breaking it into individual sentences or changing some of the independent clauses into subordinate clauses or phrases.

Stringy sentence:	We hiked into the woods for about five miles and it began to get dark and we decided we had better turn around and we thought we were reversing our footsteps but somehow we got mixed up and became completely lost.
Corrected:	We hiked into the woods for about five miles, until it began to get dark. Then we decided we had better turn around. Although we thought we were reversing our footsteps, somehow we got mixed up. We became completely lost.

T

than, then *Than* is used to point out comparisons; *then* is used as an indicator of time. Notice the use of *than* and *then* in the following examples.

◆ Younger than she are happy mothers made.
   from *Romeo and Juliet* by William Shakespeare

◆ Then Leon painted with yellow under the old man's broad nose. . . .
   from "The Man to Send Rain Clouds" by Leslie Marmon Silko

HINT: Remember that *there* has the word *here* in it; these two words are related in that they can both be indicators of place.

their, there, they're *Their* is a possessive, *there* is an introductory word or adverb of place, and *they're* is the contraction for "they are."

◆ The last graveyard flowers were blooming, and their smell drifted across the cotton field. . . .
   from "The Scarlet Ibis" by James Hurst

◆ A great black stove is its main feature; but there is also a big round table and a fireplace. . . .
   from "A Christmas Memory" by Truman Capote

◆ I have about a dozen pupils down there now. They're from the Spanish bark *San Lucar* that had the bad luck to go on the rocks out there.
   from "The Most Dangerous Game" by Richard Connell

to, too, two *To* is a preposition that means "toward, in that direction" or is used in the infinitive form of the verb, as in "to follow" or "to run." *Too* means "also" or "more than enough." *Two* means "more than one."

◆ Are they going to stay for two more days too?

verb A verb is a word that tells about an action or a state of being. The form or tense of the verb tells whether the action occurred in the past, is occurring in the present, or will occur in the future.

verb shifts in tense Use the same tense to show two or more actions that occur at the same time.

Incorrect: Rita pays *(present)* for her ticket and went *(past)* in.

Correct: Rita paid *(past)* for her ticket and went *(past)* in.

When the verb in the main clause is in the present tense, the verb in the subordinate clause is in whatever tense expresses the meaning intended.

- ◆ Jay thinks that the movie was too long.
- ◆ Kim agrees that the acting was remarkable.

who, whom *Who* is used as a subject; *whom* is used as a direct object or the object of a preposition.

- ◆ Give the zucchini to whomever you wish.
- ◆ José couldn't decide whom to ask to the movie.
- ◆ Lisa, who is my best friend, has borrowed all my CDs.

who's, whose *Who's* is a contraction meaning "who is." *Whose* is a possessive.

- ◆ Who's the teacher with the beard and dark glasses?
- ◆ Whose frozen yogurt melted all over the chair?

would of This expression is often used mistakenly because it sounds like *would've,* the contraction for *would have.* In formal writing, write out *would have,* and you won't be confused.

- ◆ I would have cleaned my room, but I overslept.

your, you're *Your* is the possessive form of the personal pronoun *you; you're* is a contraction meaning "you are."

- ◆ "We've been all through that," she said, getting out of the car. "You're not a young man any longer."
  from "The Secret Life of Walter Mitty" by James Thurber

- ◆ "Your conversation is most entertaining," said he.
  from "The Adventure of the Speckled Band" by Arthur Conan Doyle

Index of Skills and Strategies

Writing Forms, Modes, and Processes

Reading/Thinking Strategies

Comprehension. *See* Cause and effect, Compare/contrast, Details, Draw conclusions, Fact and opinion, Main idea, *and* Visualize.

Connect, xix, xxii, xxvi, 15, 35, 44, 50, 56, 61, 81, 87, 94, 104, 113, 119, 139, 144, 145, 146, 158, 166, 176, 184, 190, 218, 229, 235, 240, 276, 298, 312, 320, 327, 330, 347, 355, 363, 377, 398, 406, 416, 430, 436, 442, 449, 458, 480, 503, 504, 525, 527, 532, 550, 552, 564, 579, 588, 620, 629, 639, 647, 655, 674, 679, 688, 693, 705, 779, 788, 792, 800

Critical thinking, 667–668. *See also* Cause and effect, Draw conclusions, Evaluate, Infer, Predict, *and* Question.

Details
  in literature, 87, 88, 95, 114, 119, 124, 125, 127, 196, 237, 384, 431, 444, 499, 607, 620, 661, 715, 730, 727, 783
  in art, 23, 43, 55, 100, 615, 654

Draw conclusions, 489, 515, 523, 531, 535, 556, 719, 722, 723, 750, 757, 717, 722

Evaluate, xix, xxi, xxiv, xxv, xxvi, xxvii, xxviii, 15, 35, 44, 50, 56, 61, 87, 94, 104, 113, 119, 145, 158, 166, 176, 229, 235, 240, 276, 298, 312, 285, 327, 347, 355, 363, 377, 398, 406, 413, 430, 436, 442, 449, 458, 504, 525, 542, 545, 549, 550, 557, 560, 579, 588, 620, 629, 639, 647, 655, 674, 679, 688, 693, 702, 714, 738, 751, 759, 770, 779, 788, 792, 800

Fact and opinion, 607

Follow directions, 66, 201

Infer, 35, 56, 87, 94, 119, 145, 158, 166, 176, 190, 218, 229, 240, 248, 276, 298, 312, 347, 377, 392, 398, 430, 442, 458, 485, 487–489, 503, 504, 511, 521, 524, 525, 527, 528, 534, 539, 543, 569, 571, 572, 576, 588, 620, 647, 688, 742, 759, 779, 788, 792, 800

Main idea, 68, 71, 190, 607, 661

Personal response, xxix, 15, 35, 44, 50, 56, 61, 87, 94, 104, 113, 119, 158, 218, 229, 230, 235, 240, 276, 298, 312, 320, 347, 355, 363, 377, 398, 406, 413, 430, 436, 442, 449, 458, 468, 504, 525, 550, 564, 579, 588, 620, 629, 639, 647, 651, 655, 674, 679, 688, 693, 714, 738, 751, 759, 770, 779, 788, 792, 800

Predict, xx, xxi, xxiii, xxiv, xxv, 35, 42, 50, 87, 94, 136, 160, 197, 203, 218, 219, 243, 253, 276, 298, 312, 504, 565, 737, 744, 768, 770, 772, 793

Preview, 17, 37

Question, xx, xxi, xxvi, xxvii, xxix, xxix, 67, 95, 133, 146, 328, 407, 476, 485, 640, 641, 657, 662, 805

Reader Response. *See* Personal response.

Reading Mini-Lessons
  cause and effect, 244
  classifying information, 805
  comparison and contrast, 593
  graphic aids, 465
  main idea and supporting details, 661
  troubleshooting strategies, 67

Review, 67, 601

Sequence, 384

Set purpose, 5, 17, 37, 46, 52, 58, 67, 68, 69, 77, 89, 96, 106, 115, 133, 147, 160, 168, 178, 185, 209, 231, 237, 253, 314, 341, 349, 357, 364, 390, 400, 407, 425, 431, 437, 444, 450, 479, 581, 609, 622, 631, 641, 649, 670, 675, 681, 689, 695, 733, 772, 794

Summarize, xxi, xxvi, xxvii, xxviii, 40, 80, 126, 131, 245, 414, 422, 471, 577, 588, 594, 674, 708, 727, 771

Use prior knowledge, 5, 17, 37, 46, 52, 58, 77, 89, 96, 106, 115, 133, 145, 147, 160, 185, 209, 231, 237, 253, 314, 341, 348, 349, 356, 357, 364, 384, 390, 407, 425, 431, 444, 525, 581, 609, 620, 622, 631, 641, 670, 675, 681, 695, 733, 794

Visualize, 67, 201, 246, 339, 420, 477, 675, 717, 807

■

Vocabulary and Study Skills

Analogies, 114, 176, 738

Antonyms, 16, 114, 176, 298, 399, 564–565, 621, 751, 779

Card catalogue, 720

Charts, 56, 69, 125, 131, 145, 159, 197, 202, 218, 229, 235, 246, 253, 312, 321, 328, 334, 335, 347, 385, 413, 420, 442, 465, 472, 579, 593, 595, 602, 620, 621, 663, 679, 714, 720, 770, 792, 812

Classifying, 805

Cliché, 400, 442

Context clues, 36, 57, 87–88, 95, 105, 159, 191, 230, 313, 320, 348, 443, 504–505, 564–565, 580, 630, 793

Diagrams, 17, 35, 89, 244, 465, 551, 565, 588, 661, 804

Dictionary, 67

Events chain, 505, 526, 551, 565. *See also* Time line.

Footnotes, 723

Glossary, 74–75, 680

Graphic aids, 465

Graphic organizers. *See* Charts, Diagrams, Graphs, Maps, Outline, Time line, Venn diagram, Webs.

Graphs, 159, 190, 465, 621

Index cards, 595

Key, 465

Keywords, 725

Library, 721, 725

Magazines, 131, 191, 348, 356, 420, 459, 719, 725

Maps, 88, 444, 462–464, 465, 769

Marginal notes, 476

Museum, 719, 721

Newspapers, 105, 131, 191, 246, 348, 420, 662–666

Note cards, 419, 423, 721

Note-taking, 201, 246, 420, 601, 657, 663

Grammar, Usage, Mechanics, and Spelling

Speaking, Listening, and Viewing

Index of Fine Art & Artists

Index of Authors and Titles

Acknowledgments

continued from page iv

171 From "The Stolen Party," by Liliana Heker, from *Other Fires: Short Fiction by Latin American Women* by Alberto Manguel. Copyright © 1982 by Liliana Heker. Translation Copyright © 1986 by Alberto Manguel. Reprinted by permission of Crown Publishers, Inc. **180** "Theme for English B" from *Collected Poems* by Langston Hughes. Copyright © 1994 by the Estate of Langston Hughes. Reprinted by permission of Alfred A. Knopf Inc. **182** "In Response to Executive Order 9066" from *Crossing with the Light* by Dwight Okita. Copyright © 1992 by Dwight Okita. Reprinted by permission of the author. **186** From *Rosa Parks: My Story* by Rosa Parks with Jim Haskins. Copyright © 1992 by Rosa Parks. Used by permission of Dial Books for Young Readers, a division of Penguin Books USA Inc. **188** "Tolerance" from *Two Cheers for Democracy*, Copyright 1951 by E.M. Forster and renewed 1979 by Donald Parry, reprinted by permission of Harcourt Brace & Company. **192** From "The Art of Diversity" by Christopher John Farley, *Time,* Fall 1993, Vol. 142, No. 21. Copyright © 1993 Time Inc. Reprinted by permission. **194** From "Treasures of the Rain Forest," *Kids Discover,* 1994. Copyright © 1994 Kids Discover. Reprinted by permission of the publisher. **210** "Sorry, Right Number," from *Nightmares and Dreamscapes* by Stephen King. Copyright © 1993 by Stephen King. Used by permission of Viking Penguin, a division of Penguin Books USA Inc. **232** "The Ghostly Rhyme" from *Tongues of Jade* by Laurence Yep. Text Copyright © 1991 by Laurence Yep. Reprinted by permission of HarperCollins Publishers. **239** "Elena" by Pat Mora is reprinted with permission from the publisher of Chants (Houston: Arte Publico Press-University of Houston, 1985). **239** "Etymology" by Amy Kashiwabara. Copyright © 1991 by Amy Kashiwabara. Reprinted by permission of the author. **241** "Symbols of Humankind" by Don Lago, *Science Digest,* March 1981, Vol. 89, No. 2. Reprinted by permission. **254** Reprinted with the permission of Scribner, an imprint of Simon & Schuster, Inc., from *The Miracle Worker* by William Gibson. Copyright © 1956, 1957 by William Gibson. Copyright © 1959, 1969 Tamarack Productions, Ltd., and George S. Klein and Leo Garel as trustees under three separate deeds of trust, renewed © 1977 by William Gibson. No performance of any kind may be given without permission in writing from the author's agent, Samuel French, Inc., 45 West 25th Street, New York, NY 10010. **317** "Hearing the Sweetest Songs" by Nicolette Toussaint from *Newsweek,* May 23, 1994, p. 10. Copyright © 1994, Newsweek, Inc. All rights reserved. Reprinted by permission. **321** "The Manual Alphabet" from *Anne Sullivan Macy: The Story Behind Helen Keller* by Nella Braddy. Copyright © 1933 by Nella Braddy Henney. Used by permission of Doubleday, a division of Bantam Doubleday Dell Publishing Group, Inc. **322** Adapted from "American Sign Language: It's not mouth stuff—it's brain stuff" by Richard Wolkomir. Copyright © 1992 by Richard Wolkomir. Reprinted from *Smithsonian* Magazine with the permission of the author. **325** Excerpts from "Navajo Code Talkers" by Harry Gardiner from *Cobblestone* Magazine's July 1989 issue: *Dine: The People of the Navajo Nation* © 1989, Cobblestone Publishing, Inc., 7 School St., Peterborough, NH 03458. Reprinted by permission of the publisher. **343** "Making a Fist" from *On the Edge of the Sky* by Naomi Shahib Nye. Reprinted by permission of the author. **344** "Knoxville, Tennessee" from *Black Feeling, Black Talk, Black Judgment* by Nikki Giovanni. Copyright © 1968, 1970 by Nikki Giovanni. Reprinted by permission of William Morrow and Company, Inc. **345** "Fifth Grade Autobiography" from *Grace Notes* by Rita Dove. Copyright © 1989 by Rita Dove. Reprinted with the permission of W.W. Norton & Company, Inc. **346** Li-Young Lee. "Mnemonic" copyright © 1986 by Li-Young Lee. Reprinted from *Rose,* by Li-Young Lee, with the permission of BOA Editions Ltd., 92 Park Ave., Brockport NY 14420. **351** "My Papa's Waltz," copyright 1942 by Hearst Magazines, Inc. from *The Collected Poems of Theodore Roethke* by Theodore Roethke. Used by permission of Doubleday, a division of Bantam Doubleday Dell Publishing Group, Inc. **353** "The Courage That My Mother Had" by Edna St. Vincent Millay. From *Collected Poems,* HarperCollins. Copyright © 1954, 1982 by Norma Millay Ellis. Reprinted by permission of Elizabeth Barnett, literary executor. **353** "The Funeral" from *Whispers of Intimate Things* by Gordon Parks. Copyright © 1971 by Gordon Parks. Reprinted by permission of Viking Penguin Inc. **354** "Like Bookends" from *If Only I Could Tell You* by Eve Merriam. Copyright © 1983 by Eve Merriam. Reprinted by permission of Marian Reiner. **358** "The Last Word" by Judith Ortiz Cofer is reprinted with permission from the publisher of *Silent Dancing: A Partial Remembrance of a Puerto Rican Childhood* (Houston: Arte Publico Press-University of Houston, 1990). **361** "Alligator" from *Mama Makes Up Her Mind: And Other Dangers of Southern Living* (pp. 92–94). Copyright © 1993 by Bailey White. Reprinted by permission of Addison-Wesley Publishing Company, Inc. **365** "A Christmas Memory" from *Breakfast at Tiffany's* by Truman Capote. Copyright © 1956 by Truman Capote. Reprinted by permission of Random House, Inc. **379** "In the Shade of a Family Tree" by Robert D. San Souci from *Faces* Magazine's April 1992 issue: *Ancestors* © 1992, Cobblestone Publishing, Inc., 7 School St., Peterborough, NH 03458. Reprinted by permission of the publisher. **392** "The Exhibit" by Lisel Mueller. Reprinted by permission of Louisiana State University Press from *Second Language: Poems by Lisel Mueller.* Copyright © 1986 by Lisel Mueller. **394** "Oye Mundo/ Sometimes" from *Street Poetry and Other Poems* by Jesús Papoleto Meléndez. Copyright © 1972 by Jesús Papoleto Meléndez. Reprinted by permission of the author. **397** "Saturday Afternoon,

When Chores are Done" from *Tree Tall Woman* by Harryette Mullen (Galveston, TX: Energy Earth Communications, 1981). Reprinted by permission of the author. **403** "Jazz Fantasia" from *Smoke and Steel* by Carl Sandburg, copyright 1920 by Harcourt Brace and Company and renewed 1948 by Carl Sandburg, reprinted by permission of the publisher. **403** Excerpt retitled "Nothing but Drums" from *The Mambo Kings Play Songs of Love* by Oscar Hijuelos. Copyright © 1989 by Oscar Hijuelos. Reprinted by permission of Farrar, Straus & Giroux, Inc. **405** "I Am Singing Now" from *A Breeze Swept Through* by Luci Tapahonso. Copyright © 1987 by Luci Tapahonso. Reprinted by permission of the author. **408** "I Have A Dream" by Martin Luther King, Jr. Reprinted by arrangement with The Heirs to the Estate of Martin Luther King, Jr., c/o Joan Daves Agency as agent for the proprietor. Copyright © 1963 by Martin Luther King, Jr. copyright renewed 1991 by Coretta Scott King. **415** "Hope Returns to the South Bronx" adapted from "On these sidewalks of New York, the sun is shining again," by Patrick Breslin, *Smithsonian,* April 1995, Vol. 26, No. 1, pp. 100–111. Reprinted by permission of the author. **427** "My Grandfather Was A Quantum Physicist" by Duane BigEagle. Reprinted by permission of the author. **428** From *The World of Gwendolyn Brooks.* Copyright © 1971 by Gwendolyn Brooks. Reprinted by permission of the author. **428** Lucille Clifton. "miss rosie" Copyright © 1987 by Lucille Clifton. Reprinted from *Good Woman: Poems and a Memoir 1969–1980,* by Lucille Clifton, with the permission of BOA Editions, Ltd., 92 Park Ave., Brockport, NY 14420. **429** "maggie and milly and molly and may" from *Complete Poems: 1904–1962* by E. E. Cummings, Edited by George J. Firmage, by permission of Liveright Publishing Corporation. Copyright © 1923, 1925, 1926, 1951, 1953, 1954, 1956, 1984, 1991 by the Trustees for the E. E. Cummings Trust. Copyright © 1976, 1985 by George James Firmage. **433** "To Look at Any Thing" from *The Living Seed,* Copyright © 1961 by John Moffitt and renewed 1989 by Henry Moffitt, reprinted by permission of Harcourt Brace & Company. **434** "Tiburón" from *Trumpets from the Islands of Their Eviction, Expanded Edition* by Martín Espada. Copyright © 1994 by Bilingual Press/Editorial Bilingüe. Reprinted by permission of Bilingual Press/Editorial Bilingüe, Arizona State University, Tempe, AZ. **435** "The Runaway" by Robert Frost from *The Poetry of Robert Frost* edited by Edward Connery Lathem. Copyright 1951 by Robert Frost. Copyright 1923 © 1969 by Henry Holt and Co., Inc. Reprinted by permission of Henry Holt and Co., Inc. **439** "Postage Stamp Connections" by Lee Douglass (Nancy Lee Pulley), *The Flying Island,* Spring/Summer 1994. Reprinted by permission of the author. **441** "Write About A Radish" from *Dogs & Dragons, Trees & Dreams* by Karla Kuskin. Copyright © 1975 by Karla Kuskin. Reprinted by permission of HarperCollins Publishers. **441** "Keeping Things Whole" from *Selected Poems* by Mark Strand. Copyright © 1979, 1980 by Mark Strand. Reprinted by permission of Alfred A. Knopf Inc. **441** Reprinted by permission of the publishers and the Trustees of Amherst College from *The Poems of Emily Dickinson,* Thomas H. Johnson, ed., Cambridge, Mass.: The Belknap Press of Harvard University Press, Copyright © 1951, 1955, 1979, 1983 by the President and Fellows of Harvard College. **445** "Nameless, Tennessee" from *Blue Highways* by William Least Heat Moon. Copyright © 1982 by William Least Heat Moon. By permission of Little, Brown and Company. **451** "The Rocket" by Ray Bradbury. Reprinted by permission of Don Congdon Associates, Inc. Copyright © 1950, renewed 1977 by Ray Bradbury. **481** Notes for "Romeo and Juliet" by William Shakespeare from *The Complete Works of Shakespeare,* Fourth Edition, edited by David Bevington. Copyright © 1992 by HarperCollins Publishers Inc. **590** "Deranged Love Mutants: The Story of Romeo and Juliet" from *How to Be Hap-Hap-Happy Like Me* by Merrill Markoe. Copyright © 1994 by Merrill Markoe. Used by permission of Viking Penguin, a division of Penguin USA Inc. **610** "Graduation" from *I Know Why the Caged Bird Sings* by Maya Angelou. Copyright © 1969 by Maya Angelou. Reprinted by permission of Random House, Inc. **619** "Lift Ev'ry Voice and Sing"—James Weldon Johnson, J. Rosamond Johnson. Used by permission of Edward B. Marks Music Company. **623** "The Village Watchman," (pp. 27–38) from *Unspoken Hunger* by Terry Tempest Williams. Copyright © 1994 by Terry Tempest Williams. Reprinted by permission of Pantheon Books, a division of Random House, Inc. **632** "Fathers and Daughters" from *When Heaven and Earth Changed Places* by Le Ly Hayslip. Copyright © 1989 by Le Ly Hayslip and Charles Jay Wurts. Used by permission of Doubleday, a division of Bantam Doubleday Dell Publishing Group, Inc. **642** "A Lincoln Preface," copyright 1953 by Carl Sandburg and renewed 1981 by Margaret Sandburg, Janet Sandburg, and Helga Sandburg Crile, reprinted by permission of Harcourt Brace & Company. **650** "The Secret Life of Walter Mitty" by James Thurber. Copyright 1942 by James Thurber. Copyright © 1970 by Helen Thurber and Rosemary A. Thurber. From *My World—And Welcome to It,* published by Harcourt Brace & Company. Reprinted by permission of James Thurber Literary Properties. **657** From *Running a School Newspaper* by Vivian Dubrovin. Copyright © 1985 by Vivian Dubrovin. Reprinted by permission of Franklin Watts Inc. **658** Adapted from "Men didn't have to prove they could fly, but women did," by David Roberts, *Smithsonian,* August 1994, Vol. 25, Number 5, pp. 72–81. Reprinted by permission of the author. **671** "What True Education Should Do" by Sydney J. Harris. Reprinted with special permission of North America Syndicate. **672** "The Struggle to Be An All-American Girl" by Elizabeth Wong. Reprinted by permission of the author. **682** Excerpt from *Woodsong* by Gary Paulsen. Reprinted with the permission of Simon & Schuster Books for Young Readers from

Woodsong by Gary Paulsen. Copyright © 1990 Gary Paulsen. **690** "The Inspector-General" from *The Sneeze* by Anton Chekhov, translated by Michael Frayn. Reprinted by permission of Reed Consumer Books Ltd. **734** From the *Odyssey* by Homer, translated by Robert Fitzgerald. Copyright © 1961, 1963 by Robert Fitzgerald and renewed 1989 by Benedict R. C. Fitzgerald. Reprinted by permission of Vintage Books, a Division of Random House Inc. **796** "Siren Song" from *You Are Happy, Selected Poems 1965–1975* by Margaret Atwood. Copyright © 1976 by Margaret Atwood. Reprinted by permission of Houghton Mifflin Company and Oxford University Press Canada. All rights reserved. **797** "An Ancient Gesture" by Edna St. Vincent Millay. From *Collected Poems,* HarperCollins. Copyright © 1954, 1982 by Norma Millay Ellis. Reprinted by permission of Elizabeth Barnett, literary executor. **798** "Sea Canes" from *Collected Poems* by Derek Walcott. Copyright © 1986 by Derek Walcott. Reprinted by permission of Farrar, Straus & Giroux, Inc.

Illustrations

Unless otherwise acknowledged, all photographs are the property of Scott, Foresman and Company. Page abbreviations are as follows: (t) top, (c) center, (b) bottom, (l) left, (r) right, (INS) inset.

Cover (detail), **ii** National Gallery of Art, Smithsonian Institution, Washington, D.C./Superstock, Inc. **vii** Edward Hopper, "Automat," 1927, 28 1/8 x 36 inches, oil on canvas, Des Moines Art Center/Permanent Collection, 1958.2, photo by Craig Anderson **ix** Javier Arévalo, "Los Encuentros," 1991, Private Collection/ Courtesy of Iturralde Gallery, Los Angeles **xi** Alex Colville, "To Prince Edward Island," 1965, (detail), National Gallery of Canada, Ottawa/Photo © NGC/MBAC **xiv** Frederick Leighton, "Reconciliation of the Montagues and the Capulets," c. 1853–55, (detail), Agnes Scott College, Decatur, GA **xv** Allan Rohan Crite, "School's Out," 1936, National Museum of American Art, Washington, DC/Art Resource, NY **xvii** J. W. Waterhouse, "Ulysses and the Sirens," 1891, (detail), oil on canvas, 100 x 201.7 cm. Purchased 1891, National Gallery of Victoria, Melbourne, Australia **xxii** The Parrish Art Museum, Southampton, NY, Gift of the Estate of Fairfield Porter, photo by Jim Strong **xxx–1** Edward Hopper, "Automat," 1927 (detail), 28 1/8 x 36 inches, oil on canvas, Des Moines Art Center/Permanent Collection, 1958.2, photo by Craig Anderson **1, 132, 192, 196, 201 (icon)** Diana Ong, "Crowd #11," (detail)/Superstock, Inc. **2(t)** Courtesy JoAnn Scott, photo by Isadore Howard **2(b)** Giraudon/Art Resource **3** Katsushika Hokusai, "In the Well of the Great Wave of Kanagawa," (detail), Christie's, London/Bridgeman Art Library, London/Superstock, Inc. **5** Photo by Robert Foothorap **7** Courtesy Dong Kingman **13** Kobal Collection **17** From *Twentieth Century Authors,* edited by Stanley J. Kunitz and Howard Haycraft. New York:

The H. H. Wilson Company, 1942 **18–19** A. K. G., Berlin/Superstock, Inc. **23** Private Collection, Courtesy Nohra Haime Gallery **32–33** © David Hockney **37** Manuscripts Dept/Lilly Library, Indiana University, Bloomington, IN **39** Giraudon/Art Resource **46(r)** © Steve Vance/ Stockworks **46(l)** Courtesy Cynthia Rylant **49** Courtesy Roger Mason, Collection Keith Carradine **52(b)** Courtesy University Press of New England, photo by Mandy Sayer **52(t)** Courtesy Fondo de Cultura Económica **54–55** Private Collection, Courtesy Marlborough Gallery. ©1995 Red Grooms/Artists Rights Society (ARS), New York **57** © Scott Mlyn **58** Courtesy of The Miami Herald **60** © C.Willinger/FPG International Corp **62–63** Electronic imaging, Courtesy Tom Miecznikowski **64** © 1995 John Livzey **77** Photo by Marian Wood Kolish **79** "The Lighthouse" ©1995 Thomas McKnight **85** The Spencer Collection/New York Public Library, Astor, Lenox and Tilden Foundations **88** © Catherine A. Koehler **89** Courtesy Viking Press **90–91** Courtesy Nahan Galleries, New York **96** The Granger Collection, NY **97** (detail), **101** Zoë Oliver Sherman Collection, Museum of Fine Arts, Boston **106** Photo by Sandra L. Swan/Random House **109** Courtesy JoAnn Scott, photo by Isadore Howard **115** Photo by Carolyn Soto **120–121** Courtesy Lane Yerkes **133** © Martin Harvey/The Wildlife Collection **134–135** Gibbes Museum of Art, Carolina Art Association **141** Fine Arts Collection, Luther College, Decorah, IA **147** Courtesy Budge Wilson **148** Courtesy Overland Gallery, Bloomington, MN **153** © Ronald Defelice/The Image Bank **160(r)** © Jack Parsons **160(l)** © 1981 Linda Fry Poverman **162–163** Courtesy Arizona West Galleries, Inc., Scottsdale, AZ **168** UPI/Corbis-Bettmann **179(b)** Dartmouth College **179(c)** Courtesy Dwight Okita **179(t)** UPI/Corbis-Bettmann **181** Courtesy of the Estate of Romare Howard Bearden **182** National Archives **183** Bayly Art Museum of the University of Virginia, photo by Robert Browning II, Charlottesville, VA **185(b)** UPI/Corbis-Bettmann **185(t)** UPI/Corbis-Bettmann **186** UPI/Corbis-Bettmann **188** National Museum of American Art, Washington, DC, Gift of the Container Corporation of America/Art Resource, NY **192** © Jonathan Atkin **193** © Malfer/Retna **194(b background)** © Barbara von Hoffmann/Tom Stack & Associates **194(b)** © Dr. Nigel Smith/Animals Animals/ Earth Scenes **194(t)** © Kevin Schafer/Tom Stack & Associates **195(r background)** © Barbara von Hoffmann/Tom Stack & Associates **195(tr)** © J. H. Robinson/Photo Researchers **195(br)** © Leonide Principe/Photo Researchers **195(l)** © Dr. Nigel Smith/Animals Animals/Earth Scenes **202** Edward Hopper, "Automat," (detail), 28 1/8 x 36 inches, oil on canvas, Des Moines Art Center/Permanent Collection, 1958.2, photo by Craig Anderson **203(t)** Courtesy Roger Mason, Collection Keith Carradine **204–205** Javier Arévalo, "Los Encuentros," 1991, (detail), Private Collection/Courtesy of Iturralde Gallery, Los Angeles **206–207** Archive Photos/ Archive Films **206** Martha Swope © Time Inc. **207** Photofest **209** Courtesy Viking Press, photo by Tabitha King **211** Courtesy John Nickle **215** © David Hockney **217** Courtesy John Nickle **220**

Courtesy Stephen and Zaida Wing **225, 226** © David Hockney **231** Photo by K. Yep **233** National Palace Museum, Peking, China **237(b)** Courtesy Amy Kashiwabara **237(t)** Courtesy Arte Publico Press **238** © 1989 Carmen Lomas Garza, photo by Judy Reed **241(c)** © Erich Lessing/Art Resource **241(r, l), 242 (l)** Ancient Art & Architecture Collection/Ronald Sheridan Photo-Library **251** Storyboard Courtesy Tom Miecznikowski **253** AP/Wide World Photos **254** UPI/Corbis-Bettmann **258, 270, 281, 285** Archive Photos/Archive Films **263** Perkins School for the Blind **277, 292, 313** Courtesy of the American Foundation for the Blind **296, 308** Photofest **311** The Kobal Collection **314(b)** Courtesy Nicolette Toussaint **314(t)** Corbis-Bettmann **315** Courtesy of the American Foundation for the Blind **318** Museum Folkwang, Essen, Germany **321** From *Anne Sullivan Macy* by Nella Braddy. Copyright 1933 by Nella Braddy Henney. Reprinted by permission of Doubleday Publishing Group. **322** © David Butow **323, 324** © Lynn Johnson **325** Department of Defense, Still Media Records Center **334** Courtesy of the American Foundation for the Blind **335** Javier Arévalo, "Los Encuentros," 1991, (detail), Private Collection/Courtesy of Iturralde Gallery, Los Angeles **336–337** Alex Colville, "To Prince Edward Island," 1965, National Gallery of Canada, Ottawa/Photo © NGC/MBAC **337, 340, 379, 384, 388 (icon)** Louis Krevek, "Group Portrait of Children with Bird and Dog," (detail), Salomon Collection/E. T. Archives, London/Superstock, Inc. **337, 424, 459, 466, 470 (icon)** Jacques Louis David, "Mademoiselle Du Val D'Oghes," (detail), Metropolitan Museum of Art/Shostal/Superstock, Inc. **338(t)** Photo by Michael Nye **338(b)** AP/Wide World Photos **339(b)** © Ann Turnbull/Retna **339(t)** © Kachaturian/ Gamma Liaison **342(b)** B. O. A. Editions, Ltd., photo by Arthur Furst **342(bc)** Vintage Books, photo by Fred Viebahn **342(tc)** Courtesy Nikki Giovanni **342(t)** Photo by Michael Nye **343** © Manfred Gottschalk/Tom Stack & Associates **344–345** Superstock, Inc. **350(bc)** Courtesy Viking Press, photo by Alfred Eisenstaedt **350(tc)** Courtesy Vassar College **350(t)** Courtesy of Doubleday and Co., photo by Imogen Cunningham **351** Brooks Memorial Art Gallery, Memphis/Lerner Fine Art/Superstock, Inc. By permission of Patricia S. Cloar. **352** Photograph © 1995 The Detroit Institute of Arts, Detroit Museum of Art Purchase, Special Membership and Donations Fund with contributions from Philip, David and Paul R. Gray, and their sister Mrs. William R. Kales **353** © 1975 by Hubert Shuptrine. Courtesy of the Collection, Mr. and Mrs. Walter T. Forbes, Jr. All rights reserved. Used with permission. **356** Lerner Fine Art/Superstock, Inc. **357(b)** Courtesy Addison-Wesley, photo by Spencer Jarnigan **357(t)** Courtesy of Arte Publico Press **359** Courtesy Collection Dr. F. Monserrate, Puerto Rico, photo by John Betancourt, San Juan. Photo courtesy of The Bronx Museum of the Arts, New York **361(b)** Metropolitan Museum of Art, The Crosby Brown Collection of Musical Instruments, 1889. (89.4.1473.) Photograph by Bob Hanson. **361(t)** Superstock, Inc. **361(c)** Superstock, Inc.

362 Superstock, Inc. **364(b)** From *Capote: A Biography,* by Gerald Clarke, New York: Simon and Schuster, 1988 **364(t)** © 1979 Irving Penn, Conde Nast Publications, Inc. **366** © 1986 by S. Hill Corporation. All rights reserved. Used with permission. **373** © Photo R. M. N. **376** Superstock, Inc. **380** © PhotoEdit **382(r)** The Metropolitan Museum of Art, Rogers Fund, 1922 (JP 1278) **382(l)** Courtesy Mike Larsen **383(tl)** Hampton University Museum, Hampton, Virginia **383(bl)** National Gallery of Art, Washington, DC/Superstock, Inc. **383(r)** Tate Gallery, London/Art Resource, NY **388** Everett Collection, Inc. **391(b)** Courtesy Harryette Mullen, photo by Judith Natal **391(bc)** © 1995 Wayne Providence/Courtesy Jesús Papoleto Meléndez **391(tc)** Culver Pictures **391(t)** Courtesy Lisel Mueller, Photo by Marty De Zeeuw **392** The Metropolitan Museum of Art, Gift of John D. Rockefeller, Jr., The Cloisters Collection, 1937 (37.80.6) © 1993 by The Metropolitan Museum of Art **395** The Metropolitan Museum of Art, Gift of Mr. and Mrs. Samuel Shore, 1978. (1978.61.1–6) © 1992 by The Metropolitan Museum of Art **396** Superstock, Inc. **401(b)** Courtesy Luci Tapahonso **401(c)** Photo by Klaus Moser **401(t)** AP/Wide World Photos **402** Superstock, Inc. **404–405** Superstock, Inc. **407** © Ernst Haas/Magnum **408–409** © James P. Blair/National Geographic Image Collection **415–417** © Camilo Jose Vergara **418** Photo by Maya Alleruzzo/The Recorder **426(b)** Corbis-Bettmann **426(tc)** Courtesy HarperCollins Publishers **426(t)** Courtesy Duane BigEagle **427** Logan Museum of Anthropology, Beloit College, The Albert Green Heath Collection, LMA 30400 **428** Courtesy Tom Heflin **429** Courtesy S. R. Brennen Gallery, Carmel, CA **432(b)** Dartmouth College **432(c)** Courtesy W. W. Norton and Company, photo by Terry Pitzner **433** © Terry Donnelly/Tom Stack & Associates **434** Superstock, Inc. **435** Superstock, Inc. **438(b)** Trustees of Amherst College **438(bc)** Photo by Douglas Keng Hall **438(tc)** Photo by Douglas Kirkland **438(t)** Courtesy Nancy Lee Pulley **440** Superstock, Inc. **444(r)** From *Blue Highways* by William Least Heat Moon. Copyright © 1982 by William Least Heat Moon. By permission of Little, Brown and Company **444(l)** AP/Wide World Photos **445** From *Blue Highways* by William Least Heat Moon. Copyright © 1982 by William Least Heat Moon. By permission of Little, Brown and Company. Photo used by permission of The Wallace Literary Agency, Inc. **450** Photo by Morris Dollens **453** Courtesy Phil Huling **454, 456** NASA **456** Mike Steirnagle **459** Courtesy Maura Donnelly **459(border)** Superstock, Inc. **460** Collection Walker Art Center, Minneapolis, Gift of Frederick R. Weisman in honor of his parents, William and Mary Weisman, 1988 **461(t)** Photo by Daniel Dancer, Courtesy Stanley J. Herd **461(c)** © Randy Taylor/Sygma **461(b)** Superstock, Inc. **462(b)** National Museum of Greenland **462(t)** Tommy Lowry Tjapaltjarri, "Two Men Dreaming at Kulunjarranya," 1984, Courtesy of the Aboriginal Artists Agency, New South Wales, Australia **463(b)** The New York Public Library, Astor, Lenox and Tilden Foundations **463(t)** Copyright British Museum **472** Alex Colville, "To Prince Edward Island," 1965, (detail),

National Gallery of Canada, Ottawa/Photo © NGC/MBAC **473(b)** Metropolitan Museum of Art, The Crosby Brown Collection of Musical Instruments, 1889. (89.4.1473.) Photograph by Bob Hanson. **473(t)** Superstock, Inc. **474–475** Frederick Leighton, "Reconciliation of the Montagues and the Capulets," c. 1853–55, (detail), Agnes Scott College, Decatur, GA **475, 478, 590, 594, 600 (icon)** Francesco Hayez, "The Kiss," (detail), Pinacoteca Di Brera, Milan/M. Magliani/Superstock, Inc. **476** Archive Photos/Archive Films **479(t)** National Portrait Gallery, London **479(b)** Scale drawing by Irwin Smith from *Shakespeare's Globe Playhouse: A Modern Reconstruction in Text and Scale Drawings* by Irwin Smith. Charles Scribner's Sons, New York, 1956. Labeling by Scott, Foresman **481** Everett Collection, Inc. **490** Motion Picture & Television Photo Archive (the Avery Collection) **495** Everett Collection, Inc. **501** Shooting Star **509** Kobal Collection **514** Everett Collection, Inc. **519** Photofest **524** Everett Collection, Inc. **530** Shooting Star **537** Photofest **543** Archive Photos/ Archive Films **554** Everett Collection, Inc. **559** Photofest **570** Everett Collection, Inc. **575** Archive Photos/ Archive Films **581(b)** Corbis-Bettmann **581(t)** Manuscripts Department, Lilly Library, Indiana University, Bloomington, IN **583** National Museum of American Art, Washington, DC. Museum purchase made possible in part by Mrs. Alexander Hamilton Rice in memory of her husband and by Ralph Cross Johnson/Art Resource, NY **584** The Metropolitan Museum of Art, Bequest of Mrs. H. O. Havemeyer, 1929. The H. O. Havemeyer Collection. (29.100.63) **590** Peter McDonnell **592** Metropolitan Museum of Art, New York City/Superstock, Inc. **602** Kobal Collection **603(t)**, detail, National Museum of American Art, Washington, DC. Museum purchase made possible in part by Mrs. Alexander Hamilton Rice in memory of her husband and by Ralph Cross Johnson/Art Resource, NY **603(b)** Frederick Leighton, "Reconciliation of the Montagues and the Capulets," c. 1853–55, (detail), Agnes Scott College, Decatur, GA **604–605** Allan Rohan Crite, "School's Out," 1936, (detail), National Museum of American Art, Washington, DC/ Art Resource, NY **605, 608, 657, 662, 667 (icon)** Courtesy Erika Hugo **606** © Mary Ellen Mark/Library **607** © Lisa Quinones/Black Star **609** AP/Wide World Photos **611** John H. Surovek Gallery **615** Superstock, Inc. **622** Photo by Michelle MacFarlane/Courtesy Terry Tempest Williams **623** © Leo Keeler/Animals Animals/Earth Scenes **625(b, t)** Courtesy Terry Tempest Williams **626** Courtesy Terry Tempest Williams **631** © David Strick/Onyx **632–633** © Alain Evrard/Photo Researchers **637** From *When Heaven and Earth Changed Places* by Le Ly Hayslip. Copyright © 1989 by Le Ly Hayslip and Charles Jay Wurts. Used by permission of Doubleday, a division of Bantam Doubleday, Dell Publishing Group, Inc. **641** AP/Wide World Photos **642** Chicago Historical Society, Neg. #ICHi–20265, photo by Alexander Hesler **643** National Portrait Gallery, Washington, DC/Art Resource, NY **649** AP/Wide World Photos **651** Museum of Modern Art, Film Stills Archive **654** Museum of Modern Art, Film Stills Archive **658–660(border)** Cynthia A. Clampitt **658–659(b)** Corbis-Bettmann **659(t)** UPI/Corbis-Bettmann **660(b)** Corbis-Bettmann **670(b)** Courtesy Elizabeth Wong **670(t)** Courtesy Chicago Sun-Times **672** Private Collection, Courtesy Ken Chu **675** North Wind Picture Archives **676** Harry T. Peters Collection, Museum of the City of New York **682–683** Applestock Art Archives **689** Corbis-Bettmann **690–691** Menninger, Topeka, KS **695(l)** National Portrait Gallery, London **695(r)** Richard Lancelyn Green **697** Stanley MacKenzie **703** © Photo R. M. N. **711** © Photo by Erich Lessing/Art Resource, NY **716(t)** © Monkmeyer/Litz **717(bl)** © Derek Trask/The Stock Market **717(br)** © Bob Daemmrich/The Image Works **717(c)** © Bob Daemmrich/The Image Works **717(tr)** © Monkmeyer/Spencer Grant **717(t)** © Bob Daemmrich/The Image Works **718** Courtesy Dakota Moon Recording **726(r)** Private Collection, Courtesy Ken Chu **726(l)** Allan Rohan Crite, "School's Out," 1936, (detail), National Museum of American Art, Washington, DC/ Art Resource, NY **727** John H. Surovek Gallery [**728–729** J. W. Waterhouse, "Ulysses and the Sirens," 1891, (detail), oil on canvas, 100 x 201.7cm. Purchased 1891, National Gallery of Victoria, Melbourne, Australia] **730–731** Philadelphia Museum of Art: The George W. Elkins Collection **733(b)** Photo by Madame Robert Champigny **745** Scala/Art Resource, NY **747** Anonymous Gift in memory of L. D. Caskey, Courtesy, Museum of Fine Arts, Boston **753** Oil on canvas, 180.7 x 87.4, Art Gallery of South Australia, Adelaide **763** Corbis-Bettmann **765** Spencer Collection, The New York Public Library, Astor, Lenox and Tilden Foundations **768** H. L. Pierce Fund, Courtesy, Museum of Fine Arts, Boston **769** Map by James Chaffee **773** Nimatallah/Art Resource, NY **781** From Homer, *The Odyssey,* Translated by George Herbert Palmer, Illustrations by N. C. Wyeth. Cambridge: Houghton Mifflin, 1929 **785** From Homer, *The Odyssey,* Translated by George Herbert Palmer, Illustrations by N. C. Wyeth. Cambridge: Houghton Mifflin, 1929 **789** Scala/Art Resource, NY **795(b)** Longfellow House Trust **795(bc)** Photo by Evan Richman/Corbis-Bettmann **795(t)** Photo by Laurence Acland **795(tc)** Courtesy Vassar College **796** Courtesy Koplin Gallery, Santa Monica, CA **799** Gallery Contemporanea, Jacksonville, FL/Superstock, Inc. **801–803** Ralph Creasman **804** James Chaffee **810** The Granger Collection, NY **811** Courtesy Romare Howard Bearden Foundation, Inc. **812(b)** H. L. Pierce Fund, Courtesy, Museum of Fine Arts, Boston **812(t)** Anonymous Gift in memory of L. D. Caskey, Courtesy, Museum of Fine Arts, Boston **813** Corbis-Bettmann

Handlettering by Eliza Schulte.

Electronic Illustrations by Bruce Burdick, Scott J. Jordan, and Steven Kiecker.